English
Through
the Ages

English
Through
the Ages

William Brohaugh

WRITER'S DIGEST BOOKS
Cincinnati, Ohio

English Through the Ages. Copyright © 1998 by William Brohaugh. Printed and bound in the United States of America. All rights reserved. No part of this book may be reproduced in any form or by any electronic or mechanical means including information storage and retrieval systems without permission in writing from the publisher, except by a reviewer, who may quote brief passages in a review. Published by Writer's Digest Books, an imprint of F&W Publications, Inc., 1507 Dana Avenue, Cincinnati, Ohio 45207. (800) 289-0963. First edition.

Other fine Writer's Digest Books are available from your local bookstore or direct from the publisher.

02 01 00 99 98   5 4 3 2 1

Library of Congress Cataloging-in-Publication Data

Brohaugh, William.
   English through the ages / by William Brohaugh.
     p.   cm.
   Includes bibliographical references and index.
   ISBN 0-89879-655-5 (hardcover: alk. paper)
   1. English language—Glossaries, vocabularies, etc. 2. English language—Lexicology. 3. English language—
   Chronology. I. Title.
PE1680.B67   1998
420—dc21
                                                             97-40771
                                                               CIP

Edited by Roseann S. Biederman
Production edited by Amanda Magoto
Designed by Angela Lennert Wilcox

ABOUT THE AUTHOR

William Brohaugh is the author of *Write Tight* (about concision in writing) and *Professional Etiquette for Writers*. He edited *Writer's Digest* from 1982 until 1990, when he became editorial director of Writer's Digest Books, his current position. Brohaugh appeared in 1953. The word *brouhaha* appeared by 1890. They are unrelated. ❦

TABLE OF CONTENTS

INTRODUCTION

Now, finally, the answer to one of the eternal questions. The really important one: *Chicken* came first, perhaps hundreds of years before *egg*.

The word *chicken* entered the English language in Old English, sometime before A.D. 950. The Humpty-come-lately *egg* didn't arrive until sometime before 1340. And, interestingly, people were egging things on before the present word for eggs came into the language. The noun *egg* and the verb *egg* originate from different sources. So, to answer that other eternal question, "Which came first—the egg or the egg?", the verb surfaced first—probably in the thirteenth century.

English Through the Ages, listing words not alphabetically but by the date of their first recorded use, answers such questions. It is not a sweeping history of the roots of language and the substantial tree it became, but a log of the appearance of each new bud upon that tree. Nor is it, to redefine our metaphor, a genealogical family tree. It is, instead, a birth list.

Yes, word history plays a critical role in this reference. Yes, we see genealogies and etymologies unfold, and we watch words develop, mutate, merge . . . and disappear. But the primary goal of this book is to answer the question: "By what time are we certain that this particular word had entered the language?" "How?" and "why?" will often be apparent as the book explicates "when?", but "when?" is the focus.

English Through the Ages pinpoints as best as can be determined when each listed word became bona fide English (for instance, the Latin immigrant *bona fide* got its papers by 1790). The dates used within certainly don't represent precisely when a word popped out of someone's mouth, because lacking time machines and very large notebooks, we can't establish such times. We can, however, determine that a word is common enough that people use it in writing, and words are listed here according to when we know by the written record that a word was being used. Some words, especially in English's infancy and toddlerhood, are likely to have been in use for *hundreds* of years before finding their way into print— books and literacy being largely inaccessible to major parts of the population until more recent times.

And, obviously this book chronicles the appearance of individual words, which often has little to do with the appearance of the thing, action or concept the word describes. Oblong white things appeared from the bottoms of chickens long before there were *eggs* or *egges* or *eggys*. So, just because the word didn't exist at a specific time doesn't imply that what the word describes didn't exist at that time; often, they just had different names. (Before they were *eggs*, they were *eyren*.)

To extend the example of the *eggs* or *egges* or *eggys*, entries are based on the appearance of the word, not on the appearance of the modern spelling of the word. For instance, the words for "mother" and "father" have been in the language for a long time, and have sported numerous spellings over the centuries, some only vaguely close to modern orthography. (In fact, the view that standardized spelling is important is a relatively modern concept.) Yet, no matter the spelling, they are the same words describing the same concepts.

So, these thoughts in mind, let's move on to answer English's version of the chicken-and-egg question ("chicken-and-egg" as an adjective, from about 1955, by the by . . .). ❧

HOW TO USE
English Through the Ages

Though the timeline of words constitutes this book's primary structure, the timeline features further internal organization to help you find specific types of words.

First, here's how the timeline works.

Words are organized first by time grouping. The first three groupings reflect the first three major stages of the English language. These are:

- Words in use by 1150—that is to say, words in use in Old English.

- Words in use by 1350—that is, words that came into use in Middle English.

- Words in use by 1470—words that came into use in Late Middle English.

The groupings that follow reflect Modern English. From 1500 to 1800, words are grouped in 50-year increments. In the 1800s, words are grouped in 25-year increments, and in 10-year increments for words appearing in the 1900s.

Within the timeline groupings, words are grouped into subject categories, such as "Geography/Places," "Plants," "The Body," "Crime/Punishment/Enforcement," "Everyday Life," "Phrases" and "Archaisms." (For a complete list of these categories, see page 5.) General words appear at the end of each timeline grouping. "General/Miscellaneous," "Actions/Verbs" and "Description" contain miscellaneous words that don't fit cleanly into any of the specific categories.

Within these categories fall nouns, verbs, adjectives and other parts of speech, so that the "Medical" category in "In Use by 1650" can contain *catheter* (noun), *medicate* (verb) and *recuperative* (adjective).

Classifications are admittedly loose. *Pediatrician* would be equally comfortable listed as a profession as it would a medical term; *bilk* would be as accurately categorized as a crime word as it would a slang word. Each word appears under only one category.

When consulting a specific category, then, such as "Love/Sex/Marriage," you might also consult other potentially related categories—"Emotions/Characteristics," "Slang" and so on.

Words are arranged within the categories by more specific dates. In the "In Use by 1825—Law" section, for instance, a word known to be in use by 1810 will appear before words known to be in use by 1815, 1820 and so on. For example:

zirconium n b1810

aluminum n 1812

iodine n 1814

anthracite n *type of coal* b1815 ["mineral resembling embers": b1605]

Under these separate date groupings, words appear in alphabetical order. For example:

coulee n (Am) b1805

escarpment n b1805

tideland n b1805

watershed n b1805 [fig. use: b1900]

The Word Listings Themselves

Now let's examine the information available in each word's listing. Listings follow this structure:

delusion n *deception* b1425 ["hallucination": b1570] (delude: b1410; delusory: b1500; delusive: b1605)

There are six elements of this listing:

- **"delusion,"** in **boldface**, is the entryword

- "n" is the part of speech

- *"deception,"* in *italics*, indicates the general meaning of the entryword

- "b1425" tells you that the word was in use by the year 1425

- "["hallucination": b1570]," in brackets, indicates that *delusion* was used to mean "hallucination" by the year 1570

- "(delude: b1410; delusory: b1500; delusive: b1605)," in parentheses, lists words related to the entryword, and the date by which these words were in use.

A couple of notes about these sections:

Entrywords: In general, only one word begins each entry. Occasionally, closely related words will appear as entrywords. For example, **gaffer, gammer** are listed as one entry head, as they appeared about the same time and have approximately the same meaning (old man, old woman). In this case, the part of speech is listed as "n," as both words are nouns. Sometimes words of different parts of speech are so joined. For example, **beast, beastly** appear together. In such cases, the part of speech is listed as "n, adj," with the part of speech in the same order as the listed words.

Date: To save space, the phrase "by 1890" is abbreviated to "b1890." Note: If the secondary date grouping (e.g., "b1900") is the same as the general date grouping (e.g., "In Use by 1900"), the "b1900" component of the listing is not repeated. If no secondary date grouping information is included, assume the word was in use by the date indicated in the general date grouping. For example, in the general grouping "In Use by 1850," "**dyne** n b1845" is followed by "**Celsius** adj"—*dyne* was in use by 1845, and *Celsius* was in use by 1850.

Definitions: Again, word "definitions" appear in *italics* shortly after the **boldfaced** entryword. I say "definitions" in quotes because these italicized sections are not always strict definitions per se. They are meant to indicate the sense of the word. So you'll see such notations as:

eccentric adj *describing circles* b1555

eccentric adj *describing people* b1630

ebb n *as in "ebb and flow"* b1000

ebullient adj *lit. boiling* b1600

ecru n *type of color* b1870

ectotherm n *cold-blooded animal* b1945

element n *i.e.: earth, fire, water, air* b1300

embassy n *the job* b1535

excandescence n *akin to incandescence* b1700

Eccentric's "definitions" indicate what the words are applied to; *ebb* uses the word in a common phrase to indicate meaning; *ebullient* indicates that it's the literal sense instead of the figurative emotional sense; *ecru* indicates that it's a type of color; *ectotherm* gives a literal definition; *element* and *excandescence* show

related words to indicate meaning; and *embassy* indicates that it means "the job of the ambassador" instead of "the building"—that is, the physical offices of the ambassador.

Parentheses around letters in meanings indicate material that has been dropped out to form a word. For example, "sm(oke)(h)azy" indicates what has been dropped out when *smoke* and *haze* were melded into *smazy*.

Some definitions include more than one word or phrase to describe the entryword. In such instances, commas separate words of basically synonymous meaning, and semicolons separate different senses of the entryword. Therefore, "cantankerous, onery" indicate one general sense of the entryword, while "small hill; obs. mountaintop" indicate two different meanings of the entryword. Semicolons are similarly used in other parts of entries to differentiate meanings or uses.

Other Meanings: The material presented in brackets—other meanings of the entryword—use the same sort of "definition" notations described above. Therefore, you'll see such listings as:

embezzle v b1600 [gen. "steal": b1425 to 1700s; obs. "make weaker": b1570 to 1600s; obs. "waste": b1600 to 1700s]

emerald n b1300 [the color: b1730]

emotion n *commotion* b1570 [modern sense: b1830]

emphysema n gen. *swelling* b1665 [spec. type of lung disease: b1870]

emu n b1830 [applied to other birds: b1615]

Related Words: Within the parentheses that display related words you'll often see such phrases as "noun use: b1825." This indicates the time by which the **boldfaced** entryword was first used as a different part of speech. "Noun use," "verb use" and so on appear before other related words are listed. Thus, in the listing for **abuse** n, the parenthetical notation reads: "(verb use: b1425; obs. abusion n: b1350 to 1700s)." Even though *abusion* appeared before *abuse* as a verb, the verb use is listed first.

Where Words Fall Into the Timeline

This book organizes words according to when we are sure the word was used with this meaning. For example, "b1750" indicates that we know the word was in use by that year. This doesn't mean that 1750 was the

birthdate of that word—it may have been used for dozens, perhaps hundreds of years before its first use on paper.

When a word's creation date is certain, no *b* appears before the date, as with *zip code*.

zip code n 1963

We know that this phrase was invented in 1963, so that date appears, instead of the more general "b1965."

Most words have separate entries for their appearance as a certain part of speech. For example, *access* as a noun appeared by 1300, and is listed in the "In Use by 1350" section. *Access* as a verb appeared by 1970, and so is listed separately much later in the book. Some words list two or more parts of speech. For example, "n/v" indicates that the word appeared in noun and verb use at—as best as can be determined—around the same time. Again, one may have been used for far longer than the other, but we're not sure of that.

Similarly, most words have separate entries for their different or changed meanings. For example, *bad* as an adjective is first listed in "In Use by 1350," and then also listed in its slang sense of "good" in "In Use by 1930."

When looking for a specific word, turn first to the index starting on page 329. If there are multiple entries for a word, the index usually indicates in what sense the index word is used. For example:

B
babe n 23; slang use 462
bank n *mound* 234, 286; n *financial institution* 45; v *turn* 567

C
city n 333
crash n/adj 34; v 34, 86

D
daff n *fool* 67
daffy adj 67
damnation n/interj 112

Summary: Hierarchy of Word Order

General date grouping (e.g., "In Use by 1850")

Category of word (e.g., "Mathematics")

Secondary date grouping (e.g., "b1835")

Alphabetically—so that "**billion** n b1835" appears before "**constant** n b1835"

Subject Categories Used in This Book

Words within timeline groupings are subgrouped into these categories:

actions/verbs	finances/money	performing arts
age/aging	food	phrases
agriculture/food-gathering	games/fun/leisure	physical description
animals	general/miscellaneous	plants
archaisms	geography/places	politics
body	government	professions/duties
business/commerce/selling	heavens/sky	religion
cloth/clothing	holidays	science
colors	insults	shelter/housing
communication	interjections	slang
contractions	language and speaking	society/mores/culture
crime/punishment/enforcement	law	sports
death	life	technology
description	literature/writing	things
drink	love/romance/sex	thoughts/perception/the mind
education	magic	time
emotions/characteristics	mathematics	tools
energy	measurement	travel/transportation
entertainment	medicine	visual arts/photography
everyday life	movies/tv/radio	war/military/violence
family/relations/friends	music	weather
fantastic/paranormal	natural things	workplace
fashion/style		

Note, however, that subject categories do *not* appear in alphabetical order within the listings. They are arranged into this order:

geography/places	fashion/style	education
natural things	tools	religion
plants	travel/transportation	society/mores/culture
animals	emotions/characteristics	government
weather	thoughts/perception/the mind	politics
heavens/sky	love/romance/sex	life
science	family/relations/friends	death
technology	games/fun/leisure	war/military/violence
energy	sports	crime/punishment/enforcement
time	professions/duties	the law
age/aging	business/commerce/selling	the fantastic/paranormal
mathematics	the workplace	interjections
measurement	finances/money	slang
the body	language and speaking	insults
physical description	literature/writing	phrases
medicine	communication	general/miscellaneous
everyday life	visual arts/photography	things
shelter/housing	performing arts	description
drink	music	colors
food	entertainment	actions/verbs
agriculture/food-gathering	movies/tv/radio	archaisms
cloth/clothing		

Word historians break English down into four major periods. This introduction is being written in Modern English. The Modern English period is generally recognized as starting around A.D. 1500.

Old English is considered to have started around A.D. 450, spanning to around 1150. Middle English takes us to around 1350, and Late Middle English (often lumped into Middle English) takes us to the beginnings of the language fully in the form that we speak it today.

The Source of All—Indo-European

Before Old English was West Germanic. And before that was Indo-European, which is considered the source of many languages, from Latin to Greek to German to Etruscan to Sanskrit. English still depends heavily on words in use in Indo-European—about 80 to 90 percent of our vocabulary, by some estimates. Some sourcewords are obvious: It's clear that the rootword *menegʰ-* is related to our word for the same concept—*many*. Some need a little more analysis: The rootword *ker-* eventually brought us *horn*. In evolving from Indo-European to Germanic, the language underwent what is called The Great Consonant Shift, which softened many of the hard Indo-European consonants. Indo-European evolving into Latin did not undergo the shift in the same way (though from *bhleu-* came the Latin *fluere*, leading to our *fluent*, among other words), so we still see *ker-* in the Latin-based word *cornucopia*—"horn" of plenty. (For more on Indo-European, see page 24.)

Of course, English's lineage is neither as tidy nor as linear as a biological family tree. Many words can be traced back to Indo-European through indirect parentage. These words slipped into Latin, for instance, and English speakers borrowed from Latin without realizing they were indirectly tapping their own English roots.

Old English, the Language of *Beowulf*

Old English was the language of Germanic tribes who had migrated to Britain around A.D. 500. These settlers called their language Englisc, the language of the Angles (whence "Anglo"). We use much of the vocabulary of Old English today—one study declared that all of the one hundred most-used English words came from Old English. Among these words are *death*, *young*, *gold*, *holy*, *weapon*, *love*, *world* and *life*. Among those that didn't survive are *sibb* (peace), *guth* (war) and *yth* (wave).

Old English was, like its Germanic brethren (or should I say *bruderen*), an inflected language, with words taking their final form based on how they are being used in a sentence, or in relationship with other words and concepts. (We have few inflections today. "I go, she goes" inflects *go*. "Who are you? You gave it to whom?" inflects *who*.)

The Christian church came to Britain not long after the English did, around A.D. 600, bringing with it Latin terminology that the English accepted into their language. So the pattern of the English language welcoming outside influences began very early on, when what was then called English was but a century or so old, and itself something of an outsider to Britain. Among the words such contact brought are expected—*hymn* and *altar*—for example, but other areas were affected, as well, leading to such words as *fever*, *grammar* and *oyster*.

Scandinavian settlers and invaders further enriched the language with vocabulary. Among their imports: *they*, *skill*, *skin*.

For a taste of Old English, this anonymous poem:

> Lenten is come with love to toune
> With blosmen and with briddes roune
> That all this blisse bringeth
> Dayes-eyes in this dales
> Notes suete of nyghtingales
> Ech foul songe singeth

> Spring is come with love to town
> With blossoms and with bird song
> That all this bliss brings
> Daisies in this dale
> Notes sweet of nightingales
> Each bird, song sings.

Middle English, the Language of Chaucer

By the time Middle English is considered to have begun, A.D. 1350, English was evolving away from the

highly inflected language it was. Migrations and invasions fueled this change. The great mix of influences in some ways simplified language rather than confused it, in that inflections were fading as languages merged, and their mutual speakers found it simply easier to stop using them.

The most significant invasion late in the Old English period was that of William the Conquerer and his Norman French armies in 1066. The French conquerers established their own nobility and church structure, making French the language of the powerful. During this time, English became fragmented and was threatened with extinction. Some thirteen English dialects were spoken, all by the lower class.

The existence of two primary languages then remains reflected in today's language, particularly in our depth of vocabulary. Many English words have living Latinate counterparts, as with the "common" *chew* and the "noble" *masticate*—similar are *swine/pork, land/nation.*

English rebounded to again become the primary language by the mid-1300s (about the time considered to be the beginning of Late Middle English). The French had lost power in years previous, and subsequent wars with the French didn't inspire the English to put the continental language over their own. England eventually became an English-speaking country again.

Middle English is characterized by a syntax that sounds archaic instead of foreign (as Old English would), and by spellings that are to us unusual and erratic. Making Middle English look more alien to the modern eye are two alphabet characters we no longer use—*thorn* (which largely mutated into *th*) and *yogh* (which largely transformed into *y*). Ironically, *thorn* looks a little like a *y*, which is how *the* has been interpreted as *ye* (*ye* actually is a form of *you*). Old English sported such now-unknown letters, as well.

For a taste of Middle English, this from Chaucer's *Troilus and Criseyde*:

> He was so fallen in despeir that day
> That outrely he shope him forto dey;
> For right thus was his argument alway:
> He seyde he nas but lorn weylaway
> For al that comth comth by necessitee
> Thus to be lorn it is my destinee.

Modern English, the Language of Shakespeare

In the late 1400s, "Modern English" began taking its place. With Modern English came stability—spelling began to become standardized, and shifts in pronunciation took final effect. Unfortunately, the standardization was perhaps too early, as the introduction of "mass" printing forced arbitrary decisions on spellings at a time when the language was still very much in flux. This caused something of a blurry snapshot that we're still looking at today—the blur primarily in spellings that made sense in Middle English but no longer do so. For example, now-silent letters were not when they were set to print—the *gh* in *light* was pronounced.

Latin and Greek heavily influenced English at this time, with the ever-present French following behind, as did other continental languages, including Italian and Spanish.

Not long after (in historical terms, anyway), the sun began not setting on the English Empire, and in that constant light across the world we began seeing new influences, new words and new Englishes, from American English to Caribbean English to Australian English.

The language now is an international language. But in a sense, it always has been, what with its myriad influences. The worldwide sources of English words through all the ages are myriad, including and hardly exclusive to:

- Philippino Tagalog (*boondocks*)
- Spanish (*alligator, vamoose, cockroach*)
- Dutch (*poppycock, daffodil, rant*)
- German (*poodle, protoplasm*)
- French (*fuselage, rendezvous, fabricate*)
- Greek (*monk, church, aesthetics*)
- Middle French (*quadrangle*)
- Portuguese (*albacore*)
- Italian (*profile, regatta, credenza*)
- Hindi (*cummerbund, bungalow*)
- Arabic (*algorithm, alcohol, assassin*)
- Scandinavian (*sky, meek, they*)
- Native American (*raccoon, caucus*)
- African (*banjo*)

But of course we do more than just borrow and adapt words. We create them, assign them and inspire them, deriving them . . .

- from place names (*jeans, corduroy, badminton*)

- from people (*boycott, smark aleck, bowdlerize*)

- from mistakes (*adder, cherry, apron*)

- from writers (*factoid, blurb, chortle*)

- from shortening (*flu, memo, mob*)

- from lengthenings (*besmirch, amaze, overwhelm*)

- from contractions (*bridal, king, e-mail*)

- from acronyms (*laser, snafu, radar*)

- or from translating letters to words (*cue, emcee, jeep*).

We see these births throughout *English Through the Ages*, though we don't see etymology in its strictest sense. Many excellent books have been published about English—consult them for full chronicles of how our flexible, vibrant, occasionally frustrating and ever-changing language was born, nurtured, beaten back and ultimately unleashed. My favorite history remains Robert Claiborne's *Our Marvelous Native Tongue*. Craig M. Carver's *A History of English in Its Own Words* is not a history per se, but its explications of the origins of some 750 words is presented in chronological order.

This in mind, then, let's begin to look at the *when* of these creations.

IN USE BY
1150

Geography/Places

cliff n b725

fen n b725

field n b725 [as in "playing field": b1770]

moor n b725 (moorland: b1100)

earth n *ground; soil; the planet; land* b750 ["gen. world": b1450] (earthly: b1000)

mount n *mountain* b750 (mountain: b1200)

ditch n b850

brook n b875

burn n *creek* b900

dale n b900

east n b900

ford n b900 (verb use: b1615)

furrow n b900 (verb use: b1470)

ground n *earth's surface; soil* b900 [obs. "dry land": u1600s]

heath n b900

island n b900 (isle: b1225; islet: b1540)

knoll n *small hill; obs. mountaintop* b900

land n *ground; nation* b900 [as in "meadowland": b1630] (verb use: b1300)

lea n *grassland* b900

marsh n b900

northland n b900

pool n *as in "pool of water"* b900 [as in "swimming pool": b1630] (verb use: b1450)

sea n b900 [on the moon: b1670]

shire n b900

slough n *muddy ground* b900 [fig., as in "slough of despond": b1350]

sound n *type of inlet* b900

south n b900

sward n *bodily surface* b900 ["grassy surface": b1450]

thorp n *arch. village* b900

woodland n b900 (adj use: b1400)

combe n (Brit) *type of valley* b1000

dell n b1000

headland n b1000

highland n b1000

hill n b1000

landmark n *lit. something marking land* b1000 [phys. "prominent feature": b1600; fig. "prominent point": b1870] (adj use: b1970)

mead, meadow n b1000 (meadowland: b1530)

salt marsh n b1000

waterfall n b1000

fenland n b1100

plot n *as in "plot of land"* b1100 [as in "burial plot": b1900]

seastrand n *seashore* b1100

seawater n b1100

strand n *shore* b1100 [obs. "wharf": b1350 to 1800s] (verb use: b1000; strandline: b1905)

weald n *spec. forest* b1100 [gen. "forest": b1570]

fosse n *ditch*

marshland n

wilderness n [fig. use: b1350]

Natural Things

chalk n b700 [used for drawing: b1500] (verb use: b1575)

flint n b700

tar n b700

dew n b725 (dewdrop: b1300)

fire n b725 [fig. "passion": b1630] (verb use: b1200)

firelight n b725

flood n *too much water; also, gen. water* b725 [fig. use: b1350] (verb use: b1665)

ice n b725

mold n *as in "soil"* b725

icicle n b750

ash n *as in "cigarette ash"* b800 ["volcanic ash": b1670] (ashen: b1400)

cinder n b800

wax n *beeswax* b810 [other waxes: b1800] (verb use: b1380)

coal n *ember* b830 [the energy source: b1200]

iron n b830 (adj use: b725)

myrrh n *type of resin* b830

salt n b830 [fig. use: b1600; chemical sense: b1790]

sand n b830 ["grain of sand": b1600]

blaze n *fire* b895 ["outburst, display": b1470] (verb use: b1200)

dust n b900 [gen. "trash": b1730]

freshwater n b900 (adj use: b1530)

frost n b900 [obs. "ice": b1470 to 1500s] (verb use: b1635)

gold n b900 [the color: b1470]

grove n b900

lead n *the metal; things made*

Abbreviations Used in This Book

adj adjective • *adv* adverb • *Am* American • *arch.* archaic • *b* by (so that "b1700" means "by 1700") • *Brit* British • *conj* conjunction • *contr* contraction • *esp.* especially • *fig.* figurative • *gen.* general • *geo.* geography • *interj* interjection • *leg.* legal • *LME* Late Middle English • *lit.* literal • *ME* Middle English • *med.* medical • *mil.* military • *n* noun • *obs.* obsolete • *OE* Old English • *opp.* opposite • *phys.* physical • *prep* preposition • *pron* pronoun • *rel.* religion • *spec.* specific • *u* until • *var.* various • *v* verb ❧

of lead b900 [as in "pencil lead": b1830]

lime n *the powder* b900

mast n *forage on a forest floor* b900

night n *time of darkness* b900 ["the darkness itself": b1350]

ore n b900

pitch n *akin to tar* b900 [as in "pine pitch": b1450] (verb use: b1150)

rust n b900 (verb use: b1300)

shade n b900 (verb use: b1400)

shadow n b900 [fig. "darkness": b1150]

silver adj/n *the metal* b900

stone n *rock; gem* b900 ["what stones are made from": b1450]

stream n *lit. and fig.* b900 (verb use: b1300; streamlet: b1550)

tin n b900

water n/v b900

wild adj *describing plants and animals* b900 [describing people: b1350] (adv use: b1550)

wold n b900

brine n b1000 (verb use: b1555)

clay n b1000 ["mud"; "human material," as in "feet of clay": b1350]

copper n b1000

crystal n *type of mineral* b1000 [obs. type of ice: u1500s; type of glass: b1670; electronic sense: b1970] (adj use: b1450; crystallize: b1670)

gemstone n b1000 (gem: b1325)

gloaming n *twilight* b1000 (gloam: b1825)

high tide n b1000

margarite n *arch. pearl* b1000

ooze n *muck* b1000 ["act of oozing": b1730] (verb use: b1400)

quicksilver n b1000 (adj use: b1570)

saltwater adj b1000

shore n *coast* b1000

smoke n/v b1000 [fig.

"something that obscures": b1570; "steam": b1600]

stick n *piece of wood* b1000 ["tooled piece of wood": b1350; fig., as in "stick of gum": b1500; as in "hockey stick": b1700]

sunbeam n b1000

wildfire n b1000

seashell n b1100

spring n *water source* b1100

brimstone n *sulfur* b1125 [fig. "passion": b1630]

bark n *tree skin*

daylight n ["open space," as in "run for daylight": b1830]

gem n [fig. use: b1350] (gemstone: b1000)

pebble n

Plants

asp n *aspen* b700

birch n b700

bough n b700

dill n b700

fern n b700

hawthorn n b700

hazel n *the tree; the color* b700 (hazelnut: b900)

hemlock n b700

ivy n b700

mew n *type of gull* b700

mistletoe n b700

oak n b700 (adj use: b1300; oaken: b1395)

ash n *the tree* b725

blade n *gen. leaf* b725 [spec. to grass, etc.: b1470]

blossom n/v *young flower* b725 [as in "in blossom": b1350] (verb use: b1100)

sap n *as in "pine sap"* b750 (verb use: b1725)

hedge n b785 (verb use: b1400; hedgerow: b940)

box n *plant* b800

cluster n *pertaining to plants* b800 [pertaining to gen. things: b1450] (verb use: b1380)

ear n *as in "ear of corn"* b800

elder n *elderberry* b800

hock n *arch. type of plant, as in "hollyhock"* b800

mint n *as in "peppermint"* b800

plant n *young plant* b830 [modern sense: b1570; "factory": b1800; slang "infiltrator": b1830]

alder n b900

beech n b900

clover n b900

grass n b900

hazelnut n b900

leaf n b900 [as in "gold leaf," "table leaf": b1450] (verb use: b1615; leave v: b1350)

leech n b900 [fig. use: b1800]

malt n b900 (verb use: b1450)

maple n b900

nettle n *type of plant* b900 (verb use: b1470)

palm n *type of tree* b900 (palmetto: b1565; palmyra: b1700)

poppy n b900

red clover n b900

reed n b900

rind n b900

ripe adj b900 (verb use: b1150; ripen: b1470)

rose n b900

rush n *as in "bullrushes"* b900

rye n *type of grain* b900

sedge n *type of plant* b900

seed n b900 ["sperm": b1350] (verb use: b1400)

stem n b900 ["word root": b1670; fig., as in "pipe stem": b1700]

thistle n b900

thorn n *on plants* b900 [on animals: b1350] (verb use: b1450)

tree n b900 [arch. "wood": concurrent; obs. "something made of wood": b1450 to 1500s] (obs. adj use "made of wood": b1450)

turf n *sod, grass* b900

weed n b900 (verb use: b900)

willow n b900

wood n *tree composition* b900 [fig. "the composition of a person": b1600] (wood/wooden adj: b1540)

woodbine n *type of vine* b900

yarrow n *type of herb* b900

yew n b900

aloe n b950

twig n b950

holly n b960

moss n b975

acorn n b1000 ["all fruit": u1600s]

berry n b1000

blackberry n b1000

blow v *blossom* b1000 (noun use: b1710)

bramble n b1000

brier n *type of plant* b1000

bush n *shrub* b1000 ["bushland": b1660] (bushland: b1830)

cedar n b1000 ["cedar wood": b1350]

clove n *as in "clove of garlic"* b1000

cockle n *type of plant* b1000

cowslip n b1000

cypress n *type of tree* b1000

daisy n b1000

dock n *type of wheat* b1000

elm n b1000

foxglove n b1000

ginger n/adj b1000

hemp n b1000 [the fiber: b1350]

hull n *husk* b1000 (verb use: b1340)

leek n *type of plant* b1000

lily n b1000

linseed n b1000

madder n *type of herbs* b1000

mallow n *type of plant* b1000

marshmallow n *type of plant* b1000

nightshade n *type of poisonous plant* b1000

peony n *type of flower* b1000

periwinkle n *type of herb* b1000

pine n b1000

pine nut n b1000

shrub n b1000

stub n *tree stump* b1000 [as in "cigar stub," etc.: b1450; as in "check stub": b1900]

thicket n b1000

thorny adj b1000 [fig. "sticky": b1350]

yeast n b1000

walnut n b1050 [the tree: b1630]

fir n b1100

liverwort n *type of moss* b1100

gladiolus n (glad: b1925; gladiola: b1930)

gouts n *arch. akin to oats*

heather n

mulberry n

root n [fig. "source": b1350] (verb use: b1350)

wood n *forest* [obs. "a single tree": until ME] (wooded: b1605)

Animals

ape n b700 (verb use: b1635)

bass n b700

beetle n *the bug* b700

boar n *male pig* b700 [type of wild pig: b1350]

butterfly n b700

claw n b700 [obs. "hoof": u1600s] (verb use: b1000)

crow n *the bird* b700

finch n b700

flea n b700

fluke n *type of fish* b700

herring n b700

horse n b700

midge n *type of fly* b700

mouse n b700

nightingale n b700 [fig. "good singer": b1350]

wasp n b700 [fig. "annoying person": b1530]

feather n b725 (verb use: b1250)

fell n *hide, skin* b725

hive n b725

horn adj/n/v b725

hound n b725 ["hunting dog": b1130] (verb use: b1530)

worm n *arch. snake; var. types of worms* b725

bird n *spec. young bird* b750 [gen. "aviarian": b1350]

fish n b750

bleat v b800 (noun use: b1505)

calf n *young cow* b800 ["young of other animals": b1470; "iceberg portion": b1830]

cat n b800 [slang "dude," as in "hep cat": b1930] (catling: b1670)

cow n b800 [applied to non-bovines: b1730]

fly n b800

smelt n *type of fish* b800

snail n b800 [fig. "slug": b1600]

weevil n b800

ass n *the animal; a stupid person* b830

hawk n *the bird* b830 (verb use: b1350)

mule n *horse crossed with donkey* b830

neat n *a bovine* b830

mussel n b850

bear n b895

hide n *skin* b895 (verb use: b1770)

ant n b900

bee n *the insect* b900

cock n b900

comb n b900 ["honeycomb": b1350]

crop n b900

deer n *gen. animals; spec. doe, etc.* b900 [modern sense: b1400]

elk n b900

fowl n *bird* b900 ["domestic bird": b1350]

fox n b900

gnat n b900

goat n b900

hare n b900

hart n b900

hind n *female of red deer* b900

hornet n b900 [type of beetle: b1390]

kite n *type of bird* b900 [arch. "predatory person": b1570] (verb use: b1840)

lamb n *fig. and lit.* b900

lark n *type of bird* b900

louse n b900 [fig. use: b1670]

mane n b900 [applied to humans: b1450]

nest n *bird's home* b900 [gen. "animal's home": b1470] (verb use: b1150)

nit n *louse egg* b900

otter n b900

owl n b900 (owlet: b1545)

ox n b900 [fig. "clod": b1570]

ram n b900

raven n b900 (adj use: b1635)

roe n *doe* b900 (roe deer: b1000; roebuck: b1400)

rook n *type of bird* b900

seal n *sea lion* b900 (verb use: b1830)

sheep n b900

shell n b900 [on snails: b1470; on turtles: b1570]

shellfish n b900

shrew n b900

sow n b900 ["fat woman": b1550]

sparrow n b900

steed n b900

stork n b900

swallow n *type of bird* b900

swan n b900

swarm n *spec. to insects* b900 [gen. "multitude": b1450] (verb use: b1400)

swine n b900 [fig. use: b1350]

thrush n b900

tick n *type of arachnid* b900

tusk n b900

weasel n *lit. and fig.* b900

whale n/v b900 (obs. whale-fish: b1530 to 1700s)

whelp n b900 (verb use: b1300)

wolf n b900

wren n b900

bullock n *young bull; castrated bull* b905 (bull: b1200)

adder n b950

camel n b950

chicken n b950 [fig. "coward": b1630]

foal n b950 [arch. gen. "horse": b1350 to 1500s] (verb use: b1390)

moth n b950

beaver n b1000 [slang "female": b1970]

bill n *beak* b1000

bitch n *female dog* b1000

brood n *litter* b1000 (verb use: b1450; brooder: b1600; brood mare: b1825)

buck n *male deer* b1000 [obs. "male goat": u1500s; other male animals: b1700]

calve v b1000

capon n b1000

colt n b1000 [spec. to horses: b1400]

crab n *the crustacean* b1000

crane n b1000

crow v e.g., "cockadoodle-doo" b1000 ["boast": b1450] (noun use: b1200; obs. "crowd": b1350 to 1700s)

cud n b1000

cuttlefish n b1000

doe n b1000

drone n b1000 [applied to people: b1530; type of missile: b1970]

duck n b1000 (verb use: b1300; duckling: b1450)

dung n/v b1000

eel n b1000

erne n *type of eagle* b1000

ewe n b1000

fin n *as in "a fish's fin"* b1000

fleece n b1000

frog n b1000

gander n *male goose* b1000

goldfinch n b1000

goose n b1000 (gosling: b1400)

greyhound n b1000

hen n b1000

hoof n b1000

kipper n b1000

lobster n b1000

low v *moo* b1000 (noun use: b1550)

mite n *type of arachnid* b1000

neigh v *horse noise* b1000 (noun use: b1530)

nestle v *make a nest* b1000 ["settle in snugly": b1670]

pelican n b1000

rat n b1000 (ratling: b1900)

roe deer n b1000

silkworm n b1000

snake n b1000 [fig. "distrustful person": b1600] (verb use: b1600)

tiger n b1000

toad n b1000

turtle n *arch. turtledove* b1000

udder n b1000

yolk n b1000 [fig. "center": b1450]

dog n b1050 (dogess: b1770)

honeycomb n b1050 [obs. "honey": b1470 to 1500s] (verb use: b1725)

limpet n *type of sea creature* b1050

shad n *type of fish* b1050
bull n *bovine male* b1100 [gen. "male animal": b1470] (bullock: b905)
mare n *horse; female horse* b1100
starling n b1100
trout n b1100
dor n *obs. type of insect* [u1600s]
hog n
nest v *create a nest* ["fit snugly together": b1900] (nestle: b1000)
spider n
vixen n *female fox*

Weather

weather n b725
mist n b875 (verb use: b1000)
hail n b900 (verb use: b1100; hailstone: b1000)
rain n b900 (verb use: b1350; rainy: b1000)
rime n b900 (verb use: b1755; rime-frost: b1350)
snow n b900 (verb use: b1350)
storm n *lit. and fig.* b900 (verb use: b1670)
thunder n/v b900
wind n b900
wintry adj b900 (winterly: b1000)
shower n *as in "rain shower"* b950 (verb use: b1500)
hailstone n b1000 (hail: b900)
rainbow n b1000 [fig. "gamut": b1870]
rainwater n b1000
zephyr n *spec. wind* b1000 [gen. "breeze": b1615]

Heavens/Sky

moon n *our moon* b725 [gen. "planetary moon": b1670]
sun n *the star; sunlight* b725 [gen. "star": b1450]
heaven n b900
star n b900 ["any heavenly body": b1350]
welkin n *sky* b900
daystar n b1000
full moon n b1000
new moon n b1000
comet n b1100

lift n *sky, heavens* b1100
Saturn n

Energy

heat n b725 (verb use: b900)
tinder n b900
ember n b1000
firestone n b1100

Time

Sunday n b700
day n *daylight hours* b725 ["daylight": b1350]
harvest n *arch. autumn* b750
month n b750
midwinter n b830
morn n b830 (morning: b1250)
week n b880
afore adv/prep/conj *before* b900 (aforehand: b1450)
late adj *behind the time; slow; as in "late in the day"* b900 [as in "late in the Victorian era": b1450; as in "the late Mr. Smith": b1450] (adv use: b1150; later: b1300)
midnight n b900 [fig. use: b1600]
midsummer n b900
Saturday n b900
summer n b900 (adj use: b1400; verb use: b1450)
tide n *time, as in "eventide"* b900
time n b900 (adj use: b1715)
today adv *this day* b900 (noun use: b1535; adj use: b1970)
winter n b900 (verb use: b1400)
wintertide n b900 (wintertime: b1400)
year n b900
yesternight adv b900 (noun use: b1515)
day n *24 hours* b950 (obs. verb use "dawn": b1350 to 1500s)
even, eventide n *evening* b950 (evening "even arriving": b1000; evening "time of day": b1450)
Thursday n b950
Wednesday n b950
yesterday adv/n b950 (adj use: b1570)

midday n b975 [obs. "south": b1470 to 1600s]
November n b1000
ago adj/adv b1000 (adj use: b1300)
fortnight n b1000
Friday n b1000
Monday n b1000
sennight n *arch. a week* b1000
tonight adv b1000 [obs. "last night": concurrent] (noun use: b1350)
January n b1000
February n b1000
December n b1000
May n b1050
Tuesday n b1050
June n b1050
July n b1050
September n b1050
October n b1050
August n b1100
long n *as in "before long"* b1100 [as in "the long and the short of it": b1530]
twelvemonth n *year* b1100
April n b1100
fernyear n *obs. long ago* [u1700s]
ides n
to-morn adv/n *tomorrow*
yester adj (obs. noun use "yesterday": b1730 to 1800s)

Age/Aging

old adj b725 [as in "old friend": b1570] (ole: b1845)
young adj b900 ["younger": b1350]
youngling adj/n b900 (youngster: b1590; younker: b1515)
youth n *being young; young people* b900 ["one young person": b1350] (youthly: b1150; youthful: b1565; youthy: b1730)
childhood n b900
elder n *older person* b975 ["authority": b1450] (elder, eldest: b900; eld: b1000; elderly adj: b1615; eldress: b1640; elderly n: b1865)
eld n *old age* b1000 [obs. "the

elderly": u1500s; "times of old": b1450; "elder": b1800] (obs. verb use: b1150; arch. adj use: b1630)
young n *young person, young people* b1100 ["litter, offspring": b1350]
younger n *opp. of elder* b1100 (adj use: b1450)
forold v *arch. age*
years n *as in "wise beyond her years"*

Mathematics

fifteen n b725
fifty n b725
four n b725
ten n b725
thirty n b725
eighty n b830
eleven n b900
nine n b900
nought adj/adv/n *nothing* b900 ["zero": b1470]
one adj/n b900
seven n b900
six n b900
sixty n b900
thirteen n b900
thousand n b900
three n b900
twelve n b900
twenty n b900
two adj/n/prep b900
forty n b950
fourteen n b950
hundred n b950
eight n b1000
eighteen n b1000
five n b1000
nineteen n b1000
ninety adj/n b1000
naught n *zero* b1100 [obs. "evil": b1150 to 1600s]
score n *20* b1100
tenth n

Measurement

fathom n b725
mile n b800
elk n *arch. length longer than a yard* b900
furlong n b900
height n b900
hide n *unit of land measure, usually 120 acres* b900
length n b900

pound n *measure of weight* b900

stride n *length of a step* b900 ["the step itself": b1350; "striding": b1700] (verb use: b1350)

talent n *weight measure* b900

yard n *measurement, of varying lengths* b900 ["cubic yard": b1870]

acre n b975

foot n b1000

inch n b1000 (verb use: b1600)

weight n b1000 [fig. use: b1450]

longness n *arch. length*

speed n *velocity* ["machine setting": b1870]

The Body

belly n b700 [obs. "purse": OE only]

bladder n b700

body n b700 ["corpse": b1350]

bone n b700

arm n *the appendage; fig., as in "arm of the government"* b725 ["chair arm": b1670]

blood, bloody n, adj b725 ["bloodlines, kin": b1350] (verb use: b1635)

bosom n *lit. breast* b725 [fig. "intimate inner portion": b1350] (arch. verb use: b1605)

breast n *mammary gland; chest* b725 ["cut of meat": b1470]

foot n b725 [as in "foot of a hill": b1350; as in "foot of the bed": b1470]

head n b725

heart n b725 [fig. "core": b1570]

nail n *as in "tooth and nail"* b725

flesh n b800 [applied to fruit: b1600; as in "in the flesh": b1630] (fleshy: b1375; obs. fleshen "fleshy": b1470)

heel n b800 [on a sock, shoe: b1350]

hip n b800 (hipbone: b1200)

navel n b800

tail n b800 ["tail-like thing": b1350; buttocks: b1305; slang "genitals": b1450; slang "sex": b1870]

wart n b800 [fig. use: b1630]

finger n b825 (verb use: b1425; fingertip: b1845)

cheek n b830 ["buttock": b1600; "cheekiness": b1870]

gall n *bile* b830 ["gall bladder": b1200; fig. use: b1200]

hand n b830

mouth n b830 (verb use: b1350)

chin n b835 (chinbone: b1000)

back n b885 [gen. use: b1350]

bleed v *lose blood* b900 ["ooze": b1350; "sympathize": b1380]

ear n *for hearing* b900 [fig. "attention": b1350; as in "an ear for music": b1530]

eye n b900 [fig. "keep an eye on things": b1350] (verb use: b1500; eyeball: b1590)

fist n b900 (verb use: b1610)

gristle n b900

hair n b900

knee n b900

liver n b900

lock n *as in "lock of hair"* b900 ["little bit": b1350]

marrow n b900 [obs. applied to plants: u1700s; fig. "core": b1450]

neck n b900

nose n b900 ["front of ship, etc.": b1570]

rib n *as in "Adam's rib"* b900

shoulder n b900

sinew n b900 (sinewy: b1400)

thigh n *in people* b900 [in animals: b1350]

throat n b900 [gen. "passage": b1350] (throaty: b1645)

thumb n b900 [obs. "big toe": b1450 to 1600s]

toe n b900 [gen. "tip": b1450; as in "toe of a sock": b1450]

tongue n b900 [type of food: b1450]

tooth n b900 [fig., as in "gear tooth": b1450]

womb n b900 [obs. gen. "stomach": u1800s]

belch v b950 (noun use: b1530)

wrist n b950

ankle n b1000 (anklebone: b1400)

ass/arse n *buttocks* b1000 ["fool": b1470]

brain n b1000 [fig. "intelligence": b1350; slang "brainy person": b1970]

breastbone n b1000

brow n *eyebrow* b1000 [obs. "eyelash": b1150; "forehead": b1350]

buttock n b1000 (butt: b1470)

clot n b1000 (verb use: b1425; clod "clot": b1400)

elbow n b1000 [fig. use: b1600]

forehead n b1000

guts n b1000

ham n *arch. area behind the knee* b1000

lip n b1000 [as in "lip of a cup": b1450] (verb use: b1605)

lung n b1000

middle finger n b1000

midriff n b1000

nostril n b1000

ring finger n b1000

shin n b1000

shinbone n b1000

weapon n *slang penis* b1000

mamma n *breast, as in "mammary"* b1050

little finger n b1100

little toe n b1100

tit n *teat* b1100 ["breast": b1930] (titty: b1750)

jowl n *dewlap, jaw* ["head": b1450]

skin n *hide; epidermis* [gen. "outside layer": b1500]

sweat n [obs. "blood": u1500s; "sweating": b1350; as in "in a cold sweat": b1730]

tarse n *obs. penis* [u1700s]

Physical Description

comely adj b725

hunger n b725 [nonfood sense: b1470] (verb use: b830)

weary adj/v b725 ["wearing": b1350] (wearisome, weariless: b1450; weariful: b1475)

itch v/n b800 [fig. use: b1532]

nap v *snooze* b830 (noun use: b1355)

chill n b900 (verb use: b1175)

fair adj *as in "fair maiden"* b900

fat adj b900

swart n *swarthiness* b900

thirst n/v *lit.* b900 [fig. use: b1350] (thirsty: b950)

whole adj *unhurt, healthy* b900 [obs. "mentally healthy": u1500s; "complete, total": b1350]

wink v *as in "wink at a friend"* b900 [obs. "close eyes": b900 to 1800s; "blink": b1350] (noun use: b1530)

hungry adj b950 (hunger n: b725; hunger v: b830)

spit v *expectorate* b950 ["utter," as in "spit out": b1470; "hiss," as in "a cat spitting": b1670] (noun use: b1350)

asleep adj/adv b1000 ["numb": b1470]

athirst adj b1000

chew v b1000 (noun use: b1300)

hale adj b1000

hoarse adj b1000 (verb use: b1150; hoarsen: b1750)

lean adj *thin* b1000 ["meager": b1350; as in "lean meat": b1450; "streamlined": b1980] (noun use: b1450)

nimble adj *physically quick* b1000 ["mentally quick": b1600]

sallow adj b1000 (verb use: b1870)

swallow v *eat, drink* b1000 ["absorb, engulf": b1350; "work the throat to swal-

low": b1450; fig. "take lying down": b1600; "mum-
ble": b1800]

yell v b1000 (noun use:
b1400)

aswoon adj

fart v (noun use: b1400)

fnesen v *arch. sneeze*

kempt adj

ofhungered adj *obs. starved*
[u1500s]

reach v *obs. spit* [u1600s]

sneeze v (noun use: b1650)

snivel v

yex n *obs. sob, hiccup*
[u1600s]

Medicine

salve n b700

blind adj b725 [as in "blind
alley": b1350] (verb use:
b1100; adv use: b1780)

heal v b725 (health: b1000)

deaf adj b750 [fig. "unhearing": b1350; as in "tone
deaf": b1800] (arch. verb
use: b1450; deafen:
b1600)

halt adj *arch. lame* b900
(verb use: b830; noun use:
b1500)

lame adj *crippled* b900 [as in
"lame excuse": b1450]
(verb use: b1350)

qualm n *death, disease* b900

sick adj *phys. sense* b900
[mental sense: b1350]
(sicken: b1300; sickening:
b1715)

wound n b900

ail v b950 (ailment: b1710)

cripple n b950 (adj use:
b1300; verb use: b1400)

balsam n *balm* b1000

boil n *skin inflammation*
b1000

dumb adj *unable to speak*
b1000 ["stupid": b1350]
(verb use: b1610)

fever n b1000 [fig. use:
b1350] (verb use: b1610;
feverish, feverous: b1400)

headache n b1000

heartache n b1000 [fig. use:
b1605]

plaster n b1000 [type of
molding material: b1285;

type of building material:
b1450] (verb use: b1325)

pock n *inflammation* b1000
["pockmark caused by a
pock": b1900] (verb use:
b1845; pox: b1470; pock-
mark: b1670]

sickness n b1000

stammer n/v b1000

teen n *obs. injury* b1000
[u1600s] (verb use
"annoy": b1150)

bedridden adj b1100

sore n b1100 [var. obs.
meanings of gen. pain:
u1600s]

swathe v *bandage* b1100

toothache n b1100

canker n (verb use: b1400;
canker sore: b1910)

leech n *physician* (verb use
"cure": b1350)

paralysis n [fig. use: b1900]
(paralyze: b1805)

wind n *internal gas*

Everyday Life

bed n b700 (verb use:
b1100)

bowl n b700

chest n *type of furniture, storage* b700

comb n b700 (verb use:
b1400)

dish n b700 (verb use:
b1395)

bath n *instance of bathing*
b725 (bathe: b900)

candle n b725

lave v *wash, bathe* b900

lock n *as in "door lock"* b900
(verb use: b1400)

oven n b900

pillow n b900

settle n *type of seat* b900
(obs. verb use: b1000 to
1600s)

sew v b900

shave v b900 ["groom the
face": b1350]

taper n *type of candle* b900
["something that tapers":
b1600; "tapering": b1800]
(adj use: b1450)

well n *as in "water well"*
b900 [as in "oil well,"
"stairwell": b1700]

wick n *as in "candlewick"*
b900

gleed n *arch. ember* b950

whistle n *noisemaker* b950
[type of sound: b1450]
(verb use: b1100)

candlestick n b970

bench n b1000

box n *as in "container"*
b1000 (verb use: b1450)

bridge n/v *the structure*
b1000 ["part of nose":
b1470; "ship's control
room": b1870]

can n *container* b1000 [slang
"toilet": b1930; slang
"buttocks": b1970] (verb
use: b1865)

candlelight n b1000

cradle n b1000 [fig. "birthplace": b1600] (verb use:
b1470)

crock n *container* b1000

cup n b1000 ["cupful":
b1450; as in "loving cup":
b1670]

feather bed n b1000

leather, leathern n b1000

sack n *bag* b1000 (verb use:
b1305)

soap n b1000 (verb use:
b1570)

sponge n b1000 (verb use:
b1400)

scuttle n *type of platter* b1050
[obs. "dish": b1050 to
1700s; gen. basket: b1470]

black n *as in "boot black"*
b1100

pot n *vessel* b1100 [used
spec. in cooking: b1350]

purse n b1100 [obs. gen.
"bag": b1350 to 1800s;
obs. "scrotum": b1350 to
1700s; "pocketbook":
b1960; "prize": b1630]

tap n/v *spigot* b1100

tray n b1100

chalice n b1105

broom n b1125 [type of
plant: b700] (verb use:
b1840; broomstick:
b1685]

horn n *type of drinking container*

kettle n [geo. sense: b1870]

Shelter/Housing

den n b725 [fig., as in "den
of thieves": b1350; type of
room: b1800]

floor n b725 [as in "3rd-floor
apartment": b1470; as in
"floor of the Senate":
b1770; fig. "minimum":
b1970]

hearth n b725

home n b725

house n b725 (verb use:
b1000)

wall n b725 [fig. "obstacle":
b1350; "side": b1600]
(verb use: b1150)

yard n *obs. house* b725

nail n *as in "roofing nail"*
b800 (verb use: b950)

cot n *related to cottage* b895

catacomb n b900

door n b900 ["doorway":
b1450]

gate n b900

glass n b900 [as in "drinking
glass": b1350]

guest n b900 [obs.
"stranger": u1500s]

hall n *as in "concert hall"*
b900

lair n b900

lee n *protection* b900 ["the
protected side": b1450]
(adj use: b1450)

rafter n b900

roof n b900 (verb use:
b1470)

sill n b900

solar n *room in medieval
house* b900

stall n *cell* b900 [obs. gen.
"place": u1600s] (verb
use: b1400)

tile n b900 [type of game
piece: b1870] (verb use:
b1400)

timber n *building materials;
wood* b900 ["natural
trees": b1800; "personal
stature": b1630]

barn n *housing grains, etc.*
b950 [housing animals
and implements: b1700]

homestead n b975 [gen.
"home": b975] (verb use:
b1875]

castle n b1000

eaves n b1000 ["forest edge": b895]
guesthouse n b1000
inn n *gen. dwelling* b1000 ["student residence": b1200; "hotel": b1470]
kitchen n b1000 ["cuisine": b1700]
pile n *column* b1000 [obs. "arrow": until late ME] (verb use: b1450)
post n *timber* b1000 [as in "sign post": b1350]
stair n *stairway* b1000 ["individual stair": b1470] (stairstep: b1830)
steeple n b1000
haven n *safe place for ships* b1050 [gen. use: b1350]
hatch n *type of door* b1100
summerhouse n b1100
tower n b1100
cell n *small room* [obs. "closet": b1350 to 1500s]
hall n *mansion*
pier n *piering* ["landing": b1450]
pound n *compound* (verb use: b1450)

Drink

beer n b725
brew v b900 [fig. "engender": b1350] (noun use: b1510; brewery: b1170; brewage: b1545)
drench n *type of drink or potion* b900
drink v/n b900 ["toast," "drink alcohol": b1350; fig., as in "drink in": b1350]
mead n *type of drink* b900
milk n b900 (verb use: b975)
must n *new wine* b900
wine n *from grapes* b900
ale n b940
mash n *as in "sourmash"* [gen. use: b1580]

Food

cress n b700
fennel n b700
garlic n b700
fare n b725
feed v b725
corn n *grain* b750 ["maize": b1610]

cheese n b800
honey n b830
bake v b895 [fig. "cook by heat," as in "bake in the sun": b1450]
apple n b900
cumin n b900
eat v b900 [as in "this food eats good": b1600]
manna n b900 [fig. use: b1350]
meal n *a sitting to eat; ground grain* b900
meal n *ground grain* b900
meat n *gen. food* b900 [e.g., beef, etc.: b1350; as in "nut meat": b1450] (verb use "eat": b1450; verb use "feed": b1570)
nut n b900
pease n *arch. pea* b900 (peasecod "peapod": b1375)
plum n b900 [fig. "prize": b1830; the color: b1900]
sup v *sip* b900
wheat n b900
whey n b900
bean n b950 [applied to coffee, etc.: b1450; slang "head": b1930]
bread n b950 [slang "money": b1970]
crumb n b975 (verb use: b1400)
beet n b1000
broth n b1000
butter n b1000 (verb use: b1450)
dough n b1000
food n *food and drink* b1000 [obs. fig. "sustenance": u1600s; solid food: b1630]
jowl n *as in "hog jowls"* b1000
pear n b1000
pepper n/v b1000
peppercorn adj/n b1000
radish n b1000
raw adj *uncooked* b1000 ["natural": b1350; "unrefined": b1450; "untrained": b1500]
spit n b1000
strawberry n b1000
black pepper n b1100
eat, eats n b1100

fast v *decline to eat* b1100 (noun use: b1200)
parsley n b1100
salt v *preserve* b1100 [fig. "store": b1870]
white n *as in "egg white"* b1100
asparagus n
sweetmeat n

Agriculture/ Food-Gathering

bridle n b700 (verb use: b900)
fold n *as in "a fold of sheep"* b700 (verb use: b1300)
wain n *type of cart* b725
byre n *(Brit) cow barn* b800
mow n *haystack* b800
weedhook n b800
hay n b830 (verb use: b1560)
plant v *start a plant* b830 [fig., as in "plant an idea": b1450; as in "plant your feet": b1730; as in "plant a kiss": b1830] (noun use: b1570; plantation "planting": b1450)
heifer n b900
herd n *herder* b900
oat n b900
orchard n b900 (orchardist: b1795)
reap v b900 [fig. use: b1350] (obs. noun use: u1600s)
share n *plowshare* b900
thresh v b900
wether n b900
winnow v *applied to wheat* b900 [gen. use: b1450]
mill n b950 [as in "textile mill": b1470] (verb use: b1570)
straw n *dried grasses* b950 [type of color: b1600; "drinking device": b1870]
wean v b960 (weanling: b1535)
barley n b970
chaff n *as in "wheat and chaff"* b1000 [fig. "waste": b1450]
cole n *crop plants* b1000
cowherd n b1000
crib n *as in "corn crib"* b1000 (verb use: b1605)

fishnet n b1000
fodder n b1000 [obs. gen. "food": u1600s]
goatherd n b1000
graze v *eat grass, etc.* b1000
grist n b1000
halter n b1000
hawker n *hawkhandler* b1000
herd n *group* b1000 (verb use: b1390; herder: b1330; herdsman: b1470; herdboy: b1800; herdswoman: b1830)
hunt v b1000 [fig. use: b1350] (noun use: b1375)
seedtime n b1000
sheepfold n b1000
stud, studhorse n b1000 [sexual man: b1895]
sty n *pen* b1000 (verb use: b1150)
shepherd n b1050 (verb use: b1730; shepherdess: b1400; sheepherder: b1875)
roost n b1100 (verb use: b1530)
snare n *type of trap* b1100 (verb use: b1395)
swineherd n b1100
weed v *remove weeds* b1100 [fig., as in "weed out": b1450]
gardener n b1130 (garden: b1580)
earth n *arch. plowing*

Cloth/Clothing

hood n *type of headgear* b700 (verb use: b1200)
warp, woof n b725
web n/v *woven cloth; woven clothing* b725
cloth n *piece of cloth, as in "washcloth"* b800 ["gen. cloth": b1450]
clothes n b800
hat n b800
sock n *stocking* b800 [type of shoe: b1350]
glove n b900
lap n *flap, as in "earlap"* b900
linen adj b900 (noun use: b1350)
pall n *type of cloth* b900 [fig. "gloom": b1450] (verb use: b1450)

ring n *as in "wedding ring"* b900

sheet n *large cloth* b900 [spec. to bedding: b1350]

shoe n b900 [on horses n/v: b1350] (verb use: b1150)

silk n *type of fiber, cloth* b900 ["jockey's gear": b1900]

sock n b900

thread n b900 (verb use: b1400)

wear v *as in "wear a coat"* b900 (noun use: b1450)

weave v b900 [fig. use: b1450]

weed n b900 (weeds: b1595)

wool n b900 ["clothing made of wool": b1350] (woolen adj: b1050; woolen n: b1350)

clothe v b950

sleeve n b950

cowl n b965

belt n b1000 [as in "fan belt": b1800] (verb use: b1500)

earlap n b1000

felt n b1000

girdle n b1000 ["corset": b1930]

seam n b1000 [geo. sense: b1600] (verb use: b1585; seamless: b1485)

smock n *type of undergarment* b1000 [type of overgarment: b1930]

yarn n *as in "knitting yarn"* b1000

hose n b1100 (hosiery: b1790)

shirt n b1100

crown n *type of headwear; championship* b1115 ["fig. royalty": b1450] (verb use: b1200)

mantle n *type of cloak, or hood*

overslop n *type of loose garment*

tunic n

Fashion/Style

beard n b830

earring n b1000

fair n *obs. beauty* b1100 [u1600s]

wear v *as in "wear your hair long"* b1125

smicker adj *obs. elegant* [u1600s]

Tools

auger n b700

awl n b700

hook n b700

hurdle n b725 [sports sense: b1835; fig. use: b1930]

saddle n/v b725

cart n b800 [obs. "chariot": u1600s] (verb use: b1390)

fan n *device for winnowing grain* b800 (verb use: b1425)

adz n b830

ax/axe n b830 (verb use: b1680)

anchor n b900 [fig. sense: b1470] (verb use: b1200)

anvil n b900

beetle n *hammering instrument* b900

bellows n b900

crutch n b900 [fig. use: b1600] (verb use: b1645)

file n *as in "nail file"* b900 (verb use: b1200)

goad n b900 (verb use: b1580)

key n *lit. and fig. something that unlocks* b900

kiln n b900

mast n *as in "a ship's mast"* b900

mattock n *type of tool* b900

net n *as in "butterfly net"* b900 [as in "hair net": b1470; "network": b1600] (verb use: b1470)

pan n *type of cooking device* b900 [as in "brain pan": b1350]

rake n *as in "leaf rake"* b900 [types of similar tools: b1570] (verb use: b1300)

rope n b900 (verb use: b1350)

scythe n b900

shovel n b900 (verb use: b1500)

sieve n b900 (verb use: b1600)

spade n b900 (verb use: b1650)

spindle n b900

spur n *lit. "horse prod"* b900 ["animal claw": b1470; as

in "railroad spur": b1870] (verb use: b1300)

staff n *type of stick* b900

staple n *wood fastener* b900 ["paper fastener": b1870] (verb use: b1400)

steel n b900

stud n *type of building device* b900

tie n *rope* b900

tine n b900

tongs n b900 (tong v: b1870)

tool n *lit. and fig.* b900 ["weapon," "penis": b1450] (verb use: b1815)

twine n b900 (verb use: b1300)

wedge n b900 [fig. use: b1600] (verb use: b1425)

wheel n b900 (verb use: b1300)

whetstone n b900

yoke n/v b900

quern n *hand-tool for grinding grain* b950

seine n *type of fishnet* b950

crank n b1000 (verb use: b1900)

distaff n b1000 ["women": b1500] (adj use: b1600)

fork n *pitchfork* b1000 [eating utensil: b1470]

hammer n b1000 (verb use: b1390)

hand ax n b1000

hasp n b1000

ladder n b1000 [fig. "hierarchy": b1350]

ladle n b1000 (verb use: b1570)

line n *rope* b1000

mill wheel n b1000

mortar n *as in "mortar and pestle"* b1000

pail n b1000

rung n b1000

saw n b1000 (verb use: b1300)

shackle n b1000 [fig. use: b1350] (verb use: b1470)

sickle n b1000 (adj use: b1690)

sledge n b1000 (verb use: b1655)

millstone n b1050

reel n *as in "rod and reel"*

b1050 [on fishing rods: b1730] (verb use: b1400)

winch n b1050 (verb use: b1530)

coulter n b1100

knife n b1100 [as in "under the knife": b1900] (verb use: b1865)

pin n *as in "linchpin"* b1100 ["metal pin; type of jewelry": b1350; used in bowling: b1600; used in golf: b1930] (verb use: b1400)

shave n b1100

shear n b1100

spittle n *small spade* b1100

stay n *buttress, support* b1100

vane n *as in "weather vane"* b1100

bit n *as in "drill bit"* b1125

Travel/Transportation

boat n *small boat* b725 [gen. "water vessel": b1600; "gravy container": b1700]

fly v *as in "fly through the sky"* b725 [fig. use: b1350] (noun use: b1450)

helm n *as in "helm of boat"* b830

axle n b900

errand n *type of journey* b900 ["reason for the journey": b1350]

flight n *flying* b900 ["fleeing": b1200] (verb use: b1875)

highway n b900

lode n *road* b900 ["vein of ore": b1605]

oar n b900

path n b900 (obs. verb use "travel a path": u1800s; pathway: b1540)

port n *as in "seaport"* b900 [obs. "town": concurrent]

ride v b900 (noun use: b1760)

sail n/v b900

seaman n b900

ship n b900

street n b900 (adj use: b1500)

row v *as in "row a boat"* b950 (noun use: b1835)

hulk n *type of ship* b1000

["huge person": b1400; "rotting ship": b1675]

lane n *path, street* b1000 [as in "shipping lane": b1870; as in "fast lane": b1630]

seaway n b1000

steersman n b1000

toll n *passage fee* b1000 [fig. "cost": b1450] (verb use: b1400)

wayfaring adj *arch. traveling* b1000

wharf n b1050

ferry v b1100 (noun use: b1350)

shipwreck n b1100 (verb use: b1590)

Emotions/ Characteristics

bereave v b725

blithe adj *carefree* b725 ["careless": b1930] (blithesome: b1725)

brook v *tolerate* b725

care n *as in "cares and woes"* b725 [obs. "grief": b900; as in "health care": b1475] (verb use: b900)

fear n b725 [obs. "danger": b900] (verb use: b1390)

mood n *as in "bad mood"* b725

moody adj *obs. brave* b725 [u1700s]

tear n/v *in crying* b725 [fig. use: b1350] (teary: b1375)

eerie adj *fearful* b885 ["causing fear": b1795]

bold adj *courageous* b895 ["forward": b1350]

fright n b900 ["something frightful": b1670] (verb use: b1100; frighten: b1670)

glad adj b900 [obs. "bright": u1400s] (gladful: b1350; gladsome: b1375)

goodwill n b900

greedy adj b900 (greed: b1610)

greet v *lament* b900

hate n b900 (verb use: b1100; hatred: b1175)

laugh v b900 (noun use: b1690; laughable: b1700;

laughsome, laughworthy: b1630)

laughter n b900

long v *yearn* b900 (longing: b1000)

merry adj b900 (verb use: b1150; merriness: b1350; merriment: b1590)

rathe adj *eager* b900 ["early": b1350] (rather "sooner": b900)

shame n b900 (verb use: b1150)

shamefast adj *shy* b900 [obs. "ashamed": b1350 to 1600s]

shameless adj b900 (shameful: b1300)

smirk v b900 (noun use: b1560)

soothfast adj *truthful* b900 (soothing: b1600)

sorrow n/v b900

sorry adj *remorseful, apologetic* b900 ["sorrow-making, pitiful": b1350; as in "feel sorry for": b1470]

thank, thanks n/v b900 [obs. "nice thoughts": u1600]

thankful adj *giving thanks* b900 [obs. "warranting gratitude": u1600s] (thankless: b1470)

unfriendly adj b900

weep v b900 (obs. noun use: b1350 to 1500s)

wrath n b900 (obs. verb use: u1800s; adj use: b1535; wrathful: b1350)

wroth adj *wrathful* b900

yearn v b900 ["be compassionate": b1570]

true adj *loyal, true-blue* b900 ["accurate, not false": b1350; "phys. straight, square": b1450; as in "true to her word": b1570] (truth: b1350)

afear, afeared v, adj b1000

affright adj *frightened* b1000 (verb use: b1470; noun use: b1600)

ashamed adj b1000

bliss n b1000

callow adj b1000 ["inexperienced": b1580]

childish adj *childlike* b1000 ["immature": b1450]

(childly: b900; childlike: b1590)

chirk v *cheer* b1000

doughty adj *arch. brave* b1000

dream n *arch. joy* b1000

gast v *arch. frighten* b1000 (obs. gastness: b1400 to 1600s)

grin v b1000 ["display teeth in anger": b1000] (noun use: b1670)

guilt n *being guilty* b1000 [obs. "the act producing the guilt": u1400s; emotional sense: b1700]

pride n *vanity* b1000 ["self-esteem," "arrogance," "object of pride," "ostentation": b1350; as in "take pride in": b1600] (verb use: b1300; proud: concurrent; prideful: b1500)

proud adj *self-confident* b1000 ["taking pride": b1350; "swollen": b1450; "lustful": b1600] (pride: concurrent)

rank adj *obs. arrogant* b1000 [u1500s]

soft adj *calm, compassionate* b1000

untrue adj *disloyal* b1050 (arch. untruth: b1150)

dread v b1100 (noun use: b1350; adj use: b1450)

glad v *arch. gladden* b1100 [obs. "be glad": u1600s]

heart v *hearten* b1100 (hearten: b1530)

like v *appreciate* b1100 [arch. "please," "suit": b900]

uncouth adj *crude* b1100 [obs. "unknown": b900 to 1600s; obs. "ignorant": b1350 to 1600s; "clumsy": b1530; applied to language, etc.: b1700]

awful adj *inspiring terror, wonder* ["majestic": b1670; "bad": b1830]

bield n *obs. boldness* [u1400s]

melt n *obs. succumb to grief* [u1600s]

sloth n *laziness* (slothful: b1400)

weak adj *weak-willed* [phys. weak: b1350; weak-

minded: b1450] (obs. verb use: b1370 to 1800s; weaken: b1380)

yommer adj *obs. sad*

Thoughts/Perception/ The Mind

forget v b725

mind n b725

ween v *arch. imagine, suppose, think* b725

foresee v b900 [obs. "prepare for": u1600s] (foresight: b1300; foreseeable: b1805)

mad adj *crazed* b900 [obs. "maddening": b1570 to 1600s; as in "I'm mad about ice cream": b1350]

quick adj *mentally fast* b900 [arch. "alive": b1150; "physically fast": b1350]

slow adj *mentally dull* b900 ["not quick to accomplish something": b1350; "unhurried," "moving slowly": b1470]

sweven n *arch. dream* b900

think v *cogitate; conceive; consider; remember; believe* b900 ["picture, imagine"; opine: b1350] (noun use: b1835)

thought n *act of thinking* b900 ["spec. idea": b1350]

trow n/v *arch. believe, think* b900

understand v b900

unwise, unwisdom adj, n b900

ware adj/v/n *arch. aware/beware/wariness* b900

will n *pleasure; intention; determination; choice* b900

will v *express will* b900 (willful: b1200)

wisdom, wise n, adj b900

wise adj b900

wit n/v *arch. sanity; the mind itself; arch. know, learn* b900 [obs. "skill": u1700s]

witness n *obs. wisdom* b950 [u1400s]

brainsick adj *crazy* b1000

con v *obs. know; express* b1000 [u1600s]

mindless adj b1000

understanding n b1050 ["in-

telligence": b1450;
"agreement": b1830;
"compassion": b1870] (adj
use: b1300)

aware adj b1100 [obs. "careful": b1150 to 1800s]

wonder v *express wonder*
b1100 (adj use: b1200)

acknow v *arch. know*

foresay v *arch. predict*

forstand v *obs. understand*
[u1800s]

read v *obs. think* [u1700s]

unwares adj *arch. unawares*

willing adj

Love/Romance/Sex

banns n *public announcement
of proposed marriage* b550

bride n b725 (obs. verb use
"marry": b1600; bride-
groom: b750)

bridegroom n b750 (bride:
b725)

darling n *loved one* b900 (adj
use: b1510)

kiss n/v b900

lief adj *dear, beloved* b900

love n/v b900

lovely adj *lovable* b900 [obs.
"loving": u1600s; obs.
"passionate": b1450 to
1500s; "attractive":
b1350] (noun use: b1655)

lust n b900 [obs. gen. "pleasure": u1600s; obs. gen.
"affinity": u1500s] (gen.
verb use: b1200; verb use,
sexual sense: b1530)

wed v *marry; enter an agreement* b900 ["give the bride
away": b1450; fig. "joint":
b1830]

wedding n *being wed* b900
[type of ceremony: b1225]

wive v *marry* b900

breed v *conceive and bear*
b1000 ["create hybrids":
b1470; "be pregnant":
b1630] (noun use: b1465)

lovesome adj *lovable* b1000
["loving": b1350]

woo v b1050 [gen. use:
b1450] (noun use: b1970)

bridal n b1075 (adj use:
b1300)

whore n b1100 (verb use:
b1585; whoredom: b1175;

whorehouse: b1350;
whoremaster: b1400;
whoremonger: b1530)

cuckold n (verb use: b1590)

empty adj *arch. not married*

eunuch n [fig. use: b1600]

sleep together/sleep with v

true love n (truelove "sweetheart": b1350)

wife n (obs. verb use: b1450
to 1700s)

Family/Relations/
Friends

brother n *lit. and fig.* b715

bairn n *child* b725

daughter n b725 (adj use:
b1615)

mother n *mom* b725 (verb
use: b1545)

child n *infant; son or daughter*
b750 [fig., as in "a child of
the '60s": b1350]

father n b825 (verb use:
b1425)

friend n b900 (obs. adj use:
b1470 to 1600s; verb use:
b1300)

friendly adj b900 (noun use:
b1865; obs. friend adj:
b1470 to 1600s; friend-
like: b1570)

godson n b900 (goddaughter: b1050; godchild:
b1225)

kin n *relatives; descendents;
arch. single relative* b900
(adj use: b1600; kinsman:
b1150; kinswoman:
b1400; kinsfolk: b1475;
kinfolk: b1875)

kith n b900 [obs. "things
known": until LME; obs.
"home": u1500s; obs.
"conventions of behav-
ior": b1450 to 1800s]

sib adj/n *kin* b900

sister n b900 (adj use, as in
"sister city": b1670; sis-
terly: b1580)

son n b900

**stepdaughter, stepson, step-
father, stepmother** n b900
(stepchild: b1000; step-
brother, stepsister: b1450;
stepparent: b1890)

team n (Am) *arch. descendents* b905

offspring n *gen. descendents*
b950 ["a spec. descen-
dent": b1500]

fere n *companion* b1000
["mate, spouse": b1350]

fosterling n *foster child* b1000

godfather n b1000 (godparent: b1865)

godmother n b1000

fellow n *partner* b1020
["equal": b1350; "fella":
b1450]

goddaughter n b1050 (godson: b900; godchild:
b1225)

brethren n b1100

flesh and blood n b1100

company n *companionship;
group, as in "company of
soldiers"* [obs. "inter-
course": u1600s; "guests":
b1450; "commercial en-
terprise": b1570]

flesh n *as in "flesh and blood"*

gadling n *obs. friend*

kind n *arch. ancestry; place of
ancestry; kin* [obs. "gen-
der": u1500s; obs. "se-
men": b1450 to 1500s]

kinsman n (kin: b900; kinswoman: b1400; kinspeo-
ple: b1800)

Holidays

yule n b900

Allhallows n b1000

Allhallowmas n b1100

Christmas n b1100

Games/Fun/Leisure

game n *fun* b725

play n *opp. of work; games*
b725 ["the playing of a
game": b1350; fig., as in
"play of light on water":
b1570] (verb use: b830;
playful: b1250)

puck n b1000 (puckish:
b1875)

top n *type of toy*

Sports

angle n *fishhook* b900 (verb
use: b1450; angler: b1555;
angleworm: b1835)

links n *golf course* b1100

wrestle v b1100 [fig. use:
b1350]

Professions/Duties

cook n b700 (verb use:
b1390; cooker "cook":
b1870)

smith n/v b725 (smithy:
b1150; smithery: b1615)

chapman n *peddler* b900 (obs.
chapwoman: b1450 to
1800s)

follower n *servant* b900 ["disciple": b1350]

steward n *attendant* b900 [as
in "shop steward": b1350]
(verb use: b1625; stewardess: b1635)

wright n b900

monger n b975 (verb use:
b1800)

fuller n *cloth fuller* b1000

goldsmith n b1000

knave n *arch. servant* b1000
[obs. "boy": u1800s; "rascal": b1350]

landlord n b1000 (landlady:
b1640)

seamster n b1000 (seamstress: b1600)

silversmith n b1000

tanner n b1000

tapster n *bartender* b1000

wainwright n b1000

potter n b1100

shipwright n b1100

webster n *arch. weaver* b1100

clerk n (verb use: b1555)

graver n *engraver*

Business/Commerce/
Selling

sell v b900 [obs. "give": until ME]

business n *profession* b950
[obs. "anxiety": b950 to
1500s; obs. "busy-ness":
b1350 to 1700s; "task":
b1400]

alehouse n b1000

buy v b1000 [slang "accept":
b1930] (noun use: b1880)

guild n b1000

guild hall n b1000

pennyworth n *bargain* b1000

ware/wares n *merchandise*

b1000 [slang "genitals": b1450 to 1700s]

sale n *act of selling* b1050 ["sales event": b1700; "short-term discounts": b1870] (salable: b1530)

cheap v *var. meanings of "deal, barter"* [u1500s]

market n *commercial transactions* ["place for commercial transactions": b1350]

The Workplace

chare n *chore* b900

swink v *arch. work hard* b900

work n *work done; work to do* b900

workman n *laborer* b900 ["skilled worker": b1500] (workman: b1530)

hireling n b1000

play v *arch. work, be busy*

staff n *group of assistants* ["worker pool": b1870] (verb use: b1860)

Finances/Money

earn v b900 [fig., as in "earn a nickname": b1600]

penny n b900

rich adj *wealthy* b900 [obs. "great, powerful": u1500s] (riches: b1225)

shilling n b900

farthing n b950

scot-free adj *originally "tax-free"* b1070

worth n b1100 [applied to people: b1600]

gripple adj *arch. penurious*

mark n *English, Scottish monetary* [German unit: b1350]

scot n *type of tax*

wergild n *arch. monetary worth of a person*

Language and Speaking

speak v *talk; converse* b900 ["indicate relevance," as in "speak to a need": b1570; "give a speech": b1600]

speech n b900 (verb use: b1670)

word n *speech; single word* b900 (arch. verb use: b1300)

saw n *as in "old saw"* b950 [obs. gen. "speech": b950 to 1600s]

whisper v *speak quietly* b950 [gen. "make quiet sounds": b1530] (noun use: b1595)

byword n b1050

curse n *cuss* b1050 (cursed: b1450)

curse n/v *oath* b1050

quoth v b1100

wordy adj b1100

rune n

tongue n *a language; gen. speech*

Contractions

'em pron b1100

Literature/Writing

work v *write* (noun use: b1350)

book n b725

epistle n b900

meter n *as in "musical meter"* b900

read v b900 (adj use: b1350; noun use: b1825)

verse n *as in "a verse of a poem"* b900 [as in "a verse of a song," "gen. poetry": b1350] (verb use: b1150; versify, versifier: b1400; versification: b1605)

writ n *something written* b900

write v b900 [obs. "draw": u1500s; used in music: b1700]

scop n *OE bard, poet* b1100

foot n *poetic beat*

Performing Arts

play n *stage presentation* (verb use "perform a play": b1350; verb use, as in "play a part": b1450)

Music

harp n b725 (verb use: b1100; mouth harp: b1900)

cymbal n b825

horn n b830

anthem n b900

gleeman n *roving minstrel* b900

sing v b900 (singer: b1350)

song n b900

fiddle n b1000 (verb use: b1380)

organ n *gen. musical instrument* b1000 [spec. "type of keyboard instrument": b1325] (organist: b1595)

pipe n/v b1000 (pipes "vocal cords": b1600)

piper n b1000

songster n b1000 (songstress: b1705)

play v *as in "play an instrument"* [as in "play the radio": b1930]

Education

learn v *as in "learn the alphabet"* b900 [as in "learn bad news": b1350; as in "learn you some tricks": b1350]

school n *schooling* b900 ["school building": b1870] (verb use: b1450)

teach v *educate, show, demonstrate* b900 (teacher: b1300)

lore n *teachings* b950 [obs. "philosophy, religion": u1500s; "advice": b1350; as in "folklore": b1350]

clerk n *arch. scholar* b975

scholar n *student* b1000 ["learned person": b1300]

Religion

Christ n b675

hell n b725 [fig. use: b1350] (hades: b1600)

holy adj b725

church adj/n b750 (verb use: b1400)

minster n *type of church* b750

Satan n b750 (satanical: b1550; satanic: b1670)

devil n *demon* b800 ["Satan": b1200]

bishop n b830

cherub n *type of angel* b830 ["baby": b1570]

offer v *make an offering* b830 ["offer to give": b1420; "attempt": b1570; "propose": b1600] (noun use: b1450; offering: b1000)

temple n *place of worship* b830 ["synagogue":

b1600; "Mormon church": b1870]

archbishop n b850

abbot n b900

apostle n b900 (obs. apostless: b1470 to 1800s)

canon n b900 ["list of saints": b1730]

christen v *convert to Christianity* b900 ["baptize": b1350; "commemorate a beginning": b1450]

deacon n b900 (deaconess: b1450)

disciple n b900 [gen. use: b1350] (verb use: b1600)

Easter n b900 [obs. "Passover": u1600s] (Eastertide: b1100)

god n b900 (verb use: b1600; goddess: b1400)

ground n *God, soul* b900

hallow v b900

handbook n b900 [gen. use: b1815]

holiness n b900 [form of address: b1470]

Holy Ghost n b900 (holy spirit: b1400)

holy water n b900

hymnbook n b900 (hymnal: b1500; hymnary: b1890)

litany n b900 [fig. use: b1450]

mass n b900

monk n *type of religious figure* b900 (monkery: b1540)

nun n b900

pope n b900

priest n b900 (priestess: b1695)

psalm n b900 (psalmody: b1350; psalmist: b1485)

rood n *arch. type of crucifix* b900

Sabbath n *in Judaism* b900 [in Christianity: b1450; in Islam: b1630]

seraphim n *type of angel* b900 (seraph: b1150)

angel n b950 ["good person": b1600; "theatrical financer": b1900]

bless v b950 (blessing: b830; blessed: b1175)

gospel n b950 [fig. use: b1350]

holy day n b950

advent n *Christmas season* b965 [gen. use: b1770]

clerk n *cleric* b975

dip v *baptize* b975

cross n *symbol of Christianity* b985 ["form of punishment": b1350; secular sense: b1450] (verb use: b1350)

altar n b1000

archangel n b1000

archdeacon n b1000

believe v *have faith* b1000 ["presume as true": b1350] (belief: b1200; believable: b1400)

creed n b1000 [gen. use: b1570]

doomsday n b1000

evensong n b1000

exodus n b1000 [gen. use: b1630]

heaven n b1000 ["sky": b725]

heavenly adj b1000 [fig. use: b1470]

hellfire n b1000

hymn n b1000 (verb use: b1670)

paternoster n *Lord's Prayer* b1000 ["rosary": b1350]

shrine n b1000

Candlemas n b1050

Almighty, the n *God* b1100

Antichrist n b1100

grace n b1100

heathen n b1100 (adj use: b900)

prior n b1100 [rare "CEO": b1870] (prioress: b1300)

rabbi n b1100 (rabbinical, rabbinic: b1615)

service n b1100

chaplain n b1115

council n b1125 [gen. "meeting," "counseling body": b1350; "governing body": b1450]

saint n b1125 (verb use: b1200; sainthood: b1550; saintship: b1635)

cardinal n b1130

churchyard n b1140

apocalypse n

fear v *worship, as in "God-fearing"*

genesis n [fig. use: b1605]

high mass n

sain v *arch. make the sign of the cross*

seraph n *type of angel* (seraphim: b900)

theophany n *appearance of God to a person*

Society/Mores/Culture

folk n b725

man n *gen. person* b725

churl n *type of freeman* b800 ["boor": b1250]

alms n *donation* b810 (almshouse: b1400; almsgiver: b1635)

evil adj b900 [obs. "subpar": u1600s; obs. "botched": b1530 to 1700s]

greet, greeting v, n b900

knight n b900 [obs. meanings of "knave, boy": concurrent]

lady n *akin to lord; head of a household* b900 [akin to gentleman: b1350; type of formal rank: b1450; as in "behave like a lady": b1870]

lord n b900 [type of official title: b1350] (lording: b1200; lordling: b1275)

maidenhood n b900 (maidhood: b1100)

sin n/v b900

carl n *everyday joe* b1000 ["churl": b1350]

folkmoot/folkmote n *townspeople assembling* b1000

freeman n b1000

maiden n *girl; servant* b1000 (adj use: b1350; maid: b1200)

sot n b1000 ["dullard": b1000]

townsman n b1000

ceorl n *churl* b1100

evil n b1100 [obs. "crime": u1600s]

wise man n b1100 (wisewoman: b1400)

wrong n *as in "doing wrong"* b1100 [as in "in the wrong": b1350] (adj/adv use: b1300; verb use: b1350]

free n *obs. person of nobility* [u1500s]

justice n *getting what you de-*

serve [spec. "legal system": b1350]

lording n *lord, sir*

Government

earl n b620

queen n b725 ["chess queen": b1470; "card designation": b1600; as in "queen bee": b1630; slang "homosexual": b1900] (verb use: b1630; queenship: b1540)

alderman n b810 (alderwoman: b1570)

king n b900 [fig. "leader, ruler": b1350] (verb use: b1450; kingcraft: b1645)

lordship n b900

pharaoh n b900

town n b900 ["municipality": b1830]

wick n *arch. village* b900

atheling n *prince, male royalty* b1000

purple adj *of royal fabric; royal* b1000 ["of the color": b1450; as in "purple prose": b1600]

hamlet n b1100

chancellor n b1125 [of a college: b1300] (chancellery: b1300)

duke n (duchess: b1350; duchy: b1400)

Politics

fatherland n b1105

Life

fleshly adj *corporeal* b900 [obs. "carnal": b1350 to 1400s]

life n b900

lifeless adj b1000

quick adj *living, as in "quick silver"*

Death

dead adj/n *lit. and fig.* b725 [obs. "deadly, fatal": b1450 to 1600s; "completely": b1600] (adv use: b1400; obs. verb use "deaden": u1600s)

death n b725 ["extinction": b1450]

deathbed n *grave* b725 [the actual bed: b1300]

gallows n b725

mourn v b725 (noun use: b1300; mourner: b1395)

murder n b725 (verb use: b1150)

woelmist n *mist of death* b725

deadly adj b900 ["able to be killed": u1800s; "like death": b1350] (deathful: b1350)

fey adj *doomed to die* b900

fordo v *kill, destroy* b900

gallows tree n b900

heriot n *feudal death tax* b900

leave v *bequeath* b900

martyrdom n b900 (obs. martyry: b1300 to 1600s)

widow n b900 [obs. applied to males: concurrent] (verb use: b1350; widower: b1375)

worry v *arch. kill* b900 [obs. "choke": b1350]

grave n *burial place* b1000 (arch. verb use: b1350)

will n/v b1100

hang v

War/Military/Violence

beat v *batter, hit* b725

bow n b725

fight n b725 (noun use: b900)

hilt n/v b725

weapon n/v b725 [obs. "weaponry": u1500s] (weaponry: b1845)

arrow n *weapon* b800

flay v b800

smite v *strike* b800 [obs. "sully," obs. "smear": OE only; "kill": b1325]

cudgel n b900 (verb use: b1600)

fight v b900 [fig., as in "fight a fire": b1800] (noun use: b725)

foe n b900

harry v *raid* b900 ["harrass": b1350]

helm n *helmet* b900

reave v *plunder, rob* b900

shield n b900 [fig. use: b1350] (verb use: b1150)

shot n *act of shooting* b900 ["nasty remark": b1870]

slay v b900 [obs. "hit": b1150 to ME; obs. "execute": b1350 to 1600s]

spear n b900 [as in "broccoli spear": b1530] (verb use: b1450; spearhead n: b1400)

steel n *fig. sword, etc.* b900

stick v *stab* b900

sunder v b900

sword n b900

bolt n *crossbow bolt* b950

broadax/broadaxe n b1000

broadsword n b1000

foeman n b1000

haft n *weapon handle* b1000

harrow v *plunder* b1000 (noun use: b1300; harrowing: b1810)

scathe n *injury, harm* b1000 (verb use: b1300)

arbalest n *type of crossbow* b1100

flail n b1100 (verb use: b1500)

hit v b1100 ["encounter": b1075] (noun use: b1600)

wound v b1100 [fig. use: b1350] (wounded adj/n: b1000)

war n *warfare* b1125 [a spec. conflict: b1350; obs. "invasion": b1450 to 1600s] (verb use: b1160)

fast adj *obs. militarily unassailable* [u1600s]

hack v *cut* (noun use: b1350)

ram n *ramming machine* (verb use: b1350)

reach v *obs. hit* [u1800s]

sax n *type of knife*

swordplay n

Crime/Punishment/Enforcement

steal v b900

theft n b900

thief n b900 (thieve: b950; thievish: b1450; thievery: b1570)

lawbreaker n b1050

outlaw adj/n/v *fugitive* b1100 ["criminal": b1900]

prison n *jail; imprisonment* (verb use: b1350; prisoner: b1350)

unlaw n *crime*

The Law

ordeal n *as in "trial by ordeal"* b950 [gen. "trying circumstance": b1670]

law n b1000 ["gen. laws," "the legal profession": b1350; "police": b1530; as in "natural law": b1670; as in "Murphy's law": b1970] (obs. verb use: b1150 to 1600s; lawful: b1500)

sheriff n b1050 (sheriffwick: b1470)

outlaw v b1100

outfangthief n *arch. type of feudal right of jurisdiction*

right n *entitlement*

The Fantastic/Paranormal

fiend n *demon* b725 [obs. "foe": until ME; "wicked person": b1350] (fiendish: b1530)

firedrake n *type of dragon* b900

ghostly adj b900

hellhound n b900

mare n *as in "nightmare"* b900

phoenix n b900 [fig. "standard of beauty": b1450; fig. "something resurrected": b1600]

wight n b900 [obs. gen. "living thing": u1500s; obs. "human": b1350]

elf n b1000 ["dwarf": b1570] (elvish: b1200; elven: b1300; elfish: b1545; elvin: b1570)

werewolf n b1000

thurse n *arch. type of giant*

Magic

witch n b900 [fig. "crone": b1450] (verb use: b1350; witchcraft: b950)

Interjections

odso interj

hosanna interj/n/v b900

lo interj b900

wellaway interj b900

woe interj b900

yes adv/interj b900 (noun use: b1715; verb use: b1830)

amen interj *finis* b1000 ["so be it": b1350]

ha-ha interj b1000 (ha: b1350)

well interj b1100

alleluia interj

good day interj (good morning, good-morrow: b1470; good evening: b1870; good afternoon: b1930)

he interj

heavens interj

hehe interj (verb use: b1870)

welcome interj [used in greeting: b890]

Slang

heavy n b900

Insults

quean n *hussy* b1000

turd n b1000

witless adj b1000

badling n *bad person*

dull adj *stupid* [phys. unsharpened: b1350; gen. descriptive: b1470] (verb use: b1300; dullard: b1350)

nithing n *arch. cur*

scold n *quarrelsome person* (verb use: b1400)

worm n *jerk*

Phrases

evil eye n b1000

fast lane n b1080

far and wide adv b1100

hand and foot adv b1100

night and day adv b1100

General/Miscellaneous

bristle n b700

fetter n/v b700 (verb use: b1100)

foam n b700 (verb use: b1100)

hole n b700

answer n/v b725

bare adj/v b725

beam n *wood beam, beam of sunlight* b725 (verb use: b1425)

bolster n *type of phys. support* b725 (verb use: b1510)

bottom n b725 ["buttocks": b1800]

cold adj/n *lit. and fig.* b725 ["dead": b1350; "unrehearsed": b1900] (noun use: b1300)

deed n *as in "good deed"* b725 [type of document: b1340]

edge n *knife-edge* b725 [lit. "sharpness": b1450; fig. "sharpness": b1600] (verb use: b1300)

heap n b725 (verb use: b900)

help v/n b725

hoard n b725 (verb use: b1100)

ilk n *kind, sort* b725

limb n b725

name n/v b725 ["reputation": b1350] (verb use: b1000)

oath n *promise* b725 ["profanity": b1350]

rest n/v *sleep; music rest* b725

bellow v/n b750

blast n *as in "blast of cold air"* b750 ["blare": b1200; "explosion": b1870; slang "party": b1960; "rollicking time": b1965]

hue n b750

warning n *portent* b800 [obs. "precaution": u1500s; "being warned": b1350; type of signal, as in "tornado warning": b1930] (adj use: b1555)

way n b800 (obs. verb use: b1600 to 1700s)

team n *as in "team of horses"* b825 [applied to people: b1530] (verb use: b1555; adj use: b1990)

ark n *coffer; Noah's Ark* b830

burden n b830 (verb use: b1545; burdenous: b1530; burdensome: b1580)

craft n *as in "arts and crafts"; skill* b900 [obs. "strength": u1500s; obs. "deceit": u1600s; obs. "magic": b1350 to 1400s; "craftiness": b1350] (verb use: b1440)

deal n *portion, quantity, as in*

"great deal of trouble" b900 (verb use: b1150)

din n b900

doom n *judgment* b900 ["destruction": b1600] (verb use "judge": b1450; verb use "make doom certain": b1630; doomful: b1590)

dwarf n b900 [type of mythical creature: b1350; type of plant: b1770; type of star: b1915] (adj use: b1600; verb use: b1630)

either adj/conj/pron *each, both* b900 ["one or the other": b1350] (adv use: b1450)

end n *extent; final part; termination; ending* b900 ["goal": b1350] (adj use: b1300)

enough adj/adv/pron/n b900 (enow: b1050)

foretoken n *harbinger* b900

freedom n b900

gathering n b900

gore n *triangular piece of cloth or land* b900

groan v/n b900

half n b900

handle n b900

harm n b900 [obs. "insult": b725] (verb use: b1100; harmful: b1000; harmless: b1570)

head n *leader* b900 (verb use: b1470)

leap v/n b900 [as in "leap up": b1350]

leave n *as in "leave of absence"* b900 [as in "take leave": b1350] (verb use: b1350)

light n *illumination* b900 (verb use: b1350)

list n *narrow strip* b900

little adj/adv/n/v b900

lye n b900

main n *as in "might and main"* b900

martyr n/v b900 (martyrize: b1450)

master n *ruler; schoolmaster* b900 ["employer," "skilled person": b1350; as in "master recording": b1930] (adj use: b1150;

verb use: b1300; masterful: b1350)

match n *equal; peer; mate* b900 ["something corresponding": b1530; as in "sporting match": b1570] (verb use: b1400)

might n b900 (mightiness: b1350)

need n b900

needle n *as in "pins and needles"* b900

neighbor n b900 (adj use: b1450; verb use: b1690)

no adv b900

oneness n b900

pit n *hole* b900 [arch. "grave": b1350; "hell": b1350; as in "pit stop": b1870]

ridge n b900

room n *available space* b900 [a spec. place: b1350]

sheaf n b900

side n b900

sleep n/v b900 [fig. "death": b1150] (sleepy: b1225)

soot n b900

sooth adj/n *true/truth* b900

soul n b900 [obs. "life itself": u1600s; "person," as in "poor soul": b1350; "embodiment," as in "soul of wit": b1630]

spark n b900 ["catalyst": b1350] (verb use: b1350)

speck n b900 (verb use: b1580; speckle: b1450)

spoke n b900

starboard n b900 (adj use: b1500; verb use: b1600)

stench n *smell* b900 [fig. "foul quality": b1350]

stitch n b900 (verb use: b1300)

strength n *phys. and mental* b900 [obs. type of fort: b1450 to 1700s; "measure," as in "at half strength": b1630] (verb use: b1300)

swell, swelling v/n b900 (noun use: b1605)

tale n b900 [obs. "tale-telling": u1500s; "story," "fiction": b1350]

threshold n *lit. and fig. border* b900 ["point of perception

or activity," as in "threshold of hearing": b1900]

token n *representation* b900 [as in "token of friendship": b1450; "substitute for money": b1600; as in "arcade token": b1970]

ward n *surveillance* b900 ["guardianship," "child under care," as in "ward of the court": b1350]

weal n b900

wellspring n b900 (wellhead: b1350)

wet adj/n/v b900

while n b900 (conj use: b1200; verb use: b1635)

woman n b900 (womanhood: b1375)

wonder n *something wonderful* b900 [as in "sense of wonder": b1350] (verb use: b1150; wonderful: b1100; wondrous: b1500; wonderment: b1535)

world n b900 [fig. use: b1600]

wrack n *wreckage* b900

wretch n b900 (obs. adj use: u1500s; wretched: b1200)

yelp n b900 [obs. "bragging": until LME] (verb use: b1555)

yon n b900 (adv use: b1450)

yore n b900 (obs. adv use u1600s)

dead n *as in "the dead of night"* b950

liar n b950

likeness n b950

loaf n *as in "loaf of bread"* b950

lot n *as in "draw lots"* b950

outland n b950 (outlandish "foreign": b1000; outlander: b1605)

sheath n b950 (verb use: b1400)

sight n *something to be seen* b950 ["ability to see": b1350; "pupil of the eye": b1470] (verb use: b1630)

thrall n b950

boot n *in addition, as in "to boot"* b1000 (verb use: b1470)

cop n *top* b1000

deep n b1000 [as in "the deep of night": b1570]

dot n *spot* b1000

drop n *as in "water drop"* b1000 (droplet: b1610)

dye n/v b1000

earnest n b1000 (adj use: b1100)

ebb n *as in "ebb and flow"* b1000 [fig. use: b1450] (verb use: b1150; obs. adj use: b1450)

filth n b1000 [applied to language: b1770] (filthy: b1385)

fit n *as in "fit of anger"* b1000 [phys. sense: b1550]

gleam n b1000 (verb use: b1510)

grit n b1000 [slang use: b1830]

handiwork n b1000

hire n/v b1000

lid n b1000

man n *adult male* b1000

mote n b1000

night watch n b1000 (night watchman: b1865)

paradise n b1000 [gen. "heavenly place": b1450] (paradisal: b1560; paradisiac: b1615; paradisiacal: b1650)

part n/v *portion* b1000 ["separate," as in "part company": b1350]

prick n/v *as in "pinprick"* b1000 [obs. "sting": b1350 to 1600s; arch. "goad": b1350]

riddle n b1000 [fig. sense: b1470] (verb use: b1470)

shaft n b1000

shard n b1000

shred n/v b1000

slime n b1000

smack n *taste* b1000 [obs. "smell": b1150 to 1500s] (verb use: b1200)

streak n b1000 [as in "streak of luck": b1870] (verb use: b1600)

throng n b1000

top n b1000

trap n b1000 [type of plumbing feature: b1870]

dross n *spec. to metallurgy* b1050 [gen. use: b1470]

horoscope n b1050

shag n b1050 (adj use: b1595; shaggy: b1590)

knell n b1100 (verb use: b1450)

knob n b1100 (knobble: b1450; knobby: b1545)

loudness n b1100

peace n b1100

right n *opp. of wrong* b1100

soft n b1100

sting n b1100 [slang "con, entrapment": b1930]

miracle n b1140

wassail n b1140 (verb use: b1300; wassail bowl: b1610; wassailer: b1635)

accord n

band n *shackles; obligations*

eye n *fig., as in "keep an eye on things"* [lit. use: b900]

kind n *grouping; variety*

mark n/v *as in "landmark"*

mo adj/n *more*

place n (verb use: b1450)

procession n *act of parading* ["the parade itself": b1350; obs. "proceeding": b1600] (arch. verb use: b1695; process v: b1830)

rim n *coast* ["lip": b1470]

row n *as in "ducks in a row"*

share n *portion* [gen. use: b1670] (verb use: b1590)

slit n (verb use: b1400)

tiding n *as in "glad tidings"*

witness n *giving testimony; person who watches* (verb use: b1350)

word n *notification, news as in "receive word"*

wrack n *as in "wrack and ruin"* (obs. verb use: b1350)

Things

bin n b750

bell n b900

board n *wood plank* b900 (verb use: b1440)

mat n b900

pike n *type of spike* b900

rick n *stack* b900 (verb use: b1625)

stake n *spike* b900 (verb use: b1350)

string n b900 (verb use: b1450)

thing n b900 [obs. type of meeting, matter brought before a meeting: b900; as in "sweet thing": b1350; as in "gather your things": b1350; as in "music is my thing": b1870]

trough n b900 ["gutter": b1450; type of coffin: b1500; "natural depression": b1530; as in "peaks and troughs": b1930]

wire n b900 (verb use: b1450)

thong n *strap* b950

knot n *in rope* b1000 [fig. "bond": b1350; obs. "obligation": b1450 to 1800s; "type of tied ribbon": b1450] (verb use: b1550)

stirrup n b1000

tape n *ribbon* b1000 [as in "magnetic tape," "adhesive tape": b1970] (verb use: b1610)

wreath n *gen. round ornament* b1000 [spec., as in "Christmas wreath": b1450] (wreathe: b1530)

pole n *stick* b1050 [type of tree: b1770; in pole vault: b1900; "ski pole": b1930; racing "pole position": b1970]

bat n *club or stick* b1100 [type of sports equipment: b1630] (verb use: b1450)

brass n *the metal* b1100 ["bronze": b1000]

rod n b1100

vat n b1100

irons n *shackles* (iron v: b1630)

pipe n *tube*

Description

black adj *opp. of white* b700

brown adj *tanned, dark complected* b700 ["of the color brown": b1350] (noun use: b1300; verb use: b1350)

almighty adj b725 (adv use: b1835)

any adj b725

bitter adj b725

born adj b725 [as in "a born comedian": b1350]

broad adj b725 ["overstated": b1870; "wide-ranging": b1900] (broaden: b1730)

cool adj *phys. cool; calm* b725 [fig. "unfriendly": b1600] (verb use: b750; noun use: b1400)

dark adj *lit. and fig. unilluminated* b725 [as in "dark blue": b1450] (noun use: b1225)

dear adj *severe, expensive* b725 [obs. "noble": u1600s; obs. "valued": u1600s]

deep adj b725 [as in "deep feelings": b1350; applied to sound, color: b1450] (noun use: b1000; deepen: b1600)

fallow adj *brownish, yellowish* b725

foremost adj b725 [obs. "firstmost": u1500s]

heavy adj *lit. and fig.* b725

idle adj b725

mid adj b725

mild adj b725 (milden: b1630)

more adj b725

most adj b725 (adv use: b895; noun use: b1150)

naked adj b725 ["unconcealed": b1350] (nake v: b1350)

narrow adj b725

welcome adj *acceptable* b725 ["eagerly accepted": b1350]

after adj/adv/conj/prep b735

bright adj b740 ["intelligent": b1770] (noun use: b1970; brighten: b1200)

careful adj b750 [obs. "grieving": u1700s]

clean adj/adv b750 ["fresh," as in "a clean copy": b1700; "not obscene": b1870]

middle adj b785 (noun use: b1150)

tame adj b800 ["dull": b1630] (verb use: b900)

high adj b825

mighty adj b830 (mightful: b1350)

sweet adj *sweet-tasting; fragrant; not spoiled; melodious; indicating affection* b830 (adv use: b1300)

fresh adj *salt-free; new* b895 ["refreshed": b1350]

alway adv *always* b900 (always: b1250)

childly adj b900 (childish: b1000; childlike: b1590)

dry adj/v b900 ["thirsty": b1470; "alcohol-free": b1500; "boring": b1630; "applied to wine": b1730]

empty adj b900 ["without substance": b1350] (verb use: b1530)

even adj *flat; fair* b900

fast adj *fastened* b900

forsooth adv b900

foul adj b900

full adj b900 (verb use: b1470)

good adj b900 (noun use: b1200)

great adj *large; texturally coarse; comparatively large* b900 ["grand": b1350; "talented": b1630; "very good, exceptional": b1830]

green adj b900 (noun use: b1300)

grim adj b900 (arch. verb use: b1470)

hard adj *physically hard* b900 ["too long": b1350]

long adj/adv *opp. of short* b900 ["too long": b1350]

longsome adj *tedious, boring* b900

loud adj/adv b900 [as in "a loud bar": b1600; applied to smells: b1670; applied to colors: b1800] (loudness: b1000)

many adj b900

mean adj *inferior* b900

natheless adv *nonetheless* b900

nether adj b900 (nethermost: b1300)

never adv b900

new adj/adv b900

newly adv b900 [obs. "right now": b1350 to 1600s]

nowhither adv *toward nowhere* b900

only adj b900 (adv/conj use: b1350)

Our Verbal Antiquity

In a day when our speech is sprinkled with *cyberspace*, *downsizing*, *lifestyle*, *byte*, *subtext* and other kinda-now-kinda-wow words (including *kinda-now-kinda-wow*), it's both comforting and surprising to realize that perhaps as much as 90 percent of our vocabulary has its roots not in medieval England but ultimately in Europe, thousands of years B.C.

As briefly discussed in the introduction to this book, we generally regard a hypothetical language called Indo-European as the great-great-great-etc.-mother of our mother tongue. Certainly, the language was then vastly different, with different grammar rules and consonants we no longer use, yet if we go all the way back to Indo-European and its vocabulary as reconstructed by linguists, we still find a variety of words that are recognizable—almost on sight—as English ancestors.

In the following list of Indo-European words, we see clearly words not only common in our language, but also critical to it. (Words with hyphens are roots whose final form would be dictated by the context of the word, much as Latin was. And not all words here had the literal meaning that we now associate with the root words.)

- in *abel-* we see *apple*
- in *bʰreu-* we see *brew*
- in *dʰel-* we see *dell* and *dale*
- in *en* we see *in*
- in *gʰosti-* we see *host* and *guest*
- in *kneighwh-* we see *connive*
- in *laku-* we see *lake*

- in *math-* we see *moth*
- in *newn* we see *nine*
- in *ors-* we see *arse* and *ass*
- in *papa* we quite clearly see *father*
- in *reudʰ-* we see *ruddy* and *red*
- in *skipam* we see *ship*
- in *tragh-* we see *drag*
- in *wai* we see *woe*
- in *yek* we see *joke*
- . . . and in *we-* we see *we*

Other words that reach all the way back to centuries B.C. include *me*, *I*, *you*, *milk*, *bee*, *snow*, *wolf*, *oxen*, *cow*, *elm*.

We also see Indo-European in less-obvious forms today. For example, *denk-*, meaning "bite," ultimately gave us *tongs*, a tool that bites, and *tough*, from a figurative use much akin to "hanging tough"—since tongs are tough because they hold their bite. And in the list above, *kneighwh-* meant "to lean toward one another," which you must do in order to connive with someone.

(We don't date such words back to years B.C. in this book because they were not by any sense English at the time. The body of language, with vocabulary and structure specific to English alone, didn't start forming until much later. Also, Indo-European roots may not have a direct lineage into English, many having first evolved into such languages as Greek or Latin and then into French or Spanish or Sanskrit or whatever before ultimately being adapted into English.)

---

open adj *not closed; not covered* b900 ["not clogged, not obstructed, clear": b1450; as in "open for business": b1830] (verb use: b1100; ope adj: b1470)

our adj b900 ["plural of editorial we": b1350] (ours: b1300; ourself: b1350; ourselves: b1500)

reckless adj b900 ["neglectful": u1600s]

right adj *correct, appropriate, acceptable* b900

righteous adj b900

sere adj *dried, withered* b900

sharp adj *lit. and fig.* b900

sheen adj *beautiful, resplendent* b900 (noun use: b1605)

short adj *opp. of long* b900

silken adj b900 (silky: b1605)

silvern adj b900 (silvery: b1400)

sinless adj b900

small adj b900

sore adj b900 ["great," as in "sore amazement": b1350; "angry": b1700]

still adj/v *quiet, motionless* b900 (noun use: b1300)

strong adj *powerful; able; defensible; harsh*, as in "strong measures"; as in "strong drink" b900 ["healthy": b1350; pertaining to pulse: b1450; pertaining

to language: b1700] (adv use, as in "come on strong": b1150)

such adj/adv/pron b900

swift adj b900 (arch. adv use: b1400; rare verb use: b1630)

thick adj *broad; dense; congealed* b900 [obs. "deep": u1600s; obs. "frequent": b1450 to 1600s; "stuffy": b1630; slang "excessive": b1900] (adv use: b1200;

noun use: b1300; verb use: b1150)

thin adj *slim; meager; watery* b900 [obs. "few": b1530 to 1800s; of crowds: b1670; of sound or color: b1670] (verb use: b1100; adv use: b1300)

thine adj b900

third adj/n b900

tough adj *phys. tough* b900 ["difficult; strenuous; stringent": b1350] (verb use: b1830; noun use: b1870; toughen: b1575)

upright adj *as in "stand upright"* b900 ["morally upright": b1570; as in "upright piano": b1800] (adv use: b1600)

utmost adj *furthermost* b900 ["greatest": b1350] (uttermost: b1350)

utter adj *total* b900 (utterance: b1450)

warm adj/adv/v b900 ["protecting from cold": b1350; as in "a warm welcome": b1500] (noun use: b1350)

white adj b900 [describing hair, wine: b1350] (noun use: b1150; whiten: b1300)

wide adj b900 [obs. "big": b1350 to 1500s] (width: b1630)

worldly adj *of this world* b900 ["experienced": b1350]

worst adj b900 (noun use: b1350)

yare adj b900

aft adv b950 (adj use: b1820)

betwixt adv/prep b950

least adj b950 (noun use: b1100; adv use: b1300)

first adj b965

hot adj b975 [fig. "fresh": b1350] (verb use: b1150)

accursed adj b1000

afloat adj/adv b1000

alive adj b1000

anon adv *soon* b1000 [obs. "immediately": b1000]

anywise adv b1000

baleful adj b1000 (arch. baleless: b1350)

brickle adj *brittle* b1000

busy adj *occupied at the moment* b1000 ["consistently occupied": b1350; pertaining to design, etc.: b1970]

dim adj b1000 ["unclear," "not clear-sighted," "stupid": b1350] (verb use: b1100; noun use: b1400)

dusk adj *dusky* b1000 (dusky: b1560)

ice-cold adj b1000

lank adj b1000 ["limp": b1700] (lanky: b1670)

leaden adj *made of lead* b1000 ["resembling lead": b1450; "lifeless": b1600]

manifold adj b1000

needs adv b1000

nowhere adv b1000 (noun use: b1835; nowheres: b1870)

rough adj *e.g., of a surface* b1000 [e.g., of an action: b1350]

sour adj *opp. of sweet* b1000 ["spoiled," "cantankerous": b1350]

steadfast adj b1000

stern adj b1000

stiff adj *rigid* b1000 [slang "dead": b1350; "formal": b1630; "drunk": b1740]

enow adj/adv *enough* b1050

midway adj b1050 (adv use: b1200)

smooth adj b1050 [spec. of liquor: b1770; as in "smooth operator": b1600] (verb use: b1340; smoothen: b1635)

dear adj *precious* b1100 ["sweet": b1770]

every adj b1100

head adj b1100

laden adj b1100

light adj *not heavy; as in "a light color"* b1100 ["below weight": b1500]

ruddy adj b1100

smart adj *causing pain* b1100 (verb/noun use: b1300)

thankfully adv *as in "he thankfully returned the favor"* b1100 [obs. "done to garner thanks": b1450 to 1500s; as in "thankfully, the storm quit": b1970]

wayless adj b1100

wonderful adj b1100 [obs. "expressing wonder": b1450 to 1500s]

wont adj b1100 (noun use: b1350; verb use: b1450)

yawning adj b1100

etcetera adv

grisly adj [obs. "touched by grisliness": u1600s]

huge adj (hugeous: b1470)

ill adj *bad* ["sick": b1460] (noun use: b1300)

landed adj

lite adj

neither adj (adv use: b1560)

nevermore adv

rife adj

right adj *opp. of left* (noun use: b1350)

spare adj *spartan*

token adj (tokenism: b1960)

untimely adj/adv *poorly timed* ["prematurely": b1600]

unwholesome adj

Colors

gray adj b900 (noun use: b1900)

red adj/n b900

dun adj *having the color dun* b1000 (noun use: b1570)

iron gray adj b1000

yellow n *the color* b1100 ["something colored yellow": b900] (adj use: b1350)

purpurine adj *obs. purple* [u1800s]

Actions/Verbs

ask v *as in "ask a question"* b725 [as in "ask for help": b1350; "invite," as in "ask for trouble": b1870]

bear v *carry; endure; yield; drive* b725 [as in "bear ill will": b1350; as in "bear left": b1600] (bearance: b1730)

behoove v b725 (arch. behoof n: b1000)

beset v b725

bide v b725

bind v *tie* b725 (noun use: b1000)

blow v *as in "winds blowing"* b725 (noun use: b1660)

bow v *bow before someone* b725 (noun use: b1655)

breach n b725 (verb use: b1550)

break v b725 [fig. use: b1500] (noun use: b1300)

bring v b725

burst v *explode* b725 [obs. "break": u1800s] (noun use: b1300)

busy v b725 [obs. "disrupt": u1500s]

call v *pertaining to people* b725 [pertaining to animals: b1500; "visit": b1600; "telephone": b1900] (noun use: b1325)

care v *as in "I don't care to participate"* b725

carve v b725 ["divide up": b1730] (arch. carven: b1380)

choose v *select* b725 ["decide": b1350]

clip v *hold or fasten* b725 [arch. "hug": concurrent] (noun use: b1355)

could v b725

dare v *brave* b725 ["challenge": b1600] (noun use: b1595; daring: b1385; rare dareful: b1605; daredevil: h1795)

feel v b725 (noun use: b1225; feeling: b1175)

find v b725 (noun use: b1825)

follow v b725 ["occur after": b1350; "understand": b1700]

heed v b725 (noun use: b1300)

miss v b725 [as in "miss the bus": b1630] (noun use: b1555)

say v b725 [as in "the speedometer says 45": b1970; as in "the details say luxury": b1990] (noun use: b1575)

set v b725 (noun use: b1340)

waken v b725 (wake: b1350)

wane v b725 (noun use: b1325)

wax v *opp. of wane* b725 (noun use: b1350)

weigh v b725 [fig. use: b1350; as in "he weighs

180": b1350] (weight: b1000)

fell v *knock down* b800 [obs. "lower": b1350 to 1600s]

handle v b800 [fig. use: b1530]

hear v b800

flee v b825

beckon v b830 (beck v: b1350)

come v b830

delve v *phys. excavate* b830 ["investigate": b1450]

flow v b830 (noun use: b1470)

might v b830

quake v b830 (quaky: b1870)

yawn v *gen. open wide, as in "yawning cavern"* b830 [obs. gen. "open the mouth": b1300 to 1600s; "open the mouth in sleepiness": b1450] (noun use: b1605; yawning: b1200; yawner: b1690)

tear v *rip* b850 [as in "tear down": b1350; fig., as in "tear yourself away": b1600; as in "tear around": b1600; as in "the loss tears him up": b1670]

hold v b855

mar v b900 [obs. "spoil": u1500s; obs. "confound": b1350] (noun use: b1555)

may v b900

ache n/v b900

arise v b900

awake/awaken v b900

bark n/v *sharp report* b900

bathe v b900 ["swim fig. in something," as in "sunbathe": b1450]

beg v b900 [as in "begs the question": b1570]

behold v b900

belay v b900

bleach v b900

bore v *pierce with a tool* b900

borrow v b900 [fig. "adapt": b1350]

burn v *flame; oxodize; feel passion; feel inflammation* b900 (noun use: b1525)

cleave v *cling, remain loyal; split* b900 (cleavage: b1820)

cling v b900 [arch. "shrivel": concurrent; fig. use: b1600] (noun use: b1625)

creep v *crawl; increase slowly* b900 ["sneak": b1350] (noun use: b1500)

deem v b900

dive v b900

do v b900

draw v *pull* b900 [as in "draw the curtains": b1450]

drive v b900 [as in "drive away": b1350; as in "drive a wagon": b1470]

fall v *drop* b900 [as in "fall down": b1350; as in "fall on hard times": b1350; "become quieter": b1450] (noun use: b1300)

fill v b900 [as in "fill a job": b1600; as in "fill a tooth": b1870] (noun use: b725)

fold v *as in "folding paper"* b900 (noun use: b1300)

forego v *go before* b900

forgive v b900 [obs. "give": u1400s]

forsake v b900 [obs. "decline, renounce, steer clear of": u1500s] (foresaken: b1470)

forswear v *renounce, swear falsely* b900

free adj/v b900 ["made free": b1600; "without financial cost": b1350]

gather v b900 (noun use: b1555)

give v b900

glide v b900

go v b900

grip v/n b900

grope v b900 [obs. gen. "feel": u1500s] (noun use: b1530)

grow v b900 [as in "grow plants": b1470]

grunt v b900 (noun use: b1555)

hang v b900

have v b900

hew v b900

hide v *conceal* b900 (hid: b1200; hidden: b1300)

hope v b900 (noun use: b1000)

lade v *load* b900 (laden adj: b1200; laden v: b1515)

last v *continue* b900 [as in "as long as supplies last": b1350] (adj/noun use: b1300; lasting adj: b1175)

lay v *as in "lay down"; put down; as in "lay eggs"; "lay on hands"; "lay carpet"* b900

lead v *provide leadership for; as in "lead a good life"* b900 [fig. use: b1350; "follow someone else's lead": b1630; as in "lead a witness": b1870] (verb use: b1600)

lean v *as in "lean over"* b900 [as in "lean against": b1350; fig. "rely": b1350; as in "lean on": b1770] (noun use: b1780)

lend v b900

let v *hinder—something of an opp. of let, allow* b900

lie v *prevaricate; as in "lie in bed"* b900 [as in "lie down": b1350] (noun use: b1700)

light v *alight; dismount* b900

list v *please; listen* b900 (noun use: b1300)

live v b900 ["survive": b1770]

look v *examine; watch; consider* b900 (noun use: b1300)

lose v *as in "lose the car keys"* b900 (lost: b1450)

make v *construct* b900 [as in "make a mess": b1350]

mean v *intend; imply, signify* b900

meet v b900

melt v b900 [fig. "dissipate": b1630] (noun use: b1855)

mote v *may or might* b900

mow v *cut* b900

overcome v b900 [obs. "overtake": b900 to 1100s]

overflow v b900 (noun use: b1590)

oversee v b900 ["spy": b1770]

reach v b900 [as in "reach a destination," "reach the phone number": b1350; as in "reach up": b1600] (noun use: b1540)

rear v *raise, as in "a horse rears her head"* b900

reck v b900 (noun use: b1500)

ring v *as in "ring a bell"* b900 (noun use: b1550)

roar v b900 (noun use: b1400)

rot v b900 (noun use: b1400)

run v b900 (noun use: b1350)

sate v b900

sear v *become parched* b900 ["parch": b1470; "burn; cook": b1600]

see v b900

seek v b900

send v b900

shake v b900 (noun use: b1570)

shape v *form* b900 ["give structure to": b1350] (noun use: b1100)

shear v b900

shine v b900

shoot v *go fast* b900

shove v b900

shrink v b900 (shrink away: b1470)

sift v b900 (verb use: b1300)

sit v b900

sow v b900

spare v *refrain from killing, punishing, etc.* b900 ["forgo," as in "spare expense": b1350; "refrain from other things," as in "spare me the details": b1700]

spew v b900 [gen., as in "spew out": b1600] (noun use: b1500)

spin v *as in "spin thread"* b900 [fig., as in "spin a tale": b1570]

spring v *as in "spring forth," "spring up"; sprout; bound* b900

stand v *stand erect; stay in one place* b900

stare v b900 (noun use: b1730; stare down: b1925)

steer v b900

sting v b900 [slang "con": b1830; "feel a sting": b1870] (noun use: b1100)

stink v b900 [obs. gen. "ex-

ude odor": until ME; fig. "be bad": b1450] (noun use: b1300)

stir v *mix; move; rouse; arouse; start to move* b900 (noun use: b1450)

stoop v b900 (noun use: b1575)

stretch v *as in "stretch out"* b900 [as in "stretch your legs": b1350; as in "stretch over": b1350]

stroke v *caress* b900 [fig. use: b1530]

suck v b900 ["perform oral sex": b1900; fig. "stink": b1975] (noun use: b1300)

swear v *as in "swear to God"; promise; affirm; use a swear word* b900

sweat v b900 [fig., as in "sweat it out": b1450]

swim v b900 ["be immersed in": b1450] (noun use: b1600)

tell v b900 [obs. "list": until LME; "recognize": b1370; as in "tell him what to do": b1600; "tattle": b1930]

thrash v *thresh; beat* b900

time v *set a time for* b900

tire v b900 [obs. "wear out, collapse": u1600s] (tired: b1400; tiresome: b1500; tireless: b1590)

tithe n/v b900

tread v *walk; oppress* b900 ["step on": b1450] (noun use: b1450)

twinkle v b900 (noun use: b1670)

wake v *stay awake; stay on watch* b900 ["awaken": b1350] (noun use: b1150; waken: b900)

wallow v b900 [fig., as in "wallow in glory": b1350] (noun use: b1500)

wander v b900 [as in "mind wandering": b1450; as in "wandering gaze": b1600; as in "wandering river": b1770]

wash v *clean* b900 [fig. "make pure": b1350] (noun use: b1150)

welcome v b900 [as in "wel-

come the prospect"] (adj use: b1200; noun use: b1525)

whet v b900 [obs. "foment": u1700s] (noun use: b1630)

wield v b900

win v *take* b900 [as in "win a race": b1350] (obs. noun use "work, conflict": b1150; gen. noun use: b1865)

wish v b900 (noun use: b1350; wish for: b1350)

withstand v b900

wizen v b900 (adj use: b1790)

wreak v b900 [as in "wreak vengeance": b1500; as in "wreak havoc": b1830]

wring v b900

art v *conjugation of be* b950

braid v *twist into braids* b950 (noun use: b1530)

forgo v b950

gird v *as in "girding one's loins"* b950 [fig. use: b1470]

grind v b950 ["grind at": b1670]

knead v b950

listen v b950 (list v: b900)

misdo v b950 (misdoing: b1500)

rend v b950

slide v b950 [obs. "sleep": b1350 to 1500s] (noun use: b1570)

abide v b1000

begin v b1000 (beginning n: b1125; beginner: b1400)

bemoan v b1000

bequeath v b1000 (bequest: b1300)

bode v *augur* b1000 (bodement: b1600)

bury v b1000 ["forget," "conceal": b1350]

choke v b1000 ["obstruct": b1630] (noun use: b1565)

churn n b1000 (verb use: b1440)

climb v b1000 (noun use: b1890)

crack v *make noise* b1000 [as in "crack a whip": b1670] (noun use: b1300)

cram v b1000 [as in "cram for a test": b1830]

drip v b1000

fare v b1000

fetch v b1000

flutter v b1000 [obs. "float on water": u1700s] (noun use: b1645)

forbid v b1000 (forbidden: b1300)

freeze v *as in "it's freezing out"* b1000 ["freeze solid"; "cause to freeze": b1350; fig. "stop": b1570] (noun use: b1470)

glisten v b1000 (noun use: b1840)

glow v b1000 (noun use: b1470)

gnaw v b1000

grave v *engrave, dig* b1000

hop v *leap* b1000 (noun use: b1510)

kneel v b1000

knock v b1000 [as in "an engine knocking": b1900] (noun use: b1350)

lap v *as in "dog lapping up water"* b1000 [as in "lapping waves": b1830] (noun use: b1400)

lick v b1000 (noun use: b1600)

mash v *crush* b1000

narrow v b1000

overdo v b1000 [arch. "outdo": b1667]

pen v *shut in* b1000

pluck v b1000 [as in "pluck guitar strings": b1350]

pull v b1000 (noun use: b1350)

rise v b1000

shut v b1000 (adj use: b1500)

singe v b1000 (noun use: b1660)

sink v b1000

soak v b1000

sop v b1000

sprawl v *pertaining to people* b1000 [pertaining to things: b1600] (noun use: b1730)

stop v *block* b1000 ["clog": b1450]

strew v b1000

take v b1000 (noun use: b1655)

tan v *as in "tan leather"*

b1000 [as in "tan in the sun": b1530]

tease v *fray* b1000 ["bait, provoke": b1630; "be a sexual tease": b1900; as in "tease hair": b1930] (noun use: b1695)

temper v b1000

thaw v b1000 [fig. "get warmer": b1600] (noun use: b1450)

tow v b1000 (noun use: b1600)

turn v *rotate* b1000 ["cause to rotate": b1350] (noun use: b1500)

wipe v b1000 (noun use: b1670)

build v b1020 ["grow": b1350]

float v *on water* b1035 [in the air: b1350; "cause to float": b1630]

clatter v b1050 (noun use: b1600)

tap v *as in "tap a keg"* b1050 [as in "tap funds": b1575]

bell v *bay, bellow* b1100

beseech v b1100 (obs. noun use: 1600s only)

better v *improve* b1100

drench v *soak* b1100 ["force to drink": b900]

dub v *name* b1100

end v b1100

further v b1100 (furtherance: b1450)

harken v b1100 (hark: b1200)

hearken v b1100

let v *lease; permit* b1100

own v b1100 [obs. "obtain": until ME]

peel v b1100 [obs. "pillage": b1100 to 1700s; as in "sunburned skin peeling": b1600; "remove clothes": b1800] (noun use: b1570)

puff v b1100 ["praise": b1450; "smoke cigarettes, etc.": b1800] (noun use: b1350)

reek v b1100

right v b1100

rock v *as in "rock the boat"* b1100

shield v b1100

shimmer v b1100 (noun use: b1825)

should v b1100

slither v *slide* b1100 ["move like a snake": b1870]

speed v *expedite* b1100

spurn v *reject* b1100 [obs. "trip with the foot": u1700s]

stand up v b1100

step v *take a step* b1100 [as in "step in something": b1570; as in "step off": b1870]

tie v *bind with something* b1100 [as in "tie a shoe-lace": b1450; as in "tie a knot": b1670]

wave v *as in "a flag waving"* b1100

would v b1100

accord v b1125

can v *is able to* b1125 [obs. "know": b900 to 1800s; "is allowed": b1870]

fasten v *attach* b1125 [obs. "stabilize": b900 to 1600s]

allay v [obs. "discard": b1150 to LME]

cover v *overlay; conceal; protect* (noun use: b1225)

dip v ["baptize": b975; as in "dip in the road": b1800] (noun use: b1600)

forthcome v *come forth* (forthcoming: b1500)

gild v (gilded: b1150; gilt: b1350; obs. gilden: b1570 to 1800s)

keep v *as in "keep a promise"* [as in "keep Christmas": b1450]

leave v *as in "leave behind"*

man v *as in "man your station"*

mete v [arch. "measure": b725]

pound v *crush* ["hit repeatedly": b1595]

quench v *extinguish* ["quench thirst, etc.": b1350]

root v *as in "root around"*

slink v

spend v

stand v *endure, continue; refuse to yield*

stick v *stay*

sweep v *broom action* ["move," as in "sweep away": b1600]

swerve v *veer* [obs. "leave": until LME] (noun use: b1770)

whine v *make a whining sound* [obs. applied to arrows: b1150; "grouse": b1570] (noun use: b1635)

Archaisms

bale n *great evil* b725 (baleful: b1000)

warp v *throw; propel; hit* b725

weird n *destiny* b725 ["prognosticator": b1630; "prognostication": b1800]

moot n *assembly for discussion* b750

wif n (Am) *woman* b800

clepe v *name or call* b900

eke adv *also* b900

gang v *as in "gang aft agley"* b900

ghost n *soul* b900 [obs. "evil person": u1600s; obs. gen. "spirit": u1600s; modern sense: b1470; obs. "corpse": b1350 to 1500s] (ghostly "spiritual": b1150)

inly adv *obs. inwardly* b900 [u1600s]

iwis adv *surely* b900

ken v *obs. tell* b900 [u1600s]

kind n *nature; natural condition* b900 (obs. adj use "natural": u1600s; obs. kindly "naturally": u1500s; obs. kindly "natural": u1600s)

lose v *obs. destroy; be destroyed* b900 [u1600s]

mark n/v *border* b900

meed n *reward* b900

methinks n *it seems to me* b900 (meseems: b1400)

mislike v *displease* b900

or adv/conj/prep *before, ere* b900

overwade n *wade across* b900

somedeal adv *somewhat* b900

well v *boil* b900

won v *dwell* b900

wood adj *in a rage; wild; crazy* b900 (obs. noun use: b1350; obs. verb use: b1450)

writhen adj *contorted* b900

yield v *pay, repay* b900

braid v *obs. move suddenly* b950 [u1600s]

eftsoons adv *obs. again* b950 [u1600s] (arch. "soon after": b1350)

latch v *obs. grab* b950 [u1600s]

behoof n *benefit* b1000

drain v *obs. strain* b1000 [u1600s]

eft adv *obs. after, again* b1000

erst adv *obs. first; previous* b1000 ["long ago": b1200]

livelihood n *obs. lifetime* b1000 [u1500s]

round v *whisper* b1000

sad adj *obs. satiated* b1000 [obs. "learned": b1350 to 1500s; obs. "determined": b1350 to 1600s]

tide v *happen* b1000

lightness n *obs. light* b1050 [u1800s]

eath adj *easy* b1100

hest n *command* b1100

knee v *obs. kneel; bend the knee* b1100 [u1600s]

lout v *bow before respectfully* b1100

selcouth adj b1100 [u1800s]

thorough adv/prep *through* b1100

white v *obs. whiten* b1100 [u1400s]

worthful adj b1100

blindfell v *obs. make blind* [u1500s] (blind: b1100)

cover v *recover*

drubly adj *agitated* [u1500s]

endlong adv *lengthwise*

fair v *obs. beautify*

fang n *booty*

fathom n/v *embrace*

fern adj *old, yester*

flyte v *obs. argue* [u1700s]

follow v *obs. be similar to* [u1600s]

for-thy conj *obs. therefore* [u1800s]

forlese v *obs. lose; destroy* [u1600s]

foryield v *pay*

frayn v *ask*

full adj *obs. complete, foresworn, as in "a full enemy"*

gilden adj *obs. golden* [u1500s]

hard v *obs. harden* [u1600s]

haveless adj *obs. having nothing*

lease n/v *obs. lie, prevarication* [u1500s]

light adj *obs. bright* [u1700s]

long v *obs. lengthen* [u1400s]

mail n *payment, as in "blackmail"*

make n *mate, match*

make v *obs. do* [u1700s]

make v *behave*

manswear v *lie under oath*

math n *as in "aftermath"*

miss n *lack*

nill v *won't*

other adv/conj *or* [u1500s]

ping v *prod, push*

queme adj *pleasing*

right adj *straight* (obs. verb use: b1100)

shake v *obs. pass, leave* [u1500s]

shend v *place in disgrace*

sloom n *nap* (noun use: ME)

tell v *count*

think v *experience*

thrum n *obs. crowd*

to-break v [u1600s]

to-name n *nickname*

truck v *fail*

unright n *wrong*

uver adj *upper* (uvermost: b1570)

wark n *pain*

wary v *obs. curse* [u1700s]

wer n *male*

what interrogative *obs. why?* [u1600s]

what interrogative *how much?*

work n *commotion*

yborn adj *born*

Geography/Places

flat, flats n *flatland* b1170 (flatland: b1735)

north n b1200

west n b1200

bank n *mound, ridge* b1200 (verb use: b1590)

city n b1200

desert n *e.g., the Sahara* b1200

harbor n *spec. to the sea* b1200 ["any refuge": b1150]

lake n b1200 [obs. "stream": b1000; "small pool": b1150]

mountain n b1200 (mount: b750)

northeast n b1200

waste n *wasteland* b1200

cave n b1225 (cavern: b1380)

isle n b1225 (island: b900; islet: b1540)

country n *area, as in "rough country"* b1250 (adj use: b1350)

earthquake n b1280

quabbe n *bog* b1290

abysm n *abyss* b1300 (abyss: b1400; abysmal: b1660)

forest n b1300

ocean n b1300 [fig. "expanse," "a lot": b1500]

pinnacle n *natural peak* b1300 [fig. "apex": b1450]

plain n b1300

pond n b1300

river n b1300

valley n b1300 [fig. use: b1630]

crag n b1325 (craggy: b1400)

midstream n b1325

vicinage n *vicinity, area* b1325 (vicine "nearby": b1530; vicinity: b1560; vicinal: b1625)

yard n *area of ground* b1325 [as in "lumberyard": b1350]

coast n *waterside* b1340 [obs. "side of anything": b1125 to 1800s; obs. "border": b1450 to 1600s]

bog n (verb use: b1600)

common n *common area*

crevice n

downs n [type of hill: b1000]

fell n (Am) *hill; moor*

green n *as in "village green"*

gulf n [fig. sense: b1570]

hemisphere n

hillock n

hollow n

leap n *as in "Lover's Leap"*

pass n *as in "Donner pass"*

seacoast n

shoal n *shallows* (adj use: b900)

space n *area*

spring n *effluent water source*

Natural Things

oil n *olive oil* b1175 [gen. "grease": b1305] (verb use: b1425)

agate n b1200 [type of marble: b1870]

air n *what we breathe* b1200

birth n *applied to living things* b1200 (verb use: b1610)

marble n b1200

sunlight n b1200

hatch v *as in "hatch an egg"* b1250 [fig. use: b1670] (noun use: b1605)

metal n b1250 (metallic: b1425)

natural adj *of nature; physical; uncorrupted* b1250

sapphire n b1250

sunshine n b1250

topaz n b1275

amethyst n b1300

azure n *type of stone* b1300

element n *i.e.: earth, fire, water, air* b1300 [as in "periodic table of elements": b1670] (elementary: b1450; elemental: b1500)

emerald n b1300 [the color: b1730]

gravel n b1300 [obs. "sand": u1700s]

jasper n *type of mineral* b1300

ocher n b1300

onyx n b1300

rosin n b1300

smaragd n *emerald* b1300

suckling n *suckling animal, child* b1300 (sucker "suckling": b1450)

flame n/v b1305 [as in "old flame": b1670]

camphor n b1315 (camphor ball: b1595)

alum n *the chemical* b1325

diamond n *the gem* b1325

garnet n b1325

quicksand n b1325

ruby n b1325

saltpeter n b1325

turpentine n b1325 [type of oil: b1600]

echo n b1340 [literary sense: b1600; musical sense: b1730] (verb use: b1560)

mire n b1340 (verb use: b1400; mirepit: b1220)

mud n b1340

charcoal n [type of color: b1930]

crystalline adj

jet n *type of coal*

pearl n [the color: b1700] (pearlescent: b1940)

peat n

rock n *massive stone feature* ["stone material": b1600; "piece of rock": b1730]

sal n *salt*

slate n *type of rock* ["writing board made of slate": b1470]

soil n *lit. dirt*

suet n

sulfur n

Plants

fruit n b1175

bloom n/v *in flowers* b1200

fig n *fruit or tree* b1200

flower n/v b1200

saffron n b1200

grape n b1250

ivory n b1265 (adj use: b1330)

hollyhock n b1275

honeysuckle n b1275

lavender n b1275 [type of potpourri: b1600; type of

color: b1870] (verb use:
b1820)

anise, aniseed n b1300 (anisette: b1840)

bur n b1300

flourish v *of plants* b1300 [fig.
use: b1570; obs. "deco-
rate": u1600s; "show off":
b1470]

henbane n *type of plant*
b1300

herb n b1300

laurel n *type of tree* b1300
["honor": b1450] (verb
use: b1635)

leave n *spring leaves* b1300

plantain n *type of plant* b1300

verdure n b1300

vine n b1300 (verb use:
b1800)

watercress n b1300

cork n b1305

flax n b1325 ["flaxen cloth":
b900]

gourd n b1325

mandrake n *type of plant*
b1325 [obs. fig. "weed":
b1530 to 1600s]

popinjay n *arch. parrot* b1325
[fig. "vain person": b1530]

quack v b1325 (noun use:
b1840)

underwood n *undergrowth*
b1325

sapling n b1330 [fig. "a
youth": b1600]

brush n b1340 (brushland:
b1855)

asp n *the snake*

cattail n *type of plant*

chickweed n

crab n *crab apple tree*

fleur-de-lis n

ground ivy n

gum n *as in "tree gum"*

kernel n *as in "kernel of
grain"* ["inside of nut":
b1000; gen. "core":
b1570]

litmus n

log n *as in "tree stem"* (verb
use: b1700)

marigold n

poplar n

puffin n

self-heal n *type of plant*

sprig n

sycamore n

violet n

wainscot n *type of oak* [type
of oak panelling: b1570]
(verb use: b1570)

Animals

wing n b1175

beast, beastly n, adj b1200

coney n *rabbit fur* b1200

corbie n *carrion crow* b1200

cur n *applied to dogs* b1200
[applied to people: b1590]

dove n b1200

ermine n b1200

flock n *as in "flock of geese"*
b1200 [applied to people:
b895] (verb use: b1350)

kid n *young goat* b1200
["young child": b1600]
(verb use: b1450; kiddie:
b1600)

lion n b1200

locust n *type of insect* b1200

scorpion n b1200

stag n *male deer* b1200

beak n b1225 [slang "nose":
b1450]

ostrich n b1225

pig n b1225 ["piggish person": b1570; slang "police
officer": b1830]

snout n b1225

venom n b1225 (venomous:
b1300)

whalebone n b1225

salmon n b1230

cuckoo n *type of bird* b1250
["looney person": b1585]
(verb use: b1630)

falcon n b1250 (falconer:
b1400; falcon-gentle:
b1450; falconet: b1855)

palfrey n *horse other than a
warhorse* b1250

pie n *magpie* b1250

web n *cobweb* b1250 [fig. use:
b1600] (verb use: b1870)

fawn n b1275 [type of color:
b1900]

blackbird n b1280

creature n b1280 [obs.
"something created":
u1600s]

hake n *type of fish* b1280

anthill n b1300

blubber n b1300 [as in
"whale blubber": b1470]

bull adj *male* b1300

bunting n *type of bird* b1300
[term of endearment:
b1570]

buzzard n *Old World bird*
b1300 [fig. "coot": b1470;
"New World condor":
b1830]

chanticleer n *rooster* b1300

cloven foot n b1300 (cloven
hoof: b1870)

coot n *type of bird* b1300

coral n b1300

courser n *horse* b1300 [type
of dog: b1595; type of bird:
b1770]

crocodile n b1300

croup n *animal's tail end*
b1300

drake n *male duck* b1300

dromedary n b1300

eagle n b1300 (eaglet:
b1575)

eggshell n b1300

elephant n b1300

game n b1300

heron n b1300

howl v *applied to animals*
b1300 [applied to things:
b1700] (noun use: b1600)

jay n *type of bird* b1300

lamprey n b1300 (lamper
eel: b1710)

leopard n b1300 (leopardess:
b1570)

lioness n b1300

mackerel n *type of fish* b1300

monster n *deformed creature*
b1300 ["fantastic crea-
ture": b1470; applied to
people: b1500] (mon-
strous: b1380)

oyster n b1300

panther n b1300

pard n *leopard* b1300

partridge n b1300

peacock, peahen n b1300

pheasant n b1300

roach n *type of fish* b1300

scale n *as in "fish scales"*
b1300 (verb use: b1450)

serpent n b1300

slough n *shed snake skin*
b1300 (verb use: b1720)

sole n *type of fish* b1300

sturgeon n b1300

teal n *type of duck* b1300 [the
color: b1930]

tree snail n b1300

turtledove n b1300

volatile n *obs. birds* b1300
[u1600s]

waterfowl n b1300

flounder n b1305

haddock n b1310

baleen n *whalebone* b1315
[obs. "whale": b1350 to
1600s]

cockle n *type of shellfish*
b1315

crayfish n b1315 (crawfish:
b1625; crawdad: b1905)

crest n b1315 (crested:
b1400)

baboon n b1325 [obs. "grotesque architectural fig-
ure": b1300 to 1500s]

cobweb n b1325

cricket n *the insect* b1325

dam n *opp. of sire* b1325

fetlock n b1325

four-footed adj b1325

grasshopper n b1325 (obs.
grasshop n: b1150 to
1600s)

mallard n *type of duck* b1325

pelt n *hide* b1325 (verb use:
b1600; peltry "pelts":
b1450)

pike n *type of fish* b1325

plover n b1325

polecat n b1325

porpoise n b1325

ray n *the fish* b1325

sheldrake n *type of duck*
b1325 (shelduck: b1710)

snipe n b1325 ["worthless
person": b1630]

titmouse n b1325

animal n *lit. and fig.* b1330
(adj use: b1615)

cormorant n *type of bird*
b1330 [fig. "glutton":
b1530]

quail n b1330

egg n b1340 ["ovum":
b1900]

hyena n b1340

chick n b1345 [arch. "child":
b1325; slang "woman":
b1930]

beehive n [fig. "active environment": b1630]

bloodhound n

cete n *arch. sea creature*

chameleon n [fig. "changeable person": b1590]

cod n (codfish: b1275)
dock n *part of a tail* (verb use: b1400)
dolphin n
down n *on birds* [on plants: b1450]
ferret n *type of animal*
fry n *spawn*
fur n
gill n *as in "fish gills"*
glowworm n
gosling n
hackney, hack n *type of horse*
hippopotamus n (hippo: b1875)
kingfisher n
lynx n
mastiff n
merlin n *type of falcon*
mole n *the burrowing animal*
nuthatch n *type of bird*
paw n *animal foot*
perch n *type of fish*
rhinoceros n (rhino: b1885)
shrimp n
skate n *type of sea ray*
sorrel n *type of horse* [type of color: b1570]
spaniel n
squirrel n
talon n
tercel n *male hawk*
vermin n [applied to people: b1570] (verminous: b1620)
weave v *applied to spiders*

Weather

tempest n b1250 (verb use: b1400; tempestuous: b1510)
hoarfrost n b1300 (hoar: b1470)
lightning n b1300
sleet n b1300 (verb use: b1350)
snowdrift n b1300
weathercock n *weathervane* b1300
drought n [gen. "dryness": b1000; fig. use: b1630]
elements n
snowball n
thunderlight n *arch. lightning*
whirlwind n [fig. use: b1450] (adj use: b1615)

Heavens/Sky

cloud n b1200 [obs. "type of geographical feature": b895; gen., as in "cloud of smoke": b1450] (verb use, lit. and fig.: b1420)
cloudy adj *clouded over* b1200 [gen. "indistinct": b1450]
cosmos n b1200
sky n b1225 [obs. "clouds": b1350 to 1500s]
firmament n b1250
solstice n b1250
eclipse n/v b1280
moonlight n b1300 (moonshine: b1425)
planet n *ancient concept of celestial bodies; astrology: influence of the planets* b1300 [modern sense: b1670]
constellation n *astrological star grouping* b1325 [astronomical star grouping: b1450]
element n *obs. celestial object* [u1600s]
lodestar n
starlight n
sunrise n

Science

alloy n *mixture of metals* b1325 ["measure of gold's purity": b1600] (verb use: b1665)

Energy

kindle v b1200
furnace n b1225
fuel n b1300 [fig. use: b1600] (verb use: b1595)

Time

March n b1200
anniversary n b1200
calendar n *measure of a year* b1200 ["phys. chart of the year," as in "wall calendar": b1350; "schedule," as in "calendar of events": b1470] (verb use: b1500)
hour n b1200
term n *length of time; arch. end* b1200 [leg. eduntiluse: b1455; "length of pregnancy": b1870]
bedtime n b1250

eve n *as in "New Year's Eve"* b1250
morning n *dawn* b1250 ["dawn to noon": b1470; obs. "dawn to evening": b1770] (morn: b830)
morrow n/interj *tomorrow* b1250
tomorrow adv *the next day; the future* b1275 (noun use: b1350)
antiquity n *as in "times of antiquity"* b1280 ["antique item": b1530]
afternoon n b1300
betimes adv *in good time, soon* b1300
cockcrow n *dawn* b1300 (cockshut: b1595)
curfew n *lights out* b1300 ["time to be indoors": b1900]
noon n b1300 [obs. "nine hours after daybreak": b1900 to late ME] (noontide: b1200; noontime: b1400)
season n b1300
date n *spec. time designation* b1325 ["appointment": b1900] (verb use: b1450)
age n *as in "Age of Reason"*
forenight n *arch. evening*
moment n
point n *as in "that point of time"*
present adj/n *now* [obs. "presence," "something that is present": u1700s]
quotidian adj *daily* ["daily to the point of triviality": b1470]
to-year adv *arch. akin to tonight*
today n *this day* (adj use: b1970)

Age/Aging

age n *how old you are* b1275 (noun use: b1400)
ancient adj (noun use: b1505)

Mathematics

figure n b1200
seventy n b1200
tally v b1200

arithmetic n b1250 (adj use: b1670)
dozen n b1300
number n/v b1300
count v/n *1,2,3; as in "counts for something"* b1325 [as in "I'm counting on it": b1670; as in "every little bit counts": b1870]
geometry n
mean adj *middle*
seventeen n (adj use: b900)

Measurement

gallon n b1225
measure n b1300 (verb use: b1400)
pace n *a step* b1300 ["rate," as in "keeping pace": b1450] (verb use: b1515)
peck n *measure* b1300
dial n *compass dial* b1340 ["sundial": b1420; gen. "meter face": b1770]
cubit n [obs. "forearm": b1450 to 1800s]
gauge n *standard* ["measuring tool": b1700] (verb use: b1425)
measure v
mite n *a bit*
ounce n
quart n *two pints* ["quart container": b1325]
rule n *measure, as in "as a rule"; ruler* (ruler: b1470)
standard n

The Body

stones n *testicles* b1155
breath n b1200 [obs. "aroma, odor": b900] (breathe: b1470)
carbuncle n *boil* b1200 [type of gem: b1200]
eyesight n b1200 [obs. "range of vision": 1600s]
haunch n b1200
hipbone n b1200 (hip: b900)
throe n *phys. spasm* b1200 [fig. "spasm": b1700]
fingernail n b1225
skull n b1225
eyelid n b1250
nature n b1250 [as in "human nature": b1665]
teat n b1250 ["artificial teat": b1450]

leg n b1275 [in furniture: b1630] (verb use: b1605)

urine n b1275 (urinate: b1600)

backbone n *spine* b1300 ["mainstay," "courage": b1870]

blister n b1300 (verb use: b1425)

bowel n b1300 [gen. "interior": b1530]

chine n *spine* b1300 (verb use: b1450)

entrails n b1300 [fig. "place of internal feelings": b1450 to 1700s] (obs. entrail "intestines": u1600s)

face n b1300 [of a watch: b1700]

joint n *in bodies* b1300 [gen. use: b1450] (adj use: b1350)

member n b1300

nape n b1300

pain n b1300

phlegm n b1300

shoulder blade n b1300

spleen n *lit.* b1300 [obs. fig. "melancholy source": u1600s; "temper": b1600] (splenetic: b1545)

tress n b1300

vein n b1300 [as in "coal vein": b1450]

visage n b1300

tail n *buttocks* b1305

balls n *testicles* b1325

calf n *back of the leg* b1325 (calve: b1000)

cough v b1325 (noun use "coughing": b1350; noun use "one cough": b1770)

cunt n b1325

gums n *as in "dental gums"* b1325 (gum "interior of mouth": b1100 to 1700s)

kidney n *bodily part; fig. "temperament"* b1325

loin n b1325

pate n *head* b1325

slaver n/v *drool* b1325 [fig. "drivel": b1830]

sole n b1325 ["part of shoe": b1470]

temple n *facial feature* b1325

conception n b1335 (conceive: b1280)

humor n *type of body fluid*

b1340 ["mood": b1525; "funny perspective": b1600]

armpit n

dewlap n

fetus n (fetal: b1815)

gorge n *throat*

hangnail n (agnail: b950)

knot n *tense muscle* [as in "tree knot": b1450]

lap n *as in "sit on Santa's lap"* [obs. "bosom": u1600s]

molar n (adj use: b1630)

palm n *part of the hand* [part of the foot: b1900]

pulse n *as in "take your pulse"* [fig. "heart": b1450; gen. "beat": b1670] (verb use: b1450; pulsation: b1425; pulsate: b1795)

share n *arch. groin*

shoulder v *press against with shoulder* ["assume responsibility": b1600]

stomach n ["belly," "predilection": b1450; obs. "pride": b1530 to 1700s] (stomachic: b1650)

uvula n

waist n [fig. "middle": b1630]

Physical Description

feeble adj b1175

smell v/n b1175

gape v b1225 (noun use: b1535)

yowl v b1225 (noun use: b1450)

sob v b1250 (noun use: b1350)

piss v b1290 (noun use: b1390)

bald adj *hairless* b1295 [obs. "round": ME only; "worn": b1630]

awake adj b1300

brawn n b1300 ["boar meat": b1470] (brawny: b1400)

countenance n *facial expression; calm bearing* b1300 [obs. gen. "bearing": u1700s; "face": b1450; "blessing, support": b1600]

craving n b1300 (crave: b1450)

nourish v b1300 [obs. "nur-

ture": u1600s] (nourishment: b1370; nourishing: b1400)

pale adj *pertaining to people* b1300 [pertaining to colors: b1450] (verb use: b1400)

pore v *stare* b1300 ["study": b1450]

purblind adj b1300 ["mentally blind": b1570] (verb use: b1600)

appetite n b1305

handy adj *dexterous* b1315

yammer v *chatter* b1325 ["yowl, lament": b1325; "grouse": b1830]

mutter v b1335 (noun use: b1635)

dizzy adj *feeling spinning* [fig. use: b1530; as in "dizzy heights": b1630] (verb use: b1505)

fist n *arch. fart*

frail, frailty adj, n

galp v *obs. gawk* [u1500s]

grace n

great adj *pregnant* (greaten: b1375)

lithe adj ["gentle": b900] (lithy: b1150)

lively adj [obs. "living": b1000 to 1600s]

meager adj *emaciated* ["scanty": b1530]

pant v *breathe heavily* (noun use: b1515)

quick adj *physically fast* (adv use: b1400)

rift v *arch. belch*

slake v *quench* [var. meanings of "slacken": b1150 to 1600s]

weak adj *phys. weak* ["weak-willed": b1150]

Medicine

circumcision n b1175 (circumcise: b1250)

healer n b1200

wan adj b1200 [describing the sea: b900; morose: b1450; describing heavenly bodies: b1630]

bloodletting n b1225

leprous adj b1225 (leper: b1400; leprosy: b1535)

medicine n b1225 (verb use: b1450)

physician n b1225 [obs. "physicist": b1450 to 1600s]

malady n b1250

scab n *type of disease* b1250

sicken v *make ill* b1250 ["disgust": b1630] (sickening: b1715)

sightless adj *blind* b1250 ["invisible": b1600]

stump n *remains of amputated limb* b1250 ["stub": b1530] (verb use: b1600)

ointment n b1280

ague n *type of fever* b1300

caudle n *type of potion* b1300

chirurgeon n *surgeon* b1300 (chirurgery: b1400)

deliver v *as in "deliver a baby"* b1300 (obs. "deliverance": b1450 to 1600s; delivery: b1600)

dropsy n *edema* b1300 [obs. "yen": b1570 to 1700s]

gout n b1300

idiot n *med.* b1300 [gen. sense: b1470]

litter n b1300 [obs. gen. "bed": u1400s]

midwife adj/n b1300 [fig. use: b1600] (verb use: b1470; midwifery: b1485)

palsy n *paralysis, the shakes* b1300 (verb use: b1615)

physic n *the art of healing; a spec. medicine* b1300 [obs. "natural science": u1800s; "people in medicine": b1450] (verb use: b1400; physician: b1225; physical: b1450)

surgeon n b1300

surgery n b1300 ["where surgery takes place": b1870] (surgical: b1770)

jaundice n b1305 [fig. use: b1600] (jaundiced: b1640)

measles n b1325 (measly: b1600)

melancholy n b1325 [gen. "depression": b1450] (adj use: b1400; obs. verb use: b1450 to 1800s; melancholic: b1400; melancholious: b1450; melancholize:

b1600; melancholia:
b1695)

black-and-blue adj

drug n ["addictive substance, stimulant": b1900] (verb use: b1605)

gown n

incurable adj

lazar n *diseased person*

malease n *obs. disease* [u1500s]

medicinal adj (medicinable: b1400)

mute adj *unspeaking* (noun use: b1600; verb use: b1885)

pimple n

sickly adj (verb use: b1765)

unwell adj [slang "menstruating": b1870]

walleyed adj *speckle-eyed* ["white-eyed": b1590] (walleye n: b1525)

yblent adj *obs. blinded* [u1500s]

Everyday Life

gear n *clothing, equipment* b1200

lamp n b1200

mazer n *type of bowl* b1200

seat n b1200 ["buttocks": b1630; as in "seat of the pants": b1870] (verb use: b1630)

chair n b1225

mildew n b1225 ["honeydew": b1000 to 1600s] (verb use: b1555)

mirror n b1225 (verb use: b1595)

urinal n *type of porcelain facility* b1225 [obs. "med. container for urine": b1275 to 1800s; "chamberpot": b1450]

cistern n b1250

ink n b1250 [in squid: b1600]

platter n b1280

blanket n b1300 ["blanketing layer": b1630] (fig. verb use: b1605)

cauldron n b1300

coverlet n *bedspread* b1300

curtain n b1300 [fig. "concealing device": b1450; "theatrical use": b1600]

mattress n b1300

pantry n b1300

pavement n b1300 (pave: b1325)

pitcher n *type of water container* b1300

pocket n *type of bag* b1300 [as in "pants pocket": b1450; "pouch," as in "notebook pocket": b1830; as in "pockets of resistance": b1930]

quilt n b1300 (verb use: b1555)

sampler n *type of needlework* b1300

table n *piece of furniture; tablet; people sitting at a table* b1300 ["slab": b900] (verb use: b1450)

towel n b1300

vessel n b1300

cushion n *as in "seat cushion"* b1305 [as in "pin cushion": b1600; other types of cushioning things: b1800] (verb use: b1740)

pewter n b1310

hamper n b1320

charger n *platter* b1325

cupboard n *sideboard* b1325 [obs. type of table equipment: b1530 to 1600s; type of cabinet: b1530]

lace n *as in "shoelace"* b1325 (verb use: b1225)

pink v *as in "pinking shears"* b1325

spool n b1325 (verb use: b1605)

satchel n b1340

bath n *spa*

bottle n ["baby's bottle": b1870] (verb use: b1600)

carpet n [fig. "layer": 1500s] (verb use: b1450; carpeting: b1760)

colander n

counter n *e.g., gamepiece*

crotchet n

doubler n *arch. type of plate*

goblet n *drinking bowl* ["stemmed glassware": b1900]

grindle stone n *arch. grindstone*

hand towel n

latrine n

lavender, lavendry n *obs. launder, laundry* [u1500s]

paper n [type of document: b1450] (papers "credentials": b1700)

pouch n [spec. for carrying money: b1400; as in "animal's pouch": b1450] (verb use: b1570)

privy n *bathroom*

rose water n

screen n *on a fireplace* (verb use: b1485)

shelf n [in geology: b1470] (shelving: b1820)

shuttle n *bobbin*

sink n *as in "kitchen sink"*

skillet n

spigot n

spoon n [obs. "splinter": b900 to 1500s] (verb use: b1715)

tub n *type of container* [as in "tub of butter": b1970]

varnish n *varnishing substance* [type of finish: b1570] (verb use: b1400)

whisk n (verb use: b1500)

wicker n

work v *create needlework*

Shelter/Housing

court n *courtyard* b1175 [as in "tennis court": b1530]

booth n *stall* b1200

cellar n b1200 (verb use: b1530)

chamber n *room* b1200 ["group of rooms": b1670]

shingle n b1200 (verb use: b1565)

throne n b1225 [representing power: b1570]

window n b1225 [gen., as in "window envelope": b1450]

hostel n b1250

mortar n *building material* b1250

palace n b1250 (palatial: b1755)

belfry n b1275 (bell tower: b1615)

coal cellar n b1285

arbor n *shelter of shrubs or vines* b1300 [obs. "lawn": b1350 to 1400s; "tree": b1650] (arboreal: b1670)

building n b1300

cookhouse n b1300

dungeon n b1300

gutter n b1300

housing n *accommodations* b1300

lodge n/v b1300

loft n b1300 [obs. "heavenly vault": b1000 to 1500s]

manor n b1300 [obs. gen. "shelter": b1450 to 1500s]

masonry n *work of the mason; stonework* b1300

pavillion n *type of tent* b1300 [type of building: b1700]

porch n b1300

postern n *back door* b1300

store n *storehouse* b1300 (verb use: b1275)

tent n b1300

bay n *recessed area, as in "bay window"* b1325 [as in "sick bay": b1600] (bay window: b1405)

tenant n b1325 ["property owner": b1300] (verb use: b1635)

buttress n b1330 (verb use: b1380)

chimney n b1330 [obs. "fireplace": b1350]

jamb n b1335

buttery n *storeroom*

cabin n *room on a ship, etc.* [type of building: b1470]

closet n *small room* [as in "water closet": b1500; "storage room": b1630] (verb use: b1595; adj use: b1615)

donjon n

doornail n

drawbridge n

fortress n (arch. verb use: b1500)

gable n

garret n [obs. type of fortified turret: u1500s]

garth n *courtyard, yard*

hall n *as in "dining hall"* ["hallway": b1670]

lintel n

live v *reside*

louver n

mansion n [obs. "act of dwelling": u1700s; obs. "stopover place": b1450 to 1700s]

molding n

nook n

outhouse n *detached building* [spec. "toilet": b1830]

penthouse n *type of building* ["room at the top": b1900]

portal n

portcullis n

saucery n *spec. type of kitchen*

storehouse n

study n *type of room*

turret n [obs. "apex": u1600s; mil. use: b1870]

vault n *arch; arched space; treasury*

Drink

liquor n b1225 (verb use: b1505)

beverage n b1300

white wine n b1300

bib v *imbibe* b1325 (bibble: b1530; bibulous: b1870)

booze n/v b1325 (boozy: b1530; boozer: b1630)

red adj *as in "red wine"*

sec adj *somewhat dry (of champagne)*

Food

mustard n b1190

bit n *morsel of food* b1200 ["mouthful": b900; gen. "small portion": b1000]

cake n *type of bread* b1200 ["dessert cake": b1470] (verb use: b1610)

clove n *the spice* b1200 (cloves: b1400)

diet n *regular food* b1200 [type of weight control: b1450] (verb use: b1380)

feast n b1200 (verb use: b1300)

flour n b1225

glutton, gluttony n b1225 (gluttonous: b1350; obs. glutton v: b1630 to 1800s)

licorice n *the plant* b1225 [the food: b1450]

pottage n *type of soup* b1225

savory n *type of mint* b1225

spice n b1225 [obs. "species": u1600s] (verb use: b1400)

lentil n *type of legume* b1250

candy n *crystallized sugar*

b1275 ["confection": b1830] (verb use: b1535)

supper n b1275

chitterlings n b1280 (chitlins: b1845; chitlings: b1880)

cider n b1280

morsel n b1280 (verb use "divide": b1600)

caraway n b1285

almond n b1300

bran n b1300 [obs. "dandruff": b1350 to 1500s]

cherry n b1300 [type of wood: b1800]

date n *the fruit* b1300

delicious adj b1300 [obs. "hedonistic": u1600s]

dine v b1300 (obs. noun use: b1450)

dinner n b1300 (verb use: b1770; dinnertime: b1375)

fry v b1300 (noun use: b1670)

gingerbread n b1300

glair n *egg white* b1300

gorge v *stuff yourself* b1300

grease n *melted fat* b1300 [obs. "animal fat": u1600s] (verb use: b1400)

kale n b1300 (kaleyard: b1570)

lettuce n b1300

mace n *type of spice* b1300

mess n *food* b1300 (verb use: b1385)

mutton n b1300

pasty n *type of meat pie* b1300

pork n b1300

rice n b1300

roast v b1300 (noun use: b1350)

sugar n b1300

sup v *eat* b1300

tripe n b1300 [arch. "beer gut": b1450]

venison n b1300

vinegar n b1300 [fig. use: b1630] (vinegarish: b1650; vinegary: b1730)

crust n *on bread* b1325 ["outside": b1350; as in "pie crust": b1450; as in "crust of a planet": b1555; obs. "shell": b1630]

devour v b1325

munch v b1325

pie n *baked dish* b1325 [fig. treat: b1870]

pomegranate n b1325

quince n b1325

sage n *type of mint* b1325

sourdough n b1325

victual n b1325

bacon n b1330 [obs. "rube": 1500s only]

biscuit n b1340

brisket n b1340

sauce n b1340 (verb use: b1440)

board n *food, as in "room and board"* (verb use: b1530)

broil v (noun use: b1585)

comfit n *type of candy*

coriander n

cream n [fig., as in "cream of the crop": b1600] (verb use, as in "cream off": b1630)

currant n

gravy n *type of dressing* [modern sense: b1600]

jujube n

lard n/v [obs. "bacon": u1700s]

leaven n *leavening substance* (verb use: b1450; leavening: b1610)

nutmeg n

onion n

orange n

origanum n *type of seasoning*

pancake n

paste n *dough*

peach n *type of fruit* [as in "a peach of a person": b1770]

potage n *type of soup*

potion n

prune n

raisin n [obs. "grapes": u1700s]

repast n (obs. verb use: b1470 to 1600s)

rich adj *sumptuous, filling*

roast n

shoulder n

soup n

spinach n

steak n *cut of beef* [cuts of other types of meat: b1900]

substantial adj *ample, pertaining to food* [pertaining to other things: b1450]

thyme n

veal n

white bread n

Agriculture/ Food-Gathering

garner n *granary, accumulation* b1175

garden n b1185 (verb use: b1580; gardener: b1130)

plow/plough n b1200 (verb use: b1450; plowshare: b1400)

cattle n b1225 [obs. "assets": u1400s]

gooseherd n b1250

harvest n b1250 ["autumn": b750] (verb use: b1400)

hunter n b1250 (hunt v: b1000; hunt n: b1375; obs. hunt "hunter": b1135 to 1800s; huntress: b1400; huntsman: b1570; huntswoman: b1630)

stable n *lit.* b1250 [fig. "collection": b1900] (verb use: b1350)

park n *hunting area* b1275 [as in "city park": b1670; as in "ballpark": b1870; as in "industrial park": b1970] (parkland: b1910)

plowman n b1275

cotton n *the plant, the cloth* b1290

beef n b1300

bellwether n b1300

bushel n b1300 [fig. "a lot": b1470]

cornfield n b1300

crop n b1300

dairy n b1300

fishpond n b1300

geld v *castrate* b1300 (gelding: b1400)

grandsire n *animal's grandparent* b1300

haycock n b1300

herd v b1300

husbandry n b1300

millhouse n b1300

pasture n b1300 (verb use: b1400; pasturage: b1535; pastoral: b1450)

pitchfork n b1300 (verb use: b1870)

stray n *spec. separated animal*

b1300 [gen. "separated thing": b1800] (verb use: b1350; adj use: b1450)

stubble n *cut growth of grain* b1300 [other types of stubble, as in "beard stubble": b1600]

till v *cultivate* b1300 [obs. "work hard": b900 to 1400s]

warrener n *gamekeeper* b1300

forage n *fodder* b1325 (verb use: b1420)

pitfall n *type of trap* b1325 [obs. "ambush": b1325; fig. "trap": b1770]

provender n *animal feed* b1325

herder n b1330

coop n b1345 [type of basket: b1250] (verb use: b1585)

grain n *oats, etc.*

hawk v *hunt with a hawk*

horseshoe n

husband n *obs. farmer* [u1700s]

husbandman n *farmer*

kennel n *pet shelter* ["animal den": b1770] (verb use: b1555)

manger n

mew n *type of enclosure*

oxbow adj/n *type of yoke* ["type of river feature": b1800]

pickfork n *arch. pitchfork*

pilcorn n *type of oat*

poultry n [obs. "poultry farm or store": u1500s]

pullen n *arch. poultry*

rust n *type of plant disease*

shepherdess n (shepherd: b1050)

vineyard n (vinery: b1450)

Cloth/Clothing

breech/breeches n *trousers* b1200 [obs. "breech-cloth": b1000 to 1600s]

cap n *headgear* b1200 [obs. "hood": b1000]

chemise n *woman's garment* b1200

clothing n b1200 [rare "making cloth": b1570]

habit n *including habit as in clothing* b1200

cloak n b1225 [gen. "cover": b1530] (verb use: b1510)

hank n b1225

veil n b1225 (verb use: b1450)

button n *fastener* b1250 ["device," as in "on-off button": b1630] (verb use: b1380)

damask n *type of fabric* b1250

flock n *type of wool* b1250 (verb use: b1530)

scarlet n *type of cloth* b1250 ["red": b1300; type of official dress: b1500]

canvas n b1275 ["painting surface": b1730]

corset n *gen. type of clothing* b1275 ["fat inhibitor": b1795]

robe n b1275

russet n b1275 [the color: b1470]

apparel n b1300 [arch. broader "equipment, including clothing": b1350] (verb use: b1250)

attire n/v b1300

boot n *footwear* b1300 (verb use: b1470)

buckle n b1300 (verb use: b1390)

coat n b1300 [as in "a coat of fur": b1390; "coating," as in "coat of paint": b1630]

coif n *type of cap* b1300

collar n b1300 [as in "dog collar": b1450]

drapery n *cloth* b1300 ["curtain": b1700]

garment n b1300

gray n *gray clothing* b1300

kerchief n b1300 [as in "handkerchief": b1450] (kercher: b1450)

miniver n *type of fur* b1300

samite n *type of fabric* b1300

shod adj *wearing shoes* b1300

skirt n b1300

surcoat n *type of outer coat* b1300

visor n *on a helmet* b1300 [on a hat: b1870]

worsted n b1300

flannel n b1305 ["washcloth": b1830] (flannels: b1630; flannelette: b1890)

apron n b1310 (apron string: b1545)

bolt n *cloth measure* b1310

buckskin adj/n b1310

dud n *clothing, failure* b1310 (duds: b1530)

armhole n b1325

purfle v *ornament* b1325 (noun use: b1450)

unbutton v b1325 (unbuttoned: b1585)

velvet n b1325

wrap v b1325 [gen. use: b1450] (noun use: b1350)

fringe n [gen. use: b1670]

frock n

gambeson n *type of tunic*

garter n

gown n *robe* ["dress": b1470; in hospitals: b1930]

habergeon n *type of armor*

kilt v *tuck up* (noun use: b1730)

knit v *as in "knit a sweater"; fig.* [arch. "knot": b1000; obs. method of gelding: b1630 to 1700s]

linen n *linen clothing* [the cloth: b1450]

mitten n

nake v *arch. make naked*

skein n/v *coil of yarn*

taffeta n

tapis v *obs. type of cloth*

tire n/v *obs. attire* [u1700s]

tongue n *flap, as in "tongue of a shoe"*

twill n

vesture n *clothing* (verb use: b1555)

wadmal n *type of fabric*

web n *type of band*

white n

woolward adj *obs. wearing wool* [u1800s]

Fashion/Style

brooch n b1200

jewel n *piece of jewelry* b1300 ["gem": b1600] (jeweler, jewelry: b1350)

ouch n *clasp or brooch*

sheen n *obs. beautiful person* [u1500s]

Tools

hoop n b1175

balance n *measuring tool* b1200 (verb use: b1585)

bar n/v *rod, pole* b1200

cable n *type of rope* b1200

crook n *hooked tool* b1200 [type of staff: b1450]

firebrand n b1225 [fig. use: b1450]

floodgate n b1225

grindstone n b1225

basket n b1230

bucket n b1250

cog n *gear tooth* b1250

maul n *type of weapon* b1250 [type of tool: b1450] (verb use "strike": b1300)

hopper n b1280

brad n b1295

andiron n b1300

barrel n b1300

buoy n b1300 (verb use: b1600)

crane n b1300 (verb use: b1570)

gridiron n b1300 (grid: b1840)

harness n/v b1300

harrow n *cultivating tool* b1300

hinge n b1300 (verb use: b1610)

lantern n b1300

lever n *type of pry* b1300 [type of control device: b1870] (verb use: b1870)

limekiln n b1300

linchpin n b1300

mold n b1300 (verb use: b1400)

plumb n *lead weight* b1300 (verb use: b1450; plumb line: b1500)

razor n b1300 (verb use: b1350; raze "shave": b1450)

roller n b1300

square n b1300 (adj use: b1600)

torch n b1300 [as in "blowtorch": b1930]

washer n *connecting disk* b1300

windmill n b1300

clasp n *as in "jewelry clasp"*

b1310 ["embrace": b1670] (verb use: b1395)

hatchet n b1310

brace n *support; clasp* b1315 (verb use: b1350)

chisel n b1325 (verb use: b1510)

creel n b1325

dam n *water barrier* b1325 (verb use: b1450)

gaff n *type of hook or spur* b1325 [spec. to fish: b1660]

manacle n/v b1325

pickax n b1325 (pick: b1350)

pulley n b1325

scoop n *ladle* b1325 [as in "sugar scoop": b1490; as in "ice cream scoop": b1730; "scoopful": b1770] (verb use: b1340)

cotter n *type of pin* b1340

hose n *as in "water hose"* b1340 (verb use: b1890)

bolt n *as in "door bolt," "nuts and bolts"*

clamp n (verb use: b1680)

compass n *drawing tool; "perimeter," "area"*

dowel n

edge tool n

gimlet n

gouge n (verb use: b1570)

grapple n (verb use: b1530)

hoe n (verb use: b1450)

hone n *whetstone* [gen. "stone": b950] (verb use: b1930)

horsewhip n

lathe n

level n

pestle n (verb use: b1450)

pick n *as in "pickax"* (pickax: b1325)

pincers n [type of claws: b1670]

plane n/v *smoothing tool* ["bladed shaving tool": b1450]

rein n (verb use: b1470)

roofing nail n

scaffold, scaffolding n

sealing wax n

solder n [fig. use: b1600] (verb use: b1450)

stanchion n

trace n *type of harness gear*

trowel n [spec. for gardening: b1800] (verb use: b1670)

vise n (verb use: b1605)

weight/weights n *used in measurement* [used to propel mechanisms: b1450]

wheelbarrow n

whip n (verb use: b1450)

wisp n [as in "wisp of smoke": b1870]

Travel/Transportation

seafaring adj b1200 (noun use: b1595; seafarer: b1515; seagoing: b1830)

walk v *travel on foot* b1200 [obs. "roll": b1000 to late ME; obs. gen. "travel": b1000 to 1500s] (noun use: b1250)

galley n *type of ship* b1225

journey n b1225 [obs. "day": u1600s; obs. "distance traveled in a day": u1500s; "other things done in a day, such as work": concurrent] (verb use: b1350)

gig n *as in "whirlygig," light boat* b1250 (verb use: b1810)

sojourn n b1250

walk n *action of walking* b1250 ["path": b1450; "paved path": b1570]

ferry n b1290 (ferryboat: b1450)

amble n/v *of beasts of burden* b1300

course n *as in "the course of the ship"* b1300 [obs. "gallop": u1600s; obs. "motive power": u1500s] (verb use: b1470)

land v *as in "land a ship"* b1300 [as in "land a fish": b1630; as in "land a plane": b1870]

mariner n b1300

passage n *travel, path, access* b1300

stern n b1300

trithing n *arch. riding* b1300

trot n/v b1300

voyage n b1300 (verb use: b1500)

chariot n b1325 (charioteer: b1350)

coxswain n b1330

byway n (bypath: b1325; by-road: b1570)

car n *carriage* ["automobile": b1900]

causey n *causeway* [obs. "embankment": u1700s]

crossway n

ferriage n *carriage on a ferry*

hackney n

hoy n *type of ship*

keel n *as in "ship's keel"; type of boat*

rudder n [obs. "oar": b900 to 1600s]

sled n (verb use: b1710)

tollbooth n

travel v (noun use: b1400; traveler: b1400; traveled: b1425)

vessel n

Emotions/ Characteristics

hatred n b1175 (hate: b900)

mercy n b1175 (merciless: b1350; merciful: b1400)

ruth n b1175 (ruthful: b1225; ruthless: b1350)

troth n *arch. loyalty* b1175 [obs. "truth": concurrent] (verb use: b1450)

anguish n b1200 (verb use: b1400)

awe n/v b1200 [obs. "terror": b1150 to 1700s]

blunt adj *dull, applied to people* b1200 ["frank": b1600] (verb use: b1400)

cheer n *disposition* b1200 ["cheeriness": b1395; "audible encouragement": b1600] (verb use: b1400; cheerful: b1400; cheery: b1450; cheerless: b1580)

comfort n/v *solace, relief* b1200 ["being comfortable": b1830]

cruelty, cruel n, adj b1200

delight n/v b1200 (delightable: b1350; delightsome: b1500; delightful: b1530; delighted: b1700)

devotion n b1200 (devote: b1590; devoted: b1595; devotee: b1645)

hue n *arch. outcry* b1200

impatience n b1200 (impatiency: b1570)

indignation n b1200 (indignity: b1585; indignant: b1590)

loath adj *deeply reluctant* b1200 [obs. "belligerent": b900 to late ME; obs. "loathsome": b1150 to 1500s]

meek adj b1200 [obs. "kindly": u1600s; obs. "nonviolent": u1500s] (meek, meeken v: b1350)

obedience, obedient n, adj b1200

scare v b1200 [as in "I scare easily": b1930]

scorn n/v b1200

tempt, temptation v, n *entice; test* b1200

carp v *complain* b1225 ["talk": b1350 to 1600s] (noun use: b1905)

coward n b1225 (cowardice: b1300)

dreadful adj *dreaded* b1225 [obs. "in awe": u1600s; "bad": b1730]

fear v *instill fear* b1225 ["experience fear": b1390]

foolhardy adj b1225

gent adj *obs. elegant; graceful; genteel* b1225 [u1700s] (obs. gentle "graceful": b1350 to 1500s)

grief n b1225 [obs. "phys. pain": u1700s; obs. "grievance": u1800s]

guile n b1225 (guileful: b1350; guileless: b1730)

jealous, jealousy n b1225 [obs. "zealous," "desirous": b1450 to 1600s; "protective," as in "jealous of my time": b1450]

joy n b1225 (verb use: b1350; joyful: b1300; joyous: b1325; joyless: b1350; joyance: b1590)

largesse n b1225

lusty adj *arch. merry* b1225 [obs. "lustful": u1600s; "robust": b1450]

malicious adj b1225 [obs. "vile": u1400s; obs. "injurious": b1450 to 1700s;

obs. "wiley": b1450 to 1500s) (malice: b1300)

pity n b1225 [obs. "pitifulness": u1600s; obs. "piety": u1600s] (verb use: b1500)

rancor n b1225 [obs. "bad smell": b1450 to 1500s] (verb use: b1570; rancorous: b1590)

treachery n b1225 (obs. treacher: u1700s; obs. treacherer: b1600 to 1600s)

trust n/v *faith* b1225 [arch. "trusted person": b1450] (trusty: b1225; trusting: b1450; trustless: b1530; trustworthy: b1830)

wight adj *valorous* b1225

repentant adj b1230 (repent, repentance: b1300)

anger n b1250 [obs. "distress, vexation": concurrent] (verb use: b1200; angry: b1325)

bearing n *deportment, carriage* b1250

bounty n *generosity* b1250 [spec. "reward for services rendered": 1700s]

humble adj *self-deprecating* b1250 ["not grand": b1470] (verb use: b1380)

orgulous adj *proud* b1250

temperance n *self-discipline* b1250 [obs. "nice weather": b1450 to 1600s] (temperate: b1450)

vanity n *vainness* b1250

aghast adj b1275

annoy v b1275 (annoying: b1375; annoyance: b1390)

eager adj b1275

wicked adj b1275 ["impish": b1630]

cry n *shout, wail, plea, announcement* b1280 [as in "battlecry": b1570; "weeping": b1830]

avarice n b1300 (adj use: b1470)

contrite, contrition adj, n b1300 [obs. "phys. worn": b1670 to 1700s]

cower v b1300

daft adj *gentle* b1300 [obs.

"timid": b1000; "insane": b1450] (daffy: b1885)

desirous adj b1300 [obs. "desirable": b1450 to 1700s]

despite n *despising, contempt* b1300 (arch. verb use: b1400)

dismay v/n b1300

distress n b1300 [med. sense: b1830] (verb use: b1280)

enmity n b1300

envy, envious n, adj b1300 [obs. "malevolence": u1700s] (verb use: b1400; enviable: b1605)

faint adj *as in "faint of heart"* b1300 [as in "a faint odor": b1450; "feeble": b1600]

fickle adj *changeable* b1300 ["deceitful": b1000]

frank adj b1300 [obs. "unbound": b1300 to 1600s]

fray v *arch. make afraid* b1300

gladden v b1300 (arch. "glad" v: b1100)

gracious adj b1300

gree n *arch. goodwill* b1300 (verb use: b1470)

honest adj *worthy of honor* b1300 ["truthful": b1325]

humility n b1300

ill will n b1300

ire n b1300 (irate: b1840)

jollity n b1300 (jolly: b1325; jolliment: b1600)

lief adv *gladly* b1300

lower/lour v *frown* b1300 (noun use: b1400)

lunatic adj/n b1300 (lunacy: b1545)

mad adj *angry* b1300

penance n b1300 (verb use: b1600)

piteous adj *pitiful* b1300 [arch. "pitying": concurrent; obs. "pious": b1450 to 1500s]

prowess n *courage* b1300 ["talent, skill": b1930]

quality n b1300

rage n/v *anger; obs. madness; obs. foolishness* b1300 ["lust, passion": b1450; "fad": b1800]

rage v b1300 [as in "raging battle": b1450]

rebel n/adj/v *rebellious person* b1300 ["person in rebellion": b1450] (rebellion: b1350; reb: 1862)

sad adj *morose* b1300 [arch. "somber": b1350; "saddening": b1450; "sorry," as in "a sad performance": b1600] (sadden: b1630)

shameful adj b1300 [obs. "shy": b950]

sigh v b1300

smile v b1300 ["smile with the eyes": b1770; "be favorable," as in "smile on": b1450] (noun use: b1350)

snub v b1300 (noun use: b1400)

spite n *contempt* b1300 [obs. "spiteful act": u1600s] (verb use: b1560)

thrall v *arch. enthrall* b1300

thrill v b1300 [obs. "pierce": 1200s to 1700s] (noun use: b1700)

understanding adj b1300

uneasy adj b1300 (unease: b1300)

vainglory n b1300 (vainglorious: b1480)

venial adj b1300

wanton adj *uncontrolled* b1300 ["lewd," "extravagant": b1380] (verb use: b1585)

woe, woeful n, adj b1300

affray v *frighten* b1305 (noun use: b1400; afraid: b1300)

please v *satisfy* b1305 ["delight": b1380] (adv use: b1670; pleasing: b1400)

arrogance n b1325 (arrogant: b1390)

defamation n *shame* b1325 ["libel, slander": b1450]

despair v b1325 (noun use: b1300)

gay adj *merry* b1325 ["light": b1800; "homosexual": b1915] (gaysome: b1630)

horror n b1325

jolly adj b1325 [obs. "youthfully exuberant": u1600s; obs. "lustful": b1450 to 1600s; "attractive": b1450; "fat": b1670] (jollity: b1300; jollify: b1825)

malign adj *evil* b1325 (verb use: b1450; malignity: b1400; obs. malignation: b1450)

pomp n b1325 (verb use: b1450; pompous: b1375; pomposity: b1450)

pout v b1325 (noun use: b1595; pouty: b1865)

solemn adj b1325 (solemnity: b1300)

valiant adj *valorous; robust; strong* b1325 (noun use: b1600; valiance: b1450; valiancy: b1500)

affront v b1330 (noun use: b1535)

affiance n *trust* b1340

ambition n b1340 (ambitious: b1400)

austere adj *stern* b1340 ["self-disciplined": b1470; "stoic": b1600] (austerity: b1380)

bash v *arch. be abashed* b1340 (bashful: b1550)

compassion n b1340 [obs. "grief": u1500s; obs. "empathy": u1600s] (compassionate n: b1590; arch. compassionate v: b1595)

compunction n b1340 [obs. "pity": b1450 to 1700s]

courage n *bravery* b1340 [obs. fig. "heart, core," "tendencies": b1300 to 1600s; obs. "brazenness": b1450 to 1600s; obs. "lust": b1530 to 1600s] (courageous: b1300)

fair adj *objective* b1340 ["equal": b1770]

scowl v b1340 (noun use: b1500)

amiable adj [full meaning of "sociable": b1770]

astonied adj *arch. astonished*

benevolence n (benevolent: b1445)

cardinal virtue n

cordial adj *fig. from the heart* [obs. "lit. from the heart": u1600s] (cordiality: b1600)

courtly adj (adv use: b1500)

covetise n *arch. coveting*

discreet adj

dotage n (obs. dote "dot-

ard": b1350 to 1800s; dot-ard: b1400)

faint n *obs. cowardice* [u1500s]

frenzy n *craziness* [fig. use: b1470] (verb use: b1795; obs. frenzical: b1570 to 1700s)

gentilesse n *arch. courteous manner*

gladful adj

glee n *happiness* [obs. "fun": b900 to 1600s] (gleeful: b1590; gleesome: b1605)

green adj *jealous*

heartless adj

kind adj *compassionate; loving* [obs. "of good ancestry": u1800s; obs. "amiable": u1700s] (kindness: b1300; kindly adv: b1350; kindly adj: b1530)

loathe v [obs. "be loathesome": b900 to 1500s] (loathly: b900; loathsome: b1300; loathing: b1350; loathful: b1450)

love v *as in "I love to play poker"*

mad v *arch. be mad* ["madden": b1450]

madding adj *frenzied*

malapert adj *arch. impudent*

malease n *arch. malaise*

merciless adj [obs. "receiving no mercy": u1500s] (mercy: b1175; merciful: b1400)

mirth n (obs. "source of mirth": b900 to 1600s)

miss v *rue absence*

mow n *arch. grimace*

open adj *frank* ["receptive": b1450]

outcry n

painful adj *causing mental pain* ["causing physical pain": b1450; arch. "painstaking": b1600]

perplexity n [obs. "bother": u1600s] (perplexed: b1400; perplex v: b1595)

pitiful adj *evoking pity* ["pitying": b1350]

pleasant adj *pleasureable* ["mild": b1450; obs. "silly": b1600 to 1700s] (pleasance: b1400; pleasureable: b1580; pleasantry: b1600)

port n *bearing, comportment*

prudence n (prudent: b1400; prudential: b1645)

rebellion n *rebelling* ["act of rebelling": b1450]

recreant adj *cowardly* (noun use: b1450)

regret v (noun use: b1590)

reputation n *good reputation* [gen. "opinion": b1470] (repute v: b1400; repute n: b1555; reputable: b1675)

scoff n (verb use: b1300)

smart adj *insolent*

sober adj *moderate; somber*

["not intoxicated": b1470] (verb use: b1400)

soft adj *lacking resolve, firmness*

soft adj *sentimental* (softy: b1865)

stubborn adj

sullen adj *alone by choice* [obs. gen. "alone": u1500s; obs. "unique": u1400s]

surquidry n *arch. haughtiness*

virtuous adj [obs. "manly": u1600s]

wanhope n *lack of hope*

woebegone adj (woeful: b1300)

Thoughts/Perception/ The Mind

wile n b1175 (verb use: b1350; wily: b1300)

belief n b1200

cogitation n b1200 (cogitate: b1565)

conscience n b1200 [obs. "deepest feelings": u1600; obs. "consciousness": b1450 to 1800s]

contemplation n b1200 ["study": b1500] (contemplative: b1340; contemplate: b1540)

crafty adj *sly* b1200 [arch. "powerful": b900; arch. "skilled": b975]

hypocrisy, hypocrite n b1200 (hypocritical: b1565; hyp-

ocritic: b1570; hypocrital: b1670)

ignorance n b1200 (ignorant: b1375)

insight n b1200

logic n b1200 (logical: b1470)

thoughtful adj *cogitative* b1200 ["considerate": b1470] (thoughtless: b1585)

judge v *sit in judgment* b1225 ["opine," "evaluate": b1450]

meditation n b1225 (meditate: b1560)

presumption n b1225 (presume, presumptuous: b1350; presumptive: b1500)

prophecy n b1225 (obs. prophetize: u1700s; prophesy: b1350)

reason n *ability to think; motive; being reasonable; statement* b1225 [obs. "sentence," "motto": b1450 to 1500s]

sly adj b1225 ["secretive": b1470]

memory n b1250 (memorable: b1440)

cognizance n b1300 (cognizable: b1680; cognizant: b1820)

conceivable adj *possible to imagine* b1300

dream n/v b1300 [as in "day-

What English Is Not

Many words that were once in the language we now know only by what they are not. That is, we know their opposites, while the words themselves have sunk into obscurity. We know *ruthless* (by 1350), but have largely forgotten *ruthful* (by 1225). *Inclement weather* is a staple phrase of grade-schoolers, but how often do we use inclement's opposite—*clement*—which was in use by 1460?

We might say that using such words as *ruthful* and *clement* are evitable—they are not inevitable. *Evitable*, by the way, in use by 1505. So that we don't continue eviting them, let's look at a list of "lost opposites":

- *mediate* (by 1425), *immediate* (about the same time)

- *mancipate* (by 1500 to 1800s), *emancipate* (by 1615)

- *vincible* (by 1550), *invincible* (by 1420)

- *inhume* (by 1605), *exhume* (by 1450)

- *alienable* (by 1615), *inalienable* (by 1645)

- *pervious* (by 1615), *impervious* (by 1650)

- *discommodate* (by 1630), *accommodate* (by 1525)

- *peccable* (by 1630), *impeccable* (by 1535)

- *outgo* (by 1640), *income* (by 1600)

- *gainly* (by 1855) follows *ungainly* (by 1615)

dream": b1450; as in "the job is a dream": b1900; "goal": b1930]

foresight n b1300

forethought n b1300 (obs. forethink: b1150; forethoughtful: b1810)

free will n b1300

opinion n b1300 [type of formal declaration: b1450] (opinionated: b1605)

philosophy n b1300 (philosophe "philosopher": b1150; philosopher: b1350; philosophical: b1530; philosophize: b1595)

reckon v b1300 [obs. "count": u1500s; obs. "retell": b1000 to 1500s; as in "I reckon you're right": b1530; as in "I reckon I'll be going": b1570] (reckoning: b1400)

sage adj *wise* b1300 [well-advised, as in "sage advice": b1570] (noun use: b1350)

study n/v *revery* b1300 [obs. "uncertainty": u1600s]

suspicion n b1300 ["hint," as in "a suspicion of salt": b1830] (verb use: b1350; suspicious: b1350)

cunning adj *knowledgeable; skilled* b1325 ["crafty": b1455; "intelligent": b1700] (noun use: b1375)

curious adj *inquisitive* b1325 [obs. "careful": b1450 to 1700s; obs. "precise": b1630 to 1800s; "odd": b1715] (curiosity: b1400)

profound adj *applied to people* b1325 [applied to thoughts: b1450; fig. "intense": b1530] (profundity: b1425)

rote n *as in "by rote"* b1325 (adj use: b1645)

suppose v *assume, as in "suppose you do go"* b1325 ["presume": b1600]

conceive v *picture in mind* b1340

imagination n b1340 (imagine: b1350)

mindful adj b1340 (obs. mindly: b1470)

moral adj b1340 (verb use: b1630)

remember v b1340 (remembrance: b1300)

science n *knowledge* b1340

daffy adj (arch. daff "fool": b1350)

distract adj *arch. crazy; distracted*

guess v/n

judgment n *decision*

justice n *being just*

ken v *know; arch. see* ["tell": b900 to 1600s]

know v *as in "know a friend"; as in "know pain"; be aware; have sex; learn; be educated; understand* (noun use: b1595; knowledge: b1300)

madman n (madwoman: b1450)

misknow v

philosopher n [obs. "conjurer": u1400s] (philosophe: b1150; philosophess: b1670)

record n *obs. memory* [u1600s] (obs. verb use: u1700s)

sophistry n

spack adj *arch. quick and wise*

suspicious adj *causing suspicion* ["exhibiting suspicion": b1450]

unkenned adj *unknown*

unweeting adj *arch. unwitting*

weet v *arch. know*

will n *as in "will of the people"*

wit n *mental agility, penchant for humor* ["humorous person": b1450; "humor": b1570] (witticism: b1655)

wonder v *ponder, speculate* [obs. "make wonder": b1570 to 1700s]

Love/Romance/Sex

lecher n b1175 (lechery: b1250; lecherous: b1325)

affection n b1200 ["lust": b1350 to 1700s] (affect "show affection": b1400)

chaste, chastity adj, n b1200 [obs. "not married":

u1500s; fig. "untainted": b1630] (chastity: b1225)

spouse n b1200 [obs. "fiance/fiancee": u1500s)

virgin n b1200 (adj use "chaste": b1450; virginity: b1350; virginal: b1450)

wedlock n *marriage* b1200 ["marriage vow": b1100 to 1600s]

lover n b1225

misthink v *obs. have lewd thoughts* b1225 [u1600s]

trousseau n b1225 [obs. "bunch": b1225]

maidenhead n *virginity; hymen* b1250

conceive v *get pregnant* b1280 ["picture in mind": b1340] (conception: b1335)

sweetheart n *loved one* b1290 [obs. "mistress": b1600 to 1700s] (arch. sweeting: b1350; sweetikins: b1600; sweetie: b1800; sweetie pie: b1930)

amour n b1300 (amorous: b1305)

bachelor n b1300 (bachelorette: b1905)

bawdstrote n *obs. bawd* b1300 [u1400s]

beau n b1300

concubine n *man's lover* b1300 ["woman's lover": b1450 to 1500s]

dowry n b1300

husband n *married to wife* b1300 [obs. "head of household": b1000]

marriage n b1300 ["wedding": b1450]

marry v *be married* b1300 ["take a spouse": b1450]

matrimony n b1300 (matrimonial: b1450)

betroth v *get engaged to a woman* b1305 [gen. "get engaged": b1570] (betrothed n: b1540; betrothal: b1850)

conquest n b1325

espousal n *arch. marriage* b1325 [obs. "married person": b1500 to 1600s] (espouse "marry": b1475)

adultery n (adulterer, adulteress: b1400)

fornication n (verb use: b1555)

heart n *as in "dear heart"*

heat n *as in "in heat"*

hot adj *erotic* ["excited": b1500]

lie v *arch. have sex*

lovable adj (lovely: b900; lovesome: b1000)

luxury n *obs. lechery* [u1800s]

multiply v *obs., as in "go forth and multiply"* [u1700s]

ride v *have sex*

single n *unmarried person*

stallion n *promiscuous person* ["male horse": b1440]

strumpet n *prostitute*

swive v *have sex with*

trothplight adj/n/v *arch. engagement to marry*

Family/Relations/Friends

childbed n *state of a woman in childbirth* b1200

half sister n b1200 (half brother: b1340)

strain n *stock, ancestry; descendents* b1200 [type of germ variety, etc., as in "Andromeda Strain": b1630]

godchild n b1225 (godson: b900; goddaughter: b1050)

heir n b1225 (heiress: b1610)

ancestor n b1300 (ancestry: b1350; ancestral: b1450; ancestress: b1580)

aunt n b1300 [obs. "prostitute": b1630 to 1800s]

brother-in-law n b1300

companion n *friend, associate* b1300 [obs. "churl": b1600 to 1700s] (verb use: b1625; companionship: b1550)

compeer n *companion* b1300

cousin n *spec. relative* b1300 [gen. "relative": b1225; "pal": b1450; type of royal address: b1450] (adj use: b1450; cousinage: b1400; cousinry: b1845)

cousin-german n b1300

forefather n b1300 (foremother: b1500)

foundling n *orphan* b1300

genealogy n *spec. ancestry* b1300 ["study of ancestry": b1830]

generation n b1300

junior adj *as in "John Smith, Junior"* b1300 (noun use: b1525)

nephew n b1300 [obs. "grandson": b1350 to 1600s; obs. "niece": b1470 to 1600s]

niece n b1300 [originally meant "granddaughter"; obs. "nephew": late ME to 1600s]

progeny n b1300 (progenitor: b1400)

uncle n b1300

affinity n *kindredness* b1305 ["predilection": b1630]

lineage n b1325

coat of arms n b1340

half brother n b1340 (half sister: b1200)

adopt v *as in "adopt a child"* (adoption: b1340)

ancestry n

descent n

get n *child*

kinswoman n (kin: b900; kinsman: b1150; kinspeople: b1800)

line n *as in "family lines"*

son-in-law n

stock n *breeding, ancestry, as in "he comes from good stock"* ["human torso": b1450 to 1500s]

twin n [fig. use: b1570] (verb use: b1600)

Holidays

Christmas Eve n b1300

birthday n

holiday n *vacation day* ["holy day": b950] (verb use: b1870)

Games/Fun/Leisure

chess n *the game* b1200 (chessman: b1325; chessboard: b1450)

mate n/v *checkmate* b1225

playful adj b1225 (playsome: b1605)

tournament n b1225 (tourney: b1300)

ace n *in dice, cards* b1250 [in tennis: b1830; in golf: b1930]

ambs-ace n *lowest throw of dice; something worthless* b1300

check n *in chess* b1300

die, dice n b1300 (verb use: b1400)

leisure n b1300

wager n *stake, obs. pledge* b1305 [obs. "prize": b1450 to 1600s; "bet": b1570] (verb use: b1450; obs. wage v: b1350 to 1700s)

disport n *diversion* b1325 ["sport": b1400] (verb use: b1380)

drawing n *lottery* b1325

checkmate interj/n (verb use: b1375)

gamesome adj *fun-loving* (obs. gameful: b1350 to 1700s)

knight n *in chess* (verb use: b1300; knighthood: b1300; knightly: b1400)

play n *playing a game, as in "play starts in ten minutes"*

play v *toy with*

rook n *chess piece*

tourney n/v

Sports

bearbaiting n b1300

joust n/v b1300

race v *compete* b1300 [as in "race the engine," "my heart races": b1770]

tumble v *perform a type of gymnastics* b1325 ["fall": b1300; "collapse, destroy": b1450]

venery n *hunting* b1325

angler n

course n *as in "race course"; as in "in the course of time"* ["golf course": b1900]

fight n *as in "bullfight"*

game n [as in "Olympic games": b1470]

lose v *as in "lose a football game"*

put n *as in "shot put"*

ring n *as in "boxing ring"*

tennis n *arch. form of the game* [modern form of the game: b1900]

trotter n

tumbler n *gymnast* (obs. tumblester "woman tumbler": b1450 to 1800s)

Professions/Duties

harbinger n *obs. servant forerunner* b1175 [u1500s]

hired man n b1175 (hireling: b1000)

baker n b1200 (bakery "baker's work": b1545; bakery "type of shop": b1820)

chamberlain n *male chambermaid* b1200

cordwainer n *tooler of cordovan leather* b1200 ["shoemaker": b1400]

counselor n b1200

craftsman n b1200 (craftswoman: b1890; craftsperson: b1920; craftspeople: b1955)

menestral n *arch. servant* b1200

mercer n *fabric seller* b1200

wait n *arch. watchman, post* b1200 (obs. "waiter": b1450 to 1600s)

boy n *servant* b1225 [derogatory sense: b1630]

foreman n *primary servant* b1225 [type of supervisor: b1600; on a jury: b1630]

mason n b1225

profession n b1225

servant n b1225 (service: b1350)

blacksmith n b1250

butler n b1250

locksmith n b1250

sawyer n b1260

grazier n b1275

marshal n *obs. horse servant* b1275 [u1700s] (obs. verb use: b1450 to 1500s)

collier n *charcoal maker* b1280 ["miner": b1570]

cobbler n b1290 (cobble v: b1500)

barber n b1300 (verb use: b1610; barbershop: b1580; barber pole: b1685)

butcher n *lit. and fig.* b1300 (verb use: b1565)

carpenter n b1300 (verb use: b1470; carpentry: b1380)

currier n *currier of leather* b1300 ["currier of horses": b1570]

dispenser n *type of servant* b1300

footman n *servant* b1300 ["infantry soldier": b1300; "pedestrian": b1470]

forester n b1300

hosteler n b1300

nurse n *nanny* b1300 ["med. employee": b1600]

page n *servant; knight in training* b1300 ["errand boy": b1800]

porter n *doorman* b1300 (portress: b1350)

saddler n b1300 (saddlery: b1450)

tailor n b1300 (verb use: b1670)

wheelwright n b1300

brazier n *brassworker* b1310

chandler n b1325

councillor n b1325

notary n b1325 [obs. "secretary": u1600s] (notary public: 1490s; notarize: b1925)

whitesmith n b1325

broker n/v (brokerage: b1470)

clothier n

cooper n *type of metalworker* ["wine dealer": b1530] (verb use: b1730)

coppersmith n

courier n

cutler n (cutlery: b1340)

fishmonger n

fletcher n

furrier n

glazier n

hatter n (hatmaker: b1500)

henchman n [pejorative sense: b1840]

hosier n (hosiery: b1790)

ironmonger n

jeweler n

maltster n

miller n (obs. millward: b1150 to 1800s)

occupation n *profession* ["owning": b1325; "forceful occupation": b1570] (occupational: b1855)

painter n *one who paints* (painteress: b1450)

pavior n *road paver*

peddler n (peddle: b1535)

pewterer n

porter n *package carrier* ["doorman": b1300; *type of drink*: b1730] (verb use: b1610)

portress n *female doorkeeper* (porter: b1300)

servitor n *male servant* (servitrix: b1570; servitress: b1870)

sewer n *type of medieval servant*

usher n [in weddings: b1900] (verb use: b1595; usherette: b1925)

wakeman n *arch. guard*

woodmonger n

Business/Commerce/ Selling

brewery n b1170

huckster n *salesperson* b1200 [pejorative sense: b1555] (verb use: b1595)

merchant n b1200 (verb use: b1400)

price n *lit. cost* b1225 [obs. "esteem": u1600s; fig. "cost": b1450; "bounty": b1770] (verb use: b1450)

fair n *as in "county fair"* b1250

merchandise n b1250 (verb use: b1385)

forge n *smithy* b1280 [type of tool: b1600]

tavern n *wine shop* b1290 ["bar": b1440] (taverner: b1350)

exchange n *trade* b1300 (verb use: b1450)

shop n b1300

mine n *as in "gold mine"* b1305

overcharge v b1325

deal v *as in "wheel and deal"* (noun use: b1870)

make n *brand*

mart n

quarry n *related to stonework* (verb use: b1745)

trade n *business dealings*

["profession": b1670; "exchange": b1830]

warehouse n ["outlet store": b1730] (verb use: b1800)

The Workplace

workaday n *workday* b1200

labor n *hard work; the result of hard work* b1300 [in childbirth: b1600; "workingpeople": b1870] (verb use: b1605; laborious: b1400)

prentice n *apprentice* b1300

apprentice n b1310 (verb use: b1600)

wage n b1325 (obs. verb use "hire": u1600s; wages: b1380)

corvee n *forced road labor*

help n *as in "the help"*

livelihood n [obs. "lifetime": b1000 to 1500s]

living n *livelihood*

man n *worker, servant*

work v *have a job* (noun use: b1600)

Finances/Money

treasure n *wealth; something precious* b1200 (verb use "save": b1400; verb use "cherish": b1930)

debt n b1225 (obs. adj use: u1600s; debtor: b1200; debtee: b1570)

riches n b1225

bursar n b1235 (bursary "treasury": b1695)

money n b1250 (adj use: b1940)

thrift n *savings; obs. thriving, hard work* b1250

wealth n b1250 (wealthy: b1375)

halfpenny n b1275

usury n b1275 (obs. usure v: b1350 to 1500s; usurious: b1610)

salary n b1280 [obs. "fee": u1600s] (verb use: b1480)

account n b1300

duty n *financial obligation* b1300 [gen. "obligation": b1385] (dutiful: b1555; duteous: b1595)

exchequer n b1300

levy n *as in "tax levy"* b1300 (verb use: b1450)

sum n *amount of money* b1300 [obs. "group of people": u1800s]

tax v/n *assess tax; appraise* b1300 [obs. "assign a task": b1450 to 1800s; fig. "burden": b1700] (taxation: b1450)

treasury, treasurer n b1300

pence n b1325

penniless adj b1325

value n b1325 (verb use: b1500; valued: b1595; valuable: b1775; valuate: b1875)

rent n *rent payment* b1330 [obs. "income; properties earning rent": b1140 to 1600s]

poverty n *dearth of money, other things* b1175 (obs. "poor people": b1450 to 1500s)

earnest n *as in "earnest money"* b1200

pay v b1200 [obs. "satisfy": u1500s] (noun use: b1400)

tax n/v b1330 ["task": b1450 to 1600s; fig. "burden": b1330] (taxation: b1300)

payment n *act of paying* ["what is paid": b1450]

principal adj (noun use: b1450)

tail n *obs. type of tax* [u1600s]

tribute n *financial payment* ["honor, compliment": b1600]

Language and Speaking

clause n *part of grammar* b1200 ["section of document": b1300]

letter n *e.g., ABC . . .* b1225

language n b1300 [jargon: b1530; as in "body language": b1630; "cursing": b1870]

loquacity n b1300 (loquacious: b1670)

Old English n b1300

romance n b1300

saying n b1300

character n *letter, symbol, etc.* b1325

consonant n b1325

vowel n b1325

tense n *as in "verb tense"* b1335

gender n

rhetoric n (rhetor: b1350; rhetorician: b1425; rhetorical: b1470)

Contractions

way adv *'way* b1225

'tween prep b1300

e'en adv b1300

e'er adv b1300

ne'er adv b1300

o' prep *as in "o'clock"* b1300

'twixt prep

tone, tother adj/pron *t(he)one, t(he)other*

Literature/Writing

chapter n b1200 [fig., as in "a chapter in her life": b1630; as in "club chapter": b1830]

dialogue n b1200 [gen. use: b1450] (verb use: b1600)

roll n *scroll, list* b1225 ["register," as in "roll call": b1470]

story n *tale of history* b1225 [obs. "history book": u1700s] (verb use: b1450)

writing n b1225

gloss n *explanation—related to glossary* b1300 (verb use: b1600; glossary: b1400)

pen n *writing instrument* b1300 [obs. "feather": b1450]

poet n b1300 [gen. obs. "writer": b1450 to 1700s] (poetess: b1530)

prologue n b1300 (verb use: b1630)

rhyme n b1300 (verb use: b1400)

sign v *mark with a sign, place signature on* b1300

tablet n *writing tool* b1300 ["paper tablet": b1880; as in "aspirin tablets": b1470]

transcript n b1300 (transcribe: b1550)

chronicle n *record* b1305 ["story": b1450] (verb use: b1400)

indite v *compose* b1305
fable n *tale; myth* b1325 ["lie": b1300; "something legendary": b1600]
parable n b1325 (verb use: b1670)
parchment n *animal skin for writing* b1325 ["paper for writing": b1900]
proverb n b1325 (verb use: b1400)
copy n *spec. document copy* b1340 [gen. use: b1600; obs. "copiousness": b1450 to 1600s; "single copy of a newspaper, etc.": b1570] (verb use: b1400)
bard n
bill n *list, as in "bill of lading"* (arch. verb use: b1350)
dite n *obs. writing* [u1500s]
exposition n (expositive: b1500; expository: b1600)
letter n *type of correspondence*
library n
light adj *as in "light reading"*
mark n *substitute for signature; as in "trademark"; indicator; evidence*
poesy n *poetry* [obs. "poem": u1800s]
prose n [fig. "unpoetic writing": b1570]
read adj *as in "well-read"*
romance n *heroic narrative* (romantic: b1700)
rubric n
scrivener n
text n *writing*
title n *subhead; name for book, etc.* ["titling caption, placard": b950 to 1600s; "book": b1900] (verb use: b1450)

Communication
sign n *gesture, portent* b1225
message n b1300 (verb use: b1585; messenger: b1200)
beacon n *signal fire* b1340 [obs. "omen": b1150 to 1400s; gen. type of guide light: b1450]
soliloquy n (soliloquize: b1760; soliloquacity: b1900)

Visual Arts/Photography
carving n *act of carving* b1200 ["carved item": b1450]
painting n b1225
draw v
line n *as in "draw a line"* (verb use: b1570)
work n *as in "work of art"*

Performing Arts
interlude n b1305 [gen. sense: b1755]

Music
lyre n *type of stringed instrument* b1225
minstrel n b1225
music n *the art of music* b1250 ["the music itself": b1630]
bugle n b1300 ["type of ox": u1600s] (verb use: b1885; bugle horn: b1300)
carol n *type of song and dance, then the song* b1300 ["holiday song": b1470; spec. to Christmas: b1505] (verb use: b1305)
ditty n b1300
instrument n b1300 [gen. sense: b1325]
lute n b1300
melody n b1300 [obs. "song": u1500s; "primary song line": b1900]
note n b1300
tabor n *type of drum* b1300
flute n b1325 ["flutist": b1570] (flutist: b1605)
treble n b1325 (adj use: b1450)
bagpipe n
psaltery n *type of musical instrument*
shawm n *arch. type of musical instrument*
trumpet n [as in "ear trumpet": b1700; "trumpeting sound": b1870] (verb use: b1530; trumpeter: b1500)

Entertainment
dance n/v *dancing* b1300 [spec. type of dancing; social occasion: b1450; "song for dancing": b1530] (dancer: b1340)
make v *obs. entertain* [u1500s]

Education
lesson n b1225 [obs. "lecture": u1700s; as in "let that be a lesson to you": b1450] (arch. verb use: b1555)
schoolmaster n b1225 (schoolmistress: b1350)
ABC's n b1300
university n b1300 [arch. "universality": b1450; obs. meanings of "everything, the universe": b1450 to 1600s]
doctor n *learned person* b1325 ["physician," "teacher": b1450]
lettered adj *educated* b1325 (letterless: b1630)
art n *area of knowledge, as in "liberal arts"* ["aesthetic pursuit": b1600]
doctrine n *what is taught* [obs. "teaching": u1700s]
learned adj
principal n
schoolmistress n (schoolmaster: b1225; schoolmarm: b1835)
studious adj ["very careful": b1450]
study n/v *learning* ["the thing studied": b1570]
unlettered adj

Religion
orison n *arch. prayer* b1175
passion n *Jesus' suffering; strong emotion* b1175 ["sexual emotion": b1450] (passionate: b1425; passional: b1450)
synagogue n b1175
blasphemy n b1200 (blaspheme: b1340; blasphemous: b1415)
chapel n b1200
collect n *brief prayer* b1200
credo n b1200 [gen. use: b1590]
crucifix n b1200
devout adj b1200
feast n b1200
heresy n b1200 (heretic: b1340)
hermit n b1200 [gen. use: b1670]
Lord's day n *Sunday* b1200
nativity n b1200 [astrological sense "time of birth": b1470]
prophet n b1200 ["something prophetic": b1600] (prophecy: b1225; prophetess: b1350; prophetic: b1500)
religion n b1200 (religious: b1225)
sacrament n b1200 (sacramental: b1400)
sacren v *arch. make sacred* b1200 (sacred: b1325)
salvation n b1200 [gen. use: b1450]
sermon n b1200 [obs. gen. "speech, discussion": u1500s; fig. "preaching": b1600] (sermonette: b1815)
canticle n b1225
commendation n *type of religious tribute* b1225 ["eulogy": b1200; gen. "praise": b1450]
convent n *religious order* b1225 [obs. "convening," "convention": b1425 to 1600s; "nunnery": b1450]
misbelief, misbelieve n, v b1225
parlor n *room in a church* b1225 [type of room in a home: b1450; "business," as in "beauty parlor": b1900]
preach v b1225 [gen. "pontificate": b1450] (preacher: concurrent; preachment: b1350; preachify: b1775; preachy: b1820)
prelate n b1225 (prelatess: b1670)
primate n b1225 [rare gen. "important person": b1450; zoological sense: b1900]
purgatory adj/n b1225
purity n *spiritual cleanness* b1225 ["phys. cleanness": b1450]

Trinity n b1225

beadsman n *one who prays for another* b1250

godhead n b1250

idol n b1250 [gen. sense: b1570]

idolatry n b1250

parson n b1250

pilgrimage n *religious journey* b1250 [gen. "journey": b1450]

tabernacle n *type of sanctuary* b1250 [type of place of worship: b1715]

vigil n b1250 [gen. use: b1450; type of demonstration: b1970] (vigilant: b1480)

churchman n b1260 (churchwoman: b1725)

nunnery n b1275 [arch. slang "bordello": b1600]

sacrifice n *as in "animal sacrifice"* b1275 [gen. use: b1595] (verb use: b1300)

baptize v b1280 (baptism: b1300)

abbess n b1300

abbey n b1300

acolyte n *priest's attendant* b1300 [gen. use: b1830]

adore v *worship* b1300 [gen. sense: b1470] (adoration: b1530)

Christianity n b1300

clergy n b1300 [obs. "knowledge": b1200]

creator n b1300

cruet n *type of container* b1300

deadly sin n *pride, sloth, etc.* b1300

deity n *divinity* b1300 ["a spec. god": b1450]

friar n b1300

incarnation n b1300

judgment n b1300

majesty n *majesty of god* b1300 [as in "his majesty": b1450; "grand dignity": b1450] (majestical: b1600; majestic: b1605; majestuous: b1700)

missal n b1300

ordain v *appoint to ministry; decree* b1300 [obs. "arrange": u1500s]

parish n b1300 [gen. "governmental district": b1670] (parishioner: b1470)

pray v b1300 [obs. "invite": u1600s]

prayer n *praying; worship* b1300

prioress n b1300 (prior: b1100)

resurrection n b1300 [fig. use: b1470] (resurrect: b1775)

satisfaction n *as in "satisfaction of debts"* b1300 [as in "can't get no satisfaction": b1385] (satisfy: b1415)

scripture n b1300 [arch. gen. writing: b1470]

secular adj b1300

sign of the cross n b1300

testament n *covenant between God and man; as in "Old Testament"* b1300

vestment n b1300 (obs. vestiment: u1800s)

vicar n b1300

confirmation n b1305

inspiration n b1305 [gen. use: b1670] (inspire: b1340)

miter n *type of hat* b1305

requiem n b1305

sacrilege n b1305 (verb use: b1570; sacrilegious: b1450)

bible n b1325 [gen. "authority": b1830] (biblical: b1775)

decree n b1325 [leg. sense: b1450] (verb use: b1400)

divine adj *lit. and fig. heavenly* b1325 (noun use: b1400; divinity: concurrent)

epiphany n b1325 [gen. use: b1870]

host n *the eucharistic bread* b1325 [obs. "sacrifice": u1600s]

mystic adj b1325 (noun use: b1680; mystical: b1475; mysticism: b1740)

revelation n b1325 [gen. sense: b1870]

sacred adj b1325 (obs. sacren v: b1200; arch. sacre v: b1350)

sanctuary n b1325 [gen. use: b1380]

spiritual adj b1325

official n b1330

conversion, convert n, v b1340 [gen. "switch": b1425] (convert n: b1325)

deify v *make godlike* b1340 ["promote to god status": b1450; "treat as if godlike": b1600]

diocese n b1340

Old Testament n b1340

temporal adj *secular* b1340 ["of present life": b1450; describing time: b1800] (arch. temporaneous: b1670)

hierarchy n b1345 [gen. use: b1670] (hierarch: b1470; hierarchical: b1565; hierarchic: b1685)

ascension n *the ascension of Christ* [gen. "ascent": b1470]

catholic adj *pertaining to the Catholic church* ["Roman Catholic": b1555; gen. "universal": b1555]

clear v *make spirtually clean*

curate n

evangel n *gospel of Christ* ["evangelist": b1595] (evangelize: b1400; evangelical adj/n: b1535)

festival adj *related to a feast day* [obs. "festive": b1600 to 1600s] (noun use: b1590)

fold n

grace n [obs. graces "gen. thanks": u1500s]

grail n

Hail Mary n

illumination n *spiritual enlightenment* ["enlighten with light": b1570; "enlighten with knowledge": b1670] (illuminate v: b1425)

kyrie n *type of prayer*

laud n [gen. "prace": b1450]

lay adj *secular, as in "lay person"* ["not professional": b1830]

limbo n [fig. use: b1670]

messiah n (Messyass: b1200; Messie: b1300; messianic: b1830)

minister n (ministress: b1500)

order n *as in "religious order"*

original sin n

pantheon n

pastor n [lit. "shepherd": concurrent] (verb use: b1625)

predestination n [gen. "fate": b1530] (predestine: b1400; predestinate v: b1450)

prophetess n (prophet: b1200)

providence n (provident: b1450)

pulpit n

redemption n [var. gen. uses: b1470]

sect n

serpent n *the Devil*

worship n/v [arch. "importance; honoring importance": b900]

Society/Mores/Culture

goodman n *Master, Mr.* b1175 (goodwife: b1325)

underling n b1175

beggar n b1200 (verb use: b1450)

courtesy n b1200 (courteous: b1300)

dame n *woman's title* b1200 [obs. gen. title, "opp. of sire": u1700s; gen. "woman": b1570]

damsel n b1200

gentleman n b1200 (gentlewoman: b1250; gentleperson: b1945; gent: b1565)

honor n b1200 (verb use: b1250)

layman n *secular person* b1200 ["not-professional person": b1500] (lay adj: b1350; laypeople: b1500; laywoman: b1530; lay sister: b1710; layperson: b1975)

maid n *girl; virgin; servant* b1200 [as in "old maid": b1630] (maiden: b1000)

gentle adj *arch. high-born* b1225 (noun use: b1400)

gentrice n *arch. high birth* b1225

housewife n b1225 (housewifery: b1450; househusband: b1955)

lowborn adj b1225 (lowbred: b1760)

mankind n b1225 [obs. "being human": u1600s; "men as a group": b1450]

noble adj *virtuous* b1225

peer n *social equal* b1225 [obs. "companion" or "foe": u1800s; "age equal": b1970] (verb use: b1400; peeress: b1690)

person n *individual* b1225 ["body," as in "on my person": b1470]

villainy n b1225 [obs. "humiliation": u1500s; obs. "crassness": u1600s]

virtue n b1225 [obs. "act of God": u1530]

dishonor n/v b1250

gentlewoman n b1250 (gentleman: b1200; gentleperson: b1945)

manhood n *being human* b1250 ["being a man," "manliness": b1450]

lordling n b1275

people n b1275 (verb use: b1450)

bastard n/adj b1300 ["jerk, asshole": b1870] (bastardize: b1590)

brotherhood n b1300 ["group of fellows": b1470]

countryfolk n b1300

courtier n b1300 [obs. "aspiring lover": b1630 to 1700s]

franklin n *landowner* b1300

freeborn n b1300

goodwife n *Mrs.* b1300 (goodman: b1275; goody: b1560)

handmaiden n b1300

highborn adj b1300

host, hostess n *entertainer* b1300 (verb use: b1470)

lad n b1300 (laddie: b1550)

lass n b1300 (lassie: b1725)

liege adj b1300 (noun use: b1400)

madam n b1300

manful adj *acting like a man* b1300

manly adj b1300 [obs. "human": u1600s]

mistress n *female master* b1300 ["concubine": b1470]

noblesse n b1300

purify v *clean morally* b1300 ["clean physically": b1450] (obs. pure v: b1350 to 1600s)

sir n b1300

slave n b1300

squire n *nobleman* b1300 ["servant": b1470; "escort": b1600]

urchin n *mischievous child* b1300 ["poor child": b1570]

wench n *gen. female* b1300 [arch. "mistress": b1450] (verb use: b1600)

gentry n *noble birth* b1325 ["persons of noble birth": b1600]

sinner n b1325

villain n *rustic, rube* b1325 (villainy: b1225; villainous: b1350; villainess: b1590)

villein n *type of peasant, villain* b1325

commonweal n *public good* (commonwealth: b1425)

frape n *obs. riffraff* [u1700s]

fraternity n ["college organization": b1800]

knight-errant n (knight-errantry: b1655)

liege man n *vassal*

maid n *obs. virgin man* [u1700s]

man n *mature man, as in "act like a man"*

man of the world n

manners n (mannered: b1400; mannerable "mannered": b1450; mannerless: b1475)

master n *designating rank or status* [applied to young men: b1600]

noble n (noblewoman: b1300; nobleman: b1350)

ragamuffin adj/n

suburb n

vassal n

whole adj *obs. wholesome* [u1500s]

Government

countess n b1175 (count: b1425)

empress n b1175 (emperor: b1125)

baron n b1200 (barony: b1300; baroness: b1450)

burgh n *borough* b1200

court n *royal residence; royal entourage* b1200

overlord n b1200 (verb use: b1630)

emperor n b1225 (empress: b1175; empire, empery: b1300)

patriarch n b1225 (patriarchy: b1635)

prince n *gen. ruler; son of king or queen; fig. leader* b1225 [slang, as in "prince of a guy": b1930] (princess: b1400; princelet: b1685; princeling: b1620; obs. adj principal: b1450 to 1500s)

senate, senator n b1225

office n *job, esp. in public service* b1250

tribe n b1250 (tribal: b1635; tribesman: b1800; tribespeople: b1890)

reign n b1275 [obs. "kingdom": u1700s] (verb use: b1350)

chief n b1300

chieftain n b1300

citizen n *pertaining to cities* b1300 [pertaining to larger governments: b1450] (citizenship: b1615; citizeness: b1800; citizenry: b1820)

constable n *type of administrator; peace officer* b1300 ["household administrator": b1200] (police officer: b1835)

country n *type of municipality; nation; rural area* b1300

empire, empery n *place ruled* b1300 ["act of ruling": b1450]

govern v b1300 (governance: b1375; government: b1400)

governor n b1300

marquis n b1300 (marquess: b1400)

mayor n b1300

nation n b1300 (national adj: b1600)

parliament n b1300 [obs. "conversation": u1600s] (parliamentary: b1620)

sovereign n *ruler* b1300

tyrant n b1300 [obs. gen. "sovereign": u1700s] (tyranny: b1325; tyrannous: b1485; tyrannical, tyrannize: b1500)

count n *title of nobility* b1305 (countess: b1175)

officer n *officeholder* b1325 [as in "club officer": b1730]

chair n *position of authority* (verb use: b1555; chairman: b1650; chairwoman: b1700)

duchess n (duke: b1150; duchy: b1400)

frankpledge n

kingdom n ["ruling as a king": b1000; as in "animal kingdom": b1700]

noble adj (noun use: b1350; noblesse: b1300; nobility: b1400)

prefect n

principality n *rule by a prince* ["the place ruled": b1450]

regal adj

rule n *reign, control* (verb use: b1470; ruler: b1375)

signet n *official seal*

sovereignty n

state n *central government; nation* ["segment of a nation": b1570]

subject adj/n/v *as in "subject of the crown"*

ward n *district*

Politics

election n b1275 (elect adj/n/v: b1450)

fealty n b1300

Life

barren adj *infertile* b1200 [as in "barren land": b1450]

lifeful adj *lively* b1225 (lifesome: b1700)

spirit n *source of life* b1250

[fig. life, as in "team spirit": b1700]

newborn adj b1300 (noun use: b1880)

quicken v *come alive* b1300

Death

carrion n *dead flesh* b1200 [obs. "carcass": u1800s]

die v *applied to animals, things* b1200 [applied to plants: b1450]

sepulchre n *tomb* b1200 (verb use: b1595)

gibbet n b1225 [gen. "execution by hanging": b1470]

gravestone n b1225

kill v b1225 [fig., as in "this job is killing me": b1530; as in "kill time": b1730] (noun use: b1815)

homicide n *murder* b1230 ["murderer": b1375]

burial n *the act of burying* b1250 [obs. "burying place": b750]

poison n b1250 [slang "liquor": b1830] (verb use: b1350; adj use: b1530; poisonous: b1570)

coroner n b1275

corse n *arch. corpse* b1275

tomb n b1275 (verb use: b1350)

monument n *obs. burial vault* b1280 [u1600s]

testament n *as in "last will and testament"* b1290

carcass n b1300 [fig. "remains of inanimate thing": b1600]

deathbed n b1300 ["grave": b725]

dower n *widow's inheritance* b1300

drown v b1300

execution n b1300 (execute: b1450)

hearse n *type of coffin cover* b1300 [type of vehicle: b1650]

sepulture n *burial* b1300

inter v b1305

empoison v b1325

decease n b1340 (verb use: b1435; deceased adj: b1490; deceased n: b1625)

immortality n b1340 (immortal adj: b1375)

murderer n b1340 (murderess: b1400; murderee: b1920)

hangman n b1345 (hanger: b1450)

balm v *embalm*

chrisom child n *child that dies early*

deathly adj/adv *as in "deathly ill"* [obs. "capable of dying": b1000; arch. "causing death": b1350]

embalm v

end v *obs. kill* [u1600s]

fine n *obs. death* [u1500s]

fork n *obs. gallows* [u1800s]

ghost n *obs. corpse* [u1500s]

head v *behead* (headsman: b1605)

low adj *arch. dead*

mortality n *being mortal* ["death itself": b1470]

weeper n *hired mourner*

War/Military/Violence

arm v *equip with weapons* b1200

assail v *assault physically* b1200 ["assault verbally": b1470; obs. "woo": b1350 to 1600s] (assailant: b1535)

club n b1200 [pertaining to sports: b1450] (verb use: b1600)

conquer v b1200 [fig. "overcome": b1450] (conquest: b1325)

destroy v b1200

fleet n (Am) *many ships* b1200 ["one ship": b1000; as in "fleet of trucks": b1400]

hurt v *cause pain* b1200 ["feel pain": b1870]

sergeant n b1200 [obs. "servant": b1200 to 1500s; "police sergeant": b1870]

legion n b1225 (adj use: b1680)

quarrel n *bolt* b1225

scourge n *type of whip* b1225 [fig. use: b1385] (verb use: b1300)

siege n/v *type of attack* b1225

arm, arms n *weapons* b1250 (arm v: b1250)

assault n b1250 ["sexual attack": b1970] (verb use: b1410)

battle n b1250 [obs. "war": b1450 to 1500s] (verb use: b1300)

centurion n b1275

admiral n b1300 (admiralty: b1350)

ambush v b1300 (noun use: b1490; arch. ambushment: b1350)

archer n b1300 (archery: b1400)

armed adj *having weapons* b1300

armor n *body armor* b1300 (armored: b1605)

besiege v *lit. siege* b1300 [fig. "inundate": b1630]

bowman n *archer* b1300

box n *hit* b1300 (verb use: b1520; boxer: b1475)

buckler n *small shield* b1300

chevalier n b1300

chivalry n *gen. knights* b1300 ["the code of the knights": b1730] (chivalrous: b1350; chivalric: b1800; chivalresque: b1830)

commander n *leader* b1300 [spec. mil. title: b1450] (commandress: b1600)

company n b1300

dart n *type of weapon* b1300 (verb use: b1450)

destrier n *warhorse* b1300

destruction n b1300 (destructive: b1490; destructful: b1670; destruct v: b1670)

ding v *arch. hit hard* b1300

dismember v b1300

encounter v/n *battle* b1300 ["come across": b1530; "experience": b1830]

glaive n *type of sword* b1300

hauberk n *type of chain mail* b1300

herald n b1300 ["messenger": b1830] (verb use: b1380)

lance n b1300 [type of soldier: b1450]

mace n *type of weapon* b1300

mail n/v *type of armor* b1300 [obs. "mail armor piece": u1700s]

maim v b1300 (noun use: b1350; adj use: b1500)

maul v *mangle* b1300 (obs. "hit": b1300 to 1600s)

quiver n *arrow holder* b1300

ravish v *carry off; plunder* b1300 [rape: b1450]

scabbard n b1300

slaughter n b1300 (verb use: b1535)

soldier n b1300 (verb use: b1650)

spy n/v b1300 (spier: b1225)

target n *arch. type of shield* b1300 (targe: b1300; targeteer: b1600)

violence n b1300 (adj use: b1350)

warrior n b1300 (warrioress: b1600)

battlement n b1325

conquest n b1325

cripple v *phys. harm* b1325 ["walk lamely": b1250; fig. "obstruct": b1700]

deface v *destroy* b1325 ["mar": b1385; obs. "defame": b1450 to 1600s]

falchion n *type of sword* b1325

feud n *hostility* b1325 ["war": b1450] (verb use: b1675; feudist: b1905)

manslaughter n b1325 (manslaht: b900)

socket n *type of spearhead* b1330

navy n b1340 [obs. gen. "ships": b1350 to 1400s]

anlace n *type of dagger*

armorer n

armory n *arsenal* ["storage place": b1470]

bait v *harass, attack*

draw v *obs., as in "draw and quarter"* [u1700s]

engine n *weapon* (engineer: b1350; enginery: b1605)

forayer n *raider* (foray n/v: b1375)

gin n *obs. stone-thrower* [u1500s]

greave n *piece of armor*

gun n [obs. "any large weapon": u1500s]

gunner n

handgun n

lame v *cripple*

mank v *arch. maim*

manslayer n

marshal n

no man's land n

poleax n [type of butcher's tool: b1730] (verb use: b1885)

rap n/v *hit* [type of knock: b1670]

sharp n *sharp weapon*

skirmish n/v

sling n *type of weapon*

spoil n *war booty* [gen. "reward": b1800]

strike v *hit* ["attack," as in "we will strike at night": b1630] (noun use: b1450)

truncheon n *type of weapon* (verb use: b1600)

Crime/Punishment/Enforcement

cucking stool n *type of punishment* b1200

discipline n *punishment* b1200 ["training": b1450; as in "maintain discipline in the classroom": b1670] (verb use: b1300)

incest n b1200 (incestuous: b1535)

lawless adj b1200

ransom n b1200 (verb use: b1400)

rob, robber, robbery v, n, n b1200

traitor n b1225 (traitorous: b1350; traitress: b1400; obs. traitorly: b1530 to 1600s)

treason n *betrayal of another or of country* b1225 (rare verb use: b1350; treasonable: b1375; treasonous: b1595)

bigamy n b1250 (bigamist: b1635; bigamous: b1835)

jail n b1275 (verb use: b1605; jailhouse: b1815)

pillory n b1275 (verb use: b1600)

felony n b1290 [obs. "evil": u1500s; obs. gen. "sin": u1500s]

extortion n b1300 (extort: b1425)

felon adj/n b1300 [obs.

"demon": u1800s] (felonous: b1340; felonious: b1575)

forfeit n *type of criminal penalty* b1300

imprison v b1300

jailer n b1300

justify v *obs. mete justice* b1300 [u1600s]

pirate n b1300 [fig. "plagiarist": b1630] (verb use: b1530; piracy: b1540)

sodomy n b1300 (sodomite: b1390; sodom: b1600; sodomize: b1870; sodomist: b1900)

unlawful adj b1300

bob v *arch. cheat/filch*

drawlatch n *arch. type of thief*

inlaw n *opp. of outlaw*

malefactor n

opium n

principal n *perpetrator*

prisoner n

privateer n *pirate; pirate ship* (private man of war: b1650)

stock n *pillory*

war n *arch. part of a castle; prison; section of a prison*

The Law

article n *clause or portion of leg. document* b1200 ["portion of any document": b1470]

handfast n *arch. contract* b1200

innocent, innocence adj, n *not guilty* b1200 ["untainted": b1385] (noun use: b1200; innocency: b1275)

common pleas n b1225

default n b1225 (verb use: b1385)

rule n *as in "rules and regulations"* b1225 ["regulation": b1470]

bailiff n b1245

hue and cry n *leg. sense* b1250 [gen. "commotion": b1500]

plead v b1250 ["beg": b1630]

attorney n b1300 (attorney-at-law: b1540)

citation n b1300 ["praise": b1930] (cite "summon":

b1450; cite "quote": b1535; citation "quote": b1550)

deforce v *take or keep by force* b1300

demesne n b1300

executor n b1300 (executrix: b1400)

high court n b1300

inquest n b1300

judgment n b1300

jurisdiction n b1300 [gen. "province": b1450]

juror n b1300 [obs. "false accusor": u1500s]

jury n b1300 [nonlegal sense: b1870]

mortmain n b1300

pardon n b1300 (verb use: b1450)

perjury n b1300

statute n b1300

summons n *gen. and leg.* b1300 (verb use: b1800)

try v *subject to leg. or gen. trial* b1300 ["test": b1380; "strain," as in "try the patience": b1570] (noun use: b1610)

verdict n b1300 [gen. use: b1535]

arraign v b1325

code n *Roman statutes* b1325 [gen. code of law: b1770] (verb use: b1815)

condemn v *convict* b1325 ["blame": b1340; "rebuke": b1450; "assign to a fate": b1670; as in "condemn a building": b1730] (condemnation: b1385)

contract n b1325 (verb use: b1425; contractual: b1865)

culpable adj *legally guilty* b1325 ["deserving blame": b1600]

defendant n b1325 (adj use: b1300)

indictment, indict n, v b1325 [fig. use: b1900]

ordinance n *law* b1325

quitclaim n/v b1325

testator n *one who dies testate* b1325 (testate adj: b1430; testate n: b1450; testatrix: b1595)

warrant n *as in "search war-*

rant" b1325 [type of directive: b1225]

appeal v b1340

attach v *seize legally* b1340

convict v b1340 [gen. "show guilt": b1450; obs. gen. "prove": b1450 to 1700s; arch. "disprove": b1570] (adj use: b1400; conviction: b1440)

deed n b1340 (verb use: b1810)

warranty n *type of legal guarantee* b1340 [gen. "guarantee": b1450]

action n (actionable: b1595)

bench n *judicial sense*

bind v *make a formal agreement* (binding adj: b1400)

common law n

constitution n

court n

judge n [as in "let me be the judge": b1450] (judger: b1450; judgess: b1570)

justice n *leg. system*

justice n *judge, etc.*

recognizance n ["recognition": b1400]

record n *as in "on the record"* [gen. use: b1535]

sufficient adj *satisfactory in leg. sense* ["satisfactory in gen. sense": b1450]

suit n *lawsuit* (obs. verb use: b1530 to 1700s)

testimony n

title n

writ n

The Fantastic/Paranormal

demon/daemon n b1200 ["evil person": b1630; as in "demon rum": b1730; "whiz," as in "speed demon": b1900] (demoniac/demoniacal: b1400; demoness: b1630; demonic: b1665]

hag n b1200 [gen. insult: b1470]

otherworld n b1200 (otherworldly: b1875)

dragon n b1225 [obs. "python": u1700s] (dragonet: b1350)

incubus n *type of demon* b1225

unicorn n b1225 [obs. type of rhinoceros: b1450 to 1600s]

gargoyle n b1290

basilisk n *type of fantastic creature* b1300 [type of cannon: b1530]

fairy n *fairyland* b1300 ["inhabitant of fairyland": b1395; fig. "pixie": b1870; "homosexual": b1900]

giant n b1300 (adj use: b1470; giantess: b1400)

nightmare n *spectre bringing bad sleep* b1300 ["bad dream": b1830]

phantom n b1300 [obs. "something illusionary": u1600s] (adj use: b1450)

sprite n *ghost, pixie* b1300 [arch. fig. "spriteliness": concurrent]

superstition n b1300

vision n *something supernatural* b1300

hob n *hobgoblin* b1310 (hobgoblin: b1530)

fantasy n b1325 ["daydream": b1930] (verb use: b1430)

diviner n (divine, divination: b1400)

dwarf n *mythical creature* [small person: b900]

goblin n

griffin/griffon/gryphon n (obs. "gripe": b350 to 1600s)

leviathan adj/n

manticore n *type of legendary beast*

mermaid n (merman: b1605; merwoman: b1830)

seer n (seeress: b1845)

shadow n *something unreal*

siren n *mythical creature*

spirit n *ghost, demon*

warlock n *magician; male witch* [obs. "evil person," "demon," "Satan": b900]

Magic

bewitch v b1225 (bewitchment: b1610)

charm n *spell* b1300 ["charisma": b1600; as in

"good-luck charm": b1600] (verb use: b1350)

enchanter, enchantment n b1300 (enchant, enchantress: b1375)

sorcery n b1300 (sorcerer, sorceress: b1400; sorcerous: b1550)

curse n *type of spell* [gen. "bane": b1600] (verb use: b1450; cursed: b1300)

magus n

necromancy n *conjuring spirits*

witch v *enchant* [obs. "use magic": by OE to 1600s; "bewitch": b1600]

Interjections

O interj/n *as in "O ye of little faith"* b1175 (oh: b1550)

hail interj b1200

hey interj b1200

ho interj *as in "land ho"* b1260

alas interj b1275

ah interj b1300

eh interj b1300

fie interj b1300

Godspeed interj b1300

tehee interj b1300 (verb use: b1300; noun use: b1600)

avaunt adv/interj *onward* b1325

aha interj

ay interj

gramercy interj *thanks* ["mercy me!": b1630]

ha interj (ha ha: b1000)

heigh interj *used to call attention, give encouragement*

ho interj *whoa*

oho interj

pardie interj *by God*

perfay interj *'tis true*

shame interj

Slang

grope v *cop a feel* b1250

pass away v b1300

mare n *woman* b1305

charged adj b1325

head n *as in "drughead," "motorhead"*

nose n *ability to sense things, as in "a nose for news"*

wind n *as in "catch wind of something"; breath; prattle*

Insults

fool n b1200 (adj use: b1300; foolhardy: b1225; foolish: b1300)

hardhearted adj b1225

shrew n *shrewish woman; arch. villain of either sex* b1250 (shrewish: 1300s)

ugly adj *not attractive* b1250 ["horrifying": b1250; "indicating trouble": b1670; "threatening": b1770; "cantankerous": b1700] (adv use: b1400; uglify: b1680)

whoreson n b1250

lurdane adj/n b1300

blab n *gossipmonger* (verb use: b1470; blabber v: b1400; blabber n "blather": b1915; blabbermouth: b1940)

daff n *arch. fool*

dog n

dullard n

fon n *obs. foolish person* [u1500s] (obs. adj/v use: b1470 to 1500s)

frog n *base person*

gig n *obs. bimbo* [u1700s]

giglet n *slut*

knave n *rascal* [obs. "boy": b1000 to 1800s] (knavery: b1530)

misspeak v *obs. insult* [u1600s] (obs. misspeech: u1400s)

mop n *arch. fool, child* (verb use: b1710)

slime n *disgusting person or substance* (verb use: b1630)

sluggard n [obs. "sloth, the animal": b1670 to 1700s] (adj use: b1530)

slut n *unkempt woman, maid, prostitute* (sluttery: b1600)

trot n *arch. crone*

yahoo n

Phrases

day-to-day adj b1200

high-and-mighty adj b1200

good fellow n b1225

fire and brimstone n b1300

in a twinkling n b1300

more and more adv b1300

more or less adv b1300

side by side adv b1300

such and such adj b1300 (pron use: b1500)

olive branch n *token of peace* b1325

out-and-out adv b1325 (adj use: b1815; out-and-outer: b1815)

at bay adj

child's play n

face-to-face adj/adv

to and fro adv (adj use: b1750; toing and froing: b1845; to-fro adj: b1900)

treasure trove n

General/Miscellaneous

fastening n b1175

gift n b1175 [obs. "bribe": b1470 to 1600s] (verb use: b1550)

low adj/n *lit. and fig.* b1175 [applied to rivers, sound, temperature, etc.: b1450; applied to prices: b1630]

needy adj/n b1175

opening n *gap, hole* b1175

privilege n b1175 (verb use: b1350; privileged: b1450)

skill n b1175 [arch. "knowledge": b1150; "ability to reason": b1350 to 1400s]

smother n/v b1175 [fig., as in "smother with affection": b1600]

use n/v *using; purpose; etc.* b1175 [as in "have a use": b1450] (useful, useless: b1595)

absolution n b1200 (absolve: b1425)

acquaint, acquaintance v, n b1200

adventure n/v b1200 (verb use: b1350; adventurous: b1350)

adversity n b1200 (adverse: b1385)

authority n *information source* b1200 ["authoritative person": b1540]

babe n b1200 (baby: b1400)

behest n b1200 [obs. "guarantee": b1000 to 1500s]

bond n *something that ties, confines* b1200 ["bail money": b1670]

brim n gen. border b1200 ["edge," as in "brim of a cup": b1470; "hat brim": b1600] (verb use: b1615)

buffet n/v a blow b1200

burrow n b1200 (verb use: b1605)

cage n b1200 (verb use: b1580)

carriage n carrying b1200 [obs. "type of toll": u1700s]

cause n impetus, as in "cause and effect"; calling, as in "political cause" b1200 (verb use: b1400; causative: b1415)

champion n hero b1200 ["winner of competition": b1730] (verb use: b1830)

charter n agreement b1200 (verb use: b1425)

circumstance n b1200 [obs. "surrounding area": u1800s; as in "pomp and circumstance": b1450; "details, events," as in "extenuating circumstances": b1530]

cost n b1200 ["what is spent": b1450 to 1700s] (verb use: b1380)

counsel n advice, advice-giving b1200 (verb use: b1350)

cry v/n beg b1200 ["cry out": b1280; "weep": b1570] (noun use: b1280)

custom n habit b1200

degree n step; level b1200 (obs. verb use: b1450 to 1600s)

ease n as in "ease of entry" b1200 [obs. "opportunity": u1400s; "easy life": b1450] (verb use: b1300)

fall n as in "rainfall" b1200 [as in "waterfall": b1600; as in "nightfall": b1670]

fame n b1200 (verb use: b1450; famous: b1400; famed: b1535)

flight n fleeing b1200 ["flying": b900]

folly n b1200

fortitude n b1200

heritage n b1200

image n phys. b1200 ["men-

tal sense": b1380; "outward impression": b1910] (verb use: b1400)

intent n b1200

lightness n opp. of heaviness b1200

load n b1200 [obs. "act of carrying": b1000 to 1500s] (verb use: b1500)

loan n b1200 (verb use: b1300)

manner n b1200

merit n b1200 [obs. "just deserts": u1700s] (verb use: b1600; meritorious: b1425)

moan n complaint b1200 [suffering aloud: b1675] (obs. verb use: b1250 to 1600s)

mold n as in "in the mold of" b1200 [type of tool: b1300]

narrow n b1200

nonce n b1200

pilgrim n b1200 (pilgrimage n: b1250; pilgrimage v: b1400)

ruin n b1200 [fig. use: b1470] (verb use: b1570; ruination: b1665)

sake n b1200

savor n b1200 (verb use: b1400; savory: b1350)

shiver n/v splinter b1200

spot n blotch b1200 ["pimple": b1350] (verb use: b1400)

wait n waiting; as in "lie in wait" b1200

want n as in "for want of a nail" b1200 ["dire need": b1470]

want v/n lack, need b1200 ["desire, yearn": b1710; as in "wanted by the police": b1770]

aroma n b1225 [obs. "aromatic plant": b1225 to 1800s] (aromatic adj: b1400; aromal adj: b1870)

art n skill b1225 ["aesthetic pursuit": b1600]

balm n b1225

brink n b1225

broach n b1225

charge n/v duty b1225 [obs. phys. "burden": u1700s]

couple n pertaining to people

b1225 [gen. use: b1340; obs. "coupling": u1600s] (verb use: b1200)

crouch v b1225 (noun use: b1600)

dark n darkness b1225 ["state of being uninformed," as in "kept in the dark": b1630] (obs. verb use: b1150; darken: b1300)

double adj/v b1225 (noun use: b1350; adv use: b1400; duple adj/n: b1500)

form n b1225 (verb use: b1300)

guise n b1225 [obs. "gen. style": u1700s]

gyve n/v fetter b1225

hardship n b1225

haste n b1225 (verb use: b1350; hasty: b1470; hasten: b1570)

homage n b1225 (obs. verb use: b1470 to 1600s)

lifetime n b1225

loose adj/v free b1225 ["limber": b1350] (loose v: b1300; loosen: b1350)

mastery n b1225

matter n b1225

noise n b1225 (obs. "group of musicmakers": 1500s to 1600s)

observance n b1225

ornament n b1225 [obs. "useful accessory," such as furniture: u1700s] (verb use: b1720; ornamental: b1650)

pack n/v package b1225 [as in "pack of cards": b1600; "packet," as in "pack of cigarettes": b1930]

patience n endurance b1225 ["willingness to wait": b1450; "perseverance": b1530] (patient adj: b1350)

perfection n b1225 ["something perfect": b1500] (perfect adj: b1300; perfect v: b1400)

peril n danger; source of danger b1225 (verb use: b1570; perilous: b1300)

piece n section, part; part of a collection, as in "piece of

furniture"; sexual object, as in "piece of ass" b1225 [as in "down the road a piece": b1450; as in "game piece": b1570; "gun": b1600]

plenty n copiousness b1225 ["a lot": b1630]

preeminence n b1225 (preeminent: b1450)

present n gift, presentation b1225 [obs. "presence," obs. "something that is present": u1700s] (presentation: b1400)

press n/v as in "the press of the crowd"; arch. troubles b1225 [fig. "pressure": b1450]

proof n confirming evidence; result b1225

prosperity n b1225 (prosper: b1400; prosperous: b1450)

recluse adj/n b1225 (obs. verb use: b1450 to 1700s; obs. reclude: b1600; reclusion: b1400)

route n b1225

seal n as in "seal of approval" b1225 (verb use: b1350; sea lion: b1700)

silence n b1225 (verb use: b1600)

sire n b1225

state n phys. condition b1225 ["mental condition": b1450]

strife n b1225

tribulation n b1225 (tribulate v: b1640)

trifle n trifling matter b1225 [obs. "joke": u1600s; "trifling thing": b1450] (verb use: b1400; trifling: b1400)

truce n b1225

discord n b1230 (verb use: b1350)

clear n b1240

calling n b1250

case n situation b1250 ["example": b1300; med. sense: b1470; leg. sense: b1630]

chase n as in "the chase is on" b1250 (verb use: b1300)

chatter v/n b1250 [as in

"chattering teeth": b1450]
(chat: b1450)

clench n/v b1250

close n *enclosed area* b1250

commandment n b1250

contrary n b1250

dearth n b1250

delay n *procrastination* b1250
["obstacle": b1770] (verb
use: b1300)

faith n *loyalty, belief* b1250
[obs. "promise": 1600s]
(obs. verb use: b1250 to
1600s)

first name n b1250

mishap n b1250

muck n b1250

outlet n *exit* b1250 [fig., as in
"an outlet for expressing
rage": b1700]

prey n b1250 [arch. "booty":
concurrent; rare "prey-
ing": b1530] (verb use:
b1350)

respite n b1250 (verb use:
b1330)

sort n b1250

stealth n *furtiveness* b1250
[obs. "stealing": u1700s;
"moving furtively":
b1600] (stealthy: b1605)

tackle n *gen. equipment*
b1250 [spec. "fishing
gear": b1450; as in "block
and tackle": b1500] (obs.
verb use: b1450 to 1600s)

travail n b1250

wreck n b1250

account n/v b1275

beauty n b1275 (beautiful:
b1445; beauteous: b1450;
beautify: b1530)

commencement n b1275
["graduation ceremony":
b1450] (commence:
b1300)

dais n b1275 [obs. type of table: u1500s]

deceit n b1275 (deceive:
b1300; deceitful: b1450)

falsity n b1275

interest n b1275 ["loan payment": b1545; as in "spe-
cial interest": b1700]
(verb use: b1610)

cornerstone n b1280 [fig. use:
b1325]

fault n *lack* b1280 ["flaw":
b1350]

scarf n *type of joint* b1280
(verb use: b1630)

march n *border* b1300 (verb
use: b1400)

abstinence n b1300

access n b1300 (verb use:
b1970)

ado n *as in "much ado about
nothing"* b1300

advantage n b1300 (verb
use: b1550)

advice, advise n, v b1300
[obs. "wisdom": u1500s]

affair n *gen.* b1300

alliance n b1300

ally, allied v, adj b1300 (ally
n: b1470)

appeal n *leg. and gen.* b1300
(verb use: b1340)

arch n b1300 ["foot arch":
b1870] (verb use: b1400)

assembly n *gathering* b1300
[legislative sense: b1470;
"mil. call to assemble":
b1730]

base n *bottom of a statue, column* b1300 [gen. use:
b1450]

being n *existence; something
that is* b1300

benefice n b1300

bequest n b1300

bicker n/v b1300 (verb use:
b1500)

bound n *as in "out of bounds"*
b1300 (verb use: b1395)

boy n *young male* b1300 [obs.
"cad": b1300 to 1600s;
"fellow," as in "one of the
boys": b1470]

branch n *tree limb; fig. offshoot, as in "river branch"*
b1300

burst n *a bursting* b1300 [obs.
"harm": b1000 to late ME;
"sudden instance," as in
"burst of laughter": b1470;
"spurt": b1800]

case n *box; casing* b1300

caution n *warning* b1300
["guarantee": b1300;
"carefulness": b1605]
(verb use: b1645; cautionary: b1570; cautious:
b1640)

cement n *spec. to making con-*

crete b1300 [gen. "gluing
agent": b1450] (verb use:
b1350)

certain, certainty adj, n *fixed;
inevitable* b1300 ["un-
doubtable," "convinced":
b1470]

chain n *lit. series of links;
bonds* b1300 [fig. "some-
thing that restricts"; fig.
"series": b1450] (verb use
"fetter": b1400; verb use
"link": b1970)

chance n *fortune* b1300 ["a
possibility": b1800] (verb
use: b1395; adj use:
b1700)

channel n b1300 [as in "radio
channel": b1870] (verb
use: b1450)

charity n *contributions* b1300
["Christian love": b1140;
gen. "good will": b1500]
(charitable: b1200)

choice n *choosing; the power
to choose* b1300 ["some-
thing chosen": b1450; "selection," as in "a large
choice": b1600] (adj use:
b1350)

chosen n b1300 (adj use:
b1350)

circle n b1300 [fig. "ring,"
"orbit": b1000; as in "circle of acquaintances":
b1470] (verb use: b1400;
circular adj: b1425)

concord n b1300 (concor-
dance: b1390)

conduit n b1300

consent n b1300 [arch. empathy: b1450; arch. con-
census: b1530]

corner n b1300 [as in "far
corners of the earth":
b1450]

covenant n/v b1300 (covenanter: b1600; covenan-
tee: b1650)

damage n b1300 (verb use:
b1330)

damnation n b1300 (interj
use: b1630)

dear n b1300

defense n b1300

desert n *as in "just deserts"*
b1300

device n *plan, fancy* b1300
[type of tool: b1450]

dirt n *feces; filth; fig. inde-
cency* b1300 ["soil":
b1700]

downfall n b1300 ["rainfall":
b1630]

dreg n b1300

drift n *as in "snowdrift"*
b1300

edict n b1300

enemy n b1300

error n b1300 [obs. "defect":
b1450 to 1700s]

evidence n b1300 [leg. sense:
b1450] (verb use: b1610)

falsehood n b1300 [obs. "deceit": u1500s] (falset:
b1450)

fashion n *form* b1300 (verb
use: b1415)

favor n *as in "in good favor"*
b1300 [as in "do me a fa-
vor": b1380; as in "party
favor": b1600] (verb use:
b1350; favorable: b1350;
favored: b1400)

fender n *defender* b1300
["bumper": b1615]

figure n *form* b1300 ["human form": b1450]

foison n *cornucopia* b1300
(arch. verb use: b1470)

force n b1300 [as in "gravitational force": b1670] (verb
use: b1300)

forerunner n *predecessor*
b1300

fortune n b1300 (fortunate:
b1400)

fundament n *foundation; basis; buttocks* b1300

general adj b1300

grain n *as in "grain of sand";
kernel* b1300 [as in "grain
of truth": b1470]

grievance n b1300 [obs.
"hardship": u1700s; obs.
"distress": u1500s]

grime n b1300 (grimy:
b1615)

hazard n *dangerous obstacle*
b1300 [type of game:
b1300] (verb use: b1530)

hermitage n b1300

holocaust n *conflagration*
b1300 [mass destruction:
b1630]

impair, impairment v, n b1300

iniquity n b1300 (obs. iniquе: b1530 to 1700s; obs. iniquous: b1630 to 1700s; iniquitous: b1730)

interval n b1300

issue n *outflow* b1300 (verb use: b1350)

juice n b1300 [arch. "bodily fluid": b1450] (verb use: b1605; juicy: b1450)

leash n b1300

lieu n b1300

like n *as in "the likes of you"* b1300

lump n *mass* b1300 [as in "a cancerous lump": b1450]

marvel n/v b1300 [obs. "tale of marvel": u1400s; obs. "miracle": u1500s] (marvelous: b1350)

meaning n b1300

menace n/v *threat* b1300 ["endangerment": b1870]

mention n b1300 (verb use: b1530)

minister n b1300

misadventure n b1300

mischance n b1300 (verb use: b1570)

obligation n b1300

odor n b1300 (odorous: b1450; odoriferous: b1475)

office n *responsibility* b1300

outcast adj/n b1300

pair n b1300 (verb use: b1610; pairing: b1615)

pane n *as in "window pane"* b1300 ["section of cloth": b1350 to 1500s; gen. "panel": b1570]

partner n *associate* b1300 [obs. "participant": u1500s] (partnership: b1580)

party n *group, as in "political party"; individual, as in "party of the first part"* b1300 [obs. "part of the body": u1600s; "social gathering": b1730; "people banded together": b1800]

perch n/v *roost* b1300

plate n *as in "steel plate," "plate armor"; type of metal*

coating b1300 [type of coin: b1250; used in printing: b1670; as in "nameplate": b1670; type of denture: b1870; as in "photo plate": b1870]

plight n *tough situation* b1300 [obs. "attire": b1600]

portion n/v b1300

power n *authority; capability; control; strength* b1300 [as in "electrical power": b1730] (verb use: b1540)

predecessor n b1300

print n *as in "footprint," "fingerprint"; gen. impression* b1300 (verb use: b1400)

prize n *something won* b1300 ["something to try to win": b1630] (verb use: b1375; adj use: b1800)

profit n/v *gen. benefit; revenue* b1300 ["what's left after expenses": b1500] (profitable: b1325)

purpose n *goal; intent* b1300 ["reason for existence": b1450]

quantity n b1300

quarter n b1300 (verb use: b1355)

question n b1300 (verb use: b1470)

realm n b1300

release n/v b1300

respond, response v b1300

rift n b1300 [obs. "tear": b1300; fig. "split": b1630]

savior n *gen. and rel.* b1300

scarcity n b1300 [obs. "stinginess": u1500s]

scion n b1300

self n b1300

semblance n b1300 (obs. semblant n: b1350 to 1600s; obs. semble v: b1350 to 1700s)

show n *display, demonstration* b1300 ["pageant": b1570; "formal entertainment": b1770]

significance n b1300 (significant adj, significantly adv: b1580; significancy: b1595)

size n b1300

sound n b1300 [obs. "mu-

sic": u1500s; "musical style": b1930]

stack n/v b1300

stage n *phys. phase, step* b1300 [fig. "phase, step": b1630]

stature n *phys. presence* b1300 [fig. "social presence": b1870]

stink n *smell* b1300 ["commotion," as in "cause a stink": b1815] (verb use: b1150)

streamer n b1300

stroke n *a hit* b1300

substance n *essence; phys. material* b1300 ["wealth," "quality of character": b1450]

surfeit n b1300 (verb use: b1450)

sustenance n b1300

task n b1300 [obs. type of tax: b1450 to 1700s]

tenor n *gist, tone* b1300

theme n *subject* b1300 [type of essay: b1570; in music: b1700]

torment n/v b1300 [obs. "severe storm": u1600s] (obs. noun, verb use "shake up": b1450)

tour n *turn, as in "tour of duty"* b1300 [as in "tour of the country": b1670]

trace n/v *track* b1300 ["evidence": b1450; "tiny remaining amount": b1830; "instance of tracking": b1970]

trespass n/v *transgression; phys. invasion* b1300

trouble n *distress* b1300 [as in "you're in trouble": b1570; "cause of troubles": b1600] (troubled: b1350; arch. troublous: b1450; troublesome: b1545)

trump n/v *trumpeting* b1300

unity n b1300 (unite, unition: b1450)

unknowing adj/n b1300

unrest n b1300 (verb use: b1450)

vantage n b1300

vengeance n b1300 (arch.

venge v: b1350; vengeful: b1590)

vermillion n *type of pigment* b1300 ["the color of the pigment": b1450]

vice n b1300

voice n *lit. and fig.* b1300 (verb use: b1450)

vow n/v b1300

wail v/n b1300 (wailful: b1545)

waste n *misuse, overuse* b1300

aim n *as in "take aim"* b1305 ["target": b1325] (noun use: b1380)

barb n b1305 [fig. "pointed remark": b1800]

behalf n b1305

defame, defamation v, n b1305 (defamation: b1450)

fallacy n b1305 [obs. "guile": b1400 to 1700s] (fallacious: b1510; fallacion n: b1570)

murk n b1305 (murky: b1340)

welfare n b1305

administration n b1325 (administrator: b1450; administrate: b1650)

asphalt n *petroleum product* b1325 ["road-paving material": b1860] (verb use: b1860)

barrier n *phys. block* b1325 [fig. block: b1730]

bubble n/v b1325

bunch n *group, cluster* b1325 (verb use: b1400)

captivity n b1325 (captive adj/n: b1350; captor: b1650)

challenge n *dare* b1325 [obs. "accusation": u1600s; "dispute": b1450] (verb use: b1450)

cleft n b1325 (adj use: b1400)

condition n *prerequisite; state* b1325 [obs. "mental constitution": b1450 to 1800s; "illness," as in "tuberculatory condition": b1930] (conditional: b1380)

core n *of apples, etc.* b1325

[gen. use: b1400; fig. use: b1450] (verb use: b1450)

daze v b1325 (noun use: b1825)

debate n b1325 [arch. "fight": b1300] (verb use: b1380)

dissension n b1325 (dissent v: b1425; dissent n: b1470; dissenter: b1640)

equity n b1325

female n b1325 (adj use: b1385; feminine: b1380; feminal: b1450; masculine: b1600)

founder n *one who founds, as in a city* b1325 (foundress: b1470)

gap n b1325

gossamer n b1325 (adj use: b1810)

label n *identifier* b1325 ["ribbon": b1325; arch. "band, esp. around a document": b1500] (verb use: b1605)

maintenance n b1325

marking n b1325

midst n b1325

multitude n b1325 (multitudinous: b1605)

murmur n b1325 (verb use: b1325)

mystery n *secret* b1325 (mysterious: b1600)

natural n b1325 ["talented person": b1925]

offend, offense v, n b1325 (offensive adj: b1550)

pestilence n b1325 (pestilent adj: b1400; pestiferous: b1475)

prohibition n b1325 (prohibit, prohibitory: b1450)

property n *something owned; characteristic* b1325 [obs. "being proper": b1450 to 1700s; spec. "land owned": b1730; "theatrical prop": b1450]

protection n *act of protecting* b1325 ["something that protects": b1450] (protect: b1470)

quake n b1325 ["earthquake": b1645]

quest n/v b1325

restitution n b1325 (restitute: b1470)

rite n b1325 (ritual: b1570)

stalk n b1325

stepping-stone n b1325

swivel n b1325 (verb use: b1795)

tallow n b1325 (verb use: b1450)

victory n b1325 (victor: b1350; victorious: b1400)

way n *as in "go this way"* b1325

argument n *argumentation* b1330 ["dispute": b1500] (argumentation, argumentative: b1450)

bundle n b1335 [slang "a lot of cash": b1930] (verb use: b1600)

terms n *conditions* b1335

abundance n b1340

adversary n b1340 (adj use: b1400; adversarial: b1930)

alien n *stranger* b1340 (adj use: b1300; verb use: b1400)

bargain n b1340 (verb use: b1400)

chip n *shard* b1340 (verb use: b1425)

comparison n b1340

corruption n *phys., moral decay* b1340 ["selling out": b1450]

credence n b1340 (credent: b1600)

detraction n b1340 (detract: b1425)

fervent, fervor adj, n b1340 (fervency: b1425)

gang n *group* b1340 [applied to people: b1400] (verb use: b1860)

invisible adj/n b1340

obstacle n b1340

quarrel n *disagreement* b1340 ["altercation": b1600] (verb use: b1395; quarrelsome: b1600)

reproof n b1340 [obs. "shame": u1600s] (reprove v: b1305)

request n b1340 (verb use: b1470)

scum n b1340 [obs. "foam": b1250 to 1600s; fig. use: b1590]

commission n *authority* b1345

[spec. "mil. authority": b1450; type of governmental body: b1495] (verb use: b1665)

teeter n/v b1345

abuse n (verb use: b1425; obs. abusion n: b1350 to 1700s)

advocate n (verb use: b1600)

back n *as in "the back of the house"* [on the body: b885]

balance n *as in "hangs in the balance"*

blade n *flat part of knives, etc.* ["bon vivant": b1600]

block n *as in "block of wood"*

body n *group, as in "legislative body"*

boon n *blessing* [obs. type of prayer: b1150 to 1600s]

break n *gap*

brush n *as in "a brush with the law"* (verb use, as in "brush past": b1475)

chock n (adv use: b1835; verb use: b1855)

clump n *clod* ["lump": b1300; "grouping": b1600]

coin n *corner*

commend, commendable v, adj (commendation: b1450)

congregation n [as in "church congregation": b1530]

consideration n [obs. "seeing": u1600s; "payment": b1630]

continence, continent n, adj *self-restraint* ["opp. of incontinence": b1930]

continuance n

covey n

crown n *top* [about hats: b1500; geo. sense: b1600; about plants: b1600]

decline n *decay, withering* (verb use: b1450)

description n (describe: b1425; descriptive: b1755)

distribution n (distribute: b1425)

drain n [as in "a drain on the economy": b1730] (verb use: b1570)

drunkard n (drunk: b1870)

entirety n

exercise n *as in "exercise of duties"; practice* (verb use: b1400)

exile v *exiling; person in exile* ["state of exile": b1450]

feat n

field n *as in "field of operations"*

form n *mold*

fraud n (fraudulent: b1425; fraudulence: b1500; fraudulency: b1670)

gash n (verb use: b1470)

glory n (verb use: b1400; glorious: b1300)

grounds n *as in "coffee grounds"; as in "grounds for divorce"* [obs. phys. sense: b900 to 1700s; obs. "tenets": b1570 to 1700s]

head n *source; as in "come to a head"*

heap n *many, a lot, as in "a heap of trouble"*

honor n *something awarded*

hostage n ["hosted lodger": b1300]

hurly-burly n (hurly: b1595)

illusion n *mockery* ["something deceptive": b1380]

irreverence n (irreverent: b1470)

jeopardy n [obs. "puzzle": u1400s; obs. "scheme": u1500s] (jeopard v: b1375; jeopardize: b1650)

knock n

knoll n/v *sound a knell*

lack n [obs. "offense": u1500s; gen. "want, need": b1570]

larboard adj/n *port*

lash n (verb use: b1450)

lattice n (latticework: b1490)

leavings n

legend n *as in "the legend of the Lone Ranger"* ["tale of saint's life": b1350]

letter n *as in "letter of the law"*

loop n *loophole* [as in "loop of rope": b1400]

lozenge n *type of shape* [obs. type of pastry: u1400s; "tablet": b1570]

lure n *in falconry* [gen. use: b1450] (verb use: b1450)

magnificence n *tasteful spending* [obs. "plentitude," "glory": b1450 to 1600s; "grandeur": b1450] (magnificent: b1450; magnificency: b1570)

male n (adj use: b1450)

mark n *target, as in "hit your mark"; goal*

meantime n (adv use: b1450; meanwhile: b1400)

medley n

member n *as in "member of the party"* (membership: b1650)

midden n

moisture n [obs. "moistness": u1700s]

negligence n

note n/v *notableness* (noteworthy: b1555)

novice n

nurture n (verb use: b1450)

omission n

order n/v *sequence*

oversight n *overseeing* ["negligence": b1500]

overture n *proposal, suggestion* ["musical beginning": b1670]

pattern n [spec., as in "dress pattern": b1800]

perdition n ["hell": b1450 to 1600s]

persecution n (persecute: b1450)

perseverance n (persevere: b1375; perseveration: b1450)

petition n *request* [type of document: b1450] (verb use: b1610)

ply n *layer*

point n *argument, topic, as in "make a point"; sharp tip, as in "point of a sword"* ["primary intent of a story": b1700]

possession n *ownership; property owned*

powder n [obs. "dust": u1500s] (verb use: b1300)

precept n [obs. gen. "command": u1500s]

presence n *being here/there* [obs. "group of people": b1450 to 1700s] (obs.

present "presence": b1350)

privation n *deprivation*

process n [obs. "story": u1700s]

provision n *providing; supply; prerequisite, condition* ["preparation": b1500] (verb use: b1810)

puddle n

purveyor n

quiet n *calm* ["lack of noise": b1470] (quietude: b1600)

ray n *as in "ray of light"* (verb use: b1600)

rear n *back* (adj use: b1350; adv use: b1450)

recoil n (verb use: b1450)

reconcile, reconciliation v, n [as in "reconcile the two stories": b1570] (obs. reconciliate: b1570)

region n (regional: b1470)

remedy n *cure* ["temptation prevention": b1200] (verb use: b1400)

renown n [obs. "rumor": u1600s] (verb use: b1300; renowned: b1375)

reproach n/v

residue n (residual: b1570)

respect n *as in "in that respect"* ["admiration": b1530] (verb use: b1560)

score n *mark* (verb use: b1400)

shock n *items drawn together* (verb use: b1470)

shore n *prop*

simulation n

singular, singularity adj, n (singularity: b1300)

slab n

slander n *defamation* [obs. meanings of "shame" or "source of shame": b1350 to 1600s] (verb use: b1250)

slot n [as in "coin slot": b1900] (verb use: b1750)

sluice n (verb use: b1595)

solitude n

soothsayer n *prognosticator* [obs. "truthteller": b1350 to 1600s]

spectacle n (spectacular: b1685)

stability n *fig.* [lit. "fixed": b1570]

station n *calling*

stopple n (noun use: b1795; stopper n: b1600)

strait n *tough times, as in "dire straits"*

style n *way of doing things* ["fashionable way of doing things": b1600]

surname n *name addition, e.g., "Eric the Brave, William of Orange"* ["family name": b1450] (verb use: b1450)

swath n

sway n *power* [obs. "rotation": b1400 to 1600s; "swaying": b1870] (verb use: b1500)

taste n *fig. and lit.* [obs. "touch": b1300; "a bit," "inclination," "good judgment," "sense of taste": b1450]

threat n *menace* [gen. "oppression": b900 to LME] (obs. verb use: u1600s; threaten: b1300)

touch n ["little bit," as in "a touch of spring": b1600; as in "lose touch": b1900]

trance n [obs. "debilitating apprehension": u1500s] (obs. verb use: b1350 to 1600s)

treatise n [obs. "story": u1600s; obs. "treaty": u1500s] (obs. treaty: u1700s)

trestle n *gen. support* ["bridge support": b1500]

trip n *act of stumbling* [as in "trip a lever": b1900] (verb use: b1450)

truth n *reality; truthfulness; arch. being true-blue* [obs. "pledge, troth": b900; as in "tell the truth": b1450; type of game, as in "truth or dare": b1870] (true: b900)

tuft n

turn n *as in "one good turn deserves another"*

utility n (utile adj: b1500)

variance n *varying* ["difference": b1450]

vigor, vigorous n, adj *phys.* [fig. "energy": b1570; fig. "decisiveness": b1630]

warble n (verb use for birds: b1500; verb use for people: b1530)

wellhead n

whoop n (verb use: b1400)

wink n *as in "40 winks"* (obs. verb use "sleep": b1450 to 1600s)

witness n/v *as in "witness to a murder"*

Things

standard n *type of flag* b1175

stave n b1175

bag n *sack* b1200 [slang "primary interest": b1970] (verb use: b1415)

ball n *round object* b1200 (verb use: b1660)

band n *as in "rubber band"* b1200

banner n b1200

basin n *bowl* b1200

cord n *string* b1200

pale n *stake, fence, as in "beyond the pale"* b1200 ["area enclosed by pales": b1450] (verb use: b1350)

gewgaw n b1225

pillar n b1225

relic n b1225

coffer n b1250 [obs. "coffin": u1600s] (verb use: b1400)

fagot/faggot n *bundle* b1280

incense n b1280

plank n b1295 (verb use: b1435; planking: b1495)

garland n b1300 (verb use: b1470)

latch n b1300 (verb use: b1450)

poke n *sack, as in "pig in a poke"* b1300

rack n *as in "hatrack"; instrument of torture* b1300 [as in "off the rack": b1970]

rail n *as in "fence rail"* b1300 [for railroads: b1630]

remnant n b1300 (adj use: b1550)

scepter n b1300

spar n *pole* b1300

spike n *as in "railroad spike"* b1300 ["attached spike":

b1470; as in "golf spikes": b1870] (verb use: b1700)

style n *stylus* b1300

bauble n b1325

flake n *chip, bit* b1325 ["snowflake": b1400; "layer": b1470; "fluff": b1670] (verb use: b1420)

foil n *as in "aluminum foil"* b1325

lectern n b1325

rag n *as in "rags to riches"* b1325

splint n *strip of wood* b1325 [med. sense: b1400]

bale n *bundle* (verb use: b1760)

beaker n

glue n (verb use: b1400)

sphere n *globe; ball* ["the apparent universe": b1150]

splinter n (verb use: b1470)

statue n [type of child's game: b1930] (statuette: b1845)

vial n

Description

fair adj *mild, light, as in "fair weather," "fair-haired"* b1175

former adj b1175

lasting adj b1175

left adj *on the weak side; on the left side* b1175 [obs. "weak": b1150] (left-hand adj: b1200; left-handed: b1400)

my adj b1175

nay adv *no* b1175 (noun use: b1300)

thy adj b1175

twofold adj b1175

unstable adj b1175

aye/ay adv *for ever, continually* b1200

early adj *as in "early morning"* b1200 [as in "early inhabitants of North America": b1600; "opp. of late": b1770]

easy adj *easeful; quiet* b1200 ["not difficult": b1280; as in "free and easy," "easy money": b1450]

lower adj b1200

needful adj b1200

poor adj *not rich; not good;*

pitiable b1200 ["deficient," as in "iron-poor blood": b1450; gen. "sickly": b1500]

ready adj b1200 (verb use: b1350)

same adj b1200 (pron use: b1350; adv use: b1770)

soft adj *opp. of hard* b1200

stormy adj b1200

tender adj *soft; frail; immature* b1200 ["gentle, loving": b1325] (verb use: b1400; tenderize: b1735)

their adj b1200

unworthy adj *without worth* b1200 ["undeserving": b1530]

wholesome adj *healthful* b1200

false adj b1200 [as in "one false move," "false hope": b1730] (obs. verb use: b1350 to 1500s; arch. adv use: b1300)

bad adj b1205 ["good": b1970] (noun use: b1450; adv use: b1685)

closed adj b1225

evermore adv b1225

everywhere adv b1225

lesser adj b1225 (adv use: b1540)

privy adj b1225

simple adj *uncomplicated* b1225 [obs. "pitiful": b1350 to 1400s; "mentally deficient": b1470] (noun use: b1400; simplicity: b1375; simplify: b1655)

special adj/adv b1225

trusty adj *trusting; trustworthy* b1225 (noun use "trusted person": b1575; trustworthy: b1810)

worthy adj b1225 (obs. verb use: u1600s)

blank adj *without color* b1230

minor adj b1230 (noun use: b1400)

divers adj *various and sundry* b1250 [obs. "diverse": u1700s; obs. "perverse": u1600s]

faraway adj b1250

fine adj *delicate, excellent* b1250 ["very small," as in "fine mist": b1570;

"large": b1600] (verb use: b1350)

foreign adj b1250

frore adj *cold, frozen* b1250

fulsome adj *abundant, "full some"* b1250 ["plump": b1470; "effusive": b1630]

knotty adj *knotted; fig. intricate* b1250

unseemly adj/adv b1250

very adj *arch. genuine, truthful, exact* b1250 [precise, as in "this very place": b1450; obs. "loyal": b1450 to 1600s]

wrought adj b1250 [as in "wrought iron": b1570]

fiery adj *lit. and fig.* b1275

stable adj b1275

unsound adj b1275

clear adj b1280 ["unencumbered," as in "free and clear": b1500]

odd adj *left over* b1280

alien adj b1300

bay adj *the color* b1300

bounden adj *beholden* b1300

brief adj b1300

broken adj *not functional* b1300

chief adj b1300

common adj *shared; ordinary* b1300 ["vulgar": b1870]

counterfeit adj b1300 [var. obs. meanings of "deformed, deceiving": u1700s] (verb use: b1300; noun use: b1400)

desert adj *deserted, forsaken* b1300

dilatory adj *delaying* b1300 (obs. dilate "delay": u1600s)

everlasting adj b1300 (noun use: b1400)

faithful adj b1300 (noun use: b1560)

fell adj *savage* b1300 [obs. "angered": u1500s]

flat adj b1300

glorious adj b1300

horrible adj b1300

impossible adj b1300

keen adj *sharp; intense* b1300

last adj *final* b1300 ["most recent": b1450]

likely adj b1300 [obs. "similar": b1450 to 1600s] (adv

use: b1450; likelihood: b1400)

lorn adj *doomed* b1300 [as in "forlorn": b1500]

near adj *fig. close by* b1300 [lit. close by: b1570] (adv use: b900)

nice adj b1300

not adv b1300

noway adv b1300 (no way interj: b1965)

patent adj *open, obvious* b1300

peaceful adj b1300

perfect adj b1300 (verb use: b1400; perfection: b1225)

perilous adj b1300

plain adv *plainly* b1300 ["absolutely": b1535]

plenteous adj b1300 (plentiful: b1470)

precious adj b1300

present adj *here* b1300

principal adj b1300

proper adj *appropriate; suitable; as in "proper name"* b1300 ["decorous, decent": b1705]

pure adj/adv *unadulterated, physically and morally* b1300 [as in "pure mathematics": b1670] (obs. verb use: u1600s; purify: b1300; purist: b1710)

quit adj *freed from obligation* b1300

ragged adj b1300 ["unfinished, rough": b1500] (raggedy: b1890)

rank adj *luxuriant, excessive* b1300

reasonable adj *as in "a reasonable assumption"* b1300 [as in "a reasonable person," "a reasonable price": b1450]

safe adj *protected; healthy* b1300 ["redeemed": b1280; obs. "sane": b1450 to 1800s; "protecting": b1450; "not risky": b1600]

savage adj *of the wild* b1300 ["uncivilized": b1450; "frenzied": b1830] (noun use: b1400; savagery: b1595; savagism: b1800)

scraggy adj *rough* b1300

(scraggly: b1870; scragged:
b1600)

second adj *after the first*
b1300

slight adj b1300

sound adj *in good shape*
b1300 [valid, well-
reasoned, as in "a sound
decision"; "financially
sound": b1630]

span-new adj b1300

straight adj/adv *without
curves* b1300 (straighten:
b1545)

strange adj *not known, not
familiar; not normal* b1300
[obs. "foreign, from an-
other land": u1700s]

subtle adj b1300 (subtlety:
b1350; subtile: b1375)

sudden adj b1300 [obs.
"soon to be": b1450 to
1700s] (noun use: b1660)

sundry adj *miscellaneous*
b1300 [obs. "discrete":
b900]

supple adj/v b1300

sure adj *certain; guaranteed;
reliable* b1300 [obs. "safe,
protected": u1600s] (adv
use: b1400)

suspect adj b1300 (verb use:
b1450; noun use: b1595;
suspicious: b1350)

swith adv (Brit) b1300

timely adj b1300 (adv use "in
a timely fashion": b1350;
arch. adv use "quickly":
b1000)

undying adj b1300

unknown adj b1300 [obs.
"not knowing": u1600s]

upcoming adj b1300

upper adj b1300

uttermost adj b1300

vacant adj *as in "a vacant
job"* b1300 ["empty":
b1450; as in "a vacant
house": b1530; "on vaca-
tion": b1630; as in "va-
cant stare": b1730] (va-
cancy: b1630)

vile adj b1300 [obs. "inexpensive": b1500 to 1600s]

void adj *vacant* b1300

wasteful adj *destructive*
b1300 ["squanderous":
b1450]

would-be adj b1300

yonder adv b1300 (adj/pron
use: b1400)

covert adj b1305 (noun use
"cover, shelter": b1300)

hideous adj b1305 (hideosity: b1470)

able adj b1325 [obs. "suitable," "easily handled":
u1700s]

bald adj *undisguised* b1325

benign adj b1325 [med.
"opp. of malignant":
b1770] (benignant:
b1785)

bottomless adj b1325

cardinal adj *primary* b1325

continual adj b1325

diverse adj *varied* b1325
["separate": b1300] (di-
versity: b1340; diversify:
b1485; diversification:
b1605; diversified: b1615)

due adj b1325 (noun use:
b1470)

express adj/adv b1325

ghastly adj b1325 (ghastful:
b1400; ghast adj: b1625)

nameless adj b1325

omnipotent adj b1325 (omnipotence: b1450)

overt adj b1325 [rare "not
closed": concurrent]

peerless adj b1325

reverse adj b1325 (noun use:
b1400; verb use: b1470)

single adj *solitary; unmarried*
b1325 (verb use: b1630)

trenchant adj *lit. and fig.
sharp* b1325 (trenchancy:
b1870)

unscathed adj b1325

halfway adj b1330

actual adj *real* b1335

ardent adj *lit. and fig. fiery*
b1335

abominable adj b1340
(abomination: b1350)

active adj b1340

contrary adj *opposite, opposing* b1340 ["ornery":
b1770] (obs. verb use:
b1350; adv use: b1470)

corrupt adj *perverted* b1340
[arch. "decayed," "morally
corrupt": b1450]

final adj b1340 (noun use:
b1610)

abysmal adj *of the abyss*
["atrocious": b1830]

asunder adj/adv

authentic adj

beholden adj

bestead adj *situated*

contrariwise adv

copious adj

dainty adj *tasty; delicate*

defective adj (defect: b1425)

desolate adj (verb use:
b1385; noun use: b1450;
desolation: b1385)

done adj

drunk adj

empty adj *without substance,
as in "empty argument"*

errant adj *roving, as in
"knight-errant"* ["deviat-
ing": b1450] (obs. erroneous "roving": b1670 to
1700s; errantry: b1655)

essential adj *of essence* (noun
use: b1450; essence:
b1400)

familiar adj (noun use:
b1300; familiarize: b1610)

fat adj *as in "a fat paycheck"*

faulty adj

feat adj *attractive, trim, smart*

firm adj [applied to people:
b1450] (verb use: b1305)

firstborn adj

fruitless adj

furious adj (furibund: b1500;
furied: b1630)

goodly adj ["handsome":
b1000]

great adj *as in "the great one"*

green adj *inexperienced*

hard adj *difficultly accomplished*

hardy adj ["bold": b1225]

harsh adj *to the touch* [to
other senses: b1470;
"strict": b1600]

high adj *as in "high noon"*

hind adj *as in "hind legs"*

homely adj

immobile adj (immobilize:
b1875)

imperfect adj (imperfection:
b1390)

incorrigible adj

kindred adj *similar* ["related,
kin": b1570] (noun use
"kinship": b1600)

latter adj [obs. "slower":
b1000]

liberal adj

light adj *as in "a light pastry"*

lightsome adj *elegant* ["lighthearted": b1570]

lofty adj

loose adj *as in "loose
speech," "loose woman"*

major adj (noun use: b1620)

manifest adj (verb use:
b1400; manifestation:
b1425)

marvelous adj

material adj *phys.* ["relevant": b1500]

mighty adv *as in "I'm mighty
cold"*

moist adj (obs. verb use:
b1350 to 1400s; obs. noun
use: b1470 to 1700s; moisture: b1350; moisty:
b1470; moisten: b1580)

nevertheless adv

notable adj

obstinate adj

peaceable adj [obs. "quiet":
b1500 to 1800s]

perchance adv

perpetual adj (perpetuity:
b1425; perpetuate: b1530)

pied adj *piebald* (piebald:
b1590)

plain adj *obvious*

pliant adj (pliancy: b1700)

possible adj ["potential," as
in "possible outcome"]
(possibility: b1375)

prostrate adj (verb use:
b1450)

quaint adj [obs. "wise,
skilled": b1225 to 1700s;
arch. "cunning": b1350]

red adj *bloody*

red-hot adj [fig. use: b1630]

resident adj (noun use:
b1465)

rough adj *unskilled, unrefined*

round adj (verb use: b1300)

rude adj *insolent, uneducated*
["simple": b1280]

said adj

scant adj/adv (scanty:
b1660)

slack adj *not taut*

slick adj *smooth* ["smoothly
cunning": 1800s] (verb
use: b1350)

solitary adj (noun use: b1350)

spotty adj *spotted* ["intermittent": b1830]

steady adj (verb use: b1530; adv use: b1605)

steep adj *sloping* [rare "high up": b900]

stiff adj *strong, as in "stiff wind"* [as in "stiff drink," "stiff fee": b1830] (adv use: b1300)

tattered adj (tatter v: b1425; tatter n: b1450)

tawny adj (tawn: b1770)

treble adj/adv/v *triple* (noun use: b1450)

unruly adj

unspeakable adj

untold adj *not yet told* ["incapable of being told": b1450]

usable adj

usual adj (noun use: b1590)

vicious adj *pertaining to vice* ["faulted": b1450; "injurious": b1600; "mean" applied to animals: b1730; "mean" applied to people: b1830]

visible adj

whole adj *complete, total* (adv use: b1350; noun use: b1400)

true adv *honestly* ["accurately," as in "the pendulum swings true": b1570]

Colors

blue adj/n *colored blue* b1300 ["depressed": b1390]

color n *tint; paint* b1300 ["skin color": b1225] (verb use: b1400)

green n b1300

scarlet adj/n *red* b1300

lily-white adj b1325 [slang "Caucasian": b1930]

sanguine adj *colored red* b1325 ["related to blood": b1450; "happy": b1510]

rose n *the color* (adj use: b1600; rose-color: b1470)

rose-red adj

sorrel adj (noun use: b1570)

Actions/Verbs

scatter v b1160 (noun use: b1645; scatteration: b1780)

backbite/backbiter v/n b1175

betide v *happen* b1175

crook v *bend* b1175

lack v b1175 (noun use: b1350)

prove v *test; experience; demonstrate to be true* b1175 [obs. "try": u1600s; obs. "succeed": u1600s]

scream v b1175 (noun use: b1460)

serve v b1175

thrust v b1175

uphold v *phys. hold up* b1175

acquit v b1200 (acquittal: b1430)

advance v/n b1200

amend v b1200 (amendment: b1200; amends: b1300)

arrive v b1200 (arrival: b1380)

avow v b1200 [obs. "approve": b1350 to 1600s]

bait v *use bait to lure* b1200 (noun use: b1300)

beware v b1200

blame n/v b1200

bruise v b1200 ["crush": b900] (noun use: b1545)

butt v *as in "butt heads"* b1200 (noun use: b1650)

cackle v b1200 (noun use: b1680)

cast v *throw; fling; evoke, as in "cast a spell"; vomit; shape* b1200 ["create with a mold": b1600] (noun use: b1250)

catch v *capture* b1200 [obs. "chase": u1600s; as in "catch a cold": b1470] (noun use: b1400)

change v/n *exchange; alter* b1200 ["make change (money)": b1450; as in "change clothes": b1500]

clip v *trim* b1200 ["cut out": b1900]

close v b1200

consent v b1200 (noun use: b1400)

crawl v *lit.* b1200 [fig. "move slow": b1450] (noun use: b1920)

cringe v b1200 ["bow": b1600] (noun use: b1600)

crop v *trim* b1200 [as in "crop a photo": b1530]

deliver v *rescue* b1200 ["hand over": b1280; as in "deliver a speech": b1450; as in "deliver a punch": b1600; deliverance: b1300; delivery "handing over": b1450; arch. delivery "rescue": b1500]

desire v *gen. want* b1200 ["desire sexually": b1450] (noun use: b1400; desirous: b1300; desirable adj: b1400)

devise v b1200 [obs. "divide": u1400s; obs. "study": u1800s]

dig v *as in "dig a hole"* b1200

egg v *as in "egg on"* b1200

fail v b1200 (fail n: b1275; failure: b1645)

flatter v b1200 (flattery: b1325)

flicker v b1200 (noun use: b1850)

get v b1200

gin v *begin* b1200

harden v b1200 (obs. hard v: b1150)

hark v b1200 (harken: b1100)

haunt v *frequent* b1200 ["weigh upon": b1470] (noun use: b1300)

hoot v b1200

long v *be suitable, appropriate* b1200

mend v b1200

need v b1200

ought v b1200

pill v *extort* b1200

put v *place* b1200

quell v *suppress* b1200 [rare "kill": b1150]

rid v b1200 (riddance: b1535)

rue v b1200 [obs. "cause rue": b1150 to 1500s] (noun use: b900; rueful: b1225)

save v *rescue* b1200 [obs. "spare": u1600s; "store, keep": b1450]

scald v b1200

scour v *as in "scouring pad"* b1200

seem v b1200 [obs. "be appropriate": u1600s]

show v *display* b1200 [obs. "inspect," "read": b1150 to ME]

spread v b1200

sprout v b1200 (noun use: b1400)

stamp v *crush* b1200

talk v b1200 (noun use: b1380; talkative: b1400)

tap v *strike lightly* b1200 (noun use: b1340)

tend v *pay attention to* b1200 [obs. "listen to": u1800s; "cultivate," "take care of": b1500] (tendance: b1575)

undertake v b1200 [obs. "seize": u1400s; obs. "understand": u1500s; obs. "reprove": b1450 to 1500s]

wag v *applied to people* b1200 [obs. "teeter": u1500s; obs. "wander": u1600s; applied to tails: b1450; as in "wag your tongue": b1570; "leave": b1600] (noun use: b1590)

wake v *rouse from sleep; fig. awaken* b1200

watch v *guard; "watch for"; remain on watch* b1200 [obs. "stay awake": b725; as in "watch the kids": b1570] (noun use: b975)

withhold v b1200

befall v *happen* b1225

beguile v *delude* b1225 ["fascinate": b1570]

covet v b1225 [obs. "covet sexually": u1500s] (covetous: b1250)

cull v b1225

cut v *lit. and fig.* b1225 (noun use: b1530)

depart v *leave* b1225 [obs. "divide": u1700s; "die": b1530] (departure: b1445; obs. department "leaving": b1450 to 1600s)

A Language Turning on Itself

Tracking English becomes more difficult by the fact that words not only change meaning—they often end up contradicting themselves. For example, *champion* as a verb once meant "challenge" (by 1605 to the 1800s), and now means "advocate" (by 1850 in that sense).

Here are examples of other linguistic flip-flops over the ages:

- In Old English, *with* meant "in opposition to."

- From Middle English to the 1800s, a *maid* was a virgin man.

- *Clamor* as a verb meant "make noise" by 1385, but it could mean "silence" by 1615.

- *Capitulate* once meant "negotiate" from before 1450 to the 1600s. Now it means "to cave in, back off from negotiation," and has since before 1580.

- *Stomach*, meaning "to tolerate," was in use by 1700, but meaning exactly the opposite, it was in use by 1530 to the 1800s.

- *Egregious* has meant "remarkably bad" since before 1575, and meant "remarkably good" since before 1535.

- By 1540, *bully* meant "sweetheart" or "lover." Use in reference to someone more contemptible dates from before 1690.

- From before 1570 to the 1700s, *elevate* could mean "lower."

- A *prick* was once a nice guy—from before 1570 to the 1600s. Since before 1930, though, a *prick* is, well, not a nice guy.

- The *in-* in *inhabitable* once meant "not" (as in *incredible*). So by 1600, inhabitable meant "uninhabitable."

- Before *chuckle* meant "quiet laughter" by 1805, it meant "uproarious laughter" from before 1630 to the 1800s.

- *Nice* couldn't help but contradict itself somewhere along the line, as it has changed meanings so many times. Its present meaning of "pleasant, agreeable" dates from before 1770, but it had early not-nice meanings ranging from "stupid" from before 1340 to the 1500s, "wanton" from before 1350 to the 1600s, and "unmanly" from before 1470 to the 1700s.

---

deserve v b1225 [obs. "earn": u1700s] (deserved adj: b1555; deserving: b1570)

despoil v b1225

dote v *act stupid* b1225 ["lavish affection": b1500]

doubt n/v b1225 [obs. "fear": u1600s; obs. "reason to fear": u1500s]

enjoin v *prescribe* b1225 ["proscribe": b1600]

espy v *see* b1225 ["spy": b1400]

excuse v b1225 (noun use: b1400)

fawn v b1225

grant v b1225 (noun use: b1300)

grieve v b1225 [obs. "cause grief," "hurt": u1800s]

hurl v b1225

lace v *as in "lace up shoes"* b1225 (noun use: b1400)

order v b1225

overtake v b1225

overturn v b1225 [obs. "revolve": u1600s]

pass v *as in "pass through"; hand off; exceed; go past; occur; as in "pass a test"* b1225

pitch v *as in "pitch a tent"* b1225 [as in "pitch camp": b1450]

praise v b1225 [obs. "appraise": concurrent] (noun use: b1350)

scrape v b1225 [obs. "scratch, claw": b1150 to 1600s] (noun use: b1450)

skulk v b1225

sling v *fling—with or without sling* b1225

slumber v b1225 (noun use: b1350)

soil v b1225

strip v *remove clothing, bark, etc.* b1225

strive v *fight; attempt; struggle* b1225

summon v b1225 (summons "summon": b1685)

toll v *as in "for whom the bell tolls"* b1225 (noun use: b1450)

trouble v *disturb* b1225 [as in "don't trouble yourself": b1900] (troubled: b1350)

tug v b1225 ["struggle": b1630] (verb use: b1530)

visit v b1225 (noun use: b1625; visitor: b1450)

wiggle v *as in "the worm wiggled"* b1225 [as in "wiggle your nose": b1700]

withdraw v b1225 (withdrawal: b1750; withdrawment: b1670)

banish v b1235

abut v b1250 (abutment: b1645)

assemble v *gather* b1250

["construct": b1870] (assembly: b1300; assemblage: b1690)

await v b1250 [obs. "lie in wait": b1350 to 1600s]

babble v b1250 [as in "babble like a brook": b1450] (noun use: b1500)

beget v b1250 [obs. "get": b1000 to 1600s]

betray v b1250

bulge v b1250

confirm v b1250 (confirmation: b1385)

defend v b1250 [obs. "prevent": u1800s]

enter v b1250

flush v *as in "flush birds"* b1250 [as in "flush a toilet": b1800] (noun use: b1600)

honor v b1250 ["adhere to": b1730]

maintain v b1250

move v *change position* b1250

perish v b1250 ["degrade": b1450; arch. "destroy," as in "perish the thought": b1450]

quash v *suppress* b1250 ["crush": b1390]

ransack v b1250 [obs. "frisk": u1400s] (obs. ransackle v: b1630)

rasp v b1250 (noun use: b1515)

signify v b1250

suffer v *hurt; tolerate* b1250 (arch. sufferance: b1300; suffering: b1450)

upheave v b1250 (upheaval: b1840)

uprise v *rise: from sitting, from bed, from the dead* b1250 (uprising: b1300)

wade v b1250 [obs. "go": b900 to 1600s; obs. "pierce": b900 to late ME] (noun use: b1665)

amount v b1275 (noun use: b1710)

appear v b1275 ["seem": b1450] (appearance: b1380)

multiply v b1275

store v b1275

usurp v b1275 [arch. "use unjustly": b1450; obs. "steal": b1450 to 1600s] (usurper: b1450)

warrant v b1275

wear v *as in "wear away"* b1275 ["erode": b1450] (noun use: b1670)

comfort v/n b1280 [obs. "entertain": u1600s]

conjure v *bind by oath* b1280 ["bring about magically": b1590] (conjurer: b1350)

damn v *condemn fig. or spiritually* b1280 [obs. "sentence legally": u1800s] (adj/adv use: b1775; noun use: b1870)

oblige v *bind* b1280 ["perform a favor": b1470; "make necessary": b1670] (obligation: b1300; obligate v: b1535; obligatory: b1400)

waver v b1280 ["sway": b1450; "quaver": b1630]

(noun use: b1520; wave: b1000)

accuse v b1300 (accusation: b1390)

achieve v b1300 (achievement: b1475)

affirm v b1300 (affirmation: b1410)

allege v *accuse, claim* b1300 (allegation: b1425; alleged: b1450; obs. "allevate" v: b1470 to 1600s)

appease v *calm* b1300 ["placate": b1470]

approach v *phys.* b1300 [*fig.* use: b1470] (noun use: b1400)

array v b1300 (noun use: b1340)

assay v/n b1300

assent n/v b1300

assign v b1300

assoil v *pardon, expiate* b1300

assuage v b1300

attain v b1300 (attainment: b1385)

attend v *heed, listen, deal with* b1300

avail v b1300 (noun use: b1400)

avoid v b1300 [obs. "make void, empty": b1470 to 1800s] (avoidance: b1400)

award v/n b1300

bate v b1300

bend v *opp. of straighten* b1300 ["tighten": b1000; as in "bend the rules": b1870] (verb use: b1435)

bewray v *reveal or expose* b1300

blacken v b1300 (black v: b1200)

blend v b1300 (noun use: b1885)

bob v *as in "bobbing the head"* b1300 (noun use: b1500)

boil v b1300

bolt v *move suddenly* b1300 (noun use: b1550)

cease n/v b1300

chafe v *warm, esp. by rubbing* b1300 ["grate": b1530] (noun use: b1555)

claim v b1300 (noun use: b1325)

clap v b1300 (noun use: b1600)

command v b1300 ["be in charge": b1450]

conclude v *end; settle* b1300 [obs. "convince": b1350 to 1700s; obs. "prove": b1450 to 1700s] (conclusion: b1350)

confound v *bring to ruin; shame* b1300 ["confuse": b1380] (confounded: b1375)

contain v *comprise; quell* b1300 ["hold": b1470]

convert v b1300 [obs. "turn": u1700s; obs. "translate": b1570 to 1600s; as in "convert dollars to yen": b1570] (noun use: b1565; convertite n: b1565)

corrupt v b1300

counterfeit v b1300 [obs. "impersonate": u1600s; "pretend": b1450]

crack v *snap* b1300 ["put cracks in": b1450; fig., as in "crack under interrogation": b1670] (noun use: b1450)

curry v *comb, groom* b1300

daresay v b1300

darken v *become darker* b1300

dash v *phys. smash* b1300 [fig. "smash": b1530] (noun use: b1390)

daunt v b1300 [obs. "stop": u1700s] (dauntless: b1595)

deceive v b1300 (deceit: b1275; deception: b1450)

defy v b1300 [obs. "distrust": u1700s; "challenge to battle": b1300; as in "I defy you to answer": b1700]

deign v b1300

delay v *put off* b1300 ["hinder": b1450]

denounce v b1300 [arch. "announce": b1380; "turn someone in": b1500; arch. "warn": b1600] (denunciate: b1595; denunciation: b1845)

deny v *contradict* b1300 ["re-

fuse to acknowledge," "refuse to allow," "say no": b1450] (denyance: b1470; denial: b1530; deniable: b1550)

depose v b1300 ["make a deposition": b1450]

descend v *sink* b1300 ["incline downwards": b1450; "pounce": b1450] (descent: b1450)

descry v *discover* b1300 [obs. "reveal": u1600s]

despise v b1300 (despicable: b1555)

destine v *preordain* b1300 ["point toward": b1570; "travel toward": b1800] (destiny: b1325; destination: b1400; destined: b1600)

disguise v b1300 [obs. "dress up": u1500s]

display v *show; unfold* b1300 [obs. "tell about": b1450 to 1800s; "demonstrate," as in "display intelligence": b1500] (noun use: b1665)

dispraise v b1300

dispute v *lit. and fig. fight* b1300 ["contest": b1530] (noun use: b1595)

disturb v *create a disturbance; worry* b1300 ["stop": b1200; as in "disturb sediment": b1600] (disturbance: b1280)

droop v b1300

duck v b1300 (noun use: b1555)

ease v *phys. ease* b1300 [obs. "be hospitable": u1600s; "mentally ease": b1450] (noun use: b1200)

elect adj/n/v b1300

entice v b1300 [obs. "provoke": u1600s]

escape v b1300 (noun use: b1400)

even v *smoothen* b1300 [obs. "flatten, raze": b1150 to 1600s; "equalize": b1570]

exile v b1300 [arch. "throw away": b1450]

expound v b1300

extend v *appraise* b1300 [lit. and fig. "stretch out":

b1450; as in "extend congratulations": b1500]

filch v b1300

fire v *fig. inspire* b1300

fling v b1300 (noun use: b1550)

flock v *as in "flock together"* b1300 [obs. "bring together": u1500s]

foretell v b1300 (foresay: b1150)

found v *start the foundation* b1300

gainsay v b1300

glare v b1300 ["stare": b1630] (noun use: b1470)

hail v *greet* b1300 [as in "hail a cab": b1500]

halve v b1300

hook v *catch with a hook* b1300

inquire v b1300 (inquiry: b1430)

join v b1300 ["take up battle": b1450; as in "join a club": b1730] (join with: b1470; join in: b1570)

languish v b1300 (languid: b1600)

lessen v b1300 (less v: b1350)

lift v *raise up* b1300

lurk v b1300 [obs. "peek": b1450 to 1500s; obs. "be lazy": b1570 to 1700s]

mantle v *cover up, cloak* b1300

maze v *amaze* b1300

meddle v *interfere* b1300 [obs. "intermix": b1300 to 1600s; obs. "have sex": b1350 to 1600s; obs. "combat": b1350 to 1600s; obs. "be concerned": b1350 to 1500s]

mount v *climb* b1300

obey v b1300

perceive v *sense* b1300 ["hold an opinion of": b1830]

perform v b1300 ["create": b1450 to 1700s] (performance: b1495)

pick v *hit with a pick; pluck; pick at; choose; steal* b1300 [as in "pick a fight," "pick a lock": b1450; as in "pick your way through the

mess": b1730; "play a stringed instrument": b1870]

pierce v b1300 (piercing: b1400)

pinch v b1300 [obs. fig. "hurt": u1600s; obs. "grouse": b1450 to 1500s; as in "pinch pennies": b1570; as in "pinch off": b1700]

polish v b1300 (noun use: b1600)

powder v b1300 [obs. "season": u1700s] (noun use: b1350)

procure v b1300 [obs. "try hard": u1600s; obs. "bribe": b1450 to 1600s]

purge v *clean phys. and morally* b1300

pursue v *hunt* b1300 [fig. "follow": b1450] (pursuit: b1350)

push v *shove* b1300 [arch. "stab at": b1450; fig. "drive, press," as in "push it to the limit": b1730] (noun use: b1565)

rattle v b1300 (noun use: b1520)

reave v *break, rend* b1300

receive v *get* b1300

recover v *regain; get well* b1300

remove v b1300 (removal: b1530)

repair v *go* b1300

restore v b1300 (restoration: b1400)

ruffle v b1300

scape v *escape* b1300

scour v *search thoroughly* b1300

seize v b1300 (seizure: b1470)

shift v b1300 [obs. "arrange": b1000] (noun use: b1470)

shrill v *shriek* b1300 (noun use: b1595)

shudder v b1300 (noun use: b1610)

skip v *gambol, as in "skip rope," "skip about"; as in "skip town"* b1300

slander v *defame* b1300 [obs. meanings of "shame" or

"source of shame": b1350 to 1600s] (verb use: b1350)

slip v *move stealthfully* b1300

solace v b1300 (noun use: b1350)

sound v *make sound* b1300 ["cause to make sound": b1470]

specify v b1300

spill v b1300 [arch. "kill": b1100; obs. "destroy": b1100 to 1600s] (noun use: b1845)

squeal v b1300 [slang "tattle": b1850]

stalk v *pursue* b1300 ["walk haughtily": b1530]

stone v b1300

strain v *stretch* b1300

strangle v b1300

stun v b1300 (noun use: b1730)

succor n/v b1300

supplant v b1300 [obs. "overthrow": u1800s]

suspend v *halt, cease; remove from duty* b1300 (suspension: b1450)

sustain v b1300

swoon n/v b1300 (swound "swoon": b1450)

tarry v b1300 [obs. transitive use: u1600s] (noun use: b1470; arch. tarriance: b1475)

taste v b1300 [obs. "test by touch": u1600s; obs. "have sex": b1570 to 1700s; "test for poison": b1600] (noun use: b1325)

thrive v b1300

touch v b1300

transfigure v b1300

translate v *interpret; transport* b1300 ["explain, clarify": b1600] (translation, translator: b1350)

tumble v *fall* b1300 ["make fall": b1570] (noun use: b1730)

uplift v *phys. lift up* b1300 ["inspire": b1450; as in "uplift your voices": b1830]

whelm v b1300

whirl v b1300 (noun use: b1500)

whiten v b1300

wither v b1300

abash v b1305

abridge v b1305 (abridgement: b1430)

adjoin v b1305

anoint v b1305

argue v b1305 [as in "argue for" or "argue against": b1500; "contend," as in "argue that": b1570] (argument: b1330)

save v *store, keep* b1305

abate v b1325 (abatement: b1340)

abet v b1325 ["encourage to do good": u1700s]

abound v b1325

admonish v b1325

allow v *permit* b1325 [obs. "praise": b1300 to 1700s] (allowance: b1390)

arrest v *stop, apprehend* b1325 [obs. "rest": b1470 to 1600s; "capture," as in "arrest one's attention": b1830] (noun use: b1375)

blemish v b1325 (noun use: b1530)

brandish v b1325 (noun use: b1600)

burnish v b1325 (noun use: b1650)

carry v b1325

chastise v b1325 [obs. "reform": u1600s] (chasten: b1530)

cherish v *nurture* b1325 ["hold dear": b1450]

clarify v *phys. clarify, e.g., butter* b1325 [obs. "be clear": ME only; fig. "make clear": b1400]

clink v *make a clinking sound* b1325 (noun use: b1400)

clog v *gen. encumber* b1325

clutch v *grab* b1325 [obs. "bend finger joints or other joints": b1125 to LME; obs. "clench": b1600 to 1700s; "hold tightly": b1630]

compile v b1325 [obs. "write": b1450 to 1500s; obs. "pile up": b1600 to 1800s] (compilation: b1450)

conceal v *fig. hide* b1325 [lit. "hide": b1450]

constrain v *force* b1325 ["restrain": b1700; obs. "strain with effort": b1450 to 1800s] (constraint: b1385)

contrive v *plot* b1325 ["concoct a solution": b1450] (contrived: b1470)

croak v b1325 (noun use: b1565)

crucify v b1325 (crucifixion: b1410)

crumple v b1325 (noun use: b1500)

daub v b1325 (noun use: b1450)

declare v b1325 ["state a position": b1670] (declaration: b1350)

defile v *corrupt* b1325 (defoulen: b1280)

degrade v *demote; detract from* b1325 ["debase": b1670; "wear out": b1830] (degradation: b1535)

depress v b1325 (depressed: b1600; depression: b1670)

deprive v b1325 (deprivation: b1445; deprived: b1555)

dispense v *disburse* b1325

enamel v b1325 (noun use: b1470)

enclose v b1325

endure v *as in "endure pain"* b1325 [obs. "make durable": b1450 to 1500s; as in "music that endures": b1450] (enduring: b1450)

enforce v *as in "enforce a law"* b1325 [obs. "make forceful": b1325 to 1500s; obs. "use force": b1350 to 1600s]

err v *wander; make mistake* b1325 (erroneous: b1500)

examine v b1325 (examination: b1410)

fade v b1325 [as in "fade away": b1600] (arch. adj use: b1325)

glut v *as in "glut the market"* b1325 (noun use: b1550)

increase v b1325 (noun use: b1380; arch. increasement: b1470)

inherit v b1325

liken v b1325 [obs. "grow similar": u1800s]

mew v *make a mewing sound* b1325 (noun use: b1600)

mumble v b1325

occupy v *seize; keep busy* b1325 ["reside in": b1450; obs. "have sex with": b1530 to 1600s]

pare v b1325

pry v *investigate* b1325 ["be nosy": b1600]

rebuke v *upbraid* b1325 [obs. "rebuff": u1600s] (noun use: b1450)

rejoice v b1325 (noun use: b1470; rejoicing: b1375)

repeal v b1325 (noun use: b1530)

return v *go back* b1325 ["bring back": b1470] (noun use: b1400)

revel v b1325 (noun use: b1470; revelry: b1450; reveler: b1470)

reward v b1325 (noun use: b1400)

scorch v b1325 [obs. "destroy by flames": b1500 to 1600s] (noun use: b1400)

stanch v b1325

strain v *filter* b1325 (noun use "strainer": b1435)

stumble v b1325 (noun use: b1650)

suffice v b1325

trail v *be dragged behind* b1325 ["drag behind": b1450]

tremble v *quiver* b1325 ["fear to the point of trembling": b1450] (noun use: b1610; tremblement n: b1700)

vanish v b1325

verify v b1325 ["claim to be true": b1530] (verification: b1570)

batter v *beat* b1330 ["browbeat": b1500] (battery: b1535)

tend v *phys. lean, be inclined* b1330 [fig. "be inclined": b1450; obs. "offer, tender": b1500]

twist v *as in "twist an ankle"* b1330

try v *attempt* b1335 (noun use: b1400)

adjourn v *as in "adjourn for the day"* b1340 [obs. "summon to appear": b1350 to 1600s] (adjournment: b1610)

belong v b1340 [as in "belong to a book club": b1450]

certify v b1340 (certified: b1615)

chime v b1340 ["indicate time with chimes": b1450] (noun use: b1445)

comprehend v b1340 [arch. "experience with senses": b1450; obs. "summarize": b1450 to 1600s; "contain": b1450] (comprehension: b1450; comprehensible: b1500)

continue v *be continuous; not end* b1340 ["extend": b1450] (continuation: b1380; continuity: b1425; continuous: b1640)

discharge v *as in "discharge an obligation"* b1340 (noun use: b1400)

distract v b1340 [obs. "draw apart": u1600s; obs. "craze": u1700s] (distraction: b1450; distracted: b1590)

edify v *build, teach* b1340

inflame v b1340 [med. sense: b1670]

muse v b1340 (museful: b1630)

refrain v *restrain, reserve* b1340 ["abstain": b1530]

resemble v b1340 [arch. "compare": b1470] (resemblance: b1395; resemblant: b1400)

snatch v *grab* b1340 ["snap": b1200; "steal": b1770]

tangle v *lit. snarl* b1340 ["fig. snarl": b1770] (noun use: b1615; tangled: b1580)

address v *approach*

approve v [obs. "prove": b1325 to 1600s] (noun use: b1620)

ascribe v

bay v *howl* ["speak sharply": b1300]

beat v *win*

beat v *pulsate* (noun use: b1770)

become v *come to be; suit* [obs. "arrive, come": b900 to 1800s]

begrudge v

believe v *presume to be true* ["have faith": b1000]

bid v *say, tell, as in "bid goodbye"* [obs. "beseech": b725]

blanch v *whiten* [method of cooking: b1470; "go pale": b1770]

blunder v *as in "blunder about"* ["goof up": b1715] (noun use: b1390)

boast v *brag* [obs. "make threats": b1400; "feature": b1700] (noun use: b1265)

brace v *tighten* ["prepare for": b1500; "support with a brace": b1800]

burgeon v

burn v *redden in the sun; aggravate, as in "she burns me up"*

bustle v (noun use: b1635)

butt v *abut—as in "butt up against"*

call v *name*

cense v *burn incense* (censer: b1250)

chide v ["argue": b1000 to 1800s]

clamber v *climb clumsily*

company v *accompany* ["associate with": b1450]

compel v

confess v (confession: b1380)

correct v (adj use: b1600; correction: b1340)

counsel v

crack v *as in "crack a joke"* (noun use: b1900)

crush v [as in "crush against," "crush the opposition": b1600] (noun use: b1600)

dash v *as in "dash about"* (noun use: b1830)

depute v *delegate*

discern v (discernible, discerning: b1590)

discomfort v/n *make uncom-*

fortable [obs. "dismay": b1350 to 1700s]

discuss v *examine* [obs. "dispel": u1800s; obs. "declare, decide": u1600s; "talk"; b1450]

divide v *cut up* ["diverge," "separate": b1450] (noun use: b1645; division: b1375)

doff v [as in "doff one's hat": b1630]

draw v *as in "draw breath"; attract* [entertainment sense: b1600]

drudge v (noun use: b1500; drudgery: b1550; drudger: b1770)

eat v *erode*

embellish v (embellishment "embellishing": b1595; embellishment "ornament": b1625)

embrace v *surround*

enamor v

encompass v

end v *finish up*

enfeeble v

engender v *bring about*

enlarge v

enroll v

environ v *surround* ["enclose": b1450] (environment: b1630)

eschew v

estrange v

excite v (excitation: b1400; excitative: b1490; excitatory: b1805)

faint v *weaken* ["swoon": b1400]

falter v [fig. use: b1530] (noun use: b1835)

finish v *end* [as in "finish a chair": b1450]

forewarn v

forfeit v [obs. "commit a wrong": b1300 to 1500s]

forge v *shape* ["fake": b1325]

fulfill v [arch. "fill up full": b1000] (fulfillment: b1775)

get v *beget*

glean v

glimmer v *shine dimly* [obs. "shine brightly": u1500s] (noun use: b1590)

glitter v (noun use: b1605)

gloom v *look gloomy* (noun use: b1630; gloomy: b1590)

glorify v

grind v *as in "grind your teeth"* [obs. "grind with your teeth": b1150 to 1500s]

gut v

happen v (hap v: b1350)

hear v *as in "hear about"*

hip v *hop*

hitch v *jerk* (noun use: b1665)

hum v *um* [music sense: b1885] (noun use: b1470)

inhabit v

keep v *continue, as in "keep talking"; store, maintain possession* [var. obs. meanings of "take, acquire": b1000]

knock v *hit, collide, as in "knees knocking"*

lash v *as in "lash a tail," "rain that lashes"; dish out liberally*

launch v *propel* [as in "launch a boat": b1450; "begin": b1630; "set off, introduce": b1900] (noun use: b1750)

lay v *as in "lay down a bet," "lay a trap," "lay in waiting"; hit*

lead v *as in "where does this road lead?"*

lean v *rely*

leave v *depart; abandon*

light v *as in "light a room," "light a match"* [obs. "be bright": b1100 to 1700s]

lighten v *illuminate*

loiter v

loll v

look v *as in "look tired"*

loosen v *release* ["unfasten": b1350]

low v *lower, diminish*

lug v *carry* (noun use: b1620)

lull v (noun use: b1720)

lumber v *move clumsily*

marvel v [obs. "inspire marveling": b1450 to 1800s]

mouth v

move v *as in "I'm moved to reply"*

overthrow v *knock down; depose*

overwhelm v *phys. bury* [fig. "bury": b1530] (overwhelming adj: b1675)

owe v [obs. "own": b900; "is the result of": b1600]

parch v (parched: b1450)

peace v *silence*

peck v ["nag": b1670; "kiss": b1970] (noun use: b1595)

pertain v

pervert v [obs. "overturn": u1600s] (noun use: b1665; perversion: b1400)

pitch v *as in "pitch forward"* (noun use: b1770)

poison v ["contaminate with something destructive": b1450]

poke v *jab* [as in "poke out": b1630; as in "poke your head through the door": b1730; "dawdle": b1800; slang "have sex": b1870] (noun use: b1800; poker: b1535)

portray v [obs. gen. "create artwork": b1450 to 1600s]

pose v *offer, as in "pose a question"* [as in "pose for a photo": b1830; "pretend": b1870]

pour v [fig. use: b1600; "rain heavily": b1730]

present v *introduce; give a present* [as in "present oneself": b1450] (presentation: b1400; presentable: b1630)

prompt v

pronounce v *declare* ["articulate": b1450] (pronouncement: b1595)

propose v *suggest* ["present": b1450; "nominate": b1600; "propose marriage": b1770]

punish v [gen. use: b1450] (punishment: b1300; punition: b1450; punitive: b1625)

ram v *pack with a ram* [as in "ram a car into the wall": b1530; as in "ram the

wall": b1870; as in "ram into the wall": b1900]

rattle v *prattle*

rave v ["praise": b1700] (noun use: b1600)

receive v *as in "receive guests"*

reel v *revolve or turn* [fig. "spin": b1800] (noun use: b1575)

refuse v (refusal: b1500)

regard v ["regard highly": b1530] (regard: b1470)

relieve v

repair v *fix* [obs. "decorate": u1500s] (repair: b1470)

repress v (repressive: b1425)

require v [obs. "inquire": u1600s] (requirement: b1665)

rescue v (noun use: b1380; obs. rescous n/v: b1300 to 1600s)

reserve v (noun use: b1650)

restrain v (restraint: b1400)

revile v

revoke v [obs. "return to a belief": u1600s] (revocation: b1425; revocable: b1500)

rifle v *ransack*

roam v

roll v

rub v

say v *as in "say mass"*

scout v *reconnoiter* (noun use: b1535)

search v (noun use: b1470)

seethe v *applied to things* [arch. "cook, boil": b900; applied to people: b1600]

serve v *as in "serve food"*

sever v (severance: b1425)

shed v *as in "shed light," "shed tears"*

shiver v *tremble* (noun use: b1730)

shore v *prop—as in "shore up"*

shorten v

shun v *avoid* [var. meanings of "hide from": b1150 to 1600s]

skim v *take off the top* ["read glancingly": b1600; as in "skim a stone": b1630]

skin v *flay*

slip v *escape* (noun use: b1600)

smell v *emit odor* ["stink": b1450]

sniff v (noun use: b1770)

snore v (noun use: b1630)

spring v *leap* (noun use: b1470)

squirt v *squirt out* ["squirt into": b1570] (noun use: b1500)

stand v *take a stand* (noun use: b1600)

start n/v *move suddenly* [obs. "jump about": b1150 to 1500s; "start from sleep": b1470; "begin": b1800] (noun use: b1400)

steal v *move away by stealth*

steep v

stick v *adhere* ["affix": b1450] (noun use: b1870)

stow v [obs. "imprison": u1600s; "stop": b1700]

strike v *collide*

sun v ["sunbathe": b1600]

support v *tolerate; provide fig. support* (noun use: b1450; supportive: b1595)

swallow v *engulf, absorb*

swelter v (noun use: b1855; sweltering: b1575; sweltry: b1600)

throw v *fling, toss* (noun use: b1530)

tickle v (noun use: b1805)

touse v *tousle* (noun use: b1795)

transcend v (transcendent: b1470; transcendency: b1585; transcendence: b1605)

transform v (transformation: b1450)

treat v *discuss, approach, as in "treat the topic in an essay"* (treatment: b1870)

trickle v [fig. use: b1630] (noun use: b1580)

trill v *trickle*

turn v *as in "turn right, turn left"* [as in "the road turns here": b1570; as in "turn a corner": b1700] (noun use: b1300)

turn v *change, as in "turn the page," "turn the channel," "turn lead into gold"*

unclose v *open*

undergo v

undermine v [fig. use: b1450]

upbraid v ["present for upbraiding": b1000 to 1700s]

utter v *express, speak* [obs. "sell": u1800s; "circulate money": b1500] (utterance: concurrent)

vanquish v [fig. use: b1450]

vary v *cause change* ["waiver," "experience change," "differ," "stray": b1450; "exhibit discrepancy": b1570; "switch from one to another": b1700] (noun use: b1630)

waste v *as in "waste away"* (noun use: b1450)

weigh v *as in "weigh anchor"*

weigh down v

well v *as in "well up"*

wind v *meander; wrap, coil*

work v *function properly*

worry v *as in "a dog worrying a rag"* [fig. "vex, bedevil": b1570; "disturb": b1830]

wrench v *as in "wrench someone away"* ["turn abruptly": b1050] (noun use: b1530)

writhe v *twist about* ["twist something else about": b900]

yawp v (noun use: b1825)

yield v *as in "yield fruit," "yield results"; capitulate, acquiesce* [applied to traffic: b1630] (noun use: b1450)

Archaisms

chastien v *chastise* b1200

efface n *obs. efficacy* b1200 [u1700s]

hap n *luck, happening* b1200 (verb use: b1350)

kindless adj *obs. unnatural* b1200 [u1600s]

estate n *condition; status* b1225 [obs. "health": b1450 to 1500s]

groom n *boy, man* b1225

seemly adj *opp. of unseemly* b1225

whiles conj b1225

certes adv *certainly, truthfully* b1250 (certainly: b1300)

malison n *curse* b1250

beforetime adv *formerly* b1300

compass v *devise* b1300 ["encompass": b1450]

current adj *flowing* b1300

discover v *disclose* b1300 [obs. "confess," arch. "display": b1450; "find": b1570]

emprise n *type of enterprise* b1300

engine n *tool; ingenuity* b1300

erewhile adv *a while ago* b1300

faint adj *pretended, feigned* b1300

feint v *obs. deceive* b1300 [u1600s]

foil v *trample* b1300

miscarry v *obs. get hurt or destroyed* b1300 [u1700s]

monish v *admonish* b1300

peradventure adv *perchance* b1300 (noun use: b1570)

plain v *complain* b1300

spouse v *obs. marry* b1300 [u1500s]

stithy n b1300 ["smithy": b1630]

vair n *type of fur* b1300

vale n b1300 [fig., as in "vale of tears": b1450]

verily adv b1300

whilom adv *formerly* b1300 [obs. "while": b1900 to 1600s]

word v *speak* b1300 (arch. wording: b1630)

clumse v *be clumsy* b1325

apert adj *arch. out in the open*

beck v *beckon*

beforesaid adj *obs. aforementioned* [u1700s]

clam v *clam up* (clam up: b1920)

comeling n *new kid on the block*

common v *fraternize* [u1500s]

counsel n *secret, as in "keep counsel"*

default n *fault* [obs. "mistake": b1450 to 1800s]

deliver adj *nimble*

down-coming n

downbear v *bear down*

drive v *kill time* [u1800s]

drivel n *type of tool; type of servant* [u1500s]

eager adj *sharp, sour, tart* [obs. "hungry": b1500 to 1700s]

empt v *empty*

enlighten v *obs. cause to give off light* [u1800s] (enlightenment: b1675)

erenow adv *before now*

fade adj

faitour n *sham, pretender*

fame n *rumor* (verb use: b1350)

fame v *famish*

far-fet adj *obs. fetched from afar* [u1600s]

fellow n *obs. female companion* [u1600s]

fine v *obs. end* [u1500s]

folly n *obs. crime; insanity* [u1600s]

forweary adj (forworn: b1510)

gab v *obs. mock* [u1500s]

gainstand v *resist*

gaw v *obs. gape* [u1800s]

gender v *engender*

gentle adj *obs. graceful* [u1500s]

gestoning n *obs. hospitality*

get v *win*

gillery n *con, trick*

gnast v *obs. gnash* [u1500s]

gradely adj *worthy of praise*

gree n *degree*

grope v *obs. investigate* [u1600s]

haste v *make haste* (hasten: b1570)

have, havings n *possessions*

having n *owning* (haviour: b1470 to 1600s)

hethen adv *obs. hence* [u1400s]

inlet n *letting in*

instance n *urgency* [gen. use: b1600] (instancy: b1515)

keep n *custody, charge*

lodesman n *obs. leader* [u1500s]

loser n *obs. something that destroys* [u1600s]

luke adj *as in "lukewarm"*

mark n *obs. trace* [u1500s]

mark n *obs. type of marker* [u1700s]

mastery n *obs. show of skill* [u1600s]

mightful, mightless adj

mischieve v *obs. harm* [u1600s]

misdeem v *deem wrongly*

multiply v *speak profusely*

oppone v [u1700s]

outly adv *absolutely*

publish v *obs. create a public—populate* [u1500s]

read v *tell*

ream n *stretch out the sleep*

renable adj *eloquent*

renovel v *obs. renew* [u1500s]

roke n *smoke, fog, etc.*

sad adj *heavy; firm; deep*

say v *obs. test* [u1800s]

semblable adj *obs. similar* [u1800s]

semble v *obs. resemble* [u1700s]

sentence n *obs. sense, significance* [u1500s]

speedful adj *helpful*

terms n *boundary* [obs. "menstruation": b1570 to 1700s] (terminal adj: b1745)

train n *obs. scheme* [u1700s]

turn v *obs. return* [u1500s]

uprist n *resurrection* ["sunrise": b1150 to 1600s]

venge v *avenge*

view n *obs. type of inspection*

virtue n *obs. power, magical power* [u1500s]

waste adj *obs. wasted, destroyed* [u1800s]

whatso pron *whatever*

workful *obs. functional* [u1600s]

wrong *obs. phys. crooked* [u1600s]

wrongous adj [u1600s]

ysame *obs. together* [u1500s]

IN USE BY
1470

Geography/Places

antarctic n b1375 [fig. "opposite": b1670 to 1700s]

cavern n b1375 (cave: b1250; cavernous "of a cavern": b1400; cavernous "huge": b1870)

mainland n b1375 (main: b1570)

millpond n b1375

pole n b1380 (North Pole, South Pole: b1400; polar: b1555)

horizon n b1385

cape n *jutting land* b1395

distance n b1395 ["emotional distance": b1600] (verb use: b1580; distant: b1400)

abyss n b1400

bay n *inlet* b1400

champaign n b1400

clime n *area defined by climate* b1400

equator n gen. b1400 [spec. "The Equator": b1630] (equatorial: b1665)

firth n *estuary* b1400

fissure n b1400

fountain n *natural spring* b1400 [manmade: b1530] (verb use: b1900)

loch n *lake* b1400 (lochan: b1670)

planisphere n *type of map* b1400

site n b1400

territory n *city property* b1400 [gen. area: b1610; "animal's range": b1800; as in "sales territory": b1930; akin to state: b1800]

tropic n b1400 [obs. astronomical use: b1400 to 1600s] (adj use: b1800; tropical: b1700; tropicopolitan: b1900)

village n b1400 [gen. "district": b1870; type of municipality: b1900] (villager: b1570)

wasteland n b1400

alp, alpine n, adj b1425

rural adj b1425 (arch. noun use: b1470)

countryside n b1450

neighborhood n b1450 ["proximity": b1570; "vicinity": b1700]

topography n b1450

watering place n b1450

depths n

geometry n obs. *land-measurement* [u1600s]

glade n

grounds n *as in "palace grounds"*

mappemonde n *arch. world map*

morass n *marsh; lit. and fig. swamp* [fig. use: b1870]

part n *area, as in "parts unknown"*

petrify v *lit. "turn to stone"* [fig. "scare": b1800]

race n *fast current* [type of channel: b1600]

range n *as in "home on the range"* (verb use: b1870)

rough n *rough ground* [golf sense: b1930]

space n *unoccupied place*

spot n *small place*

strait n *narrow body of water* [obs. "other narrow places, such as a mountain pass": u1700s; "isthmus": b1570]

tongue n *type of geo. formation*

zone n *latitudes* [gen. "band": b1600; gen. "region, area": b1830]

Natural Things

climate n *as in "equatorial climate"* b1375 [obs. type of area: b1400 to 1700s; "climatic conditions": b1615; fig. "atmosphere": b1670] (clime: b1400; climatic: b1830; climatology: b1470)

deluge n b1375 (verb use: b1595)

iris n *rainbow* b1375

marine adj b1375 [describing shipping: b1570]

vapor n b1375 (verb use: b1450)

crystal adj b1380

natal adj b1385 (obs. verb use: b1730)

resin n b1385

aurora n *dawn* b1390

hermaphrodite n b1390

arsenic n b1395

crude adj *natural* b1395 [arch. "not ripe": b1570; "jury-rigged": b1630; "boorish": b1670]

anthrax n b1400

ashfall n b1400

gypsum n b1400

limestone n b1400

natural law n b1400

opal n b1400

sex n b1400 ["love-making": b1930]

tourbillion n *whirlwind, vortex* b1400

turquoise n *the stone* b1400 [the color: b1830]

vitriol n *type of chemical* b1400 [fig. "acrimony": b1770]

flag n *type of stone* b1420

antimony n b1425

boulder n b1425 (boulder-stone: b1300)

fertility n b1425 (fertile: b1475)

mineral n/adj b1425

twilight n b1425 [fig. use: b1600] (twilit: b870)

magnet n *magnetic rock* b1450 ["magnetized item": b1630] (magnetism: b1620)

molehill n b1450

quintessence n *theoretical underriding fifth element* b1450 ["gist": b1600] (quintessential: b1630)

silt n b1450 (verb use: b1670)

spate n *lit. flood* b1450 [fig. use: b1630]

eddy n b1455 (verb use: b1770)

green adj *verdant*

mercury n *the metal*

natural adj *as in "natural father"*

steam n *spec.* *"water vapor"* [rare gen. "liquid vapor": b1150]

tide n

Plants

dandelion n b1375

iris n *the flower* b1375

sorrel n *type of plant* b1375

plane n *type of tree* b1385

filbert n b1390

myrtle n *type of shrub* b1395

bud n/v *as in "rosebud"* b1400 [fig. "spring up" v: b1570]

cane n b1400 ["walking aid": b1590]

cedarwood n b1400

chestnut n b1400 ["type of color, type of horse": b1600; "hoary joke": b1900]

chickory n b1400 ["source of coffee flavoring": b1830]

conifer n b1400

crocus n b1400

ebony n b1400

fig leaf n b1400

frankincense n b1400

gaggle n *of geese* b1400

hornpipe n b1400

husk n b1400 (verb use: b1665)

ibis n b1400

juniper n b1400

kelp n b1400

lemon n b1400

melon n b1400

mold n *as in "bread mold"* b1400 (verb use "permit molding": b1500; verb use "get moldy": b1570)

primrose n b1400 [obs. "the best": u1600s]

pulp n b1400 [gen. "goo": b1700] (verb use: b1685)

rape n *type of herb* b1400 (rapeseed: b1535)

rhubarb n b1400 [type of food: b1800]

rose of Jericho n *resurrection plant* b1400

rosemary n *type of mint* b1400

spike n *ear of corn* b1400

spruce n b1400 (spruce pine: b1685)

toadstool n b1400

safflower n b1410

coppice n *group of small trees* b1425

maidenhair fern n b1425

millet n *type of grass* b1425

creeper n b1440

mushroom n b1440

elderberry n b1450

flaxen adj *made from flax* b1450 [the color of flax: b1520]

foliage n *plants* b1450 (painted/carved leaves: b1450)

germ n *something that can germinate* b1450 [fig. use: b1570] (germen: b1605)

oak apple/oak gall n b1450

shoot n b1450 (verb use: b1470)

vert n *arch. vegetation* b1450

aromatic n *aromatic plant* (adj use: b1400)

bulb n [as in "light bulb": b1860]

date palm n

fog n *type of grass*

fungus n

king n *obs. queen bee* [u1700s]

knot n *as in "tree knot"*

pansy n *the flower* [the color: b1900; "sissy": b1930]

roil n *obs. type of horse* [u1500s]

sesame n

Animals

egret n b1355

forefoot n b1375

gizzard n b1375

hobby n *type of falcon* b1375

minnow n b1375

pullet n b1375

vulture n b1375 [fig. use: b1600] (vulturous: b1625; vulturine: b1650)

behemoth n b1385

horsefly n b1385

muzzle n *halter* b1385 (verb use: b1430)

cicada n b1390 (obs. cigala: b1630 to 1700s; cicala: b1820)

jade n *useless horse* b1390

carp n *the fish* b1395

musk n b1395 [type of perfume: b1670]

reptile n b1395 (obs. adj use: b1610 to 1700s; reptilian: b1840)

sardine n b1395

antler n b1400

bestiality n *being a beast* b1400 ["sex with animals": b1630]

bird of prey n b1400

bison n b1400

bloodsucker n b1400 ["parasitic person": b1630]

boa n *snake* b1400 [as in "feather boa": b1870] (boa constrictor: b1810)

camelopard n *giraffe* b1400

cowhide n b1400

cygnet n *young swan* b1400

dun n *horse* b1400 [the color: b1570]

earthworm n b1400

gib n *gelded cat* b1400

gullet n b1400 ["throat": b1670]

halibut n b1400

horned owl n b1400

king of beasts n b1400

kitten n *applied to cats* b1400 [applied to other animals: b1500] (kit: b1565; kittenish: b1755; kitty: b1820)

lizard n b1400

maggot n b1400

marmoset n *type of monkey* b1400 [obs. type of figurine: u1700s]

mouser n b1400

nag n *horse* b1400

nestling n *bird that hasn't left the nest* b1400 [fig. "baby of the family": b1600]

oryx n *type of antelope* b1400

peregrine n *type of falcon* b1400

pigeon n *the bird* b1400

pismire n *type of ant* b1400

plumage n b1400

plume n *feather* b1400 [as in "plume of smoke": b1600]

pounce n *talon* b1400 ["act of pouncing": b1850]

rabbit n b1400 ["rabbit fur": b1930]

reindeer n b1400

reynard n *fox* b1400

roebuck n b1400

school n *as in "school of fish"* b1400 (verb use: b1470)

sleuthhound n *bloodhound* b1400

spawn v b1400 [fig. "engender": b1600] (noun use: b1500)

swordfish n b1400

tadpole n b1400

tortoise n b1400

wildcat n b1400

filly n b1405 [fig. slang use: b1630]

cob n *male swan* b1410

conch n b1410 [type of bowl: b1395]

hock n *as in "ham hocks"* b1410

muzzle n *snout* b1410

terrier n b1410

antelope n b1420

bevy n *of quail* b1425 [gen. use: b1450]

caprine adj *relating to goats* b1425

marten n b1425 [type of fur: b1300]

newt n b1425

porcupine n b1425

redbreast n b1425

rump n b1425

rut n/v *estrus for males* b1425

sable n b1425 (adj "black": b1400; adj "made of sable": b1450)

garfish n b1440 (gar: b1765)

scallop n b1440 [type of shell: b1350]

stallion n b1440 ["promiscuous man": b1350]

bulrush/bullrush n b1450

catamountain n *type of wild cat* b1450 (catamount: b1665)

caterpillar n b1450

chub n *type of fish* b1450

dormouse n b1450

duckling n b1450

falcon-gentle n *falcon* b1450

fitch n *skunk* b1450 (fitchet: b1535)

gull n b1450

hedgehog n b1450 (hedgepig: b1605)

housefly n b1450

humblebee n *bumblebee* b1450

pollywog n b1450

prawn n b1450
rail n *type of bird* b1450
sparrow hawk n b1450 (spar-hawk: b1150)
mongrel n b1460 [applied to people: b1570] (adj use: b1580; mong "mixture": b1150)
dab n *type of fish*
dorsal adj
grub n
litter n
mange n (mangy: b1530)
martin n *type of bird*
osprey n
philomel n *type of bird*
pride n *group of lions*
robin redbreast n
roe n *fish eggs*
sepia n *cuttlefish*
shark n *sea creature*
shed v [gen. use: b1870]
whitefish n

Weather
humidity n b1395 (humid: b1400)
thunderclap n b1400
windstorm n b1400
thunderbolt n b1450 ["zigzag drawing": b1730]
hoar n *hoarfrost* (hoarfrost: b1300)
mizzle n/v *kind of misty drizzle*
puft n *obs. bit of wind* [u1700s]
weather n *obs. precipitation* [u1600s]

Heavens/Sky
meridian n b1355
conjunction n b1375
celestial adj b1380 (noun use: b1575)
galaxy n *Milky Way* b1380 [gen. use: b1850] (galactic: b1840)
Milky Way n *stars in the Milky Way* b1380 ["our galaxy": b1870]
ecliptic n b1395
sunset n b1395 [fig. use: b1630]
ether n *assumed contents of the heavens* b1400 ["the sky": b1600; type of chemical: b1770] (ethereal: b1515)

North Star n b1400
northern lights n b1400
retrograde adj b1400
zenith n b1400 [gen. "apex": b1630]
zodiac n b1400
half-moon n/adj b1425
interstice n b1425 [gen. sense: b1605]
moonshine n *moonlight* b1425 (moonlight: b1300)
mobile n *outer sphere of the universe* b1430
solar adj b1450
constellation n
dragon n *obs. shooting star* [u1700s]

Science
amber n b1365
alchemy, alchemist n b1375
astrolabe n b1375
azimuth n b1390
cosmography n b1390
natural science n b1395
elixir n *alchemical preparation* b1400 [type of drug: b1500]
ambergris n b1425
sciential adj

Energy
firewood n b1380
fuelwood n b1400
waterwheel n b1410
bonfire n b1415
coke n *fuel residue* b1425
combustion n b1425 [obs. med. "inflammation": u1600s] (combust v: b1375; combustible adj: b1530)

Time
clock n b1370 [obs. "type of bell": u1700s] (verb use: b1885)
autumn n b1375
eternity n b1375 (eterne adj/n: concurrent; eternal: b1400)
horologe n *any timekeeping device* b1375
midyear adj/n b1375
temporal adj b1375 ["secular": b1340]
minute n b1380

annual adj b1385 (noun use: b1400)
diurnal adj *daily* b1390
quarter n *quarter of a year* b1390
agone adv/adj *ago* b1400
equinox n b1400
high noon n b1400
indiction n *15-year unit (like a decade)* b1400
instant n b1400
leap year n b1400
luster n *half a decade* b1400
nighttime n b1400
posterity n b1400 (rare posterior n: b1530)
summertime n b1400
half hour n b1420
daily adj b1425
forenoon n *opp. of afternoon* b1425
octaves n *8 days following a celebration* b1425
trice n *as in "in a trice"* b1450
quarter n *as in "quarter past the hour"* b1460
evening n ["process of evening arriving": b1000 to 1500s]
hours n *as in "1300 hours"*
moon n *slang month*
point n *obs. measure of time*
spring n *type of season*
stroke n *as in "at the stroke of midnight"*
vernant adj *obs. arising in the spring* [u1800s]
week n *a week from now, as in "Tuesday week"*
weeks n *a long time*

Age/Aging
middle age n b1380 (middle-aged: b1610; midlife: b1800)
senior adj/n b1400
adolescence n b1425 (adolescent n: b1460; adolescent adj: b1785)
aged adj b1425 [as in "aged wine": b1870]
nonage n *being under legal age* b1425 [fig. "youth": b1600]
whitebeard n *old man* b1450

grown-up adj (noun use: b1815)
yearling n

Mathematics
corollary n b1375
quadruple v b1375 (noun use: b1425; adj use: b1560)
million n b1380
abacus n b1390
diameter n b1390
cipher n *zero* b1400 ["code": b1530, "gen. numbers": b1530] (verb use: b1530)
cube n b1400 ["cube-shaped thing": b1630] (verb use: b1970)
digit n b1400
fraction n b1400 [var. meanings of "fracture": b1570]
geometrical adj b1400 (geometric: b1630)
irrational adj b1400 (noun use: b1700; irrational number: b1555)
quadrangle n b1400 ["courtyard": b1630]
right angle n b1400
digital adj b1425
mathematical adj b1450
mathematician n b1450 (obs. mathematic: b1570 to 1700s)
product n b1450
quotient n b1450
ternary adj/n *threefold* b1450
divide, division v, n (divisor: b1475; dividend: b1570)
even adj *divisible by 2*
multiply v
odd adj *opp. of even*
root n
square n *type of shape* (adj use: b1350; verb use: b1400)
sum n *total of addition* [obs. "number": u1700s] (verb use: b1350)
table n/v *akin to chart*
unity n *number 1*

Measurement
infinity n b1380 (infinitude: b1645)
depth n *phys. sense* b1385 [fig. use: b1600]
circumference n b1395

altitude n b1400

dimension n b1400 [obs. "measuring": b1570 to 1700s]

dram n b1400

gross n *144* b1400

latitude n *opp. of longitude; gen. area* b1400 ["variance range": u1700s; "leeway": b1630]

league n *measure of distance* b1400

longitude n *opp. of latitude; gen. length* b1400

pennyweight n *measure of weight* b1400

pint n b1400 ["glass of beer": b1770]

second n *unit of measurement* b1400

ton n b1400 [slang "a lot": b1800]

breadth n b1425

hairbreadth n b1450

barrel n

carat n

finger n *as in "a finger of scotch"*

grain n

height n *arch. altitude*

piece n *as in "down the road a piece"*

scale n *e.g., Fahrenheit scale* ["measurement standard": b1630]

score n *arch. type of weight measure*

spot n *little bit, as in "a spot of trouble"*

velocity n

yardland n

The Body

cramp n *muscle contraction* b1375 (verb use: b1425)

jaw n b1375 (slang verb use: b1750)

paunch n b1375 (paunchy: b1600)

chest n b1385

crow's-feet n b1385

bum n (Brit) *buttocks* b1390

choler n *yellow bile* b1390 ["bilious disposition": b1570]

thing n *slang penis* b1390

digestion, digest n, v b1395

inside/insides n b1395

muscle n b1395

nervous adj *pertaining to nerves* b1395 ["sinewy": u1700s; "anxious": b1740] (nervosity: b1790)

organ n *internal body part* b1395 ["penis": b1905]

respiration n b1395 (respire v: b1385)

retina n b1395

artery n b1400 ["thoroughfare": b1870] (arterial adj: b1425)

asshole n b1400 ["jerk": b1935]

botch n *boil, blemish* b1400

canine n *the tooth* b1400 ["dog": b1870]

cartilage, cartilaginous n, adj b1400 (cartiligenous: b1400)

colon n *part of intestines* b1400 (colonic adj: b1885; colonic n: b1940)

cornea n b1400

corporal adj *pertaining to the body* b1400 ["secular": b1390; obs. "possessing a body": b1500 to 1600s]

cranium n b1400

diaphragm n b1400

dimple n *on people* b1400 [on things: b1670] (verb use: b1600)

earwax n b1400

esophagus n b1400

feces n b1400

fiber n *obs. part of the liver* b1400 [u1600s]

freckle n b1400 (verb use: b1570; freck v: b1630)

genital, genitals adj, n b1400 (genitories: b1470; genitalia: b1880)

groin n b1400

hemorrhoid n b1400

index n *index finger* b1400 (index finger: b1850)

knuckle n b1400

ligament n *type of binding* b1400 [type of body section: b1425]

matter, mattery n, adj *pus* b1400

menstrual adj b1400

mole n *skin spot* b1400 [obs. "gen. spot": b1000 to 1800s]

nerve n *part of nervous system* b1400 ["sinew": b1385] (nervous system: b1750; neural: b1840; nerve cell: b1860; nerve net: b1905)

optic adj b1400 [arch. "optical": b1700]

orbit n *eyesocket* b1400

organic adj *pertaining to body organs* b1400 [arch. "instrumental": b1530; "biological": b1700; "of a whole": b1830]

palate n b1400 ["liking, preference": b1870]

physiognomy n b1400

puberty n b1400

pudendum n b1400

semen n b1400

snot n b1400 (snotty: b1570)

sperm n b1400

thorax n b1400

tiptoe n b1400 (adv use: b1595; adj use: b1595; verb use: b1665)

trachea n b1400

ventricle n b1400

anus n b1425

auricle n b1425

cervix n b1425

congestion n b1425 [gen. "crowdedness": b1870]

corn n *as in "toe corns"* b1425

follicle n b1425

intestine, intestinal n, adj b1425

iris n *part of the eye* b1425

mandible n b1425 [applied to birds: b1700; applied to insects: b1830]

membrane n b1425

nasal adj b1425

noddle n *head* b1425 ["simpleton": b1730]

pile n *hemmorhoid* b1425

saliva n b1425 (salivate: b1660)

teethe v b1425

testicle n b1425 ["female ovary": u1600s]

cardiac adj b1450

complexion n *skin; outer appearance* b1450 [pertaining to body humors: b1340]

forefinger n b1450

instep n b1450

kneepan n *kneecap* b1450 (kneecap: b1870)

spine n *spinal column* b1450 [fig. "central support": b1670; as in "book's spine": b1930]

thighbone n b1450

whisker n b1450 [obs. "whisking tool": concurrent]

chamber n *as in "chamber of the heart"*

crane n *arch. cranium*

cuck n *arch. defecate*

dogtooth n *canine tooth*

embryo n (obs. embryon: u1800s; embryonal: b1655; embryotic: b1770; embryonic: b1845)

epiglottis n

eyebrow n

ferntickle n *arch. skin blemish*

gender n *sex*

genitories n *arch. testicles*

grinders n *slang teeth*

gut n *as in "beergut"; as in "catgut"*

lobe n

mail n *arch. film in the eye*

morphew n *skin blemish*

os n *bone*

pericardium n

pubescence n (pubescent: b1650)

pupil n *part of the eye*

pus n

tendon n

tibia n

ulna n

uterus n

vessel n *as in "blood vessel"*

vulva n

Physical Description

misery n *phys. misery* b1375 ["mental misery": b1530] (miserable: b1415; miser "miserable one": b1545)

snort v *expel air* b1375 (noun use: b1810)

voluptuous adj *sensual* b1375 ["comely": b1870] (voluptuary adj/n: b1605)

scab n b1395 (verb use: b1635)

scar n b1395 [fig. use: b1600] (verb use: b1555)

Words and Wordesses

Modern sensibility leads us to "de-sexing" the language—removing bias against either gender by neutralizing words. But this is a book about the past and what was, and what was was a myriad of words indicating that the person described by the word was female, usually with such suffixes as -ess, -ette and -ix.

Often, the opposite of a female-specific word wasn't necessarily male-specific. The jocular *farmerette* (by 1905) is certainly female, but the *farmer* can be of either sex. The same is oddly true of *maness*, from before 1600—its opposite, *man*, could refer to people of either sex until the meaning of "male adult" came about around 1000.

What's more, some "obviously" gender-specific words didn't begin as such. For example, a *girl* (by 1350) could be a young female or a young male; its present meaning didn't firm up until before 1570. And *fellow* carried the now-obsolete meaning of "female companion" from Old English to the 1600s.

So, without commentary on the appropriateness of such gender-tagged words, let's compare when male- and female-specific words appeared in English:

- *empress* (by 1175), *emperor* (by 1125)
- *gentlewoman* (by 1350), *gentleman* (by 1200)
- *kinswoman* (by 1350), *kinsman* (by 1150)
- *prophetess* (by 1350), *prophet* (by 1200)
- *executrix* (by 1400), *executor* (by 1300)
- *huntress* (by 1400), *hunter* (by 1250), *huntsman* (by 1570)
- *murderess* (by 1400), *murderer* (by 1340)
- *authoress* (by 1500), *author* (by 1470)
- *foremother* (by 1500), *forefather* (by 1300)
- *poetess* (by 1530), *poet* (by 1300)
- *landlady* (by 1540), *landlord* (by 1000)

- *actress* (by 1600), *actor* (by 1585)
- *Mrs.* (by 1615), *Ms.* (by 1950), *Mr.* (by 1450)
- *conductress* (by 1625), *conductor* (by 1500)
- *taskmistress* (by 1650), *taskmaster* (by 1530)
- *clergywoman* (by 1675), *clergyman* (by 1580)
- *proprietress* (by 1695), *proprietrix* (by 1840), *proprietor* (by 1500)
- *editress* (by 1800), *editor* (by 1715)
- *visitress* (by 1830), *visitor* (by 1450)
- *businesswoman* (by 1845), *businessman* (by 1715)
- *seeress* (by 1845), *seer* (by 1400)
- *policewoman* (by 1855), *policeman* (by 1805)
- *comedienne* (by 1860), *comedian* (by 1605)
- *cowgirl* (by 1885), *cowboy* (by 1870)
- *aviatrix* (by 1910), *aviator* (by 1890)
- *congresswoman* (by 1920), *congressman* (by 1780)
- *assemblywoman* (by 1970), *assemblyman* (by 1650)

A couple of additional notes:

Usually the male-specific or the neutral form precedes the female-specific version, with rare exception. For example, *protegée* preceded *protegé* by about ten years (by 1780 versus by 1790). *Countess* is recorded by 1175, while *count* is recorded by 1305. *Housewife* arrives before 1225 (though more in the sense of house manager); *househusband*, before 1955. And as seen in the list above, *huntswoman* came after *hunter* but before *huntsman*.

Also, some feminine forms survive where the masculine does not. *Seductor*, in use by 1500 into the 1600s, is obsolete; *seductress*, in use by 1805, is still with us.

---

awk adj *obs. backward, awkward* b1400 [u1800s]

blubber v *cry* b1400

callous adj b1400 [fig. "insensitive": b1670] (verb use: b1835)

carnal adj b1400 ["blood relative": u1500s]

corpulent adj b1400 [obs. gen. "solid," "corporeal": u1600s] (corpulence: b1500)

costive adj *constipated* b1400 [obs. "constipating": b1570 to 1600s]

famish v b1400 [obs. "starve to death": b1570 to 1700s] (famished: b1425)

goggle-eyed adj b1400

gulp v *as in "gulp down"* b1400 ["swallow hard in fear": b1570] (noun use: b1500)

left-handed, right-handed adj *using the left or right hand; awkward* b1400

nod v *give phys. assent; nod off* b1400 (noun use: b1545)

pain v *feel pain* b1400 [obs. "hurt someone else": b1400 to 1600s]

pall v *become pale* b1400

pine v *waste away* b1400 [obs. "cause pain": b900; "yearn": b1600] (obs.

noun use "pain, punishment": b1150)

pulchritude n b1400

ravenous adj b1400

sip v b1400 (noun use: b1500)

slobber v b1400 ["fawn": b1830] (noun use: b1760)

toothless adj *lit. lacking teeth* b1400 ["lacking power": b1600]

agility n b1415 (agile: b1580)

gesture n b1425 [obs. "general bodily carriage, motion": u1800s] (verb use: b1600)

graceful adj b1425 (graceless: b1375)

livid adj b1425 ["enraged": b1930]

visual adj *pertaining to seeing* b1425 ["meant to be seen": b1670; "optical": b1730]

yawn v *open mouth sleepily* b1430 (noun use: b1730)

decrepit adj b1440 (decrepitude: b1600)

bare-handed adj/adv b1450

couchant adj *reclining* b1450

deft adj b1450 [obs. "gentle": b1225]

gait n b1450 (gate n "journey": b1300)

gaunt adj b1450 [obs. "slim": u1700s]

queasy adj *unsettled* b1450

short-winded adj b1450

shrug v *as in "shrug your shoulders"* b1450 [obs. "fidget": b1440 to 1600s] (noun use: b1600; shrug off: b1930)

stale n/v *urinate* b1450

eructation n *burp* [of volcanoes: b1670] (eruct: b1670; eructate: b1800)

lather n *heavy sweat* (verb use: b1350)

office n *arch. bodily function*

ravishing adj *as in "a ravishing beauty"*

vision n *ability to see*

Medicine

apothecary n *druggist* b1375

arthritic adj b1375 (noun

use: b1400; arthritis: b1545)

infection n b1375 (infect: b1380)

migraine n b1375 (megrim: b1470)

pertussis n *whooping cough* b1375

contagion, contagious n, adj b1380

cure n b1380 [obs. "gen. treatment": u1700s; obs. "concern": b1300 to 1600s] (verb use: b1385)

immunity n b1385 (immune: b1450)

apoplexy n *stroke* b1390 (apoplectic adj: b1615)

delicate adj *medically fragile* b1390 [gen. "fragile": b1570] (delicacy: b1670)

hernia n b1390

disease n b1395 ["unease": b1340; obs. "something that discomforts": u1700s]

incision n b1395 (incise v: b1545)

inveterate adj b1395 [gen. sense: b1530]

sclerosis n b1395

acute adj b1400 [gen. sense: b1570]

anatomy n b1400 (anatomist: b1545)

asthma n b1400 (asthmatic adj/n: b1545)

bulimia n b1400

catalepsy n b1400

cataract n b1400 ["waterfall": b1600]

cautery, cauterize, cauterization n, v, n *cauterizing tool* b1400

chap n/v *sore or rough skin* b1400 (verb use: b1325)

chord n *cord, as in "spinal chord"* b1400

clyster n *enema* b1400

constipation n b1400 (constipate: b1535; constipated: b1550)

consumption, consume n, v b1400 [spec. "tuberculosis": b1660; "spending, using": b1665] (consumptive: b1665)

contusion n b1400 (contuse: b1425)

cup v *draw blood* b1400

diarrhea n b1400

dislocation n b1400 (dislocate: b1600)

diuretic adj/n b1400 (diuresis: b1685)

dysentery n b1400

faint v b1400 ["weaken": b1300] (noun use: b1810)

fester v b1400 (noun use: b1325)

herpes n b1400 (herpes zoster: b1810; herpes simplex: b1910; herpesvirus: b1925)

impetigo n *type of skin infection* b1400

indigestion n b1400

indisposed adj *ill* b1400 [obs. "unorganized": u1600s]

julep n *drink spiked with medicine* b1400 [type of alcoholic drink: b1800]

king's evil n *type of disease* b1400

laxative adj b1400 (noun use: b1450; lax "not constipated": b1400)

leper n b1400 [obs. "leprosy": b1350; fig. use: b1830] (obs. adj use: u1500s)

lousy adj *infested with lice* b1400 [slang use: b1450]

patient n b1400

phlebotomy n *blood-letting* b1400

plague n *gen. affliction, pestilence* b1400 [obs. "wound": u1500s; spec. "sweeping disease": b1570] (verb use: b1500)

pleurisy n b1400

polyp n b1400

regimen n b1400

rheum, rheumatic n, adj b1400 (rheumy: b1595)

rigor n b1400

sand-blind adj *partially sighted* b1400

sciatica n b1400

shingles n b1400

sickbed n b1400

spasm n b1400 [fig. use: b1830] (verb use: b1930)

splint n b1400

suppository n b1400

symptom n b1400 [gen. use: b1630]

syringe n b1400

tetanus n b1400

ulcer n b1400 (obs. ulcerate adj: u1700s; ulcerate v: b1425; ulcerous: b1470)

vomit n b1400 (verb use: b1450; vomitory adj: b1605; vomition: b1670)

aneurysm n b1425

antidote n b1425

cerate n *type of medicinal ointment* b1425

chronic adj *med. lingering* b1425 [gen. "constantly recurring": b1870]

colic adj/n b1425 (colicky: b1745)

conserve n *medicinal fruit perserve* b1425

crisis n b1425 [gen. "focal problem": b1630] (critical: b1550)

curative adj *medical* b1425 ["curing": b1670] (noun use: b1870)

debility n b1425 (debilitate v: b1535)

eruption n *as in "eruption of a rash"* b1425 ["eruption of a volcano": b1770; "eruption of a tooth": b1870]

hemorrhage n b1425 (verb use: b1930)

inflammation n b1425 ["setting afire": b1535]

lancet n *type of surgical instrument* b1425 [obs. "small lance": u1700s]

liniment n b1425

medication n *use of medicine* b1425 ["medicine": b1970]

method n b1425 [gen. sense: b1590]

nausea n b1425

period n *course of a disease* b1425

pill n b1425 (verb use: b1740)

pregnant adj b1425 (pregnancy: b1530)

remission n b1425 ["pardon": b1200; "decrease": b1400]

ringworm n b1425

sedative adj b1425 (sedation: b1545; sedate v: b1945)

childbirth n b1450

craze v *become physically ill* b1450 [obs. "break": b1370 to 1800s; become mentally ill: b1500] (crazy adj: b1630)

sanative adj *healthful* b1450

stut n *arch. stutter* b1450

unguent n *salve* b1450

whole blood n b1450

infirmary n b1455

calamine n

care n *as in "health care"* [as in "cares and woes": b725] (verb use: b1350)

concussion n (concuss: b1600)

doctor n (verb use: b1730; doctress: b1600)

dose n [gen. use: b1630] (verb use: b1665)

easement n *obs. bowel or bladder relief* [u1700s]

enema n

enlighten v *obs. cure blindness* [u1700s]

ephemera n *obs. type of short-lived illness* [u1800s]

fermery n *arch. infirmary*

fig n *obs. hemorrhoids* [u1500s]

frog n *mouth disease, as in "frog in the throat"*

gallipot n *type of pot used by pharmacists*

grievance n *obs. disease* [u1700s]

kyle n *obs. boil*

left-handed adj *obs. disabled* [u1600s]

lesion n

medicament n *medication*

mediciner n *arch. doctor*

paroxysm n [gen. "outburst": b1670]

peripneumony n *obs. pneumonia* [u1800s]

pilule n *small pill*

poultice n (verb use: b1730)

pox n (verb use: b1605)

priapism n *continual erection*

purgative n

quick adj *pregnant*

repercussion n *obs. medicine for reducing infection* [u1700s]

rot n

serrate v *obs. amputate* [u1500s]

set v

sunburn v (noun use: b1655; sunburnt: b1400)

suture n (verb use: b1780)

tablet n (tabloid: b1900)

torture n *agony* [type of punishment: b1570] (verb use: b1590; torturous: b1500)

treat v (treatment: b1770)

tumor n [obs. fig. "swelled ego": b1630 to 1800s]

varicose adj

vertigo n (vertiginous: b1610)

void v

Everyday Life

desk n b1365 [obs. "bookcase": b1570 to 1700s]

lavatory n *bath* b1375

trash n *something worthless* b1375 [obs. slang "cash": b1600 to 1800s; "worthless person," as in "white trash": b1605; "garbage": b1930] (trashy: b1620)

urn n b1375

napkin n b1385

fan n *cooling device* b1390

tack n/v *pin* b1390 [gen. type of fastener: b1300; sewing term: b1730] (verb use: b1200)

cheesecloth n b1400

container n b1400

couch n *type of living room furniture* b1400 [arch. "sleeping place": b1340]

laundry n *washing clothes* b1400 ["place to wash clothes": b1600; "clothes to be washed": b1930] (verb use: b1500; launder: b1600)

ream n *quantity of paper* b1400

receipt n *arch. recipe* b1400

rubbish n b1400

wallet n *type of pouch* b1400 [modern sense: b1835]

carving knife n b1415

plate n b1415 ["plateful": b1600; as in "collection plate": b1800; as in "home plate": b1870]

closestool n *seat above chamberpot* b1425

coalbin n b1425

contour n *quilt* b1425

dentifrice n b1425

plaster of paris n b1425

purse strings n b1425

spinning wheel n b1425

bung n *stopper* b1440 (verb use: b1590)

bedstead n b1450

chafing dish n b1450

ironware n b1450

penknife n b1450

cask n/v b1460

flagon n *type of bottle* b1460

economic n *obs. home economics* [u1600s] (obs. adj use: b1595 to 1700s)

glass n *mirror*

lamplight n

larder n *type of storage* ["what is stored": b1375 to 1400s]

mousetrap n

range n *cooking device*

sideboard n

spectacles n *glasses* (specs: b1805)

stool n *three-legged stool* [obs. "seat of authority": b900 to 1800s; obs. "pcw": b1630]

tablecloth n

thimble n

tick n *ticking*

tin foil n

vase n

Shelter/Housing

hovel n b1360

bathhouse n b1365

bedchamber n b1375

hospitality n b1375 (obs. hospital "hospitality": b1470 to 1800s)

joist n b1375

moat n b1375 ["embankment": b1300]

newel n *staircase post* b1375 (newel post: b1800)

pinnacle n *turret* b1375

transom n b1375 [obs. type of bed support: u1500s]

trapdoor n b1375

wine cellar n b1375

edifice n b1380

household n b1380

sanctuary n *refuge* b1380 [as in "wildlife sanctuary": b1900]

canopy n b1385 [pertaining to vehicles: b1900]

cottage n *housing for the poor* b1390 [gen. type of small house: b1770]

country house n b1400

dwelling n b1400 [act of dwelling: b1300] (dwell: b900)

gatehouse n b1400

rabbet n *as in "rabbet joint"* b1400 (verb use: b1500)

refuge n b1400 (verb use: b1595)

saltcellar n b1400 (saltshaker: b1895)

story n *building level* b1400

tenement n *residence building* b1400 [leg. "property": b1300; spec. type of building: b1600]

thatch n *type of roofing* b1400 ["covering, such as hair": b1670; "type of grass": b1700; as in "lawn thatch": b1970]

thatch v/n b1400 [obs. "cover": b900]

valve n *arch. type of door* b1400

clerestory n *pertaining to churches* b1415 [pertaining to other buildings: b1530]

brick n *baked clay* b1420 ["blocks of baked clay": b1530; gen. "brick-shaped block": b1770] (verb use: b1595)

casement n *window* b1420

renovation n *rehabbing housing* b1425

stronghold n b1425

asylum n *phys. refuge* b1440 [fig. "refuge": b1730; "mental institution": b1780]

gallery n b1440

safe n *as in "wallsafe"* b1440

column n *type of architectural feature* b1450

garderobe n *arch. type of storeroom* b1450

parlor n *living room* b1450

["room in a church":
b1225]
safekeeping n b1450
sconce n *wall light* b1450
[obs. type of candle: b1395
to 1700s]
subtenant n b1450
water pipe n b1450
fence n b1465 [obs. "defense": b1340 to 1500s]
(verb use: b1435)
resident n b1465 (adj use:
b1385)
abode n [obs. "wait, sojourn": b1200]
coverture n *shelter; cover;
covering; disguise* ["bedspread": b1225 to 1600s]
(covert n: b1350)
domestic adj *describing the
home* ["homey": b1670]
domicile n
dormitory n *sleeping room*
["college housing": b1870]
entry n *entryway* (entryway:
b1745)
hostage n *obs. hostel*
[u1800s]
inn n *public lodging*
lair n *animal den* [gen.
"sleeping place": b900]
lean-to n *type of building*
["type of shelter": b1900]
(adj use: b1650)
light n *as in "skylight"*
partition n *wall* (verb use:
b1745)
plaster n *type of building material* [type of molding material: b1285]
refectory n *dining hall*

Drink

hippocras n *type of mulled
wine* b1375
cordial n *drink for the heart*
b1390
libation n *pouring* b1400
["drink": b1770] (libate:
b1870)
barleycorn n b1425
grind n *spec. to coffee*
moisture n *obs. drink*
[u1700s]
raspis n *obs. type of wine*
[u1500s]
wet v *drink*

Food

wafer n b1370 [rel. sense:
b1560]
bun n b1375
endive n b1375
famine n b1375
batter n *food coating* b1385
(verb use: b1975)
cold cream n *type of custard*
b1385
cucumber n b1385 (cuke:
b1905)
eatable adj b1385 (noun use:
b1675; edible: b1595)
chive n b1390 ["sauce with
chives": b1800]
cinnamon n b1390
cook v b1390 ["be cooked":
b1870]
scallion n b1390 ["leek":
b1830]
cabbage n *vegetable* b1395
[slang "money": b1930]
oatmeal n b1395
tartar n *as in "cream of tartar"* b1395 [as in "tartar-
control toothpaste":
b1630]
cardamom n b1400
farina n b1400
filet n b1400 (fillet: b1475)
fritter n b1400
frumenty n *type of oatmeal*
b1400
jelly n b1400 [gen. "jelly-
like material": b1630]
marjoram n *type of mint*
b1400
muscatel n b1400 (muscat
wine: b1570)
nurse v *breast-feed* b1400
["help as a med. nurse":
b1770; as in "nurse a
drink": b1970]
oatcake n b1400
pamper v *spec. feed well*
b1400 [gen. "treat well":
b1570]
parboil v *par(tially)boil*
b1400 [obs. "boil com-
pletely": u1600s]
parsnip n b1400
poach v *as in "poach an egg"*
b1400 (poacher "type of
utensil": b1865)
pome n *type of fruit* b1400
poppy seed n b1400

refect v *arch. refresh with food*
b1400 (refection: b1350)
salad n b1400
season v b1400
spun sugar n b1400
stew v *cook* b1400 [obs.
"bathe": u1600s; "fret,
ponder": b1930]
sweet n *sweet-tasting thing*
b1400 ["sweet eats":
b1450; "candy": b1870]
(adj use: b900)
syrup n b1400
tart n *pastry* b1400 (tartlet:
b1425)
vittles n b1400
wheat bread n b1400
white pepper n b1400
conserves n *confections*
b1425
haggis n b1425
nutriment n *nourishment*
b1425
nutrition n b1425 (nutritious: b1665)
red herring n b1425
scullery n *area of kitchen responsibility* b1445 [spec.
place: b1770]
basil n b1450
batch n *spec. to baking* b1450
[gen., as in "a batch of orders": b1730] (verb use:
b1880)
bay leaf n b1450
cheesecake n b1450
delicacy n b1450 [obs. "hedonism": b1375 to 1700s]
dish n *type of food, as in
"meat dish"* b1450
gourmand n *glutton* b1450
["gourmet": b1870]
pap n b1450 [gen. "pablum": b1570]
pickle n b1450 [slang "jam,
predicament": b1570;
"bleach": b1800] (verb use
"preserve": b1570; verb
use "bleach": b1870; pickled: b1555)
potation n *drinking potables;
the potables themselves*
b1450 (potable adj:
b1575; potable n: b1625)
sausage n b1450
umbles n *entrails* b1450
breakfast n b1465 (verb use:
b1680)

chip n *as in "fish and chips"*
chop n *as in "pork chop"*
condiment n [type of pickling
juice: b1340]
confection n *sweets* [obs. type
of medicine: b1350; obs.
type of potion: b1500 to
1600s] (verb use "mix,
prepare": b1400)
cut n *as in "cut of meat"*
decoct v *obs. cook by boiling*
[u1600s]
form n *obs. recipe* [u1600s]
gruel n [obs. "flour, etc.":
b1325]
heat n *hot spiciness*
junket n *type of cream dish*
lamb n
link n *as in "sausage links"*
nibble v *eat* (noun use:
b1500)
pistachio n
potable adj (noun use:
b1625; potation: b1450)
puff n *as in "cheese puff"*
roll n
say n *obs. food-testing*
[u1600s]
sirloin n
starch n/v [fig. "inflexibil-
ity": b1730]
stuff n *obs. edible stuffing*
[u1500s]
sugar candy n
toast n

Agriculture/
Food-Gathering

hunt n b1375 [obs. "hunter":
b1135 to 1800s]
slaughterhouse n b1375
fallow adj b1380 (noun use:
b1100; verb use: b1500)
warren n *breeding ground*
b1380
quarry n *object of the hunt*
b1390
barnyard n b1400
carthorse n b1400
corn-fed adj b1400
drover n b1400
huntress n b1400 (hunter:
b1250; huntsman: b1570;
huntswoman: b1630)
neatherd n b1400
plowshare n b1400

seed v b1400 (noun use: b900)

weeder n b1400

arable adj *suitable for farming* b1410

farmer n b1415 ["rent collector": b1385] (farmerette: b1905)

poult n *young fowl* b1425

sod n/v b1425

spay v b1425

agriculture n b1440 (agricultural: b1780)

culture n *land cultivation* b1440 ["growing crops, etc.": b1630; "growing bacteria, etc.": b1900] (cultural: b1870)

hop n *as in "barley and hops"* b1440

stump n *as in "tree stump"* b1440

browse v *eat browse* b1450 [fig. "scan": b1870]

fisherman n b1450 (fisherwoman: b1820)

harvestman n *reaper* b1450

packhorse n b1450

shepherd dog n b1450

transplant v *replant* b1450 [fig. "move": b1570; as in "transplant an organ": b1800] (noun use: 1760)

vintage n *wine crop; wine harvest* b1450 ["good wine": b1770; fig. use: b1900] (adj use: b1600)

vintner n b1450 (obs. vinter: b1350 to 1400s)

earmark n b1460 [gen. use: b1600] (verb use: b1595)

agricultor n *obs. farmer* (obs. agricole: b1670 to 1800s)

herdsman n (obs. herdman: b1000 to 1600s; herdswoman: b1830)

horseflesh n

manure v [obs. "manage land": u1600s; obs. "dwell": b1600 to 1600s; obs. "cultivate mentally": b1570 to 1700s]

pastoral adj *pertaining to herding* [as in "pastoral song": b1585]

pitch v *as in "pitch hay"*

rear v *applied to plants and animals* [applied to children: b1600]

wash n *as in "hogwash"*

Cloth/Clothing

galosh n b1355

clog n b1370

satin n b1370 (adj use: b1450)

bonnet n *headwear for men* b1375 ["headwear for women": b1425]

lambskin n b1375

lint n *flax; type of cloth* b1375 ["fuzz": b1630]

motley n *obs. type of cloth* b1375 [u1500s]

threadbare adj *lit.* b1375 [fig. "worn": b1600]

neckerchief n b1385

sandal n b1385

tassel v b1390

bedclothes n b1400

bracer n *wristband* b1400

breastplate n b1400

broider v *arch. embroider* b1400

camel hair/camel's hair n b1400

chimere n *type of garment* b1400

cordwain n *cordovan leather* b1400

coronet n *small crown* b1400 [type of headdress: b1600]

cotton wool n *unprocessed cotton* b1400

embroider, embroidery v, n b1400 [fig., as in "embroider a tale": b1630]

frieze n *type of wool* b1400

hair shirt n b1400

kersey n *type of fabric* b1400

kidskin n b1400

mantelet n *type of cloak* b1400

nightcap n b1400 [type of drink: b1830]

nightgown n b1400 (nightie: b1875)

plait n *braid* b1400 (verb use: b1385)

raiment n b1400

ribbon n b1400

serge n *type of fabric* b1400

slop n *type of outerwear* b1400

spun yarn n b1400

wardrobe n *clothing* b1400 [type of furniture: b1600]

broadcloth n b1415

hatband n b1425

lining n b1425

linsey-woolsey n *type of fabric* b1425

petticoat n *type of skirt* b1425 [obs. type of men's garment: u1500s; slang "woman": b1630] (adj use: b1660)

mink n *type of fur* b1435 [the animal: b1630]

aglet n *part of a shoelace* b1450

codpiece n b1450

elegant adj *natty* b1450 ["graceful": b1530; "cultured": b1730] (elegancy: b1500; elegance: b1510)

jacket n b1455

tartan adj/n b1455

back v *arch. clothe*

color n *as in "wearing colors"* ["flag," as in "flying the colors": b1600]

cutwork n

disrobe v

gipser n *belt-hung bag*

habit v *clothe*

leg n

loose adj *obs. unclothed* [u1700s]

loose adj *loose-fitting*

ray n *obs. clothing* [u1600s]

slipper n

suit n (verb use: b1600)

toe n *as in "toe of a sock"*

tuck v *create pleats*

undight v *undress*

Fashion/Style

fashion n b1380 [gen. "form": b1300]

preen v b1400

solitaire n *type of gem setting* b1400

stately adj b1400

nosegay n *type of bouquet* b1425

popular adj *common* b1425 ["of the populace": b1550; "for lay people": b1600; "liked by most": b1630; "for popular consumption": b1870]

dapper adj b1440

bracelet n b1450 [slang "handcuff": b1630]

fard v *paint with cosmetics* b1450 (noun use: b1570)

accessory n

compt adj *obs. with adorned hair* [u1700s]

form n *obs. beauty* [u1600s]

formosity n *arch. beauty*

gaud n *ostentatious trinket* (obs. verb use: b1570 to 1600s; gaudy: b1500; gaudery: b1600)

pendant n *type of jewelry* [type of architectural feature: b1350]

pretty adj *attractive, beautiful* [arch. "clever": b1000] (adv use: b1565; noun use: b1740; verb use: b1830)

stud n *type of ornament*

Tools

cleaver n b1360

dibble n b1375

brush n *brushing tool* b1380 [as in "artist's brush": b1500] (verb use: b1470)

scissors n b1380 (scissor n: b1500; scissor v: b1615)

mortise n b1390

cartwheel n b1395 [type of gymnastic move: b1855]

scale n *obs. ladder rung* b1395 [u1600s]

waterspout n b1395

bail n *pail* b1400 (verb use: b1615)

eyelet n b1400

faucet n b1400 [obs. "stopper": u1700s]

fishhook n b1400

frying pan n b1400

griddle n b1400 ["grill": b1225]

guy n *guyline* b1400

handsaw n b1400

inkhorn n b1400

money changer n b1400

perspective n *type of optical glass* b1400

plummet n *plumb* b1400

rivet n b1400 (verb use: b1500)

rock n *distaff* b1400

whittle n *arch. type of knife* b1400 (verb use: b1555)

windlass n b1400

screw n b1405 [in construction: b1630] (verb use: b1605)

cramp n *clamp* b1425

crucible n b1425

funnel n b1425 (verb use: b1595)

mallet n b1425 [obs. fig. "oppressor": b1530 to 1800s]

scale n b1425 [type of bowl: b1200; "pan on a scale": b1390] (verb use: b1605)

handbarrow n b1450

pump n *as in "water pump"* b1450 (verb use: b1510)

clip n *shears* b1465 (clipping shears: b1435; clipper: b1600; clippers: b1880)

block n *as in "block and tackle"*

cap n *sealer* (verb use: b1600)

crop n *as in "riding crop"*

crow n *crowbar* [obs. type of hook: b1570; obs. type of knocker: b1600]

loom n *weaving machine* [gen. "tool": b900; obs. "penis": b1450 to 1500s]

press n/v *as in "garlic press"* [spec. "printing press": b1570]

probe n [type of investigation: b1930] (verb use: b1650)

rattrap n [fig. use: b1870]

skewer n (verb use: b1705)

spring n *metal coil*

stilt n *walking devices* [type of handle: b1325; as in "a house on stilts": b1730]

turnstile n

whorl n

Travel/Transportation

alley n b1365 ["bowling alley": b1500] (alleyway: b1790)

dray n *type of wagon* b1375 (verb use: b1860)

footbridge n b1375

galiot n *type of sailing vessel* b1375

halyard n b1375

shipmaster n b1375

transport v b1375 [obs. "move residence": b1570 to 1600s] (noun use:

b1615; transportation: b1540)

argonaut n b1400

carriage n *vehicle* b1400

hull n *as in "ship's hull"* b1400

lighter n *type of barge* b1400

packsaddle n b1400

perk v *walk insolently* b1400 ["raise," as in "perk one's ears": b1600; as in "perk up": b1670] (perky: b1855)

sailer/sailor n b1400

ship v b1400

skipper n *captain* b1400 (verb use: b1895)

thoroughfare n *pathway* b1400 ["main highway": b1570]

tramp v *walk* b1400 ["stomp": b1600] (noun use: b1800)

wayside n b1400

forecastle n b1410

bow n *bow of a boat* b1415

mizzen n *type of sail* b1420 (mizzenmast: b1450)

compass n *navigation tool* b1425

fare n *first a paid journey, then the cost of the journey* b1425 [obs. "travel": b1120 to 1700s; obs. "travelers": b1350 to 1600s; obs. "road": b1450 to 1700s]

gallop v b1425 (noun use: b1525)

itinerary n *route* b1425 ["plan of travel": b1870] (adj use: b1570)

naval adj b1425 [gen. "of ships": b1630]

portage n b1425 (verb use: b1865)

tiller n *part of steering mechanism* b1425

departure n b1445 ["deviation": b1700]

causeway n b1450 (causey: b1350)

paddle n *type of oar* b1450 ["stirring tool"; "gaming device": b1670] (verb use: b1680)

slip n *boat landing* b1450

tollhouse n b1450

wayfarer n b1450 (arch. wayfare n: b1450; wayfaring: b1540; arch. wayfare v: b1570)

barge n *river transport* [type of sailing vessel: b1350]

catch n *type of boat*

craft n *vehicles, as in "spacecraft"*

deck n *on ships* [gen. "platform": b1870; slang, as in "hit the deck": b1930]

dock n *place near the pier* ["the pier itself": b1830; applied to land transport: b1930] (verb use: b1600)

oarsman n (oarswoman: b1825)

perambulate v

pram n *type of boat* ["dinghy": b1870]

range v *roam*

sleigh n (Am) (verb use: b1730)

traverse v *travel across*

Emotions/ Characteristics

complain v b1370 [fig., as in "the car complained in cold weather": b1670] (complaint: b1380)

feeling n *emotion* b1370

pleasure n *desire, as in "what's your pleasure"* b1370 ["something pleasing": b1450] (verb use: b1540; pleasance: b1400; pleasureable: b1580)

consolation n b1375 (obs. consolate v: b1500 to 1800s; console: b1670)

delicacy n *obs. hedonism; luxury* b1375 [u1700s]

delicate adj *obs. hedonistic, luxurious, indulgent* b1375 [u1700s]

derring-do n b1375

disposition n *mood, temperament* b1375

felicity n b1375

fury n b1375 ["inspiration": b1570]

gladsome adj b1375

hearty adj b1375

just adj *righteous; fair; legal; deserved* b1375 [obs. "precise": u1800s]

lamentation n b1375 (lament

v: b1450; lament n: b1570)

lethargy n b1375 (lethargic: b1400)

niggard adj/n b1375 (niggardly adj/adv: b1530)

perturb v b1375

pompous adj *stately; arrogant* b1375 (pomposity "stateliness": b1450; pomposity "arrogance": b1620)

remorse n b1375 [arch. remord "cause remorse": b1470; remorseful, remorseless: b1595]

terror n b1375 [fig., as in "a terror on the golf course": b1900]

tremor n *obs. extreme fear* b1375 [u1400s]

alarm n *gen. concern* b1380 ["signal of alarm": b1550; "signal sound": b1600] (verb use: b1590)

boon adj *genial, as in "boon companion"* b1380

fierce adj b1380 ["proud": b1240]

impatient adj b1380 [obs. "testing patience": u1600s]

pleasance n *pleasure* b1380

blue adj *depressed* b1385 (blues: b1745)

ecstasy n b1385 [obs. type of psychological state: b1600 to 1800s] (ecstatic adj: b1590; ecstatic n: b1660)

ardor n b1390

coy adj b1390 [obs. "still": b1340 to 1600s] (arch. verb use: b1585)

humiliation n b1390 (humiliate: b1535)

insolent, insolence adj, n b1390 (insolency: b1500)

temerity n b1390 ["chance": b1700] (temerarious: b1525)

terrible adj *terrifying* b1390 ["inspiring dread": b1600; "atrocious": b1930]

contempt n b1395 (obs. verb use: u1800s; contemptible: b1385; contemn v: b1425; contemptuous: b1595)

distraught adj b1395 (dis-

tract adj "distraught": b1340)

poignant adj *sharp to emotions or senses* b1395 [obs. "pointy": u1600s]

adulation n b1400 (adulate: b1780)

allegiance n b1400 (allegiant adj: b1615)

coltish adj b1400

confidence n *trust of someone else; trust in oneself* b1400

delightful adj b1400 [obs. "delighted": b1600 to 1600s]

demerit n *quality, both bad and good* b1400 ["demerit point": b1930]

demure adj b1400

desperate adj b1400 (desperation: b1370; obs. desperacy: b1630 to 1800s)

diabolic adj b1400 (diabolical: b1505; diabolism: b1610)

doubtful adj *causing doubt; feeling doubt* b1400 ["unlikely": b1870]

enjoy v b1400 [obs. "be joyful": u1500s] (enjoyment: b1535; enjoyable: b1645)

fleer v *sneer* b1400 [obs. "grin". u1700s] (noun use: b1605)

freehearted adj *frank, generous* b1400

frown v b1400 (noun use: b1585)

glout v *scowl, frown* b1400

greathearted adj b1400

habitude n *arch. character* b1400

headstrong adj b1400

heavy-hearted adj b1400

ill at ease adj b1400

impetuous adj b1400

infelicity n b1400 (infelicitous: b1835)

jocund adj b1400

jubilation n b1400 (jubilate: b1645; jubilant: b1670; jubilize: b1670)

lickerish adj *greedy, hungry* b1400

loyalty n b1400 (loyal: b1635)

mansuetude n *arch. docility*

b1400 (mansuete adj: b1450)

peevish adj *irritable* b1400 [obs. "silly"; "malevolent": u1700s] (peeved: b1910)

pleasing adj b1400

proudhearted adj b1400

quiddity n b1400

rash adj *describing people* b1400 [describing actions: b1570] (obs. adv use: b1450)

set adj *determined* b1400

simplehearted adj b1400

sneer v b1400 (noun use: b1710)

stoic n b1400 (adj use: b1600; stoicism: b1630)

temper n *mood* b1400 [arch. "compromise": b1600; "calmness": b1600; "tendency toward anger": b1830]

unfaithful adj b1400 ["not of religious faith": b1350]

vexation n b1400 (vex: b1425; vexatious: b1535)

whim-wham n b1400

zeal n b1400 (zealous: b1530; gen. zealot: b1650; zealotry: b1660)

agog adj b1405

behave v b1410 (behavior: b1425)

disloyalty n b1410 (disloyal: b1420; obs. disleal: b1590)

content v *sated* b1420 (adj use: b1400; contentment: b1440; contented: b1445)

dejection n *depression* b1420 [obs. "humiliation": u1600s] (deject: b1500; dejected: b1585)

abhor v b1425 (abhorrent: b1620)

audacity n *boldness* b1425 ["obnoxious boldness": b1570] (audacious: b1550)

bellicose adj b1425

contemn v *treat with contempt* b1425 (contempt: b1400)

credulity n b1425 (credulous: b1580)

fidelity n b1425 [fig., as in "high-fidelity reproduction": b1570]

halfhearted adj b1425

heartsease n *serenity* b1425

irksome adj b1425

lighthearted adj b1425

obsequious adj *gen. serving* b1425 ["servile": b1630]

tenacity n b1425 ["toughness": b1570] (tenacious: b1610)

saturnine adj *given to inertia* b1435 ["related to Saturn": b1380]

complacence n b1440 (complacency: b1645; complacent: b1770)

cupidity n *greed* b1440

fainthearted adj b1440

scrupulous adj b1445 (scruples: b1500)

amity n b1450

averse adj b1450 (aversion: b1600)

bawl v *weep* b1450

calumny n b1450 (calumniate v: b1555)

devilish adj b1450

esperance n *arch. hope, anticipation* b1450

gallant adj b1450 ["ostentatious": b1440] (noun use: b1390)

gratitude n b1450

incredulity n b1450

listless adj *without craving* b1450

parsimony n *cheapness* b1450 (parsimonious: b1600)

personable adj b1450

serious adj *solemn* b1450 ["critical": b1600]

squeamish adj b1450 (rare squeam v: b1600; rare squeam n: b1800)

strain v *stress* b1450 (noun use: b1400)

unhappy adj *sad* b1450 ["troublesome": b1300; "unfortunate": b1670]

vivacity n b1450 (vivacious: b1645)

misbehave v b1455 (misbehavior: b1470)

alacrity n b1460

frantic adj b1465 ["crazy": b1375; "frenzied": b1530]

affable adj

brass n *audacity*

cheer v *cheer up; encourage* (noun use: b1600)

difficile adj *obs. difficult (stubborn sense)* [u1600s]

diligence, diligent n, adj *perseverance* [obs. "caution": b1340 to 1700s; obs. "expeditiousness": b1500 to 1700s]

discontent adj [obs. "annoyed": b1500 to 1600s] (verb use: b1530; noun use: b1595; discontented: b1494)

dreadless adj *fearless* (obs. adv use: u1500s)

duress n [obs. "cruelty": b1325 to 1600s]

earthy adj *crude* [obs. "dull," from earth, wind, fire, water: b1450 to 1600s]

familiar adj *obs. polite* [u1700s]

gally adj *arch. galled*

glow v *arch. glower*

good nature n (good-natured: b1580)

grovel v (noun use: b1900; groveling adv: b1350; groveling adj: b1470)

habit n *obs. gen. bearing; gen. character, repeated act* [u1500s] (verb use: b1595)

haught adj *arch. haughty* (haughty: b1500)

heartburnings n *jealousy*

heartful adj *arch. with all my heart*

humblesse n *obs. humility* [u1700s]

irascible adj

irk v ["be irked": b1300] (irksome: b1425)

malevolence n (malevolent: b1510; obs. malevolous adj: b1530 to 1700s)

motion n *obs. emotion* [u1700s]

outrage n [obs. "lack of control": b1300 to 1500s] (outrageous: b1325)

pitiable adj

positive adj *optimistic, advantageous* (noun use: b1830)

prejudice n *negative prejudgment* ["harm because of a judgment": b1300] (verb use: b1450; prejudicial:

b1425; prejudge v, preju-
diced adj: b1580)

probity n *good character*

pusillanimous adj

rail v *erupt verbally* [obs.
"joke around": b1530 to
1600s] (noun use: b1530)

remord v *arch. cause remorse*

sincerity n

spirit n *emotion, as in "high
spirits"*

torpor, torpid n, adj (torpefy:
b1830)

unpiteous adj

unpleasant, unpleasing adj
(unpleasantness: b1550;
unpleasure: b1800)

vain adj ["worthless": b1400]

vituperation n (vituperate:
b1545; vituperatory:
b1590; vituperative:
b1730)

wary adj

Thoughts/Perception/ The Mind

attention n b1375

deliberation n b1375 (arch.
deliber v: b1375; deliberate v: b1400; deliberate
adj: b1425)

mystery n *puzzle* b1375

pensive adj b1375

pretend v b1375 [obs. "present, tender": u1600s; obs.
"rationalize": u1700s; obs.
"lay claim": u1700s; obs.
"portend": u1600s] (adj
use: b1915)

unknowable adj b1375 (noun
use: b1730)

verity n b1375

conception n *imagination*
b1380 ["concept": b1630]
(concept: b1560; concep-
tual: b1665)

indifferent adj *impartial*
b1380 [obs. "the same as":
u1700s; "diffident":
b1520] (indifference:
b1445; indifferency:
b1450)

intelligence n b1380 (intelligent: b1510)

agony n *mental suffering*
b1385 ["phys. suffering":
b1730]

attentive adj b1385

dialectic n *type of logic* b1385

inquisitive adj b1390

conjecture n *guess* b1395
[obs. "prophecy": b1385
to 1600s] (verb use:
b1425; conjectural:
b1535; obs. conject:
b1450 to 1700s)

decide v *resolve* b1395
["make a judgment":
b1770; "come to a deci-
sion": b1870] (decision:
b1455)

imaginary adj b1395

aim n/v *obs. conjecture*
b1400 [u1800s]

apprehend v *comprehend*
b1400

curiosity n *nosiness* b1400
["inquisitiveness": b1615;
"being curious": b1600;
"something curious":
b1670] (curious: b1470)

predict v b1400 [obs. "preordain": b1400] (noun use:
b1700)

foreknow v b1400 (foreknowledge: b1535)

idea n *ideal* b1400
["thought": b1590]

incontinence n *lack of emotional control* b1400 [med.
sense: b1770]

intellect n b1400 (intellectual: b1400; obs. intellec-
tion: b1450 to 1700s; in-
tellective: b1500)

mania n *psychiatric sense*
b1400 [gen. use: b1700]
(maniac adj: b1600; mani-
acal: b1605; maniac n:
b1765; manic: b1905)

ponder v b1400 [var. obs.
meanings of "evaluate,
weigh": b1350 to 1600s]
(obs. ponderate v: b1450
to 1700s; ponderous:
b1425)

rapt adj *fig. carried away, to
heaven; obs. phys. carried
away, raped* b1400 ["mes-
merized": b1530]

rational adj *able to reason*
b1400 ["sane": b1450]

surmise n *conjecture* b1400
[obs. type of leg. claim:

b1400 to 1700s] (verb use:
b1600)

syllogism n b1400

touched adj *crazy* b1400

unthinkable adj b1400 (un-
think: b1600)

wish n *something desired*
b1400 ["making a wish":
b1450]

worldly-wise adj b1400

assume v *take for granted*
b1420 (assumption:
b1630)

instinct n b1420

acuity n b1425

certitude n b1425

cognition n *knowing* b1425

forecast n *obs. forethought,
plan* b1425 [u1700s]

mental adj b1425

metaphysical adj b1425
(metaphysic: b1390;
metaphysician: b1470;
metaphysics: b1570)

mind's eye n b1425

talent n *mental ability* b1430
[obs. "inclination": b1300
to 1600s; gen. "aptitude":
b1700; "talented person,"
"star": b1830]

memorable adj b1440

madwoman n b1450 (madman: b1350)

maturity n *obs. deliberation*
b1450 [u1700s]

mother wit n *natural wit*
b1450

oblivious adj b1450

permission n b1450

estymate n *mind power* b1465

cogitable adj *able to be cogi-
tated upon*

decern v *obs. decide* [u1600s]

dream v *hope* (noun use:
b1900)

insense v *impart understanding*

intent adj

lenity n *leniency* (leniency:
b1780; lenience: b1800)

logical adj *related to logic*
["reasoning": b1670; "reasonable": b1870]

notion n *concept* ["inkling":
b1630]

perpend v *arch. ponder*

prevision n *foresight* (verb
use: b1895)

recognizance n *obs. cognizance* [u1700s]

reject v *ignore* ["say no to":
b1570]

rememoration n *arch. memory, remembrance*

riddle v *ponder* ["quiz":
b1575]

study n/v *examination, scrutiny*

stupefy v *make stupid*
["stun": b1590]

suspect v (suspicion: b1300)

unknow v *not know* ["forget":
b1600]

vision n *foresight* ["imagination, goal": b1930]

wit n *as in "have your wits
about you"*

Love/Romance/Sex

bawd n *madam or prostitute*
b1375 (obs. bawdstrote:
b1300 to 1400s; obs. baw-
dry: b1400 to 1700s)

married adj b1375

tryst n *dalliance; obs. gen.
meeting* b1375

wedding ring n b1395

beloved adj/n b1400

cantharsis n *Spanish fly*
b1400

contract v *get engaged* b1400

deflower v *take virginity*
b1400 (defloration:
b1450)

divorce n b1400 (verb use:
b1450)

heartbreak n b1400 (heartbreaking: b1595; heart-
breaker: b1665)

love knot n b1400

sex act n b1400

truelove n *sweetheart* b1400

unmarried adj b1400

lascivious adj b1450

libidinous adj b1450

lovemaking n b1450

passion n b1450 ["desire":
b1250; "enthusiasm":
b1640]

valentine n *sweetheart* b1450
[type of card: b1830]

venereal adj b1450 [describ-
ing disease: b1670]

wittol n *arch. knowing cuckold*
b1450 [gen. "fool": b1600]

assure v *obs. betroth* [u1500s]

callet n *prostitute*

couple v *have sex* (obs. couplement: b1550 to 1700s)

dove n *term of endearment*

gender v *arch. copulate*

honest adj *chaste*

honey n *term of endearment*

leap v *arch. have sex* (noun use: b1630)

lewd adj *lascivious, vulgar* [obs. "secular": b900 to 1800s; obs. "bumbling": b1450 to 1700s]

love n *obs. lover; sex* [u1600s] (verb use: 1900)

lovesick adj

paramour n *lover* (obs. "love": u1500s; obs. adv use "for love": b1300 to 1600s)

procreate v (procreant: b1590)

satyriasis n *male nymphomania*

sole adj *arch. celibate*

sterile adj *unable to reproduce* ["germ-free": b1670]

union n *wedding*

venery n *seduction*

Family/Relations/Friends

baby n b1380 (verb use: b1745)

daughter-in-law n b1385

infant n b1385 (infancy: b1400)

blood brother n b1400

consanguinity n *blood relationship* b1400

family n *lineage* b1400 ["household": b1530; as in "family of nations": b1600] (adj use: b1605)

father-in-law n b1400

mother-in-law n b1400

stepdame n *arch. stepmother* b1400

clan n *spec. to Scots* b1425 [gen. use: b1530]

fraternal adj b1425

grandfather n b1425 (granddaddy: b1760; grandpapa, grandpappy: b1770; granddad: b1785; grandpa: b1890; grandpop: b1900)

grandmother n b1425

(granny: b1565; grandmamma: b1770; grandma: b1800)

parent n b1425 (adj use: b1670; parental: b1625)

granduncle n b1450 (grandaunt: b1830)

paternal adj b1450

paternity n b1450

sister-in-law n b1450

stepbrother, stepsister n b1450 (stepdaughter, stepson, stepfather, stepmother: b900; stepchild: b1000; stepparent: b1890)

breed n *line of ancestry* b1465 ["lineage": b1500]

fall v *be borne* (noun use: b1900)

genetrix n *mother*

genitor n *arch. parent*

legitimate adj *as in "a legitimate child"* [gen. use: b1670] (verb use: b1500)

only-begotten adj *arch. being the only child*

orphan n (verb use: b1815)

Holidays

jubilee n *type of celebration; time of celebration* b1400 ["celebratory joy": b1530]

Games/Fun/Leisure

pawn n *in chess* b1375 [gen. "tool": b1600]

recreation n b1400 [obs. lit. and fig. "nourishment": u1600s]

straight n *type of poker hand* b1400

trey n b1400 [gen. "threesome": b1900]

draughts n (Brit) *checkers* b1425

king n *in chess* [in cards: b1570]

man n *marker, game piece*

stake n *wager* [interest, as in "a stake in the outcome": b1800] (verb use: b1570)

whirligig n

Sports

bowl n *related to bowling* b1400 (verb use: b1440; bowls: b1495; bowler, bowling: b1500)

cartwheel n b1400 (verb use: b1920)

football n b1400

olympiad n b1400

quoit/quoits n b1400

athlete n b1425 (athletics: b1605; athletic adj: b1640)

relay n *fresh hunting dogs* b1425

handball n *in a game similar to football* b1450 [the game: b1600]

exercise n

furlong n *obs. running track* [u1500s]

golf n

javelin n (javelot: b1440)

rod n *in fishing*

Professions/Duties

draper n (Brit) *cloth dealer* b1375

lapidary n *gem cutter* b1375 [obs. "gem expert": u1700s]

lieutenant n b1375 [type of mil. title: b1570]

packer n b1375

spinster n *spinner* b1375 [obs. "unmarried woman": b1700 to 1900s; "old maid": b1730]

interpreter n b1385 (interpretress: b1800)

logician n b1385

arbiter n b1390

menial n *servant* b1390 (adj use: b1390)

ranger n *as in "forest ranger"* b1390

mercenary n *hired hand* b1395 ["hired gun": b1530] (adj use: b1535)

alewife n *keeper of an alehouse* b1400

comptroller n b1400

falconer n b1400

glover n b1400

manservant n b1400

metalsmith n b1400

registrar n b1400

secretary n b1400 [obs. "confidant": u1800s]

shoemaker n b1400

skinner n *skin-seller* b1400 ["remover of skins": b1700; "teamster": b1870]

substitute n *pertaining to people* b1400 [pertaining to things: b1600]

umpire n b1400 [in sports: b1730] (verb use: b1610; ump n: b1915; ump v: b1930)

watchman n *guard* b1400

inquisitor n b1405

fishwife n b1425

guard n *person or thing that guards* b1425 [obs. "guardianship": u1700s; "safeguard": b1600] (verb use: b1500)

plumber n b1425 (plumbery: b1450; plumb v: b1900)

historian n b1440

bricklayer n b1445

assistant n b1450 (assistance: b1425)

clockmaker n b1450

governess n b1450

ironworker n b1450

magnate n b1450

standard-bearer n b1450

director n b1455 (directress: b1580)

caterer n

grocer n [obs. "wholesaler": b1375 to 1600s]

scoutwatch n *arch. guard*

sewster n *arch. seamstress*

supervisor n (supervise: b1590; supervision: b1650)

Business/Commerce/Selling

hawk v *as in "hawking wares"* b1390

freight n/v b1400

marketplace n b1400

customer n b1410 ["customs officer": b1400; fig., as in "a tough customer": b1590]

retail n b1420 (noun use: b1415; adj use: b1605)

hawker n *vendor* b1425

mint n *coin factory* b1425 [obs. "coin": b700] (verb use: b1550)

wholesale n b1425 (adj use: b1645; verb use: b1800; wholesaler: b1860)

barter n/v b1440

market price n b1450

retainer n *as in "a lawyer on retainer"* b1455

incorporate v b1465 [gen. use: b1400]

market v

merchandry n

price v *set cost* ["find out the cost": b1870]

The Workplace

pension n b1375 [obs. "wages": b1375 to 1800s]

workmanship n *craftsmanship* b1375 [obs. "work done": b1375 to 1800s]

mystery n *craft* b1390

office n *workroom* b1395

servile adj *appropriate for slaves* b1400 ["slavish": b1570] (servility: b1600)

recompense n/v b1425 (obs. recompensation: u1700s)

workday n b1450 (workaday n: b1200)

discharge v *fire, remove from duty*

emolument n *compensation*

industry n ["manufacture": b1570]

journeyman n ["tyro": b1570] (journeywoman: b1770)

servitude n

shop n *as in "workshop"*

varlet n *arch. worker* ["scoundrel": b1570] (varletry: b1610)

Finances/Money

cent n b1375 ["100": b1375]

wealthy adj *prosperous* b1375 [obs. "happy": u1500s; rich: b1430]

coin n *money* b1380 ["wedge": b1305] (verb use: b1340)

contribution n *tribute, tax* b1390 [gen. use "payment": b1600] (contribute: b1530)

customs n b1390

fee n b1395 ["feudal estate": b1300]

inheritance n b1395 (inherit: b1325)

accounting n b1400 (accountant: b1455)

enrich v *make rich* b1400 ["add to": b1600]

expense n b1400 (verb use: b1910)

lucre n b1400 (obs. lucrous: b1530 to 1700s; lucrative: b1425)

mammon n *wealth* b1400 (mammonist: b1550)

mortgage n b1400 ["dead pledge": b1395] (verb use: b1500)

nest egg n b1400

paper money n b1400

penury n *poverty* b1400 ["stinginess": b1670]

sixpence n b1400

bill n *payment due* b1405 (verb use: b1870)

annuity n b1415

control v *audit* b1425

revenue n b1425

audit n/v b1435 (verb use: b1560; auditor: b1935)

implement n b1445 ["tool": b1540]

countinghouse n b1450

creditor n b1450

net adj *as in "net earnings"* b1450 (verb use: b1760; noun use: b1905; net income: 1760s)

purser n b1450

stipend n b1450

surcharge v b1450 (noun use: b1500)

accountant n b1455

charge n *credit* b1460 (verb use: b1800)

moneyed adj b1460

book n *as in "financial books"*

crown n

even adj *square*

indebted adj [gen. sense of obligation: b1225]

liable adj

monies n ["coins": b1300]

principal n (adj use: b1300)

purchase v *buy* [var. obs. meanings of "procure" by var. means: b1325 to 1800s] (noun use: b1600)

return n *as in "return on investment"*

white n *money*

Language and Speaking

construe v b1375 (noun use: b1845)

grammar n *study of grammar* b1375 ["grammar rules": b1870]

term n b1380 (verb use: b1570)

asterisk n b1385 ["tiny star": b1700]

adjective adj/n b1390

adverb n b1400

circumlocution n b1400

conjunction n b1400

contumely n b1400

eloquence, eloquent n, adj b1400

etymology n *a word history* b1400 ["study of word histories": b1670] (etomologize: b1530)

grammarian n b1400

mother tongue n b1400

noun n b1400

participle n b1400 (participial: b1570)

plural adj b1400 [gen. "multiple": b1600]

preposition n b1400 [obs. "prefix": b1570 to 1600s]

present tense n b1400

preterit n *the past tense* b1400

quote n *quotation* b1400

sense n *as in "the sense of a word"* b1400

simile n b1400 ["similarity": 1600s only] (similize: b1630)

singular n b1400

syllable n b1400 (verb use: b1400; syllabic adj: b1730)

synecdoche n *type of figure of speech* b1400

verb n b1400 (verb use: b1940; verbal: b1495)

word for word adv b1400

hyperbole n b1425

capital, capital letter n b1430 (cap: b1900)

derivative n b1450

imperative n b1450 (adj use: b1530)

locution n b1450

pronunciation n b1450

synonym n b1450 (synonymous, synonymy: b1610)

misnomer n b1455

article n *as in "definite article: the"*

colloquy n

diphthong n

orthography n *spelling*

possessive adj/n

pronoun n

sentence n

Contractions

'cause contr b1450

Literature/Writing

script n *gen. writing* b1375 [in theatre: b1900] (verb use: b1935)

allegory n b1385 (allegoric: b1395; allegorical: b1530; allegorize: b1590; allegorist: b1690)

inscription n b1385

scribe n b1385 [gen. "writer": b1535]

almanac n b1390

blank adj *not written on* b1400 [obs. "without color": b1350 to 1600s; as in "blank stare": b1570] (noun use: b1555)

doggerel adj b1400 (noun use: b1630)

farce n b1400

finis n b1400 [gen. use: b1700]

glossary n *a collection of glosses* b1400 (gloss: b1550)

glossator n *gloss writer* b1400 (glossarist: b1775)

legible adj b1400

pamphlet n b1400 (pamphleteer n: b1600)

poet laureate n b1400

poetry n b1400 [obs. "tale, fiction": u1600] (poesy: b1350; poetic: b1530)

preamble n b1400 [leg. sense: b1600]

preface n b1400 (verb use: b1620; prefatory: b1675)

register n/v *type of book* b1400

scan v *as in "scan poetry"* b1400 [as in "the poetry scans": b1870]

schedule n *list* b1400 [obs. "note": u1600s; "appen-

dix": b1420; "timetable":
b1865]

scroll n b1400

volume n *book* b1400 ["part
of a series": b1530]

compose v *write, create*
b1405 [obs. gen. "build":
concurrent; "compose
music": b1600] (composi-
tion: b1570)

alphabet n b1425 (alphabetize: 1800)

analogy n b1425

commentary n *written com-
ments* b1425

edition n b1425 [gen. use:
b1630]

epilogue n *in books* b1425 [in
plays: b1600]

fabulous adj *like a fable*
b1425 [superlative use:
b1610] (fabular: b1685)

figment n b1425

handwriting n b1425 (handwrite v: b1830)

illiterate adj b1425 (noun
use: b1630; illiteracy:
b1660)

quill n *type of pen* b1425

certificate n *type of document*
b1440 [obs. "certification,
assurance": b1420 to
1600s] (verb use: b1770;
certification: b1425)

column n *space for copy on a
newspaper* b1440 ["section
written by a columnist":
b1785] (columnist: b1920;
column inch: b1940)

introduction n b1440

document n b1450 [obs.
"something taught," "doc-
umentation": u1800s]

epigram n b1450

folio n *page* b1450 [size of
book: b1535; type of book:
b1630]

literate adj b1450 (noun use:
b1550; literacy: b1885)

prosody n b1450

vellum n b1450 (adj use:
b1565)

scribble v b1460 (noun use:
b1580)

author n *writer* [gen. "creator": b1350; arch. "fa-
ther": late ME] (authoress:
b1500)

enchiridion n *handbook*

entry n *as in "encyclopedia
entry," "journal entry"*

manual n

margin n *as in "margin of a
page"* (marginal: b1575;
marginalia: b1835)

measure n

minutes n *as in "minutes of a
meeting"* (verb use: b1570)

spell v *use letters to construct
a word* ["read laboriously,
letter by letter": b1400]

story n *entertaining tale* [as in
"newspaper story": b1900]

Communication

communication n b1385 [obs.
"discourse": u1700s]
(communicative: b1400;
communicate: b1530;
communicatory: b1650)

protest n *declaration of dissent*
b1400 [gen. "declaration":
b1400; "picketing, etc.":
b1970] (verb use "declaration": b1400; verb use
"dissent": b1600; protesta-
tion "declaration":
b1350)

publication n *gen. dissemination* b1400 [spec., as in
"magazine publication":
b1600]

salute v/n *greet* b1400
["greet with gesture":
b1440]

bill n *ad, as in "post no bills"*

sign n *as in "street sign"*

Visual Arts/ Photography

portraiture n *portraits; portrayal* b1375 (portrait:
b1570; portraitist: b1870)

muse n *one of the Muses*
b1380 [gen. "source of inspiration": b1630]

sculpture n b1395 (verb use:
b1645; sculpt: b1865)

artificer n b1400

tapestry n b1400 ["panorama": b1595]

cameo n *type of carving*
b1425 [as in "cameo ap-
pearance": b1855]

depict v *paint* b1430 [dis-

guise: b1420; fig. "de-
scribe": b1770] (depicture
"depiction": b1530; de-
picture v: b1600)

master n *as in "old masters"*

vignette n *type of design* [type
of photo: b1855; in literature: b1900]

Performing Arts

theater n *the building* b1375
["the art": b1670; "histrionics": b1930] (theatrical:
b1560; theatricals: b1585;
theatrics: b1810)

tragedian n *type of writer*
b1375 [type of actor:
b1600]

tragedy n *type of play* b1375
["sad occurrence": b1510]
(tragic, both senses:
b1535)

amphitheater n b1400

mummer n *actor* b1430
(mum v: b1400)

enact v *act on stage*

part n *theatrical role*

Music

chorister n *choir singer* b1375

cornet n *made of horn* b1375
["type of brass instru-
ment": b1870]

refrain n b1375

chant v *sing; recite in song*
b1390 ["repeat rhythmi-
cally": b1600] (noun use:
b1675)

fingering n b1390 (finger v:
b1450)

strain n *as in "a strain of
song"* b1390

tenor n b1390 ["tenor
singer": b1500]

ballad n b1395

cradlesong n b1400

descant n b1400 (verb use:
b1450)

gittern n *a medieval guitar*
b1400

kithara n *type of stringed instrument* b1400

melodious adj b1400 (melodic: b1825)

musician n b1400

tune n *melody, etc.; as in "in
tune"* b1400 (verb use

"sing": b1500; tuneful:
b1595)

choir n b1405 ["place for
singing": b1300] (verb
use: b1600)

monochord n *type of musical
instrument* b1425

bass n *akin to alto, baritone*
b1450

counterpoint n b1450 (verb
use: b1875)

fiddlestick n b1450

clavichord n b1460

chimes n

drum n (verb use: b1585)

key n *as in "key of G"* [as in
"piano key": b1500]

rebec n *type of stringed instrument*

recorder n

roundelay n

tone n

unison n [fig. "harmony":
b1670]

whew n *obs. type of musical
instrument* [u1400s]

Entertainment

comedy n *story with happy
ending; comedic story*
b1385 [gen. "humor":
b1900] (comedian:
b1605)

comic adj *pertaining to comedy* b1390 ["funny":
b1770] (comical: b1425)

festivity n b1390 (festival:
b1590; festive: b1655)

delectation n *arch. entertainment* b1400

foot v *dance* b1400 ["walk":
b1600; "kick": b1600]

pageant n b1400 (pageantry:
b1610)

tale-teller n b1400

applause n b1425 (applaud:
b1475)

morris dance n b1460

Education

informer n *obs. teacher* b1385
[u1600s]

grammar school n b1400

hook it v *play hookey* b1400

instruction n b1400 (instruct:
b1425; instructive:
b1615)

liberal arts n b1400

pedagogue n b1400 (pedagogy: b1585)

philosophical adj *educated* b1400 ["pertaining to philosophy": b1530]

primer n *reader* b1400 ["introductory text": b1630]

professor n b1400 [arch. "professional": b1570] (prof: b1840)

pupil n *student* b1400 ["orphan": b1400]

schoolhouse n b1400

student n b1400 (rare studentess: b1870)

tutor n b1400 [obs. "guardian": u1600s] (verb use: b1595; tutoress: b1615; tutee: b1930)

erudite adj b1425

graduate n b1425 (grad: b1875)

graduation n b1425

school v *attend school* b1425 ["teach": b1445]

faculty n b1450

spelling n b1450

commencement n

degree n (verb use: b1570)

fellow n

graduate v *award a degree* ["earn a degree": b1830] (graduation: b1425)

truant n [obs. "Fagin-type beggar": b1300 to 1600s] (adj use: b1565; verb use: b1580; truantry: b1500; truancy: b1785)

Religion

devilry n b1375 (deviltry: b1790)

graceless adj b1375 ["inelegant": b1670] (graceful: b1425)

infernal adj b1375 [gen. use: b1770]

pagan n b1375 (paganism: b1450)

theology n b1375 ["non-Christian theology": b1670]

confessor n *type of priest* b1380

induct v *spec. to rel.* b1380 [gen. use: b1605; mil. use: b1935]

canonize v b1385

communion n b1385 [secular use: b1630]

dedication n b1385 (arch. dedicate adj: b1425; dedicate v: b1450)

schism n b1385

consecrate v b1390 (consecration: b1385)

sanctity, sanctitude n b1390

sanctify v b1395

benediction n *blessing* b1400

burnt offering n b1400

custode n b1400

decalogue n *the Ten Commandments* b1400

enlighten v b1400 [gen. use: b1590] (enlightenment: b1675)

Eucharist n b1400

exorcism n b1400 (exorcise: b1540)

fane n *temple or church* b1400

first cause n *the creator* b1400

gentile n b1400 (adj use: b1470)

goddess n b1400 [fig. use: b1350] (god: b900)

grey friar n b1400

high priest n b1400 (high priestess: b1645)

holy city n b1400

Holy Spirit n b1400 (holy ghost: b900)

Last Judgment n b1400

Law of Moses n b1400

Lord's Supper n b1400

man of God n b1400

monastery n b1400

neophyte n *religious convert* b1400 [gen. "beginner": b1600]

papacy, papal n, adj b1400

parochial adj *of a parish* b1400 ["provincial": b1870]

Passion Sunday n b1400

Passion Week n b1400

pew n b1400

prince of peace n b1400

profane v b1400 (adj use: b1450; profanation: b1555; profanity: b1570; profanatory: b1853)

sequence n b1400 [gen. use: b1600]

synod n b1400

tract n *type of Scripture* b1400

unction n *act of anointing* b1400

venial sin n b1400

crucifixion n b1410

excommunicate v b1425 (adj use: b1530)

gradual n *type of hymnal* b1425

spirituality n b1425 [arch. "clergy": concurrent]

motor n *motive force—God; mover* b1450

tract n *as in "religious tract"* b1450

vocation n *religious calling* b1450

antipope n

christen v *commemorate a beginning* (christening: b1300)

deaconess n [modern sense: b1630] (deacon: b900)

dispense v

episcopal adj

laity n

ministry n

mosque n

piety n [obs. "pity": b1425 to 1630]

pious adj [arch. gen. "loyal": b1630] (piosity: b1930)

presbytery n

priesthood n *the clergy* ["being a priest": 900]

pseudapostle n *obs. false apostle* [u1700s]

semigod n

spirit n *as in "Holy Spirit"*

Society/Mores/Culture

commoner n b1360 ["citizen": b1325 to 1600s]

morality n b1375 (morals: b1615)

obeisance n *type of bow* b1375 [obs. "obedience": u1600s]

pollute v *corrupt morally* b1375 ["corrupt physically": b1570] (polluted, pollution: b1400; pollutant: b1895)

simple n b1375

womankind n b1375 [obs. "an individual woman":

u1800s] (womenkind: b1400)

humble v *bow* b1380 ["humiliate": b1500]

humanity n b1385 (humankind: b1645)

femininity, feminity n b1390 (femineity: b1830)

jack n *Everyman* b1390 [way to address a stranger: b1900]

castellan n *occupant of a castle* b1400

converse n arch. *social interaction* b1400 (verb use "talk": b1630; obs. verb use "communicate": b1585)

ethic n *ethics* b1400 ["principles," as in "work ethic": b1900]

evildoer n b1400

geste n *deportment* b1400

injustice n b1400 (obs. injust adj: b1470 to 1700s)

man-child n b1400

moralize v *discuss moral aspects* b1400 ["preach": b1670] (moral v: b1630)

private adj *as in "private citizen"; not public; personal, as in "private property"* b1400 ["secret, unpublicized": b1500; "reclusive": b1600] (noun use: b1500; privacy: b1450)

provincial adj *not worldly* b1400 (provincialism: b1830)

public adj b1400 [opp. of private: b1750; related to government: b1900] (noun use: b1500)

refuse n *outcast people* b1400 ["garbage": b1470] (adj use: b1470)

social adj b1400 ["friendly": b1670; "related to society": b1830]

unmanly adj b1400

virtual adj arch. *related to virtue* b1400

vulgar adj *common* b1400 ["ordinary": b1570; "base": b1670]

wisewoman n b1400 (wise man: b1100)

yeoman n *type of landholder*

b1400 [type of servant: b1350] (yeomanry: b1400; yeowoman: b1870)

landholder n b1425

native adj *born in slavery* b1425 ["innate": b1385] (noun use: b1460)

peasant n b1425 [fig. insult: b1570] (peasantry: b1555)

politic adj b1425

courtesan n b1430

freemasonry n b1450

Mr. n b1450 (Mrs.: b1615; Ms.: b1950)

unmannered adj b1450

vagrant adj/n b1450 (vagrancy: b1730)

chatelain n *occupant of a castle* (castelain: b1450; chatelaine: b1845)

compeer n *peer* (obs. verb use: b1630 to 1800s)

mademoiselle n

personage n

Government

community n b1375 [obs. "commoners": u1700s; "things shared": b1570; "group togetherness": b1600]

governance n b1375 (government: b1400)

imperial adj b1375

president n b1375 (rare adj use: concurrent; presidency: b1595; presidential: b1605; presidentess: b1800)

royal adj b1375 (royalty: b1400)

colony n b1385 [Roman mil. settlement: b1400] (colonize: b1625; colonist: b1705; colonial: b1865)

civil adj *pertaining to citizenry* b1390

consul, consulate n b1390

commonweal n *type of governing district, nation* b1400 ["public good": b1350] (commonwealth: b1530)

confederacy n b1400 (confederate adj: b1400; confederation: b1425; confederate n: b1495; confederate v: b1535)

coronation n b1400 (coronate: b1450)

duchy n b1400 (duke: b1150)

dynasty n b1400 [obs. "single instance of ruling": u1800s] (dynast: b1635)

government n b1400

magistrate n b1400

marquess n b1400 (marquis: b1300)

potentate n b1400 (obs. adj use: b1570 to 1700s)

princess n *arch. female sovereign; daughter of a sovereign* b1400 (prince: b1225)

regent n b1400 [educational use: b1900]

treaty n *accord between nations* b1400 ["accord between individuals," obs. "discussion": concurrent] (treat v: b1300; obs. treat n "agreement": b1450 to 1500s; rare treatment: b1830)

viscount n b1400 (viscountess: b1475)

deputy n b1410 (depute: b1400; deputize: b1730)

confederation n *act of uniting* b1425 [type of organization: b1630] (confederacy: b1400)

praetor n b1425

monarch n b1440 (monarchy: b1350)

administrator n b1450 (administratrix: b1625)

baroness n b1450 (baron: b1200)

mayoress n *mayor's wife* b1450 ["female mayor": b1900]

patrician n b1450

regency n b1450

bill n *unapproved law*

province n *municipality* [gen. "region": b1350; "bailiwick": b1630] (provincial adj/n: b1450)

Politics

ambassador n b1375 (ambassadress: b1595)

sedition n *anti-authority action* b1385 (seditious: b1450)

The Adjectived Language

To show how convolute English word evolution can be, we often see longer words replacing perfectly acceptable roots. One example—*care* becoming *carefulness*—is covered elsewhere in this book. Here we'll briefly examine something more subtle, like our tendency to prefer *convoluted* to *convolute* as an adjective in the sentence opening this discussion. *Convolute* was in use by 1700; *convoluted*, by 1770. In some cases like this, adjectives have been converted to verbs, and then converted back to adjectives by adding *-ed*.

In the following list, all italicized words are adjectives. So, in times past, something or someone could be . . .

- *distract* by 1350, *distracted* by 1590

- *fade* by 1350, *faded* by 1500

- *elevate* by 1400, *elevated* by 1555

- *intoxicate* by 1550, *intoxicated* by 1580

- *infuriate* by 1670

vote n (verb use: b1555; voter: b1580)

Life

lifelike adj b1400

long-lived adj b1400

Death

mortal adj b1370 (noun use: b1470)

homicide n *murderer* b1375 ["murder": b1230]

immortal adj b1375 (noun use: b1670; immortality: b1340)

memorial adj b1375 (noun use: b1385; memorialize: b1800)

obit n *memorial service* b1375 [obs. "death": u1600s; obs. "funeral": u1700s; "obituary notice": b1875]

widower n b1375 (widow: b900)

mortification n b1390

capital adj *as in "capital punishment"* b1395

charnel n b1400 (charnel house: b1560)

epitaph n b1400

exequies n *funeral rites* b1400

expire v b1400 [obs. "release the soul": u1700s]

funeral adj b1400

murderess n b1400 (murderer: b1340)

obsequy n *type of funeral rite* b1400

sudden death n *dying suddenly* b1400 [sports sense: b1835]

fatal adj *causing death* b1420 ["fated, preordained": b1380]

cemetery n b1425 [obs. "churchyard": 1400s to 1800s]

extinction n b1425 (extinct: b1450)

mausoleum n b1425

cerecloth n b1450 (cerement: b1605)

black adj *funereal*

corpse n *dead body* [obs. "body, dead or alive": b1275 to 1700s] (corps: b1275; slang verb use: b1870)

entomb v

execute v *kill*

finishment n *death*

funeral n (adj use: b1400; funerary: b1695)

go v *die*

hangment n *arch. execution by hanging*

late adj

lyke-wake n *watch over the dead*

spirit n *soul after death*

starve v *die of lack of food* [gen. "die from var. causes": b1000]

wake n *as in "Irish wake"* (verb use: b1350)

War/Military/Violence

dagger n/v b1375

disarm v b1375 [fig. "render harmless": b1630]

foin n/v *stab at* b1375

man-at-arms n b1375

martial adj b1375

stab n/v *lit. stabbing* b1375 [fig. stabbing: b1570]

brain v *hit in the head* b1385

injury n b1385 (injure, injurious: b1425)

mortify v *obs. destroy strength, kill* b1385 [u1700s]

altercation n b1390 (altercate v: b1530)

wartime n b1390

dent v *hit* b1395 (noun use: b1570)

archery n b1400

army n b1400

arrowhead n b1400

artillery n *projectile weapons* b1400 ["gen. weapons": b1470 to 1700s]

battle-ax n *the weapon* b1400

cannon n b1400 (cannonade n: b1555; cannonball: b1665; cannonade v: b1670)

concussion n *as in "a bomb's concussion"* b1400 (concuss: b1600)

espial n *spying* b1400

fortalice n *fortress* b1400 (fort: b1470)

fray n *as in "fracas"* b1400

gore v *pierce* b1400 (noun use: b1565)

longbow n b1400

ordnance n b1400

pillage n b1400 (verb use: b1595)

pipe bomb n b1400

review n b1400 [gen. use: b1565]

set on v *attack* b1400

spearhead n b1400

broil v *brawl, embroils* b1405 (noun use: b1525)

militant adj *in battle* b1415 ["aggressive": b1630] (noun use: b1610; militancy: b1650; militance: b1950)

warlike adj b1420 [obs. "prepared for war": u1700s]

march v b1425 [fig. use: b1670] (noun use: b1575)

cohort n *mil. group* b1425 ["individual friend": b1955]

conflict n/v b1425

gauntlet n *armored glove* b1425

gunpowder n b1425

gunshot n b1425

hostility n *hostile feelings* b1425 ["hostile act": b1630]

incursion n b1425

insurrection n b1425 (insurrect v: b1830)

mangle v b1425

raid n b1425 [nonmilitary sense: b1900] (verb use: b1865; raider: b1865)

rapine n *plundering* b1425

court-martial n b1435 (verb use: b1860)

bombard n *type of cannon* b1440 (noun use: b1600; bombardment: b1705)

civil war n b1440

impregnable adj b1440

invasion n b1440 (invade: b1495)

sallet n *type of helmet* b1440

salute n/v b1440

bloodshed n b1450

crossbow n b1450

culverin n *type of early gun* b1450

dudgeon n *wood used to make a dagger* b1450 [the dagger itself: b1600]

fortification n b1450

helmet n b1450

quartermaster n b1450

military adj b1460 (noun use: b1740)

warfare n b1460

cuirass n *type of armor* b1465 (cuirassier: b1555)

armipotent n *effective as a fighter*

battailous adj *arch. battle-ready*

battery n *artillery* ["gun emplacement": b1450]

blow n *as in "a blow to the head"* [fig., as in "a blow to the ego": b1700]

booty n (adj use: b1440; arch. boot n: 1590s)

column n *type of troop arrangement*

commission n

do v *as in "do in"*

enforce v *obs. ravish, conquer* [u1600s]

escarmouche n *obs. skirmish* [u1800s]

fort n

garrison n [obs. gen. defense: b1300 to 1600s] (verb use: b1570)

gladiator n

hammer n *on a gun*

mine n (verb use: b1670; minefield: b1890)

officer n *mil. leader*

pilliwinks n *type of torture instrument*

pop n/v *hit* ["shoot": b1770]

receive v *obs. accept surrender* [u1400s]

riot n *violent disturbance* [obs. "debauchery": b1225] (verb use: b1770; riotous: b1470)

sally n *origin of attack* ["the attack itself": b1560] (verb use: b1560)

scale n *part of scale armor*

skean n *type of dagger*

slap v *hit* (noun use: b1650)

stock n *as in "stock of a gun"*

swordsman n (sworder: b1600)

trident n

vanguard n [fig. sense: b1870]

wing n

withdraw v

Crime/Punishment/Enforcement

cutpurse n *pickpocket* b1375

defraud v b1375

fob v *cheat, trick* b1375

heinous adj b1375

crime n b1385 [arch. "sin": b1250; obs. "accusation": b1450 to 1600s; fig. use: b1530] (criminal adj: b1400; criminous: b1450; criminal n: b1630)

brigand n *freebooter* b1390 [obs. type of soldier: b1400 to 1700s]

sodomite n b1390 (sodomist: b1895)

false imprisonment n b1400

fine n *monetary penalty* b1400 [arch. gen. "penalty": b1200] (verb use: b1560)

flagitious adj *criminal, villainous* b1400

high treason n b1400

traitress n b1400 (traitor: b1175)

accessory adj b1415 (adj use: b1630)

accessory n *criminal partner* b1415

clemency n b1425 (clement adj: b1460)

penitentiary n b1425

capias n *warrant* b1450

purloin v b1450 [obs. "put away": b1350 to 1600s]

rosary n *arch. counterfeit money* b1450

delict n *minor offense*

gang n (gangster: b1900)

latrociny n *obs. robbery* [u1600s]

multiplier n *obs. counterfeiter* [u1500s]

pickpurse n *arch. pickpocket*

receipt n *obs. receiving stolen goods* [u1700s] (obs. verb use: b1530 to 1700s)

roundhouse n *arch. prison*

The Law

bylaw n b1370 ["group of laws": b1260]

justice of the peace n b1375

license n *freedom; approval;*

written permission b1375 (verb use: b1450)

civil law n b1380

default v b1385 [as in "default on a loan": b1600]

dispense v b1385

motion n *as in "a motion before the court"* b1385 [gen. use: b1570]

client n *leg. client* b1390 ["customer": b1630] (clientele: b1590; clientage: b1625; cliency: b1670)

easement n b1390

court of law n b1400

deposition n b1400

dissolve v b1400

executrix n b1400 (executor: b1300)

habeas corpus n b1400

intestate adj *lacking a will* b1400 (noun use: b1660)

judicial adj b1400

lawmaker n b1400

lawyer n b1400

lease n b1400 (verb use: b1500)

lessor n b1400 (lessee: b1495)

litigious adj b1400

plaintiff n b1400

real adj *as in "real property"* b1400

reversion n b1400 [gen. use: b1600]

sue v *file suit* b1400 [var. obs. meanings of "pursue," including "follow," "court," "proceed": b1150 to 1600s]

codicil n b1420

complainant n b1425

enact v b1425 [obs. "record publicly": u1600s]

subpoena n b1425 (verb use: b1640)

inheritor n b1430 (inheritrix: b1485; inheritress: b1530)

conviction n *guilty verdict* b1440

detention n b1445

evict v *repossess property* b1450 ["remove people": b1570]

exhibit v *show* b1450 (noun use: b1630)

pact n b1450

penal adj b1450 ["incurring penalty": b1630]

probate n b1450 [obs. "proof": u1800s]

recite v *cite* b1450 (recitation: b1485)

triable adj b1450

act n

bar n *lawyer's organization*

barrister n

composition n *arch. formal agreement*

counsel n *leg. advisors* [obs. "gen. group of advisors": b1300 to 1500s; "a single leg. advisor": b1700] (counselor: b1450)

decree n (verb use: b1400)

disable v *leg. sense* [phys. sense: b1500]

discharge v *obs. clear of legal charges* [u1700s]

embracer n *jury-tamperer*

legality n

legist n *leg. expert*

libel v *obs. sue* [u1500s]

panel n *jury list* [gen. "jury, group": b1600]

patent n

premises n *property, as in "occupy the premises"* [gen. use: b1630]

ruling n

serve v *as in "serve papers"*

trial n [as in "trials and tribulations": b1570]

void adj (verb use: b1350)

The Fantastic/ Paranormal

centaur n b1375

fantasy n *obs. phantasm* b1375 [u1500s]

faun n b1375

harpy n b1375 [gen. use as insult: b1400]

Hydra n b1375 [fig. use: b1495]

prescience n b1375 (prescient: b1630)

satyr n b1380 [type of ape: b1375; fig. "horny guy": b1800]

fantastic adj b1385 ["whimsical": b1500; "incredible": b1970]

chimera n *spec. type of mythi-* *cal monster* b1390 [gen. "monster": b1600] (chimerical: b1640)

bug n *obs. bugbear* b1395 [u1800s]

cockatrice n *legendary creature* b1400

dryad n b1400

genius n *type of supernatural guardian* b1400 ["guardian angel": b1600] (genius loci: b1605)

giantess n b1400 (giant: b1300)

gorgon n b1400

halcyon n b1400

lamia n *type of monster; witch* b1400

naiad n *type of nymph* b1400

nymph n b1400 ["young woman": b1600]

succubus n b1400 [arch. "prostitute": b1630]

transubstantiation n *changing one substance to another* b1400

water nymph n b1400

palmistry n b1425

sphinx n b1425

precognition n *ESP* b1450 (precognize: b1615)

chiromancy n *palm reading*

cyclops n

ghost n *apparition* [obs. "soul": b900] (verb use: b1610; ghostess: b1870)

monster n *fantastic creature* ["deformed creature": b1300]

phantasm n [obs. "something deceptive": b1225 to 1800s; obs. "charlatan": b1600 to 1600s]

shade, shades n *demon, hell*

supernatural adj

Magic

enchantress n b1375 [fig. use: b1730] (enchanter: b1300)

pyromancy n *divining by fire* b1375

incantation n b1395 (obs. incant v: b1570 to 1600s)

divine, divination v, n b1400

geomancy n b1400

mage n b1400

magic n/adj *magical* b1400

[obs. "spell": u1800s; fig. use: b1630; "producing magic": b1700; "sleight of hand": b1870] (verb use: b1910; magical: b1555)

magician n b1400 [fig. use: b1830]

philosopher's stone n b1400

pythoness n *diviner* b1400

sorcerer, sorceress n b1400

sortilege n b1400

weird adj *magical* b1400 ["odd, strange": b1815]

legerdemain n *magic tricks* b1450 [gen. "trickery": b1570]

raise v *conjure*

spell n *incantation* ["narrative": b900; fig. "heavy influence": b1580] (verb use: b1625)

Interjections

marry interj b1375

oyez interj b1375

Jesus interj b1380

all hail interj b1400

hoy interj b1400

yo interj b1425 ["yes": b1970]

huff interj b1450 [u1600s]

tush interj b1450

yow interj b1450

alack interj

good morning interj (good day: b1150; good-even, good-morrow: b1470; good evening: b1870; good afternoon: b1930)

heave ho interj

heh interj

heigh-ho interj

man interj

mea culpa n

mum interj

shoo interj

what ho interj

whew interj

whoa interj

whoop interj

Slang

chop n *as in "punch in the chops"* b1400

hellhole n b1400

newfangled adj *impressed with new things* b1400 ["new": b1570] (oldfangled:

b1845; newfanglement: b1890)

procurer n *pimp* b1400 (procuress: b1425; procureur: b1600; procure v: b1630)

procuress n *madam* b1425 (procurer: b1400)

butt n *buttocks; end, as in "gun butt"*

chaw v *chew* (noun use: b1710)

easy adj *easily persuaded; promiscuous* (adv use: b1400)

head n *as in "a head for figures"*

lousy adj *bad*

mackerel n *pimp, madam*

pander n *matchmaker, pimp* (verb use: b1605)

rush n *buzz, high, thrill*

walk v *leave, die*

water v *as in "water down a drink"*

whistle n *as in "wet your whistle"*

words n *argument, as in "have words"* (obs. wording "having words": b1565 to 1600s)

yard n *penis*

Insults

losel n *wastrel* b1375

lubber n *clumsy person* b1375 [as in "landlubber": b1600] (lubberly: b1600)

crone n b1390 [used for men: b1670]

shrimp n b1390

chicken n *coward* b1400 (adj use: b1945; chicken out: b1945)

grig n *obs. little person* b1400 [u1600s]

looby n *clod* b1400

milksop n b1400 [obs. "milk and break": u1600s]

ugsome adj *vile* b1400 (ugglesome: b1570)

virago n *mean woman; arch. virile woman* b1400 [obs. gen. "woman": b1000 to 1500s]

harlot n b1425 [obs. "vagabond": b1200 to 1600s; obs. "male worker": u1500s]

pinchpenny adj b1425

slug n *dull person* b1425 ["hateful person": b1970]

cracker n *liar* b1440

dastard n *dastardly person* b1440 [obs. "dolt": b1450 to 1500s] (dastardly: b1570]

beldam n *hag* b1450 [obs. "grandmother": b1450 to 1800s]

chuff n *boor* b1450

gill n *girl* b1450

jackanapes n b1450

bitch n *applied to women* [applied to men: b1350] (bitchy: b1940)

doddypoll n *arch. deadhead*

flibbertigibbet n

gallous adj *deserving of hanging*

grub n *obs. short person* [u1700s] (grubby: b1630)

hag n ["fantastic creature": b1225]

hotspur n *hothead*

precious adj

want-wit adj/n *arch. dimwit*

Phrases

heir apparent n b1375

high time n b1390

sweet tooth n b1395

graven image n *engraved, sculpted image* b1400

here and there adv b1400

high and low adv b1400

mother-naked adj b1400

piping hot adj b1400

salt of the earth n b1400

sergeant at arms n b1400

sleight of hand n b1400

sum total n b1400

thick and thin n b1400

tree of life n b1400

high horse n b1425

hand-to-hand adj b1450

red-letter adj b1450

second best n b1450 (adj use: b1400)

skin and bones n b1450

snail's pace n b1450

have a baby v

General/Miscellaneous

determination, determine n, v *decision, decide* b1355 ["reaching a decision": b1500] (verb use: b1450)

conspiracy n b1360 (conspiration: b1325; conspire v: b1375)

adorn, adornment v, n b1375 (adornment: 1470s)

appropriation n *commandeering* b1375

attribute n b1375

attrition n *wearing down by friction* b1375 ["gradual loss": b1915] (attrite v: b1625; attrit v: b1970)

audience n *as in "audience with the king"* b1375 ["spectators": b1770]

border n/v b1375 (border on v: b1550; borderland: b1815; border line: b1870)

byname n *nickname* b1375

captain n b1375 [naval sense: b1555] (verb use: b1600)

casual adj/n *chance; irregular* b1375 ["unobligated": b1670; "unpressured": b1900; "informal": b1970]

center n *middle; pivot; core* b1375 (verb use: b1590)

demonstration n b1375 ["protest": b1870] (demonstrative: b1395; demonstrate: b1600)

digression n b1375 (digress: b1530)

ensign n *type of badge, symbol* b1375

estimation n b1375 [obs. "estimate": u1700s] (estimate n: b1600; estimate v: b1670)

extremity n b1375 (extreme: b1475)

fate n b1375 (verb use: b1600)

feature n *arch. shape* b1375 [obs. "creature": u1600s; obs. "part of the body": u1700s; "beneficial part": b1695]

guide n b1375 (verb use: b1400; guidance: b1570)

homecoming n b1375

indigence n b1375 (indigent: b1400)

indulgence n b1375 (indulgent: b1510; indulgency: b1570; indulge: b1625)

interchange v/n b1375

legacy n *something bequeathed* b1375 [fig. use: b1600]

liberty n b1375

limit n b1375 (verb use: b1400)

midpoint n b1375

necessity n *something necessary* b1375 [as in "by necessity": b1350; "state of need": b1350]

notify, notification v, n b1375 [obs. "notice": u1600s]

payer n b1375 (payee: b1760)

permutation n b1375

plurality n *being numerous* b1375 ["majority": b1600]

position n b1375 (verb use: b1820)

premise n b1375

proselyte n b1375 (verb use: b1625; proselytess: b1630; proselytize: b1680)

purgation n b1375 [obs. "laxative": u1600s; obs. "menstruation": b1570 to 1700s]

regress n b1375 (verb use: b1555; regression: b1600)

report n *rumor* b1375

resort n *as in "last resort"* b1375

retinue n b1375 [obs. "being in a retinue": u1600s]

rumor n b1375 (verb use: b1595)

scent n *as in "bloodhound following a scent"* b1375 [gen. "odor": b1500] (verb use "feel": b1400; verb use "smell": b1410)

sliver n b1375 (verb use: b1605)

solution n *as in "solution to a problem"; "solid dissolved in liquid"* b1375

stranger n b1375 (verb use: b1605)

submit, submission v, n b1375 (submissive: b1580)

subsidy n b1375

surplus n b1375 (surplusage: b1425)

tranquility n b1375 (tranquil: b1450; tranquilize: b1625)

twosome, threesome n b1375

undertaking n b1375

absence, absent n, v b1380 (absent v: b1400)

accident n b1380

act n b1380

addition n b1380

angle n b1380 (angular: b1600; obs. angulous: b1470)

appearance n *act of appearing* b1380 ["how something looks": b1470]

cadence n *rhythm* b1380 ["rhythm in speech": b1600] (cadency: b1630)

celebrity n *being famous* b1380 [obs. "ceremony": u1700s; "famous person": b1985] (celebrated: b1590; celeb: b1915)

censure n b1380 ["leg. judgment": b1400 to 1800s] (verb use: b1590)

consequence n *result* b1380 ["weight, importance": b1570] (consequent adj: b1410; consequential: b1630)

conservation n *gen. preservation* b1380 ["creating fruit preserves": b1900; "preservation of natural resources": b1930]

continuation n b1380

cycle n b1380 (verb use: b1845)

danger n *possible harm* b1380 [obs. "dominion, arrogance": b1225 to 1800s; obs. "reluctance": b1225 to 1500s] (verb use "endanger": b1500)

difficulty n b1380 [as in "financial difficulty": b1730]

faculty n *ability* b1380

harmony n b1380

talk n *gen. speech* b1380 [spec. "single discussion": b1570]

alter, alteration v, n b1385

auditory n *audience/auditorium* b1385 (auditorium: b1730)

ceremony n b1385 (ceremo-

nial: b1400; ceremonious: b1555)

circuit n *circle* b1385 [as in "electrical circuit": b1750; as in "making the golf circuit": b1870] (verb use: b1450; circuitous: b1650)

clamor n/v *ruckus* b1385

commemoration n b1385 (commemorate, commemorative: b1600)

concourse n *meeting—of water, people, etc.* b1385 [as in "airport concourse": b1865]

connection n *connecting* b1385 (connect: b1450)

contention n *battling* b1385

contradiction n b1385

controversy n b1385 (obs. "controverse": b1600 to 1700s; obs. controversion: 1700s; controversial: b1585)

diffusion n *scattering* b1385 ["dissemination": b1770]

effect n b1385 [obs. "goal": u1600s; obs. "reality": u1700s]

inquisition n b1385 [as in "Spanish Inquisition": b1505]

intrusion n b1385 (intrusive: b1425)

narcotic n b1385 ["illegal drug": b1930] (adj use: b1525; narcotize: b1525)

occasion n b1385 ["special event": b1870] (verb use: b1445)

satisfaction n *contentment* b1385 (satisfy: b1420)

arbitration n b1390 [obs. "authority to make decisions": b1470 to 1600s] (arbitrate: b1590; arbitrator: b1430)

collusion n b1390 (collude: b1525)

comment n b1390 [obs. "commentary": u1800s] (verb use: b1450)

commotion n *public hubbub* b1390 [obs. "mental commotion": u1700s; "fuss": b1630]

compensation n b1390

["pay": b1800] (compensate: b1650)

construction n b1390 (construct v: b1425)

hodgepodge, hotchpotch n b1390

information n b1390

nasty adj/n b1390

objection n b1390 [obs. "attack": u1500s] (object v: b1450)

scrap n *fragment* b1390

augur n *type of oracle* b1395 (verb use: b1605)

calculation n b1395

congruity n b1395 (congruent: b1425; congruous: b1600)

craw n b1395

history n b1395

inclination n b1395 (obs. incline n: b1630)

inspection n b1395 (verb use: b1625; obs. inspect n: b1500 to 1700s)

introduction n b1395 (introduce: b1425; intro: b1830)

mesh n *the spaces in a net* b1395 [the net itself: b1630]

nadir n *opp. of zenith* b1395 [fig. "low point": b1900]

oblivion n b1395 (oblivious: b1450)

retention n b1395

ability n b1400

accent n b1400 (verb use: b1530)

acquisition n b1400 (acquist n: b1630)

activity n b1400

aggregate adj/n/v b1400

amalgam n b1400 (verb use: b1450; amalgamation: b1615; amalgamate: b1620)

amazon n b1400 [gen. "woman warrior": b1550; gen. "muscular woman": b1630]

amenity n b1400

antecessor n *predecessor* b1400

arctic adj/n b1400 [gen. "cold," "remote": b1700]

assistance n b1400 (assistant: b1450; assist v: b1430)

associate adj/n *join* b1400 [as in "associate with criminals": b1670] (noun use: b1535; association: b1535)

augment n/v b1400 (augmentation: b1400)

axis n b1400

backside n *hind part* b1400 ["buttocks": b1530]

backwater n b1400

badge n b1400

beginner n b1400

cancel v *obliterate* b1400 ["stop": b1445] (cancellation: b1425)

caustic adj *lit. burning* b1400 [fig. "burning, sarcastic": b1775] (noun use: b1470)

check n *part of checkered pattern* b1400

chink n *as in "chink in the armor"* b1400 (verb use: b1555)

cinquefoil n *type of plant, architectural design* b1400

close n *as in "bring to a close"* b1400

coequal adj/n b1400 [obs. "of equal age": u1600s]

college n *group, as in "electoral college"; university; clerical community* b1400 ["educational institution": b1565; "charity organization": b1700] (collegian: b1400; collegiate: b1450)

colossus n *Colossus of Rhodes* b1400 [fig. use: b1630] (colossal: b1710)

command n *commandment, order; area of authority* b1400 ["mastery," as in "command of English"]

commentator n b1400 (commentate: b1795)

confine, confines n b1400 (verb use: b1525; confinement: b1650)

consolidation n *gathering* b1400 ["compacting"; "strengthening": b1630] (consolidate v: b1515)

constriction n b1400 [constrict: b1425]

consummation n b1400

contrariety n b1400

convenience n b1400 ["something providing convenience," as in "modern conveniences": b1700] (verb use: b1670; convenient: b1500; conveniency: b1605)

cooperation n b1400 (cooperate applied to things: b1585; applied to people: b1605; cooperative: b1605)

corrode, corrosion v, n b1400 (corrosive: b1395)

crate n *grate* b1400 [type of box: b1670] (verb use: b1875)

crescent n b1400

current n *as in "river current"* b1400

delegate n b1400 (verb use: b1470; delegation: b1820)

designation n b1400 (designate: b1795)

discussion n *conversation* b1400 [obs. "leg. decision": b1340 to 1500s]

disguise n *act of disguising* b1400 [type of outfit: b1600]

domination n b1400 [obs. "region under domination": u1600s] (dominant: b1470; dominate: b1615)

dominion n b1400

drivel n b1400 [arch. "drool, dribble": b1400]

duality n b1400

duration n b1400 (obs. durance: b1450 to 1600s)

effusion, effuse n, v b1400 (effusive: b1665)

elongation n b1400 (elongate v: b1580; elongate adj: b1755)

embattle, embattled v/n b1400

equality n b1400

equation n *equalizing* b1400

evacuate, evacuation v, n *as in "evacuate the bowels"* b1400 [as in "evacuate the town": b1630; "retreat": b1730]

exaltation n b1400 (exalt: b1425; exalted: b1595)

examination n b1400 (examen: b1610)

example n b1400 (verb use: b1450)

excellence, excellent adj/n b1400 (excellency: b1325; excel: b1450)

excess, excessive n, adj b1400 (adj use: b1450)

exclamation n b1400 (exclaim: b1570)

exemplar n b1400

exhalation n b1400

exhortation n b1400 (exhort: b1425)

existence n *reality; state of existing* b1400 ["a being": b1630; "the universe": b1770] (existent: b1565; exist: b1605)

experience n b1400 ["skill gained by experience": b1500; "knowledge gained by experience": b1570] (verb use: b1600)

experiment n b1400

explanation n b1400 (explain: b1425)

exploit n b1400 [obs. "progress": b1400 to 1500s]

expulsion, expel n, v b1400 (expulse: b1450)

extension n *extending* b1400 ["expansion": b1600]

farewell n b1400 (verb use: b1200; adj use: b1670)

ferment, fermentation v, n *be fermented* b1400 ["cause to ferment": b1500] (ferment n: b1450)

fiction n *something invented* b1400 [literature sense: b1600]

filling n b1400

foreboding n b1400 (adj use: b1680; forbode v: b1515)

foundation n *various* b1400

frontier adj/n *border* b1400 ["unexplored border": b1700]

froth n/v b1400 (frothy: b1500)

fugitive adj/n b1400

fume n b1400

gaze n b1400 (verb use: b1560)

gob n b1400

grate n *grating* b1400

hero n b1400 (heroine: b1660)

hesitation n b1400 ["pause": b1730] (hesitance: b1605; hesitancy: b1620)

host n *large group* b1400 ["large army": b1250] (host v: b1425; hostess v: b1930)

imitation n b1400 ["counterfeit": b1670] (adj use: b1840; imitate: b1535)

impediment n b1400 (impede: b1600)

incorporate v b1400 [corporate use: b1465]

infidelity n b1400

institution n *as in "institution of a rule"* b1400

integrity n *phys.* b1400 [moral sense: b1550]

juncture n b1400

labyrinth n b1400 [fig. use: b1550] (verb use: b1830; labyrinthian: b1590; labyrinthine: b1635)

lector n b1400 (lectrice: b1900; lecturess: b1830)

likelihood n b1400 [obs. "likeness": u1600s]

limitation n *limiting* b1400 [obs. "territory": u1500s; "something that limits": b1530]

lop n *material lopped off* b1400 (verb use: b1520)

lotion n b1400

magnitude n b1400 [astronomic sense: b1670]

malediction n b1400 (maledict adj: b1550; maledict v: b1625)

margin n *border* b1400 (margent: b1485; marge: b1555; marginal: b1670)

mass n *large form* b1400

mate n *match* b1400 [type of mil. title: b1500; "spouse": b1570; "part of a pair": b1600]

matron n b1400

maze n *puzzling structure* b1400 (obs. "delirium": b1300)

mediation n b1400 (mediate: b1600)

motion n *moving* b1400

novelty n b1400 ["gadget, doodad": b1930]

obscurity n *something obscure* b1400 [gen. "indistinctness": b1570]

offal n b1400

opportunity n b1400 (opportune: b1425)

oracle n b1400

origin n b1400 (originate: b1655; originality: b1745)

overplus n *overage* b1400

particle n *small part—diminutive of part; tiny bit* b1400

patch n b1400 (verb use: b1450)

peal n b1400 (verb use: b1635)

pentangle n b1400

perception n *perceiving* b1400 ["opinion, image": b1670] (perceptual: b1880; percipience: b1775)

persuasion n b1400 ["type," as in "of the human persuasion": b1870] (persuade, persuasive: b1500)

perversion n b1400

pigment n b1400 [arch. type of spice: concurrent] (verb use: b1900; pigmentation: b1870)

pittance n *tiny amount* b1400 [type of allowance: b1225]

policy n *stated way of handling things; political shrewdness; gen. shrewdness* b1400 [obs. "government": u1700s; obs. "deception": u1800s]

pollution n *polluted state* b1400 ["ejaculation without sex": b1350]

pore, porous, porosity n, adj, n b1400

precinct n b1400 ["headquarters of police precinct": b1900]

preparation n *getting ready* b1400 (preparatory: b1425; prepare: b1450; preparedness: b1590)

prerogative n b1400

presage n *omen* b1400 (verb use: b1565)

presentation n b1400 ["speech, demonstration": b1630; "manner of presenting": b1970]

pressure n *lit. and fig.* b1400

(verb use: b1940; pression
"pressure": b1570)

primacy n b1400

principle n b1400 ["concept
behind": b1830] (princi-
pled: b1645; principles:
b1670)

priority n *preceding; primary
importance* b1400 (prioritize: b1965)

problem n b1400 ["created
challenge," as in "math
problem": b1600] (adj use:
b1895)

prognostic n *sign, omen*
b1400 (prognostication:
b1450; prognosticate:
b1500)

project n *enterprise* b1400
[obs. "plan, design":
b1400 to 1600s; obs. "vi-
sion": b1600 to 1700s]
(obs. verb use: b1450)

proportion n/v b1400 (proportionate: b1400; pro-
portional: b1450)

proscription n b1400 (proscribe: b1425)

provocation, provocative n
b1400 (provoke: b1450)

puncture n *act of puncturing;
the hole itself* b1400 (obs.
punction "puncture":
b1450 to 1700s)

pygmy n b1400

rank n *informal position
achieved* b1400 [formal position achieved: b1600]

readiness n b1400

recapitulation n b1400 (reca-
pitulate: b1570; recap v:
b1930; recap n: b1945)

reception n *receiving* b1400

relapse n b1400 [med. sense:
b1600] (noun use: b1500)

relief n *as in "relief from
pain"* b1400 [type of payment: b1350]

renunciation n b1400 (renounce: b1380; renunci-
ate: b1830)

retribution n b1400

revolution n *one turn* b1400
(revolve: b1670)

rote n *crowd* b1400

rubble n b1400 (verb use:
b1930)

salutation n b1400

second n *the one after first*
b1400

secret adj/n b1400 (obs. verb
use: b1600 to 1700s; se-
crecy: b1470)

session n b1400

shout n/v b1400

shove n b1400

signal n b1400 (verb use:
b1805)

siren n *warning sound* b1400

spout n b1400

stricture n b1400

stupor n b1400 (stuporous:
b1895)

supplement n b1400 (verb
use: b1830; supplemental:
b1605)

susurration n *murmur* b1400
(susurrate: b1630; susurrus
n: b1825)

tag n *as in "rag tag"* b1400

third n *as in "divide into
thirds"; in music* b1400
(verb use: b1450)

tradition n b1400

transmutation n b1400
(transmute: b1450)

triangle n b1400 [fig., as in
"romantic triangle":
b1630]

triumph n *victory* b1400 [obs.
"type of celebration":
b1530 to 1800s] (verb use:
b1510)

undoing n b1400

updraft n b1400

variation n *variance* b1400
["varying": b1530]

verge n *edge* b1400 ["furthest
end": b1600; "brink":
b1630; fig. "end of life":
b1770] (verb use: b1785)

wrongdoer n b1400 (wrongdoing: b1480)

monstrosity n *abnormality*
b1405 ["monstrous crea-
ture": b1670]

correspondence n *correlation*
b1415 (correspond:
b1530; corresponding adj:
b1580; correspondency:
b1590; correspansive:
b1610)

deception n b1415 (deceive:
b1300; deceptive: b1615)

inventory n b1415 (verb use:
b1530)

tenet n b1415

appointment n *scheduled
meeting* b1420

brunt n *full effect, as in "bear
the brunt"* b1420 ["force,
attack": b1380]

consort n *associate* b1420
[obs. "association": b1585
to 1700s; "lover": b1600]
(verb use: b1590)

denizen n b1420 (verb use:
b1570; obs. denize v "naturalize": b1600 to 1700s)

incident n b1420

reprisal n b1420

advocacy n b1425

assertion n b1425 (assert:
b1605)

bygone, bypast adj/n b1425

calamity n *adversity* b1425
["catastrophe": b1570]
(calamitous: b1545)

capacity n b1425 ["potential": b1670] (adj use:
b1900)

catalog n b1425 (verb use:
b1600)

catholicon n *panacea* b1425

collision n b1425 (collide:
b1625)

complication n b1425

compulsion n *compelling*
b1425 [psychological
sense: b1910] (compul-
sive: b1590; compulsory:
b1520)

confluence n b1425 (confluent: b1475)

consultation n b1425 (consult: b1530; consultant:
b1700; consultancy:
b1955)

contaminate, contamination v,
n b1425 (contaminant:
b1925)

content n *as in "the contents
of a box"* b1425

contort, contortion v, n b1425

contraction n b1425 [e.g.,
"can't": b1730]

convene, convention v, n *come
together* b1425 ["bring together": b1570]

crick n b1425

delusion n *deception* b1425
["hallucination": b1570]
(delude: b1410; delusory:
b1500; delusive: b1605)

denunciation n *accusation*
b1425 ["castigation":
b1845] (denounce: b1325;
denunciate: b1595)

detestation, detestable n, adj
b1425 (detest: b1500)

detriment n b1425 (detri-
mental: b1590)

disruption n b1425 (disrupt
v: b1660; disruptive:
b1845)

dissipate, dissipation v, n
b1425

dissonant, dissonance adj, n
b1425

donation n *donating* b1425
["something donated":
b1600] (donor: b1450; do-
nate: b1785)

efficacity n b1425 (efficacy,
efficacious: b1530)

evasion n b1425 (evade:
b1500; evasive: b1725)

exclusion n *act of excluding*
b1425 ["something ex-
cluded": b1670]

excoriate, excoriation v, n
b1425

extraction n b1425

fracture n b1425 (verb use:
b1600)

fragment n b1425 (verb use:
b1820; fragmentize:
b1815)

guardian adj/n b1425

heirloom n b1425

incentive n *something that in-
censes or incites* b1425 ["reward": b1970]

inception n b1425

increment n b1425

indication n b1425 (indicative: b1450; indicate:
b1610)

inequality n b1425

ingredient n b1425 (arch. adj
use: b1470)

injection n b1425 (inject:
b1630)

injunction n b1425 [leg.
sense: b1570] (injunct v:
b1900)

instability, instable n, adj
b1425

intervention n b1425 (intervent v: b1600; intervene
"step in": b1670)

investigation n b1425 (investigate: b1510)

jettison n b1425 (verb use: b1550)

link n *as in "link in a chain"; fig.* b1425 (verb use: b1450)

liquefy, liquefaction v, n b1425 (obs. liquate: b1670 to 1700s)

machination n b1425

mixture n b1425

moderation n b1425

narration n b1425 (narrative adj/n: b1450; narrate: b1660)

negation n b1425 (negate: b1625)

nomination n *proposing for a post or honor* b1425 [obs. "a name": u1700s] (verb use: b1550)

object n *objective* b1425

paucity n b1425 (obs. paucify: b1670 to 1700s)

pedigree n b1425

plenitude n *perfection* b1425 (plentitude: b1615)

precursor n b1425

pretense n *pretending; excuse* b1425

probation n b1425 [leg. sense: b1900]

promise n/v *commitment; portent* b1425 (promissory: b1450)

pulsation n b1425 (pulsate: b1795)

purport n b1425 (verb use: b1530; purported: b1895)

rate n/v *grade, value* b1425

receptacle n b1425

repetition n b1425 (repetitious: b1675)

sobriety n b1425

socket n *mechanical fitting* b1425 [anatomical use: b1630; as in "light socket": b1900]

spangle n b1425 (verb use: b1430)

suspense n b1425 (suspend: b1630; rare suspension: b1670)

trick n/v *deception* b1425 (adj use: b1530; tricker: b1555; trickery: b1800)

tumult n *describing crowds* b1425 [gen. use: b1590] (tumultuous: b1550; tumultuate v: b1630; tumultuary adj: b1670)

wrinkle n *in clothes, etc.* b1425 [on a face: b1450] (verb use: b1525)

commissioner n b1430

inquiry n b1430 [official sense: b1530]

interjection n b1430 (interject: b1580)

microcosm n b1430 (microcosmos: b1200)

mockery n *action of mocking* b1430 ["something that mocks": b1630]

alias adv b1435 (noun use: b1605)

bend n *something curved, curved portion* b1435

crease n b1435 (verb use: b1590)

offer n *result of offering* b1435 ["bid, attempt": b1570]

baggage n b1440

bribe n b1440 [obs. "something stolen": b1400 to 1500s; "something given to a beggar": b1425] (verb use: b1530; bribery: b1580)

clod n *as in "dirt clod"* b1440 [obs. "coagulation": b1400 to 1700s]

congratulation n b1440 (congratulate: b1540; congratulations interj: b1635)

corporation n b1440 ["trade guild": b1570]

cranny n b1440

disclaimer, disclaim n, v b1440

economy n *handling resources* b1440 ["thrift": b1700]

hearsay n b1440

innovation n b1440 (innovate: b1550; innovative: b1610)

insistence n b1440 (insist: b1590; insistent: b1870; insistency: b1860)

motive n b1440 [obs. "proposition": b1374 to 1600s]

nap n *hair or fiber surface* b1440 (verb use: b1620)

rest n *as in "the rest of the story"* b1440

conduct n *leading* b1445 [obs. "leader": u1700s; as in "good conduct": b1570] (verb use: b1425)

decay n *deteriorating* b1445 ["the deterioration itself": b1530] (verb use: b1475)

indemnity n b1445 (indemnify: b1615)

set n *group* b1445 ["group of people": b1390]

allocation n b1450 (allocate: b1645)

aperture n b1450

bedfellow n b1450

cluster n *gen.* b1450 [pertaining to plants and animals: b800]

custody n b1450 ["incarceration": b1500]

diet n *confab* b1450 ["lawmaking body": b1565]

duplicity n b1450 (duplicitous: b1900)

emblem n b1450 (verb use: b1585; emblematic: b1645)

enterprise n b1450 ["company": b1900] (verb use: b1500)

flinders n *splinters* b1450

foretaste n/v b1450

generality n b1450

globe n *sphere* b1450 ["round map": b1570; "our planet": b1600]

grantee n b1450

harangue n b1450 (verb use: b1660)

imprint n b1450

inhabitant n b1450

intercession n b1450 (intercede: b1600)

intercourse n b1450 ["sex": b1800]

intermission n *gen. "pause"* b1450 ["theatrical sense": b1570]

interspace n *interval* b1450 (verb use: b1685)

landing n *landing place* b1450 [type of platform: b1800]

liberation n b1450 (verb use: b1600)

longanimity n *endurance* b1450

loon n *rapscallion* b1450 ["whore": b1570; "everyday fellow": b1570; "lout": b1630; "loony person": b1900]

luck n b1450

luminary n *lit. and fig.* b1450

mediocrity n *in the middle* b1450 ["moderate success": b1400; "being mediocre": b1600] (mediocre: b1590)

misfortune n b1450 (misfortunate: b1530)

neutral adj/n b1450 ["asexual": b1670] (neutrality: b1475)

nickname n b1450 (verb use "use a nickname," "use a wrong name": b1540)

notice n *warning* b1450

ort n *scraps* b1450

patentee n b1450 (patentor: b1890)

pause n/v b1450

peacemaker n b1450

peep n/v *sound* b1450

peg n b1450 [fig. "level": b1600]

perforation n b1450 (perforated: b1490; perforate: b1540)

permanent, permanence adj, n b1450 (permanency: b1555)

pitter-patter n *spoken repetition* b1450 [as in "pitter-patter of little feet": b1870] (verb use: b1500; adv use: b1700)

prop n *support* b1450

proviso n b1450

proxy n b1450

speckle n b1450 (verb use: b1570)

splendor n *lustrousness* b1450 ["sumptuousness," "glory": b1630] (splendid: b1620)

sprinkling n *smattering* b1450 ["the result of sprinkling": b1450]

supporter n b1450

transgression n b1450 (verb use: b1500)

transit n/v b1450 [as in "public transit": b1830]

(transitory: b1375; transition: b1555)

trunk n *as in "tree trunk";* *torso* b1450 [type of box: b1450; obs. "corpse": b1600 to 1700s]

ullage n *amount needed to fill* b1450

unanimity n b1450 (unanimous: b1625)

uniformity n *conformity* b1450 (uniform adj: b1540; uniformal: b1600; uniform v: b1685)

union n *joining* b1450

venerable, veneration adj, n b1450 (venerate: b1625)

violate, violation v, n b1450

visitor n b1450 (visitator: b1570; visitress: b1830)

wastewater n b1450

benefactor n b1455 (benefaction: b1665; benefactress: b1715; benefact v: b1900)

bulk n b1455 (bulky: b1450)

counterpart n *complement* b1455 ["duplicate": b1700]

multiplicity n b1455

resonance n b1460 [fig. use: b1630] (resonant: b1595; resonate: b1875)

concession n *conceding* b1465

fancy n *taste* b1465 [obs., as in "young man's thoughts turning to fancy": b1570 to 1700s; "fanciful thought": b1500; "delusion": b1600]

infraction n b1465

absurdity n (absurd: b1560)

agent n *as in "agent of change"*

ally n

annotation n

article n *as in "article of clothing"*

assimilate, assimilation v, n

bar n *stripe*

bent n *inclination*

body n *as in "body of work"*

challenge n *dispute* (verb use: b1450)

clank n (verb use: b1615)

clap n/v *sound, as in "clap of thunder"* ["clapper": b1350; "applause": b1600]

clasp n/v *embrace*

commission n *as in "commission of a crime"*

complice n *accomplice* [obs. gen. "colleague": u1800s]

composition n *as in "the compositon of one's character"*

crest n *as in "crest of a hill," "crest of a wave"* (verb use: b1870)

depilation n (depilate: b1560; depilatory: b1605)

directions n *how to proceed* (direct v: b1630)

dissimilitude n (dissimilarity: b1705)

domain n

donator, donor n (donee: b1525; donatrix: b1570; donatee: b1730)

duplication n [spec. mathematical sense: b1450]

ebriety n *drunkenness* (ebrious: b1570)

edge n *border, extent, rim*

element n *constituent part; basics* (elementary: b1570)

eligible adj/n

emission n (emit: b1630)

enclosure n *act of enclosing* [type of structure: b1540]

enormity n *abomination* ["immensity": b1800]

equivalence n (equivalency: b1535)

esquire n

essentials n

euphony n (euphonious: b1775)

features n *as in "facial features"*

fig n *whit, as in "I don't give a fig"*

foil n *counterpoint*

fork n *as in "fork in the road"*

forum n

foundress n (founder: b1325)

front n *as in "put on a good front"; opp. of rear* [obs. "forehead, face": b1350]

gesticulation n (gesticulate: b1605)

grain n *graininess* [spec. to photos: b1900]

ground n *base coat, as in of paint*

groundwork n [fig. use: b1670]

gurgle n/v

head n *as in "heads and tails"*

intake n

lapse n/v *something that has lapsed* ["inattentive goof": b1500]

larum n *alarm*

league n *confederation* [as in "National League": b1870] (verb use: b1600)

litter n *as in "kitty litter"*

looks n *as in "good looks"*

lyam n *leash*

magnification n ["something magnified": b1870]

material n

means n

median n *type of vein* [geometric sense: b1900] (adj use: b1600)

modicum n

monument n [obs. "burial place": b1280 to 1600s]

neck n *narrow passage, as in "bottleneck"*

negative n *negative statement*

newcomer n

news n [obs. "something new": u1500s; "broadcast news program": b1930]

nick n [as in "the nick of time": b1600; as in "shaving nick": b1630] (verb use: b1530)

note n/v *as in "make a note"*

nothing n *as in "that is nothing"* [as in "he is a nothing": b1540] (nothingness: b1635)

opiate n (adj use: b1545)

orifice n

overlay n (verb use: b1300)

pacification n

pack n *as in "pack of dogs"*

pallor n

panel n *distinct part of a surface* ["pane": b1570] (verb use: b1530; paneling: b1630)

parcel n/v *as in "parcel of land"* [obs. "thing": b1325 to 1600s; "package": b1700]

part n *as in "her part in the proceedings"*

particular n *detail*

percussion n *striking hard* [musical sense: b1800; mil. sense: b1830] (obs. percuss: b1560 to 1600s)

perimeter n

pivot n [fig. use: b1830] (adj use: b1800; verb use: b1845; pivotal: b1845)

point n *spot, position*

port n *opening*

potent, potency adj, n *powerful* ["strong," as in "potent argument": b1600; "strong," as in "potent drink": b1630; "able to get an erection": b1900] (potence: b1425)

practice n *doing* [as in "law practice": concurrent; as in "the practice of showering daily": b1570] (verb use: b1400; practicing adj: b1625)

precedent n

preservation n

preservative n [obs. "preventive medicine": concurrent] (verb use: b1400)

prime n *beginning* ["time of excellence," as in "the prime of life": b1570] (adj use: b1400)

principal n *as in "one of the principals of the firm"*

probability n [statistical sense: b1730]

prognostication n (prognostic n: b1425; prognosticate: b1500)

progress n *improvement* [arch. type of journey, as in "Pilgrims' Progress": b1450; "headway": b1530] (verb use: b1540; progression: b1450; progressive: b1610)

radiation n *radiating* [as in "energy radiation": b1600]

receipt n *receiving* ["statement of receipt": b1630]

remain, remains n

repair n [as in "good repair": b1600]

revolution n *upheaval, change* ["political rebellion": b1630] (revolt: b1550)

ruins n

rupture n (verb use: b1740)
sample n [obs. "example": b1300 to 1500s] (verb use: b1770; adj use: b1820)
seat n center
section n (verb use: b1820)
shadow n a foreshadow
shame n as in "that's a shame"
sheet n covering, as in "sheet of ice"
slant n incline (verb use: b1695)
soda n chemical substance (soda water: b1805)
solid n [as opposed to a liquid: b1700]
spissitude n thickness
spoliation n plunder (spoliate: b1725)
stock n/v supply (adj use: b1625)
stop n/v bringing something to a halt ["prevent from beginning": b1570]
strip n as in "strip of wood" [as in "landing strip": b1970]
stripe n/v [indicating mil. rank: b1830; "classification," as in "of a professional stripe": b1870]
subject n topic
summit n phys. top [fig. "top": b1830]
superior n (superioress: b1700)
surrender n/v surrender of property; surrender oneself to the enemy
testament n testimony
tip n end (verb use: b1400)
title n designation, e.g., "Lord, Lady," etc. (verb use: b1770; titled: b1595)
tooth n taste, as in "sweet tooth" (obs. verb use "teethe": b1450; verb use "bite": b1600)
trumpery n bunk; deception
turn n as in "it's your turn"
tyro n
untrue, untruth adj, n (untruthful: b1845)
version n
vestige n
waste n refuse, overage (adj use: b1870)

whit n as in "not a whit"
word n promise, as in "give your word"

Things

alabaster n b1375 (adj use: b1530)
object n thing b1375 [obs. "obstacle": u1500s]
pellet n globule; type of shot b1375 ["animal dropping": b1930] (verb use: b1600)
butt n type of cask b1385
cock n/v as in "haycock" b1390
bead n b1400 [obs. "prayer": b900]
card n b1400 [gen., as in "calling card": b1600]
gum arabic n b1400
hogshead n type of cask b1400
locker n b1400
tether n type of rope b1400 [fig. "limit": b1600; fig. "shackle": 1630] (verb use: b1450)
commodity n item b1420 [obs. "commodiousness": u1800s]
jetty n b1425
cobblestone n b1450 (cobble n: b1600)
noose n b1450 [spec. "hanging rope": b1670] (verb use: b1600)
capsule n [med. sense: b1860; as in "space capsule": b1960] (verb use: b1860; adj use: b1940; capsulize: b1950)
gimcrack n (gimcrackery: b1780)
needle n as in "compass needle"
paste n goo; type of glue (verb use: b1565)
pyramid n
sell n saddle
siphon n (verb use: b1860)
stamp n as in "rubber stamp"
tab n flap (verb use: b1875)
wrapper n

Description

aromatic adj b1375 (noun use: b1470; aroma: b1815)

awry adj/adv b1375 ["wrong": b1500]
bounteous adj benevolent b1375 ["copious": b1570] (bountiful: b1510; bountied: b1790)
complete adj b1375 (verb use: b1390)
confounded adj b1375
cumbersome adj b1375 (cumber v: b1300; obs. cumbrous: b1325 to 1800s)
easeful adj peaceful; comforting b1375
erratic adj b1375 ["unpredictable": b1870] (noun use: b1635)
exempt adj b1375 (verb use: b1450; exemption: b1450)
expert adj b1375 (noun use: b1535; verb use: b1890)
fit adj apt b1375 (verb use: b1420)
future adj b1375 (noun use: b1470)
interminable adj b1375
lone adj b1375 ["lonely": b1870]
nowadays adv b1375
perverse adj b1375
petty adj small; not of primary importance b1375 ["frivolous": b1600]
redoubtable adj b1375
subtile adj subtle b1375
transitory adj b1375
universal adj pertaining to all; pertaining to the universe b1375 (noun use: b1555; universality: concurrent)
unlikely adj b1375
unsightly adj b1375
unsung adj b1375
variant adj b1375 (noun use: b1850)
absolute adj b1380
big adj large b1380 [obs. "strong": b1300 to 1500s]
calm adj b1380 (noun/verb use: b1400)
close adj closed b1380 ["confining": b1500; "stuffy": b1600] (adv use: b1450)
colorless adj b1380
conservative adj b1380 [political sense: b1835]

credible adj believable b1380 [obs. "believing": u1600s] (credibility: b1570)
famous adj b1380 (fame: b1225)
feminine adj b1380
infamous adj b1380 (infamy: b1425)
infinite adj b1380 (noun use: b1535)
motley adj multicolored b1380 [gen. "varied": b1600]
necessary adj b1380 (noun use: b1340)
wayward adj b1380
brittle adj b1385
desirable adj b1385 (noun use: b1645)
headlong adv b1385 (adj use: b1530)
native adj innate b1385 ["born in slavery": b1425; as in "native of Nebraska": b1535]
odious adj b1385
pregnant adj convincing b1385 ["meaningful": b1405; "with child": b1425]
replete adj b1385
reprehensible adj b1385 (reprehend v: b1340; reprehension: b1375; reprehensive: b1590)
representative adj b1385 (noun use: b1650)
temperate adj not extreme, physically or emotionally b1385 ["of mild temperature": b1310]
artificial adj opp. of natural b1390
base adj debased b1390
confederate adj confederated b1390 (noun use: b1500; verb use: b1535)
constant adj steadfast b1390 [unchanging: b1570]
distinct adj individual; blatant b1390 ["obtrusive": b1530; "discrete": b1600] (distinctive: b1425)
happy adj as in "happy accident" b1390
irregular adj b1390
tart adj sour b1390 [obs. "severe": b1000 to 1600s;

obs. "phys. sharp": b1500 to 1600s; applied to speech: b1630]

terrestrial adj *of the real world* b1390 ["of the Earth": b1570; "land-living": b1600; "resembling Earth": b1900] (noun use: b1600; obs. terrestrious: b1630 to 1700s)

watertight adj b1390

apparent adj *obvious* b1395 ["seeming": b1670] (apparently: b1570)

compendious adj b1395 [obs. "time-saving": u1700s] (compendium: b1585)

direct adj *phys. straight* b1395 [fig. "blunt": b1570] (adv use: b1400)

effectual adj b1395 (effective: b1400)

effeminate adj b1395 (obs. verb use: b1450; noun use: b1600; effeminacy: b1605)

fast adj *quick, speedy* b1395 ["vigorous": b1325]

impotent adj b1395 [sexual sense: b1445]

improper adj *incorrect* b1395 ["socially incorrect": b1630]

moderate adj b1395 (verb use: b1425; noun use: b1795)

abstract adj b1400

adjacent adj b1400

aforesaid adj b1400

ajar adj/adv b1400

akimbo adj/adv *skewed* b1400

arbitrary adj b1400

auld adj *old* b1400

bleary adj b1400 (blear v: b1300; blear-eyed: b1380; blear adj: b1390; bleary-eyed: b1930)

boisterous adj *rambunctious* b1400 [obs. "physically rough, coarse": b1400 to 1700s] (boistous: b1300)

bound adj *as in "bound for glory"* b1400 ["ready," as in "bound and determined": 1200s]

checkered adj *as in "a checkered past"* b1400 (checked: b1425)

chill adj/v b1400

chock-full adj b1400

clammy adj b1400 (clam adj "sticky": b1340)

colorable adj *apparently real, true* b1400

compact adj b1400 (verb use: b1450; compaction: b1400)

concentric adj b1400

concrete adj *solid, specific* b1400 ["made of concrete": b1900] (verb use: b1590)

consonant adj *fig. harmonious* b1400

cross adj b1400

delectable adj b1400 (noun use: b1925; delectation: b1400; delectate v: b1805)

dependent adj b1400 (depend: b1410)

deviant adj b1400 (deviate v: b1635)

devoid adj b1400

difficult adj *as in "difficult job"* b1400 [as in "difficult person": b1530; as in "difficult problem": b1570] (obs. verb use: b1450 to 1800s)

dirty adj b1400 ["pornographic": b1530] (verb use: b1595)

disagreeable adj *offensive* b1400 ["difficult," as in "a disagreeable person": b1730]

discrete adj b1400 (obs. verb use: b1670 to 1800s; discretion: b1300; discretionary: b1700)

dormant adj b1400 (dormancy: b1780)

dulcet adj b1400 (obs. dulce: b1500 to 1700s)

durable adj b1400

earthshaking adj b1400 (earthshaker: b1955; earthshattering: b1970)

earthy adj b1400 [fig. "crude"]

entire adj b1400 (noun use: b1600; entirety: b1350)

equal adj b1400 ["on the same level, corresponding": b1530] (verb use:

b1590; noun use: b1600; equality: b1400; equalize: b1625)

erect adj b1400 (verb use: b1450)

erroneous adj b1400 [obs. "morally wrong": u1800s]

especial, especially adj, adv b1400

evident adj b1400 (evidence: b1670)

excessive adj b1400

expectant adj b1400

expedient adj b1400 (expedience: b1470; expediency: b1615)

figurative adj b1400 (figural: b1450; figurate "speak figuratively": b1670)

fortunate adj b1400 (obs. verb use: u1700s)

fusty adj *musty, out of date* b1400

giddy adj *dizzy* b1400 [obs. "crazy": b1000 to 1300s; "lightheaded:": b1570] (verb use: b1605; giddify: b1630)

hapless adj b1400

hasty adj b1400 [arch. speedy: b1280] (obs. hastive: b1350 to 1400s)

hazel adj b1400

healthful adj b1400

human adj *related to homo sapiens* b1400 ["exhibiting human foibles": b1570] (noun use: b1535)

immaterial adj b1400 ["irrelevant": b1700]

immoderate adj b1400

imprudent adj b1400

indign adj *unworthy* b1400

inevitable adj b1400

inflexible adj b1400

inordinate adj b1400

instant adj b1400 ["urgent": b1400]

instrumental adj *critical* b1400

intense adj b1400 [describing people: b1670] (intensity: b1665; intensify: b1820)

irrevocable adj b1400

leonine adj b1400

lineal adj b1400

liquid adj b1400

literal adj *as in "literal translation"* b1400

livelong adj b1400

lukewarm adj b1400

malleable adj *applied to metals* b1400 [fig. use: b1630]

massy adj b1400

measureless adj b1400

mechanic adj *manual, mechanical* b1400 [arch. "lowly": b1570]

moth-eaten adj b1400

mum adj b1400 (noun use: b1405)

negative adj/adv *saying no* b1400

neuter adj b1400 (noun use: b1470)

noisome adj b1400

now adj b1400 [slang "modern, hip": b1970]

nowise adv b1400

numb adj b1400 (verb use: b1600)

numeral adj b1400

obscure adj *dark* b1400 (verb use: b1425; obscurity: b1400)

olden adj b1400

onerous adj b1400

opposite adj *on the other side* b1400 ["reversed": b1600] (noun use: b1450; adv use: b1670; prep use: b1760)

original adj *native; originative* b1400 ["clever, creative": b1770] (originality: b1745)

palpable adj b1400

parlous adj *perilous* b1400 (adv use: b1600)

partial adj *opp. of impartial* b1400 ["liking," as in "partial to green": b1700] (partiality: b1425)

particular adj *specific* b1400 [obs. "pertaining to a small part": u1600s; "fastidious": b1670]

passive adj *not active; being acted upon* b1400 [obs. "suffering": u1600s; "submissive": b1630]

personal adj b1400 (personalize: b1730)

persuasive adj b1400

pertinent adj b1400 [obs. "belonging to": u1600s]

pliable adj b1400

potential adj b1400 [rare "potent": b1500] (noun use: b1820)

powerful adj b1400 (adv use: b1830)

precise adj b1400 ["strict": b1570] (precision: b1870)

pregnable adj opp. of impregnable b1400

preservative adj b1400 (noun use: b1500)

primitive adj primal b1400 ["crude, unsophisticated": b1700] (noun use: b1800)

primordial adj b1400 [biological sense: b1800]

probable adj likely to happen; arch. trustworthy b1400

prone adj tending toward b1400 ["opp. of supine": b1600]

quiet adj b1400 ["discreet, subdued": b1530]

rampant adj fierce; not restrained b1400 ["on hind legs": b1350; applied to plants: b1770]

rare adj scarce b1400 [obs. "spaced out": u1800s; obs. "far apart": u1600s]

redolent adj b1400 [fig. sense: b1830] (redolence: b1470)

regular adj b1400

rigorous adj b1400

second-best adj b1400

secondary adj b1400

seething adj b1400

sensitive adj b1400

serpentine adj b1400 ["curving": b1630] (verb use: b1800; serpent adj: b1600; serpentiform: b1800)

shallow adj b1400 [fig. use: b1600] (verb use: b1510)

shrill adj b1400

slender adj b1400 (verb use: b1570; slenderize: b1925)

sole adj only b1400

solid adj as opposed to liquid, or hollow b1400 [as in "solid food": b1600] (solidify: b1800)

spacious adj b1400

storied adj decorated b1400

styptic adj b1400

superior adj b1400 (noun use: b1450)

superlative adj b1400 (noun use: b1500)

tepid adj b1400

thankworthy adj b1400

thriftless adj useless b1400 (thriveless: b1530)

tired adj b1400 ["cliched, weak": b1770]

tortuous adj b1400

total adj b1400 (noun use: b1560; adv use: b1605; verb use: b1720; totalize: b1820)

trifling adj b1400

trine adj three b1400 (noun use: b1555)

undue adj b1400

unjust adj b1400 ["not honest": b1500; obs. "wrong": b1570 to 1700s]

variable adj varying b1400 ["possible to vary": b1500; "able to be varied": b1600]

virgin adj pure b1400 ["chaste": b1450] (virginal: b1450)

virtual adj b1400

virulent adj b1400

viscous adj b1400 (viscosity: b1425; viscid: b1635)

vital adj b1400 ["necessary": b1630] (vitality: b1595; vitalize: b1680)

vocal adj b1400 ["able to speak," "articulate": b1630; "outspoken": b1900]

voluntary adj b1400

weak adj as in "a weak drink" b1400

weighty adj heavy b1400 ["important," fig. "weighing down": b1490]

worm-eaten adj b1400 [fig. use: b1600]

comparable adj b1410

finite adj b1410

ideal adj b1410 (noun use: b1500; idea "ideal": b1400)

miraculous adj b1410 [fig. sense: b1600] (obs. miracular: b1730 to 1800s)

tedious adj b1410 (tedium: b1665)

abject adj b1415

fallible adj b1415 (fallibility: b1635)

flexible adj b1415 (flex v: b1525; flexile: b1635)

innate adj b1415

auburn adj b1420

circumspect adj b1420 (circumspection: b1390)

infallible adj b1420

prolix adj b1420

appropriate adj b1425

brute adj as in "brute force" b1425 (noun use: b1615)

coarse adj b1425 [obs. "ordinary": b1300; "indelicate": b1510; "rough, bawdy": b1715] (coarsen: b1805)

collective adj b1425

commodious adj b1425

concave adj b1425 [obs. "hollow": u1600s]

corporate adj b1425 [obs. "corporal": b1600 to 1800s]

corporeal adj material b1425 [opp. of "spiritual": b1630] (corporeity: b1625; corporeality: b1655)

dense adj b1425 [fig. use "difficult": b1770] (density: b1605)

derivative adj b1425

fecund adj b1425 (fecundate v: b1635)

fetid adj b1425 (fetor n: b1500)

fluid adj b1425 (noun use: b1660)

frangible adj breakable b1425

fulgent adj resplendent b1425

hereditary adj b1425 (heredity "inheritance": b1540)

historical adj b1425 (historic: b1610)

immediate adj b1425

immutable adj b1425

implacable adj b1425

increate adj uncreated b1425

incredible adj unbelievable b1425 [obs. "unbelieving": b1470 to 1700s; "surprising": b1500]

ineffectual adj b1425 (ineffective: b1650; inefficacious: b1660)

inferior adj lit. "below"

b1425 [fig. "below, lesser": b1500] (inferiority: b1600)

internal adj b1425 (arch. intern adj: b1500)

intricate adj b1425 (intricacy: b1605)

irreparable adj b1425

lenticular adj b1425

light-footed adj b1425

lucrative adj b1425 (obs. luciferous "lucrative": b1670 to 1700s)

luscious adj b1425 ["cloyingly luscious": b1570; sexual sense: b1630]

maculate adj spotted b1425 (macula "spot": b1450; macule "blemish": b1500)

massive adj b1425

mechanical adj machine-related b1425 ["machine-like": b1570; "by rote": b1630] (mechanic adj: b1400)

mediate adj intermediate b1425 (verb use "divide": b1570; verb use "moderate": b1600)

mellifluous adj b1425 (mellifluent: b1605)

oblique adj lit. and fig. b1425 (adv use: b1670)

oblong adj b1425

opportune adj timed well b1425 [obs. "useful": u1600s]

ornate adj lit. and fig. b1425

ponderous adj heavy b1425 [fig. "difficult": b1730]

portable adj b1425 [obs. "tolerable": b1450 to 1600s] (noun use: b1885; portative: b1400)

practical, practic adj b1425

preparatory adj b1425

profuse adj abundant b1425 ["wasteful": b1545] (profuseness: b1600; profusive: b1640; profusion: b1700)

putrid adj b1425 (putrefy: b1400)

resounding adj b1425

several adj b1425

sinister adj b1425 (sinistrous: b1550)

stalwart adj/n b1425

superficial adj b1425 (superficiality: b1530)

tolerable adj b1425

transparent adj *see-through* b1425 ["without guile": b1600]

tripartite adj b1425

unnatural adj b1425

unsubstantial adj b1425

immense adj b1430

ample adj b1440

imminent adj b1440

impure adj b1440 ["not chaste": b1570] (noun use: b1450)

inverse adj b1440 [mathematical use: b1670]

resplendent adj b1440 (resplendence: b1425; resplend v: b1500; resplendency: b1615)

feasible adj b1445 (feasibility: b1625)

habitual adj b1445

immaculate adj b1445

important adj b1445 (importance: b1505)

infantile adj b1445 (infantine: b1605)

requisite adj b1445 (verb use: b1840; required: b1630)

aureate adj *grandiose* b1450

brutal adj *vicious* b1450 [obs. "pertaining to animals": b1500 to 1800s; "brutish": b1570] (brutality: b1550; brutalize: b1705)

consummate adj *of the highest degree* b1450 [obs. "finished": b1450 to 1800s; arch. "perfect": b1530] (verb use: b1530; consummation: b1400)

discrepant adj b1450 (discrepancy: b1525)

duplicate adj b1450 (verb use: b1500; noun use: b1535)

excusatory adj b1450

extended adj b1450

external adj *tangible* b1450 ["opp. of internal": b1660]

extinct adj *extinguished* b1450 ["obsolete": b1500; "wiped out": b1700] (obs. verb use: b1450 to 1600s)

formidable adj b1450

fragrant adj b1450 (fragrancy: b1580; fragrance: b1670)

fundamental adj b1450 (noun use: b1640; fundament: b1300)

gratis adv b1450 (adj use: b1670)

impenetrable adj b1450

indicative adj b1450

intolerable adj b1450

inutile adj *having no use* b1450 (inutility: b1600)

lightsome adj *illuminated* b1450

luminous adj b1450 (luminosity: b1635)

manual adj b1450 (manuary: b1570)

mature adj/v b1450 (maturation: b1400; maturate: b1570)

mellow adj *ripe, mature* b1450 [fig. "mature": b1600; "drunk": b1630; "easy-going, laid-back": b1730] (verb use: b1575)

nonpareil adj *without equal* b1450 (noun use: b1595)

pearly adj b1450

peculiar adj *distinguished* b1450 ["odd": b1630] (peculiarity: b1610)

permeable adj b1450 (permeate: b1660)

populous adj b1450

premier adj *foremost* b1450

propitious adj b1450

prosperous adj *causing prosperity* b1450 ["enjoying prosperity": b1500]

putative adj b1450

radiant adj b1450 [fig., as in "a radiant personality": b1630] (noun use: b1730; radiant: b1570; radiancy: b1650)

ready-made adj b1450 (noun use: b1885)

remiss adj b1450 [obs. "weak": b1425 to 1600s]

rustic adj b1450 (noun use: b1470; rusticate: b1500)

satiate adj/v *satiated* b1450

sensual adj b1450 ["carnal": b1500]

sluggish adj b1450 ["slow in responding": b1670] (slugged adj: b1470)

stationary adj b1450

summary adj *summarizing* b1450 ["immediate": b1730]

superfluous adj b1450

towering adj b1450

triplicate adj b1450 (verb use: b1625; noun use: b1800)

vagabond adj b1450 (noun use: b1500; verb use: b1600)

wasted adj b1450

wearisome adj *wearying* b1450 [obs. "wearied": u1600s]

wee adj b1450 (obs. noun use: b1325)

corrigible adj *correctable* b1455 [obs. "needing correction, punishment": b1450 to 1600s]

mundane adj b1455

compatible adj b1460

incendiary adj b1460 (noun use: b1405)

incessant adj b1465

advisable adj

animal adj

auxiliary adj *assisting* ["adjunct": b1700]

balmy adj [applied to weather: b1630]

beneficial adj

brick adj *brick-colored* (brick red: b1810)

conglomerate adj

dappled/dapple adj (noun use: b1555; verb use: b1600)

darkling adv (adj use: b1740; darkle: b1800)

disparate adj *different* ["unequal": b1770] (disparity: b1555)

dominant adj

elective adj

exorbitant adj *excessive; beyond the law* [obs. "crazed, frantic": b1630 to 1700s] (exorbitance: b1615)

extraordinary adj

extreme adj (noun use: b1555; extremity: b1375)

exuberant adj *abundant* ["showing exuberance": b1530]

frigid adj [sexual sense: b1670] (frigidity: b1470)

fusk adj *dusky*

incorporeal adj

indubitable adj (obs. indubious: b1630 to 1800s)

informal adj

inhuman adj (inhumanity: b1480; inhumanism: b1930)

intermediate adj

large adj *big* [obs. meanings of "lavish," "ample," "broad," "abundant," "extensive": b1275; obs. "generous": b1450] (obs. adv use: b1350)

latent adj (latency: b1640)

lateral adj

lavish adj *profuse* ["sumptuous": b1900] (verb use: b1545)

level adj *horizontal* ["even": b1570] (verb use: b1450)

lew-warm adj *lukewarm*

limpid adj

lost adj

lucent adj *shining*

lucky adj *experiencing good luck* ["bringing good luck": b1570]

lunar adj *shaped like a crescent* ["related to the moon": b1630]

molten adj ["dissolved": b1150]

odd adj *occasional, as in "the odd complaint"*

operant adj

operative adj *as in "the operative clause"* ["significant": b1930]

ordinary adj *normal* ["plain": b1600]

orthodox adj (orthodoxy: b1630)

overwrought adj

partial adj *being a portion of*

pernicious adj

pestiferous adj *causing pestilence*

plain adj *simple, unadorned; candid; ordinary* [obs. "flat": b1300; "direct," as in "plain speaking":

b1500; as in "plain Jane":
b1770]

plentiful adj (plenteous:
b1300)

praiseworthy adj (arch. praise
"praiseworthiness":
b1530)

preponderant adj

present adj *as in "the present
topic of discussion"* [obs.
"having presence of
mind": concurrent]

primary adj *first* ["most important": b1570]

prodigal adj (noun use:
b1600; prodigality:
b1350)

profane adj [opp. of sacred:
b1500] (verb use: b1400)

prominent adj *protruding*
["obtrusive": b1770]

promissory adj

prompt adj *on time* (promptitude: b1450)

pseudo adj

questionable adj *open to question* ["dubious": b1830]

recent adj (recency: b1630)

receptive adj

relative adj

right adj *perpendicular*

rigid adj [applied to people:
b1600] (rigidity: b1625; rigidify: b1845)

ruly adj *opp. of unruly*

scarce adj [obs. "sparse":
b1300 to 1500s; obs.
"stingy": b1350 to 1600s]
(adv use: b1450; scarcity:
b1350)

serene adj [applied to people: b1670] (serenity:
b1450)

sidelong adj

sightly adj

sober adj *not intoxicated*
(verb use: b1400; soberize:
b1710)

somnolent adj

spare adj *duplicate, in reserve*

spent adj *pertaining to things*
[pertaining to people:
b1570]

stale adj ["aged," pertaining
to liquor: b1300] (verb
use: b1770)

sturdy adj *solid* [obs. "fierce":
b1300 to 1600s]

subordinate adj

subsequent adj

supine adj

surely adv [obs. "without
risk": b1350 to 1600s; as
in "surely you jest":
b1600]

tempting adj

terminate adj

thick adj *as in "thick accent"*

tight adj *compacted, close* [as
in "watertight": b1510]
(adv use: b1680)

tonguey adj *chatty*

turbulent adj *gen.* [describing
air and liquid: b1900] (tur-
bulence: b1590; turbu-
lency: b1610)

twin adj

unfit adj

unkempt adj [obs. fig.
"crude": u1600s]

unsavory adj *objectionable*
[obs. "bland": b1225 to
1700s]

various adj

vast adj (noun use: b1605;
vasty adj: b1600; vastness:
b1600; vastitude, vastity:
b1630)

velvety adj

weariful adj *wearying* ["wearied": b1870]

whilom adj

worn adj

Colors

dapple-gray adj/n b1400

crimson adj/n b1420 (verb
use: b1605)

eggshell adj

general n *obs. neutral color*
[u1600s]

purple adj/n/v *of the color*

violet adj/n *the color*

Actions/Verbs

annex v b1370 (noun use:
b1505)

impress v *mark with pressure,
influence* b1370

resign v b1370 (resignation:
b1390)

abandon v *give up* b1375
[obs. "subdue": b1470;
"leave behind": b1500]

add v b1375

adjudge v b1375

administer v b1375 (administrate v: b1650)

appoint v b1375 (appointee:
b1730; appointment:
b1670)

assure v *comfort, certain*
b1375

avenge v b1375

begone v b1375

compare v *demonstrate a comparison* b1375 [as in "contrast and compare":
b1500] (noun use: b1590)

conjoin v b1375

conserve v b1375

consider v b1375 (consideration: b1400; considered
adj: b1605)

crave v *yearn for* b1375 [obs.
"demand": b1000; "ask
for": b1350] (craving:
b1300)

defeat v *as in "defeat the purpose"* b1375 [obs. "deface,
demolish": b1450 to
1600s; "win over, beat":
b1570] (noun use: b1570;
obs. defeature "defeat":
b1590 to 1800s)

defer v *postpone* b1375

define v b1375 [obs. "confine": b1530 to 1600s; obs.
"end": u1600s; as in "he is
defined by his attitude":
b1670] (definition:
b1400)

differ v *be different; rare make
different* b1375 ["dis-
agree": b1570] (difference
n: b1340; different adj:
b1385; difference v:
b1500; different adv:
b1745)

direct v *as in "direct a letter";
"direct an aim"; counsel*
b1375 (direction: b1385)

disfigure v b1375 [obs. "disguise": u1700s]

distill v *concentrate; let drip;
extract* b1375 (distillation:
b1400)

enhance v *exaggerate* b1375
[obs. lit. and fig. "raise
up": b1350 to 1600s;
"make better": b1530]

establish v b1375 [obs. "stabilize": b1500 to 1800s]

exceed v b1375 [as in "ex-

ceed your authority":
b1570]

glaze v *install glass* b1375
["apply glassy layer":
b1600] (noun use: b1755)

hamper v b1375

impugn v b1375 [obs.
"fight": u1600s]

induce v b1375

mitigate v b1375 [as in "mitigating circumstances":
b1730]

muck v *clean muck* b1375
["make mucky": b1835]

overlook v *look over* b1375
(noun use "vantage
point": b1865)

peek v b1375 (noun use:
b1845)

plunge v b1375 [fig. "become deeply involved":
b1700; gen. "fall": b1870]

prance v b1375 (noun use:
b1755)

precede v *precede in time*
b1375 [obs. "outdo":
u1700s; "phys. precede":
b1500] (precedent adj:
b1400; preceding adj:
b1495; precedent n:
b1500; precedence:
b1590; precedency:
b1600)

preserve v *protect; retain;
maintain* b1375

prize v *value; appraise* b1375

ratify v b1375

refer v b1375 (reference:
b1590; referral: b1930)

renew v b1375 (obs. renovel:
b1350 to 1500s)

renounce v b1375 (renunciate: b1830)

represent v b1375

resist v b1375 (resistance:
b1350)

resolve v b1375 (noun use:
b1595)

reveal v b1375

rumble v b1375 (noun use:
b1400)

rush v *move fast* b1375
["charge": b1570; "force
to hurry": b1830; "hurry":
b1870]

soar v b1375 [fig. "rise, increase": b1600]

soften v b1375

ENGLISH THROUGH THE AGES

subvert v *undermine* b1375 [obs. "destroy": u1700s]

succeed v *opp. of precede; replace* b1375 ["follow physically": b1500 to 1700s] (successor: b1300; successive: b1450)

supply v *provide supplies, etc.* b1375 [obs. "supply troops": u1500s; obs. "assist": u1700s]

throb v b1375 (noun use: b1580)

triple v b1375 (triplicate v: b1625)

twitter v b1375 (noun use: b1680)

wait v *anticipate; postpone; await* b1375 [obs. "lie in wait": b1200 to 1500s; obs. "watch out": b1350 to 1600s; "attend," as in "wait tables": b1500]

wave v *fashion into waves* b1375 ["vacillate": b1000]

wester v *move west* b1375 (west v: b1450)

abstain v b1380

accept v b1380 (acceptable: b1385; accepted: b1495; acceptance: b1575)

accomplish v b1380 (accomplishment: b1425)

adjust v b1380 (adjustment: b1645)

apply v *as in "apply glue"* b1380 ["have relevance": b1500; as in "apply for a job": b1670] (applicator: b1660; application: b1425)

back v *back up, reverse* b1380

ban v *prohibit* b1380 [obs. "call to arms": b1150 to late ME; arch. "curse": b1150] (noun use: b1670)

brawl v b1380 (noun use: b1445)

chop n/v *as in "chop wood"* b1380 ["mince," as in "chop celery": b1450]

compound v *mix into a compound* b1380 [obs. "join": u1600s; var. meanings of "settle, agree": b1450] (noun use: b1570)

compress v b1380

congeal v b1380

consume v *destroy; enthrall; spend* b1380 ["eat, drink": b1600]

copy v *duplicate* b1380 ["mimic": b1670] (noun use: b1600)

cost v b1380 ["appraise, estimate": b1900]

create v b1380 ["invent": b1600] (arch. adj use: b1450; creative: b1500)

curl v b1380 [spec. "curl hair": b1570] (noun use: b1600)

deprave v b1380 ["speak ill of": b1375] (depraved: b1595; depravity: b1645)

desert v *leave* b1380 ["abandon": b1670; as in "desert one's post": b1700] (desertion: b1470)

discolor v b1380 (discoloration: b1645)

disdain v b1380 (obs. verb use "cause disdain": b1450 to 1800s; noun use: b1340)

dissolve v b1380 [fig., as in "dissolve into laughter": b1530]

herald v b1380

reduce v b1380

resound v b1380

scale v *as in "scale a wall"* b1380

scold v *quarrel* b1380 ["reprove": b1730]

tatter v b1380 (noun use: b1400; tattered: b1350)

agree v *concur, accept* b1385 ["harmonize": b1500] (agreeable: b1380; agreement: b1425)

ascend v b1385 (ascent: b1600)

authorize v b1385 (authorization: b1500)

circumscribe v b1385

declaim v b1385 ["speak vigorously": b1600] (declamatory: b1585)

demand v *ask* b1385 ["require": b1435] (noun use: b1280)

hinder v b1385 [obs. "hurt": b1000 to 1700s; obs. "insult": b1470 to 1500s] (hindrance: b1530)

hiss v b1385 (noun use: b1515)

intend v b1385

interpret v b1385 (obs. interpretate: b1630; interpretation: b1300)

involve v b1385

mince v b1385

modify v b1385 (modification: b1605)

reply v b1385 (noun use: b1560)

savor v *relish* b1385 ["give pleasure": b1250; "season": b1350] (noun use: b1225)

admit v *allow in* b1390 (admission: b1430; admittance: b1450)

afford v *have the wherewithal to* b1390

brag v b1390 (braggart: b1580)

commit v *assign to another's care* b1390 [as in "commit a crime": b1450; "dedicate oneself": b1800]

commune v *discuss, experience "intimate rapport"* b1390 ["associate with": b1325]

crash v *make noise* b1390 ["break": b1400; "collide," "collapse": b1910; as in "crash a party": b1930; "go to sleep": b1940] (noun use: b1580; adj use: b1945)

crinkle v b1390 (noun use: b1600)

disparage v *dishonor* b1390 [obs. "marry below position": b1375 to 1700s; "insult": b1530] (disparaging: b1645)

plead v *beg* b1390

retain v b1390 [obs. "restrain": u1700s]

testify v b1390

annul v b1395

attempt v b1395 (noun use: b1535)

bumble v *buzz, as in "bumblebee"* b1395

convey v *carry; communicate* b1395 [obs. "lead": b1300; arch. "steal": b1450]

disclose v b1395 [obs. "open": u1700s] (disclosure: b1600)

mistake v *make a mistake* b1395 (noun use: b1630; transgress: b1340; mistaken: b1570)

mollify v b1395

observe v *as in "observe a holiday"* b1395

sag v b1395

scarify v *scratch, lacerate* b1395

aid v b1400 (noun use: b1430)

append v b1400 (appendage: b1650)

apprehend v *capture* b1400 [obs. "seize": b1470 to 1800s]

apprize v *appraise* b1400

arch v b1400

aspire v b1400

baste v *sew up temporarily* b1400

buzz v *hum* b1400 (noun use: b1630)

cannot v b1400

caterwaul v b1400

caulk v b1400

champ v *as in "champing at the bit"* b1400

check v *obstruct, stop* b1400 ["hold in check, restrain": b1600] (noun use: b1530)

coagulate v b1400 (coagulat adj: b1395; coagulation: b1400; coagulant adj/n: b1770)

counter v *run counter* b1400 (adv/n use: b1450; adj use: b1700)

croon v b1400

cross v *as in "cross a bridge," "cross the room"* b1400 [as in "the bridge crosses the river": b1600]

decrease n/v b1400 (decrement n, decrescent adj: b1610)

deform, deformed, deformity v, adj, n b1400

design v b1400

dice v *chop* b1400

diffuse v *scatter* b1400 [obs. "flow": b1600 to 1700s] (adj use: b1415; diffusion: b1385)

digest v *lit. and fig.* b1400

dilate v b1400 [obs. "delay": u1600s]

discontinue v b1400 [obs. "disrupt": u1800s]

dispel v b1400

disperse v *disburse; distribute* b1400 [as in "disperse the smoke": b1570]

dock v *cut short* b1400

don v b1400

earth v *opp. of unearth* b1400

emboss v b1400

encircle v b1400

endeavor n/v *labor* b1400 ["try": b1600]

endow v b1400 (endowment: b1475)

enshrine v b1400

ensue v b1400 [var. obs. meanings of "follow," lit. and fig.: u1600s]

entail v *require* b1400

entitle v *give a title; give permission* b1400

envelop v b1400

exclude v b1400 (exclusion: b1425)

execute v *do* b1400 (execution: b1450)

expel v b1400

express v *press out; state; portray* b1400

extol v b1400 [obs. lit. "lift up": u1600s]

forfend v b1400 [obs. "forbid": u1800s]

furbish v b1400

gain v b1400

garner v *fig. collect* b1400 ["collect in a granary": b1400]

gasp v b1400 (noun use: b1600)

glister v *glisten* b1400

goggle v b1400

grasp v *as in "grasp at"* b1400 ["take hold": b1600] (noun use: b1600)

grate v b1400 [fig. use: b1570]

growl v b1400 (noun use: b1730)

gush v b1400 (noun use: b1685)

hover v b1400 (hoven: b1250)

hush v b1400

incur v b1400

indwell v *dwell within* b1400

inform v b1400 [obs. "give form to": b1325 to 1600s]

interrogate v b1400

interrupt v *temporarily stop* b1400 [obs. "completely stop": u1600s]

jingle v b1400 (noun use: b1600)

kick v b1400 [fig., as in "kick yourself": b1900] (noun use: b1530)

leak v b1400 [as in "light leak": b1830] (noun use: b1500)

lengthen v b1400

lighten v *unload* b1400 ["make lighter": b1500]

line v *as in "line a coat"* b1400

magnify v *glorify; make larger* b1400 [as with a magnifying glass: b1670; "exaggerate": b1770] (magnification: b1450)

mass v *amass* b1400

misspend v b1400

nip v *bite* b1400 (noun use: b1550)

oppose v b1400

patter v b1400 (noun use: b1760)

perfect v b1400 [obs. "complete": u1600s]

pile v *heap* b1400 (noun use: b1450)

possess v *own* b1400 [arch. "take": b1530; "make love": b1600] (possessive: b1530)

practice v *do; work at; repeat to learn or polish* b1400 (noun use: b1450)

prefer v b1400 [as in "prefer charges": b1570] (preference: b1670; preferential: b1850)

press v *as in "press down"* b1400 (noun use: b1450)

prevail v *win; succeed* b1400 [obs. "get stronger": u1700s; "be common": b1630; "be prevalent": b1800] (prevalent "powerful": b1580; prevailing adj: b1590)

proceed v b1400 (procedure, procedural: b1600)

proclaim, proclamation v, n b1400

promote v *as in "promote an employee"; help, publicize* b1400 (promotion "elevation": b1450; promotion "publicizing": b1930)

provoke v b1400 [obs. "invite": u1700s; obs. "pick a fight": b1500 to 1600s]

prowl n/v b1400

prune v *preen, spiff up* b1400

putrefy v b1400 [obs. "type of alchemical process": b1500 to 1600s]

ramp v *menace* b1400 [arch. "be rampant": b1350] (noun use: b1600)

rarefy v b1400 (rarefied: b1600)

rate v *berate* b1400

recommend v *as in "recommend someone for a job"* b1400 ["advise": b1770] (recommendation: b1450)

rectify v b1400

relent v b1400 ["physically melt": b1400 to 1700s]

remain v b1400

requite v *repay* b1400

revenge v b1400 (noun use: b1470)

rinse v b1400 [obs. religious sense: b1350] (noun use: b1840)

rustle v *make rustling sounds* b1400 (noun use: b1760)

scratch v b1400 (noun use: b1590)

shroud v b1400

skew v b1400 (adj use: b1610)

slash v b1400 (noun use: b1580; slashing: b1590)

smirch v *sully* b1400 ["besmirch": b1830] (noun use: b1690)

snarl v *tangle* b1400 [fig. use: b1390] (noun use: b1610)

sophisticate v *dilute, adulterate* b1400 ["rob of simplicity": b1630; "bring culture to": b1970] (sophistication: b1470; sophisticated: b1630)

sort v b1400 [obs. "assign": u1500s]

sprinkle v b1400

squeak v *pertaining to living things* b1400 [pertaining to things: b1570]

stain v *color, dye; spot; taint* b1400 [obs. "bleach": u1700s] (verb use: b1400)

straggle v b1400

struggle v *fig. and lit. fight* b1400 ["try hard": b1600] (noun use: b1695)

subdue v b1400 (subdued: b1595)

suckle v b1400

suppress v *stop* b1400 ["restrain," as in "suppress laughter": b1570] (suppression: b1500; suppressor: b1530)

swirl v b1400 (noun use: b1450)

throttle v b1400 [mechanical sense: b1900] (noun use: b1550)

throw v *fashion, shape* b1400

tingle v b1400

tinkle v b1400 (noun use: b1700)

tip v *fall, as in "tip over"* b1400 ["tilt": b1670]

toast v *make toasty* b1400

toil v b1400 (noun use: b1600)

trace v *track* b1400 [obs. "walk about": b1450; as in "trace a chronology": b1670; "copy by tracing": b1770]

transfer v b1400 (noun use: b1675)

transmit v b1400 [as in "transmit radio signals": b1900]

transpose v *switch order* b1400 (transposition: b1540)

twin v *pair* b1400 ["bear twins": b1600; "mirror": b1630]

unhair v *remove hair* b1400

varnish v b1400 [fig. use: b1600]

vent v b1400 (noun use: b1510)

whip v *go fast* b1400

whirr v *make whirring sound* b1400 [obs. "throw": u1600s]

wrangle v *squabble* b1400 (noun use: b1470)

allure v b1405 (noun use: b1550; alluring: b1535; allusion: b1550)

jabber v *blather* b1405 ["speak in nonsense": b1830] (noun use: b1730)

affect v *change* b1410

concur v *agree* b1410 [obs. "crash together": u1600s; "happen simultaneously": b1600]

deduce v *figure out; arch. bring* b1410 [obs. "deduct": b1410 to 1800s] (deduction: b1500; deductive: b1650)

bag v *put in a bag* b1415 ["droop," "capture/kill": b1830]

obtain v b1415 [obs. "win": u1600s]

appraise v b1420 (appraisal: b1820)

combine v *unite* b1420

concern v b1420 ["become involved": b1670; "distress": b1830]

countermand v b1420 (noun use: b1500)

deduct v b1420 ["deduce": b1570] (deduction: b1425)

derogate v b1420 (derogatory "detracting": b1505; derogatory "insulting": b1600)

diminish v b1420

impoverish v b1420

include v b1420 ["hide, enclose": b1405]

offer v *as in "offer a ride"* b1420

abbreviate v b1425

absorb v b1425

accustom v b1425 (accustomed: b1450)

adapt v b1425

advertise v *call attention to* b1425 [obs. "pay heed": u1500s; commercial sense: b1730] (advert v: b1420; advertisement: b1470)

affect v *as in "affect airs"* b1425 [arch. "show affection": b1470] (affectation: b1550)

alleviate n b1425 [obs. "reduce weight of": b1400 to 1600s]

amplify v b1425 (amplification: b1550)

assess v *as in "assess a tax"* b1425 (assessor: b1400; assessment: b1545)

attenuate adj/v *thin* b1425

attract v *attract physically* b1425 ["attract emotionally": b1630]

beam v *direct a beam* b1425 ["smile": b1900]

collect v *gen. use* b1425 [as in "collect one's thoughts": b1630; spec. "collect as a hobby": b1870] (collection: b1400)

comprise v b1425 [obs. "seize": u1600s; obs. "write": b1500 to 1600s; "compose, be part of": b1800]

conduct v *lead* b1425 [as in "conduct business": b1670; as in "conduct electricity": b1770; as in "conduct an orchestra": b1800]

corrugate v b1425 (corrugation: b1530; corrugated: b1590)

curve v b1425

denude v b1425

detain v b1425 [obs. "be sick": b1450 to 1600s; "stop": b1570] (detainee: b1930)

dignify v b1425 (obs. dignation: b1450 to 1700s; dignified: b1765)

dissimulate v *disguise or conceal* b1425 (dissimulation: b1380)

eject v b1425 (ejecta: b1890)

equate v *compare* b1425 [obs. "equalize": b1425 to 1700s]

evaporate v b1425 [fig. use: b1670]

exsiccate v *dry* b1425

extract v b1425 (noun use: b1600)

finger v *touch* b1425

fray v *wear* b1425 ["unravel": b1730]

illuminate v b1425 [fig. use: b1570] (illumine v: b1340; illume v: b1470)

impel v b1425

implant v b1425 [med. sense: b1900] (noun use: b1890)

infest v *give pain* b1425 ["swarm": b1605]

inflate v b1425 (inflation: b1340; inflate adj: b1350; inflated: b1655; inflatable: b1880)

infuse v *phys.* b1425 [fig. sense: b1530] (infusion: b1400)

install v *of people* b1425 [of things: b1870] (installation: b1465)

instill v *physically introduce* b1425 [gen. "introduce": b1670]

laud, laudable v, adj b1425 (laudative: b1450; laudation: b1475; laudatory: b1555)

muffle v b1425

prate v *prattle* b1425 (noun use: b1600)

redeem v b1425 (redemption: b1470; redeeming: b1635)

repel v b1425 [obs. "extinguish": b1400 to 1500s]

repulse v b1425 (noun use: b1470; repulsion: b1420)

resume v b1425 ["take again": b1405]

resuscitate v b1425 (resusciten v: b1450)

retrieve v *in hunting* b1425 [fig. use: b1570]

revive v b1425 (revival: b1630)

smudge v *mar* b1425

terminate v *end* b1425 ["form a border": b1700; "be part of the end": b1800; "fire": b1980] (termination: b1630)

thicken v b1425 [obs. "compact": u1800s; "get wider": b1630; as in "the plot thickens": b1700] (thick v: b1150)

unsay v b1425 (unswear: b1585; unspeak: b1605)

vest v *as in "the powers vested in me"* b1425

abjure v b1430

accompany v b1430

assist, assistance v *help* b1430 (assist n: b1600)

boom v b1430 (noun use: b1500)

repeat v *say, do again* b1430 [obs. "return": b1375 to 1600s; repetition: b1425]

condescend v b1435 [obs. "descend": u1600s; obs. "yield": b1340 to 1700s] (condescendence: b1640; condescension: b1650)

dismiss v *release* b1435 ["send away": b1570] (dismissal: b1810)

impound v b1435 [leg. sense: b1655]

accrue v b1440

commute v *change* b1440 [as in "commute a sentence": b1635; "travel": b1890]

connect v b1440 [fig. "put 2 and 2 together": b1930]

contend v *rival, be in the running* b1440 ["assert": b1570] (contention: b1400; contender: b1550)

discourage v *deter; remove courage* b1440 ["caution against": b1670]

tarnish v *phys. dull* b1440 [fig. "stain": b1700] (noun use: b1715)

waggle v b1440 (noun use: b1870; waggly: b1895)

constitute v *form* b1445 [as in "that constitutes fraud": b1870] (adj use: b1400)

cross v *as in "cross out"* b1445

acquire v b1450 (acquisition: b1400; acquirement: b1630)

alienate v b1450 (adj use: b1420; alien v: b1400; alienation: b1395)

approbate v *sanction* b1450

chat v b1450 (noun use: b1530; chatter: b1250)

chirp v b1450 (noun use: b1805)

circumvent v b1450

clean v *as in "clean a fish," "clean your plate"* b1450

["wash, tidy": b1730; as in "clean out": b1870]

crackle v b1450 (noun use: b1885)

defer v *delegate* b1450

divert, diversion v, n b1450 (arch. diversive: concurrent)

encourage v *instill courage* b1450 ["urge": b1500; "aid": b1670] (encouragement: b1570; encouraging: b1595)

exact v b1450

exhume v b1450

expand v *as in "expand a map"* b1450 ["enlarge": b1800; "elaborate": b1870] (expansion: b1615)

expend v *spend* b1450 ["eplete": b1770]

exploit v b1450 ["perform exploits": b1450 to 1700s] (exploitation: b1805; exploitative: b1885; exploitive: b1925)

fabricate v b1450 ["lie": b1780] (fabric v: b1630)

fault v *find fault; fail* b1450

fillip v *flick with your fingernail* b1450 (noun use: b1520)

foreordain v *preordain* b1450

fortify v b1450

frequent v b1450

frustrate v b1450 (frustration: b1555; frustrating: b1875)

furnish v b1450 (furnishing: b1470)

glance v *as in "glance off"* b1450 ["look": b1600]

heighten v b1450 [obs. "exalt": b1450 to 1600s; "intensify": b1600]

immix v *commingle* b1450

incite v b1450

inebriate v b1450 (adj use: b1450; noun use: b1800; inebriated: b1610)

intact adj b1450

interfere v b1450 (interference: b1785)

invoke v b1450 (invocation: b1375; invocate: b1530)

jounce v *bounce* b1450

(noun use: b1790; jouncy: b1945)

lash v *as in "lash a rope"* b1450 ["lace," as in "lash a corset": b1450 to 1600s] (noun use: b1450)

manumit v *emancipate* b1450

mock v b1450 ["trick": b1430] (noun use: b1500)

portend v b1450 (portentous: b1500; portent: b1565)

prohibit v *fig. prohibit* b1450 ["phys. prohibit": b1570]

prune v *gen. trim* b1450 [spec. "trim trees": b1570]

remand v b1450 (noun use: b1800)

retract v *physically withdraw* b1450 [fig. use: b1545]

separate v b1450 (adj use: b1450)

solicit v b1450 [obs. "cause anxiety": b1470 to 1700s; as in "solicit prostitutes": b1600] (solicitation: b1495; solicitous: b1565)

stem v *curtail* b1450

subdivide, subdivision v, n b1450

subjugate v *defeat* b1450 ["take control over": b1600]

surcease v b1450

tousle v b1450 (touse v: b1350)

unite v *phys. join* b1450 [gen. "join in": b1570; "marry": b1730] (unity: b1300; united: b1554)

venture v b1450 [as in "venture an opinion": b1670] (noun use: b1570)

coerce v b1455 (coercion: b1415)

control v *wield power, handle* b1455 [obs. "reproach": b1530 to 1700s; "restrain": b1570; "place in check": b1870] (noun use: b1590; controlment: b1500)

abolish v b1460

act v b1460 (noun use: b1380)

desist v b1460 ["resist": b1970]

gad v *as in "gad about"*

b1460 (gadabout n: b1840)

wage v *conduct, as in "wage war"* b1460

bluster v *lit. and fig.* b1465 (noun use: b1585)

celebrate v *perform a ceremony* b1465 ["observe," as in "celebrate an occasion": b1530; "praise": b1570; "rejoice, party": b1930] (celebration: b1530)

face v *confront* b1465 ["look toward": b1670]

abrogate v

action n

address v *as in "address an envelope"* (noun use: b1715)

admit v *confess* (admission: b1570)

advantage v

affix v

appall v *shock* [obs. "become pale": b1325 to 1800s] (appalling: b1820)

apply v *as in "apply knowledge"; as in "apply oneself"* (application: b1475)

appropriate v

attach v *join together* ["join to": b1830]

attend v *as in "attend a rally"*

balk v [obs. "plow into ridges": b1325 to 1600s] (balky: b1850)

bar v *prevent*

beat v *flap*

beshrew v *curse*

bind v *put together, e.g., "bind a book"*

blather v (noun use: b1525)

block v *prevent* (noun use: b1650)

board v *enter by force* [gen. "enter": b1600]

bumble v *bungle, blunder*

calculate v (obs. calculen "calculate": b1380; obs. calk "calculate": b1400)

catch v *as in "catch a cold"*

clear v *demonstrate innocence; lit. and fig. clarify* (adj use: b1300)

cloak v (noun use: b1295)

cocker v *indulge, pamper*

comment v *make comment* [obs. "concoct": u1500s]

confer v [obs. "gather": u1600s; obs. "compare": b1530 to 1700s; "present, award": b1570]

confide v *trust* [as in "confide a secret": b1735] (confidant: b1620; confidante: b1700)

confuse v *confound* [obs.

"ruin": b1330; "mistake one for another": b1630] (confusion: b1350; confusticate "confuse": b1900)

crumble v

decollate v *behead*

defense v [in sports: b1950]

delegate v (delegation: b1615)

deliver v *as in "deliver a speech"* (delivery: b1600)

depreciate v *insult*

dilacerate v *tear up*

dip v *drop*

disappear v

discommend v

dispeople v

drag v

drain v *as in "drain a glass of beer"*

ease v *make easy*

eclipse v *surpass, obscure*

embrace n/v *hug; accept*

employ v *use* ["hire": b1600]

enfranchise v

ensnarl n

entangle v *make entangled* ["make tangled": b1540] (entanglement: b1535)

enter v *as in "enter the priesthood"*

eradicate v *uproot* ["eliminate": b1630]

eviscerate v [fig. "deprive of strength": b1870]

exonerate v ["take away": b1525; obs. "purge": b1570 to 1800s]

expose v (exposure: b1605)

fall v *fell*

fend v *as in "fend off"* ["defend against": b1300; as in "fend for yourself": b1630]

foreshow n *foretell* [obs. "make provision": b1000]

frig v *wiggle* ["fuck": b1600]

full v *make full*

fumble v (noun use: b1635)

generalize v

gnash v

guess v *as in "I guess"*

halt v *vacillate* (halting: b1585)

have at v

incline v *fig. "be inclined"* ["phys. lean in": b1380]

infringe v ["encroach":

b1770] (infringement: b1595)

inscribe v

inspire v [religious sense: b1340]

knell v *ring a bell* [obs. "hit": b950]

knit v *as in "knitted brow"*

lacerate v (adj use: b1545; laceration: b1600)

lead v *be in first place* [in sport: b1800]

louse v *delouse*

mark v *as in "mark my words"*

marshal v

mingle v

molt v [spec. biological sense: b1595] (noun use: b1815)

move v *as in "I move to adjourn"*

muster v [obs. "explain": b1325 to 1600s]

neglect v (noun use: b1590)

obfuscate v (obfuscation: b1610)

object v *express disagreement* [obs. "create an obstacle": u1800s]

oppress v *subjugate* [obs. "suppress": b1350 to 1800s; obs. "surprise," "rape": u1600s] (oppression: b1350; oppressive: b1600)

outspeak v

patch v

peep v *peek* [as in "peep out": b1600]

pitch v *throw, toss* [used in sports: b1770] (noun use: b1870)

play v *as in "play the fool"*

plenish v *replenish*

point v *indicate, as in "point with your finger"*

prepare v *make ready* [as in "prepare dinner": b1500] (noun use: b1570)

project v *cause to protrude* ["protrude": b1700]

promise v ["foreshadow": b1600; "be promising": b1630]

pulse v

pulverize v [fig. "destroy":

b1670] (obs. "pulver": u1700s)

raise v *rise*

ramble v *express yourself wanderingly* ["travel aimlessly": b1620]

ramify v *branch out* (ramification: b1665)

rap v *knock* (noun use: b1670)

rattle v *as in "rattle off six wins"*

receive v *as in "receive an injury"*

recoil v [obs. "push back": b1225 to 1700s]

record v [obs. "tell," "recite," "remember": b1225 to 1700s; pertaining to sound: b1900]

recount v *relate*

redouble v

reflect v *mirror* ["deflect": b1400; "think": b1630] (reflection: b1400)

regulate v (regulation: b1665)

reinforce v [mil. sense: b1500]

relax v *as in "relax a muscle"* [obs. "loosen": b1400 to 1600s]

relinquish v

retreat v

rip v (noun use: b1715)

roof v

shatter v *smash* ["scatter": b1350]

situate v (adj use situated, situation: b1500)

snuff v *snort, sniff*

sound v *fathom*

squat v (noun use: b1590)

squench v *quench, extinguish*

stagger v ["astonish": b1520; "arrange in a staggered way": b1870]

stamp v *as in "stamp your foot"; as in "stamp a coin"* ["walk heavily": b1500] (noun use: b1600)

strike v *miscellaneous meanings, as in "strike a match"; "the clock strikes nine"; "strike a coin"; "strike an agreement"*

strut v *swagger* [obs. "protrude": b1000 to 1800s;

obs. "bloat": b1350 to 1800s]

submerse v

succeed v *be successful* (noun use: b1600)

support v *as in "support a family"* (noun use: b1600)

survey v *look over* ["perform a land survey": b1570; "conduct a survey of opinion, etc.": b1970] (noun use: b1550)

survive v [as in "survive a birthday party": b1500] (survival, survivor: b1600)

sweeten v (rare sweet v: b1150)

swing v *as in "swing a bat"* (noun use: b1670)

thwack v (noun use: b1590)

totter v [obs. "swing": b1225 to 1600s] (noun use: b1750)

trail v *track*

train v *as in "train a plant"* ["teach, educate": b1570; as in "train for the Olympics": b1870] (training: b1450; trainer: b1600; trainee: b1845)

treat v *handle, deal with, as in "treat your children well"* [obs. "treat with kindness": b1450 to 1500s; "give treats": b1730] (treatment: b1560)

trip v *as in "trip the light fantastic"* (noun use: b1350; tripple: b1630; tripsome: b1870)

trip v *stumble; cause to stumble* (noun use: b1350)

unbe v *cease to be*

unveil v

vivify v

waive v *as in "waive a right"* ["outlaw": b1300; arch. "avoid": b1350; obs. "abdicate": b1350 to 1600s; obs. "reconsider": b1450 to 1800s; as in "waive a rule": b1670] (waiver: b1630)

warm v *as in "warm up to someone"*

warp v *bend, distort* ["pervert": b1600] (noun use: b1700)

weep v excrete, drip, as in "weeping pipes"
wheeze v
witness v as in "witness a wedding" [gen. "see": b1600]
work v as in "work the controls"

Archaisms

habit v obs. reside b1375 [u1600s]
jeopard v jeopardize b1375
peasecod n arch. peapod b1375
range v arrange b1375
repugn v oppose b1375
suasion n persuasion b1375 (suasible: b1600)
monstrous adj obs. unnatural b1380 [u1700s] ("huge": b1520; "egregiously villainous": b1600)
disjoint n dilemma b1385
repugnance, repugnant n, adj opposition; opposed b1385
determinate v obs. determine b1395 [u1800s] (adj use: b1395)
commove v move violently b1400
definition n arbitration, decision b1400
denomination n naming b1400
fable v obs. tell tall tales b1400 [u1800s] (obs. fabulize: b1630 to 1800s)
grudge v/n complain b1400 ["begrudge": b1500]
grutch v begrudge b1400
howbeit conj although b1400
irascible n hateful part of the soul b1400
meseems v it seems to me, methinks b1400 (methinks: b900)
moderator n obs. ruler b1400 [u1800s]
poetical adj fictitious b1400
somewhither adv b1400
term v obs. terminate b1410 [u1500s]
alienate adj b1420
commix v blend b1425 (commixture: b1595)

deject adj dejected b1425 (dejection: b1450)
eminent adj high-up b1425
facture n quality of manufacture b1425 ["manufacture": b1500]
lowlihead n lowliness b1425
lurch v obs. lurk b1425 [arch. "steal": b1570]
tenebrous adj dark, gloomy b1425 (obs. tenebres "darkness": b1350 to 1600s; arch. tenebrific: b1785)
repulsive adj repelling b1430 [fig. "uninviting": b1600]
factor n obs. perpetrator b1435 [u1800s] (verb use: b1615)
face v boast b1440
molsh adj moist b1440
con v study b1450
durance n duration b1450 (obs. dure v: b1350 to 1500s)
gust n liking, taste b1450 ["gusto": b1670]
import v imply b1450
influent adj exerting astrological influence b1450 (influential: b1570)
swound n swoon b1450 (verb use: b1530)
troublous adj b1450
allegate v obs. allege [u1600s]
apostless n obs. female apostle [u1800s] (apostle: b900)
complicate adj complicated
confeder v confederate [u1600s]
decore v arch. decorate
decurtation n obs. trimming [u1700s]
defamous adj infamous
delay v obs. alleviate [u1600s]
demand n inquiry
demy adj half
deprehend v obs. surprise [u1600s]
despect n obs. something that causes contempt [u1800s]
diminue v obs. diminish, disparage [u1500s] (obs. diminute "diminished": u1700s)
disadventure n obs. misadventure [u1600s]

enchase v [u1700s]
enlarge v let go, liberate
enorm n obs. abomination [u1500s]
ensample v obs. exemplify [u1600s]
entertain v maintain
entire adj obs. righteous, beyond reproach; honest [u1700s]
envy v obs. vie with [u1600s]
everylike adj always the same
everywither adv
expugn v obs. conquer [u1700s]
fee v obs. bribe [u1800s]
fellow n obs. conspirator [u1600s]
feracity n prolificity
force n obs. farce [u1700s]
force v obs. strengthen [u1800s]
fort adj obs. strong [u1700s]
frequence n gathering
frisk adj [u1800s] (verb use: b1520; noun use: b1525; frisky: b1525)
frumple v wrinkle
full v obs. fulfill [u1500s]
geal v obs. congeal [u1800s]
gest n gesture
get v arrive at
gleimy adj obs. sticky [u1700s]
gnar v snarl (obs. gnarl v: b1600 to 1800s)
great adj myriad
gride v hurt, wound
hand v handle
happiness n prosperity, success ["gladness": b1600]
headsman n leader
het adj heated
incarn v heal
incontinently adv immediately
increasement n
infrigidation n cooling (infrigidate: b1570)
inquiet adj obs. tumultuous [u1500s]
instinction n obs. instigation [u1600s]
instore v obs. restore [u1500s]
intestine adj internal
jet v obs. strut [u1600s]
large adj not strict, unrestrained
lead v obs. steer [u1500s]

licentiate v arch. license
light v make lighter
lightful adj
like v obs. liken [u1600s]
like adv equally
likelihood n obs. likeness [u1600s]
likely adj obs. similar [u1600s]
livelihead n obs. liveliness [u1700s]
lumine v illuminate
man v obs. populate [u1500s]
man v obs. escort [u1700s]
marrow n colleague
masculine n man
mash v obs. mix [u1700s]
moist adj obs. new [u1700s]
mysterial adj mysterious
pike v obs. leave quickly [u1500s]
plum n plump up (adj use: b1600)
precellence n excellence (obs. precel v: u1700s)
race n journey [u1500s]
radious adj obs. radiant [u1600s]
reason n obs. process [u1600s]
reason v obs. discuss [u1500s]
reasonable adj articulate
refel v obs. refute [u1700s]
sad adj dark, as in "a sad red" (sadden: b1800)
say-well n saying nice things
scrawl v obs. sprawl [u1500s]
sensate adj
towardly adj
tuggle v jerk around
uberty n fecundity
unpossible adj
violate adj
visive adj obs. seeing [u1800s]
voice n obs. speech [u1600s]
walter v wallow
wave v obs. waver [u1700s]
white adj obs. plausible [u1800s]
whosomever pron [u1600s]
wilderness n obs. wildness [u1600s]
will v obs. ask, request [u1600s]
work v ache
ypent adj penned up

IN USE BY
1500

Geography/Places
sinkhole n b1475
glen n b1490
low country n
lowland n (adj use: b1510)
wave n *on the ocean* [gen. "surge": b1870] (verb use: b1570; waw: b1200)

Natural Things
fox fire n b1475
atom n b1480 (atomic: b1680; atomy "atom": b1600)
touchstone n *type of stone* b1485 [fig. "standard, benchmark": b1530]
dawn v *of the sun* [gen. "begin": b1730] (noun use: b1600; daw: b1150; dawning: b1250)
deadwood n *lit.* [fig. "useless things": b1730]
springwater n

Plants
aerie n b1475
rocket n *type of plant*
rosebud n
water lily n

Animals
beagle n b1475
dogfish n b1475
greenhorn n *young animal* b1475 [fig. use: b1685]
red deer n b1475
sea horse n b1475
bruin n b1485
aquatic adj b1490 (aquatile adj: b1670)

barnacle n [type of goose: b1350]
bulldog n [fig. use: b1870]
clam n ["clamp": b1450]
fallow deer n
field mouse n
greenfinch n
honeybee n
lyamhound n *bloodhound*
pizzle n *animal penis*
sea mew n

Weather
meteor n *arch. weather phenomenon* b1475
hailstorm n

Science
projection n *arch. type of alchemical process* b1480
astronomy n [obs. "astrology": b1225 to 1700s]
geography n (geographical: b1560; geographic: b1670)

Energy
petroleum n

Time
weekday n *opp. of weekend* b1480 [obs. "day": b900 to LME; obs. "weekday including Saturday": b1600]
springtime n b1495 [fig. "beginning": b1600]
grass n *the time when grass grows*
hourglass n

Age/Aging
overage adj *too old*

Mathematics
geometrician n b1485

Measurement
avoirdupois weight n
jot n *little bit*
karat n
point n *compass position*
troy weight n

The Body
spittle n b1480
heartstring n b1485
jawbone n b1490
trundle-tail n *arch. dog with curled tail* b1490
axle-tooth n *arch. molar*
collarbone n
false rib n
hams n *as in "hamstrings"* (hamstring: b1565)
ichor n *blood*
musculature n
pectoral adj (noun use: b1770; pecs: 1970)
rectum n

Physical Description
bonny adj *pretty* b1475
clean-limbed adj b1475
blond/blonde adj b1485 (noun use: b1825)
drowsy adj (drowse v: b1575; drowse n: b1700)
egest v *opp. of ingest; defecate* (egestion: b1470; egesta: b1730)

impuissance n *weakness* (impuissant: b1630)
manducation n *arch. chewing* (manducate: b1630)
portly adj *grand, stately* ["fat": b1600]
suspiration n *sigh* (suspire: b1570)

Medicine
bonesetter n b1475
diabetes n (diabete: b1425; diabetic adj: b1800; diabetic n: b1840)
dress v *as in "dress a wound"*
hives n
knit v *heal*
leprosy n
limewater n
nursling n (arch. nursle: b1600)

Everyday Life
pomander n b1475
pothook n b1475
truckle bed n *trundle bed* b1475
dishwater n b1485
flag n *banner* b1485 (verb use: b1860)
tankard n b1485 [obs. type of container: b1325 to 1600s]
birdcage n b1490 (birdhouse: b1870)
toothpick n b1490
bedsheet n
kennel n *street gutter*
mop n *cleaning tool*
needle n *as in "knitting needle"*

rolling pin n
warming pan n *bedwarmer*

Shelter/Housing
padlock n b1475 (verb use: b1670)
repository n b1485 (repertory "repository": b1595; reposit v: b1645)
shed n *small building* b1485
entertain v *as in "entertain guests"* b1490
manse n *obs. mansion* b1490 [u1700s]
bar n *counter, as in "snack bar"*
bulkhead n
crossbeam n
linseed oil n
nursery n ["nurturing": b1450 to 1600s]

Drink
rack v *wine-making term* b1475
ambrosia n
buttermilk n
dry adj *alcohol-free*
spruce beer n

Food
baste v *pour liquids over* b1475
comestible adj *obs. consumable* b1485 [u1600s]
seedcake n b1490
bone v *debone* b1495
marchpane n *marzipan* b1495
caper n *garnish* [type of bush: b1400]
carrot n [fig. "incentive": b1900]
curd n/v (crud: b1380; verb use: b1470; curdle: b1650)
French bread n
ham n
marmalade n
marzipan n
steam v *cook by steaming*
zest n *as in "lemon zest"* [fig. use: b1730; "gusto": b1800]

Agriculture/ Food–Gathering
trawl v b1485
beeyard n *apiary*

domestic adj *tame*
graft v/n
haystack n (haycock: b1300)
sugarcane n

Cloth/Clothing
crewel n *type of yarn* b1495 [type of embroidery: b1600]
calfskin n
chapeau n *hat*
cuff n *as in "shirtcuff"* [obs. type of mitten: b1380; as in "pant cuffs": b1915] (verb use: b1530)
disattire v *arch. undress*
haircloth n
headgear n

Fashion/Style
coif n (verb use: b1835; coiffure: b1625; coiffured: b1910)
posy n *bunch of flowers* [arch. "sentimental bon mot": b1450]

Tools
handbasket n b1495
sledgehammer n b1495 (verb use: b1635; adj use: b1845)
candlelighter n
distillatory n *obs. type of still* [u1700s]
eightpenny nail n
masher n *as in "potato masher"*
tenpenny nail n
utensil n

Travel/Transportation
castaway n b1475 (adj use: b1535)
mainsail n *sailing term* b1475 (mainmast, mainsheet: b1485)
wagon n b1475 (verb use: b1610)
ketch n *type of boat* b1485
moor v b1495
sidesaddle adv/n b1495
backstreet n
caravan n (verb use: b1885; caravanner: b1895)
gunwale/gunnel n
longboat n
merchant ship n

merchantman n *type of ship*
pink n *type of ship* (pinkie: b1840)
raft n *boat* [arch. "rafter": b1300] (verb use: b1700)
skiff n
wreck n *destroyed ship* ["wreckage": b1730; "something wrecked": b1800]
yardarm n

Emotions/ Characteristics
demeanor n b1475 (demean v "conduct oneself": b1300)
fair-spoken adj b1475
frivolous adj b1475 (obs. frivlol adj: b1500 to 1600s)
querulous adj *complaining* b1475 ["litigious": b1400]
truehearted adj b1475
vigilant adj b1480 (obs. vigilancy: b1570 to 1700s; vigilance: b1535)
brave adj b1485 (bravery: b1550)
vehement adj *violent* b1485 [describing feelings: b1530]
turpitude n b1490
incense v *anger* b1495 ["excite": b1410]
amicable adj *friendly* [obs. "benign": b1425]
cheerly adj *arch. cheerful*
delightsome adj
dour adj
enfire v *obs. impassion* [u1800s]
enjoy v *obs. make joyful* [u1600s]
enrage v
foolishness n (foolery: b1555)
frivol n *frivolity*
furor n [obs. "madness": b1470]
gravity n *seriousness*
grudge n
haughty adj ["noble": b1400] (arch. haught adj: b1470)
humane adj ["human": b1470 to 1700s]

misdemean v *arch. have a bad demeanor*
penitence n [rare "penance": b1200]
polite adj [obs. phys. "polished": b1450 to 1700s; obs. "phys. clean": u1700s]
presence n *bearing, stature, as in "stage presence"* ["someone with presence": b1830]
raving adj/adv
stare n *being frozen in astonishment*
timorous adj *timid* [rare "scared": b1450]
warmhearted adj

Thoughts/Perception/ The Mind
permissive adj *giving permission; received permission* b1475
premonition n b1475 (premonish v: b1530; premonitory: b1650)
sharp-witted adj b1490
stratagem n b1490
addle adj *addled* ["rotten": b1250] (verb use: b1600; addled: b1750)
asinine adj
creative adj
determine v *obs. deduce* [u1800s]
enigma n *riddle* ["mystery, something unknown": b1630] (enigmatic: b1630)
humor n *state of mind* [mood: b1525; type of body fluid: b1340; "funny perspective": b1600]
incertitude n (obs. incertain: b1470 to 1700s; obs. incertainty: b1500 to 1700s)
justification n *reason, rationalization* ["law": b1400 to 1600s]
obtuse adj *dull-witted* [geometry sense: b1500]
position n *point of view, opinion*
studied adj
supposed adj

Love/Romance/Sex

heart-whole adj *not in love* b1475 (heartfree: b1750)

nuptial adj b1490 (noun use: b1510)

virile adj b1490 ["lusty": b1530; "able to father children": b1570; arch. describing manly attire: b1630] (virility: b1590)

lubricity n *lust* b1495 (lubric adj: b1500; lubricious: b1535)

affiance v *betroth*

intended n

marital adj

minion n *lover* (servant: b1530)

mixture n *obs. sex* [u1700s]

mount n *slang sex* (verb use: b1700)

seductor n [u1600s] (seductress: b1805)

see v *as in "seeing a girl-friend"*

union n *sexual union*

Family/Relations/Friends

paterfamilias n *head of the household* b1475

maternal adj b1485

agnate n *male relative on father's side*

dad, daddy n

extraction n

forbear n *ancestor*

foremother n (forefather: b1300)

only child n

Games/Fun/Leisure

deuce n *playing card* b1475 [in tennis: b1600]

pastime n b1490

rack v *as in "rack pool balls"*

Sports

cockfight n b1495

bowling n (bowls: b1495; bowling alley: b1545)

racquet n (racket: b1565)

Professions/Duties

ferryman n b1475

scullion n *scullery worker* b1475

teller n b1475

nightwalker n b1485

farrier n (obs. farry v: b1700 to 1800s)

hatmaker n (hatter: b1350)

innkeeper n

Business/Commerce/Selling

coal mine n b1475

gold mine n b1475

bar n *tavern* (barroom: b1800)

cheap adj *inexpensive* ["flimsy": b1600] (arch. noun use: b725; cheapen: b1670)

pawn n *as in "pawn shop"* (verb use: b1570)

proprietor n (proprietress: b1695)

shop window n

taphouse n

The Workplace

workfolk n b1475

industrial adj *related to work*

vocation n (vocational: b1565)

working day n

Finances/Money

bank n *financial institution, storage place* b1475 (verb use: b1755)

treasure-house n b1475

customhouse n b1490

excise n *tax* b1495 (verb use: b1655)

pauper n b1495 (pauperize: b1835)

journal n *bookkeeping record*

rate n *charge, as in "the going rate"*

spending money n

Language and Speaking

metaphor n b1480

legend n *motto*

possessive pronoun n

proper noun n

Literature/Writing

misprint v b1495 (noun use: b1830)

authoress n (author: b1470)

bookseller n

copy n *written work* (copy-edit: b1955)

moral n (obs. moralize: b1500 to 1700s)

paragraph n

poem n (poet: b1300; poetry: b1400; poetic: b1530; poetics: b1730)

Visual Arts/Photography

chalk n [the substance: b700]

mosaic n *type of artwork* ["process of creating mosaics": b1400] (adj use: b1585)

picture n [obs. "art of picturing": b1425 to 1800s; as in "the picture of health": b1600; as in "the big picture": b1930]

picture v *create a picture* ["imagine": b1770]

potter's clay n

Performing Arts

exeunt v b1485

Music

windbag n *part of a bagpipe* b1475

harmonize v b1485

tambour n *type of drum* b1485

viol n b1485

chanson n *type of song*

dulcimer n

fret n *as in "guitar fret"* (verb use: b1605)

key n *as in "piano key"* [as in "typewriter key": b1870]

sackbut n *arch. trombone*

timbrel n *type of percussion instrument*

tune v *sing* [as in "tune the piano": b1530; fig. "put on the same wavelength": b1600; as in "tune an engine": b1830; as in "tune the radio": b1930]

Entertainment

banquet n b1475 [obs. "between-meal snack": b1530 to 1600s]

Education

advanced degree n b1475

go up v *(Brit) attend a university*

master of arts n *the degree* (master of science: b1905)

schoolfellow n (schoolmate: b1565)

Religion

infidel n b1475 (adj use: b1470; infidelity: b1425)

yuletide n b1475

theologian n b1485 (theologician: b1570)

breviary n

clerical adj ["pertaining to clerks": b1800]

dismal n *obs. satan* [u1500s]

godling n

hymnal n (hymnbook: b900; hymnary: b1890)

irreligious adj (irreligion: b1600)

laying on of hands n

ministress n (minister: b1350)

sacrosanct adj

Society/Mores/Culture

serf n b1485 [obs. "slave": b1485]

conductor n *gen. leader* [spec. "band leader": b1785; as in "electrical conductor": b1740; as in "train conductor": b1830] (conductress: b1625)

distaff n *women*

laypeople n

maidservant n

Government

regina n *queen* b1475

viscountess n b1475 (viscount: b1400)

ochlocracy n *mob rule* b1485

town hall n b1485

commission n

great seal n

oligarchy n (oligarch: b1610)

police n *arch. government*

Politics

Election Day n

embassage n *embassy*

Life
livingly adv *vitally*

Death
dance of death n b1480
deceased adj b1490 ["someone dead": b1625]
fatality n b1490
cadaver n (cadaverous: b1425)
fratricide n *someone who kills* ["killing a brother": b1570]
ratsbane n *type of poison*
suffocate v

War/Military/Violence
combatant n b1475 (adj use: b1450)
surprise n *surprise attack* b1475 ["something that surprises": b1595; "feeling of surprise": b1610] (verb use: b1390)
man-of-war n *type of warship* b1485
rear guard n b1485
halberd n *type of weapon* b1495
invade v b1495 [obs. "assault": b1470]
belt v *hit with a belt* [gen. "hit": b1870] (noun use: b1900)
commissioned officer n
convoy v *escort militarily* [gen. "guide": b1375]
crossbowman n
dub v *drub*
duel n *leg. challenge* [gen. challenge: b1595] (verb use: b1645; duelist: b1600; duello: b1600)
gunnery n ["all guns": b1500]
mate n
mayhem n
molest v *hurt, abuse* [obs. "bother, annoy": b1375 to 1700s]
pelt v *hit* (noun use: b1450)
victim n *human sacrifice* [gen. "injured party": b1670; as in "victim of a joke": b1800] (victimize: b1830)
waste n *as in "lay waste"*

Crime/Punishment/Enforcement
larceny n b1475 (larcener: b1635; larcenous: b1745; larcenist: b1805)
offender n b1475
misdemeanor n b1490 (misdemeanant: b1820)
fact n *as in "after the fact"*
foul play n
misbegotten adj
order n *as in "law and order"*
rape n *sexual assault* ["taking away by force": b1400] (verb use: b1600)

The Law
courthouse n b1475
droit n *leg. right* b1480
bail n b1485 [var. obs. meanings related to jurisdiction: b1340 to 1800s] (verb use: b1550)
inheritrix n b1485 (inheritor: b1450; inheritress: b1530)
jurist n b1485 ["leg. expert": b1630]
reversal n b1490
chance-medley n *related to self-defense* b1495
repossess v b1495
charge n *accusation* (verb use: b1350)
grand jury n
legal adj *pertaining to law* ["allowed by law": b1670]
legislator n
lex n *law*
material adj
parole n (verb use: b1670; parolee: b1905)
petit jury n
recognition n *obs. type of real estate repossession* [u1700s]

The Fantastic/Paranormal
brownie n *type of goblin*
rotation n *alchemy term*

Interjections
ach interj
bon voyage interj
gad/gads interj
go to interj
hem interj/v *as in "hem and haw"*

hi interj *hello* [used to get attention, akin to "hey": b1470]

Slang
beat off v *masturbate*
bender n *alcoholic fling*
fuck v ["destroy, spoil": b1970]
kingmaker n
shrinking violet n *shy person*

Insults
riffraff n b1475
hardhead n (hardheaded: b1585)
ruffian n

Phrases
fool's paradise n b1475
all fours n
article of faith n
back-to-back adj/adv
bred-in-the-bone adj *deep-seated*
double-edged adj
helping hand n
hue and cry n *commotion*
mortal sin n
now and then adv
open house n
over and above prep
over and over adv
part and parcel n
rhyme or reason n
then and there adv
through and through adv
time out of mind n
upper hand n
white elephant n

General/Miscellaneous
entrance n *right to enter* b1475 ["entering": b1530]
mishmash n b1475
neutrality n b1475 (neutralism: b1580)
ostentation n b1475 [obs. "omen": b1450 to 1600s] (ostentatious: b1660)
predation n *plunder* b1475
recognition n *honor* b1475 (recognize: b1570)
talebearer n b1480
accomplice n b1485
axiom n b1485 (axiomatic: b1800)
celerity n *speed* b1485

delinquent n b1485 (adj use: b1605)
emery n b1485
paradigm n b1485
proximity n b1485
registry n b1485
accumulation, accumulate n, v b1490 (accumulate: b1500)
band n *troop or group* b1490 ["musical group": b1665] (verb use: b1570)
effort n b1490 [obs. "power": u1600s; "result of effort": b1870] (effortless: b1805; effortful: b1895)
situation n *placement* b1490 ["difficult circumstance": b1770; "job": b1830] (situational: b1905)
endurance n *duration* b1495 ["patience": b1600; "ability to endure": b1900]
acceleration, accelerate n,v (accelerate: b1530)
all n *as in "gave his all"* (adj/other uses: b725)
antagonist n (antagonism: b1830)
attribute n (verb use: b1525)
base n *basis*
bilge n [fig. "nonsense": b1900] (bilgewater: b1630)
bite n *act of biting* ["portion of food": b1570; "piquance": b1900] (verb use: b725)
brevity n
end n *remnant*
extent n *phys. scope* ["land appraisal": b1300; fig. "scope": b1600]
fabrication n *something fabricated* ["prevarication": b1800]
fetor n *stench* (fetid: b1450)
havoc n [type of battle cry: b1420] (verb use: b1580)
housing n *ornamental enclosure* [for a machine: b1885]
idlesse n *idleness*
mainstay n
must n *mustiness*
packet n
pang n (verb use: b1505)
pass n *as in "it came to pass"*

penalty n

public n as in "out in public" ["people": b1670]

reality n [opp. of perception: b1870]

romance n fabrication (verb use: b1675)

scale n as in "the scale of a production"

shortcoming n

simulacrum n representation

slice n [as in "slice a golf ball": b1900]

sparkle n [fig. "ebullience": b1630] (arch. spark: b1400)

stall n/v delay

standard n an example to be met ["criterion": b1570] (adj use: b1830)

stop n pause

strand n filament

tier n [fig. "rank": b1600] (verb use: b1890)

track n as in "animal track" [gen. "route": b1570; as in "railroad tracks": b1830; as in "racetrack": b1870; as in "tank tracks": b1900] (verb use: b1565)

train n procession [fig. "sequence," as in "train of thought": b1670; as in "drive train": b1800; as in "railway train": b1830]

trench n [obs. "path": b1400 to 1500s; "ocean channel": b1970]

trepidation n trembling (trepid adj: b1650; trepidant adj: b1895)

troglodyte n

variety n being varied; varied collection ["difference": b1570]

wake n as in "the wake of a boat" [gen. "track, evidence of passing": b1500]

Things

oriflamme n type of banner b1475 [spec. "banner of St. Dennis": b1475]

book n something bound, as in "matchbook"

rattle n as in "baby rattle"

Description

becoming adj b1475

cornerwise adv b1475

integral adj b1475

splendent adj lit. lustrous b1475 ["resplendent": b1550]

stock-still adj b1475

verbatim adv b1475 (adj use: b1740; noun use: b1900)

mutual adj reciprocal b1480

commanding adj b1485

licit adj opp. of illicit b1485

nocturnal adj of the night b1485 [pertaining to animals: b1600]

sumptuous adj luxurious b1485 [obs. "expensive": b1450 to 1600s]

tardy adj slow b1485 ["late": b1670] (verb use: b1630; noun use: b1960; obs. tardation: b1530 to 1600s; tardity: b1450)

furtive adj b1490

interior adj b1490 (noun use: b1600)

magnific adj magnificent b1490

mobile adj b1490

urgent adj b1490 (urgency: b1540)

degenerate adj b1495 (verb use: b1545; noun use: b1555)

amber adj (noun use: b1770)

askance adv (askant: b1670)

audible adj

authentic adj genuine [obs. "commanding obedience": b1350 to 1800s] (authenticate, authenticity: b1660)

convenient adj [obs. "befitting": b1380 to 1600s; obs. "proper," "suitable": b1450 to 1700s] (convenience: b1425)

definite adj (definitive: b1400)

everduring adj everlasting

expeditious adj

experimental adj untested ["experiential": b1530]

far-off adj

fitting adj

furibund adj furious

gaudy adj (gaud: b1470; gaudery: b1600)

gorgeous adj

imperceptible adj (imperceivable: b1620)

inhabited adj

involuntary adj

knee-deep adj

lax adj not strict ["not constipated": b1400; "relaxed": b1670]

lily adj

main adj primary [var. obs. meanings of "large, powerful, great": b1150 to 1600s]

native-born adj

newfound adj

nocent adj harmful

novel adj [obs. "freshly created": b1450 to 1600s]

noxious adj

numerous adj ["copious, multi-faceted": b1450]

occult adj hidden [pertaining to mystical arts: b1670] (occultation: b1425)

open adj unprotected, as in "open to attack"

perishable adj (noun use: b1770)

perpendicular adj (arch. adv use: b1400; noun use: b1575)

plumb adv absolutely

possessed adj (possess: b1530; possession: b1600)

prodigious adj awe-inspiring [obs. "portentous": b1500 to 1700s; "huge": b1630]

russet adj (noun use: b1470)

separate adj [obs. "separated": b1450 to 1600s]

silent adj (silentious "typically silent": b1830)

slippery adj [fig. "unreliable": b1570] (slippy: b1550)

so-called adj

sterling adj pertaining to silver [fig. "excellent": b1670]

strict adj [rare "restricted": b1450]

supreme adj

thorough adj carried through

tiresome adj

tragic adj

trim adj/v spiffy [gen. "in good shape": b1570] (verb use: b1530)

undisguised adj

unhabited adj uninhabited

well-favored adj attractive

wondrous adj (obs. wonders "wondrous": b1350 to 1600s)

Colors

jet-black adj b1485

azure n the color (adj use: b1530)

ruby adj

silver n the color

Actions/Verbs

cleanse v clean physically, spiritually b700

allot v b1475 (allotment: b1575; allotee: b1850)

benefit v b1475

curtail v restrict b1475 ["shorten": b1555] (curtailment: b1795)

dredge v b1475 (noun use: b1475)

ennoble v b1475

expedite v handle expediently b1475 ["promote": b1630]

intermingle v mix b1475

pacify v b1475

permit v b1475 ["present opportunity": b1570]

prescribe v decree b1475 (prescription: b1300; prescriptive: b1750)

mix v b1480 (noun use: b1590; mixed: b1425; mixture: b1470)

retard v b1480

seduce v b1480 [sexual sense: b1570] (seduction: b1530; seducement: b1590; seductive: b1775)

tinge v b1480 (noun use: b1755)

acknowledge v b1485 (acknowledgement: b1595)

amass v b1485

announce v b1485 (announcer: b1605; announcement: b1800)

cluck v b1485 [fig. "fuss": b1600] (noun use: b1705)

convalesce v b1485 (convalescence: b1490; conva-

lescent adj: b1560; conva-
lescent n: b1770)

diversify v *make diverse*
b1485 [obs. "be diverse":
b1450 to 1800s]

plump v *fatten* b1485 (adj
use: b1570; plumpen:
b1670)

quiver v *shake* b1490 [obs.
"numbering system to ref-
erence text": b1530 to
1600s] (noun use: b1790)

rig v *as in "rig a sail"* b1490

scandalize v *publicize a scandal* b1490 ["offend":
b1650]

disappoint v b1495 ["remove
from an appointment":
b1435] (disappointing:
b1530; disappointed:
b1540; disappointment:
b1615)

dispossess v *take away things*
b1495 ["exorcise": b1600]
(dispossessed: b1500)

abandon v *leave behind* ["give
up": b1375; obs. "subdue":
b1470)

address v *speak to* (noun use:
b1670)

admire v

agree v *harmonize*

animate v (adj use: b1400;
animated: b1535)

apply v *have relevance* (applicable: b1600)

call v *visit*

concede v [as in "concede
the run" in baseball:
b1670; as in "concede the
election": b1900] (concession: b1450)

dissuade v

distemper v *obs. get drunk*
[u1500s]

draggle v *bedraggle* ["straggle": b1600]

elevate v (elevation: b1400;
elevated: b1555)

embitter v

endorse v *as in "endorse a
check"* ["support," as in
"endorse a candidate":
b1670] (endorsement:
b1550)

engorge v

engrave v (obs. engraven v:
b1630 to 1700s)

evade v *escape* ["work to escape": b1630]

eye v [obs. "see": b1600 to
1700s]

fit v *as in "fitted for a suit"*
(noun use: b1825)

forgather v

incinerate v

insert v (noun use: b1895)

lance v *as in "lance a boil"*

linger v *dawdle* ["stay":
b1570; as in "lingering illness": b1770]

near v

occur v [as in "it occurs to
me": b1630] (occurrent:

b1500; occurrence:
b1540)

participate v

persuade v ["convince":
b1530]

ply v *as in "ply a trade"* [gen.
"work hard": b1350; as in
"ply with liquor": b1570]

postpone v

recite v [obs. gen. "narrate":
u1700s] (recital: b1570)

retort v [obs. "physically rebuff": u1700s] (noun use:
b1600)

rival v *be approximately equal*
(adj use: b1670)

screak v *screech*

shriek v (noun use: b1590)

site v

slacken v *slow down* ["relax":
b1630]

slice v [obs. "fragment":
1300s to 1500s]

stuff v *cram*

sully v

thwart v *oppose successfully*
[arch. gen. "oppose":
b1250]

wait v *attend, as in "wait tables"*

wriggle v [lit. and fig., as in
"wriggle into": b1595]
(noun use: b1700)

Archaisms

fabric n *something built* b1485
["factory": b1670; "tex-
tile": b1770]

raven v *pillage/eat greedily*
b1495 ["eat ravenously":
b1570]

tristful adj b1495

bashaw n *muckamuck*

dispiece v *divide*

enormity n *obs. abnormality*
[u1800s] (obs. enormous:
b1530 to 1800s)

entertainment n *obs. pay*
[u1700s]

foy n *sendoff gift*

indeficient adj *obs. constant*
[u1800s]

intern adj *internal*

intoxicate adj *intoxicated*

lubric adj *smooth*

malheur n *obs. bad luck*
[u1700s]

mancipate n *obs. opp. of
emancipate* [u1800s]

mastiff n *obs. massive*
[u1700s]

mirific adj *wonderful* (obs.
mirifical: b1630 to 1800s)

pickthank n *sycophant*

practice n *treachery*

rate v *obs. allot, divide*
[u1600s]

resplent v *be resplendent*

utile adj *useful, utilitarian*

variation n *vacillation*

worser adj/adv

IN USE BY
1550

Geography/Places
archipelago n b1505
meadowland n b1530
quarter n *as in "French quarter"* b1530 [gen. "region": b1300]
seashore n b1530
whirlpool n b1530
islet n b1540 (island: b900; isle: b1225)
peninsula n b1540
rill n *brook* b1540 (verb use: b1610)
promontory n

Natural Things
grot n *grotto* b1510 (grotto: b1620)
mother-of-pearl n/adj b1510
lodestone n b1515
smolder v *smoke* b1530 ["smother": b1325]
woodnote n *natural music* b1535
brackish adj b1540

Plants
buttercup n b1515 ["cup for holding butter": b1700]
sandalwood n b1515
cornflower n b1530 [type of color: b1910]
service tree n *type of tree* b1530
carnation n b1535
forget-me-not n b1535
gooseberry n b1535
daffodil n b1540
spearmint n b1540
tendril n b1540
witch hazel n b1545

geranium n [modern use: b1770]
larch n
oleander n *type of shrub*
sea wrack n *seaweed*
wintergreen n [type of flavor: b1870]

Animals
dolphinfish n b1515
flying fish n b1515
torpedo n *type of fish* b1520
badger n b1525 (verb use: b1795)
parrot n b1525 [fig. "mimic": b1600] (verb use: b1600)
stinging nettle n b1525
bumblebee n b1530
carrion crow n b1530
cub n *young fox* b1530 [other animal young, including bear: b1630]
grampus n *type of dolphin* b1530
grouse n b1530 (verb use: b1870)
lamper eel n b1530
monkey n b1530 (monk: b1845)
periwinkle n *type of mollusk* b1530
puss n *cat* b1530 [slang "girl": b1630]
tumbler n *arch. type of dog* b1530
viper n *type of snake* b1530 [fig. "mean person": b1600]
woodpecker n b1530

bay n *bay-colored animal* b1535 (bayard: b1450)
civet n *type of wild cat* b1535 (civet cat: b1610)
snapper n *type of fish* b1535
spiderweb n b1535 ["mesh": b1650]
ringtail n b1540
starfish n b1540
ursine adj b1540
varmint n *applied to animals* b1540 [applied to people: b1800]
buffalo n *Asian buffalo* b1545 ["American buffalo": b1670]
harrier n *type of hawk* b1545
jackdaw n *type of bird* b1545
moo n/v b1545
owlet n *small owl* b1545
seagull n b1545
shrike n *type of bird* b1545
anemone n
crab louse n
fleabane n
head louse n
pen n *female swan*
robin n

Weather
overcast adj b1540 (verb use: b1225)
drizzle n b1545 (verb use: b1570)
fog n b1545 (verb use: b1600)
weatherman n b1545 (weatherperson: b1975)
gale n

Heavens/Sky
evening star n b1535
morning star n b1535
vernal equinox n b1535

Energy
kindling n *material to start fires* b1515 ["act of starting fires": b1300]
oil n *petroleum* b1530

Time
anno Domini n b1530
daybreak n b1530
peep n *dawn* b1530
daytime n b1535
noonday n b1535
vernal adj *of the spring* b1535
foretime n b1540
gnomon n *sundial pointer*

Age/Aging
age of consent n b1505
younker n *youth* b1515 ["child": b1605] (youngling: b900; youngster: b1515)
junior n b1525

Mathematics
cipher v b1530
quadrant n *square* b1530 ["a quarter day": b1400 to 1600s]
semicircle n b1530
algebra n b1545 [obs. "med. treatment of broken bones": late ME to 1500s] (algebraic: b1665)
cone n *type of geometric shape* b1545 [obs. "type of

angle": b1490 to 1700s; type of mountain: b1870] (conic, conical: b1570)

denominator n b1545

numerator n b1545

parallel adj [fig. "closely similar": b1630] (adv use: b1670)

Measurement

hundredweight n b1530

The Body

bun n *buttocks* b1530

nipple n b1530 ["nipple for baby bottle": b1900]

scruff n *dandruff* b1530

trillibubs n *arch. guts* b1530

windpipe n b1530

foreskin n b1535

hicket n *obs. hiccup* b1540 [u1600s]

abscess n b1545

aorta n b1545

cerebellum n b1545

dandruff n b1545

eyetooth n b1545

umbilical adj b1545

bile n (bilious: b1545)

tailbone n

throttle n *throat* [type of valve: b1830] (verb use: b1400)

Physical Description

awkward adj *clumsy, out of synch* b1530 [obs. "backward": b1350] (obs. "awk" adj: b1400 to 1800s)

clear-eyed adj b1530

sense n *taste, etc.* b1530 (verb use: b1535)

toothy adj b1530

tension n *bodily tension* b1535 ["mental tension": b1770] (verb use: b1895; tense adj: b1670)

Medicine

smallpox n b1520 (obs. small-pock n: b1470 to 1800s)

walleye n b1525

asthmatic adj/n b1530

cast n *as in "leg cast"* b1530

druggery n *arch. pharmaceuticals* b1530

gonorrhea n b1530

ingredience n *obs. med. ingredients* b1530 [u1600s]

miscarry v b1530 (miscarriage: b1665)

mithridate n b1530

phthisis n *type of consumptive disease* b1530

pregnancy n b1530 [fig. "fertility, creativity": b1500]

qualm n *nausea* b1530 ["misgiving": b1570] (qualmish: b1550)

communicable adj b1535

immedicable adj *incurable* b1535

clubfoot n b1540

cold n *as in "the common cold"* b1540 ["symptoms of being in the cold": b1340; "pain from being cold": b1300]

light-headed adj *dizzy* b1540 ["frivolous": b1450]

anodyne adj *pain-killing* b1545 [fig. "soothing": b1800] (noun use: b1560)

arthritis n b1545 (arthritic adj: b1375)

compound fracture n b1545

epilepsy n b1545 (epileptic adj: b1605)

gangrene n b1545 (cancrene: b1400)

infectious adj b1545 [fig. use: b1630] (infective: b1400)

malignant adj b1545 [gen. "rebellious": concurrent; "evil": b1600] (obs. malign: b1450; malignancy, malignance: b1605)

recuperate v b1545 [gen. use: b1870]

sedation n b1545

syndrome n b1545

therapeutics n b1545 (therapeutic adj: b1650)

convulsion n [gen. use: b1670; applied to laughter: b1770] (convulse: b1645)

hospital n ["guest house": b1300] (obs. hospitality "hospital": b1570 to 1700s)

panacea n (panace "nonexistent cure-all herb": b1530)

salubrious adj *healthful*

Everyday Life

dog collar n b1525

spatula n b1525

bushelbasket n b1530

dish clout n b1530 (dishcloth: b1830)

footstool n b1530

fountain n *as in "water fountain"* b1530 ["natural spring": b1425] (verb use: b1900)

glass n *as in "eyeglass"* b1530

handkerchief n b1530 (hankie: b1895)

looking glass n b1530

mug n b1530 [type of bowl: b1570]

porcelain n b1530 ["something made of porcelain": b1630] (adj use: b1600)

sheet n *piece of paper* b1530

tinderbox n b1530

washbowl n b1530

jakes n *bathroom* b1535

pacifier n b1535

chamber pot n b1540

housekeeping n b1540 (arch. householdry: b1600)

jug n *type of container* b1540

tea service n b1545

tooth powder n b1545

trundle bed n b1545

cabinet n *type of furniture* [type of political group: b1615] (cabinetmaker: b1685; cabinetry: b1930)

nutcracker n

Shelter/Housing

blockhouse n b1515

terrace n b1515 [type of geog. feature: b1700] (verb use: b1615)

clapboard n b1520

mantel n *support beam* b1520 ["mantelshelf": b1770] (manteltree: b1450; mantelshelf: b1830)

back door n b1530

camp n *temporary residence* b1530 [fig. "group," as in "the opposing camp": b1900] (verb use: 1545)

cohabit v b1530 (cohabitation: b1455)

residence n *home* b1530 ["re-

siding": b1400] (resident n: b1465; residential: b1655)

rough-hew, rough-hewn v, adj b1530

stand n *as in "fruit stand"* b1530

town house n b1530

truss n *architectural support* b1530 ["hernia support": b1670]

wing n *as in "wing of a building"* b1530

ceiling n b1535 [gen. "room lining, paneling": b1380] (ceil v: b1450)

platform n b1535 [as in "party platform": b1805]

vaulted adj *as in "vaulted ceiling"* b1535

rampart n b1540 (arch. rampire: b1570)

basilica n b1545

watchtower n b1545

cupola n

Drink

quaff v b1525 (noun use: b1580)

sack n *type of wine* b1530

syllabub n *type of drink* b1540

swig n (verb use: b1650)

Food

scone n *type of bread* b1515

artichoke n b1530

citron n *type of fruit* b1530 (citronade: b1395)

gigot n *leg of meat* b1530

candy v b1535

metheglin n *type of mead* b1535

porridge n b1535 [fig. "potpourri": b1670]

turnip n b1535

chawbacon n b1540

mother n b1540 (mother of vinegar: b1605)

Parmesan n b1540

pastry n *gen. pastry* b1540 ["pastry dough": b1450; a single piece of pastry: b1930]

potherb n b1540

salad oil n b1540

tarragon n *type of herb* b1540

buckwheat n

gormandize v *gorge*

kidney bean n

Agriculture/Food-Gathering

henhouse n b1515 (hencoop: b1700)

knot garden n *elaborate garden* b1520

browse n *shoots and twigs eaten by animals* b1525

farm n b1525 [type of tax, payment: b1300; "leased land": b1335] (farmhouse: b1600; farmery: b1670; farmyard: b1750)

fatling n b1530

granary n b1530

head n *as in "16 head of cattle"* b1530

stock n *livestock* b1530

leister n/v *spear used to catch fish* b1535

dragnet n b1545

workhorse n b1545

manure n

Cloth/Clothing

buskin n *type of boot* b1505

calico adj/n *type of cloth* b1505

toque n b1505

deck v b1515

Kendal green n *type of cloth* b1515

plaid n b1515

gabardine n *type of dress* b1520 [type of cotton: b1905]

jerkin n *type of jacket* b1520

waistcoat n *type of man's clothing* b1520 [type of woman's clothing: b1730]

duds n b1530

farthingale n *hoop structure for hoop skirts* b1530

headpiece n b1530

peak n *peak of a hat* b1530 [as in "mountain peak": b1635; fig. use: b1785]

textile n b1530

undergarment n b1530

headband n b1535

mask n b1535 [fig. "disguise": b1600; as in "deathmask": b1800] (verb use: b1565)

muffler n *type of scarf* b1535 ["wrap against cold": b1600]

swaddling clothes n b1535

drab n *cloth* b1545

inkle n *type of cloth* b1545

accouterment n

tawdry lace n [u1700s]

waistband n

Fashion/Style

trig adj (Brit) *prim and proper* b1515

periwig n *type of wig* b1530

affected adj *feigned, adopted* b1535

Tools

printer n b1505

punch n/v *as in "metal punch"* b1505

spokeshave n b1510

peen v *work with a peen hammer* b1515

rasp n b1515 (verb use: b1250)

bobbin n b1530

cast n *mold* b1530

gear n *gear mechanisms* b1530 ["individual gear": b1900] (gearwheel: b1875)

rest n *on which something rests* b1530

strainer n b1530 (strain n: b1435)

poker n *type of fire tool* b1535 (verb use: b1800)

grappling iron n b1540 (grapple: b1350)

implement n b1540

whipsaw n b1540 (verb use: b1845)

boom n/v *spar* b1545

magnifier n

Travel/Transportation

caravel n *type of ship* b1530

footpath n b1530

forridden adj *obs. weary from riding* b1530 [u1800s]

galleon n *type of ship* b1530

navigation n b1530 (navigate: b1590)

passenger n *rider* b1530 [obs. "ferry": b1350 to 1600s; "pedestrian": b1350]

pilot n b1530 [as in "balloon pilot": b1870; "test," as in "TV pilot": b1930] (verb use: b1600)

roll v *move on rollers* b1530

embark v b1535

pinnace n *type of ship* b1540

rove v b1540

rowboat n b1540

gondola n (gondolier: b1605)

maritime adj

runabout n

tall ship n

Emotions/Characteristics

suave adj b1505 ["nice": b1470 to 1500s] (suaviloquence "suave talk": b1670)

maudlin adj *crying because of drunkenness* b1510 ["sentimental": b1670]

ribald adj b1510 (arch. noun use: b1250; ribaldry: b1350]

sanguine adj *hopeful* b1510 ["red": b1325; arch. "of a hopeful constitution": b1450]

bawdy adj b1515 [obs. lit. "dirty": b1380 to 1600s] (baud n: b1375)

mien n b1515

misgive v b1515

anxiety n b1525 (anxious: b1620)

boohoo n/v b1525

dumps n b1525 (obs. dump v "be in the dumps": b1570 to 1800s; dumpish: b1520; dumpy: b1620)

fanatic n *madman* b1525 [obs. spec. "religious madman": u1800s] (adj use: b1535; fanatical: b1550; fanaticism: b1655)

astonish v *amaze* b1530 [obs. "terrify, stupefy": 1530s to 1700s; obs. "paralyze": b1570 to 1600s] (astonishing: b1545; astonishment: b1580)

brainish adj *hotheaded* b1530

cock-a-hoop adj *triumphantly boastful* b1530

coronach n *dirge, lament* b1530 [obs. "public outcry": b1500 to 1600s]

darksome adj b1530

debonair adj b1530 [obs. "gentle": b1200 to 1600s]

fiendish adj b1530

finesse n b1530 ["delicateness": b1450] (verb use: b1750)

fume v *express anger* b1530

grave adj *somber* b1530

happy adj *joyful, satisfied* b1530 ["lucky": b1350]

hearten v b1530 (heart v: b1100)

idiocy n b1530 (idiotism: b1595)

inquiet adj *obs. anxious* b1530

leer v b1530 (noun use: b1600)

long-suffering n b1530 (adj use: b1570; long-suffrance: b1530)

mare n *obs. melancholy* b1530 [u1600s]

misery n b1530 ["phys. misery": b1375]

pert adj *perky* b1530 ["attractive, jaunty": b1350; obs. "adept": b1350 to 1500s]

respect n *admiration* b1530 [as in "respect your privacy": b1630] (verb use: b1570; respectable: b1770)

skittish adj *hesitant* b1530 ["frivolous": b1470] (skittery: b1905)

supercilious adj b1530

testy adj *irritable* b1530 ["obstinate": b1375]

tongue-tied adj b1530

touching adj b1530

atrocity n *wickedness* b1535 ["wicked deed": b1800] (atrocious: b1670)

brown study n b1535

exasperate v *annoy; exacerbate* b1535 [obs. "worsen": b1670 to 1700s] (adj use: b1545; exasperation: b1550)

hopeless adj *without hope* b1535 ["undeserving of hope": b1870]

infatuate v *make silly* b1535

["inspire obsession":
b1570] (adj use: b1475; infatuation: b1650)

kindhearted adj b1535

licentious adj b1535

pique n b1535

secure adj b1535 ["safe": b1600] (verb use: b1595)

thanksgiving n b1535 (thanksgive: b1670)

alter ego n b1540

exhilarate v b1540 (exhilaration: b1625)

ignominy n b1540

imperious adj b1540

sedulous adj *perseverant* b1540 (sedulity: b1545)

tenderhearted adj b1540

truculent adj b1540 (truculency: b1570; truculence: b1730)

snappish adj b1545

thick-skinned adj b1545

bashful n *shy* [obs. "unconfident": b1500 to 1700s]

brutality n *viciousness* [obs. "primitiveness": b1550]

decadence n (decadency: b1635; decadent adj: b1840; decadent n: b1890)

disrelish v *dislike* [obs. "destroy flavor": b1550 to 1700s] (noun use: b1625)

dubious adj *doubtful* ["doubting": b1670] (dubitable: b1620)

glum adj (obs. verb use: b1470)

lazy adj [as in "lazy river": b1570; as in "lazy day": b1630] (verb use: b1615; laze v: b1595; laze n: b1870)

sarcasm n (sarcast "sarcastic person": b1670; sarcastic: b1695)

scare n [obs. "being scared": b1450 to 1600s]

timid adj

weakhearted adj

white-livered adj *lily-livered*

Thoughts/Perception/ The Mind

intelligent adj b1510 (intelligence: b1380; obs. intelli-

gible "intelligent": b1385 to 1700s)

intelligible adj *understandable* b1510 ["understanding": b1385]

wis, wist v *arch. know—be wise* b1510

inkling n b1515 [obs. "suggestion made in low voice": b1470]

shrewd adj *sagacious* b1520 ["mischievous": ME only; var. obs., arch. meanings of ominous, evil: b1350 to 1800s]

choplogic adj/n *specious logic* b1530

dexterity n *mental skill* b1530 ["phys. skill": b1670] (dexterous: b1625)

excogitate v *think through; concoct* b1530

foxy adj *crafty* b1530

like-minded adj b1530

misthink v *think mistakenly* b1530 [obs. "have lewd thoughts": b1225 to 1600s]

quick-witted adj b1530

reckon v *as in "I reckon you're right"* b1530 ["account": b1300; as in "I reckon I'll be going": b1570]

acumen n b1535

common sense n *horse sense* b1535 [obs. "sense uniting smell, touch, taste, sight, hearing": b1635]

evil-minded adj b1535

facility n *aptitude* b1535 ["gentleness": b1425]

obsess v b1535 [rare "possess": b1450; "besiege": b1505] (obsession: b1680; obsessive adj: b1905)

ruminate v *ponder* b1535 ["chew cud": b1550]

stupid, stupidity adj, n b1545 ["not worth the time": b1800] (noun use: b1715)

conscionable adj

cynic adj/n (cynical: b1585; cynicism: b1675; cynism: b1870)

garboil n *arch. confusion*

insane adj [fig. use: b1870]

(noun use: b1800; insanity: b1590)

misinterpret v

premeditate v (premeditation: b1450; premeditated: b1590)

Love/Romance/Sex

court v b1515 [as in "court disaster": b1575]

drab n *slang prostitute* b1515 (verb use: b1600)

hothouse n *obs. bordello* b1515 [u1600s]

brokenhearted adj b1530

conjugal adj b1530

dirty adj *pornographic* b1530

fond v *obs. dote on* b1530 [u1600s]

heartsick adj b1530 (heartbroken: b1590)

mouse n *term of endearment* b1530

mutton n *arch. sex, prostitution* b1530

prostitute v b1530 [fig. use: b1600] (noun use: b1615; prostitution: b1555)

remarry v b1530

romount n *romance* b1530

sheep's eyes n b1530

fleshpot n b1535

loving-kindness n b1535

strange woman n *prostitute* b1535

bully n *arch. lover* b1540

repudiate v *divorce* b1545 [gen. use: b1545] (adj use: b1465)

cocky adj *arch. lecherous*

honeymoon n/v [fig. use: b1600]

Family/Relations/ Friends

affine n *relative by marriage* b1510

great-grandfather n b1515 (great-grandmother: b1530; great-grandparent: b1885)

cater-cousin n *arch. intimate friend* b1520

September n *unit of a clan* b1520

mammy n b1525 [in slave culture: b1870]

relation n *relative* b1530 (relative: b1670; related: b1730)

yokefellow n *arch. companion* b1530

comrade n b1545

Games/Fun/Leisure

blackjack n *type of card game* b1515

playfellow n b1515 (playmate: b1645)

tilt n *joust* b1515 (verb use: b1600)

stalking horse n b1520

shuttlecock n b1525

acrostic n b1530

bopeep n *peekaboo* b1530

flush n *as in "royal flush"* b1530

suit n *spades, clubs, etc.* b1530

trump n b1530 (verb use: b1590)

shuffleboard n b1535

bacchanal n *decadent celebration* b1540 (bacchanalia: b1635)

cockhorse n *rocking horse* b1540

playing card n b1545

jest n (verb use: b1530; jester: b1530)

Sports

racket n *sports gear* b1520 ["game played with rackets": b1450]

fairway n b1525

coursing n *a type of hunt* b1530

court n *as in "tennis court"* b1530

divot n b1530

hockey n b1530 [on ice: b1900]

race n *competition* b1530 ["moving forward": b1150; as in "space race": b1870] (verb use: b1300)

somersault n b1530 (verb use: b1860)

goal n b1535 [obs. "border": b1325; fig. use: b1630]

golf ball n b1545

hippodrome n

Breef Thawts on Spellling

Do you take umbrage at spelling *light/night* as *lite/nite*? Or *through* as *thru*? We actually have little historical foundation for such complaints.

We can't complain on a general basis, because as we'll see in a moment, we've been changing our spelling vigorously since the very beginnings of the language.

And we can't complain on a specific basis. For example, *light*'s silent *g* was added to the word in the early 1300s. Before then, the word carried such spellings as *leoht* around 725, *leht* before 830 and *liht* around 1175. In comparison, *lite* seems almost anchored in time. *Night* similarly took its spelling around 1300. In Old English, the word was spelled *niht* and *nigt*, and *niht* was derived from such regional words as *neaht* and *neht*. And do those that decry *thru* similarly decry the poetic *thro'*? (And as an aside, the adjective *lite* meaning "few" appeared in Old English.)

And if we want to reach way back to the days when Old English wasn't even young yet, we can trace the word *father* back to the Sanskrit *pitr*, which led to such variations as Latin *pater*, Old High German *fater*, German *Vater* and Old English *foeder*. Similarly, *matr* and *mater*, *muoter*, *Mutter* and *modor* in the respective languages.

Important to remember is that a concern for "good spelling" is relatively recent. Chaucer might spell the same words different ways in the same document. And one argument for the theory that Shakespeare was actually more than one person is that extant signatures are spelled different ways. Fact is, Shakespeare and his contemporaries didn't care about "proper spelling," since there was really no such thing, so the "evidence" of differing signatures is based on modern values only. Robert Claiborne, in *Our Marvelous Native Tongue*, notes: "Nowadays, if we want to know how to spell a word, we look it up in the dictionary; in the sixteenth century, there was no such resource, and many people tended to spell pretty much as the spirit moved them at the moment: the writer Robert Greene, in one of his popular pamphlets on 'coney catching' (we'd say 'trimming a mark' or, more formally, 'fleecing a victim') managed to spell 'coney' nine different ways."

As recently as the 1800s, we were sent to *gaol* (still the British spelling) instead of *jail*. Noah Webster arbitrarily decided we needed to spell it more phonetically when he compiled his dictionary—and his spelling alterations live with Americans still, as in *center* vs. *centre*. So if the more commonsensical *jail* is good, why is *thru* bad?

Even some of our common words are based on spelling errors. For example, *pea* (by 1615) is based on *pease*, a singular word thought to be a plural (itself spelled variously as *piose*, *pise* and *pese*). *Cherry*, *coho*, *asp* and others came about the same way. And *nickname* (by 1440) was based on misdividing the Middle English phrase "an eke name," meaning "an extra name." So it was too with *adder* and *umpire*.

So, how's your *knowledge* of spelling?—spelled *knowlege* by 1400, *knoweleche* by 1330, *knowlych* by 1305. Let's have a little bee. Here are just a few words you're "misspelling" using modern spelling. Which of the spellings is *betst* (the spelling of *best* in Old English)?

- *gallon* (by 1425)—*galun* (by 1225).

- *king* (by 1125)—is a contraction of *cyning* (by 725), itself a shorter version of *kuningaz* in Proto-Germanic.

- *elephant* (around 1550)—*olyfaunt* (by 1300).

- *heaven* (by 1150)—*heofonum* (by 725).

- Even a simple word like *pock* (as in "pockmark") has evolved from *pocc* before 1000 to *poke* (by 1325) to *pokkes* (by 1280) and finally *pox* (by 1505).

Again, words in *English Through the Ages* are categorized by their first recorded appearance in any spelling (although the ages of some spelling variants are noted), so that *gallon* in the list above appears in the list of words appearing before 1350, even though the modern spelling arrives sometime before 1425.

So, what about the verb *spell* itself? Its own spelling is unchanged since it took its present meaning before 1400, and has changed little since it arrived in its original meaning of "read laboriously" when the verb was spelled *spellen*.

Professions/Duties

informer n b1510 [obs. "instructor": b1385 to 1600s]

costermonger n (Brit) *fruit vendor* b1515 (coster: b1855)

salesman n b1525 (saleswoman: b1705; salesperson: b1905)

contractor n b1530

equerry n *type of stableworker* b1530

jester n b1530

marketer n b1530 (marketeer: b1830)

milliner n b1530 (millinery: b1690)

scavenger n *garbageman* b1530 ["garbage picker": b1565; applied to animals: b1600] (scavager: b1500; scavenge: b1645)

waiter n b1530 [obs. type of watchman: b1385 to 1600s; obs. gen. "servant": b1500 to 1700s] (waitress: b1835; waitperson: b1980; waitron: b1985)

censor n b1535 (verb use: b1885; censorious: b1535; censorship: b1590)

poulterer n b1535

landlady n b1540 (landlord: b1000)

maître d'hôtel n b1540

redcap n b1540

spokesman n b1540 (spokeswoman: b1650; spokesperson: b1970; spokespeople: b1975)

geographer n b1545

laundress n

Business/Commerce/Selling

traffic n *trade* b1505 ["illegal trade": b1670; "vehicle movement": b1830] (verb use: b1540)

import v *as in "import a car"* b1510

caveat emptor n b1525 (caveat: b1535)

gratuity n b1525

distributor n b1530 (distributress: b1670)

keep v *as in "shopkeeper"*

b1530 [as in "housekeeper": b1450]

shopkeeper n b1530

monopoly n b1535 (monopolist: b1605; monopolize: b1615)

commerce n b1540 [gen. "interaction": b1540] (commerce v "interact": b1600; commercial adj: b1600)

bakery n b1545 ["baker's profession": b1545] (bakeshop: b1780)

rialto n

The Workplace

overseer n *supervisor* b1525 ["watcher": b1400 to 1600s]

payday n b1530

taskmaster n b1530 (taskmistress: b1605)

workwoman n b1530 (workman: b900)

foundry n *the founding business* b1540 [the building: b1670]

overtime n b1540 (adv use: b1850)

workmanly adj b1545

day layborer n

hackney n *obs. scutworker* [u1800s] (hack: b1700)

paymaster n

piecework n

Finances/Money

pecuniary adj b1505 (pecunious "rich": b1450)

tuppence n b1515

disburse v b1530 (disbursement: b1600)

gelt n *money* b1530 [slang use: b1895]

guaranty n b1530

sovereign n *type of coin* b1530

thrifty adj *frugal* b1530 ["thriving": b1425]

assets n b1535 (asset: b1900)

banker n b1535

bankrupt n *bankrupt person* b1535 (adj use: b1570; verb use: b1590; bankruptcy: b1700)

lien n b1535

interest n b1545 [gen. use: b1425]

pin money n b1545

ha'penny n

Language and Speaking

part of speech n b1510

gerund n b1515

collective noun n b1520

interrogative n b1525

apostrophe n *punctuation* b1530 [obs. "the material omitted": b1570 to 1600s]

cipher n *code* b1530

compound n *as in "compound word"* b1530 (verb use: b1570)

conjugate v b1530 (conjugation: b1450)

gibberish n b1530 (obs. adj use: b1600 to 1800s; gibber v: b1605; gibber n: b1870)

person n *as in "first person singular"* b1530

phrase n *phraseology; type of linguistic unit* b1530 [as in "a phrase of music": b1800] (verb use: b1570; phrasing: b1615; phraseology: b1665)

King's English n b1535

periphrasis n b1535

ellipsis n b1540 (elliptical: b1800)

non sequitur n b1540

abusage n *misuse of words*

adage n

colon n *punctuation*

paraphrase n (verb use: b1700; paraphrastic: b1625)

Literature/Writing

elegy n b1505

irony n b1505 (ironical: b1580; ironic: b1630)

georgic n *poem about agriculture* b1515

first person n b1520

herbal n b1520

postscript n *used in letters* b1525 [used in books, etc.: b1670; "appendix": b1900]

squib n *fig. fiery remark; lit. firework* b1525

conceit n b1530

dictionary n b1530 [obs. "vocabulary": b1600 to 1700s]

poetess n b1530 (poet: b1300)

print v *as in "print a newspaper"* b1530 (noun use: b1630)

publish v *as in "publish a book"* b1530 [obs. "accuse": b1450 to 1500s; gen. "make known," "distribute": b1350] (publisher: b1740)

rondeau n b1530

exordium n *beginning* b1535

peruse v b1535 [obs. "use up": b1600 to 1600s]

platonic adj *pertaining to Plato* b1535

scribe n *writer, copyist* b1535 (verb use: b1470)

signature n b1535

vocabulary n *type of word list* b1535 ["words available": b1770]

autograph n *signature* b1540 ["handwritten manuscript": b1645; "handwriting": b1870] (verb use: b1840)

penman n b1540

annals n b1545 (annal n: b1700; annal v: b1630)

appendix n *book supplement* b1545

rhapsody n b1545 [fig. use: b1670] (rhapsodist: b1770; rhapsodic: b1785)

writing paper n

Communication

missive n b1505 (adj use: b1445)

communicate v b1530 [arch. "share": b1530; obs. "give": b1600 to 1700s] (communication: b1385)

trialogue n *akin to monologue, dialogue, polylogue* b1535

dispatch n *type of message* b1540

Visual Arts/Photography

artisan n b1540

oil color n b1540

Performing Arts

drama n b1515 [fig. use: b1730]
masque n b1515
act n b1530 (verb use: b1600)
entertainer n b1535
catastrophe n *turn of events in drama* b1540 ["disaster": b1750]
exit v *as in "exit, stage left"* b1540 [gen. "leave": b1910]
scene n b1540 [gen. "location," as in "scene of the crime": b1600] (scenical: b1450; scenic: b1625)

Music

kit n *type of violin* b1520
dirge n b1530 [type of service: b1200]
harmonious adj b1530 [gen. use: b1570] (obs. "harmonical": b1500 to 1700s)
instrumental adj b1530
rest n b1530
trumpet v *play the trumpet* b1530 ["proclaim, hype": b1630; "make a trumpet-like sound": b1830]
virginal n *type of spinet* b1530
wait n *obs. type of musician* b1530 [u1600s]
fife n b1540
paean n *type of song* b1545
twang n *from a musical instrument* b1545 [from a voice: b1630; "tang": b1630] (verb use: b1970; twangle v: b1570)

Entertainment

satire n *work of satire* b1505 [gen. "mockery": b1700] (verb use: b1930; satiric: b1510; satirical: b1530)
hay n *type of dance* b1530
sequel n *as in "sequel to a book"* b1530
puppet n *marionette; doll* b1540 [fig. use: b1600] (puppeteer: b1925)
carnival n *a spec. festival* [gen. "festival": b1600]

Education

dean n b1525 [type of religious leader: b1300; type of guild leader: b1450]
night school n b1530
practice n *repeating to learn* b1530 (verb use: b1450; practiced: b1570)
autodidact n *self-taught person* b1535
education n *gen. rearing* b1535 ["teaching in school": b1630] (educate: b1450; educator: b1570)
scholarship n *financial aid* b1535 ["scholarliness": b1590]
inkhorn adj *learned, pedantic* b1545
monitor n

Religion

catechism n b1505 (catechist: b1670; catechesis: b1755)
plainsong n *chant* b1515 (plainchant: b1730)
papist, papistry n b1525
congregation n b1530 (congregate v: b1400)
demigod n b1530 (demigoddess: b1630)
godless adj b1530
Jehovah n b1530
monkery n b1530
Passover n b1530
rosary n b1530
sanctimonial n *arch. nun* b1530
shaveling n *monk* b1530
Armageddon n b1535 [fig. use: b1815]
Garden of Eden n b1535
Lord's table n b1535
cantor n b1540
crossbearer n b1540
exorcise v *drive away a spirit* b1540 ["call up a spirit": b1400]
protestant adj/n b1540
atheism n (atheist: b1575)
Holy Communion n
Lord's Prayer n
puritan n (adj use: b1590; puritanism: b1575; puritanical: b1610)

Society/Mores/Culture

illicit adj b1505
culture n *personal refinement* b1510 (cultural: b1875)
utopia n 1516 (utopian: b1545)
demoiselle n *young woman* b1520
upbringing n b1520 [obs. "build": b1500] (arch. upbring v: b1350)
neighborly adj b1525
dove n *symbol of peace* b1530
dowager n b1530
laywoman n b1530 (layman: b1200; lay adj: b1350; laypeople: b1500; lay sister: b1710; layperson: b1975)
old maid n b1530
rabble n b1530 [obs. "verbal babble": b1400 to 1600s; obs. "animal pack": b1450] (verb use: b1600; rabblement: b1550; rabblerous: b1845)
sirrah n b1530
wholesome adj *morally proper* b1530
birthright n b1535
entertainment n *manners* b1535
plebeian n *spec. to Rome* b1535 [gen. use: b1590] (adj use "of the common people": b1570; adj use "vulgar, ordinary": b1630)
society n b1535 ["the fashionable": b1830]
sorority n *gen. women's group* b1535 [spec. "university women's group": b1905]
illegitimate adj *bastard* b1540 [gen. sense: b1600]
naughty adj *saucy* b1540 ["mischievous": b1635]
comity n *manners, civility* b1545
curtsy n *show of respect* [type of bow: b1575] (verb use: b1555)
laddie n
worldling n

Government

viceroy n b1525 (viceroyalty: b1705; vicereine: b1825; viceregal: b1840)
archduke n b1530 (archduchess: b1620; archduchy: b1680)
enthrone v b1530 (enthronize: b1450)
politics n *administration of government* b1530 ["political maneuvering": b1670] (politic adj: b1425; political: b1955; politician: b1630; politick v: b1935)
vice president n b1530
attorney general n b1535
democracy n b1535 (democratic: b1605)
anarchy n b1540 [fig. "chaos": b1670] (anarchic: b1650)
abdicate v b1545 (abdication: b1555)
civic adj *pertaining to a city* b1545 ["pertaining to type of Roman honor": b1555; "pertaining to citizenship": b1800]
county n *obs. count* [u1800s]
doge n

Politics

embassy n *the job and the home of ambassadors* b1535 (embassage: b1500)
loyal adj *loyal to country* b1535 [gen. use: b1600]
protocol n *official courtesy, course of action* b1545 [type of official document: b1545]
ballot n (ballot box: b1680)

Life

live adj *alive* b1545 [as in "real live": b1900]

Death

coffin n b1525 [obs. gen. "box": b1340 to 1600s] (coffer: b1250)
potter's field n b1530
headstone n b1535
executioner n b1540
exterminate v b1545 [obs. "banish": b1450 to 1600s] (obs. extermine: b1540; exterminator: b1615)
swing v *die by hanging* b1545
starveling n

War/Military/Violence

veteran n b1505 [gen. use: b1600] (adj use: b1630)

tuck n *arch. type of weapon* b1510

pike n *type of spear* b1515 (verb use: b1800; pikeman: b1550)

waylay v b1515

redcoat n b1520

embowel v *disembowel* b1525

pioneer n *mil. forerunner* b1525 [gen. "forerunner": b1605] (verb use: b1780; adj use: b1840)

bloody v b1530

cope n *obs. skirmish* b1530 [u1700s] (verb use: b1350)

cuff v *hit* b1530 (noun use: b1570)

discharge v *as in "discharge a gun"* b1530 (noun use: b1600)

encounterer n *arch. enemy* b1530

field v *arch. fight* b1530

lance-knight n b1530

mercenary n *hired gun* b1530 ["hired hand": b1395]

munition n b1530 ["privilege": b1450; "rampart": b1510]

rapier n b1530

trim v *beat up* b1530 (trimming: b1700)

0.22 n *type of gun* b1530

armada n *spec., Spanish Armada* b1535 [gen. "navy": b1730]

assailant n b1535 (assail: b1200)

baste v *beat* b1535

bloodthirsty adj b1535

grenade n b1535 [obs. "pomegranate": b1535 to 1600s]

harquebus n *type of gun* b1535

mutilate v b1535 (adj use: b1530; mutilation: b1525)

powder horn n b1535

provost marshal n b1535

shoot n *shooting* b1535 [as in "turkey shoot": b1870] (verb use: b1150)

warship n b1535

wipe out v *destroy* b1535

forlorn hope n b1540

raze v *destroy* b1540 [scratch, erase: b1400]

combat n b1545 (verb use: b1665; adj use: b1825; combatant: b1475)

galleass n *type of fighting ship* b1545

troop n b1545 ["trooper": b1870] (verb use: b1565; troops: b1600)

camisado n *night attack*

cavalry n

colonel n

conquistador n

corsair n

demolition n *fig. destruction* [phys. "destruction": b1630] (demolish: b1570)

encamp v (encampment: b1600)

firelock n *type of gun*

flank n/v [gen. use: b1100]

inroad n [gen. sense: b1670]

offensive adj (offensive n: b1720)

pikeman n

quarterstaff n

sack n/v *plunder*

scimitar n

wipe n *sweeping blow* (verb use: b1530)

Crime/Punishment/Enforcement

prowler n b1520

contraband n *smuggling; the smuggled material itself* b1530 (verb use: b1570; contrabandist: b1820)

durance n b1530

incestuous adj b1530 (incest: b1200)

lift v *steal* b1530

lurcher n *thief* b1530

officer n *as in "police officer"* b1530

poach v b1530 (poacher: b1615)

assassin n b1535 (obs. verb use: b1670 to 1700s; assassinate: b1610)

incarceration n b1540 (incarcerate: b1530)

piracy n b1540

burglar n b1545 (burgler: b1520; burglary: b1525;

burgle: b1870; burglarize: b1875)

The Law

survivor n *leg.* b1505 [gen. "someone who survives something": b1600]

inheritress n b1530 (inheritor: b1450; inheritrix: b1485)

legal n b1530

plat n *type of map* b1530

settle v b1530 (settlement: b1670)

pandect n *body of law* b1535

peremptory challenge n b1535

attorney-at-law n b1540 (attorney: b1300)

illegal adj b1540

aggravated adj *leg.*

law of nations n *international law*

law-abiding v

The Fantastic/Paranormal

bogle n *spectre* b1505

wraith n b1515

hobgoblin n b1530 [hob n: b1310]

Magic

witchery n b1540

ensorcell v *bewitch* b1545

Interjections

quotha interj *indeed!* b1520

why interj b1520

heyday interj *hey!* b1530

please adv *as in "please go away"* b1530

tut, tut-tut interj b1530

hallelujah interj b1535 (noun use: b1625)

faugh interj b1545

lullaby interj b1545 [type of song: b1590]

oh interj (O: b1175; oh-oh: b1730)

Slang

double-dealing n b1530 (adj use: b1590)

fulham n *loaded die* b1530

fumble v *have bad sex* b1530

grease v *as in "grease his

palm"* b1530 (noun use: b1800)

pilgarlic n *bald head or man* b1530

saucy adj *insolent* b1530 ["tasty": b1510; "bawdy": b1630]

smellfeast n *arch. party crasher, who "smells the feast"* b1530

tittle-tattle n b1530

tosh n *nonsense* b1530

wipe v *trounce* b1530

hobbledehoy n b1540

light-fingered adj

Insults

brat n *snotty child* b1505 (bratling: b1670)

eldritch adj b1510

shit n b1510 ["excrement": b1585]

slouch n *indolent person* b1515 (slouchy: b1695)

termagant n *shrew, bully* b1520 (adj use: b1600)

trull n *whore* b1520

busybody n b1530

disable v *arch. insult* b1530

dizzy adj *ditzy* b1530 [obs. "foolish": b900] (dizzard "dolt": b1570)

doxy n *floozy, bimbo* b1530

gib n *obs. old woman* b1530 [u1600s]

hop-o'-my-thumb n *small person* b1530

poltroon n *wretch, coward* b1530 (adj use: b1645; poltroonery: b1590)

twit n *teasing, insult* b1530 ["dope": b1935] (verb use: b1150)

cutthroat n b1535 (adj use: b1570)

dolt n b1535 (obs. verb use: b1570 to 1800s)

feebleminded adj b1535

good-for-nothing adj/n b1535

harebrained adj b1535

laughingstock n b1535

she-devil n b1535

parasite n *parasitic person* b1540 [parasitic animal: b1730] (parasitism: b1615; parasitical: b1590; parasitic: b1630)

lout, loutish n b1545 (lout v: b1830)

blockhead, blockish n, adj (blockish: b1550)

gull n/v *a gullible person* (gullish: b1600; gullible: b1820)

patch n *blockhead*

weakling n [obs. "effeminate person": b1530 to 1600s; "unreligious person": b1550]

Phrases

curry favor v b1510

hand-to-mouth adj b1510

clink n *slang jail* b1515

per diem adv b1520 (adj use: b1810; noun use: b1815)

alpha and omega n b1530

by and by adv b1530 (noun use: b1600)

grass widow n *unmarried woman who has enjoyed the "fruits" of marriage* b1530

peace offering n b1530

per accidens adv *opp. of per se* b1530 (per se: b1575)

pig in a poke n b1530

rife in mouth adj *cliched* b1530

blood money n b1535

ex officio adj/adv b1535

off and on adv b1535

tabula rasa n b1535

tooth and nail adv b1535

dog days n b1540

hot water n *trouble* b1540

per annum adv b1540

wild card n b1540

of course b1545 (bi course: b1300)

sure enough adv/adj b1545

ipso facto adv

loose end n

General/Miscellaneous

importance n b1505 (important: b1445; importancy: b1540; import: b1590)

mandate n b1505 (verb use: b1630)

oration n b1505 [obs. type of prayer: b1375] (oration: b1375; oratorical: b1590; oratory: b1630; orate "speak": b1670)

outside n *outer surface; area*

beyond the outer surface b1505 (adj use: b1635; adv use: b1815; prep use: b1830)

rencounter n/v *hostile meeting* b1505 ["casual meeting": b1550]

ringleader n b1505

soil n *fig. dirt* b1505 (verb use: b1225)

cornucopia n b1510 [fig. use: b1630]

faction n *group* b1510

inventor, inventress n b1510 (inventrix: b1630)

opulence n b1510 (opulent: b1570)

pet n *favorite* b1510 [type of animal: b1600] (adj use: b1830)

post n *relay; related to postal* b1510 [gen. "mail": b1600] (post "mail": b1870)

summary n b1510

hardware n b1515 [in computing: b1965]

interview n b1515 (verb use: b1870)

plash n *splash* b1515 ["puddle": b1000] (verb use: b1545)

pretext n b1515

runaway n b1515 (adj use: b1550)

taunt n b1515 (verb use: b1540)

thud n b1515 (verb use: b1800)

turmoil n/v b1515

epitome n b1520

rattle n *sound* b1520

rumple n b1520 (verb use: b1605)

trimming n b1520 [as in "all the trimmings": b1630; "scraps, cuttings": b1830] (trimmings "scraps, cuttings": b1830)

uproar n b1520 (uproarious: b1820)

abstention n b1525

burn n *burned area, act of burning* b1525

colleague n b1525

conclave n *gen.* b1525 [type of religious meeting:

b1395; type of room: b1450]

dilemma n b1525

lackey n b1525 (verb use: b1670)

luster n b1525 (verb use: b1585; lustrous: b1605)

pit-a-pat adv b1525 (noun use: b1585; verb use: b1630; adj use: b1670)

welcome n *act of welcoming* b1525 [obs. "welcome person": b725]

abeyance n b1530

aborigines n b1530 (aborigine: b1860)

accidence n *happenstance* b1530

adventurer n b1530 (adventuress: b1755)

anathema n b1530

antic, antics n b1530

antique n b1530 (adj use: b1535; verb use: b1925)

antithesis n b1530 (antithetical: b1585)

ballast n b1530

benefit n *perk, advantage* b1530 ["a favor, a kindness": b1400] (verb use: b1475)

bound n *as in "leaps and bounds"* b1530 (verb use: b1590)

brabble n/v *squabble* b1530

business n *concern, as in "none of your business"* b1530

combustible adj b1530 (noun use: b1700)

compare n b1530

competitor n b1530 [obs. "someone who competes with you—and not against": b1600 to 1600s] (competition: b1605)

compromise n b1530 [rare "arbitrated settlement": b1430] (verb use: b1450)

conference n *meeting* b1530 ["organized meeting," as in "a med. conference": b1600; "division of a league," as in "National Football Conference": b1900]

congress n *meeting* b1530 ["group of servants":

b1400; "meeting of armies": b1460; "governing group": b1765]

dazzle v *confound* b1530 [arch. "lose eyesight": b1485]

denial n b1530 (denyance: b1450)

drone n *droning sound* b1530 ["droning speech": b1800]

entrance n *entering* b1530

equivalent adj/n *describing value* b1530 ["describing similarity": b1670]

essence n *e.g., perfume* b1530 (verb use: b1670)

eyesore n b1530 [obs. lit. "sore in the eye": b1350 to 1500s]

fetch n *act of fetching; arch. "trick"* b1530

hugger-mugger n *secrecy* b1530

insinuate, insinuation v, n b1530

kick n b1530 [fig. use: b1630] (verb use: b1400)

map n b1530 (verb use: b1590)

nuzzle n/v b1530 [obs. "grovel": b1350 to 1400s]

offscouring n *discards* b1530

participant n b1530 (adj use: b1470)

pasteboard n b1530

pest n b1530 ["pestilence": b1500]

quick n *essence* b1530

recognition n *recognizing* b1530

sequel n *consequence* b1530 ["sycophant": b1425]

stuffing n *as in "knock the stuffing out of"* b1530

tattle n *prattle* b1530 (verb use: b1550)

ticket n *note* b1530

time n *as in "have a good time"* b1530

valuation n b1530

voracity n b1530 (voracious: b1635)

artifice n *deceit* b1535 [obs. "craftsmanship": b1470 to 1700s]

associate n *colleague* b1535

association n b1535

auspice n b1535 (auspicious:

b1595; auspicate v:
b1650)

basis n *phys. base* b1535
[gen. use: b1630]

commonplace n b1535 (adj
use: b1610)

connotation n b1535 (connote: b1655)

cumulate n/v b1535 (cumulative: b1605)

disfavor n b1535 (verb use:
b1570)

excrement n b1535 (excrete
v: b1670; excreta: b1860;
obs. excretion "excre-
ment": b1630 to 1700s)

firstling n b1535

forename n *first name* b1535

function n b1535 (verb use:
b1850; functional: b1635)

human n b1535 (adj use:
b1400; human being:
b1800)

impunity n b1535

infinite n b1535 (adj use:
b1380)

invention n *a thing invented*
b1535 ["process of invent-
ing": b1500]

ledge n b1535 [obs. type of
barring device: b1350]

metamorphosis n b1535 [bio-
logical sense: b1670]
(metamorphose: b1580)

minority adj/n *being in the minority* b1535 ["a minority
group": b1770]

native n b1535

obstruction n *act of obstructing* b1535 ["something
that obstructs": b1500]
(obstruct: b1590)

perfume n/v *pleasant odor;
source of pleasant odor*
b1535

practitioner n b1535 [obs.
"schemer": u1600s] (prac-
ticant "practitioner":
b1670)

quip n b1535 (verb use:
b1580; quipster: b1880)

rent n *tear* b1535

scope n *range, extent, sphere*
b1535 ["target": b1535;
"goal": b1555]

stopgap n b1535 [obs. type
of argument: b1535 to
1500s]

absentee n b1540

aqueduct n b1540

area n b1540

changeling n *traitor; something exchanged* b1540

clearance n b1540

credit n *trust, believability*
b1540 ["acknowledge-
ment": b1630]

discovery, discover n, v b1540

effigy n b1540

elbowroom n b1540

expectation n b1540

extrusion n b1540 (extrude:
b1570)

eyewitness n b1540

fatuity n *something fatuous*
b1540

flimflam n b1540 (verb use:
b1660)

gloss n *glaze* b1540 (verb
use: b1660)

gradation n b1540

Gypsy n b1540 [gen. use:
b1630]

looker-on n *onlooker* b1540

paradox n b1540 (paradoxical: b1585)

penult n *next to last* b1540

posthaste n *great haste* b1540
(adv use: b1595; adj use:
b1605)

smattering n b1540 (adj use:
b1600)

supremacy n b1540

sycophant n b1540 ["informer": b1540] (syco-
phancy: b1670; syco-
phantism: b1825)

tinsel n b1540 [gen. "glitz":
b1670] (adj use: b1500)

torchbearer n b1540

wad n b1540 (verb use:
b1580; wadding: b1630)

acclamation n b1545

archetype n b1545

backer n *supporter* b1545
(back v: b1530)

bout n b1545

capture n b1545 (verb use:
b1795)

cavity n b1545

defection n *switching allegiance; rare being defective*
b1545 (defect: b1600)

emulation n b1545 [obs. "rival, envy": u1700s] (emu-
late: b1585)

erosion n b1545 (erode:
b1615)

gurgitation n b1545 (gurgitate: b1670)

hanger-on n b1545

infundibulum n *something
funnel-shaped* b1545

machine n *gen. something
built* b1545

pitch n *slope, rake* b1545

rostrum n b1545

scrag n *scrawny thing* b1545
(scraggy: b1615)

stamina n b1545

strangulation n b1545

archenemy n

bang n/v *noise*

barbarian adj/n *savage* ["infidel": b1340; "alien":
b1385] (barbaric: b1395;
barbarous, barbarism:
b1450; barbarity: b1670)

Christian name n

citation n *quote* (cite: b1535)

climax n ["uppermost point":
b1780; "orgasm": b1930]
(climactic: b1875)

endorsement n

freshman n *newcomer* [edu-
cational sense: b1600]

interim n ["meantime":
b1630]

islander n

loser n [slang "screwup":
b1970]

malversation n *corruption*
(malversate: b1900)

paragon n [obs. "companion"; "foe": u1800s]

parenthesis n *parenthetical
material* [type of punctuation: b1730] (parentheti-
cal: b1630; parenthetic:
b1780)

plea n *entreaty* (verb use:
b1440; plead: b1250)

round-robin n

rudiment n (rudimentary:
b1840)

satellite adj/n *minion* [e.g.,
the moon: b1670; fig. use:
b1800]

sediment n [geological sense:
b1700]

suds n (verb use: b1835)

sweep n

telltale n (adj use: b1580)

triad n

twaddle n

twinkle n *brief time* ["twinkling": b1670]

vacuum n

yaw n (verb use: b1590)

Things

baton n b1520

orb n *sphere* b1530 ["circle":
b1400; spec. "spheres that
carry the planets": b1530]

sawdust n b1530

trellis n *as in "garden trellis"*
b1530 [gen. "lattice":
b1400] (trelliswork:
b1715)

still n *as in "moonshiner's
still"* b1535 (verb use:
b1300; stillatory "still":
b1450)

trinket n *bauble* b1535 [obs.
type of tool: u1700s; obs.
type of food: b1600 to
1800s] (trinketry: b1810)

fiber n b1540 (fibril: b1665)

obelisk n

Description

evitable adj b1505

multifarious adj b1505

slope adj b1505

darling adj b1510 (noun use:
b900)

emerald adj b1510

fallacious adj b1510

forworn adj *spent* b1510

queer adj *odd* b1510 ["bad":
b1570; slang "homosex-
ual": b1900]

steely adj b1510

alternate adj b1515 (verb
use: b1600; noun use:
b1720)

inborn adj b1515 [obs. "native": b1000 to 1800s]

sceptered adj *endowed with
authority* b1515

specious adj *ultimately false*
b1515 [obs. "beautiful":
b1400 to 1800s]

unfriended adj b1515 (un-
friend "foe": b1350)

widdershins adv *contrary*
b1515

compulsory adj b1520

crystal-clear adj b1520

gingerly adj b1520

monstrous adj *huge* b1520

[obs. "unnatural": b1380 to 1700s; "egregiously villainous": b1600]

frisky adj b1525 (obs. frisk adj: b1500 to 1800s)

industrious adj b1525 ["clever": b1500]

pointed adj b1525

wry adj lit. twisted b1525 [fig. "twisted": b1590; obs. "awry": b1600]

apt adj liable, inclined b1530 (aptitude: b1450)

behindhand adj b1530

compelling adj b1530

contiguous adj b1530

crisp adj as in "a crisp cookie" b1530 ["curly": b900; as in "a crisp pace": b1830; as in "a crisp day": b1870] (crispy: b1615)

cross adj across b1530

cross-legged adj b1530

destitute adj describing people b1530 [describing places: b1385] (verb use: b1450; destitution: b1425)

essential adj necessary b1530

exterior adj b1530 (noun use: b1595)

fleet adj b1530 (verb use: b1200; fleet-footed: b1595)

hollow adj fig., as in "hollow promises" b1530 (hollow-hearted: b1570)

initial adj b1530

long-lasting adj b1530

matchless adj without equal b1530

missing adj b1530 (noun use: b1325)

obstepterous adj clamorous b1530

outworn adj b1530

pithy adj concise b1530 ["strong, potent": b1350]

premature adj b1530 [med. sense: b1770]

rank adj foul-smelling b1530 [gen. "foul": b1600; gen. "offensive": b1300]

resolute adj resolved b1530 ["dissolved": b1425] (resolution: b1590; resolve n: b1595)

rusty adj out of practice b1530 [lit. use: b900]

silver adj dulcet b1530

tall adj opp. of short b1530 [obs. "prompt": b1000; obs. "brave": b1400; obs. "handsome": b1450]

tan adj b1530

threatening adj b1530

topsy-turvy adv b1530 (noun use: b1600; adj use: b1615; topsy-turn v: b1600; topsy-turviness: b1845)

ungodly adj b1530

unlucky adj b1530

weather-beaten adj b1530

wild adj crazy, as in "wild ideas" b1530 ["unconventional": b1670] (obs. noun use "wild thing": b1350 to 1500s; noun use, as in "the wild": b1600)

winding adj b1530

contradictory adj b1535 (noun use: b1385; contradictious: b1605)

dissident adj b1535 (noun use: b1770; dissentientious "dissenting": b1560; dissidence: b1660)

egregious adj remarkably good b1535 ["remarkably bad": b1575]

enormous adj b1535 [obs. "abnormal": u1800s]

exact adj exacting; detailed b1535 (verb use: b1565; exacting: b1585)

exanimate adj inanimate b1535

frequent adj b1535

impeccable adj b1535 (impeccancy: b1630; impeccant: b1770)

labored adj difficult b1535 [obs. "worn": b1525; obs. "well worked": u1700s]

notorious adj b1535 [obs. "obvious": b1630 to 1700s] (notoriously: b1500)

paramount adj b1535 (noun use: b1620)

parti-color/parti-colored adj b1535

posterior adj opp. of prior b1535 ["behind": b1600]

roundabout adj b1535

so many adj b1535

sopping adj b1535

top-heavy adj b1535

unlooked-for adj b1535

arduous adj b1540

bleak adj barren b1540 [obs. "white, pale": b1150 to 1400s; "hopeless": b1720]

crapulous adj binging b1540

flinty adj b1540

halcyon adj b1540

incondite adj crude b1540

termless adj endless b1540

wooden adj lit. and fig. b1540

anterior adj b1545

astringent adj inducing contraction b1545 ["harsh": b1830] (noun use: b1630; astringe v: b1570)

conspicuous adj b1545 (conspicuity: b1605; conspicuousness: b1770)

diagonal adj b1545 (noun use: b1575)

extant adj b1545

garish adj b1545

insidious adj b1545

longwise adj/adv b1545 (longways: b1590)

neat adj pure b1545 ["tidy": b1580]

orange adj b1545 (noun use: b1600)

preposterous adj b1545 [rare "reversed": concurrent]

subsidiary adj b1545 (noun use: b1605)

torrid adj lit. hot b1545 [fig. "hot, passionate": b1670]

troublesome adj b1545

unmanned adj b1545

workable adj able to be worked b1545 [doable: b1770]

arcane adj

cloying adj

fortunately adv

gainful adj

immature adj premature

incumbent adj (noun use: b1410)

jolly adv very

mock adj fake (verb use "trick": b1430)

operable adj working [med. "able to be operated on": b1930]

pacific adj peace-making ["peaceful": b1670]

proverbial adj as in "the proverbial cat that ate the ca-

nary" [pertaining to proverbs: b1450]

puny adj small ["junior": b1600; obs. "callow": b1600 to 1700s] (obs. noun use: "someone's junior": b1550 to 1600s)

reputed adj respected ["said to be": b1580]

ridiculous adj laughable ["unbelievable": b1870] (ridicule n/v: b1700)

robust, robustious adj

severe adj (severity: b1485)

temporary adj [obs. "temporal": b1630 to 1700s]

trite adj

vague adj describing statements, etc. [as in "vague idea": b1730]

vincible adj

weightless adj

Colors

roan adj b1530 (noun use: b1580)

rose-colored adj b1530 [fig. use: b1865] (rosy: b1375; roseate: b1590; rose adj: b1590)

Actions/Verbs

unify v b1505 (unification: b1855)

upbuild v b1505

gag v silence b1510 [fig. use: b1630]

gambol v leap b1510 ["make merry": b1605] (noun use: b1530)

giggle v b1510

lounge v slouch about b1510 ["dally": b1700; "lay about": b1660] (noun use: b1775)

pump v b1510 [as in "pump for information": b1670; slang "have sex": b1770]

toot v b1510 (noun use: b1645; tootle: b1820)

toss v buffet; throw; fling or overturn b1510 [as in "toss your head": b1600; as in "toss a salad": b1730] (noun use: b1635)

cheep v b1515 (noun use: b1775)

damnify v damage b1515

pace v *step* b1515 [as in "pace off": b1600; "set the pace," "maintain a speed": b1900]

stifle v *suppress* b1515 [phys. "choke, suffocate": b1350]

surge v b1515 [obs. phys. "stream": b1490 to 1500s] (noun use: b1520)

whimper v b1515 (noun use: b1700; whimp v: b1570)

bounce v *rebound* b1520 [obs. "beat, pound": b1225 to 1800s; "reject a check": b1900] (noun use: b1525)

cuddle v b1520

dispatch v *send* b1520 (obs. noun use: b1570 to 1600s; dispatch "type of message": b1540)

dog v b1520

implore v b1520

accommodate v b1525

beard v *confront boldly* b1525

buckle v *collapse* b1525

equip v b1525 (equipment: b1720)

exhaust v *use up* b1525 ["tire": b1670] (exhaustion: b1630)

remunerate v *repay* b1525 ["pay": b1600] (remuneration: b1400)

renovate v b1525 (adj use: b1440; renovation: b1400)

sling v *hoist with a sling* b1525

splice v b1525 (noun use: b1630)

addict v b1530 [obs. "to serve": u1700s]

adhere v b1530 (adherence: b1535)

adulterate v b1530

aggravate v *exacerbate* b1530 ["annoy": b1600]

air v *ventilate* b1530

attest v b1530

back v *support* b1530 (backer: b1600)

bechance v *befall* b1530

blindfold v b1530 (noun use: b1880; blindfelled: b1485)

botch v *mess up* b1530 ["repair": b1385] (noun use: b1605)

bungle v b1530 (bunglesome: b1890)

captivate v b1530 [obs. "control": b1530 to 1800s]

cede v b1530

coil v *position in coils* b1530 (noun use: b1600)

consist v *as in "this book consists of a lot of words"* b1530 [obs. "reside": b1450 to 1800s; obs. "be compatible": b1870; "be consistent": b1700]

contract v *shrink, shrivel* b1530

contribute v b1530 [fig. use: b1630]

couch v *as in "couch in delicate terms"* b1530 [lit. sense: b1300]

curry v *as in "curry favor"* b1530 [obs. "flatter": b1450 to 1800s]

denigrate v b1530 [obs. "phys. blacken": b1450]

drib v *dribble* b1530 (dribble v: b1590)

dust v *make dusty; remove dust* b1530 [obs. "turn to dust": b1470 to 1600s; "apply powder": b1600]

empty v b1530 (arch. empt v: b1150)

falsify v b1530 ["show to be untrue": b1450] (falsen v: b1200)

favor v *as in "favor a sore leg"* b1530

flip v b1530 (noun use: b1695)

found v *create, as in a foundry* b1530

gargle v b1530 (noun use: b1660)

grapple v b1530

harp v *as in "harp on"* b1530

illustrate v *illuminate* b1530 [obs. "enlighten": b1375; "give examples": b1615; "create art": b1640]

infer v b1530 [obs. "wage war": b1500 to 1700s; obs. "mention": b1500 to 1600s] (inference: b1595)

infuse v *fig.* b1530 [phys. sense: b1425] (infusion: b1630)

inveigh v *rail* b1530

jar v b1530 ["clash," phys. "grate against": b1670] (jarring: b1570)

jumble v *be confused* b1530 ["mix together": b1570]

jump v b1530 ["start in surprise," as in "jump to conclusions": b1730; "rise quickly," as in "a price jumping"] (noun use: b1555)

leave v *as in "leave me alone"* b1530

lower v *reduce* b1530 ["make physically lower": b1670]

matter v b1530

mention v b1530 (noun use: b1300)

milk v *fig.* b1530 [lit. use: b975]

misbecome v b1530

off v *take off, remove* b1530 ["be off": b1530; "kill": b1870]

oppugn v *impugn* b1530 [obs. "to fight against": b1450 to 1800s]

outrun v b1530

overlook v *ignore* b1530 (obs. overhear "ignore": OE only)

penetrate v b1530 ["begin intercourse": b1630] (penetration: b1450)

perpetuate v b1530

profess v *proclaim* b1530 ["commit to a religious order": b1350; "claim": b1570]

promulgate v b1530 (arch. promulge v: b1500)

quiet v *make quiet* b1530 ["make free": b1350 to 1400s] (quieten: b1830)

relate v *tell* b1530 (relation "story": b1400)

repine v *grieve* b1530 [obs. "give trouble": b1450]

riddle v *as in "riddled with mistakes"* b1530

roost v b1530 (noun use: b1100)

slip v *as in "slip into something more comfortable"* b1530 [as in "slip some pants on": b1350]

snap v *bite quickly* b1530 (noun use: b1495)

startle v *inspire a start* b1530 [obs. "struggle": b1100 to 1300s; "start": b1570]

stutter v b1530 (noun use: b1850; stut "stutter": b1450)

suggest v b1530 [obs. "lead to temptation": b1600 to 1670; "bring to mind": b1670] (suggestion: b1350)

swagger v b1530 (noun use: b1725; adj use "vogue": b1900)

swash v *swashbuckle* b1530 (noun use: b1595; swasher n: b1590)

throng v b1530 [obs. "crush": b1350 to 1800s]

tolerate v *endure* b1530 ["accept, permit": b1570] (tolerable: b1425; tolerant: b1780)

toy v *as in "toy with the prey"* b1530 ["phys. fiddle with": b1830]

whinny v b1530 (noun use: b1825)

accredit v b1535

afflict v *trouble* b1535 [obs. "deject": b1350 to 1600s]

allude v b1535 [obs. "hint at": b1500 to 1600s]

anticipate v b1535 (anticipation: b1400; anticipatory: b1670)

constipate v b1535 [fig. "clog up": b1900] (constipat adj: b1425)

effect v b1535 (effectuate: b1580)

encroach v b1535 [obs. "take, confiscate": b1325 to 1600s]

entrap v b1535 (entrapment: b1600)

explicate v b1535 (explicatory: b1625)

inhibit v *hinder* b1535 ["forbid": b1425]

invent v b1535 [obs. "discover, find": b1475] (invention: b1500)

invest v *clothe; bequeath authority* b1535 [financial sense: b1620]

invite v b1535 [as in "open doors invite robbery":

b1600] (noun use: b1660; invitation: b1600)

iterate v b1535 (iteration: b1500)

molder v b1535

nullify v b1535

overbear v *fig. and lit. apply pressure* b1535 (overbearing: b1600)

pester v b1535

prattle v b1535 (noun use: b1555)

prod v b1535

quaere v *question* b1535 (noun use: b1950)

qualify v *as in "qualify a statement"* b1535 (qualified: b1600)

recant v b1535

recognize v b1535 [obs. "repossess real estate": b1475 to 1600s; obs. "proofread": b1570 to 1700s]

restrict v b1535 (restriction: b1415)

retire v *retreat* b1535 [as in "retire to the parlor": b1640; work sense: b1670] (retirement: b1600)

solve v *as in "solve a problem"* b1535 ["dissolve": b1450; obs. "untie": b1450 to 1600s]

surrogate v b1535 (noun use: b1605; surrogacy: b1820)

tender v *offer* b1535 (noun use: b1545)

unpeople v b1535

decent adj *appropriate; proper* b1540 [as in "decent wages": b1730]

fleece v *rob* b1540 ["clip a sheep": b1630]

gratify v b1540 [obs. "grate," "make pleasant": b1400 to 1600s] (gratification: b1580; gratifying: b1615)

intercept v b1540

intimate v *hint* b1540 ["tell boldly": b1625]

inveigle v *finagle* b1540 [obs. "deceive": b1495 to 1700s]

mount v *as in "mount a picture"* b1540

pepper v *sprinkle, spray* b1540

perpetrate v b1540

persist v b1540 [fig. "survive": b1770] (persistence: b1550; persistency: b1600; persistent: b1870)

progress v *make phys. headway* b1540 ["improve": b1630] (progression: b1450)

revolt v b1540 (revolute v: b1900)

scrabble v *scribble* b1540 (noun use: b1800)

sheer v *as in "sheer away"* b1540

squander v *scatter; spend* b1540 (noun use: b1710)

subtract v *remove; retract* b1540 ["perform a math function": b1670]

swear in v b1540 (swearing-in: b1895)

thump v b1540

twiddle v *waste time* b1540 [as in "twiddle your fingers": b1700]

vault v *leap* b1540 (noun use: b1580)

cavil v b1545

clinch v *phys. nail in* b1545 [fig., as in "clinch a deal": b1720] (noun use: b1630)

coalesce v b1545

extinguish v b1545 (extinct v "extinguish": b1450)

flag v *as in "flagging interest"* b1545

flounce v *move broadly* b1545 (noun use: b1585)

incise v b1545

intermit v *cause to be intermittent* b1545 (intermittent: b1605)

loom v b1545 (noun use: b1840)

meliorate v b1545 (melioration: b1450; meliorative: b1830)

peg v b1545 ["hit": b1900; "stereotype, describe": b1930]

piddle v b1545 [slang "urinate": b1800] (piddling: b1560; piddly: b1970)

segregate v b1545 (adj use: b1470; segregation: b1555)

smelt v *melt* b1545

berate v

brave v [arch. "dare": b1550]

dampen v *diminish*

gird v *mock* [obs. "hit": b1225]

immolate v

inculcate v

jog v *shake* ["nudge": b1600]

jostle v ["have sex with": b1450] (noun use: b1615)

overhear v *eavesdrop* [obs. "ignore," as in "overlook": OE only; obs. "hear": b1150 to late ME]

pilfer v (noun use: b1450)

pummel v

shuttle v (noun use: b1900)

skirr v *flee*

tattle v [obs. "blather": b1485 to 1700s] (tattler: b1550)

trudge v ["travel": b1670] (noun use: b1835)

urge v (noun use: b1620)

whiz v (noun use: b1620)

Archaisms

mate v *match, equal* b1510

reflex n *reflection* b1510

convent v *convene* b1515

mound n *fence* b1515 (verb use: b1515)

prenominate adj *obs. aforementioned* b1515 [u1600s]

recess n *type of agreement* b1520

cap-a-pie adv *head-to-toe* b1525

straiten v *narrow* b1525

equal adj *obs. fair* b1530 [u1700s] (obs. equality: b1450 to 1600s)

grate adj *obs. pleasing* b1530 [u1600s]

hare v *obs. harass* b1530 [u1600s]

incend v *incite* b1530

inchmeal adv *bit by bit* b1530

irrision n *derision* b1530

makebate n *inciter* b1530

makepeace n b1530

oblectation n b1530 [u1800s]

woulder n *wisher, not doer* b1530

mayhap adv b1535

vindicate v *be vengeful* b1535 [obs. "punish": b1630 to 1700s] (obs. vindication: b1485 to 1600s; vindictive: b1620)

explode v *obs. disapprove noisily* b1540 [u1800s]

feasance n *obs. opp. of malfeasance* b1540 [u1700s]

insult v *brag* b1540 ["deprecate": b1620]

pelting adj *paltry* b1540

saturate v *obs. satisfy* b1540 [u1800s] (obs. saturation: b1555 to 1800s)

acrimony n *arch. acrid taste* b1545 ["causticity": b1620] (acrimonious: b1615)

caliginous adj *misty, dim*

cotquean n *loosely, a manly woman or a womanly man*

disclose n *disclosure* [u1700s] (disclosure: b1600)

dup v *open*

eximious adj *excellent*

flirt n *obs. witticism* [u1700s]

insincerity n *corruption* ["lack of sincerity": b1700]

runagate n *vagabond* [obs. "renegade": b1530 to 1600s]

IN USE BY
1600

Geography/Places

cardinal points n *compass points* b1555

hammock n *hummock* b1555

isthmus n b1555 [med. sense: b1730]

New World n b1555

savanna n b1555

temperate zone n b1555

tropic of Cancer n b1555 (tropic of Capricorn: b1545)

antarctic circle n b1560

continent n *Asia, Europe, etc.* b1560 ["land mass": b1425; obs. "large section of land": b1545] (lit. and fig. continental: b1760)

geographical adj b1560 (geographic: b1670)

maelstrom n b1560

piazza n *public square* b1565

riverbank n b1565

delta n b1570

inland n b1570

inlet n b1570

main n *as in "the Spanish Main"* b1570

point n b1570

projection n *type of map* b1570

sierra n b1570

tract n *area, etc.* b1570 [obs. "length of time": b1450; as in "digestive tract," etc.: b1700]

chart n *map* b1575 [type of graph: b1870] (verb use: b1845)

lee shore n *shore at ship's leeward side* b1580

quagmire, quag n b1580 ["complex situation": b1775] (quaggy: b1630)

fountainhead n b1585

torrent n b1585 (adj use: b1670; torrential: b1850)

ashore adv b1590

cove n *bay* b1590 [type of closet: b800; type of valley: b1400]

rivulet n b1590

torrid zone n b1590

quadrangle n *courtyard* b1595

underground n *area below the ground* b1595 [fig. type of secret group: b1970] (adj use: b1610)

beach n *the shore area* [arch. "sand on the beach": b1535] (verb use: b1840)

chasm n

crosscurrent n

estuary n [type of inlet: b1540]

patch n *area, as in "patch of ground"*

tundra n

Natural Things

cat's-eye n *type of gem* b1555

trace element n b1555

ignis fatuus n *"foolish fire"— swamp gas* b1565

afterbirth n b1570

shallow n b1575

copse n b1580

reef n *as in "coral reef"* b1585

sylvan adj *pertaining to the woods* b1585

moonbeam n b1590

naturalist n b1590

whitewater n b1590

atomy n *atom* b1595

carnivorous adj b1595 (carnivore: b1840)

connatural adj *inborn* b1595 (connate adj: b1570)

jade n *the stone* b1595

shooting star n b1595

albumen n *egg white*

aquamarine n *the rock*

canary seed n

crystallize v *form crystals* [obs. "turn into crystal": b1600 to 1700s; fig. "take form": b1830]

ebon adj (noun use: b1400)

fairy ring n

ray n *ray of light*

vivarium n *type of terrarium* [obs. "habitat": b1600]

Plants

alga n b1555 (algae: b1795)

cacao n b1555 (cacao bean/cocoa bean: b1840)

chrysanthemum n b1555

clematis n b1555

evergreen n b1555 (adj use: b1675)

ground pine n b1555

tuna n *type of plant* b1555

jasmine n b1565 [type of perfume: b1700]

lily of the valley n b1565

palmetto n *type of palm tree* b1565

ripen v *get ripe* b1565 ["make ripe": b1470]

sunflower n b1565

sweet william n b1565

thistledown n b1565

goldenrod n b1570

hardwood n b1570

manioc n b1570

mayflower n b1570

nasturtium n b1570 [earlier type of plant: b1150]

sumac n b1570 [type of mixture for tanning: b1300]

muskmelon n b1575

papaw/pawpaw n *type of tree* b1575

pink n *type of plant* b1575

rampion n b1575

shamrock n b1575

snapdragon n b1575

bluebell n b1580

coca n b1580

deadly nightshade n b1580

honeydew n b1580

larkspur n *type of plant* b1580

linden n *type of tree* b1580

love apple n *tomato* b1580

pondweed n b1580

sassafrass n b1580

sea grass n b1580

seaweed n b1580

thorn apple n b1580

tulip n b1580

wallflower n b1580

mango n b1585

vegetable n *as in "fruits and vegetables"* b1585 [arch. gen. "plant": b1580]

bamboo n b1590

rosebush n b1590

topiary adj b1595

truffle n b1595 [type of sweet: b1930]

aspen n

banyan n
belladonna n
calabash n *type of gourd*
club moss n
daylily n
dogbane n
dogwood n
henna n (verb use: b1920)
horse chestnut n
horsetail n *type of plant*
huckleberry n (Am)
hyacinth n [type of gem: b1555]
lady's slipper n (Am)
milkweed n
mountain ash n
papaya n *type of tree*
pip n *small seed*
pissabed n *dandelion* ["bed-wetter": b1645]
poke n *pokeweed* (pokeweed: b1755)
ramp n *type of wild onion*
sorghum n
squid n
twitch n *type of grass* (twitch grass: b1690)
undergrowth n
vegetable adj *as in "animal, vegetable or mineral?"*

Animals

antbear n *aardvark* b1555
dog tick n b1555
fang n b1555 (verb use: b1830)
iguana n b1555
manatee n b1555
stingaree n *stingray* b1555 (stingray: b1615)
turkey n b1555 [type of guinea fowl: b1545]
water rat n b1555
duckbill n b1560
toucan n b1560
flamingo n b1565 [type of color: b1900]
kit n *kitten or small animal* b1565 (kitten: b1450)
roundworm n b1565
tarantula n b1565
alligator n b1570
bullfinch n b1570
calamary n *type of squid* b1570
fledge v *grow the feathers that allow a bird to fly* b1570 (fledgling: b1830)

geir n *obs. vulture* b1570 [u1800s]
haggard n *male hawk, or "an intractable person"* b1570
leopardess n b1570 (leopard: b1300)
parakeet n b1570
porkling n b1570
remora n *type of fish* b1570
sea star n *starfish* b1570
trunk n *as in "elephant's trunk"* b1570
turtle n b1570
water spaniel n b1570
bat n *flying mammal* b1575
gazehound n *kind of the opp. of bloodhound* b1575
wolverine n b1575
albacore n b1580
armadillo n b1580
aviary n b1580
coyote n b1580
lambkin n b1580
penguin n b1580 [obs. "great auk": u1700s]
pigeonhole n b1580 [type of desk feature: b1700; "category, stereotype": b1870]
scarab n b1580 [type of gem: b1900]
web n *as in "web-toed"* b1580
gazelle n b1585
mosquito n b1585
pussy n *cat* b1585
water flea n b1585
baa v b1590 (noun use: b1630)
caw v b1590 (noun use: b1670)
seabird n b1590
bill v *as in "bill and coo,"* applied to birds b1595 [applied to people: b1730]
chinchilla n b1595
gadfly n b1595 (fig. use: b1630; gadbee: b1570)
giraffe n b1595
lovebird n *type of bird* b1595
puppy n b1595 [obs. "wench": b1600 to 1600s; "obnoxious man": b1600] (puppy dog: b1595)
sailfish n b1595
screech owl n b1595 (screech n: b1570)
sea urchin n b1595
anchovy n

dobbin n
flycatcher n *type of bird* [type of plant: b1870]
foil n *animal trace*
grimalkin n *type of cat*
guinea hen n
jenny n *female animal*
kibble n *type of dog*
llama n
magpie n *type of bird* [fig. use: b1670]
man-eater n
meow n/v
rockfish n
zebra n [slang "striped thing": b1830]

Weather

hurricane n b1555
halo n b1565 [religious sense: b1650]
trade wind n b1570
monsoon n b1585
veer v *applied to the wind* b1585 ["change direction": b1630] (noun use: b1615)
gust n *as in "gust of wind"* b1590 (verb use: b1815)
sultry adj *pertaining to weather* b1595 [pertaining to people: b1900]
whiff n/v *small breeze* b1595
aweather adv *on the weather side*
shift n *windshift* (verb use: b1670)
typhoon n

Heavens/Sky

polestar n b1555
falling star n b1565
fixed star n b1565
meteor n b1590 ["any weather phenomenon": b1475] (meteorite: b1825; meteorolite: b1830; meteoroid: b1865)
perigee n b1595
asterism n *constellation*
macrocosm n *the universe* [opp. of microcosm: b1870]

Science

etiology n *study of sources of diseases* b1555
genus n b1555

chemist n b1565
conservatory n *botanical building* b1565 [obs. "preservative": b1565 to 1600s; as in "conservatory of music": b1830]
empirical adj b1570 (empiric: b1530)
optics n b1570
auditory adj b1580
chemic adj *alchemical, chemical* b1580
chemical adj b1580 [obs. "alchemical": u1700s] (noun use: b1750)
parallax n b1580
anthropology n b1595
perpetual motion n b1595
precipitate n b1595 (verb use: b1670; precipitation: b1500)

Energy

energy n b1570
stove n b1570 [obs. "type of hot-air bath": b1450 to 1700s] (stovepipe: b1700)
radiation n (radiate: b1570)

Time

peacetime n b1555
forepassed/forepast adj *bygone* b1560
sandglass n *hourglass* b1560
ante meridiem adj A.M. b1565 (post meridiem: b1650)
biennial adj b1565 (noun use: b1800; biennium: b1900)
fall n *autumn* b1570
hand n *on a clock* b1570
past n b1570
ephemeral adj *day-long* b1580 [gen. use: b1670]
sundial n b1580
watch n b1590 [obs. "alarm clock": b1440 to 1500s; obs. types of clock works: b1600 to 1800s]
chronology n b1595 (chronologer: b1575; chronologist: b1615; chronological: b1615)
cockshut n *twilight* b1595 (cockcrow: b1400)
Iron Age n b1595
aftertime n *the future*

Abbreviations Used in This Book

adj adjective • *adv* adverb • *Am* American • *arch.* archaic • *b* by (so that "b1700" means "by 1700") • *Brit* British • *conj* conjunction • *contr* contraction • *esp.* especially • *fig.* figurative • *gen.* general • *geo.* geography • *interj* interjection • *leg.* legal • *LME* Late Middle English • *lit.* literal • *ME* Middle English • *med.* medical • *mil.* military • *n* noun • *obs.* obsolete • *OE* Old English • *opp.* opposite • *phys.* physical • *prep* preposition • *pron* pronoun • *rel.* religion • *spec.* specific • *u* until • *var.* various • *v* verb ❦

midnoon n
second n *unit of time*

Age/Aging

golden age n b1555 (golden-ager: b1965)
majority n *as in "age of majority"* b1570
youngster n *youth* b1590 ["child": b1770] (young-ling: b900; younker: b1515)
underage adj *not old enough* b1595

Mathematics

eccentric adj *describing circles* b1555 [describing people: b1630] (noun use: b1400)
irrational number n b1555
isosceles adj b1555
theorem n b1555
arithmetician n b1560
cube n b1560 (adj use: b1570; verb use: b1590)
square root n b1560
whole number n b1560
cylinder n *geometric shape* b1570 [type of chamber: b1700] (cylindrical: b1650; cylindric: b1700)
hexagon n b1570 (hexagonal: b1675)
obtuse angle n b1570
octahedron n b1570
oval adj/n b1570
parallelogram n b1570
pentagon/pentagonal n/adj b1570
percent adv b1570 (noun use: b1670; adj use: b1890;

percentage: b1790; percentile: b1890)
polygon n b1570
polyhedron n b1570
prime number n b1570 [prime: b1600]
rhomboid n b1570
rhombus n b1570
square n/v *as in "2 × 2"* b1570
unit n 1570
value n b1570
hypotenuse n b1575
integer n b1575 (adj use "whole": b1510)
rectangle n b1575 (rectangular: b1625)
parabola n b1580
mathematics n b1585 (mathematic: b1400; math: b1880; maths (Brit): b1915)
arithmetic progression n b1595
cardinal number n b1595
common denominator n b1595
secant n b1595
baker's dozen n
chiliad n *group of 1,000* ["1,000 years": b1450]
entrance n *obs. bookkeeping* [u1800s]
equation n *lit. and fig.*
finite adj
octagon n (obs. octangle: b1570 to 1700s; octagonal: b1820)
power n *as in "10 to the third power"*
radius n *in geometry*

remainder n
teens n

Measurement

glass n *hourglass* b1570
head n *akin to foot* b1570
quantum n *quantity, amount* b1570 [as in "quantum mechanics": b1910]
score n *obs. 20 paces* b1570 [u1600s]
pica n *unit of measure* b1590
span n *time, distance from one end to another* ["space between thumb and little finger": b900; "part of a bridge": b1830]

The Body

bowleg n b1555
callus n b1565 [callosity: b1940] (verb use: b1865)
hamstring n b1565 (verb use: b1645; hams: b1500; hamstring muscle: b1890)
blink v *close and open eyes* b1570 (noun use: b1595)
courses n *menstruation* b1570
ducky n *arch. female breast* b1570 [u1800s]
fat n b1570
prat n *buttocks, as in "prat fall"* b1570 (pratfall: b1940)
pubes n b1570 (pubic: b1835)
purgation n *obs. menstruation* b1570 [u1700s]
quadriceps n b1570 (quads: b1970)
time n *menstrual period* b1570
windbags n *lungs* b1570
crotch n b1575 [obs. type of tool: b1540]
birthmark n b1580
glottis n b1580
larynx n b1580
lifeblood n b1580
pancreas n b1580
proboscis n b1580 [slang "schnozz": b1670]
skeleton n b1580
sphincter n b1580
vertebra n b1580
shit n b1585 [obs. "diarrhea": b1000; "worthless

person": b1510] (verb use: b1310)
chops n *jowls* b1590 (chop: b1400; chaps: b1555)
eyeball n b1590 (verb use: b1900; adj use: b1975)
eyestrings n *assumed body parts that don't exist* b1590
blush n *facial flush* b1595 ["glance," as in "at first blush": b1350] (verb use: b1405)
dental adj b1595
pinkie n *little finger* b1595
prick n *penis* b1595
agnail n *hangnail* [obs. "toe corn": b1150 to 1800s]
chancre n
cowlick n
curl n *of hair* [gen. use: b1630]
dentition n *cutting teeth*
fibula n
glabella n *area between the eyebrows*
heelbone n
jugular vein n
puke v (noun use: b1740)
radius n *type of bone*
root n *slang penis*
scalp n *hair and skin* ["obs. "pate": b1300; lit. type of trophy: b1630; fig. type of trophy: b1730]
scapula n
scrotum n
stool n *excrement* (rare verb use: b1570)
tonsil n
vagina n (vaginal: b1730)

Physical Description

androgyne n b1555 (androgynous: b1630)
forspent adj *exhausted* b1565
redheaded adj b1565 (redhead: b1870)
sharp-nosed adj b1565 (sharp-sighted: b1575; sharp-eyed: b1670; sharp-eared: b1895)
aptitude n *ability* b1570 ["inclination": b1425]
dryth n *dryness, thirst* b1570
gap-toothed adj b1570
gaze v b1570 ["stare blankly": b1470]
stubby adj *squat* b1575

ejaculate v b1580 [obs. "exude": b1670 to 1800s; "spout verbally": b1670] (ejaculation: b1605)

swarthy adj b1580 (swart "swarthiness": b900)

buxom adj *full-bodied* b1590 [obs. "obedient": b1150; obs. "gracious": b1375 to 1800s]

empty-handed adj b1590

handsome adj *attractive* b1590 ["handy": b1400; "large": b1580]

long-winded adj b1590

nose v b1590

urinate v b1590

bright-eyed adj b1595

muliebrity n *opp. of virility* b1595

clumsy adj (clumse v: b1325; clums adj: b1630)

lynx-eyed adj *sharpsighted*

masculine adj *manly* [grammatical sense: b1350; "male": b1450] (arch. noun use: b1450; feminine: b1400; masculinity: b1770)

pinguedinous adj *fat, fatty* (pinguefy: b1600)

sinewy adj *fig. sense of tough* [phys. sense: b1400]

spawl v *arch. spit*

swift-footed adj

unman v *emasculate*

vacillate v [emotional sense: b1625] (vacillation: b1400)

whip v *drink fast*

young-eyed adj

Medicine

bellyache n b1555 (verb use: b1885)

healthy adj b1555 (obs. healsome: b1470; healthless: b1570)

prosthesis n b1555 [rare grammatical use: b1555]

delirium n b1565 (obs. delire v: b1450; delirious: b1600; obs. delirancy: b1670 to 1700s)

hard-of-hearing adj b1565

pica n *abnormal food craving* b1565

pomade n *type of ointment* b1565

scurvy n b1565

abort v *terminate pregnancy prematurely* b1570 (abortion: b1550)

debile adj *debilitated* b1570

dispense v b1570 (dispensary: b1700; dispenser: b1870)

dry nurse n b1570 (dry-nurse v: b1585)

elephantiasis n b1570

harelip n b1570

laudanum n *morphine medication* b1570

lozenge n b1570

lubricity n *loose bowels* b1570 [u1700s]

seasick adj b1570 (seasickness: b1625)

strain n *as in "muscle strain"* b1570 (verb use: b1630)

urinary adj b1570

wamble n *arch. stomach trouble* b1570

well adj b1570

welt n b1570 [type of leather strip: b1425]

wrench v *as in "wrench a muscle"* b1570

prophylactic adj b1575

angina n b1580

broken-winded adj *having the heaves* b1580

cholera n *spec. type of disease* b1580 [gen. "diarrhetic disease": b1605]

recipe n b1585 [gen. "formula": b1670; "way to prepare food": b1730] (verb use: b1400)

valetudinary adj *sickly* b1585 (valetudinarian: b1705)

clap n *slang gonorrhea* b1590

philter n/v *type of potion* b1590

anorexia n (anorexic: b1910; anorectic adj: b1900)

atrophy n (verb use: b1865)

caries n (cariogenic: b1930)

compress n

doctress n (doctor: b1450)

dummy n *unspeaking person* ["stupid person": b1800]

experiment n *obs. type of medicine* [u1700s]

heartburn n [obs. "passion": b1250] (obs. heartburning: b1470 to 1700s)

hygiene n (hygienic: b1835)

incider n *obs. type of med. tool* [u1700s]

infirm adj [gen. "weak, not firm": b1380]

labor n (obs. verb use: b1450 to 1700s)

measly adj *afflicted with measles; small* [slang "small": b1870]

mumps n

obstipation n *obsti(nate) (consti)pation*

oculist n

pathology n (pathological: b1590; pathologist: b1650)

prescribe v (prescription: b1600)

rabies n (rabid: b1830)

raw adj *as in "raw skin"*

simple fracture n

stroke n

vulnerary adj/n *conducive to healing*

Everyday Life

hammock n b1555

pad n *as in "mattress pad"* b1555

rose oil n b1555

woodpile n b1555

placard n *poster* b1560 [obs. "license": b1485 to 1700s]

mineral water n b1565

tobacco n b1565 ["the source plant": b1600]

file n *as in "file cabinet"* b1570 ["string on which papers are strung": b1525] (verb use: b1475)

pet n b1570 (adj use: b1600)

portmanteau n *type of traveling bag* b1570

armoire n b1575

cooler n *as in "camping cooler"* b1575

bracket n *shelf* b1580 ["support for shelf": b1630]

daybook n b1580

dead letter n b1580

housework n b1580

master key n b1580

silverware n b1580

spic-and-span adj b1580

washhouse n *laundry* b1580

bedpan n b1585

garbage n b1585 [obs. "dung": b1425 to 1800s]

wastepaper n b1585

detersive adj *detergent* b1590 (noun use: b1670)

homespun adj *lit. "made at home"* b1590 ["homey, simple": b1630]

blotter n b1595 ["daily record": b1680; as in "police blotter": b1890] (blotting paper: b1500)

daybed n b1595

doghouse n b1595

jar n *type of container* b1595

keg n b1595

keyhole n b1595

paring knife n b1595

pinhead n *head of a pin* b1595 [slang "dolt": b1900]

armchair n

bedpost n

china n (China-dishes: b1580; chinaware: b1635)

darn v *as in "darn socks"*

diurnal n *diary, journal*

drawer n

dustheap n

escritoire n *writing desk*

flowerpot n

footbath n

furniture n *chairs, etc.* [obs. "act of furnishing": b1520 to 1600s; var. meanings of equipment: b1570]

hairbrush n

luggage n *baggage* ["suitcases": by1930]

pipe n *smoking instrument*

pot n *chamberpot* (potty: b1850; potty chair: b1945)

stopper n (verb use: b1830; stopple "bung": b1350)

toilet n *haircare*

wardrobe n *piece of furniture* [obs. "bedroom": b1300 to 1600s; "dressing room": b1450 to 1800s; "clothing": b1400]

water glass n

wax light n *candle*

wineglass n

Shelter/Housing

courtyard n b1555

frame house n b1555

quarry n *square tile or stone* b1555 ["square glass": b1450]

citadel n b1565

compartment n b1565 (verb use: b1870)

cornice n b1565

dovetail n/v b1565

fascia n b1565

flue n b1565

frieze n *type of architectural detail* b1565

Ionic adj *type of architecture* b1565

coping n *walltop* b1570

entrance n *entryway* b1570 (entranceway: b1865)

hospitable adj b1570

keep n *part of a castle* b1570

manor house n b1575

model n *obs. architect's plans* b1575 [u1700s]

public house n *public building* b1575 ["hotel": b1660; "pub": b1730]

strut n *support* b1575

atrium n b1580

chimney corner n b1580

magazine n *storehouse* b1585

parapet n b1585

shelter n b1585 [fig. sense: b1630] (verb use: b1590)

cockloft n b1590

inmate n *roommate* b1590 ["prisoner": b1834]

waterworks n b1590

back room n b1595 (backroom adj: b1940)

dormer n b1595

jalousie n *type of shutter* b1595

lobby n b1595

soffit n b1595

withdrawing room n *drawing room* b1595

alcove n

arena n

caravansarai n *inn or hotel*

galley n

garden n *as in "Madison Square Gardens"*

lodgement n *lodging* (lodging house: b1765)

lodger n [obs. "tent-dweller": b1300]

quarters n

recluse n *obs. place of recluse* [u1700s]

spire n *type of architectural feature* [rare "plant stem": b1000]

stucco n *type of plaster* [type of exterior covering: b1770] (stuc: b1670)

sudatory n *type of steam bath* (sudatorium: b1760)

Drink

nectar n *spec. drink of the gods* b1555 ["drink fit for gods": b1600]

bordeaux n b1570

head n *as in "the head on a beer"* b1570

winebibber n b1570

coffee n

crush v *arch. drink*

rotgut n

sherry n

skim milk n

wash down v *as in "wash it down with water"*

Food

apricot n b1555

cacao butter n b1555

cassava n *type of plant* b1555

guava n b1555

maize n b1555

pettitoes n b1555

plantain n *type of fruit* b1555

potato n *sweet potato* b1555 ["white potato": b1600]

torte n b1555

caviar n b1560

tipple v b1560 [obs. "sell alcohol": b1500 to 1600s] (noun use "drink": b1585)

epicure n *hedonist* b1565 ["gourmet": b1600]

spicy adj *tasting of spice* b1565 ["pertaining to spice": b1560; fig. "tart": b1870]

sweetbread n b1565

crude adj *obs. uncooked* b1570 [u1700s]

dessert n b1570

epulation n *arch. feast* b1570

fricassee n/v b1570

giblets n b1570

glut v *eat greedily* b1570

ingurgitate v *guzzle—kind of the opp. of regurgitate* b1570

pudding n b1570 ["animal intestines as food": b1325]

rack n *cut of meat* b1570

stuffing n b1570 (stuff v: b1450)

feed n *feeding* b1575 [as in "horse feed": b1590; as in "direct feed": b1870]

frijole n b1580

grits n b1580

guzzle v b1580

kitchen garden n b1580

luncheon n b1580 (lunch: b1815)

rye bread n b1580

sarsaparilla n *plant, drink* b1580

seasoning n b1580

cream cheese n b1585

molasses n b1585

piecrust n b1585

sorbet n b1585

antipasto n b1590

carbonado n *style of cooking meat* b1590 (verb use: b1600)

trencherman n *good eater* b1590

yam n b1590 ["type of sweet potato": b1800]

edible adj b1595 (noun use: b1670; eatable: b1385)

intenerate v *arch. tenderize* b1595

red pepper n b1595

rusk n *type of bread* b1595

shortcake n b1595

banana n [as in "top banana": b1930]

candied adj

cashew n (cashew nut: b1800)

cauliflower n

compote n [type of pigeon dish: b1770] (obs. compost: b1400 to 1700s)

couscous n

curry n *spice* [type of sauce: b1685]

custard n [type of pie: b1355]

dumpling n

flapjack n

hasty pudding n

horseradish n

jaggery n *type of sugar*

kickshaw n *fancy chow*

loblolly n *gruel, mire*

macaroni n

neat adj *straight, as in "scotch neat"*

olive n ["olive tree": b1200]

preserve n/v *jam*

puff paste n

salt v *flavor with salt*

spareribs n

tack n *hardtack*

watermelon n

Agriculture/ Food-Gathering

brand n *lit. burn mark* b1555 ["torch," as in "firebrand": b950; fig. "mark": b1600] (verb use: b1425)

fishing rod n b1555 (fishing pole: b1790)

folder n *arch. shepherd* b1555

crowkeeper n b1565

farmhouse n b1570

huntsman n b1570 (obs. hunt: "hunter": b1135 to 1800s; hunter: b1250; huntswoman: b1630)

harvest home n b1575

hayloft n b1575

poultryman n b1575

scarecrow n b1575 ["person who scares crows": b1555]

corral n b1585 (verb use: b1850)

milk house n b1590

pastureland n b1595

pigsty n b1595 (piggery: b1785)

blight n *as in "plant blight"* ["skin rash": b1615; gen. "pestilence": b1665] (verb use: b1670)

dairymaid n (dairywoman: b1610; dairyman: b1615)

paddy n *rice* ["where rice is grown": b1970]

smut n *fungal infection*

wallow n *as in "hog wallow"*

Cloth/Clothing

lace n b1555

pump n *type of shoe* b1555

scarf n *sash, headscarf* b1555

tiara n b1555

chamois n *type of leather* b1560 ["goat providing chamois leather": b1535]

brocade n *type of fabric* b1565

buttonhole n b1565
gauze n b1565
mule n *type of slipper* b1565
turban n b1565
bodice n b1570 [use as singular: b1900]
cape n *type of garment* b1570 [type of religious clothing: b1200]
contex v *obs. weave* b1570 [u1700s]
drawers n b1570
dress n *clothing* b1570 [spec. article of clothing: b1610] (verb use: b1450)
goggles n b1570
grogram n b1570
sheer adj b1570
shirtsleeve n b1570
shroud n *as in "death shroud"* b1570 [obs. "clothes": b1150 to 1600s; obs. "shelter": b1470 to 1600s; "covering": b1570]
wear n *as in "sportswear"* b1570
strap n *as in "bootstrap"* b1575 [type of fastening tool: b1700] (verb use: b1715)
wristband n b1575 (wristlet: b1870)
bib n b1580
buff n *type of leather* b1580
chopine n *type of shoe* b1580
galligaskins n *type of loose breeches* b1580
overshoe n b1580
jersey n *type of cloth* b1585 ["top made of jersey": b1870]
stocking n *sock* b1585
brogue n *type of shoe* b1590
necklace n b1590
pantaloon n b1590 [type of clown: b1590]
sleave silk n *arch.* b1590
topless adj b1590 [gen. "immeasurably high": b1590]
velure n *arch. velour* b1590
caftan n b1595
cordovan adj/n *type of leather* b1595
drawnwork n b1595
plush n *type of fabric* b1595 (adj use "made of plush": b1630)
trousers n b1595

burnoose n
chain stitch n
coattail n
denim n [modern use: b1850]
gathers n
jackboot n
knit n
muff n *handwarmer*
shift n
tabby n *type of fabric*
toga n
undress v (noun use: b1685)
waist n [obs. type of belt: b1570 to 1600s]

Fashion/Style

tricksy adj *fashionable* b1555 ["playful": b1600] (verb use: b1500; arch. trick "fashion": b1570)
grotesque n *art style* b1565 (adj use: b1605)
frowze n *obs. frizzy wig* b1570 [u1700s]
vogue n *fashion* b1575 [obs. "inclination": b1575]
disheveled adj *describing hair* b1585 [obs. "hatless": b1410 to 1600s; describing other things: b1570]
mustache n b1585 (mustachio: b1555)
elflock n *type of hair* b1595
frill n *spec. type of ornament* b1595 [gen. "luxury": b1900] (verb use: b1575)
genteel adj *arch. stylish*
primp v

Tools

candlesnuffer n b1555
hayfork n b1555
retort n *distilling vessel* b1560
forceps n b1565
moneybag n b1565
water level n b1565
burning glass n b1570
cork n *type of stopper* b1570 (verb use: b1580)
cracker n *as in "nutcracker"* b1570
pliers n b1570
press n *printing press* b1570 ["publishing house": b1600; "the journalism business": b1800; "journalists as a group": b1930]
shaver n b1570

sight n *as in "gunsight"* b1570 (verb use: b1930)
turnspit n b1570
currycomb n b1575
hod n b1575
walking stick n b1580
oilstone n *whetstone* b1585
caliper n b1590 (verb use: b1880; calliper compasses: b1580)
cane n *walking aid* b1590 (verb use: b1670)
hobnail n b1590
printing press n b1590
shoehorn n b1590 (verb use: b1930)
reaphook n b1595
switch n *type of whip* b1595 ["type of stick": b1730] (verb use: b1615)
appliance n *gen. tool* ["application": b1565]
easel n
mouthpiece n

Travel/Transportation

canoe n b1555 (verb use: b1795)
nautical adj b1555 (nautic: b1630)
pad n/v *travel on foot* b1555
bareback adj/adv b1560
coach n *carriage* b1560 [type of train car: b1870; type of bus: b1930] (verb use: b1615)
yacht n b1560 (yachtsman: b1865; yachtswoman: b1890)
equitation n *riding a horse* b1565
foredeck n b1565
riverboat n b1565
junk n *type of ship* b1570
junket n/v b1570
passport n *travel document* b1570 [gen. "clearance to leave port": b1500 to 1600s]
port n *opp. of starboard* b1570 (verb use: b1580; adj use: b1870)
short cut/shortcut n *obs. short journey* b1570 [u1600s]
track n *route* b1570
broadside n *part of ship's side* b1575 ["attack from the

broadside": b1600] (verb use: 1985)
jaunt v *trudge about* b1575 ["take a short trip": b1670] (noun use: b1595)
argosy n *type of ship* b1580
flyboat n *speedy boat* b1580
shallop n *type of boat* b1580
dirigible adj *steerable* b1585
disembark v b1585
careen v *tilt a ship* b1595 ["dash madly": b1930]
caroche n *type of carriage* b1595
hold n *as in "ship's hold"* b1595
jaunt n *tiresome trip* b1595 ["short journey": b1680]
phaeton n *type of carriage* b1595 [type of charioteer: b1595]
pontoon n *type of boat, sometimes used as bridge support* b1595 (pontoon bridge: b1705)
porthole n *ship entry* b1595 ["ship window": b1900]
expedition n [obs. "expediting": b1450 to 1600s]
itinerate v *travel*
lock n *on a waterway* [obs. "water barrier": b1350 to 1700s; obs. "under-bridge passage": b1570 to 1800s]
meander v [fig. "wander": b1830] (noun use: b1580)
road n [obs. "travel by horseback": b875 to 1600s]
roadway n
seaport n
sledge n *sled*
trajectory n (adj use: b1670)
yawl n

Emotions/ Characteristics

despicable adj b1555
distemper n *emotionally sick* b1555
good-hearted adj b1555
grateful adj b1555
impulsive adj b1555
quail v *shy away* b1555 ["wither": b1450; "intimidate": b1530]
stouthearted adj b1555
sybarite n *hedonist* b1555

assertive adj b1565 (assert: b1605)

crocodile tears n b1565

jeer v b1565 (noun use: b1625)

morose adj b1565 [obs. "slow": b1470 to 1600s]

shiftless adj b1565 (shift: b1570)

appreciate v *recognize, display gratitude* b1570 (appreciation: b1605; appreciative: b1700; appreciatory: b1820)

bristle v *take offense* b1570

critical adj *picky, insulting* b1570 [pertaining to criticism: b1770]

cry v *weep* b1570

decorum n b1570 ["appropriateness": b1570] (decorous: b1665)

ferocity n b1570 (ferocious: b1650)

frenetic adj *hyper* b1570 [obs. "insane": b1400 to 1700s]

fret v *as in "fret over a problem"* b1570 [obs. "eat": b900 to 1500s; "gnaw" physically: b1350]

genial adj *cheerful* b1570 ["related to reproduction": b1570; "contributing to growth": b1670]

gentle adj *kindly, easy* b1570 ["highborn": b1225]

immodest adj b1570

impudent adj b1570 [obs. "blunt, immodest, shameless": b1390 to 1700s] (impudency: b1570; impudence: b1630)

inhiate v *arch. gape open-mouthedly* b1570

lout v *be sarcastic* b1570 [u1600s]

mettle n b1570

negative adj *pessimistic* b1570

passionate v b1570 [u1600s]

plainful adj *arch. plaintive* b1570

riant adj *cheerful* b1570

snotty adj b1570

spiritless adj b1570

stonyhearted adj b1570

surly adj *cantankerous* b1570

[obs. "lordly, sirly": b1570 to 1700s]

value v *cherish* b1570 (valued: b1670)

waspish adj b1570 (wasp: b1530)

brood v *sulk* b1575 ["sit on to hatch": b1390] (broody: b1870)

cock v *swagger* b1575

crotchet n *quirk* b1575 (crochety: b1825)

dudgeon n *indignation, offense* b1575

false-hearted adj b1575

terrify v b1575

belligerent adj b1580 (belligerence: b1815; belligerency: b1865; obs. belligerous adj: b1570 to 1700s)

braggart n b1580 (bragger: b1370)

bravado n b1580

horn-mad adj b1580 ["horny": b1895]

incredulous adj b1580 [obs. "religiously unbelieving": b1535; obs. "incredible": b1570 to 1600s]

libertine n *free spirit* b1580

plaintive adj *sad* b1580 ["grieving": b1395]

pleasurable adj b1580 [obs. "pleasure-seeking": b1600 to 1700s] (pleasant: b1375; pleasing: b1400)

silly adj *foolish* b1580 ["blessed": b900; "innocent": b1200; "weak": b1300; "ignorant": b1550] (noun use: b1858)

single-hearted adj b1580

softhearted adj b1580

feckless adj b1585 (feck: b1500)

frown n *gen. expression of concern* b1585 ["phys. expression": b1630] (verb use: b1400)

garrulity n b1585 (garrulous: b1615)

lycanthropy n *delusions of being an animal* b1585 ["werewolfism": b1870] (lycanthrope: b1630)

magnanimous adj b1585 (magnanimity: b1670)

scary adj *scaring* b1585 ["scared": b1830]

braggadocio n *braggart* 1590 ["bragging": b1770]

childlike adj b1590 (childly: b900; childish: b1000)

dishearten v b1590

fancy-free adj b1590

grumble v/n b1590

heyday n *high spirits, excitement* b1590 ["best of times": b1755]

jovial adj b1590 [obs. astrological "Jovian": u1800s]

low-spirited adj b1590

merriment n b1590 [obs. "type of entertainment": b1580 to 1800s]

miscarriage n *obs. misbehavior* b1590 [u1600s]

self-sufficient adj b1590 (self-sufficiency: b1600; self-subsistent: b1670; self-sufficing: b1700)

spleenful adj *splenetic* b1590

wry adj *fig. twisted* b1590 [lit. "twisted": b1525]

arouse v *excite* b1595

bloodguilt, bloodguilty n, adj b1595

capricious adj *whimsical* b1595 [obs. "improbable": b1590 to 1700s] (noun use: b1670)

cold-blooded adj b1595

commiserate v b1595

compassionate v *arch. be compassionate* b1595

dauntless adj b1595

dismal adj *dolorous* b1595 [obs. "foreboding": b1400 to 1600s; pertaining to unlucky days: b1325] (dismale n "unlucky days": b1300)

dispassionate adj b1595 (obs. dispassion v: b1630 to 1700s; dispassion n: b1695)

disturbed adj b1595

esprit n b1595

finical adj *finicky* b1595 (finicking: b1665; finicky: b1825)

frolic v b1595 (adj use: b1540; noun use: b1570)

glib adj b1595

heartrending adj b1595

moody adj *dour* b1595 [obs. "brave": b725 to 1700s; obs. "angry": b1350 to 1600s]

overjoy, overjoyed v, adj b1595 (overjoy n "too much joy": b1600)

perfidy n *disloyalty* b1595

aggravate v *annoy* ["burden, worsen": b1530]

air n *style, disposition*

amaze v *astound* [obs. "stupefy": b1150 to 1700s; obs. "terrify": b1570 to 1700s] (amazement: b1595; amazing: b1830)

apology n *regretful admission* ["defense against accusation": b1535] (apologize: b1600)

astound v *amaze* ["stun": b1300; obs. "stupefy": b1470 to 1700s] (adj use: b1400; astounding: b1590)

aversion n *repulsion* ["averting": b1600] (averse: b1450; arch. aversation: b1600s)

awesome adj *awe-filled* ["awe-filling": b1700; "great, fabulous": b1980]

bland adj *gentle, applied to people* [applied to things: b1670]

careless adj *sloppy* ["carefree": b1000]

carriage n *bearing*

chapfallen adj

charm n *charisma* (verb use: b1450)

chicanery n (chicane v: b1675)

comportment n (comport v: b1590)

disgust n (verb use: b1605; disgustful: b1615; disgusting: b1755)

dishonesty n *lack of honesty* [obs. "lack of honor": b1400 to 1500s; obs. "promiscuity": b1450 to 1600s; obs. "ugliness": b1450 to 1500s]

distance n *emotional distance* (distant: b1730)

encheer v

facetious adj ["sophisti-

cated": b1595] (arch. fa-
cete adj: b1605)
foulmouthed adj
greed n (greedy: b900)
green-eyed monster n
gruntle v *complain*
high-lone adj *very alone*
honesty n (adj use: b1325)
hot-blooded adj (hotblood:
b1800)
humor n *funny perspective*
[type of body fluid: b1340;
"mood": b1525] (humor-
ous: b1705)
impolitic adj
indiscreet adj [obs. "demon-
strating lack of judgment":
b1425 to 1600s] (indiscre-
tion: b1350)
ironfisted adj
maniac adj (noun use:
b1765; maniacal: b1605)
miserable adj *in mental misery*
["in phys. misery": b1415]
naif adj *naive* (noun use:
b1895)
officious adj *obnoxiously official* [obs. "helpful": b1565
to 1800s]
pathological adj *pertaining to
pathology* [as in "pathological liar": b1870]
pet n *peeve* (pettish: b1595)
phlegmatic adj ["pertaining
to phlegm": b1350]
possess v *cause obsession*
puerile adj
rapture n *intense joy* [obs.
"seizing, carrying off,
rape": b1600 to 1700s;
"religious rapture": b1670]
(verb use: b1640)
rave n *raving* [as in "the
show received raves":
b1930]
relevate v *obs. cheer up*
[u1700s]
salt adj *lusty*
self-contempt n
self-respect n (self-
respecting: b1790)
settle v *as in "settle down"*
spleen n *temper* [obs. "melancholy source": b1350
u1600s] (spleenful, sple-
netic: b1590)
thin-skinned adj
uncourtly adj *rude*

valor n *honor, bravery* [obs.
type of self-esteem: b1350
to 1500s; obs. "value":
b1350 to 1800s] (valorous:
b1500)
virtue n *chastity*
whim n [obs. "wordplay":
b1645; obs. "quirky idea":
u1800s]

Thoughts/Perception/
The Mind
qualm n *misgiving* b1555
dissentious adj *dissenting*
b1560 (dissentient adj:
b1625)
high-minded adj b1560 [arch.
"arrogant": b1505]
preconceive v b1560 (pre-
conception: b1625)
recollect v *remember* b1560
paralogism n *false argument*
b1565
plausible adj b1565 ["acceptable": b1545; obs.
"applaudable": u1700s;
obs. "popular": u1800s]
(plausive "plausible":
b1630; plausibility:
b1650)
bookish adj b1570
design n *scheme* b1570 (verb
use: b1630; designing:
b1620; designs: b1700)
dogma n b1570 (dogmatism:
b1605; dogmatic: b1685)
erect adj *obs. alert* b1570
[u1700s]
incurious adj *arch. not notic-
ing* b1570
judgment n *judiciousness*
b1570
ken n *range of knowledge*
b1570 [obs. "range of
sight": u1600s] (verb use:
b1350)
preoccupy v b1570 (preoccupied: b1845; preoccupa-
tion: b1870)
sconce n *arch. head, sense or
wit* b1570
tamper v *scheme* b1570
["meddle": b1600]
vafrous adj *obs. shrewd*
b1570 [u1700s]
enterprising adj *scheming*

b1575 ["go-getting":
b1615]
observant adj *perceptive*
b1575 [obs. "servile":
b1570 to 1600s]
forefeel v *have prescience*
b1580
quandary n b1580
single-minded adj b1580
unriddle v *solve* b1580
analysis, analyze, analytic n,
v, adj b1585 ["psycho-
analysis": b1930] (analyst:
b1660; analyze: b1605)
ready-witted adj b1585
unwish v *arch. retract a wish*
b1585
cognitive adj b1590
fantast n *visionary* b1590
(fantastry: b1670)
logos n *philosophical term*
b1590
prenotion n *premonition*
b1590
reminiscence n b1590 (reminisce: b1830)
synthesis n *logic sense* b1590
[chemical sense: b1770]
contemptuous adj b1595
[akin to "contempt of
court": b1530; contempt-
ible: b1570] (contempt-
ible: b1385)
theorist n b1595 (theorician:
b1870; theoretician:
b1890)
theory n b1595 [obs. "contemplation": b1630 to
1700s; as in "music the-
ory": b1630; "guess":
b1800] (theorize: b1640)
afterthought n
alert adj (noun use: b1800;
verb use: b1870)
arcanum n *arcane knowledge*
barmy adj *looney*
bias n *prejudice* ["phys.
slant": b1530] (obs. adj
use: b1555 to 1600s)
broad-minded adj
canny adj *knowing* ["cunning": 1640]
conviction n *being convinced*
["convincing others":
b1670]
creator, creatress, creatrix n
inventor
forgetive adj *inventive*

judicious adj
notice n *awareness of something* (verb use: b1770)
obstrupescence n *stupefication* [u1800s]
ominate v *predict* [u1600s]
outsight n *opp. of insight*
plot n/v *devious plan* [as in
"plot of a novel": b1670]
reason v *think* [as in "reason
with someone": b1870]
(noun use: b1225; reason-
able "able to reason":
b1300)
sense n *perception; as in
"common sense"* (verb use:
b1900)
senses n *as in "come to your
senses"*
subdolous adj *arch. cunning*
suppose v *presume, as in "I
suppose it's true"* [obs. "believe": b1325; obs. "sus-
pect": b1450 to 1700s]
symbolism n
thesis n *supposition*
vision, visions n *dream* [as in
"a vision of radiance":
b1830]

Love/Romance/Sex
bawdy house n b1555
bridesmaid n b1555 (bridesman: b1830)
self-love n b1565
bed v b1570
buss v *kiss* b1570
cuckquean n *female cuckold*
b1570
keep v *akin to "kept woman"*
b1570
magdalen n *former prostitute*
b1570
mate n *spouse* b1570
pucelage n *obs. female virginity* b1570 [u1700s]
smack n *kiss* b1570
turtledove n *term of endearment* b1570
light-o'-love n *lover, whore*
b1580
smooch n *kiss* b1580 (verb
use: b1585)
dowsabel n *sweetheart* b1585
courtship n b1590 [obs.
"courteousness"; "diplo-
macy": b1600 to 1700s]

epithalamium n *type of wedding song* b1590

heartbroken adj b1590 (heartsick: b1530; heartsore: b1595)

maid of honor n *compare matron of honor* b1590

uxorious adj *wife-loving* b1590 (uxorial: b1800)

bordello n b1595 (bordel: b1325)

brothel n b1595 [obs. "cur": b1380; obs. "whore": b1495 to 1600s]

have v *have sex with* b1595

heartsore adj b1595 (heartbroken: b1590)

inamorato n *male lover* b1595 (inamorata: b1655)

love affair n b1595

lovelock n *lock of hair of a loved one* b1595

polygamy n b1595 (polygamous: b1615; polygamist: b1670; polyandry, polygyny: b1780)

streetwalker n b1595

temptress n b1595 (tempter: b1450)

amatory adj

cyprian adj/n *prostitute*

duck/ducky n *term of endearment*

favors n *as in "sexual favors"*

fondling n *loved person*

fornicatrix n

frig v *fuck* (frigging: b1925)

inamorate v *obs. infatuate* [u1800s]

inchastity n *arch. unchasteness*

poplet n *obs. darling* [u1600s]

punk n *arch. prostitute*

salute n *arch. kiss*

siren n *seductive woman*

suit n *wooing*

suitor n ["follower": b1450 to 1800s]

unmaiden v *deflower*

vault v *obs. mount sexually* [u1700s]

wench v

Family/Relations/Friends

half blood n b1555 (half-breed: b1760)

mama n b1555 [slang, as in "hot mama": b1930]

befriend v b1560

coz n *arch. cousin* b1560

akin adj *family* b1570 ["fig. related": b1670]

ancestress n b1580 (ancestor: b1300)

comate n *mate* b1580

great-nephew n b1585 (great-niece: b1885)

grandchild n b1590 (grandbaby, grandkid: b1920)

grandson n b1590 (granddaughter: b1615)

sonship n b1590 (sonhood: b1470)

truepenny n *trusted person* b1590

affriended adj *obs. befriended*

compatriot n

descendant n (adj use: b1460; descent: b1350; descend v: b1450)

kin adj

Holidays

maypole n b1555

Halloween n b1560

orgy n *decadent celebration* b1565 [type of ancient worship: b1565]

All Saint's Day n b1580

vacancy n *arch. vacation* b1580 [obs. "lull": b1630]

saturnalia n *type of festival* b1595 [gen. "bacchanal": b1800]

Games/Fun/Leisure

hobbyhorse n b1560 [type of horse costume: b1350; "rocking horse": b1770]

hoodman-blind n *blindman's bluff* b1565

cut v *as in "cut the cards"* b1570

king n *in cards* b1570 [in chess: b1450]

knave n *in cards: jack* b1570

lottery n b1570

pall-mall n *type of game* b1570

billiard/billiards n b1580

ninepin n b1580

ducks and drakes n *skipping stones* b1585

all hid n *hide-and-seek* b1590

blindman's bluff n b1590

gleek v *joke* b1590 (obs. noun use: b1570 to 1800s)

horseplay n b1590

deck n *pack of cards* b1595

muss n *arch. type of game* b1595

cricket n *the game*

diamond n *card suit*

even adj *of odds*

hand n *as in "poker hand"*

jackstraw n *a nobody*

leapfrog n (verb use: b1875)

logograph n *type of word puzzle*

peekaboo n

plaything n

prank n *harmless deception* [obs. "malicious deception": b1530 to 1700s; obs. "magic trick": b1570 to 1800s] (verb use: b1570; prankster: b1930)

see v *in poker*

spade n *on cards*

tenpins n (tenpin: b1810)

toy n *child's toy* [arch. "joke": b1450; obs. "friskiness": b1500 to 1700s; "something trivial": b1570] (verb use: b1530; adj use: b1805)

trick n *used in card games*

tricksy adj *playful* ["fashionable": b1555] (tricksome: b1830)

Sports

fly-fishing n b1565 (fly rod: b1685; fly-fish v: b1755; fly casting: b1890)

horsemanship n b1565

fall n *wrestling term* b1570

match n *as in "sporting match"* b1570

bullbaiting n b1580

fencing n b1585 (fence: b1600)

playing field n b1585

cockpit n *arena for cockfights* b1590 ["pertaining to airplanes, etc.": b1915]

gymnast n b1595 (gymnasiast: b1860)

rubber n *as in "rubber game"* b1595

diversion n *recreation* ["separation": b1425] (divert: b1630)

gymnasium n (gym: b1875)

pin n *in bowling*

set n *in tennis*

sport n *gaming* ["pastime": 1400s; arch. "jest": b1470; "sportsperson," as in "good sport": b1900] (adj use: b1855)

stroke n *as in "breaststroke"; stroke of the oars*

volley n (verb use: b1900)

Professions/Duties

actuary n *clerk* b1555

architect, architecture n b1555 (architectonic: b1645; architectural: b1765)

letter carrier n b1555

milkmaid n b1555 (milkman: b1590)

superintendent n b1555

moderator n *arbiter* b1560

scrutineer n *scrutinizer* b1560

antiquary n *antiquarian* b1565 (antiquarian n: b1610; antiquarian adj: b1775)

agent n *as in "literary agent"* b1570

housekeeper n b1570 [obs. "householder": b1425 to 1800s]

mechanician n b1570 (mechanist: b1610)

pantryman n *butler* b1570

valet n b1570 [type of mil. position: b1500] (valet de chambre: b1650)

chronologer n b1575 (chronologist: b1615; chronology: b1895)

gatekeeper n b1575

papermaker n b1575

cashier n b1580

coachman n b1580

directress n b1580 (director: b1455; directrix: b1600; directrice: b1635)

glassmaker n b1580

gownsman n b1580

scoutmaster n b1580

sentinel n b1580 (verb use: b1795)

chambermaid n b1590

footboy n *page* b1590

gunsmith n b1590

herbalist n b1590 (herbarist: b1600)

linguist n *foreign language expert* b1590 [gen. "language expert": b1630] (linguistician: b1895)

milkman n b1590 (milkmaid: b1555)

navigator n b1590

ragman n b1590 ["raggedy person": b1400]

skinker n *barkeep* b1590

washwoman n b1590 (washerwoman: b1630)

confectioner n b1595

charwoman n (charlady: b1910)

curatrix n

packman n *peddler*

pimp n (verb use: b1640)

seamstress n (seamster: b1000)

smoker n *type of cook*

Business/Commerce/Selling

company n b1555

cookshop n b1555

sawmill n b1555

truck n *trade* b1555

invoice n b1560 (verb use: b1700)

haggle v *barter, argue* b1585 [obs. "hack at": b1585] (noun use: b1860)

trader n b1585

bazaar n b1590

emporium n b1590

auction n b1595 (verb use: b1800; auctioneer: b1710)

vendor n b1595 (vendee: b1540; vendeuse: b1915)

market n *as in "the market for dry goods"; as in "I'm in the market for a car"*

marketable adj

seconds n *manufacturer's rejects*

tradesman n (tradeswoman: b1710; tradespeople: b1730)

The Workplace

workaday adj b1555

workroom n b1565

workshop n b1565

industry n *manufacture* b1570 [gen. "hard work": b1470]

job n *duty* b1570 ["duty, challenge": b1700; "occupation": b1870] (verb use: b1695)

daywork n b1580

paperwork n b1590

spell n/v *relief shift* b1595 ["period of time," as in "dry spell"; "attack of illness," as in "fainting spell": b1870]

employ v *hire* (noun use: b1700; employer: b1600; employee: b1825)

employer n

novitiate n *apprenticeship* ["neophyte": b1630]

salaried adj *earning a salary* ["paying a salary": b1870]

work n *job, workplace*

Finances/Money

bookkeeper n b1555 (bookkeeping: b1690)

dollar n b1555 [American, Canadian, etc.: b1800]

miser n b1560 [obs. "miserable person": b1545 to 1800s]

capital n *related to worth* b1570

fortune n *a lot of money* b1570

frugal adj b1570

imprest n *type of loan* b1570 (obs. verb use: b1570 to 1800s)

liquidate v b1570

mass n *obs. mass of cash* b1570 [u1700s]

refund v *return money* b1570 [gen. "return": b1400] (noun use: b1870)

remit v *pay* b1570 ["forgive": b1375; "send back": b1415]

chink n *money* b1575

gross n *as opposed to net* b1580

scattergood n *arch. spendthrift* b1580

mortgagee, mortgagor n b1585

ledger n b1590 [obs. "type of

bible": b1485 to 1600s; gen. "recordbook": b1570]

penurious adj *poor* b1590 ["stingy": b1630]

profit and loss n b1590

cash n b1595 [obs. "cashbox": u1700s] (adj use: b1625; verb use: b1815)

flush adj *rich* b1595 ["perfect": b1550; "even": b1630]

insolvent adj b1595

tariff n b1595 [obs. type of math table: u1700s]

affluence n *wealth* ["profuse flow": b1470] (affluent: b1450)

balance n/v *as in "balance sheet"*

cheeseparing n *penny-pinching, miserliness*

compound v *as in "compound interest"*

driblet n

empty adj *obs. penniless* [u1700s]

fisc n *state treasury, and source of the word "fiscal"* (fiscal year: b1845)

impecunious adj *broke* (impecuniary: b1830)

income n ["arrival": b1325]

purchase n *buying; the thing bought* [obs. "hunt": b1400 to 1700s; obs. "procurement, attempt to procure": b1400 to 1500s]

Language and Speaking

apothegm n *maxim* b1555

catachresis n *misuse of words* b1555

interrogation point n *question mark* b1555 ["question": b1390]

solecism n *grammar goof* b1555

circumflex n b1565 (adj use: b1565)

bibble-babble n *blather* b1570

bombast n b1570 (bombastical: b1650; bombastic: b1705)

dash n b1570 [used in Morse Code: b1870]

define v *as in "define a word"* b1570 (definition: b1630)

maxim n b1570 [obs. mathematical term: b1450 to 1600s]

pleonasm n *type of verbosity* b1570

profanity n b1570

roll v *as in "roll the r"* b1570

tautology n b1570 (tautological: b1620; tautologous: b1715)

tralatitious adj b1570

idiom n b1575 (idiomatic: b1715)

syntax n b1575

cacography n *badd spellling* b1580

conversation n *chat, exchange* b1580 [obs. "intimacy": b1340 to 1700s; "behavior": b1350] (arch. converse n: b1600; conversational: b1780)

dialect n b1580 [type of examination: b1555]

epexegesis n b1580

epithet n *descriptive phrase* b1580 ["insulting phrase": b1900]

gnome n *aphorism* b1580

onomatopoeia n b1580 (onomatopy: b1670; onomatop: b1830; onomatopoesis: b1870)

paronomasia n *punning* b1580

hieroglyphic, hieroglyphics adj, n b1585 (hieroglyph: b1600)

quote v *as in "quote a source"* b1585 [as in "quote a price": b1830]

comma n b1590 ["sentence fragment": b1530]

idiotism n *idiom* b1590

motto n b1590

queen's English n b1590

third person n b1590

wordmonger n b1590

labial adj *related to the lip* b1595

phrase book n b1595

silver-tongued adj b1595

aphorism n *maxim*

euphemism n *use of euphemism* ["the euphemism itself": b1800] (euphemize: b1860)

full stop n *period*

period n ["complete sentence"; "pause between sentences": concurrent]

Contractions

I'll contr b1570
'll contr *will* b1580
we'll contr b1580
's contr *contr of is, has, does* b1585
's contr *contr of us* b1590
'twas contr b1590
'twere contr b1590
'm contr *am* b1595
're contr b1595
I'm contr b1595
she'll contr b1595
they're contr b1595
you'll contr b1595
you're contr b1595

Literature/Writing

rhythm n b1560 [obs. "rhyme": 1600s] (rhythmic: b1580; rhythmicity: b1905)
sonnet n b1560 (sonneteer: b1590)
nomenclator n *book listing words like, um, this one?* b1565 ["creator of names": 1600s]
wording n *phrasing* b1565
composition n *the act of writing* b1570 ["the writing itself": b1600]
context n b1570 [lit. and fig. "weaving": b1425]
digest n *type of compendium* b1570 [leg. sense: b1390; type of magazine: b1930]
geld v *obs. expurgate, bowdlerize* b1570 [u1700s]
license n *as in "poetic license"* b1570
line n *as in "line of poetry"* b1570
note n *explanation, as in "footnote"* b1570
passage n *book excerpt* b1570 ["music excerpt": b1700]
index n b1575 [gen. "pointer": b1575; as in "economic index": b1830] (verb use: b1720)
commonplace book n *book of excerpts* b1580

couplet n b1580 ["couple": b1630]
notebook n b1580
Cimmerian n *mythical people in Homer* b1585 (adj use: b1580)
diary n *keeping a diary* b1585 ["the book itself": 1605]
lyric n *type of poetry* b1585 ["song's words": b1900] (adj use: b1590; lyrical: b1530)
poetize v b1585
anagram n b1590 (verb use: b1630; anagrammatize: b1590)
blank verse n b1590
canto n b1590
epic adj *describing literature* b1590 [gen. description: b1770] (noun use: b1710)
heroic verse n b1590 (heroic poem: b1695; heroic couplet: b1905)
hornbook n b1590
idyll n b1590 (idyllian adj: b1730; idyllic: b1860)
ode n b1590
page n *as in "page of a book"* b1590
rhymester n b1590
satirist n b1590
stanza n b1590
euphuism n *purple prose* b1595
fabulist n *teller of fables* b1595 ["liar": b1630]
newsmonger n b1595
paper v *put on paper, write* b1595 ["wallpaper": b1800]
plotline n b1595
analphabet adj *illiterate*
cover n *as in "can't judge a book"*
dedication n *e.g., "This book is dedicated to my mom"* (dedicate: b1530)
depencil v *obs. write with a pencil* [u1700s]
display n *obs. written description* [u1700s]
essay n (essayist: b1605)
fiction n (fictionist: b1830; fictionalize: b1920; fictioneer: b1925)
frontispiece n (front: b1600 to 1700s)

hackney v *create cliches*
inscroll v *arch. write on a scroll*
list n *as in "grocery list"* (verb use: b1615)
manuscript n (adj use: b1600)
matter n *as in "printed matter"*
neoteric adj *modern, trendy*
newsman n (newswoman: b1930; newspeople, newsperson: b1975)
note n *brief letter*
pamphleteer n (verb use: b1700)
parody n [fig. "unintentionally funny imitation": b1870] (verb use: b1745; parodist: b1745)
pencil n [type of brush: b1400; slang "penis": b1600]
press n *publishing house*
publication n
purple adj *as in "purple prose"*
read out v *read out loud*
remembrancer n *fact book*
skim v *read quickly*
tome n *huge book* [obs. "individual volume of larger work": b1520 to 1700s]
wordbook n
write v *as in "write a letter"*

Communication

word of mouth n b1555
lecture n b1570 [arch. "reading": b1425] (verb use: b1590)
converse v *talk; occupy oneself with* b1590 [obs. "live with": b1380 to 1700s; obs. "deal with," "have sex with": b1450 to 1800s]
intercommunicate v b1590
symbol n (verb use: b1835; symbolism: b1600; symbolize: b1605; symbolic: b1610)

Visual Arts/ Photography

oil n *oil paint* b1570 ["oil painting": b1870] (oil paint: b1790)

portrait n b1570 [obs. "statue, bust": u1600s; gen. "painting": b1560; fig. "verbal description": b1600] (portraitist: b1870)
artist n b1585 [obs. "educated person": b1530 to 1700s]
gallery n *for art display* b1595
art n *aesthetic pursuit and skill* ["skill," "area of knowledge": b1325]
cartoon n/v *type of drawing* [spec. type of humorous drawing: b1845]
composition n *artistic arrangement in paintings and photos*
fresco n *style of painting* ["a fresco painting": b1700]
landscape n ["the land being painted": b1630] (landscapist: b1845)
pastel n *art material* ["pastel drawing": b1870; type of color: b1900] (adj use: b1884)
pyrography n *woodburning* (pyrogravure: b1900)
tableau n *picture* ["table, chart": b1800]
wash n *in painting* (verb use: b1630)
watercolor n *type of paint* [type of painting: b1700]

Performing Arts

theatrical adj b1560 ["demonstrative": b1600]
chorus n b1565
dumb show n b1565
stage n *as in "theatrical stage"* b1570 [rare "story of a building": b1350; "boxing ring": b1830] (adj use: b1825; verb use: b1880)
zany n *secondary clown, merry-andrew* b1570 (adj use: b1600)
tragicomedy n b1580
actor n b1585 (actress: b1630)
harlequin n b1590
masquerade n b1590 [gen. "disguise": b1630; gen. "put-on": b1870] (verb use: b1595)

pantomime n *type of performer* b1590 [type of performance: b1670] (verb use: b1770; pantomimist: b1840)

act v b1595

personate v *perform a role* b1595 ["impersonate": b1600] (obs. adj use: u1800s)

book n *performance script*

clown n/v *as in "circus clown"* ["rube": b1565] (clownery: b1590)

curtain n *stage curtain* ["end of play": b1900]

entrance n *as on a stage*

eurythmy n

hand n *applause*

rehearse, rehearsal v, n *practice* [gen. "repeat": b1350]

Music

cittern n *type of stringed instrument* b1560

bass n *type of musical instrument* b1570

hautbois n *oboe* b1570

kettledrum n b1570

organist n b1570 [obs. "organ-maker": b1530 to 1600s]

reed n b1570

regal n *arch. type of musical instrument* b1570

drummer n b1575

tablature n b1575

clef n b1580

tambourine n b1580

violin n b1580

wind instrument n b1585

air n b1590

choral adj/n b1590

drumstick n b1590

duo n b1590 [gen. sense: b1900]

gong n b1590

lullaby n b1590

madrigal n *type of poem, song* b1590

wind v *play a wind instrument* b1590

flat adj/n b1595

Jew's harp n b1595

bow n *as in "violin bow"* (verb use: b1870)

chorus n *part of a song*

["something sung or spoken in unison": b1700]

color n

compose, composer, composition v, n, n ["compose writing": b1450]

contrabass n

drinking song n

drum major n

F clef n

fugue n

giraffe n *type of piano*

half note n

lutenist, lutist n *lute player*

measure n

octave n

part-song n *song in parts*

pitch n *as in "perfect pitch"*

scale n

sharp n *musical note*

syncopation n

vocal adj *opp. of instrumental* (noun use: b1930)

voice n

Entertainment

jig n *type of dance* b1560 (verb use: b1605)

country-dance n b1580

housewarming n b1580

reel n *type of dance* b1585 (verb use: b1530)

festival n b1590 [as in "film festival": b1870] (adj use: b1350; festivity: b1400)

humorist n *1599*

ring dance n

Education

college n b1565 [gen. "group": b1400]

schoolmate n b1565 (schoolfellow: b1500)

academy n b1570 [spec. place: b1480] (academe "academy": b1590)

class n *occupants of one classroom* b1570 ["students at the same level," as in "graduating class": b1700]

course n b1570

erudition n *learnedness* b1570 [obs. "what is learned": b1400 to 1700s] (erudite: b1425)

exercise n b1570

natural history n b1570

headmaster n b1580 (headmistress: b1875)

matriculate v *attend school* b1580

public school n b1580

academic adj b1590

educate v (Am) *teach* b1590 ["raise children": b1450] (education: b1620; educator: b1675)

educated adj b1590

pedant n *learned showoff* b1590 [obs. "teacher": u1700s] (pedantry: b1585; pedantic, pedantism: b1600; pedanticism: b1900)

school day n b1590

schoolboy n b1590 (schoolfellow: b1500; schoolmate: b1565; schoolgirl: b1780; schoolchild: b1840; schoolkid: b1940)

doctorate n ["person holding a doctorate": b1670]

scholarity n *obs. being a scholar* [u1800s]

science n *as in "arts and sciences"*

tenure n ["owning a tenement": b1415]

thesis n

Religion

aspersion n *as in "cast aspersions"* b1555 [religious sense: b1450] (asperse: b1490)

divinity school n b1555

Xmas n b1555

gift of tongues n b1560

liturgy n b1560

druid n b1565

gnostic n b1565 (gnosis: b1600; gnosticism: b1665)

satanism n b1565

evangelist n *preacher* b1570 [Matthew, Mark, Luke or John: b1175]

God-man n *God in human form* b1570

Magian n b1570

Monad n *God* b1570

testimony n b1570

vote v *devote* b1570

apotheosis n *deification* b1580 [gen. "triumph": b1670]

clergyman n b1580 (clergywoman: b1675)

sanctum n b1580 [gen. use: b1830]

service book n b1580

Torah n b1580

Allah n b1585

seminary, seminarian n b1585

capuchin n b1590

cathedral n *primary diocesan church* b1590 [gen. "large church": b1830] (adj use "pertaining to bishop's throne": b1300)

ecumenical adj b1590

Holy Grail n b1590

afterlife n b1595

evangel n *evangelist* b1595

god v b1595

judgment day n b1595

afterworld n

Hades n (hell: b900)

iconoclast n [gen. use: b1870]

Jack-a-Lent n *Lent puppet; insignificant person*

mischief, the n *the devil*

monsignor n

pontiff n *high-ranking priest* ["the Pope": b1700] (pontificate n: b1450)

prayer book n

presbyter n (presbytery: b1475; presbyteress: b1670)

priestess n (priest: b900)

reborn adj

ubiquity n [gen. use: b1630]

Society/Mores/Culture

mister n *Mr.* b1555 [abbreviation used: b1450]

sociable adj *given to group activity* b1555 ["friendly": b1600]

straitlaced adj *formal* b1555 [obs. "constrained": u1600s] (straitlace: b1670)

inequity n b1560 (inequitable: b1670)

staid adj b1560

bourgeois adj b1565 (noun use: b1565; bourgeousie: b1710; bourgeoise "female bourgeois": b1790)

gent n b1565 (gentleman: b1200)

sylvan n *one who lives in the woods* b1565

immorality n b1570 (immoral: b1660)

ladylike adj b1570

madame n b1570

public opinion n b1570

society n *type of group* b1570

somebody n *someone of note* b1570

gaffer, gammer n *arch. goodfellow, old man; old woman* b1575 (noun use: b1555)

populace n b1575 (populous: b1450)

nomad n b1580 (nomadic: b1820)

woman of the world n b1580

modern adj *up-to-date* b1585 ["of the present day": b1470]

nobody n b1585

right-minded adj b1585

roturier n *socially low person* b1590

unsociable adj b1590 (unsocial: b1735)

villainess n b1590

bantling n *young child* b1595

disciplinarian n b1595 [type of Puritan: b1685]

gentlefolk n b1595

grace cup n b1595

titled adj b1595

tomboy n b1595 [obs. "assertive woman": u1700s; obs. "rough boy": b1570 to 1500s]

unblooded adj *inferior* b1595

bawcock n *arch. a fine fellow*

canaille n *rabble*

cosmopolite n

ethics n ["writing about ethics": b1450]

milord n (milady: b1840)

nonentity n

Old World n (adj use: b1715)

patriot n (patriotism: b1730; patriotic: b1760)

refined adj *cultured*

vagrom adj *arch. vagrant*

Government

confiscate v *take for government treasury* b1555 [gen. "take": b1830] (adj use: b1535; confiscation:

b1545; obs. confisk v: b1450 to 1600s)

czar n b1555

official n b1555

political adj *pertaining to government* b1555 [pejorative sense: b1770]

sultan n b1555

townlet n b1555

aristocracy n *government by the most powerful* b1565 ["government by the best": b1500] (aristocratic: b1605; aristocrat: b1780)

despot n *spec. type of ruler* b1565 [gen. "tyrant": b1800]

alderwoman n b1570 (alderman: b810)

crownation n *arch. coronation* b1570

hegemony n *leadership, domination* b1570 (hegemon: b1930)

inauguration n b1570 (inaugurate: b1610; inaugural adj: b1690; inaugural n: b1835)

public service n b1570 (public servant: b1680)

gynarchy n b1580 (gynocracy: b1615)

queen mother n b1580

lieutenant governor n b1585

triumvirate n b1585 (triumvir "member of a triumvirate": b1450)

dictatorship n b1590 (dictator: b1600)

embargo n b1595 (verb use: b1755)

county n *government jurisdiction* [arch. type of jurisdiction: b1300; "count's domain": b1380]

dictator n [type of Roman ruler: b1390] (dictatorship: b1590; dictatorial: b1705; dictation "being a dictator": b1870)

divine right n

duarchy n

fasces n *Roman symbol of authority*

imperator n *emperor* (imperatrix: b1630)

inaugurate v [gen. "begin": b1770]

municipal adj ["domestic": b1540]

regnant adj (regnancy: b1870)

republic n (republican: b1715)

Politics

purge n b1565

Machiavellian n b1570 (adj use: b1580)

suffrage n *pertaining to voting* b1570

balance of power n b1580

ambassadress n b1595 (ambassador: b1375)

statesman n b1595 (stateswoman: b1630)

Life

life-giving adj b1565

short-lived adj b1590

life n *liveliness*

Death

parricide n *murder of parents or close relative* b1555

tombstone n b1565

dispatch v *kill; finish* b1570 (noun use: b1600)

engrave v *obs. place in a grave* b1570 [u1600s]

scaffold n *place of execution; execution itself* b1570

stillborn adj b1570 (stillbirth: b1755)

vidual adj *arch. pertaining to widows* b1570

bane v *arch. kill with poison* b1580 [arch. "harm": b1350]

earn v *obs. grieve* b1580 [u1700s]

massacre n b1580 (verb use: b1585)

amort adj *almost dead* b1590

deathless adj b1590

deathsman n *executioner* b1590

memento mori n *reminder of death* b1590

eulogy n b1595 [gen. "praise": b1450] (eulogize: b1810)

gravedigger n b1595

matricide n *the deed* b1595 ["the victim": b1670]

patricide n *act of killing a par-*

ent b1595 ["victim of patricide": b1630]

sepulchre v *bury* b1595 (noun use: b1300)

unlive v *obs. kill* b1595 [u1700s]

carnage n

death's-head n

encoffin v

extinguish v *arch. kill, obliterate*

fetch-light n

ghost v *arch. die*

panegyric n *tribute, eulogy* (panegyrist: b1605)

tuck up v *execute by hanging*

War/Military/Violence

arsenal n b1555 [obs. "dock serving ships": b1510 to 1800s]

captain n b1555 [gen. use: b1375]

phalanx n b1555

bombardier n *cannon operator* b1560 ["bomber crewmember": b1945]

bullet n b1560 ["typographical device": b1970]

dirk n b1560 (verb use: b1600)

falconet n *type of cannon* b1560

mortar n b1560 (verb use: b1930)

partisan n *type of weapon* b1560

strappado n *type of torture* b1560

gore n *blood, esp. clotted blood* b1565 [obs. "dung, offal": b900] (verb use: b1400; gory: b1480)

shock n *arch. type of battle* b1565 (obs. verb use: b1570 to 1700s)

annihilate v *completely destroy* b1570 [arch. "cancel": b1525] (adj use: b1400; annihilation: b1570)

butchery n *carnage* b1570 ["butcher shop": b1350]

charge n *as in "charge of the Light Brigade"* b1570

corporal n *mil. rank* b1570

douse n (Brit) *hit* b1570

enlist v b1570

exercise n b1570 (verb use: b1450)

lick v *drub* b1570 (noun use: b1600; licking: b1760)

lieutenant n b1570

mount v *prepare to fire guns* b1570

muzzle n *part of a gun* b1570

pistol n b1570 (pistoleer: b1835)

poniard n *type of dagger* b1570

punch v *hit* b1570 ["poke, stab": b1400] (noun use: b1600)

recoil n/v b1570

ruin v *destroy* b1570 ["spoil": b1585] (noun use: b1350)

tactical adj b1570

tangle n *fight* b1570

torture n b1570

heraldry n b1575 (obs. heraldy: b1470 to 1700s)

sconce n *detached defensive work* b1575

volley n b1575 (verb use: b1770)

battalion n b1580

cartridge n b1580 [gen. use "container": 1900s]

catapult n b1580 (verb use: b1850)

escort n *guard* b1580 (verb use: b1710)

field marshal n b1580

havoc v b1580 (noun use: b1500)

hostile adj b1580

infantry n b1580 (infantryman: b1885)

intelligencer n *arch. spy* b1580 ["conveyor of news": b1600]

leaguer n *siege* b1580

legionary n *legionnaire* b1580

petronel n *type of gun* b1580

scuffle v b1580 (noun use: b1610; scuff "type of hit": b1825)

tattoo n *drumbeat* b1580 ["beating sound": b1770] (verb use: b1780)

ambuscade n *ambush* b1585

caliber/calibre n *on a gun* b1590

cavalier n b1590

cossack n b1590

defeature n *obs. defeat* b1590 [u1800s]

fieldpiece n b1590

fire ship n *kind of a kamikaze ship* b1590

lame n *armorplates* b1590

lancer n b1590 (lance: b1450)

militia n b1590 (militiaman: b1780)

musket, musketeer n b1590 (musketoon "type of musket": b1670)

rear admiral n b1590

battering ram n b1595

cutlass n b1595

foil n *type of sword* b1595

forearm v *prepare arms* b1595

guardhouse n b1595

paladin n b1595

salvo n b1595 [type of salute: b1720] (verb use: b1840)

speargun n b1595

surprise v *attack by surprise* b1595 ["startle": b1595; "cause surprise": b1700; "be surprised": b1970]

adjutant general n

ammunition n [fig. use: b1630] (ammo: b1915)

attack v *assault physically* ["assault verbally": b1670] (noun use: b1665)

chamber n *part of a gun*

cock v *as in "cock a gun"*

commandress n (commander: b1300)

corps n ["group of people": b1430; "group of knights": b1465] (corpsman: b1905)

cudgel v

detonation n (detonate: b1730)

discreate v *arch. destroy*

escalade n *scaling walls*

fence v

fire n *as in "gunfire"* (verb use: b1530)

fowling piece n *type of shotgun*

general n (generaless: b1870)

harpoon n (verb use: b1800; obs. harping-iron: b1470 to 1800s)

impress v *as in "impress into the service"*

machete n

magazine n *armory* [as in "gun magazine": b1770]

marine n

militate v [fig. use: b1645]

parry v *in swordplay* [fig. "defend": b1830]

piece n *gun*

rank and file n *type of formation* [gen. "group members": b1800]

ranks n *arrangement of soldiers* (rank v: b1575)

regiment n ["governmental rule": b1400] (verb use: b1620)

rout v/n *defeat*

squadron n (squad: b1650)

sworder n *swordsman*

trireme n *type of warship*

volunteer n [gen. use: b1670] (adj use: b1650; verb use: b1700)

warrioress n (warrior: b1300)

white flag n

Crime/Punishment/Enforcement

ill-gotten adj b1555

picklock n *akin to pickpocket* b1555 ["tool of the picklock": b1600]

fine v *levy a fine* b1560 [obs. "pay a fine": b1300 to 1500s]

turncoat n b1560 (verb use: b1630)

freebooter n b1570 (freeboot v: b1600; obs. free-booty: b1630 to 1700s)

lurch v *arch. steal* b1570

order n/v *command* b1570

rook v *steal* b1570 (noun use: b1600)

sea robber n *pirate* b1570

snaphance n *obs. robber* b1570 [u1600s]

forgery n *fakery* b1575 ["counterfeiting": b1595] (forge v: b1325)

amnesty n b1580

house of correction n b1580

mutiny n *rebellion* b1580 [obs. "discord": b1570 to 1600s] (mutinous: b1580; mutineer n: b1610; mutineer v: b1700)

sea rover n b1580

posse n b1585 [slang "gang": b1990]

miscreant n *criminal* b1590 ["heathen": b1385] (adj use: b1595; miscreancy: b1830)

bandit n b1595

catamite n *youth having sex with a man* b1595

pickpocket n b1595 (verb use: b1700; arch. pickpurse: b1450)

bravo n *thug for hire* b1595

detention n

ducking stool n

embezzle v [gen. "steal": b1425 to 1700s; obs. "make weaker": b1570 to 1600s; obs. "waste": b1600 to 1700s]

enter v *as in "breaking and entering"*

hashish n (hash: b1960)

marshal n *type of law enforcement officer*

mittens n *slang handcuffs*

monstrous adj *egregiously villainous* [obs. "unnatural": b1380 to 1700s; "huge": b1520]

pinch v *steal* ["arrest": b1840] (noun use: b1770)

receive v *as in "receive stolen goods"*

whipping post n

The Law

affidavit n b1570

judgess n b1570 (judge: b1350)

lawman n *arch. lawyer* b1570

martial law n b1570

prefer v *as in "prefer charges"* b1570

resolution n b1570

solicitor n *lawyer* b1570 (solicitress "woman who solicits": b1565)

valid adj b1575 [fig. use: b1670] (validity: b1550; validate: b1650; validation: b1660)

breach of promise n b1590

criminal law n b1590 (criminal lawyer: b1870)

dock n b1590

tort n b1590

sentence v b1595 [obs. gen. "judge, opine": b1470 to 1700s] (noun use: b1870)

statute book n b1595

testatrix n *woman who dies testate* b1595 (testator: b1325)

criminal court n

hearing n

nonfeasance n

pass n *document allowing passage* ["free ticket": b1870]

prosecute v [gen. "persist": b1450; obs. "pursue": b1570 to 1600s; "practice, execute": b1600] (prosecution, prosecutor: b1670)

The Fantastic/ Paranormal

familiar spirit n b1565

fantasied adj b1565

seaman n *obs. merman* b1570 [u1700s]

bugbear n *imaginary goblin* b1580

elysian fields n b1580

loup-garou n *werewolf* b1580

roc n b1580

wood nymph n b1580

faerie n b1590

fairyland n b1590

apparition n *ghost* [gen. "unexpected appearance": b1425]

demonology n

genius n

haunt v

manitou n (Am) *type of supernatural spirit*

orc n *type of land creature* [obs. "type of sea creature": b1600 to 1800s]

phantasma n

poker n *type of goblin* (pokerish: b1830)

tarot n

wyvern n [obs. type of snake: b1450]

Magic

toadstone n b1560

abracadabra n b1565

goety n *type of magic* b1570

theurgy n *type of magic* b1570 (theurgist: b1655)

wizard n b1570 [arch. "wise man": b1450]

bedevil v *bewitch* b1575 ["torment": b1770]

amulet n b1585

periapt n b1585

conjure v b1590

fortune-teller n b1590

Interjections

eureka interj b1570

hallo interj/n/v b1570 (verb use: b1570; noun use: b1900; hello: b1885)

ho ho interj b1570

humph interj b1570

slam v *obs. euphemism for damn* b1570 [u1700s]

st interj *shh* b1570

there interj b1570

umph interj/v b1570

vale interj *goodbye* b1570

welladay interj b1570

cock-a-doodle-doo interj b1575

goodbye interj/n b1575

huzzah interj/n/v b1575

bowwow interj *the sound* b1580

prithee interj b1580

ding interj *sound* b1585 (noun use: b1770; verb use: b1830)

hollo interj b1590

law interj b1590

well met interj b1590

pish interj b1595

'sblood interj ('sbud: b1700)

bah interj

begad interj

gar interj

hell interj

indeed adv/interj *truly?* ["harrumph": b1835]

la interj

od/odd interj

oons interj

pah interj

pooh interj

presto adj/adv

ready interj

'snails interj *(God)'s nails*

zounds interj

Slang

collar v *capture* b1555 (noun use: b1870)

fast and loose adv b1560

arsy-varsy adj *assbackwards* b1570

fucking adj/adv b1570

full adj *intoxicated* b1570

gemman n *gentleman* b1570

hitty-missy adj (Am) *arch. hit-or-miss* b1570

mill v *rob* b1570

mouth n *arch. mouthpiece, spokesperson* b1570 (mouthpiece: b1830)

shifty, shift, shifter adj, n, n b1570

to-do n *commotion, event* b1570

windfall n *unexpected gain* b1570 ["something blown down by the wind": b1475]

dog in the manger n b1575

magnifico n *bigshot* b1575

graybeard n b1580

mare's nest n b1580

fuddle v *get drunk* b1590 ["befuddle": b1630] (noun use: b1770)

lamps n b1590

roaring boy n *type of ruffian* b1590

saucebox n *naughty person* b1590

bookworm n b1595

dildo n b1595

earwitness n b1595

meat n *male sexual organ; sexual conquest* b1595 ["female sexual organs": b1615]

minx n b1595 [type of dog: b1545]

peccadillo n b1595

tetchy adj *touchy* b1595 (techous "touchy": b1900)

blasted adj *damned* ["drunk": b1975]

blow v *mess up*

bugger v *sodomize*

cover n *assumed identity*

dickens n

die v *as in "die laughing," "die for a chance"*

fry n *as in "small fry"*

grandee n

henpeck v

illuminati n

jig n *game, as in "the jig is up"*

kid n *child* (kiddie: b1870)

leak v *urinate* (noun use: b1970)

liver n *source of cowardliness*

moneybags n

mouse n *quiet person* (mousy: b1815)

parrot v

powder n *as in "take a powder"* (verb use: b1635)

royal adj *as in "he's a royal pain"*

smock n *obs. woman, akin to slang "skirt"* [u1700s]

stinking adv

tit n *woman*

use n *as in "drug use"* (verb use: b1970)

warm adj *rich*

worm v *as in "worm the truth out of them"*

Insults

mome n *arch. dolt* b1555

goody n *goodwife* b1560

clown n *rube* b1565 [as in "circus clown": b1630]

hick n b1565 (adj use: b1920)

mad-brained adj b1565

makeshift adj *obs. shifty person* b1565 [u1800s] (obs. adj use: b1600)

bum n *cad* b1570

bumpkin n b1570

coax n *arch. simpleton* b1570 (verb use: b1590)

coxcomb n *jester's cap; fool* b1570 (coxcombry: b1610)

crackbrain n *crackpot* b1570

double-faced adj *hypocritical* b1570

drumble n *slothful person* b1570 (verb use: b1600)

flea-bitten adj b1570

gander n *idiot, fool* b1570

mab adj *arch. slut* b1570

shark n *scoundrel* b1570 ["lawyer": b1800] (verb use: b1600)

sloven n *slovenly person* b1570 (adj use: b1815; slovenly: b1570)

softling n b1570

cullion n *grouch* b1575 [obs. "testicle": b1400]

mealymouthed adj b1575

slow-witted adj b1575

toadeater n *toady* b1575

coistrel n *varlet, scamp* b1580

crab n *grouch* b1580 ["complaint": b1900] (verb use: b1500; crabber: b1930)

do-nothing n b1580 (adj use: b1835; do-nought: b1600)

hayseed n b1580

mountebank n *snake oil salesman* b1580

pettifogger adj b1580

quacksalver n *charlatan* b1580 (quack: b1630)

sleepyhead n b1580

turkey-cock n *blowhard* b1580 [obs. type of bird: b1535 to 1600s]

cuckoo n b1585 (adj use: b1920)

dowdy n *dowdy woman* b1585 (dowd n: b1350; dowdy: b1680)

hilding n *worthless person* b1585

dunce n b1590 [obs. "disciple of John Duns Scottus": b1530; obs. "book of Scottus's principles": b1570; obs. "boring educated man": b1600 to 1700s] (verb use: b1600; duncery: b1600)

lazybones n b1590

loggerhead n b1590

mouthy adj b1590

nit n (Brit) *nitwit* b1590

scab n *rascal* b1590

scoundrel n b1590

scum n b1590

vixen n b1590

clod n *dolt* b1595 (clodpoll: b1605)

ninny, ninnyhammer n b1595

rat n *as in "you dirty rat"* b1595

slugabed n *arch.* b1595

wiseacre n b1595

belswagger n *obs. bully* [u1700s]

boor n [obs. "common person": b1555] (boorish: b1565)

cousin n *obs. whore; blockhead* [u1800s]

draggle-tail n *slut*

fat-witted adj

fig n *arch. type of insulting gesture*

froth n *scum*

frothy adj *frivolous* (froth "something worthless": b1470)

fucker n

gowk n *idiot* [type of bird: b1325]

incult adj *arch. rubish*

ironhearted adj

jolt-head n *dolt*

macaroon n *obs. dimwit* [u1800s]

nigger n

numps n *arch. dolt*

poetaster n *bad poet* (poetast v: b1930)

scald n *rascal*

stinkard n (stinker: b1600)

tartar n *irritable person*

thick adj *dimwitted* (noun use: b1870)

wildcat n *volatile person*

Phrases

high-water mark n b1555

fullness of time n b1560

hip and thigh adv *ruthlessly; as in "smite hip and thigh"* b1560

line of sight n b1560

piece by piece adv b1560

tit for tat n b1560

last word n b1565

quid pro quo n *substitute* b1565

Pandora's box n b1570

siren song n b1570

spread eagle n b1570 (verb use: b1830; adj use: b1860)

table talk n b1570

per se adv b1575 (per accidens: b1530)

castle in the air n b1580

dyed-in-the-wool adj b1580

ex nihilo adj/adv *from nothing* b1580

false alarm n b1580

rainy day n b1580

sooner or later adv b1580

blind alley n b1585

gentler sex n b1585

laughing matter n b1585

stone's throw n b1585

horn of plenty n b1590

king's ransom n b1590

mother country n b1590

stumbling block n b1590

alurums and excursions n b1595

burden of proof n b1595

by-and-by n b1595 (adv use: b1530)

fair play n b1595

nine day's wonder n *flash in the pan* b1595

short shrift n b1595

wild-goose chase n b1595

black-and-white adj (noun use: b1600)

Gordian knot n

hammer out v

saving grace n

single file adv/n

so-and-so n [as in "that dirty so-and-so": b1900]

subject matter n *topic* [phys. "source material": b1570]

hiccup/hiccough n b1580

hawk v *as in "hawk up phlegm"* b1585 (noun use: b1605)

General/Miscellaneous

mar n b1555

billow n b1555 (verb use: b1600)

blank n *as in "fill in the blanks"* b1555

cannibal n b1555 (cannibalism: b1800)

cue n *starting signal* b1555 (verb use: b1925)

gallimaufry n *potpourri* b1555

grunt n b1555 (verb use: b900)

happening n b1555 (hap n: b1305)

horde n b1555

horizontal adj *related to horizon* b1555 ["opp. of vertical": b1670]

hubbub n b1555 (hubble-bubble: b1635)

implication n *something implied* b1555

indigo n b1555 [the color: b1630]

lumber n *furniture discards* b1555 ["timber": b1670]

majority n *larger part* b1555 [obs. "state of being major": u1700s]

miss n *opp. of hit* b1555 (verb use: b725)

parallel n/v *parallel line; mapping convention* b1555 ["close analogy": b1600]

partisan n *fanatic of sorts* b1555 ["armed insurgent": b1700] (adj use: b1730)

prototype n *first* b1555 ["sample of a product": b1970] (prototypical: b1650; prototypal: b1695)

repute n b1555 (verb use: b1400; reputation: b1350)

sullage n *sewage* b1555 ["silt": b1700]

swill n b1555

transition n b1555

universal n b1555

upstart n b1555

crossbar n b1560

dingdong n b1560 (verb use: b1660)

edging n b1560

luxe n *luxury* b1560 (luxury: b1670)

network n *netting* b1560 [fig. "interconnected things": b1830; as in "TV network": b1930]

recipient n b1560

screech n b1560 (verb use: b1580; animal that screeches: b1670)

stargazer n b1560 (stargaze: b1600)

start-up n b1560

swashbuckler n b1560 ["swashbuckling entertainment": b1940] (swasher: b1590; swashbuckling adj: b1695; swashbuckle: b1900)

bastion n b1565 [fig. use: b1600]

brickbat n b1565

carking adj *burdensome, vexing* b1565

comedown n b1565

component n b1565 (adj use: b1665)

correlation n b1565 (correlate: b1745)

dent n *as in "a dent in a fender"* b1565 [obs. "blow that causes a dent": b1225 to 1600s]

down v *put down* b1565 ["go

down": b1830; "knock down": b1800]

filter n b1565 [obs. "felt": b1425] (verb use: b1580; filtration: b1605)

freak n *abnormal* b1565 ["instance of capriciousness": b1565] (adj use: b1890; freakish: b1665; freaky: b1825)

hiatus n *phys. gap* b1565 [gen. "gap": b1630]

levity n b1565

nimiety n *excess* b1565

perspective n *as in "drawing in perspective"* b1565 [obs. type of optical instrument: b1400 to 1700s; "panoramic view": b1630; "perspective picture": b1670]

pickaback adj/adv/v *piggyback* b1565 (piggyback: b1565)

plod v b1565 (noun use: b1900)

policy n *as in "insurance policy"* b1565

prediction n b1565 (predict: b1630)

prelude n b1565 [used in music: b1670] (verb use: b1655)

racket n *noise* b1565 (racquet: b1500)

random n *as in "select a contestant at random"* b1565 [obs. "speed, power": b1325 to 1800s; obs. "gun range": b1600 to 1700s] (adj use: b1565; adv use: b1620)

reciprocation n b1565 (reciprocal: b1570; reciprocate: b1600; reciprocity: b1770)

rogue n *vagrant* b1565 ["rascal": b1600] (roguery: b1595)

snatch n *bit* b1565

arrow n *pointer* b1570

backslide v/n b1570

board n *group, as in "board of directors"* b1570

bump n *protuberance* b1570 ["knock": b1630; as in "bump and grind": b1900] (verb use: b1615)

bystander n b1570

caliber/calibre n *level* b1570 [pertaining to guns: b1590]

cast n *character, as in "the day had a strange cast to it"* b1570

chaos n *disorder* b1570 [obs. "the void": b1400 to 1600s] (chaotic: b1715)

characterization n b1570

complot n *plot* b1570 (verb use: b1600)

congeries n *miscellany* b1570

constitution n *build, structure* b1570 (constitutional adj: b1700; constitutional n: b1830)

converse adj *reverse* b1570

crowd n b1570 (verb use, as in "crowd around": b1450; verb use "invade someone's space," "jam people in": b1630)

cut n *as in "roadcut"* b1570

demise n *collapse* b1570 [leg. sense: b1445; "death": b1755]

emanation n b1570 (emanate: b1760)

encomium n b1570 (encomiast: b1610)

event n b1570 (eventful: b1600)

falling-out n b1570

friction n b1570 [scientific sense: b1705]

girl n b1570 ["male or female child": b1300]

glare n (Am) *smooth surface, as in "glare ice"* b1570

gossip n *gossipy person* b1570 [obs. "godparent": b1050; "result of gossiping": b1830] (verb use: b1630)

harbinger n *omen* b1570 [obs. "servant forerunner": b1175 to 1500s]

import n *importance* b1570 (importance: b1505)

irrelevance, irrelevant n, adj b1570 (irrelevancy: b1595)

level n *as in "the topmost level"* b1570 [as in "sea level": b1900]

line n *queue* b1570

look n *as in "a look of danger"* b1570

lurch n *as in "in the lurch"* b1570 (verb use: b1535)

minikin n *slight or insignificant thing* b1570

needcessity n b1570

notoriety n b1570 ["someone with notoriety": b1870]

onset n b1570 ["attack": b1535]

optical adj b1570

option n *act of choosing* b1570 ["ability to choose": b1670; "accessory": b1970] (opt: b1880)

order n *normal, tidy state* b1570

paltry adj/n b1570

passerby n b1570

peel n *as in "orange peel"* b1570 [type of shovel: b1400]

perquisite n *gen.* b1570 [obs. spec. type of property transfer: b1450 to 1700s]

pitch n *as in "at fever pitch"* b1570

play n *as in "the play of light on water"* b1570 (verb use: b1600)

plot n *type of diagram* b1570 ["theatrical lighting diagram": b1870] (verb use: b1600)

pop n *sound* b1570

prime n *as in "the prime of life"* b1570 (adj use: b1450)

proceedings n b1570

progression n *series of steps* b1570

promenade n *walk* b1570 ["place to promenade": b1650] (verb use: b1590)

propensity n b1570 (propense adj: b1530; propension: b1630)

prospect n *view* b1570 [obs. "viewing": b1450; "what is viewed," fig. "chance of happening": b1670] (verb use: b1845; prospective n: b1600)

rascal n b1570 [obs. "rabble": b1350] (rascality: b1580; rascally: b1595; rascalry: b1870)

rebate n b1570

recital n *recitation* b1570

spoil v *ruin* b1570 [as in "spoil a child": b1700]

stab n *attempt* b1570

start n *beginning* b1570 ["starting place": b1900] (verb use: b1800)

station n *spec. place of duty, as in "battle stations"* b1570 (verb use: b1600)

stuff n *as in "the right stuff"* b1570

talk n *rumor* b1570

tergiversation n *equivocation, lying* b1570 (tergiversate: b1655)

ticket n *tag* b1570 (verb use "tag," "designate": b1670)

tie n *bond, as in "family ties"* b1570

tilt n *angled position* b1570 (verb use: b1595)

tip n *hint, inside info* b1570 (verb use: b1885; tipster: b1865)

toil n *hard work* b1570 [arch. "strife": b1400]

trial n *as in "trials and tribulations"* b1570

trip n *goof* b1570 (verb use: b1600)

venture n b1570

verification n b1570 ["substantiation": b1625]

anomaly n b1575

dodge n *act of dodging* b1575 [fig. use: b1630] (verb use: b1680)

emphasis n b1575 (emphatic: b1710; emphasize: b1810)

haphazard n *chance* b1575 (adj use: b1675)

item n b1575 ["statement, warning": b1570] (adv use: b1400)

jerk n *quick motion; twitch; stupid person* b1575 [obs. "whip lash": b1550 to 1700s] (jerky: b1860)

noisemaker n b1575

parity n *equality* b1575

periphery n b1575 [type of atmospheric layer: b1400] (peripheral adj: b1810)

screen n *type of mesh* b1575

subterfuge n b1575

whiplash n b1575

windup n b1575

aye/ay n yes b1580

capriole n/v type of leap b1580

chamber-fellow n b1580

compliment n b1580 (verb use "praise": b1735; complimentary: b1720)

counterbalance v b1580 (noun use: b1605)

curmudgeon n b1580

dislike n b1580 [obs. "disapproval": b1555 to 1700s] (verb use: b1580)

enforcer n b1580

fiddle-faddle n b1580

film n coating b1580 [obs. "membrane": b1000 to 1700s]

hail-fellow adj hail-fellow-well-met b1580

inherent, inherence adj, n b1580

jactation n bragging b1580

jag n something jagged b1580 ["ornamental cut in clothing": b1400]

mash n something mashed b1580

masterpiece n b1580

meander n b1580 (verb use: b1600)

medal n b1580 (verb use: b1830)

neat's foot oil n b1580

notch n b1580 ["level," as in "take it up a notch": 1600s] (verb use: b1600)

ostracism n type of Greek exile b1580 [fig. "banishment": b1670] (ostracize: b1650)

panoply n b1580 (panoplied: b1835)

review v b1580 (noun use: b1400)

rival n b1580 ["equal": b1670] (adj use: b1590)

rut n b1580 [fig. use: b1870]

shoal n crowd b1580

showplace n b1580

slavery n subjugation b1580 [gen. "hard work": b1555]

split n/v b1580 [obs. "splinter": u1600s] (adj use: b1650)

transfusion n process of transfusing b1580 [as in "trans-

fusion of blood": b1670] (verb use: b1425; spec. "transfuse blood": b1670)

chink n sound b1585 (verb use: b1590)

compendium n b1585

critic n censor b1585 ["reviewer": b1605] (critical: b1590; criticism: b1610; criticize: b1650)

dervish n b1585

designment n plan b1585

dissection n b1585 (dissect: b1600)

distortion n b1585 (distort: b1590; distorted: b1635)

elision n b1585 (elide: b1870)

favorite n b1585 (adj use: b1715; favoritism: b1765)

formula n b1585 ["recipe": b1730; mathematical sense: b1800; chemical sense: b1870]

malcontent n b1585 (adj use: b1590; malcontented: b1590)

medium n average b1585 (adj use: b1715)

nemesis n avenger b1585 ["persistent foe": b1970]

nonplus n b1585 (verb use: 1595)

omen n/v b1585

ownership n b1585

parley n meeting b1585 [arch. "conversation": b1450]

renegade n b1585 (verb use: b1615; adj use: b1705; renegat: b1390)

stain n spot b1585 (verb use: b1400)

wag n quipster b1585 [obs. "puckish boy": b1555 to 1600s] (waggish: b1590; waggery: b1593)

caduceus n Mercury's staff; med. symbol b1590

caper n/v leap b1590

category n b1590 (categorize: b1705; categorization: b1890)

compact n pact b1590

compost n composition; type of organic disposal b1590 [obs. "compote": b1400 to 1700s] (verb use: b1830)

concern n concernment b1590

deletion n b1590 [arch. "destruction": b1500] (delete: b1605; dele v: b1705; dele n: b1730)

dong v as in "dingdong" b1590 (noun use: b1900)

errata n errors b1590 ["list of errors": b1635] (erratum: b1570)

failing n flaw b1590

flaw n b1590 ["flake": b1325]

grandiloquence, grandiloquent n, adj b1590

influence n gen. b1590 [obs. "influx": u1700s; astrological sense: b1375] (verb use: b1670)

loneliness n being alone b1590 ["being alone unhappily": b1830] (lonelihood: b1870)

madcap adj/n b1590

maybe n b1590

method n b1590 [spec. to medicine: b1425]

mimic n b1590 (adj use: b1600; verb use: b1690; mimicry: b1690)

miniature n b1590 (adj use: b1715)

no n b1590

opponent n someone with an opposing point of view b1590 (adj use: b1650)

otherness n b1590

posture n b1590 (verb use "phys. pose": b1870; verb use "fig. pose": b1900)

proficient adj/n b1590 (proficiency: b1640)

proponent n b1590

report n type of noise b1590

short n as in "the long and the short" b1590

snag n b1590 ["setback": b1830] (verb use: b1810)

spectator n b1590 (spectate "see": b1730)

stigma n phys. brand b1590 [fig. "brand": b1630] (stigmatize: b1585; obs. stigmatic "blemished": b1570 to 1800s)

symposium n conference b1590 ["party": b1590]

universe n everything b1590

[fig., as in "the universe of book publishing": b1670]

usual n b1590

well-wisher n b1590

aberration n b1595

accused n b1595

ancient history n b1595

apogee n b1595

bet n b1595 (verb use: b1600; bettor: b1610)

callant n lad b1595

carrel n b1595 [spec. in library: b1930]

cavalcade n b1595 [obs. "horseride": b1690 to 1700s]

class n b1595

disaster n b1595

earthling n b1595

filament n b1595 [in light bulbs: b1900]

hurly n hurlyburly b1595 (hurlyburly: b1350)

location n being located b1595 ["place": b1800]

loophole n portal b1595 [fig. use: b1670]

mainspring n b1595

mulatto n b1595

obscene adj b1595 (obscenity: b1590)

panelist n b1595

pother n bother, fuss b1595 (verb use: b1695)

potluck n b1595 [style of serving food: b1900]

proclivity n b1595

pullback n b1595

rendezvous n b1595 (verb use: b1645)

savagery n b1595

settlings n sediment b1595

spurt n/v as in "spurt of energy" b1595

suspect n b1595

tangent adj/n b1595

test n as in "a test of accuracy" b1595 [type of container: b1395] (verb use: b1750)

transparence n b1595 (transparency: b1600)

whitewash n/v b1595 [fig. use: b1770] (noun use: b1700)

acme n

ambiguity n uncertainty [obs. "hesitation": b1450 to

1500s] (ambiguous: b1530)

appointments n *equipment*

arc n *curve* [obs. "path of the sun": b1390; "arch": b1570 to 1800s] (verb use: b1970)

ascent n

assist n (verb use: b1430)

bandage n (verb use: b1775)

bane n [arch. "killer," "something that kills": b1000]

bar n *as in "bar of soap"*

bay n *as in "sickbay"*

candidate n *aspirant* ["possibility": b1770] (candidature: b1855; candidacy: b1865)

cast n *composition, as in "cast of characters"*

clue n ["ball of thread": b750; "guide": b1390] (obs. verb use "follow clues": b1665)

committee n *type of group* [opp. of comitor: b1475] (committeeman: b1655; committeewoman: b1855)

composition n *compromise*

configuration n [type of astronomical relationship: b1560] (configurate: b1575; configure: b1660)

countersign v

crankle n/v *zigzag*

crew n *group* [obs. "group of soldiers": b1440 to 1500s; as in "road crew," "ship crew": b1630] (verb use: b1935)

cut n *as in "short cut"; as in "haircut," "the cut of one's jib"*

dash n *smidgeon*

delicacy n *delicate beauty* ["med. fragility": b1700; gen. "fragility": b1800]

dereliction n *abandonment* [as in "dereliction of duty": b1800] (derelict adj: b1650; derelict n: b1670)

determination n *identification*

dichotomy n *division into two* ["contrast": b1970]

dictum n

dispatch n/v *speed*

disservice n (disserve: b1630)

division n *as in "sales division," "17th Airborne Division," "Central Division of the NFL"*

do n *ado* ["to-do": b1830]

element n *as in "someone is in his element"; bit, small portion, as in "an element of disgust"*

entity n *an existing thing* [gen. "existence": b1500]

entreaty n *plea* [obs. "treatment, handling": b1500 to 1600s]

equal n

eruption n *as in "an eruption of emotion"*

eyeshot n *akin to earshot*

fastener n

file n/v *as in "single file"*

filler n

forefront n *fig.* ["building front": b1475]

glance n/v *as in "glance at"*

go-between n

halt n *stop* (verb use: b1660)

heat n *as in "the heat of the moment"*

hurry n *commotion* [as in "in a hurry": b1670] (verb use: b1590)

hypothesis n [scientific sense: b1650] (hypothetical: b1600; hypothesize: b1740)

impedimenta n *appurtenances*

improbable, improbability adj, n

inexperience n (inexperienced: b1630)

inflection n *of the voice*

influx n

informality n

invective n ["use of invective": b1450] (adj use: b1450)

invitation n *phys. invitation* ["act of inviting": b1445] (invite v: b1535)

juniority n *opp. of seniority*

knack n *talent* ["trick": b1375]

lackluster adj/n

lampblack n

lather n *as in "soap lather"* [obs. type of froth: b950;

type of sweat: b1670; "tizzy": b1870] (verb use: b1150)

main n *the main part*

management n [business sense: b1770]

mate n *part of a pair*

materials n

mightiness n *as in "Your Mightiness"*

minimum n [obs. "atom": b1665]

miscellany n (miscellanea: b1575)

mission n (verb use: b1695)

offscum n *scum*

outskirt n

palisade n *row of pales* (verb use: b1635)

panel n *as in "panel of inquiry"* ["jury list": b1450] (panelist: b1595; panel discussion: b1940)

par n *equality* ["average": b1800; "golf average": b1900]

pattern n *repeated design* ["repeated actions, etc.," as in "pattern of violence": b1930]

phenomenon n (phenomena: b1580)

pinch n *act of pinching; little bit* [type of tool: b1700; slang "theft": b1770; slang "arrest": b1930]

pip n *dot*

plausive adj *applauding* (obs. plausible "applaudable": b1570 to 1700s)

poke n *as in "a poke in the eye"*

post n *as in "manning one's post"* ["fort, station": b1730] (verb use: b1685)

precaution n

precipice n

predicament n *sticky situation*

procedure, procedural n, adj

product n *something produced*

prominence n *something prominent* ["being prominent": b1630]

pucker n/v

pull n *lit. and fig. the power to pull* ["the force of pulling": b1800]

rack n *as in "rack and ruin"*

range n *distance, extent, as in "range of sight"* (verb use: b1670)

reflection n *mirror image*

rivalry n (rivality: b1600; rivalship: b1630)

scandal n [spec. to rel.: b1225; obs. "slander": b1630 to 1800s; "cause of scandal": b1630] (verb use: b1595; scandalous: b1600)

sequence n [religious use: b1400] (verb use: b1945)

silencer n

slip n *as in "slip of a girl"*

sodom n *gen.*

something n *as in "isn't that something?"*

stamp n *influence, affect, as in "shows the stamp of oppression"*

stratum n

stuff n *what composes, as in "the stuff of dreams"*

success n *good outcome* [obs. "gen. outcome.": b1535 to 1700s; "person who has success": b1900]

supply n *stock* ["supplying": b1800]

survival n (survivance: b1625)

symmetry n [obs. gen. "proportionate": b1535] (symmetrical: b1755; symmetrize: b1780)

totality n

trappings n *adornment, characteristics*

tribute n *honor, compliment*

trick n *prank; secret, as in "the trick to opening the door"*

triviality n (trivialize: b1850; trivia: b1905)

twirl n/v *spin* ["cause to spin": by1630]

vastness n

view n *what can be seen; range of vision; opinion* ["viewing": b1500; as in "in view of the situation": b1730]

whatnot n (pron use: b1540)

wherewithal n

whorl n *type of pattern*

yin/yang n

Things

slag n b1555 (verb use: b1900)

firework n b1560 [type of mil. device: b1560]

pedestal n b1565 [fig. use: b1870]

bow n *type of knot* b1570

jetsam n b1570

prism n *type of solid figure* b1570 ["optical device": b1630] (prismatic: b1710)

trophy n *plaque, cup* b1570 [type of battlefield victory symbol: b1500; fig., as in "the fish was taken as a trophy": b1530]

sandbag n b1590 (verb use: b1860)

gonfalon n *type of banner* b1595

catgut n (catling: b1630)

ingot n [obs. "mold": b1395 to 1700s]

patch n *as in "eyepatch"*

shooting stick n *portable seat*

temporaries n *obs. temporal things* [u1600s]

tube n

Description

aflame adj b1555

articulate adj *clear* b1555 (verb use: b1595; articulation: b1630)

chestnut adj b1555

enchanting adj b1555

futile adj b1555 (futility: b1625; futilitarian: b1830)

humdrum adj b1555

inexorable adj b1555

noteworthy adj b1555

skilled adj b1555

spiral adj b1555

toothsome adj *lit. tasty; fig. appealing, attractive* b1555

unskilled adj b1555

vivific adj *making vivacious* b1555

ad hoc adj b1560

brisk adj *quick* b1560 ["invigorating": b1600; "brusque": b1630] (verb use: b1630)

dusky adj b1560 (dusk adj: b1000)

explicable adj b1560

relevant adj b1560 (relevancy: b1565; relevance: b1700)

senseless adj b1560

vertical adj b1560

breakneck adj b1565

capable adj b1565 [obs. "having sufficient capacity": b1660 to 1700s] (capability: b1590)

current adj *accepted, prevalent* b1565 ["contemporary": b1610] (noun use: b1600; currency: b1830)

dexter adj *to the right* b1565

down adj *downward* b1565

existent adj b1565

fleeting adj b1565 [obs. "not stable," "flowing": b1325 to 1600s]

girlish adj b1565

grating adj *irritating* b1565

justifiable adj b1565 ["subject to adjudication": b1525 to 1600s]

limber adj b1565

midcourse adj b1565

modest adj b1565 ["inconspicuous": b1800] (modesty: b1535)

null adj *as in "null and void"* b1565 (noun use: b1610; null and void: b1670)

pretty adv b1565

select adj b1565 (verb use: b1570; noun use: b1610; selected: b1590)

unconscionable adj b1565

abusive adj b1570

acute adj b1570 [med. sense: b1400]

apt adj *fitting* b1570 [arch. "prepared": b1350]

base adj *scurrilous* b1570

brand-new adj b1570

chary adj b1570 [obs. "grieving": b750 to ME]

chilly adj b1570

clandestine adj b1570

constant adj b1570

corneous adj *horny* b1570

cross adj *opposing, as in "at cross purposes"* b1570

delicate adj *sensitive* b1570 (delicacy: b1730)

dire adj b1570 [diluted modern sense: b1930] (direful: b1585)

domestic adj *home-grown* b1570

downtrodden adj b1570

dry adj *as in "dry wit"* b1570

duplex adj b1570 (verb use: b1835)

elementary adj *basic* b1570

elysian adj b1570

entertaining adj b1570 [obs. "hospitable": b1570]

equidistant adj b1570

equilateral adj b1570

equitable adj b1570

erstwhile adv b1570 (adj use: b1905)

experienced adj b1570 (obs. experient "experienced": b1450 to 1600s)

exquisite adj *delicious; at the apex* b1570 [obs. "exacting, precise": b1450 to 1700s; obs. "verbose": b1500 to 1600s; "intense": b1670]

fancied adj *imagined* b1570

forlorn adj *deserted* b1570 [obs. "morally adrift": b1150 to 1600s; "pitiful": b1600] (obs. noun use: b1530 to 1800s)

fragile adj b1570 [obs. "morally breakable": 1500s]

gruesome adj b1570 (grue v: b1350)

harmless adj *not causing harm* b1570 ["unharmed": b1280]

hazardous adj b1570 [obs. "risktaking": u1600s]

illustrious adj b1570

impassable adj b1570

irresponsible adj b1570

itinerant adj b1570 (noun use: b1570)

kenspeckle adj *conspicuous* b1570

limp v b1570 (noun use: b1820)

maiden adj *as in "maiden voyage"* b1570

many-sided adj b1570

orderly adj b1570

plump adj *rounded* b1570 [obs. "frank, vulgar": b1500 to 1600s] (plump v: b1535)

practiced adj b1570

predominant adj *dominating* b1570 ["most common, most important": b1630] (predominate adj: b1595; predominate v: b1595; predominance, predominancy: b1600)

professed adj *as in "professed expert"* b1570

quick adj *occurring fast* b1570

real adj *actual, true, not fake* b1570 [leg. sense: b1400; not imagined: b1600; correct: b1700] (noun use: b1630; reality: b1500)

reliable adj b1570 (noun use: b1890)

ritual adj b1570 (noun use: b1650)

rugged adj *rough* b1570 [obs. "shaggy": b1350 to 1700s; obs. "rough like a rug (blanket)": b1570 to 1800s; "rough around the edges": b1630; "manly": b1770]

scenic adj *fake* b1570 ["dramatic": b1625; "pretty": b1870]

spare adj *extra, in excess* b1570

stupendous adj b1570

stygian adj b1570

transnatural adj b1570

ugglesome adj b1570 (ugsome: b1400)

uncorrect adj b1570

unfleshed adj *inexperienced* b1570

waking adj *as in "every waking moment"* b1570

true adj *as in "true to her word"* b1570 (adv use: b1350)

benighted adj *in the dark* b1575

brazen adj *fig. hardened* b1575 ["made of brass; hardened by fire": b1000] (brazen v: b1555; brazenfaced: b1575)

closefisted adj b1575

convex adj b1575

crescent adj *growing, as the moon* b1575 ["crescent-shaped": b1630]

dank adj *cold, clammy* b1575 ["moist": b1400]

point-blank adj b1575

sweltering adj b1575

unusual adj b1575

visceral adj *deeply felt* b1575

voluble adj *talkative* b1575 ["changeable": b1470]

brassy adj *made of brass* b1580 ["loud": b1865]

bulbous adj b1580

buoyant adj b1580

Cimmerian adj *dark, gloomy* b1580

conciliatory adj b1580 (conciliate v: b1545)

confident adj b1580 [obs. "gen. trusting": u1600s]

jagged adj b1580

lengthwise adv b1580 (lengthways: b1600)

limiting adj b1580

multiple adj b1580

neat adj *tidy* b1580 ["pure": b1445; obs. "clean": b1550 to 1600s] (neaten: b1900)

next door adv b1580 (next-door adj: b1750)

obsolete adj b1580 (verb use: b1640)

offensive adj *grating, insulting* b1580

plus adj/prep b1580 (noun use: b1655; conj use: b1950)

preternatural adj *not natural* b1580 ["supernatural": b1800]

prickly adj b1580

sinuous adj *winding* b1580 (sinuate: b1870; sinuosity: b1600)

tenable adj *defensible* b1580 [fig. use: b1715]

thumping adj b1580

tipsy adj b1580

well-thought-of adj b1580

withering adj b1580

abrupt adj b1585

deficient adj b1585 (deficiency: b1635)

desultory adj b1585

direful adj b1585 (dire: b1570)

exacting adj b1585

farfetched adj *straining credibility* b1585 ["fetched from afar": b1565] (arch. farfet: b1350)

limitless adj b1585

longtime adj b1585

lucid adj *luminous* b1585 ["transparent": b1630; "sane": b1630; "easy to understand": b1800] (luculent "luminous": b1425; luculent "clearly understood": b1550)

munificent adj b1585 (munificence: b1425)

perfunctory adj b1585 (obs. perfunctorious: b1630 to 1800s; rare perfunctionary: b1870)

ticklish adj *susceptible to tickling; fig. sensitive, as in "a ticklish situation"* b1585

toilsome adj b1585

unbeseeming adj *unbecoming* b1585

unsettled adj b1585 (unsettled: b1670)

useful, useless adj b1585 (usefulness: b1500; uselessness: b1670)

verdant adj b1585

withindoors, withinside adv *indoors* b1585 (withoutdoors: b1620)

aforementioned adj b1590

alternative adj b1590 (noun use: b1830)

apocryphal adj b1590 (apocrypha: b1390)

artless adj b1590

bosom adj *as in "bosom buddies"* b1590

categorical adj *direct* b1590

ceaseless adj b1590

celebrated adj b1590 (celebrious: b1630)

classical adj b1590

concise adj b1590 (conciseness: b1660; concision: b1800)

countless adj b1590

crestfallen adj b1590

disastrous adj *causing disaster* b1590 [obs. "experiencing disaster": b1590 to 1800s]

disjointed adj b1590

exemplary adj b1590 (noun use: b1450)

fond adj *showing fondness* b1590 ["foolish": b1340]

generous adj b1590 (generosity: b1620)

gloomy adj b1590

hardhanded adj b1590

hypothetical adj b1590 (hypothetic: b1700)

impartial adj b1590

indigested adj *without form, random* b1590

inviting adj b1590

laconic adj b1590 (laconism: b1570)

legendary adj b1590

mediocre adj b1590

obvious adj b1590

odd adj *unusual* b1590 [obs. "unique, remarkable": b1450 to 1600s]

ominous adj *gen. predictive* b1590 [obs. "indicating good signs": u1700s; "indicating bad signs": b1570]

pallid adj b1590

piebald adj *motley* b1590 (pied: b1350)

placable adj b1590

predatory adj *destructive* b1590 [pertaining to animals: b1670]

promethean adj b1590

quondam adj *former, one-time, has-been* b1590 (noun use: b1540)

saw-toothed adj b1590

shaggy adj b1590 (shag adj: b1595)

sleek adj b1590 (verb use: b1450; sleeken: b1625)

spiny adj *like a spine or thorn* b1590 ["covered with spines or thorns": b1630]

stainless adj *unstained* b1590

submissive adj b1590

tangible adj *phys. graspable* b1590 ["fig. graspable": b1710] (noun use: b1890)

tentative adj b1590

terrifying adj b1590

unbitted adj *uncontrolled* b1590

unquestionable adj b1590

varied adj b1590 ["varicolored": b1450]

worn-out adj b1590

worthless adj b1590 (worthful: b1100)

chanceful adj *causal, or eventful* b1595

changeful adj *variable* b1595 (changeless: b1580)

defamatory adj b1595

exclamatory adj b1595

gargantuan adj b1595

herculean adj b1595

ill-boding adj b1595

impressive adj *impressionable* b1595 ["making an impression": b1775]

lated adj *belated* b1595

new-fashioned adj b1595

paper adj *flimsy* b1595 ["existing only on paper": b1670]

priceless adj *treasured* b1595 ["worthless": b1800; as in "his reaction was priceless": b1930]

rawboned adj b1595

relentless adj b1595

smooth-tongued adj b1595

spirited adj b1595

squalid adj b1595 (squalor: b1525)

star-crossed adj b1595

star-spangled adj b1595

supportive adj b1595

time-honored adj b1595

tireless adj b1595

unfamiliar adj b1595

unhealthy adj *harmful* b1595 ["not healthy": b1630] (unhealth: b1150; unhealthful: b1580)

unheard-of adj b1595

unparalleled adj b1595

unreal adj b1595 (unrealistic: b1865)

unvarnished adj *crude* b1595 ["not varnished": b1770]

wide-spreading adj b1595

abstruse adj

accurate adj (accuracy: b1665)

acknowledged adj

affined adj *closely related*

amenable adj *liable* ["willing": b1830]

anonymous adj *from an unknown creator* ["lacking a name": b1600]

articulate adj *jointed* (articulation: b1425; articulated: b1550)

artificial adj *imitation* [obs. "skillful": b1470 to 1700s]

blatant adj *noisy* ["the blatant beast," coined by Spenser: b1600; "unoverlookable": b1900]

circumstantial adj *incidental*

close adj *as in "close friends"*

consentaneous adj *unanimous*

correct adj ["proper": b1600]

cyclopean adj *large*

damning adj (damnatory: b1685)

defunct adj *no longer used* ["dead": b1550] (noun use: b1550)

diminutive adj

dissimilar adj

divisive adj

ebony adj

ebullient adj *lit. boiling* [fig. use: b1665] (ebulliency: b1670; ebullience: b1750)

eminent adj [arch. "high-up": b1425]

eventful adj

exotic adj *foreign* ["interestingly strange": b1630] (noun use: b1645)

extravagant adj *excessive* ["divergent, straying": b1400]

filling adj

flatulent adj *causing gas*

fraught adj [arch. "laden": b1350]

full tilt adv

furry adj

gone adj

higgledy-piggledy adv/adj

ignoble adj ["not of noble birth": b1450]

illusory adj (illusive: b1610)

implicit adj

infertile adj

inflated adj (inflate adj: b1350)

infrangible adj

inhabitable adj *uninhabitable*

innocuous adj

intertissued adj *interwoven*

irresistible adj

laughable adj (laughsome, laughworthy: b1630)

leading adj

liable adj *as in "liable to explode"*

lonely adj *alone* ["saddened by being alone": b1830] (lonesome: b1650)

manageable adj

mercurial adj (mercuric: b1835)

moving adj *touching*

mysterious adj (arch. mysterial: b1470)

niggling adj

obstreperous adj

old-fashioned adj

omnipresent, omnipresence adj

opposed adj *against*

oppressive adj [fig., as in "oppressive heat": b1730]

outlandish adj *preposterous* ["foreign": b1000; "rural": b1800]

overblown adj *blown out of proportion* ["blown over": b1600]

peachy adj [slang use: b1930]

pitch-black adj (pitch-dark: b1830)

planet-stricken adj *affected by astrological forces*

pointed adj *as in "pointed remarks"*

positive adj *without question, as in "proof positive"*

punctual adj ["punctilious": b1600; "exact": b1630]

pungent adj *painful* ["sharp-tasting": b1670] (obs. pungitive: b1450 to 1700s; pungency: b1650)

registered adj

remote adj *far away* ["far apart": b1425; "slight," as in "remote chance": b1730] (remotion "remoteness": b1400)

scanty adj

scrutable adj

serious adj *critical* ["solemn": b1450]

sheer adj *pure*

similar adj (noun use: b1670; similitude: b1375; b1665)

Sisyphean adj *futile* (Sisyphism n: b1870)

skimble-skamble adj *confused* (noun use: b1630)

slap adv *directly*

soggy adj

sordid adj [obs. med. "discharging pus, etc.": b1470;

obs. "lowly": b1600 to 1700s]

sprightly adj (sprightful: b1595)

stolid adj

straw n *type of color* (straw yellow: b1900)

strenuous adj *active* ["demanding": b1700]

stumpy adj

tameless adj

telling adj

tenuous adj

terminable adj *endable* [obs. "determinable": b1425]

tight adj *taut*

tiny adj

to-be adj *as in "bride-to-be"*

transient adj (transitory: b1375; transiency: b1655; transcience: b1745)

translucent adj *partially transparent* [obs. "transparent": b1610; obs. "bright": b1600 to 1700s] (translucency: b1610; translucid: b1630; translucence: b1755)

truebred adj

uncanny adj *seemingly not real* [supernatural: b1600]

unfathered adj

unlightsome adj *dark*

velvet adj *velvety*

vintage adj

virid adj *verdant*

volatile adj (noun use: b1690; volatility: b1630)

wieldy adj *not cumbersome* [obs. "nimble, agile": b1375 to 1600s]

world-shaking adj

Colors

red ocher n b1575

ivory adj *ivory-colored*

sea green n

ultramarine n (adj use: b1655)

Actions/Verbs

bepaint v *tinge* b1555

canvass v *poll* b1555 [obs. "beat up in a canvas bag": b1510 to 1600s] (noun use: b1620)

deflect v b1555 (deflection: b1605)

dilute v b1555 (adj use: b1605)

disproportion v b1555 (noun use: b1595; disproportionate: b1545; disproportional: b1610)

engulf v b1555

entrench v b1555 [fig. "dig in": b1600]

fatten v b1555

overload v b1555 (noun use: b1670)

surpass v b1555

trounce v b1555 [obs. "trouble": u1600s]

wash out v *rinse* b1555 ["clean": b1770]

whittle v b1555

delineate v b1560 [fig. "sketch out": b1630] (delineation: b1670)

discredit v b1560 (noun use: b1565)

echo v b1560 [fig. use: b1600]

furl v b1560

ingather v b1560

naturalize v b1560

sally v *as in "sally forth"* b1560

slop v *spill* b1560 [as in "slop the hogs": b1870]

slow v *impede* b1560 [obs. "be slow": ME only; "reduce speed": b1600]

smack v *as in "smack your lips"* b1560 ["kiss": b1580]

sparge v *splash* b1560 ["spatter": b1790]

wobble v b1560 (noun use: b1670)

abscond v b1565

butcher v b1565 [fig., as in "butcher a song": b1700]

cozen v *deceive, cheat* b1565 (cozen: b1565)

dab v b1565 ["hit hard with a weapon": b1310; "strike lightly": b1535]

distinguish v b1565

emerge v b1565 (emergence: b1705)

foil v *stop* b1565 ["trample": b1300; "overthrow": b1550]

jut v b1565 (noun use: b1790)

overwatch v b1565

A Language in Flex

An evidence that English is a flexible language is that it's also a flexile language. We experiment with words, and if *flexible* (by 1415) isn't working, we'll experiment with *flexile* 1635). If we don't think *punishment* (by 1385) does the job, we'll dabble with *punition* (by 1470). We aren't completely happy with *expel* (by 1400), so we tinker with *expulse* (by 1500). *Benign* (by 1325) isn't benign enough? How about *benignant* (by 1785)? *Infamous* (by 1380) doesn't quite do the job? How about *defamous* (by 1470)?

As these miscellaneal examples demonstrate, sometimes flexility doesn't stick, but sometimes it does, as with *finicky* (by 1825), replacing its earlier form, *finical* (by 1595). *Miscellaneal* is one of those that didn't survive. It came about by 1670, and short-lived into the 1700s. Meantime, *miscellaneous* (by 1630) is still with us.

One area ripe for experiment (but not *experimence* or *experimency*) is with the *-ce* or *-cy* ending. Look at this brief list of variants, and we see that the only *consistency* is lack of *consistence* (by 1595 and by 1605, respectively), with *inconsistency* leading them both—in use by 1550).

- *innocency* (by 1375), *innocence* (by 1340)

- *elegancy* (by 1425), *elegance*, which seems so much more *elegant* (by 1510)

- *inconveniency* (by 1450), *inconvenience* (by 1400) and *conveniency* (by 1605), *convenience* (by 1400)

- *indifferency* (by 1450), *indifference* (by 1445)

- *equivalency* (by 1535), *equivalence* (by 1545)

- *importancy* (by 1540), *importance* (by 1505)

- *correspondency* (by 1590), *correspondence* (by 1415)

- *significancy* (by 1595), *significance* (by 1400)

- *extravagancy* (by 1605), which seems so much more extravagent than *extravagence* (by 1645)

- *militancy* (by 1650), which seems a little less powerful than *militance* (by 1950)

- *incoherency* (by 1685), *incoherence* (by 1615)

As something of an aside, *dependency* (by 1595) is alive and well, as is *dependence* (by 1415). As is *independence* (by 1640). Yet not *independency* (by 1615).

Then there are our mad-scientist experiments with the uns and outs of the language:

We have *insanitary* (by 1875) and *unsanitary* (by 1900), and *insane* (by 1550), but not *unsane* (we experimented with it only fleetingly by 1700).

We generally use *unstable* (by 1175), yet *instability* (by 1425), while we have pretty much given up on *instability*'s contemporary, *instable*.

Then there's *impossible* (by 1350) and *unpossible* (by 1470).

And finally, consider *habit*, an obsolete verb from Late Middle English to the 1600s meaning "to reside." It lead to an opposite of sorts—*inhabitable* (by 1600), which means "uninhabitable," with *in-* meaning "not." Then came *inhabitable* (by 1700), meaning "habitable," because you can "habit in" the place, I suppose. What's next on the progression? *Ininhabitable*?

---

shell v *as in "shell peanuts"* b1565

simper v b1565 (noun use: b1600)

squash v b1565 ["quash": b1770]

trundle v *roll* b1565 ["walk": b1700]

assume v *as in "assume responsibility"* b1570 (assumption: b1500)

bawl v *yell, cry out* b1570 ["bark": b1440]

bestow v *give* b1570

blow v *as in "blow your nose"* b1570

buckle down v *get to work* b1570

carouse v b1570 (noun use "drinking bout": b1600; carousal: b1765)

castrate v b1570 (castration: b1425)

catch v *ignite, start* b1570

cheat v b1570 ["confiscate": b1440] (noun use: b1645)

clear v *clean up or out, as in "clear a piece of land"* b1570 ["clear the table": b1870] (adj use: b1300)

confront v *stand before* b1570 ["challenge": b1580]

(confrontation: b1630)

contend v *assert* b1570 (contention: b1670)

contradict v b1570 [obs. "oppose": u1700s] (contradictory n: b1385; contradictory adj: b1535)

countenance v b1570

crane v *use a crane* b1570 [as in "crane your neck": b1800]

cut v *as in "cut through a parking lot"* b1570

debase v b1570 ["demote," "deprecate": b1565 to 1800s]

deplore v b1570 [obs. "bewail": b1660 to 1700s] (deplorable: b1615)

deter v b1570

differ v *disagree* b1570 (difference: b1450)

dilapidate v b1570 [arch. "squander": b1530] (dilapidation: b1425; dilapidated: b1810)

discover v *find* b1570

dissociate v b1570 (adj use: b1550)

dodge v *deceive* b1570 (noun use: b1630; dodgery: b1670)

edge v *put pan edge on* b1570
elucidate v *lit. and fig.* b1570
enable v *make capable* b1570 ["empower": b1425; obs. "become capable": b1450 to 1600s]
esteem v *hold in high regard* b1570 [obs. "estimate": b1450 to 1700s; gen. "regard": b1530]
eternize v b1570
excruciate v b1570 (excruciating: b1600)
exult v b1570 [obs. "jump for joy": u1700s] (exultation: b1425)
gabble v b1570 (noun use: b1580)
gather v *deduce, know* b1570
generate v b1570
gibe v b1570 (noun use: b1600)
gouge v b1570
happen v *find, as in "happen upon"* b1570
hug v b1570 (noun use: b1620)
immortalize v b1570
inflict v b1570 ["afflict": b1530] (infliction: b1535)
initiate v *as in "initiate a frat member"* b1570 [gen. "begin": b1630] (adj use: b1605; noun use: b1815; initiation: b1585)
intersperse v b1570
justify v *show reason* b1570 ["clear of wrongdoing": b1450; "prove true": b1450]
keep v *"maintain," as in "keep the books"* b1570
knock v *as in "knock around"* b1570
look v *as in "look out"* b1570
lord v *as in "lord over"* b1570 [obs. "rule over": b1350 to 1400s]
make v *achieve* b1570
march out v b1570
mediate v b1570
observe v *watch* b1570 (observer: b1550)
override v *overrule* b1570 ["ride over": b900; "take over manually": b1970]
quantify v b1570
rescind v b1570

scant v *skimp* b1570
season v *make mature, experienced* b1570
shrivel v b1570
shuffle v *rearrange, walk slowly* b1570 (noun use: b1630)
sipple v b1570
spurt v *squirt* b1570
squeeze v b1570 ["extract money from": b1610] (noun use: b1620)
stamp v *imprint* b1570 (noun use: b1570)
stay v *remain* b1570 [obs. "come to a stop": b1450; "prevent, postpone": b1530]
stick out v b1570
storm v *be stormy, lit. and fig.* b1570 ["assault": b1670]
strike v *afflict* b1570 (stricken: b1770)
swing v *as in "swing back and forth"* b1570
trample v *crush underfoot* b1570 ["tramp": b1400]
trim v *clip off; put trimmings on* b1570 (noun use: b1670)
turn v *as in "turn your stomach"* b1570
view v *inspect* b1570 ["formally review": b1525; "see": b1600]
wear v *continue, as in "the idea wears well"* b1570
worm v *de-worm* b1570
apportion v b1575
blurt v b1575
chamfer v *bevel* b1575 [arch. "groove": b1605] (noun use: b1850)
cock v *tilt* b1575 (noun use: b1715)
coup v *overturn* b1575
creak v b1575 ["speak with a creak": b1325] (noun use: b1605; creaky: b1835)
desiccate v b1575
deteriorate v *degrade* b1575 ["become degraded": b1700] (deterioration: b1660)
drowse v b1575 [obs. "droop": b900] (noun use: b1700)
exude v b1575

heel v *tip, lean* b1575 (noun use: b1760)
rank v *arrange in an order* b1575
rely v *depend* b1575 [obs. "gather": b1350 to 1600s]
reprieve v b1575 [obs. "send to prison": 1500s] (noun use: b1570; reprieval: b1590)
tree v *as in "tree a raccoon"* b1575
accost v b1580
bandy v b1580
block v *plan, as in "block out"* b1580
broach v *bring up, address* b1580 ["phys. pierce": b1470]
capitulate v *cave in* b1580 [obs. meanings of negotiate: b1540 to 1600s] (capitulation: b1535)
cashier v *discharge, dismiss* b1580
clang v b1580 (noun use: b1600)
dart v *go fast* b1580 (noun use: b1730)
dismantle v b1580
effectuate v b1580
ensnare v b1580
enthrall v b1580 [arch. "enslave": b1450]
excise v *cut out* b1580
flinch v b1580 [obs. "slink away": b1565 to 1600s]
foreshadow v b1580 (noun use: b1870; foreshadowing: b1855)
goad v b1580 (noun use: b900)
grabble v b1580
huddle v b1580 [obs. "hide": u1800s] (adv use: b1565; noun use: b1590)
interject v b1580 (interjection: b1430)
interweave v b1580
metamorphose v b1580
moderate v *as in "moderate a panel"* b1580 (moderator: b1600)
moisten v b1580 (obs. moist v: b1350 to 1400s; moist n: b1375)
outstrip v b1580

populate v b1580 (populous: b1450)
rehabilitate v *gen. restore* b1580 [as in "rehabilitate a criminal": b1970]
temporize v *compromise; delay* b1580
browbeat v b1585
click v b1585 [slang "fall into place," "get along": b1915] (noun use: b1615)
defrock v b1585
detect v *discover, notice* b1585 [obs. "reveal": b1425 to 1800s] (detection: b1430)
enshroud v b1585
entoil v *capture* b1585
explore v *investigate* b1585 [as in "explore the New World": b1830]
grab v b1585
grace v b1585
gratulate v *congratulate* b1585 ["greet": b1560]
hang back v b1585
huff v b1585 (noun use: b1600; huffy: b1680)
hunch v *as in "hunch your shoulders"* b1585 ["push": b1500]
impose v *as in "impose a tax"* b1585 [fig. "impinge": b1600]
open up v b1585
partake v b1585 [obs. "give": b1565 to 1600s] (partaking "taking part": b1450)
recall v *call back; resuscitate; cancel* b1585 (noun use: b1615)
refine v *as in "refine oil"* b1585 (refined: b1565)
scramble v *as in "scramble to your feet"* b1585 [as in "scramble eggs": b1870; "jam a radio signal": b1930] (noun use: b1675)
serry v *press together* b1585 (serried: b1670)
shake up v *scold* b1585
snail v b1585
snuffle v b1585
snug v b1585 (adj use: b1870)
spatter v b1585
tower v b1585

transact v b1585 (transaction: b1650)

wind up v b1585

agitate v b1590

alarm v b1590 ["call to arms": b1600] (alarming: b1680)

analyze v b1590

baffle v *befuddle* b1590 [obs. "ridicule": b1530 to 1600s; obs. "swindle": b1570 to 1700s]

base v b1590

bastardize v b1590 (arch. abastardize: b1580)

beleaguer v b1590

budge v *yield* b1590

dangle v b1590 (noun use: b1760)

discard v *dismiss* b1590 ["throw away": b1600] (verb use: b1745)

dispart v *separate* b1590

distaste v b1590 (noun use: b1600; distasteful: b1610)

dribble v b1590 (noun use: b1680; drib v: b1530)

emblazon v b1590

embosom v *embrace* b1590

enlighten v *lit. and fig.* b1590

ensconce v *gen.* b1590 [obs. mil. sense: u1800s]

enwomb v *arch. impregnate* b1590

equal v b1590

equivocate v b1590 [obs. "use double meaning": b1425 to 1600s]

foist v *impose* b1590 [obs. "perform trickery with dice": b1545; obs. "deceive": b1600 to 1700s]

humor v b1590 (noun use: "whim": b1565)

impend, impendent, impending v, adj, adj b1590

inundate v b1590 [fig. use: b1625] (inundation: b1425)

mope v *sulk* b1590 [arch. "act dazed": b1570] (noun use: b1695)

obstruct v *lit. get in the way* b1590 [fig. sense: b1650]

operate v b1590

patronize v *support* b1590 ["shop at": b1830]

peacock v b1590

pocket v *take* b1590 ["put in a pocket": b1590]

procrastinate v b1590

qualify v *as in "qualify for a job"* b1590 (qualification, qualified: b1560)

rebuff v b1590 (noun use: b1630)

relish v b1590 (noun use: b1700)

roil v b1590 (noun use: b1700)

second v *as in "I second the motion"* b1590

snarl v *growl* b1590 ["speak harshly": b1695] (noun use: b1615)

snip v *cut quickly* b1590 (noun use: b1560)

spruce v *as in "spruce up"* b1590 (adj use: b1600)

suffuse v b1590

supervise v *be a supervisor* b1590 [obs. "read over": b1500 to 1700s] (supervisor: b1475; supervision: b1650)

thunderstrike v b1590 [thunderstruck: b1605]

topple v b1590

unseat v *lit.* b1590 ["overthrow": b1630]

vouchsafe v b1590

barricade n/v b1595

chuck v *throw* b1595

closet v *hide* b1595

concenter v *draw to the center* b1595

confine v *restrict* b1595 ["border": b1525] (confinement: b1650)

counterpose v b1595

debauch v b1595 [obs. "turn loyalty": u1800s] (noun use: b1605; debauched: b1600; debauchery: b1630; debauchee: b1665)

denote v b1595

dictate v *as in "dictate a letter"* b1595 (dictation: b1730)

dirty v b1595

disgrace v (Am) b1595 [obs. "disfigure": b1550 to 1700s] (noun use: b1590; disgraceful: b1595)

domineer, domineering v, adj b1595

entrance v *put in a trance* b1595

epitomize v *condense* b1595 ["typify": b1630]

flounder v *struggle* b1595

fool v *deceive; as in "fool around"* b1595 [obs. "be a fool": b1350]

fuel v b1595 [as in "fuel up": b1900]

fuse v *meld* b1595 (fusion: b1555)

impassion v b1595 (impassioned: b1605)

lam v *thrash* b1595

overpower v *phys. overwhelm* b1595 [fig. sense: b1670]

peer v *gaze* b1595

peregrinate v b1595

predecease v b1595

puzzle v b1595 ["make puzzling": b1670] (noun use: b1615; puzzling: b1665; puzzlement: b1825)

rally v *as in "rally the troops"* b1595 [as in "rally courage": b1670; as in "rally round a friend": b1830; "recover from illness": b1870] (noun use: b1670)

rummage v *arrange* b1595

scandal v b1595

secure v *make safe* b1595 (security: b1450)

side v *as in "side with"* b1595

smoke out v b1595

tinker v *fix* b1595 ["fiddle": b1670]

traipse v *wander; dress poorly* b1595

unsex v b1595

waddle v b1595 [obs. "fall": b1400] (noun use: b1695)

womanize v *feminize* b1595

actuate v

adopt v *as in "adopt an attitude"*

alternate v (adj use: b1515; noun use: b1720)

antiquate v (arch. adj use: b1500; antiquated: b1630)

apologize v

ascertain v *find out for certain* [obs. "inform": b1450 to 1700s]

attune v *lit. bring into tune*

[fig. bring into tune: b1730]

aver v *affirm* [obs. "judge or find true": b1425 to 1600s]

avert v *turn away* ["prevent": b1630]

besmirch v

bewilder v (bewilderment: b1820)

bog v

breast v *handle boldly*

brush up v

catch v *notice, as in "did you catch that?"*

chunter v (Brit) *mutter*

command v *deserve, as in "command respect"*

connive v [arch. "ignore": b1605] (connivance: b1595; conniver: b1670; connivery: b1960)

cope v *handle* [obs. "hit, fight": b1350; "purchase": b1450 to 1500s]

counteract v [obs. "oppose": b1730 to 1800s]

cow v *make a coward of*

crossbreed v (noun use: b1775; crossbred: b1860)

crown v *as in "the crowning touch"*

cut v *leave*

daff v *push aside, put off*

decimate v *kill one in ten* [gen. "kill a portion of": b1660]

defect v

demonstrate v [obs. "point out": b1555 to 1600s; "protest": b1900]

detach v ["shoot a gun": b1480] (detached: b1705)

dismiss v *forget* ["ignore": b1700]

dispense v *as in "dispense with a problem"*

disrump v *disrupt*

dissect v ["analyze": b1630]

do v *be adequate, as in "that will do"*

double back v

douse v *drench* ["extinguish": b1800]

drawl v (noun use: b1760)

dwindle v *shrink*

eke out v (eke v "add to": b1000)

embrace v *comprise*

enjoy v *experience*

excavate v [as in "excavate the ruins": b1870] (excavation: b1615)

expect v *anticipate; suspect* [obs. "wait, stay": b1560 to 1700s] (expectant: b1400)

extravagate v *diverge* ["be extravagant": b1830]

fantasticate v

fathom v *measure* ["embrace": b1150; fig. "understand": b1625] (arch. noun use: b1630)

festinate v *hasten* (adj use: b1605; festination: b1570)

flush v *blush*

fob off v *pass off fraudulently*

foreshorten v

frizz v *curl tightly* ["groom with pumice stone": b1470] (noun use: b1670; frizzle: b1565; frizzly: b1710; frizzy: b1865)

gall v *chafe, vex*

germinate v

get v *achieve, as in "get drunk"*

give v *yield* (noun use: b1870)

glass v *look into a mirror*

go v *as in "how the story goes"*

graze v *brush against*

gum v *as in "gum up the works"*

hazard v *venture, as in "hazard a guess"*

hear v *as in "hear of"*

hedge v *dodge*

hound v *fig. pursue doggedly*

idolize v (idolatrize: b1630)

implicate v

imply v [obs. "entwine": b1375 to 1800s]

inch v (noun use: b1000)

inlay v [obs. "hide": b1570 to 1600s] (noun use: b1670)

intercede v [veto: b1580] (intercession: b1450)

intoxicate v ["poison": b1450 to 1800s] (intoxication: b1650)

irradiate v *bathe in light* [bathe in radiation:

b1905] (irradiation: b1590; irradiance: b1670)

irritate v *annoy, exasperate* [obs. "exacerbate": b1535 to 1800s; obs. "aggravate": b1630 to 1800s]

jade v *wear out or dull* (jaded: b1670)

jolt v [fig. use: b1900] (noun use: b1600)

manage v *gen. handle* [obs. "handle a horse": b1560]

mince v *as in "don't mince words"*

negotiate v *discuss compromise* (negotiation: b1580; negotiable: b1970)

obliterate v (obliterative: b1815)

obviate v *dispose of*

occlude v (occlusion: b1645)

outdo v [obs. "eject": b1350 to 1600s]

overshadow v *steal the spotlight* ["cast a shadow over": b900]

pop v *as in "pop corn"*

prick v *as in "prick up your ears"*

prime v *as in "prime an explosive"* [applied to painting: b1630; to pumps: b1830; to engines: b1930]

project v *throw* (projection: b1600; projectile: b1665)

propel v *cause to move* [obs. "expel": b1450 to 1600s] (propellant: b1645)

push v *make effort* ["prod": b1600] (noun use: b1600)

raffle v (noun use: b1770)

rake v *as in "fingernails raking the blackboard"*

rant v *as in "rant and rave"* ["be unruly": b1600] (noun use: b1650)

reach v *as in "reach a decision"*

redo v

refute v *disprove* [obs. "refuse": b1515 to 1600s; "deny": b1970]

regurgitate v (regurgitation: b1605)

reinstate v

reside v *live* (residence: b1400)

retrench, retrenchment v, n

reverberate v [obs. "dispel, repel": b1500 to 1700s] (adj use: b1605; reverb v: b1605)

screw v *as in "screw your face up"*

settle v *relocate* ["colonize": b1700]

slight v [obs. "level, raze": b1350 to 1600s]

snake v *wind about* ["crawl": b1870]

snap v *make snappish remarks*

sneak v

sophisticate v *corrupt with devious reasoning*

sparkle v (arch. spark: b1200)

speculate v ["speculate financially": b1800] (speculation: b1375; speculative: b1400; speculatist: b1630)

sputter v *pertaining to things* ["speak with a sputter": b1700; "come to a halt": b1700] (noun use: b1675)

square v *reconcile, jibe*

squint v *look through partially closed eyes; look cross-eyed* (noun use: b1655)

steel v *brace, prepare*

strike v *be striking*

sunbathe v

swap v (noun use: b1625)

tantalize v (tantalizing: b1685)

teem v [obs. "give birth": b900 to 1600s]

toddle v

top v *outdo, as in "top this"* [as in "top off": b1530]

topsy-turn v *turn topsy-turvy*

trend v *go in a phys. direction* ["go in a gen. direction": b1870]

unskin v *skin*

unthaw v

uproot v *phys. pull out by the roots* [fig. "dislocate": b1620]

vilify v *insult* [obs. "devalue": b1450; "make vile": b1630 to 1700s]

vociferate v (vociferous: b1615)

ward n *as in "ward off"* [arch. "guard": b1150]

wash away v *erode*

watch v *observe* ["keep abreast of": b1700]

weave v *totter, sway*

weigh against v

Archaisms

futile adj *chatty* b1555

mutine v b1555 [u1600s]

offset n *outset* b1555

roister n *carouser* b1555 (verb use: b1585)

misventure n b1565

prostitute adj *prostituted, corrupted* b1565

bedim v *dim* b1570

coil n *as in Shakespeare's "this mortal coil"* b1570

cotton v *succeed* b1570

crank n *cranny* b1570 [u1800s]

dell n *slang woman* b1570

elevate v *obs. fig. lower* b1570 [u1700s]

embetter v *make better* b1570

emotion n *obs. commotion* b1570 [u1700s]

encounter v *obs. oppose* b1570 [u1700s]

estray v b1570

excrement n *obs. something that issues forth—e.g., fingernails* b1570 [u1700s]

exonerate v *obs. purge, excrete* b1570 [u1800s]

experience v *obs. test, experiment* b1570 [u1700s] (noun use: b1450)

fall v *obs. get smaller* b1570 [u1800s]

fedity n *obs. repulsiveness* b1570 [u1700s]

fratry n *fraternity* b1570

goodlike adj b1570 [u1800s]

imburse v *save, store, place in pocket* b1570

indiligent adj b1570 [u1700s]

lavish v *exaggerate* b1570 [u1600s]

loud adj *blatant* b1570 [u1600s]

lowmost adj *lowest* b1570

main n *obs. goal* b1570 [u1700s]

misagree v b1570

misthrive v b1570

outscourer n *scout* b1570

persue n *obs. trail of a*

wounded deer b1570 [u1600s]

ration n *reasoning* b1570

seminate v *disseminate* b1570

servitrix n b1570 (servitor: b1350; servitress: b1870)

submiss adj *submissive* b1570

visitator n b1570

wareless adj *not careful* b1570

whimp v *whine* b1570

sir-reverence n *obs. begging your pardon* b1575 [u1600s]

transshape v *change shape* b1575

erelong adv *before long* b1580

bestead v *help* b1585

entwist v b1590

scientific adj *not mechanical* b1590

disvelop v *unwrap* b1595

gadfly n *gadabout* b1595

jaunce v *prance* b1595

lunch n *chunk* b1595

[u1800s] (obs. luncheon: b1580 to 1800s)

oeillade n *glance* b1595

senseful adj *obs. sensible, reasonable* b1595 [u1700s]

tucket n *type of fanfare* b1595

abastardize v *obs. debase* [u1700s]

abbess n *obs. brothel madame* [u1800s]

absume v *obs. consume slowly* [u1700s]

ambigu n *obs. ambiguity*

bandy v *obs. unite* [u1800s]

bosom v *embrace*

controverse v [u1700s]

current adj *real* [u1700s]

decays n *ruins* [u1700s]

diapasm n *type of scented powder*

dislike adj *obs. unlike* [u1600s]

dot n *obs. lump* [u1800s] (verb use: b1740)

elapse v *obs. sneak away* [u1700s]

fimble v *fumble with fingers*

fogger n *pettifogger*

foible adj *obs. feeble* [u1700s]

foutre n *slang "something worthless"*

gape-seed n *something gaped at*

gild v *"gild" with blood*

gilt n *gold*

grandity n *obs. grandeur* [u1800s]

grisy n *obs. grisly* [u1800s]

homeling n *native*

indigena, indigene n *aborigine*

inopinate adj *obs. unexpected* [u1800s]

intersert v *obs. insert* [u1700s]

lutulent adj *clouded, muddied*

machine n *obs. machination* [u1700s] (obs. verb use: b1450 to 1600s)

maledicent n *calumnious*

managery n *obs. management* [u1700s]

maness n *woman*

mathematician n *obs. astrologer* [u1700s]

mistreading n *obs. transgression* [u1700s]

rampallion n *obs. rapscallion* [u1800s]

regreets n *obs. greetings* [u1600s]

rub n *as in "there's the rub"*

secluse adj *secluded*

sneap n *snub*

sottery n [u1700s] (sottish: b1570)

subduce v *obs. subtract* [u1600s]

sulter v *obs. swelter* [u1600s]

terminate v *obs. determine* [u1700s] (obs. determination: b1450 to 1600s)

tireling n *obs. something tired* [u1600s]

way v [u1700s]

wontless adj *not usual*

IN USE BY
1650

Geography/Places

subterranean adj/v b1605 (rare subterrestrial: concurrent)

terra firma n *land* b1605

underworld n *the earth* b1610 ["crimeland": b1870]

crater n b1615 (verb use: b1885)

oasis n b1615 [fig. "refuge": b1830]

volcano n b1615

aboveground adj b1620

terra incognita n *unexplored territory* b1620

atoll n b1625

creek n b1625 [type of inlet: b1250; obs. "cleft": u1600s; type of port: b1500]

eastern hemisphere, western hemisphere n b1625 (northern hemisphere, southern hemisphere: b1775)

frigid zone n b1625

landlocked adj b1625

swamp n b1625 (verb use: b1785; swampland: b1665)

cave in v *lit. collapse* b1630 [fig. "give in": b1837] (cave-in n: b1860)

range n *as in "mountain range"* b1630

peak n *mountaintop* b1635

worldwide adj b1635 (adv use: b1895)

gully n *trench* b1640 ["gullet": b1540]

Natural Things

galena n b1605

Mother Nature n b1605

sea salt n b1605

talc n b1605 (talcum: b1560)

wooded adj b1605

asbestos n b1610 [obs. "mineral that burns perpetually": b1400 to 1800s]

will-o'-the-wisp n b1610

driftwood n b1615

grotto n b1620 (grot: b1510)

dewfall n b1625

half-light n b1625

species n *spec. biological grouping* b1630 [gen. "grouping": b1400] (specie: b1715)

friar's lantern n *swamp gas* b1635

moonstone n b1635

quartz n b1635

atmosphere n *air* b1640 ["ambiance": b1800] (atmospheric: b1785; atmospheric pressure: b1665)

gravitation n b1645 (gravitate: b1695)

zinc n b1645

granite n [fig. use: b1870]

parturition n *giving birth* (parturient adj: b1600)

Plants

lichen n b1605

rhodendendron n b1605

sea cucumber n b1605

taproot n b1605

coconut n b1615 [slang "head": b1870]

mangrove n b1615

passionflower n b1615

prickly pear n b1615

rose of Sharon n b1615

redwood n b1620

lilac n b1625 [the color: b1800]

lime n *type of tree* b1625

efflorescence n *blooming* b1630 (verb use: b1775)

ligneous adj *woody* b1630

locust n *type of tree* b1630

plantage n *obs. plants* b1630 [u1800s]

squash n b1635

baobab n b1640

green corn n (Am) b1645

chestnut oak n (Am)

cranberry n (Am)

puffball n

pumpkin n

Animals

bobtail n b1605 [type of arrow: b1540]

centipede n b1605

chrysalis n b1605 (chrysalid: b1625)

condor n b1605

feral adj *bestial* b1605 (ferine: b1670)

guano n b1605

hedgepig n b1605 (hedgehog: b1450)

insect n b1605

jackal n b1605

jaguar n b1605

millipede n b1605

moose n (Am) b1605

nautilus n *type of mollusk* b1605

purr n b1605 (verb use: b1620)

river horse n b1605

water snake n b1605

raccoon n 1608

hamster n b1610

house cat n b1610

ibex n b1610

Indian elephant n b1610

lemming n b1610

marmot n *type of rodent* b1610

monkfish n b1610

muskrat n b1610 (mushrat: b1900)

opossum n (Am) b1610

queen bee n b1610

simian adj *apelike* b1610 (noun use: b1880; simious: b1885)

slink n *prematurely born animal* b1610

watchdog n b1610 [fig. use: b1870] (verb use: b1905)

whippet n *type of dog* b1610 [type of wine: b1500; "small person": b1570]

wolf spider n b1610

catfish n b1615

meadowlark n (Am) b1615

nighthawk n b1615

possum n (Am) *oppossum* b1615

salamander n b1615 [type of fantastic creature: b1340]

sea cow n b1615

sea turtle n b1615

stingray n b1615 (stingaree: b1555)

tanager n b1615

terrapin n (Am) b1615

wood louse n b1615
basset n b1620 (basset hound: b1885)
chinch n *bedbug* b1620
cockatoo n b1620
birdcall n b1625
bug n *bedbug* b1625 ["any insect": b1670; "germ": b1930]
cockroach n b1625
crawfish n b1625 (crayfish: b1315; crawdad: b1905)
flying squirrel n b1625
gray squirrel n (Am) b1625
moray eel n (Am) b1625
carnivora n *gen. carnivores* b1630 (carnivore: b1840)
coati n b1630 (coatimundi: b1680)
dodo n b1630 [slang use: b1900]
dragonfly n b1630
grouper n b1630
jack n *male animal, as in "jackass"* b1630
kittiwake n b1630
knuckle n *as in "pig's knuckles"* b1630
macaw n *type of parrot* b1630
mink n b1630 [type of fur: b1435]
rattlesnake n (Am) b1630 (rattler: b1830)
sheltie n *type of horse* b1630 [type of dog: b1930]
sloth n *type of animal* b1630
sunfish n b1630
vulpine adj *foxlike* b1630
alewife n (Am) b1635
dung beetle n b1635
hummingbird n (Am) b1635
loon n *type of aquatic bird* b1635
pilot fish n b1635
skunk n (Am) b1635 ["nasty person": b1870]
amphibious adj b1640 (noun use: b1840)
bird of paradise n b1640
red fox n (Am) b1640
red squirrel n (Am) b1640
lapdog n b1645
biped n
carrier pigeon n
crustaceous adj (crustacea: b1815; crustacean: b1835)
narwhal n *type of sea animal*
quadruped n

Weather

weathercaster n b1610
meteorology n b1620 (meteor: b1475)
nimbus n b1620 (nimbostratus: b1890)
weatherproof adj/v b1620
breeze n b1630 [obs. "wind from the north": b1560 to 1700s; slang "piece of cake": b1930]
haze n b1630 [fig. use: b1780] (hazy: b1625)
precipitation n *rain, etc.* b1630 (precipitate v: b1870)
tornado n *cyclone* b1630 [type of tropical storm: b1960]
slush n b1645

Heavens/Sky

aerial adj *happening in the air* b1605 ["ephemeral": b1600]
aster n *obs. star* b1605 [u1700s]
astral adj b1605
satellite n b1615 [fig. use: b1800] (adj use: b1900)
unearthly adj *phys. heavenly* b1615 [fig. "otherworldly": b1830]
aurora borealis n b1625 (aurora australis: b1745)
astrologer n *astrologist* b1630 [obs. "astronomer": b1400 to 1700s] (astrologist: b1970)
interstellar adj b1630
sidereal adj *astral* b1635
sun dog n *parhelion* b1635
disk/disc n *applied to heavenly bodies* b1645 [gen. use: b1730]
parhelion n *sun dog*

Science

acoustic adj b1605
laboratory n b1605
refract v b1615 (refraction: b1630)
family n *type of grouping* b1630
physiology n b1630 ["gen. science": b1565]
variety n *classification* b1630

alkahest n *alchemist's universal solvent* b1645
focus n b1645 [fig. "point of concentration": b1770]
chemistry n ["alchemistry": b1600]
icthyology n *study of birds*
myology n *study of muscles*

Technology

automaton n *something self-propelled* b1615 ["machine": b1670; "machine-like being": b1700]

Energy

motive power n b1625
cordwood n b1640
electric adj *producing electricity* ["using electricity": b1675; fig. "exhilarating": b1830]
electricity n

Time

decade n b1605 ["ten books": b1475; gen. "group of ten": b1600] (decennium: b1685)
immemorial adj b1605
time immemorial n b1605
centenary n *hundredth anniversary* b1610 ["century": b1610] (centennial adj: b1800; centenarian: b1845; centennial n: b1875)
epoch n b1615 [geological sense: b1830]
era n b1615 [geological sense: b1900]
middle ages n b1620
sundown n b1620
ultimo adj *the previous month* b1620 [describing last day of the month: b1585 to 1600s]
antecede v *precede* b1625
dusk n b1625
century n *100 years* b1630 [obs. land measure: b1400; obs. type of Roman mil. group: b1450; gen. "group of 100": b1615]
forever/forevermore adv b1630 (for ever: b1350; noun use: b1860)

period n *as in "period of time"* b1630
winter solstice n b1635
millenium n b1640
weekend n b1640 (adj use: b1900; verb use: b1905)
anachronism n ["chronologically incongruous": b1830] (anachronistic: b1800; anachronous: b1830)
eon n
Gregorian calendar n
nightfall n
per mensem adv
post meridiem adj *P.M.* (ante merediem: b1565)
quadrennial adj *lasting four years* ["every four years": b1705]

Age/Aging

middle-aged adj b1610 (middle age: b1380)
minor n *underage person* b1615
juvenile adj *young* b1625 ["immature": b1670] (noun use: b1735; juvenility: b1635)
out-of-date adj b1630

Mathematics

figure eight, figure of eight n b1605
plane n *in geometry* b1605 (adj use: b1730)
zero n b1605
decimal adj *related to ten* b1610
logarithm n b1615
monad n *one* b1615
trigonometry v b1615
calculus n b1620 [obs. gen. "calculation": b1700 to 1800s]
cosine n b1620
enumerate v b1620
numerical adj b1625
cotangent n b1630
log n *logarithm* b1635
nonagon n *nine-sided polygon* b1640
ratio n b1640
decimal n b1645 (adj use: b1610)
median adj b1645

quadrilateral n (adj use: b1660)

Measurement
half-pint n b1615
thermometer n b1625
cord n b1630
volume n *phys. measure* b1630
width n b1630
nautical mile n b1635
iota n *bit, whit* b1640 ["Greek letter": b1470]
infinitude n b1645

The Body
abdomen n b1605 ["belly fat": b1600] (abdominal: b1740)
thumbnail n b1605 ["thumbnail sketch": b1870] (adj use: b1855)
underbelly n b1610
vitals n b1610
cerebrum n b1615
clavicle n b1615
clitoris n b1615 (clit: b1970)
flexor n b1615
gestation n b1615 [obs. gen. "carrying": b1570] (gestate: b1870)
menstruum n *arch.* b1615
pectoral muscle n b1615 (pecs: b1970)
pelvis n b1615 (pelvic adj: b1830)
phallus n b1615
cock n *penis* b1620
pedal adj *of the foot* b1625
Roman nose n b1625
urethra n b1625
appendix n b1630
buff n *birthday suit, as in "in the buff"* b1630
drum n *as in "eardrum"* b1630
epidermis n b1630
hand n *obs. hand and arm* b1630 [u1700s]
oral adj *pertaining to the mouth* b1630
posterior n *behind* b1630 (adj use: b1600)
seat n *buttocks* b1630 ["sitting place": b1200; as in "seat of the pants": b1870]
thymus n *type of gland* b1630

[obs. type of growth: b1570 to 1600s]
biceps n b1635
eardrum n b1645
elevator n *type of muscle*
glans n *head of penis or clitoris*
prostate n (prostate gland: b1830)
sensorium n
sneeze n (nesing "sneeze": b1385)

Physical Description
excretion n b1605 (excrete: b1670)
gesticulate v b1605 (gesticulation: b1470)
idiosyncrasy n *phys. quirk* b1605 ["personality quirk": b1665]
soft-spoken adj b1610
chuffy adj *chubby* b1615
magnetic adj *attractive* b1615 ["magnetized": b1635] (magnetical: b1600)
obesity n b1615 (obese: b1655)
owlish adj b1615
ungainly adj b1615
dodder v b1620 (doddering: b1670; doddery: b1870)
able-bodied adj b1625
dexterous adj b1625 ["convenient": b1605]
gracile adj *slim* b1625
hirsute adj b1625
stocky adj *heavyset* b1625 [rare "made of wood": b1400]
Apollonian adj b1630
fair-haired adj b1630
motion n *gesture* b1630 (verb use: b1800)
perspiration n *act of perspiring* b1630 [obs. "respiration": u1700s; "sweat": b1730] (perspire: b1685)
sedentary adj *lethargic* b1630 ["not migratory": b1600]
skinny adj *slim* b1630 ["composed of skin": b1580]
squat adj *short and stocky* b1630 ["squatting": b1450]
tip v *obs. make tipsy, drink* b1630 [u1700s] (tipsy: b1580)

sniffle v b1635 (noun use: b1900; the sniffles: b1830)
surefooted adj b1635
mundungous n *reeking tobacco* b1640
appendage n
exhaustion n *tiredness*
intoxication n ["poisoning": b1410]
masticate v

Medicine
backache n b1605
black eye n b1605
cancer n b1605 [obs. type of sore: b1000; fig. use: b1670]
catheter n b1605
epidemic adj b1605 (noun use: b1770)
epileptic adj b1605 (noun use: b1670)
flat-footed adj b1605
glass eye n b1605
nauseous adj *feeling nausea, causing nausea* b1605 ["creating nausea": b1615]
nostrum n *snake oil* b1605
pneumonia n b1605
sprain n b1605 (verb use: b1625)
farsighted adj b1610
cesarean section n b1615 (cesarean n: b1905)
druggist n b1615 [obs. drugster: b1630 to 1700s]
insalubrious adj *unhealthy* b1615
pesthouse n b1615
shaking palsy n b1615
grume n *clot* b1620
sty n *type of inflammation* b1620
diagnostic adj/n b1625 (diagnosis: b1685; diagnose: b1860)
goiter n b1625
insomnia n b1625 (insomniac: b1910)
lisp n b1625 (verb use: b1100)
medicate v b1625
bloodshot adj *describing eyes* b1630
crinkum n *obs. slang VD* b1630 [u1800s]
infusion n b1630

junk n *arch. type of splint* b1630
medicaster n *arch. phony doctor* b1630
obstetricate v *help a birth* b1630 [u1800s]
quack n *fake doctor* b1630 (adj use: b1660; quacksalver: b1580; quackery: b1700)
recuperative adj b1630
topical adj b1630 [gen. "local": b1600]
twinge n *pain, pang* b1630
ward n *section of a hospital* b1630
lues n *syphilis* b1635
rickets n b1635 (rickety: b1685)
nauseate, nauseating v, adj *feel nausea* b1640 ["create nausea": b1655] (nausea: b1425)
tarantism n *type of malady* b1640
bill of health n b1645
germ n b1645 ["something that germinates": b1450] (germ cell: b1855)
glaucoma n b1645
invalid adj *bedridden* b1645 (noun use: b1710)
prophylactic n b1645 [slang "condom": b1970]
repellent adj b1645
coma n (comatose: b1700)
medical adj
pharmaceutical adj (noun use: b1885)
spotted fever n

Everyday Life
counterpane n *bedspread* b1605 (counterpoynte: b1470)
facecloth n b1605
tripod n *type of stool* b1605 [as in "photo tripod": b1830]
washtub n b1605
saucer n b1610 [obs. "type of condiment holder": b1350 to 1700s]
umbrella n b1610 [fig. "protection": b1970]
weed n *tobacco* b1610 ["cigar": b1870; "marijuana": b1930]

flagstaff n b1615 (flagpole: b1885)

iron n b1615 (ironing: b1710)

liner n *lining* b1615

redecorate v b1615

valise n b1615

curling iron n b1620

parasol n b1620

Persian carpet/Persian rug n b1620

smoker n *cigarette consumer* b1620

deterge v *wash* b1625 (detergent adj: b1620; detergent n: b1680; detergency: b1710)

everyday adj b1625 ["ordinary": b1770]

streetlight n b1625 (streetlamp: b1800)

cooler n b1630

cover n *place setting* b1630

leg n *in furniture* b1630

lint n *fuzz* b1630 ["flax": b1375]

nipperkin n *type of liquor bottle* b1630

pad n *as in "knee pad"* b1630

pincushion n b1630

shade n *windowshade* b1630

smoke v *smoke a cigarette* b1630 (noun use "a cigarette": b1870)

staple n *needed item* b1630 ["center of commerce": b1400; obs. "storehouse of staples": b1550 to 1700s] (adj use: b1615)

wash n *as in "eye wash"* b1630 (verb use: b1570)

cigar n b1635 (cigarillo: b1835)

cot n *portable bed* b1635 [gen. type of bed: b1635]

ticking n *type of fabric* b1645

chest of drawers n

crib n *as in "baby crib"*

earthenware n

night-light n

Shelter/Housing

dining room n b1605

fretwork n b1605

ground floor n b1605

portico n b1605

standing room n b1605

tarpaulin n *type of covering*

b1605 [arch. slang "sailor": b1670; type of hat: b1870] (tarp: b1910)

spa n b1610

bell tower n b1615 (belfry: b1275)

ghetto n *Jewish quarter* b1615 [gen. use: b1900]

girder n b1615

grating n b1615

rooftop n b1615

saltbox n *type of house design* b1615

stockade n *barricade* b1615 ["mil. jail": b1870] (verb use: b1680)

storage n b1615

villa n b1615

balcony n b1620 ["theatre area": b1730]

bedroom n b1620

awning n b1625

lighthouse n b1625

longhouse n b1625

staircase n b1625 (stairway: b1770; stairwell b1920)

blind n *concealment device* b1630

occupant n *resident* b1630

outbuilding n b1630

register n *as in "cold air register"* b1630

rotunda n b1630

sewer n b1630 ["marsh drainage": b1425]

structure n *building* b1630 [obs. "process of construction": b1450; "organization, composition": b1600] (verb use: b1695)

vault n *obs. bathroom* b1630 [u1800s]

wigwam n b1630

earthwork n b1635

meetinghouse n b1635

putty n *type of mortar* b1635 [type of cement: b1710] (verb use: b1735)

campanile n *bell tower* b1640

apartment n b1645

drawing room n b1645

superstructure n b1645

Turkish bath n b1645

Dutch door n

passageway n

Drink

mull v *as in "mulled wine"* b1610

absinthe n b1615

brandy n b1615 (brandy-wine: b1625)

John Barleycorn n b1620

cola n b1630

spirit n *distillation* b1630 ["alcohol": b1700]

Food

chili n *the pepper* b1605 [the stew: b1850]

chocolate n *type of drink* b1605 [as in "chocolate bar": b1670]

gobble v *eat quickly* b1605

lemonade n b1605

mother of vinegar n b1605 (mother: b1540)

tomato n b1605

corn n *maize* b1610 [gen. "grain": b750]

Indian meal n (Am) b1610

sugarplum n b1610

persimmon n 1612

cod-liver oil n b1615

macaroon n *type of cookie* b1615

omelette n b1615

pea adj/n b1615

pilaff n b1615

pone n (Am) *as in "corn pone"* b1615

puff pastry n b1615

ravioli n b1615

spoon-feed v b1615

tapioca n b1615

Indian corn n (Am) b1620

nectarine n b1620

raspberry n b1620 (arch. rasp "raspberry": b1570)

sauerkraut n b1620

table d'hôte n *meal at a fixed price* b1620

allspice n b1625

flummery n b1625 ["nonsense": b1770]

powdered sugar n b1625

yogurt n b1625

bread v *cover with crumbs* b1630

charqui n *jerky* b1630 (jerky: b1845)

cure v *as in "cure a fish"* b1630

gherkin n b1630

hominy n (Am) b1630

mum n *type of beer* b1630

snap n *biscuit, as in "ginger snap"* b1630

punch n *type of drink* b1635

culinary adj b1640

lime n *citrus fruit* b1640

pot marjoram n *oregano* b1640

Jerusalem artichoke n b1645

marinate v b1645 (marinade n: b1725; marinade v: b1730)

a la mode adj *stewed in wine (of beef)* ["fashionable": b1600; "served with ice cream": b1930]

bisque n

plum pudding n

roasting ear n

slurp n/v *consume quickly* ["the sound of consuming quickly": b1970]

sweet basil n

sweet corn n (Am)

Agriculture/Food-Gathering

gristmill n b1605

incubation n b1615 (incubate: b1645)

cultivate v *lit. and fig.* b1620 (cultivation: b1700)

pot v *as in "pot a flower"* b1620

inseminate v *implant seed* b1625 ["implant with semen": b1925] (insemination: b1660)

irrigate v b1625

hotbed n b1630 [fig. use: b1770]

domesticate v b1640

cornstalk n (Am) b1645

porker n b1645 [slang "fat person": b1900]

bowery n (Am) *type of farm*

fertilize v *as in "fertilize a field"* [as in "fertilize an egg": b1860] (fertilizer: b1665)

veterinarian n (veterinary surgeon: b1805; veterinary n: b1865)

Cloth/Clothing

anadem n *headband* b1605
galloon n *type of trim* b1605
mobled adj *arch. wrapped* b1605
nightclothes n b1605
tiffany n b1605
muslin n b1610
backstitch n/v b1615
chador n b1615
chintz n *type of fabric* b1615 (chintzy: b1855)
dungaree n b1615
gingham n b1615
moccasin n b1615
tawdry n *type of necktie* b1615
vest n b1615 [type of gown: b1615; "waistcoat": b1670]
cummerbund/cumberbund n b1620
mohair n *type of fabric* b1620 (mocayare: b1570)
mourning band n b1620
shoestring n b1620
coonskin n b1625
garb n b1625 [obs. "fashion": b1595] (verb use: b1600)
montero n *type of hunting cap* b1625
percale n *type of cloth* b1625
duroy n *arch. type of fabric* b1630
foolscap n *type of cap* b1630 [type of paper: b1700]
shawl n b1630
tuck v *as in "tuck up a dress"* b1630
duck n *type of cloth* b1640
life preserver n b1640 (life buoy: b1805; life belt: b1860; life jacket: b1870; life ring: b1910; life vest: b1915)
pocket-handkerchief n b1645
Sunday best n b1645
duffel n *fabric*
shoelace n
undershirt n

Fashion/Style

fashionable adj b1610 ["able to be fashioned": b1600 to 1600s]
arabesque adj *ornamental style* b1615

gothic adj b1615
peruke n *type of wig* b1630 ["hair": b1540]
trim n *haircut* b1630
coiffure, coiffured n, adj b1635
mode n b1645
plush adj *posh* b1645 ["made of plush": b1630] (plushy: b1615)
cosmetic n/adj ["art of using cosmetics": b1605]

Tools

depilatory adj b1605 (noun use: b1610)
bevel n b1610 ["angle created by a bevel": b1600] (adj use: b1560; verb use: b1680)
drill n/v *type of tool* b1615
pruning hook n b1615
clockwork n b1630 (adj use: b1770)
glass n *telescope* b1630
hook and eye n *type of fastener* b1630
key n *type of winding or grasping tool* b1630
mariner's compass n b1630
marlinespike n *type of tool* b1630
nut n *as in "nuts and bolts"* b1630
sextant n *type of measuring instrument* b1630 [obs. type of measure: b1600 to 1700s]
works n *mechanism* b1630
flambeau n *torch* b1635
drawknife n b1640
grout n b1640
handcart n b1640
crosscut saw n (Am) b1645
fuse n *as in "dynamite fuse"* b1645
handcuff n b1645 (verb use: b1720)
dark lantern n
fire irons n
hub n [fig. "center": b1860]
telescope n

Travel/Transportation

gondolier n b1605
leg v *run* b1605
footer n *pedestrian* b1610
sea captain n b1615

transport n *transporting* b1615 [as in "mass transport, troop transport,": b1700] (transportation: b1540)
boulevard n b1620
hackney coach n b1620 (hack: b1705)
ramble v *travel wanderingly* b1620 (noun use: b1670)
sampan n *type of boat* b1620
side street n b1620
catamaran n b1630
dry dock n b1630
easting n *progress toward the east* b1630
engineer n *as in "train engineer"* b1630
founder v *of ships* b1630
landfall n *landing* b1630
peripatetic n *traveler* b1630 ["type of follower of Aristotle": b1450] (peripatetic "wandering": b1670)
quay n *landing place on a waterway* b1630 (caye: b1310)
rail n *as in "ride the rails"* b1630
relay n *fresh horses* b1630
sloop n b1630
tack n *ship movement* b1630 [type of ship equipment: b1450; gen. "course": b1700] (verb use: b1560)
trunk n *type of luggage* b1630 [obs. gen. box: b1450]
tub n *dilapidated ship* b1630
circumnavigate v b1635
sedan n *sedan chair* b1635 [type of car: b1930] (sedan chair: b1750)
corvette n *type of ship* b1640
stagecoach n b1640
cargo n
locomotion n (locomotive adj: b1615; locomotory adj: b1825; locomote v: b1835)
promenade n *place to walk*

Emotions/Characteristics

animosity n b1605 [obs. "courage": b1425]
antipathy n b1605

apathy n b1605 (apathetic: b1745)
assuming adj *presumptuous* b1605
chopfallen adj b1605
conceit n *vanity* b1605 [obs. "ability to conceive thoughts": b1380 to 1800s; literary sense: b1530] (self-conceit: b1590; conceited: b1611)
condolence n b1605 (condolent adj: b1500; condole v: b1590)
contradictious adj b1605
deportment n b1605 (deport: b1485)
evenhanded adj b1605
felicitate adj *happied* b1605 (verb use: b1605)
fleshment n *excitement from getting off to a good start* b1605
frontless adj *shameless* b1605
gaingiving n *misgiving* b1605
gambol v (Am) *make merry* b1605 (noun use: b1600)
ill-natured adj b1605
ill-tempered adj b1605
lily-livered adj b1605
milk-livered adj *arch. cowardly* b1605
misgiving n b1605 (misgive: b1515)
touchy adj b1605 (touchous: b1870)
unnerve v b1605
worldly-minded adj b1605
aloof adj b1610
coldhearted adj b1610
concernment n *arch. concern* b1610
enrapt adj b1610 (enrapture: b1740)
rankle v *bother* b1610 ["fester, cause wounds": b1300]
surprise n b1610 ["surprise attack": b1460; "surprising thing": b1595] (verb use: b1595)
consternation n b1615 (consternate v: b1555)
disinterest v b1615 (noun use: b1660; disinterested: b1670)
disinterested adj *uninterested* b1615 ["unconcerned":

b1605; "impartial": b1610] (disinterest n: b1600)

fastidious adj b1615 [obs. "repulsive, haughty": b1425 to 1700s; obs. "disgusted": b1570 to 1600s]

fellow feeling n *compassion* b1615 ["common ground": b1715]

meddlesome adj b1615

openhearted adj b1615

passionless adj b1615

quibble v b1615 [obs. "pun": b1630 to 1700s] (noun use: b1670; obs. quib "quibble" n: b1570 to 1600s)

rabid adj *"furious"* b1615 ["afflicted with rabies": b1830]

self-preservation n b1615

withdrawn adj b1615 (withdrawal: b1930)

anxious adj b1620 ["eager": b1770]

good humor n b1620 (goodhumored: b1665)

hardmouthed adj *stubborn* b1620

mendacious adj b1620 (mendacity: b1650)

misogynist n b1620 (misogyny: b1660; mysognymism: b1830; misandry: b1930)

pigheaded adj b1620

pomposity n *arrogance* b1620 ["stateliness": b1450]

congenial adj *pertaining to people* b1625 [pertaining to things, situations: b1770]

depress v *make sad* b1625 (depression: b1400; depressing: b1790; depressed: b1800; depressant: b1880)

droll adj b1625 (noun use "jester": b1645; verb use: b1665)

free-spoken adj b1625

funk n b1625

magniloquence n *bombast* b1625 (magniloquent: b1655)

miff n *a state of miffment; tiff* b1625 (verb use: b1800)

self-pity n b1625

vacillate v b1625 (vacillation: b1400)

affinity n *predilection* b1630 ["kindredness": b1305]

apprehend, apprehension v, n *fear* b1630

carp n *complaint* b1630 (verb use: b1225)

character n *composite characteristics; reputation* b1630

compose v *as in "compose oneself"* b1630 ["compose oneself physically": b1570; arch. "make quiet": b1670] (composed: b1485; composure: b1650)

curt adj b1630 [gen. "short": b1425]

devious adj b1630 ["out of the way": b1600]

diffidence n b1630 ["distrust": b1400] (adj use: b1730)

dishonest adj b1630 [obs. "dishonorable," "unchaste": b1390 to 1700s] (obs. verb use: b1450; dishonesty: b1600)

disrespective adj *obs. disrespectful* b1630 [u1700s]

down adv *depressed* b1630

downcast adj b1630 (noun use: b1300)

dyspathy n *opp. of sympathy* b1630

eccentric adj *describing people* b1630 [describing circles: b1555] (noun use: b1830; eccentricity: b1660)

esteem n b1630 [obs. "worth": b1350 to 1800s; arch. "opinion": b1600]

hauteur n *haughty airs* b1630

insuavity n b1630

irritation n *annoyance, anger* b1630 ["exacerbation": b1425]

jocular adj b1630 (jocose: b1675)

quirk n *peculiarity* b1630 ["evasion": b1570; "quip": b1600]

reservation n *hesitation* b1630

respectuous adj *arch. respectful* b1630

sheepish adj *embarrassed* b1630 ["related to sheep": b1200; obs. "timid": b1350 to 1600s]

sympathy n *appreciation of another's feelings* b1630 ["affinity": b1570; obs. "agreement": b1600] (sympathize: b1630; sympathetic: b1700)

vapor n/v *bombast* b1630

awestruck adj b1635

budge adj *pompous* b1635

exuberance n b1635 (exuberant: b1530)

gaiety n b1635

high-spirited adj b1635

imbrute v *become brutish* b1635

naughty adj *mischievous* b1635 [obs. "needy": b1380; arch. "evil": b1380; obs. "inferior": b1530 to 1700s; "saucy": b1540]

obliging adj b1635

beatific adj b1640 (beatitude: b1500; beatify: b1535)

cross adj *angry* b1640 [obs. "quarrelsome": b1565 to 1800s]

fastuous adj *arch. arrogant* b1640

sardonic adj b1640

self-confidence n b1640 (self-confident: b1630)

selfish adj b1640 (selfful: b1670)

sentiment n *gen. feeling* b1640 [obs. "sensation": b1374 to 1800; "emotional feeling": b1730]

dispirit v b1645 [obs. "dilute alcohol": u1700s]

hotheaded adj b1645 (hothead: b1770)

irrational adj b1645 ["incapable of reason": b1500] (noun use: b1670)

largehearted adj b1645

mortify v *cause deep concern* b1645 [obs. "kill": b1385 to 1600s]

pugnacious adj b1645

salacious adj b1645

crude adj *boorish*

down in the mouth adj

lonesome adj (noun use: b1900)

lymphatic adj *frantic, crazed* [u1800s]

selfhood n

shy v *as in "shy away"*

transfix v *freeze; fascinate* [phys. "hold in place by piercing": b1590]

Thoughts/Perception/ The Mind

appreciation n *assessment* b1605 ["recognition": b1570; "rise in value": b1800] (arch. appreciate n: b1770)

considered adj b1605

intension n *mental intensity* b1605

lunes n *arch. lunatic spells* b1605

omniscient adj b1605 (omniscience: b1615)

opinionated adj b1605

preoccupation n *being preoccupied* b1605 ["something that preoccupies": b1900]

sanity n *mental health* b1605 [obs. "gen. health": b1425; "reasonableness": b1870] (sane: b1630; sanify "make sane": b1870)

tender-minded adj b1605

vatic, vaticination adj, n *prophetic, prophesy* b1605 (vaticinate v: b1625; vaticinal: b1590)

whimsy n *whim* b1605 ["whimsical thing": b1730]

equilibrium n *mental equilibrium* b1610 ["equilibrium of force": b1670; "net lack of change": b1700] (obs. equilibre: b1630 to 1800s; equilibrize: b1870)

ethical adj *pertaining to ethics* b1610 ["principled": b1900]

gorgonize v *mesmerize, petrify* b1610

interest v b1610

mind v *object* b1610

non compos mentis adj *not of sound mind* b1610

cathartic adj *mentally stimu-*

lating b1615 [med. sense: b1615] (catharsis: b1875)

conscientious adj b1615

cracked adj *crazy* b1615 (crackers: b1930)

intellectual n *arch. intellectual powers, wits* b1615

nescience n *ignorance* b1615

soul-searching adj b1615

crazy adj b1620 ["phys. sick": b1530 to 1800s; "phys. cracked": b1580] (noun use: b1865)

designing adj b1620

perspicacious adj b1620 (perspicuous: b1590)

dissentient adj *dissenting* b1625 (noun use: b1655; dissentious: b1560)

hypnotic adj b1625

narrow-minded adj b1625

shortsighted adj b1625

conscient adj *conscious* b1630

conscious adj b1630 [obs. "expressing conscience": b1600 to 1800s] (noun use: b1920; conscient adj: b1630)

figment n b1630 [lit. sense: b1425]

genius n *aptitude* b1630

incoherent adj b1630 [fig. use: b1670]

insulse adj *arch. dull, witless* b1630

intelligential adj *arch.* b1630

opiniatre n *opinionated person* b1630 [u1700s] (obs. verb use: b1670 to 1700s)

reflect v *think* b1630 (reflection: b1470)

sense n *as in "that makes sense"* b1630

skeptic n *doubter* b1630 [philosophical sense "unconvinced of certainty of anything": b1570]

smart adj *intelligent* b1630

strike v *occur, as in "it strikes me that . . ."* b1630

unfathomable adj b1630

brainchild n b1635

consciousness n *being conscious* b1635 (conscience: b1635)

second thought n b1635

demented adj b1645 (dement adj: b1500; de-

mency: b1530; dement v: b1545; dementate v: b1630; dementia: b1800)

gifted adj b1645

ratiocinate v b1645

deductive adj

designer n *schemer* ["creator": b1665]

fascinating adj

forehanded adj *looking ahead*

unbalanced adj

uninterested adj *not interested* [obs. "disinterested": b1650 to 1770]

visionary adj *able to envision* [pertaining to visions; futuristic: b1730] (noun use: b1705)

Love/Romance/Sex

groom n b1605 (groomsman: b1700)

heartache n b1605 [lit. use: b1000]

ruttish adj *lusting* b1605

sixty-nine n b1605

tumble v *have sex with* b1605 (noun use: b1905)

coition n *coitus* b1615

monogamy n *marrying only once* b1615 ["faithfulness to one person at a time": b1730] (monogamist: b1650)

pederasty n b1615 (pederast: b1670)

prostitute n b1615 [fig. use: b1630] (prostitution: b1555)

erotic adj b1625

commerce n *arch. sex* b1630

copulate v b1630 [obs. "link": b1425 to 1800s] (copulation: b1485)

digamy n *second marriage* b1630

elope v b1630 [gen. "escape": b1600]

enter v *insert sexually* b1630

flirt v b1630 [obs. "sneer": b1550; "flick": b1580] (noun use: b1550; flirtation: b1720)

hippomanes n b1630

intermarriage, intermarry n, v b1630 [gen. "marriage": b1580]

matchmaker, matchmake n, v b1630

mix with v *have sex* b1630

philogyny n *love of women* b1630 (philogynist: b1870)

solicitrix n *prostitute* b1630

spend v *ejaculate* b1630

triangle n b1630

tweak n *obs. slang whore, john* b1630 [u1700s]

lovelorn adj b1635

platonic love n b1635

orgasm n b1640 [fig. use: b1765]

nubile adj *marriageable* b1645 ["attractive": b1970]

come v *achieve orgasm* (noun use: b1925)

grind v *have sex* (noun use: b1900)

impregnate v *make pregnant*

infatuation n (infatuate: b1570)

racy adj *blue*

wedding cake n

Family/Relations/ Friends

genealogist n b1605

heiress n b1610 (heir: b1225)

matriarch n b1610

granddaughter n b1615 (grandson: b1590)

maternity n b1615 (adj use: b1895)

patronymic n *name derived patrilineally* b1615

heir presumptive n b1630

papoose n (Am) b1635

grandnephew n b1640 (grandniece: b1830)

Holidays

April Fool's Day n b1605

Christmastide n b1630

Games/Fun/Leisure

marionette n b1605

rebus n b1605

twenty-one n b1615

chronogram n *type of cryptogram* b1625

popgun n b1625

cribbage n *type of card game* b1630

deal n *in cards* b1630 (verb use: b1530)

mumblety-peg n b1630

playsome adj b1630

trick n *stunt, display, as in "magic trick"* b1630

skittles n b1635

curler n b1640

backgammon n b1645

playmate n b1645 (playfellow: b1515)

carousel n *type of tournament*

handicap n *arch. type of game*

Sports

athletics n b1605

Olympic Games n b1605 (Olympian Games: b1595)

pentathlon n b1605 (pentathlete: b1830)

curling n b1620 (curler: b1640)

hug n *used in wrestling* b1620 [gen. use: b1670]

toreador n b1620

decoy n *place for hunting with decoys* b1625 ["the decoy itself": b1645] (verb use: b1570)

dumbbell n b1630

racehorse n b1630

serve v *in tennis* b1630 (noun use: b1690)

skate n *as in "ice skate"* (verb use: b1700)

Professions/Duties

inspector n b1605 [in the police: b1870] (inspectress: b1800)

town crier n b1605

upholsterer n b1605 (obs. upholster n: b1450 to 1700s; upholstery: b1650; upholster v: b1855)

chimney sweep n b1615 (chimney sweeper: b1500)

domestic n b1615 [obs. "someone living at home": b1570 to 1700s]

helpmeet n *helper* b1615 (helper: b1300; helpmate: b1715)

storekeeper n b1620

underwriter n b1620

wet nurse n b1620 (verb use: b1785)

florist n b1625
trapper n b1625 (trappist "trapper": b1900)
dun n *dunner* b1630
engineer n *as in "civil engineer"* b1630 (verb use: b1845)
garcon n b1630
haberdasher n b1630 ["gen. vendor": b1315 to 1700s]
speculatist n *theorist* b1630
watchmaker n b1630
curator n *manager* b1635 [type of guardian: b1375; "museum head": b1665] (curatrix: b1600)
stewardess n b1635 (steward: b900)
washerwoman n b1635 (washwoman: b1590; washerman: b1715)
wine taster n b1635
cryptographer n b1645 (cryptograph: b1850)
wagon master n b1645
chairman n (verb use: b1890; chairwoman: b1685; chairperson: b1975)
concierge n
lifeguard n [in swimming: b1900]

Business/Commerce/ Selling
monopolist n b1605
overprice v b1605
bill of sale n b1610
coffeehouse n b1615
indemnify v b1615
showroom n b1615
factory n b1620 ["job of a factor": b1560; "trading post": b1585]
vend v *be sold* b1620 ["sell": b1670]
bid v *propose an offer* b1630 [in card games: b1900] (noun use "offer": b1790; noun use "attempt": b1900)
dun v *persist for payment* b1630 (noun use "dunner": b1630; noun use "act of dunning": b1700)
score n *amount due* b1630

(obs. verb use "run up a tab": b1600 to 1700s)
cabaret n *type of tavern* b1635 ["type of performance": b1930]
colliery n *coal mine and environs* b1635
printery n *print shop* b1640
mercantile adj b1645

The Workplace
journeywork n b1605
taskmistress n b1605 (taskmaster: b1530)
extern n *opp. of intern* b1610 (externship: b1945)
outlier n *someone who lives far from work* b1610
shorthanded adj *understaffed* b1625
manage v b1630
coolie n b1640
workingman n b1640
coworker n b1645
manufactory n *factory* [obs. "something manufactured": b1630 to 1700s]

Finances/Money
spendthrift n b1605
penny-wise adj b1610
piece of eight n b1610
invest, investment v, n *invest money* b1615
autarky n *financial independence* b1620
financier n b1620
doubloon n b1625
expensive adj *spending much* b1630 ["costing much": b1670]
post v *as in "post a bookkeeping entry"* b1630
proceeds n b1630
scrib n *arch. parsimonious person* b1630
solvent adj b1630
wastethrift n *arch. spendthrift* b1630
pocket money n b1635
pound sterling n b1635 (pound: b1150)
outgo n *opp. of income* b1640
wampum n b1640 (wampumpeag: b1630)
letter of credit n b1645

depreciate v (depreciation: b1740)
exciseman n

Language and Speaking
hyphen n b1605 (verb use: b1815)
vernacular adj *native, applied to language* b1605 [native, applied to art, architecture, etc.: b1870]
expletive n *filler* b1610 ["cussing," "interjection": b1830]
grave n *type of accent mark* b1610
nomenclature n *name; creation of names* b1610 ["system of names": 1600s; "terminology": 1700s]
verbalize v *use verbiage* b1610 ["convert to verb": b1670; "put into words": b1900]
intransitive adj b1615
philology n *study of language* b1615 ["love of learning": b1400]
phrasing n b1615
sesquipedalian adj b1615 (sesquipedal: b1630)
lingua franca n b1620
oral adj *verbal* b1625
initial n b1630
palindrome n b1630
word v *choose words* b1630
etymologist n b1635 (etymologer: b1630)
metaphrase n *type of translation* b1640
say-so n *word* b1640
shibboleth n *type of code* b1640
Anglicism n b1645
cryptology n *mysterious communication* b1645 ["codes": b1935]
homonym n b1645 (homonymy: b1600)
patois n *type of dialect* b1645
polyglot adj *multilingual* b1645
repartee n b1645
semicolon n b1645
loose-tongued adj
prefix n ["title of honor": b1870]

Contractions
we'd contr b1605
you'd contr b1605
they'll contr b1610
they've contr b1615
it's contr b1625
don't contr *also means does not* b1640
who'd contr b1640
couldn't v

Literature/Writing
stenography n 1602 [stenographer: b1800; steno: b1915]
gazette n b1605
versification n b1605
album n *type of book* b1615 ["phonographic recording": b1930]
illegible adj b1615
italic adj *of the typeface* b1615 [in handwriting: b1565] (italics: b1680; italicize: b1790)
writing desk n b1615
amanuensis n *type of assistant* b1620
exegesis n b1620
bestiary n b1625
epigraph n b1625 [obs. type of book imprint: b1600 to 1800s]
holograph n *related to handwriting* b1625 (holography: b1805)
juvenilia n b1625
literati n b1625 (literatus: b1705)
alliteration n b1630 (alliterative: b1765)
allusion n b1630 [obs. "pun," "metaphor": b1550 to 1700s]
doggerel n b1630
excerpt n b1630 (verb use: b1900)
florilegium n *collection, anthology* b1630
Grub Street n b1630
guide n b1630 (guidebook: b1815)
journal n *diary* b1630 [obs. "traveler's guide": b1375 to 1600s; "financial books": b1500; "newspaper, etc.": b1730]

Assorted Lost Verbs

In the title above, how could we have "assorted" lost verbs if we couldn't assort them in the first place? Well, we could—by 1490, though you won't hear the word today. Pity, that—as well as not being able to hear a variety of other verbs that once invigorated English.

Look back to the past for wonderful verbs that have slipped away from us, including:

- *fright* (by 1100), leading to the longer *frighten* (by 1670)

- *insurge* (by 1150), thus *insurgent* (by 1765)

- *clumse* (by 1325), thus *clumsy* (by 1600)

- *conduce* (by 1400), thus *conducive* (by 1650)

- *permute* (by 1400), from *permutation* (by 1375)

- *contuse* (by 1425), from *contusion* (by 1400)

- *restitute* (by 1470), from *restitution* (by 1325)

- *asperse* (by 1490), thus *aspersion* (by 1555)

- *assort* (by 1490), thus *assortment* (by 1615)

- *reluct* (by 1530), thus *reluctance* (by 1645)

- *resile* (by 1530), thus *resilient* (by 1645)

- *extermine* (by 1450), growing to *exterminate* (by 1545)

- *excruciate* (by 1570), thus *excruciating* (by 1600)

- *fledge* (by 1570), thus *fledgling* (by 1830)

- *inhere* (by 1580), about the same time *inherent* appeared

- *convoke* (by 1600), from *convocation* (by 1390)

- *misgive* (by 1615), from *misgiving* (by 1605)

- *belate* (by 1630), about the same time *belated* appeared

- *consternate* (by 1655), from *consternation* (by 1615)

- *insurrect* (by 1850), from *insurrection* (by 1425)

- *obsolesce* (by 1875), from *obsolescent* (by 1755)

- *exposit* (by 1885), from *expository* (by 1600)

---

marker n *type of writing utensil* b1630
print n *printed matter* b1630 (verb use: b1530)
proof n *test run in printing* b1630 [in coinage: b1770; in engraving: b1800; in photography: b1870]
anthology n *collection of poems* b1640 ["gen. collection": b1800] (anthologize v, anthologist n: b1830)
atlas n *book of maps* b1640 [fig. "supporter": b1590]
novel n *book-length fiction* b1640 ["fiction of shorter length": 1560s] (novelist: b1730; novelette: b1800; novella: b1900)
shorthand n/adj b1640
correspondence n *letter-writing* b1645 (correspond, correspondent: b1630)
encyclopedia n *book of learning* b1645 ["learning": b1535] (encyclopedist: b1655)
manifesto n

Communication
express n *fast messenger* b1620 ["fast train": b1870]
press gallery n b1620
account n *story, report* b1630
medium n *as in "the medium of television"* b1630
quotation n *something quoted* b1630 ["numerical method of referencing text": b1530 to 1600s]
post office n b1635
signboard n b1635

Visual Arts/ Photography
calligraphy n b1605 (calligrapher: 1760)
realist n b1605 (realistic: b1830; realism: b1870)
relief n *as in "relief painting"* b1610
technic n *arch. pertaining to art* b1615
technology, technological n, adj *describing the arts* b1615

chef d'oeuvre n *masterwork* b1620
diagram n b1620 (verb use: b1840)
palette n *artist's tool* b1625 ["range of color": b1900]
bas-relief n b1630
illustrate v b1630 (illustration: b1830)
sculptor n b1635 (sculptress: b1665; sculpt: b1865)
plastic art n b1640
crayon n b1645 (verb use: b1665)
intaglio n *type of engraving* b1645

Performing Arts
comedian n b1605 (comedienne: b1860)
groundling n b1605
mime n b1605 (verb use: b1620; mimic n: b1590)
odeum n b1605
verisimilitude n b1605 (verisimilar: b1685)
low comedy n b1610

proscenium n *stage* b1610 ["forestage": b1830]
overact v b1615
playbill n b1620
actress n b1630 (actor, describing both men and women: b1585)
playwright n b1630 (playwriting: b1810; playwrighting: b1900)
gallery n *theater sense*
histrionic adj (histrionics: b1865)

Music
concert n b1605 ["musical harmony": b1605; gen. "harmony, cooperation": b1670]
flutist n b1605 (flute "flutist": b1570)
theorbo n *type of stringed instrument* b1605
baritone n b1610 (adj use: b1730)
chord n b1610
singsong n b1610

harpsichord n b1615 (obs. harpsical: b1630 to 1700s)
warbler n *singer* b1615
intonation n b1620
guitar n b1625
threnody n *elegy* b1625
march n b1630
castanet n b1630
perform v *sing* b1630 [gen. "put on a performance": b1870] (performance: concurrent)
raise v as in *"raise your voice in song"* b1630
requiem n b1630
balladeer n b1640
opera n *the form* b1645 ["opera company": b1670]
serenade n (verb use: b1670)

Entertainment

sword dance n b1605
reviewer n b1615
ropewalker n b1615 (ropedancer: b1650; ropewalk: b1675)
ball n *formal dance* b1630 ["fun," as in "having a ball": b1970]
entertain v *amuse* b1630 (entertainment: b1615)
saltation n *dance* b1630 ["leap": b1650]

Education

tutoress n b1615 (obs. tutrix: b1500 to 1700s; tutor: b1400)
baccalaureate n b1625
indoctrinate v b1630 [fig. "brainwash": b1870] (obs. indoctrine v: b1450 to 1800s)
senior n b1630
undergraduate adj b1630 (noun use: b1700)
curriculum n b1635
scholarly adj b1640 (adv use: b1600)
alumnus n b1645 (alumna: b1880; alum: b1930)
didactic adj/n b1645 (didact: b1955)
man of letters n b1645

Religion

clerical n b1605 (cleric: b1615)
demigoddess n b1605 (demigod: b1530)
prince of darkness n b1605
fakir n b1610
reverend n b1610 (adj use: b1450)
kaddish n *type of prayer* b1615
Koran n b1615
polytheism n b1615
precentor n b1615
theogony n *origins of the gods* b1615
cult n *worship* b1620 ["organized worship": b1680; "fanatical group": b1730]
God's acre n *churchyard* b1620
nonconformist n *spec. rel. sense* b1620 [gen. sense: 1600s] (nonconform v: 1680s)
cleric adj/n b1625 (clerical: b1605)
apocalyptic adj b1630
evangelism n b1630
inheaven, inhell v b1630
mother n as in *"Mother Teresa"* b1630
papess n b1630
prayer beads n b1630
prayerful adj b1630
sanctimony n *religiosity* b1630 [obs. "truly religious": b1470 to 1700s]
theologaster n *bad theologian* b1630
guardian angel n b1635
eldress n b1640
juggernaut n *referring to Krishna* b1640 [fig. use: b1845]
charisma n *God-given talent* b1645 [gen. "aura of authority": b1950; "charm": b1965]
high priestess n b1645 (high priest: b1400)
Second Coming n b1645
antediluvian adj *before the Flood* [fig. "ancient": b1770]
devotional adj (noun use: b1660)
halo n [gen. sense: b1565]
mitzvah n
theosophy n *type of way of seeing God*

Society/Mores/Culture

dissociable adj *asocial* b1605 (dissocial: b1765)
freedman n b1605 (freedwoman: b1870)
ill-bred adj b1605
civil adj *mannerly* b1610 [arch. "civilized": b1555; obs. "kind": 1600s only]
peon n b1610
philanthropy n b1610 (philanthropism: b1730; philanthropic: b1790)
sisterhood n *commonality* b1610 [feminist sense: b1970]
tatterdemalian n *ragamuffin* b1610 (adj use: b1615)
uncivilized adj b1610
urban adj b1610
caste n *social level* b1615 ["breed": b1555]
coquette n b1615 (coquet: b1700)
fief n b1615
indecent adj *obscene* b1615 [gen. "unseemly": b1590]
morals n b1615 (morality: b1375)
Mrs. n b1615 (Mr.: b1450; Ms.: b1950)
nowness n b1615
pariah n *spec. Indian caste* b1615 [gen. "shunned person": b1830]
population n *residents; number of residents* b1615 [obs. "populated place": b1580 to 1600s; "act of populating": b1800]
public health n b1620
unsophisticated adj b1620
belle n b1625
chit n *kid, young woman* b1625
conductress n b1625 (conductor: b1500)
immigrate v b1625 (immigration: b1660; immigrant: b1790)
poor box n b1625
urbane adj *sophisticated* b1625 [obs. "urban": b1535]
waif n *urchin* b1625 ["property not claimed": b1380]
black n *Negro* b1630

genteel adj b1630 [arch. "stylish": b1600] (noun use: b1700)
playboy n b1630 (playgirl: b1935)
poll n *counting votes* b1630 ["head": b1300; obs. "census, headcount": b1630; "vote": b1870; "survey": b1930] (pollster: b1940)
propriety n *properness* b1630 ["true nature": b1400]
thoroughbred adj *of people* b1630 [of horses: b1800]
census n *spec. to Roman census* b1635 [obs. "tax": b1615 to 1800s; gen. "counting": b1770]
country gentleman n b1635
women's rights n b1635 (woman's rights: b1840)
toast v *propose a toast* b1640 (noun use: b1770)
cosmopolitan n b1645 (adj use: b1845; cosmopolite: b1620)
humankind n b1645
emigration n
townspeople n

Government

Caesarism n *totalitarianism* b1605
quorum n *minimum needed for voting* b1605 ["spec. members needed for group decision": b1450]
triarchy n *triumvirate* b1605
dethrone v b1610
citizenship n b1615
district n b1615 [gen. "region": b1730]
gynecocracy n b1615 (gynarchy: b1580)
mesne lord n *lord subserviant to another lord* b1615
nabob n b1615
archduchess n b1620 (archduke: b1530)
autonomy n *self-government* b1625 ["free will": b1800; "independence": b1830] (autonomous: b1800)
crown land n b1625
emir n b1625 (emirate: b1865)
junta n b1625

theocracy n b1625 (theocrat: b1830)

imperatrix n *female emperor* b1630 (imperator: b1600)

regalia n *phys. manifestations of royalty* b1630 ["royal privilege": b1540]

patriarchy n b1635

representative n b1635

councilman n b1640 (councilwoman: b1930; councilperson: b1980)

dyarchy n b1640

queen regnant n *reigning queen* b1640

town meeting n b1640

city hall n (Am) b1645

envoy n b1645

assemblyman n (assemblywoman: b1970; assemblyperson: b1975)

crown jewel n

prime minister n

Politics

foreign affairs n b1615

politician n b1630 [obs. "cunning schemer": b1590 to 1700s] (politico: b1630; pol: b1945)

politico n b1630

stateswoman n b1630 (statesman: b1595)

anarchism n b1645 (anarchy: b1540; anarch: b1670; anarchist: b1680)

demagogue n (verb use: b1660; demogogy: b1655; demogoguery: b1855)

loyalist n

Life

birthplace n b1610

graveless adj *without a grave, deathless* b1610

sire v b1615

Death

cerement n *death shroud— cerecloth* b1605 (cerecloth: b1450)

headsman n *beheader* b1605

inhume n *opp. of exhume* b1605

lethal adj b1605 [describing spiritual death: b1585]

felo-de-se n *suicide "victim"* b1610

kill off v b1610

posthumous adj b1610

deicide n b1615

mummy n b1615 ["medicine made from mummies": b1395] (mummify: b1630)

sepulchral adj b1615

cremation n b1625 (cremate: b1875)

garrote/garote/garotte/ garrotte n b1625 (noun use: b1855)

feral adj *arch. deadly* b1630

finish v *kill* b1630 [obs. "die": b1450 to 1600s]

ganch v b1630

self-homocide n *suicide* b1630 (self-murder: b1565; self-slaughter: b1605; self-violence: b1700)

catafalque n b1645

suicide n b1645 ["victim of suicide": b1770] (suicidal: b1780)

War/Military/Violence

Cadmean victory n *victory with equal losses* b1605

carbine n b1605

disembowel v b1605

fistfight n b1605

fisticuffs n b1605

impale v b1605 ["fence in": b1530]

beefeater n *guard* b1610

exenterate v *disembowel* b1610

militant n *combatant* b1610 [fig. use: b1930]

redoubt n b1610

reinforcement n b1610

aegis n *shield* b1615 [fig. sense: b1795]

aggression n b1615 (aggress v: b1715)

decapitate v b1615 (decapitation: b1650)

drill v *as in "drill instructions"* b1615 (noun use: b1670)

sentry n b1615 (verb use: b1830)

stiletto n b1615

tomahawk n b1615 (verb use: b1650)

explosion n b1620 (explosive adj: b1670)

dragoon n b1625 (verb use: b1690)

foot soldier n b1625

furlough n b1625 (verb use: b1785)

gun v *hunt* b1625 [as in "gun down": b1700]

gunman n b1625

sanguinary adj *bloodthirsty* b1625

sciamachy n *fighting an imaginary enemy* b1625

divell v *obs. pull asunder* b1630 [u1800s] (divellicate v: b1670)

flag of truce n b1630

insult n b1630 (verb use: b1700)

level v *raze, destroy* b1630

load v *as in "load a gun"* b1630

midshipman n b1630

slug n *as in "bullet slug"* b1630

tactics n b1630 (tactical: b1670; tactic: b1800)

drub v b1635 [fig. use: b1830] (noun use: b1630; drubbing: b1650)

brigade n b1640 (brigadier: b1670)

lambaste v *beat, hit* b1640

matchlock n b1640

platoon n b1640 [sports sense: b1730]

breastwork n b1645

commander in chief n b1645

field artillery n b1645

hamstring v b1645

recruit n b1645 [obs. "reinforcements": u1700s]

reveille n b1645

aggressor n

campaign n [gen. use: b1770; election use: b1810] (verb use: b1705)

clash n [fig. use: b1785]

coup d'etat n (coup: b1855)

firearm n

forte n *strongest part of a sword* [applied to people: b1700]

headquarters n [gen. use: b1800]

melee n (arch. mellay: b1450)

Crime/Punishment/ Enforcement

jailbird n b1605

fence v *sell stolen items* b1610 (noun use: b1700)

mutineer n b1610 (verb use: b1700)

consigliere n b1615

criminality n b1615

housebreaking n *as in "breaking and entering"* b1620

picaroon n/v *pirate, rascal* b1625

plagiarism n b1625 (obs. plagiary: b1600 to 1600s; plagiarist: b1700; plagiarize: b1720)

punitive adj b1625 (punitory: b1730)

criminal n b1630 (adj use: b1400)

criminate v *incriminate* b1645

workhouse n *poorhouse* b1645

desperado n ["someone in despair": b1610 to 1700s] (desperate n: b1565)

highwayman n

The Law

process server n b1615

adjudication n b1620 (adjudicate: b1700)

counselor-at-law n b1620

legalize v b1620

libel n/v b1620 [type of document: b1300; obs. "libelous publication": b1530 to 1700s]

lawsuit n b1625

case n *leg. proceedings* b1630 ["argumentation," as in "state your case": b1600]

dismiss v *as in "dismiss a claim"* b1630

foreman n b1630 (forewoman: b1730; foreperson: b1975)

jurisprudent n *jurist* b1630 (jurisprudence: b1660)

mischief n *as in "malicious mischief"* b1630

mistrial n b1630

disbar v b1635

civil liberty n b1645

court order n

The Fantastic/ Paranormal

genius loci n b1605
leprechaun n b1605
merman n b1605 (mermaid: b1350; merwoman: b1830)
specter n b1605 [fig., as in "the specter of bankruptcy": b1800] (arch. spectrum: b1615; spectral: b1815)
underworld n *land of the dead* b1610
mythological adj b1615 (mythologic: b1630)
spectrum n *arch. specter* b1615
troll n b1620 [obs. type of witch: b1450]
hippocampus n b1630 ["seahorse": b1610]
numen n *type of supernatural force* b1630 (numinous: b1650)
pixie n b1630
kobold n *type of gnome* b1635
sea devil n b1635
netherworld n b1640
hippogriff n
sea serpent n

Magic

fascination n *arch. spell-casting* b1605 ["ability to fascinate": b1700; "preoccupation": b1870]
hellbroth n b1605
fetish n b1615 ["preoccupation": b1840; sexual sense: b1900] (fetishism: b1805)
osteomancy n *divining with bones* b1630
psychomancy n b1630
talisman n b1640
love potion n
rhabdomancy n *divination by wands*

Interjections

hush interj b1605 (husht: b1470)
old boy interj b1605
phew interj b1605
uh interj b1605
huh interj b1610
gardyloo interj b1625

hocus-pocus interj b1625 (noun use: b1670; verb use: b1700; hokeypokey: b1850)
avast v *imperative stop* b1630
ave interj/n *greetings* b1630
damnation interj b1630
death interj b1630
fiddlesticks interj b1630
gee interj/v *as in "gee and haw"* b1630 (gee-ho interj: b1670)
gramercy interj *mercy me* b1630 ["thanks": b1350]
hillo interj b1630
rubbish interj b1630
'sdeath interj *God's death* b1630
um interj b1630
wounds interj b1630
wow interj b1630
yah interj *yay* b1630
congratulations interj b1635
zooks interj b1635

Slang

hellcat n b1605
moll n *prostitute* b1605 [as in "gun moll": b1825] (molly: b1730)
upshot n *result* b1605 [fig. and lit. "last shot": b1535; "end": b1600 to 1600s]
cock-and-bull story n b1610
jockey v *as in "jockey for position"* b1610
pound-foolish adj b1610
powwow n 1624 (verb use: b1645)
half-baked adj b1625
whopping adj b1625
bull n *ridiculousness; nonsense* b1630
cook up v *concoct* b1630
egg n as in "he's a good egg" b1630
ferret n *detective* b1630
high adj *as in "living high"* b1630
infantry n *infants* b1630
poppy n b1630
rhino n *money* b1630
ring v *as in "ring true"* b1630
screw up v *as in "screw up courage"* b1630 ["botch": b1680]
trim v *cheat* b1630

whip up v *create fast* b1630 ["excite": b1830]
wizard n *skilled person* b1630 (adj use: b1580; verb use: b1630; wizardry: b1585)
worm v *lit., as in "worm your way in"* b1630 [fig. use: b1730]
ape v b1635
hoof v b1645

Insults

charlatan n *snake-oil salesman* b1605 ["faker": b1700]
clodpoll n *dolt* b1605
hunks n *a Scrooge* b1605
kinglet n b1605
pigeon-livered adj b1605
trash n b1605
whey-face n b1605
has-been n b1610
slur n b1610 ["thin mud": b1500] (verb use: b1660)
stinker n *nasty person* b1610 ["something bad," as in "the play was a stinker": b1920] (stinkeroo: b1935)
two-faced adj b1610
butterfingered adj b1615 (butterfingers: b1840)
ignoramus n b1615
trollop n b1615
faineant n *do-nothing* b1620 (adj use: b1855)
insult v *deprecate* b1620 ["brag": b1540] (noun use: b1675)
dunderhead n b1625 (arch. dunderpate: b1700)
oaf n b1625 (oafish: b1610)
addlepated adj b1630 (addled: b1715; addle-brained: b1870)
buffoon n *clownish person* b1630 [obs. type of dance: b1550; "professional jester": b1585] (buffoonery: b1625)
lickspittle n *brownnoser* b1630
loudmouthed adj b1630 (loudmouth: b1670)
meretricious adj *related to prostitution* b1630
mullipuff n *arch. vile person* b1630
poopnoddy n *arch. dolt* b1630

slubberdegullion n *arch. slob* b1630
fatuous adj *imbecilic* b1635 ["without phys. taste": b1610]
louse n b1635
thick-witted adj b1635
half-wit n b1640
slattern n *slut* b1640 (adj use: b1700)
sneak n *sneaky person* b1645
empty-headed adj
hatchet face n
hussy n ["housewife": b1505]
simpleton n (simp: b1905)

Phrases

be-all and end-all n b1605
coign of vantage n *corner of vantage* b1605
eagle eye n b1605
foregone conclusion n b1605
primrose path n b1605
pull in v b1605
yeoman's service n b1605
ad infinitum adv b1610
arm's length n b1610
hit-or-miss adj b1610 (hit-and-miss: b1900)
pitched battle n b1610
salad days n b1610
sea change n b1610
back and forth adv/adj b1615 (noun use: b1950)
dead reckoning n b1615
point of honor n b1615
in effigy adv b1620
iron man n b1620
jack-of-all-trades n b1620
ex post facto adv *after the fact* b1625 (adj use: b1790)
little woman n b1625
man of straw n b1625
bread and butter n/adj b1630
chapter and verse n b1630
creature comfort n b1630
end-all n b1630
long run n *as in "in the long run"* b1630
young blood n b1630
Hobson's choice n *no choice at all* b1635
how-do-you-do n *as in "that's a fine how-do-you-do"* b1635
elbow grease n b1640
staff of life n b1640

lip service n b1645

pot-valiant adj *drunkenly brave* b1645

second childhood n b1645

tag, rag and bobtail n *rabble* b1645

ad nauseum adv

bed of roses n

breathing space n

grain of salt n

heaven-sent adj

humble pie n (eat humble pie: b1830)

moot point n

ups and downs n

whipping boy n

General/Miscellaneous

accommodation n b1605

apex n b1605

archive n b1605 (verb use: b1900; archives: b1840; archivist: b1755; archival: b1830)

coincidence n *correspondence; being in the same place* b1605 ["things happening simultaneously": b1700] (coincidental: b1800)

competition n b1605 (compete: b1615; competitive: b1830)

condensation n *e.g., water condensing* b1605 [literary condensation: b1800] (condense: b1450)

contexture n *weaving* b1605

defensive n b1605 [obs. type of medicine, preventive: b1450 to 1700s]

density n *being dense* b1605 [in physics: b1670; as in "population density": b1870]

detail n *attention to detail* b1605 [the detail itself: b1800] (verb use: b1650; detailed: b1740)

divestiture, divest n, v b1605

emmissary n b1605

exposure n b1605

gibber v b1605

hint n b1605 (verb use: b1650; henten v "tell": b1400)

individual adj/n *spec. to an individual* b1605 [obs. "indivisible": b1425 to 1600s]

(individuality: b1615; obs. individuity: b1630 to 1800s)

moppet n b1605 (obs. mop: b1425 to 1500s; mopsy: b1600)

odium n *odiousness* b1605

outbreak n b1605

pioneer n *forerunner* b1605 [mil. sense: b1525]

premium n *prize* b1605 [as in "insurance premium": b1670; "bonus," etc.: b1700] (adj use: b1845)

prolusion n *prelude* b1605

redundancy n b1605 (redundance: b1600)

reticence n b1605 (reticency: b1620; reticent: b1835)

retrospect n b1605 (retrospection: b1635)

scrutiny n *examination* b1605 [rel. term: b1415]

sheen n b1605 (adj use: b900)

splotch n b1605 (verb use: b1655; splodge n/v: b1870)

squabble n/v b1605

surface n b1605 [fig. use: b1730] (adj use: b1665)

swoop n b1605

system n b1605

topic n *subject* b1605 (topical: b1870)

tutelage n *guardianship* b1605 ["tutoring": b1870]

adaptation n b1610

appetence n *appetite, desire* b1610 (appetency: b1630)

blind side n b1610 (verb use: b1970)

colloquium n *conference* b1610 [obs. "conversation": b1610 to 1700s]

earshot n b1610

equanimity n b1610 [obs. "fairness": u1700s]

excitant n b1610

heroine n b1610 (hero: b1400)

impropriety n b1610

incrustation n b1610

inlander n b1610

masterwork n b1610

mountaineer n *mountain dweller* b1610 ["mountain climber": b1870; slang "rube": b1900]

onlooker n b1610

reliance n b1610 (reliant: b1860)

reunion n b1610 [as in "family reunion": b1830]

role n b1610

separator n b1610

spilth n *spillage* b1610

syndicate n *group of sindics* b1610 [type of business group: b1870; "crime mob": b1930] (verb use: b1885)

trichotomy n *akin to dichotomy* b1610

assortment n b1615 (assort v: b1490; assorted adj: b1800)

beat n *as in "drumbeat"* b1615

beneficiary n b1615

bump v/n *as in "bump your head"* b1615 [slang "push out," as in "bump from a flight": b1930]

burr n *ragged edge* b1615

cabal n *conspiracy* b1615 ["secret organization": b1660] (verb use: b1690)

cabinet n *group* b1615

caress n b1615 (verb use: b1660)

coalition n *result of coalescing* b1615 [political sense: b1715] (coalize "form coalition": b1800)

coloration n b1615

criterion n b1615

curb n *gen. restraint* b1615 (verb use: b1530)

deferment n b1615

delegation n *delegating* b1615 ["group of delegates": b1800]

emulsion n b1615 (emulsify: b1860)

expediency n b1615 (expedience: b1470)

generalist n b1615

guru n b1615

gyration n b1615 (gyrate: b1830)

ignition n b1615 (ignite: b1666)

jumble n b1615 (verb use: b1570)

longevity n b1615

niche n b1615 (verb use: b1760)

nonsense n b1615

puzzle n *puzzlement* b1615 ["challenge": b1670; as in "crossword puzzle": b1830]

quarter n *reprieve* b1615

ravage n/v b1615

reaction n *as in "for every action there's a reaction"* b1615

repatriate n b1615 (noun use: b1930; repatriation: b1595)

resource n b1615

revision, revisal n *revising* b1615 (revise n: b1570)

say n *as in "have your say"* b1615

sensation n *sensing* b1615 (arch. sensate adj: b1470)

series n b1615

slope n b1615 (verb use: b1595)

smear n *smudge* b1615 [obs. "ointment": b800 to 1600s; "slander": b1970] (verb use: b1100)

stimulus n b1615

suction n b1615

synopsis n b1615 (synopsize: b1885)

transmission n *transfer* b1615 ["transmitting": b1730] (transmit: b1400)

tremor n *quiver* b1615 [obs. "extreme fear": b1375 to 1400s; "small earthquake": b1670] (tremulous: b1615)

vehicle n *agent, facilitator* b1615 [cars, etc.: b1670]

well-being n b1615

whatness n b1615

whitener n b1615

avocation n b1620

blacklist n b1620 (verb use: b1720)

generosity n b1620 ["noble birth": b1425]

gusto n b1620

quota n b1620 ["ration": b1670]

signpost n *the post itself* b1620 [post and sign: b1870]

yogi n b1620 (yogini: b1970)

abduction, abduct n, v b1625

accolade n b1625

adhesion n *sticking* b1625

bedlam n *chaos* b1625 [obs. "mentally ill person": b1525 to 1700s] (bedlamite: b1590)

bulge n b1625 [obs. "wallet": b1250 to 1600s]

condonation n *official condoning* b1625

convection n b1625 (convect: b1885)

facet n b1625 [fig. use: b1820]

flux n *change* b1625 ["outflow": b1350]

foothold n b1625

frontage n b1625

horripilation n b1625

impostor n b1625 ["conniver": b1590]

inexistence n b1625

ingrate n b1625 (obs. adj use: b1400 to 1500s)

onslaught n b1625

plaudit n b1625

scintillate, scintillation v, n b1625 (scintilla: b1695)

scuttle n *quick shuffle* b1625 (verb use: b1450)

selection n *selecting* b1625 ["something selected": b1830]

spray n *as in "water spray"* b1625 (verb use: b1830)

squalor n b1625

taction n *contact* b1625

trigger n b1625 (verb use: b1920)

veracity n *truthfulness* b1625 ["truth": b1770]

acquirement n b1630

agenda n b1630 (agendum: b1850)

aim n *goal* b1630

apparatus n b1630

attachment n *predilection* b1630

boundary n b1630

cataclysm n b1630

confrontation n *meeting* b1630 ["hostilities": b1970] (confrontational: b1970)

contact n b1630 [as in "a business contact": b1970]

continuant adj/n b1630

cut n *edit* b1630 (verb use: b1350)

discharge n *act of excretion* b1630 [the excretion itself: b1700]

disposal n *as in "at one's disposal"* b1630

dwarfling n b1630

exhibit n b1630

exodus n b1630

fortunes n *experiences* b1630

gamut n b1630 [spec. music sense: b1450]

gloom n b1630

grain n *as in "wood grain"* b1630

helix n b1630 [architectural sense: b1565]

incidence n b1630 ["something incidental": b1425]

intimate n b1630

jig-a-jig n b1630

kilter n (Am) b1630

layer n b1630 (verb use: b1930)

locality n *being local* b1630 ["neighborhood": b1870]

main n *as in "water main"* b1630 (obs. adj use "flowing": b1350 to 1600s)

manufacture n *act of creating* b1630 ["something created": b1570 to 1700s]

mass n *massiveness* b1630

misapprehension n b1630

miscarriage n *as in "miscarriage of justice"* b1630

mistake n b1630 (verb use: b1395; mistaken: b1570)

model n *smaller version* b1630

nib n b1630 ["beak": b1590]

plunder n/v b1630 (plunderage: b1800; plunderous: b1845)

proselytess n b1630 (proselyte: b1375)

rake n *incline* b1630

recess n *as in "lunch recess"* b1630 (verb use: b1900)

respects n *as in "last respects"* b1630

settlement n b1630 [a place: b1700]

shock n *jolt, blow* b1630

sludge n b1630

snap n *snapping sound* b1630 (verb use: b1700)

station n b1630

story n *hearsay* b1630

tendency n b1630

tone n *as in "tone of voice"* b1630 [arch. "accent": b1700]

trail n *evidence of passage* b1630 ["path": b1830]

trial n *act of trying* b1630

tussle n b1630 (verb use: b1640)

vastitude, vastity n *vastness* b1630 [obs. "devastation": b1545]

veto n b1630 (verb use: b1710)

wedge n *fig., as in "a wedge of pie"* b1630

bagatelle n *trifle* b1635 [type of game: b1830]

bilk n b1635 (verb use: b1675)

conformist n b1635

contemporary adj/n b1635 [type of design: b1870] (contempo: b1980)

craunch n/v *crunch* b1635

culmination n b1635 (culminate: b1650)

efficiency n b1635 [obs. "source of efficiency": b1595] (efficient: b1800)

emergency n b1635 ["emerging": b1670] (adj use: b1900; obs. emergence "emergency": b1670 to 1800s)

equipoise n *equilibrium* b1635 (verb use: b1665)

fact n b1635 [as in "after the fact": b1500] (factual: b1835)

farrago n *potpourri* b1635

fiat n b1635

ivory black n b1635

prerequisite adj/n b1635 (prerequire: b1630)

query n b1635 (verb use: b1655)

apologist n b1640

chaff n *banter* b1640 (verb use: b1830)

fundamental, fundamentals n b1640

imprimatur n b1640

independence n b1640 (independency: b1770)

model n *something to emulate, example* b1640

onus n b1640

polemic n b1640 (polemicize: b1950)

reprimand n b1640 (verb use: b1685)

research n b1640 [gen. "search": b1580] (verb use: b1595)

tidbit n b1640

archaism n *use of the archaic; the archaic thing itself* b1645

cascade n b1645 (verb use: b1705)

clinker n *slag* b1645

complex n b1645

compliant, compliancy, compliance adj, n, n b1645 (compliable: b1670)

extravagance n b1645

failure n b1645 ["person who fails": b1870]

identification n b1645

impetus n b1645

intimacy n b1645 ["sex": b1700]

lampoon n b1645 (verb use: b1660)

monotone n b1645

phosphorus n b1645 ["anything phosphorescent": b1630] (phosphorescent: b1770; phosphoresce, phosphorescence: b1795)

repugnance n *repulsion* b1645

retrieval n b1645

save-all n b1645

spare n *something extra* b1645

trill v *warble* b1645 (noun use: b1650)

undersigned n *as in "we the undersigned"* b1645

vista n b1645

antenna n b1645

ascetic n/adj (ascesis: b1865)

boss n *chief* ["political leader": b1870] (verb use: b1860; bossy: b1885; boss man: b1935)

club n *organization* [obs. "secret organization": u1800s] (clubbable "sociable": b1785; clubber "so-

cialite": b1635; clubby "sociable": b1860)

clutter n *junk, litter* [obs. "clotted material": b1560 to 1600s] (verb use: b1675)

coexistence n (coexist: b1670)

confinement n ["childbirth": b1800]

continuum n

cortege n

data, datum n [applied to numbers: b1900]

deference n (defer: b1700; deferent, deferential: b1825)

dissolvent adj/n

dubiosity n

impulse n (verb use: b1615)

insignia n *gen. badges* ["one badge": b1800]

intrigue n (verb use: b1615)

mechanics n

membership n *being a member* ["group of members": b1870]

namesake n

protuberant, protuberance adj, n (protuberate: b1580; protuberancy: b1655; protruberance: b1830)

recession n

result n (verb use: b1425)

scheme n *plan* [obs. "map of the heavens": b1600 to 1800s] (verb use: b1770)

sobriquet n

somewhere n

squad n [gen. "group": b1800]

squish n/v *smoosh* ["make a squishing sound": b1800] (squishy: b1850)

swatch n

trustee n (verb use: b1820)

Things

knapsack n b1605

flotsam n b1610

nozzle n *projection* b1610 ["spout": b1690]

pedal n b1615 (verb use: b1890)

podium n b1615

rocket n b1615

tank n *reservoir* b1620

kiosk n b1625

festoon n *type of garland* b1630 (verb use: b1800; festoonery: b1840)

plug n *e.g., a stopper* b1630 (verb use: b1630)

sheepshank n *type of knot* b1630

unit n *item* b1630

enginery n *engines* b1645

handhold n b1645

Description

authoritative adj b1605

classic adj *excellent* b1605 ["related to Greek/Roman arts": b1630] (noun use: b1715; classical: b1590)

cryptic adj b1605

cursory adj b1605

de facto adv b1605 (adj use: b1700)

earthborn adj b1605

earthbound adj *bound to the earth* b1605 ["bound for the earth": b1935]

enervate adj b1605 (verb use: b1615)

enviable adj b1605

extensive adj *common, wide-ranging* b1605 ["extending": b1425]

full-blown adj b1605

horrid adj b1605 ["bristling": b1590; "unpleasant": b1670]

ill-starred adj *ill-fated* b1605

immane adj *huge, monstrous* b1605

inept adj b1605

inflammable adj b1605 [obs. med. sense: b1425]

interim adj b1605 (noun use: b1630)

majestic adj b1605

mellifluent adj b1605

monumental adj b1605

nefarious adj b1605

open-eyed adj b1605

opposeless adj *incapable of being opposed* b1605

outward-bound adj b1605

panic adj b1605

pendulous adj b1605 [obs. "overhanging": b1605 to 1700s] (pendulum: b1660)

perceptible adj b1605 [obs.

"able to perceive": b1645 to 1700s]

periodical adj b1605 (periodic: b1645)

primal adj b1605

provisional adj b1605

redundant adj *duplicating* b1605 ["abundant": b1595]

remarkable adj b1605 (obs. remark "remarkableness": b1635 to 1700s)

seamy adj *fig.* b1605 [lit. "seamed": b1600]

searchless adj *impenetrable* b1605

secluded adj b1605 (seclusion: b1300)

septic adj b1605

stealthy adj b1605

stentorian adj b1605 [stentor: b1610] (stentorious: b1530)

succulent, succulence adj, n b1605

susceptible adj b1605

tacit adj *silent* b1605 ["implied": b1670]

unique adj *one-of-a-kind* b1605

unpregnant adj *clumsy, ineffectual* b1605

vice versa adv b1605

vulnerable adj b1605

bucolic adj b1610 (noun use "type of poem": b1530; bucolical: b1525)

conflicting adj b1610

customary adj *normal* b1610 ["by habit instead of by law": b1525] (customable: b1350 to 1600s)

dual adj b1610

elephantine adj b1610

explicit adj b1610

fabled adj b1610

fabulous adj *superlative sense* b1610 ["like a fable": b1425]

facial adj *face-to-face* b1610 ["related to the face": b1820]

fatidic adj *prophetic* b1610 (fatiloquent: b1670)

historic adj b1610 (historical: b1425)

honorary adj b1610

hydraulic adj b1610

inebriated adj b1610 (inebriety: b1790; inebriate n: b1800; inebrious: b1870)

innovative adj b1610

insipid adj *without flavor* b1610 [fig. "dull": b1630]

invidious adj b1610

involved adj *complex* b1610

irredeemable adj b1610

limited adj b1610 [obs. "fixed": b1555 to 1600s]

lush adj b1610 [obs. "soft": b1450]

made-up adj b1610

precipitant adj b1610 (noun use: b1700)

problematic adj b1610

progressive adj *involving steps in a progression* b1610 (progression: b1570)

synonymous adj b1610

thriving adj b1610

uncalled-for adj b1610

underground adj b1610 [fig. use: b1700] (adv use: b1575)

weatherworn adj b1610

willy-nilly adv b1610 (adj use: b1900; william-nilliam: b1930)

admissible adj b1615

alienable adj b1615

astute adj b1615

certified adj b1615

closet adj *secret* b1615

comprehensive adj b1615

consecutive adj b1615 (consecution: b1535)

daughter adj b1615

decisive adj *deciding* b1615 ["determined": b1770]

directional adj b1615 (noun use: b1885)

feudal adj b1615 (feud "fee": b1350; feudal system: b1780; feudalism: b1820)

fictitious adj b1615

fragmentary adj b1615 (fragmental: b1800)

gigantean adj b1615 (gigantic: b1655; gigantesque: b1825)

handmade adj b1615

independent adj b1615 (independence: b1640)

jejune adj *not nutritive, not significant, dull* b1615 [obs. "starved": u1700s]

livable adj b1615

pervious adj b1615

productive adj b1615

retroactive adj b1615

self-made adj b1615

sizable adj b1615

skin-deep adj b1615

striking adj b1615

tactile adj b1615 (tact "touch": b1655)

tremulous adj b1615 (tremulant: b1840)

vociferous adj b1615 (vociferant: b1610)

voluminous adj b1615

whirlwind adj b1615

aboveboard adj b1620

adequate adj b1620 (adequacy: b1810)

belated adj b1620

considerable adj *large* b1620 [obs. "ponderable": b1450 to 1600s]

explanatory, explanative adj b1620

flaccid adj b1620

groundless adj *without foundation* b1620 [obs. "bottomless": b900 to 1600s]

irrefutable adj b1620

jury adj *makeshift* b1620

outdated adj b1620 (outdate v: b1650)

pressing adj *urgent* b1620 ["oppressive": b1600]

superordinate adj *opp. of subordinate* b1620

tasty adj b1620 ["showing refined taste": b1730]

trashy adj b1620

turgid adj b1620 (obs. turgent: b1450)

assumed adj b1625

ghast adj *ghastly* b1625

hazy adj b1625 (haze: b1710)

heterogeneous adj *opp. of homogeneous* b1625 (heterogeneal: b1605)

practicing adj b1625

previous adj b1625

put-on adj b1625 (noun use: b1930)

roomy adj b1625

sapid adj *flavorful, opp. of insipid* b1625

selective adj b1625

splendid adj *magnificent,*

wonderous b1625 ["excellent": b1670]

stock adj *on-hand* b1625 (noun use: b1450)

swimmingly adv b1625

taut adj b1625 [obs. "overextended": b1425] (tauten: b1815)

territorial adj *pertaining to territory* b1625 ["protecting territory": b1930]

unerring adj b1625

acid adj b1630 (noun use: b1700; acidity: b1620; acidic: b1880)

aimless adj b1630

all right adj *satisfactory* b1630

anywhither adv b1630

astride adv b1630

aweigh adj b1630

bluff adj *with a smooth front* b1630 ["frank": b1730]

consequential adj *resulting* b1630 ["weighty, important": b1730]

corroborant adj *invigorating* b1630

crude adj *jury-rigged* b1630

delible adj *opp. of indelible* b1630

drear adj *dreary* b1630 (obs. noun use: b1570 to 1800s)

effable adj b1630

elaborate adj b1630 ["well-put-together": b1585; obs. "created laboriously": b1595 to 1800s]

exciting adj b1630

expressive adj *communicative* b1630

fanciful adj b1630 ["not real," "whimsical": b1670]

flat adj *as in "flat beer"* b1630

furthersome adj *aiding* b1630

galore adv b1630

germane adj b1630 ["akin": b300]

great adj *talented, accomplished, as in "she's great at math"* b1630

high-handed adj b1630

impertinent adj *impudent* b1630 ["not pertinent": b1395] (impertinence: b1715)

intangible adj b1630 (noun use: b1915)

ironic adj b1630 (irony: b1505; ironical, ironically: b1580)

minute adj *small* b1630 ["chopped small": b1475]

miscellaneous adj b1630 (miscellany: b1600; obs. miscellany adj: b1630 to 1700s; obs. miscellaneal adj: b1670 to 1700s)

nominal adj *pertaining to names; in name only* b1630 ["pertaining to nouns": 1400s]

olive adj b1630 (olive green: b1760; olive drab: b1900)

parenthetical adj b1630 (parenthetic: b1780)

pasty adj b1630

peccable adj *opp. of impeccable* b1630

placid adj b1630

profligate adj b1630 (profligacy: b1740)

rancid adj b1630

sensory adj b1630

shoreless adj *limitless* b1630

snug adj *comfortable* b1630 ["fitting tightly": b1840]

spurious adj *false* b1630 [lit. "bastard": b1500]

submarine adj b1630

succinct adj *brief* b1630 [arch. "surrounded": b1450]

summarily adj *right now* b1630

superable adj *overcomeable* b1630

surreptitious adj *stealthy, secretive* b1630 ["obtained by misrepresentation": b1450]

tangential adj *lit.* b1630 [fig. use: b1825]

timeless adj b1630 [obs. "poorly timed": b1560]

turbid adj *phys. not clear* b1630 [fig. "not clear": b1450]

ungainsayable adj *undeniable* b1630

white adj *Caucasian* b1630 (noun use: b1700)

disaffected adj b1635 (disaffect: b1645)

feverish adj *fig.* b1635 [lit. use: b1400]

fugacious adj *quickly gone* b1635 (fugacity: b1630)

heavy-handed adj b1635 (heavy-footed: b1625)

identical adj b1635

intimate adj b1635 (noun use: b1630; intimacy: b1645)

nocuous adj *opp. of innocuous* b1635

numbing adj b1635

occasional adj *every once in a while* b1635 [pertaining to an occasion: b1640]

plastic adj *supplying shape* b1635 ["pliable": b1715; "made of plastic": b1930] (noun use: b1905; plasticity: b1785)

rapid adj b1635 (rapidity: b1620)

specific adj *peculiar, as in "specific to" someone or something* b1635 (noun use: b1665)

subservient adj b1635 (subserve: b1620; subserviency: b1665; subservience: b1680)

suggestive adj *making a suggestion* b1635 ["naughty": b1900]

superhuman adj b1635

tremendous adj *awe- and fear-inspiring* b1635 [modern sense of "great, wonderful": b1830]

unblenched adj *undaunted* b1635

brummagem adj *tawdry, spurious* b1640

continuous adj b1640 (continuate adj: b1425)

extraneous adj b1640

fathomless adj b1640

fireproof adj b1640 (verb use: b1870)

genuine adj b1640 ["sincere": b1870]

graphic adj b1640

inconsiderable adj b1640 [obs. "unimaginable": b1600]

satisfactory adj *adequate* b1640

scrannel adj *cacophonic* b1640

sensuous adj b1640

transpicuous adj *obvious; transparent* b1640

unbeknownst adj b1640

unpopular adj b1640

untenable adj b1640

vicarious adj *substitute* b1640 ["imagined": b1930] (vicarial: b1620)

vivid adj *bright; clear; vivacious* b1640 [as in "vivid memory": b1830]

airborne adj b1645

aqueous adj b1645

backstairs adj b1645

commensurate adj b1645

deleterious adj b1645

disposable adj *at one's disposal* b1645

emblematic adj b1645

homogeneous adj b1645

inalienable adj b1645

instantaneous adj b1645

intrinsic adj *essential* b1645 ["inner": b1490] (intrinsical: b1550)

linear adj b1645

opaque adj b1645 [obs. "in the dark": b1425 to 1700s; rare "nonreflecting": b1700s]

periodic adj b1645 (periodical adj: b1605)

pointy adj b1645

quasi adj b1645 (adv use: b1485)

retardant adj b1645 (noun use: b1955)

second-string adj b1645

shipshape adj b1645

slow-footed adj b1645

steamy adj b1645

supposable adj *conceivable* b1645

tantamount adj b1645

wholesale adj *lit. and fig.* b1645 (adv use: b1760)

ambidextrous adj (ambidexter, ambidexterity n: b1600)

analogous adj

bizarre adj [obs. "irascible": b1300] (bizarrerie: b1750)

canorous adj *euphonious*

central adj (noun use: b1890; centric: b1590)

complicated adj

conclusive adj ["summarizing": b1540; "ending": b1615]

conducive adj (conduce v: b1500)

derelict adj *abandoned* ["negligent": b1870]

designate adj *as in "judge designate"*

discriminating adj

dispensable adj *able to be dispensed with* ["eligible for dispensation": b1530]

erumpent adj *erupting*

experiential adj

exsanguine adj *bloodless*

fancy adj *fanciful* [opp. of "plain": b1755]

florid adj *ruddy* ["covered with flowers": b1645]

handy adj *nearby*

impervious adj

incognito adj/adv (noun use: b1640; incognita: b1670)

indigenous adj

ineffective adj (ineffectual: b1425; inefficacious: b1660)

inert adj [chemical sense: b1830]

luciferous adj *illuminating*

nutrient adj (nutrient: b1830)

overactive adj

pat adj *as in "pat answers"*

pictorial adj

precocious adj [lit. "flowering prematurely": b1650]

prolific adj [applied to people: b1970] (prolificity: b1725; prolificacy: b1800)

reversible adj (noun use: b1865)

ulterior adj

Colors

tortoiseshell n b1605

flesh color n b1615

primary color n b1615

raven adj *black* b1635

emerald green n

Actions/Verbs

aroint v *away with thee* b1605

blanket v b1605

civilize v b1605 (civilized: b1615; civilization: b1775)

comingle v b1605

confabulate v *talk* b1605 (confab: b1705)

contest v *fight* b1605 ["question": b1670] (noun use: b1645; contestant: b1665)

demean v *degrade* b1605 ["to exhibit demeanor": b1300]

disquantity v *lessen* b1605

disseminate v b1605 (adj use: b1425)

elbow v *nudge* b1605

elicit v b1605

embroil v b1605

enliven v *fig. and lit.* b1605

enmesh v b1605

ensky v *exalt, elevate* b1605

exist v b1605 ["sustain": b1800]

expunge v b1605

flop v *make a flopping sound* b1605 ["fall": b1840]

forebode v b1605

foredoom v *condemn* b1605 ["preordain": b1565] (noun use: b1570)

hanker v b1605 (hankering: b1665)

humanize v b1605

immerse v b1605

impact v *as in "impacted tooth"* b1605 ["make phys. impact": b1920; "make fig. impact": b1935] (noun use: b1785)

instate v b1605

label v *attach label* b1605 ["characterize, stereotype": b1870]

lancinate v *pierce* b1605

palter v *waffle* b1605

pander v b1605

recriminate v b1605 (recrimination: b1615)

resent v b1605

satirize v b1605

sizzle v b1605 (noun use: b1825)

skirt v *border* b1605 (noun use, as in "outskirts": b1470)

snap v *break* b1605

succumb v *give way* b1605 ["cause to give way": b1490 to 1500s]

torrefy v *scorch* b1605

tweak v *as in "tweak a nose"* b1605 ["hone": b1970] (tweak: b1610)

vegetate v b1605

yap v b1605

cake v b1610

castigate v b1610 (castigation: b1390)

convince v b1610 [obs. "conquer," "win an argument," "disprove": b1530 to 1700s] (convincing adj: b1615)

eavesdrop v b1610 (eavesdropper: b1450)

emasculate v *lit. and fig.* b1610 (adj use: b1630)

evidence v b1610

exit v b1610 (noun use: b1590)

familiarize v b1610

harass v b1610

immingle v *intermingle* b1610

indicate v b1610

preside v b1610

size v *measure* b1610

submerge v b1610

taper v *as in "taper off"* b1610 [obs. "rise": b1590] (noun use: b900)

dabble v/n *work without dedication* b1615 ["sprinkle": b1580]

disinter v b1615

dominate v *lord over* b1615 ["be conspicuous": b1830]

elaborate v *decide details* b1615 ["build up": b1600; "explain in more detail": b1970]

emancipate v b1615 (emancipation: b1635)

enisle v *make an island of* b1615 [fig. "isolate": b1870]

ensphere v b1615

extricate v b1615

facilitate v b1615 (facile: b1485)

foment v *incite* b1615 ["apply poultice": b1400]

fraternize v b1615

guggle v *gurgle* b1615

immerge v *immerse* b1615

intersect v b1615 [geometry sense: b1670] (intersection: b1560)

irrigate v *dampen* b1615 [agricultural sense: b1625] (irrigat adj: b1450)

list v *tilt* b1615 (noun use: b1635)

modulate v b1615 (modulation: b1570)

monopolize v b1615

muzzle v *silence* b1615

outpace v b1615

patter v *pat* b1615 (noun use: b1845)

realize v *make real* b1615 (realization: concurrent)

refurbish v b1615

reimburse v b1615 (imburse: b1570)

retaliate v b1615

scrawl v b1615 (noun use: b1695)

specialize v *make special* b1615 ["concentrate on a specialty": b1900] (specialization: b1845)

unsight v *block the view* b1615

compete v b1620 (competition: b1605; competitive: b1830)

disgust v *repulse* b1620 [obs. "be repulsed": b1605 to 1800s] (disgustful: b1615)

improve v *better* b1620 ["cultivate": b1475; "turn a profit": b1530]

ingest, ingestion v, n b1620

niggle v b1620 [slang "have sex with": b1570; "nag": b1800] (niggling: b1600)

preclude v b1620 [obs. "phys. preclude, block": b1500 to 1700s]

preface v b1620 (prefatory: b1675)

protrude v b1620 [obs. "thrust forward": u1800s]

radiate v *fan out from a single source* b1620 ["emit light": b1670; "emit heat, energy": b1870]

squelch v b1620

stimulate v *excite* b1620 [rare "sting": b1550]

surround v b1620 [obs. "flood": b1450]

tease v *make fun* b1620 ["be a sexual tease": b1900] (noun use: b1870)

titter v b1620

titilate v b1620 (titilating: b1715)

collide v *force a collision* b1625 ["experience a collision": b1700] (collision: b1425)

colonize v b1625

constellate v *join in a group* b1625 [obs. "prophesy horoscopically": b1600 to 1800s]

degust v *savor* b1625 (degustate v: b1600; degustation: b1660)

deposit n/v *something deposited* b1625 ["in deposit": b1600]

dictate v *order* b1625 (noun use: b1595; dictation: b1670)

enunciate v *announce* b1625 ["speak clearly": b1770]

equalize v b1625 [obs. "be the equal of": b1590 to 1800s]

evoke v b1625 (evocation: b1635; evocative: b1660; evocatory: b1730)

flagellate v b1625 (adj use: b1860; noun use: b1880; flagellation: b1415; flagellant: b1565)

hesitate v b1625

indulge v b1625 (indulgence: b1380)

ingratiate v b1625 (ingratiating: b1655)

inspect v b1625 (inspection: b1395)

lubricate v b1625 (lubric adj: b1500)

lump v *as in "lump together"* b1625

migrate v b1625 [spec. to animals: b1730] (migration: b1615; migratory: b1755)

palpitate v b1625

recalcitrate v *kick* b1625 ["be obstinate": b1770] (recalcitrant: b1845)

steward v *manage, direct* b1625

synchronize v *happen coincidentally* b1625 ["make happen at the same time": b1830; "align," as in "synchronize watches": b1900]

(synchronous: b1670; synchronization: b1830; synchronicity: b1890)

tranquilize v b1625 (tranquilizer: b1500)

ululate v b1625 (ululant: b1870)

acclaim v b1630 [obs. "lay claim to": b1600 to 1700s] (noun use: b1670)

activate v b1630

assure v *ensure* b1630

belate v b1630

buzz v/n *gossip* b1630 (noun use: b1900)

catch v *as in "catch up"; as in "catch in the act"* b1630

clear v *phys. pass over or through, as in "clear a hurdle"* b1630

complicate v b1630 [obs. "enmesh": b1625 to 1700s] (complication: b1450; complicated: b1650)

crack v *as in "his voice cracked"; as in "crack a code"* b1630

cramp v *as in "cramp your style"* b1630 [obs. "apply a type of torture": b1570 to 1700s] (cramp, cramped: b1675)

discriminate v *have a difference* b1630 ["see a difference"; "be picky": b1800; "practice discrimination": b1870] (discrimination: b1650)

divulge v *reveal* b1630 [obs. "publish": b1470 to 1700s]

dwarf v *make smaller* b1630 ["tower over": b1870]

ease v *as in "ease off"* b1630

emaciate v b1630 (emaciated, emaciation: b1665)

emit v b1630

encrust v b1630

enslave v b1630

ensoul v b1630

espouse v *support* b1630 (espousal: b1900)

evolve v b1630 (evolution: b1700)

exaggerate v b1630 [obs. "heap," lit. and fig.: b1535 to 1600s; obs. "emphasize": u1700s] (exagger-

ated: b1555; exaggeration: b1565]

explode v *as in "explode a myth"* b1630

favor v *resemble* b1630 (arch. noun use: b1500)

fib v b1630 (noun use: b1570)

fuzzle v *get drunk; befuddle* b1630

glare v *stare* b1630

gossip v b1630 (noun use: b1570)

grind v *as in "grind down"* b1630

hoodwink v b1630 ["blindfold": b1565]

inject v b1630 [obs. "throw": b1600 to 1700s]

land v *as in "land a fish"* b1630 [as in "land a good job": b1870]

lap v *overlap* b1630 (noun use: b1800)

live v *as in "live it up"* b1630

lodge v *wedge* b1630

masculate n *make masculine* b1630

master v *as in "master the art of chicanery"* b1630 (masterful: concurrent; masterly: b1570)

necessitate v b1630

negotiate v *arrange, as in "negotiate a deal"* b1630

observe v *state an observation* b1630

paw v *handle rudely* b1630

percolate v b1630 ["make coffee": b1970]

pet v *treat with favoritism* b1630 ["caress": b1830]

precipitate v *cause* b1630 ["throw down": b1530; chemical sense: b1670]

prime v *as in "prime a house for painting"* b1630 (primer: b1700)

purse v *as in "purse your lips"* b1630

push v *as in "sprouts pushing up"* b1630

read v *fig. "interpret"* b1630 [as in "read into": b1900]

recede v b1630 [obs. "deviate": b1480] (recession: b1650)

recoup v *reimburse* b1630
["be reimbursed": b1870]
recover v *rediscover* b1630
refine v *hone* b1630
replenish v *restock* b1630
[obs. "stock in the first
place": b1350]
revise v b1630 [obs. "resee,
review": b1570 to 1600s]
(noun use: b1595; revi-
sion: b1615)
ride v *as in "shorts riding up"*
b1630
shine v *polish* b1630 (noun
use: b1470)
shoo v b1630
sophisticate v *rob of simplicity*
b1630 (sophistication:
b1400; sophisticated:
b1605)
stand v *endure, abide* b1630
strain v b1630
suit v *be suitable* b1630
syndicate v b1630
vie v *rival, strive* b1630 [obs.
card game term: b1535 to
1600s; obs. "pit against":
b1580 to 1800s; arch.
"match": b1600]
wash v *as in "wash ashore"*
b1630
wind v *as in "wind a watch"*
b1630
wrangle v *cajole* b1630
aggrandize v b1635
decant v *pour off* b1635
["transfer to decanter":
b1770]
decline v *say no* b1635
devastate, devastating v, adj
b1635 (devastation:
b1465; devast "devas-
tate": b1540)
encase v b1635

equilibrate v b1635
etch v b1635 (noun use:
b1900)
fluctuate v *waver* b1635
["undulate": b1635] (fluctuation: b1450)
haw v *as in "hem and haw"*
b1635 (noun use: b1700)
higgle v *haggle* b1635
insure v b1635 ["ensure":
b1415] (insurance: b1655;
insurant: b1870)
post v *as in "post an announcement"* b1635
rifle v *cut grooves in* b1635
squall v *squawk* b1635
(noun use: b1710)
amputate v b1640 (amputa-
tion: b1615)
concentrate v *draw to the center* b1640 ["make
stronger": b1700; "focus
attention": b1930] (con-
center v: b1595; concen-
tration: b1635)
prevaricate v b1640 [obs.
"stray": b1585 to 1600s]
(prevarication: b1670)
worst v *better, best, defeat*
b1640
bronze v b1645 (noun use:
b1725)
cajole v b1645 (cajolery:
b1650)
complement v b1645 ["exchange formalities":
b1605]
deprecate v b1645 [arch.
"pray against": b1625;
"depreciate": b1900]
desiderate v *desire, want*
b1645 (desideratum:
b1655)
elapse v b1645 [obs. "kill
time": u1700s]
extemporize v b1645

ingrain v b1645 (adj use:
b1870; ingrained: b1600)
intertwine v b1645
react v *respond* b1645
["move opp.": b1900] (re-
action: b1645)
recruit v b1645
scuttle v *scrap* b1645
bask v *revel* [obs. fig. "bathe
in blood": b1395 to 1500s]
comply v ["fulfill": b1335;
obs. "observe courtesies":
1600s]
criticize v
curdle v (crudle: b1590)
empower v
enfever v
intimidate v (intimidation:
b1660)
invalidate v (invalid: b1545)
invigorate v
jeopardize v
misrepresent v
posit v *position* ["postulate":
b1700]
state v *say, specify*
weave v *as in "weave through
the trees"*
weight v *weigh down*
["weigh": b1730]
widen v [obs. "open wide":
b1610]

Archaisms

facete adj *facetious* b1605
hush adj *hushed* b1605
implausible n *not applaudable*
b1605
roly-poly adj *useless* b1605
["plump": b1820]
scout v *obs. mock, scoff*
b1605 [u1700s]
stranger v *estrange* b1605
miss n b1610

depeople v b1615 (depopu-
late: b1535)
fox v b1615
intrigue v *cheat* b1615
simular adj *bogus* b1615
(noun use: b1530)
wilder v *make lost* b1615
["bewilder": b1670]
diploma n *gen. type of document* b1615
indagate v *investigate* b1625
deepsome adj b1630
deliquium n *faint* b1630
discommodate v *opp. of accommodate* b1630 (dis-
commode: b1730)
dispeed v b1630 [u1800s]
disventure n *obs. misadventure* b1630 [u1700s]
dormitory adj *obs. inducing
sleep* b1630 [u1800s]
exolete adj *obsolete* b1630
in-a-door adv *indoors* b1630
innoxious adj *obs. innocent*
b1630 [u1700s]
memorables n *memorabilia*
b1630
milden v *make mild* b1630
onewhere adv *akin to everywhere, nowhere* b1630
quackle v *choke* b1630
shorthanded adj *obs. inefficient* b1630
warm v *obs. as in "house warming"* b1630 [u1800s]
otherguess adj *of another sort*
b1635
vegete adj *strong, healthy*
b1640
trepan n/v *trap; trickster*
b1645 (arch. verb use:
b1660)
eradiate v *radiate*
factitious adj *manmade*
gantelope n *gauntlet*

IN USE BY
1700

Geography/Places

water hole n b1655
butte n (Am) b1660
pineland n (Am) b1660
environs n b1665
swampland n (Am) b1665
bluff n *cliff* b1670
heliocentric adj b1670
hot spring n b1670
kill n (Am) *creek, channel* b1670
lot n *as in "vacant lot"* b1670
Mercator projection n *type of map form* b1670
orthographic projection n b1670
real estate n b1670
slide n *landslide* b1670
terranean adj *of the earth* b1670
tremor n *small earthquake* b1670
lagoon n *tropical lagoon* b1675 [*type of standing water*: b1615]
steppe n b1675
clearing n *clear space* b1680
landslip n b1680 (landslide: b1840)
seaquake n b1680
grassland n (Am) b1685
plaza n b1685
prairie n b1685
undercurrent n b1685 [fig. use: b1800]
geocentric adj b1690
caldera n b1695
cay n
chain n *as in "mountain chain"*
key n *type of island, reef*

settlement n *colony* (settler: b1670)
square n *as in "town square"*
superterranean adj *opp. of subterranean*
tableland n

Natural Things

sump n *pit* b1655 ["swamp": b1425]
timberland n (Am) b1655
vortex n b1655
obsidian n b1660
geyser n b1665
nature n *natural surroundings* b1665
lactation n b1670 (lactate v: b1890)
loam n *type of soil* b1670 [type of clay: b900; gen. "soil": b1350]
ripple n b1670
rock oil n b1670
sandstone n b1670
shellac n b1670 (verb use: b1880)
white gold n b1670
whitecap n b1670
daze n *mica* b1675
teak n b1675 (teakwood: b1785)
vascular adj *applied to plants* b1675 [applied to animals: b1730]
atomic adj b1680
autumnal equinox n b1680
geode n b1680
manganese n *type of mineral* b1680 [the element: b1785]

stalactite n b1680 (stalagmite: b1680)
cobalt n b1685
soapstone n b1685
surf n b1685
mineral kingdom n b1695
dirt n *soil*
gravity n
ossification n (ossify: b1715)

Plants

boxwood n b1655
ginseng n b1655
grapevine n b1655
mayfly n b1655
spindly adj *pertaining to plants* b1655 [pertaining to other things: b1830] (spindling adj: b1750)
ironwood n b1660
mahogany n b1660
rosewood n b1660
seedling n b1660
latex n *type of plant secretion* b1665 [obs. "bodily fluids": b1665 to 1700s; type of artificial mixture: b1970]
leaf bud n b1665
vanilla n b1665
yucca n *North American plant* b1665 [type of South American plant: b1570]
annual n b1670
hickory n (Am) b1670
Judas tree n b1670
shagbark hickory n b1670
tuber n b1670
twatchel n *arch. earthworm* b1670

Virginia creeper n (Am) b1670
floret n b1675
morel n *type of fungus* b1675
overripe adj b1675
shuck n *husk* b1675 (verb use: b1775)
legume n b1680
bluebonnet n b1685
cob n *corncob* b1685
red cedar n (Am) b1685
white ash n *type of tree* b1685
white pine n (Am) b1685
deciduous adj b1690
pod n *as in "pea pod"* b1690
pinecone n b1695 (pineapple: b1450)
wilt v *applied to plants* b1695 [gen. use: b1800] (noun use: b1855)
arrowroot n ["the starch thereof": b1830]
dumbcane n *dieffenbachia*
gum n *type of tree*
palmyra n *type of palm tree*
peppermint n ["oil of peppermint": b1770; "peppermint-flavored candy": b1830]
perennial adj *blooming every year* ["evergreen": b1645 to 1700s] (noun use: b1770)
ring n *tree ring*
shaddock n *type of fruit*
skunk cabbage n (Am)
tumbler n *obs. porpoise* [u1800s]

Animals

canary n b1655 [type of wine: b1585] (canary bird: b1580)

collie n b1655
walrus n b1655
equestrian adj b1660
firefly n b1660
gray fox n b1660
green turtle n b1660
groundhog n (Am) b1660
lupine adj *wolflike* b1660
mantis n b1660 (mantid: b1895)
mealworm n b1660
omniverous adj b1660 (omnivore: b1890)
pony n b1660 [slang "glassful": b1870; slang "racehorse": b1930]
porcine adj b1660
walking leaf n b1660
animalcule n *microbe* b1665 [obs. "small creature": b1600 to 1800s]
caribou n (Am) b1665
catamount n *type of wild cat* b1665 (catamountain: b1450)
cowrie n b1665
feelers n b1665
guinea pig n b1665
insectivorous adj b1665 (insectivore: b1840)
jaybird n (Am) b1665
jerboa n *type of rodent* b1665
mountain cat n b1665
scorpion fish n b1665
sea otter n b1665
squab n b1665 [obs. "tyro": b1540]
angelfish n b1670
cobra n b1670
gadbee n b1670
gallinipper n *biting insect* b1670
gregarious adj *describing animals* b1670 [describing people: b1790]
hexapod n *insect* b1670
Irish wolfhound n b1670
lake trout n b1670
pirouette n *pertaining to horses* b1670 [pertaining to dance: b1710] (verb use: b1830)
red ant n b1670
redbird n b1670
sea eagle n b1670
shearwater n *type of bird* b1670
song thrush n b1670

swift n *type of bird; type of lizard* b1670
valve n b1670
water beetle n b1670
wood tick n b1670
albatross n b1675
auk n b1675
barn owl n b1675
house sparrow n b1675
red-eye n *type of fish* b1675
sandpiper n b1675
shorebird n b1675
white shark n b1675
woodchuck n (Am) b1675
barracuda n b1680
beeswax n b1680
cardinal bird n b1680 (cardinal: b1730)
corn snake n (Am) b1680
ephemera n *a type of insect* b1680
gamecock n b1680
grosbeak n *type of bird* b1680
menagerie n b1680
mockingbird n b1680
spoonbill n b1680
tern n b1680
feline adj b1685
freemartin n *type of calf* b1685
rhinoceros beetle n b1685
sand fly n b1685
stag beetle n b1685
tarpon n *type of fish* b1685
white ant n *termite* b1685
bald eagle n (Am) b1690
bluebird n b1690
bunny n *rabbit* b1690 [term of endearment: b1610]
cabbageworm n b1690
flying frog n b1690
lop-eared adj b1690
skylark n *type of bird* b1690
white whale n b1690
orangutan n b1695 (orang: b1780)
prairie chicken n (Am) b1695
sled dog n b1695
bullfrog n (Am)
cocoon n (verb use: b1870)
doggy n
eider n *eiderduck or down*
garefowl n *great auk*
goldfish n
king crab n
ladybug n
macaque n
mammoth n [fig. "something

large": b1900] (adj use: b1805)
mongoose n
scavenger n
sea lion n (seal: b900)
sucker n *suction device on an animal*
swallowtail n *type of butterfly* ["other things shaped like a swallow's tail": b1545]
tumbler n *type of pigeon*
white fox n

Weather

thunderstorm n b1655
fog bank n b1660
semantic adj *arch. related to weather* b1665
mackerel sky n *type of cloud formation* b1670
crosswind n b1680
flurry n *applied to air* b1690 [gen. use: b1700] (verb use: b1885)
squall n *lit.* [fig. "squabble": b1830] (verb use: b1900)
thundercloud n
thundershower n

Heavens/Sky

corona n b1660 [type of architectural feature: b1565]
stellar adj b1660 [fig., as in "stellar performer": b1900]
extramundane adj *extraterrestrial* b1665 ["supernatural": b1730]
blue n *the sky, nowhere, as in "out of the blue"* b1670
perihelion n b1670 [gen. "apex": b1830]
planet n *modern concept of celestial bodies* b1670 [ancient concept: b1300]
ring n *e.g., on Saturn* b1670
space n *outer space* b1670
void n b1670 [as in "feeling a void": b1800]
observatory n b1680
interplanetary adj b1695
orbit n *as in "a planet's orbit"* (verb use: b1945)
system n *as in "solar system"*

Science

ornithology n b1655
botanical adj b1660 (botany: b1690)
cosmology n b1660
phytology n *botany* b1660
pneumatics n b1660
spontaneous generation n b1660
armillary sphere n b1665
barometer n b1665
element n *as in "periodic table of elements"* b1670
principle n *arch. basic element* b1670
zoology n b1670
spectrum n *range of color* b1675
mineralogy n b1690
botany n (botanist: b1685)
cosmogony n *study of universal beginnings* ["beginning of the universe": b1770]
kingdom n *as in "animal kingdom"*
scientific adj

Technology

pneumatic adj b1660 (obs. pneumatical: b1630 to 1800s)
hydraulics n b1675

Energy

engine n *as in "steam engine"* b1670
campfire n b1675

Time

yestermorning adv/n b1655
Christian era n b1660
chronograph n b1665
hesternal adj *arch. yesterday* b1670 (obs. hestern: b1600 to 1700s)
hour hand n b1670 (minute hand: b1730; second hand: b1760; sweep-second hand: b1940)
betweenwhiles adv b1680
decennium n *decade* b1685 (decennial adj: b1660)
time v *measure time*

Age/Aging

adult n b1660 (adj use: b1535)

coeval adj *of equal age* b1665 (noun use: b1605)

senescence n *old age* b1695 (senescent: b1660; senesce v: b1670)

Mathematics

plus n *plus sign* b1655

plus sign n b1655 (minus sign: b1670)

decimal system n b1660

parameter n *geometric sense* b1660 ["boundary, definition": b1930]

slide rule n b1665

estimate v *predict a number* b1670

hyperbola n b1670

minus sign n b1670 (plus sign: b1655)

percent n b1670

polynomial n b1675

quadrillion n b1675

inverse n b1685 (adj use: b1670)

multiple n b1685

numeral n *number* b1690 ["word representing a number": b1570]

trillion n b1690

algorithm n

cube root n

ellipse n (elliptical: b1660)

factor n [gen. "contributing element": b1820] (verb use: b1850)

Measurement

cubic measure n b1660

direction n *e.g., north, south* b1670

knot n b1670

measurement n b1670

micrometer n *type of measuring instrument* b1670

rate n *as in "rate of speed"* b1670

scale n *as in "4:1 scale"* b1670

temperature n b1670 [obs. "something mixed": b1450 to 1800s; arch. "complexion": b1570; obs. "temperament": b1670 to 1700s]

dry measure n b1690

scintilla n *trace, bit* b1695

The Body

circulation n b1655 [obs. type of alchemical process: b1450 to 1600s; as in "magazine circulation": b1700] (circulate: b1630)

subcutaneous adj b1655

viscera n b1655

blackhead n b1660

gastric adj b1660

lumbar adj b1660

ovary n b1660 (ovarian: b1835)

salivate v b1660 (salivation: b1600)

twat n *vagina* b1660

mucous n b1665 (adj use: b1650)

build n *as in "a man's build"* b1670

capillary n b1670

digit n b1670

expectorate v b1670

incisor n b1670

sternum n b1670

wisdom tooth n b1670

lymph n b1675 [gen. "water": b1600]

coronary adj b1680

gall bladder n b1680

penis n b1680 (penile: b1865)

placenta n b1680

fornix n b1685

ganglion n b1685 [type of swelling: b1685]

gluteus n b1685 (gluteus maximus: b1890)

mammary adj b1685

muscular adj b1685 (obs. musculous: b1470 to 1700s)

testis n b1685 [obs. "female ovary": u1800s]

bubby n *slang breast* b1690

blood vessel n b1695

gland n b1695

pharynx n b1695

sputum n b1695

thyroid adj b1695 (noun use: b1840)

trapezius n b1695

cerumen n *ear wax*

mons veneris n [part of palm: b1625]

muff n *slang female genitals*

peepers n *slang eyes*

red rag n *slang tongue*

roger n *obs. penis* [u1800s] (verb use: b1711)

Physical Description

adroit adj b1655

ageless adj b1655

tope v *tipple* b1655

lurid adj *pale* b1660 ["vividly red": b1730; "graphic": b1870]

olfactory adj b1660 (olfaction: b1850)

overhand adj b1660 (adv use: b1870)

slim adj *physically slight* b1660 [fig. "slight": b1700] (verb use: b1865)

brunette n *dark-haired Caucasian* b1670 ["dark-skinned Caucasian": b1540] (adj use: b1755)

haggard adj *drawn, gaunt* b1670 [applied to hawks: b1570]

lanky adj b1670 (lank: b1000)

maladroit adj b1675

moan n *suffering aloud* b1675 [complaint: b1200] (verb use: b1725)

perspire v b1685 [obs. "evaporate": b1650 to 1700s] (perspiration: b1630)

bandy-legged adj *bowed* b1690

doze v *snooze* b1695 ["make sleepy": b1650]

fatigue n *weariness* b1695 ["the cause of weariness": b1670] (verb use: b1695)

gawp v *gape*

Medicine

febrile adj b1655 (febrific: b1710)

pharmacy n *the profession* b1655 ["using drugs": b1450; "apothecary": b1870]

prognosis n b1655 [gen. "prediction": b1730]

wellness n b1655

earache n b1660

intumescence n *swelling* b1660 (intumesce v: b1800)

medic n b1660

morbid adj b1660 ["funereal": b1870] (morbidity: b1725)

otalgia n *earache* b1660

paraplegia n b1660 (paraplegic adj/n: b1830)

polydipsia n *abnormal thirst* b1660 (polyphagia "abnormal appetite": b1695)

emphysema n *gen. swelling* b1665 [spec. type of lung disease: b1870]

miasma n b1665 [fig. use: b1870]

miscarriage n b1665 (miscarry: b1530)

quarantine n *40 days of isolation for a ship* b1665 ["widow's right to stay in husband's house for 40 days": b1525; gen. use: b1680] (verb use: b1805)

sleeping pill n b1665

thrush n *type of disease* b1665

toxic adj *poisonous* b1665 ["caused by poison": b1900] (noun use: b1890)

consumptive n *tuberculosis victim* b1670

hospitalize v b1670

inflame v b1670

inpatient n b1670

monocle n b1670

nervine adj *arch. medically soothing nerves or tendons* b1670

osteology n *study of the skeleton* b1670

pandemic adj *sweeping through the population* b1670 [gen. "universal": b1830] (noun use: b1855)

preparation n *as in "Preparation H"* b1670 (prepare: b1570)

vapors n *arch. conception of a med. condition* b1670 (vapor "unhealthy exhalation": b1450)

whooping cough n b1670

autopsy n b1680 [rare "seeing for yourself": b1655]

rheumatism n b1680 [obs. "effluence of water": b1605]

scarlet fever n b1680 [scarletina: b1805]

acupuncture n b1685 (acupressure: b1860)

diagnosis n b1685 [gen. use: b1870] (verb use: b1860)

diuresis n b1685

neurology n b1685 (neurologist: b1835)

nyctalopia n b1685

psoriasis n b1685

spasmodic adj *pertaining to spasm* b1685 ["irregular": b1870] (spasmatic: b1630; spastic: b1760)

waiting room n b1685

medico n b1690

nearsighted adj b1690

overdose n b1690 (verb use: b1730)

pimping adj *sickly; insignificant* b1690

sore throat n b1690

drastic adj b1695 [gen. use: b1830]

lumbago n *type of rheumatism* b1695

melancholia n b1695

myopia n b1695 (myope n: b1730; myopic: b1800)

paresis n *partial paralysis* b1695

polyphagia n *abnormal appetite* b1695 (polydipsia "abnormal thirst": b1660)

tinnitus n *ringing in the ears* b1695

tourniquet n b1695

trauma n *phys.* b1695 [psychological sense: b1900] (arch. traumatism: b1860; traumatic: b1870; traumatize: b1905)

comatose adj [fig. "sluggish": b1830]

disorder n (obs. verb use: b1600 to 1800s)

dispensary n

operate v (operation: b1600)

wheelchair n

Everyday Life

fob n *as in "watch fob"* b1655

rummer n *type of drinking glass* b1655

siesta n b1655

swab n *mop* b1655 (verb use: b1720; swabber: b1595)

toothbrush n b1655

backyard n b1660

doormat n b1665

india ink n b1665

cheroot n b1670

crystal n *type of glass* b1670

cutthroat n *obs. type of lantern* b1670 [u1800s]

dentiscalp n *toothpick* b1670

frippery n *finery* b1670 [obs. "clothes": b1570 to 1800s] (obs. fripper "frippery": u1600s)

lavatory n *bathing room; rest room* b1670 ["bath": b1375; "toilet": b1970] (lave "wash": b900; lavation: b1470)

roaster n *type of cooking pan* b1670

service n *set of utensils* b1670

ticket n *pass, as in "meal ticket," "airline ticket"* b1670 (verb use: b1870)

toilet n *toiletry* b1670

tumbler n *type of glass* b1670

hutch n *piece of furniture* b1675 ["chest": b1200; as in "rabbit hutch": b1400]

canister/cannister n b1680 ["basket": b1475]

common salt n b1680

finery n b1680

table linen n b1680

grill n b1685 ["food that has been grilled": b1770; type of restaurant: b1885] (verb use: b1670)

knicknack n b1685

microphone n *arch. ear trumpet* b1685

snuff n *type of smokeless tobacco* b1685 (snuffbox: b1690)

stoneware n b1685 (stone china: b1825)

grille/grill n *grate* b1690

saucepan n b1690

tank n (Am) *type of container* b1690 ["pool": b1620]

tea table n b1690

teaspoon n b1690 ["teaspoonful": b1800]

dressing table n b1695

flask n b1695 [type of case: b1360]

punch bowl n b1695

watering can n b1695

alarm clock n

bureau n *piece of furniture*

chopstick n

counter n *as in "kitchen counter"* ["counting desk": b1345 to 1500s]

glim n *type of lamp*

lacquerware n

light n *e.g., matches*

needlepoint adj/n/v

oilcloth n *waterproofed cloth* [type of covering: b1795]

pocketbook n *purse* ["book with a pocket": b1620]

teacup n

teapot n

toaster n

toilet n *dressing table*

Shelter/Housing

fireplace n b1655

hut n b1655 [mil. use: b1570]

antechamber n b1660

depository n b1660

facade n b1660 [fig. use: b1900]

rattan n b1660

banister n b1670

common room n b1670

dome n b1670 ["domicile": b1515]

flying buttress n b1670

hall n *hallway* b1670 (hallway: b1880)

plumbing n b1670 ["plumb work": b1450]

reservoir n b1670

ticket office n b1670

dressing room n b1675

smokehouse n b1675

bungalow n b1680

compound n *type of enclosure* b1680 [gen. "pound": b1930]

fire engine n b1680 (fire truck: b1935)

fire escape n b1680

skylight n *roof window; light from the sky* b1680

sash n *as in "window sash"* b1685

mantelpiece n b1690

arcade n

attic n (attic storey: b1725)

bathroom n

capitol n (Am)

exit n *exitway*

great room n

lifeline n

mall n *promenade* ["alley for type of game": b1645]

salon n

shutter n *as in "window shutters"* [photographic shutter: b1870]

Drink

rum n b1655

champagne n b1665 [type of color: b1900] (Brit slang "champers": b1955)

Chablis n b1670

imbibe v *drink* b1670 [fig. "absorb": b1395]

rosin n *slang alcoholic beverage* b1670

rumbullion n *arch. rum* b1670

stout n *type of ale* b1680

flip n *type of drink* b1685

saki n *type of alcoholic beverage* b1690

malt liquor n b1695 (malt: b1730)

port n *type of wine* b1695

nip n *drink* (verb use: b1870)

scotch n *type of whiskey*

sparkling wine n

Food

appetizing adj b1655

rare adj *describing meat* b1655 [obs. describing eggs: b1670 to 1800s]

tea n b1655

bouillon n b1660 (bouillon cube: b1935)

grub n *food* b1660 (grubbery: b1830)

pimento n b1660

ragout n b1660

celery n b1665

cheddar n b1665

ghee n b1665

hash n *as in "corned beef hash"* b1665 (verb use: b1590)

Irish potato n b1665

pineapple n b1665 [obs. "pinecone": b1450]

shallot n b1665

anthropophagy n *cannibalism* b1670

avocado n b1670

broccoli n b1670
burgundy n b1670
gratin n *the crust on au gratin* b1670
grill v b1670 (noun use: b1685)
halvah n b1670
ladyfinger n b1670
pabulum n b1670 [fig. "food for the soul": b1735; "insipidity": 1900s]
palatable adj *tasty* b1670 [fig. "enjoyable": b1700]
piquant adj *sharp* b1670 [arch. pertaining to emotions: b1630]
refreshment n b1670
relish n *as in "eating with relish"* b1670 ["odor, taste": b1350] (verb use: b1590)
round n *as in "round of beef"* b1670
vermicelli n b1670
whisk n b1670 (verb use: b1570)
eatable n b1675
kabob n b1675
mush n b1675 [fig. use: b1830] (verb use: b1785)
saccharine adj b1675 ["sickeningly sweet": b1845]
salmagundi n *type of salad plate* b1675
okra n *type of plant* b1680
sea biscuit n *hardtack* b1680
soy n b1680
hotcake n (Am) b1685
underdone adj b1685
barbeque v b1690 ["dry on a barbeque": b1665] (noun use: b1710)
catchup n b1690
forcemeat n *type of stuffing* b1690
ketchup n b1690
Worcestershire sauce n b1690
crumpet n b1695 (crompid cake: b1385)
tamale n (Am) b1695
breadfruit n
burgoo n
callaloo n
cos lettuce n
Dutch cheese n *cottage cheese*
flavor n *taste* ["aroma": b1350]
fondant n *type of candy*
green pepper n

kumquat n
sage cheese n
spoil v *go bad* (spoilage: b1600)
sponge cake n
tortilla n
vinaigrette n *type of sauce* [obs. type of stew: b1450; type of salad dressing: b1900]
whip v (noun use: b1770)

Agriculture/ Food-Gathering

apiary n *beehive* b1655
cowbell n b1655
livestock n b1660
mulch n b1660 (verb use: b1730)
greenhouse n b1665
orangery n b1665
saddle horse n b1665
agricole n *obs. farmer* b1670 [u1800s]
gamekeeper n b1670
raise v *as in "raise flowers"* b1670 [as in "raise kids": b1770]
whaleboat n b1675
cowman n b1680
horticulture n b1680
corncrib n b1685
cornhusking n (Am) b1695
produce n b1695
sterilize v *rend unfruitful* b1695 ["make germ-free": b1900]
hencoop n (henhouse: b1515)
podder n *peapicker*

Cloth/Clothing

cravat n b1660
gambado n *type of boot* b1660
flip-flop n/v b1665
greatcoat n b1665
point lace n b1665
shalloon n *type of fabric* b1665
snowshoe n (Am) b1665 (verb use: b1880)
cross-stitch n b1670
fall n b1670
hem n *stitched edge* b1670 [gen. "edge": b1000]
kimono n b1670

lapel n b1670
straitlace v *lace up* b1670
suede n b1670
cocked hat n b1675
high heels n b1675
manteau n *type of outerwear* b1675
furbelow n b1680
cashmere n *type of fabric* b1685
duffle coat n b1685
sash n *clothing* b1685 ["turban": b1600]
skullcap n b1685
undress n b1685
commode n *type of headdress* b1690
kid leather n b1690 (kid: b1500)
shoulder strap n b1690
burlap n b1695
domino n *type of costume* b1695
double-breasted adj
lift n *in elevator shoes*
morning dress n *morning coat and pants*

Fashion/Style

beauty spot n b1660
modish adj b1660 (modistic: b1930)
fall n *type of hairpiece* b1670
frost v *as in "frost hair"* b1670
grandeur n b1670 ["phys. height": b1530; "power": b1630] (obs. grandity: b1600 to 1800s)
paste n *stuff of fake jewelry* b1670
ringlet n b1670 ["small ring": b1555]
wig n b1675
locket n b1680 [obs. type of locking device: b1450 to 1500s]
kick n *fad*
loo n *type of mask*

Tools

hacksaw n b1655
microscope n b1655 (microscopy: b1665)
ratchet n b1655
tweezers n b1655 (verb use: b1830; tweeze: b1935)
air pump n b1660

eyeglass n b1665 [obs. "eye lens": b1615]
holster n b1665
magnifying glass n b1665
bob n *as in "plumb bob"* b1670
cantilever n *type of bracket* b1670 ["projection": b1870] (verb use: b1905)
coupler n b1670
machine n *mechanical device* b1670 [gen. something built: b1550; fig. use: b1700]
pointer n b1670
protractor n b1670
spud n b1670 ["potato": b1845] (verb use: b1425)
valve n b1670
fulcrum n b1675
lag n *barrel stave* b1675
miter square n b1680 (mitrum: b1200)
miter, miter box n *in construction* b1680 (miter joint: b1690; miter v: b1735)
shillelagh n *type of club* b1680
peen n b1685
scrub brush n b1685
brazier n *coalpan* b1690
punk n (Am) *stick for lighting fuses* b1690
soldering iron n b1690
counterweight n b1695
hunting horn n b1695
die n *as in "die cast"*
face n *as in "type face"*
grinder n
mangle n *laundry machine* (verb use: b1775)
weld v *join with welding tools* ["be joined": b1600] (noun use: b1835)

Travel/Transportation

avenue n *roadway* b1655 [fig. "way somewhere": b1630; "city street": b1800]
cruise v *in sailing* b1655 [gen. use: b1700; as in "cruising altitude": b1930] (noun use: b1710)
debark v *disembark* b1655
flatboat n b1660
post road n b1660
diving bell n b1665
jib n/v *type of sail* b1665

calash n *type of carriage* b1670

chaise n b1670

corsair n b1670

cross street n b1670

crossing n *as in "river crossing"* b1670 [as in "railroad crossing"]: b1700]

dogcart n b1670

machine n *obs. vehicle* b1670 [u1800s]

saunter v *walk ramblingly* b1670 [obs. "talk ramblingly": b1450 to 1500s] (noun use: b1770)

scow n (Am) b1670

tour n *visit; inspection* b1670 ["visit": b1890]

trip v *take a trip* b1670 (noun use: b1700)

vehicle n *e.g., train, plane* b1670

canal n b1675 ["tube": b1425; "natural waterway": b1570]

jaunt n *short trip* b1680 ["tedious trip": b1595]

stroll v *walk* b1680 [obs. "move nomadically": b1605 to 1700s] (noun use: b1800)

paddle wheel n b1685

go-cart n *baby carriage* b1690

jibe n/v *related to ship movement* b1695

keelboat n b1695

diligence n *type of stagecoach*

excursion n [obs. "digression": b1600]

jolly boat n

launch n *type of boat*

post chaise n *type of carriage*

railway n

shipyard n

Emotions/ Characteristics

atrabilious adj *melancholy* b1655

brusque adj b1655 (brusquerie: b1755)

disingenuous adj b1655

disrepute n b1655 (disreputable: b1685)

dogged adj *persistent* b1655 [obs. "mean": b1350 to 1600s]

downhearted adj b1655

fanaticism n b1655 (obs. fanatism: b1700 to 1800s)

fanfaronade n *bluster* b1655 (verb use: b1870; fanfaron: b1630)

grimace n b1655 (verb use: b1770)

naive adj b1655 (naivete: b1675; naivety: b1730)

psychology n b1655 (psychics "psychology": b1830)

rapacious adj b1655

reserve n *self-restraint* b1655 (reserved: b1605)

self-destructive adj b1655 (self-destruction: b1590; self-destroying: b1670; self-destruct: b1970)

cavalier adj b1660 ["gentlemanly": b1640]

concerned adj b1660

eccentricity n b1660 (eccentric n: b1830)

freehanded adj *generous* b1660

hedonic adj b1660 (hedonist: b1825; hedonism: b1860)

misanthropy n b1660 (misanthrope: b1565; misanthropic: b1765)

pavid adj *timid* b1660

self-esteem n b1660

charming adj *charismatic* b1665 ["magical": b1300]

idiosyncrasy n *personality quirk* b1665 ["phys. quirk": b1605]

rapport n b1665

revere v b1665 (reverence: b1300; reverent: b1400; reverend adj: b1450)

unsettling adj b1665

acrimony n b1670 ["acrid taste": b1545]

agape adj/adv b1670

arch adj *roguish* b1670 ["primary," akin to "arch-enemy": b1550]

atrocious adj *wicked* b1670 ["awful": b1900]

convivial adj b1670

dignity n b1670 ["worthiness": b1200] (dignify: b1425; dignified: b1765)

disgruntle v b1670

dry-eyed adj b1670

ennui n b1670

frighten v b1670 (fright v: b1100)

honor n *arch. promise made on honor* b1670

human nature n b1670

hypochondria n *unexplained melancholia* b1670 ["self-convinced illness": b1840]

impersonal adj b1670 (impersonalize: b1880)

impolite adj b1670

infuriate v/adj b1670

jocoserious adj *semi-serious* b1670

jubilant adj b1670 (jubilance: b1865)

magnanimity n *being magnanimous* b1670 ["magnanimity because of feelings of superiority": b1350]

mean adj *malicious* b1670

micrology n *picking nits* b1670

panic n b1670 ["commotion": b1710]

pathos n b1670 [rare "something pathetic": b1590]

randy adj *crude* b1670 ["unruly": b1700; "bawdy": b1870]

reality n *obs. loyalty* b1670 [u1700s]

restive adj *restless* b1670 [obs. "resting": b1410 to 1800s] (restless: b1000)

sarcast n *sarcastic person* b1670

satanic adj b1670 (satanical: b1550)

selfful adj *arch. selfish* b1670

shock v *surprise, horrify* b1670 (noun use: b1730)

sniveling adj b1670

staggering adj *astonishing* b1670

stress n *psychological pressure* b1670 ["phys. pressure": b1870] (verb use: b1570)

stunning adj *confounding* b1670 ["gorgeous": b1870]

terrific adj *terrifying* b1670 ["huge": b1810; "very good": b1930] (terrification: b1630)

wistful adj b1670 [obs. "attentive": b1615 to 1800s]

candid adj *frank* b1675 [obs. "white": b1630 to 1800s; arch. "pure": b1630] (candor: b1770)

cockles of the heart n b1675

easygoing adj b1675

fidget n b1675 (verb use: b1755; fidgety: b1740; the fidgets: b1755)

foible n b1675 [fencing term: b1650]

happy-go-lucky adj b1675

jaunty adj *devil-may-care* b1675 [obs. "stylish": b1665 to 1800s]

moonstruck adj b1675

obnoxious adj b1675 ["susceptible to injury": b1585; obs. "submissive": b1600 to 1700s]

shy adj *bashful* b1675 ["skittish": b1000; "cautious": b1600]

true-blue, true blue adj, n b1675

huffy adj b1680 (huffish: b1755)

mischievous adj *naughty* b1680 (mischiefful: b1350)

nonchalance n b1680 (adj use: 1730s)

plainspoken adj b1680

self-centered adj b1680 (self-centering: b1700)

self-righteous adj b1680

chagrin n b1685 [obs. "despondency": b1660 to 1800s] (verb use: b1670)

purse-proud adj b1685 (pursy: b1630)

laugh n b1690 [as in "that's a laugh": b1900] (verb use: b900)

unselfish adj b1690

mean-spirited adj b1695

mope n *moper* b1695 ["idiot": b1570]

snicker v b1695 (noun use: b1835)

wishy-washy adj b1695 (wish-wash n "swill": b1790)

attrist v *obs. sadden* [u1800s]

brave n *one who is brave/bully, arch. assassin* [obs. "thug": b1600 to 1800s; "warrior": b1770]

delighted adj [obs. "delight-ful": b1605 to 1700s]

effrontery n

euphoria n gen. good feeling ["ecstasy": b1885]

forte n fig. strong point [applied to swords: b1650]

fractious adj

gruff adj ["physically coarse": b1500]

guilt n [absolute sense: b1000]

intrepid adj

priggish adj (prig n: b1580)

rampage v (noun use: b1865; ramp v "menace": b1400; rampageous: b1825)

sore adj angry

stomach v tolerate ["don't tolerate": b1530 to 1800s]

tasteless adj lacking good judgment ["bland": b1605]

Thoughts/Perception/The Mind

dumbfound v b1655

hallucinate v b1655 [obs. "trick": b1605] (hallucination: b1630)

noetic adj intellectual b1655

weakheaded adj b1655

witticism n b1655

remind v b1660 ["remember": b1645] (reminder: b1655)

reverie n b1660 [arch. "revelry": b1350 to 1500s]

conceptual adj b1665 (conceptualize: b1880)

frame of mind n b1665

presence of mind n b1665 (obs. present "having presence of mind": b1450)

daydream n b1670 (verb use: b1820)

desipience n foolishness b1670

fascinate v captivate attention b1670 ["put under a spell": b1600 to 1600s] (fascination: b1870)

lucidity n b1670

philosophess n b1670

positive adj certain b1670

recall v/n b1670 ["remember": b1700]

theoretical adj b1670 [obs. "theorizing": b1605]

unthinking adj b1670

volition n as in "of his own volition" b1670 [arch. "wishing": b1615]

innuendo n b1680 [leg. phrases: b1565]

introspection n b1680 (introspect v: b1900)

obsession n b1680 [obs. "siege": b1515 to 1600s; "something haunted": b1605]

orphic adj prophetic b1680

riveting adj b1680

romantics n arch. romantic philosophy b1680

self-conscious adj self-aware b1680 ["feeling awkward": b1870]

self-perception n b1680

witling n arch. lesser wit b1685

free thinker n b1695

conundrum n puzzle [obs. "caprice": b1600 to 1700s; obs. "pun": b1645 to 1700s]

mind v pay attention to

recollection n remembering ["concentration": b1625; "a memory": b1800] (recollect: b1560)

rethink v

think v as in "think of me if you want to sell"

Love/Romance/Sex

alimony n b1655 ["gen. provision": b1630]

inamorata n female lover b1655 (inamorato: b1595)

sexual adj related to sex b1655

connubial adj b1660

misogamy n b1660

celibacy n b1665

heartbreaker n b1665 (heartbreak: b1400)

knock up n slang impregnate b1665 (knock: b1600)

smitten adj b1665

assignation n tryst b1670

charivari n shivaree b1670

engagement n b1670 (engaged: b1615; engage: b1730)

flame n b1670

frigid adj b1670

girl n girlfriend b1670 (girlfriend: b1860)

gallant v court b1675

jilt v/n b1675 ["be disloyal": b1660]

fuck n act of intercourse b1680 ["intercourse partner": b1900] (verb use: b1500)

trade n prostitution b1680

philander v b1685 (obs. noun use "lover": b1700 to 1800s; philanderer: b1841)

hubby n b1690

maiden name n b1690

eros n

groomsman n (groom: b1630)

mixed marriage n

polyandry n marrying multiple husbands (polygamy: b1595; polygyny: b1780; polyandrous: b1830; polyandrist: b1835)

proposal n (propose: b1770)

rampant adj obs. lusting [u1800s]

separate v prelude to divorce

spinster n old maid [obs. "unmarried woman": b1700 to 1900s]

Family/Relations/Friends

great-aunt, great-uncle n b1660

second cousin n b1660

first cousin n b1665

granny n b1665 (grandmother: b1425; granny: b1565; grandmamma: b1770; grandma: b1800)

parent v sire or bear b1665 ["rear": b1900]

folks n b1670

mum/mummy n (Brit) mother b1670 (mumsy: b1900)

nepotism n b1670 [spec. "favoring the Pope's nephew": 1650s]

relative n b1670 (relation: b1530)

chum n b1685 (verb use: b1730; chummy: b1835)

pal n b1685 (verb use: b1880)

papa n b1685 (pappy: b1765)

tot n child b1690

family name n

Holidays

Father Christmas n b1660

Valentine's Day n b1670

Games/Fun/Leisure

festive adj b1655

gambit n chess term b1660 [gen. use: b1855]

move n as in "checker move" b1660

playtime n b1665

whist n b1665

joke n/v jest b1670 ["something trivial": b1730; "something mockable": b1800] (joker: b1730; jokist: b1830)

kite n as in "fly a kite" b1670 (verb use: b1870)

merry-andrew n clowning person b1670

face card n b1675

hide-and-seek n b1675

loo n type of card game b1675

tug-of-war n b1680 (tug n: b1670)

hoity-toity adj playful b1690 ["haughty": b1900]

pool n pot in a card game b1690 [as in "office football pool": b1930] (verb use: b1880)

trictrac n type of game b1690

doll n type of toy [obs. "mistress": b1550 to 1600s; "babe": b1800]

jack n card

marble n

swing n as in "swingset"

Sports

gymnastics n b1655 (gymnastic: b1575)

regatta n b1655 [spec. "Venetian boat race": b1630]

backhand n b1660 (verb use: b1935)

discus n b1660

goalkeeper n b1660 (goal-

Two by Two

English words like to travel hand-in-hand in tried-and-true phrases, such as, well, "tried and true."

The time by which such words join hands has little to do with the actual age of the words themselves. For example, take "here and there." *Here* was in use by 725, and *there* by 800. The phrase "here and there" appeared before 1400. On the other hand, "here and now" joins two words in use by 725, yet the phrase wasn't recorded until before 1830.

Nor do the words need to have appeared in the language near one another to be paired. The phrases above sport words of Old English antiquity, but then there's "vim and vigor," with the spry young *vim* (by 1845) joining the more experienced *vigor* (by 1350). A May-December marriage, that.

Let's examine some other word pairs to see how closely their component words match up in age.

- *now* (by 725) and *then* (also by 725)

- *kith* and *kin*, both before 900, with the phrase arriving before 1230

- *first* (by 965) and *foremost* (by 725)

- *bits* (by 1000) and *pieces* (by 1225)

- *to* (by 1100) and *fro* (by 1200)—the phrase by 1350

- *hue* (by 1200) and *cry* (by 1280)—the full phrase (by 1250) predates *cry* meaning "outcry," because the phrase arrived from French with a specific legal sense, and *cry* split out from it

- *rules* (by 1225) and *regulations* (by 1715)

- *nook* (by 1300) and *cranny* (by 1440)

- *pomp* (by 1325) and *circumstance* (by 1200)

- *hem* (by 1500) and *haw* (by 1635)

- *prim* (by 1710) and *proper* (by 1705)

Interestingly, some of these word pairs team a bit of foundation English ("bit," "rule") with a piece of later Latinate synonymy ("piece," "regulation").

And, oh, yes: "tried and true"? *Tried* by 1470, *true* by 725, and the full phrase by 1935.

---

tender: b1910; goalie: b1925)

footrace n b1665

champ n b1670

heat n b1670

jockey n b1670 ["horse trader": b1670] (verb use: b1770)

matador n b1670

putt n b1670 (verb use: b1770)

backstroke n *swimming* b1675

shinny n/v *type of hockey* b1675

feint n b1680 (adj use: b1290; verb use: b1810)

fly rod n b1685

ice-skate v [common use: b1950] (noun use: b1665)

sportsman n (sportswoman: b1745)

tee n/v *golf tee* (teaz: b1675)

tie n/v *draw, as in "a 10-10 tie"*

Professions/Duties

spokeswoman n b1655 (spokesman: b1540;

spokesperson: b1970; spokespeople: b1975)

turnkey n *jailer* b1655

barmaid n b1660

linkboy n *type of servant* b1660 (linkman: b1730)

nursemaid n b1660

tobacconist n b1660

draftsman n b1665

informant n *information provider* b1665 ["squealer": b1800] (informer: b1510)

dapifer n *food server* b1670

hand n *as in "farmhand"* b1670

jobber n b1670

mechanic n *as in "auto mechanic"* b1670 [arch. "manual laborer": b1565; "skilled laborer": b1670]

stationer n *seller of stationery* b1670 [obs. "bookseller": b1350 to 1800s]

axman n (Am) b1675

explorer n b1685 (obs. explorator: b1450 to 1600s)

whaler n b1685 ["whaling ship": b1830]

fortune hunter n b1690

housepainter n b1690

pawnbroker n b1690

timekeeper n b1690

woodsman n b1690

housemaid n b1695

chairwoman n (chairman: b1650; chairperson: b1975)

consultant n (consulter: b1600; consultor: b1630)

lookout n [as in "on the lookout": b1770]

model n (verb use: b1930)

mourner n *professional lamenter* [gen. use: b1395]

shipbuilder n

Business/Commerce/Selling

concern n *as in "business concern"* b1655

dry goods n b1660

piece goods n b1665

creamery n (Am) b1670

distributress n b1670 (distributor: b1530)

manufacture n *arch. factory* b1670

premium n *as in "insurance premium"* b1670

stock-in-trade n b1670

balance of trade n b1690

duty-free adj b1690

icehouse n b1690

teahouse n b1690

market value n b1695

proprietress n b1695 (proprietor: b1500; proprietrix: b1840)

consumer n (consumption: b1665; consumerism: b1945)

discount n [obs. gen. "reduction": b1625 to 1700s] (verb use: b1625)

print shop n (printery: b1640)

sell off v

The Workplace

girl n *female worker* b1670

office n *company, workplace, as in "branch office"* b1670

operose adj *hardworking* b1670

retire v b1670 (retirement: b1600; retired: b1830)

unemployed adj *not working* b1670 ["not used": b1600] (noun use: b1800; unemployment: b1890)

hack n *drudge worker* b1690

staffer n b1690

dogwatch n *night shift*

Finances/Money

economy n *as in "the nation's economy"* b1655 (economic adj: b1835)

compound interest n b1660

currency n *circulation of money* b1660 [gen. "flow": b1660; "the money itself": b1730] (current adj: b1500)

denomination n b1660

hardfisted adj b1660

honorarium n b1660

stingy adj *cheap* b1660 ["small," as in "a stingy raise": b1870] (stinge "stingy person": b1930)

amortization n b1670 (amortize: b1470)

bill n *as in "dollar bill"* b1670

export v b1670 [obs. "carry away": b1485 to 1700s] (noun use: b1690; exporter: b1695)

note n *official IOU* b1670 (note of hand: b1740)

fund n b1680 [obs. "bottom; foundation": b1600]

debit v b1685 (noun use: b1780)

quid n (Brit) b1690

banknote n b1695

bit n *as in "two bits is a quarter"*

dividend n ["the divided portion": b1480]

draw v *withdraw*

drawback n *type of refund*

economy n *being thrifty*

land bank n

negotiate v *convert negotiable assets* (negotiable: b1760)

run n *as in "a run on the bank"*

securities n

settle v

stock n *as in "stock market"*

Language and Speaking

esoteric adj *jargonistic* b1655 ["mysterious": b1870] (esoterica: b1930)

jargon n *argot, industry-specific terms* b1655 [arch. "warbling": b1350; "nonsense": b1450; obs. type of code: b1600 to 1700s; "pidgin": b1670]

misspell v b1655

raillery n *repartee* b1655

badinage n *banter* b1660 (verb use: b1830)

dactylology n *sign language* b1660

lingo n b1660

oxymoron n b1660

phraseology n b1665

pun n b1665 (verb use: b1670; obs. pundigrion: b1700 to 1800s; punster: b1700)

etymologicon n *word-origin book* b1670

etymon n *source word* b1670 [obs. "original form of a word": b1600 to 1700s; obs. "original meaning": b1630 to 1800s]

loquacious adj b1670 (loquacity: b1300)

predicate n b1670

double entendre n b1675

lingua n b1675

second person n b1675

verbose adj b1675 (verbosity: b1570)

caret n ^ b1685

anecdote n b1690 ["bit of history": b1680] (anecdotage: b1830; anecdotal: b1840)

brogue n *type of accent* b1690

poignancy n b1690

chitchat n (verb use: b1825; chitter-chatter n: b1715)

diction n [obs. "word": b1450 to 1600s; obs. "description": b1585 to 1600s]

subject n *grammatical sense*

vernacular n *native tongue* ["jargon": b1900] (adj use: b1605)

Contractions

can't contr b1655

won't contr b1655 (noun use: b1930)

I'd contr b1665

shan't v b1665

ma'am n b1670

they'd contr b1680

you've contr b1695

Literature/Writing

chirography n *handwriting* b1655

dissertation n b1655 [obs. "debate": b1615 to 1700s] (dissert v: b1625; dissertate v: b1770)

dialogist n b1660

epistolary adj b1660

illiteracy n b1660

lexicographer n *creator of dictionaries* b1660 (lexicography: b1680)

mythographer n b1660

opuscule, opusculum n *minor work* b1660

tetralogy n b1660

character n *as in "character in a novel"* b1665

palimpsest n *type of writing material* b1665 [obs. type of parchment writing service: b1665 to 1700s]

belles lettres n b1670

copyist n b1670

emit v *obs. publish* b1670

lexicon n *vocabulary* b1670 [type of dictionary: b1605]

line n *as in "drop me a line"* b1670

longhand adj/n b1670

memoir n *autobiography* b1670 ["official notation": b1575]

miscellany n b1670

mock-heroic adj b1670 (noun use: b1715)

newspaper n b1670 ["pulp paper": b1930] (verb use: b1945)

paper n *(news)paper* b1670

plot n *narrative events* b1670 ["devious plan": b1600] (verb use: b1590; plotline: b1595)

read v *copyread; be readable,* as in *"the novel reads well"* b1670

romance n *love story* b1670

scripturient adj *crazy about writing* b1670

protagonist n b1675 [gen. "leader, primary player": b1870]

dramatist n b1680

logbook n b1680

scribe v *mark* b1680

stationery n b1680

biography n b1685 [gen. "written histories of people": 1500s] (biographer: b1715; biographical: b1740; biographee: b1845; bio: b1950)

lowercase adj/n b1685 (verb use: b1910)

font n *as in "type font"* b1690 ["act of metal-casting": b1580]

lead pencil n b1690

machine, machinery n *plot device* b1690

heroic poem n b1695 (heroic verse: b1590; heroic couplet: b1905)

journalist n b1695 (journalism: b1835)

penmanship n b1695

alphabetize v (alphabet: b1425)

annual n *annual book*

criticism n

foolscap n *type of paper* [type of cap: b1630]

rule n *type of printing line* (verb use: b1470)

space n *break between words*

story n *tall tale*

Communication

bulletin n b1655 [as in "news bulletin": b1765] (verb use: b1840)

postage n *cost of posting* b1655 [obs. "messenger service": b1590 to 1600s; obs. "postal service": b1670 to 1700s]

postpaid adj b1655

general post office n b1660

dulciloquent adj *pleasantly eloquent* b1670

mail n *related to postal* b1670

[type of bag: b1225] (verb use: b1830)

postmark n b1680 (verb use: b1720)

Visual Arts/ Photography

profile n *type of drawing; view from the side* b1660 [type of writing: b1770; "public image": b1970] (verb use: b1715)

monochrome n b1665 (adj use: b1850)

sculptress n b1665 (sculptor: b1635; sculpt: b1865)

woodcut n b1665 (woodblock: b1840)

chiaroscuro n b1670 (chiaroscurist: b1800)

dirty adj *describing colors* b1670

graphic arts n b1670

museum n b1670 [type of university building: b1615]

print n *type of artwork* b1670 [as in "photographic print": b1870]

sketch n b1670 ["short comedic scene": b1800] (verb use: b1700)

unities n *the 3 unities: of time, place, action* b1670

colorist n b1690

bust n *in the statue* b1695

art n *artwork*

atelier n *type of studio*

drawing n *type of artwork* ["act of drawing": b1450]

Performing Arts

revival n b1655

ventriloquist n b1660 (ventriloquy: b1585; ventriloquism: b1800)

acting n b1665

ballet n b1665 (ballerina: b1795)

juggle n *magic trick* b1665 [juggle "perform magic": b1450] (jugglery: b1350)

burlesque n b1670 (adj use: b1560; verb use: b1680)

entertainment n *show* b1670 ["amusement": b1615]

house n *audience* b1670

monologue n b1670 ["person who controls conversation": b1550]

opening n *gen. beginning* b1670 ["first chess move": b1770; as in "opening of a play": b1930]

production n b1670

punchinello n *type of clown* b1670

represent v *arch. perform on stage* b1670

thespian adj b1675 (noun use: b1830)

episode n b1680 ["incidence": b1800] (episodic: b1715)

dramatics n b1685

theatricals n b1685

deus ex machina n

Music

symphonious adj b1655

spinet n b1665

bar n *musical unit of meter* b1670

fingerboard n b1670 (fingering: b1390)

glee n b1670

harmonic adj b1670 [obs. "musical": b1570]

overture n *musical beginning* b1670 ["proposal, suggestion": b1350; obs. gen. "beginning": b1600 to 1700s]

prelude n b1670 [gen. use: b1565] (prelusion: b1600)

staff n b1670

chant n *song* b1675 ["repetitious song or recitation": b1830] (verb use: b1400)

minuet n b1675

campanology n *art of ringing bells* b1680

timbal n *kettledrum* b1680

French horn n b1685

piano adj/adv b1685

violinmaker n b1685

roll n *as in "drum roll"* b1690

snare n *part of snare drum* b1690

tempo n b1690 [gen. "pace": b1900]

diatonic adj b1695

solo n *composition for one* b1695 ["performance of

solo": b1800] (verb use: b1870; soloist: b1865)

sonata n b1695

tom-tom n b1695

krummhorn n *type of woodwind instrument*

major adj

minor adj (noun use: b1800)

oboe n

write v *compose*

Entertainment

master of ceremonies n b1665

amuse v *entertain* b1670 [arch. "deceive": b1480; obs. "command attention": b1630 to 1700s] (amusement: b1605; amusing: b1715; amusive: b1770)

carousel n *merry-go-round* b1675 [type of tournament: b1650]

fire-eater n b1675

vanity fair n b1680

round dance n b1685

barker n *as in "carnival barker"*

hero n *protagonist* (heroine: b1730)

lido n *chichi resort*

Movies/TV/Radio

magic lantern n *type of projector*

Education

sophomore n b1655

common school n (Am) b1660

syllabus n b1660

educator n (Am) b1675 ["raiser of children": b1570]

verse v *learn* b1675

boarding school n b1680

diploma n b1685 [gen. type of document: b1625]

homework n b1685

mortar cap n *mortarboard* b1690 (morter: b1605; mortarboard: b1855)

alma mater n b1695 [gen. "provider": b1670]

Religion

lama n *lamaist monk* b1655

national church n b1655

religionist n b1655

sabbat n *medieval satanist rite* b1655

virgin birth n b1655

afflatus n *divine inspiration* b1660

established church n b1660

missionary n b1660 (adj use: b1645; missioner: b1665; missionist: b1930)

monotheism n b1660 (monotheist: b1700; monotheistic: b1850)

coven n b1665 [gen. "meeting": b1520]

forbidden fruit n b1665

divinify v b1670

hymn v b1670

majestatic adj *divinely majestic* b1670

Old Nick n *the devil* b1670

prelatess n b1670 (prelate: b1225)

presbyteress n b1670 (presbyter: b1600)

pyrolatry n *fire worship* b1670

clergywoman n b1675 (clergyman: b1580)

desecrate v b1675 (desecration: b1720)

mystic n b1680 (adj use: b1385; mystical: b1475)

theism n b1680

tritheism n b1680

deism n b1685 (deist: b1625)

churchgoer n b1690

Immaculate Conception n b1690

Supreme Being n

Society/Mores/Culture

countrified adj b1655

rake n *libertine* b1655 (verb use: b1730; rakehell adj/n: b1550; rakish: b1710)

immoral adj b1660 (immorality: b1570)

proletarian n b1660 (adj use: b1845; proletaire: b1830; proletariat: b1855; prole n: b1890)

bigot n b1665 [type of religious follower: 1590s to 1600s] (bigotry: b1675)

cultivated adj *refined* b1665 (cultural: b1865; cultivation: b1870)

tramp n *hobo* b1665 (verb use: b1870)

decency n b1670 [obs. "appropriateness": b1565 to 1700s; "honor": b1770] (decent: b1540)

fellow man n b1670

hermit n b1670 [religious use: b1200]

hoi polloi n b1670

materialist n b1670 (materialism: b1750)

miss n *unmarried woman* b1670

faux pas n b1675

highbred adj b1675

indentured servant n b1675

johnny n *guy, chap* b1675

fop n b1680 ["fool": b1440]

public-spirited adj b1680

haut monde n *high society* b1685

refugee n b1685 (verb use: b1770)

townswoman n b1685

fair sex n b1690

gentleman-commoner n b1690

peeress n b1690 (peer: b1225)

bon vivant n b1695

society adj b1695

scarlet letter n (Am)

station n *rank*

Government

autocracy n b1655 [obs. "autonomy": b1660 to 1800s] (autocrat: b1805)

monocracy n b1655 (monocrat: b1800)

plutocracy n b1655

stratocracy n b1655

federal adj *U.S. type of government sense* b1660 ["related to a treaty": b1645]

autarchy n b1665

capital n *seat of government* b1670

constitution n *as in "U.S. Constitution"* b1670 [gen. "rule, set of rules": b1400] (constitutional: b1770)

feudalism n b1670

interregnum n *interval between regimes* b1670 [obs. "temporary rule": b1690 to 1700s] (interrex "ruler during interregnum": b1600)

commune n *spec. type of French municipality* b1675 ["place for communal living": b1930] (communize: b1890)

signet ring n b1685

inaugural adj b1690 (noun use: b1835)

forestry n *the royal forest* b1695

grand duke n b1695 (grand duchess: b1760; grand duchy: b1835)

bureau n *government office* [gen. "agency": b1930] (bureaucracy: b1820)

patent office n

township n *type of municipality*

Politics

anarch n *revolutionary* b1670 ["anarchist": b1900]

politics n *political maneuvering* b1670 ["administration of government": b1530]

dignitary n b1675 (adj use: b1730)

ship of state n b1675

poll tax n b1695

Life

immortal n b1670 (adj use: b1375)

longevous adj *achieving longevity* b1680

Death

reliquiae n *relics* b1655

infanticide n b1660

ossuary n *resting place for bones of the dead* b1660

crypt n b1670 [obs. "cave": b1565]

deathwatch n b1670

kick v *as in "kick the bucket"* b1670

pass n *arch. death* b1670 (verb use: b1350)

death warrant n b1695

die off v

extinct adj *as in "extinct species"* ["extinguished": b1450; "obsolete, archaic": b1500]

frummagemed adj *obs. slang* "hanged" [u1800s]

undertaker n *funeral director* [obs. "aide": b1400 to 1600s; "one who undertakes": b1450; "subcontractor": b1630; obs. "editor, publisher": b1700 to 1800s]

War/Military/Violence

blunderbuss n b1655

self-defense n b1655

warhorse n b1655

fustigate v *beat, cudgel* b1660 (fustigation: b1600)

gunfight n b1660

marksman n b1660 (markswoman: b1805)

missile n *thrown weapon* b1660 ["long-range weapon": b1740] (adj use: b1615)

armistice n b1665

hand grenade n b1665

projectile n b1665

aide-de-camp n b1670 (aide: b1780)

birch n *flogging tool* b1670 (verb use: b1830)

carabineer/carbineer n b1670

destruct v b1670

engage v *as in "engage the enemy"* b1670 (engagement: b1670)

frigate n b1670 [gen. "fast ship": b1585]

machine n *arch. type of war machine* b1670

major, major-general n b1670

range n b1670

reserve n b1670

screw n *torture device* b1670

shell n *cartridge* b1670 (verb use: b1830)

storm v *assault* b1670

battle royal n b1675

bayonet n b1675 [obs. type of dagger: b1615 to 1700s] (verb use: b1700)

chiv n *knife* b1675 (verb use: b1725)

flagship n b1675

flesh wound n b1675

scalp v b1675

shiv n *knife* b1675

burn in effigy v b1680

counterattack n/v b1680

cruiser n b1680

flog v b1680

fusil, fusilier n *type of flintlock, soldier using a fusil* b1680

grenadier n b1680

nom de guerre n b1680

prisoner of war n b1680

saber n b1680 (sabreur: b1870)

bomb n b1685 [obs. type of fire weapon: b1590; fig. "failure": b1965] (verb use: b1690; bome: b1590)

flintlock n b1685

barracks n b1690

commandant n b1690

side arm n b1690

small arms n b1690

strategy n *spec. mil. strategy* b1690 [gen. "planning": b1870] (strategic: b1825; strategist: b1840)

armed forces n b1695

commodore n b1695

holy war n b1695

howitzer n b1695

outgun v b1695

bayonet v *stab with a bayonet* (noun use: b1675)

buzz v *strafe*

grape n (grapeshot: b1750)

guard n *group of guards*

gun down v

maraud, marauder v, n (noun use: b1870; marauder: b1700)

shooting iron n (Am)

sock n/v *hit*

Crime/Punishment/Enforcement

modus operandi n *method of operation* b1655

peeper n *peeping Tom* b1655

cat-o'-nine-tails n b1665

vandal n b1670 [vandalism: 1793] (vandalize: b1805)

arson n b1680 (arsonist: b1680)

shoplifter n b1680 (shoplift: b1820)

foodpad n *type of highwayman* b1685

kidnap v b1685 (kidnapper: b1670)

buccaneer n *French or English*

pirate b1690 [obs. "boucan cook": b1660 to 1700s; gen. "pirate": b1900]

ganja n b1690

smuggle v b1690 (smuggler: b1665)

halfway house n b1695

culprit n *defendant* ["guilty person": b1770]

dirty adj *illegal*

fork v *arch. slang* "pick a pocket"

furacious adj *thieving*

order n *as in "money order"*

The Law

legislation n *making laws* b1655 ["a law itself": b1870]

compurgation n *acquittal using character witnesses* b1660

forensic adj b1660 (forensical: b1581)

Roman law n b1660

cross-examine v b1665 (cross-question: b1695; cross-examination: b1825)

brief n b1670 ["gen. letter": b1340] (verb use: b1870)

litigation n b1670 ["dispute": b1570] (litigate: b1615; litigant: b1640)

malpractice n b1675

courtroom n b1680

legislature n b1680

probable cause n b1680

voir dire n b1680

permit n *type of document* b1685 ["permission": b1530]

court of common pleas n b1690

superior court n b1690

court of claims n b1695

cross-question n/v b1695

bench warrant n

degree n *as in "first-degree murder"*

malfeasance n (malfeasant: b1830)

The Fantastic/ Paranormal

larva n *arch. type of ghost* b1655

sylph n b1660 ["slim woman": b1870]

demoness n b1670 (demon: b1200)

demonolatry n b1670

gnome n b1670

presence n *as in "ghostly presence"* b1670

ultramundane adj *supernatural* b1670

clairvoyant adj b1675 [gen. "perceptive": b1700] (noun use: b1855; clairvoyance: b1840)

draconic adj *related to dragons* b1680

dowse, dowsing rod v, n b1695 (dowser: b1840)

banshee n

demonism n

kelpie n *folklore spirit*

Magic

witches' Sabbath n b1680

shaman n (shamanism: b1780)

Interjections

gadzooks interj b1655

viva interj b1670

egad interj b1675

pshaw interj b1675

son of a bitch interj b1675 (noun use: b1710)

haw interj *similar to ha!* b1680

stow it interj b1680

hurrah/hurray interj/n/v b1690 (huzzah: b1595)

au revoir interj/n b1695

dear interj b1695

jingo interj *as in "by jingo"* b1695

lackaday interj *expression of regret* b1695 (lackadaisy: b1800)

'sbodikins interj

'slidikins interj *obs. (God)-slid-ikins* [u1700s]

criminy interj

dad interj *gad*

gadso interj *gadzooks*

halloo interj

hear him, hear hear interj

Slang

deuce n *little dickens* b1655

hector v *swagger* b1655 (noun use: b1660)

cat's-paw n *dupe, puppet* b1660 ["light breeze": b1660]

tub-thumper n *vociferous speaker* b1665

bloody adv (Brit) *damned* b1670 (bleeding: b1860)

bro n *brother* b1670

Bucephalus n *riding horse* b1670

cuffs n *handcuffs* b1670 (cuff v: b1695)

fiddle away v b1670

flap n *loose woman* b1670

game n *as in "play games with the truth"* b1670

lose v *as in "you've lost me"* b1670

needle n *penis* b1670

sappy adj b1670

screw v *fleece, rob* b1670

tan v *as in "I'll tan your hide"* b1670

warming pan n *bedmate* b1670 [slang "fill-in": b1870]

whippersnappper n b1675

ism n b1680 (ist: b1830)

mogul n *hotshot* b1680 ["Mongol": b1590]

screw up v *botch* b1680 [as in "screw up courage": b1630] (screwup n: b1960)

spitfire n *ardent person* b1680

whip hand n b1680

greenhorn n b1685 [lit. use: b1475]

sharper n *cheat* b1685

chophouse n b1690

heeltop n *liquor remaining after drinking* b1690

madhouse n b1690

yawner n b1690

dab n (Brit) *skilled person* b1695

devil n *as in "poor devil"*

drag out v

fudge n *nonsense*

moggy n *wench*

slyboots n

swing-swang n *swinging back and forth*

they *them*

tripe n *junk* [arch. "person full of tripe": b1600]

Insults

anile adj *old-womanesque* b1655

bully-ruffian n b1655

potbellied adj b1660 (potbelly: b1715)

cully n *gullible person* b1665 (obs. verb use: b1680 to 1800s)

fribble n *trifler* b1665 (fribble v: b1630)

pissant n b1665

scaramouche n *rascal* b1665

doddering adj b1670

gill-flirt n *arch. slut* b1670

grotesque n/adj b1670

hobnail n *rube* b1670

Janus-faced adj *two-faced* b1670

skinflint n b1670

softheaded adj b1670

thumbless adj *inept* b1670

tomfool n *fool* b1670 ["mentally challenged person": b1375] (adj use: b1770; verb use: b1830; tomfoolery: b1815)

bullyhuff n *bully* b1680

hangdog adj b1680 (noun use: b1890)

hoyden adj/n *tartish woman* b1680 [obs. "rude man": b1595 to 1700s]

nincompoop n b1680 (ninny: b1600; nincompoopery: b1930)

chickenhearted adj (Am) b1685

criticaster n *bad critic* b1685

April fool n b1690

clodhopper n b1690

schoolboy adj b1690 (schoolboyish: b1835; schoolgirl adj: b1870)

backward adj *not up to date*

cow n *ugly woman*

crosspatch n *grouch*

dunderpate n

harridan n

landlubber n

maggot n *erratic person*

rapscallion n

snake in the grass n

Phrases

carte blanche n b1655
touch and go adj b1655
annus mirabilis n *year to remember* b1660
center of gravity n b1660 (center of mass: b1880)
dead weight n b1660
je ne sais quoi n b1660
old wives' tale n b1660
sit out v b1660
harm's way n b1665
make mincemeat of v b1665
second nature n b1665
umble pie n *humble pie* b1665
all along adv b1670
grand tour n b1670
in and in adv b1670
ins and outs n b1670
moon blindness n b1670
null and void adj b1670
promised land n b1670
wear and tear n b1670
labor of love n b1675
living death n b1675
noble savage n b1675
salient point n b1675
gift of gab n b1685
court of honor n b1690
life-and-death/life-or-death adj b1690
par excellence adj b1695
rule of thumb n b1695
coup de grace n
free and easy adj
lantern jaw n

General/Miscellaneous

blue ribbon n b1655
collective n *collective group, farm* b1655 (collectivism: b1860; collectivize: b1895)
craftsmanship n b1655
granule n b1655 (obs. granula: b1670 to 1800s; granular: b1795)
juxtaposition n b1655 (juxtapose: b1855)
melange n b1655
proposal n *suggestion* b1655 ["marriage proposal": b1700; "contractual proposal": b1770]
regulator n b1655
sponsor n *supporter; esp. godparent* b1655 ["nomina-

tor": b1700; "financial supporter": b1970] (verb use: b1885)
spontaneity n b1655 (spontaneous: b1650)
vibration n b1655 (vibrate: b1620)
abrasion n b1660 (abrade: b1680)
aftermath n *repercussion* b1660 ["second mowing": b1500]
agency n b1660
cacophony n b1660 (cacophonous: b1800)
cohesion n b1660 (cohesive: b1730)
complicity n b1660 (complice n: b1475; complicitous: b1860; complicit: b1975)
composite n *something composed of multiple elements* b1660 (adj use: b1400)
conflagration n *great blaze* b1660 [gen. fire: b1545] (conflagrant adj: b1660)
critique n b1660 (verb use: b1755)
dictation n *command* b1660
divergence n b1660 (diverge: b1665; divergent: b1700; divergency: b1710)
duad n *couple* b1660
groove n b1660 ["mineshaft": b1400; fig. use: b1870] (verb use: b1690)
half-truth n b1660
invite n b1660 (verb use: b1535)
outburst n b1660
parade n *showiness* b1660 ["mil. display": b1670; type of procession: b1700] (verb use: b1690)
preliminary n b1660 [sports sense: b1900] (adj use: b1670)
prodigy n *as in "child prodigy"* b1660 ["something unusual, portentous": b1475; "something inspiring awe": b1600]
pyre n b1660
rationale n b1660 ["excuse": b1700]
slam n/v *blow* b1660
slipknot n b1660

togetherness n b1660
characteristic adj/n b1665 (characteristical: b1625)
concert n *as in "working in concert"* b1665
contour n b1665 (verb use: b1875)
crony n b1665 (cronyism: b1840)
defector n b1665 (defect: b1600)
elasticity n b1665 (elastic adj: b1675)
facsimile n b1665 [obs. "making of copies": b1600 to 1600s] (adj use: b1770; verb use: b1870)
gauntlet n *as in "run the gauntlet"* b1665
intensity n b1665
mechanism n *way of working* b1665 ["machine": b1700]
nominee n *one nominated* b1665 ["person named": b1660]
outline n b1665 [as in "book outline": b1770] (verb use: b1790)
patrol n *patroling* b1665 ["something that patrols": b1700] (verb use: b1695)
pervert n b1665 (verb use: b1350)
reform n b1665
requirement n *something required* b1665 ["request": b1530]
risk n b1665 (verb use: b1670; risky: b1830)
similarity n b1665
smut n *soot* b1665 (verb use: b1470)
snippet n b1665
stinkpot n b1665
archfiend n b1670
aspect n *point of view* b1670 [astronomical sense: b1385]
balance n *equilibrium, stability, as in "mental balance"* b1670
ban n *prohibition* b1670 [arch. "official proclamation": b1350; "excommunication": b1600]
capitalize v *set value; benefit* b1670

class n *category, classification* b1670
collectanea n b1670
consistency n *as in "the consistency of oil"* b1670 ["ability to hold form": b1595; "being consistent": b1670] (consistent: b1650)
credential n b1670 (adj use: b1475; verb use: b1890)
cross-purposes n b1670
cut n *as in "woodcut"* b1670
derelict n *something abandoned* b1670 ["bum": b1730]
design n *invention; pattern* b1670 (verb use: b1450; designment: b1585)
doyen n *senior member* b1670 (doyenne: b1870)
duct n b1670 ["instance of guiding, conducting": b1650] (ductwork: b1935)
endorse, endorsement v, n *support* b1670
exertion n *exerting* b1670 ["laboring": b1800]
exit n *leaving* b1670 ["place to leave": b1700]
expanse n b1670
fragrance n b1670 (fragrancy: b1580)
frequency n b1670
hallmark n *fig.* b1670 [type of seal: b1725]
hurry n *rush* b1670 (verb use: b1590)
identity n b1670 ["being identical": b1570]
incognita adj/adv/n b1670 (incognito: b1650)
incompetent adj/n b1670 [leg. sense: b1600] (incompetency: b1615; incompetence: b1665)
jackadandy n b1670
leeway n b1670
levitation n b1670 (levity "lightness": b1600; levitate: b1675)
luxury n *as in "life of luxury"* b1670 [obs. "lust": b1350 to 1800s; "item of luxury": b1730] (luxe: b1560; luxuriate: b1625)
mainstream adj/n b1670

mentor n b1670 (verb use: b1985)

mischief n *naughtiness* b1670 [misfortune, evil: b1300] (mischievousness: b1570; mischievous: b1680)

mode n *as in "mode of behavior"* b1670

moderate n b1670

nuisance n *annoyance* b1670 [leg., as in "public nuisance": b1400]

order n *rank, level, as in "on the order of . . ."* b1670

outlook n *phys. perspective* b1670 [fig. "point of view": b1770]

play n *looseness, as in "play in a steering wheel"* b1670 (verb use: b1600)

prospects n *chances, potential* b1670 (obs. prospect "mentally viewing": b1570 to 1700s; prospective adj: b1830)

range n *as in "range of discussion"* b1670

rascallion n b1670

realty n b1670 [obs. "reality": b1450 to 1600s]

reception n *as in "warm reception"* b1670

round n *as in "round of drinks"* b1670

solidarity n b1670 (solidarism: b1920)

spring n *give, elasticity* b1670

stand n *as in "nightstand"* b1670

stop n *sojourn* b1670 (verb use: b1770)

stretch n *as in "stretch of road"* b1670 [as in "home stretch": b1870]

stroke n *as in "brushstroke"* b1670

support n *phys. support* b1670

system n *organized plan* b1670 (systematize: b1765; systemize: b1780; systematic: b1830)

texture n *surface feel* b1670 [obs. "weaving": b1450 to 1700s; "character": b1630] (verb use: b1695)

thread n *sequence* b1670

tone n *as in "muscle tone"* b1670

ubication n *being in a place* b1670

union n *organization, group* b1670

variation n *deviation* b1670

warrantee n b1670 (warrantor: b1685)

background n *as in "the background of a photo"* b1675 ["history": b1870] (verb use: b1770)

balderdash n *nonsense* b1675 [obs. "liquid" or "concoction of liquids": 1590s to 1600s]

dyad n b1675

fuzz n *as in "peach fuzz"* b1675 [type of fungus: b1600] (verb use: b1705)

group n b1675 (verb use: b1720)

migrant adj b1675 (noun use: b1760)

penchant n b1675

pockmark n b1675 (verb use: b1760)

ridicule n *something ridiculous; the ridicule itself* b1675 (verb use: b1700)

self-evident adj/n b1675 (self-evidencing: b1670)

setback n b1675

solvent n b1675

suite n *entourage* b1675

transfer n *act of transferring* b1675

blockade n/v b1680

kink n b1680 (verb use: b1700; kinkle: b1870)

masterstroke n b1680

missy adj/n b1680

mottle n/v b1680 (mottled: b1700)

penultimate adj/n b1680

routine n b1680 (adj use: b1820)

tick n *as in "ticktock"* b1680 [obs. "touch": b1450] (verb use: b1725)

tinplate n b1680 (verb use: b1890)

tubule n b1680

acoustics n b1685 (acoustic adj: b1605)

addendum n b1685

backlog n *log at the back of the fire* b1685

complexity n *complexness* b1685 ["something complex": b1725]

douche n b1685 (verb use: b1870)

helter-skelter n b1685 (adv use: b1595; adj use: b1785)

nascency n b1685 (nascence: b1575; nascent: b1625)

peephole n b1685

ratatat n b1685

renewal n b1685

ultimate n *the end* b1685 ["the best, the apex": b1970]

upright n b1685

warrantor n b1685 (warrantee: b1670)

bully n *ruffian* b1690 [arch. "sweetheart": b1540] (verb use: b1710; bully-ruffian: b1655)

lacquer n/v b1690 [obs. type of secretion: b1580 to 1700s]

mimicry n b1690

mob n b1690 (verb use: b1710; mobile: b1630; mobility: b1700)

patchwork n b1690 (adj use: b1730; verb use: b1970)

turnout n b1690

wave n *as in "wave of the hand"* b1690 (verb use: b1830)

chunk n b1695

foreground n b1695

lowlander n b1695

tease n b1695

tête-à-tête n *talk* b1695 (adv use: b1700; adj use: b1730; verb use: b1870)

additive adj

aspect n *component*

branch n *subdivision, as in "branch of government"*

dive n

drive n *as in "cattle drive"* [as in "Sunday drive": b1785]

evolution n [mil. sense: b1620; Darwinian sense: b1870]

excandescence n *akin to incandescence*

exhibition n

fetch n *doppelganger*

incumbent n *gen. sense* [religious sense: b1425]

jet n *jets of air*

lurch n *sudden movement* (noun use: b1830)

measure n *as in "take measures to stop the bleeding"*

momentum n

monogram n [type of sketch: b1610] (verb use: b1870)

premium n *surcharge; bonus*

relations n *dealings with*

remark n [obs. "remarkableness": b1635 to 1700s] (verb use: b1675)

run n *as in "run of good luck"*

shade n *as in "a shade of pink"* (verb use: b1730)

slip n *as in "slip of paper"*

smut n *pornography*

spirit n *fig. life, as in "team spirit"*

spring n *springiness*

squeak n

sweep n *as in "the sweep of a line," "the sweep of the land"*

thread n *continuity* (verb use: b1875)

tingle n *tingling*

trial n

trilemma n *dilemma with three choices*

vagrancy n *wandering* ["daydreaming": b1645; "homelessness": b1730]

world n *as in "the animal world"*

Things

bedroll n b1655

arbor n *spindle, shaft* b1660

medallion n b1660

pendulum n b1660 (pendulous: b1605; pendular: b1880)

rawhide n b1660

trangam n *obs. trinket, doodad* b1660 [u1800s]

calumet n *type of Native American tobacco pipe* b1665

cast iron n b1665 (cast-iron adj: b1700)

pig iron n b1665

alcohol n *liquid distillate* b1670 ["powder": b1570]

compressed air n b1670

fizgig n *type of firework or noisy toy* b1670 [arch. "flirt": b1530]

jack n *flag, as in "Union Jack"* b1670

prong n *tine* b1670 ["tined utensil": b1450]

specimen n *sample* b1670 ["model": b1630; scientific use: b1700; fig., as in "a fine specimen of a man": b1830]

cesspool n b1675 (cesspit: b1780)

union jack n b1675

wrought iron n b1680

strongbox n b1685

gangway n b1690 [obs. "road": b1100]

skyrocket n b1690

lens n b1695 [applied to the eye: b1730]

drop n *as in "cough drop"*

pennant n

till n *tray, as in "cash register till"* [gen. "compartment": b1450]

Description

arid adj b1655

compleat adj b1655

complex adj *made of many parts* b1655 ["complicated": b1715] (arch. verb use: b1680; complexity: b1685; complicated: b1730; complexify: b1830)

cordate adj *heart-shaped* b1655 [obs. "savvy": b1645 to 1700s]

crass adj *fig. coarse* b1655 ["physically coarse": b1435] (crassitude: b1680)

expansive adj b1655

fiddling adj *piddling* b1655

fortuitous adj b1655

gigantic adj b1655 ["related to giants": b1605 to 1700s] (gigantean: b1615; gigantesque: b1825)

horrific adj b1655

impracticable adj *impassable* b1655 ["impractical": b1670]

influential adj *gen.* b1655

(influence n: b1590; influence v: b1670)

informative adj b1655 ["giving form": b1400] (informatory: b1470)

ingratiating adj b1655

malefic adj b1655

quicksilver adj *fig. mercurial* b1655 [spec. to mercury: b1570]

remedial adj b1655 [educational sense: b1925] (remediate: b1605)

ridden adj *as in "lice-ridden"* b1655

salvable adj *salvageable* b1655

secondhand adj b1655 (adv use: b1850)

skewbald adj b1655

ultimate adj b1655 (noun use: b1685; verb use: b1830; ultimacy: b1845)

vacuous adj b1655

valedictory adj *saying goodbye* b1655 (noun use: b1780)

veridical adj *veracious* b1655

cogent adj b1660 (cogency: b1670)

constituent adj *part of* b1660

contemporaneous adj b1660

extemporaneous adj b1660 (obs. extemporary: b1600 to 1700s; extempore: b1555; extemporal: b1570)

glacial adj *cold* b1660 ["related to glaciers": b1870]

gratuitous adj *gratis* b1660 ["unnecessary": b1700]

homemade adj b1660

horrendous adj b1660

momentous adj b1660 ["having momentum": b1655]

petticoat adj b1660

pluvial adj b1660 (pluvious: b1450)

simultaneous adj b1660

strapping adj b1660

strident adj b1660

tertiary adj b1660

unorthodox adj b1660

vapid adj *flavorless* b1660 ["vacuous": b1770]

august adj b1665

ancillary adj b1665 (noun use: b1770)

effusive adj b1665

igneous adj b1665 [geologic sense: b1800]

irritable adj b1665 (irritability: b1755)

nutritious adj b1665 (nutritive: b1400)

outlying adj b1665

primeval adj b1665

reluctant adj b1665 (reluct v: b1530; reluctancy: b1635; reluctance: b1645; reluctate v: b1645)

soporific adj *causing sleep* b1665 ["sleepy": b1870] (noun use: b1730; sopor "sleep": b1570)

varicolored adj b1665

adept adj b1670 (noun use: b1710)

adhesive adj b1670 (noun use: b1900)

all-powerful adj b1670

apropos adv b1670 (adj use: b1690)

astraddle adv *astride* b1670

cerulean adj b1670

close adj *as in "pay close attention"* b1670

competent adj *able* b1670 [obs. "appropriate": b1400 to 1700s] (competence: b1730)

destructful adj b1670

dreary adj b1670 [obs. "gory, horrid": b900 to 1600s] (drear adj: b1630)

ephemeral adj b1670 (noun use: b1820)

equal adj *equally distributed* b1670

ethereal adj *nebulous* b1670

exact adj *precise* b1670 [applied to people: b1600]

explosive adj b1670 (noun use: b1875)

extra adj b1670 (noun use: b1795; adv use: b1825)

farewell adj b1670

fast adj *as in "colorfast"* b1670

first-rate adj b1670

gradual adj b1670 [obs. "in stages, gradated": b1470 to 1700s]

hard adj *as in "hard water"* b1670

impromptu adv b1670 (noun

use: b1700; adj use: b1765; verb use: b1830)

jaded adj b1670

malapropos adv *inappropriate; opp. of apropos* b1670 (adj use: b1730; noun use: b1870)

minimal adj b1670

obtrusive adj b1670 (obtrude: b1555; obtrusion: b1780)

off adj b1670

practicable adj b1670

prevalent adj b1670 [arch. "powerful": b1580] (prevalence: b1715)

puzzling adj b1670

second-rate adj b1670

seminal adj b1670 ["related to semen": b1400]

shabby adj b1670

sibilant adj b1670 (sibilate v: b1660; sibilous: b1770)

soft adj *easy, as in "a soft job"* b1670

soulful adj b1670

spanking adv *as in "brand spanking new"* b1670 (adj use: b1670)

spartan adj b1670

stagnant adj *lit. motionless* b1670 [fig. "undeveloping": b1770] (stagnate: b1670)

stringy adj b1670

synchronous adj b1670

tense adj *applied to things* b1670 [applied to people: b1825] (verb use: b1680; tension: b1535; tensity: b1660)

unbeauteous adj b1670

unseldom adv *often* b1670

versatile adj b1670 ["fickle": b1605] (versatility: b1800)

vulgar adj *base* b1670

worthwhile adj b1670

advertent adj b1675

cramp, cramped adj *cramped* b1675

elastic adj b1675 [obs. use describing gas: b1655 to 1700s; fig. "resilient": b1870] (noun use: b1850; elasticity: b1665)

engaging adj b1675 (engage: b1770)

esurient *adj hungry, greedy* b1675

excursive *adj digressing* b1675

feeblish *adj* b1675

reputable *adj* b1675

colorific *adj* b1680

generic *adj* b1680

implausible *adj* b1680

legion *adj* b1680

mythical *adj* b1680 (mythic: b1670)

omnificent *adj having ultimate power to create* b1680

slapdash *adj done hastily* b1680 ["done poorly": b1800] (verb use: b1830)

swaybacked *adj* b1680

tawdry *adj* b1680 (noun use: b1680)

veracious *adj truthful* b1680 ["true": b1800]

brilliant *adj* b1685 (brilliancy: b1750; brilliance: b1755)

eventual *adj* b1685 [obs. "conditional": b1685 to 1700s]

frowsy *adj* b1685

nondescript *adj* b1685 [obs. scientific "not easily classified": b1680 to 1800s]

spectacular *adj* b1685 (noun use: b1890)

asymmetrical *adj* b1690

flashy *adj showy* b1690

instanter *adv* b1690

lengthy *adj* (Am) b1690

roughshod *adj* b1690

bulk *adj* b1695

existential *adj existing* b1695 [philosophical sense: b1945]

focal *adj* b1695

noisy *adj* b1695

rustproof *adj* b1695 (verb use: b1930)

shocking *adj* b1695

delicate *adj subtle*

equal *adj as in "equal to the task"* (obs. equalize: b1590 to 1800s)

firsthand *adj*

flabby *adj* (flab n: b1925; fig. use: b1800)

footloose *adj*

hulking *adj*

irretrievable *adj*

lump *adj*

makeshift *adj* (noun use: b1815)

marsupial *adj pouchlike* ["of the marsupials": b1830]

painstaking *adj* (rare verb use: b1640)

precarious *adj unstable* ["not certain": b1650]

rattling *adj very* (adv use: b1830)

rewarding *adj*

shilly-shally *adv* (adj use: b1735; noun use: b1770; verb use: b1785)

split-new *adj brand-new*

thematic *adj*

unfair *adj* [obs. "not beautiful": b900 to 1600s]

unswerving *adj*

unworldly *adj*

Colors

royal purple *n* b1665

pink *adj/n the color* b1680 [as in "in the pink": b1770]

Actions/Verbs

capacitate *v make capable* b1655

cultivate *v fig. nurture, as in "cultivate a taste"* b1655 [as in "cultivate a relationship": b1700]

despond *v* b1655 (noun use: b1670; despondency: b1655; despondence: b1680; despondent: b1700)

originate *v* b1655

outwit *v* b1655

pervade *v* b1655 (pervasive: b1750)

simmer *v* b1655 (noun use: b1810; simmer down: b1875)

simulate *v* b1655 (simulated: b1625)

variegate *v* b1655 (variegated: b1665)

weather *v survive* b1655

dawdle *v* b1660

erupt *v gen.* b1660 [spec. to volcanoes: b1770; spec. to new teeth: b1870]

exacerbate *v* b1660

grade *v arrange into grades or categories* b1660

harangue *v* b1660 (noun use: b1450)

incapacitate *v* b1660 (incapacity: b1615)

perk *v* (Am) *percolate* b1660

regale *v* b1660 (noun use: b1670)

repristinate *v make pristine again* b1660

slur *v pass over quickly* b1660 ["fumble words": b1900]

stunt *v inhibit* b1660 ["irk": b1585 to 1600s] (verb use: b1725)

substantiate *v provide substance* b1660 ["prove": b1830]

transmogrify *v* b1660

coax *v* b1665 ["fondle, pet": b1590]

coordinate *v cause to work together* b1665 ["make equal": b1665] (coordinator: b1865)

deaden *v* b1665

embrangle *v entangle* b1665

exscind *v cut off* b1665

hagride *v torment, harass* b1665

laminate *v* b1665 (adj use: b1670; lamination: b1680)

stratify *v* b1665

tailor *v* b1665 [fig. "customize": b1945]

tiptoe *v stand on tiptoes* b1665 ["walk on tiptoes": b1770]

travesty *n/v disguise; parody* b1665

waft *v float* b1665 ["escort": b1515]

wheedle *v* b1665

wrack *v ruin, hurt* b1665

apply *v as in "apply for a job"* b1670 (application: b1670; applicant: b1790)

banter *v* b1670 (noun use: b1690)

bob *v trim* b1670

carnify *v turn into flesh* b1670

cheapen *v* b1670 [arch. "inquire about price": b1565]

coo *v* b1670 (noun use: b1730)

diabolify *v* b1670 (diabolize: b1705)

disinfect *v* b1670 [obs. "cure of infection": b1600 to 1700s] (disinfectant: b1840)

dupe *v* b1670 (noun use: b1685; dupery: b1760)

ejaculate *v exclaim* b1670

elude *v* b1670 ["confuse": b1540 to 1700s] (elusion: b1550)

engage *v as in "engage in an activity"* b1670

estimate *v assess* b1670 (noun use "assessment": b1600; noun use "numerical prediction": b1630)

hand *v as in "hand over"* b1670

heckle *v* b1670 (heckler: b1885)

identify *v* b1670 ["view as identical": b1665; "empathize": b1800]

indenture *v* b1670 [gen. "contract": b1660]

intervene *v step in* b1670 [obs. "prevent": b1590 to 1800s; as in "the intervening time": b1630] (intervent v: b1600)

keelhaul *v* b1670

lead *v officiate, set a trend* b1670

leaf *v as in "leaf through a book"* b1670

lose *v as in "lose weight"* b1670

make *v force, as in "make me do that"* b1670

maroon *v* b1670

oust *v* b1670 [leg. sense: b1425]

outnumber *v* b1670

part *v as in "part your hair"* b1670

pique *v* b1670

play *v as in "play one against the other"* b1670

project *v as in "project a picture"* b1670 (projection: b1900)

quit *v as in "quit complaining"* b1670 [var. meanings of "release from obligation": 1200s]

raise *v as in "raise a question"* b1670

rally *v as in "rally courage"* b1670 (noun use: b1830)

reflect v *as in "the behavior of one reflects on the group"* b1670

relate v *connect* b1670 (related: b1665)

relax v *make less stringent* b1670

resort v *as in "resort to other measures"* b1670 (noun use: b1385)

revolve v *spin* b1670 [var. meanings of "turn figuratively": b1400 to 1600s] (revolution: b1400)

ripple v b1670 (verb use: b1800)

sandbag v b1670 [fig. use: b1900]

scrape v *as in "bow and scrape"* b1670

serve v *as in "if memory serves"* b1670

stoke v b1670 [fig. use: b1870]

suspend v *hang in the air* b1670 ["keep in suspense": b1630]

truckle v *suck up* b1670

twist v *as in "twist two wires together"* b1670

vindicate v *exonerate* b1670 [obs. "rescue": b1570 to 1700s] (vindictive: b1630; vindication: b1670)

vocalize v b1670

whiff v b1670

fudge v *fake, dodge* b1675

hedge v *as in "hedge a bet"* b1675 (noun use: b1770)

hocus v *trick or hoax* b1675 (hoax: b1800)

nap v *nab, as in "kidnapper"* b1675 (nab: b1685)

nudge v b1675 (noun use: b1870)

palm v *as in "palm a coin"* b1675

remark v b1675 ["notice": b1600]

revivify v b1675 (reviviscence: b1630)

scrutinize v b1675 (scrutiny: b1605)

char v b1680 (noun use: b1880)

expurgate v b1680 [obs. "defecate": b1625 to 1600s]

gobble v *make turkey noises* b1680 (noun use: b1800)

mechanize v b1680

minify v *opp. of magnify* b1680

muddle v b1680 [obs. "wallow in mud": b1350; obs. "make physically cloudy": b1600] (noun use: b1820; muddy: b1605)

ogle v b1680 (noun use: b1715)

placate v b1680

slump v *collapse into water* b1680 [gen. "collapse": b1870]

tote v (Am) b1680

exert v b1685

manufacture v *make usable* b1685 ["create": b1770]

marble v b1685 (marbleize: b1860)

nab v b1685 (nap v, as in "kidnap": b1675)

prim v b1685 (adj use: b1710)

retouch v b1685

disconcert v b1690

mimic v b1690 (noun use: b1590)

scamper v b1690 [obs. "escape": u1800s] (noun use: b1700)

snuggle v *lie snugly* b1690 ["work to fit snugly": b1800]

align v b1695 (alignment: b1790)

apprise v b1695

converge v b1695 (converge-ncy: b1710; convergence: b1715; convergent: b1730)

garble v *miscommunicate* b1695 ["remove garbage": b1420]

gravitate v b1695 [obs. "affect with gravity": b1645 to 1800s]

squirm v *lit. wriggle* b1695 [fig. use: b1830]

structure v b1695

Americanize v (Am)

buoy v *support, lift* ["set a buoy": b1600]

check v *test, inspect* (noun use: b1630)

compromise v *endanger*

cross v *as in "paths cross"*

cut v *as in "cut a tooth"*

deposit n *lay down*

ease v *make gradual progress, as in "ease into"*

enter v *as in "enter a contest"*

erase v (erasure: b1735; eraser: b1790)

fizz v ["cause to fizz": b1665] (noun use: b1815)

give v *as in "give a damn"*

holler v (Am) (noun use: b1825)

hook v *fig. catch* [lit. "catch": b1300]

kick out v

lace v *as in "lace a drink with strychnine"*

lose v *as in "lose the pursuers"*

officiate v [rel. sense: b1635]

offset v

pack v *as in "pack your bags"*

regiment v *make regimented* ["assign to mil. regiments": b1620] (regimentation: b1900)

retrace v

rotate v *alternate, as in "rotating shifts"* ["spin": b1810]

scratch v *as in "scratch out"*

sidle v

slipper v *beat with a slipper*

snuff v *extinguish*

soothe v [obs. "prove": b950 to 1500s; obs. "flatter": b1600 to 1800s]

spirit v *as in "spirit away"*

split v *share*

stick v *as in "stick him with an unpleasant job"*

suppose v *as in "you're supposed to be on time"*

tiff v *quarrel* ["drink": b1770] (noun use: b1755)

twist v *as in "twist a dial"*

volunteer v *sign up* ["offer things, information": b1830]

Archaisms

lenient adj *soothing* b1655

consarcination n *hodgepodge* b1670

cotemporary adj/n *contemporary* b1670

emane v *obs. emanate* b1670 [u1800s]

exsuccous adj *dry* b1670

flirt v *blurt* b1670

flurr v *scatter* b1670

fortune n *rich woman* b1670

fracid adj *obs. overripe* b1670 [u1800s]

griph n *obs. conundrum* b1670 [u1800s]

manuductor n *obs. conductor* b1670 [u1800s]

panchestron n *obs. cure-all* b1670 [u1700s]

proruption n *erupting forth* b1670

schemist n *astrologer* b1670

tache n *type of fastening device* b1670

inane n *void* b1680

jobe v *obs. upbraid* [u1700s]

saint-errant n *obs. akin to knight-errant* [u1800s]

IN USE BY
1750

Geography/Places
magnetic pole n b1705
backwoods n/adj (Am) b1710
motherland n b1715
flood tide n b1720
bottomland n b1730
crop n *outcropping* b1730
subterrain n *subterranean area* b1730
coral reef n b1745
backcountry n

Natural Things
gold dust n b1705
phosphor n b1705 ["Satan": b1635]
rock salt n b1710
ice water n b1725
gas n b1730 [mystical sense: b1660]
phlogiston n *arch. fire as a substance* b1730
aura n *phys. emanation* b1735 ["nonphysical emanation": b1860; arch. "breeze": b1400]
fossil n *fossilized animal* b1740 ["fossilized fish": b1570; gen. "rock": b1630] (adj use: b1665; fossilize: b1795)
waterspout n b1740
glacier n b1745
lava n
shale n

Plants
gram n *chickpea and other such plants* b1705
petal n b1705
tulip tree n (Am) b1705
cornhusk n b1710
hibiscus n b1710
phlox n *type of flower* b1710
catnip n (Am) b1715
crab apple n b1715 (crab: b1300)
Norway pine n b1720
aster n *type of flower* b1730
gill n *on a mushroom* b1730
kola tree n b1730
China rose n b1735
Norway spruce n b1735
Scotch pine n b1735
sugar maple n b1735
weeping willow n b1735
beechnut n b1740
chess n *type of grass* b1740
timothy n b1740
coffee tree n b1745
crabgrass n b1745 [type of marine grass: b1600]
flowering plant n b1745
poison oak n (Am) b1745
magnolia n
pond lily n (Am)
ryegrass n
shrubbery n
wintersquash n

Animals
cheetah n b1705
silverfish n b1705
skipjack n *type of fish* b1705 [arch. "fop": b1550]
blue jay n (Am) b1710
brain coral n b1710
catbird n (Am) b1710
constrictor n b1710
devilfish n b1710
fiddlercrab n (Am) b1710
fish hawk n (Am) b1710
green snake n (Am) b1710
king snake n b1710
marsh hen n (Am) b1710
mosquito hawk n (Am) b1710
Portuguese man-of-war n b1710
praying mantis n b1710
shelduck n *type of duck* b1710 (sheldrake: b1325)
spider crab n b1710
staghound n b1710
stone crab n b1710
tit n *type of bird* b1710 [type of horse: b1550; "woman": b1600]
trumpeter swan n b1710
whippoorwill n (Am) b1710
yellow pine n b1710
gecko n b1715
hawksbill turtle n b1715
parrot fish n b1715
predaceous adj *predatory* b1715
kitty n *kitten* b1720
finback n *fin whale* b1725
humpback whale n b1725
right whale n b1725
tomcat n b1725
whalebone whale n b1725
cardinal n b1730 (cardinal bird: b1670)
jackass n b1730 [fig. insult: b1830]
mako shark n b1730
man-of-war n *type of jellyfish* b1730
parasite n b1730 ["parasitic person": b1550]
pigeonhawk n (Am) b1730
runt n *smallest in litter* b1730 ["type of tree stump": b1505; "small cow": b1570; "small person": b1700]
slug n *akin to snail* b1730
whirligig beetle n b1730
whooping crane n (Am) b1730
Canada goose n b1735
hermit crab n b1735
killdeer n (Am) b1735
Arabian horse n b1740
chimpanzee n b1740 (chimp: b1880)
frigate bird n b1740
gobbler n *turkey* b1740
Italian greyhound n b1740
tree frog n b1740
black bear n b1745
chigger n (Am) b1745
coon n (Am) (rac)coon b1745
honey locust n b1745
mandrill n *type of baboon* b1745
musk ox n b1745
purple martin n (Am) b1745
red snapper n (Am) b1745
sea anemone n b1745
sea trout n b1745
bantam n *the fowl* (adj use: b1785)
fire ant n
kingfish n *type of fish*
water bug n

Weather
weather vane n b1725
muggy adj b1735

northwester n b1735
snowflake n b1735

Heavens/Sky

nucleus n *core of a comet*
b1705 [gen. "central
part": b1765; biological
"center of cell": b1835;
"center of atom": b1915]
solar system n b1705
harvest moon n b1710
primary n *primary planet*
b1725
aurora australis n b1730 (aurora borealis: b1625)
moonrise n b1730 (moonset:
b1845)
nebula n b1730 ["cloudi-
ness": b1550; "eye film":
b1665]
zodiacal light n b1735
lunar eclipse n b1740

Science

centripetal force n b1710
(centrifugal force: b1720)
dendrology n *study of trees*
b1710
vivisection n b1710 (vivisect:
b1865)
inertia n b1715 [fig. use:
b1825]
physics n b1715 ["gen. science": b1580]
centrifugal force n b1725
(centripetal force: b1710)
science n b1725 ["knowl-
edge": b1340]
teleology n b1740
chemical n (adj use: b1580)
freezing point n

Technology

engineering n b1720
android n b1730
circuit n *as in "electrical circuit"* ["circle": b1385]
sprocket n *part of a gear* ["element of construction":
b1540]

Energy

power n b1730 (verb use:
b1900)
electrify v *lit. and fig.* b1745
battery n *source of electricity*

Time

midweek adj/adv/n b1710
chronometer n b1715 [obs.
"metronome": b1730 to
1800s]
sunup n (Am) b1715
yesterevening adv/n b1715
(yester-even: b1450)
stopwatch n b1740

Age/Aging

juvenile n b1735 (adj use:
b1625; obs. juvenal:
b1600 to 1800s)
sexagenarian n b1740
boyhood n b1745
school-age adj b1745

Mathematics

trapezoid n b1705 [type of
wrist bone: b1870]
infinitesimal n b1710
monomial n b1710
coefficient n b1715
mil n b1725
pi n b1730
positive adj b1730
Roman numerals n b1735
solid geometry n b1735
tabulate v b1735 ["put down
a plank": b1660] (tabula-
tion: b1840)
plane geometry n

Measurement

sliding scale n b1710
pedometer n 1723
drib n *as in "dribs and drabs"*
b1730
mass n b1730
electrometer n
milestone n

The Body

pulmonary artery/pulmonary
vein n b1705
triceps n b1705 (adj use
"having three heads":
b1580)
extensor n *type of muscle*
b1710
fallopian tube n b1710
mug n *slang face* b1710
plantar adj *pertaining to feet*
b1710
salivary gland n b1710
in utero adj/adv b1715

pineal gland n b1715
urinary bladder n b1720
auditory nerve n b1725
inhale v b1725 (inhalation:
b1625)
torso n b1725
bust n *chest* b1730
forearm n b1730
gag v *retch* b1730
gastric juice n b1730
milk tooth n b1730
sinuses n b1730
slouch n *type of posture*
b1730 (verb use: b1755)
bollocks n *testicles* b1745
coronary artery n b1745
encephalon n *the brain* b1745
eustachian tube n b1745
frontal bone n b1745
poop n/v *slang excrement*
b1745 (poo, poopoo:
b1970)
sac n b1745
sciatic nerve n b1745
titty n (tit: b1930)

Physical Description

eupnea n *breathing* b1710
shovel-nosed adj b1710
gawky adj b1725 (noun use:
b1725; gawkish: b1880)
husky adj *as in "a husky
voice"* b1725
underhand adj *as in "an underhand throw"* b1730
(adv use: b1830)
throw up v *vomit* b1740

Medicine

beriberi n b1705
ailment n b1710 (ail v: b950;
ail n: b1300)
dyspepsia n b1710
extrauterine adj b1710
invalid n *one who is bedridden*
b1710 (adj use: b1645)
rash n b1710 [fig., as in "a
rash of injuries": b1830]
scoliosis n b1710
scratchy adj *suffering from
scratching disease* b1710
cystic adj b1715 ["pertaining
to the gall bladder":
b1635] (cyst: b1715)
hunchback n b1715 (hunch-
backed: b1600)
outpatient adj/n b1715
apnea n b1720

bunion n b1720
officinal adj *medicinal* b1720
syphilis n b1720 (syph:
b1915)
witch doctor n b1720
anesthesia n b1725 (anes-
thetic n/v: 1840s)
carcinoma n b1725
inoculate v b1725 [obs.
"graft": b1450] (inocula-
tion: b1715)
pharmacology n b1725
albino n b1730 (albinism:
b1840)
antiseptic adj/n b1730
chicken pox n b1730
evacuate v b1730
hepatitis n b1730
logodiarrhea n *diarrhea*
b1730
pillbox n b1730
thrombosis n *blood clot* b1730
[gen. "coagulation":
b1710]
tonsillitis n b1730
tracheotomy n b1730 (tra-
cheostomy: b1970)
antacid n b1735
noctambulist n *sleepwalker*
b1735 (obs. noctambulo
"noctambulist": b1630 to
1700s; noctambulism:
b1860)
malaria n b1740 (malarial,
malarious: b1870)
nettle rash n b1740
prickly heat n (Am) b1740
yellow fever n b1740
colicky adj b1745
influenza n b1745
obstetric/obstetrical adj
b1745
scalpel n b1745
stasis n *med. stagnation*
b1745 ["equilibrium":
b1930]
caster oil n
Hippocratic oath n
invalidism n *chronic invalidity*
sleepwalker n (sleepwalk,
sleepwalking: b1800)
snow blindness n

Everyday Life

chopping block n b1705
coffee pot n b1705 (coffeemaker: b1930)

pier glass n *type of mirror* b1705

powder puff n b1705

reading desk n b1705

soupspoon n b1705

cold cream n b1710

crown glass n b1710

envelope n *postal sense* b1710 [gen. sense: b1570]

tureen n b1710

address n *as in "home address"* b1715 (verb use: b1470)

bunting n *decorative material* b1715

carboy n *type of bottle* b1715

card table n b1715

decanter n b1715 (verb use: b1825)

fireplug n b1715 (fire hydrant: b1945)

glassware n b1715

lowboy n *type of furniture* b1715

sheeting n *bedsheets* b1715 (sheet: b1350)

bouquet n b1720 [aroma, as in "a wine's bouquet": 1800s; fig. "compliment": 1900s]

buffet n *sideboard* b1720

corkscrew n b1720

crockery n b1720

settee n *type of seat* b1720

sofa n b1720 ["raised seating area": b1620]

boiler n b1725

emery board n b1725

pillowcase n b1725

straight razor n b1725

Windsor chair n b1725

bookcase n b1730

cream n *as in "facial cream"* b1730

divan n b1730

headboard n b1730

jorum n *type of drinking vessel* b1730

plateglass n b1730

recipe n b1730

shakedown n *type of bed* b1730

wash n *washing laundry* b1730 [the laundry itself: b1800]

window blind n b1730

cuspidor n b1735

chandelier n b1740

sunscreen n b1740

fauteuil n *type of chair* b1745

flatiron n b1745

traveling case n b1745

curler n

potpourri n *type of scenting substance* [obs. type of stew: b1615 to 1700s; "hodgepodge": b1870]

sauceboat n

Shelter/Housing

field house n b1705

windowsill n b1705

camera n *chamber* b1710 ["photographic instrument": b1870]

coliseum n b1710

gateway n b1710

mezzanine n b1715 [in a theater: b1930]

veranda n b1715

colonnade n b1720

hacienda n b1720

levee n (Am) b1720

pad n *bed, residence* b1720

terra-cotta n b1725 [the color: b1900]

auditorium n b1730

basement n b1730

boardinghouse n b1730 (boarder: b1530)

condemn v b1730 ["close permanently": b1570]

hip roof n b1730

skyscraper n b1730

suite n *group of rooms* b1730

vestibule n *lobby* b1730 [in Greek architecture: b1625]

vomitory n *type of entrance* b1730 (vomitorium: b1755)

ground plan n b1735

adobe n b1740

ballroom n b1740

chateau n b1740

fire company n (Am) b1740 (fire department: b1825; fire brigade: b1835)

Gothic arch n b1740

shed roof n b1740

tepee n (Am) b1745

entryway n *(Am)*

loge n *booth*

storeroom n

Drink

green tea n b1705

orangeade n b1710

bitters n b1715

gin n b1715

sauternes n *type of wine* b1715

whiskey n b1715

dram v *tipple* b1730

dry adj *applied to wine* b1730

liqueur n b1730

malt n *malt liquor* b1730

proof n *in alcohol* b1730

sangria n b1740

pot liquor n b1745

proof spirit n *liquor with 50% plus ethanol* b1745

eau-de-vie n

Food

brown sugar n b1705

cookie n b1705

crabstick n b1705

muffin n b1705

pate n *as in "liver pate"* b1705

bell pepper n b1710

blueberry n b1710

casserole n b1710

cocoa n b1710 (cacao: b1555; cocoa bean: b1855)

croquette n b1710

cutlet n b1710

fatback n (Am) b1710

grenadine n *poultry dish* b1710

meringue n b1710

puree n b1710

savoy cabbage n b1710

sugar pea n *snow pea* b1710

beefsteak n b1715

caramel n b1715

half-and-half n b1715

pea soup n b1715 ["fog": b1870]

pecan n (Am) b1715

pekoe n *type of tea* b1715

ration n b1715 (verb use: b1860)

maple sugar n (Am) b1720

chickpea n b1725 ["chickpea plant": b1550]

chuck n *cut of beef* b1725 [gen. "chunk of meat": b1675]

milk chocolate n b1725

praline n *type of confection* b1725

rarebit n b1725

rock candy n b1725

salt pork n b1725

side dish n b1725

Welsh rabbit n b1725

white sauce n b1725

black-eyed pea n b1730

cayenne pepper n b1730

greens n b1730

ice n *type of ice cream* b1730

ice n *icing* b1730

icing n b1730

jam n *as in "peach jam"* b1730

marinade v b1730 (verb use: b1700; marinate v: b1645)

matelote n *type of stew* b1730

miso n *type of food paste* b1730

shortbread n b1730

toss v *as in "toss a salad"* b1730

vanilla n *vanilla extract* b1730

hot cross bun n b1735

sweet pea n b1735

tenderize v b1735 (tender v: b1400)

applesauce n b1740

cantaloupe n b1740

cock-a-leekie n *type of soup* b1740

cracker n b1740

johnnycake n (Am) b1740

scallop v b1740

butternut n (Am) b1745

hoecake n (Am) *type of pancake* b1745

hors d'oeuvre n b1745 (adv use: b1715)

ice cream n b1745 [ice cream cone: b1910]

pemmican n *type of rations* b1745

seltzer n b1745

waffle n b1745

cornbread n *(Am)*

cornmeal n

jug v *as in "jugged chicken"*

picnic n [slang "piece of cake": b1830] (verb use: b1830)

pound cake n

sweet potato n *(Am)*

wild rice n

Yorkshire pudding n

Agriculture/ Food-Gathering

county agent n (Am) b1705
dray horse n b1710
plantation n b1710 ["planting": b1450; "colonizing": b1570]
seed plant n b1710
farm v b1720 ["pay rent": b1435]
georgic adj *agricultural, pastoral* b1720 (georgical: b1670)
cowboy n *cowherder* b1725 ["young cowhand": b1625] (verb use: b1970; cowherd: b1000; cowgirl: b1885)
gig n *type of fishing gear* b1725 (verb use: b1805)
drill n *furrow for seeding* b1730 (verb use: b1740)
greenskeeper n b1730
layer n *hen* b1730
poularde n *spayed hen* b1735
beast of burden n b1740
salt lick n (Am) b1745
farmyard n
tenant farmer n

Cloth/Clothing

cassimere n *type of fabric* b1705
headdress n b1705
overdress v b1710
poplin n *type of fabric* b1710 (poplinette "fake poplin": b1870)
etamine n *type of fabric* b1715
flounce v *fabric edging* b1715 (verb use: b1615)
nightdress n b1715
mantilla n *type of scarf* b1720
poncho n b1720
glove leather n b1725
pea jacket n (Am) b1725
seersucker n b1725
kilt n b1730 (verb use: b1350)
porkpie hat n b1735
chenile n *type of yarn* b1740
fitted adj b1740 ["apt": b1670] (fitting n: b1610)
bandana n b1745
frock coat n b1745
haversack n

uniform n ["a single uniform": b1800; "someone wearing a uniform": b1800]

Fashion/Style

costume n *gen. dress of a time* b1715 ["style": b1830; "stage costume": b1900] (verb use: b1825)
eardrop n *type of earring* b1720
smart adj *snappy, stylish* b1730
toupee n b1730
cue n *pigtail* b1735

Tools

teakettle n b1705
spyglass n b1710
jackknife n (Am) b1715 [type of dive: b1930]
pantograph n *earlier copying tool* b1725
shim n *type of plough* b1725
jack n *as in "automobile jack"* b1730 (verb use: b1845)
pocketknife n b1730
potter's wheel n b1730
regulator n b1730
strop n *for sharpening razors* b1730 (verb use: b1845)
steel trap n b1735
conductor n *electrical conductor* b1740
opera glass n b1740
mosquito net n b1745
tappet n b1745
caster n *type of wheel*
crowbar n (Am)
dumbwaiter n

Travel/Transportation

dockyard n b1705
hack n *taxi* b1705 (verb use: b1890; hackie: b1930)
pontoon bridge n b1705
canter v b1710 (noun use: b1755; Canterbury v: b1675)
dory n (Am) *type of boat* b1710
ship of the line n b1710
bearings n *awareness of location* b1715
brig n *the ship* b1715 (brigantine: b1500)

carryall n (Am) *type of carriage* b1715
free port n b1715
schooner n (Am) b1715
sea legs n b1715
Conestoga wagon n b1720
crossroad n *a road that crosses* b1720 ["crossing": b1800]
shay n *chaise* b1720
boathouse n b1725
fly n *type of coach* b1730
manifest n *as in "ship's manifest"* b1730 ["manifestation": b1565]
run n *regular route* b1730 (verb use: b1800)
detour n b1740 (verb use: b1840)
dockmaster n b1740
flying machine n b1740
sidewalk n b1740
covered wagon n (Am) b1745
crosswalk n b1745
landau n *type of carriage* b1745
roadster n *type of ship* b1745
underway adj *applied to ships* b1745 [gen. use: b1830]
window seat n b1745
outrigger n
oxcart n
shipmate n
steering wheel n

Emotions/ Characteristics

down-at-the-heels adj b1705
humorous adj *funny* b1705
smug adj b1705 ["smooth": b1555]
sobersides n *somber person* b1705
condescending adj b1710 [obs. "yielding": b1640]
eupepsia n *good disposition, good digestion* b1710
guarded adj *on one's guard* b1710
hipped adj *arch. depressed* b1710
indolence, indolent n, adj b1710 [obs. "unsusceptibility to pain": b1630 to 1700s]
lionhearted adj b1710

snigger v b1710 (noun use: b1825)
syrupy adj *maudlin* b1710
horselaugh n b1715
matter-of-fact adj b1715
self-assured adj b1715
self-control n b1715 (self-government: b1700)
tantrum n b1715
flustrated, flustrate adj b1720 (fluster: b1730; flustration: b1770)
guffaw n/v b1720
gumption n b1720
hopeful n b1720 (adj use: b1200)
blithesome adj b1725
hard-boiled adj b1725
clean-handed adj *innocent* b1730
considerate adj *thoughtful* b1730 [arch. "careful": b1575] (consideration: b1450; obs. considerative: b1450 to 1800s)
dash n *state of being dashing* b1730 (dashing: b1800)
enthusiasm, enthusiast n b1730 ["possession by a deity": b1580 to 1700s; "religious fervor": b1670]
flippant adj *disrespectful* b1730 ["flexible": b1605; obs. "loquascious": b1630 to 1700s]
glower v b1730 ["gaze": b1400]
guileless adj b1730 (guileful: b1350)
malbehavior n b1730
mellow adj *laid-back* b1730
adventuresome adj b1735
fatalism n *resignation* b1735 ["belief in fate": b1680] (fatalist: b1650)
felicitous adj *happy* b1735 ["appropriate": b1790]
heartfelt adj b1735
madden v *get mad* b1735 ["make mad": b1800]
nerveless adj b1735
uppish adj *snooty* b1735 [obs. "flush, rich": b1680]
nervous adj *anxious* b1740 ["suffering nerve problems": b1735]
self-satisfaction n b1740

blues n (Am) *depression* b1745 (blue adj: b1385)

sulky adj b1745 (sulk v: b1785; sulk n: b1800)

elation n *raised spirits* ["raised thoughts": b1400] (elated: b1615; elate: b1620)

frumpy adj *irascible*

high-strung adj

on tenterhooks n

sentimental adj (sentiment: b1730; sentimentality: b1770; sentimentalism: b1820)

wince v ["express impatience": b1300] (noun use: b1870)

Thoughts/Perception/ The Mind

idealist n b1705 (idealism: b1800)

outthink v b1705

visionary n b1705

clearheaded adj b1710

mnemonics n b1710 (mnemonic adj: b1755; mnemotechny: b1870)

addled adj b1715

egotism n b1715

egotist n b1715

presentiment n *a touch of prescience* b1715

unconscious adj *unaware* b1715 ["done without thinking": b1830; "out cold": b1870] (noun use: b1900)

guesswork n b1720

mastermind n *smart person* b1720 ["leader, creator": b1900] (verb use: b1940)

large-minded adj b1725

ontology n b1725

clever adj *mentally agile* b1730 ["physically agile": b1595]

coherent adj *logical* b1730 [obs. "in accordance with": b1555 to 1600s]

low-minded adj b1730

mystify v b1735 (mystification: b1815; mystified: b1870)

wrongheaded adj b1735

daymare n b1740

predilection n b1745

distrait adj *absent-minded* [obs. "distracted": b1470]

Love/Romance/Sex

lothario n b1705

condom n b1710

marriage of convenience n b1715

aphrodisiac n b1720

screw v/n *have intercourse* b1725 (noun use: b1930)

adorable adj *cute* b1730

affair n *tryst* b1730

onanism n b1730

pump v *slang have sex* b1730

spark n *lover* b1730 (verb use: b1790)

unite v *marry* b1730

flirt n (Am) b1735 [obs. "trollop": b1630 to 1700s] (verb use: b1630; flirtation: b1720; flirtatious: b1830)

ladylove n b1735

demirep n *prostitute*

heart-free adj *not in love* (heart-whole: b1475)

Family/Relations/ Friends

great-grandson n b1720 (great-granddaughter, great-grandchild)

pater n b1730 ["The Lord's Prayer": b1350]

related adj b1730 (relation: b1530; relative: b1670)

Holidays

All Fool's Day n b1715

yule log n b1725

Games/Fun/Leisure

jack-in-the-box n b1705

checkers n b1715

rocking horse n b1725 (rocker: b1870)

dibs n b1730

fun n b1730 [obs. "trick": b1685] (verb use: b1835; adj use: b1850)

merry-go-round n b1730

party n *social gathering* b1730 (verb use: b1920)

point n *as in "scoring points"* b1730

quadrille n *type of card game* b1730

croupier n *in gambling* b1735 [obs. "gambling kibbitzer": b1710]

peg top n *type of toy* b1740

tag n *the game* b1740 (verb use: b1880)

casino n b1745

fairground n b1745

roulette n b1745 ["small wheel": b1735]

cue n *in pool*

prize money n

Sports

prizefighter, prizefight n b1710 (prize-ring: b1830)

riposte n *counter in fencing* b1710 ["retort": b1870]

boxing n *the sport* b1715 (boxer: b1475; boxing glove: b1875)

hop, step and jump n *triple jump* b1720

lacrosse n (Am) b1720

letterman n b1725

champion n b1730 ["hero": b1200] (champ: b1870)

umpire n b1730 (ump: b1915)

inning n b1735

gundog n *hunting dog* b1745

putter n *golf club* b1745

sportsmanship n b1745

Professions/Duties

inspector general n b1705

librarian n b1705 [obs. "copier": b1670 to 1700s]

auctioneer n b1710 (verb use: b1770)

dustman n (Brit) *garbageman* b1710

janitor n b1710 ["doorman": b1585]

laundryman n b1710 (laundrywoman: b1865)

machinist n b1710

barkeep n b1715

fireman n *extinquisher* b1715 ["fire tender": b1380]

helpmate n b1715 (helper: b1300; helpmeet: b1615)

washerman n b1715 (washerwoman: b1635)

chaperon n b1720 [arch. type of hood: b1410] (verb use: b1800)

gentleman's gentleman n b1725

greengrocer n b1725 (greengrocery: b1830)

nanny n b1730

stableboy n b1730

sweep n *as in "chimney sweep"* b1730

bodyguard n b1735

logger n (Am) b1735

roughrider n b1735 (roughride v: b1900)

signalman n b1740

friseur n *hairdresser*

lamplighter n

toastmaster n (toastmistress: b1925)

Business/Commerce/ Selling

livery stable n b1705

saleswoman n b1705 (salesman: b1525; saleslady: b1860; salesperson: b1905)

tradeswoman n b1710 (tradesman: b1600; tradespeople: b1730)

businessman n b1715 (businesswoman: b1845; businesspeople: b1865; businessperson: b1975)

canteen n *type of establishment; type of water bottle* b1715

carriage trade n b1720

dramshop n *barroom* b1725

pothouse n *drinking establishment* b1725

advertise v b1730 (advertising: b1765)

consignment n b1730

manager n b1730 (manageress: b1800)

refinery n b1730

store n *commercial establishment* b1730 [storehouse: b1300] (stores "things stored": b1670)

vint v *arch. sell wine* b1730

wholesale v b1730

standing order n b1740

firm n *company* b1745 [obs. "signature": b1575 to 1700s; obs. "company name": b1770 to 1800s]

The Newfangled Oldfangled (and Vice Versa)

Everything oldfangled is newfangled again, or so it seems with much of our vocabulary.

Let's take a look at a couple of words in the sentence above as a for-instance. *Newfangled* seems such a newfangled word, yet it was used before 1400. *Oldfangled* is the newfangled word—used before 1845. Other old "new" words include:

- *Spew*, meaning "vomit," has been with us since before 900. Its more general sense was in place by 1600.

- *Suburb* was first recorded in Middle English.

- One could *blab* by 1400, *blabber* by 1470, and be a *blab* by 1350.

- *Weathercaster* was used before 1610—the word combines *weather forecaster*, not *weather broadcaster*, as many assume.

- The phrase *women's rights* was recorded before 1635.

- *Salad days* was in use by 1650.

- One could be *anti-American* before there was a United States to be anti—by 1775.

- *Fly* as an adjective was in use by 1815—though as "alert" or "crafty," and not in the modern slang sense.

- *Credit card* was used before 1900.

- *Mushroom cloud* was used before 1910, though not in the military sense, which came before 1945.

- The phrase *baby boom* was recorded by 1945, before the boom is generally regarded to have begun resounding.

Surprisingly, it's slang—those words from which we anticipate faddish volatility and fragility—that shows some of the most remarkable durability. As examples:

- *Hot* meaning erotic has been with us since before 1350.

- *Man* has been used as an interjection since Late Middle English, as has *yo* as an interjection.

- *Clap* referring to gonorrhea was in use by 1590.

- *Frig* as a euphemism for something harsher has been around since before 1600.

- *Knock up* as slang for "impregnate" by 1665.

- *Bro* as slang abbreviation for brother was in use by 1670.

- The phrase *on the fritz* was in use by 1725.

- *Old man* meaning "father" was in use by 1770—and *old lady* by 1870.

- *Crib* as slang for a place to stay, live or sleep was in use by 1870. Even earlier—*pad*, in roughly the same senses by 1720.

- *Coffin nail* as slang for cigarette proves that we didn't need a Surgeon General to see the dangers—the phrase was in use by 1890.

Zeroing in on slang, we might observe that the '60s seems to have been with us for decades, even centuries. So much of the slang vocabulary that seems tied to that decade has been around for some time. "Tune in, turn on, drop out"? One could *tune in* and *tune out* by 1910, *turn on* by 1905, *drop out* by 1850.

Of course, the senses are somewhat different—context of the times and all that, as we'll see with other words that seem to be of our youthful past but are actually much older:

- *Mellow* meaning "laid back" has been with us since before 1730.

- The phrase *free love* was used before 1825.

- *Boss* ("cool," "neat," "nifty") was pre-hippie slang—used by 1840.

- *Freak* as in "aficionado" was used before 1910.

- *Easy rider* (by 1915) isn't much older than motorcycles, though the phrase was used as slang for "lover" and not as a premonition of Jack Nicholson movies.

- And "what's the haps?", meaning "what's happening?" "what's going on?"—has an aged ancestor: *Hap*, meaning "luck, event, happening," has been with us since before 1350.

Finally, a couple of intriguing notes that have to do more with words than strictly with meanings:

- *No way!* is a relatively recent interjection—by 1965—but as an adverb *noway* has been used since before 1300.

- *Laser* has been with us since Middle English, though it described a type of plant resin.

The Workplace

understrapper n *underling* b1705

night shift n b1710

workpeople n b1710

manufacturer n *obs. laborer* b1720 [u1800s]

char v *work as a charwoman* b1730

raise v *pay increase* b1730

shift n b1730

slave v *work hard* b1730 ["enslave": b1550]

payroll n b1740

self-employment n b1745 (self-employed: b1950)

chore n [obs. "chorus": b1425 to 1600s]

Finances/Money

bear v b1710 (bearish: b1885; bull: b1715)

broke adj *having no money* b1710

promissory note n b1710

stockbroker n b1710

bankbook n b1715

counting room n b1715

medium of exchange n b1715

double entry n b1725

hallmark n *mark to establish purity* b1725 [fig. use: b1870]

copper n *coin* b1730

hard adj *as in "hard currency"* b1730

rate of exchange n b1730

solvency n b1730

two bits n (Am) b1730

budget n b1735 [obs. type of wallet: b1425] (verb use: b1900)

legal tender n b1740

poorhouse n b1745

Language and Speaking

minuscule n *type of writing style* b1705 (adj use: b1745)

phonography n *phonetic spelling* b1705

diesis n *double dagger* b1710

double dagger n *diesis* b1710

chitter-chatter n b1715 (verb use: b1930; chitchat n: b1710)

idiomatic adj b1715

verbiage n b1725

bon mot n b1730

catchword n b1730

contraction n *e.g., "can't"* b1730

logodaedalist n *articulate person* b1730

slogan n *catchphrase* b1730 ["battle cry": b1520]

uppercase adj b1730 (noun use: b1920; verb use: b1950; upper case "typesetter's drawer": b1685)

watchword n b1740 [obs. "password": b1400 to 1600s]

bracket n

Contractions

o'clock adv b1720 (of the clock: b1390)

wa'n't contr b1730

I've contr b1745

mustn't contr b1745

she'd contr b1745

we've contr b1745

Literature/Writing

authorship n *the writing profession* b1710 ["the act of writing": b1830]

epic n b1710 [gen. use: b1870]

fountain pen n b1710

lending library n b1710

pseudonymous adj b1710

saga n b1710

storyteller n b1710 ["liar": b1770]

yearbook n *as in "high school yearbook"* b1710 [type of law record: b1590]

antihero n b1715 (antiheroine: b1910)

biographer n b1715 (biographee: b1845)

classics n b1715

editor n b1715 ["publisher": b1650] (editress: b1800)

storybook n b1715 (adj use: b1845)

plagiarize v b1720

readership n b1720

jot v b1725

companion n b1730

cyclopedia n b1730 [gen. "learning": b1640]

journal n *periodical publication* b1730

majuscule n CAPITAL LETTER b1730

memo n b1730

novelist n b1730 [obs. "creator of the new": 1500s to 1700s]

papyrus n *writing material* b1730 [type of plant: b1400]

poetics n b1730

type n *as in "type writer"* b1730

bibliomania n b1735

rag n *bad newspaper* b1735

editorial adj b1745

parodist n b1745

picture writing n b1745

schoolbook n b1745

brochure n

fairy tale n

literary adj [obs. "of the alphabet": b1650 to 1700s]

Communication

postrider n b1705

first class n

Visual Arts/Photography

pastiche, pasticcio n b1710

stencil n *pattern* b1710 ["result of stenciling": b1900]

caricature n b1715 (verb use: b1750)

contrast n *in artwork* b1715 [obs. "conflict, resistance": b1600 to 1700s; gen. use: b1770; in photos: b1930] (verb use: b1695)

focal point n b1715

low relief n *bas relief* b1715

profile v *draw a profile* b1715 ["write a profile": b1970]

drawing board n b1725

sgraffito n *decoration style* b1730

style n *as in "impressionist style"* b1730

Performing Arts

greenroom n b1705

leading man n b1705 (leading lady: b1875)

benefit n *charity performance* b1730

dramatis personae n b1730

orchestra n *place in theater where musicians sit* b1730 [arch. "part of the theater": b1610]

performer n b1730

run n *as in "the run of a play"* b1730 (verb use: b1830)

skit n b1730 ["satirical observation": b1730]

showman n b1735

entr'acte n

Music

bass drum n b1705

marimba n b1705

opus n b1705 (opuscule "minor opus": b1660)

score n b1705 (verb use: b1870)

songstress n b1705 (songster: b1000)

clavier n *keyboard* b1710 ["keyboard instrument": b1845]

harmonics n b1710

mandolin n b1710

roulade n b1710

pitch pipe n b1715

opera house n b1720

orchestra n *group of musicians* b1720 (orchestral: b1815; orchestrate: b1880)

alto n b1725

aria n b1725

bassoon n b1725

cantata n b1725

fantasia n b1725

finale n b1725 [gen. use: b1785]

forte adj/adv b1725 (noun use: b1760)

fortissimo adj/adv b1725 (noun use: b1860)

maestro n b1725 [fig. use: b1870]

pastorale n *type of opera* b1725

toccata n b1725

tremolo n b1725

trombone n b1725

viola n b1725

violoncello n b1725

concerto n b1730

contralto n b1730

double bass n b1730

entree n b1730

mandola n *type of lute* b1730

reprise n b1730
soprano adj/n b1730
troubadour n b1730
banjo n b1740
duet n b1740 (verb use:
b1825; duettino: b1870)
libretto n *the book of a musical*
b1745
timpani n b1745
hurdy-gurdy n

Entertainment
pirouette n b1710
cotillion n *type of dance*
b1730 ["type of social
event": b1815]
heroine n *protagonist* b1730
(hero: b1700)
hop n *type of dance* b1730
saloon n *ballroom* b1730
["bar": b1845; "ship, plane
passenger space": b1870]
at home n *at-home reception*
b1745
fandango n

Education
classmate n (Am) b1715
savant n b1720
self-taught adj b1725

Religion
crusade n b1710 [gen. use:
b1710] (verb use: b1735)
lay sister n b1710
denomination n b1720
patron saint n b1720
vulgar era n *Christian era*
b1720
churchwoman n b1725
(churchman: b1350)
confessional n b1730
revival n b1730
Zen n b1730
pantheism n b1735
family Bible n b1740
mysticism n b1740 (mystic:
b1385)
Scratch, Old Scratch n *the devil*
b1740

Society/Mores/Culture
proper adj *as in "prim and
proper"* b1705
prude n b1705 (verb use:
b1770; prudery: b1710;
prudish: b1720)
connoisseur n b1715

conversation piece n b1715
chap n *fellow* b1720 ["customer of a chapman":
b1580]
politesse n *formal politeness*
b1720
lassie n b1725
toast n *as in "toast of the
town"* b1730
American Indian n b1735
(Amerindian: b1900)
man-about-town n b1735
modernism n b1740
townsfolk n b1740
grand dame n b1745
Main Street n b1745
etiquette n
gentleman-farmer n

Government
colonist n (Am) b1705 (colonizer: b1785)
secretary-general n b1705
John Bull n *English Uncle Sam*
b1715
premier n b1715
federation n b1725 (federate
adj: b1675)
minister n b1730
gubernatorial adj (Am)
b1735
self-government n b1735
democrat n b1740
secret service n b1740

Politics
foreign minister n b1710
coalition n *political sense*
b1715 ["coalescing":
b1615]
nationalist n b1715 (adj use:
b1890; nationalism:
b1840)
general election n (Am)
b1720
ticket n *as in "party ticket"*
b1730

Death
sarcophagus n b1705
obituary n *list of obit-days*
b1710 ["newspaper item":
b1770] (adj use: b1710;
obit: b1875)
pallbearer n b1710
top v *slang kill* b1720
footstone n *opp. of headstone*
b1725

funereal adj b1725 (fune-
brial: b1600; funebrious:
b1630)
homicidal adj b1725
martyry, martyrion n *memor-
ium for a martyr* b1725
moribund adj b1725
necrology n *list of the dead*
b1730 ["obituary": b1800]
postmortem adj b1735 (noun
use: b1850; verb use:
b1900; postmortem exam-
ination: b1840)

War/Military/Violence
caisson n b1705
noncommissioned officer n
b1705 (noncom: 1880s)
sentry box n b1705
staff officer n b1705
submarine n b1705 (subma-
rine v, submariner: b1915)
bombshell n b1710
double-barrelled adj b1710
(double-barrel n: b1815)
enfilade v b1710 (noun use:
b1800)
reconnoiter v b1710 [gen.
use: b1770]
flotilla n b1715
thumbscrew n b1715
war dance n (Am) b1715
commanding officer n b1720
claymore n *type of sword*
b1725
enlisted man n b1725 (en-
listee: b1960; enlisted
woman: b1975)
smash n *hit* b1725
armament n *war equipment*
b1730 [arch. "naval
force": b1700]
bludgeon n b1730 (verb use:
b1870)
cut n *stroke, blow, as in "uppercut"* b1730
detail n b1730 (verb use:
b1730)
discruciate v *obs. torture*
b1730 [u1800s]
handicuffs n *arch. fisticuffs*
b1730
regular adj b1730 (noun use:
b1770)
round n *shot* b1730
samurai n b1730
services, service n *branch of
the military* b1730

tack v *arch. attack* b1730
gunflint n b1735
lunge n *weapon thrust* b1735
[gen. use: b1870] (verb
use: b1825)
military n b1740 (adj use:
b1460)
missile n *long-range weapon*
b1740 ["thrown weapon":
b1740]
set-to n b1745
crown v *bop on the head*
field day n
grapeshot n (grape: b1700)
row n *disturbance* (verb use:
b1800)
war cry n

Crime/Punishment/Enforcement
cop v *steal* b1705
cop v (Am) *arrest* b1705
(cap "arrest": b1590)
bondsman n b1715
peace officer n b1715
police n b1720 [obs. "government": b1500]
con n *con(vict)* b1725
job n *crime* b1725
crack v *as in "safecracking"*
b1730
deputize v b1730
incriminate v b1730 (incrimination: b1655; inculpate:
b1800)

The Law
circuit court n (Am) b1710
(circuit judge: b1805)
forewoman n b1710
supreme court n b1710
gist n b1715 [gen. use:
b1830]
leasehold v b1720
civil rights n b1725
appellate adj b1730
copyright n b1730 (verb use:
b1810)
foreclose v b1730 [obs. "restrain": b1300; "hinder,
prevent": b1500] (foreclosure: b1730)
merger n *leg.* b1730 [corpo-
rate sense: b1870]
probate court n b1730
rap v *obs. testify against*
b1730 [u1800s]

regulation n *law* b1730 (adj use: b1840)

circumstantial evidence n b1740

eminent domain n b1740

sanction n b1740 ["enacting a law": b1425] (verb use: b1780)

search warrant n b1740

alibi n b1745 (verb use: b1910)

judge advocate n

power of attorney n

The Fantastic/ Paranormal

fairyism n *magical power* b1715

ogre, ogress n b1715

little people n b1730

lunarian n *lunar native* b1730

phantasmagoria n b1730

vampire n b1735

bugaboo n *bugbear* b1740 ["peeve": b1900]

genie n *jinn* [obs. "genius": b1655]

Magic

thaumaturge n *magician* b1715 (thaumaturgy: b1730; thaumaturgist: b1830)

sympathetic ink n *invisible ink* b1725

Interjections

kiss my ass interj b1705

by/bye interj b1710 (bye-bye: b1720)

son of a gun interj b1710

encore n b1715 (noun/verb use: b1750)

howdy interj b1715

bye-bye interj b1720 (adv use, as in "go bye-bye": b1920)

pow interj/n b1725 (noun use: b1885)

aloha interj b1730

oh-oh interj b1730

hey presto interj *(Brit) kind of "voila"* b1735

voila interj b1740

Slang

bamboozle v b1705

rep n *reputation* b1705

scrape n *tough time* b1710

argufy v b1715

hogwash n b1715 [lit. use: b1470]

pudding n *penis* b1720 (pud: b1940)

scandalmonger n b1725

speechify v b1725

butter up v b1730

malt v *drink malt liquor* b1730

roast v *upbrade* b1730

seedy adj b1730 [lit. sense: b1575]

bigwig n b1735

clinker n *(Am) sour note* b1735 ["first-rate" (Brit): b1840]

rigmarole n b1740

rocky adj *shaky* b1740

stewed adj *drunk* b1740

deadeye n

jaw v *talk*

Insults

biddy n *old woman* b1710 ["chicken": b1630; "cleaning woman": b1730]

rattlebrain n b1710

thickheaded adj b1710 (thick adj: b1600; thickhead: b1825)

cockalorum n *stuck-up person* b1715

stupid n b1715

numskull n b1720

namby-pamby adj/n b1730 (noun use: b1765)

chucklehead n b1735

stick-in-the-mud n b1735

blackguard n *rascal* b1740

ne'er-do-well n b1740

simpleminded adj b1745

catchpenny adj *cheap*

dumpy adj *pudgy*

quiz n *strange person* (verb use: b1800; quizzical: b1800)

scatterbrained adj (scatterbrain: b1790)

Phrases

iron hand n b1705

mum's the word interj b1705

number one n b1705 (adj use: b1840; numero uno: b1970)

step-by-step adj/adv b1705

sweetness and light n b1705

by and large adv b1710

cut-and-dried adj b1710

flying colors n b1710

hammer and tongs adv/adj b1710

hush money n b1710

single-handed adj b1710

behind-the-scenes adj b1715

bone of contention n b1715

man Friday n b1720

point of view n b1720

local color n b1725

nota bene v b1725

Tweedledum and Tweedledee n b1725

dark age n b1730

head-to-head adj/adv b1730

on the fritz adj *(Am)* b1730

open sesame n b1730

poetic justice n b1730

pro bono adj b1730

red tape n b1730 [fig. use: b1740]

sounding board n b1730

land of Nod n *sleepland* b1735

cats and dogs adv b1740

hornet's nest n b1740

matter of course n b1740

kettle of fish n b1745

kiss ass v

odds and ends n

old school n

capful of wind n b1720

General/Miscellaneous

emergence n b1705 ["emergency": b1650]

falderal/folderol n b1705

fuss n b1705 (verb use: b1795; fussy: b1835)

metallurgy n b1705

standstill n b1705

tip-top n b1705 (adj use: b1725; adv use: b1885)

veneer n b1705 [fig. "guise": b1870] (verb use: b1730)

amount n b1710 (verb use: b1275)

anticlimax n b1710 (anticlimactic: b1900)

blunder n *goof* b1710 (verb use: b1715)

counterfoil n b1710

damp adj/n *wetness, dampness* b1710 [type of vapor: b1320; obs. "fog": b1630]

to 1800s; obs. "daze": b1570 to 1700s]

debris n b1710

hump n b1710

incidental n b1710

inclined plane n b1710

institution n *as in "charitable institution"* b1710

marplot n *plot-spoiler* b1710

misconduct n b1710 (verb use: b1770)

offshoot n b1710

panic n *commotion* b1710 ["panicked emotion": b1670] (verb use: b1830)

plan n *as in "floor plan," "plan of action"* b1710 [part of a perspective drawing: b1680] (verb use: b1730)

purist n b1710

truism n b1710

benefactress n b1715 (benefactor: b1455)

clique n b1715

hair ball n b1715

locus n b1715

oddity n b1715

rip n *tear* b1715 (verb use: b1480)

trickster n b1715 (tricker: b1555)

yes n b1715

zigzag n b1715 (adv use: b1730; adj use: b1750; verb use: b1780; zigzaggery: b1770)

alternate n b1720 (adj use: b1515; verb use: b1600)

crux n *type of riddle* b1720 ["ankh": b1635; "gist": b1890]

equipment n b1720 (arch. equippage: b1580)

out n b1720

pyrotechnics n *art of fireworks* b1720 ["the fireworks themselves": b1870] (pyrotechnic adj: b1825)

tint n b1720 (verb use: b1795; tintless "colorless": b1790)

blob n b1725 (verb use: b1430)

clutch n *group* b1725

naysayer n b1725

portfolio n b1725 [as in "stock portfolio": b1970]

trio n b1725
accompaniment n b1730
appointee n b1730
aside n b1730
berm n *ledge* b1730 ["road-side area": b1900]
claptrap n *nonsense* b1730 ["applause-provoking tool": b1730] (adj use: b1815)
consistency n *being consistent, regular, reliable* b1730
coterie n b1730
currency n *being up-to-date* b1730 (current n: b1600)
down n *as in "ups and downs"* b1730
drawback n *disadvantage* b1730
fracas n b1730
go n *as in "on the go"* b1730
indentation n b1730
ingesta n *ingested material* b1730
ironist n *user of irony* b1730
joker n b1730
knothole n b1730
mass n *as in "the masses"* b1730
mound n *small pile* b1730 ["small hill": b1830] (verb use: b1860)
palaver n b1730 (verb use: b1770)
plethora n *plenty* b1730 [rare med. sense: b1545]
position n *phys. placement, arrangement, as in "missionary position"* b1730
purchase n *foothold* b1730
quid n *something for chewing* b1730
renascence, renascent n, adj b1730
roster n b1730
salvage n b1730 ["payment for saving a ship": b1645] (verb use: b1890; salve v: b1710)
self-abuse n b1730 ["self-deceiving": b1605]
sham n *fake* b1730 [obs. "trick": b1680 to 1800s] (adj use: b1685)
stimulant n b1730 (adj use: b1800)
tag n *addition* b1730
thrust n *force* b1730 ["at-

tack": b1570; "gist": b1965]
tread n *as in "shoe tread"* b1730 [as in "tire tread": b1900]
average n b1735 (verb/adj use: b1770)
demulcent adj/n *soothing* b1735 (obs. demulce "sooth": b1570)
department n b1735 ["departure": b1450]
dilettante n b1735
hurry-scurry adj/adv/n b1735 (verb use: b1800)
ultimatum n b1735
aspirant n b1740 (adj use: b1815; aspire: b1400)
clincher n *deciding factor* b1740
humbug interj/n/v *fraud* b1740 ["nonsense": b1830]
maximum n b1740 (max: b1870)
precision n b1740 [obs. "slicing off": b1640] (adj use: b1875)
swipe n *as in "take a swipe at someone"* b1740 (verb use: b1825)
wham n b1740 (verb use: b1925)
airiness n b1745
flashing n b1745
originality n b1745
relationship n b1745
transience n b1745 (transiency: b1655)
unreality n b1745
catastrophe n *disaster* ["turn of events in drama": b1540]
catcall n *raucous noise* ["noisemaker": b1660]
dubiety n *dubiousness*
fortuity n
headway n *progress* [type of road: b1300; type of mining passage: b1710]
impresario n
launch n *the result of launching*
patina n
planning n
squeal n
toss-up n

Things

picket n *stake* b1705 [type of mil. punishment: b1690; "guard": b1770; "someone on strike": b1870] (noun use: b1745)
piston n b1705
trelliswork n *latticework* b1715
Greek cross n b1725
effects n *things* b1730
mannequin n b1730
package n *parcel* b1730 ["the action of packing": b1615] (verb use: b1925)
plug n *as in "plug of tobacco"* b1730
canteen n b1740
saddle blanket n b1740

Description

flimsy adj b1705
laggard adj b1705 (noun use: b1810)
out-of-the-way adj *atypical* b1705 ["remote": b1800]
picturesque adj b1705 ["descriptive": b1770]
quality adj *high-quality* b1705
recumbent adj b1705 (recumbency: b1650)
schematic adj b1705 (noun use: b1930)
serrated adj b1705
well-defined adj b1705
widespread adj b1705
consumedly adv *excessively* b1710
cozy adj *applied to people* b1710 [applied to places: b1800; "friendly": b1930]
emphatic adj b1710
flagrant adj b1710 [arch. "fiery": b1450] (flagrancy: b1600; flagrance: b1615)
full-length adj b1710
ill-fated adj b1710
infinitesimal adj b1710
limp adj b1710
sloppy adj *physically messy* b1710 [as in "sloppy work": b1830]
titanic adj b1710
yellow-bellied adj b1710 (yellowbelly: b1790)
acrid adj b1715

colossal adj *huge* b1715 ["wonderful": b1900]
connected adj *phys. connected* b1715 [fig. "related": b1800]
curious adj *odd* b1715 ["inquisitive": b1325; obs. "excellent," "remarkable": b1450 to 1800s]
distinguished adj b1715 [obs. "discrete": b1610 to 1800s]
exhaustless adj *perpetual* b1715
fateful adj *predictive* b1715 ["deadly": b1770; as in "that fateful day": b1830]
forbidding adj b1715
fuzzy adj *covered with fuzz* b1715 ["blurry": b1800]
indoor adj b1715
inflammatory adj b1715 (noun use: b1700)
lopsided adj b1715
medium adj b1715
miniature adj b1715 (noun use: b1590)
pent-up adj b1715
prior adj b1715
showy adj b1715
unflagging adj b1715
absorbent adj b1720
concerted adj b1720
elusive adj *uncaught* b1720 ["tough to catch": b1770]
farcical adj b1720
leery adj b1720
man-made adj b1720
overarching adj b1720
pedestrian adj *dull* b1720
trying adj b1720 (try: b1570)
wispy adj b1720 (wispish: b1895)
chubby adj *short and thick* b1725 ["resembling a chub": b1615 to 1800s; chuffy: b1615]
evasive adj b1725
outre adj b1725
snub, snub-nosed adj b1725
staccato adj b1725
Brobdingnagian adj 1726
lilliputian adj 1726
all-around adj b1730
corkscrew adj b1730
curly adj b1730
exclusive adj *as in "mutually exclusive"* b1730

grand adj *awe-inspiring, large* b1730

indecisive adj *as in "an indecisive battle"* b1730 [as in "an indecisive person": b1800] (indecision: b1765)

intentional adj *on purpose* b1730

interesting adj b1730 ["important": b1715]

likable adj b1730

loose adj *unconnected* b1730

muzzy adj b1730

pointless adj *meaningless* b1730

pronounced adj *noticeable* b1730

providential adj *fortunate* b1730 [obs. "foresightful": b1650 to 1800s]

renewable adj b1730

solid adj *pure, as in "solid gold"* b1730 [as in "solid color": b1900]

sticky adj b1730 ["humid": b1900; slang "ticklish, difficult": b1930]

storied adj *having an interesting background* b1730

superb adj *excellent* b1730 ["stately": b1550]

thickset adj *fat* b1730 ["close together": b1375]

tidy adj *neat* b1730 [obs. "timely": b1250 to 1700s; attractive: b1250; "ordered": b1830] (verb use: b1825)

timeworn adj b1730

versicolored adj b1730

wavy adj b1730

alfresco adj/adv *outside* b1735

amorphous adj b1735

dated adj b1735

dependable adj b1735

latterly adv *later, lately* b1735

mass adj *as in "mass hysteria"* b1735

microscopic adj b1735 ["related to the microscope": b1680]

rotary adj b1735 (noun use: b1890)

singsong adj b1735

well-off adj b1735

dingy adj *dirty* b1740 (dinginess n/v: b1830)

fair-weather adj b1740

scintillant adj b1740

snap adj *immediate* b1740

waterproof adj b1740 (noun use: b1800; verb use: b1845; water-repellent: b1900; water-resistant: b1925)

deep-seated adj b1745

indelicate adj *indecent* b1745 ["tactless": b1830] (indelicacy: b1715)

knee-high adj (Am) b1745

streaky adj *streaked* b1745 ["patchy, irregular": b1900]

unobtrusive adj b1745

automatic adj *mechanical; working without help*

creole adj (noun use: b1605)

emeritus adj (arch. emerited: b1700)

hackneyed adj (hackney adj: b1600 to 1700s)

harum-scarum adj *reckless* (adv use: b1700)

nary adj

outdoor adj (outdoors adv: b1820; outdoors n: b1845)

poorly adj *as in "feeling poorly"* (adv use: b1300)

prescriptive adj

spry adj

Colors

oxblood n *type of color* b1705

carmine n *the color* b1715 (adj use: b1760)

indigo blue n b1715

Prussian blue n b1725

sky blue n b1730

Actions/Verbs

bemuse v b1705

chorus v b1705

defile v *march in single file* b1705

ensure v b1705 [arch. "assure": b1400; obs. "insure": b1670 to 1700s]

overhaul v b1705 ["overtake": b1800]

escort v b1710

jam v b1710 [as in "jam radio signals": b1930] (noun use: b1805)

maltreat v b1710

secrete v *exude* b1710 (secretion: b1650)

aggress v b1715 ["commit aggression": b1715]

coincide v *correspond; be in the same place* b1715

disembody v b1715

document v b1715 [obs. "teach": b1670 to 1700s]

fanaticize v *be fanatic* b1715 ["make fanatic": b1815]

impersonate v b1715 ["personify": b1625] (impersonation: b1825)

laugh off v b1715

splash v b1715 [fig., as in "splash with color": b1870; "exhibit boldly": b1970] (noun use: b1740)

tackle v *harness* b1715 ["involve": b1340]

touch up v *fix* b1715 ["seek a loan": b1770]

hinge v *depend on* b1720 [lit. use: b1610]

hunker v b1720

leaguer v *beleaguer* b1720

whack v b1720 (noun use: b1940)

backtrack v (Am) b1725

sap v *drain of sap* b1725 [fig. "drain energy": b1755]

snaffle v (Brit) *take, snitch* b1725

belie v *distort* b1730 [obs. "malign": b1350; "disprove": b1670]

broaden v b1730

corroborate v b1730 [obs. phys. "strengthen": b1530 to 1800s] (corroboration: b1770)

deflagrate v *burn down* b1730

dip v *make a candle* b1730

discount v *deem insignificant* b1730

disembarrass v b1730

eliminate v *eradicate* b1730 [obs. "drive away": b1570] (elimination: b1605)

establish v *prove* b1730

exhibit v *put on exhibit* b1730 (noun use: b1670)

fritter v *as in "fritter away"* b1730 (fritters n: b1700)

gab n/v *chat* b1730 ["babble": b1370]

gabber v b1730

gamble v *risk* b1730 ["wager": b1900] (noun use: b1825)

honor v b1730 ["bequeath honor": b1250]

implement v b1730 (implementation: b1930)

insulate v *isolate* b1730 ["isolate": b1540; electrical sense: b1770]

liven v *enliven* b1730

manage v *as in "manage to get the work done"* b1730

merge v *intertwine, coalesce* b1730 [obs. "be immersed": b1640 to 1800s]

orient v *position to face East* b1730 (orientation: b1840; orientate v: b1850)

oscillate v *vibrate* b1730 [fig. sense: b1800] (oscillation: b1660)

overlap v b1730 (noun use: b1830)

personalize v b1730

personify v b1730 (personification: b1755)

plan v *design a building, etc.* b1730 ["prepare": b1770]

push v *promote, sell* b1730 (noun use: b1670)

rate v *rank* b1730 [fig. "regard": b1570; as in "that rates a second look": b1930]

shepherd v b1730 [fig. use: b1830]

spank v b1730 (spanking n: b1870)

subside v b1730

table v *postpone* b1730

accentuate v b1735 (accent: b1530)

chowder v (Am) b1735 (noun use: b1755)

collapse v b1735 [fig. use: b1830] (noun use: b1805)

conduct v *as in "conduct heat"* b1740

cushion v *phys. give cushions* b1740 ["provide fig. cushion": b1830]

fix v *repair* b1740 ["attach": b1390; "arrange": b1665]

funk v *retreat, shrink back*
b1740 (noun use: b1745)
rag v *scold* b1740 ["tease":
b1830] (noun use: b1830)
baby v b1745
bother v *annoy* b1745 ["confound": b1720] (noun use:
b1835)

correlate v *be correlated*
b1745 ["make correlated":
b1870]
dillydally v b1745 (obs. noun
use: 1600s)
partition v b1745
picket v *fence in* b1745 [as in
"picket a business":

b1870]
pounce v b1745
secrete v *secret away* b1745
blaze v *as in "blaze a trail"*
buck v *as in "bucking trends"*
develop v ["unfold": b1660]
(development: b1755)
limber v

modernize v (modernization:
b1770)

Archaisms
quidnunc n *gossip* b1710
bything n *something inconsequential* b1730
fast adj *frozen* b1730

IN USE BY
1800

Geography/Places

continental adj b1760

mesa n (Am) b1760

ravine n b1760

thermal adj *pertaining to hot springs* b1760 [pertaining to heat: b1870] (thermic: b1845)

bayou n b1765

rapids n b1765

salt lake n b1765

cross-country adj b1770

gorge n b1770

sandbar n b1770

terrain n b1770 ["place for horse training": b1730; fig. use: b1825]

horse latitudes n b1775

locale n b1775

northern hemisphere, southern hemisphere n b1775 (eastern hemisphere, western hemisphere: b1625)

scape n *as in "city scape"* b1775

tidewater n b1775

Davy Jones's locker n b1780

international adj b1780

scrubland n (Am) b1780

wetland n b1780

scenery n *as in "viewing the scenery"* b1785 (scenic: b1870)

dune n b1790 (duneland: b1925)

embankment n b1790 (embank v: b1575)

moraine n *glacial feature* b1790

kame n *glacial feature* b1795

plateau n b1795 [fig. "flattening out": b1900] (verb use: b1940)

deposit n (verb use: b1700)

fault line, fault n

lakeshore n

neck n *area, as in "this neck of the woods"*

oxbow n *type of river feature*

veldt n

Natural Things

nickel n *the metal* b1755

avalanche n b1765 (verb use: b1875)

habitat n b1765

windbreak n b1765

eddy v b1770

feldspar n b1770 (feldspath: b1760)

hornblende n b1770

interbreed v b1770

pitchblende n b1770

salt n *as in "Epsom salts"* b1770

tungsten n b1770

wave n *as in "sound waves"* b1770

boiling point n b1775

iceberg n b1775 [obs. type of glacier: b1775 to 1800s]

volcanic adj b1775 (noun use: b1895)

brush fire n (Am) b1780

cotyledon n b1780

mica n b1780 [obs. "type of crystal": b1710]

coal tar n b1785

marsh gas n (Am) b1785

polymorphous adj b1785 (polymorph: b1820; polymorphism: b1840)

carbon n b1790

hard coal n b1790

nitrogen n b1790

oxygen, oxygenate n, v b1790

red tide n b1790

uranium n 1790

hydrogen n b1795

inorganic adj b1795

molecule n b1795 (molecula: b1680; molecular: b1800)

oxidation n b1795 (oxidate v: b1800; oxidize: b1830)

schist n *type of rock* b1795

spontaneous combustion n b1795

zircon n b1795

ammonia n (ammunition: b1630)

citric acid n

ferric adj (ferrous: b1865)

fieldstone n

gaseous adj (gassy: b1760)

graphite n

humus n

macrobiotic adj

rubber n *as in material*

timber n *trees*

turn v *as in "leaves turning"*

Plants

azalea n b1755

begonia n b1755

bluegrass n (Am) b1755

camellia n *type of shrub or tree* b1755

frond n b1755

fuchsia n b1755

mimosa n *type of plant* b1755

summer squash n b1755

gardenia n b1760

indigo plant n b1760

inflorescence n b1760

loblolly pine n (Am) b1760

mesquite n (Am) b1760

pollen n b1760 [obs. gen. "powder": b1525 to 1700s] (pollen grain: b1835; pollinate, pollination: b1875)

alligator pear n b1765

buckeye n (Am) b1765 ["resident of Ohio": b1830]

century plant n (Am) b1765

farkleberry n (Am) b1765

silver maple n b1765

cactus n b1770 [type of artichoke: b1610]

Lombardy poplar n b1770

red maple n (Am) b1770

scrub oak n b1770

summer cypress n b1770

tupelo n b1770

vegetation n *plant growth* b1770

Venus's flytrap n (Am) b1770

zinnia n b1770

English walnut n b1775

flytrap n *type of plant* b1775

gingko n b1775

maidenhair tree n b1775

underbrush n (Am) b1775

balsa n b1780 [type of boat: b1595]

chokeberry n (Am) b1780

cowpea n (Am) b1780

cranberry bush n (Am) b1780

flora n b1780 ["personification of plant fertility": b1665] (floral: b1755)

hard maple n (Am) b1780

herbarium n b1780

jungle n b1780 [fig. use: b1870]

cannabis n b1785

cucumber tree n (Am) b1785

poison ivy n (Am) b1785

silkweed n (Am) *milkweed* b1785

box elder n b1790

eelgrass n (Am) b1790

puff adder n b1790

ragweed n b1790

amaryllis n b1795

dahlia n b1795

florescence n b1795

quaking aspen n b1795

sapwood n b1795

scrub pine n (Am) b1795

Dutch clover n

fiddlehead n

Georgia pine n (Am)

impatiens n *type of plant*

needle n *evergreen leaf*

Norway maple n

teaberry n

wildflower n

Animals

claybank n *yellowish horse, or the color* b1755

fruit fly n b1755

harvest fly n *cicada* b1755

katydid n (Am) b1755

lantern fish n b1755

Norway rat n b1755

painted lady n *type of butterfly* b1755

quahog n *type of clam* b1755

ruffed grouse n (Am) b1755

sea snake n b1755

tapeworm n b1755

tapir n b1755

flying fox n b1760

jigger n *chigger* b1760

octopus n b1760

oyster crab n b1760

Pomeranian n b1760

anteater n b1765

foxhound n b1765

gar n (Am) b1765 (garfish: b1450)

painter n (Am) *type of cougar* b1765

sea bass n b1765

spider monkey n b1765

tentacle n b1765

tom n *male animal* b1765

webfoot n b1765

anaconda n *type of snake* b1770

charger n *horse* b1770

coral snake n b1770

dragonet n *type of fish* b1770

eiderdown n b1770

flatworm n b1770

garter snake n (Am) b1770

gibbon n b1770

grebe n *type of bird* b1770

harp seal n b1770

kangaroo n b1770

larva n b1770

mynah n *type of bird* b1770

pintail n *type of duck* b1770

piranha n b1770

punkie n (Am) *type of insect* b1770

sphinx moth n b1770

walking stick n b1770

arctic fox n b1775

copperhead n (Am) *type of snake* b1775

cougar n b1775

electric ray n b1775

Eskimo dog n b1775

fauna n b1775

fur seal n b1775

grackle n b1775

great dane n b1775

hornbill n b1775

horseshoe crab n b1775

marsh hawk n (Am) b1775

ocelot n b1775

pangolin n b1775

prairie dog n (Am) b1775

pup n b1775 ["obnoxious man": b1590]

rooster n b1775

sheepdog n b1775

snow goose n (Am) b1775

songbird n b1775 [slang "songstress": b1900]

squirrel monkey n b1775

steenbok n b1775

Welsh pony n b1775

zebrafish n b1775

animal kingdom n b1780

equine adj b1780

garpike n *type of fish* b1780

gemsbok n *type of antelope* b1780

gnu n b1780

lightning bug n (Am) b1780

oriole n b1780

pompano n *type of fish* b1780

puma n b1780

red spruce n b1780

red-winged blackbird n b1780

sandworm n b1780

sea slug n b1780

tree toad n (Am) b1780

wood duck n (Am) b1780

American eagle n (Am) b1785

bighorn sheep n (Am) b1785

brown bear n b1785

bull snake n (Am) b1785

canvasback n (Am) *type of duck* b1785

donkey n b1785

gallows bird n b1785

game fowl n b1785

golden plover n b1785

great laurel n b1785

indigo bunting n (Am) *type of bird* b1785

mollusk n b1785

mud turtle n (Am) b1785

mute swan n b1785

pileated woodpecker n (Am) b1785

polar bear n b1785

prehensile adj b1785

rubythroat, rubythroated hummingbird n b1785

snapping turtle n (Am) b1785

termite n b1785 (termitary: b1830)

tiger shark n b1785

two-toed sloth n b1785

whistling swan n b1785

yellow warbler n b1785

zebrawood n b1785

dingo n 1789

barn swallow n (Am) b1790

Clydesdale n *type of horse* b1790 [type of terrier: b1900]

guinea fowl n b1790

hartebeest n *type of antelope* b1790

ivorybill n b1790 (ivorybilled woodpecker: b1815)

kangaroo rat n b1790

muskellunge n (Am) b1790 (muskie: b1895)

nanny goat n b1790

vampire bat n b1790

wolfhound n b1790

yak n b1790

chow chow n *type of dog* b1795 (chow: b1890)

electric eel n b1795

gopher n b1795

grizzly bear n b1795

lemur n b1795

liver fluke n b1795

mason wasp n b1795

Rocky Mountain sheep n (Am) b1795

warm-blooded adj b1795

wood thrush n b1795

aardvark n

alpaca n

bobolink n (Am) (bob o' lincoln: b1775)

burro n

cheviot n *a type of sheep or wool*

chickabiddy n *chick*

darter n

duck-billed platypus n

gorilla n [fig. use: b1900]

hard-shell clam n (Am)

howler n

hydra n

kinkajou n

moccasin n

platypus n

sand flea n

secretary bird n

Shetland n *pony or dog*

soft-shell clam n

soldier ant n

wallaby n

warbler n

wombat n

yellow jacket n *type of wasp*

Weather

northeaster n b1775

sandstorm n b1775

snowstorm n (Am) b1775

cold snap n (Am) b1780

Indian summer n (Am) b1780

norther n (Am) b1780

snowbank n b1780

headwind n b1790

sheet lightning n b1795

freezing rain n

southeaster n

Heavens/Sky

sunspot n *spot on the sun* b1770 ["skin spot caused by the sun": b1805]

terminator n *nightline* b1770

Ptolemaic system n b1775

southern lights n b1775

double star n b1785

Science

ballistics n b1755 (ballista "thrower of projectiles": b1530; ballistic adj: b1775)

neutralize v *make chemically neutral* b1760 [obs. "stay neutral": b1660; "nullify": b1800]

entomology n b1770

ballistic adj b1775

social science n b1785

dynamics n b1790

nitrate n b1790

caloric n *supposed source of heat* b1795 (adj use: b1830)

nitric acid n b1795

geology n [obs. gen. "earth study": b1735] (geologic/geological: b1795)

methodology n

nitrous oxide n

toxicology n

Technology

cam n *as in "overhead cam"* b1780

vacuum tube n b1785

Energy

energize v b1755

steam engine n b1755

charge n/v *as in "electrical charge"* b1770

current n *as in "electrical current"* b1770

discharge n *electrical discharge* b1770

insulation, insulate n, v b1770 (insulator: b1805)

negative, positive adj *electrical terms* b1770

resistance n *in electricity* b1770

shock n/v *electrical jolt* b1770

gas n *natural gas* b1780

radiant heating n b1795

galvanism n (galvanize: b1805)

generator n

Time

timepiece n b1765

early adj *before appointed time* b1770

jiffy n *very short period of time* b1780 (jiff: b1800)

cuckoo clock n b1785

Roman calendar n b1790

age of reason n b1795

semiannual adj b1795

centennial n (noun use: b1875)

Age/Aging

juvenescence n (juvenescent: b1825)

Mathematics

average n b1755

carry v *as in "carry the four"* b1770

statistics n *study of numerical data* b1770 [the data itself: b1870] (stat: b1965; statistic: b1880)

calculator n *calculating machine* b1785

percentage n b1790

decillion n

function n

Measurement

Fahrenheit adj b1755

elevation n *altitude* b1770

milepost n (Am) b1770

soupcon n b1770

Roman mile n b1780

calorimeter n b1795

odometer n (Am) b1795

centimeter, centigram, centiliter n

gram n

kilogram n

kilometer n

liter n

meter n *in metrics*

sea mile n

The Body

Adam's apple n b1755

birthday suit n b1755

bucktooth n b1755

deltoid adj/n b1755

eyelash n b1755

umbilical cord n b1755

gallstone n b1760

hunkers n *haunches* b1760

anal adj b1770 [psychologically "retentive": 1900s] (anality: b1940)

conceptus n *embryo, fetus* b1770

corpuscle n b1770 [gen. "something small":

b1660] (arch. corpuscle: b1670)

grub n *arch. pimple* b1770

noggin n *head* b1770 ["mug": b1630; "mugful of drink": b1700]

small intestine n b1770

system n *as in "digestive system"* b1770

tan n *suntan* b1770 ["tan color": b1900] (verb use: b1570)

derriere n b1775

femur n b1775

hair follicle n b1775

private parts n b1775

solar plexus n b1775

menstruation n b1780 (menstruate: b1800)

pug nose n b1780

trap n *slang mouth* b1780

horn n *slang erection* b1785 (horny adj: b1890)

ivories n *slang teeth* b1785

jock n *slang genitals, male or female* b1790

phallic adj b1790

priapic adj *phallic* b1790

hip joint n b1795

behind n *buttocks*

dick n *slang penis*

fin n *slang hand*

lashes n *eyelashes*

menstruate v (adj use: b1385)

pump n *heart*

rear n *buttocks*

tissue n [type of cloth: b1375]

Physical Description

gimlet-eyed adj *sharp-eyed* b1755 (gimlet eye: b1825)

pilose adj *hirsute* b1755

squabby adj *squat* b1755 (squab "squat person": b1700)

beat adj *exhausted* b1770

blond/blonde n b1770 [type of silk: b1760] (adj use: b1485)

lithesome adj *lissome* b1770 (lissome: b1800)

wet v *as in "wet one's pants"* b1770

spit up v b1780

starvation n b1780

backbreaking adj b1790

meaty adj *lit. "fleshy"* b1790 ["substantial": b1870]

scruff n *as in "scruff of the neck"* b1790

aftertaste n

blirt n *sudden crying*

eliminate v *urinate, defecate*

lissome adj (lithesome: b1770)

physical adj *bodily; material* ["medical": b1450]

regular adj *having regular body functions*

retch n/v *vomit* ["clear throat": b1550 to 1600s]

snook v *thumb the nose*

tic n *spasm, twitch*

Medicine

dentist n b1755 (dentistry: b1840)

eczema n b1755

spastic adj *med. sense* b1755 (noun use: b1900; slang spaz: b1965)

aftercare n b1765

croup n b1765 (obs. verb use: b1515)

stomachache n b1765

benign adj b1770

caducity n *senility* b1770

distemper n b1770 (verb use: b1555)

expectorant n b1770

incontinence n b1770

optician n b1770 [rare "optical expert": b1690]

patent medicine n b1770

peg leg n b1770

pyrexia n *fever* b1770

surgical adj b1770

tonic adj *restorative* b1770 ["pertaining to tone": b1650] (noun use: b1800)

asphyxia n *suffocation* b1780 (asphyxiation, asphyxiate: b1840)

asylum n b1780

clinical adj b1780 [fig. "impersonal": b1930]; fig. "sterile": b1970] (clinic adj: b1630)

cretin n b1780 [slang "idiot": b1900] (cretinism: b1805)

cystitis n b1780

ear trumpet n b1780

grippe n *the flu* b1780

mal de mer n *seasickness* b1780

menorrhagia n *heavy menstruation* b1780

sick headache n *migraine* b1780

airsickness, airsick n, adj b1785

chiropodist n *foot doctor; arch. hand doctor* b1785 (chiropody: b1890)

orderly n *mil. aide* b1785 ["hospital aide": b1830]

rheumatic fever n b1785

amnesia n b1790 (amnesiac: b1870)

common cold n b1790

game adj *lame* b1790

ipecac n (Am) b1790 (ipecacuanha: b1610)

multiple sclerosis n b1795

vaccine n 1798 (adj use: b1800; vaccination: b1800; vaccinate: b1805; vaccinee: b1890)

cowpox n

cranial adj

enuresis n *bedwetting*

exsanguinate v *drain blood*

placebo n [type of prayer: b1225]

seizure n

somnambulism n (somnambulate: b1835; somnambulant: b1870)

tonic n

tranquilizer n (tranquilize: b1625)

tubercular adj

typhoid adj (noun use: b1865; typhus: b1800; typhoid fever: b1845)

typhus n [obs. "pride": b1610]

Everyday Life

clothes moth n b1755

dessertspoon n b1755

roundabout n *type of chair* b1755

shoeblack n *bootblack* b1755

stepladder n b1755

sundries n *miscellanea* b1755

washing machine n b1755

water closet n b1755

bunk n *as in "bunk bed"* b1760 (verb use: b1840; bunk bed: b1925)

duvet n *comforter* b1760

rocking chair n (Am) b1760 (rocker: b1870)

tinware n b1760

chiffonier n b1765

darning needle n b1765

sadiron n *type of flatiron* b1765

shop v *as in "go shopping"* b1765

tablespoon n b1765

afghan n b1770

bidet n b1770 ["horse": b1630]

commode n *type of furniture* b1770 [type of toilet: b1855]

demijohn n *type of bottle* b1770

Dutch oven n b1770

Epsom salts n b1770

head n *bathroom* b1770

lawn n *as in "front lawn"* b1770 [arch. "laund, glade": b1400; obs. "grassy land": b1630]

lounge n *type of furniture* b1770

tallboy n *type of furniture* b1770 [type of drinking glass: b1680]

tin can n b1770

venetian blind n b1770

cedar chest n (Am) b1775

china closet n b1775

eggcup n b1775

music box n b1775

sitting room n b1775

tea tray n b1775

card paper n *cardboard* b1780

hairpin n b1780

tissue paper n b1780 (tissue: b1930)

dustpan n b1785

greenbrier n (Am) b1785

meerschaum n b1785

shower bath, shower n b1785

spinning jenny n b1785

carafe n b1790

carton n/v b1790

chewing tobacco n (Am) b1790

deck chair n b1790

Franklin stove n (Am) b1790

hand glass n *small mirror* b1790

india rubber n b1790

lamppost n b1790

magnum n *type of wine bottle* b1790

night table n b1790

oil paint n b1790

tea caddy n b1790

window dressing n b1790

hatbox n b1795

lace pillow n b1795

lady of the house n b1795

manhole n b1795

matchstick n b1795

shithouse n *outhouse* b1795 (shitter: b1970)

toggle bolt n b1795

walkway n (Am) b1795

chaise longue n (chaise lounge: b1905)

cut glass n

double bed n

flush v *flush a toilet*

jenny n *as in "spinning jenny"*

kit n *group of items* [type of container: b1375; as in "model kit": b1870] (verb use: b1920)

pottery n *pots* ["potter's workshop": b1485; "art of potmaking": b1730]

pottle n *type of container* [arch. type of measurement: b1300]

shade n *lampshade*

soap bubble n

tin n *container*

tub n *bathtub*

washboard n [type of ship protection: b1745]

wringer n

Shelter/Housing

gazebo n b1755

stoop n *porch* b1755

fire wall n (Am) b1760

anteroom n b1765

dooryard n (Am) b1765

gambrel roof n (Am) b1765

hotel n b1765

lodging house n b1765

slat n *strip of wood* b1765

strong room n b1765

aisle n *as in "grocery aisle"* b1770 ["church wing": b1470]

doorstep n b1770

estate n *e.g., plantation* b1770

stairway n b1770

sublet v b1770 (noun use: b1910; sublease: b1830)

carillon, carillonneur n b1775

inglenook n b1775

boudoir n b1780

ramp n *as in "launch ramp"* b1780

tea room n b1780

chalet n b1785

houseboat n b1790

roommate n (Am) b1790 (roomie: b1930)

depot n *storage place* b1795 [as in "train depot": b1870]

handrail n b1795

den n *room in a house*

doorway n

picket fence n (Am)

reservation n *as in "Indian reservation"*

station n *as in "railroad station," "gas station"*

Drink

alcohol n b1755

cognac n b1755 [type of wine: b1595] (cognac brandy: b1690)

red wine n b1755

cafe au lait n b1765

bracer n *stiff drink* b1770

grog n b1770

sling n (Am) *type of drink* b1770

dessert wine n b1775

Jamaica rum n b1775

mocha n *type of coffee* b1775

corn whiskey n (Am) b1780

rye whiskey n b1785

lactic adj *related to milk* b1790

lush n *alcohol* b1790 ["drinking": b1870; "drunk": b1890] (verb use: b1815; lushy: b1830)

ardent spirits n *strong liquor*

hard adj *as in "hard liquor"*

julep n

toddy n *type of drink* ["type of tree sap": b1610]

Food

collard n b1755

passion fruit n b1755

succotash n (Am) b1755

garbanzo n b1760

lima bean n b1760

pumpernickel n b1760

snack n b1760 ["a taste": b1350] (verb use: b1810)

string bean n (Am) b1760

tater n *potato* b1760

chewing gum n (Am) b1765

entree n b1765

lobster pot n b1765

sandwich n b1765

drumstick n b1770

eggplant n b1770

frizzle v *frizz, sizzle* b1770

frost v b1770

pole bean n b1770

smoke v *cook with smoke* b1770 (smokehouse: b1670)

snap bean n (Am) b1770

stew n b1770 ["state of vexation": b1830] (verb use: b1400)

stock n *broth* b1770

whip n *as in "dairy whip"* b1770

apple butter n (Am) b1775

calf's-foot jelly n b1775

eggnog n (Am) b1775

mandarin orange n b1775

oregano n b1775

tofu n b1775

wheat cake n b1775

gum v *chew with gums* b1780

noodle n *the pasta* b1780

black raspberry n (Am) b1785

griddle cake n b1785

lollipop n b1785

mock turtle soup n b1785

mulligatawny n *type of soup* b1785

Welsh rarebit n b1785

aspic n b1790

black tea n b1790

cuisine n b1790

hard cider n (Am) b1790

hulled corn n b1790

waterbiscuit n b1790

black bean n b1795

breadstuff n (Am) b1795

chowchow n *type of relish* b1795 (chow: b1860)

cold slaw n b1795 (coleslaw: b1870)

corn flour n (Brit) *cornstarch* b1795

cottage pie n b1795

maraschino n b1795

potpie n (Am) b1795

soy sauce n b1795

waffle iron n b1795

yeast cake n b1795

bonbon n

brussels sprout n

buffet adj *in the style of a buffet*

cashew nut n

elevenses n (Brit) *morning snack*

hominy grits n (Am)

Irish whiskey n

jerk n (verb use: b1710)

nog n

peanut n (Am)

relish n

rhubarb n [gen. type of plant: b1400]

scoff v *slang eat greedily*

seconds n

shipbiscuit n *hardtack*

shortening n

slapjack n *pancake*

slaw n (Am)

turnover n

vegetable oil n

Agriculture/ Food-Gathering

springhouse n (Am) *cooling-house* b1755

pinery n b1760

yard v *herd* b1760

gin n *as in "cotton gin"* b1770 (cotton gin: b1800)

hothouse n b1770

lasso n b1770 (verb use: b1810)

roundup n b1770

threshing machine n b1775

slaveholder n b1780

botanical garden n b1785

piggery n b1785

applecart n b1790

boss n (Am) *cow* b1790 (bossy n: b1845)

corncob n (Am) b1790

fishing pole n (Am) b1790 (fishing rod: b1555; fish pole: b1830)

veterinary adj b1790 (noun use: b1865)

orchardist n b1795

roof garden n (Am) b1795

blinkers n *blinders* ["glasses": b1830] (verb use: b1865)

cotton gin n (Am)

elevator n *as in "grain elevator"*

herd-boy n

nose bag n *feedbag* [slang "food": b1875]

Cloth/Clothing

dickey n b1755

leggings n b1755

breechclout n *loincloth* b1760 (breechcloth: b1795)

spun silk n b1760

full-dress adj b1765 (full dress: b1790)

mitt n b1765 [in baseball: b1905]

blues n b1770

dress coat n *tail coat* b1770

dressy adj b1770

fancy dress n *costume* b1770

jaconet n *type of cloth* b1770

muffler n *boxing glove* b1770 (obs. muffle: u1800s)

print n b1770 (verb use: b1600)

slip n *type of undergarment* b1770

tie n *as in "necktie," "bowtie"* b1770

Vandyke collar n b1770

bathing suit n b1775

clotheshorse n b1775

gaiter n *type of shoe* b1775

polonaise n *type of overdress* b1775

dressing gown n b1780

parka n b1780

togs n b1780 (tog v: b1790; toggery: b1805)

velveteen n b1780

epaulet/epaulette n b1785

kerseymere n *type of fabric* b1785

pinafore n b1785 (pinny: b1870; pinafore dress: b1900)

stockinette n b1785

terry n *as in "terry cloth"* b1785

bustle n *woman's garment* b1790

corduroy n b1790

half boot n b1790

hosiery n b1790

peacoat n (Am) b1790

Shetland wool n b1790

upper n *shoe top* b1790

breechcloth n b1795 (breechclout: b1760)

camisole n *type of men's garment* b1795 [type of women's garment: b1870]

corset n b1795 [type of bodice: b1300]

crossover n b1795

fabric n b1795

scrim n b1795

argyle n

armband n

bootie n (Am) *baby footwear*

capote n (Am) *long cloak or overcoat*

cardinal n *type of cloak*

cord n *corduroy*

crepe n

evening dress n

overall n

pajamas n

pot hat n *type of hat*

single-breasted adj

sombrero n [type of umbrella: b1600]

velour n *type of fabric* [type of hatmaking tool: b1710] (velure: b1590)

waterproof n

zephyr n

Fashion/Style

rouge n b1755 ["red": b1475] (verb use: b1780)

tattoo v *mark with a tattoo* 1769 (noun use: b1780)

pigtail n b1770 ["coil of tobacco": b1690]

scent n *spec. perfume* b1770 (verb use: b1700; scented: b1570)

earlock n *type of lock of hair* b1775

good-looking adj b1780

natty adj b1785 [slang use: b1560]

stylish adj b1785

haute adj b1790

nose ring n b1790

fashionable n

nouvelle adj *novel*

rage n *fad*

style n *fashion*

Tools

clasp knife n b1755

compressor n b1755

derrick n *boom* b1755 [obs.

"hangman": b1630; obs. "gallows": b1730; type of crane, framework: b1870]

palette knife n b1760

rocker n b1760

refracting telescope n b1765

claw hammer n b1770

eyebolt n b1770

machinery n b1770

prod n b1770 ["act of prodding": b1830]

hod carrier n b1775

loupe n *type of magnifier* b1775

pile driver n b1775

inhaler n b1780 (inhalant: b1900)

keyhole saw n b1780

sawhorse n b1780

screwdriver n b1780

brake n *as in "car brakes"* b1785 (verb use: b1870)

dipper n b1785

flywheel n b1785

parachute n b1785 (verb use: b1810; parachutist: b1890)

T square n b1785

trip-hammer n (Am) b1785

workbench n b1785

eraser n b1790

eyepiece n b1790

lightning rod n (Am) b1790

snowplow n (Am) b1795

bearing n *as in "ball bearing"*

male adj

plunger n *piston; plumber's helper* (plumber's helper: b1955)

wrench n (verb use: b1600)

Travel/Transportation

iceboat n b1755

vis-à-vis n *type of carriage* b1755

kayak n b1760

sulky n b1760

cabriolet n *type of carriage* b1765

buggy n *carriage* b1770

circus n b1770

right-of-way n b1770

seamanship n b1770

truck n *type of transportation device* b1770 ["motorized transport": b1930] (verb use: b1750)

tunnel n *man-made* b1770

[obs. type of fishnet: b1450; obs. "tube": b1550 to 1800s; natural tunnel: b1900] (verb use: b1795)

turnpike n *type of road* b1770 [type of defensive setup: b1375; obs. "turnstile": b1535 to 1700s]

coast v *as in "coast on a bicycle"* b1775 ["travel the coast": b1390; slang "rest on laurels": b1935]

saddlebag n b1775

toll bridge n b1775

tollgate n b1775

en route adj/adv b1780

raftsman n b1780

tourist n b1780 (tourism: b1815)

wayworn adj *tired because of traveling* b1780

aeronaut n b1785 (aeronautics: b1825)

aerostat n *lighter-than-air craft* b1785

finger post n *sign with finger pointers* b1785

steamboat n (Am) b1785

tandem n *type of carriage* b1785 ["par": b1870] (adv use: b1795; adj use: b1805)

way station n (Am) b1785

destination n b1790 ["intention": b1655] (destine: b1800)

steamship n b1790

curbstone n b1795

dinghy n b1795

four-in-hand n *four-horsed vehicle* b1795

landaulet n *small carriage* b1795

pedestrian n b1795 (adj use "by foot": b1800; obs. pedestrious: b1670 to 1800s)

carriageway n (Brit)

cul-de-sac n *blind street* [anatomical term; type of container: b1740]

sailboat n

sleigh-ride n

switch n *as in "railroad switch"* [as in "light switch": b1870; gen. "change": b1930] (verb use: b1870)

tire n [obs. "wheel plating": b1495 to 1800s]

Emotions/ Characteristics

kittenish adj b1755

self-indulgence n b1755 (self-indulgent: b1795)

funny adj *hilarious* b1760 ["off-kilter," as in "I feel funny": b1800; "odd": b1830]

somber adj b1760 (sombrous: b1730)

sour grapes n b1760

dignified adj b1765 [obs. "serving as a dignitary": b1670 to 1800s]

favoritism n b1765

tension n b1765

candor n *frankness* b1770 [rare "whiteness": b1400; rare "fairness": b1610] (candid: b1630)

cantankerous adj b1770

character n *moral fortitude* b1770

cocky adj b1770

comfortable adj *experiencing comfort* b1770 ["pleasant": b1340 to 1700s; "comforting": b1450; as in "comfortable margin": b1970] (comfy: b1830)

complacent adj b1770 [obs. "pleasant": b1660 to 1700s]

contrary adj *ornery* b1770 (obs. contradictious: b1605 to 1700s)

enthusiastic adj b1770 ["possessed by religious fervor": b1605 to 1800s]

fearsome adj b1770

gloat v b1770 ["glance at": b1575]

good-tempered adj b1770

horrors, the n *depression* b1770

inconsiderate adj *rude* b1770 ["without thinking": b1470]

lackadaisical adj b1770 (lackadaisy adj: b1800)

malaise n b1770

nettlesome adj *irritable* b1770 ["irritating": b1930]

nostalgia n *homesickness for a place* b1770 ["homesickness for a time": b1930] (nostalgist: b1955)

pathetic adj b1770 [obs. "stirring emotions": b1600 to 1700s]

tasteful adj *possessing good judgment* b1770 ["tasty": b1615]

trait n *characteristic* b1770

worldweary adj b1770

feelings n b1775

flabbergast v b1775

flighty adj *capricious* b1775 ["fast": b1555; "loony": b1830]

self-importance n b1775 (self-important: b1770)

taciturn adj b1775 (taciturnity: b1500)

adulate v b1780 (adulation: b1400)

bonhomie n *congeniality* b1780

coolheaded adj b1780

crabby adj b1780

frisson n *shudder of excitement* b1780

grumpy adj b1780 (grumpish: b1800)

jeremiad n b1780

rumbustious adj b1780

blue devils n *despondency* b1785 (blue-devil v: b1820)

depressing adj b1790 (depressed: b1800)

ego n *the self* b1790 ["conceit": b1895] (egotism, egotist: b1715; egoism, egoist: b1785; egotize: b1800; egomania: b1825; egocentric: b1895)

furore n *furor* b1790

long face n b1790

spunk, spunky n, adj *spirit* b1790 ["tinder": b1540] (spunk v: b1840)

teardrop n b1790

carefree adj b1795

devil-may-care adj b1795

eerie adj *causing fear* b1795 ["fearful, cowardly": b885]

pessimism n b1795 [obs. "bad conditions": b1795 to 1800s] (pessimist, pessimistic: b1870)

unscrupulous adj b1795
alarmist n (alarmism: b1870)
bearing n pertinence, affect
depressed adj (depressing: b1790)
frivolity n (frivolous: b1475; frivol n: b1500; frivol v: b1870)
homesick adj
insouciance n (insouciant: b1830)
lift n as in "give your spirits a lift"
ornery adj
personality n character ["being a person": b1400; "personal insult": b1770; "celebrity": b1870]
pluck n verve (plucky: b1830)
poise n cool behavior ["importance": b1400 to 1700s]
polrumptious adj cocky
rattle v fluster
self-discipline n
selfless adj
slaver v fawn
tact n sensitive, skillful handling ["sense of touch": b1655] (tactless: b1840; tactful: b1860)
weeps n tears
wild adj as in "I'm just wild about Harry" [gen. "excited": b1830]

Thoughts/Perception/ The Mind

mythos n b1755
absorbed adj b1765 (absorbing: b1755)
pococurante n uncaring person b1765 (adj use: b1815)
neurosis n b1770 (neurotic adj: b1875; neurotic n: b1900)
percipience n perception b1770
sensibilities n b1770
view v hold an opinion, regard b1770
egoism n b1785
egoist n b1785
mesmerism n b1785 (mesmerize, mesmeric: b1830; mesmerian: b1870)

savvy n/v knowledge/know b1785 (adj use: b1905)
longsighted adj farsighted b1790
phobia n b1790
tricky adj cunning b1790 ["complex": b1870]
philosophism n specious philosophy b1795
strong-minded adj b1795 (strong-willed: b1900)
vision v b1795
dementia n (demency: b1530)
evaluation n assessment ["placing a value": b1755] (evaluate: b1845)
forward-looking adj
lenient adj [arch. "soothing": b1655]
obliviscence n forgetfulness
prime v mentally prepare
realize v come to understand
spellbound adj (spellbind: b1810; spellbinding: b1935)
uninterest n

Love/Romance/Sex

spliced adj married, hitched b1755
declaration n marriage proposal b1770 (declare: b1870)
fast adj slang promiscuous b1770
love n b1770
masturbation n b1770 (masturbate: b1860; masturbatory: b1865)
prurient adj lustful b1770 ["mentally desirious": b1595; "phys. itching": b1640] (prurience: b1785; pruriency: b1795)
nymphomania n b1775 (nympho: b1915)
polygyny n having more than one wife b1780 (polygamy: b1595; polyandry: b1780)
tail v slang have sex b1780 (noun use: b1870)
best man n b1785
bundling n unmarried couple sleeping together fully clothed b1785
hump v have sex b1785 (noun use: b1935)

lady's man/ladies' man n b1785
mesalliance n marriage to someone of lower status b1785
shag v have sex b1790
steady n b1795
connection n arch. "lovemaking"
Darby and Joan n long-married couple
harem n ["secluded house quarters": b1625]
intercourse n [gen. "dealings": b1450]
mavourneen n darling
sexual adj carnal
sexual intercourse n
sexuality n
sweetie n ["type of candy": b1700] (sweetheart: b1300; arch. sweeting: b1350; sweetikins: b1600; sweetie pie: b1930)
tasty adj sexually attractive

Family/Relations/ Friends

great-grandchild, great-granddaughter n b1755 (great-grandson: b1720)
materfamilias n woman running the household b1760
pappy n b1765 (papa: b1685)
granddaddy n b1770 (grandfather: b1425; grandpapa, grandpappy: b1770; granddad: b1785; grandpa: b1890; grandpop: b1900)
grandmamma n b1770 (grandmother: b1425; granny: b1565; grandma: b1800)
next of kin n b1770
poppa n b1775
family man n b1790
quadruplet n b1790 (quad: b1955)
auntie n b1795
toddler n b1795
kinspeople n (kin: b900; kinsman: b1150; kinswoman: b1400)
triplet n

Holidays

resort n vacation spot b1755
Santa Claus n (Am) b1775
jubilarian n celebrant b1785

Games/Fun/Leisure

stalemate n/v spec. to chess b1765 [gen. impasse: b1900]
wheel of fortune n b1765
cat's cradle n b1770
dummy n b1770
raffle n b1770 [type of dice game: b1450]
romp n play b1770 ["playful person": b1710] (verb use: b1710)
solitaire n b1770 ["reclusive person": b1730]
charade n b1780 ["farce": b1900] (charades: b1870)
lotto n type of game of chance b1780
playground n b1780
dollhouse n b1785
sweepstakes n b1785 (obs. sweepstake "winner who takes all": b1495 to 1600s)
turnabout n carousel b1790
numismatic adj b1795 (numismatics: b1830)
caddie n as in "golf caddie" [obs. "cadet": b1630 to 1800s; "worker of any odd job": b1870] (verb use: b1710)
domino n
pachisi n type of board game
shooting gallery n
treat n something special

Sports

bullfight n b1755 (bullfighting: b1755)
handicapper n b1755
ski n b1755
sportswoman n b1755 (sportsman: b1700)
unsportsmanlike adj b1755
medalist n b1760 ["medal expert": b1780]
racecourse n b1765
field n as in "playing field" b1770
field n competitors b1770 (field event: b1900)
green n b1770

play v *as in "play the Packers"* b1770 ["allow a player to participate": b1900]

pugilist n b1770 (pugilism: b1795)

score n b1770 [obs. "mark used to keep score": b1700 to 1800s] (verb use "make scores": b1770; verb use "record scores": b1870)

spar v *box* b1770 ["fight with spurs," as in a cockfight: b1540]

stroke n *action of hitting, as in "golf stroke"* b1770

turf n *in horseracing* b1770

lightweight n b1775 [fig. use: b1900]

balloon, ballooning, balloonist n b1785

rink n *ice rink* b1790 [obs. "jousting area": b1375 to 1600s]

equestrian n b1795 (equestrienne: b1865)

sporting dog n b1795

steeplechase n b1795

dead heat n

handicap n *type of horserace* [fig. use: b1900]

jock n *jockey*

picador n (picara: b1930)

round n *in golf* [in boxing: b1830]

trampoline n

Professions/Duties

decorator n b1755

electrician n (Am) b1755

equilibrist n *high-wire artist* b1760

fabricant n *manufacturer* b1760

stonemason n b1760

landscape gardener n b1765

woodcutter n (Am) b1765 (wooder: b1150)

cognoscenti n *expert* b1770

escort n *guide* b1770

hairdresser n b1770

harbormaster n b1770

middleman n b1770

postman n *mail carrier* b1770

mapmaker n b1775

rainmaker/rainmaking n (Am) b1775

protégée n b1780

teamster n *horse-team driver* b1780 ["truck driver": b1930]

frontiersman n (Am) b1785

mail carrier n (Am) b1790

protégé n b1790

stevedore n (Am) b1790

stockkeeper n b1790

callboy n *bellhop* b1795

civil engineer n b1795

geologist n b1795 (geologer: b1870)

potboy n *type of tavern servant* b1795

roundsman n *someone who makes rounds* b1795

coiffeuse n (coiffeur: b1850)

interpretress n (interpreter: b1380)

professional adj *working in a profession* ["of a profession": b1750; "with a professional attitude": b1930] (professionalism: b1860)

restaurateur n (restaurant: b1830)

stenographer n (Am)

Business/Commerce/Selling

asking price n b1755

embargo v b1755 ["seize": b1670] (noun use: b1595)

tip n *gratuity* b1755 (verb use: b1730)

distillery n b1760 [obs. "distillation": b1680 to 1800s] (distiller: b1580)

advertising n b1765

steak house n b1765

boutique n b1770 [as in "bout of measles": b1900]

estimate n *predicted cost* b1770 (verb use: b1670)

option n *as in "stock option," "movie option"* b1770 (verb use: b1970)

variety store n (Am) b1770

mercantile system n b1780

corporator n *part of a corporation* b1785

bakeshop n b1790 (bakery: b1820)

cafe n b1790

chamber of commerce n b1790

executive officer n b1790

lumberyard n (Am) b1790

plant n *factory* b1790

high-priced adj b1795

newsstand n (Am) b1795

commission merchant n

guarantee n ["guarantor": b1680] (verb use: b1795)

line n *as in "railroad line"*

manageress n (manager: b1730)

mark n *as in "trademark"*

monger v (noun use: b975)

notions n *goods*

trading post n (Am)

wet adj *able to sell alcohol*

The Workplace

engage v *hire* b1770

flunky n b1770 ["yes-man": b1855]

journeywoman n b1770 (journeyman: b1470)

manufacturer n b1770 [obs. "laborer": b1720 to 1800s]

strike v *stop work* b1770 (noun use: b1900)

fag v *toil* b1775 (noun use: b1780)

laborsaving adj b1775

leave of absence n b1775

division of labor n b1780

scab n *person who doesn't join a union* b1780 ["strikebreaker": b1810] (verb use: b1810)

working class n b1790

worktable n b1790

clerical adj ["pertaining to the clergy": b1500]

transfer n *change to new job*

unionist n

Finances/Money

schilling n b1755

stockholder n b1755

write-off n b1755

negotiable adj *liquid, as in "negotiable bonds"* b1760

payee n b1760 (payer: b1375)

appropriation n *financial allocation* b1770

credit n *opp. of debit* b1770 (verb use: b1700)

deposit n b1770 (verb use: b1670)

drawee n b1770

eagle n *type of coin* b1770

expenditure n *spending* b1770 ["what is spent": b1800]

finance n *as in "high finance"* b1770 [obs. "payment": b1400 to 1500s; obs. "tax": b1500 to 1600s] (finances: b1730; financial: b1770)

balance sheet n b1775

stock exchange n b1775

checkbook n (Am) b1780

debit n *opp. of credit* b1780 [obs. "debt": b1350 to 1600s] (verb use: b1685)

installment n b1780

trust fund n b1780

deficit n b1785

national debt n (Am) b1785

quarter n *the coin* b1785

bob n *shilling* b1790

dime n (Am) b1790 [gen. "tenth": b1380]

half eagle n (Am) *$5 coin* b1790

half-dollar n b1790

national bank n (Am) b1790

picayune n *small coin* b1790 (adj use: b1830)

scrip n b1790 [type of receipt: b1765]

disme n *short-lived 10-cent U.S. coin* 1792

capitalist n b1795 (adj use: b1850; capitalism: b1855; capitalistic: b1875)

due bill n (Am) b1795

economics n b1795 [as in "home economics": b1590]

half dime n b1795

half disme n *type of coin* b1795

IOU n b1795 (IOU replacing "I owe you": b1630)

shareholder n b1795

appreciation, appreciate n, v *rise in value* ["recognition": b1570; "assessment": b1605]

check n *financial instrument*

draft n

income tax n

stamp tax n

tender n *as in "legal tender"*

withdraw v (withdrawal: b1870)

Language and Speaking

cognate n b1755 (adj use: b1645)
colloquial adj b1755 (colloquialism: b1800)
burr n *as in "a Scottish burr"* b1760
slang n b1760 (slanguage: b1880)
definite article n *the* b1765
adnoun n *obs. adjective* b1770 [u1800s]
ampersand n *&* b1770
filth n *bad language* b1770
vocabulary n b1770 [type of word list: b1535]
suffix n b1780
Americanism n (Am) b1785
cursive adj b1785 (noun use: b1865)
cacology n *bad pronunciation* b1785
colloquialism n (colloquial adj: b1755)
hard adj *as in "hard G"*
mixed metaphor n
neologism n *creation of a word, the word itself*
parlance n *idiom, phrasing* [gen. "speech, parlaying": b1580]
past participle n

Contractions

ain't v b1780
swan v (Am) *swear, short for "I shall warrant"* b1785

Literature/Writing

calligrapher n b1755 (calligraphist: b1820)
denouement n b1755
handbill n b1755
letterpress n b1760
lyricism n b1760 (lyrism: b1860)
precis n b1760
bookstore n (Am) b1765 (bookshop: b1865)
casebook n b1765
newsboy n b1765 (newsie: b1875)
directory n b1770 (adj use: b1450)
draft n *as in "first draft"* b1770 (verb use: b1830; adj use: b1900)
duologue n b1770

journalize v b1770
magazine n b1770 [type of book: b1670 to 1800s]
remainder n *bargain book* b1770 (verb use: b1905)
rewrite v b1770 [obs. "write in reply": b1570] (noun use: b1915)
autobiography n b1775 (autobiographical: b1830)
colophon n *type of inscription* b1775 [publisher's imprint: b1930]
glossarist n b1775 (glossator: b1400)
chit n *note* b1780 (chitty: b1760)
postface n *opp. of preface* b1785
rhapsodic adj b1785 (rhapsode n: b1835)
in medias res adv b1790
poetic license n b1790
book club n b1795
edit v b1795
longueur n *dull reading* b1795
alliterate v (alliteration: b1660)
athenaeum/atheneum n *library* ["temple of Athena": b1730]
chapbook n
circular n
condensation n (condense: b1830)
editress n (editor: b1715)
imprint n *publisher's name* (verb use: b1375)
literature n ["learnedness": b1425]
nonsense verse n
novelette n
organ n *publication*
periodical n *magazine*
press n *journalism business* ["journalists as a group": b1930]
return n *on a typewriter, etc.*
scan v *skim*
series n

Communication

postbox n b1755
public speaking n b1765
enunciate v *speak clearly* b1770
letter box n b1775
telegraph n 1792 [type of

semaphore: b1730] (telegram: b1850)
publicity n b1795 (publicist: b1970)

Visual Arts/ Photography

papier-mâché adj/n b1755
bravura n b1760
baroque adj b1765 [fig. "convoluted, complex": b1870] (noun use: b1780)
figurehead n *type of carving* b1765 [fig. use: b1885]
elevation n *type of drawing* b1770
etching n b1770
fine art n b1770
study n *preliminary* b1770
oil painting n b1785
silhouette n *type of portrait* b1785 (gen. use: b1870; verb use: b1880)
magnum opus n b1795
stained glass n b1795
stylist n b1795
commission v *as in "commission a sculpture"*
panorama n *type of photograph* [gen. "scenic view": b1830]
seascape n
value n
vanishing point n

Performing Arts

comic opera n b1765
musical comedy n b1765
scenery n b1770 [obs. "stage action": b1740 to 1800s]
song and dance n (Am) b1770
dramatize v b1780 [fig. use: b1830]
harlequinade n b1780
stage door n b1780
theatricalize v b1780
arabesque n *ballet position* b1790
box office n b1790
choreography n *dance notation* b1790 ["dance design": b1930] (choreograph v: b1945)
improvisation n b1790 (improvise: b1830)
ballerina n b1795

monodrama n b1795
flat n *type of scenery*
grand finale n
portray v *as in "portray a role"* (portrayal: b1850)

Music

coda n b1755
Gregorian chant n b1755
mezzo-soprano n b1755 (mezzo: b1815)
castrato n b1765
harmonica n b1765
clarinet n b1770
fanfare n b1770
fortepiano n b1770
keynote n b1770 [gen. use: b1800]
operetta n b1770
prima donna n *primary singer* b1770 ["self-centered person": b1870]
round n b1770 ["song alternating singers": b1530 to 1600s]
suite n b1770
symphonist n b1770
electric organ n b1775
falsetto n b1775
intermezzo n b1775
quartet n *musical group* b1775 [gen. "group of four": b1630]
strum v b1775
tuning fork n b1775
afterpiece n b1780
crescendo adj/n/v b1780
conduct, conductor v, n b1785
waltz n b1785 (verb use: b1795)
bolero n b1790
chamber music n b1790 (chamber adj: b1710)
melodist n b1790
songsmith n b1795
trouvere n *type of troubadour* b1795
grind v *as in "organ grinder"*
hand organ n (Am)
percussion n (percussionist: b1820)
quintet n *type of musical composition* ["group of five": b1900]
side drum n *snare drum*
symphony n *e.g., "Beethoven's 9th"* [obs. types of musical instruments:

b1450; gen. "agreement":
b1600; type of overture:
b1670] (symphonic:
b1860)

Entertainment

heroicomic adj b1760 (heroi-comical: b1730)
quadrille n *type of square dance* b1775
souvenir n b1775
masked ball n b1780
tea party n b1780
pigeonwing n *type of dance* b1785
seriocomic adj b1785
tarantella n *type of dance* b1785
MC n b1790
circus n *type of show* b1795 [type of arena: b1380; "traffic roundabout": b1770]
daredevil n b1795 (adj use: b1835)
funambulist n b1795 (funam-bulo: b1630; funambula-tor: b1700; funambulism: b1825)
waltz v *dance* b1795 ["ca-vort, move": b1870]
review v *as in "review a movie"* (reviewer: b1655)
soiree n

Movies/TV/Radio

animation n

Education

parochial school n b1755
valedictorian n (Am) b1760 (valedictory n: b1780)
junior n b1770
schoolroom n b1775
military school n (Am) b1780
schoolgirl n b1780 (school-fellow: b1500; school-mate: b1565; schoolboy: b1590; schoolchild: b1840; schoolkid: b1940)
textbook n b1780 (text: b1900)
day school n b1785
fraternity n (sorority: b1905)
honors n

Religion

lay reader n b1755
totem n (Am) b1760
mission n *seat of missionaries* b1770
altar boy n b1775
biblical adj b1775
scriptorium n *monastery copy-ing room* b1775 (scriptory: b1500)
prayer meeting n b1780
avatar n b1785
kingdom come n b1785
Sunday school n b1785
creche n b1795
totemism n (Am) b1795
dharma n
iconoclasm n
mantra n
Sabba-day n
serious adj *devout*
theodicy n

Society/Mores/Culture

emigrant n (Am) b1755 (adj use: b1795; emigration: b1650; emigrate: b1780; emigre: b1795)
lowbred adj b1760
tea time n b1760
Yankee n b1760 (Yank: b1780)
au courant adj b1765
chivalry n *courteousness, etc.* b1770 ["gen. knights": b1300]
civilization n b1770 [spec. leg. sense: b1705] (civilize: b1615)
class n *social status, as in "lower-class"* b1770
conventional adj *normal* b1770 (conventionality: b1835)
fellow n *obs. African-Ameri-can* b1770 [u1800s]
have n *as in "haves and have-nots"* b1770 (obs. have-less: b1150 to late ME; have-not: b1840)
masculinity n b1770
middle class n b1770 (adj use: b1840)
tea n *type of social event* b1770
anti-American adj (Am) b1775

lower class n/adj b1775
colonial adj (Am) b1780 (noun use: b1865)
p's and q's n b1780
pureblood n/v b1780
taboo adj/n/v b1780
visiting card n b1785
effete adj b1790 [obs. "infer-tile": b1625 to 1800s; obs. "no longer unique": b1660 to 1800s]
gregarious adj b1790 [de-scribing animals: b1670]
immigrant n (Am) b1790
black sheep n b1795
human rights n b1795
antisocial adj
dystopia n *opp. of utopia*
elite n (adj use: b1825)
haut noblesse n (haut bour-geoisie: b1900)
milady n (milord: b1600)
milieu n
race n *i.e., Caucasians, Ne-groids, etc.* ["family, de-scendents": b1570; gen. "kindred group": b1600; as in "the human race": b1600] (racial: b1865; rac-ism: b1870; racialism: b1910)
roue n *rake, Don Juan*

Government

burg n *ancient town* b1755
grand duchess n b1760 (grand duke: b1695; grand duchy: b1835)
congress n b1765 ["meet-ing": b1765]
lame duck n b1765
queen consort n b1765
queen regent n b1765
executive n b1775 [business sense: b1930]
aristocrat n b1780 (aristoc-racy: b1565; aristocratic: b1605)
congressman n (Am) b1780 (congresswoman: b1920; congressperson: b1975)
feudal system n b1780 (feu-dalism: b1820)
regime n b1780
civil service n b1785
confederal adj b1785
city council n b1790

federalist n (Am) b1790 (federalism: b1790)
municipality n b1790
crown prince n b1795
citizeness n (citizen: b1300)
civil servant n
colonialism n
presidentess n (president: b1375)
squirearchy n
states' rights n (Am)

Politics

politicize v *be a politician* b1760 ["give a political twist": b1850] (political-ize: b1870)
caucus n (Am) b1765 (verb use: b1790)
party politics n b1775
political science n b1780
Republican n b1785
electioneer n/v b1790
favorite son n (Am) b1790
libertarian adj/n b1790
demo n *democrat* b1795
functionary n b1795
diplomacy n *profession of a diplomat* ["diplomatic be-havior": b1870] (diplo-mat: b1815)
metapolitics n

Death

post-obit adj b1755
scrag v *execute by hanging or choking* b1760
pop off v *die* b1765 ["kill": b1830]
euthanasia n b1770 [gen. "peaceful death": b1650] (euthanitize: b1875; eu-thanize: b1965)
graveyard n b1775
resurrect v b1775 (resurrec-tion: b1300)
black death n b1780
blow away v *kill* b1780
future life n *afterlife* b1780
kick the bucket v b1785
fetch n *wraith* b1790
deathblow n b1795
crossbones n *as in "skull and crossbones"*
heroon n *hero's monument*
memorialize v (memorial v: b1770)

stiff n (adj use "dead": b1350; verb use: b1975)

War/Military/Violence

air gun n b1755
misfire v b1755 (noun use: b1840)
striking distance n b1755
war party n (Am) b1755
warpath n (Am) b1755
coup de main n *attack* b1760
present arms n b1760
ramrod n *for loading guns* b1760
wardroom n b1760
guardroom n b1765
insurgent n b1765 (adj use: b1815; obs. insurge v: b1570 to 1600s; insurgency: b1805; insurgence: b1850)
outflank v b1765
brave n b1770
irregular n b1770
operation n b1770
pit v *lit. and fig. throw into a pit for battle* b1770
ricochet n b1770 (verb use: b1770)
rifle n *the weapon* b1770 ["groove in a rifle gun": b1700]
slungshot n (Am) b1770
smack n *hit* b1770 (verb use: b1870)
buckshot n b1775
cadet n b1775 ["young son": b1610]
mantrap n b1775
minuteman n (Am) b1775
rifleman n (Am) b1775
singlestick n b1775
snickersnee n *type of knife* b1775
aide n (Am) *aide-de-camp* b1780 [gen. "assistant": b1870] (aide-de-camp: b1670)
gunboat n b1780
marching orders n b1780
military academy n (Am) b1780
militiaman n b1780
shotgun n (Am) b1780
smash v *hit* b1780
sortie n b1780
first lieutenant n b1785
deploy v b1790 [obs. "un-

fold": b1480; gen. use: b1870] (deployment: b1800)
lance corporal n b1790
whale v *as in "whale on your head"* b1790
battleship n b1795
body blow n b1795
disarmament n b1795
espionage n b1795
guillotine n b1795
subsidize v *mil. sense—hire mercenaries* b1795 [gen. "support": b1830] (subsidy: b1375)
attention n *as in "at attention"*
conscription n *forced enlistment* [gen. "written list": b1385; obs. gen. "enlistment": b1530 to 1600s] (obs. conscribe "enlist": b1570 to 1600s; conscript n: b1800)
draft n *conscription* (verb use: b1715)
echelon n [gen. use: b1945] (verb use: b1860)
explode v
position n
rifling n
shot n *shotgun ammunition*
smoothbore gun n
snipe, sniper v, n ["take fig. potshots": b1900]
tactician n
terrorism n ["government by terror": b1795] (terrorize: b1825; terrorist: b1865)
torpedo n (verb use: b1880)
war hawk n

Crime/Punishment/Enforcement

bagman n b1765 ["tax collector": b1380]
arrestee n b1770
criminal conversation n *adultery* b1770
snatch v *steal* b1770
want v *as in "wanted by the police"* b1770
highway robbery n b1780
resurrectionist n *body snatcher* b1780
Jolly Roger n b1785
snitch n *informant* b1785

["nose": b1700] (verb use: b1770)
solitary confinement n b1785 (solitary: b1855)
swindle v b1785 (noun use: b1835; swindler: b1800)
vandalism n 1793 (vandalize: b1805)
calaboose n (Am) *jail* b1795
swag n *loot* b1795
breaking and entering n
cracksman n *safecracker*
inculpate v *incriminate*
peeping Tom n
police officer n
time n *as in "doing time," "serving time"*

The Law

hearsay evidence n b1755
false pretense n b1760
quitclaim deed n b1760
malicious mischief n b1770
statute of limitations n b1770
statutory adj b1770
in flagrante delicto adv b1775
court of appeals n b1780
inadmissible adj b1780
blue law n (Am) b1785
district attorney n (Am) b1790
district court n (Am) b1790
federal court n b1790
moot court n b1790 (moot n: b1570; moot case: b1590)
due process n b1795
convict n *prisoner* ["person convicted": b1500]
gag law n (Am)
state's evidence n

The Fantastic/Paranormal

Davy Jones n b1755 (Davy Jones's locker: b1880)
divining rod n b1755
kraken n *mythical monster* b1755
sixth sense n b1765
tricorn n *three-horned creature* b1770
nympholepsy n *possessed by nymphs* b1775 (nympholept: b1815)
transmundane adj *beyond the ordinary world* b1780

ghoul n b1790 (ghoulish: b1845)
mythology n *gen.* myths [obs. "mythtelling or analysis": b1420 to 1600s; "a myth": b1605] (mythological: b1615; myth: b1830)
supernaturalism n (supernaturals "supernatural beings": b1600; supernaturalism: b1800; supernature: b1845; the supernatural: b1870)
supersensible adj *supernatural* (supersensual: b1700; supersensory: b1885)
water sprite n

Magic

diablerie n *black magic* b1755
rune n

Interjections

ahoy interj b1755
hip interj *as in "hip hip hooray"* b1755
gosh interj b1760
ahem interj b1765
bravo interj/n b1765 (brava: b1805)
capital interj b1770
Christ n b1770
fudge interj b1770
hushaby interj b1770
lackadaisy interj b1770 (lackaday: b1695)
or what? interj b1770
oy interj *hey* b1770
rabbit n *drat it* b1770
tallyho interj/n/v b1770
ugh interj b1770
yoho interj b1770
yoicks interj b1770
golly interj b1775
excelsior n b1780
darn adj/adv/v b1785 (noun use: b1840; darned: b1815)
fiddle-de-dee interj b1785 (noun use: b1870)
dang interj/v b1790 (adj/adv use: b1915)
botheration interj/n (bothersome: b1835)
chin chin interj (Brit) *type of toast*
goody interj

hooray interj
pillaloo interj

Slang

mobocracy n b1755
panjandrum n *big wheel* b1755
peach n *something good* b1755
goody n *as in "goodies"* b1760
sugarcoat v b1765
blackball v b1770
cutie n (Am) b1770
dive in v *get heavily involved* b1770
doggess n b1770
dozens n *many* b1770
fundamental adj *of the buttocks* b1770
hotbed n b1770 [lit. use: b1630]
immense adj *great, swell* b1770
machine n *penis* b1770
rich adj *as in "that's rich"* b1770
scene n *as in "make a scene"* b1770
thick adj *as in "thick as thieves"* b1770
vegetate v *be a couch potato* b1770
chatterbox n b1775
French leave n *rapid departure* b1775
preachify v b1775
spadework n *legwork* b1780
blind staggers n (Am) b1785
deuced adj *euphemism for "damned"* b1785
gam n *leg* b1785
jack-tar n *sailor* b1785 (jack: b1700)
nuts adj *enthusiastic* b1785
tarnation n b1785 (tarnal adj: b1800)
whopper n b1785
bluestocking n *learned woman* b1790
diddle v *waste time* b1790
leggy adj b1790
loot n b1790
missus n b1790
nobby adj (Brit) b1790
nose n *informant* b1790
Philadelphia lawyer n (Am) b1790

toot n *drinking spree* b1790 ["cocaine": b1970] (verb use: b1700)
dandy adj b1795
gal n b1795
lump v (Am) *as in "like it or lump it"* b1795
pardner n (Am) b1795
scarify v *scare* b1795
beanpole n
bona fides n
character n *quirky person*
covess n *female*
cut v *as in "cut a class"*
frisk v/n *pat down*
hang v *as in "keeping the crowd hanging"*
happy adj *tipsy*
jug n *prison*
leak v *as in "the secret leaked out"* [as in "leak a secret": b1870] (noun use: b1930)
lech, letch n *lust* ["lecher": b1970] (verb use: b1915)
lick v *as in "lick a problem"*
mace v *bamboozle*
mag n *chitchat*
moon-eyed adj *drunk*
mother n *madame*
quixotic adj (quixote: b1650)
taradiddle n *lie* ["nonsense": b1980]

Insults

fatheaded adj b1755 (fathead: b1840)
gauche adj b1755 (gaucherie: b1800)
noodle n *simpleton/head* b1755
codger n b1760
half-breed n (Am) b1760 (half-blood: b1555)
muddleheaded adj b1760
goodie two-shoes n/adj b1765
misanthropic adj b1765 (misanthropical: b1670; misanthrope adj: b1770)
stupe n *blockhead* b1765
coot n b1770
cowheart n *coward* b1770
cracker n *Southern white* b1770
deadbeat adj/n b1770
fidfad adj/n *arch. persnickety person* b1770

flat n *arch. not-sharp person* b1770
tabby n *old maid* b1770
tufthunter n *golddigger, hanger-on* b1770
cuss n b1775
fogey n *as in "old fogey"* b1780
fubsy adj (Brit) *fat* b1780
killjoy n b1780
rap n *critical remark* b1780 [incrimination, reputation: b1930] (verb use: b1930)
rip n *worthless person, horse* b1780
puzzleheaded adj b1785
bleeder n *foolish person* b1790
hellion n (Am) b1790 (heller: b1895)
laughing jackass n b1790
lowlife adj b1795 (noun use: b1915)
backhanded adj
dummy v *twit*
fly-by-night n (adj use: b1915; fly-by-nighter: b1950)
frog n *Frenchman*
hard-shell/hard-shelled adj
joskin n *rube*
saphead n
shark n *lawyer* [gen. "unscrupulous person": b1570]

Phrases

close quarters n b1755
hatchet man n (Am) b1755
old hat n b1755
devil's advocate n b1760
hop, skip and a jump n b1760
hot stuff n b1760
Indian file n (Am) *single file* b1760
peace pipe n b1760
all-or-nothing adj b1765 (all-or-none: b1900)
bird's-eye view n b1765
call of nature n b1765
catch-as-catch-can adj b1765
cause célèbre n b1765
country cousin n b1770
eye view n *as in "bird's-eye view"* b1770
give-and-take n b1770
John Doe n b1770 (Jane Doe: b1940)

old man n *father, husband* b1770 (old lady: b1870)
goings-on n b1775
head over heels adv b1775
hero worship n b1775 (verb use: b1885)
roll call n b1775
apple-pie order n b1780
esprit de corps n b1780
red flag n b1780
animal magnetism n b1785
old country n b1785
old hand n b1785
old lady n b1785
sick and tired adj b1785
checks and balances n b1790
lion's share n b1790
niminy-piminy adj b1790
stamping ground n b1790
cure-all n b1795
en masse adv b1795
optical illusion n b1795
pump up v b1795
rough-and-tumble n *unorganized fight* b1795 (adj use: b1835)
show off v b1795
vicious circle n b1795
pleasure dome n 1797
close order n
family way n
in toto adv
neck and neck adj/adv
pièce de résistance n ["main entree": b1840]
poke around v
round of applause n
yours truly n

General/Miscellaneous

serendipity n 1754 (serendipitous: b1945)
adventuress n b1755 (adventurer: b1540)
debut n b1755 (verb use: b1800)
ephemera n b1755 [type of short-lived illness: b1770; type of insect: b1680]
expiry n *expiration, end* b1755
hegira n *exodus* b1755 [spec. "exodus of Muhammed": b1600]
heyday n *best of times* b1755 ["excitement": b1590]
interlude n b1755 [theatrical sense: b1305]

interrogator n b1755 (inter-
ogee: b1920)
minutia n b1755
repulsion n *repugnance*
b1755
small talk n b1755
eventuality n b1760
maneuver n b1760 [obs.
"handwork": b1500] (verb
use: b1780)
outpost n b1760
outpouring n *fig.* b1760 [lit.
use: b1450] (outpour v:
b1675; outpour n: b1865)
outset n *beginning* b1760
[obs. "opp. of income":
b1540 to 1700s]
ride n b1760 (verb use:
b900)
summation n *addition* b1760
["summary": b1900] (sum-
mate v: b1900)
tailwater n b1760
fancier n b1765
generalization n b1765
guidepost n b1765
hullabaloo n b1765
outfit n *act of outfitting* b1765
["clothes," "group":
b1870] (verb use: b1850)
prospectus n b1765
rumpus n b1765
advent n *arrival* b1770
audience n *as in "audience of
a play"* b1770 ["meeting":
b1380]
balance n *aesthetic counterposition* b1770 (verb use:
b1930)
bee n *as in "spelling bee"*
b1770
blarney n b1770
confrere n *colleague* b1770
[obs. "fraternity brother":
b1470 to 1600s]
contrast n *comparison* b1770
(verb use: b1730)
cover n *as in "first-day cover"*
b1770
endorsee n b1770
entree n *entry* b1770
expatriate v/n b1770 (adj
use: b1815)
field n *as in "field of vision"*
b1770
gala n/adj b1770 [obs.
"clothing worthy of a
gala": b1625]

genre n b1770
highjinks n b1770
interference n b1770 (interfere: b1450)
keep n *as in "for keeps"*
b1770
letdown n b1770
litter n *garbage* b1770 (verb
use: b1730)
mark n *as in "high water
mark"* b1770
mount n *as in "jewelry
mount"* b1770 (mounting:
b1565)
nipper n *as in "little nipper"*
b1770
notice n *as in "give notice"*
b1770
paraphernalia n *miscellanea*
b1770 [type of leg. allocation: b1655]
pat n *as in "pat of butter"*
b1770
pick n *selection* b1770
pitfall n *fig. trap* b1770 [lit.
"trap": b1450]
ramification n *consequence*
b1770 ["organic branch":
b1665]
rattle n *as in "death rattle"*
b1770
responsibility n *obligation,
charge* b1770 ["being re-
sponsible": b1800] (re-
sponsible: b1645)
rinse n b1770 (verb use:
b1400)
rosette n b1770
scheme n *describing related elements* b1770
segment n b1770 [geometry
sense: b1570] (verb use:
b1860)
slop n b1770 ["bad food":
b1670; "maudlinness":
b1870; "nonsense":
b1970]
stain n *staining material*
b1770
toggle n b1770
undertone n *sound* b1770
["undercurrent": b1870]
vitriol n b1770 (vitriolic:
b1870)
ways n *as in "the ways of the
wild"* b1770
backwash n b1775
beastie n b1775

bonus n b1775
campus n (Am) b1775
conferee n (Am) b1775
devilment n b1775
fulfillment n b1775
statement n b1775
utilitarian n b1775
valuable n b1775 (adj use:
b1590)
carom n b1780 (verb use:
b1860; carombole: b1775)
dandy adj/n b1780 (Jack
O'Dandy: 1635; dandy-
ism: b1820)
deadlock n *impasse* b1780
(verb use: b1900)
drunk n *drunken binge* b1780
["drunken person":
b1870]
fare-thee-well n b1780
finish n b1780
gimcrackery n b1780 (gimcrack: b1470)
offing n *as in "in the offing"*
b1780 [type of nautical
term: b1630]
scatteration n b1780
spun glass n b1780
trend n *tendency, style* b1780
[phys. "direction of a
river": b1780] (verb use
"go in a phys. direction":
b1600; verb use "go in a
gen. direction": b1870;
trendsetter, trendy:
b1965)
amateur adj/n b1785 (ama-
teurism: b1865)
apologia n b1785
backup n *auxiliary* b1785 [as
in "traffic backup": b1970]
(back up: b1985)
bushman n b1785
dump n *as in "garbage dump"*
b1785 [slang "hovel":
b1900] (verb use: b1800)
impact n b1785 [fig. use:
b1830] (verb use: b1605)
nuance n b1785
puffery n b1785
squatter n b1785
truancy n b1785 (truantry:
b1500)
bangle n b1790
counteroffer n b1790
downdraft n b1790
fluff n b1790 ["flub": b1900;
"triviality": b1930]

keepsake n b1790
listen n *as in "give a listen"*
b1790 [obs. "sense of hearing": b1450]
nix n b1790 (adv use: b1930;
verb use: b1940)
outcome n *resolution* b1790
[obs. "coming out":
b1225]
phosphate n b1790
screed n *discourse* b1790
sulfuric acid n b1790
wonderland n b1790
aegis n b1795 ["shield":
b1615]
commitment n *obligation*
b1795
counterrevolution n b1795
curb n *as in "street curb"*
b1795 [other types of border: b1530]
dry rot n b1795 (dry-rot v:
b1870)
initiative n *action of initiation*
b1795 ["will to initiate":
b1930]
intermediary n b1795
intonation n b1795
liability n *accountability*
b1795 ["debit": b1870]
metier n b1795
phosphoric acid n b1795
plus n *bonus* b1795
scrabble n *scramble* b1795
thank-you n b1795
zag n b1795 (verb use:
b1800; zigzag n: b1715)
zig n b1795 (verb use:
b1940; zigzag n: b1715)
alert n (adj use: b1600; noun
use: b1800)
announcement n (announce:
b1485)
atmosphere n *ambience* (atmospheric: b1930)
block n *as in "city block"*
cache n
chiller n
concision n ["cut": b1400]
(conciseness: b1660)
connection n *as in "political
connections"*
cross n *as in "a cross between
a horse and a donkey"*
dip n *as in "dip in the road"*
disrepair n
double n *lookalike*

Abbreviations Used in This Book

adj adjective • *adv* adverb • *Am* American • *arch.* archaic • *b* by (so that "b1700" means "by 1700") • *Brit* British • *conj* conjunction • *contr* contraction • *esp.* especially • *fig.* figurative • *gen.* general • *geo.* geography • *interj* interjection • *leg.* legal • *LME* Late Middle English • *lit.* literal • *ME* Middle English • *med.* medical • *mil.* military • *n* noun • *obs.* obsolete • *OE* Old English • *opp.* opposite • *phys.* physical • *prep* preposition • *pron* pronoun • *rel.* religion • *spec.* specific • *u* until • *var.* various • *v* verb ❦

enormity n *immensity* (enormous: b1535)

extravaganza n ["extravagance": b1755]

fixity n *stability* [obs. "unevaporatability": b1670] (fixidity: b1770)

fondle v/n [obs. "pamper": b1695]

grade n *stage, level* [as in "gradation in color": b1730]

hang n *as in "the hang of a dress"*

headquarters n [mil. use: b1650]

human being n

inebriate n *drunkard*

kudos n

lap n *overlap* (verb use: b1630)

like n *liking*

malformation n

malpractitioner n

memorabilia n

misstep n

mobilization n

oddment n

opening n *opportunity, chance*

organization n *act or result of organizing* ["organic internal structure": b1425; "organism": b1730; "group": b1830] (verb use: b1670)

outsider n *one on the outside* [fig. use: b1870]

outturn n *output; outcome*

propulsion n [obs. "repelling": b1615 to 1700s]

recess n *niche* [gen. use: b1870] (verb use: b1810)

seclusion n ["exclusion": b1620]

shipment n

spree n

stance n *as in "batting stance"* ["phys. standpoint": only in ME; "fig. standpoint": b1970]

surveillance n (surveillant n: b1820; surveil: b1950)

trickery n

unluck n *bad luck*

yoga n

zest n *gusto, as in "zest for life"*

Things

target n *with bull's-eye* b1760 [obs. "small shield": b1300; "goal": b1970] (verb use: b1840)

memento n *souvenir* b1770 [type of prayer: b1400; "reminder": b1580]

snap n *fastener* b1770

thingamabob n b1770 (thingummy: b1800; thingamajig: b1830)

sleigh bell n b1775

chrome n 1797 (verb use: b1880; chromium: b1810)

false bottom n

gelatin n (gel: b1900)

raw material n

silver paper n *tin foil*

springboard n *lit. and fig.*

Description

chunky adj (Am) b1755

consensual adj *related to consent* b1755 ["by mutual consent": b1800]

descriptive adj b1755

destructible adj b1755

disgusting adj b1755

fancy adj *ornate* b1755

gimlet adj b1755

nonessential adj b1755

obsolescent adj b1755 (obsolescence: b1830; obsolesce: b1875)

sparse adj b1755

symmetrical adj b1755 (symmetric: b1800)

toilworn adj b1755

unsymmetrical adj *asymmetrical* b1755

airtight adj b1760

confidential adj b1760 [obs. "confident": b1655]

gassy adj b1760 (gaseous: b1800)

lifelong adj b1760 ["livelong": b1760]

nee adj *female ne* b1760 (ne "applied to men": b1930)

pear-shaped adj b1760

isolated adj b1765 (isolate adj: b1820)

aberrant adj b1770

avid adj b1770 (avidity: b1450)

convoluted adj b1770 (convolution: b1545; convolve v: b1650; convolute v: b1700)

decided adj b1770

delicate adj *sticky, as in "a delicate situation"* b1770

dense adj *difficult* b1770

interdependent adj b1770 (interdepend: b1870)

literal adj *opp. of figurative* b1770

nation adj *very large* b1770

nowhence adv/pron b1770

prosaic adj *bland* b1770 [pertaining to prose: b1660]

raucous adj b1770

rickety adj *shaky, unstable* b1770 ["afflicted with rickets": b1685]

specific adj *concrete, exact* b1770

stout adj *solid* b1770 [obs. "arrogant": b1300 to 1800s; obs. "fierce": b1350 to 1600s; "robust": b1700; "pudgy": b1830] (stouten: b1830)

subjective adj *opp. of objective* b1770

synthetic adj *artificial* b1770 ["pertaining to logical synthesis": b1700] (noun use: b1950)

tight adj *hard to handle, as in "tight spot"* b1770 ["lacking maneuvering space," as in "tight curve": b1970]

warm adj *as in "a warm blue"* b1770 (verb use: b1870)

waterlogged adj b1770 (waterlog: b1780)

bilateral adj b1775

damn adj/adv b1775 (damned: b1400)

euphonious adj b1775 (euphonic: b1815)

fake adj *counterfeit* b1775 (noun use: b1830; verb use: b1855)

flyaway adj b1775

nohow adv *anyhow* b1775

pesky adj b1775

rackety adj b1775

revolutionary adj b1775 (noun use: b1850)

two-fisted adj (Am) b1775

unattractive adj b1775

advisory adj b1780 (noun use: b1940)

backslapping adj b1780 (backslap v: b1930)

far-gone adj b1780

manque adj *failed in aspirations* b1780

monotonous adj *characterized by monotone* b1780 ["boringly repetitious": b1830]

terse adj *curt* b1780 [obs. "neat and clean": b1600 to 1800s; obs. "cultured": b1625 to 1700s]

hard-bitten adj b1785

ludicrous adj *ridiculous* b1785 [obs. "witty, frivolous": b1600 to 1800s]

milk-and-water adj *weak* b1785

objectionable adj b1785

petite adj b1785

rotate adj *round* b1785

smack adv *hard, with a smack* b1785 ["directly": b1830]

swell adj b1785

unimpeachable adj b1785

alcoholic adj *related to alcohol* b1790 ["addicted to alcohol": b1930]

bona fide adj b1790

exhaustive adj b1790

first-class adj/adv b1790

imposing adj *impressive* b1790

indoors adv b1790

tacky adj *sticky* b1790

arresting adj b1795

boughten adj b1795

businesslike adj b1795

crack adj *as in "a crack shot"* b1795 (noun use: b1640)

incandescent adj b1795 (incandescence: b1660; incandesce: b1875)

iridescent adj b1795 (iridescence: b1805)

myriad adj *many* b1795 (noun use: b1555)

optional adj *not necessary* b1795 [pertaining to choice: b1765]

orotund adj *clear, pertaining to voice* b1795

otiose adj *ineffective* b1795 ["unnecessary": b1870]

piggish adj b1795

scathing adj *phys. injurious* b1795 ["harsh, caustic": b1870]

subhuman adj b1795 (noun use: b1940)

acting adj *temporary*

adaptable adj (adaptable: b1825)

assorted adj

astir adj

autonomous adj

axiomatic adj (axiom: b1485)

coincidental adj (coincident adj: b1565)

congenital adj

dashing adj

dinky adj ["neat": b1790]

docile adj *tame* ["teachable": b1485]

economical adj/adv *thrifty; related to economics* (econo-mist "thrifty person": b1730)

edacious adj *eating* (verb use: b1770)

efficient adj ["causal": b1380]

energetic adj [arch. "effective": b1655] (energetical: b1670; energic: b1730)

getable adj *get-at-able*

lilting adj

meaningless adj (meaningful: b1855)

noticeable adj

old-time adj (old-timey: b1850; old-timer: b1860)

patchy adj

prize adj

quizzical adj

repellent adj *repulsive* (repel: b1830)

repugnant adj *repulsive* ["opposed": b1385] (repugnance: b1645)

rosy adj *optimistic*

scintillating adj (scintillant: b1740)

self-appointed adj

sporting adj *fair* [obs. "playful": b1600 to 1700s]

statuesque adj

stricken adj *afflicted*

sweeping adj

tacky adj *shabby* ["in poor taste": b1885]

taxing adj

tight adj *tight-fitting*

unprofessional adj

washed-out adj *faded* ["pale": b1840]

Colors

Indian red n b1755

pea green n b1755

olive green adj/n b1760

almond n *the color* b1770

amber n *the color* b1770

puce n b1790

royal blue n b1790

maroon n *the color* b1795

cream n *the color*

lemon n *the color* (adj use: b1600)

lilac n *the color*

pearl gray n

slate blue n

straw yellow n

turquoise blue n

Actions/Verbs

coat v *paint; plate* b1755 ["give a coat to": b1380]

decompose v *break down* b1755 ["rot": b1800]

secede v b1755

slouch v b1755

stet v *let stand* b1755

wash up v b1755

infiltrate v *lit. "filter into"* b1760 [fig. use: b1970]

saturate v *drench* b1760 [obs. "satisfy": b1540 to 1800s]

scoot v b1760

swish v b1760 (noun use: b1820)

weather v *become weathered* b1760 (weathered: b1780)

affiliate v b1765 (noun use: b1880; affiliated: b1795)

home v b1765

rough v *as in "roughing it"* b1765

touch off v b1765

ameliorate v b1770 (ameliorative adj: b1830)

arrange v b1770 [purely mil. sense: b1375; "plan," as in "arrange a visit": b1800]

assemble v *construct* b1770

background v b1770 (backgrounder: b1960)

bore n/v *causing boredom* b1770 (boring adj: b1840; boredom: b1855)

braise v b1770

chip v *as in "the vase was chipped"* b1770 [as in "chip off": b1870] (noun use: b1900)

engage v *as in "engage your attention"* b1770

forge v *as in "forge ahead"* b1770 [gen. use: b1900]

infringe v *encroach* b1770 ["break a law": b1470] (infringement: b1675)

jell v b1770 [fig. "take shape, come together": b1930] (jelly v: b1590; jellify: b1830)

knuckle under v b1770

log v *as in "become water-logged"* b1770 (logged adj: b1820)

louden v *make louder* b1770 ["get louder": b1805]

overcompensate v b1770 (overcompensation: b1915)

ream v *bore, enlarge* b1770

stamp v *place a stamp on* b1770

support v *provide evidence for, as in "support a claim"* b1770 (noun use: b1800)

tar v *as in "tar and feather"* b1770

trace v *copy* b1770 [gen. "draw, diagram": b1450] (tracing paper: b1825)

weep v *droop, as in "weeping willow"* b1770

focus v b1775

honeycomb v b1775

underscore v b1775 (noun use: b1905)

derange v *rearrange* b1780 ["make crazy": b1825]

embed v b1780

surface v *apply a surface* b1780 ["come to the surface": b1900; fig. "arise": b1970]

belittle v (Am) b1785

cue v *queue/strike with a pool cue* b1785

donate v (Am) b1785

effervesce v *bubble* b1785 [obs. "react chemically": b1705] (effervescence: b1685)

fumigate v b1785 [obs. "scent, perfume": b1520] (fumigant: b1890)

gawk v b1785 (noun use: b1760)

jink v *move quickly, jerk* b1785

splatter v b1785 (noun use: b1820)

squatter v *splash about* b1785

stash v b1785 (noun use: b1915)

swamp v b1785

bullyrag v *badger* b1790

capsize v b1790

diddle v *cheat* b1790

economize v b1790

eventuate v (Am) b1790

experiment v *as in "experiment with drugs"* b1790 [obs. "experience": b1450 to 1700s; "try": b1500] (noun use: b1450)

jury-rig v b1790
kibble v *grind* b1790
remodel v b1790
scrunch v b1790
seep v b1790 (noun use: b1825; seepage: b1825)
snooze v b1790 (noun use: b1800)
acclimate v b1795 (acclimatize: b1840)
aerate v b1795 (aerator: b1865)
badger v b1795
capture v b1795 (noun use: b1555)
cavort v (Am) b1795
commentate v b1795
defoliate v b1795 (defoliation: b1660)
designate v *select for office* b1795 ["signify": b1830]
disorganize v b1795 (disorganized: b1815)
district v b1795
horrify v b1795
jaundice v *affect* b1795
legitimatize v b1795 (legiti-mate v: b1535; legitimize: b1850)
superimpose v b1795
approximate v *guess* ["bring into phys. proximity": b1425] (approximation: b1670)
centralize v
classify v ["categorize as secret": b1970] (classification: b1790)
clunk v (noun use: b1825)
crank v *bend* (noun use: b1600)
cross v *as in "cross in the mail"*
decorate v *ornament* ["honor": b1425]
devil v *annoy*
disintegrate v
doctor v *alter*
dump v ["fall": b1400] (noun use: b1785)
glimpse v *see briefly* ["glimmer": b1400]
hoax v (noun use: b1810; hocus v: b1675)
honk v (Am) *make a honking sound* (noun use: b1855)
hulk v
institute v *start* ["appoint": b1325]
paralyze v
pull v *restrain, as in "pull punches"*
rationalize v
reel v *fig. spin, as in "the mind reels"*
renege v *welch* ["renounce": b1550]
revolutionize v
run v *as in "it runs in the family"*
scale v *as in "scale up, scale down"*
shirk v *avoid* ["sneak, trick": b1635] (shirk n: b1830)
start v *begin* (noun use: b1570)
stereotype v
swat v (noun use: b1800)
transpire v *happen*
twist v *as in "twist your face"*
upset v *knock down* [obs. "set up": by 350 to 1700s; "mentally distress," "disrupt": b1830; as in "upset your stomach": b1870] (adj use: b1805; noun use: b1830)
utilize v
weigh on v
zag v (noun use: b1795; zigzag v: b1780)

Archaisms

groggy adj *drunk* b1770 ["cloudy": b1830]
hum v *slang "con"* b1770
make n *making, manufacture* b1770
make-game n *target of ridicule* b1770
vigilance n *insomnia* b1770
refreshen v b1785
defeature n *disfigurement*
gruel n *something grueling* (grueling: b1855)

IN USE BY
1825

Geography/Places
coulee n (Am) b1805
escarpment n b1805
tideland n b1805
watershed n b1805 [fig. use: b1900]
arroyo n (Am) b1810
intermontane adj (Am) *between mountains* b1810
sea level n b1810
communal adj *pertaining to a commune* b1815 ["intended for all": b1870] (communalism: b1875)
crevasse n (Am) b1815
magnetic north n b1815
groundswell n b1820
heathland n b1820
quad n *quadrangle* b1820
saltflat n b1820
couloir n
everglade n (Am)
skyline n

Natural Things
anthropic adj *human* b1805
iridium n b1805
mirage n b1805
calcium n b1810
chlorine n 1810 (chlorinate: b1860)
magnesium n b1810
potassium n b1810
sodium n b1810
zirconium n b1810
aluminum n 1812
iodine n 1814
anthracite n *type of coal* b1815 ["mineral resembling embers": b1605]
chloride n b1815

platinum n b1815 [the color: b1930] (platina: b1750)
sea fire n *ocean bioluminescence* b1815
lithium n 1818
azurite n b1820
cadmium n b1820
fire opal n b1820
floe, ice floe n b1820
nicotine n b1820
silicon n b1820
strychnine n b1820
undertow n b1820
berg n *iceberg*
gloam n *twilight* (gloaming: b1000)
sepia n *ink of cuttlefish, or the color thereof*

Plants
balsam fir n (Am) b1805
cocklebur n b1805
cottonwood n (Am) b1805
eucalyptus n b1805 (eucalypt: b1885)
forsythia n b1805
heartwood n b1805
lemongrass n b1805
calla n b1810 (calla lily: b1875)
red pine n (Am) b1810
shade tree n (Am) b1810
bladderwort n b1815
calico bush n (Am) b1815
grapefruit n b1815
gul n *rose* b1815
lily pad n (Am) b1815
morning glory n (Am) b1815
chlorophyll n 1818
wisteria n 1818
balsam poplar n b1820

jackfruit n b1820
pitcher plant n b1820
plantlet n b1820
poison hemlock n (Am) b1820
poison sumac n b1820
quack grass n b1820
citrus n
petunia n
saw grass n
succulent n
tiger lily n

Animals
box turtle n (Am) b1805
chickaree n (Am) *red squirrel* b1805
cowbird n (Am) b1805
Hereford n *type of cattle* b1805
hoofprint n b1805
koala n b1805
mountain sheep n (Am) b1805
mule deer n b1805
panfish n (Am) b1805
passenger pigeon n (Am) b1805
peafowl n *type of pheasant* b1805
plant louse n *aphid* b1805
prairie wolf n b1805
pussycat n b1805 [fig. use: b1870]
sapsucker n b1805
Shetland pony n b1805
speckled trout n (Am) b1805
woof v *bark* b1805 (noun use: b1840)
yellow perch n b1805
bedbug n b1810

boa constrictor n b1810
cocktail n *bobtail horse* b1810
downy woodpecker n (Am) b1810
Exmoor n *type of sheep* b1810
field sparrow n (Am) b1810
flicker n (Am) *type of woodpecker* b1810
horned lizard n (Am) b1810
mustang n (Am) b1810
rose-breasted grosbeak n (Am) b1810
scarlet tanager n (Am) b1810
Scotch terrier n b1810 (Scottish terrier: b1840)
song sparrow n (Am) b1810
bandicoot n *type of marsupial* b1815 [type of rat: b1790]
bobwhite n (Am) b1815
critter n b1815
daddy longlegs n b1815
damselfly n b1815
deerhound n b1815
gray wolf n b1815
great horned owl n b1815
heehaw n (Am) b1815 (verb use: b1825)
hellbender n (Am) *type of salamander* b1815
ivorybilled woodpecker n b1815 (ivorybill: b1790)
loggerhead turtle n (Am) b1815
mastodon n b1815
mudhen n (Am) b1815
pronghorn n *type of antelope* b1815
rock bass n b1815
water boatman n *type of insect* b1815

waterthrush n (Am) b1815
Angora cat n b1820 (angora: b1835)
bovine adj b1820 (noun use: b1865)
cicala n *cicada* b1820 (cicada: b1390)
diamondback n b1820 (diamondback rattler: b1895)
gypsy moth n b1820
lammergeier n *type of vulture* b1820
mackerel shark n b1820
mudcat n (Am) *type of catfish* b1820
poodle n b1820
seventeen-year locust n b1820
silver perch n (Am) b1820
small game n b1820
spiny lobster n b1820
striped bass n (Am) b1820 (striper: b1940)
tiger moth n b1820
waxwing n b1820
cliff swallow n
dalmatian n
firebird n *brightly colored bird*
flipper n
fox terrier n
Persian cat n
razorback n *type of hog*
Spanish moss n (Am)
turkey vulture n (Am)
water moccasin n
wildebeest n

Weather
cirrus, cirrocumulus, cirrostratus n b1805
cumulus n b1805 ["accumulation": b1660]
thunderpeal n b1805
zero n *zero degrees* b1805 (adj use: b1810)
brume n *mist, fog* b1810
downpour n b1815 (verb use: b1800; downfall: b1630)
St. Elmo's Fire n b1815
cloudburst n (Am) b1820
rainstorm n b1820
relative humidity n b1820
gullywasher n
snowfall n

Heavens/Sky
asteroid n b1805
planetoid n b1805

cloudland n b1820
sunbow n *akin to rainbow* b1820
sunburst n b1820
meteorite n (meteor: b1590; meteorolite: b1830; meteoroid: b1865)

Science
atom n b1805
Homo sapiens n b1805
litmus paper n b1805
physical science n b1805
zoological adj b1810
agronomy n *study of soil management* b1815
biology n b1815 (biological adj: b1860)
gemology n b1815 (gemologist: b1935)
petrology n *study of rocks* b1815
polarize, polarization v, n b1815 [fig. "divide": b1970]
taxonomy n *study of classification* b1815
horology n b1820
paleography n *study of ancient writings* b1820
suspended animation n b1820
atomic number n
herpetology n
selenology n *study of the moon*
vitalism n

Energy
galvanic battery n b1805
induction n b1805 (inductance: b1890)
tension n *as in "high-tension wire"* b1805
calorie n b1810 (calorimeter: b1795; caloric: b1830)
coal gas n b1810
horsepower n b1810
coalfield n b1815
gas burner n b1815
gas meter n b1815
propellant n b1815 (adj use: b1645)
refuel v b1815
gasworks n b1820
waterpower n b1820
electromagnetic adj (electromagnet, electromagnetism: b1830)

natural gas n
thermoelectricity, thermoelectric n, adj
turbine n

Time
evenfall n b1815
sidereal time n b1815
antenatal n *prenatal* b1820
mean solar day n b1820
trimester n

Age/Aging
nonagenarian n *someone in their nineties* b1805
septuagenarian adj/n b1805 (adj use: b1715)
grown-up n b1815 (adj use: b1470)
octogenarian adj/n b1815
teen adj/n *teenager* b1820

Mathematics
linear equation n b1820
triangulation n b1820 (triangulate: b1835)
coordinate n
statistician n

Measurement
centigrade adj b1805
galvanometer n b1805
dynamometer n b1810
kiloliter n b1810
millimeter, milliliter n b1810
tachometer n b1810
dollop n b1815 (verb use: b1860)
meter n *as in "water meter"* b1815 (verb use: b1885)
atomic weight n b1820 (atomic mass: b1900)
yardstick n b1820

The Body
cerebral adj *pertaining to the brain* b1805 ["intellectual": b1930]
mucous membrane n b1810
blood heat n *body temperature* b1815
fetal adj b1815
physique n b1815
smegma n b1820
cockeye n
innards n [gen. "insides": b1925] (inwardes "innards": b1400)

large intestine n
motor adj
nictitate v *wink*
snaggletooth n

Physical Description
drool v b1805 (noun use: b1870)
sinistral adj *left-handed* b1805
butterball n b1815
mousy adj b1815 (fig. mouse: b1600)
au naturel adj b1820
svelte adj b1820
wide-awake adj *not sleeping* b1820 ["watchful": b1870]
bedraggled adj [bedraggle: b1730]
popeyed adj (Am) (pop v: b1700; pop eye: b1830)
ramshackle adj *describing people* [describing buildings: b1870]

Medicine
asthenia n *weakness* b1805
extravascular adj b1805
hysteria n *of women only* b1805 [gen. use: b1870] (hysterical: b1615)
jungle fever n b1805
lockjaw n b1805
medicine man n b1805
pigeon-toed adj b1805
rubeola n *measles* b1805
sarcoma n *type of tumor* b1805
scarlatina n *scarlet fever* b1805
specs n *glasses* b1805
ambulance n *mobile hospital* b1810 ["evacuation vehicle": b1860]
anemia n b1810 (anemic: b1840)
bronchitis n b1810
faint n b1810 (verb use: b1400)
family physician n b1810 (family doctor: b1850; family practice: b1975)
gastritis n b1810
herpes zoster n b1810 (herpes: b1400; herpes simplex: b1910; herpesvirus: b1925)
mustard plaster n b1810

breech presentation n b1815
delirium tremens n b1815
frostbite n b1815 (verb use: b1600; frostbitten: b1595)
hematology n b1815
scabies n *type of rash* b1815 [obs. type of disease: b1400]
sick bay n b1815
straitjacket n b1815 (verb use: b1865)
dermatology n b1820 (dermatologist: b1865)
limp n b1820 (verb use: b1570)
obstetrics n b1820
paralysis agitans n *shaking palsy* b1820
passive resistance n b1820
roseola n *rubella* b1820
stethoscope n b1820
homeopathic, homeopathy adj, n
laryngitis n
milk sickness n (Am)
mutism n
neuralgia n
painter's colic n *lead poisoning*
phlebitis n
sniffles, the n

Everyday Life

centerpiece n b1805
chairbed n b1805
chute n *as in "coal chute"* b1805 (verb use: b1885)
peroxide n b1805 (verb use: b1910; adj use: b1920)
pier table n *used with pier glass* b1805
sheet glass n b1805
tea garden n b1805
water main n b1805
cookbook n (Am) b1810 (Brit cookery book: b1640)
gaslight n b1810
housemate n b1810
hydrant n b1810
interior decoration n b1810 (interior decorator: b1870; interior design: b1930)
mailbox n b1810
skeleton key n b1810
slop bowl n b1810
washer n b1810
washroom n (Am) b1810

window shade n b1810
bed table n b1815
candelabrum, candelabra n b1815
cologne n b1815
console table n b1815
cookstove n b1815
doorbell n b1815
matchbook n b1815
penholder n b1815
washbasin n b1815
water wagon n b1815
belonging n *possession* b1820 (belongings: b1605)
bookshelf n b1820
dry-clean v b1820 (dry-cleaner, dry-cleaning: b1900)
gas main n b1820
hat tree n (Am) b1820
jeroboam n *type of bottle* b1820
passkey n b1820
shelving n *shelves* b1820
sofabed n b1820
Chinese lantern n
cutting board n
doorplate n
flacon n *type of bottle*
four-poster n
latchkey n
plate rail n
scrapbook n
spittoon n
stone china n (stoneware: b1685)
wineskin n

Shelter/Housing

campground n (Am) b1805 (campsite: 1910)
flat n *apartment* b1805
French window n b1805
life buoy n b1805
lifeboat n b1805
swinging door n b1805
cellarette n *wine storage* b1810
rest house n b1810
studio n *as in "artist's studio"* b1810 [place for filmmaking: b1930]
corridor n *hallway* b1815 [gen. "passageway": b1595; fig., as in "Boston–New York corridor": b1930]

slum n b1815 [obs. "room": b1830] (verb use: b1885)
butler's pantry n b1820
clubhouse n b1820
engine company n (Am) *fire squad* b1820
fanlight n *type of window* b1820
hidey-hole n b1820
hospice n b1820 [med. sense: b1900]
parquet n *type of flooring* b1820 (verb use: b1680)
playroom n b1820
room v b1820 [obs. "make room": b1470] (roomer: b1875)
shanty n b1820
toolhouse n b1820
windowpane n b1820
dayroom n
double-hung adj
fire department n (fire company: b1740; fire brigade: b1835)
igloo n
lanai n *porch*
living room n
lunchroom n
root cellar n

Drink

soda water n b1805
vodka n b1805
cocktail n (Am) *drink* b1810
ginger beer n b1810
marsala n *type of wine* b1810
vermouth n b1810
curacao n b1815
swizzle n *type of drink* b1815
applejack n b1820
firewater n (Am) b1820
kirsch n *type of brandy* b1820
mountain dew n b1820
red-eye n *strong whiskey* b1820
amontillado n *type of wine*
caffeine n

Food

American cheese n (Am) b1805
carbonate v b1805 (noun use: b1795; carbonation: b1885)
consumable n b1805
cruller n (Am) b1805
doughnut n b1805

gingersnap n b1805
Gruyere n *type of cheese* b1805
gumbo n *type of stew, soup* b1805
hand-feed v b1805
pandowdy n (Am) *type of dessert* b1805
soybean n b1805
au gratin adj b1810
citron melon n (Am) *type of melon* b1810
crouton n b1810
curry powder n b1810
diner n *one who dines* b1810 [type of restaurant: b1970]
English breakfast n b1810
kohlrabi n b1810
mint julep n (Am) b1810
Swedish turnip n *rutabaga* b1810
chutney n b1815
consomme n b1815
gastronomy n b1815 (gastronome: b1825)
hard wheat n b1815
Irish stew n b1815
lunch n b1815 (verb use: b1825)
pot cheese n (Am) *type of cottage cheese* b1815
sauté n b1815 (verb use: b1860)
scuppernong n (Am) *type of grape* b1815
soufflé n b1815 [med. type of body sound: b1900]
sweet pepper n b1815
butter bean n b1820
dine out v b1820
foie gras n b1820
gourmet n b1820 (adj use: b1930)
lemon drop n b1820
Limburger n *type of cheese* b1820
popcorn n (Am) b1820
schnapps n b1820
sugarbeet n b1820
taffy n b1820
creme n
dropped egg n *poached egg*
fish fry n
gastronome n (gastronomy: b1815)
graham cracker n (Am)
inedible adj
mouth-watering adj

poi n
pretzel n (Am)
sour cream n (Am)
Swiss cheese n
toffee n [the color: b1970]

Agriculture/ Food-Gathering

pigpen n b1805
pith v type of cattle slaughter b1805
plainsman n b1805
stockyard n b1805
veterinary surgeon n b1805
farmstead n b1810
husking bee n b1810
ranch n (Am) b1810 [as in "ranch house": b1935] (verb use: b1840)
winter-kill v b1810
winemaking n b1815
abattoir n b1820
beekeeper n b1820
fisherwoman n b1820 (fisherman: b1450)
grainfield n b1820
pomology n science of growing fruit b1820
floriculture n
forestry n
gaucho n
stampede n (Am) lit. [fig. sense: b1870; "rodeo": b1930] (verb use: b1840)

Cloth/Clothing

britches n b1805
fez n b1805
overcoat n b1805
overshirt n b1805
spat n b1805
topcoat n b1805
chemisette n woman's garment b1810
dreadnought n type of overcoat b1810 [type of battleship: b1910]
Hessian boot n b1810
opera hat n b1810
top hat n b1810
camise n type of shirt b1815
chambray n (Am) fabric b1815
mufti n style of dress b1815
slip-on n b1815
toggery n togs b1815

chaps n (Am) b1820 (chapajaros: b1865)
deerstalker n b1820
poke bonnet n b1820
pouf n type of headdress b1820 [type of furniture: b1900]
coverall n
melton n type of fabric
sartorial adj well-tailored (sartin n: b1200; sartor n: b1660; sartorian adj: b1670)

Fashion/Style

eau de cologne n b1805
trinketry n b1810
side-whiskers n b1815
anklet n b1820
arbiter elegantiarum n lit. "arbiter of refinements" b1820
curlpaper n b1820
beglamour v
cosmeticize v
paisley n
rakish adj jaunty

Tools

copying machine n b1805
insulator n b1805
refrigerator n b1805 [gen. "something that cools": b1615]
scuttlebutt n type of cask b1805 ["rumor": b1905]
sunglass n b1805
blinder n b1810
chuck n as in "drill chuck" b1810 (chock: b1705)
steamer n b1815
straightedge n b1815
circular saw n b1820
ice ax n b1820
template n shaping tool b1820 (temple "template": b1690)
boomerang n
holystone n
pry n prying tool
sandpaper n (verb use: b1850; sand v: b1870)
suction pump n

Travel/Transportation

barouche n type of carriage b1805

hike v b1805 (noun use: b1865; hiker: b1915)
jaunting car n b1805
marina n b1805
stanhope n type of buggy b1805
covered bridge n b1810
dogsled n (Am) b1810
second class n b1810 (adj use: b1840)
wagon train n b1810
bridle path n b1815
pike n (Am) (turn)pike b1815
tourism n b1815
towboat n b1815
traps n luggage b1815
wheelhouse n b1815
airship n b1820
charabanc n (Brit) type of bus b1820
crow's nest n b1820
life raft n b1820
roadster n type of horse b1820
roadworthy adj b1820
rotary engine n b1820
running board n (Am) b1820
velocipede n type of bicycle b1820
viaduct n b1820
aeronautics n (aeronaut: b1785)
locomotory adj
macadam n macadamized road
oarswoman n (oarsman: b1450)
outboard adj (adv use: b1850; noun use: b1935)
railroad n for trains [for wagons: b1760] (verb use: b1880)
slaver n slave ship
suspension bridge n
toll road n
train n rail transportation (verb use: b1870)
tramway n
trolley n

Emotions/ Characteristics

bumptious adj arrogant b1805
chuckle n quiet laughter b1805 [obs. "uproarious

laughter": b1630 to 1800s] (noun use: b1730; chuck: b1600)
dispiteous adj cruel b1805 ["merciless": b1530]
doldrums n b1805 [obs. "dolt": b1800]
fetishism n b1805
mannerism n b1805
panic-stricken adj b1805
raffish adj b1805
red-blooded adj b1805
self-sacrifice n b1805
tirade n b1805
gooseflesh n b1810 [lit. sense: b1425] (goose pimples: b1890; goose bumps: b1935)
outspoken adj b1810 (rare outspeak: b1450)
pernickety adj b1810 (persnickety: b1890)
pins and needles n b1810
belligerence n b1815 (belligerent: b1560; belligerency: b1865)
fly adj (Brit) alert, artful b1815
horror-struck/horror-stricken adj b1815
lark n/v whim b1815 (larky: b1830)
nerve-wracking adj b1815
savoir faire n b1815
stiff upper lip n b1815
animus n animosity b1820 [psychological sense: b1930]
appalling adj b1820
blasé adj b1820
bullheaded adj b1820
cold shoulder n/v b1820
creep n as in "gives me the creeps" b1820
dither n b1820
draconian adj b1820 (draconic: b1710)
false face n b1820
free-living adj b1820
gullible adj b1820 (gull: b1550; gullish: b1600)
preachy adj b1820
self-possessed adj b1820
stilted adj haughty; labored b1820 (stiltified: b1830)
wild-eyed adj b1820
aggressive adj (aggression:

b1615; aggressor: b1650; aggress v: b1715]

brash adj *brazen* ["fragile": b1570]

cachinnate v *laugh loudly* (cachinnation: b1625)

collywobbles n *butterflies in the stomach*

consuming adj *deeply felt* ["engrossing": b1920]

cranky adj *sour* ["infirm": b1790]

derange v *make crazy* ["re-arrange": b1780]

finicky adj (finical: b1595; finicking: b1665; finick v: b1870]

hedonist n (hedonic: b1660; hedonism: b1860)

hilarious adj (hilarity: b1870)

jollify v (jollification: b1830)

maddening adj

narcissism n (narcissistic: b1930)

temperament n [obs. "blend": b1400 to 1600s; "weather conditions": b1600; obs. "temperature": b1670 to 1700s] (temperamental: b1910)

tense adj *applied to people* [applied to things: b1670] (verb use: b1950)

Thoughts/Perception/ The Mind

foreseeable adj b1805

objectivity n b1805

romanticism n b1805 (romanticize: b1800; romantic: b1900)

transcendentalism n b1805

calculating adj b1810

forethoughtful adj b1810

craze n *state of craziness* b1815 [obs. "something wrong": b1600 to 1800s]

make-believe n b1815 (adj use: b1825; make-belief: b1870)

mystification, mystify n b1815 (mystify: b1735; mystified: b1870)

paranoia n b1815 (paranoid adj/n: b1905)

appraisal n b1820

clerisy n *intelligentsia* b1820

cognizant adj b1820 (cognizance: b1350)

daydream v b1820 (noun use: b1685)

envisage v b1820

intellectual adj *pedantic* b1820 ["related to intellect": b1400] (noun use: b1670)

introspective adj b1820 (introspection: b1680; introspect v: b1900)

nihilism n b1820 (nihilist: b1870)

realism n *pragmatism; philosophical outlook* b1820 (realistic: b1860; realist n: b1870)

visualize v b1820 (visualization: b1835)

egomania n

egotistical adj (egotistic: b1860)

heuristic adj

monomania n

negativism n

Love/Romance/Sex

love child n *illegitimate child* b1805

seductress n b1805 [obs. "seductor": b1500 to 1600s]

disorderly house n *whorehouse* b1810

easy virtue n b1810

postnuptial adj b1810

divorce, divorcee n *divorced man* b1815

fancy man, fancy woman n *slang lover* b1815

lady-killer n b1815

antenuptial adj b1820

lovey-dovey n *term of endearment* b1820 (adj use: b1890)

mismarriage n b1820

anaphrodisiac adj

bisexual adj/n

calf-love n *puppy love*

cuddle n (verb use: b1520; cuddly: b1865; cuddlesome: b1880)

free love n

neck v ["hit in the neck": b1490]

soul mate n

Family/Relations/ Friends

clansman n b1810 (clanswoman: b1900)

family tree n b1810

pa n *pa(pa)* b1815

pure-blooded adj

Holidays

Easter egg n b1805 (pace egg: b1615)

Games/Fun/Leisure

hopscotch n b1805 (verb use: b1920; hop-scot: b1780)

jackstraws n *pick-up-sticks* b1805

peashooter n b1805

squirt gun n (Am) b1805

peewee n *small marble* b1810 ["small person": b1890] (adj use: b1890)

keno n (Am) b1815

kaleidoscope n 1817

hobby n b1820

toboggan n b1820 (verb use: b1850)

bunker n *golf sandtrap* ["bench": b1760]

monte n *type of card game*

ringer n *in horseshoes*

sightsee, sightseeing v, n

thimblerig n *the shell game* (verb use: b1840)

trump card n

Sports

jump rope n b1805

mountaineering n b1805 (mountaineer: b1870)

loving cup n b1810

diving board n b1815

false start n b1815

featherweight n b1815

English saddle n b1820

infighting n b1820 [fig. use: b1970]

turfman n *railbird* b1820

acrobat n (acrobatics: b1885)

championship n

Professions/Duties

dressmaker n b1805

headwaiter n b1805

cameleer n b1810

commercial traveler n *traveling salesman* b1810 (commercial n: b1870)

longshoreman n b1815 (longshoring: b1930)

professional n b1815 [slang "whore": b1870]

tinsmith n b1815

tonsorial adj b1815

couturiere n b1820 (couture: b1910; couturier: b1900)

lumberman n (Am) b1820 (lumberjack: b1835)

patternmaker n b1820

taxidermy n b1820

gasman n

maitre d' n

Business/Commerce/ Selling

dicker v *barter* b1805 (noun use: b1825)

drugstore n (Am) b1810

life insurance n b1810

taproom n b1810

estaminet n *type of cafe* b1815

per diem n b1815

pourboire n *gratuity* b1815

wareroom n b1815

free trade n

soda fountain n (Am)

stockroom n

The Workplace

career n *life's calling* b1805 [obs. lit. "course for running," "gallop": b1530 to 1700s] (verb use "gallop": b1635)

resume n b1805 (obs. verb use: b1800)

tickler file n (Am) b1805

general strike n (Am) b1810

slave driver n (Am) b1810

slavey n (Brit) *scutworker* b1810

breadwinner n b1820

overwork n b1820 ["overtime": b1770] (verb use: b1900)

employe, employee n

sack n *dismissal* (verb use: b1845)

walking papers n (Am)

Finances/Money

monetary adj b1805

money order n b1805

poverty-stricken adj b1805

property tax n b1810

stock market n b1810

treasury note n (Am) 1812

diminishing returns n b1815

savings bank n b1820

small change n b1820

taxpayer n b1820

coupon n *investment statement* [as in "sales coupon": b1865]

shinplaster n (Am) *privately issued currency*

Language and Speaking

diatribe n *long rebuke* b1805 [arch. "discourse": b1585]

jargonize v b1805

postfix n *suffix* b1805

terminology n b1805 (term: b1450)

American English n b1810

code n *as in "Morse code"* b1810 (verb use: b1885)

ipsissima verba n *exact quote* b1810

cuss v (Am) b1815 (cussword: b1875)

hyphen v *hyphenate* b1815 (hyphenize: b1870; hyphenate: b1890)

past tense n b1815

phrasemonger n b1815

platitude n *trite speech; trite word or phrase* b1815 (platitudinarian n: b1855; platitudinous: b1865; platitudinize: b1885)

cuneiform adj b1820 (noun use: b1865)

logogram n *as in "&" for "and"* b1820

password n b1820

punctuate v b1820 ["point out": b1635]

schwa n b1820

stereotype n *cliche* b1820 ["duplicating tool": b1800; "cliched depiction": b1930] (verb use: b1805)

exclamation point n

figure of speech n (figure: b1450)

malaprop n (malaprop/malaproprian: b1840; malapropism: b1850)

phrasemaker n

Contractions

'tain't contr *it ain't* b1820

Literature/Writing

anthologist, anthologize n, v b1805

bibliography n b1805 [obs. "act of writing books": b1680 to 1700s] (bibliographer: b1775)

excursus n *narrative digression—e.g., appendix, sidebar* b1805

passim adv *something sprinkled through a text* b1805

prosaist n b1805

upset n *draft, translation* b1805

hack n b1810

litterateur n *writer* b1810

newspaperman n b1810 (newspaperwoman: b1885)

picaresque adj b1810 (noun use: b1895)

characterization n b1815

forensic n *type of speech* b1815

guidebook n b1815 (guide: b1630)

handbook n b1815 [religious sense: b900]

lithography n b1815 (lithograph n/v: b1830; litho: b1890)

yarn n/v *tall tale* b1815

autograph v *handwrite* b1820 ["sign": b1840]

diarist n b1820

endpaper n b1820

auctorial adj *authorial*

bibliophile n

footnote n (verb use: b1865)

headline n (head: b1930)

headword n

monograph n (verb use: b1880)

nom de plume n

read n

subtitle n *secondary title* [pertaining to movies: b1930]

thesaurus n *as in "Roget's"* ["dictionary": b1600]

Communication

word-of-mouth adj b1805

addressee n b1810

public relations n b1810

mailbag n b1815

semaphore n b1820 (verb use: b1895)

dial v *as in "dial a telephone"*

Visual Arts/Photography

applique n b1805

snapshot n b1810 ["rushed gunshot": b1830]

sketchbook n b1820

wood engraving n b1820

xylography n *wood engraving* b1820

aesthetic, aesthetics adj/n, n [obs. "sensual": b1800] (aesthetical: b1800; aesthete: b1885)

artiste n

diorama n [type of three-dimensional display: b1930]

old master n

replica n [gen. use: b1870]

tracing paper n

Performing Arts

dramaturgy n b1805 (dramaturge: b1860)

show bill n b1805

summer theater n b1805

melodrama n b1810 (melodramatics: b1915)

playwriting n b1810 (playwrighting: b1900)

promptbook n b1810

theatrics n b1810

little theater n b1815

stagestruck adj b1815

ad lib n b1820 (verb use: b1920)

comedy of manners n

musical n ["musical instrument": b1500; "musical performance": b1580]

playgoer n

troupe n (Am) (verb use: b1900)

Music

cantatrice n *female opera singer* b1805

cemballo n *harpsichord* b1805

grand opera n b1805

piano n b1805

treble clef n b1805

organ-grinder n b1810

second fiddle n b1810 [slang use: b1835]

glee club n b1815 (glee "type of song": b1670)

metronome n b1815

ivories n *on a piano* b1820

keyboard n b1820 [as in "typewriter keyboard": b1870]

panpipe n b1820

pennywhistle n b1820

percussionist n b1820

glockenspiel n

instrumentalist n

maraca n

melodic adj (melodious: b1425)

patter song n

songwriter n

taps n (Am)

Entertainment

Highland fling n *type of dance* b1805

tightrope n b1805

hit n b1815

yarn v *tell yarns* b1815

season ticket n b1820

Virginia reel n (Am) b1820

hula n

Education

polytechnic adj b1805 (noun use: b1840)

primary school n b1805

reeducate v b1810

school district n b1810

dame school n *home school* b1820

sciolism n *pretending to learn* b1820 (sciolist: b1615)

associate professor n

blackboard n

flunk v (Am) *gen. fail* [as in "flunk a course": b1845]

high school n

preparatory school n

Religion

nirvana n b1805
noel n b1815
sermonette n b1815 (sermon: b1200)
bar mitzvah n b1820 (verb use: b1950; bas mitzvah: b1955)
revivalist n b1820
true believer n b1820
voodoo n (Am) b1820 (verb use: b1880; voodooism: b1865)
requiescat n *type of prayer*

Society/Mores/Culture

debutante n b1805 (debutant: b1825)
menfolk n b1805
parvenu adj/n *nouveau riche* b1805 (parvenue: b1830)
golden rule n b1810
un-American adj (Am) b1810
nouveau riche n b1815
pluralism n b1820
overpopulation n (overpopulate v: b1870)

Government

autocrat n b1805 (arch. autocrator: b1770)
county seat n (Am) b1805
vice presidency n b1805
rapprochement n b1810
diplomat, diplomatist n b1815
Uncle Sam n (Am) b1815
bureaucracy n b1820 (bureaucrat: b1845)
citizenry n b1820
vicereine n *wife of viceroy*

Politics

platform n *as in "party platform"* b1805 ["plan": b1550]
campaign n b1810 [mil. use: b1650]
gerrymander n/v (Am) 1812
iron curtain n b1820
liberal, liberalism n b1820
laissez-faire n
suffragist n (suffragette: b1905)
ultraliberal adj

Death

eulogist n b1810
eulogize v b1810

croak v *slang die* b1815 ["kill": b1930]
keen n *funeral lament* b1815 (verb use: b1845)
kill n *result of killing* b1815
necropolis n *burial ground* b1820
buy it v (Am) *die*
death rattle n
morgue n

War/Military/Violence

bash n *hit* b1805 (verb use: b1645)
emplacement n b1805 (emplace v: b1865)
fugleman n *model soldier* b1805
fusillade n b1805
gunfire n b1805
insurgency n b1805 (insurgence: b1850)
markswoman n b1805 (marksman: b1660)
plate armor n b1805
sharpshooter n b1805
blowgun n (Am) b1810
fistic adj *pugilistic* b1810
franc-tireur n *civilian irregular* b1810
goose step n b1810 (verb use: b1880)
guerrilla n b1810 (adj use: b1815)
hair trigger n b1810 (adj use: b1835)
Quaker gun n *fake gun* b1810
reconnaissance n b1810 (recon n/v: b1920)
shrapnel n b1810
torpedo boat n (Am) b1810
warbonnet n b1810
battle cry n b1815
battle line n b1815
battlefield n b1815
bivouac n b1815 ["night watch": b1705]
shako n *type of mil. hat* b1815
free lance, freelance n *mercenary* b1820 (verb use: b1905; freelancer: b1940)
guardsman n b1820
legionnaire n b1820
middy n b1820
primer n *explosive or paint primer* b1820 ["priming wire": b1500]

chain mail n
color guard n
combat adj
field of honor n
Greek fire n
hide v *flog*
wallop n/v *blow* [gen. "boiling": b1570]

Crime/Punishment/Enforcement

bushranger n *outlaw living in the bush* b1805
have v *cheat, con* b1805
peculate v *embezzle* b1805 [obs. "steal public money": b1750 to 1800s]
policeman n b1805 (policewoman: b1855; policeperson: b1970)
bushwhacker n (Am) b1810 (bushwhack: b1840)
chisel v *cheat* b1810 (chiseler: b1920)
thug n *member of Indian crime organization* b1810 [gen. "hooligan": b1870] (thuggee, thuggism, thuggery: b1870)
body snatcher n b1815
jailhouse n (Am) b1815
racket n *scam; occupation* b1815 (racketeer: b1930)
contrabandist n *smuggler* b1820
juvenile delinquent n b1820 (juvenile delinquency: b1820)
misdemeanant n *perp of misdemeanor* b1820 (misdemeanor: b1490)
petty larceny n b1820
red-handed adj/adv b1820
hot adj *stolen*
hustle, hustler n *con*
moll n *as in "gun moll"* ["prostitute": b1605]
safecracker n (Am)
secret police n

The Law

jurywoman n b1805
legislate v b1805
patent right n b1805
copyright v b1810
deed v b1810 (noun use: b1340)

gag rule n (Am) b1810
lynch law n (Am) b1815 (lynch v: b1835)
illegalize v b1820
subcontract n b1820 (subcontract v, subcontractor: b1845)
cross-examination n
indirect evidence n
traverse jury n *petit jury*

The Fantastic/Paranormal

phrenology n *skull reading* b1805
seance n b1805 [gen. governmental or royal meeting: b1800; portrait sitting: b1900]
spook n (Am) b1805 ["spy": b1970] (verb use: b1970; spooky: b1850; spookery: b1895)
spectral adj b1815 ["able to see specters": b1720]
ghost story n b1820
water witch n (Am) b1820
Jack Frost n

Interjections

brava interj/n *"bravo" for women* b1805 (bravo: b1765)
lo and behold interj b1810
drat interj/v b1815
boo interj/n b1820 (verb use: b1885; obs. bo "boo": b1500)
glory/glory be interj b1820
bejabbers interj/n
my interj
poof interj

Slang

boiled adj *drunk* b1805
shell out v *pay* b1805
simon-pure adj b1805 (noun use: b1800)
two-bit adj (Am) b1805
weirdie n b1805 (weirdo: b1955)
bang-up adj *great* b1810
burn v (Am) *rip off* b1810
fix n *bad situation* b1810
one-two n b1810
bitch n *as in "life's a bitch"* b1815

boner n *gaffe* b1815

cheese v *as in "cheese it—the cops!"* b1815

cleaned out adj (Am) b1815

darned adj/adv b1815

gasper n (Brit) *cigarette* b1815

hang v *as in "hang around, hang out"* b1815

kid v *josh* b1815 (noun use: b1900; kidder: b1900)

mop up v b1815

plant n *infiltrator* b1815 (verb use: b1710)

queer n *counterfeit money* b1815 [slang "homosexual": 1900s]

rat v *desert* b1815

stink n *ruckus* b1815

dreamworld n b1820 (dreamland: b1835)

drop off v *fall asleep* b1820

ducky adj b1820

eye-opener n (Am) b1820

fish story n (Am) b1820

rag n *money* b1820

ragbag n b1820

screwy adj *drunk* b1820

skin v *cheat, con* b1820

sod n (Brit) b1820

wallflower n b1820

waterloo n b1820

advisee n

bitch v *bungle*

blowout n

bluebeard n

feller n (fella: b1870)

hornswoggle v

joint n *as in "let's blow this pop joint"* ["penitentiary": b1970; "marijuana cigarette": b1970] (verb use: b1530)

lip n *backtalk*

nibs n *as in "his nibs"*

paleface n

perk n *perquisite*

rattletrap n ["bauble": b1770]

raw n *as in "in the raw"* (adj use: b1970)

ripe adj *drunk*

ripped adj *drunk* ["high": b1975]

scapegoat n *blame-taker* [lit. use: b1530] (verb use: b1945)

shocker n

sirree n

slam-bang adj (Am)

teeny adj

turps n *turpentine* [slang "booze": b1865]

Insults

imbecile n b1805 (adj use "physically weak": b1550; adj use "mentally weak": b1830)

muttonhead n b1805 (mutt: b1905)

tight adj *cheap* b1805 (tightwad: b1895)

vulgarian n b1805 (adj use: b1650)

dummkopf n (Am) b1810 (dumbhead: b1890)

highbinder n (Am) *cheat, ruffian* b1810

scapegrace n *rascal* b1810

snot n *impudent person* b1810 (snotty: b1870; snotnose: b1945)

underhanded adv *fig. low* b1810 (adj use: b1830; underhand: b1600)

wet blanket n b1810

galoot n *rookie marine* b1815 ["oaf": b1870]

louche adj *disreputable, shifty* b1815

sap n *dolt* b1815 (sapskull: b1735)

yokel n b1815

exquisite n b1820

frump n b1820 ["instance of mocking": b1555] (frumpy: b1840; frumpish: b1850)

blighter n (Brit)

crotchety adj

dense adj *stupid*

gump n *idiot*

know-nothing n (know-nothingism: b1855)

spoilsport n

toploftical, toplofty adj *snooty*

Phrases

done for adj b1805

Irish bull n *non sequitur* b1805

middle ground n b1805

reign of terror n b1805

silver spoon n b1805

tour de force n b1805

Achilles' heel n b1810

camp follower n b1810

Dutch courage n b1810

growing pains n b1810

infernal machine n b1810

rough-and-ready adj b1810

spur-of-the-moment adj b1810

stay-at-home adj b1810

trial and error n b1810

feet of clay n b1815

field of view n b1815 (field of vision: b1865)

Tom, Dick and Harry n b1815

carpe diem n b1820

godsend n b1820

heel-and-toe adj b1820

ragtag and bobtail n b1820

riot act n b1820 [lit. leg. use: b1715]

seventh heaven n b1820

sword of Damocles n b1820

vested interest n b1820

bad blood n

baptism of fire n

blue moon n

cloud-cuckooland n

comic relief n

dirt cheap adj/adv

every which way adv

forty winks n

gimlet eye n *sharp eye, look* (gimlet-eyed: b1755)

hand over fist adv

high and dry n

homebody n (Am)

infra dig adj

leading question n

out loud adv

pony up v

second wind n

General/Miscellaneous

bobbery n *hubbub* b1805

differentiation n b1805 (differentiate: b1820)

expose n b1805

hustle n *as in "hustle and bustle"* b1805

invitee n b1805 (invitant: b1600)

irreality n b1805 (irreal: b1945)

irritant n b1805 (adj use: b1870)

jam n *as in "traffic jam"* b1805 (verb use: b1710; jam-up: b1945)

kowtow n b1805 (verb use: b1830)

lapboard n b1805

lockstep n b1805

mineral oil n b1805

spat n b1805

stratus n b1805

adequacy n b1810

centerline n b1810

cognomen n *name* b1810 [limited use: b1630]

dido n *antic* b1810

dismissal n b1810

flotation n b1810

guy n *effigy, man* b1810

hoax n b1810 (verb use: b1800)

jumbo n b1810 (adj use: b1885)

lope n b1810 [arch. "leap": b1375] (verb use: b1825)

productivity n *productiveness* b1810 ["measure of productiveness": b1900]

scamp n *rascal* b1810 [obs. "highwayman": b1785 to 1800s]

uptake n *as in "quick in the uptake"* b1810

anonym n *anonymous person* b1815 ["pseudonym": b1870] (anonymity: b1820)

backlash n/v *phys. recoil* b1815 [fig. "negative reaction": b1930]

borderland n b1815

byplay n b1815

coming-out n b1815

fixture n *as in "he's a fixture in the club"* b1815 ["process of fixing": b1600; "fixity": b1830]

hunk n b1815

in-between n b1815 (adj use: b1900; inbetweener: b1930)

initiate n b1815

materiel n b1815

notable n *someone notable* b1815

phase n *as in "phase of the moon"* b1815 ["stage," as in "he's going through a phase": b1870]

slosh n b1815 ["the sound of water sloshing": b1900] (verb use: b1845)

technicality n b1815

tomfoolery n b1815 (tomfool n: b1710)

anonymity n b1820 (anonymous: b1600)

breakout n b1820 (break out v: b1100)

cleavage n *split* b1820 [pertaining to breasts: b1970]

conglomerate n *mixture* b1820 [type of rock structure: b1730; "business group": b1970]

crawl n *act of crawling* b1820

delegation n *group* b1820

dig n b1820

dominance n b1820

drop-in adj/n b1820

enactment n b1820

habitue n b1820

imbroglio n b1820 ["hodgepodge": b1750]

inebriant n *intoxicant* b1820

inrush n b1820

macedoine n *potpourri* b1820

muddle n b1820 (verb use: b1690)

pose n *as in "photo pose"* b1820 (verb use: b1830)

potential n b1820 (adj use: b1400)

rapeseed oil n b1820

reliability n b1820

rowdy adj/n (Am) b1820

shock n *as in "shock of hair"* b1820

subclass n b1820

technique n b1820

variable n b1820

wiggle n b1820

abandon n

artifact n

backdraft n

bull's-eye n

catnap n/v (Am)

comeback n *retort* ["return": b1930]

concoction n ["digestion": b1535] (concoct "cook": b1675; concoct "create": b1795)

cubbyhole n

desirability n

dispersal n

esurience n *hunger, greed*

find n (verb use: b725)

gamble n

leadership n

local n *someone assigned to a locality* ["resident": b1870]

lubricant n

luminous paint n

makeup n *composition*

malodor n (malodorous: b1850)

misfit n

norm, normal n, adj

outing n *field trip*

precondition n *prerequisite*

pullout n

puzzlement n

resilience n ["returning to position": b1630] (resilient: b1675; resile v: b1730; resiliency: b1840)

rig n *rigging*

ruction n (ruckus: b1890)

shimmer n (verb use: b1100)

treadmill n

yap n [obs. "barking dog": b1630; slang "mouth": b1900]

yawp n

Things

confetti n b1815

fluorine n b1815

safety valve n b1815

contraption n

plaster cast n

rice paper n

Description

backdoor adj b1805

catchy adj b1805

documentary adj b1805 (noun use: b1935)

effortless adj b1805 (effortful: b1895)

expendable adj b1805 (noun use: b1945)

hardscrabble adj (Am) *meager* b1805

imprecise adj b1805

inappropriate adj b1805

riley adj b1805

sketchy adj b1805

terminal adj *at the end* b1805 ["at the boundary": b1425; "final, last": b1830]

toy adj b1805

unilateral adj b1805

wirehaired adj b1805

dilapidated adj b1810

gangling adj b1810 (gangly: b1875; gangle v: b1970)

gossamer adj b1810

half-cocked adj b1810

harrowing adj b1810

irreplaceable adj b1810

lightweight adj b1810

multifold adj b1810

peripheral adj b1810 [fig. "tangential": b1970]

revolting adj *disgusting* b1810 (revolt: b1770)

straightforward adj/adv b1810

trustworthy adj b1810 (trusty: b1225)

uproarious adj *tumultuous, hilarious* b1810

whacking adj b1810 (adv use: b1855)

appealing adj *attractive* b1815 (appeal: b1900)

eclectic adj *wide-ranging* b1815 [describing type of philosopher: b1685] (noun use: b1820)

flammable adj b1815 (flammability: b1650)

irrepressible adj b1815

long-standing adj b1815 (noun use: b1605)

nouveau adj b1815

one-sided adj b1815

opalescent adj b1815

quotable adj b1815

slipshod adj *shoddy* b1815 ["wearing loose or worn shoes": b1580]

sophomoric adj (Am) b1815

stuffy adj *unventilated* b1815 [obs. "stuffed": b1545 to 1600s; haughty: b1900]

talky adj b1815

third-rate adj *inferior* b1815 ["type of naval designation": b1650]

wearing adj *tiring* b1815

weird adj *odd* b1815 ["magical": b1400]

aglow adj b1820

awful adv *as in "awful silly"* b1820

broken-down adj b1820

deluxe adj b1820

dried-up adj b1820

dynamic adj b1820

escape adj b1820

hawkeyed adj b1820

inane adj b1820 ["empty": b1665] (inanity: b1755)

organized adj *orderly* b1820

repulsive adj *repugnant* b1820

roly-poly adj b1820 [obs. "useless": b1605]

routine adj b1820 (noun use: b1680)

runny adj b1820

sample adj b1820

small-fry adj *inconsequential* b1820

sobering adj b1820

thereinafter adv b1820

tumbledown adj b1820 [obs. applied to horses: b1800]

ultra adj b1820

underarm adj *underhand* b1820 (adv use: b1910)

white-hot adj b1820 (white heat: b1710)

wide-ranging adj b1820

adaptive adj (adaptable: b1800)

available adj *accessible* [obs. "effective": b1420]

bone-dry adj

encyclopedic adj (encyclopedian: b1870)

far-reaching adj

freaky adj

gigantesque adj (gigantean: b1615; gigantic: b1655)

hard up adj

hard-pressed adj

high-pressure adj (verb use: b1930)

imperative adj *critically important*

king-size adj

lattermost adj

monochromatic adj

plangent adj *loud*

pyrotechnic adj

self-perpetuating adj

self-styled adj

untiring adj

well-to-do adj

womanfully adv

Colors

brick red n b1810 (brick adj: b1470)

forest green n b1810

lemon yellow n b1810

magpie adj *black and white* b1810

chrome yellow n b1820
steel blue n b1820

Actions/Verbs

cotton to v b1805
crunch v b1805 ["crush":
b1870] (noun use: b1840;
craunch: b1635)
enounce v *announce* b1805
galvanize v b1805 [fig. use:
b1855]
haze v *make hazy* b1805
hibernate v b1805 (hibernation: b1665)
ignore v b1805 ["be unin-
tentionally ignorant":
b1500]
integrate v *add to the whole*
b1805 ["make whole":
b1640]
magnetize v b1805 [arch.
"attract, fascinate":
b1785]
maximize v b1805
minimize v *make small* b1805
["regard as insignificant":
b1900]
plunk v b1805 ["shoot":
b1890]
poeticize v b1805 (poetize:
b1585)
stomp v b1805
tell off v b1805
titivate v *spruce up* b1805
vaporize v b1805 ["turn to

smoke": b1635] (vapor v:
b1570)
waffle v *quibble* b1805
book v *schedule* b1810
bust v *break* b1810 (noun
use: b1765)
emphasize v b1810
gulf v *engulf* b1810
isolate v b1810 (adj use:
b1820; noun use: b1890;
isolation: b1835)
lionize v b1810
provision v b1810
pry v *lever* b1810
rejuvenate v b1810 (rejuve-
nize: b1830)
rhapsodize v b1810
rotate v *spin* b1810 ["alternate": b1700] (rotation:
b1555)
scurry v b1810 (noun use:
b1825; hurry-scurry adj:
b1735)
swank v *swagger* b1810
boost v (Am) b1815 (noun
use: b1825; booster:
b1890)
cash v b1815
coddle v *mollycoddle* b1815
["parboil": b1600]
humph v b1815 (interj use:
b1570)
hustle v *hurry* b1815
["shake": b1685; "push":
b1755; "con": b1840]
jibe v (Am) *agree, confirm*
b1815

orphan v b1815
peter v *as in "peter out"; stop*
b1815
queer v *spoil* b1815
tauten v *make taut* b1815
upend v b1815
volume v b1815
crisscross v b1820 (adj use:
b1850; noun use: b1880)
dehumanize v b1820
demarcate v b1820 (demar-
cation: b1730; demark:
b1835)
flick v b1820
furcate v b1820
gallivant v b1820
hitch up v b1820
intensify v b1820
malinger v b1820
mutate v *change* b1820 ["mutate genetically": b1915]
(mutation: b1380)
pontificate v *serve as a pontiff;
be a blowhard* b1820
position v b1820
potentiate v *make potent*
b1820 ["make possible":
b1870]
retrogress v b1820 (retro-
gression: b1770; retro-
gressive: b1805)
section v b1820 (noun use:
b1470)
squiggle v b1820
tootle v b1820

wangle v b1820 (noun use:
b1915)
yank v b1820 (noun use:
b1865)
chitchat v (noun use: b1700;
chitter-chatter v: b1930)
corner v *trap*
crosshatch v
dandify v
frazzle v (noun use: b1865)
harshen v
holler n *yell* (verb use:
b1700)
jab v ["punch": b1930]
(noun use: b1875)
lunge v
nag v (noun use: b1900)
palm off v
plop v [as in "plop on the
couch": b1930] (noun/adv
use: b1870)
rehash v (noun use: b1850)
rile v
scotch v *as in "scotch a project"* ["cut": b1415]
skive v *pare*
squawk v [slang "complain":
b1900] (noun use: b1850)
tide over v
tidy v
understate v (understated:
b1910)

Archaisms
delectate v *delight* b1805

IN USE BY

1850

Geography/Places

arete n *type of mountain ridge* b1830

bushland n b1830 (busy: b1660)

divide n b1830

environment n b1830 [obs. "being enclosed": b1630; "environs": b1870; "ecosystem": b1975]

hogback n b1830

megalopolis n b1830

tributary n b1830

upheaval n *geo.* b1830 [fig. use: b1900]

uptown adj *geo.* b1830 [fig. "upscale": b1870]

arctic circle n b1835

canyon n (Am) b1835

drumlin n *glacial feature* b1835

gulch n b1835

mountain range n b1835

riverbed n b1835

landslide n (Am) b1840 ["big political victory": b1900] (verb use: b1930; landslip: b1680)

seabed n b1840

tar pit n b1840

barrio n b1845

cartography n b1845

interstate adj (Am) b1845

metamorphism n b1845

subtropical adj b1845 (subtropic adj/n: b1900)

uptown n b1845 (adj use: b1830)

bedrock n

esker n *type of glacial feature*

foothill n (Am)

forest floor n

incline n ["slope": b1600]

orography n *mountain geology*

Wild West n (Am)

Natural Things

arboretum n b1830

asexual adj b1830

auric adj *of gold* b1830

coprolite n b1830

ebb tide n b1830

gabbro n b1830

hydrocarbon n b1830

pothole n *natural feature* b1830 ["hole in the road": b1930]

sedimentary adj b1830

tidal wave n b1830

animalism n b1835

atavism n b1835

ion n b1835

loess n *type of loam* b1835

nucleus n (Am) *center of cell* b1835

volcanic glass n b1835

coconut oil n b1840

glycerine n b1840 (glycerol: b1885)

topsoil n b1840

ultraviolet adj b1840 (noun use: b1875)

cell n *unit of life* b1845 [arch. type of biological subsection: b1675] (cellular: b1740)

halogen n b1845

low tide n b1845

melting point n b1845

outdoors n b1845 (out-of-doors: b1800; outdoorsy: b1930)

methyl alcohol n

parthenogenesis n *type of reproduction*

soundwave n

Plants

bottle gourd n b1830

diefenbachia n b1830

flower bud n b1830

gymnosperm n b1830

sandbur n (Am) b1830

bitterroot n (Am) b1835

elephant grass n b1835

gingerroot n b1835

kiwi n b1835

Monterey pine n b1835

pollen grain n b1835

sagebrush n (Am) b1835

softwood n b1835

poinsettia n 1836

coconut palm n b1840

jack-in-the-pulpit n (Am) b1840

pinesap n (Am) b1840

spore n b1840

chaparral n (Am) b1845

cycad n *type of palm tree* b1845

daisy chain n b1845

flowering dogwood n b1845

frondescence n *foliation* b1845

leaf mold n b1845

loco n (Am) *locoweed* b1845

orchid n b1845

pit n (Am) *as in "peachpit"* b1845 (verb use: b1915)

rhizome n b1845

sequoia n 1847

four-leaf clover n

ivory nut n

Manila hemp n

pieplant n (Am)

rubber tree n

tea rose n

Animals

beeline n (Am) b1830 (verb use: b1940)

bloodstock n *thoroughbred horses* b1830

bushmaster n *type of snake* b1830

chickadee n b1830

chicken hawk n (Am) b1830

chihuahua n b1830

cooter n (Am) *type of turtle* b1830

crappie n (Am) b1830

decapod n b1830

emu n b1830 [applied to other birds: b1615]

fledgling n b1830

gastropod n b1830

great auk n b1830

ichthyosaur n b1830

invertebrate adj b1830 (noun use: b1840)

june bug n b1830

mammal n b1830

ovine adj/n *relating to sheep* b1830

pincer n *type of claw* b1830

point n *as in "eight-point buck"* b1830

racer n *snake* b1830

rattler n *rattlesnake* b1830

rhesus monkey n b1830

spiny anteater n b1830

star-nosed mole n (Am) b1830

termitary n *termite's nest*

b1830 (termitarium: b1865)

tetrapod n b1830

trap-door spider n b1830

vertebrate adj/n b1830

wallaroo n b1830

weaverbird n b1830

amphibian n b1835 [rare "dualistic": b1670] (adj use: b1640)

angleworm n (Am) b1835

anthropoid n b1835

California condor n b1835

chacma baboon n b1835

cottonmouth n (Am) b1835 (cottonmouth moccasin: b1880)

deer mouse n (Am) b1835

harvest mite n (Am) *chigger* b1835

house mouse n b1835

hyperparasite n *the parasite's parasite* b1835

kookaburra n b1835

longhorn n *type of cattle* b1835

lyrebird n b1835

marsupial n b1835

mountain goat n (Am) b1835

mourning dove n (Am) b1835

panda n b1835

pod n (Am) *grouping of animals* b1835

quarter horse n b1835

ring-necked duck n b1835

ring-necked pheasant n b1835

rodent n b1835

sperm whale n b1835 (sperm oil: b1830)

trilobite n b1835

tufted titmouse n (Am) b1835

anthropoid ape n b1840

brachiopod n b1840

brine shrimp n b1840

brook trout n b1840

budgerigar n b1840 (budgie: b1930)

bushpig n b1840

carnivore n b1840 (carnivorous: b1595; carnivora: b1630)

carpenter bee n b1840

coach dog n *dalmatian* b1840

cocker spaniel n b1840

gnatcatcher n *type of bird* b1840

goggle-eye n *type of fish* b1840

gopher snake n (Am) b1840

insectivore n b1840 (insectivorous: b1665)

joey n *baby kangaroo* b1840

leopard frog n (Am) b1840

lobo n *type of wolf* b1840

pachyderm n b1840

python n b1840

red wolf n b1840

scaly anteater n *pangolin* b1840

Scottish terrier n b1840 (Scotch terrier: b1810; Scottie: b1900)

skeeter n *mosquito* b1840

surfbird n (Am) b1840

treehopper n *type of insect* b1840

warthog n b1840

dinosaur n 1841

cayuse n *type of horse* b1845

cedar waxwing n (Am) b1845 (cedarbird: b1885)

chipmunk n (Am) b1845 (chitmunk: b1835)

elephant seal n b1845

gator n (Am) b1845

grass snake n (Am) b1845

jellyfish n b1845 [fig. "wimp": b1900]

lake herring n b1845

measuring worm n (Am) b1845

orthopteran n *type of insect* b1845

pike perch n (Am) b1845

pill bug n (Am) b1845

pinniped adj/n *flipper-footed* b1845

Rocky Mountain goat n (Am) b1845

scrod n (Am) b1845

soft-shell crab n b1845

spitz n b1845

thoroughbred n b1845 (adj use: b1800)

wading bird n b1845

wirehair n b1845

woolly bear n *type of caterpillar* b1845

abalone n

Angora rabbit n

aquarium n

bacterium n (bacterial: b1870; bacteria: b1885)

black rhinoceros n

bronco n (broncobuster: b1890; bronc: b1895)

bullterrier n

chimney swift n

dachshund n

digger wasp n

endoskeleton n

exoskeleton n

gam n (Am) *school of whales*

gerbil n

higher animals n

Kentucky bluegrass n

no-see-um n *type of insect*

pack animal n

rat-kangaroo n

reptilian adj (obs. reptile adj: b1610 to 1700s)

saber-toothed tiger n

shark sucker n *remora*

shavetail n (Am) *pack mule*

water strider n

white-tailed deer n (whitetail: b1875)

Weather

barometric pressure n b1830

dew point n b1835

fogbow n *similar to rainbow* b1835

heat lightning n b1835

southwester n b1835

cyclone n 1848

line storm n

rainfall n

Heavens/Sky

starlet n *small celestial object* b1830 [celebrity sense: b1920]

Uranus n b1830

earthlight n b1835

earthshine n b1835

moonlet n b1835

galactic adj b1840

moonset n b1845 (moonrise: b1730)

stardust n *the stars looking like dust* b1845 ["poetic substance": b1930]

binary star n (binary system: b1805)

cosmic adj [obs. "earthly": b1650] (cosmical: b1585)

galaxy n *star grouping* [spec.

"Milky Way": b1380] (galactic: b1850)

multiple star n

Science

electrostatics n b1830 (electrostatic: b1860)

ethnology n b1830

morphology n b1830

electrolysis, electrolyte n b1835 [type of hair removal: b1930]

ethnography n b1835

infrared adj b1835

mammalogy n b1835

oology n b1835 (oologist: b1865)

scientist n b1835

aerodynamics n b1840

archeology n *scientific study* b1840 [arch. "gen. ancient history": b1610]

kinematics n *study of motion* b1840

mycology n *study of fungi* b1840

ozone n b1840

paleontology n b1840

physicist n b1840

phytochemistry n *plant chemistry* b1840

symbology n b1840

magnetic field n b1845

pseudoscience n b1845

atomic theory n (atomism: b1680)

Darwinism n (Darwinian: b1860)

dioxide n

embryology n

histology n

inorganic chemistry n

nuclear adj *gen. pertaining to the nucleus* [pertaining to the atomic nucleus: 1800s; pertaining to atomic energy: 1900s] (nuke: b1950)

test tube n

thermodynamic adj (thermodynamics: b1855)

topology n [obs. type of plant science: b1660]

Technology

electrode n 1834

cathode n b1835

Energy

arc n *electrical discharge* b1830 (verb use: b1895)

energy n *e.g., electrical energy, kinetic energy* b1830 ["what's supplied by a utility": b1930]

fossil fuel n b1835

thermostat n b1835 (verb use: b1925)

alternating current n b1840

induction coil n b1840

scuttle n *coal bucket*

woodstove n

Time

medieval adj b1830 (noun use: b1860)

season n *arch. year* b1830

semester n b1830

timetable n b1830

local time n b1835

witching hour n b1835

Renaissance n *the renaissance* b1840 [gen. use: b1875]

seasonal adj b1840

small hours n b1840

antebellum adj

moyen-age n *Middle Ages*

Age/Aging

pastness n b1830

quadragenerian n *40-year-old* b1840

centenarian n b1845

shirttail adj (Am) *young* b1845

spring chicken n (Am) b1845

Mathematics

geodesic adj b1830

long division n b1830

billion n b1835 [obs. "trillion": b1690]

constant n b1835

pentagram n b1835 (pentangle: b1400)

complementary angle n b1840

Arabic numeral n

vector n

Measurement

index of refraction n b1830 [refractive index: b1875] (refractive index: b1875)

magnetometer n b1830

unit n *in phys. measurement*

b1830 [in other measurement, e.g., electricity: b1900]

volume n *sound measure* b1830

benchmark n *surveying term* b1845 [fig. use: b1900]

dyne n b1845

smidgen n b1845 (smidge: b1930)

tape measure n b1845 (tape: b1830)

absolute zero n

Celsius adj (Celsius's thermometer: b1800)

magnetograph n

wavelength n [fig. use: b1930]

The Body

acne n b1830

crown n *as in "crown of a tooth"* b1830 (verb use: b1900)

dermis n b1830

embryogenesis n b1830

lingua n *tongue* b1830

motor, motor nerve n b1830

nocturnal emission n b1830

prostate gland n b1830 (prostate: b1650)

change of life n b1835

double chin n b1835

floating rib n b1835

gastrointestinal adj b1835

genial adj *related to the chin* b1835

intrauterine adj b1835

mammary gland n b1835

pollex n *thumb* b1835

pubic adj b1835

sacroiliac adj b1835 (noun use: b1940)

veinlet n b1835

protein n 1838

adenoid n b1840 (adj use: b1840)

funny bone n b1840

gray matter n b1840

involuntary muscle n b1840

permanent tooth n b1840

white matter n *akin to gray matter* b1840

embryonic adj b1845

fat cell n b1845

fingertip n b1845

gourd n *head* b1845

melanin, melanism n *type of pigment* b1845

toenail n b1845

aural adj *related to the ear*

blood cell n

bronchial tube n

crap v *defecate* (noun use: b1900)

heartbeat n

index finger n (index: b1470)

ovulation n (ovulate adj/v: b1865)

protoplasm n

widow's peak n

Physical Description

reaction n *phys. response* b1830 ["mental response": b1930] (react: b1645)

towhead n (Am) b1830

wiry adj *describing people* b1830

double-jointed adj b1835

eupeptic adj *digesting well* b1835 ["cheery": b1970]

peaked adj *pale* b1835 (peak v: b1605; peaky: b1825)

scrawny adj (Am) b1835 (scranny: b1820)

sculpturesque adj b1835

ill-being n b1840

pudgy adj b1840 (pudge: b1830)

clean-cut adj b1845

interdigitate v *lock fingers*

logy adj (Am) *lethargic*

olfaction n *sense of smell*

pep n (verb use: b1925; peppy: b1920)

Medicine

cirrhosis n b1830

cross-eye n b1830 (cross-eyed: b1795)

farsightedness n b1830

hay fever n b1830

herb doctor n b1830

knock-knee n b1830

leech v *apply leeches* b1830 ["act as a parasite": b1930]

melanoma n b1830

meningitis n b1830

morphine n b1830 (morphia: b1820)

obstetrician n b1830

ophthalmologist n b1830 (ophthalmology: b1845)

pediculosis n *lice infestation*

b1830 (pediculous "lousy": b1570)

prenatal adj b1830

shock n b1830

autonomic adj *autonomous* b1835

colicroot n (Am) b1835

conjunctivitis n b1835

cough drop n b1835

green soap n b1835

housemaid's knee n b1835

mental health n b1835 (mental illness: b1965)

pharmacist n b1835 (pharmaceutist: b1800)

albinism n b1840 (albino: b1780)

asphyxiate v b1840 (asphyxia: b1780)

black lung n b1840

chloroform n b1840 (verb use: b1850)

codeine n b1840

deaf-mute n b1840

diabetic n b1840 (adj use: b1800)

disinfectant n b1840

flu n b1840

hypochondria n b1840 ["unexplained melancholia": b1670]

orthopedic adj b1840 (orthopedics: b1855)

plastic surgery n b1840 (plastic surgeon: b1950)

sanatorium n b1840 (sanative: b1450; sanatory: b1700)

sawbones n b1840

smelling salts n b1840

snakebite n b1840

clinic n *teaching medicine* b1845 [gen. "educational experience," as in "put on a clinic": b1930] (clinical: b1980)

color-blind adj b1845

dipsomania n b1845 (dipsomaniac: b1860; slang dipso: b1880)

encephalitis n b1845

forensic medicine n b1845

hydropathy n b1845 (hydrotherapy: b1880)

infantile paralysis n *polio* b1845

lead poisoning n b1845

mastitis n b1845

plasma n *as in "blood plasma"* b1845 [type of gas in phys. science: b1930]

resuscitator n b1845

rhinoplasty n *nose job* b1845

typhoid fever n b1845

water cure n b1845

anesthetic, anesthetize adj/n, v (Am)

anesthetize v

astigmatism, astigmatic n, adj

cardiology n

cleft palate n

dietitian/dietician n

doc n *doctor*

dosage n *giving doses* ["amount of dose," "dose": b1900]

emesis n *throwing up*

family doctor n (family physician: b1810)

geophagy n *eating dirt*

German measles n

gynecologist, gynecology n

hematoma n *collection of blood internally*

hyperkinesis/hyperkinesia n

intravenous adj

leprosarium n *leprosy sanitarium*

leukemia n

medical examiner n

mountain sickness n

nosebleed n

orthodontia n (orthodontics: b1910)

palpate v *diagnose by touch*

paregoric n *type of elixer* (adj use "soothing": b1700)

postpartum adj (postnatal: b1860)

relaxant n (adj use: b1775)

strawberry mark n *type of birthmark*

swamp fever n (Am)

therapy n

vaginitis n

Everyday Life

carpetbag n b1830 (verb use: b1870)

cheval glass n *type of mirror* b1830

cigarette n b1830 (cigar: b1635; cigarito: b1830; cigarillo: b1835; cig: b1870)

clothesline n b1830

cover n *bedcover* b1830

dishcloth n b1830 (dish clout: b1530)

lead n *as in "pencil lead"* b1830

mackinaw n (Am) *type of blanket* b1830

ottoman n b1830

pillow slip n b1830

rug n *carpet* b1830 [obs. type of cloth: b1555 to 1700s; "blanket": b1595]

secretary n *type of writing desk* b1830

shoe tree n b1830

suite n *as in "bedroom suite"—set* b1830

toilet n *place to dress* b1830

bathtub n b1835

cigarillo n b1835 (cigar: b1635)

corncob pipe n b1835

crisper n b1835

drawstring n b1835

hook and ladder truck n (Am) b1835

kitchen cabinet n (Am) b1835

party line n (Am) *type of telephone system* b1835

quilting bee n b1835

sewage n b1835

tableware n b1835

toiletry n b1835

toothpaste n (Am) b1835

wallet n (Am) b1835 [type of pouch: b1395]

camera n b1840

carryall n *type of luggage* b1840

diaper n b1840 [gen. type of fabric: b1350; "towel": b1600]

dishrag n (Am) b1840

door chain n b1840

friction match n (Am) b1840

icebox n b1840

layette n *baby stuff* b1840

mouthwash n b1840

paraffin n b1840

patchwork quilt n b1840

personal property n b1840

rock garden n b1840

scrap heap n b1840

screen n *as in "screen door"* b1840

shampoo n b1840 ["massage": b1765] (verb use: b1870)

toby jug n b1840

toilet powder n b1840

toilet soap n b1840

traveling bag n b1840

tub chair n b1840

artesian well n b1845

bedspread n b1845

butcher block n b1845

chair rail n b1845

housekeep v b1845

ice chest n (Am) b1845

jardiniere n *ornamental plant stand* b1845

percolator n b1845

personal effects n b1845

tatting n b1845

venetian glass n b1845

water bed n b1845

wax paper n b1845

bleaching powder n

butter knife n

cardboard adj/n (adj use "flimsy": b1895)

cased glass n

clothespin n

crochet n (verb use: b1860)

dustbin n

flypaper n

ground glass n

highchair n

maduro adj/n *type of cigar*

panatela/panetela n *type of cigar*

potty n (potty-chair: b1945)

practical joke n

pressboard n *ironing board*

sewing circle n (Am)

sleeping bag n

stogie n *cigar* ["type of shoe": concurrent]

tampon n

tea set n

washday n

wastebasket n

watercooler n (Am)

willow pattern n (willowware: b1855)

Shelter/Housing

drywall n/v b1830

fire tower n b1830

mantelshelf n b1830

open-air adj b1830

patio n (Am) b1830

pied-à-terre n *temporary residence* b1830

preserve n *as in "wildlife preserve"* b1830 (verb use: b1630)

rabbet joint n b1830

restoration n *of a building* b1830

steam bath n b1830

sublease n b1830 (verb use: b1845)

wallpaper n b1830 (verb use: b1925)

concrete n *cement* b1835 ["something concrete": b1660]

fire brigade n b1835 (fire company: b1740; fire department: b1825)

guardrail n b1835

stairstep n b1835

brownstone n b1840

cabana n b1840

companionway n b1840 (companion: b1765)

doorjamb n b1840

double door n b1840

fire door n b1840

fire extinguisher n b1840

radiator n b1840 (radicalism: b1820)

retaining wall n b1840

soup kitchen n b1840

toolshed n b1840

downstairs n b1845

firebreak n b1845

upstairs n b1845

woodshed n b1845

doorknob n

fireboat n

gable roof n

garden city n

weather strip n (Am)

Drink

nightcap n b1830 [type of nightwear: b1400]

table wine n b1830

wine v b1830

branch water n b1835

Chianti n b1835

liebfraumilch n *type of wine* b1835

Riesling n b1835

anisette n b1840

bay rum n (Am) b1840

malt whiskey n b1840

café noir n b1845

demitasse n b1845

lager n b1845

Rhine wine n b1845
root beer n (Am) b1845
java n *coffee*
joe n *coffee*
oolong n *type of tea*
planter's punch n
tequila n

Food

a la carte adj/adv b1830
apple pandowdy n (Am) b1830
avocado pear n (Brit) b1830
borscht n b1830
Brazil nut n b1830
brioche n *type of pastry* b1830
catawba n *type of wine* b1830
cupcake n (Am) b1830
dip n *as in "chip dip"* b1830
drawn butter n (Am) b1830
Edam n *type of cheese* b1830
gazpacho n b1830
kiss n b1830
mayonnaise n b1830 (mayo: b1960)
nougat n *type of confection* b1830
pâté de foie gras n b1830
pop n *as in "soda pop"* b1830
porterhouse n b1830 ["ale-house, steakhouse": b1760]
restaurant n (Am) b1830 (restaurateur: b1800)
soda biscuit, soda cracker n (Am) b1830
sucker n *lollipop* b1830
tea cake n (Am) b1830
tenderloin n (Am) b1830 [slang, as in "tenderloin district": b1900]
Tom and Jerry n b1830 (rare verb use "drink rowdily": concurrent)
tuck-out n *slang pig-out, big meal* b1830
baked beans n b1835
beet sugar n b1835
clambake n (Am) b1835
corn dodger n *type of corn-meal cake* b1835
European plan n (Am) b1835
goober n *peanut* b1835
graham flour n (Am) *whole wheat flour* b1835
grape sugar n b1835
high tea n b1835
tutti-frutti n (Am) b1835

comestible n b1840 (obs. adj use: b1585 to 1600s)
duff n *type of pudding* b1840
friedcake n (Am) *donut* b1840
hardtack n b1840
jawbreaker n b1840
meatball n b1840
menu n b1840
pilot biscuit n b1840
roly-poly n *type of pudding* b1840
Roquefort n *type of cheese* b1840
salad dressing n b1840
seafood n (Am) b1840
square meal n b1840
vegetarian n b1840 (adj use: b1850; vegetarianism: b1855)
amandine adj b1845
cannelloni n b1845
charlotte russe n *type of dessert* b1845
chitlins n b1845 (chitterlings: b1280; chitlings: b1880)
chorizo n *type of sausage* b1845
cornball n b1845
flavoring n b1845
headcheese n b1845
ice milk n b1845
luau n b1845
pimiento n b1845
potato chip n b1845
tangerine n b1845 [type of color: b1900]
ziti n *type of pasta* b1845
baking powder n
bologna n (bolognian sausage: b1600; bologna sausage: 1750)
cane sugar n
cherry tomato n (Am)
chili n *the stew* [the pepper: b1605]
chili con carne n (Am)
chuck n *as in "chuck wagon"*
corn sugar n (Am)
cottage cheese n (Am)
flan n
fruitcake n
glace adj *candied, frosted*
green bean n (Am)
green onion n (Am)
jerky n (Am) *as in "beef*

jerky" (jerk v: b1710; jerk n: b1800)
kugel n *type of pudding*
lasagna n
maple syrup n
matzo n *type of bread*
milk sugar n
mocha n *flavoring*
slumgullion n (Am) *type of stew* ["fish offal": b1870]
swizzle v *guzzle* (swizzled "drunk": b1900)

Agriculture/Food-Gathering

herdswoman n b1830 (herdsman: b1470)
ring v *kill a tree by removing bark* b1830
cereal n *grain* b1835 [as in "breakfast cereal": b1870] (adj use: b1820)
cowshed n b1835
guernsey n *type of cow* b1835
rodeo n *roundup* b1835 [type of competition: b1930]
root crop n b1835
silo n b1835
feedbag n (Am) b1840
halterbreak v b1840
seine v *fish with a seine* b1840 (noun use: b950)
alfalfa n b1845
farmhand n b1845 (farmworker: b1950)
fencerow n b1845
cropland n
gang plow n

Cloth/Clothing

beret n b1830
blouse n *gen.* b1830 [spec. to women's clothing: b1900]
cossack n *type of boot* b1830
crinoline n *type of fabric* b1830
foulard n *type of fabric* b1830
madras n *type of kerchief* b1830
monkey jacket n b1830
organdy n *type of muslin* b1830
patent leather n (Am) b1830
raincoat n (Am) b1830
roundabout n *type of jacket* b1830
sarong n b1830

serape n (Am) b1830
skimmer n (Am) b1830
suspenders n b1830
brogan n *type of shoe* b1835
decollete adj b1835
featherstitch n b1835
galluses n *suspenders* b1835
getup n b1835
knee breeches n b1835
lingerie n b1835
panama n *type of hat* b1835
pantalets n *type of drawers* b1835
peignoir n *type of negligee* b1835
shoddy n *"reclaimed wool"* b1835
silk hat n b1835
swallowtailed coat n b1835
tailor-made adj b1835
underclothes, underclothing n b1835
underdrawers n b1835
watch pocket n b1835
challis n *fabric* b1840
costumery n b1840
footgear n b1840 (footwear: b1885)
mackintosh n b1840 (mac: b1905)
necktie n b1840
pants n *as in "pair of pants"* b1840 (singular use: b1900)
shimmy n b1840
slouch hat n b1840
sou'wester n *type of raingear* b1840
tights n *akin to leggings* b1840 [type of breeches: b1830]
wideawake n *type of hat* b1840
corsage n *bodice* b1845 [obs. "the body": b1485 to 1600s; type of flower: b1915]
cotton flannel n b1845
cutaway adj b1845 (noun use: b1850)
eyeshade n b1845
fly n *on pants* b1845 [on tents, etc.: b1810]
glengarry n *type of cap* b1845
guipure n *type of lace* b1845
kiltie n *person in kilts* b1845
lei n b1845
tweed n b1845
Chantilly lace n

denim n [type of serge: b1600]

elastic fabric n

gum boot n (Am) (gum: b1870)

knickerbockers n (knickers: b1885)

moneybelt n (Am)

monk's cloth n

nightshirt n

strapless adj

tailcoat n *formal coat*

tam-o'shanter n *type of hat*

underthings n

Fashion/Style

bouffant n b1830 (adj use: b1880)

passe adj *out of vogue* b1830

dandiacal adj *dandified* b1835

fad n *whim* b1835 ["craze": b1870]

wiglet n b1835

modiste n *creator of fashionable wear* b1840

goatee n (Am) b1845

rose cut n *type of gem cut* b1845

swank/swanky adj b1845 (noun use: b1855)

Tools

drawshave n b1830

egg beater n (Am) b1830

lighter n *something that lights* b1830

machine shop n (Am) b1830

milking stool n b1830

paintbrush n b1830

paper cutter n b1830

router n b1830

ticker n *producer of tickertape* b1830

grader n (Am) b1835

lariat n b1835

lazy tongs n b1835

meat-ax n b1835

plumb bob n b1835

toolbox n b1835

turntable n b1835

block and tackle n b1840 (block: b1470)

dyestuff n b1840

field glass n b1840

oilcan n b1840

pinch bar n b1840 (pinch: b1700)

pipette n b1840

respirator n *type of mast* b1840 [med. sense: b1930]

screw propeller n b1840

semiconductor n b1840

stroboscope n b1840 (strobe: b1945)

rheostat n 1843

fly whisk n b1845

freezer n b1845

hot plate n b1845

ironing board n b1845

squeegee n b1845 (arch. squeege: b1800)

chain saw n (Am)

filter paper n

jimmy n *type of crowbar* (verb use: b1895)

oil well n (Am)

reata, riata n (Am) lariat

ripsaw n

snips n

vaporizer n

Travel/Transportation

bus n b1830 (verb use: b1840)

cab n/v *type of carriage* b1830 ["taxicab": b1900] (cabriolet: b1765; cabbie: b1860)

cabdriver n b1830 (cabbie: b1860)

car n *as in "train car"* b1830 ["automobile": b1900]

clipper n b1830

cover v *as in "cover six miles"* b1830

excursionist n b1830

inboard adv b1830 (adj use: b1850; noun use: b1950)

locomotive n b1830

omnibus n b1830

propeller n b1830

ride n *horse* b1830

rumble seat n b1830

seagoing adj b1830

sidecar n *on a motorcycle* b1830

track n *as in "railroad tracks"* b1830

traffic n *vehicle movement* b1830

tram n b1830 (tramway: b1825)

tugboat, tug n (Am) b1830 (tug "pull with a tugboat": b1870)

van n b1830 ["caravan": b1870]

brakeman n b1835

camshaft n b1835

coupe n *type of carriage* b1835 [type of automobile: b1930]

go-devil n (Am) *type of sled* b1835

horsecar n (Am) b1835

iron horse n b1835

railcar n b1835

rocketeer n b1835

sidetrack n (Am) b1835

backfire n (Am) *engine irregularity* b1840 (verb use: b1870)

bobsled n (Am) b1840

buckboard n (Am) b1840

bumper n *on a train* b1840 [on a car: b1930]

clarence n *type of carriage* b1840

corniche n *type of road* b1840

cowcatcher n (Am) b1840

graving dock n *dry dock* b1840

lightship n *floating lighthouse* b1840

lorry n (Brit) *type of wagon* b1840 [type of truck: b1910]

poop deck n b1840

port of entry n b1840

rocket v *travel fast* b1840 ["launch a rocket": b1830]

sleeping car n (Am) b1840

terminus n b1840 [gen. "end": b1555]

truss bridge n (Am) b1840

yacht v b1840

commutation ticket n b1845

deckhand n (Am) b1845

freight train n b1845

main line n b1845

prairie schooner n *type of wagon* b1845

rockaway n (Am) *type of carriage* b1845

taillight n b1845

trunk line n b1845

aircraft n

cabstand n

dashboard n (dash: b1870)

dinkey/dinky n *type of locomotive*

exhaust n

fourgon n *luggage wagon*

gangplank n (Am)

hand brake n

handcar n (Am)

hansom n

pilothouse n (Am)

red light n (red light: b1850; green light: b1940; yellow light: b1975)

return ticket n

stowaway n (stow away v: b1880)

Emotions/Characteristics

aplomb n b1830

change of heart n b1830

cheeky adj b1830

determination n *being determined* b1830 ["the goal of being determined": b1700] (determined: b1515)

diplomatic adj *tactful* b1830 ["related to documents": b1715]

eccentric n b1830 (adj use: b1630; eccentricity: b1660)

emotion n *anger, sorrow, etc.* b1830 [arch. "commotion": b1570 to 1700s; "mental commotion": b1670] (emotional: b1835)

enthuse v b1830

eudaemonism n *hedonism* b1830

fight n *determination* b1830

floor v *as in "I was floored by the news"* b1830

grit n *determination* b1830

grouse v *grumble* b1830 (noun use: b1920)

indelicate adj *tactless* b1830 (indelicate: b1745)

insouciant n b1830 (insouciance: b1800)

insubordinate adj b1830 (noun use: b1900)

larky adj b1830

laughful adj b1830

misogynism n b1830

mopes, the n b1830

optimism n *positive outlook* b1830 [type of philosophy: b1770] (optimist: b1770)

perky adj b1830 (perk v: b1400)

quick-tempered adj b1830

rambunctious adj (Am) b1830

sensitive adj b1830

temper n (Am) *tendency toward anger* b1830 [gen. "mood": b1400; "placidity": b1600]

verve n b1830 ["writing skill": b1700]

atwitter adj b1835

conniption n (Am) b1835

dander n *as in "get your dander up"* b1835 ["dandruff": b1790]

fussy adj b1835

infelicitous adj b1835

mad n *madness, bad mood* b1835

offish adj (Am) *standoffish* b1835

purehearted adj b1835

sass, sassy n, adj (Am) b1835 (sass v: b1855)

self-reliance n b1835 (self-reliant: b1850)

whole-souled adj b1835

worriment n b1835

antsy adj b1840

chipper adj *lively* b1840

decadent adj b1840 (decadence: b1650)

defiant adj b1840 (defiance: b1300)

disenchanted adj b1840 (disenchant v: b1590)

fantod n *state of apprehension and irritability* b1840

irate adj b1840 (ire: b1300)

moon v *as in "moon about"* b1840 [as in "moon over a lover": b1930]

pretentious adj b1840

sharp-tongued adj b1840

wholehearted adj (Am) b1840

buck fever n (Am) *nervous excitement* b1845

dysphoria n b1845

grump n *grumpy mood* b1845 ["grumpy person": b1930] (verb use: b1845; grumpy: b1780; grumpish: b1800)

interpersonal adj b1845

recalcitrant adj b1845

self-involved adj b1845

spring fever n (Am) b1845

angst n

demoralize v *lower morale* [arch. "make immoral": b1795]

effervesce v *be spirited* (effervescence: b1750; effervescent: b1835)

flip adj *flippant*

procrustean adj

self-absorbed adj

self-doubt n

snippy adj ["stingy": b1730]

tactless adj

Thoughts/Perception/The Mind

deontology n *type of ethics* b1830

faze v (Am) b1830 (obs. feeze: b890)

groggy adj b1830 ["drunk on grog": b1770]

judgmatic adj *judicious* b1830 (judgmatical: b1800)

knowledgeable adj b1830 [obs. "perceivable": b1610]

mesmerize v b1830 (mesmerism: b1785)

nightmare n *bad dream* b1830 ["feelings of suffocation during sleep": b1570]

open-minded adj b1830

reminisce v b1830 (reminiscence: b1590)

right-thinking adj b1830

scheming adj b1830

stump v *puzzle, confound* b1830 ["dare": b1770]

upset v *mentally distress* b1830 (adj/noun use: b1870)

discombobulate v (Am) b1835

horse sense n (Am) b1835

impressionable adj b1835

subconscious adj b1835 (noun use: b1890)

think n b1835

attitude n *mental attitude* b1840 ["phys. orientation": b1670]

caper n *scheme* b1840

conceptualism n b1840

headwork n b1840

know-how n (Am) b1840

memorize v *learn by heart* b1840 ["make memorable": b1595]

semiconscious adj b1840

sentience n b1840 (sentient adj: b1605; sentient n: b1630)

hypnotism n 1842

hypnotist, hypnotize n, v 1843

brainy adj b1845

preoccupied adj b1845

propagandize v b1845 (propaganda: b1930)

serious-minded adj b1845

mentation n

nuts adj *loony* (nutty: b1900; nutsy: b1945; nutso: b1975)

parochialism n

psychiatry n (obs. psychiater: b1870; psychiatrist: b1900)

psychopathology, psychopathy n (psychopathic adj: b1850; psychopathic n: b1890; psychopath: b1885)

psychosis n

small-minded adj

Love/Romance/Sex

celibate adj b1830 (arch. noun use "celibacy": b1630; noun use "celibate person": b1870; celibacy: b1665)

The Way We Worded

Words change, disappear, are replaced. Here are some examples of words and phrases you use now and how your ancestors would have referred to the same concepts:

- *Nicknames* (by 1440) were once *bynames* (by 1375).

- A *loaded die* was a *fulham* (by 1530).

- The *question mark* (by 1870) was once called an *interrogation point* (by 1555).

- A *flash in the pan* (by 1905) was once known as a *nine day's wonder* (by 1595).

- Your *last name* (by 1900) was once your *family name* (by 1700), and before that was your still-in-use *surname* (which meant family name by 1450, but "extra name," as in "Olaf the Bold," by 1350).

- *Ponytails* (by 1875) were once *cues* (by 1735). *Pigtail* was used by 1770.

- *Oxygen* (by 1790) was briefly called *dephlogisticated air* (by 1775).

- Before you had a *green thumb* (by 1945), you had *green fingers* (by 1935).

- And because we are speaking of these words in the *past tense* (by 1815), this language term replaced the *preterit* (by 1400).

cute adj *adorable* b1830
["acute": b1625]
liaison n *tryst* b1830
love n *term of endearment*
b1830 (lovey n: b1770;
lovey-dovey n: b1830)
romance n *romantic actions*
b1830 (verb use: b1970;
romancy adj, romantic:
b1670)
puppy love n b1835
spoon v *pitch woo* b1835
heartthrob n b1840
betrothal n b1845 (betroth:
b1305; betrothed: b1540)
hooker n *prostitute* b1845
(hook v: b1960)
philanderer n b1845
shivaree n (Am) b1845
erotism n (eroticism: b1885)
wedding march n

Family/Relations/
Friends

genealogy n *study* b1830
[spec. ancestral list:
b1300] (genealogist:
b1605)
grandaunt n b1830 (grand-
uncle: b1450)
grandniece n b1830 (grandnephew: b1640)
grandparent n b1830
pop n b1830 (poppa: b1775)
Siamese twin n b1830
avuncular adj *like an uncle*
b1835
kinship n b1835 [fig. "being
related": b1900]
mum n b1835 (momma:
b1885; mommy: b1890;
mom: b1895)
amigo n b1840
camaraderie n b1840
nana n *grandma* b1845
buddy n (Am) (verb use:
b1920; bud: b1855; buddy-
buddy: b1955)

Holidays

Kriss Kringle n b1830
Christmas tree n (Am) b1835
[type of decoration:
b1790]
celebrant n b1840
Christmastime n b1840

fiesta n (Am) b1845
off-season adj/adv/n

Games/Fun/Leisure

ante n (Am) b1830 (verb
use: b1845)
book n *applied to betting*
b1830
craps n (Am) b1830 (Brit
crabs: b1770; crapshooter:
b1895)
cutthroat n b1830
euchre n (Am) b1830
fling n *party, etc.* b1830
merrymaker n b1830 (merry-
making: b1715)
raise v *in cards* b1830 (noun
use: b1730)
rounders n b1830
seesaw n b1830 [gen. "back
and forth": b1705] (verb
use: b1715)
seven-up n *type of card game*
b1830
snowman n b1830
poker n (Am) b1835
bridge n b1845
cutup n *prank* b1845
["prankster": b1900]
hare and hounds n *type of
game* b1845
it n *in a game of tag* b1845
tiddlywinks n b1845 ["game
using dominoes": b1840]
ball game n (Am)
crisscross n (Am) *tic-tac-toe*
draw poker n (Am)
fun adj (noun use: b1730;
verb use: b1835)
misdeal n/v ["distribute
poorly": b1485]
paper doll n
world's fair n (Am)

Sports

calisthenic, calisthenics adj, n
b1830
constitutional n *type of exercise* b1830
draw n *tie game* b1830 (verb
use: b1870)
horizontal bar n b1830
iron n *in golf* b1830
let n *in tennis* b1830
pentathlete n b1830
raceway n *channel* b1830
["racecourse": b1970]
road racing n b1830

scoreboard n b1830
surfboard n b1830
trap n *as in "shooting trap"*
b1830
upset n *unexpected victory*
b1830
grandstand n b1835 (verb
use: b1920)
meet n b1835
sudden death n b1835
backstretch n b1840
derby n *race* b1840
baseball n b1845 [referring
to rounders: b1745]
Canadian football n b1845
homestretch n (Am) b1845
polo n b1845
second base n b1845
sit-up n b1845
turkey shoot n (Am) b1845
hockey stick n
rowing machine n
warm up v (warm-up: b1915)

Professions/Duties

attache n b1830
chef n b1830
conductor n *on a train* b1830
economist n b1830 [obs.
"keeper of the house-
hold": b1590 to 1800s;
"thrifty person": b1730]
field hand n (Am) b1830
forest ranger n b1830
glassblowing n b1830
hotelkeeper n (Am) b1830
(hotelier: b1905)
liaison n b1830
marketeer n b1830
raconteur n b1830
sleuthhound n *detective*
b1830 ["bloodhound":
b1400]
standby n *person on standby*
b1830 [rare "ship on
standby": b1800; "state of
readiness": b1930] (adj
use: b1885)
welder n b1830
dogcatcher n (Am) b1835
flagman n b1835 (flagger:
b1900)
house girl n b1835 (houseboy: b1900)
lumberjack n b1835
technician n *knowledgeable
person; skilled person* b1835

["operator of technical
equipment": b1970]
typesetter n b1835
waitress n b1835 [obs. type
of maid: b1590] (waiter:
b1530; waitperson: b1980;
waitron: b1985)
bartender n (Am) b1840
beachcomber n b1840
bellboy n (Am) b1840
circuit rider n (Am) b1840
dockwalloper n (Am) *type of
dockworker* b1840
expressman n (Am) b1840
famulus n *type of servant*
b1840
landscape architect n b1840
rancher n b1840
roughneck n b1840 (adj use:
b1920)
snake charmer n b1840
super n *superintendent, supervisor* b1840
futurist adj/n b1845
toolmaker n b1845
actuary n [gen. "clerk":
b1555] (actuarial: b1870)
coiffeur n (coiffeuse: b1800)
corsetiere n *corsetmaker*
patrolman n (Am)
saloon keeper n

Business/Commerce/
Selling

check n *bill* b1830
commercialize v b1830
consortium n b1830
doggery n *slang tavern* b1830
economy adj *cheap* b1830
greengrocery n b1830
(greengrocer: b1725)
grocery n *type of store* b1830
["groceries": b1450]
guarantor n b1830
lumbermill n (Am) b1830
show window n (Am) b1830
silent partner n (Am) b1830
(secret partner: b1910)
chief executive n (Am) b1835
general store n (Am) b1835
antibusiness adj b1840
boardroom n (Am) b1840
business card n b1840
cafeteria n (Am) *coffee house*
b1840 [type of eating es-
tablishment: b1940]
coffeeshop n (Am) b1840

deal n *transaction* b1840
land-office business n (Am) b1840
pay-as-you-go adj (Am) b1840
prepay v *referring to postage* b1840 [gen. use: b1930]
salesroom n (Am) b1840
trademark n b1840
ad n *advertisement* b1845
businesswoman n (Am) b1845 (businessman: b1715; businesspeople: b1865; businessperson: b1975)
cantina n (Am) b1845
private enterprise n b1845
rag trade n *the fashion industry* b1845
saloon n *bar* b1845
chain n *franchise, as in "drugstore chain"* (chain store: b1910)
commercialism n (commercialist adj/n: b1830)
horse trade n
pawnshop n (pawn ticket: b1860)

The Workplace

off adj *not working* b1830
workplace n b1830
hump v *slang work hard* b1835
industrialism n b1835
personnel n b1835
trade union n b1835
automatize v b1840 (automate: b1955)
sick leave n b1840 (sick day: b1960)
working-class adj b1840
trainee n b1845 (trainer: b1600)
unionism n b1845
unionize, unionized v, adj b1845
busywork n
industrial revolution n
slopwork n
temporary n

Finances/Money

charge n *fee* b1830 (verb use: b1870)
financing n b1830
millionaire n b1830 (millionairess: b1885)

passbook n b1830
quotation n *estimate of cost or price* b1830
secure v b1830 (security: b1470)
collateral n b1835 (collateral security: b1720)
gold standard n (Am) b1835
petty cash n b1835
silver standard n (Am) b1835
trust company n (Am) b1835 (trust: b1900)
bust/busted adj *bankrupt* b1840
fiver n b1840
four bits n (Am) b1840
inflation n b1840 (inflationary: b1920)
red cent n (Am) b1840
slush fund n (Am) b1840
trial balance n b1840
budgeteer n b1845
fiscal year n b1845
inheritance tax n b1845
common stock n
double eagle n (Am) *type of coin*
sawbuck n (Am)

Language and Speaking

double negative n b1830
glyph n b1830
lexicology n b1830
Middle English n b1830
monoglot adj *unilingual* b1830
pidgin English n b1830
cliche adj/n b1835 [manufacturing term: b1835] (cliched: b1930)
ideograph n b1835
royal we pron b1835
trilingual adj b1835
baby talk n b1840
double-u n *W* b1840
gumbo n (Am) *creole* b1840
lexical adj *related to words* b1840
multilingual adj b1840
standard English n b1840
virgule n / b1840
Arabic alphabet n b1845
bilingual adj b1845
dirty word n b1845
catchphrase n
eponym, eponymous n (eponymy: b1865)

linguistics n
phonetic alphabet n
sign language n

Contractions

wouldn't contr b1830
shouldn't contr
wasn't contr

Literature/Writing

authorship n *act of writing* b1830 ["writing profession": b1710]
causerie n b1830
editorial n b1830
fictionist n b1830 (fictioneer: b1925)
first edition n b1830
hack writer n b1830
handwrite v b1830 (handwriting: b1425)
installment n b1830
log n/v *as in "ship's log"* b1830
lyrical adj *fig. poetic* b1830 ["pertaining to lyric poetry": b1530]
novelize v b1830 [obs. "create novel things": late ME]
program n *written program, as in "play program"* b1830 [obs. "public notice": b1635 to 1800s; "scheduled events": b1870; as in "radio program": b1930; as in "computer program": b1970]
quarterly n *periodical published quarterly* b1830
reminiscences n b1830
report n *prepared account* b1830 (verb use: b1730)
trilogy n b1830 [arch. "writing in three sections": b1665]
cross-reference n b1835 (verb use: b1905; cross-refer: b1880)
daily n *type of newspaper* b1835
fictionize v b1835 (fictionalize: b1920)
flyleaf n b1835
journalism n b1835 (journalist: b1695)
marginalia n b1835
monthly n b1835

nursery rhyme n b1835
proofreader n b1835 (proofread: b1920)
pseudonym n b1835 (pseudonymous: b1710; pseudonymity: b1880)
rhapsode n b1835
speechwriter n b1835
weekly n *weekly publication* b1835
bookmark n b1840
bowdlerize v b1840
format n b1840 (verb use: b1965)
initial rhyme n *alliteration* b1840
foreword n b1845
iamb n b1845 (iambus: b1590)
pictorial n b1845
prose poem n b1845
serif n b1845
folklore n 1846
John Hancock n *signature* (John Henry: b1915)
lit n *short for "literature"*
notepaper n (notepad: b1925)
pen name n
picture book n
pornography n *writing about prostitutes; obscene material* (porn: b1965)
serial n *magazine*
trade edition n

Communication

mail v *send via the mail* b1830
bulletin board n (Am) b1835
speaking tube n b1835
general delivery n (Am) b1840
Morse code n b1840
parcel post n b1840
postage stamp n b1840
free speech n
pony express n (Am)
self-addressed adj
telecommunication n

Visual Arts/ Photography

danseur, danseuse n b1830
engraving n *type of artwork* b1830
illustration n b1830 (illustrate: b1640)

landscapist n *type of painter* b1830

mezzotint n *type of engraving style* b1830 [obs. "half tint": b1740]

self-portrait n b1835

tempera n b1835

work of art n b1835

daguerrotype n *1839*

photograph, photographic, photography n/v, adj, n 1839 (photographer: b1850; photogram: b1860)

rococo n b1840 (adj use: b1845)

woodblock n *woodcut* b1840

box camera n b1845

cartoon n *humorous drawing* b1845 [gen. type of drawing: b1675] (cartoonist: b1880)

darkroom n b1845

ferrotype n *type of photograph; akin to tintype* b1845

film n *in photography* b1845 (verb use: b1900)

rubbing n b1845

bohemian n *artistic person*

motif n

photographer n

pictureize v *make pictures*

wood carving n

Performing Arts

dress rehearsal n b1830

improvise v b1830 (improvisation: b1790)

lead n *primary role* b1830

limelight n b1830 [fig. use: b1900] (verb use: b1910)

thespian n b1830 (adj use: b1665)

vaudeville n b1830 [type of song: b1740]

villain n *antagonist* b1830 [arch. "rube": b1350]

costumier n (Brit) b1835

mise-en-scène n b1835

tragic irony n b1835

cyclorama n b1840

footlights n b1840

showgirl n b1840

prop n *property* b1845

repertory n *repertory theater* b1845 [obs. "catalog": b1555 to 1700s; "reposi-

tory": b1595; "a repertory company": b1930]

ingenue n

matinee n

repertoire n (repertory: b1870)

show business n (showbiz: b1945)

Music

accompanist n b1830

arrange v *arrange music* b1830

concertina n b1830

conservatory n b1830

cornist n *horn player* b1830

pianist n b1830

recital n b1830

register n b1830

yodel v b1830 (noun use: b1850)

accordion n b1835

brass band n b1835

grand piano n b1835

hemidemisemiquaver n b1835

vocalist n b1835 ["speaker": b1615]

choirboy n b1840

English horn n b1840

étude n *musical term* b1840

grand n *grand piano* b1840

hornist n b1840

kapellmeister n *choir director* b1840

chorale n *type of song* b1845 ["choral group": b1970]

instrumentation n b1845

music hall n b1845

philharmonic n b1845 ["music lover": b1765]

pianism n b1845

saxhorn n b1845

sitar n b1845

bass horn n

folk song n (folksinger: b1885; folk music: b1890)

harmonium n

melodeon n (Am) *type of musical instrument*

musicale n (Am)

timbre n [part of a helmet: b1375]

zither n

Entertainment

star n *celebrity* b1830 (adj/verb use: b1835; stardom: b1865; starstruck: b1970)

zoological garden n b1830 (zoo: b1850)

barn dance n (Am) b1835

gallopade n *type of dance* b1835

galop n *type of dance* b1835

box seat n b1840

turkey trot n (Am) b1840

county fair n b1845

hoedown n (Am) b1845

polka n/v b1845

cancan n

funnyman n

schottische n *type of dance*

sideshow n (Am)

takeoff n *parody*

zoo n [fig. use: b1930] (zoological garden: b1830)

Movies/TV/Radio

screen n *as in "movie screen"* b1830

Education

educational adj b1830 ["resulting from education": b1655 to 1800s]

graduate v *earn a degree* b1830 ["award a degree": b1470] (graduation: b1425)

institute n b1830

mark n *grade* b1830 (verb use: b1900)

philistine n *someone not educated* b1830 (philistia: b1860)

physical education n b1830

private school n b1830

school board n b1830

three R's n b1830

training school n b1830

tuition n *fee for teaching* b1830 [obs. "custody, care": b1300 to 1700s; "teaching": b1600]

undergrad adj/n b1830

misology n *hatred of knowledge* b1835

nursery school n b1835

schoolmarm n (Am) b1835

secondary school n b1835

ivory tower n 1837 (ivory-towered: b1940)

dunce cap n b1840 (dunce: b1590)

finishing school n b1840

housemother n b1840

(housefather: b1845; houseparent: b1955)

progressive education n b1840

schoolchild n b1840 (schoolfellow: b1500; schoolmate: b1565; schoolboy: b1590; schoolgirl: b1780; schoolkid: b1940)

educable adj b1845

elementary school n b1845

coach n *tutor* ["sports coach": b1865] (verb use: b1730)

elective n

groves of academe n

haze v *as in "frat hazing"* [gen. "terrify": b1680; nautical sense: b1840] (hazing: b1855)

hooky n (Am)

industrial arts n

salutatorian n (Am) (salutatory n: b1780)

schoolteacher n

study hall n

Religion

archdiocese n b1830

heliolatry n *worship of the sun* b1830

karma n b1830

animism n b1835

apocalyptist n b1835

God-fearing adj b1835

inferno n b1835

messianic adj b1835 (messiah: b1350)

nonsectarian adj b1835

churchianity n b1840

counterreformation n b1840

ecclesiology n b1840

eschatology n b1845

Holy Roller n b1845

oversoul n (Am) b1845

creationism n (creation science: b1980)

Society/Mores/Culture

colleen n *lass* b1830

conversationalist n b1830

gay adj *immoral* b1830

individualism n b1830 (individualist: b1840)

moralism n b1830 (moralist: b1625; moralistic: b1865)

parvenue n *a female parvenu* b1830 (parvenu: b1805)

retiracy n *retir(ement) (priv)acy* b1830

socialize v *indoctrinate to society* b1830 (socialization: b1870)

status n *social stature* b1830 ["condition": b1870]

unwashed n b1830

teetotal, teetotaler, teetotalism adj/v, n, n 1833

blue blood n b1835

breadline n b1835

conventionality n b1835

entitlement n b1835

man in the street n b1835

status quo n b1835

womenfolk n b1835

yacht club n b1835

gamin n *boy urchin* b1840 (gamine: b1890)

hombre n b1840

middle-class adj b1840 (noun use: b1770)

noblesse oblige n b1840

time capsule n b1840

upper-class adj b1840 (upper class: b1840)

woman's rights n b1840

Americana n (Am) b1845

chatelaine n *mistress of a castle* b1845 (chatelain: b1450)

classism n b1845

communitarian adj b1845

cosmopolitan adj b1845

humanitarian n b1845 [obs. "believer in nondivine Christ": b1820]

sociology n b1845

ultramodern adj b1845

class struggle n

joe n *as in "average joe"*

mountain man n

prohibitionist n *someone seeking alcohol bans* (prohibitory: b1595)

temperance n *not drinking alcohol*

who's who n

Government

system n *fig. the government, the establishment* b1830

constituency n b1835 (constituent n: b1715)

first lady n b1835

grand duchy n b1835 (grand duke: b1695; grand duchess: b1760)

inaugural n b1835 (adj use: b1690)

native son n (Am) b1835

communism, communist n b1840 (communize: b1890)

executive session n (Am) b1840

slavocracy n b1840 (slavocrat: b1870)

bureaucrat n b1845 (bureaucratic: b1840)

city father n (Am) b1845

crown colony n b1845

territorial waters n b1845

plutocrat n

Politics

lobby n b1830 (verb use: b1840)

radical adj b1830

right n *the conservatives* b1830

run v *as in "run for office"* b1830

socialism, socialist n b1830

conservative adj b1835

conservativism n b1835 (conservative adj/n: b1835)

separationist n b1835

antidemocratic adj b1840

reactionary adj/n b1840

protectionist n

extremist n (extremism: b1865)

politicalize v *make political*

progressive adj/n (progressivism: b1895)

referendum n

woman suffrage n

Death

muff v *arch. die* b1830

death trap n b1835

gravesite n b1840

happy hunting ground n (Am) b1840

hara-kiri n b1840

postmortem examination n b1840 (postmortem n: b1840)

rigor mortis n b1840

feticide n b1845

mourner's bench n (Am) b1845

thanatology n b1845

casket n *coffin* ["box for valuables": b1465]

goner n

in memoriam prep

postmortem n (postmortem examination: b1840)

rub out v *kill* (noun use: b1930)

War/Military/Violence

birch v *flog* b1830 (noun use: b1670)

blank cartridge n b1830

cap n *as in "cap gun"* b1830

civilian n *nonmilitary person* b1830 ["worker in civil law": b1400] (civil: b1595)

commandeer v b1830

gingall n *type of gun* b1830

gun n *as in "hired gun"* b1830 (gunman: b1625)

insurrect v b1830 (insurrection: b1425)

investment n *arch. laying seige* b1830

kick n *as in "kick of a gun"* b1830 (verb use: b1870)

military police n b1830

military science n b1830

percussion n b1830

slug n (Am) *hard hit* b1830 (verb use: b1865)

snapshot n *rushed gunshot* b1830

suit n *as in "suit of armor"* b1830

war game n b1830 (wargame v: b1945)

war paint n (Am) b1830

warmonger n b1830 ["mercenary": b1590]

wing v *wound* b1830

coast guard n b1835

drumhead court-martial n b1835

Kentucky rifle n b1835

muster out v b1835

pistoleer n b1835

revolver n (Am) b1835

squirrel rifle n b1835

bowie knife n (Am) b1840

fatigues n *uniform* b1840 (fatigue "duty": b1780)

misfire n b1840 (verb use: b1755)

sheath knife n b1840

shooter n *gun* b1840

sidewinder n *type of punch* b1840

square off v b1840 (obs. square "fight": b1570 to 1700s)

uppercut n b1840

casualty n *victim of accident or war* b1845 ["chance," "accident": b1425]

disorderly conduct n b1845

outrank v (Am) b1845

scale armor n b1845

six-shooter n b1845 (six-gun: b1915)

weaponry n b1845

billy n (billy club: b1950)

booby trap n

cease-fire n

comrade in arms n

powder burn n (Am)

revolutionary n (adj use: b1775; revolutionist n: b1710)

riflery n

sea power n

slingshot n (Am)

thalassocracy n *"maritime supremacy"*

vet adj/n (Am) vet(eran)

Crime/Punishment/Enforcement

blackmail n *extortion* b1830 ["protection money": b1555] (verb use: b1900)

grand larceny n b1830

habit n *as in "drug habit"* b1830

heist v (Am) b1830 (noun use: b1930)

kleptomania n b1830 (kleptomaniac: b1865)

magsman n *con man* b1830

skull and crossbones n b1830

chain gang n b1835

constable n b1835 ["peacekeeper for the king": b1300]

inmate n *prisoner* b1835 ["roommate": b1590]

lynch v (Am) b1835

police reporter n b1835

reformatory n b1835

station house n b1835

swindle n b1835 (verb use: b1785)

extradition n b1840 (extradite: b1840)

felonry n b1840

penology n b1840

pinch v arrest b1840

police force n b1840

bobby n (Brit) policeman b1845

pyromania n b1845

confidence man n (Am) (confidence game: b1860)

copper n (Am) police officer (verb use "arrest": b1900; cop: b1860)

detective n (adj use: b1845)

first offender n

flash v expose [gen. "show off": b1630] (flasher: b1975)

police station n

squeal v inform (squeak: b1690; squealer: b1865; squawk: b1875)

stool pigeon n (stool: b1910; stoolie: b1925)

The Law

flagrante delicto adj/adv b1830

in camera adv in chambers b1830

international law n b1830

judiciary n b1830

municipal court n b1830

corpus delecti n b1835

prosecuting attorney n b1835 (prosecutor: b1670)

public domain n (Am) b1835

visa n b1835 (verb use: b1950)

penal code n b1845

shyster n (Am) b1845

common-law adj

field trial n

homestead law n (Am)

hung jury n (Am)

The Fantastic/ Paranormal

eidolon n phantom, spectre b1830

merwoman n b1830 (mermaid: b1350; merman: b1605)

planetarian n native of another planet b1830

thunderbird n b1830

zombie n living dead b1830 [slang use: b1940]

nixie, nix n mythical water sprite b1835

spiritualism n belief in communicating with the dead b1835 ["belief in the spirit": b1800] (spiritism: b1860)

bogey n as in "bogeyman" b1840 (boogeyman: b1850; bogeyman: b1890)

clairvoyance n b1840 (clairaudience "hearing the beyond": b1865)

dowser n b1840

seeress n b1845 (seer: b1400)

supernature n the supernatural b1845

mantic adj related to divination (mantical: b1590)

poltergeist n

sensitive n

Magic

hex v perform witchcraft b1830 (noun use: b1860; hexerei "witchcraft": b1900)

thaumaturgist n b1830 (thaumaturge: b1715)

illusionist n magician b1845

Interjections

gum interj as in "by gum" b1830

hurroo interj b1830

maa interj sheep sound b1830

thankee interj b1830

tra-la-la interj b1830

yo-heave-ho interj b1830

chop-chop adv/interj b1835

hawhaw interj b1835

indeed interj harrumph b1835 ["truly?": b1600]

begorra interj b1840

crikey interj b1840

fire away v start talking b1840

nuff said interj (Am) b1840

ouch interj (Am) b1840

scat interj/v (Am) scoot b1840

thunderation interj (Am) b1840

yep/yup adv b1840

haw interj as in "gee and haw" b1845 (verb use: b1780)

my word interj b1845

whoopee interj (Am) b1845

no siree, yes siree interj (Am)

prosit interj toast to health

sh interj

shucks interj

so long interj (Am)

Slang

absquatulate v abscond b1830

blazes n Hades b1830

buckaroo n (Am) b1830

citify, citified v, adj (Am) b1830

comfy adj b1830

complexify v b1830

crack n try b1830

cracking adj great b1830 (adv use: b1870)

cram v as in "cram for a test" b1830

crib n as in "crib notes" b1830 (verb use: b1780)

cross n/v as in "double cross" b1830

damnedest n b1830

doggone v (Am) b1830 (adj/ adv use: b1855; noun use: b1930; doggoned: b1870)

double-cross v b1830 (noun use: b1835)

drab n as in "dribs and drabs" b1830

electric adj exciting b1830

ex n as in "ex-wife" b1830

fess v b1830

flapdoodle n b1830

hair-splitting n b1830 (hairsplitter: b1850)

hang around v b1830 (hang: b1870)

hoss n b1830

ist n b1830 (ism: b1680)

kerfuffle n (Brit) disturbance, commotion b1830

lifer n b1830

ma n b1830

mag n b1830

monkeyshines n (Am) b1830

mosey v (Am) b1830

mouthpiece n spokesperson, lawyer b1830

muscle n power, influence b1830

nab n cop b1830

plum n prize b1830 [£100,000: b1700]

raft n a lot b1830

rap n as in "don't care a rap" b1830

rummy adj odd b1830

sack n bed b1830 (verb use, as in "sack out": b1950)

screw v break and enter b1830

shake n as in "three shakes of a monkey's tail"; as in "a fair shake" b1830

smithereens n b1830 (smithereen v: b1930)

sockdolager n (Am) decider b1830

stuck-up adj b1830

stunner n good-looker b1830

sub n sub(stitute) b1830 ["subordinate": b1700] (verb use: b1855)

sucker n dupe b1830 (verb use: b1970)

tight adj drunk b1830

warm adj saucy, blue b1830

whole-hog adj/n b1830

wig n as in "bigwig" b1830

wire-puller n (Am) influence peddler b1830

wrinkle n as in "a new wrinkle" b1830 [obs. "devious move": b1450 to 1500s]

all-fired, all-firedly adj/superlative/adv hell-fired b1835

blamed adj/adv darned, confounded b1835

bosh n nonsense b1835 (interj use: b1855)

clean up v (Am) b1835

double cross n b1835 (verb use: b1905)

dreamland n b1835 (dreamworld: b1820)

fleabag n b1835

fun v joke with b1835

goldarn adj (Am) b1835 (goldarned: b1860)

kibosh v b1835 ["bunk": b1900] (noun use: b1885)

locomote v b1835

mugwump n muckamuck b1835

vamoose v b1835

wheeze n old joke b1835

A1 adj b1840

booby hatch n *jail* b1840 ["asylum": b1925]

boss adj *cool* b1840

bub, bubby n (Am) *informal address* b1840

bust n *bash/flop* b1840

chicken feed n b1840

Cinderella n *fig.* b1840

clinker n (Brit) *first-rate* b1840 ["sour note": b1970]

corker n b1840 (corking adj: b1895)

cussed adj (Am) b1840

fishy adj *suspicious* b1840

flummox v b1840

have-not n b1840 (have n: b1770)

henchman n b1840

highfalutin adj b1840

jiggered adj *as in "I'll be jiggered"* b1840

K.G. adj (Am) *no go* b1840

leg up n b1840

monster adj b1840

peanut adj *worthless* b1840

prof n (Am) b1840

reel off v b1840

ripsnorter n b1840 (ripsnorting adj: b1850)

Sam Hill n *hell* b1840

sell n *hoax* b1840

soft-soap v b1840 (noun use: b1830)

tap v *borrow from, beg from* b1840

thataway n b1840

tin-pot adj *small-potatoes* b1840

weather eye n b1840

bodacious adj b1845

coon's age n (Am) b1845

crawfish v *back out* b1845

dunno v b1845

hanky-panky n b1845 [sexual sense: b1940]

josh v (Am) b1845 (noun use: b1880)

lickety-split adv (Am) b1845

mix-up n b1845

monk n *monkey* b1845

ole adj *old* b1845

pickled adj *drunk* b1845

pied piper n b1845

scare up v b1845

scorcher n *hot day* b1845

splendiferous adj *wondrous* b1845

spud n b1845

stag adj *male-only* b1845

thing n *as in "do your own thing"* b1845

bustup n

caboodle n (Am)

crappy adj (Am)

doll n *woman*

drag n *something boring*

furriner n *foreigner*

gringo n

gunk n (Am)

hairy adj *difficult, rough*

katzenjammer n *hangover, clamor* ["confusion": b1900]

muck-a-muck n (Am)

nut n *head*

pack rat n

paper tiger n

paste v *smack around*

pissed n *drunk* ["angry": b1950]

Podunk n (Am) *nowhere*

prettify v

pro adj/n *professional*

rep n *representative*

rot interj, n *rubbish, baloney*

scrap n *fight* [obs. "scheme": b1700 to 1800s] (verb use: b1875)

thank-you-ma'am n

wolf n/v *masher*

Insults

bastard n b1830

dud n *worthless sort* b1830 ["fizzled explosive": b1900]

futilitarian adj/n b1830

jackass n b1830 (jackassery: b1835)

loafer n (Am) *slaggard* b1830 (loaf: b1835)

redneck n (Am) b1830

toady n b1830 (verb use: b1830)

whitey n b1830

windbag n b1830

cad n *lout* b1835 (caddish: b1870)

chowderhead n b1835

crank n *cranky person* b1835

do-nothing adj b1835

featherhead n b1835

foozle n *bungler* b1835 ["instance of bungling": b1890] (verb use: b1870)

Indian giver n b1835

jackassery n b1835

lotus-eater n *idle person* b1835 (lotusland: b1845)

old fogey n b1835

white trash n (Am) b1835

woodenhead n b1835 (woodenheaded: b1855)

yellow dog n *coward* b1835

barrelhead n b1840

fathead n b1840

featherbrain n b1840 (featherhead: b1835)

gossipmonger n b1840

money-grubber n b1840

weaselly adj b1840 (weasel adj: b1930)

hawkish adj b1845

no-account adj b1845

swellhead n (Am) b1845 (swelled head: b1895)

tightfisted adj b1845

wastrel n *spendthrift* b1845 ["bit of wasteland": b1590] (waster: b1355)

black-hearted adj

hair-splitter n (hair-splitting: b1830)

low-down adj

mama's boy n

scalawag n (Am)

skeezix n *arch. rascal*

slowpoke n

snollygoster n *shrewd person*

sorehead n

tenderfoot n (Am)

Phrases

beat a dead horse n b1830

blue streak n b1830

crime against nature n b1830

dead duck n (Am) b1830

Dutch uncle n b1830

eat humble pie v b1830

eleventh hour n b1830

fair shake n b1830

gold digger n (Am) b1830 (gold-dig v: b1930)

gone goose n (Am) *dead duck* b1830

hand-me-down adj/n b1830

here and how n b1830

jumping-off place n (Am) b1830

knock-down-drag-out adj b1830

open secret n b1830

polish off v b1830

secret society n b1830

still and all adv b1830

trigger finger n b1830

upper crust n b1830

betwixt and between adj/adv b1835

close shave n (Am) b1835

dark horse n b1835

de rigueur adj b1835

dog-eat-dog adj b1835

hole-and-corner adj *secret* b1835

johnny-come-lately n b1835

nip and tuck adj/adv b1835

object lesson n b1835

small potato n b1835

Sunday-go-to-meeting adj (Am) b1835

swan song n b1835

vigilance committee n (Am) *vigilantes* b1835 (vigilante: b1835)

better half n b1840

clarion call n b1840

fine-tooth comb n b1840

forked tongue n b1840

hook, line and sinker adv b1840

leg-of-mutton adj *describing a shape* b1840

Occam's razor n b1840

sure thing n (Am) b1840

tinker's damn n b1840

Trojan horse n b1840

vital statistics n b1840

whole cloth n b1840

black mark n b1845

cloak-and-dagger adj b1845

exact science n b1845

fait accompli n b1845

free lunch n b1845

Good Samaritan n b1845

hell on wheels n b1845

higher law n (Am) b1845

lock, stock and barrel adv b1845

lousy with adj *as in "the stands were lousy with hecklers"* b1845

manifest destiny n b1845

open-and-shut adj (Am) b1845

rhetorical question n b1845

shove off v (Am) *leave* b1845

soft spot n *vulnerable spot* b1845

bitter end n

chamber of horrors n

conscience money n
crème de la crème n
freak of nature n
hot potato n
judgment call n
last straw n
night owl n
old guard n
Prince Charming n
set piece n
two cents n

General/Miscellaneous

acolyte n *novice* b1830 [religious sense: b1300]
alternative n *choice* b1830 (adj use: b1590)
analog/analogue n b1830
antagonism n b1830
autonomy n *freedom* b1830 ["self-government": b1625]
backseat n *lit. and fig.* b1830
bonanza n (Am) b1830
brand n *trademark; type* b1830
breakdown n b1830 (break down v: b1400)
cahoots n (Am) b1830
check n *ticket, as in "hat check"* b1830 (verb use: b1870)
classicism, classicist n b1830
clip n *something clipped* b1830
cooperative n b1830 (co-op: b1875)
cyanide n b1830
deniability n b1830
deterrent adj/n b1830 (deterrence: b1865)
doubleganger n b1830
downtown adv (Am) b1830 (adj/noun use: b1855)
embodiment n b1830 (embody: b1900)
engagement n *appointment* b1830
escapade n *adventure* b1830 [obs. "escape": b1655 to 1800s]
exploration n b1830 [obs. "investigation": b1540 to 1600s]
fake n *trick* b1830 ["something counterfeit": b1870; "faker": b1890] (fakery: b1890)

given name n (Am) b1830
gossip n *result of gossiping* b1830 ["gossipy person": b1570] (verb use: b1630; gossipmonger: b1840)
grade n *slope, gradation* b1830 (verb use: b1870)
hairspring n *type of fine spring* b1830
hydrochloric acid n b1830
interface n b1830 (verb use: b1965)
intro n b1830
keep n *as in "earn your keep"* b1830
kismet n *fate* b1830
lay n *as in "lay of the land"* b1830
leverage n b1830 ["using a lever": b1725; fig. use: b1870] (verb use: b1940)
lull n *quiet period* b1830 ["something that lulls": b1720]
manipulation, manipulate n, v b1830 [technical use: b1730; "chemical experimentation": b1800]
mess n *something jumbled* b1830 ["entanglement": b1835; "something dirty": b1855] (verb use: b1853)
monolith n *lit.* b1830 [fig. sense: b1940]
move n *instance of moving* b1830
myth n b1830 (mythical: b1670)
natter n/v *chatter* b1830 ["nibble": b1750; "grumble": b1825] (noun use: b1870; gnatter: b1807)
notice n *sign* b1830
organization n *group* b1830
pat n *as in "pat on the head"* b1830 (verb use: b1730)
prestige n b1830 [obs. "prestidigitation": b1670 to 1700s]
pundit n *gen.* b1830 ["Hindu expert": b1675]
rebuttal n b1830
revulsion n *repugnance* b1830 [med. sense: b1545]
ribbons n *something torn* b1830

rollick v/n b1830 (rollicking: b1815)
ruse n b1830
self-help adj/n b1830
septet n *group of 7* b1830
spirit n *intent, as in "the spirit of the law"* b1830
splurge n (Am) *big show* b1830 ["spending spree": b1930] (verb use: b1845)
standpoint n *phys. point of perspective* b1830 ["mental point of view": b1870]
stipulation n *requirement* b1830 ["contract": b1555] (stipulate: b1625)
susurrus n *susurration* b1830
teamwork n b1830
thrashing n b1830
visitress n b1830 (visitor: b1450)
worry n/v *disturb* b1830
tintinnabulation n *bell-ringing* 1831 (tintinnabulum "type of bell": b1600)
better *as in "you'd better behave"* b1835 (best: b1945)
buffer n *intermediary* b1835 (verb use: b1895; buff v: b1425)
clearinghouse n b1835
cottonseed oil n b1835
cross section n b1835 [as in "a cross-section of America": b1930]
double-decker n b1835
entourage n b1835
extensity n b1835
eyeful n b1835
finality n b1835 ["final goal": b1545]
gradient n b1835
handout n b1835 (hand out v: b1880)
interaction, interactive n, adj b1835 (interact: b1840)
isolation n b1835 [med. sense: b1900]
maladjustment n b1835 (maladjusted: b1885)
middle name n b1835
passel n b1835
pileup n b1835
ping n b1835 (verb use: b1770)
resurgence n b1835 (resurge v: b1575; resurgent: b1810)

showcase n b1835 (verb use: b1945)
simulator n *person who simulates* b1835 ["simulation device": b1930]
vigilante n (Am) b1835
waterjet n b1835
blowoff n b1840
bric-a-brac n b1840
carapace n b1840
catchall n b1840
chirpy adj/adv b1840
chuckhole n b1840
claquer n *one paid to applaud* b1840 (claque: b1865)
cock n *as in "Cock Robin"* b1840
cronyism n b1840
definitude n b1840
ethyl n b1840
flare-up n b1840
gadabout n b1840 (adj use: b1820)
glucose n b1840
grid n b1840 [on paper: b1930] (gridiron: b1300)
holdup n (Am) *delay* b1840
inflow n b1840
letup n (Am) b1840
lockup n b1840
orientation n *phys. position* b1840 [fig. "position": b1900; "introduction": b1970]
outgrowth n b1840
pathfinder n (Am) b1840
percept n b1840
poster n *placard; person who posts placards* b1840
pyrotechnic n b1840
rebirth n b1840
sachet n b1840 [obs. type of bag: b1485]
sequitur n *consequence* b1840
slew n (Am) *a lot* b1840
split-up n b1840
turndown n *something phys. turned down* b1840
wreckage n *being wrecked* b1840 ["remains of a wreck": b1900]
aficionado n b1845 (aficionada: b1955)
brightwork n (Am) *chromework, etc.* b1845
bunkum/buncombe n b1845 (bunk: b1900)

catch-up adj/n (Am) b1845

consensus n b1845 [brief use: b1635; consensual: b1755]

curlicue/curlycue n/v b1845

dissymmetry n b1845

earpiece n b1845

inbreeding n b1845 (inbred: b1595; inbreed: b1925)

laughing gas n b1845

pacemaker n *leader* b1845

patter n *as in "pitter-patter"* b1845

peek n b1845 (verb use: b1375)

pounce n *act of pouncing* b1845 (verb use: b1710)

rabblerouser n b1845

rowdyism n (Am) b1845 (rowdy: b1820)

runner-up n b1845

spill n b1845

standoff n b1845

tweet n/v b1845

ultimacy n b1845

agendum n (agenda: b1630)

backlight n/v

biff n *whack or blow*

bonemeal n (Am)

building block n

bypass n (verb use: b1870)

canard n *falsehood*

cosmopolis n

debacle n [phys. "onrush of water": b1805]

decentralization n (decentralize: b1845)

flumadiddle n (Am) *type of food; nonsense*

insider n

lacework n

lagniappe n (Am)

layout n (Am)

manhunt n (Am)

mecca n *hub*

metalwork n (metalworking: b1885)

peyote n (Am)

pinpoint n (adj use: b1870; verb use: b1920)

plaque n

poppycock n (Am)

portrayal n

rataplan n *beating sound*

sensationalism n (sensational: b1840; sensationalize: b1870)

shake-up n

shut-in n (Am) (adj use: b1910)

slick n *as in "oil slick"* [slang "slick person": b1870]

sonny n

spitball n (Am) *spitwad*

synchrony n

ticktock n (ticktack: b1550; tick-a-tick: b1830)

variant n

vulcanize, vulcanization v, n

whoosh n (verb use: b1870)

Things

firecracker n (Am) b1830

fluoride n b1830

slide n *as in "microscope slide," or transparency* b1830

split rail n b1830

Roman candle n b1835

tag n *as in "name tag"* b1835 [fig. use: b1970]

terminal n *as in "electrical terminal"* b1835

dingbat n *thingamajig* b1840

galvanized iron n b1840

statuette n b1845

elastic n

Description

aflutter adj b1830

aglimmer adj b1830

aglitter adj b1830

almighty adv *as in "I'm almighty tired"* b1830

anthropomorphic adj b1830 (anthropomorphism: b1753; anthropomorph: b1895)

aplenty adj b1830 (adv use: b1850)

approximate adj *almost equal* b1830

armchair adj b1830

awful adj *bad* b1830

bang adv *as in "smack bang in the middle"* b1830

breathless adj *as in "breathless description"* b1830 ["dead": b1400]

careworn adj b1830

ceramic adj b1830 (noun use: b1860; ceramist: b1855; ceramics: b1860)

competitive adj b1830

complementary adj b1830 [obs. "formal": 1600s]

crucial adj b1830 [related to the cross: b1710]

custom adj b1830

damaging adj b1830

demonstrative adj *open emotionally* b1830

discriminatory adj b1830

down-home adj (Am) b1830

drastic adj b1830 [med. use: b1695]

erosive adj b1830

fornicate adj *arched* b1830

great adj *very good, as in "the play was great"* b1830

headfirst adv b1830 (headforemost: b1700)

homegrown adj b1830

hourglass adj b1830

in extenso adv *at full length* b1830

inconspicuous adj b1830 ["invisible": b1625 to 1700s]

incorrect adj *wrong, not correct* b1830 [obs. "uncorrected": b1425 to 1600s; "socially unacceptable": b1700]

indomitable adj b1830 ["untrainable": b1635]

lead adj *first or foremost* b1830

low-pressure adj b1830

mandatory adj *required* b1830

markworthy adj *remarkable* b1830

meticulous adj b1830 [obs. "timid": b1535 to 1600s]

monotonous, monotony adj, n *boringly repetitive* b1830 ["characterized by monotone": b1780]

multilateral adj b1830 [lit. "many-sided": b1700]

nebulous adj *indistinct* b1830 ["cloudy": b1425; "pertaining to nebulas": b1790]

negligible adj b1830

off-putting adj b1830 (offput v: b1870)

omnicompetent adj b1830

picayune adj b1830 (noun use: b1790)

pitch-dark adj b1830

pro tem adv b1830 (pro tempore: b1470)

relieved adj b1830 (relieve: b1470; unrelieved: b1570)

repellent adj *water-repellent* b1830

restricted adj b1830

risky adj b1830 (risk: b1665)

scrumptious adj *sumptuous* b1830 ["delicious": b1885]

self-serving adj b1830

sporadic adj *gen. intermittent* b1830 [med. "isolated": b1690]

standard adj *unexceptional* b1830

strong-arm adj (Am) b1830

tight adj *close, as in "tight race"* b1830

top-notch adj b1830

tremendous adj *modern sense of great, wonderful* b1830 ["awe- and fear-inspiring": b1635]

undangerous adj b1830

unmentionable adj b1830

viable adj *able to live* b1830 ["workable": b1870]

walloping adj b1830

wild adj *as in "a wild throw"* b1830

abnormal adj b1835

archaic adj b1835 (archaical: b1805)

awash adj b1835

combative adj b1835

creaky adj b1835

creepy adj b1835

eurythmic adj b1835

factual adj b1835

full-size adj b1835

gastight adj b1835

go-ahead adj (Am) *energetic* b1835 (noun use: b1840)

hair-trigger adj b1835

hell-bent adj (Am) b1835

long-ago adj b1835

newsy adj b1835

reticent adj b1835 (reticence: b1605)

rip-roaring adj (Am) b1835 (riproarious: b1870)

smashing adj b1835

sneaky adj b1835

splashy adj *bold, showy* b1835

structural adj b1835

trustful adj *trusting* b1835

[obs. "trustworthy": b1580 to 1700s]

OK adj 1839 (noun use: b1845; verb use: b1890; adv use: b1900)

all-important adj b1840

banal adj b1840 ["related to ban, call to arms": b1755] (banality: b1865)

banner adj (Am) as in "banner year" b1840

bogus adj (Am) b1840 (noun use "type of counterfeiting machine": b1830; noun use "bogus money": b1840)

burned-out adj b1840

catercorner/catercornered/cattycorner adj/adv b1840

chockablock adv b1840 (adj use: b1890)

cramfull adj b1840

featherlight adj b1840

frumpy adj b1840 ["irascible": b1750] (frumpish: b1850)

grandiose adj b1840

hard-hitting adj b1840

head-on adv (Am) b1840 (adj use: b1905)

imitation adj b1840

inexpensive adj b1840

naturalistic adj b1840

onetime adj b1840 (adv use: b1890)

pioneer adj b1840

real-life adj b1840

regulation adj b1840 (noun use: b1730)

relief adj b1840

repetitive adj b1840 (repetitious: b1675)

rudimentary adj b1840 (rudiment: b1550)

scrappy adj composed of scraps b1840

second-class adj b1840 (noun use: b1810)

sensational adj b1840

serial adj b1840

shopworn adj b1840

sit-down adj as in "sit-down dinner" b1840

snug adj fitting tightly b1840 [spec. applied to ships: b1595; "comfortable": b1630]

straight-ahead adj b1840

straight-out adj (Am) b1840

telluric adj earthly b1840 (tellurium: b1800)

third-class adj b1840 (noun use: b1845)

ubiquitous adj everywhere b1840 (ubiquitary "someone who is everywhere": b1600; gen. ubiquity: b1630)

unconventional adj b1840

basic adj fundamental b1845 (noun use: b1930)

challenging adj b1845

die-hard adj b1845 ["conservative": b1925] (adj use: b1875)

disruptive adj b1845

gamey adj plucky b1845

ghoulish adj b1845 (ghoul: b1790)

hard-won adj b1845

incommunicado adj/adv (Am) b1845

latter-day adj b1845

letter-perfect adj b1845

life-size adj b1845

liminal adj perceptible, as in "subliminal" b1845

messy adj b1845

model adj b1845

oldfangled adj b1845 (newfangled: b1570)

omnibus adj varied b1845

oncoming adj b1845 (noun use: b1450; oncome n: b1350)

one-man adj b1845

overdue adj b1845

piggy adj b1845

plunderous adj b1845

polychromatic adj multicolored b1845

premium adj b1845

sanitary adj b1845

sledgehammer adj b1845

slimsy adj (Am) b1845

spang adv (Am) directly, smack b1845

storybook adj b1845

worrisome adj b1845

balky adj

detective adj (detective police: b1845)

diversionary adj

drafty adj

exceptional adj

foxed adj stained

high-stepping adj

holus-bolus adv all at once

incisive adj fig. cutting, sharp [lit. use: b1425]

infrahuman adj

intramural adj

jackleg adj (Am) amateur

monochrome adj

nonetheless adv

phenomenal adj extraordinary ["related to phenomena": b1825]

preferential adj

shoddy adj second-rate

spatial adj

vanilla adj lit. and fig.

vest-pocket adj

viridescent adj green

way adv very

Colors

coffee n the color of coffee b1830

complementary color n b1830

drab n color b1830 (adj use "of drab color": b1800; adj use "not bright": b1900)

honey n the color b1830

peachblow n (Am) type of color b1830

cobalt blue n b1835

secondary color n b1835

burnt sienna n b1845

cerise n b1845

steel gray n b1845

Actions/Verbs

bat v as in "batting your eyelashes" b1830

chalk up v b1830

champion v b1830 [obs. "challenge": b1605 to 1800s]

clear v leave, as in "clear out" b1830

clomp v b1830

cover v as in "five dollars will cover it"; provide insurance coverage b1830

crack up v as in "not all it's cracked up to be" b1830

cup v as in "cup the hands" b1830

devitalize v b1830

embarrass v humiliate b1830 ["obstruct": b1630; "confuse": b1670; "make harder": b1770]

fluidize v b1830 (fluidify: b1870)

foot v as in "foot the bill" b1830

gyrate v b1830 (gyration: b1615)

hark back v b1830

hone v b1830 (noun use: b1350)

innerve v invigorate b1830

keel v as in "keel over" b1830

loot v plunder b1830

manage v get by, cope b1830

optimize v b1830 (optimization: b1860)

pad v supply with a pad b1830

parlay v (Am) b1830 (noun use: b1905)

picnic v b1830

pooh-pooh v b1830

prime v as in "prime a pump" b1830

rally v as in "rally round a friend" b1830

renunciate v b1830 (renounce: b1380; renunciation: b1400)

ricochet v bounce around b1830 ["fire at with ricochets": b1770]

scrimshaw v b1830 (noun use: b1865)

show up v b1830

skip v as in "skip school" b1830

slate v schedule b1830

sleep in v b1830

supplement v b1830

synthesize v b1830

tackle v phys. grab b1830 [fig. "handle": b1850]

tough v as in "tough it out" b1830

twist v as in "twist and turn"; as in "twist the truth" b1830 (noun use: b1800)

ultimate v b1830

unhappen v b1830

upset v disrupt, as in "upset a schedule" b1830

vault v rise quickly, as in "vault into prominence" b1830

ventriloquize v b1830

victimize v b1830

climax v b1835

contact v cause to touch

b1835 [fig. "get in touch with": b1930]

fix up v b1835

gate v *confine by curfew* b1835

handpick v b1835

mollycoddle v b1835 (noun use: b1865)

pawn off v b1835

snoop v (Am) *spy* b1835 (noun use: b1900; snoopy: b1900)

turn on v *activate* b1835

use up v b1835

acclimatize v b1840 (acclimate: b1795)

beach v b1840

bluff v b1840 (noun use: b1875)

brief v b1840 [leg. sense: b1870] (briefing: b1910)

burke v *suppress* b1840 [arch. "kill and dispose of victim quietly": b1830]

cave in v *give in* b1840 [lit. "collapse": b1710]

check off n/v b1840

detour v b1840 (noun use: b1740)

diagram v b1840 (noun use: b1620)

fool around v b1840

jiggle v b1840 (noun use: b1900; jigger: b1870)

keep back v b1840

kick around v b1840

liquidize v b1840

mobilize v b1840 [mil. sense: b1855]

muss v b1840 (noun use: b1870)

pan v *as in "pan gold"* b1840

parenthesize v b1840

pigeonhole v *lit. place in a pigeonhole* b1840 [fig. "stereotype": b1900]

salvo v b1840

sanitize v b1840 (sanitary: b1845; sanitation: b1850; sanitate v: b1885)

scamp v b1840 ["roam": b1755]

suck in v b1840

target v *choose a target* b1840 ["set a goal," "take aim": b1970]

toilet v b1840

trot out v b1840

walk out v b1840

balloon v *swell* b1845

bootlick v (Am) b1845

buck up v b1845

cycle v *as in "cycle through"* b1845

engineer v *create; design; orchestrate* b1845

fizzle v/n *fail* b1845 ["break wind": b1440 to 1700s; "make a fizz sound": b1860]

head off v b1845 (head v: b1730)

ill-use v b1845

live down v b1845

muff v b1845 (noun use: b1870)

pitch in v b1845

pivot v b1845

pock v b1845 (pockmark v: b1760)

prospect v *search, mine* b1845 [obs. "see, view": b1570 to 1600s]

rework v b1845

rigidify v b1845

round up v b1845

shoot down v b1845

sic v *as in "sic the dogs"* b1845

skitter v b1845

skunk v *defeat handily* b1845

slap down v b1845

watch out v b1845

whipsaw v b1845

true v *make square* b1845

buck v *as in "a horse bucking"* ["butt with head": b1750; "resist, go against": b1860] (noun use: b1880)

chomp v

corral v

derail v

drape v [obs. "weave": b1450 to 1600s]

electroplate v

gam v *talk*

hang about v

historicize v (obs. history v: b1470 to 1500s)

jettison v

off-load v

piffle v (noun use: b1890; piffling: b1870)

pipe down v

preempt v (preemption: b1605; preemptive: b1795)

reproduce v *copy* (reproduction: b1830)

revamp v (Am)

salt away v

taper off v

trivialize v

upholster v (Am)

water down v

x v *as in "x out"*

Archaisms

lumbersome adj *cumbersome* b1830

earwig v *bother* b1840

IN USE BY
1875

Geography/Places

badlands n (Am) b1855
coastland n b1855
cwm n b1855
extramural adj *beyond the city* b1855 [educational sense: b1900]
ice cap n b1855
intercontinental adj b1855
piedmont adj *related to foothills* b1855
riverfront n b1855
seafloor n b1855
shoreline n b1855
cityscape n (Am) b1860
coastline n b1860
downgrade n (Am) b1860 (verb use: b1930)
landmass n b1860
low-lying adj b1860
mare n *lunar and martian "seas"* b1860
panhandle n *as in "Texas panhandle"* b1860
prime meridian n b1860
rimrock n (Am) b1860
seismic adj b1860
streambed n b1860
tidal basin n b1860
contour map n b1865
frostline n (Am) b1865
riptide n b1865
subcontinent n b1865
tell n *mound, hill* b1865
cirque n b1870
continental divide n (Am) b1870
extinct adj *as in "extinct volcano"* b1870
great divide n b1870
kettle n b1870
semitropical adj b1870
water level n *level of groundwater, gen. water* b1870
floodplain n
ghost town n
seven seas n

Natural Things

eolian adj b1855
ferrite n b1855
megalith n b1855
ball lightning n b1860
fertilization n *as in "fertilization of an egg"* b1860 [gen. "making fertile": b1790]
natural selection n b1860
survival of the fittest n 1864
cesium n b1865
man ape n b1865
Neanderthal man n b1865 (Neanderthal: b1925)
volcanism n b1865 (volcanicity: b1840; vulcanity: b1875)
carbohydrate n b1870
fertilize v *as in "fertilize an egg"* b1870
field n *as in "magnetic field"* b1870
glaciate v b1870 ["freeze": b1625]
halite n *rock salt* b1870
helium n b1870
magma n *molten rock* b1870 [obs. "dregs": b1450 to 1800s]
methane n b1870
monoxide n b1870
natural resource n b1870
nature worship n b1870
organism n *living thing* b1870

["organization": b1665; "something that resembles the living": b1775]
osmosis n b1870 (osmose n "osmosis": b1855; osmose v: b1900)
timberline n (Am) b1870
alpenglow n
carbon dioxide n
carbon monoxide n
fool's gold n
ice sheet n
isopropyl alchohol n
life cycle n
oil shale n
wood fiber n

Plants

American beauty n (Am) *rose* b1860
citronella n *type of grass* b1860
coralberry n (Am) b1860
corn poppy n b1860
Douglas fir n b1860
navy bean n b1860
saguaro n (Am) *type of cactus* b1860
star fruit n b1860
corn silk n b1865
edelweiss n b1865
ficus n b1865
leaf rust n b1865
opium poppy n b1865
brier/brierroot/brierwood n *source of briar pipes* b1870
coleus n b1870
kola nut n b1870
penicillium n b1870 (penicillum: 1929)
pine needle n b1870

plant food n b1870
pussy willow n (Am) b1870
sweet clover n b1870
vinca n b1870
crazyweed n *locoweed*
deforestation n (deforest: b1540)
houseplant n
Monterey cypress n
pollinate, pollination v, n

Animals

amoeba n b1855
blue whale n b1855
chinook salmon n (Am) b1855
deerfly n (Am) b1855
dogdom n b1855
ecdysis n *shedding* b1855
eider duck n b1855
falconet n *type of falcon* b1855
herbivore n b1855 (herbivorous: b1665)
husky n *type of dog* b1855
lacewing n *type of insect* b1855
leafhopper n (Am) b1855
leatherback turtle n b1855
luna moth n (Am) b1855
paper wasp n (Am) b1855
coelacanth n b1860
driver ant n b1860
English setter n b1860
fairy shrimp n b1860
furcula n *wishbone* b1860
gray whale n b1860
ground sloth n b1860
Irish terrier n b1860
Manx cat n b1860
mountain lion n (Am) b1860

mud dauber n (Am) *type of wasp* b1860

northern pike n (Am) b1860

pinto n (Am) *type of horse* b1860

rat snake n b1860

red salmon n b1860

roadrunner n b1860

spider plant n b1860

timber wolf n b1860

timberdoodle n *type of bird* b1860

Barbary ape n b1865

Bengal tiger n b1865

big game n b1865

billy goat n b1865

click beetle n b1865

game fish n b1865

inchworm n b1865

jackrabbit n b1865

mamba n *type of snake* b1865

Old World monkey n b1865

protozoan n b1865 (protozoon: b1855; protozoology: b1905)

skewbald n *type of horse* b1865

tsetse fly n b1865

arachnid n b1870

avian adj b1870

canine n b1870 (adj use: b1610)

cattle tick n (Am) b1870

chuckwalla n (Am) b1870

cloven hoof n b1870

coho n b1870

cottontail n (Am) b1870

crocodile bird n b1870

doodlebug n b1870

game bird n b1870

homeothermic adj *warmblooded* b1870

hydrozoan n b1870

Irish setter n b1870

leghorn n b1870

orca n b1870

peeper n *type of frog* b1870

piebald n *motley animal* b1870 ["mongrel": b1765]

pilot whale n b1870

rangy adj *describing animals* b1870 [describing people: b1880]

retriever n b1870

snow leopard n b1870

Tasmanian devil n b1870

walleyed pike n (Am) b1870 (walleye n: b1900)

ant cow n

army ant n

baleen whale n

bullmastiff n

duck call n

hippo n (hippopotamus: b1350)

impala n

jack salmon n

Russian wolfhound n

Siamese cat n

surgeonfish n

tree squirrel n

tree swallow n

Yorkshire terrier n

Weather

fogbound adj b1855

thunderhead n b1855

acid rain n b1860

blizzard n (Am) *snowstorm* b1860 ["violent hit": b1930]

hydrometeor, hydrometeorology n *precipitation* b1860

ice fog n b1860

isobar n b1865

airstream n b1870

precipitate v *rain* b1870

weathercast n b1870

williwaw n *type of storm* b1870

electric storm n

howler n *big storm*

weather map n (Am)

Heavens/Sky

extragalactic adj b1855

globular cluster n b1860

magnetic storm n b1860

midnight sun n b1860

minor planet n b1865

Big Dipper n b1870

celestial pole n b1870

extraterrestrial adj b1870 (noun use: b1960)

island universe n *galaxy* b1870

Milky Way n *our galaxy* b1870 ["the stars above": b1380]

rill n *valley on the moon* b1870

celestial equator n

Science

biochemical adj b1855 (biochemistry: b1885)

energetics n b1855

heliotropism n b1855

nonscience n b1855

pteridology n *the study of ferns* b1855

scientific method n b1855

albedo n *level of surface reflection* b1860

ecology n b1860

evolutionist n b1860

kinetics n b1860 (kinetic: b1855; kinesis: b1905)

nitroglycerin n b1860 (nitro n: b1930)

oceanography n b1860

rhythmics n b1860

seismology n b1860

entropy n b1865

geologic time n b1865

oceanology n (Am) b1865

formaldehyde n b1870

heredity n b1870

heterogeny n *spontaneous generation* b1870

trichology n *study of hair* b1870

apparent magnitude n

biologist n

Brownian motion n

controlled experiment n

cryogen n (cryogenic: b1900)

fourth dimension n

geothermal adj

geotropic, geotropism adj

organic chemistry n

physical anthropology n

psychodynamics n

Technology

technology n b1860 (technological: b1800)

cell n *as in "dry cell battery"* b1870

tube n *as in "radio tube"* b1870 ["TV": b1960]

Energy

conservation of energy n b1855

Coulomb's law n b1855

kerosene n b1855

short circuit n b1855

coal oil n (Am) b1860

motor n *mechanical engine* b1860

shale oil n b1860

gasoline n (Am) b1865 (gas: b1930)

gusher n b1865

propane n 1866

element n *as in "heating element"* b1870

kinetic energy n b1870

short-circuit v b1870 (short v: b1905)

circuit breaker n (Am)

octane n

volt n (voltage: b1890)

Time

proximo adj *next month* b1855

forever n b1860

lunchtime n b1860

weeknight n b1860

Bronze Age n b1865

neolithic adj b1865 [fig. "out of date": b1970] (neolith "stone tool": b1885)

schedule n/v *timetable* b1865

Stone Age n b1865

yesteryear adv/n 1870

ice age n

postbellum adj

year end n (year-end adj: b1900)

Age/Aging

prehistoric adj b1855 (prehistory: b1875; prehistorian: b1895)

elderly n b1865

equaeval adj *contemporary* b1870

junior adj *for kids, as in "junior sizes"* b1870

Mathematics

geometric progression n b1860

prorate v (Am) b1860 (pro rata: b1575)

third dimension n b1860

decimal point n b1865

euclidean geometry n b1865

hexagram n b1865

long dozen n *13* b1865

non-euclidean adj b1865

figure v b1870 (noun use: b1200)

goose egg n *slang zero* b1870

range n b1870

set n b1870

trig n *trigonometry* b1870

aught n

Measurement

geographical mile n b1855
isometric adj *as in "isometric drawing"* b1855
liquid measure n b1855
acreage n b1860
fluid dram n b1860
fluid ounce n b1860
seismograph n b1860 (seismometer: b1845; seismogram: b1895)
telemeter n b1860 (verb use: b1925; telemetry: b1885)
water meter n b1860
ohm n 1861 (ohmmeter: b1890)
calibrate v b1865 (calibration: b1860)
colorimeter n b1865
farad n *unit of measure* b1865
manpower n *akin to horsepower* b1865 ["available workforce": b1930]
metric adj b1865
metric system n b1865
molar adj *related to mass* b1865
pressure gauge n b1865
spectroscope n b1865 (spectroscopy: b1870)
statute mile n b1865
cup n b1870
kilo n b1870
kymograph n *measurer of fluid pressure* b1870
erg n
oscillograph n
spectrometer n

The Body

amniotic fluid n b1855 (amniotic sac: b1885)
bicuspid n b1855
crazy bone n (Am) b1855
diastema n *gap in teeth* b1855
genu n *knee* b1855
middle ear n b1855
periodontal adj b1855
sense organ n b1855
tootsy n *slang foot* b1855
vocal cords n b1855
earlobe n b1860
kisser n *slang mouth* b1860
liver spots n b1860
long bone n b1860
lymph gland n b1860
menorrhea n *menstrual flow*

b1860 (menstruum: b1470; menses: b1600; menstruation: b1800)
rectal adj b1860
tricuspid n *type of tooth* b1860 (adj use: b1670)
tumescence n b1860 (tumescent: b1870; tumesce: b1970)
circulatory system n b1865
collagen n b1865
hemoglobin n b1865
neuromuscular adj b1865
penile adj b1865 (penis: b1680)
snoot n *slang nose* b1865
white cell n b1865 (white corpuscle: b1870; white blood cell: b1885)
booger n b1870
comedo n *blackhead* b1870
gestate v b1870 (gestation: b1615)
innervate v *furnish with nerves* b1870
jism n *slang semen* b1870
kneecap n b1870 ["knee covering": b1660] (kneepan: b1450)
reflex, reflexes n b1870
tummy n b1870
adrenal gland n (adrenalin: b1905)
blood pressure n
bloodstream n
body cavity n
dukes n *slang hands*
menopause n
metabolism n (metabolic: b1845; metabolize: b1890)
scar tissue n

Physical Description

jasm n *energy* b1860
malnutrition n b1865
sashay v (Am) b1865 (noun use: b1900)
sprint n/v *run fast* b1865 [obs. "spring": b1570]
wolf v *eat quickly* b1865
adoze adj b1870
almond-eyed adj b1870
bibulous adj *fond of drink* b1870
bushed adj *exhausted* b1870
defecate v *go to the bathroom* b1870 ["purify": b1500] (defecation: b1830)

exhale v *breathe out* b1870 ["evaporate": b1400; "expel with breath": b1600]
flatulence n *gastric sense* b1870 [fig. "inflation, pomposity": b1715] (flatulent adj: b1600; flatuosity: b1630; flatulency: b1660)
husky adj *burly, strong* b1870
maunder v *talk meanderingly* b1870 [obs. "grouse": b1625 to 1800s]
redhead n b1870
rotund adj *stocky, large* b1870 [gen. "round": b1705]
gangly adj (Am) (gangling: b1810; gangle v: b1970)
halitosis n
hypersensitive adj
jowly adj

Medicine

artificial respiration n b1855
carcinogen n b1855 (carcinoma: b1725; carcinogenesis: b1925; carcinogenic: b1930)
counterirritant n b1855
craniology n b1855 ["phrenology": b1810 to 1800s]
diphteria n b1855
etherize v b1855
germ cell n b1855 (germ: b1645)
hemophilia n b1855 (hemophilic: b1865; hemophiliac: b1900)
painkiller n (Am) b1855
pathogenic adj b1855 (pathogen: b1880)
pinkeye n b1855 [type of potato: b1795]
rose fever n (Am) *type of allergy* b1855
sanitarium n b1855
saturnism n *lead poisoning* b1855
sports medicine n b1855
sunstroke n b1855
writer's cramp n b1855
acupressure n b1860 (acupuncture: b1685)
alcoholism n b1860 (alcoholic n: b1890; alcoholic adj: b1930)
ambulance n *type of vehicle*

b1860 ["mobile hospital": b1810]
arrhythmia n b1860
auscultate v *diagnose by listening to the sounds of the organs* b1860
breakbone fever n b1860
bursitis n b1860
capsule n b1860
colitis n b1860
croaker *slang doctor* b1860
diagnose v b1860
double vision n b1860
DTs n b1860
epidemiology n b1860
false pregnancy n b1860
fever blister n b1860
mental deficiency n b1860
oncology n *study of tumors* b1860
paresthesia n *skin sensation without apparent cause* b1860
partial denture n b1860
physiatrics n b1860 (physiatry: b1940; physiatrist: b1950)
postnatal adj b1860 (postpartum: b1850)
pseudopregnancy n b1860
rheumatoid arthritis n b1860
therapeusis n *arch. therapeutics* b1860
traumatism n b1860
tuberculosis n b1860 (tuberculosed adj: b1900)
alienist n *psychiatrist* b1865
bedsore n b1865
blood poisoning n b1865
dermatologist n b1865
dialysis, dialyze n, v b1865 [in logic: b1550]
dwarfism n b1865
endoscope n b1865
foot-and-mouth disease n b1865
heart disease n b1865
Hodgkin's disease n b1865
hypodermic adj b1865 (noun use: b1875)
urethroscope n b1865
aphasia n *speech loss* b1870
bedside manner n b1870
bicarbonate of soda n b1870
calmative n/adj b1870
cardiograph n b1870 (cardiogram: b1880)
cholic n b1870

cocaine n b1870 (cocainize: b1890)

colostomy n b1870

defervescence n *fever subsiding* b1870

degree n *as in "third-degree burns"* b1870

diagnostician n b1870

embolism n b1870

emphysema n *describing lung disease* b1870

expectant adj *expecting* b1870

gastralgia n b1870

hurt v *feel pain* b1870 ["cause pain": b1200]

hyperactive adj b1870 (hyperactivity: b1890; hyper: b1975)

hypodermic injection n b1870

induce v *as in "induce labor"* b1870

muscular dystrophy n b1870

myalgia n *muscle pain* b1870

obstetrix n *midwife* b1870

ocularist n *maker of artificial eyes* b1870 (oculist: b1600)

plate n *type of denture* b1870

rally n/v *recover from illness* b1870

stretcher n *litter* b1870

trichinosis n b1870

turn v *as in "turn your ankle"* b1870

upset n/v *as in "stomach upset"* b1870

20/20 adj

abortionist n

achy adj

agoraphobia n

analgesic n

anorexia nervosa n

bed rest n

clinician n

eyecup n (Am)

eyestrain n

fibrosis n

germ theory n

gingivitis n

heatstroke n

hypodermic n *type of treatment* [the needle itself: b1895] (adj use: b1865)

skin graft n

sleeping sickness n

Everyday Life

abrasive n b1855 (adj use: b1875)

bassinet n b1855 [obs. type of flower: b1600 to 1700s]

combination lock n b1855

commode n *type of toilet* b1855 [type of furniture: b1770]

curio n b1855

davenport n *writing desk* b1855 ["couch": b1905]

end table n (Am) b1855

flatware n b1855

headrest n b1855

homey adj b1855

ice pack n b1855

mopboard n b1855

packsack n (Am) b1855

slop jar n b1855

stein n b1855

stockpot n b1855

toilet water n b1855

vesuvian n *type of match* b1855

women's room n b1855

backrest n b1860

breadboard n b1860

bulb n *as in "light bulb"* b1860

ditty bag n b1860

dog biscuit n b1860

drinking fountain n b1860

finger bowl n b1860

lead glass n b1860

paperweight n b1860

pepper mill n b1860

pillow lace n b1860

rummage sale n b1860

safety pin n b1860

Saratoga trunk n (Am) *type of traveling trunk* b1860

sponge bath n b1860

spring cleaning n b1860

swivel chair n b1860

tire iron n b1860

can v *store in cans* b1865

cozy n b1865

gunnysack n b1865 (gunny: b1730)

handbag n b1865

hibachi n b1865

houseclean/housecleaning v b1865

kitchen midden n *"refuse heap"* b1865

lunchbox n b1865

safety match n b1865

steam table n b1865

Turkish towel n b1865

vinyl n b1865

wood alcohol n b1865

accident insurance n b1870

baby carriage n b1870

birdhouse n (Am) b1870

blender n b1870

briar n *type of smoking pipe* b1870

comforter n *type of quilt* b1870 [type of scarf: b1830] (comfortable n: b1870)

deadlock n *deadbolt* b1870

deodorant n b1870 (deoderize: b1860)

dip v *use snuff or chewing tobacco* b1870

doily n *type of ornamentation* b1870 [type of napkin: b1800] (adj use: b1680)

driveway n (Am) b1870

excelsior n (Am) b1870

form n *something to be filled out* b1870

junk n *trash* b1870 [obs. "bad rope": b1490 to 1700s; type of shipboard food: b1770] (verb use: b1920)

ladies' room n b1870

lampshade n b1870

lights-out n b1870

match n *m lighting fires* b1870 [obs. "wick": b1400 to 1600s; type of fuse: b1550]

matchbox n b1870

perambulator n *baby buggy* b1870

pipe cleaner n b1870

queue n *line* b1870 ["hair worn in pigtail": b1750] (verb use: b1930)

rocker n *rocking chair, rocking horse* b1870

stamp n *as in "postage stamp"* b1870

straw n *drinking device* b1870

tête-à-tête n *type of sofa* b1870

top n *stopper, as in "bottle top"* b1870

batting n *quilt lining* (batt: b1830)

cachepot n *flowerpot holder*

denture n (denturist: b1965)

dishpan n (Am)

doorstop n (Am)

exhaust fan n

manila paper n

milk glass n

safety razor n (Am)

student lamp n (Am)

tea towel n

white goods n

Shelter/Housing

baseboard n (Am) b1855

cloakroom n b1855

doorframe n b1855

family room n b1855

headroom n b1855

recreation room n b1855 (rec room: b1965)

solarium n b1855 ["sundial": b1820]

air lock n b1860

dance hall n (Am) b1860

drainpipe n b1860

foyer n b1860

life belt n *life preserver* b1860

roadhouse n b1860

roofline n b1860

tenement house n b1860

concourse n *as in "airport concourse"* b1865

entranceway n (Am) b1865

lake dwelling n b1865

linoleum n b1865

mess hall n b1865

pup tent n (Am) b1865

ranch house n (Am) b1865 (ranch-style adj: b1965)

shelter tent n (Am) b1865

throne room n b1865

annex n *building* b1870 ["appendix of a document": b1670]

carbarn n b1870

center n *building/area, as in "center of commerce"* b1870

coatroom n b1870

crib n *pad* b1870

cubiculum n *arch. bedroom* b1870

domestic science n b1870

floor plan n b1870

Gothic revival n b1870

life jacket n b1870

lift n *elevator* b1870

orphanage n b1870 [obs. "caring for orphans": b1540 to 1700s; "state of being an orphan": b1600]

Bad English

One of the tenets of English is that, ultimately, commonness of usage determines whether a new word is a "real" word. Every word we speak was at one time new, and if enough people use it and understand it, newness fades and the word is accepted among its peers.

This isn't always true, of course. Some words just ain't welcome, as they say—*ain't* being high on the list of the unwelcome.

Ain't, say the purists, is bad because technically it is not a contraction. *Aren't* contracts "are not," yet no one says "I ai not." For that matter, no one says "I amn't," either. Disdaining *ain't* on a technicality seems odd from speakers of a language that still allows such irregular word conjugations as *be/is/am/are/were*. If there's no *are* in *were*, why must there be an *are* in *ain't*? And the people who decry such "bad" grammar as "Hopefully, I'll get a raise" have no compunction about saying "Gratefully, I never misuse hopefully"— even though *gratefully* in the second phrase is used the same way *hopefully* is in the first.

Besides, some bad grammar has been around too long to be dismissed entirely. For example:

- *Hisself*. Men have been referring to "hisself" since before 1200.

- *Invite* as a noun. "Send him an invite" sounds so backwoods—but the woods were likely in England, as this noun was in use by 1660.

- *Eats* as a noun. A bit earlier than *invite* as a noun— in use by 1100.

- *Irregardless*. People carp about this lengthening of *regardless* as a recent corruption. It's been in use since 1915, irregardless of what people think.

- *Learn* as a synonym of *teach*. Would it surprise you if I learned you that *learn* has been used as a transitive verb since Middle English?

- *Loan* as a synonym of *lend*. The fact that this word, too, has been used as a transitive verb since Middle English loans it some credibility.

- *Persuade* as a synonym of *convince*. Purists remain unpersuaded of this usage, even though it's been around since before 1530.

- *Preventative*. Despite preventive strikes against this word ballooning, people have been preventating since before 1670.

- *Hopefully*. This word's literal meaning of "in a hopeful manner" was first recorded before 1630. The meaning of "it is hoped that," which purists will hopefully accept someday, is indeed relatively new—in use by 1930. And fortunately, people have been using such nonliteral interpretations of adverbs for many many years—for example, "fortunately" in this sentence has been used in this sense since before 1550.

- *Ongoing* as a modern monstrosity. Modern? Perhaps, if you think that being in use by 1860 is modern. Monstrosity? No more so than the adjective *incoming* (by 1755—and by 1325 as a noun), the verb *outgo* (by 1530), or the more common verb *uplift* (by 1300) and other words constructed by the same mechanism we used to create *ongoing*.

- *Impact* and *access* as verbs. Such usages impact purists right in the jaw. As well it should. Technically, *impact* as a verb has been with us since before 1605—as in "impacted tooth." The more modern sense surfaced before 1920 in its literal sense and before 1935 in its figurative sense. *Access* as a verb has no pedigree, however, as it first surfaced around 1965. *Contact* has been with us as a verb since before 1840 in the sense of "cause to touch." The figurative sense of "get in touch with" was in use by 1930.

- *Ax* as a variant of *ask*. Disdain of this usage flared in the flap about Ebonics (what some called "Black English") some years ago. "Pure" English speakers pointed out that if you're axing questions, you're grammatically incorrect. These days, yes, but *ax* was once an accepted variant, and only these days is it considered dialect.

- *Reckon*, similarly less common than in days previous. What sounds so colloquial in the United States is very much in the British mainstream, and has been with us since before 1300.

- *Like* used as a conjunction. The biggest controversy about cigarette advertising in the '60s seemed to be that cigarettes caused bad grammar, not lung cancer. "Winston tastes good like a cigarette should" was declared illiterate, though *like*'s use in this way has been around longer than cigarettes—in use by 1400.

And finally . . .

- *Ain't*. It ain't that new—it was in use by 1780.

pent-roof n *shed roof* b1870

protectory n *shelter for homeless children* b1870 (obs. adj use: b1660)

register v *announce hotel arrival* b1870

shelterbelt n *akin to greenbelt* b1870

stadium n b1870 [type of distance measure: b1470; "stadium-length race course": b1630]

subdivision n *housing development* b1870

trap n *type of plumbing feature* b1870 (verb use: b1400)

apartment house/apartment building n (Am)

boardwalk n (Am)

facility n *as in "health care facility"*

hideout n

homestead v (noun use: b975)

lockbox n (Am)

roomer n (Am)

sanitary ware n *ceramic plumbing*

summer kitchen n

woodworking, woodworker n

Drink

cream soda n (Am) b1855

home brew n b1855

shandygaff n (Brit) *type of drink* b1855 (shandy: b1890)

Turkish coffee n b1855

bock n b1860

condensed milk n b1860

macon n *type of wine* b1865

tarantula-juice n (Am) *bad booze* b1865

bourbon n b1870

collins n *type of drink* b1870

evaporated milk n b1870

gamay n *type of wine* b1870

gingerade n b1870

granita n *type of drink* b1870

heavy wet n *type of alcohol* b1870

hooker n *type of drink* b1870

popskull n (Am) *slang rotgut* b1870

slug v *drink quickly* b1870 (noun use: b1765)

sour n (Am) *type of drink* b1870 (verb use: b1400)

straight adj *without mix, as in "vodka straight"* b1870

zinfandel n *type of wine* b1870

brewer's yeast n

moonshine n *illegally created liquor* ["smuggled liquor": b1785] (verb use: b1900; moonshiner: b1860)

Food

Boston baked beans n (Am) b1855

bouillabaisse n b1855

butterscotch n b1855

cider vinegar n b1855

cornstarch n (Am) b1855

fryer n b1855

greenstuff n *green foodstuff* b1855

grenadine n *type of syrup* b1855

kraut n *sauerkraut* b1855

kuchen n *type of coffee cake* b1855

liver sausage n b1855

lolly n (Brit) *candy* b1855

long pig n *cannibalized human flesh* b1855

quick bread n b1855

salami n b1855

schnitzel n (Am) b1855

scrapple n (Am) b1855

self-rising flour n (Am) b1855

tartar sauce n b1855

water chestnut n b1855

wishbone n b1855

wurst n b1855

appetizer n b1860

beer and skittles n b1860

Brunswick stew n b1860

chipped beef n b1860

chow n (Am) *slang food* b1860 (verb use: b1920; chowchow: b1795)

cobbler n b1860

corn pone n (Am) b1860

frangipane n *type of dessert* b1860

frosting n b1860

gumdrop n (Am) b1860

half shell n (Am) b1860

pomelo n b1860

safflower oil n b1860

sucrose n b1860

Valencia orange n b1860

Boston cream pie n (Am) b1865

bottle-feed v b1865

brown Betty n (Am) *apple pudding* b1865

button mushroom n b1865

cottage pudding n b1865

eclair n b1865

fructose n b1865

malt sugar n b1865

pate n *pastry* b1865

soda pop n (Am) b1865

store cheese n *cheddar cheese* b1865

blood sausage n b1870

Brie n *the cheese* b1870

cereal n *breakfast cereal* b1870 ["grain": b1835]

coleslaw n b1870 (cold slaw: b1795)

enchilada n b1870

fondue n b1870

Gouda n b1870

goulash n b1870

gum n *chewing gum* b1870

hollandaise n b1870

liverwurst n (Am) b1870

mincemeat n b1870 (minced meat: b1580)

palm sugar n b1870

salsa n b1870

sesame oil n b1870

sowbelly n b1870

spaghetti n b1870

Turkish delight n b1870

bird's nest soup n

foodstuff n

French toast n

granola n

jambalaya n (Am)

marble cake n (Am)

margarine n (Am) (margarin "source of margarine" b1870; marge: b1930)

oleomargarine n (oleo: b1885)

oyster cracker n

pasta n (pastina: b1950)

Peking duck n

vanilla bean n

Agriculture/Food-Gathering

bullwhip n (Am) b1855

cow horse n (Am) b1855 (cow pony: b1875)

cowhand n (Am) b1855

domestic animal n b1855 (domesticate n: b1955)

fisherfolk n b1855

grain elevator n b1855

hen fruit n (Am) *eggs* b1855

barn raising n b1860

chum n/v (Am) *bait* b1860

crossbred adj b1860

feedstuff n (Am) b1860

field corn n (Am) b1860

field crop n b1860

pisciculture n *raising fish* b1860

barbed wire n b1865

fish farm n b1865

harness horse n b1865

holstein n b1865

rosarian n *rose grower* b1865

sheep-dip n b1865

vet n *vet(erinarian)* b1865

veterinary n b1865

aquiculture n b1870

cash crop n (Am) b1870

chip n *as in "cowchips"* b1870

maverick n (Am) *type of calf* b1870 ["independent person": b1900]

purebred adj b1870

rosarium n *rose garden* b1870

rotate v *alternate crops* b1870

terraculture n b1870

truck farm n (Am) b1870

live trap n

mixed farming n

sheeperder n (Am) (shepherd: b1050)

snow fence n (Am)

viniculture n *wine-making*

Cloth/Clothing

bloomer n (Am) *as in "bloomers"* b1855 (bloomers: b1895)

blue jeans n b1855

chesterfield n *type of overcoat* b1855

coatdress n b1855

grass cloth n b1855

insole n b1855

sandshoe n *tennis shoe* b1855

sharkskin n b1855

black tie n b1860 (adj use: b1935)

earflap n b1860 (earlap: b1000)

earmuff n (Am) b1860

hoopskirt n (Am) b1860
hug-me-tight n (Am) *type of women's jacket* b1860
khaki adj/n *pertaining to the color and the cloth* b1860 (khakis: b1970)
kneepad n b1860
lockstitch n b1860
loincloth n b1860
overclothes n b1860 (overgarment: b1475)
tailored adj b1860
weskit n b1860
bowler n *the hat* b1865
espadrille n *type of shoe* b1865
garibaldi n b1865
inverness n *type of coat* b1865
plug hat n *type of hat* b1865
reversible n b1865
shepherd's check n *type of pattern* b1865
underskirt n b1865
arctic n *a type of overshoe* b1870
bathing cap n b1870
boa n b1870
business suit n b1870
cardigan n b1870
denims n *jeans* b1870
derby n (Am) b1870
drag n *transvestite's clothes* b1870 (adj use: b1890)
fagoting n *type of embroidery* b1870
faille n *type of fabric* b1870 [obs. type of hood: b1530 to 1600s]
G-string n (Am) b1870 [musical sense: b1870]
herringbone n b1870
jeans n b1870 (jean "denim": b1580)
lap robe n (Am) b1870
material n b1870
mukluk n (Am) *type of boot* b1870
nude adj *naked* b1870 [obs. "plain, obvious": b1530 to 1600s] (noun use: b1710)
outfit n b1870
rags n *slang clothes* b1870
rubbers n *galoshes* b1870
seat n b1870 ["sitting place": b1200; "buttocks": b1630]
tutu n b1870

waders n b1870
crepe de chine n *type of fabric*
godet n *clothing term*
nightie n (nightgown: b1400)
shirttail n
tuque n
underwear n
wing tip n

Fashion/Style
fashion plate n b1855
spiffy adj b1855 (spiffing adj: b1865; spiff v: b1880)
chic n b1860 (adj use: b1865)
face poser n *type of makeup* b1860
frangipani n *type of perfume* b1865
frizzy adj b1865 (frizzly: b1710)
muttonchops n b1865
up-to-date adj b1865
boutonniere n b1870
makeup n *using cosmetics* b1870 ["cosmetics": b1900]
redo v *redecorate* b1870
uptown adj *upscale* b1870
brilliantine n (Am) *hair dressing*
burnsides n (Am) *sideburns*
demode adj *declasse* (demoded: b1890)
ponytail n

Tools
emery wheel n b1855
scroll saw n b1855
Archimedes' screw n b1860
bucksaw n (Am) b1860
buzz saw n (Am) b1860
carpet sweeper n (Am) b1860
eyewash n b1860
foghorn n b1860
gavel n (Am) b1860 [type of mallet: b1805] (verb use: b1925)
gyroscope n b1860
incubator n b1860
lightning arrester n b1860
microtome n b1860
monkey wrench n b1860
putty knife n b1860
rocker arm n b1860
roller bearing n b1860

sand v *use sandpaper* b1860
shim n *type of wedge* b1860
whisk broom n b1860
aerator n b1865
atomizer n *sprayer* b1865 (atomize: b1850)
band saw n (Am) b1865
cherry picker n b1865
drill press n (Am) b1865
drop hammer n b1865
fretsaw n b1865
fuller n *type of hammer* b1865 (verb use: b1820)
headlight n (Am) b1865 (headlamp: b1885)
ice pick n b1865
locknut n b1865
machine v b1865
machine tool n b1865
slop pail n b1865
dynamite n 1867 [fig. use: b1930] (verb use: b1885)
typewriter n (Am) 1868 (typewrite: b1885)
Bunsen burner n b1870
buttonhook n b1870
distributor n b1870
dumpcart n (Am) b1870
key n *as in "typewriter key"* b1870 [as in "piano key": b1500]
keyboard n *as in "typewriter keyboard"* b1870 [as in "piano keyboard": b1820] (verb use: b1965)
lawn mower n b1870
lever n *type of control device* b1870 [type of pry: b1300] (verb use: b1870)
relay n *type of circuit* b1870
rig n *as in "oil rig"* b1870
rucksack n b1870
seeder n b1870
steamroller n b1870 [fig. "juggernaut": b1900] (steamroll: b1880)
time lock n b1870
tumbler n *part of a lock* b1870
adding machine n
binocular n (binoculars: b1880)
extension ladder n
gearwheel n
inkwell n
jigsaw n/v
nail file n
paper clip n
pipe wrench n

rangefinder n
sandblast n (verb use: b1890)
scope n *as in "microscope"*

Travel/Transportation
brougham n *type of carriage* b1855
crankshaft n b1855
hangar n b1855 [rare use: b1700] (verb use: b1945)
round-trip n (Am) b1855
side road n b1855
square-rigger n b1855
sternwheeler n (Am) b1855 (sternwheel: b1830)
turnoff n *road outlet* b1855
wanderlust n b1855
zip v *as in "zip along"* b1855
ahorse adj/adv *on horseback* b1860
boxcar n (Am) b1860
commuter n (Am) b1860 (commute v: b1890; commute n: b1955)
hayride n (Am) b1860
mount n *horse* b1860 (verb use: b1570)
muffler n b1860
parlor car n b1860
safety belt n b1860
sharpie n (Am) *type of boat* b1860
shunpike n (Am) b1860
surfboat n b1860
wagonette n b1860
caboose n *train car* b1865 ["ship's kitchen": b1750]
carburetor, carburetion n b1865 (carburet v: b1870)
chuck wagon n b1865
corner v b1865
double-ender n *type of boat* b1865
flatcar n (Am) b1865
mush v *used with dogsled* b1865 (noun use: b1905)
portage v b1865
stopover n b1865
streetcar n (Am) b1865
touch down v b1865
two-wheeler n b1865
artery n *major thoroughfare* b1870
automobile n b1870 (adj use: b1870; automotive: b1900; automobility: b1905)

aviation n b1870 (aviate, aviator: b1890; aviatrix: b1920)

bicycle n/v b1870 (bike: b1885)

bridge n *on a ship* b1870

connection, connect n, v *transfer* b1870

conning tower n b1870

elevated railway n (Am) b1870 (elevated n: b1885; el: b1910)

freighter n b1870 ["person who moves freight": b1625]

hitch v *hitchhike* b1870 (hitchhike: b1925)

intersection n b1870

itinerary n *plan of travel* b1870 ["route": b1425]

jet propulsion n b1870

junction n *crossing* b1870 ["act of joining": b1715]

main n *main railroad line* b1870

monocycle n *unicycle* b1870

park v *as in "park a car"* b1870

picketboat n b1870

Pullman n *type of railroad car* b1870

reaction engine n b1870

rig n b1870

roadwork n b1870

Rob Roy n *type of canoe* b1870

roundhouse n *locomotive switcher* b1870

schoon n *move like a schooner* b1870

screw n *type of propeller* b1870

sinuate v *travel windingly* b1870

spinnaker n *type of sail* b1870

touristy adj b1870

trawler n *type of boat* b1870

trucker n b1870 (truck-driver: b1895)

unicycle n (Am) b1870

aeroplane n [obs. "aerofoil": b1870 to 1900s]

air brake n (Am)

biplane n

cable car n (Am)

hit the road v (hit the bricks: b1935)

hydraulic brake n

icebreaker n (Am) *fig. ship* [fig. use: b1900]

lakeport n (Am)

paddleboat n

rapid transit n (Am)

rule of the road n

standard gauge n

Emotions/ Characteristics

berserk adj b1855 (noun use "type of warrior": b1820; berserker: b1825)

jimjams n *nervousness* b1855

stressful adj b1855

wax n (Brit) *anger* b1855

wide-eyed adj b1855

hedonism n b1860 (hedonic: b1660; hedonist: b1825)

perfervid adj *fervent* b1860

sidesplitting adj b1860

standoffish adj b1860 (stand-off adj: b1840)

acerbic adj b1865 (acerbity: b1575)

blue funk n b1865

choosy adj (Am) b1865

choppy adj *fickle* b1865

elan n b1865

emotionless adj b1865

felicific adj *happy-making* b1865

pouty adj (Am) b1865

self-assertive adj b1865

self-fulfillment n b1865

snippety adj *snappish* b1865

tactful adj b1865

alarmism n b1870 (alarmist: b1800)

amok n *gen. frenzy* b1870 ["a Malaysian in a frenzy": b1670] (adv use: b1675; adj use: b1945)

anserine adj *silly* b1870

apologetic adj b1870 ["vindicating": b1650] (apology, apologize: b1600)

beamish adj b1870

bighearted adj b1870

chauvinism n *patriotism* b1870 ["sexism": b1970]

edgy adj *nervous* b1870 ["phys. sharp": b1775]

erotomania n b1870

expressionless adj b1870 ["unexpressed": b1835]

fresh adj *impudent* b1870

gush v *speak gushingly* b1870 (gushy: b1845)

heart-to-heart adj b1870 (noun use: b1910)

hehe v b1870 (interj use: b1150)

het up adj *excited, heated up* b1870

hilarity n b1870 ["peaceful joy": b1440] (hilarious: b1825)

infuriation n b1870 (infuriate: b1670)

kick n *fig. "shock, thrill," as in "getting your kicks"* b1870

morale n *attitude* b1870 ["morals": b1755] (moral n: b1900)

morbid adj *dark, funereal* b1870 ["diseased": b1660] (morbidity: b1725)

picky adj b1870

self-conscious adj *feeling awkward* b1870 ["self-aware": b1680]

self-dependence n b1870 (self-dependent: b1700)

shifty adj *pejorative sense* b1870 [gen. "resourceful": b1570]

snotty adj *uppity* b1870

stick-to-it-iveness n b1870

unfazed adj b1870

upset adj *angry* b1870

weathercockism n *fickleness* b1870

chortle v 1871 (noun use: b1905)

even-tempered adj

frustrating adj

indeterminism n *theory of human action*

puckish adj

self-actualize v (self-actualization: b1940)

self-realization n

uppity adj (Am)

weltschmerz n

Thoughts/Perception/ The Mind

absent-minded adj b1855

ethos n b1855

hindsight n b1855

intuit v b1855 ["teach": b1780] (intuition: b1600)

objective adj *unbiased* b1855 [obs. "related to objects": 1600s only]

objectivism n b1855

philosophy of life n b1855

positivism n b1855

senile dementia n b1855 (senile: b1870)

epistemology n *type of philosophy* b1860

mnemonic n *memory device* b1860

worldview n b1860

logistics n b1865

mixed-up adj b1865

psychosomatic adj *related to mind and body* b1865 ["bodily effects caused by the mind": b1970] (noun use: b1940)

brain wave n b1870

catharsis n b1870 ["cleansing": b1775] (cathartic: b1615)

epiphany n *sudden idea* b1870 (epiphanic: b1955)

expertise n b1870 (expertize v: b1900)

fascination n b1870 ["spell-casting": b1605; "ability to fascinate": b1700]

mentality n b1870

perceptive adj *discerning, wise* b1870 ["able to perceive": b1660]

perspective n *point of view* b1870

psychotherapy n b1870 (psychotherapeutics: b1875)

reason with v b1870

recognize v *come to understand* b1870

reminiscent adj *reminding one of something else* b1870

senile adj *mentally decrepit* b1870 ["related to agedness": b1665] (senility: b1780)

visuality n *mental picture* b1870 ["ability to see": b1930]

will v *make happen by force of will* b1870

creativity n (creativeness: b1830)

egoistic hedonism n

extrapolate v [obs. "delete": b1835]

fair-minded adj
mull v *ponder* [lit. "grind over": b1470]
neurotic adj (noun use: b1900; neuroticism: b1900)
passivism n
psychotherapeutics n
solipsism n
trappy adj *tricky, devious*
willpower n

Love/Romance/Sex

coitus n b1855 (coite: b1425; coition: b1615)
dot n *dowry* b1855
fiancé, fiancée n b1855
monandry n *monogamy for women* b1855
other woman n b1855
Cupid's bow n b1860
girlfriend n b1860 (girl: b1670)
hitched b1860
exogamy n *marriage outside tribe* b1865
loved one n b1865
agape n *nonerotic love* b1870 [type of feast: b1630]
baby n *term of endearment* b1870 (babe: b1930)
cocotte n *type of prostitute* b1870
gamahuche n/v *oral sex* b1870
lesbianism n b1870 (lesbian adj/n: b1900)
poke v *slang have sex* b1870 (noun use: b1905)
prenuptial adj b1870
tail n *slang sex* b1870 (verb use: b1780)
masher n *flirt* (mash v: b1880)

Family/Relations/Friends

ancestor worship n b1855
mater n (Brit) *mother* b1860
parenthood n b1860
sororal adj b1860
big brother n *older brother* b1865
godparent n b1865 (godfather: b1000)
spear adj *opp. of distaff* b1865

trilling n *triplet* b1870
kinfolk n (kinsfolk: b1475; kinspeople: b1800)
quintuplet n (quint: b1935)

Holidays

jamboree n (Am) b1865
jubilance n b1865
holiday v b1870 (noun use: b950)
jack-o-lantern n b1870 [obs. "night watchman": b1665 to 1700s; "swamp fire": b1700]
legal holiday n (Am) b1870
national park n (Am) b1870
reception n *as in "wedding reception"* b1870
bank holiday n

Games/Fun/Leisure

penny ante n (Am) b1855 (penny-ante adj: b1870)
rag doll n b1855
three-card monte n (Am) b1855
cardsharp/cardsharper n (Am) b1860
croquet n b1860
pool table n b1860
sack race n b1860
baby doll n b1865
baccarat n b1865
gag n *joke* b1865 ["prank": b1805] (verb use: b1780)
philatelist, philately n b1865
pinochle n (Am) b1865
poolroom n b1865
skat n b1865
straight poker n b1865
stud poker n (Am) b1865 (studhorse poker: b1860)
bagatelle n b1870 ["trifle": b1635]
balloon n *child's toy* b1870 [obs. "tetherball": b1580 to 1800s; obs. type of firework: b1630 to 1800s]
block n *type of child's toy* b1870
chip n/v *as in "poker chips"* b1870
collect v *as in "collect stamps"* b1870 [gen. use: b1425]
escape n *e.g., a fantasy, a hobby* b1870
mallet n *in croquet* b1870
old maid n b1870

play v *as in "play your cards"* b1870
pool n *billiards* b1870
royal flush n b1870
Simon says n b1870
tic-tac-toe n b1870
tricycle n b1870 [rare type of coach: b1830]
badminton n [type of drink: b1840]
parlor game n
ringtoss n (Am)

Sports

basketry n b1855
clay court n b1855
figure skating n b1855 (figure v: b1775; figure eight: b1890)
sport adj b1855
captain n b1860
goalpost n b1860
gymnasiast n *gymnast* b1860 (gymnast: b1595)
Indian club n b1860
jig n/v *as in "fishing jigs"* b1860
jujitsu n b1860
racetrack n b1860
rematch v b1860 (noun use: b1945)
spectate v *watch a spectator sport* b1860 [gen. "watch": b1730]
stock car n b1860
coach n b1865 ["tutor": b1850]
equestrienne n b1865 (equestrian: b1795)
grand prix n b1865
jumping jack n (Am) b1865
roller skate n (Am) b1865
rugby n b1865
touchdown n *football score* b1865 ["landing": b1970]
black belt n b1870
breaststroke n b1870
caving n *spelunking* b1870
corner n *in boxing* b1870
dribble v b1870 (noun use: b1900)
glaciarium n *type of skating rink* b1870
lap n/v *once around the track* b1870
misplay n (Am) b1870 (verb use: b1970)
parallel bars n b1870

pitcher n *baseball player* b1870
plate n b1870
referee n b1870 [gen. use: b1615] (verb use: b1890)
ringside n b1870
run n *score* b1870
scratch n/v *sink a cue ball; withdraw* b1870
spinning rod n b1870 (spinning reel: b1950)
straight n *straight part of a racecourse* b1870 (straightaway: b1880)
strike n *in bowling and baseball* b1870
throw v *lose on purpose* b1870
track n *course for runners, horses* b1870 [gen. "track and field sports": b1930]
broad jump n
gym n (gymnasium: b1600)
lawn tennis n
middleweight n (adj use: b1930)
trapshooter, trapshooting n (trap n: b1830)
vaulting horse n

Professions/Duties

forty-niner n b1855
occupational adj b1855
road agent n b1855
scrimshander n *scrimshaw maker* b1855
bar girl n b1860
caretaker n b1860
contortionist n b1860
costumer n (Am) b1860
doorman n b1860
enumerator n *census taker* b1860
gas fitter n b1860
mixologist n (Am) b1860 (mixology: b1950)
ragpicker n b1860
railsplitter n b1860
shantyman n *lumberjack* b1860
shipping clerk n b1860
shirtmaker n b1860
stationmaster n (Am) b1860
bouncer n *bar guard* b1865 ["braggart": b1760]
cattleman n (Am) b1865
coordinator n b1865
laundrywoman n b1865 (laundryman: b1710)

mailman n b1865
newsdealer n b1865
night watchman n b1865
tracklayer n (Am) b1865
yardmaster n b1865
aide n (Am) *assistant* b1870
[mil. sense: b1780]
conservationist n b1870
hygienist n b1870
interior decorator n b1870
(interior decoration:
b1810; interior designer:
b1940)
mule skinner n b1870
private detective n b1870
roustabout n (Am) b1870
sanitary engineering n b1870
servitress n b1870 (servitor:
b1350; servitrix: b1570)
shingle n *type of professional
sign* b1870
handyman n
junkman n (Am)
newsy n *newspaper dealer*
repairman n
scrubwoman n
sleuth n [obs. "trail": b1350
to 1400s] (verb use:
b1900)

Business/Commerce/ Selling

cash on delivery n b1855
entrepreneur n *businessperson*
b1855 [spec. type of musical organizer: b1830]
job lot n b1855
merchant marine n b1855
American plan n b1860
blind tiger n *speakeasy* b1860
charcuterie n *pork store*
b1860
Gresham's law n *economic theory* b1860
hock n *pawn* b1860 (verb
use: b1880)
pay adj *as in "pay toilet"*
b1860
pub n b1860
saleslady n (Am) b1860
shopper n *one who shops*
b1860
brasserie n *type of restaurant*
b1865
gin mill n (Am) b1865
grubstake n (Am) b1865
(verb use: b1880)

receivables n b1865
trade name n b1865
cannery n (Am) b1870
carry v *keep in stock* b1870
club n *as in "nightclub"*
b1870
drum n *cathouse, tavern*
b1870
futures n b1870
hash house n (Am) b1870
(hash slinger: b1870; hash
joint: b1895)
jerry shop n *public house*
b1870
lunch counter n b1870
mail order n (Am) b1870
(mail order house: b1910)
order n *as in "place an order"*
b1870 (verb use: b1770)
refund n b1870
regular n *regular customer*
b1870
special n *as in "blue plate special"* b1870
bucket shop n (Am) *saloon
where alcohol is served in
buckets and other containers*
dive n *dumpy drinking establishment*
guildsman n
hockshop n
list price n
mercantilism n

The Workplace

goldbrick n (Am) b1855
(verb use: b1905)
hard labor n b1855
headhunter n b1855 (head-
hunt v: b1970)
lockout n b1855
workingwoman n b1855
minimum wage n b1860
picket line n b1860
industrial n b1865
industrialist n b1865
nonunion adj b1865
grind n/v *hard work* b1870
labor n *workingpeople* b1870
labor union n b1870
lock out v *mainly in the employee relations sense* b1870
picket v b1870
report v *sign in* b1870 [as in
"report to the boss":
b1900]
sweatshop n b1870

workful adj *dedicated to work*
b1870
company store n (Am)
day shift n
lifework n
time card n (Am)
union card n (Am)

Finances/Money

call loan n b1855
capitalism n b1855 (capitalist n: b1795)
dough n *cash* b1855
first mortgage n b1855
stake v *savings* b1855
billionaire n (Am) b1860
buck n *dollar* b1860
century n (Am) *slang $100*
b1860
dollar sign n (Am) b1860
tycoon n b1860
fractional currency n (Am)
change from your dollar
b1865
gold certificate n (Am)
b1865
greenback n (Am) b1865
monetary unit n b1865
revenue stamp n b1865
stock certificate n b1865
William n (Am) *dollar bill*
b1865
affordable adj b1870
cashier's check n (Am)
b1870
corner n *as in "a corner of the
market"* b1870
fiat money n b1870
fin n (Am) *five-dollar bill*
b1870
finance v *supply money* b1870
["ransom": b1620; "work
in finance": b1830]
gold reserve n (Am) b1870
kite v *as in "kite a check"*
b1870 (noun use: b1830)
monkey n *slang $500* b1870
nickel n *five cents, but once
meant one cent* b1870
overdraft n b1870
roll n *as in "bankroll"* b1870
royalty n b1870
thou n *thousand* b1870
arbitrage n *type of stock dealing* [arch. "arbitration":
b1490] (verb use: b1900;
arbitrageur: b1870)

expense account n
yen n *Japanese monetary unit*

Language and Speaking

braille n/v b1855
futhark, futhorc n *runic alphabet* b1855
pictograph, pictography n
b1855 (pictogram: b1910)
platitudinarian n b1855
wordplay n b1855
argot n b1860
euphemize v b1860
punctuation mark n b1860
quotation mark n b1860
rhyming slang n b1860
verbicide n b1860
dialectology n b1865
gesture language n b1865
tilde n b1865
antonym n b1870
blither v/n b1870 (blithering: b1900)
British English n b1870
grammar n *linguistic rules*
b1870 ["study of gram-
mar": b1375]
modifier n b1870 (modify:
b1730)
phonetic adj b1870
phonics n b1870 [obs. "gen.
study of sounds": b1685 to
1800s]
question mark n b1870
reflexive, reflexive pronoun n
b1870
shriekmark n *!* b1870
loanword n

Contractions

doesn't contr b1860
it'll contr b1860
we're contr b1865
'cept conj/prep b1870

Literature/Writing

cameo n b1855
card catalog n (Am) b1855
checklist n (Am) b1855
erotica n b1855
folktale n b1855
funny/funnies n b1855
graffito/graffiti n b1855
headnote n b1855
science fiction n b1855
stream of consciousness n
b1855
writer's cramp n b1855

booklet n b1860
Boswell n *chronicler* b1860
clothbound adj *hardcover* b1860
dramaturge n b1860
editorialize v (Am) b1860 (editorialist: b1905)
rose pink n *flowery writing* b1860
script n *handwriting* b1860
agony column n *newspaper "personals" related to missing friends and relatives* b1865
beast fable n b1865
book review n b1865
dime novel n (Am) b1865
initial v b1865
managing editor n b1865
manual alphabet n b1865
personal n *type of ad* b1865
potboiler n b1865 (potboil: b1867)
reportage n b1865
silly season n b1865
war correspondent n (Am) b1865
Baedeker n *guidebook* b1870
cub reporter n b1870
exclusive adj *as in "an exclusive report"* b1870 (noun use: b1930)
feature n *as in "newspaper feature"* b1870 (feature story: b1915)
graphology n *study of writing* b1870 ["study of handwriting": b1900] (graphologist: b1885)
interview n/v b1870 (interviewee: b1885)
leading n *typographical term* b1870
leaflet n b1870 (verb use: b1965)
print v *handprint* b1870
word-hoard n b1870
dreadful n *as in "penny dreadful"*
eye rhyme n
funny paper n (Am)
news agency n (Am)
penny dreadful n
scoop n/v *breaking story*

Communication

billboard n (Am) b1855
communique n b1855
telegram n (Am) b1855 (verb use: b1865)
fourth class n (Am) b1865
cablegram n (Am) b1870 (cable: b1900)
line n *as in "telephone line"* b1870
petroglyph n b1870
postcard, postal card n b1870
transmitter n *as in "radio transmitter"* b1870 ["one who transmits": b1730] (verb use: b1900)
wire n/v *telegram* b1870
lipreading n (lip-read: b1895)
switchboard n (Am)

Visual Arts/ Photography

pastoralism n b1855
photo n b1860 (verb use: b1870; adj use: b1890)
photogram n *photograph* b1860
stereograph n b1860
intarsia n *type of mosaic* b1865
objet d'art n b1865
sculpt v b1865 (sculpture v: b1645)
tintype n (Am) b1865
art form n b1870
artistry n b1870
Byzantine adj b1870 ["convoluted": b1970]
clog dance n b1870
form n *as in "form and function"* b1870
iris diaphragm n b1870
macrame n b1870
negative n *photographic negative* b1870
pen and ink n *type of drawing* b1870
portraitist n b1870
positive adj *opp. of photographic negative* b1870 (noun use: b1830)
primitive adj b1870 (noun use: b1900; primitivism: b1856)
print n/v *as in "photographic print"* b1870
realism n b1870
stop n *as in "f-stop"* b1870

tone v *color a photograph* b1870
transparency n *type of photo* b1870
cassette n *for photo film*
oeuvre n *body of work*
photoengraving n

Performing Arts

big top n b1855
busk v *entertain on the street* b1855 (busker: b1860)
fiasco n *stage disaster* b1855 [gen. "disaster": b1865]
miracle play n b1855
mystery play n b1855
tragedienne n *type of actor* b1855 (tragedian: b1600)
comedienne n b1860 (comedian: b1605)
histrionics n b1865 (histrionic: b1650)
stage whisper n b1865
deuteragonist n *second banana* b1870
minstrel show n (Am) b1870
passion play n b1870
reenact v *stage, duplicate* b1870
showboat n (Am) b1870 (verb use: b1955)
theatergoer n b1870
upstage adv b1870
billing n *as in "top billing"*
leading lady n (leading man: b1750)
revue n

Music

brass instrument n b1855
concertgoer n b1855
flue pipe n *of organ* b1855
flue stop n *of organ* b1855
flugelhorn n b1855
postlude n *opp. of prelude* b1855 [gen. "summary, ending": b1930]
reed organ n (Am) b1855
saxophone n b1855
scherzo n b1855
treble staff n b1855
tuba n b1855 [obs. type of trumpet: b1450]
bandstand n b1860
calliope n (Am) b1860
chantey/chanty n *as in "sea chanty"* b1860
flautist n b1860

orchestration n b1860 (orchestrate: b1880)
parlor grand n (Am) b1860
piano accordian n b1860
piccolo n b1860
saxtuba n b1860
sheet music n b1860
snare drum n b1860
symphonic adj b1860
a capella adj b1865
alpenhorn n b1865
euphonium n *type of instrument* b1865
librettist n *composer of librettos* b1865
nocturne n b1865
tenorist n b1865 (tenor: b1500)
upbeat n b1865
vibrato n b1865
chanteuse n *female singer* b1870
mouth organ n (Am) b1870
shanty n b1870
spiritual n b1870
xylophone n b1870
country rock n
helicon n *type of tuba*
percussion instrument n
string quartet n

Entertainment

nightlife n b1855
peep show n b1855
segue v b1855 (adv use: b1740; noun use: b1940)
strongman n b1860
cakewalk n *type of contest* b1865
country club n (Am) b1870
social n *as in "ice cream social"* b1870 (sociable: b1830)
square dance n b1870
talk n *speech, lecture* b1870
fox-trot n (Am) *the gait and the dance* (verb use: b1920)
lantern slide n
ringmaster n

Education

adult education n b1855
assistant professor n (Am) b1855
coeducation n (Am) b1855 (coed n: b1885; coed adj: b1890)

grade school n (Am) b1855
grant-in-aid n b1855
industrial school n b1855
kindergarten n b1855
mortarboard n b1855 [in bricklaying: b1900] (mortar: b1605; mortar cap: b1690)
cap and gown n b1860
postgraduate adj b1860 (noun use: b1890)
school year n b1860
schoolwork n b1860
summer school n (Am) b1860
territorial court n b1860
business college n (Am) b1865
church school n b1865
academe n *academics* b1870
classroom n (Am) b1870
dormitory n b1870
exam n b1870
extension n b1870
fox n *arch. school freshman* b1870
grade n *as in "first grade"* b1870 [as in "grade A": b1900]
higher education n b1870
midterm adj/n b1870
preparation n *study* b1870 (prepare: b1700; prep, as in "prep school": b1900)
quiz n/v *test* b1870
rep n *repetition* b1870 (repetition: b1425)
school n *the building* b1870
schoolyard n b1870
speller n b1870
upperclassman n (Am) b1870
chautauqua n
cum laude adj/adv (Am)
grad n/adj (graduate: b1425)
headmistress n (headmaster: b1560)
intercollegiate adj
spelling bee n (spelldown: b1950)
truant officer n (Am)
underclassman n (Am)

Religion

kosher adj b1855 [slang "OK": b1900] (verb use: b1875; noun use: b1890)
profanatory adj b1855

religiose adj b1855
amen corner n (Am) b1860
good book n b1860
henotheism n b1860
inner light n b1860
mandala n *symbol representing the universe* b1860
oblate n b1865
seder n *type of Jewish service* b1865
Yahweh n 1869
agnostic n b1870 (adj use: b1875)
baptismal name n b1870
genuflect v *bow in worship* b1870 [fig. sense: b1900; obs. "bend the knee": b1630]
jihad n b1870
recessional n b1870
Holy Joe n *chaplain*

Society/Mores/Culture

altruism, altruist, altruistic n b1855
bloke n b1855
demimonde n b1855 (demimondaine: b1895)
enfant terrible n b1855
ladykin n b1855
proletariat n b1855
rye n *male Gypsy* b1855
temperance movement n b1855
townie n (Am) b1855
street arab n *homeless person* b1860
traditionalism n b1860
bum n *vagrant* b1865
colonial n b1865 (adj use: b1780; colonist: b1705; colonizer: b1785)
courtesy title n b1865
demiworld n b1865
folklife n b1865
high-class adj b1865
lady-in-waiting n b1865
pop adj b1865 ["lay," as in "pop psychology": b1970]
primitivism n b1865
racial adj b1865
shirtsleeve adj *informal* b1865
culture n *heritage, society* b1870
discrimination, discriminate n, v b1870
ethnic adj b1870 [arch.

"non-Judeo-Christian": b1500] (obs. noun use "heathen": b1375 to 1700s; modern noun use: b1945; ethnical: b1500)
freedwoman n (Am) b1870 (freedman: b1605)
function n *ceremony, soiree* b1870
glamour n b1870 ["magic": b1715]
hobnob v b1870 ["give or take": b1600; "drink together": b1830]
matriotism n *patriotism* b1870
racism n b1870
womanism n *type of feminism* b1870
zeitgeist n b1870
handshake n
utopian n

Government

self-rule n b1855
collectivism n b1860 (collectivize: b1895)
home rule n b1860
crown princess n b1865
emirate n b1865
officialdom n b1865
Old Glory n b1865
police state n b1865
statehood n (Am) b1870

Politics

demagoguery n (Am) b1855 (demogogue: b1650; demogogy: b1655)
filibuster n/v b1855 [type of pirate: b1800]
red adj *type of Communist* b1855
secessionist n (Am) b1855
foreign office n b1860
foreign policy n b1860
plebiscite n b1860
world power n b1860
civil disobedience n b1870
interventionist n b1870 (interventionism: b1925)
left n b1870
lobbyist n b1870
primary n *type of election* b1870
running mate n (Am) b1870
straw vote n b1870
stump v *campaign* b1870
ultraconservative adj/n b1870

whip n b1870
runoff n (Am)

Life

birthrate n b1860
reincarnate n b1860 (verb use: b1870; adj use: b1900)
term n *length of pregnacy* b1870

Death

boneyard n (Am) b1855
die out v b1855
garrote/garote/garotte/garrotte v b1855 (verb use: b1625)
death rate n b1860
necropsy n *autopsy* b1860 (verb use: b1930)
thanatophobia n *fear of death* b1860
insecticide n b1865
mortuary n b1865 [obs. "gift from the dead": b1385; obs. "funeral": b1470 to 1600s] (adj use: b1515)
destroy v *put to sleep* b1870
estate n b1870
national cemetery n (Am) b1870
cremate v (cremation: b1625)
euthanatize v

War/Military/Violence

brass knuckles n (Am) b1855
brig n *navy guardhouse, prison* b1855
coup n *overthrow* b1855 ["blow": b1400; "successful move": b1795] (verb use: b1575)
derringer n b1855
donnybrook n b1855
powder keg n b1855
swordsmanship n b1855
breechloader n b1860
bulletproof adj/v b1860
cavalryman n b1860 (cavalry: b1550)
court-martial v b1860
cross fire n b1860
doughboy n (Am) b1860
first sergeant n b1860
gentleman-at-arms n b1860
knock out v b1860
line of fire n b1860

muzzleloader n *type of gun*
b1860 (muzzler: b1900)
rawhide v *whip* b1860
shellfire n b1860
warlord n b1860
blockade-runner n b1865
draftee n b1865
gatling gun n (Am) b1865
ironclad n *type of ship* b1865
(adj use: b1850)
Johnny Reb n (Am) b1865
militarism n b1865 (militaristic: b1905)
raid, raider v, n b1865
troopship n b1865
base n *as in "airbase"* b1870
blast n *explosion* b1870
bloodbath n b1870
bludgeon v b1870 (noun use:
b1730)
bolt n *rifle bolt* b1870 (bolt-
action adj: b1875)
cosh n (Brit) *weapon* b1870
(verb use: b1900)
draw v *as in "quick draw"*
b1870
ensign n b1870
iron n *gun* b1870
issue n *as in "government issue"* b1870 (verb use:
b1930)
left n *in boxing* b1870
machine gun n b1870
monitor n *ironclad* b1870
(verb use: b1925)
peacemaker n b1870
plug v *slang shoot* b1870
["hit": b1875]
repeater n *type of gun* b1870
(repeating: b1830)
report n *note of reprimand*
b1870
rimfire adj (Am) b1870
sabotage n b1870 (verb use:
b1915; saboteur: b1925)
sarge n b1870
self-mutilation n b1870
spoil v *as in "spoil for a fight"*
b1870
terrorist n b1870 (terrorism:
b1800)
tour of duty n b1870
turret n b1870
airman n
BB n (Am) *as in "BB gun"*
cartridge belt n
explosive n

firing pin n
pole hammer n *war hammer*

Crime/Punishment/
Enforcement
indecent exposure n b1855
policewoman n b1855 (policeman: b1805; police-
person: b1970)
stir n *as in "in stir"* b1855
(stir-crazy: b1905)
break-in n b1860 (break in
v: b1555)
confidence game n (Am)
b1860 (confidence man:
b1850)
cop n *police officer* b1860
(copper: b1850)
criminology n b1860
flatfoot n b1860
reform school n b1860
run in v *arrest* b1860
sneak thief n (Am) b1860
stickup n b1860 (verb use:
b1850)
uxoricide n b1860
white slavery n b1860 (white
slave: b1835; white slaver:
b1915)
arsonist n b1865 (arson:
b1680)
camorra n *disreputable organization* b1865 (camorrista:
b1900)
graft n *illicit profiteering*
b1865 (verb use: b1860)
hoosegow n b1865
indecent assault n b1865
mug, mugger v, n *as in rob*
b1865 ["hit in the face":
b1820; "attack": b1850]
straight adj *not criminous*
b1865
sweatbox n b1865
book v *process a criminal*
b1870
burgle v b1870 (burglarize:
b1875)
case n *job, as in "a tough case
for a detective"* b1870
(casework: b1890)
dip n *pickpocket* b1870
gouge v *cheat, soak* b1870
hook n *pickpocket* b1870
inspector n b1870 [gen. use:
b1605]

log n *type of punishment*
b1870 (verb use: b1830)
Mafia n b1870 (mafioso:
b1875)
protection n *type of racket*
b1870
skin game n (Am) b1870
skulduggery n (Am) b1870
sodomize v b1870
spanking n *corporal punishment* b1870
underworld n b1870
bunco/bunko n/v
firebug n (Am)
hoodlum n (Am) *juvenile delinquent* ["criminal":
b1880]
polygraph n *lie detector* [type
of drawing instrument:
b1805]
roll v *rob* (roller: b1915)
trick n (Am) *crime*

The Law
limited liability n b1855
witness stand n (Am) b1855
direct examination n b1860
case law n b1865
contractual adj b1865
licensee n b1865
mens rea n *criminal motive*
b1865
entrap v b1870
magistrate's court n b1870
rest v *as in "the prosecution
rests"* b1870
sentence n b1870 [obs.
"opinion": b1225 to
1600s] (verb use: b1595)
sergeant n *in the police* b1870
["mil. sergeant": b1570]
moratorium n [gen. use:
b1970] (moratory: b1895)
nolo contendere n (nolo:
b1915)
retrial n

The Fantastic/
Paranormal
crystal ball n b1855
daimon n *type of spirit* b1855
fairy godmother n b1855
aura n b1860 ["phys. emanation": b1735]
fantasie n b1860
psychic adj *supernatural*
b1860 ["clairvoyant":

b1930] (noun use: b1875;
psychism, psychist:
b1900)
clairaudience n *"hearing" the
beyond* b1865
spirit writing n b1865
ghostess n b1870 (ghost:
b1470)
hyperspace n b1870
lycanthropy n *werewolfism*
b1870 [type of delusion:
b1585]
manifestation n b1870
medium n *psychic* b1870
otherworldly adj

Magic
hex n *witch or spell* b1860
[type of spell: b1910] (verb
use: b1830)
prestidigitation n b1860
(prestigiation: b1570;
prestidigitator: b1830)
grimoire n *book of magic*
b1870
hoodoo n (Am) (verb use:
b1890)

Interjections
aw interj b1855
gee whillikins interj b1855
(gee whiz: b1885)
lordy interj b1855
whillikers interj (Am) b1855
upsy-daisy interj b1860
mazel tov interj b1865
bully interj b1870
dammit interj b1870
er interj b1870
fore interj b1870
gee interj *as in "gee whillikers"* b1870 (gee whillikins: b1870; gee whiz:
b1885)
goldarn adj b1870
good evening interj b1870
(good day: b1150; good
morning, good-morrow,
good-even: b1470; good
afternoon: b1930)
hello interj/n b1870 (hallo:
b1570)
houp-la interj b1870
(hoopla n: b1880)
OK interj b1870
ole interj/n b1870
pfui interj b1870 (phooey:
b1930)

rah interj b1870 (rah-rah adj: b1915)
rather interj b1870
say v b1870
shoofly interj b1870
whizbang n b1870
honest injun interj (Am)
sayonara interj
what the hell? interj

Slang

bird n *man* b1855 ["woman": b1915]
bud n (Am) *buddy* b1855
card n (Am) *humorous person* b1855
double-time v b1855
fag end n (Brit) *cigarette butt* b1855
full of beans adj b1855
gas n/v *chitchat* b1855 (gasbag: b1890)
grab bag n (Am) b1855
guv n (Brit) b1855 (guvnor: b1805)
heck n b1855
moniker n b1855
number n *as in "I've got your number"* b1855
pungle v *pay* b1855
rig v *as in "rig an election"* b1855 [slang "play a hoax": b1830] (noun use: b1800)
rub in v b1855
rummy n *drunk* b1855
shenanigan n (Am) b1855
beef v *as in "beef up"* b1860
biz n (Am) b1860
bleeding adj/adv (Brit) b1860 (bloody: b1670)
bust v (Am) *raid* b1860
caught adj *pregnant* b1860
comeuppance n (Am) b1860
fluke n *lucky shot, bit of luck* b1860 (verb use: b1870)
French letter n (Brit) *condom* b1860
knuckle-duster n (Am) b1860
lulu n b1860
monkey v *mimic* b1860
paper chase n b1860
pay dirt n (Am) b1860
philistia n *the class of philistines* b1860
plug-ugly n (Am) *tough, hood* b1860

sellout n (Am) b1860
shake down v *blackmail* b1860 (shakedown: b1905)
sporting house n b1860
strapped adj (Am) *as in "strapped for cash"* b1860
suck up v *brown-nose* b1860
welsh v b1860
buttonhole v *corner* b1865
dressing-down n (Am) b1865
dutch auction n b1865
johnny-on-the-spot n b1865
loony adj b1865 (loon: b1885)
mousetrap v b1865
prep n b1865 (verb use: b1915)
reb n b1865
sandman n b1865
shebang n (Am) b1865
skedaddle n/v b1865
softy n b1865
up-and-up n b1865
working girl n b1865
beaut n (Am) b1870
blue adj *pornographic* b1870
boyo n b1870
carpetbagger n (Am) b1870
case n *as in "nut case"* b1870
catawumpus adj/n b1870
chin v (Am) *discussion* b1870
do v *as in "do time," "do drugs"* b1870
dog v *as in "I'll be dogged"* b1870
doggoned adj b1870
drink n *as in "in the drink"* b1870
fest n (Am) *as in "filmfest"* b1870
fork over, fork out v b1870
get v *as in "gotcha"* b1870
get-out n *as in "all get-out"* b1870
get-up-and-go n b1870
grind out, grind away v b1870
groove n b1870
jerry n *chamber pot* b1870
kill v *as in "kill a case of beer," "kill the lights," "kill a story"* b1870 [as in "kill time": b1730] (killer: b1470)
kingpin n b1870
lady of the evening n b1870

lather n *consternation, tizzy* b1870
light out v b1870
loaded adj *drunk* b1870
long shot n b1870
look-in n *opportunity* b1870
lump n *as in "a lump in my throat"* b1870
magnolious adj *wonderful* b1870
make n *as in "on the make"* b1870
max n *maximum* b1870 (verb use: b1900; adj use: b1970)
measly adj *small* b1870
meaty adj *substantial* b1870
morass n b1870 ["marsh": b1470]
natch adv b1870
oodles n b1870
persuasion n *type, as in "of the human persuasion"* b1870
pick-me-up n b1870
pigeon n *mark* b1870 ["twit": b1595; "stool pigeon": b1850]
plant v *bury* b1870
potwalloper n *cook* b1870
rough adj *as in "a rough neighborhood"* b1870
rough n *ruffian* b1870
rut n *as in "stuck in a rut"* b1870
salt n *sailor* b1870
scads n *many* b1870
shadow n *spy, surveillant* b1870 (verb use: b1630)
sharp n *expert* b1870
shim v *borrow cash* b1870
squizzed adj *drunk* b1870
tear n *spree, binge, as in "on a tear"* b1870
theirn pron b1870
tub n (Am) *fire truck* b1870
tuckered adj (Am) *tired* b1870
twistify v (Am) b1870
Uncle Tom n (Am) b1870 (verb use: b1950)
used-to-be n *has-been* b1870
wash v *be understood, get approval, as in "his alibi will wash"* b1870
wax v *thrash* b1870
weed n *fast-growing person* b1870

well hung adj b1870
whaler n *something huge* b1870
wimmen n b1870
breezy adj
bum n *bender*
dead center n
divvy n/v
druthers n
dutch treat n
galleywest adv *into confusion*
globe-trotter n
hole up v
loverly adj
no-go n (adj use: 1900s)
oldie n
PDQ adv
runaround n (Am)
squiffed adj *drunk* (squiffy: b1855)
ventilate v *shoot*

Insults

blowhard n (Am) b1855
cheapjack n *purveyor of cheap goods* b1855 (adj use: b1865)
crybaby n (Am) b1855
dope n *twit* b1855 (dopey: b1900)
lunkhead n (Am) b1855
porky adj b1855
crummy adj b1860 [arch. slang "attractive": b1730]
guttersnipe n b1860
weak sister n b1860
brassy adj b1865 ["made of brass": b1580]
crackpot n b1865
gamey adj b1865
know-all n (Brit) *know-it-all* b1865
pinheaded adj b1865 (pinhead: b1900)
slob n b1865 ["mud": b1780]
smarty, smart aleck n (Am) b1865 (smartypants: 1910s; smartass: 1960s)
weak-kneed adj b1865
addlebrained adj b1870 (addled: b1715; addlepated: b1630)
coon n b1870
crazy n b1870
doddery adj b1870
goody-goody n b1870 (goody: b1830)

jerkwater adj (Am) b1870

lemon n *crabby person; loser* b1870

mick, micky n b1870

muggins n *fool, dolt* b1870

penny-ante adj b1870

prima donna n *self-centered person* b1870

screw n *scrooge* b1870

snob n *uppity person* b1870 ["lesser person": b1800] (snobby, snobocracy: b1850)

thumbling n *little person* b1870

tubby adj *fat* b1870 (tub "tubby person": b1900)

vacuous adj *empty-headed* b1870 [fig. use: b1870]

yellow adj *cowardly, chicken* b1870 (yellow dog: b1835; yellow-bellied: b1930; yellowbelly: b1970)

chicken-livered adj (Am)

four-eyes n

mossback n (Am) *fuddy-duddy, reactionary*

piker n

twerp n

Phrases

and/or conj b1855

dragon's teeth n b1855

fact of life n b1855

far and away adv b1855

flying start n b1855

hat in hand adv b1855

kangaroo court n (Am) b1855

missing link n b1855

name-calling n b1855

on and off adj/adv b1855

poor farm n (Am) b1855

stomping ground n b1855

turning point n *lit. and fig.* b1855

wet dream n b1855

acquired taste n b1860

act of God n b1860

back talk n b1860

breeding ground n b1860

dumping ground n (Am) b1860

grand old man n b1860

high-muck-a-muck n b1860

hole-in-the-wall adj/n b1860

holier-than-thou adj b1860

inside track n (Am) b1860

mother lode n b1860

muck about v b1860

pathetic fallacy n *personifying inanimate things—Mother Nature* b1860

point of departure n b1860

rogue elephant n b1860

rogues' gallery n b1860

staying power n b1860

strong suit n b1860

all there adj (Am) *mentally there* b1865

and how adv b1865

big time n (Am) b1865

blind spot n b1865

conspiracy of silence n b1865

field of vision n b1865 (field of view: b1815)

head and shoulders adv b1865

hill of beans n b1865

lay of the land n b1865

little guy n b1865

muddle through v b1865

raison d'être n b1865

rose-colored glasses n b1865

shoot your mouth off v b1865

vantage point n b1865

count in, count out v b1870

even-steven adj b1870

hands down adj/adv b1870

hard-and-fast adj b1870

honorable mention n b1870

iron out v b1870

it's your funeral b1870

meal ticket n (Am) b1870

nerve center n b1870

old lady n *wife, mother* b1870 (old man: b1770)

rock bottom n (Am) b1870 (adj use: b1885)

rule out v b1870

sign of the zodiac n b1870

wasp waist n b1870

dry-as-dust adj

fifth wheel n

get it v (Am) *as in "you're gonna get it!"*

going-over n (Am)

hot air n *empty talk*

inner circle n

mutually exclusive adj

off year n

silver lining n

thinking cap n

what for n *as in "I'll give him what for"*

General/Miscellaneous

bandwagon n (Am) b1855

crack-up n b1855

dehydration, dehydrate n, v b1855

doppelganger n b1855

fallback n (Am) b1855

fill-up n b1855

gambit n b1855 [chess term: b1660]

getaway n b1855

hangout n (Am) b1855

highlight n (Am) *gen. "bright moment"* b1855 [lit. use: b1670] (verb use: b1930)

impasse n b1855

lob n/v *type of throw* b1855

melt n b1855 (verb use: b900)

midget adj/n b1855

nugget n b1855

policyholder n (Am) b1855

slipup n b1855

swelter n b1855

unification n b1855

vendetta n b1855

viewpoint n b1855

boilerplate n b1860

bong n *bell sound* b1860

by-product n b1860

cageling n b1860

carry n *distance of travel* b1860

crawly adj/n *as in "creepy-crawly"* b1860

deadline n b1860

distillate n b1860

earthman n b1860 (earthling: b1595; earthwoman: b1905)

excreta n *excrement* b1860

haggle n b1860 (verb use: b1585)

kickoff n b1860

massage n b1860 (verb use: b1890; masseur, masseuse: b1880)

mooch n/v b1860 [obs. "feign destitution": b1470; "sneak": b1855]

nameplate n b1860

output n/v b1860

pipeline n b1860 [fig. use: b1930]

plate mark n *hallmark* b1860

right-hander n b1860 (right-handed: b1400; righty: b1950)

run-in n b1860 [rugby term: b1860]

sanitarian n b1860

send-off n (Am) b1860

sensibilia n *that which can be sensed* b1860

specialist n b1860 (specialty: b1870; specialize: b1900)

swastika n b1860

throwback n b1860

about-face n b1865

caveman, cave dweller n b1865

co-op adj/n b1865

deportee n b1865 (deport: b1645)

deterrence n b1865

escapee n b1865

interplay n b1865

intoxicant adj/n b1865

miscegenation n (Am) *integration* b1865

signatory n b1865

surroundings n b1865

win n b1865

Anglophile, Anglophobe n b1870

border line n b1870 (adj use: b1910)

break n *as in "coffee break"* b1870

chug n (Am) *type of sound* b1870 (verb use: b1900)

cleanup n (Am) b1870 (verb use: b1920)

clip n *rate of speed, as in "at a fast clip"* b1870

clop n/v b1870

connection n *as in "electrical connection"* b1870 [as in "telephone connection": b1900]

counterflow n b1870

crackle n b1870

damn n *as in "I don't give a damn"* b1870

definition n *clarity, as in "photographic definition"* b1870

double n *as in "on the double"* b1870

doyenne n b1870 (doyen: b1670)

drop n *as in "drop in temperature"* b1870

drunk n *drunken person*

b1870 ["drunken binge": b1780] (drunkard: b1450)
enclave n b1870
extension n *as in "an extension building"* b1870
girleen n b1870
hoopla n b1870 (houp-là interj: b1870)
hooroosh n *confused noise* b1870
institution n *tradition* b1870
issue n *point of discussion* b1870 ["result": b1440]
issue n *issuance, as in "first day issue, certificate of issue"* b1870 (verb use: b1630)
jerry-built n b1870 (jerry-build: b1885)
jog n *as in "jog in the road"* b1870 (verb use: b1955)
jump n *something to jump* b1870
kiddie n b1870
lag n *result of lagging* b1870 [obs. "last person": b1515] (verb use: b1530; obs. adj use "last": b1555)
latecomer n b1870
lead n *precedent, model* b1870
life history n b1870
lilt n b1870 [type of song: b1680]
margin n *as in "profit margin," "margin for error"* b1870 (marginal: b1900)
marker n *as in "first-down marker"* b1870
nil n b1870
notabilia n *things notable, akin to memorabilia* b1870
oil of wintergreen n b1870
opportunism n b1870 (opportunistic: b1895)
outcropping n b1870
outfit n *group* b1870
ovation n b1870
overtone n *akin to undertone* b1870 [musical term: b1870]
pandemonium n *chaos* b1870 ["hell" (in *Paradise Lost*): 1667]
phone n *a sound* b1870 (phonate v: b1880)
pigmentation n b1870

play n *maneuver, attempt* b1870
polymer n b1870
pop n *instance, as in "$3 a pop"* b1870
potpourri n *hodgepodge* b1870
rally n *as in "pep rally"* b1870
range n *as in "target range"* b1870
rascalry n b1870
rasp v/n *speak with a rasp* b1870
rendition n *version* b1870
revision n *something revised* b1870
ring n *as in "car theft ring"* b1870 (ringleader: b1505)
school n *as in "school of thought," "the deco school of architecture"* b1870
scratch n *as in "start from scratch"* b1870
shortage n b1870
skirr n *whirr* b1870
slide n *as in "log slide"* b1870
slump n *phys. slump* b1870 [fig. use: b1890]
specialty n *area of expertise* b1870 ["special quality": b1500; "state of being special": b1630]
spin n *as in "take it for a spin"* b1870
stand n *as in "stand of trees"* b1870
tough n *ruffian* b1870 (toughie: b1925)
trenchancy n b1870
turnabout n *as in "turnabout is fair play"* b1870
type n *model; kind, class* b1870
upgrade n (Am) *incline* b1870
variation n *as in "a variation of the pyramid scheme"* b1870
wisp n b1870
afterglow n
afterimage n
blockage n
case study n
Celtic cross n
ethane n
giveaway n (Am)
handspring n

hideaway n *hiding person* ["hiding place": b1930]
hydrogen peroxide n
jabberwocky n *nonsense*
linkage n
miscue n (verb use: b1895)
poseur n
renaissance n [the Renaissance: b1840]
time-out n
washout n *lit.* [slang "failure": b1930]
zip n *zipping sound*

Things
figurine, figurette n b1855
finger hole n b1855
gadget n b1855 (gadgetry: b1920; gadgeteer: b1940)
granny knot n b1855
bell jar n b1860
fingerprint n b1860 (verb use: b1905)
smokestack n b1860
decalcomania n b1865 (decal: b1940)
trapeze n b1865 (trapezist: b1875)
carbon steel n b1870
celluloid n b1870
dummy n *mannequin, etc.* b1870
ethyl alchohol n b1870
square knot n b1870
tailgate n b1870
transfer n *decal* b1870
beanbag n
dingus n *gizmo, whatchamadoodle*
doodad n (Am)

Description
all-inclusive adj b1855
arrhythmic adj b1855
atingle adj b1855
atypical adj b1855
chintzy adj b1855
clear-cut adj b1855
folksy adj (Am) b1855
gainly adj b1855
grueling adj b1855 (noun use: b1800)
kinetic adj b1855
long-range adj b1855
meaningful adj b1855 (meaningless: b1800)
purposeful adj b1855
resourceful adj b1855

small-scale adj b1855
specialized adj b1855
thumbnail adj b1855
undercover adj *covered* b1855 [as in "undercover cop": b1920]
utility adj b1855
wide-open adj b1855
abuzz adj b1860
anti adj b1860
better-off adj b1860
bum adj *as in "bum knee"* b1860
complicitous adj b1860
godforsaken adj b1860
idyllic adj b1860 (idyllian adj: b1730)
off-color adj b1860
ongoing adj b1860 (noun use: b1670)
reliant adj b1860
sic adv *as in "keeping the piece (sic)"* b1860
simplistic adj b1860 (simplism: b1885; simplist n: b1930)
susurrous adj b1860
anthropocentric adj b1865
boxy adj b1865
circa adv/prep b1865
clueless adj b1865
futureless adj b1865
impractical adj b1865 (impracticable: b1680)
irenic adj *conducive to peace* b1865
nifty adj (Am) b1865
pindling adj (Am) *spindly, frail* b1865
ranking adj *senior* b1865
ratty adj *dilapidated* b1865
simpatico adj b1865
straggly adj b1865
timesaving adj b1865
unrealistic adj b1865
agleam adj b1870
aswarm adj b1870
baroque adj *convoluted* b1870
chancy adj b1870 [Scottish "lucky": b1515]
choppy adj *as in "choppy seas"* b1870 (chop v: b1670; chop n: b1870)
close-fitting adj b1870
common adj b1870 ["ordinary": b1300]
constructive adj *helpful* b1870

["pertaining to construction": b1830]

doubtful adj *unlikely* b1870

dustproof adj b1870

escapable adj b1870

everywhen adv b1870

everywheres adv b1870

faceless adj *unidentifiable* b1870 [obs. "cowardly": b1570]

flat adv *as in "flat broke"* b1870

foudroyant adj *loud* b1870

genuine adj *sincere* b1870 ["real": b1640]

grubby adj *dirty* b1870

hefty adj b1870 (heft: b1500)

hunky-dory adj (Am) b1870

insistent adj b1870 (insist: b1590; insistence: b1440)

jumpy adj *vacillating* b1870 ["nervous": b1900]

macabre adj b1870 (noun use: b1450)

moot adj *not relevant* b1870 ["open to argument": b1570]

murky adj *fig. obscure* b1870 [lit. use: b1340]

outsize adj b1870 (noun use: b1845)

outstanding adj *excellent* b1870 ["unresolved": b1615] (outstand: b1770)

pepper-and-salt adj *salt-and-pepper* b1870

persistent adj b1870 ["opp. of deciduous": b1830]

pragmatic adj *practical* b1870 [rare "active," obs. "arrogant": b1620]

relativistic adj b1870

risque adj b1870

run-down adj b1870 ["down-trodden": b1685; "shabby": b1900]

sawed-off adj (Am) b1870

scraggly adj b1870 (scraggy: b1300)

scratchy adj *causing scratches* b1870

shaky adj b1870 ["cracked": b1705]

short-range adj b1870

solid adj *strong, as in "solid support"* b1870

stark adj *barren* b1870 [rare

"unyielding": b900] (adv use: b1300)

static adj b1870

submersible adj b1870 (noun use: b1900)

tall adj *as in "tall tales"* b1870

technical adj *detailed* b1870 ["knowledgeable": b1620; "using technical terms": b1800]

testimonial adj *as in "testimonial dinner"* b1870 [arch. "related to testimony, evidentiary": b1425] (noun use "written reference": b1600; noun use "honor": b1870)

tricky adj *complex* b1870

typical adj b1870

undermanned adj b1870

upside down adj b1870

upstanding adj *as in "morally upstanding"* b1870 [phys. "standing up": b1000]

utilitarian adj *useful* b1870 (utile adj: b1500)

vibrant adj b1870 (vibrancy: b1890; vibrance: b1925)

aglare adj

diamond adj *as in "diamond anniversary"*

equipotent adj

ersatz adj

insanitary adj

land-poor adj (Am)

lived-in adj

precision adj (noun use: b1740)

redux adj

regardless adv

rogue adj

scruffy adj

tangy adj (tang: b1440)

well-rounded adj

Colors

beige adj/n b1860 (adj use: b1880)

chrome green n b1860

magenta n b1860 (adj use: b1900)

mauve n b1860

canary yellow n b1865

aquamarine n *the color* b1870

chartreuse n b1870 [type of food dish: b1830]

ecru n *type of color* b1870

ginger n *the color* b1870 (adj use: b1830)

lavender n *the color* b1870

hunter green n

Actions/Verbs

beg off v b1855

binge n b1855 (verb use: b1870)

delimit v b1855

externalize v b1855 (externize: b1870)

fake v b1855 [slang "perpetrate": b1830] (noun use: b1830; verb use: b1855)

handicap v b1855 (noun use: b1890)

juxtapose v b1855

mug v *as in "mugging for the camera"* b1855

reify v *make real* b1855

shinny v (Am) *as in "shinny up a pole"* b1855 (shin: b1830)

skelter v b1855

skyrocket v b1855

zap v b1855

air-dry v b1860

asphalt v b1860

boss v *as in "boss around"* b1860

condone v b1860

emulsify v b1860 (emulsifier: b1890)

formulate v b1860

function v b1860 (noun use: b1535)

itemize v (Am) b1860 (item v: b1605; itemization: b1895)

loft v *lob* b1860

lose out v b1860

monumentalize v b1860

roll up v b1860

segment v b1860

slog v *as in "slog through"* b1860 ["attack by hitting": b1830] (noun use: b1890)

steam up v b1860

stymie n/v b1860

trash v *throw away* b1860 ["destroy": b1970; "insult": b1975]

best v *outdo* b1865

chip in v b1865

cosher v *pamper* b1865

dematerialize v *make immate-*

rial b1865 ["disappear": b1895]

egg v *throw eggs at* b1865

encapsulate v b1865 (encapsule: b1880)

knife v b1865 [as in "knife through the crowd": b1930]

knuckle down v b1865

lallygag, lollygag v (Am) b1865

line up v b1865

manhandle v b1865 [obs. "attack," "use a tool by hand": b1475]

mother v *nurture, care for* b1865

motivate v b1865 (motivation: b1875)

slim v b1865

stabilize v b1865

alert v b1870

antagonize v *provoke* b1870

ask v *invite, as in "ask for trouble"* b1870

bone up v b1870

bowl over v b1870

browse v *scan* b1870

buff v *polish* b1870

bull v *force* b1870

bushel v (Am) *renovate, alter* b1870

check v *mark with checkmark* b1870 (noun use: b1900; check off: b1840; check mark: b1920)

clip v *sideswipe* b1870

cocoon v b1870

crack v *as in "get cracking"* b1870

credit v *as in "credit with success"* b1870 (noun use: b1630)

crop up v b1870

customize v (Am) b1870

cut v *dilute* b1870

demobilize v b1870

depersonalize v b1870 (depersonalization: b1910)

deplete v b1870 [med. use: b1810]

detoxicate v b1870 (detoxify: b1905; detox: b1975)

drum v *as in "drum your fingers"* b1870 (drummer: b1575)

dunk v (Am) b1870

dynamize v b1870

ease v *slow down* b1870

engage v *as in "engage a gear"* b1870

get v *as in "the problems got to him"* b1870

haul off v b1870

head for v b1870

hike v *raise* b1870 (noun use: b1935)

instigate v b1870 ["urge": b1555]

lead v *as in "lead the crowd in song"* b1870

lock v *jam up* b1870

materialize v *make appear* b1870 ["represent physically": b1710; "appear": b1900]

micrify v *trivialize* b1870

miss out v *eliminate* b1870

negotiate v *maneuver through* b1870 (negotiation, negotiable: b1900)

operate v *control* b1870 (operation: b1900)

outclass v b1870

overexpose v b1870

pan out v b1870

plug v *as in "plug away"* b1870

pull v *as in "pull taffy"* b1870

range v *run a gamut, vary* b1870

receive v *as in "receive a TV program"* b1870

relax v *take a break* b1870

shed v *get rid of* b1870

sit in v b1870

slather v b1870 ["slide": b1820]

spin v *rotate* b1870 [fig., as in "head spinning": b1870]

spot v *see* b1870

squinny v *cry* b1870

stand v *measure, as in "the building stands four stories"* b1870

straighten up v b1870

strand v *leave helpless* b1870 ["run aground": b1000]

strike n/v *as in "strike gold"* b1870

stud v *as in "star-studded"* b1870

subscribe v *as in "subscribe to a magazine"* b1870

swoosh v b1870

telescope v b1870

track v *as in "track dirt into the house"* b1870

trail v *as in "trail off"* b1870

typify v b1870 ["symbolize": b1625]

underlap v *opp. of overlap* b1870

waste v *as in "waste a chance"* b1870

watch v *as in "watch out"* b1870

wear v *irritate* b1870

weigh in v b1870

galumph v 1872

boom v *surge* (noun use: b1880)

collaborate v ["collaborate traitorously": b1970] (collaboration: b1860)

contour v

counterpoint v

crate v

immobilize v (immobile: b1340)

incandesce v (incandescent: b1795)

leapfrog v

resonate v

shanghai v (Am)

simmer down v

standardize v

summarize v

understudy v (noun use: b1885)

Archaisms

manifold v *reproduce, publish* b1870

postliminary adj *opp. of preliminary* b1870

IN USE BY
1900

Geography/Places

gold coast n *upperclass residential area* b1880
relief map n b1880
sandlot n b1880
shantytown n b1880
temblor n (Am) *earthquake* b1880
water table n b1880
craterlet n b1885
crosstown adj/adv b1890
epicenter n b1890
exclave n *part of a country within another country's borders* b1890
hinterland n b1890
hydrosphere n b1890
orogeny, orogenesis n *creation of mountains* b1890
aftershock n b1895
continental shelf n b1895
equatorial plane n b1895
landform n b1895
rift valley n b1895
tectonic adj b1895 [gen. "of building": b1660] (tectonics: b1900)
boomtown n
El Niño n *warm water current*
ghetto n *gen.* ["Jewish confinement area": b1615] (verb use: b1400)
hillcrest n
tombollo n
tristate adj
tsunami n

Natural Things

ape-man n b1880
cell body n b1880
menthol n b1880

microorganism n b1880 (microbe: b1885)
phylum n b1880
water vapor n b1880
cell division n b1885
microbe n b1885
chromosome n 1888 (chromosome number: b1910)
argon n b1890
eddy current n b1890
groundwater n b1890
mitosis n b1890
rhinestone n b1890
sex cell n b1890
subculture n *biological sense* b1890 [sociological sense: b1970]
terrarium n b1890
electron n 1891
cryptozoic adj *living in secluded places* b1895
impact crater n b1895
methanol n b1895
reproduce v *breed* b1895 (reproduction: b1800)
amino acid n (amino: b1890)
biosphere n
inert gas n
life force n
neon adj/n
radium n
squidge n *the sound mud makes*
tropism n

Plants

annual ring n b1880
Easter lily n b1880
Japanese cedar n b1880
kudzu n b1880
locoweed n (Am) b1880

McIntosh n *type of apple* b1880
peat moss n b1880
philodendron n b1880
ponderosa pine n (Am) b1880
sea lily n b1880
barrel cactus n (Am) b1885
blue spruce n b1885
cloverleaf n b1885
fruitlet n b1885
giant cactus n b1885
hard pine n b1885
jack pine n b1885
Joshua tree n (Am) b1885
lanolin n b1885
Mexican jumping bean n b1885
plant kingdom n b1885
pulpwood n b1885
baby's breath n b1890
downy mildew n b1890
jumping bean n (Am) b1890
lemon balm n *type of mint* b1890
navel orange n b1890
pond scum n b1890
powdery mildew n (Am) b1890
rubber plant n b1890
sporozoan n b1890
tumbleweed n (Am) b1890
black-eyed Susan n (Am) b1895
bristlecone pine n b1895
compass rose n b1895
everblooming adj b1895
husk-tomato n (Am) b1895
plankton n b1895
aflower adj
Christmas cactus n

ground cover n
Japanese maple n
knotty pine n
mum n
photosynthesis n
phototropism n
phytoplankton n
sandspur n

Animals

Airedale n b1880
arthropod n b1880
chimp n b1880 (chimpanzee: b1740)
cockatiel n b1880
cottonmouth moccasin n b1880 (cottonmouth: b1835)
death's-head moth n b1880
diamondback terrapin n b1880
English sparrow n (Am) b1880
eohippus n b1880
fruit bat n b1880
Gila monster n (Am) b1880
ladybeetle n b1880
largemouth bass n (Am) b1880
painted turtle n b1880
potter wasp n (Am) b1880
screwworm n (Am) b1880
silver salmon n b1880
stinkbug n (Am) b1880
three-toed sloth n b1880
whooper swan n b1880
wildlife n b1880
aphid n b1885
basset hound n b1885 (basset: b1620)
bluegill n (Am) b1885

carpenter ant n b1885
cedarbird n b1885 (cedar waxwing: b1845)
croc n b1885
dik-dik n *type of antelope* b1885
ectoplasm n b1885
emperor penguin n b1885
fin whale n b1885
harvest ant n b1885
indigo snake n (Am) b1885
Irish water spaniel n b1885
jack mackerel n (Am) b1885
killer whale n b1885
king penguin n b1885
king salmon n (Am) b1885
lungfish n b1885
mud puppy n (Am) *type of salamander* b1885
piglet n b1885 (pigling: b1730)
pit viper n b1885
rainbow trout n b1885
rhino n *rhinoceros* b1885 (rhinoceros: b1350)
rock lobster n b1885
rust mite n b1885
sand dollar n (Am) b1885
smallmouth bass n (Am) b1885
soft-shell turtle n b1885
spittlebug n (Am) b1885
springer spaniel n b1885
surf fish n (Am) b1885
surfperch n (Am) b1885
tuna n (Am) *type of fish* b1885
Welsh terrier n b1885
whale shark n b1885
bird dog n (Am) b1890 (verb use: b1945)
bobcat n (Am) b1890
borzoi n *type of dog* b1890
brown trout n b1890
Cape buffalo n b1890
carpet beetle n b1890
cashmere goat n b1890
cattalo n b1890
chow n *type of dog* b1890 (chow chow: b1795)
elephant bird n b1890
elkhound n b1890
estrus n b1890 (estrous adj: b1900)
giant clam n b1890
giant squid n b1890
heartworm n b1890
homing pigeon n b1890

hominid n b1890 (adj use: b1920; hominoid: b1930)
monarch butterfly n b1890
Old English sheepdog n b1890
periodical cicada n *17-year locust* b1890
Russian blue n *type of cat* b1890
snowshoe hare n b1890
Tasmanian wolf n b1890
tiger swallowtail n *type of butterfly* b1890
water buffalo n b1890
zebra finch n b1890
blowfish n b1895
boll weevil n (Am) b1895
Boston terrier n (Am) b1895
Chesapeake Bay retriever n *type of dog* b1895
gooney bird n b1895
king cobra n b1895
leopard seal n b1895
Manchester terrier n b1895
mantid n b1895
muskie n b1895 (muskellunge: b1790)
pond skater n b1895
sweat bee n b1895
timber rattlesnake n b1895
topi n b1895
tree shrew n b1895
vervet monkey n b1895
diurnal adj *opp. of nocturnal*
earwig n [obs. "obsequious person": b1000 to 1700s]
estrous adj
estrous cycle n (estral cycle: b1945)
hatchling n
Japanese beetle n
Kodiak bear n
malamute n *type of dog*
Mexican hairless n
okapi n
primate n (primatology: b1930)
Rhode Island Red n *type of fowl*
samoyed n *type of dog*
Scottie n *type of dog*
sidewinder n
vestigial adj
virus n ["snake venom": b1600]
wahoo n *type of fish* [type of elm: b1800]
walleye n

wingspread n
wood pussy n *skunk*
zephyr n *type of butterfly*

Weather

cold wave n b1880
dust storm n b1880
heat wave n b1880
high n b1880
ice storm n b1880
westerly n b1880
cumulonimbus n b1890
dust devil n b1890
line squall n b1890
air mass n b1895
stratocumulus n b1895
weather station n b1895
depression n
low n
tailwind n
twister n

Heavens/Sky

celestial sphere n b1880
gegenschein n *light in the night sky* b1880
meteor shower n b1880
nova n b1880
outer space n b1880
Perseid n *meteor shower* b1880
cosmic dust n b1885
solar eclipse n b1890
ozone hole n

Science

cross-fertilization, cross-fertilize n, v b1880
demography n b1880 (demographic: b1885; demographics: b1970)
four-dimensional adj b1880
hydrolysis n b1880
parasitology n b1880
surface tension n b1880
toponymy n b1880 (toponym: b1970)
aerobic adj b1885
anaerobic, anaerobe adj, n b1885
conservation of mass/conservation of matter n b1885
endoplasm n b1885
enzyme n b1885
eugenic, eugenics adj, n *improving offspring* b1885
geoid n *hypothetical sphere at earth sea level* b1885

geotectonic adj b1885
hereditarian n *genetic theorist* b1885
insectarium n b1885
microphysics n b1885
null-space n b1885
steady state n b1885
astrophysics n b1890
cell theory n b1890
chemical engineering n b1890
chemiluminescence n b1890
cytology n b1890
Erlenmeyer flask n b1890
gamete n b1890
geophysics n b1890
glaciology n b1890
microbiology n b1890
volcanology n b1890
zygote n b1890
biophysics n b1895
cholesterol n b1895
geochronology n b1895
geomorphology n b1895
kinesiology n *study of anatomy and movement* b1895
periodic table n b1895
petri dish n b1895
social psychology n b1895
control n
dissecting microscope n
eunochoid n
ionize v
lepidopterology n *study of moths and butterflies*
relativity n [gen. use: b1835]
scientize v
tectonics n ["architectural science": b1635]
test n *as in "drug test"* (verb use: b1870)

Technology

satellite n b1880
electric field n b1890
mechanical engineering n b1890
roentgen ray n b1890
high frequency n b1895
x ray n 1895 ["x-ray photography": b1970]
electric eye n

Energy

British Thermal Unit/BTU n b1880
static electricity n b1880
tuck n *energy* b1880

ampere n 1881 (amp: b1890; amperage: b1895)

coulomb n b1885

fuse n as in "electrical fuse" b1885

glow lamp n b1885

hydroelectric adj b1885 [type of steam generator: b1830] (hydro n: b1920)

joule n measure of energy b1885

kilowatt n b1885

magneto n type of generator b1885

piezoelectricity n b1885

powerhouse n b1885 [fig. use: b1930]

storage battery n b1885

torque n type of force b1885 (verb use: b1960)

direct current n b1890

inductance n b1890 (induction: b1805)

photovoltaic adj b1890

power plant n b1890

radiant energy n b1890

therm n unit of heat b1890

cold light n b1895

dry cell n b1895

fuel oil n b1895

ground wire n b1895

heat engine n b1895

heat pump n b1895

petrol n (Brit) gasoline b1895 ["petroleum": b1700]

photoelectric cell, photocell n b1895

crude n oil

dynamotor n

induction motor n

juice n slang electricity

outlet n as in "electrical outlet"

plug n as in "electrical plug" (verb use: b1930)

radioactive, radioactivity adj, n (radioactivate: b1930)

wildcat n type of oil well (wildcatter: b1885)

Time

biannual adj two times a year b1880

sesquicentennial adj/n (Am) b1880

standard time n (Am) b1880

time line n b1880

antemortem adj b1885

bicentennial n b1885 (bicentennary: b1865)

central time n (Am) b1885

date n appointment b1885 (verb use: b1930)

eastern time n b1885

egg timer n b1885

mountain time n (Am) b1885

pacific time n (Am) b1885

quarter hour n b1885

time zone n b1885

Universal time n b1885

dateline n b1890

present-day adj b1890

perpetual calendar n b1895

afternoons n (Am)

curfew n time to be indoors ["time to put lights out": b1300]

midafternoon adj/n

period n as in "first period of a hockey game"; as in "third-period class"

sec n second

wristwatch n

Age/Aging

teener n teenager b1895

midlife n (middle age: b1400)

Mathematics

graph n b1880 (verb use: b1900)

math n b1880

euclidean space n b1885

linear algebra n b1885

percentile n b1885

Boolean algebra n b1890

inversely proportional adj b1890

linear space n b1890

metamathematics n b1890

short division n opp. of long division b1890

tesseract n cube in four dimensions b1890

set theory n b1895

random sampling n

summate v sum up

Measurement

candlepower n b1880

cyclometer n measurer of distance b1880 ["measurer of circles": b1815]

ergometer n b1880

molecular weight n b1880

tonne n metric ton b1880

watt n 1882

clock v b1885 ["sound a bell": b1875]

comparator n b1885

gauss n b1885

micron n unit of length b1885 (micrometer: b1880)

potentiometer n b1885

spectrograph n b1885

voltmeter n b1885 (voltameter: b1840)

impedance n 1886

light-year n b1890

linear measure n b1890

lux n measure of illumination b1890

metric ton n b1890

thermocouple n b1890

atomic mass n (atomic weight: b1820)

board foot n (Am)

graduate n type of measuring glass

The Body

belly button n (Am) b1880

brain stem n b1880

cardiovascular adj b1880

catabolism n active metabolism b1880 (catabolize: b1930)

cuspid n b1880

frontal lobe n b1880

genitalia n b1880 (genitals: b1400)

gonad n b1880

knee jerk n b1880

muscle fiber n b1880

pussy n female sex organs b1880 (puss: b1670)

taste bud n b1880

cardiopulmonary adj b1885

neuron n b1885

premenstrual adj b1885

puss n slang face b1885

tendon of Achilles n b1885

vomitus n b1885

yellow bile n b1885

Achilles tendon n b1890

big toe n b1890

duff n buttocks b1890

gingiva n b1890

gluteus maximus n b1890

hair cell n b1890

hamstring muscle n b1890

lymphocyte n type of cell b1890

parietal lobe n part of the brain b1890

port-wine stain n b1890

seminal vesicle n b1890

autotoxin n b1895

cardiorespiratory adj b1895

central nervous system n b1895

gash n slang vagina b1895

innersole n insole b1895

internal secretion n hormone b1895

lymph node n b1895

plaque n in arteries b1895 [on teeth: b1900]

platelet n b1895 (blood plate: 1885)

temporal lobe n b1895 (temporal: b1600)

antibody n

bottom n buttocks

dome n as in "chromedome"

epinephrine n

gas n flatulence

gastric gland n

menarche n start of menstruation

microanatomy n

mitts n slang hands (mittens "hands": b1830)

mons pubis n

moon n slang buttocks

period n as in "menstrual period"

potent adj able to get an erection (potency: b1930)

primary tooth n

red marrow n

synapse n

tippytoe adj/adv/noun/v

waistline n

yap n (Am) slang mouth

Physical Description

bombinate v hum b1880

gawkish adj b1880

muscle-bound adj b1880

pee v b1880 (noun use "urination": b1900; noun use "urine": b1950)

reaction time n b1880

strawberry blond adj (Am) b1880

left-hander n left-handed person b1885 ["blow from the left hand": b1865] (lefty: b1930)

mute v *silence* b1885 (adj use: b1350)
pie-eyed adj (Am) b1885
fill out v *get fat* b1890
overbite n b1890
raspberry n *slang fart* b1890
slim-jim adj b1890
visual acuity n b1890
glassy-eyed adj b1895
wind v *get winded* b1880
woozy adj (Am)

Medicine
bacillus n b1880
botulism n b1880
cough syrup n b1880
depressant n b1880
folk medicine n b1880
germicide n b1880
grand mal n *type of epilepsy* b1880
hydrotherapy n b1880 (hydropathy: b1845)
intern n (Am) b1880 [gen. use: b1930] (verb use: b1930; internship: b1905)
morning sickness n b1880
narcolepsy n b1880 (narcolept n, narcoleptic adj: b1930)
osteoarthritis n b1880
Parkinson's disease n b1880 (parkinsonism: b1925)
plumbism n *lead poisoning* b1880
poliomyelitis n b1880 (polio: b1935)
ptomaine n b1880
streptococcus n b1880 (strep: b1930)
anesthetist n b1885 (anesthesiologist: b1945)
anointing of the sick n b1885
arteriogram n b1885 (arteriography: b1845)
arteriosclerosis n b1885
breech delivery n b1885
bridgework n *dental bridge* b1885
bronchial asthma n b1885
bubonic plague n b1885 (bubonic: b1875)
clinic n b1885 ["teaching medicine": b1845]
epidural adj/n b1885
eye doctor n b1885
first aid n b1885
general practitioner n b1885

gigantism n b1885
greenstick fracture n b1885
hoof-and-mouth disease n (Am) b1885
hyperextend v b1885
pediatrics n b1885 (pediatrician/pediatrist: b1905)
pharmaceutical n b1885 (adj use: b1650)
physical examination n b1885
rheumatic n *rheumatism sufferer* b1885
rubella n b1885
tabloid n b1885 (adj use "small": b1905)
tennis elbow n b1885
toxicant n b1885
toxicity n b1885
urinalysis n b1885
alcoholic n b1890 (adj use: b1930; alcoholism: b1860)
antitoxin n b1890
bedwetting n b1890
catatonia n b1890 (catatonic n: b1900; catatonic adj: b1905)
cerebral palsy n b1890
charley horse n b1890
checkup n (Am) b1890
cold sore n b1890
contact lens n b1890
contraception n b1890 (contraceptive n: b1895; contraceptive adj: b1920)
dyslexia n b1890 (dyslexic: b1965)
dystrophy n b1890
food poisoning n b1890
gastrectomy n b1890
gastroscope n b1890
gross anatomy n b1890
heat rash n b1890
hyperthermia n b1890
hysterectomy n b1890
implant n b1890 (verb use: b1900)
inoperable adj b1890
medicinal leech n b1890
optometry n b1890 (optometrist: b1905)
ovariectomy n b1890
postoperative adj b1890
pressure sore n b1890
Rocky Mountain spotted fever n (Am) b1890
self-treatment n b1890

toxin n b1890 (toxic n: b1890)
urologist n b1890
anorectic/anoretic adj b1895 (noun use: b1960)
antibiotic adj b1895 (noun use: b1945)
appendectomy, appendicectomy, appendicitis n b1895
biopsy n b1895
cocainism n *cocaine addiction* b1895
coronary n b1895
hangover n (Am) b1895
heart failure n b1895
hypertension n b1895
hypodermic syringe n b1895 (hypodermic needle: b1910)
hypoglycemia n b1895
immunize, immunization v, n b1895 (immunity: b1900)
in vitro adj/adv b1895 (opp. in vivo: b1905)
infantilism n b1895
med adj b1895
passive immunity n b1895
prosthetics n b1895 (prosthetic adj: b1930)
ptomaine poisoning n b1895
root canal n b1895
short sight n *myopia* b1895
social disease n b1895
terminal adj *fatal* b1895
water blister n b1895
antibacterial adj
arrest n *as in "cardiac arrest"*
artificial insemination n
aspirin n
barbiturate n
braces n
chiropractic n (noun use: b1905; chiropractor: b1905)
dyspareunia n
fibrillation n (fibrillate: b1930)
fluoroscope n/v (Am)
giantism n [gen. sense: b1640]
graft n *as in "skin graft"* (verb use: b1870)
hack n *type of cough*
hemostat n
hyperthyroidism n
ingrown adj *as in "ingrown toenail"* ["native": b1670]
isolation n *quarantine; sepa-*

ration [gen. sense: b1835] (isolate v: b1810)
lower n *part of dentures*
medicine dropper n
mescaline n
mongolism, mongoloid n, adj
needle n *as in "hypodermic needle"*
neonatal adj *related to newborns* (neonate "newborn": b1935)
night terror n
nursing home n
osteopath, osteopathy n (Am)
peptic ulcer n
proctology n
radiology n (radiologist: b1910)
registered nurse n
resident n
retainer n
serum n [gen. "fluid": b1665]
stat adv
tendinitis n
tick fever n
tonsillectomy n
unit n *dosage*
vasectomize v
withdrawal n *as in "heroin withdrawal"*

Everyday Life
boatswain's chair n b1880
coffee table n b1880
credenza n b1880
ditty box n (Am) b1880
double boiler n (Am) b1880
futon n b1880
gashouse n (Am) b1880
homemaker n b1880
junkyard n (Am) b1880
milk of magnesia n b1880
onionskin n (Am) *type of paper* b1880
petrolatum n (Am) *petroleum jelly* b1880 (petroleum jelly: b1890)
push button n (Am) b1880
storm door n (Am) b1880
swizzle stick n b1880
water heater n b1880
crackleware n b1885
flagpole n b1885 (flagstaff: b1615)
gas log n b1885
ginger jar n b1885

An Etymology of *Etymology*

This is not a book of etymology, so we include but one word history—that of *etymology*.

The Greek word *etymon* or *etumon* meant, roughly, the original sense of a word, the "true" sense of a word before taking other meanings. The person who studied etymons was an *etumologos*, and subsequently his or her study became *etumologia*.

The Romans borrowed the word as *etymologia/etimologia* into Latin. In Old French, the word was used as *ethimologie*. Our peripatetic word eventually followed its own history into Middle English as *ethimologie*.

The word became a confirmed member of the English language by 1400, spelled *ethymologye*, but it didn't carry the meaning of "study of word histories." When it entered English, the word meant a specific word history, or the process of tracing a word history. By 1600 it took the obsolete meaning of "original meaning" (roughly returning to its own roots in *etumon*), and that meaning died in the 1700s.

In English, the linguistic study of word histories became known as *etymology* by 1670.

---

gladstone n *type of suitcase* b1885
incandescent lamp n b1885
lightbulb n b1885
mason jar n b1885
Oriental rug n b1885
porcelain enamel n b1885
pram n (Brit) *baby buggy* b1885
public assistance n b1885
sunlamp n b1885
tap water n b1885
tarmacadam n *type of pavement* b1885
toilet paper n b1885
trike n *tricycle* b1885
water tower n b1885
ashtray n b1890
bifocals n b1890
bleach n b1890 (bleaching powder: b1850)
fag n *cigarette* b1890
flyswatter n b1890
handlebar n b1890
kaffeeklatsch n b1890
key ring n b1890
letterhead n b1890

nutpick n b1890
petroleum jelly n b1890 (petrolatum: b1880)
pilot light n b1890
rolltop desk n b1890
rubber band n b1890
rubber cement n b1890
slipcover n b1890
steamer trunk n b1890
talcum powder n b1890
washrag n (Am) b1890
bath mat n b1895
billfold n (Am) b1895
birdbath n (Am) b1895
bone china n b1895
box spring n b1895
carbon copy n b1895
coat hanger n b1895
cocoa butter n b1895
common or garden adj (Brit) *everyday* b1895
corkboard n b1895
dinnerware n b1895
floor lamp n b1895
general-purpose adj b1895
hankie n b1895 (handkerchief: b1530)

hatpin n b1895
highboy n b1895
hurricane lamp n b1895
kit bag n b1895
longcase clock n *grandfather clock* b1895
lunchpail n (Am) b1895
nightstand n b1895
pepper shaker n b1895
perfecto n (Am) *type of cigar* b1895
saltshaker n (Am) b1895 (saltcellar: b1450)
schoolbag n b1895
scratch pad n b1895
steak knife n b1895
tea ball n b1895
teething ring n (Am) b1895
ash can n
bedspring n
bumbershoot n
can n (Am) *bathroom*
Chinese lacquer n
countertop n
drier/dryer n
dustcover n
escalator n (adj use: b1930)
fluorescent lamp n
fourniture n *furniture*
goblet n ["drinking bowl": b1350]
greeting card n
grip n *type of baggage*
home economics n (Am)
hook n *as in "phone off the hook"* (verb use: b1300)
housebroken adj
identity card n (identification card: b1900)
metalware n
morris chair n
nipple n *on baby bottle* [on body: b1530]
refrigerate v *preserve with cold* [gen. "cool": b1470]
rest room n (Am)
schooner n *type of beer glass*
scratch paper n
serial number n
sham n *part of bedclothing*
steel wool n
term insurance n
tote bag n (Am)
trifocals n
uppers n *part of dentures*
washcloth n (Am)

Shelter/Housing

bunkhouse n (Am) b1880
cold storage n b1880
eaves trough n b1880
fire station n b1880 (firehouse: b1900)
half bath n b1880
hallway n (Am) b1880 (hall: b1670)
shack n (Am) b1880
storm cellar n b1880
toolroom n b1880
catwalk n b1885
console n *type of cabinet* b1885 [type of panel: b1710; as in "instrument console": b1945]
firetrap n b1885
floorboard n b1885
linen closet n b1885
safe-deposit box n (Am) b1885
sauna n *saunahouse* b1885 ["saunabath": b1940]
sleeping porch n b1885
sprinkler system n b1885
two-by-four n (Am) b1885
water supply n b1885
window box n b1885
campcraft n b1890
cyclone cellar n (Am) b1890
fire drill n b1890
foster home n b1890
hutment n *group of huts or a single hut* b1890
I beam n b1890
natatorium n *swimming pool* b1890
rooming house n (Am) b1895
tar paper n (Am) b1895
built-in adj (noun use: b1930)
checkroom n (Am)
development n *as in "real estate development"*
downspout n
fiberboard n
firehouse n (fire station: b1880)
funk hole n
lounge n
motte and bailey n *type of castle*
plasterboard n
station n *as in "police station"*
terrazzo n

Drink

tree house n

wire v *as in "wire a house for electricity"*

orange pekoe n *type of tea* b1880

rock and rye n b1880

soft drink n b1880

pasteurize v b1885 (pasteurization: b1890)

sour mash n (Am) b1885

Tom Collins n b1885

gargle n *slang alcoholic drink* b1890

ginger ale n b1890

grain alcohol n b1890

hit the bottle v b1890

malted milk n b1890

manhattan n *type of cocktail* b1890

martini n (Am) b1890

milkshake n (Am) b1890

snort n *drink* b1890

spike v *slip alcohol into* b1890 (noun use: b1910)

whiskey sour n (Am) b1890

aperitif n b1895

limeade n b1895

rickey n (Am) *type of drink* b1895

chaser n *as in "beer chaser"*

cream n *type of sherry*

hooch n *slang liquor*

lotion n *arch. slang drink*

nondrinker n

ouzo n

rose n *type of wine*

shake n

vino n

sloe gin n b1895

Food

Bavarian cream n b1880

bearnaise sauce n b1880

brick cheese n (Am) b1880

brown sauce n b1880

Camembert n b1880

carbonnade n *type of stew* b1880

chateaubriand n b1880

chiffonade n *vegetables cut for garnish* b1880

coffee cake n (Am) b1880

crabmeat n b1880

cream puff n b1880

crepe n b1880

fish-and-chips n b1880

flatbread n b1880

French dressing n (Am) b1880

gorgonzola n *type of cheese* b1880

hard sauce n *type of dessert topping* b1880

layer cake n b1880

lemon sole n b1880

mess kit n b1880

pilsner n b1880

poor boy n (Am) b1880

popover n (Am) b1880

pousse-café n b1880

ratatouille n b1880

ricotta n *type of cheese* b1880

round steak n b1880

saccharin n b1880

shepherd's pie n b1880

sun-cured adj (Am) b1880

table salt n b1880

tournedos n b1880

whole-wheat adj b1880

angel food cake n b1885

baking soda n (Am) b1885

green vegetable n b1885

hamburger n b1885

health food n b1885

helping n *as in "2nd helpings"* b1885

jack bean n b1885

peanut oil n b1885

petit four n *type of cake* b1885

pot roast n (Am) b1885

prairie oyster n *type of hangover remedy* b1885

vinaigrette sauce n b1885

bamboo shoot n b1890

bean curd n b1890

bratwurst n b1890

butterfat n b1890

canape n b1890

casaba n *type of melon* b1890

chop suey n (Am) b1890

confectioners' sugar n b1890

crème brûlée n b1890

delicatessen n (Am) *food sold at a delicatessen* b1890 (deli: b1950)

fruit sugar n b1890

parbake v b1890

patent flour n b1890

pea bean n b1890

peanut butter n (Am) b1890

pearl onion n b1890

rib roast n b1890

rolled oats n (Am) b1890

sauerbraten n (Am) b1890

snake poison n (Am) *bad liquor* b1890

Spanish omelette n b1890

white mule n *type of alcohol* b1890

brut adj *very dry—to describe wine* b1895

chile relleno n (Am) b1895

escargot n b1895

frankfurter n (Am) b1895 (frank: b1905)

fruitarian n *fruit vegetarian* b1895

gefilte fish n b1895

gnocchi n *type of dumpling* b1895

goat cheese n b1895

Granny Smith n *type of apple* b1895

hard-boil v b1895

hasenpfeffer n b1895

iceberg lettuce n b1895

jelly roll n (Am) b1895

minestrone n *type of soup* b1895

mousse n b1895

Neapolitan ice cream n b1895

parfait n b1895

saltwater taffy n (Am) b1895

shore dinner n b1895

smorgasbord n *buffet* b1895 ["array": b1870]

strudel n b1895

sundae n b1895

sushi n b1895

zweiback n b1895

animal cracker n

brownie n (Am) *type of dessert*

brunch n

certified milk n

chow mein n (Am)

commissary n

corn oil n

crescent roll n

croissant n

din-din n *slang dinner*

eggs Benedict n (Am)

fudge n (Am) *type of confection*

hokeypokey n *type of ice cream*

hot dog n (Am)

kaiser roll n

marshmallow n *type of confection* [type of plant: b1000]

meat loaf n

paprika n

parmigiana adj

pizza n

plum tomato n

red meat n

roulade n *type of beef*

Salisbury steak n (Am)

sherbet n *type of ice dessert*

shredded wheat n

sour ball n

sweet chocolate n

wax bean n

wheat germ n

wiener n (Am) (wienerwurst: b1890; wienie: b1900)

yummy adj

Agriculture/ Food-Gathering

cowpuncher n b1880

farmwife n b1880

groundkeeper n b1880 (groundskeeper: b1905)

hatchery n b1880

potato blight n b1880

vinification n b1880

winery n (Am) b1880

cowgirl n b1885 (cowboy: b1870)

cowpoke n b1885

cross-pollination n b1885 (cross-pollinate: b1900)

cutting horse n b1885

disk harrow n b1885

disk/disc v b1885

milo n (Am) *type of grain* b1885

root rot n b1885

roughage n b1885

silage n b1885

combine n b1890 (verb use: b1930)

dogie n (Am) *as in "get along little dogie"* b1890

insectary n b1890

weedkiller n b1890

aquarist n b1895

dairy cattle n b1895

hogtie v (Am) b1895

bonsai n

herbicide n

hopperdozern n *insect killer*

tractor n

wrangle v *be a wrangler*

wrangler, wrangle n, v

Cloth/Clothing

batik n b1880
blazer n b1880
clobber n (Brit) *clothing* b1880
Egyptian cotton n b1880
handwoven adj b1880
leatherette n *simulated leather* b1880
sateen n *type of satin* b1880
shirt jacket n b1880
smoking jacket n b1880
tea gown n *gown for afternoon entertaining* b1880
dress shield n b1885
Eton jacket n b1885
filet n *type of lace* b1885
footwear n (Am) b1885 (footgear: b1840)
full-fashioned adj b1885
interlining n b1885
knickers n b1885 ["type of women's clothing": b1900]
Mother Hubbard n (Am) *type of dress* b1885
pajama n b1885
skintight adj b1885
slicker n (Am) *raincoat* b1885
slip stitch n b1885
Swiss muslin n b1885
bell-bottoms n b1890
civvy/civvies n b1890
Eton collar n b1890
fedora n (Am) b1890
fright wig n b1890
huarache n *type of sandal* b1890
inseam n b1890
jockstrap n b1890 (jock: b1955)
kid glove n b1890
larrigan n *type of moccasin* b1890
leotard n b1890
maillot n *type of clothing* b1890
oxford n *type of shoe* b1890
picture hat n *type of hat* b1890
pith helmet n b1890
separate n *a la carte clothing* b1890
tennis shoe n b1890 (tennies: b1955)

tuxedo n (Am) b1890 (tux: b1920)
bootstrap n b1895
cowboy boot n b1895
cowboy hat n b1895
dinner jacket n b1895
double knit n b1895
dress shirt n b1895
hip boot n (Am) b1895
homburg n *type of hat* b1895
leg warmer n b1895
mess jacket n b1895
mothproof adj b1895 (verb use: b1895)
peekaboo adj b1895
ready-to-wear adj (Am) b1895
single-knit adj/n b1895
string tie n b1895
sweatband n b1895
turtleneck n (Am) b1895
union suit n b1895
Windsor tie n b1895
ascot n
bow tie n
chiffon n *type of fabric* [arch. type of garment ornamentation: b1760] (adj use: b1905)
cuff link n
formfitting adj
housedress n (Am)
jodhpur n *type of riding breeches*
lid n *slang hat*
matinee n
patch n *as in "armpatch"*
reefer n *type of overcoat*
sneaker n
stocking cap n
supporter n
sweater n
tricorn n *type of hat*
trunks n *as in "swimming trunks," "boxing trunks"* [obs. "trunk-hose": b1600 to 1600s; type of underwear: b1970]
undies n
weight n *sturdiness of fabric*
wraparound n (adj use: b1930)
zug n *type of leather*

Fashion/Style

bang/bangs n *hair term* b1880

epilation n *hair removal* b1880 (epilate v: b1890)
lipstick n (Am) b1880 (verb use: b1930)
manicure n *manicurist, the manicure itself* b1880 (verb use: b1890; manicurist: b1890)
pince-nez n *type of eyeglasses* b1880
swish adj *in style* b1880
tony adj *chichi* b1880 (tonish: b1800)
eyebrow pencil n b1885
polka dot n (Am) b1885
handlebar mustache n b1890
mascara n b1890
sideburns n (Am) b1890
Early American n b1895
Gibson girl n (Am) b1895
hot adj *popular, good* b1895
maquillage n b1895
marcel n *type of hair wave* b1895 (verb use: b1910)
stickpin n (Am) b1895
upscale adj (Am) b1895 (verb use: b1970)
Vandyke beard n b1895
bun n *type of hairstyle*
conditioner n *type of hair treatment*
craze n *fad*
haircut n
pedicure n ["person who gives pedicures": b1845]
pin curl n
pinstripe n
pompadour n *hairstyle* [gen. "fashions from the reign of Marquise de Pompador": b1760]
sequin n *gaudery* [type of coin: b1585]
snappy adj *smart, snazzy*

Tools

arc light n b1880
center punch n b1880
clippers n b1880 (clipping shears: b1435; clip: b1465; clipper: b1600)
durometer n b1880
hectograph n *type of duplicating machine* b1880
megaphone n (Am) b1880 (verb use: b1905)
milling machine n b1880
mixer n b1880

periscope n b1880 [type of lens: b1825]
steam shovel n (Am) b1880
worm gear n b1880
dynamo n 1882 [fig. use: b1900]
arc lamp n b1885
ball bearing n b1885
ball joint n b1885
cooker n b1885 ["cook": b1870]
cotter pin n b1885 (cotter: b1340; cotter hole: b1650)
cyclostyle n *early copying machine* b1885
French curve n b1885
headlamp n b1885
humidifier, humidify n, v b1885
incinerator n b1885
loudspeaker n b1885
mortise joint n b1885
rubber stamp n b1885
searchlight n b1885
smudge pot n b1885
thumbtack n (Am) b1885
centrifuge n b1890 (adj use: b1805; verb use: b1900; centrifugal: b1870)
eyebar n b1890
flashlight n b1890
gearbox n b1890
leveling rod n b1890
linter n (Am) *lint-removing machine* b1890
servomotor n b1890 (servo: b1900)
socket wrench n b1890
talking machine n b1890
viewfinder n b1890
duplicator n b1895
inner tube n b1895
baffle n [obs. "confusion": b1630 to 1800s]
blowtorch n
clipboard n (Am)
computer n *calculating machine* ["person who computes": b1620; modern sense: b1945]
detonator n
drop forge n
dropper n
inhalant n
intercooler n
lead n *dog leash*
mantle n *in lanterns, etc.*

multiplier n *calculator*
part n *as in "car parts"*
ricer n (Am) *type of kitchen utensil*
sump pump n
transformer n
wing nut n

Travel/Transportation

catboat n *type of boat* b1880
crankcase n b1880
jet-propelled adj b1880
way point n (Am) b1880
windjammer n (Am) b1880
aquanaut n b1885
bike n (Am) b1885 (verb use: b1895; bicycle: b1870)
camion n *type of cart, truck or bus* b1885
coach-and-four n *type of carriage* b1885
cycle n/v *bicycle, etc.* b1885
dirigible n b1885
internal combustion engine n b1885
port of call n b1885
road map n b1885
running light n b1885
runway n (Am) *gangway* b1885 ["deer tracks": b1835; for airplanes: b1930]
aviator n b1890 (aviatrix: b1910)
club car n (Am) b1890
commute v *as in "commute to work"* b1890 (noun use: b1955; commuter: b1860)
gripman n *cable car driver* b1890
helicopter n b1890 (verb use: b1930; helicopt v: b1945)
motor vehicle n b1890
motorcar n (Am) b1890
motorman n (Am) b1890
mudguard n b1890
odyssey n b1890
parkway n (Am) b1890
pedal v b1890
rickshaw n b1890
ropeway n b1890
tandem bicycle n b1890
terminal n *as in "railroad terminal"* b1890
three-wheeler n b1890
trolley car n b1890

alternator n *automotive sense* b1895
balloon tire n b1895
busman n b1895
diesel adj/n b1895 (verb use: b1975)
horseless carriage n b1895
pushcart n b1895
road hog n b1895
roadster n *type of carriage* b1895
saddle seat n b1895
scenic railway n b1895
spaceship n b1895
speed limit n b1895
surrey n b1895
taximeter n b1895
tow car n (Am) *towtruck* b1895
truckdriver n b1895 (trucker: b1870)
two-seater n b1895
velodrome n b1895
auto n *car*
autobus n (Am)
automotive adj (noun use "self-propelled vehicle": b1870; automobile adj: b1870)
cab n *motor vehicle* ["carriage": b1830]
car n *auto* [gen. use: b1350]
clutch n *in automobiles* [in other mechanisms: b1815]
cog railway n (Am)
elevator n *for people*
emergency brake n
footslog v *march* (verb use: b1920)
fuel injection n
glider n
gurney cab n
local n *type of train route*
locomobile n
manifold n
monorail adj (noun use: b1930)
motor v
motorcycle n
motorist n
plug n *as in "sparkplug"*
quad n *type of bicycle*
rush hour n
self-propelled adj
shuttle n *type of vehicle* (verb use: b1550)
sleeper n *sleeping car*

subway n ["underground passage": b1825]
suitcase n
tanker n (tank steamer: b1890)
telpherage n *electrical transportation*
track n *as in "tank tracks"*
trailer n *towed vehicle*
transfer n *type of bus ticket, etc.*
trek n [spec. type of journey: b1835] (verb use: b1930)
victoria n *type of carriage*
zeppelin n

Emotions/ Characteristics

claustrophobia n b1880 (claustrophobic adj: b1900; claustrophobic n: b1955)
tight-lipped adj b1880
unemotional adj b1880
uninhibited adj b1880
bellyache v b1885 (bellyacher: b1930)
bossy adj (Am) *domineering* b1885
cataplexy n *freezing in fear* b1885
closemouthed adj b1885
flannelmouthed adj (Am) *boastful* b1885
gun-shy adj b1885
hero-worship v b1885 (noun use: b1775)
hubris n b1885
internalize v b1885
nosy adj b1885
poker face n (Am) b1885 (poker-faced: b1925)
spook v *startle* b1885
catty adj b1890
decadent n b1890 (adj use: b1840)
dumbstruck adj b1890
goose pimples n b1890 (goose-flesh: b1810; goose bumps: b1935)
nerve n *gall* b1890 ["strength": b1605; "courage": b1810]
persnickety adj b1890 (pernickety: b1810)
plaster saint n *unfeeling person* b1890

sadism n b1890 (sadistic: b1895; sadist: b1900)
scream n *something hilarious* b1890
short-tempered adj b1890
snifty n (Am) *slang uppity* b1890
straight face n b1890
cagey n b1895
chutzpah n b1895
cold feet n b1895
defense mechanism n b1895
exhibitionism, exhibitionist n b1895
grouch, grouchy n, adj (Am) *grouchy mood* b1895 ["grouchy person": b1930] (verb use: b1930)
guts, gutsy adj *courage* b1895 (gutty: b1940)
intrigue v *inspire interest* b1895 ["have a love affair": b1670] (intriguing: b1910)
masochism n b1895
prissy adj (Am) b1895 (priss: b1930)
scrappy adj (Am) *feisty* b1895
self-starter n b1895
swivet n *nerves* b1895
beef n/v *slang gripe*
chesty adj (Am) *haughty* ["big-chested": b1970]
chippy adj *having a chip on the shoulder*
class n *admirableness*
couth adj [obs. "known": b1000 to 1600s; obs. "courteous": b1325 to 1500s] (noun use: b1960)
feisty adj
hack off v *tick off*
heartwarming adj
inhibition n
micromania n *self-depreciation*
panache n *suaveness* [type of feather decoration: b1555]
peckish adj *ornery*
pose n *attitude, pretense* (verb use: b1870; poseur: b1875)
shamefaced adj *ashamed* ["shy": b1545]
shook-up adj *agitated*
spineless adj *cowardly*
toyful adj *arch. playful*
trauma n [med. sense: b1695;

gen. "perturbation":
b1970] (traumatic: b1900;
traumatize: b1905)

vocal adj *outspoken* ["articulate": b1630]

willies n (Am)

xenon n

Thoughts/Perception/ The Mind

conceptualize v b1880

levelheaded adj (Am) b1880
(level adj: b1870)

ontological argument n b1880

self-awareness n b1880 (self-aware: b1930)

electrotherapy n b1885

hypnosis n *mesmerization*
b1885 ["coaxing to sleep":
b1880]

hypomania n b1885

psychopath n b1885

autosuggestion n b1890

expertism n b1890

megalomania n b1890

posthypnotic adj b1890

psychotic adj b1890 (noun
use: b1930)

screwy adj (Am) b1890
["drunk": b1820;
"scroogelike": b1870]

theoretician n b1890

twisted adj *crazy, perverted*
b1890

blue-sky adj b1895

brainstorm n/v b1895

bughouse adj *crazy* b1895
(noun use: b1930; bugs
adj: b1925)

egocentric adj b1895

dementia praecox n *schizophrenia*

ethical adj *principled*

free association n

hunch n *inkling* ["hint":
b1870]

hypnotherapy n

knee-jerk adj

loony tunes adj/n

off your rocker adj

phobic adj (noun use:
b1970)

romantic n *idealist* (romanticize: b1820)

siege mentality n

statuvolism n *self-hypnosis*

swing n *change of opinion*

unconscious n

value judgment n

Love/Romance/Sex

bride-price n *opp. of dowage*
b1880

diddle v *have sex with* b1880

monogyny n *having only one
wife at a time* b1880 [monogamy in this sense:
b1730]

one-night stand n (Am)
b1880

eroticism n b1885 (erotism:
b1850)

bridal wreath n b1890

casanova n b1890

chippy n (Am) *loose woman*
b1890

cunnilingus n b1890

erogenous adj b1890 (erotogenic: b1910)

fellatio n b1890 (fellate v:
b1900)

horny adj *seeking sex* b1890
(horn-mad: b1895)

married n b1890

mash note n b1890

premarital adj b1890

sapphism n *lesbianism* b1890

stuck on adj (Am) *in love
with* b1890

conjugal rights n b1895

cunt-struck adj b1895

hard-on n b1895

heterosexual adj b1895
(noun use: b1920; hetero:
b1935)

homosexual, homosexuality
adj, n b1895 (noun use:
b1905; homo: b1930)

libido n b1895 (libidinous:
b1450; libidinal: b1925)

ménage à trois n b1895

red-light district n b1895

stud n (Am) *attractive man*
b1895

autoerotic, autoerotism, auto-eroticism adj, n

bang v *have sex*

coitus interruptus n

come-hither adj

common-law marriage n

courtly love n

curious adj *erotic*

do v *have sex*

erect adj *sexual sense* (erection: b1500)

lesbian adj/n *gay* ["of Lesbos": b1595]

meat market n *singles bar*

oversexed adj

promiscuous adj ["mixed":
b1605] (promiscuity:
b1865)

safe n *condom*

scorcher n *beautiful woman*

scrub n *whorish woman*
(scrubber: b1960)

suck v *perform oral sex*

tease v *tease sexually* (noun
use: b1980)

unattached adj *maritally single*

urning n *arch. homosexual*

womanize v *pursue women*

Family/Relations/ Friends

comradery n b1880

newborn n b1880

parity n *parenthood* b1880

great-grandparent n b1885
(great-grandfather: b1515;
great-grandmother:
b1530)

great-niece n b1885 (great-nephew: b1585)

momma n b1885 (mum:
b1825; mommy: b1890;
mom: b1895)

distaff side n b1890

grandpa n b1890 (grandfather: b1425; granddaddy:
b1760; grandpapa, grand-pappy: b1770; granddad:
b1785; grandpop: b1900)

identical twin n b1890

mommy n (Am) b1890
(mum: b1825; momma:
b1885; mom: b1895)

stepparent n b1890 (stepparenting: b1980)

adoptee n b1895

in-law n b1895

mom n b1895 (mum: b1825;
momma: b1885; mommy:
b1890)

boyfriend n

clanswoman n (clansman:
b1810)

familial adj

gramp n

grandpop n (grandfather:
b1425; granddaddy:
b1760; grandpapa, grand-

pappy: b1770; granddad:
b1785; grandpa: b1890)

grandsire n *grandfather*

parent-in-law n

Holidays

Christmas card n b1885

Roman holiday n b1890

vacation v

Games/Fun/Leisure

musical chairs n b1880

bye n *as in "a tournament
bye"* b1885 ["unscheduled
game": b1720]

cue ball n b1885

pinball n (Am) b1885 (pinball machine: 1936)

ballpark n (Am) b1890

full house n *the poker game*
b1890

glassie n *type of marble*
b1890

go n *the game* b1890

kitty n *as in "poker kitty"*
b1890 [Brit slang "jail":
b1825]

patty-cake n b1890

pinata n b1890

ring-around-a-rosy n b1890

shoofly n *type of rocker* b1890

snooker n b1890

middle game n *in chess* b1895

prizewinner n b1895

railbird n *horserace fan* b1895

slot machine n b1895

tee off v b1895

box kite n

chukker n *polo term*

game n *as in "board game"*

hearts n

joker n *in cards*

maffick v *celebrate*

reversi n

slide n *type of playground
equipment*

snap n *type of card game*

sparkler n *type of firework*

squash n

stake race n

swimming hole n (Am)

tetherball n

volleyball n (Am)

Sports

doubleheader n b1880

scorecard n b1880

scorekeeper n (Am) b1880

sumo n b1880
acrobatics n b1885
bantam-weight n b1885
cyclist n b1885
grass court n b1885
ice hockey n b1885
long jump n b1885
major league, minor league
adj/n (Am) b1885
pari-mutuel n b1885
playfield n b1885
replay v b1885 (noun use:
b1895)
roller rink n b1885
speed skating n b1885
water polo n b1885
all-American adj b1890
(noun use: b1920)
all-star adj (Am) b1890
(noun use: b1940)
barbell n b1890
bleachers, bleaching boards n
(Am) b1890
consolation prize n b1890
court tennis n b1890
figure eight n *in figure skating*
b1890
fly casting, flycast n, v b1890
fly fisherman n b1890
golf course n b1890
handball n b1890
judo n b1890
miler n b1890
nelson n *type of wrestling hold*
b1890
open season n (Am) b1890
pole vault n/v b1890 (pole
jump: b1900)
punching bag n b1890
safari n b1890
ski v b1890 (skier, skiing:
b1890)
soccer n b1890
stiff n *bad competitor* b1890
basketball n 1892
backswing n b1895
belly flop v/n b1895
benchwarmer n b1895
circus catch n b1895
high jump n b1895
locker room n b1895 (adj use:
b1950)
medicine ball n b1895
pigskin n b1895 [obs. "saddle": b1855 to 1940s]
play-off n b1895
puck n *as in "hockey puck"*
b1895

rock climbing n b1895
semifinal n b1895 (adj use:
b1885)
shot put n b1895
workout n b1895
marathon n 1896 [gen. use:
b1930] (adj use: b1930)
bangtail n *racehorse*
compete v
doubles n
down adv *losing*
field event n
finish line n
gallery n *golf, etc., audience*
golf cart n
hammer n
hammer throw n
hammerlock n
handstand n
kung fu n
mitt n *in baseball* [gen. use:
b1765]
pole n *in pole vault* ["ski
pole": b1930; racing "pole
position": b1970]
pole jump n *pole vault*
relay race n
seed v *rank in a tournament*
shoot v
single n
starting gate n
swan dive n (Am)
swimming pool n
weight lifter, weightlifting n
western saddle n
wire n *as in "wire to wire"*

Professions/Duties

estate agent n (Brit) b1880
floorwalker n (Am) b1880
masseur, masseuse n b1880
paperboy n b1880
bookie n b1885
home builder n b1885
housemaster n b1885
liftman n (Brit) *elevator operator* b1885
pipe fitter n b1885
press agent n b1885
steelworker n b1885
steeplejack n b1885
typist n b1885
wildcatter n (Am) b1885
building trades n b1890
chocolatier n b1890
craftswoman n b1890 (craftsman: b1200; craftsperson:

b1920; craftspeople:
b1955)
ethicist n b1890 (ethician:
b1630)
floor manager n (Am) b1890
garbageman n (Am) b1890
geisha n b1890
hawkshaw n *detective* b1890
manicurist n b1890
palmist n b1890 (palmistry:
b1425)
patentor n b1890 (patentee:
b1450)
steamfitter n b1890
therapist n b1890
mortician n (Am) b1895
chauffeur n (verb use:
b1920)
cleaner n *as in "dry cleaner"*
couturier n (couture: b1910;
couturiere: b1820)
ditchdigger n
dynamitard n *dynamiter*
house detective n (Am)
houseboy n (housegirl:
b1835)
lifeguard n ["bodyguard":
b1650]
panhandler, panhandle n, v
(Am) (panhandle: b1900)
waddy n (Am) *cowboy*
wine steward n

Business/Commerce/
Selling

boycott n/v 1880
buy n b1880
cash register n (Am) b1880
five-and-ten n b1880
general partnership n b1880
markdown n b1880 (mark
down: b1875)
robber baron n b1880
salesmanship n b1880
salespeople n (Am) b1880
(salesperson: b1905)
storefront n b1880 (adj use:
b1940)
trade route n b1880
traveling salesman n b1880
cut-rate adj b1885
distress sale n b1885
grillroom n b1885 (grill:
b1900)
honest broker n b1885
loaner n b1885
price tag n (Am) b1885

advertorial n b1890
beanery n (Am) b1890
book value n b1890
consumer goods n b1890
corporatism n b1890
department store n (Am)
b1890
free enterprise n b1890
rag trade n *clothing business*
b1890
restraint of trade n b1890
salesgirl n (Am) b1890
scalp v *as in "scalp tickets"*
b1890 (scalper: b1870)
shopping bag n b1890
speakeasy n (Am) b1890
(speak: b1930; speako:
b1935)
tab n *slang bill* b1890
carrying charge n (Am)
b1895
cold store n b1895
fire sale n (Am) b1895
oligopoly n *akin to monopoly*
b1895
rollback n b1895 (roll back:
b1945)
shakeout n b1895
soft goods n b1895
trade secret n b1895
vending machine n b1895
bargain basement n (adj use:
b1950)
business n *commercial company*
capital goods n
enterprise n
front office n (Am)
galleria n
odd lot n
pitch n *as in "sales pitch"*
(verb use: b1970)
rathskeller n (Am)
receivership n
register n *cash register*
sandwich board n
shopping center n
trading stamp n (Am)
trust n *type of company; cartel*
(trustee: b1650; trust company: b1835)

The Workplace

handwrought adj b1880
fire v *discharge* b1885
["eject": b1875]
industrialize v b1885
labor force n b1885

profit sharing n b1885

shoptalk n b1885

ca'canny n (Brit) *work slow-down* b1890

employment agency n (Am) b1890

forelady n (Am) b1890

layoff n b1890

living wage n b1890

sick pay n b1890

time and a half n b1890

time clock n (Am) b1890

unemployment n b1890

wage slave n b1890

walkout n (Am) b1890

collective bargaining n b1895

decasualization n *hiring permanent employees* b1895

footage n *way to determine miners' pay* b1895

pick-and-shovel adj b1895

road gang n b1895

straw boss n (Am) b1895

time sheet n b1895

differential n

full-time adj (full-timer: b1865)

labor camp n

open shop n

paycheck n

position n *job*

reference n

Finances/Money

accrual n b1880 (adj use: b1920; accrue: b1440)

certified check n (Am) b1880

installment plan n b1880

balance of payments n b1885

blank check n b1885

credit union n (Am) b1885

millionairess n b1885 (millionaire: b1830)

out-of-pocket adj b1885

silver certificate n b1885

surtax n b1885

antitrust adj (Am) b1890

bankroll n b1890 (verb use: b1930)

credit card n (Am) b1890

jack n *slang cash* b1890

price index n b1890

tax rate n b1890

long green n (Am) *cash* b1895

shortchange v (Am) b1895

traveler's check n b1895

conspicuous consumption n 1899

asset n (assets: b1535)

bounce v

certified public accountant n (Am)

cost of living n

depress v (depressed: b1625)

dollars-and-cents adj

equity n

escrow n [leg. sense: b1595] (verb use: b1950)

exchange rate n

liquid adj (noun use: b1730)

market n *stock market*

simolean n *slang $*

well-heeled adj

Language and Speaking

cryptogram n b1880 (cryptograph: b1850)

cryptonym n *code name* b1880

direct object n b1880

indirect object n b1880

pidgin n b1880 (pidginize: b1940)

Roman alphabet n b1880

Americanese n b1885

dysphemism n *opp. of euphemism* b1885

heteronym n *e.g., bow "gesture" and bow "front of ship"* b1885

journalese n b1885

nonce words n b1885

officialese n b1885

pejorative n b1885 (gen. adj use: b1890; pejorate "worsen": b1670)

portmanteau word n b1885

swear word n (Am) b1885

telegraphese n b1885

accent mark n b1890

back-formation n b1890

consonant shift n b1890

past perfect adj b1890

Esperanto n b1895

footle n/v *prattle* b1895

linguistician n *linguist* b1895

logorrhea n *rapid sesquipedalianism* b1895

phoneme n b1895

semantics, semantic n, adj b1895 (semanticist: b1905)

technobabble n b1895

decode v

four-letter word n

future perfect n

initialism n *acronym*

koine n *dialect*

logomaniac n *word maven*

morpheme n

mumbo jumbo n *nonsense* ["type of West African idol": b1740]

reformed spelling n

split infinitive n

spoonerism n

tongue twister n

weasel word n (Am) *meaningless word* (weasel v: b1900)

Contractions

mightn't contr b1890

Literature/Writing

carbon paper n b1880

dossier n b1880

echoism n *onomatopoeia* b1880

ex libris n b1880

gravure n b1880

Italian sonnet n b1880

printed matter n b1880

prosateur n *prose writer* b1880

short story n b1880

typecast v *set up type for printing* b1880 [slang use: b1930]

automatic writing n b1885

call slip n (Am) *in libraries* b1885

character sketch n b1885

curiosa n *curios; erotic books* b1885

documentation n b1885

folk etymology n b1885

literacy n b1885

newspaperwoman n b1885 (newspaperman: b1810)

write-up n (Am) b1885

afterword n b1890

bedtime story n b1890

bestseller n (Am) b1890

endleaf n b1890

hard copy n b1890

scarehead n *alarming headline* b1890

subheading, subhead n b1890

typeface n b1890

typewrite v b1890 (type v: b1900)

want ad n (Am) b1890

copyreader n (Am) b1895

picaresque n b1895 (adj use: b1810)

roman à clef n b1895

shift key n b1895

typographical error n b1895

copy editor n

cover v *as in "cover a story for a newspaper"*

double-space v

galley proof n (galley: b1670)

ghostwriter, ghost n (ghostwrite, ghost v: b1930)

haiku n

hardcase adj (hardbound adj: b1930; hardcover: b1950; hardback: b1955)

limerick n

little magazine n *magazine of the small press*

memorandum n *note* ["memory jogger": b1450] (adj use: b1435)

novella n

paperback n

proof v *proofread; create a proof*

sourcebook n (Am)

storiette n *short-short story*

story n *as in "newspaper story"*

text n *textbook*

thirty n *the end*

type v *use a typewriter*

vignette n

white paper n *report*

wordsmith n

Communication

microphone n *in telephone* b1880 ["ear trumpet": b1685; in radio: b1930]

open letter n b1880

telephone n *modern sense* b1880 [type of ship communication device: b1835; type of loudspeaker: b1850] (verb use: b1880)

phone n *telephone* b1885 (verb use: b1890)

radiophone n b1885

ring up, ring off v (Brit) *hang up* b1885

special delivery n (Am) b1885

telephone number n b1885

mimeograph n/v b1890 (mimeo: b1945)

phototelegraphy n *transmission of pictures* b1890

press box n (Am) b1890

registered mail n b1890

busy signal n b1895

dial tone n b1895

rural free delivery n b1895

telephone booth n (Am) b1895

wireless telephone n b1895

wiretapper n b1895 (wiretap v: b1905; wiretap n: b1950)

cable n *telegram* (cablegram: b1870)

exchange n *as in "telephone exchange"*

pigeongram n *carrier pigeon message*

radiotelegraph n

rural route n

wireless telegraphy n

Visual Arts/ Photography

artwork n b1880

impressionist n b1880

neoclassic adj b1880

photogravure n b1880

stereo adj *stereoscopic* b1880 (noun use: b1825; stereoscope: b1840)

wide-angle adj b1880

aesthete n b1885

gouache n b1885

telephotography n b1885 (telephoto adj: b1895; telephoto n: b1905)

airbrush n, v b1890

gallerygoer n b1890

tondo n *type of painting* b1890

trompe l'oeil n b1890

double exposure n b1895

exposure meter n b1895

f-number n b1895

kinetoscope n b1895

line drawing n b1895

neo-gothic adj b1895

neo-impressionism n b1895

roll film n b1895

time exposure n b1895

graphics n

Performing Arts

commedia dell'arte n b1880

Punch-and-Judy show n b1880

scenario n b1880 [gen. use: b1965]

stage v b1880

stage fright n b1880

audition n *tryout* b1885 (verb use: b1935)

barnstorm v b1885

comedy drama n b1885

curtain call n b1885

ham n b1885 (verb use: b1935; hambone: b1895)

playlet n b1885

stagecraft n b1885

three-ring circus n (Am) b1885

variety show n b1885

curtain-raiser n b1890

greasepaint n b1890

peanut gallery n (Am) b1890

trouper n (Am) b1890 [fig., as in "he's a good trouper": b1930]

angel n *financial backer* b1895

backstage adj (adv use: b1925)

costume n

decor n *stage setting* [as in "residential decor": b1930]

gate n *total attendance*

interpretation v *personal version*

juggle v *as in "juggle balls"* [var. gen. meanings of "entertain": b1400]

Kabuki n

line n *as in "learn your lines"*

mount v *as in "mount a play"*

playact v

principal n *principal performer*

road company n (Am)

script n *playscript*

toe dance n (toe-shoe: b1950)

Music

bull fiddle n (Am) b1880

cello n b1880 (cellist: b1890)

concertmaster n b1880

double bassoon n b1880

downbeat n b1880

humoresque n *type of musical composition* b1880

leitmotif n b1880

luthier n *maker of stringed instruments* b1880

ocarina n b1880

orchestrate v b1880 [fig. "organize": b1900] (orchestration: b1860)

phonograph n b1880

woodwind n *woodwind section* b1880 ["woodwind instrument": b1930]

diva n b1885

hum v b1885

kazoo n (Am) b1885

light opera n (Am) b1885

metallophone n *type of musical instrument* b1885

pipe organ n b1885

symphony orchestra n b1885

tone color n *timbre* b1885

gramophone n 1887

art song n b1890

disk n *phonograph record* b1890

drumroll n b1890

upright piano n b1890

world beat n b1890

bandleader n b1895

chopsticks n b1895

chorus girl n b1895 (chorine: b1925)

concert grand n b1895

contrabassoon n b1895

razzmatazz n b1895

tone-deaf adj b1895

beat n *musical beat*

celesta n *musical instrument*

direct v *as in "direct an orchestra"*

hamfatter n *hamhanded musician*

lyric n

organistrum n *type of hurdy-gurdy*

rag n *ragtime song*

ragtime n

record n *as in "phonograph record"*

rhapsody n

song cycle n

sousaphone n

swing n *type of music* (adj use: b1935)

tuning pipe n *pitch pipe*

ukulele n (Am) (uke: b1925)

Entertainment

house party n b1880

stunt n (Am) *as in "motorcycle stunt"* b1880 (verb use: b1920)

high wire n b1885

nightclub n (Am) b1885

samba n b1885

freak show n b1890

roller coaster n b1890

shadowgraph n *shadow play* b1890 (shadow play: b1895; shadow box: b1910)

spoof n/v b1890 [type of card game: b1885; "parody": b1915]

Ferris wheel n 1893

headline v b1895

high comedy n b1895

midway n b1895

prom n (Am) b1895

serialize v b1895 ["arrange serially": b1860]

two-step n *type of dance* b1895

beauty contest n

belly dance n

collectible adj *suitable for a collection* (noun use: b1955; collect: b1870)

flamenco n

hootchy-kootchy n

roast n *as in "wienie roast"*

shindig n *party, hoopla* [lit. "dig in the shins": b1860]

tango n (verb use: b1915)

Movies/TV/Radio

nickelodeon n (Am) b1890

cinematograph n 1895

motion picture n b1895

cinematography, cinematographer n 1897 (cinematograph: 1896)

cine n

grip n *in films*

moving picture n (movie: b1910)

picture n *motion picture* (verb use: b1500)

projector n

shoot v

Education

alumna n b1880 (alumnus: b1645; alum: b1930)

docent n b1880
interscholastic adj b1880
extension course n b1885
housefather n b1885 (housemother: b1840; housepar-
ent: b1955)
correspondence school n
b1890
seminar n (Am) b1890
trade school n b1890
coed n b1895 (adj use:
b1890)
frat n b1895
prep school n b1895
detention n
dorm n
interlibrary adj
junior college n (Am)
letters n
magna cum laude adj/adv
major n (verb use: b1915)
minor n (verb use: b1930)
preppy adj (Am) *pertaining to
prep school* [of a type of
fashion: b1970]
regent n [governmental use:
b1400]
report n
rush n (rushee: b1920)
summa cum laude adj/adv
unit n

Religion

totem pole n b1880
sky pilot n *chaplain* b1885
ankh n b1890
congregant n b1890
hymnary n *hymnal* b1890
(hymnbook: b900; hym-
nal: b1500)
menorah n b1890
prayer rug n b1890
theocentric adj b1890
theonomy n *being theonomous*
b1890
black mass n b1895
interdenominational adj
b1895
Christogram n
theomorphic adj *in God's
image*

Society/Mores/Culture

animal rights n b1880
bag lady n b1880
classless adj b1880
amoral adj b1885
asocial adj b1885

enserf v b1885
persona grata n b1885 (persona non grata: b1905)
socioeconomic adj b1885
undesirable n b1885
urbanite n b1885
urbanize v *make urban* b1885
[obs. "make urbane":
b1635]
class-conscious adj b1890
declasse adj b1890
fin de siecle adj *mood at century's end* b1890
Four Hundred, the n (Am)
high society b1890
gamine n *girl urchin* b1890
(gamin: b1840)
hobo n b1890
interracial adj b1890
prole n b1890 (adj use:
b1970)
quasi-public adj b1890
social work n b1890
suburbanite, suburbanize,
suburbia n b1890 [obs. sub-
urbian: b1630 to 1900s]
populist adj/n (Am) 1892
correctitude n b1895
feminism n b1895 ["feminine
qualities": b1855]
slice-of-life adj b1895
calling card n (Am)
ethnocentric adj
highbrow adj/n
hoity-toity adj ["playful":
b1690]
Jack n *akin to Mac, Bub,
friend*
last name n
mores n
peoplehood n
roadster n *hobo*
schmooze v (Am) (noun use:
b1940)
shake v *shake hands*
tyke n *tot* [lit. and fig. "dog,
cur": b1350]
underprivileged adj

Government

buffer state n b1885
civics n (Am) b1885
executive order n b1885
matriarchate, matriarchy n
b1885
national n *citizen* b1890
regnum n b1890

tribalism n b1890 (tribal:
b1635)
city-state n b1895
majority rule n b1895
electorate n *voters*

Politics

jingo, jingoism n 1878
goldbug n (Am) b1880
Americanist n b1885
disestablishmentarian n
b1885
left wing n b1885
mugwump n *political independent* b1885
paternalism n b1885
regionalism n b1885
great power n *superpower*
b1890
hunger strike n b1890
demonstrate v
expansionism n (expansionist: b1870)
floor leader n (Am) *political
term*
imperialism n *colonization*
(imperialistic: b1880; im-
perialist: b1900)
voting machine n
Zionism n

Death

cinerarium n *place to deposit
cremation ashes* b1880
crematorium, crematory n
b1880
death mask n b1880
mortality table n b1880
cash in v *die* b1885
electric chair n (Am) b1890
electrocute v (Am) b1890
floater n (Am) *dead body*
b1890
funeral director n (Am)
b1890
necrophilia n b1895 (ne-
crophilism: b1865; necro-
phobia: b1870)
plot n *as in "burial plot"*
undead n (adj use: b1450)

War/Military/Violence

bulldozer, bulldoze n, v (Am)
intimidator b1880 ["earthmover": b1930]
high explosive n b1880
iron ration n b1880
militarize v b1880

missilery n b1880
reservist n b1880 (reserve:
b1870)
state of war n b1880
theater of operations n b1880
torpedo v *lit. and fig.* b1880
crosshair n b1885
foreign legion n b1885
free-for-all n (Am) b1885
gunplay n (Am) b1885
infantryman n b1885
pogrom n b1885 (verb use:
b1915)
police action n b1885
Pyrrhic victory n b1885
air rifle n (Am) b1890
chief petty officer n (Am)
b1890
dumdum n *type of bullet*
b1890
epee n *type of rapier* b1890
gelatin dynamite n b1890
guard of honor n b1890
knockout n b1890 [slang
"type of auction": b1820]
land mine n b1890
minefield n b1890 (mine:
b1470)
nightstick n (Am) b1890
sap n *type of club* b1890
(verb use: b1930)
semiautomatic adj b1890
(noun use: b1970)
shoot up v b1890
shore leave n b1890
Springfield rifle n b1890
theater of war n b1890
cannon fodder n b1895
firebomb n/v b1895
iron maiden n b1895
time bomb n b1895
wolf pack n b1895
automatic adj *as in "automatic weapon"* (noun use:
b1905)
baton n *police nightstick* [con-
ductor's baton: b1700; relay racer's baton: b1930]
blow up v *explode*
chain of command n
charge n *as in "explosive
charge"*
conscientious objector n
counterespionage n
destroyer n
dress uniform n
firefight n

jacket n *as in "full metal jacket"*
knee v *hit with the knee*
mailed fist n
pom-pom n *as in "pom-pom guns"*
private n ["private citizen": b1500 to 1700s]
redleg n *artilleryman*
serviceman n (service-woman: b1945; service-person: b1975)
swing v *take a punch*
warhead n
woodpecker n *slang machine gun*

Crime/Punishment/ Enforcement

crook n b1880 ["trickery": b1350 to 1500s] (crooked: b1710)
holdup n b1880
involuntary manslaughter n b1880
revenuer n (Am) b1880
cooler n (Am) *slang jail* b1885
gunrunner, gunrunning n b1885
mark n *victim* b1885
pen n (Am) *prison* b1885
tong n (Am) *gang* b1885
bootlegger n b1890 (bootleg v: b1900)
con adj (Am) *con(fidence game)* b1890
patrol wagon n (Am) b1890
police blotter n b1890
recidivism n b1890 (recidivate: b1530)
second-story man n b1890
shell game n (Am) b1890
swipe v *slang steal* b1890
take n *ill-gotten gains* b1890
marijuana n (Am) b1895
bootleg v (noun use: b1970; bootlegger: b1890)
gangster n (Am)
heroin n
hit-and-run adj (Am)
hooligan, hooliganism n
john n *slang policeman*
madam n *female pimp*
penitentiary n (Am) *prison* [obs. "ecclesiastic place of punishment": b1425;

"prostitute's halfway house": b1830] (adj use: b1580)
plainclothesman n (plainclothes adj: b1870)
third degree n (Am)

The Law

probation officer n (Am) b1880
restraining order n b1880
trial jury n b1885
legal aid n b1890
punitive damages n b1890
trial court n b1890
court reporter n (Am) b1895
parliamentary law n b1895
birth certificate n
grandfather clause n (Am)
juvenile court n (Am)
probation n ["trial, trial period": b1425]
statutory rape n

The Fantastic/ Paranormal

chtonic adj *related to the underworld* b1885
faith cure, faith healing n b1885
mind reading n b1885 (mind reader: b1890)
telepathy, telepathic n, adj b1885 (telepath: b1900)
crystal gazing n b1890
ghost dance n (Am) b1890
shape-shifter n b1890
telekinesis n b1890
discarnate adj *disembodied* b1895
time machine n 1895
elemental n *conjured personification of the elements*
golem n
ray n *as in "death ray"*

Magic

witch-hunt n b1885
kahuna n *"Hawaiian witch doctor"* b1890
cartomancy n *telling fortunes with cards*
hexerei n *witchcraft* (hex "witch": b1860)

Interjections

gawd interj b1880
shoot interj *shit* b1880

yum, yum-yum interj b1880 (yummy: b1900)
auf Wiedersehen interj b1885
come again? interj b1885
congrats interj/n b1885
gee whiz interj (Am) b1885 (adj use: b1935; gee: b1895)
balls interj b1890
blimey interj b1890
kerplunk adv b1890
rats interj b1890
oy interj b1895
brrr interj
crumbs interj
curses interj
giddyap interj (Am)
gorblimey interj
hic interj *hiccup*
horrors interj
hot dog interj (hot diggety dog: b1925)
morning n *good morning*
nighty-night interj
righto interj
sooey interj
splat adv/interj *as in "fell splat on her face"*
uh-huh interj
wahey interj
whee interj

Slang

b'rer n (Am) b1880
bwana n b1880
chin-wag n/v *talk* b1880
critical point n b1880
dipso n b1880 (adj use: b1930)
dude n (Am) b1880
goose v b1880
jim-dandy adj/n b1880
nudge n/v *nag* b1880
ragged edge n b1880
richen v *enrich* b1880
shoestring adj b1880 (noun use: b1930)
snap n (Am) *something easily done* b1880
sozzled adj b1880
stonewall v b1880
tec n *detective* b1880
teeny-weeny adj b1880 (teensy-weensy: b1900)
barrelhouse n (Am) b1885
blooming adj/adv *as in "blooming idiot"* b1885

(bloomer n "blunder": b1890)
bucko n b1885
chalk talk n b1885
gimme n/v b1885
hog v b1885 (noun use: b1470)
kiddo n b1885
loco v *make crazy* b1885 (adj use: b1890)
look-see n b1885
loony bin n b1885
monkey v *as in "monkey around"* b1885
mostest adj/n b1885
pic n b1885
poo-bah n b1885
prelim adj/n b1885
q.t. n b1885
southpaw n (Am) b1885
tommyrot n *bunk* b1885
too-too adj *excessively so* b1885
whatsit n b1885
yum-yum n *sex* b1885 (yum-yum girl: b1960)
blankety-blank adj/adv b1890
bug n b1890
chuck v (Am) *stop* b1890
coffin nail n *cigarette* b1890
comp adj/n/v *comp(limentary)* b1890
dope n *drugs* b1890 [type of sauce, liquid: b1810] (dopey: b1900)
flubdub n (Am) *nonsense* b1890
frame-up n (Am) b1890 (frame v: b1930)
guff n b1890 ["bit of wind": b1825]
gyp n (Am) b1890 (verb use: b1930)
hightail v (Am) b1890
howler n *big goof* b1890
humdinger n b1890 (hummer: b1910)
Jekyll and Hyde n b1890
lefty adj b1890 (noun use: b1930)
lush n *drunkard* b1890
marker n *IOU* b1890
mingy adj b1890
phenom n b1890
plowed adj *drunk* b1890
poop v *as in "poop out"* b1890

razzledazzle adj/n/v b1890

rev n *revolution* b1890 (verb use: b1920)

ringer n *as in "bringing in a ringer to play football"* b1890 ["expert": b1850]

roughhouse n (Am) b1890 (verb use: b1900)

ruckus n (Am) b1890 (ruction: b1825)

sticky-fingered n b1890 (sticky fingers: b1930)

tenderloin n (Am) *as in "tenderloin district"* b1890

twofer n (Am) b1890

wild-and-woolly adj b1890

world-beater n b1890

all-nighter n b1895

altogether n *nude* b1895

brass hat n *muckamuck* b1895 (brass: b1900)

crackerjack/crackajack n b1895 (adj use: b1910)

dead ringer n b1895

don't n *as in "dos and don'ts"* b1895

flag-waver n b1895

flophouse n b1895

holdout n *device for cheating at cards* b1895

honkytonk n/v (Am) b1895

jag n *spree, fling* b1895

jiggery-pokery n *trickery* b1895

kaput adj b1895

lab n b1895

legwork n (Am) b1895

outasight, out-of-sight adj b1895

pally adj *being pals* b1895

prez n b1895

pussyfoot v (Am) b1895

shavetail n *rookie* b1895

shiksa n *non-Jewish girl* b1895

soak v *take money* b1895

tanked adj *drunk* b1895 (tank v: b1900)

tootsie n *woman* b1895

top-shelf adj b1895

whack n *as in "I'll take a whack at it"* b1895

wunderkind n b1895

accident n (Am) *incontinence*

beam v *slang smile*

beat n *area of concern, as in "police beat," "journalist's beat"*

belt n *blow, or drink* (verb use: b1500)

blow v *squander*

buffalo v *bamboozle*

buggery n (Am) *hell*

bunk n (Am) *bunkum*

cheapie n

cheesy adj *tacky*

cinch n *sure thing* ["saddle girth": b1860]

come-on n (Am)

comer n *as in "up-and-comer"*

crap n *dung; rubbish* [obs. "chaff": b1425 to 1400s] (verb use: b1850)

day-tripper n

dif n *as in "what's the dif?"*

donkey's years n (Brit)

drag n (Am) *clout*

dustup n *argument*

exec n

eyeball v

eyeful n (Am)

fall n *as in "take the fall"*

fart v *as in "fart around"*

fed up adj

filbert n *head*

flop n *failure* ["con": b1825] (verb use: b1920)

gabfest n (Am)

gel n/v (gelatin: b1800)

gob v *spit*

goo-goo eyes n

governor, guvner n

honey n *as in "a honey of a day"*

hoot n *as in "I don't give a hoot"*

hop n *narcotic*

hotfoot v (adv use: b1300)

jolly n *as in "get your jollies"*

juicy adj *titillating*

killing n

kitten n *girl*

knock v *insult*

lam n *as in "on the lam"* (verb use: b1890)

lollapalooza n (Am)

looker n

lump, the n *workhouse*

maverick n [type of calf: b1870] (adj use: b1890)

meat n *gist*

mop-up n

mug n *criminal, everyday joe*

needle v *annoy*

nuthouse n (nut college, nuttery: b1935)

nutty adj (nuts: b1850; nutsy: b1945; nutso: b1975)

patsy n (Am)

phony adj/n (Am) (verb use: b1945)

pooch n

qualified adj *euphemism for "damn"*

queer n/adj *homosexual*

railroad v

real adj *as in "get real"*

ringer n *doppelganger*

rinky-dink adj (Am) (noun use: b1915)

rubberneck n/v (Am)

screw out n *leave quickly*

shake v *elude*

sherlock n *detective*

shut-eye n

sleeper n *dark horse*

slug n *coin substitute*

spiel n *patter*

spring v *release*

teensy, teensy-weensy adj

throw n *as in "50 cents a throw"*

veg n

wanna, wanta v

well-heeled adj *wealthy*

wing it n *improvise*

works, the n

zero adj *as in "I have zero cash"*

zip n *energy* (zippy: b1905)

zip n *nothing*

Insults

geek n b1880

chump n *fool* b1885 ["block of wood": b1705]

cow town n b1885

geezer n b1885

mudslinging n b1885 (mudslinger: b1890)

pencil pusher n (Am) b1885

rumormonger n b1885

slam n *insult* b1885 (verb use: b1915)

tinhorn n/adj (Am) b1885

wuss n b1885

bigmouth n (Am) b1890

creep n b1890

dub n *clumsy person* b1890

dumbhead n b1890

four-flush/four-flusher v/n, n (Am) b1890

gasbag n b1890

hardnosed adj b1890 (hardnose: b1960)

meshuggener n *crazy person* b1890 (meshuga adj: b1885)

shorty n b1890

tart n *whore* b1890 [gen. "woman, lover": b1865] (tarty: b1920)

tin god n b1890

cocksucker n b1895 (cocksucking adj: b1925)

fairy n b1895

heller n (Am) *hellion* b1895 (hellion: b1790)

know-it-all n b1895

mucker n (Am) *vulgar, false person* b1895

nebbish n b1895

schlemiel n b1895

schmuck n b1895

sissy adj/n b1895 ["sister": b1850]

swelled head n b1895 (swellhead: b1845)

ambulance chaser n (Am)

bounder n *knave*

cheapskate n (Am)

copycat n (Am) (verb use: b1930)

deadhead n *blockhead* [obs. "death's head figure": b1580 to 1700s; "free rider": b1845]

dippy adj (dip: b1935)

dodo n *dolt*

dopey adj (Am)

fink n (Am) (verb use: b1925)

gutless adj

hillbilly n

jay adj (Am) *crude, backwater*

jeff n *backwater rube*

pipsqueak n

reuben n *rube*

rube n (Am)

rumdum adj/n

scrooge n

slicker n *as in "city slicker"*

tightwad n (Am) (tight adj: b1805)

wise guy n (Am)

womanthrope n *misogynist*

yellow peril n

Phrases

agent provocateur n b1880
business end n b1880
cracker-barrel adj (Am) b1880
do-or-die adj b1880
eat crow v (Am) b1880
face value n b1880
full circle adv b1880
gold rush n b1880
hat trick n b1880
incubation period n b1880
leading edge n b1880 (adj use: b1990)
long suit n b1880
merit system n b1880
modus vivendi n *method of living* b1880
nose paint n *alcohol* b1880
push-button adj (Am) b1880
short run n b1880
talking-to n b1880
all get-out n b1885
chew the fat v (Am) b1885
close call n (Am) b1885
doubting Thomas n b1885
force majeure n b1885
gentleman of fortune n b1885
good deal n b1885
hen party n b1885
high roller n (Am) b1885
Midas touch n b1885
mirror image n b1885
monkey business n (Am) b1885
morning after n b1885
never-never land n b1885
out of whack adj b1885
pull off v *accomplish* b1885
rain check n b1885
real McCoy n b1885
side effect n b1885
sphere of influence n b1885
ugly duckling n b1885
beat the band v b1890
booby prize n b1890
cat and mouse n b1890
crazy quilt n b1890
dead end n b1890 (dead-end adj: b1890; dead-end v: b1945)
down-and-out adj (Am) b1890 (noun use: b1905)
early bird n b1890
fighting chance n b1890
gentlemen's agreement n (Am) b1890

head start n b1890
hell-for-leather adv b1890 (adj use: b1920)
in absentia adv b1890
Irishman's raise n *pay reduction* b1890
kit and caboodle n b1890 (caboodle: b1850; kit and boodle: b1865)
odd man out n b1890
on the rocks adj *ruined* b1890
order of business n b1890
proving ground n b1890
radial symmetry n b1890
rare bird n b1890
steering committee n (Am) b1890
team player n (Am) b1890
thumbs-down n b1890 (thumbs-up: b1920)
top dog n b1890
Tower of Babel n b1890
waiting game n b1890
acid test n b1895
blood sport n b1895
busman's holiday n b1895
coffee klatsch n b1895
cough up v *give up* b1895
dope fiend n (Am) b1895
double standard n b1895
even money n b1895
glad hand n b1895 (verb use: b1905)
good faith n b1895
high-powered, high power adj, n b1895
knockout drops n b1895
middle-of-the-road adj (Am) b1895 (noun use: b1920)
plunk down v b1895
pot of gold n b1895
silk stocking n *bigshot* b1895 (silk-stocking adj: b1790)
spit and polish n b1895
test case n b1895
time lag n b1895
white knight n b1895
all-or-none adj (all-or-nothing: b1765)
also-ran n
ball of fire n
borrowed time n
brass tacks n
breaking point n
charmed circle n
destroying angel n
easy mark n
easy street n (Am)

frame of reference n
free ride n
glad rags n
gun for v
hit-and-miss adj (hit-or-miss: b1610)
kiss of peace n
lead-pipe cinch n (Am)
man's man n
muck up v
pipe dream n
red herring n *false clue*
small fry n *kids*
sporting chance n
tag along v (tag: b1700; tag-along: b1935)
waiting list n

General/Miscellaneous

affiliate n b1880 (verb use: b1765)
authoritarian adj/n b1880
evictee n b1880
exotica n b1880
happenchance n b1880 (happenstance: b1900; happen-so: b1930)
implosion n b1880 (implode: b1885)
knockabout adj/n b1880
Maltese cross n b1880
optimum n b1880
scatology n b1880 (scatological: b1925)
slugger n (Am) b1880
tad n *kid* b1880
toehold n b1880
upkeep n b1880
blend n b1885 (verb use: b1325)
breakaway n b1885 (adj use: b1930)
clip-clop n b1885
concentrate n b1885
conductance n b1885
counterproposal n b1885
degringolade n *rapid decline* b1885
firing line n b1885
groundwood n b1885
hindquarter n b1885
jackpot n (Am) b1885
latest n b1885
logjam n b1885
mascot n b1885
objective n *goal* b1885
phallicism n b1885
portable n b1885

pow n (Am) *sound* b1885 (interj use: b1725)
showpiece n b1885
substation n b1885
tackiness n b1885
throw-in n b1885
touch-up n b1885
underdog n (Am) b1885
ambience n b1890 (ambient adj: b1600; ambiance: b1925)
blueprint n b1890
brouhaha n b1890
central n b1890
combine n *alliance* b1890
crux n *gist* b1890
dejecta n *excrement* b1890 (obs. dejection: b1630 to 1800s)
durative adj/n *continuative* b1890
ejecta n b1890
exemplum n *example* b1890
expellee n b1890
fakery n b1890
fan n (Am) *as in "sports fan"* b1890 [gen. abbreviation of fanatic: b1685] (the fancy "fandom": b1735)
fug n/v *something stuffy* b1890
handicap n *gen. "encumbrance"* b1890 (verb use: b1855)
high hat n *type of hat; type of person* b1890
holdover n (Am) b1890
imbalance n b1890
insert n b1890
lineup n (Am) b1890
luminescence n b1890 (luminesce: b1900)
mechanical drawing n b1890
mineral spirits n b1890
refill n b1890 (verb use: b1685)
scaremonger n b1890
setup n b1890
synchronicity n b1890 (synchronous: b1670; synchronization: b1830; synchroneity: b1910)
thriller n b1890
trove n *(treasure) trove* b1890
underline n b1890 (verb use: b1570)

waffle n *prattle* b1890 (verb use: b1705)

walkaway n *runaway* b1890

anthropomorph n b1895

leftover n b1895 (adj use: b1900)

make-do n b1895 (adj use: b1925)

must n *as in "education is a must"* b1895 (adj use: b1915)

mystique n b1895

pacesetter n b1895 (pacemaker: b1845)

pollutant n b1895

record n *the top, the best* b1895

rookie n b1895 [in sports: b1930] (rook: b1930)

shortfall n b1895

stranglehold n b1895

thumb-sucker n b1895

backlog n *stock* (verb use: b1970)

ballyhoo n (Am) (verb use: b1930)

bank n *grouping or series*

battery n *grouping*

benefit n *as in "veteran's benefits"*

bite n *as in "the drink has a bite"*

bracket n *grouping, as in "tax bracket"*

color n *description, flavor, as in "color commentary," "local color"*

conk n/v *hit*

corrugated paper n

cut n *as in "price cut"*

decelerate, deceleration v, n

drifter n *transient*

drive n *as in "clothing drive"*

dupe n/v

entry n *as in "contest entry"*

ethanol n

finalist n

force-out n (Am)

fruition n [obs. "enjoyment": b1425]

glob n

goo n (Am)

hair-raiser, hair-raising n, adj

handle n *how something handles*

handoff n

happenstance n (happen-

chance: b1880; happenso: b1930)

input n (verb use: b1950)

lash-up n *something jury-rigged*

lectrice n (lector: b1475; lecturess: b1830)

life-form n

lonesome n *as in "by your lonesome"*

makefast n

pointer n *tip*

premiere adj/n (verb use: b1935)

preview n *gen. "sneak peek"* [spec. "theatrical preview": b1925]

questionnaire n

ramrod n *leader*

ready n *as in "at the ready"*

replacement n *that which replaces* ["replacing": b1790]

shear n *as in "wind shear"*

slowdown n

splat n

stand n *stay, as in "one-night stand"*

sticker n *adhesive note*

stop n *as in "bus stop"* (verb use: b1770)

symbiosis n [rare "living together": b1625]

tack n *tackiness*

tearaway n (Brit) *rebel* (adj use: b1830)

thingness n *being*

transient n *vagrant* (adj use: b1670)

voyeur n

white list n *opp. of blacklist*

Things

blindfold n b1880 (verb use: b1530)

crepe paper n b1880

gripsack n (Am) b1880

briquette n b1885

glass fiber n b1885

corrugated iron n b1890

Geneva cross n b1890

oil slick n b1890

spirit gum n b1890

sponge rubber n b1890

swagger stick n b1890

plasticine n

pom-pom/pom-pon n *as in "pom-pom girls"* [obs. type of hair ornament: b1750]

reject n *factory second*

thingy n

Description

breathtaking adj b1880

fetching adj b1880 ["scheming": b1585] (fetch: b1630)

first off adv b1880

flamboyant adj *showy* b1880 ["architecturally ornate": b1835; "colorful": b1855]

freestanding adj b1880

gesticulant adj b1880

god-awful adj (Am) b1880

high-grade adj b1880

high-level adj b1880

inflatable adj b1880

intransigent adj b1880

low-grade adj b1880

perceptual adj b1880

self-congratulatory adj b1880 (self-congratulation: b1730)

aquiver adj b1885

costume adj *fake* b1885

earsplitting adj b1885

egalitarian adj b1885 (egalite: b1795)

formulaic adj b1885

full-fledged adj b1885

growthy adj b1885

long-distance adj b1885

low-level adj b1885

maximal adj b1885

mechanistic adj b1885

medium-sized adj b1885

one-dimensional adj b1885

participatory adj b1885

pastel adj b1885

ragtag adj b1885 (noun use: b1820)

revelatory adj b1885 (revelation: b1870)

this-worldly adj b1885 (this-worldliness: b1870)

two-dimensional adj b1885

unappetizing adj b1885

alright adj/adv b1890 (all right: b1150)

blanket adj b1890

bunglesome adj b1890

clockwise adv b1890

cold adv *as in "stone cold sober"* b1890

colorful adj b1890 (colorific: b1680)

counterclockwise adj/adv b1890

dead-on adj b1890

degressive adj *reducing* b1890

discount adj b1890

dogleg adj b1890 (noun use: b1910; verb use: b1950)

electromechanical adj b1890

flameproof adj/v b1890 (flame-retardant: b1950)

hairpin adj b1890

heated adj *fig.* b1890

illusionary adj b1890

kitty-corner adj b1890

large-scale adj b1890

leadoff adj b1890 (noun use: b1890)

nope adv (Am) b1890

odds-on adj b1890

optimal adj b1890

raggedy adj b1890

rapid-fire adj b1890

semiprecious adj b1890

sporty adj *sporting* b1890 ["flashy": b1970] (sportif: b1920)

subliminal adj b1890

tattletale adj (Am) b1890 (verb use: b1930; noun use: b1890)

time-consuming adj b1890

warmed-over adj b1890

cover-all adj b1895

crunchy adj b1895

disrelated adj b1895

effortful adj b1895 (effortless: b1805)

far-flung adj b1895

hard put adj b1895

itty-bitty, itsybitsy adj b1895 (itty: b1800)

lots adv *as in "lots nicer"* b1895

low-key adj b1895

minuscule adj b1895 [typographical sense: b1745]

out-of-sight adj (Am) b1895 (adv use: b1830)

part-time adj b1895

pocketbook adj b1895

problem adj b1895

purported adj b1895

three-dimensional adj b1895

underdeveloped adj b1895

waggly adj b1895

punk adj *inferior* 1896

all-out adj/adv

anticlimactic adj (anticlimax: b1710)

anticlockwise adj/adv (Brit) *counterclockwise*

atrocious adj *awful*

blatant adj *obvious* ["noisy": b1630]

bottleneck adj (noun use: b1910; verb use: b1935)

capacity adj

cardinal adj *red*

cockeyed adj *strange, off-center* ["squinty": b1725; "drunk": b1930]

demanding adj

drab adj *colorless*

global adj *worldwide* ["related to globes": b1680]

habit-forming adj

hopping adv *as in "hopping mad"*

insular adj *isolated* ["of an island": b1615]

key adj *crucial*

marginal adj *barely productive*

multidimensional adj

multifaceted adj

neon adj *bright*

oh-so adv *as in "it was oh-so cute"*

plotty adj *complex*

pointful adj *relevant*

positive adj *as in "a positive test result"*

pushful adj

self-explanatory adj

stainless adj *stainproof*

straight adj *straightforward, direct*

substandard adj

super adj

tight adj *concise*

tin, tinny adj *cheap*

topical adj *in the news*

tough adj *like a ruffian, as in "tough guy"*

two-toned adj (two-tone: b1910)

water-repellent adj

watered-down adj

weathertight adj

weekend adj

wispish adj

Colors

cyan blue n b1880

moss green n b1885

peacock blue n b1885

salmon pink n b1885

shrimp pink n b1885

veridian n b1885

baby blue n (Am) b1890

cyan adj/n b1890

shell pink n b1890

slate black n b1890

turquoise green n b1890

jade green n b1895

burgundy n *the color*

mocha n

mustard n *the color* (adj use: b1870)

navy n *navy blue*

olive drab n

powder blue n [type of glaze ingredient: b1710]

walnut n *the color*

wine n *the color*

Actions/Verbs

befuddle v b1880

boot v *kick, give the boot to* b1880

bug v *as in "eyes bugging out"* b1880

laten v *get late* b1880

opt v b1880

pal v b1880

putter v *as in "putter around"* b1880

shellac v b1880 (noun use: b1670)

sidetrack v b1880

skimp v b1880 (adj use: b1780; skimpy: b1835)

snow under v b1880

censor v b1885 (noun use: b1535)

convect v b1885

detrain v b1885

exposit v *expound* b1885

fixate v b1885 (fixation: b1400; fixated: b1930)

fluff v *goof up* b1885

hierarchize v *prioritize* b1885

replicate v *duplicate* b1885 ["repeat": b1425] (replication: b1695)

roll out v b1885

size up v b1885

sponsor v b1885

stand pat v b1885

synopsize v b1885

tongue-lash v b1885

tromp v b1885

bus v *as in "busing tables"* b1890 (busboy: b1915; busgirl: b1945)

credential v b1890

fire off v b1890

flesh out v b1890

heel v *follow* b1890

homogenize v b1890 ["way to prepare milk": b1930]

hose v b1890

mill v *as in "mill about"* b1890 (noun use: b1900)

pipe up v b1890

resurface v b1890

root v (Am) *cheer* b1890

salvage v b1890

zoom v b1890 (noun use: b1920)

cross-index v b1895

date v *go out of date* b1895 (dated: b1735)

deflate v b1895 [fig. "dispirit": b1930]

defrost v b1895

demote v (Am) b1895 (demotion: b1905)

departmentalize v b1895

honk v *as in "honk a horn"* b1895

overnight v b1895

pigstick v *hunt wild boar* b1895 (pigsticking: b1870)

reference v b1895 (noun use: b1590)

scrap v *turn into scrap; throw away* b1895

tension v b1895

wigwag v b1895 [obs. "zig-zag": b1585] (noun use: b1890)

appeal v (appealing: b1815)

archive v (noun use: b1605)

backpedal v

barge v *as in "barge in"*

butt in v

call n/v *as in "telephone call"*

carry v *fig. support*

con v *deceive* (noun use: b1905)

confusticate v *confuse*

desensitize v

devaluate v (devaluation: b1915; devalue: b1920)

earmark v *assign a purpose to* [lit. use: b1595]

eat v *bother, annoy*

embody v *represent* ["give a phys. body to": b1550]

end up v

fall v *as in "the temperature is falling"*

fluff v *as in "fluff a pillow"*

fountain v

harness v *fig.* [lit. use: b1300]

hurdle v *fig.* ["create a hurdle": b1600]

jackknife v *as in "a jackknifed truck"*

jump v *as in "train jumping the tracks"; as in "jump ship"* (noun use: b1670)

knelt v

locate v *find*

move in v

neaten v

offbear v *take away*

pancake v *flatten* ["land an airplane flatly": b1915]

pigment v

process v *as in "process cheese"*

proof v *as in "waterproof"*

read v *as in "read into"; as in "the speedometer reads 90"*

recognize v *as in "the chair recognizes Mr. Simms"*

relay v *communicate, pass along*

ricket v *be rickety*

scrape v *as in "scrape by"*

scream v *as in "screaming heterosexual"* (screaming: b1870)

scuff v (Am) *as in "scuff a shoe"* ["walk scuffingly": b1850]

seize up v (seizure: b1930)

stack up v

straighten out v

stylize v

supercool v

swashbuckle v (swash: b1530)

switch v *exchange, as in "switch clothes"*

trip v *as in "trip a lever"*

waste v *discard*

whump v (noun use: b1930)

wile away v

work v *as in "work it so he can attend"*

IN USE BY
1910

Geography/Places
foreshock n *opp. of aftershock* b1905
heartland n b1905
krummholz n *timberline forest* b1905
life zone n b1905
scabland n b1905
strandline n *shoreline* b1905

Natural Things
alpha particle n b1905
aquifer n b1905
beta particle n b1905
gamma radiation n b1905
gamma ray n b1905
ice point n *point when water freezes* b1905
Mendel's law n *genetic theory* b1905
national forest n b1905
rain forest n b1905
gravitational wave n
human ecology n
nitrogen cycle n
tektite n *type of meteorite*

Plants
African violet n b1905
green alga n b1905
Oregon fir n b1905
chestnut blight n (Am)
growth ring n
shaggymane n *type of mushroom*
topiary n

Animals
'roo n *kanga* b1905
alley cat n b1905
boxer n *type of dog* b1905

bush baby n b1905
chum, chum salmon n b1905
crawdad n (Am) b1905 (crayfish: b1315; crawfish: b1625)
damselfish n b1905
hard-shell crab n b1905
hookworm n b1905
kelpie n *type of dog* b1905
shorthair n *type of cat* b1905
Tibetan terrier n b1905
bottle-nosed dolphin n
delta ray n
giant tortoise n
krill n *type of crustacean*
Labrador retriever n
mutt n (Am)
rottweiler n
Shetland sheepdog n
spotted owl n
Texas longhorn n (Am)
web-spinner n

Weather
easterly n b1905
smog n *sm(oke)(f)og* 1905
funnel cloud n

Heavens/Sky
astronomical unit n b1905
planetesimal adj/n *small orbital body* b1905
red star n b1905
Northern Cross n
stratosphere n

Science
atmospherics n b1905
chain reaction n b1905
clone n b1905 [fig. "replica": b1980] (verb use: b1950)

Doppler effect n b1905
euthenics n *improving humans through environment* b1905
genetics n 1905
geobotany n b1905
geochemistry n b1905
hypocenter n b1905
kinesis n *study of body reactions* b1905
protozoology n b1905 (protozoan: b1865)
sexology n b1905
shortwave adj/n b1905
subatomic adj b1905
genotype n 1909
creative evolution n
half-life n
pH n
planetology n
protohuman adj
quantum n *as in "quantum theory"* (quantum theory: b1915; quantum mechanics: b1925; quantum jump: b1930; quantum leap: b1960)
silicone n

Technology
cathode ray tube n b1905 (cathode: b1835)
cooling tower n b1905
electronic adj b1905
electronics n

Energy
gas turbine n b1905
heat exchanger n b1905
high-tension adj b1905
irradiate, irradiation v, n b1905 [bathe in light: b1600] (irradiance: b1960)
live wire n (Am) b1905
public utility n b1905
underpowered adj b1905
atomic energy n
black gold n *slang oil*
energy level n
secondary cell n *storage battery*

Time
betweentimes adv
calendar year n
daylight saving time n
elapsed time n
grandfather clock n
international date line n
microsecond n

Age/Aging
prepubescent adj/n b1905

Mathematics
Gaussian curve, Gaussian distribution n b1905
geometric mean n b1905
Mobius strip n b1905
rational number n b1905 (rational: b1700)
equal sign/equals sign/equality sign n
geometric series n *geometric progression*
imaginary number n
multiplication sign n
Pythagorean theorem n
real number n (real adj: b1730)
subtotal n/v
trigonometric function n

Measurement

gram calorie n b1905
mole n *molecular weight* b1905
curie n *unit of radioactivity*
Kelvin adj *thermometer scale* (noun use: b1930)
oscilloscope n

The Body

adrenalin n b1905
hormone n b1905
number one, number two *bathroom references* b1905
organ n *sex organ* b1905 ["internal organ": b1395]
pecker n *slang penis* b1905
peter n *slang penis* b1905
suntan n b1905 (verb use: b1830)
auditory tube n
cuticle n ["small skin": b1615]
red blood cell n
rib cage n

Physical Description

all in adj *exhausted* b1905
ash-blond/ash-blonde adj b1905
bare-knuckle adj/adv b1905
pie-faced adj b1905
sidearm adj *as in "throw sidearm"*
undernourished adj

Medicine

anticoagulant adj/n b1905
cesarean n b1905
depression n b1905 [gen. sense: b1400]
deuteranopia n *color blindness to green* b1905
electrocardiogram n b1905 (electrocardiograph: b1915)
electrosurgery n b1905
gastroenterology n b1905
hypo n *hypodermic needle* b1905
internal medicine n b1905
internist n b1905
monochromat n *color-blind person* b1905
nervous breakdown n (Am) b1905
neurosurgery n b1905

pediatrician/pediatrist n b1905
physiotherapy n b1905
prosthetist n b1905
scrub nurse n b1905
shiner n *black eye* b1905
trots, the n *the runs* b1905
allergen, allergenic, alergic, allergy n, adj, adj, n
amputee n (amputate: b1640)
anorexic adj (noun use: b1915)
antigen n
canker sore n (canker: b1150)
carsick adj
cauliflower ear n (Am)
chemotherapy n
cold pack n
depth perception n
engram n
gastric ulcer n
geriatrics n (geriatric adj: b1920)
herpes simplex n (herpes: b1400; herpes zoster: b1810; herpesvirus: b1925)
hot flash n
hyperpituitarism n
hypodermic needle n (hypodermic, hypodermic syringe: b1895)
immunochemistry n
immunology n
immunotherapy n
insomniac n (insomnia: b1625)
medicine show n (Am)
moron n (Am) (moronic: b1930)
novocaine n
orthodontics n (orthodontia: b1850)
pathobiology n
serology n *study of serums*
thiamine n *vitamin B2*

Everyday Life

ammonia water n b1905
attaché case n b1905
claw-and-ball foot n b1905
cookie cutter n b1905
davenport n b1905 ["writing desk": b1855]
earplug n b1905
enamelware n b1905

gateleg table n b1905
giftware n b1905
humidor n b1905
light housekeeping n b1905
love seat n b1905
man of the house n b1905
mercury-vapor lamp n b1905
phone book n b1905
pilot burner n b1905
sectional n *type of furniture* b1905
septic tank n b1905
torchere n b1905
towelette n b1905
Turkish rug n b1905
vacuum cleaner n b1905
vanity case n b1905
wind-bell n *wind chime* b1905
wing chair n b1905
air conditioner, air conditioning n (air condition v: b1935)
bath salts n
bookend n
chaise lounge n (chaise longue: b1800)
chifforobe n (Am)
cocktail glass n
comfort station n (Am)
dental floss n (Am)
groundsheet n (ground cloth: b1920)
identification card n (identity card: b1910; ID card: b1945)
ladder-back adj
mothball n
moving stairway n
peroxide v
photocopy n
powder room n ["gunpowder storage": b1630]
pushpin n [type of game: b1675]
repellent n *against insects*
seidel n *type of beer glass*
stapler n
styptic pencil n
tarp n (Am) (tarpaulin: b1595)
thermos n
vacuum bottle n
yellow pages n

Shelter/Housing

boiler room n b1905
dead bolt n b1905
dead-air space n b1905

garage n/v b1905
kitchenette n b1905
studio apartment n b1905
subbasement n b1905
A-frame n
apartment hotel n
bed-and-breakfast n
central heating n
cookshack n
crawlway n
life ring n *lifepreserver*
plywood n
pressboard n *type of pasteboard*
revolving door n
wallboard n

Drink

crème de cacao n b1905
crème de menthe n b1905
jolt n *slang drink* b1905
smoke n (Am) *bad alcohol* b1905
suds n *beer* b1905
Asti Spumante n
fortified wine n
near beer n (Am)
robusta n *type of coffee*

Food

blintze n b1905
bordelaise sauce n b1905
breast-feed v b1905
cilantro n b1905
club sandwich n (Am) b1905
corn syrup n (Am) b1905
cuke n *cucumber* b1905
delicious apple n b1905
devil's food cake n (Am) b1905
dill pickle n b1905
durum wheat n b1905
English muffin n b1905
flank steak n b1905
force-feed v b1905
frank n (Am) b1905 (frankfurter: b1895)
frappé n b1905 (adj use: b1850)
ice-cream cone n b1905
Italian dressing n b1905
jelly bean n (Am) b1905
maraschino cherry n b1905
muenster n *type of cheese* b1905
mulligan stew n b1905
soft-boiled adj b1905
stone-ground adj b1905

sunny-side up adj b1905
tangelo n *cross between tangerine and orange* b1905
tea bag n b1905
top round n b1905
Waldorf salad n b1905
alphabet soup n
baked Alaska n (Am)
breadstick n
cornflakes n (Am)
crème caramel n
crown roast n
en brochette adj
filet mignon n
mung bean n
peach Melba n
romaine n *type of lettuce*
Romano n *type of cheese*
saltine n (Am)
spoon bread n (Am)
streusel n
tortellini n
weenie n

Agriculture/ Food-Gathering

chicken wire n (Am) b1905
farmerette n (Am) b1905
groundskeeper n b1905
  (groundkeeper: b1880)
haywire n b1905 (slang adj
  use: b1930)
neuter v b1905
tree surgery n b1905 (tree
  surgeon: b1910)
crop rotation n
drift fence n
potting soil n

Cloth/Clothing

barrette n b1905
bathrobe n b1905
benny n *type of coat* b1905
gabardine n *type of cotton*
  b1905 [*type of dress:*
  b1520]
neckline n b1905
tie-dyed adj b1905
V neck n b1905
bush shirt n
clip-on adj/n
face mask n
granny dress n
menswear n
pantie n (Am) ["trousers":
  b1845]
Peter Pan collar n

A Word About A-Wording

As our language evolves, we tend to tangle words, and we then tend to entangle them—making them more complex by intensifying them, modifying them and ultimately not changing them. For example, the verb *tangle* was in use by 1340 in the figurative sense and by 1530 in the literal, and the verb *entangle* was in use by 1425 in the figurative and by 1570 in the literal.

Here are some other verbs in "entangled" and "unentangled" forms:

- *grave* (by 1000), meaning *engrave* (by 1500)

- *monish* (by 1300), meaning *admonish* (by 1325)

- *plain* (by 1300), meaning *complain* (by 1370)

- *scape* (by 1300), meaning *escape* (from about the same time)

- *smirch* (by 1300), meaning *besmirch* (by 1600)

- *whelm* (by 1300), meaning *overwhelm* (by 1350)

- *boss* (by 1400), meaning *emboss* (by about the same time)

- *plenish* (by 1470), meaning *replenish* (by 1630)

- *vote* (by 1570), meaning *devote* (by 1590)

Do any of these astonish you, amaze you? Do they maze you, with *maze* in use by 1350 and *amaze* in the sense of "astonish" by 1600?

---

playsuit n
polo coat n
shawl collar n
snap-brim n
vestee n

Fashion/Style

diamante n *sparkles* b1905
mission adj *describing a type
  of architecture* b1905
posh adj b1905
chichi n *elegant* (adj use:
  b1930)
couture n
doll up v
haute couture n
hep adj
millefleur adj *flowered background*

nail polish n
pearl essence n *fake pearl*

Tools

aerial n *antenna* b1905
aerial ladder n *on a fire truck*
  b1905
ionization chamber n b1905
remote control n b1905
resistor n b1905
rotor n b1905
spotlight n b1905 (verb use:
  b1910)
dictating machine n
gyro n *gyroscope* (gyroscope:
  b1860)
gyrocompass n
lie detector n
power shovel n

processor n
quartersaw n
rip cord n

Travel/Transportation

aerodrome n *airport* b1905
  ["airplane": b1900]
airspace n b1905
choo-choo n b1905
disc brake n b1905
flyover n b1905
heavier-than-air adj b1905
hubcap n b1905
hydroplane n b1905
jitney n (Am) b1905 (adj
  "two-bit": b1930)
johnboat n (Am) b1905
lighter-than-air adj b1905
limousine n b1905 (limo:
  b1970)
loop-the-loop n b1905
metro n b1905
motor bus n b1905
motorbike n/v b1905
motorboat n/v b1905
secondary road n b1905
spark plug, sparking plug n
  (Brit) b1905
speedometer n b1905
station wagon n (Am) b1905
takeoff n b1905
touring car n b1905
travelogue n (Am) b1905
two-cycle engine n b1905
underpass n b1905
windshield n b1905
ornithopter n 1908
aerodyne n *heavier-than-air
  craft*
air bus n
airline, airliner n *air transport
  company*
airplane n
aviatrix n (aviator: b1890)
bucket seat n
coachwork n *automobile body-
  work*
el n
flivver n (Am)
gyroplane n
joyride n/v (Am)
juice n (Brit) *gasoline*
ladder truck n
lemon n *bad car*
monoplane n *type of airplane*
outboard motor n
plane n *airplane*
powerboat n

road test n

roadster n *type of car* [type of ship: b1745; type of horse: b1820; type of carriage: b1895; "hobo": b1900]

shock absorber n

stake truck n

taxi, taxicab n (Am) (verb use: b1920)

town car n

triplane n

Emotions/ Characteristics

empathy n 1904 (empathic: b1910; empathize: b1925; empathetic: b1935)

bloodcurdling adj b1905

burnout n b1905

can-do adj b1905

characterful adj b1905

grief-stricken adj b1905

hog-wild adj (Am) b1905

manic adj b1905

manic-depressive adj/n b1905

repressed adj b1905

savvy adj b1905

starry-eyed adj b1905

turn on v *excite* b1905 (turnon, turnoff: b1965)

worked up adj b1905

compulsion, compulsive n, adj *neurotic need*

fixation n *obsession* (fixate: b1930)

heebie-jeebies n (Am)

interiorize v *internalize*

judgmental adj

peeve, peeved v, adj (Am) (noun use: b1915)

smarmy adj (smarm "flatter": b1930)

snarky adj (Brit) *snappish*

stir-crazy adj

tickled pink adj

Thoughts/Perception/ The Mind

abnormal psychology n b1905 (abnormality, abnormity: b1855)

androcentric adj *from the male point of view* b1905

autohypnosis n b1905

bughouse n (Am) *nuthouse* b1905 (adj use: b1895)

déjà vu n b1905 (déjà vu entendu "words"; déjà vu lu "writing": b1970)

gallows humor n b1905

multiple personality n b1905

obsessive adj b1905

paranoid adj/n b1905

self-hypnosis n b1905

wise v *as in "wise up"* b1905

ideology n [arch. "study of ideas": b1800; "speculation": b1815]

insightful adj

intelligentsia n

intriguing adj

metapsychology n

Oedipus complex n (Oedipal: b1940)

psychoanalysis, psychoanalytic n, adj (psychoanalyze: b1915)

schizophrenia, schizophrenic n, adj (schizophrene: b1925; schizophrenic n: b1930)

tough-minded adj

Love/Romance/Sex

bachelorette n b1905 (bachelor: b1300)

cruise v *look for partners* b1905

homosexual n b1905 (adj use: b1905; homosexualist: b1920; homophile: b1960)

matron of honor n b1905

snatch n *pussy* b1905 ["quick intercourse": b1600]

tumble n *sex* b1905 (verb use: b1605)

birth v (noun use: b1200)

hickey n (Am) *bitemark*

vamp n *seductress* (verb use: b1915)

Family/Relations/ Friends

fraternal twin n b1905

matrilineal adj b1905

patrilineal adj b1905 (patrilineage: b1950)

paw n (Am) *dad* b1905

sibling n *brother or sister* b1905 [obs. gen. "relative": b1000 to LME]

bloodline n

Games/Fun/Leisure

bocce (bocci) n b1905

candlepin n b1905

cheerleader n (Am) b1905 (cheerlead v: b1970)

dartboard n b1905

dopesheet n (Am) b1905

jai alai n b1905

nim n *type of game* b1905

quinella/quiniella n b1905

ring-a-levio n *type of game* b1905

teeter-totter n (Am) b1905 (verb use: b1900)

three-legged race n b1905

water pistol n b1905

teddy bear n 1906

auction bridge n

dopester n (Am) *oddsmaker*

duckpin n

jigsaw puzzle n

joystick n

penny arcade n

playgroup n

rummy n (Am) *type of card game*

Sports

Australian Rules football n b1905

bodybuilding n b1905

dog paddle n b1905

field hockey n b1905

harness racing/harness race n b1905

hill climb n b1905

light heavyweight n b1905

luge n b1905 (verb use: b1900)

table tennis n b1905

track meet n (Am) b1905

track-and-field adj b1905

Australian crawl n

backspin n

diving suit n

goaltender n

gold medal n

Hall of Fame n

mutuel n

pommel horse n

semipro adj/n (semiprofessional: b1900)

ski boot n

ski jump n

skijoring n (Am)

sportfishing n

track shoe n

water wings n

Professions/Duties

automaker n b1905

firefighter n b1905

hotelier n b1905 (hotelkeeper: b1830)

receptionist n b1905

social secretary n b1905

troubleshooter n b1905 (troubleshoot: b1920)

adman n

cameraman n (arch. camerist: b1870; camerawoman: b1975; cameraperson: b1980)

char n *charwoman*

dick n *slang detective*

gumshoe n *detective* [type of shoe: b1865] (verb use: b1930)

lobbygow n (Am) *errand boy*

Business/Commerce/ Selling

beauty shop n b1905

door-to-door adj b1905

eatery n b1905

health insurance n b1905

price-cutter n b1905

remainder v *sell at a discount* b1905 (noun use: b1770)

salesperson n b1905 (salesman: b1525; saleswoman: b1705; salespeople: b1880)

store-bought adj b1905

ten-cent store n (Am) b1905

trade discount n b1905

yard goods n *piece goods* b1905

chain store n

free market n

holding company n

limited partner n

mail order house n (Am)

marque n *brand*

secret partner n

trademark v

valorize v *fix prices*

The Workplace

closed shop n (Am) b1905

industrial union n b1905

internship n b1905

jobholder n (Am) b1905

pay envelope n b1905
shop steward n b1905
strikebreaker n b1905
sympathy strike n b1905
union shop n b1905
graveyard shift n (Am)
vertical file n

Finances/Money

big business n (Am) b1905
blue chip n (Am) b1905
  (blue-chipper: b1970)
charge account n (Am)
  b1905
fair market value n b1905
  (fair market price: b1925)
nonprofit adj b1905
reserve bank n b1905
trustbuster n (Am) b1905
working capital n b1905
checking account n (Am)
Christmas club n
commercial bank n
estate tax n
expense v
moola n (Am) money

Language and Speaking

semanticist n b1905 (semantician: b1930)
block letter n
bromide n
entry word n
great vowel shift n
lowercase v
pictogram n (pictograph:
  b1855)
tone language n

Contractions

it'd contr b1905

Literature/Writing

chain letter n b1905
editorialist n b1905
flashback n b1905 (flash
  back v: b1945; flash-
  forward: b1950)
front-page adj (Am) b1905
  (verb use: b1930)
heroic couplet n b1905 (heroic verse: b1590; heroic
  poem: b1695)
internal rhyme n b1905
limited edition n b1905
loose-leaf adj b1905
newsletter n b1905
rewrite man n (Am) b1905

scandal sheet n b1905
Shakespearean sonnet n
  b1905
sight-read v b1905
sportswriter n b1905
tabloid journalism n b1905
  (tabloid newspaper:
  b1920)
thumb index n b1905
vers libre n free verse b1905
antiheroine n (antihero:
  b1715)
bildungsroman n
classified ad n
dream vision n type of poem
form letter n (Am)
free verse n
front matter n
muckraker n (muckrake n:
  b1875; muckrake v:
  b1910)
mystery n
nonfiction n
rejection slip n
workbook n

Communication

radio n type of communication; radio receiver b1905
  (adj use: b1890; verb use:
  b1915)
telephone box n (Brit) b1905
teletypewriter, teletype n
  b1905
wireless n b1905
wiretap v b1905 (noun use:
  b1950; wiretapper: b1895)
body English n (body lan-
  guage: b1930)
keynote address n
SOS n

Visual Arts/
Photography

art nouveau n b1905
expressionism n b1905
linecut n type of engraving
  b1905
pointillism n b1905
stereophotography n b1905
avant-garde n ["mil. front
  troops": b1470] (adj use:
  b1925; avant adj: b1965)
cubism n
photog n
Postimpressionism n

Performing Arts

aerialist n b1905
chronicle play n b1905
tryout n (Am) b1905 (try
  out v: b1910)
walk-on n b1905
comic-opera adj
dramatic irony n
road show n

Music

baby grand n b1905
blues n b1905 (bluesman:
  b1965)
player piano n (Am) b1905
squeezebox n (Am) b1905
barbershop adj singing style
glass harmonica n
musicology n
phono n
Tin Pan Alley n (Am)

Entertainment

amusement park n
shadow dance n

Movies/TV/Radio

film n b1905
matinee idol n b1905
outtake n b1905
cinema n [type of projector:
  b1900] (cine, cinematic,
  cinematize: b1920)
filmmaker n (filmmaking:
  b1915)
movie n (moving picture:
  b1900)
sound effects n

Education

correspondence course n
  b1905
curriculum vitae n b1905
library science n b1905
master of science n the degree
  b1905
pledge n as in "fraternity
  pledge" b1905
sorority n b1905 (fraternity:
  b1800)
honor roll n (honor society:
  b1930)
junior high school n
senior high school n
student body n
student teacher n
teachers college n

Religion

Magen David n star of David
  b1905
prayer shawl n b1905
yarmulke n b1905
kashruth n Jewish dietary laws

Society/Mores/Culture

comstockery n censorship,
  blue-nosedness b1905
persona non grata n b1905
  (persona grata: b1885)
standard of living n b1905
war baby n b1905
welfare n social aid b1905
xenophobia n b1905 (xeno-
  phobe: b1915)
rite of passage n 1909
biracial adj
everyman n (everywoman:
  b1945)
in-group n
lowbrow adj/n
nonperson n
racialism n racism
Renaissance man n

Politics

bloc n b1905
elder statesman n b1905
factionalism n b1905 (factionalize: b1975)
geopolitics n b1905
pacifism n b1905 (pacifist,
  pacificism: b1910)
right wing n b1905
suffragette n b1905 (suffragist: b1825)
activism n
bipartisan adj
detente n
dollar diplomacy n (Am)
minimalist n Menshevik
social security n

Life

lifetime adj b1905

Death

boot hill n (Am) slang cemetery b1905
do in v b1905
wooden overcoat n coffin
  b1905
bump off v

War/Military/Violence

armlock n *hammerlock* b1905
automatic n b1905 (adj use: b1900)
blackjack v *hit with a blackjack* b1905
concentration camp n b1905
corpsman n (Am) b1905
firing squad n b1905
forty-five n *the pistol* b1905
gat n (Am) *pistol* b1905
general quarters n b1905
headlock n b1905
militaristic adj b1905 (militarism: b1865)
minesweeper n b1905
war chest n (Am) b1905
0.32 n *type of gun* b1905
air power n
bean v *hit in the head*
black powder n
counteroffensive n
dreadnought n *type of battleship* [type of overcoat: b1810]
hash mark n
minelayer n
mushroom cloud n
plastic explosive n
prison camp n
re-up v (Am)
switchblade n (switch knife: b1950)
world war n

Crime/Punishment/Enforcement

loan shark n (Am) b1905
moulage n *type of evidence gathering* b1905
rap n *as in "rap sheet"* b1905
rip v *steal* b1905 (rip off: b1970)
snitch v *steal* b1905
vice squad n b1905
yegg n *slang burglar* b1905
cat burglar n
crim n (Am) *criminal*
frame v (frame-up: b1900)
gun moll n
inside job n
jailbreak n (Am)
pedophilia n (pedophile: b1955)
police dog n
war crime n

The Law

consent decree n b1905
due diligence n b1905
legal age n b1905
parolee n b1905
alibi v (noun use: b1745)
double jeopardy n

The Fantastic/Paranormal

dybbuk n *type of demon* b1905

Magic

sympathetic magic n b1905
hex n *type of spell* ["witch": b1860] (verb use: b1830)
magic v

Interjections

touché interj b1905
whizzo interj b1905
yeah adv b1905
attaboy interj
bejesus interj/n
cheerio interj (Brit)
cripes interj
gesundheit interj (Am)
nothing doing interj
pip-pip interj (Brit)
toodle-oo interj

Slang

arty, artsy, artsy-craftsy adj b1905
carrottop n b1905
coke n/v (Am) *cocaine* b1905
dope n *inside info* b1905
dopehead n b1905
fence-sitter/fence-sitting n/adj b1905
gimp n *bravura, spirit* b1905
gongoozler n (Am) b1905
hip adj (Am) b1905
jefe n *chief, boss* b1905
jerk off v b1905
kicks n *shoes* b1905
knock off v *quit* b1905
lamster n *someone on the lam* b1905
lit adj *drunk* b1905 (lit up: b1915)
nineteenth hole n b1905
pesthole n b1905
plastered adj b1905
pross n *pros(titute)* b1905

rat n *informant* b1905 (verb use: b1935)
rod n *penis; gun* b1905
rook n *rookie* b1905
say-so n *permission* b1905
scream v *snitch* b1905
scuttlebutt n b1905 [type of cask: b1805]
shakedown n b1905 (shake down: b1860)
skiddoo v (Am) b1905
smoothie n b1905
spring v *pay* b1905
sticks, the n *boondocks* b1905
barfly n (Am)
big shot n (big wheel: b1735)
big wheel n
bilge n *nonsense, garbage*
boondocks n (Am) (boonies: b1960)
camp adj *amusingly out of date* (noun use: b1965)
can v (Am) *stop*
cheese n *bigshot, as in "big cheese"*
floozy n
freak n *aficionado*
gink n (Am) *person*
glom v (Am)
Gomorrah n *a place of sin*
groundbreaking adj (groundbreaker: b1940)
hand-holding n
helluva adj/adv
hon n
ice n *diamonds*
jane n (Am) *female*
legit adj/n
machine-gun adj
man-eater n
pushover n ["something done easily, a piece of cake": b1900]
raring adj *eager*
rock n *diamond*
soapbox n *fig. speaking platform*
speedball n (Am)
starkers, starko adj (Brit) *nude* ["crazy": b1965]
stickum n
tail n/v *surveillance*

Insults

batty adj b1905 [bats: b1920]
bluenose n (Am) b1905
buttinsky n (Am) b1905

cluck n (Am) *dumb cluck* b1905
fuddy-duddy n b1905
fussbudget n (Am) b1905
mutt n *muttonhead* b1905
nut n *loony person* 1905 (nuts adj: b1850; off your nut: b1860; nutcase: b1960)
pen pusher n b1905
simp n b1905
sissified adj b1905
wisenheimer n (Am) b1905
bonehead n (Am)
boob n (Am) *simpleton* (booby: b1605)
fraidy-cat n
meanie n
nance/nancy n *effeminate man*

Phrases

all clear n b1905
cri de coeur n *cry in the night* b1905
curate's egg n (Brit) *something with good and bad* b1905
cut-and-try adj *trial-and-error* b1905
dog's chance n b1905
earth mother n b1905
flash in the pan n b1905
grass roots n b1905 (grassroots adj: b1910)
high sign n b1905
honor system n (Am) b1905
house of cards n b1905
little bitty adj (Am) b1905
man-to-man adj b1905
museum piece n b1905
point man n b1905
rescue mission n b1905
run along v b1905
short end n *as in "short end of the stick"* b1905
spitting image n b1905
talk turkey v b1905
top drawer n b1905
trial run n b1905
advance man n
bitch goddess n *success*
brain trust n (Am) (Brit brains trust: b1935)
buffer zone n
charter member n (Am)
Cook's tour n
fall guy n (Am)

heart-to-heart n (adj use: b1870)
interest group n
lone wolf n (Am)
made-to-order adj
mug's game n *futile activity*
opposite number n
pork barrel n (Am)
pub crawler n (pub-crawl v/ n: b1940)
run off at the mouth v
sacred cow n
shock wave n
sound off v
state of the art n
tank town n (Am) *small town*
tune out, tune in v
twilight zone n

General/Miscellaneous

cartel n b1905 [type of challenge: b1560; type of agreement: b1700]
catalyst, catalyze n b1905 (catalysis: b1650; catalyze: b1890)
clinkety-clank n *sound* b1905
decompress, decompression v, n b1905
directive n b1905 [limited use: b1645] (direct v: b1570)
earthwoman n b1905 (earthling: b1595; earthman: b1860)
fandom n (Am) b1905
hookup n b1905
maquette n *small preliminary model* b1905
mutant adj/n b1905
parlay n b1905
patchup adj/n b1905
payoff n b1905 (adj use: b1935)
protohistory n b1905
sabbatical n b1905 (adj use: b1890)

safelight n b1905
sidekick n (Am) b1905
subset n b1905
superman n b1905 (superwoman: b1910)
throwaway n b1905 (adj use: b1930)
tip-off n *warning* b1905
titleholder n b1905 (titlist: b1925)
trivia n b1905 (trivial, triviality: b1600; trivialize: b1850)
turbo n b1905
folkway n 1907
addict n (verb use: b1530; addictive: b1940)
backfill n/v
boy scout n
changeover n
depersonalization n
fuselage n
futurism n
gaffe n
image n *as in "corporate image"* (imagemaker: b1930)
keystroke n (verb use: b1970)
klaxon n (Am)
national monument n
one-shot adj/n
persona n
plastic n ["something molded": b1905; rare "something pliable": b1830] (plasticize: b1920)
stabilizer n
synchroneity n (synchronous: b1670; synchronization: b1830; synchronicity: b1890)
trailblazer n (trailbreaker: b1925; trailblazing adj: b1955)
unquote n
untouchable n
yen n *gen. craving* (verb use:

b1920; yen-yen "need for opium": b1890)
yip v/n *dog sound* ["bird sound": b1450]

Things

quartz glass n b1905
ticker tape n (Am) b1905
birthstone n
hickey n *as in "doohickey"*
sheet metal n

Description

age-old adj b1905
bitsy, bitty adj b1905
crosswise adj b1905
dual-purpose adj b1905
erstwhile adj b1905
feetfirst adv b1905
foolproof adj (Am) b1905
hands-off adj b1905
head-on adj b1905 (adv use: b1840)
long-term adj b1905
mint adj *newly made* b1905
nonreturnable adj b1905
nonstop adj/adv b1905
outmoded, outmode adj, v b1905
peak adj *utmost* b1905
period adj b1905
raggletaggle adj b1905
ramrod adj *unbending* b1905
short-term adj b1905
textbook adj b1905
borderline adj (adv use: b1925)
cordless adj
flat-out adj
freewheeling adj
full blast adv
gooey adj
heatproof adj
last-ditch adj
no-good adj (Am) (noun use: 1920s)
picture-postcard adj
pocket-size adj
rubbery adj

saddlesore adj
show-me adj (Am)
small-time adj
sold-out adj
surefire adj
weather-burned adj

Colors

cornflower blue n
taupe n [type of mole: b1890]

Actions/Verbs

deactivate v b1905
detoxify v b1905
finalize v b1905
flub v (Am) b1905 (noun use: b1950)
headquarter v b1905
jack v *as in "jack up the prices"* b1905
lightning v *lighten* b1905
listen in v b1905
nix v b1905
ping-pong v b1905
reactivate v b1905
sidestep v (Am) b1905
sideswipe v (Am) b1905 (noun use: b1915)
spritz v (Am) b1905 (noun use: b1930)
talk down v b1905
torch v *set afire* b1905
traumatize v b1905
upgrade v *improve* b1905
watchdog v b1905
weekend v b1905
breeze v
choose up v
crash v *collide*
defeminize v
kick in v
outdraw v
scrounge v
sleep out v
slip up v
update v (noun use: b1965)

IN USE BY
1920

Geography/Places
coast-to-coast adj b1915
conurbation n *consolidated urban areas* b1915
countrywide adj b1915
hometown n (Am) b1915
inselberg n *type of mountain* b1915
shield volcano n b1915
oceanfront adj/n
rurban adj
shorefront n

Natural Things
histamine n b1915
isotope n b1915
mutate v *mutate genetically* b1915 [gen. "change": b1820] (mutation: b1900)
nucleus n *core of atom* b1915 ["part of an atom": b1845]
radon n 1918
bioluminescence n
freshwater pearl n
humanoid adj
photon n
proton n

Plants
tree ring n

Animals
black widow n b1915
lunker n b1915
palomino n (Am) *type of horse* b1915
predator n b1915 [fig. use: b1970] (predatory: b1670)
Alsatian n
coonhound n (Am)
corn borer n

Doberman pinscher n
English springer spaniel n
European corn borer n
giant panda n
golden retriever n
grunion n *type of fish*
marlin n (Am)

Weather
air pocket n b1915

Heavens/Sky
dwarf star n b1915
giant star n b1915 (giant: b1930)
green flash n *green light at sunrise/set* b1915
spiral galaxy n b1915
moonscape n
red dwarf n
red giant n *type of star*

Science
superconductivity n 1913
audio frequency n b1915
behaviorism n b1915
bioengineering n b1915
pedology n *study of soils* b1915
quantum theory n b1915
soil science n b1915
diode n 1919
general relativity n
human engineering n (Am)
special theory of relativity n

Technology
feedback n *electronic sense* ["response": b1970]
punched card n (punch card: b1945)
robot n

Energy
immersion heater n b1915
petrochemical adj b1915 (noun use: b1945)
hydro n *hydroelectric power*
induction heating n
rad n *dose of radiation*
service station n

Time
split second n b1915

Age/Aging
coming-of-age n
life span n

Mathematics
bar chart n b1915 (bar graph: b1925)
maths n (Brit) b1915
numerology n b1915
coordinate geometry n
Venn diagram n

Measurement
parsec n b1915
tensiometer n b1915

The Body
gene n 1911
endocrine gland n b1915
noodle n *the head* b1915
nuts n *testicles* b1915
voice box n b1915
x chromosome, y chromosome n b1915
immune system n
prepubescence n (prepubescent adj/n: b1905; prepuberty: b1925)
sex hormone n

Physical Description
handicapped adj b1915
plain-Jane adj b1915
salt-and-pepper adj b1915
shag v *lope along* b1915
upchuck v

Medicine
vitamin n 1912
Alzheimer's disease n b1915
anesthesiology n b1915 (anesthetist: b1885; anesthesiologist: b1945)
autism, autistic n, v b1915
birth control n (Am) b1915
blackout n b1915 (verb use: b1925)
blood test n b1915
cleft lip n b1915
con n *tuberculosis* b1915
hyperirritability n b1915
insulin n b1915 (insulin shock: b1925)
mental retardation n b1915
occupational therapy n b1915
periodontology n b1915
pink elephants n *DTs* b1915
podiatrist/podiatry n b1915
retardation n b1915
salmonella n b1915
serum sickness n b1915
shell shock n b1915 (fig. shell-shocked: b1970)
TB n b1915
trench fever, trench foot, trench mouth n b1915
altitude sickness n
analysand n *psychoanalytic patient*
B vitamin n
delouse v

hemorrhoidectomy n
high blood pressure n
infectious mononucleosis n
mononucleosis n
oxygen mask n
phenobarbital n
rapid eye movement n
recovery room n
shock therapy n
triage n [gen. "sorting":
  b1830]
vital signs n
vitamin A, B, C n (vitamin D:
  1921; E: 1925; B complex,
  B2: 1928; G: 1929; B6:
  1934; D2: b1935; H, K:
  1935; K2, P: b1940; B12:
  1948; K3, M: b1960)

Everyday Life
adhesive tape n b1915
antifreeze n b1915
bread mold n b1915
bubbler n *water fountain*
  b1915
cellophane n b1915
coatrack n b1915 (coat tree:
  b1945)
folder n b1915
hope chest n b1915
photostat n/v b1915
reefer n *slang refrigerator*
  b1915
running water n b1915
shopping list n b1915
club chair n
delivery boy, deliveryman n
dispatch case n
duffel bag n (Am)
ice cube n
lazy Susan n
presoak n/v
salad fork n
sanitary napkin n (Am)
tarmac n *type of pavement*
twin bed n (Am)
whirlpool bath n

Shelter/Housing
Cape Cod cottage n
houseguest n
pissoir n *public urinal*
safety glass n
stainless steel n
stairwell n
sunporch n (Am)
sunroom n (Am) (sun parlor:
  b1920)

walk-up adj (noun use:
  b1925)

Drink
cabernet sauvignon n b1915
white lightning n (Am)
  b1915
bubbly n *champagne*
daiquiri n
neutral spirits n
Rob Roy n *type of drink*

Food
brittle n *the candy* b1915
club steak n b1915
continental breakfast n b1915
fettuccini n b1915
flambé adj b1915 [applied to
  porcelain glaze: b1890]
  (verb use: b1950)
jack cheese n b1915
mixed grill n *type of meal*
  b1915
mozzarella n *type of cheese*
  b1915
nutmeat n b1915
pressure cooker n b1915
provolone n *type of cheese*
  b1915
shish kebab n b1915
short ribs n b1915
steak tartare n b1915
à la king adj
au jus adj
bagel n
banana split n
blackstrap molasses n (Am)
brown rice n
chow line n
club cheese n
deep-dish pie n
french fry n
grain sorghum n
guacamole n
honeydew melon n
hush puppy n
knish n
natural food n
pimento cheese n
pinto bean n
process cheese n
rotisserie n (Am) [type of
  restaurant: b1870]
sukiyaki n
T-bone n
tempura n
Thousand Island dressing n

upside-down cake n (Am)
vichyssoise n

Agriculture/ Food-Gathering
interplant v b1915
animal husbandry n
dirt farmer n (Am)
double-crop v
overgraze v
sodbuster n (Am)
woodlore n

Cloth/Clothing
brassiere n b1915 (bra:
  b1935)
cross-dressing n b1915
  (cross-dress v: b1925)
culotte n b1915 [type of
  breeches: b1845]
duvetyn n *type of fabric* b1915
georgette n *type of fabric*
  b1915
hobble skirt n b1915
housecoat n b1915
middy blouse n b1915
shoulder bag n b1915
sportswear n b1915
virgin wool n b1915
wing collar n b1915
women's wear n b1915
crash helmet n
French cuff n
playclothes n
plus fours n *type of knickers*
polo shirt n
pull-on n
seabag n
sheer n *a sheer fabric* (adj use:
  b1570)
slipover n *type of sweater*
soup-and-fish n *slang formal-wear*
sport shirt n
T-shirt n (Am)
trench coat n
windbreaker n

Fashion/Style
corsage n *flower* b1915 [obs.
  "the body": b1485 to
  1600s; "dress bodice":
  b1845]
cover girl n (Am) b1915
facial n b1915
hairstyle n b1915 (hairdo:
  b1925)

up-to-the-minute adj b1915
bathing beauty n
Greek Revival n
henna v (noun use: b1600)
ritzy adj (Am) (ritz n/v:
  b1930)
vanishing cream n

Tools
direction finder n b1915
gas mask n b1915
headphone n b1915
wind tunnel n (Am) b1915
decoder n
friction tape n
hand truck n
jackhammer n/v (Am)
keypunch n (verb use:
  b1960)
spray gun n

Travel/Transportation
aquaplane n b1915
cockpit n b1915 [type of ship
  quarters: b1710]
external combustion engine n
  b1915
fairing n *type of boat, airplane
  structure* b1915
flight path n b1915
flying boat n b1915
hedgehop v b1915
kickstart v b1915
life vest n (Am) b1915
motorcade n (Am) b1915
prop n *propeller* b1915
retread n *type of tire* b1915
  (verb use: b1890)
roadability n b1915
seaplane n b1915
speedboat n b1915
taxi v b1915
tin lizzie n b1915
traffic cop n (Am) b1915
traffic light n b1915
trolley bus n b1915
air taxi n
airfare n
airport n
automatic pilot n (autopilot:
  b1935)
blimp n
control tower n
convertible n
cowling n
crash dive n/v
fender n *on a car*
free fall n

freedom of the seas n
groundspeed n
gun it v *give it gas*
hydrofoil n
landing field n
motor scooter n
motortruck n
scooter n *type of boat, toy*
[*type of plow*: b1820]
semitrailer n (semi: b1945)
skyway n
speedster n
streamliner n *type of train*
superliner n
test pilot n
traffic signal n
wingspan n

Emotions/ Characteristics

Electra complex n b1915
extroversion n b1915 [med. sense: b1670] (extrovert: 1918)
livid adj *enraged* b1915
personality test n b1915
rah-rah adj *enthusiastic* b1915
tick off v b1915
ambivalence, ambivalent n, adj (ambivalency: b1915)
cabin fever n (Am)
consuming adj *engrossing* ["deeply felt": b1825]
defeatism, defeatist n
emote v (Am)
gaga adj
grouse n *complaint* (verb use: b1830)
introvert n (verb use: b1650; introverted: b1915)
pet peeve n (Am)
snooty adj

Thoughts/Perception/ The Mind

cerebrate v *think* b1915
intelligence test n b1915
mental age n b1915
pleasure principle n *psychological term* b1915
bats adj *crazy*
conscious n
envision n
industrial psychology n
intelligence quotient/IQ n

psych v *psychoanalyze* [as in "psyche up": b1970]
punch-drunk adj (Am)
superego n

Love/Romance/Sex

baby-snatcher n *person who dates someone younger* b1915
easy rider n (Am) *lover* b1915
gay adj *homosexual* b1915 (noun use: b1955)
go down v (Am) *perform oral sex* b1915
sex object n b1915
sex symbol n b1915
heterosexual n (adj use: b1895; hetero: b1935)
homoerotic, homoeroticism adj
jazz v *slang have sex* (noun use: b1925)
love life n
make v *slang bed, seduce*
newlywed n
sex play n
war bride n

Family/Relations/ Friends

grandbaby, grandkid n (grandchild: b1590)

Games/Fun/Leisure

coaster wagon n b1915
crossword puzzle n b1915
pocket billiards n b1915
yoyo n b1915 (adj use: b1935; verb use: b1970)
fun and games n
mah-jongg n *type of game*
playland n
shoot-the-chutes n
strip poker n
treasure hunt n

Sports

aerobatics n b1915
anchorman n *as on a relay team* b1915
backpack n b1915 (verb use: b1930)
decathlon n b1915 (decathlete: b1970)
Indian wrestling n (Am) *arm wrestling* b1915 (Indian wrestle: b1940)

miniature golf n b1915
push-up n b1915
ump n b1915
all-American n (adj use: b1890)
bird v *go birdwatching*
daily dozen n (Am) *type of exercise program*
kayo n (Am) (verb use: b1925)
outdoorsman n

Professions/Duties

efficiency expert n (Am) b1915
geneticist n b1915
ombudsman n b1915
craftsperson n (craftsman: b1200; craftswoman: b1890; craftspeople: b1955)
dockhand, dockworker n
file clerk n
gandy dancer n
short-order cook n
timberjack n

Business/Commerce/ Selling

massage parlor n b1915
price control n b1915
sales adj b1915
vendeuse n b1915
white sale n b1915
bill of goods n
briefcase n
business cycle n
cash discount n
cash-and-carry adj (noun use: b1925)
dealership n
duopoly n
flog v *slang sell*
loss leader n
markup n
package store n
penny stock n (Am)
price-fixing n
self-service adj/n (self-serve adj: b1930)

The Workplace

assembly line n (Am) b1915
clock-watcher n b1915
company union n b1915
man-hour n b1915 (man-year: b1920; man-day: b1925)

pink slip n/v b1915
base pay n
collective farm n
donkeywork n
man-year n
salariat n *salaried workers as a group*
white-collar adj
workmen's compensation insurance n
yellow-dog contract n (Am) *type of preemployment contract*

Finances/Money

cost-of-living index n b1915
coverage n (Am) *in insurance* b1915
credit line n b1915
overhead n b1915
profiteer n b1915 (verb use: b1830)
savings account n b1915
scratch n *money* b1915
second mortgage n b1915
surety bond n b1915
devalue v
inflationary adj (inflation: b1840)
investment company n
line of credit n
recapitalization n
revolving credit n
service charge n
smacker n (Am) *slang dollar* (smackeroo: b1940)
stop payment n

Language and Speaking

blabber n *blather* b1915 (verb use: b1400)
legalese n b1915
mot juste n *precisely the right word* b1915
run-on sentence n b1915
coordinating conjunction n
finger spelling n
uppercase n (adj use: b1740; verb use: b1950)

Literature/Writing

imagism n *type of poetry* 1912
backspace v/n b1915
blurb n/v (Am) b1915
copywriter n b1915
John Henry n *signature* b1915
pan v *give a bad review* b1915

rewrite n b1915 (verb use: b1870)
sob sister n b1915
steno n b1915
byline n (verb use: b1940)
columnist n (Am) (column: b1870)
comic strip n (Am)
complimentary close n
fictionalize v (fictionize: b1835)
newshound n
proofread v
rhyme scheme n
subplot n
superhero n
touch system n *typing system*

Communication
airmail n/v b1915
intercommunication system n b1915 (intercom: b1940)
radio frequency n b1915
telephone book n b1915
window envelope n b1915
geophone n
postal service n

Visual Arts/ Photography
depth of field n b1915
collage n
Dada, Dadaism n
mural n *wall painting*
neorealism n

Performing Arts
ensemble adj/n *type of group* b1915 [gen. "totality": b1750; "acting in unison": b1830]
eurythmics n b1915
modern dance n b1915
stooge n (Am) *stagehand* b1915 ["yes-man": b1940] (verb use: b1940)
tragic flaw n b1915
ad-lib v (noun use: b1820; adj use: b1935)
hoofer n (Am) *dancer* (hoof v: b1925)
houselights n

Music
fipple flute n b1915
jazz n b1915
songfest n b1915

work song n b1915
bongo n (Am) *the drum*
boogie-woogie, boogie n/v (Am) (boogie n: b1925; boogie v: b1930)
didgeridoo n *type of trumpet*
falling rhythm n
tin ear n

Entertainment
airshow n b1915
celeb n b1915
one-step n/v *type of dance* b1915
party v

Movies/TV/Radio
animated cartoon n b1915
call letters n b1915 (call sign: b1920)
filmdom n b1915
filmland n b1915
first-run adj b1915
movie actor n b1915
moviemaker n b1915
photoplay n (Am) b1915
scriptwriter n b1915 (scripter: b1940)
talkie n b1915
cinemagoer n
costar n/v
dissolve n *film term*
double bill n (double-bill v: b1930)
fade-in, fade-out n
filmgoer n
filmization n (Am)
footage n
moviedom n (Am)
newsreel n
photodrama n
scenarist n
screenplay n
silver screen n
starlet n ["small celestial object": b1830]

Education
consolidated school n (Am) b1915
cow college n b1915
diploma mill n b1915
frosh n b1915
homeroom n b1915
major v *as in "major in a subject in college"* b1915
Montessori method n b1915

parent-teacher association n b1915
refresher course n b1915
teacher's pet n b1915
environmentalist n *proponent of type of learning theory*
flunk out v
raw score n
report card n (Am) (report: b1900)
social studies n
survey course n

Religion
desacralize v b1915
wailing wall n

Society/Mores/Culture
community center n b1915
kultur n b1915
melting pot n b1915
community chest n (Am)
deb n
longhair n
subdebutante n (sub-deb: b1920)
underclass n

Government
city manager n (Am) b1915
city planning n b1915
nationwide adj b1915 (adv use: b1930)
soviet n 1917
technocracy n 1919 (technocrat: b1930)
city clerk n
client state n
commissar n
congresswoman n (congressman: b1780; congressperson: b1975)
fascism n
nation-state n

Politics
diplomatic immunity n b1915
guild socialism n b1915
realpolitik n b1915
segregationist n b1915
leftism, leftist n
smoke-filled room n

Death
death wish n b1915
death house n
death instinct n

murderee n (murderer: b1340)

War/Military/Violence
air base n b1915
air raid n b1915
ammo n b1915
antiaircraft adj b1915
atomic bomb n b1915 (atom bomb: b1945)
battle cruiser n b1915
bomber n b1915
escadrille n b1915
firepower n b1915
flechette n *type of weapon* b1915
haymaker n *type of punch* b1915
leatherneck n *marine* b1915 ["gen. soldier": b1890]
poison gas n b1915
rabbit punch n b1915
roscoe n *handgun* b1915
sabotage v b1915 (noun use: b1870)
six-gun n b1915 (six-shooter: b1845)
strafe v 1915
tank n b1915
TNT n b1915
U-boat n b1915
war room n b1915
war zone n b1915
warplane n b1915
selective service n 1917
air force n
aircraft carrier n
AWOL adj/adv/n
barrage n *bombardment* [type of barrier: b1860]
buck adj *as in "buck private"*
bunker n
call to quarters n
chemical warfare n
command post n (Am)
D day n
depth charge n
dog tag n
flamethrower n
flying circus n *air squadron*
foxhole n
fragmentation bomb n
front line n
GI adj *galvanized iron* (noun use: b1945)
high command n
kitchen police n
KP n (Am)

mustard gas n
nonviolence n
POW n *prisoner of war*
putsch n
recon n/v (Am)
riot gun n
roundhouse n *type of punch*
service stripe n
shadowbox v
shock troops n
shore patrol n
slugfest n (Am)
sub n *sub(marine)*
subchaser n
submachine gun n
tear gas n (verb use: b1950)
trench warfare n

Crime/Punishment/ Enforcement

can n (Am) *slang jail* b1915
case v *as in "case the joint"* b1915
gangland n (Am) b1915
grift n/v *graft* b1915
big house n *slang prison*
bust v *arrest* ["raid": b1860] (noun use: b1940)
chiseler n *cheat* (chisel: b1810)
drug addict n
jaywalk v (Am)
knock off v *rob* (knock over: b1930)
mobster n (mob: b1930)
pokey n *jail*
rumrunner n (Am)

The Law

fundamental law n b1915
trial lawyer n b1915
public defender n
traffic court n

The Fantastic/ Paranormal

death ray n
paranormal adj/n

Interjections

come off it interj b1915
hell's bells interj b1915
ow interj b1915
shoot interj *go ahead* b1915
yippee interj b1915
zowie interj (Am) b1915

ooh interj
shit interj

Slang

afterthought n (Am) *late child* b1915
big noise n *big shot* b1915
blow v *leave* b1915
broad n *woman* b1915
BS n (Am) *bull* b1915
bullshit n b1915 (verb use: b1945; bullshitter: b145)
buzz off v (Am) b1915
click v *fall into place, get along* b1915
curtains n *end, doom* b1915
cushy adj b1915
flipping adj (Brit) b1915
gander n *as in "take a gander"* b1915 (verb use: b1890)
glass jaw n b1915
gonna v b1915
highball v *go fast* b1915
higher-up n b1915
hophead n *druggie* b1915 (hopped up: b1925)
horn in v b1915
info n b1915
jam n *fig. tight spot* b1915
john n (Am) *whorer* b1915
lech, letch v b1915
lowdown n b1915
muscle v b1915
once-over n (Am) b1915
paperhanger n *forger* b1915
polluted adj *drunk* b1915
prep v b1915 (noun use: b1865)
rock hound n (Am) b1915
schlock adj/n b1915
skirt n *woman* b1915
tank n (Am) *as in "drunk tank"* b1915
whiz n *wizard* b1915
whizbang adj/n b1915 (interj use: b1870)
wisecrack n/v (Am) b1915
word salad n b1915
worm's-eye view n b1915
baloney interj/n (Am) *nonsense*
baloney n *mediocre boxer*
basket case n *person with no limbs*
beaucoup adj *many*
blotto adj *drunk*
bull session n

bushwa n (Am)
catfight n
char n (Am) *tea*
chute n/v (Am) *parachute*
clam up v (clam v: b1350)
cold turkey n (Am) (adv use: b1945)
conk v *as in "conk out"*
cootie n
copacetic adj (Am)
doozy n (Am) (adj use: b1905; doozer: b1930)
drag v *as in "drag off a cigarette"* (noun use: b1915)
earful n
funfest n
hokum n
icky-boo, icky-poo adj *sick*
iffy adj
jazz n *nonsense*
jazzy adj (Am)
level v *as in "let me level with you"*
man, the n *authority* ["police": b1965]
mean adj *as in "he plays a mean game of tennis"*
merde n
razz n (verb use: b1915; razoo n/v: b1890)
rev v *as in "rev an engine"* (noun use: b1890)
rubber-stamp v
shill n (verb use: b1915)
spill, spill the beans v
umpteen, umpteenth adj (umpty n: b1900)
wicked adj *as in "tennis player with a wicked serve"*
wow n (verb use: b1925)
wren n (Am) *woman*
Xanadu n

Insults

deviate n b1915
dingbat n (Am) *ditz* b1915
faggot n (Am) *homosexual* b1915 [gen. insult: b1570; "woman": b1595]
feeb n (Am) b1915
fud n *fuddy-duddy* b1915
goof n *dolt* b1915 ["mistake": b1955] (verb use: b1935; goofball: b1940)
gunsel n *young man; young homosexual* b1915 ["guman": b1945]
heel n (Am) *jerk* b1915

hell-raiser n b1915
lounge lizard n b1915
lowlife n b1915 (adj use: b1795)
poop n *fuddy-duddy* b1915
smartass n b1915 (adj use: b1960)
souse n *drunk* b1915 ["drinking spree": b1905] (soused: b1905)
stuffed shirt n (Am) b1915
wino n (Am) b1915
yellow streak n b1915
yes-man n b1915
apple-knocker n *rustic*
bats adj *batty* (batty: b1910)
bimbo n (Am) *dull man* ["dull woman": b1930] (bim: b1925; bimbette: b1985)
bozo n (Am)
colored n
crumb n *low person* ["louse": b1870]
cuckoo n (noun use: b1585)
dumbbell n
egghead n (eggheaded: b1940)
ham-handed adj (ham-fisted: b1930)
hick adj *backwoods* (noun use: b1565)
potshot n/v *sniping remark* ["rifle shot for food, at random": b1860]
punk n *thug* ["prostitute": b1600; "homosexual": b1905]
smartypants n
SOB n
wimp n (Am)

Phrases

bare bones n b1915
bread and circuses n b1915
by-your-leave n b1915
change of pace n b1915
closed book n b1915
duck soup n (Am) b1915
femme fatale n b1915
fever pitch n b1915
fifty-fifty adj b1915
founding father n b1915
hard knocks n b1915
hit the hay/sack v b1915
long view n b1915
lunatic fringe n b1915
pie in the sky n (Am) b1915

raw deal n b1915
sob story n b1915
square shooter n b1915
stick around v b1915
string along v b1915 (string: b1815)
Swedish massage n b1915
talking point n *common point of discussion* b1915
visual aid n b1915
asphalt jungle n (Am)
buck passer n
bum's rush n (bum-rush v: b1990)
code name n
collective unconscious n
cry uncle v
dead soldier n *empty bottle* (slang dead men: b1700)
dollar-a-year, dollar-a-year man adj, n
fighting words n
hell-for-leather adj (adv use: b1890)
home front n
honest-to-goodness/honest-to-God adj/adv
hot seat n
human relations n
last minute n
line of duty n
make-or-break adj
middle of the road n (adj use: b1895)
trip wire n
zero hour n

General/Miscellaneous

attrition n *gradual loss* b1915 ["wearing down by friction": b1375]
backdrop n (Am) b1915
bucket brigade n b1915
close-up n (Am) b1915
downwash n b1915

expo n b1915
front-runner n (Am) b1915
gelate n/v *gelatin* b1915
get-together n b1915
intangible n b1915 (adj use: b1640)
jinx n b1915 (verb use: b1920)
lead-in adj/n b1915
livability n b1915
nada n b1915
nosedive n/v b1915
rotogravure n b1915
smoke screen n b1915
static n b1915
streamline, streamlined v, adj *make efficient* b1915 (scientific noun use: b1870)
tailspin n/v b1915
teammate n b1915
throughput n *akin to input and output* b1915
troublemaker n b1915
zing n b1915 (verb use: b1920)
audio adj (noun use: b1395)
blah n *nonsense* [as in "the blahs": b1970]
breakthrough n (break through v: b1955)
camouflage n/v (adj use: b1945)
check mark n (check: b1890)
check-in n
dysfunction n
evacuee n
fill-in n
flowchart n (flow diagram: b1945)
handset n
high-hat adj/v (noun use: b1890)
internee n
interrogee n (interrogator: b1955)
kickback n (Am)
mock-up n

provocateur n
spillover n
stall n *hesitation, as in "an airplane stall"*
stockpile n *supply* [spec. "supply of coal": b1875] (verb use: b1925)
surprint n/v
svengali n
takeover n [business sense: b1945]
trade-in n
yea-sayer n
zoom n

Things

doohickey n (Am) b1915
stink bomb n b1915
gadgetry n

Description

all-time adj b1915
bush-league adj b1915 (bush adj: b1970)
cutesy adj b1915 (cutesy-poo: b1975)
five-star adj b1915 (four-star: b1925)
futuristic adj b1915
harried adj b1915
heavy-duty adj b1915
irregardless adv *regardless* b1915
must adj b1915 (noun use: b1895)
nonflammable adj b1915
over with adj b1915
pathbreaking adj b1915
prestigious adj *bearing prestige* b1915 [arch. "illusory": b1550]
pretend adj b1915
shockproof adj/v b1915
textbookish adj b1915
everyplace adj

flooey adj *as in "go flooey"*
goddamned, goddamn adj/adv
goofy adj
hush-hush adj
listenable adj
peroxide adj
put-upon adj
slinky adj

Colors

midnight blue n

Actions/Verbs

break v (Am) *as in "breaking news"* b1915
chuff n/v *make exhaust sound* b1915
churn out v b1915
keynote v b1915
landscape v *as in "landscape a yard"* b1915 (landscaper: b1965)
masculinize v b1915 (arch. masculate: b1630)
shortcut v b1915
windmill v b1915
zero v *as in "zero in"* b1915 (zeroize "set to zero": b1930)
bug v *eavesdrop*
bundle up v
check in v (check out: b1925)
crab v *move as a crab*
field-test v (Am)
grandstand v (noun use: b1895)
jazz v *as in "jazz up a car"*
junk v *discard*
level off v
pinpoint v
recondition v
shape up v
soft-pedal v
trigger v

IN USE BY
1930

Geography/Places
midlatitudes n b1925
rockfall n b1925
Big Apple n *New York*
continental drift n
gully erosion n
midtown adj/n
outback n (adv use: b1880)
tremblor n *earthquake*
wilderness area n (Am)

Natural Things
dry ice n b1925
inseminate v *implant with se-men* b1925 ["implant seed": b1625] (insemination: b1860)
living fossil n b1925
meltwater n b1925
neutron n b1925
conservation n *preservation of natural resources* (conservationist: b1870)
temperate rain forest n
tropical rain forest n

Plants
death cap n *type of mushroom* b1925
dire wolf n *type of prehistoric animal* b1925
Dutch elm disease n b1925
glad n b1925
oakmoss n b1925
strawflower n b1925
cottage tulip n
fruitwood n
gladiola n (gladiolus: b1150)
key lime n

Animals
afghan hound n b1925
Appaloosa n (Am) b1925
Dungeness crab n b1925
guppy n b1925
night crawler n (Am) b1925
Rhode Island White n (Am) *type of fowl* b1925
schnauzer n b1925
shih tzu n *type of dog* b1925
budgie n (budgerigar: b1840)
corgi n *type of dog*
dawn horse n
dragon lizard, Komodo dragon n
duck-billed dinosaur n
English foxhound n
German shepherd n
king mackerel n
Lipizzaner n
miniature pinscher n
miniature schnauzer n
mouthbreeder n *class of fish*
pinscher n
pit bull n (pit bull terrier: b1945)
Siberian husky n
swordtail n *type of fish*
Tibetan spaniel n
Welsh corgi n

Weather
cold front, warm front n b1925
microclimate n b1925
windburn n b1925
halo effect n
micrometeorology n

Heavens/Sky
cosmic ray n 1925
white dwarf n b1925
intergalactic adj
ionosphere n
metagalaxy n
ozone layer n (ozone shield: b1980)
planetarium n *building for duplicating the night sky* [type of model: b1735]
supercluster n
supergalaxy n
supernova n

Science
Coriolis force n b1925
cultural anthropology n b1925
preman n b1925
quantum mechanics n b1925
redshift n b1925
sonic adj b1925
ultrasound n b1925
bathysphere n
plasma n *type of gas* [as in "blood plasma": b1845]
primatology n
quantum jump n (quantum leap: b1960)
radio telescope n

Technology
demodulate v b1925
frequency modulation n *FM* b1925
lox n *liquid oxygen explosive* b1925
supercharger n b1925
baud n
servocontrol n

servomechanism n (servo: b1950)

Energy
fuel cell n b1925
gas station n b1925
liquefied petroleum gas n b1925
space heater n b1925
bottled gas n
gas n *gasoline*
hertz n *measurement of energy*
nuclear energy n
white gas n

Time
year-round adj b1925
dendrochronology n

Age/Aging
teenage, teenager adj, n b1925 (teen adj/n: b1820; teener: b1895; teenaged: b1955)
geriatric n *old person*
preadolescence n

Mathematics
inverse square law n b1925
line graph n b1925
lowest common denominator, lowest common multiple n b1925
circle graph n *pie chart*
graph paper n
law of averages n
logarithmic function n

Measurement
Geiger counter n b1925
kilocycle n *kilohertz* b1925

light meter n b1925
roentgen n b1925 (adj use: b1900)
altimeter n
decibel n
gram-atomic weight n
kilohertz n
leg n *as in "second leg of the race"*
Rorschach test n
sensor n

The Body

dong n *slang penis* b1925
growth hormone n b1925
inner ear n b1925
prepuberty n b1925 (prepubertal: b1860; prepubescent adj/n: 1904; prepubescence: b1920)
underarm n b1925
can n (Am) *slang buttocks*
cerebral cortex n
curse, the n *slang menstruation*
ejaculate n
estrogen n
fanny n *buttocks* ["female genitals": b1880]
laugh line n *wrinkle*
scat n *slang feces*
schnozzle n *slang nose* (schnozz: b1940)
seminal fluid n
tube n *slang penis*

Physical Description

heavyset adj b1925
accident-prone adj
barrel-chested adj
bleary-eyed adj (blear-eyed: b1380)
malnourished adj
surehanded adj

Medicine

bromo n b1925
cervical cap n *type of contraceptive* b1925
cheaters n (Am) *glasses* b1925
contaminant n b1925
dental hygienist n b1925
encephalography n b1925 (encephalogram, encephalograph: b1930)
first-degree burn n b1925

(second-degree burn, third-degree burn: b1930)
gimp n (Am) *slang cripple* b1925 (verb use: b1950)
hearing aid n b1925
hepatoma n b1925
herpesvirus n b1925 (herpes: b1400; herpes zoster: b1810; herpes simplex: b1910)
insulin shock n b1925
low blood pressure n b1925
mastectomy n b1925
oxygen tent n b1925
paramedical adj b1925 (paramedic: b1955)
parkinsonism n b1925
physical therapy n b1925
practical nurse n b1925
quadriplegia, quadriplegic n, adj/n b1925
radiation sickness n b1925
septic sore throat n *strep throat* b1925
sickle-cell anemia n b1925
truth serum n b1925
tubercular n b1925
universal donor, universal recipient n b1925
penicillin n 1929 (penicillium: b1870)
alcoholic adj *addicted to alcohol* ["related to alcohol": b1790] (noun use: b1890; alcoholism: b1860)
allergist n
analysis, analyst n *psychoanalysis, psychoanalyst*
anticancer adj
asbestosis n
athlete's foot n
bug n *slang germ, disease*
cardiac n *cardiac patient* [type of vein: b1440; obs. "cardiac medicine": b1770 to 1800s]
childbed fever n
condition n
congestive heart failure n
continence n *opp. of incontinence* (continent: b1970)
cryotherapy n
donor n
eyedrops n (eyedropper: b1940)
geriatrician n (geriatrist: b1970)
heart attack n

heliotherapy n
hemorrhage v (verb use: b1425)
holism, holistic n, adj
hyperventilation n (hyperventilate: b1935)
idiot savant n
inhalatorium n
iron n
microsurgery n
misdiagnose v
Pasteur treatment n *rabies treatment* (Pasteurism: b1900)
paternity test n
preemie n *premature baby*
preterm adj
preventorium n
respirator n
Rx n
shinsplints n
shot n *injection*
split personality n
steroid n
strep, strep throat n *strep(tococcus)*
tetralogy n
x-ray therapy n

Everyday Life

aerosol n b1925
after shave n b1925
bed warmer n b1925
bunk bed n b1925
deacon's bench n b1925
dinette n (Am) b1925
direct mail n *junk mail* b1925
earphone n b1925
household art n *household skill* b1925
housewares n b1925
indirect lighting n b1925
Murphy bed n *type of foldup bed* b1925
overnight bag n b1925 (overnighter: b1950)
tea wagon n b1925
throne n *slang toilet* b1925
toggle switch n b1925
toilet training n b1925
vacuum v b1925
wallpaper v b1925
air mattress n
chain-link fence n
chesterfield n *type of sofa*
clothes tree n
coffeemaker n (coffeepot: b1705)

cookie sheet n
decor n ["stage setting": b1900]
drapes n
facial tissue n
freezer burn n
fridge n
horn-rims n
men's room n
nappy n (Brit) *diaper*
pack n *backpack* (verb use: b1870)
place mat n
recliner n *type of furniture*
rubbing alcohol n
run n *as in "a run in my hose"*
scatter rug n
smoke detector n
springform pan n
stemware n
switch v *turn on or off* (noun use: b1870)
throw rug n
toilet n *bathroom, lavatory* (toilet paper: b1885)
trash n *garbage, discards* ["something worthless": b1325]
tube pan n
unit n *e.g., piece of a sectional couch*
utility n *electrical service, etc.*
windchime n

Shelter/Housing

duplex, duplex apartment n b1925
French door n b1925
inbuilt adj *built-in* b1925 (inbuild: b1930)
master bedroom n b1925
motel n (Am) b1925
rainspout n b1925
rest home n b1925
trailer camp n b1925 (trailer park: b1945)
wading pool n b1925
cinder block n
cubicle n [obs. "bedroom": b1450 to 1500s; "small bed": b1900]
efficiency apartment n
flood control n (Am)
hideaway n *hiding place* ["hiding person": b1875]
interior design n (interior decoration: b1810; interior designer: b1940)

railroad flat n

reservation n *as in "a hotel reservation"*

roomie n (roommate: b1780)

woodhenge n

youth hostel n

Drink

bathtub gin n b1925

corn liquor n (Am) b1925

decaffeinated adj b1925 (decaffeinate: b1930; decaf: b1985)

piña colada n b1925

alexander n *the drink*

chardonnay n

down v *slang drink*

Gibson n *type of martini*

giggle water n (Am) *slang alcohol*

gimlet n *type of drink*

glogg n *type of drink*

oenophile n *wine lover*

setup n *ingredients of a drink*

tonic water n

Food

bean sprouts n b1925

blue cheese n b1925

bottom round n *cut of beef* b1925

bouillon cube n b1925 (bouillon: b1660)

coffee ring n b1925

coffee royal n b1925

crêpe suzette n b1925

deep-fry v b1925

delmonico steak n b1925

French pastry n b1925

hard candy n b1925

melba toast n b1925

minute steak n b1925

Mornay sauce n b1925

pepperoni n (Am) b1925

rigatoni n b1925

Russian dressing n b1925

spaghettini n b1925

spumoni n b1925

sugar-free adj b1925

Swiss steak n b1925

whipping cream n b1925

white chocolate n b1925

white rice n b1925

a la mode adj (Am) *served with ice cream* ["stewed in wine (of beef)": b1650]

baloney n

A Word About *Word*

While we're considering the age of words, let's also consider the age of *word*.

The word that describes itself is, appropriately, a long-standing member of the English language, appearing in *Beowulf* around A.D. 725. (As a verb meaning "to speak," *word* has been around since before the thirteenth century.)

Word's roots are deep, traceable back to the long-pre-English Indo-European *wer-*, "to speak," which is also the root of *verb*.

And the other parts of speech? *Noun, verb, adjective* and *adverb* all joined English about the same time, by 1400. (*Adjective* used as an adjective, by the way, is recorded slightly earlier, by 1390.) *Sentence* precedes 1400, and *paragraph* was in use by 1500.

And to end this discussion, in use by 1600 was the word *period*.

---

blue plate adj (blue-plate special: b1945)

braunschweiger n

celery cabbage n

chiffon n *as in "lemon chiffon pie"*

cotton candy n (Am)

crispbread n

cube steak n

Danish pastry n

fava n *type of bean*

finger food n

fleshy fruit n

float n

food chain n

fruit cocktail n

fruit cup n (Am)

gelato n *type of ice cream*

gratine adj *au gratin* (verb use: b1935)

haute cuisine n

heavy cream n

knockwurst n

lobster thermidor n *lobster dish*

macadamia nut n

mix n *as in "cake mix"*

mole n *type of sauce*

monosodium glutamate n

nonfat adj

panfry v

patty n *as in "hamburger patty"*

precook v

prosciutto n *type of ham*

puree v

quick-freeze v

red-eye n *slang ketchup*

rib eye n

shoofly pie n (Am)

snack bar n

Spanish rice n

subgum n *type of Chinese dish*

sweet-and-sour adj

topping n [gen. top: b1350]

truffle n *type of sweet*

western sandwich n

zucchini n

Agriculture/ Food-Gathering

inbreed v b1925 [obs. "be bred": b1600]

sharecropper n (Am) b1925 (sharecrop v: b1930)

4-H n

combine v *harvest with a combine*

deworm v

ear rot n

field bed n

homogenize v *prepare milk*

seed stock n

soilage n

vegeculture n

Cloth/Clothing

broadloom adj/n *made on a wide loom* b1925

bunting n *infant clothing* b1925

cire n *type of fabric surface* b1925

coolie hat n b1925

hemline n b1925

knitwear n b1925

lame n *type of fabric* b1925

man-tailored adj b1925

muumuu n b1925

outerwear n b1925

rayon n b1925

sweatpants, sweatshirt n b1925

teddy n (Am) *type of lingerie* b1925

tracksuit n b1925

tux n b1925

underpants n b1925

zipper n b1925 (verb use: b1930; zip: b1934)

athletic supporter n

beachwear n

beanie n (Am)

bustline n

cap sleeve n

colorfast adj

drop cloth n

foundation garment n

girdle n *corset* [gen. use: b1000]

glen plaid n

hard hat n

nudism n

polyester n (adj use: b1960)

preshrink v

pullover n

rompers n

scanties n

sleeper n *nightwear*

spike heel n

sunsuit n

sweat suit n (sweatpants, sweatshirt: b1925)

swimsuit n

ten-gallon hat n

threads n

two-piece n

unmentionable n

Fashion/Style

Bauhaus adj *design style* b1925

compact n *makeup case* b1925

cultured pearl n b1925

face-lift n (Am) b1925

hairdo n b1925 (hairstyle: b1915)

permanent n b1925 (perm n/ v: b1930)

choker n *type of jewelry*

cosmetology n

emerald cut n

eye shadow n

eyewear n

hairpiece n

modistic adj (modish: b1660)

photogenic adj [obs. "photographic": b1840]

voguish adj

Tools

coping saw n b1925

dehumidifier n b1925 (dehumidify: b1930)

electron gun n b1925

electron tube n b1925

floodlight n b1925

gyrostabilizer n b1925 (gyro: b1910)

headset n b1925

inhalator n (Am) b1925

instrument panel n b1925

quartz lamp n b1925

rototiller n b1925 (rotary cultivator: b1930)

air cleaner n

backhoe n

bulldozer n *earth mover*

bungee cord n

C-clamp n

coolant n

defroster n

dump truck n (Am)

hand lens n

jumper cables n

master n *as in "master recording"*

photocopier n

postage meter n

push broom n

ring binder n

rotary cultivator n (rototiller: b1925)

rotary press n

scanner n

teleprinter n

Travel/Transportation

autogyro n b1925

cabin cruiser n b1925

deplane v b1925

filling station n b1925

flight deck n b1925

floatplane n b1925

gyropilot n *automatic pilot* b1925

hitchhike v (Am) b1925 (hitch v: b1870)

light plane n b1925

paddle wheeler n b1925

parking lot n (Am) b1925

pigboat n (Am) b1925

sailplane n/v b1925

service road n b1925

snowmobile n b1925

speed trap n b1925

sports car n b1925

superhighway n (Am) b1925

supertanker n b1925

taxi stand n b1925

trackless trolley n b1925

U-turn n b1925

whistle-stop n (Am) b1925 (verb use: b1955)

airfreight n

astronaut, astronautics n

captain n *of an airplane* [of a ship: b1650]

car park n

controls n

copilot n

derailleur n

double-clutch v

driver's license n

elevator n *airplane steering device*

field trip n

flight-test v

four-wheel drive n

freeway n (Am)

front-wheel drive n

gearshift n

hang glider n

heap n *rattletrap car*

helicopter n

in-line engine n

instrument flying n

jalopy n (Am)

land yacht n

landing strip n

license plate n

lift n *upward force on a wing*

lift truck n

miss v *as in "an engine missing"*

model n *as in "make and model"*

overdrive n

overpass n

rearview mirror n

red ball n *fast train*

rocket plane n

rocket ship n

rocketry n

roundabout n *rotary*

sedan n

shift v *as in "shift gears"*

skiplane n

spacecraft n

spacesuit n

stick n *as in "stick shift"*

stoplight n

synchromesh adj

through street n *opp. of dead end*

thruway n

transmission n *as in "automatic transmission"*

travel agent, travel agency n

truck n/v *motorized transport* [type of wheel: b1350; type of transport: b1800]

water taxi n

wind sock n

Emotions/ Characteristics

id n 1924

adamant adj b1925 ["physically unbreakable": b1390] (adamancy: b1940; adamance: b1955)

belly laugh n b1925

camera-shy adj b1925

gravitas n *deadly seriousness* b1925

hincty adj *slang conceited* b1925

inferiority complex n b1925

jitter n (Am) b1925 (verb use: b1930)

penis envy n b1925

Pollyanna n (Am) b1925

sadomasochism n b1925

self-discovery n b1925

adversarial adj (adversary adj: b1400)

bitch v *complain, act surly*

butterflies n *nerves*

deadpan adj (Am) (verb use: b1945)

drive n *ambition* (driven: b1925)

fugue n

initiative n

inkblot test n

misandry n *hatred of men* (misogyny: b1660)

misty-eyed adj

moxie n (Am)

pissy adj

project, projection n, v *engage in psychological projection*

sardonicism n *akin to sarcasm*

screaming meemies n

self-disgust n

steamed adj *slang angry*

temper tantrum n

treasure v *cherish* ["save": b1400]

warm spot n *as in "a warm spot in my heart"*

Thoughts/Perception/ The Mind

anima n b1925

depth psychology n *psychoanalysis* b1925

eidetic adj *having photographic memory* b1925

epistemic adj *related to knowledge* b1925

Gestalt psychology n b1925

guesstimate n (Am) b1925

introspectionism n b1925

outfox v b1925

outsmart v b1925

schizoid adj/n b1925

schizophrene n *schizophrenic* b1925

teched adj b1925

cerebral adj *intellectual* ["of the brain": b1805]

concentrate v *focus attention* (concentration: b1870)

dialectical materialism n

fantasize v

marbles n *as in "lost your marbles"*

obsessive-compulsive adj

potty n *crazy*

psyche n *the mind* ["the soul": b1660]

schizy adj *schizo* (schizo: b1945; schiz: b1960)

total recall n

transference n

wishful thinking n

Love/Romance/Sex
blind date n b1925
come n *slang ejaculation* b1925 (verb use: b1650)
cradle-snatcher n *person who dates young person* b1925
double date n b1925
extramarital adj b1925
flower girl n b1925
French kiss n b1925
Mr. Right n b1925
one-nighter n b1925
proposition v *suggest sex* b1925
sex appeal n b1925
sexy adj b1925 ["sensational": b1965]
SWAK *sealed with a kiss* b1925
trial marriage n b1925
trick n *sex with a prostitute* b1925 (verb use: b1970)
two-time v b1925
call house n *bordello* (call girl: b1935)
cherry n (Am) *slang virginity*
climax n *orgasm*
eat v *slang have oral sex*
foreplay n
homo n
nooky n
pansexual adj
pass n *romantic advance*
pitch v *as in "pitch woo"*
quickie adj/n
relations n *sex*
screw n *slang sex* (verb use: b1725)
sex n *love-making*
shotgun wedding n (Am)
slap and tickle n (Brit)
sleep around v
sweetie pie n (arch. sweeting: b1350; sweetikins: b1600; sweetie: b1800)
tomcat v (slang noun use: b1970)
turn a trick v *commit prostitution* ["rob": b1870]

Family/Relations/Friends
homeboy, homegirl n (Am)

Holidays
shower n *as in "baby shower"*

Games/Fun/Leisure
brainteaser n b1925
capture the flag n b1925

contract bridge n b1925
game of chance n b1925
jungle gym n b1925
pogo stick n b1925
slumber party n (Am) b1925
dart n
dreidel n
duplicate bridge n
headpin n *in bowling*
Kewpie n
pool hall n (Am)
prankster n (Am)
shapes n *loaded dice*
vacationland n
wild adj *as in "deuces are wild"*

Sports
cross-country n b1925
dodgeball n b1925
goalie n b1925 (goalkeeper: b1660; goaltender: b1910)
ice dancing n b1925
invitational adj/n b1925
jock n (Am) b1925
KO n/v b1925
marathoner n b1925
paddle tennis n (Am) b1925
slalom n b1925 (verb use: b1935)
tack n *horse equipment* b1925
technical knockout n *TKO* b1925
axel n
crawl n *type of swim stroke*
deck tennis n
field n *as in "track and field"*
lawn bowling n
length n *swimming measure*
picara n *female picaro* (picador: b1800)
pike n *type of diving position*
pin n *used in golf*
play-by-play adj/n
pull-up n ["sudden stop": b1855]
quarter n *division of game*
rodeo n *type of exhibition* ["roundup": b1835]
scissors kick n
skeet n
softball n
surf v
surf casting n
title n *championship* (titleholder: b1905; titlist: b1925)
track n *track-and-field sports*

trial n *as in "time trial"*
weight n *in boxing*

Professions/Duties
beautician n (Am) b1925
cosmetician n b1925
gigolo n b1925
puppeteer n b1925
researchist n b1925
soda jerk n (Am) b1925
toastmistress n b1925 (toastmaster: b1750)
usherette n b1925
zookeeper n b1925
bell captain n (Am)
crewman n
fact finder n
garde-manger n *preparer of cold foods*
grease monkey n
imagemaker n
model v (noun use: b1700)
nutritionist n
soundman n

Business/Commerce/Selling
bistro n b1925
brand name n b1925
case goods n *furniture designed for storage* b1925
checkout n (Am) b1925
closeout n b1925
controlling interest n b1925
double indemnity n (Am) b1925
flea market n b1925
free on board adj/adv b1925
greasy spoon n b1925
luncheonette n (Am) b1925
mass-produce v b1925
money-back adj b1925
over-the-counter adj b1925
price war n b1925
selling point n b1925
supermarket n (Am) b1925
supper club n b1925
trade agreement n b1925
trade in v b1925
window-shop v b1925
after-hours adj
black adj *as in "black market"*
dime store n (Am)
durable goods n (durables: b1945)
executive n *as in "business executive"*

factory ship n
label n *brand name*
market research n (marketing research: b1930)
outlet n *as in "outlet store"*
pitchman n (Am) (pitchwoman: b1960)
premium n *purchase enticement*
prospect n
ribbon development n *early version of strip mall*
room service n
sales check n
sales slip n
salesclerk n
salon n *as in "beauty salon"*
strip mine n/v

The Workplace
aptitude test n b1925
company man n b1925
cottage industry n b1925
craft union n b1925
make-work n (Am) *busywork* b1925
man-day n *akin to man-hour* b1925
unemployment insurance n b1925
workweek n b1925
company town n
daylighting n *opp. of moonlighting*
downtime n
grunt n *scut worker* (grunt work: b1980)
interview n
manpower n
punch in n
semiskilled adj
unemployment benefit, unemployment compensation n
working papers n
working stiff n

Finances/Money
capital gain, capital loss n b1925
cold cash n b1925
creditworthy adj b1925
do-re-mi n *slang cash* b1925
Dow-Jones average n b1925
finance company n b1925
grand n *$1,000* b1925
green n *slang money* b1925
investment bank n b1925
sales tax n b1925

savings and loan association n
b1925

tax-exempt adj b1925

black, red n *as in "in the
black, in the red"*

bundle n *slang a lot of cash*

buyer's market n

cabbage n *money*

consumer credit n

discount rate n

down payment n

escrow v

folding money n

front money n

fund v *provide money* ["pay
debt": b1780; "place in a
fund": b1830]

G, gee n *slang $1,000*

hyperinflation n

lettuce n *slang cash*

money market n

municipal bond n

recession n

reconcile v

red ink n

skin n *dollar* ["wallet":
b1790]

tax stamp n

Language and Speaking

cryptanalysis n (Am) *study of
codes and untranslated languages* b1925

hypercorrect adj *using pretty
English* b1925

linguistic atlas n b1925

nonverbal adj b1925

dialect geography n

jive n (Am) *jargon, blather*

monolingual adj

Literature/Writing

Dewey decimal classification n
b1925

eye dialect n *intentional mispelling to communicate dialect* b1925

fantasist n b1925 ["visionary": b1900]

fictioneer n b1925 (fictionist: b1830)

interior monologue n b1925

magazinist n b1925

mass media n b1925

newsmagazine n (Am)
b1925

preliterate adj b1925

skywriting n b1925

tear sheet n b1925

bookmobile n

bulldog edition n (Am) *newspaper term*

clerihew n *type of verse*

desk n *as in "city desk"*

dust jacket n (dust wrapper:
b1935)

endnote n

fan magazine n

ghostwrite v (ghostwriter,
ghost n: b1900)

hard adj *as in "hard news"*

hardbound adj (hardcase adj:
b1900; hardcover: b1950;
hardback: b1955)

head n *headline* (headline:
b1825)

human-interest adj

issue n *as in "magazine issue"*
(verb use: b1670)

lead n/v *pertaining to the top
story*

magic realism n

morgue n *newspaper archive*

newscast n

press n *journalists as a group*
["the journalism busi-
ness": b1800]

QWERTY n

single-space v

whodunit n

Communication

blower n *slang telephone*
b1925

ham radio operator v b1925

media n *as in "mass media"*
b1925

mike n b1925 (verb use:
b1940)

pie chart n b1925

public-address system n
b1925

radiocast n b1925

buzz n (Am) *slang telephone
call*

line n *as in "pickup line"*

mayday n *distress phrase*

microfilm n (verb use: b1940)

reception n *as in "TV reception"*

tap n *as in "phone tap"* (verb
use: b1870)

Visual Arts/ Photography

surrealism n 1924 (surreal-
istic: b1925; surreal:
b1930)

commercial art n b1925

construction paper n b1925

constructivism n b1925

fauvism n *painting style*
b1925

origami n b1925

practical art n b1925

freehand adj

glossy n

needle n *stylus*

photoflash n

photomural n

printmaking n

representational adj

silkscreen n/v

still n *still photo*

Performing Arts

dramatic unities n b1925

forestage n b1925

miscast adj/v b1925

offstage adj/adv b1925

run-through n b1925

straight man n b1925

bit part n (bit player: b1940)

cabaret n [type of tavern:
b1635]

comic n *comedian*

direct, director v, n *as in "direct a play"*

drill team n

ensemble acting n

folly n *type of theatrical revue*

mezzanine n [gen. use:
b1715]

morality play n

rave n *as in "rave review"*

routine n *as in "dance routine"*

satyr play n

showstopper n

slapstick n *type of comedy* ["a
stick that simulates slap-
ping noises": b1900]

summer stock n

typecast v

variety n *as in "variety show"*

water ballet n

Music

chorale prelude n b1925

chorine n (Am) *chorus girl*
b1925

combo n b1925

sax n b1925

shout song n b1925

skiffle n *type of music* b1925

steel guitar n b1925

uke n b1925

backbeat n

background music n

band shell n

bebop n (Am)

big band n

calypso n *music style*

chamber orchestra n

clave n *musical instrument*

countermelody n

Dixieland n *type of music*

gig n *musician's job* (verb
use: b1940)

gutbucket n *type of jazz*

Hawaiian guitar n

hit parade n

jam n *musical improv* (verb
use: b1970; jam session:
b1935)

jazzman n

long-playing record n

lyricist n *type of songwriter*
["master of lyric poetry":
b1885]

mariachi n

mellophone n *type of musical
instrument*

musical saw n

off-key adj/adv

offbeat n/adj

paradiddle n *drumroll*

piano roll n

recording n

rhythm section n

riff n (verb use: b1950)

scat n *type of jazz* (verb use:
b1935)

shell n *as in "bandshell"*

sound n *musical style* [obs.
"music": u1500s]

soundtrack n

string bass n

synthesizer n

theme song n (Am)

torch song, torch singer n
(Am)

track n *song*

tunesmith n

vibraphone n

wax n *phonograph record; music*

Entertainment

Charleston n *the dance* b1925

cover charge n (Am) b1925

dude ranch n b1925

fan mail n b1925 (fan letter: b1935)

punch line n (Am) b1925

rumba n b1925

superstar n (Am) b1925

tie-in n b1925

bash n *party, to-do*

box social n (Am)

cocktail party n

do-si-do n

fan club n

floor show n

mixer n *social event*

muscleman n (Am)

tap dance n

taxi dancer n *dancer on the meter*

Movies/TV/Radio

art theater n b1925

broadcast, broadcasting n/v, n *related to radio and TV* b1925 ["sow seeds widely": b1800]

Hollywood n *"the American movie industry"* b1925 (adj use: b1930)

montage n b1925 (verb use: b1945)

moviegoer n b1925

pan n *pan(orama)* b1925

preview n b1925 [gen. use: b1900]

projectionist n b1925

screen test n b1925

screenland n *filmdom* b1925

screenwriter n b1925

slow motion adj/n b1925

world premiere n b1925

air n *airwaves*

airwaves n

art film n

cineast n *film enthusiast*

double feature n (Am)

drive-in n (Am)

dub v/n *copy in film, radio*

feature n *as in "newspaper feature"* (featurette: b1940; feature-length: b1940)

filmic adj

filmstrip n

flick n *movie* (obs. flickers: b1930 to 1960s)

grind house n

horse opera n

indie n

location n

narrowcasting n (narrowcast v: b1955)

request n

rushes n

serial n

shooting script n

silent n *type of movie*

station n *as in "radio station"*

stuntman n (Am) (stuntwoman: b1945)

televise v

television n ["seeing at a distance": b1910] (televise: b1925)

trailer n

treatment n

turkey n *bad movie*

weepie n *tearjerker*

western n

Education

flash card n b1925

nonreader n b1925

preschool n b1925 (adj use: b1915; preschooler: b1950)

remedial adj b1925 [gen. sense: b1655]

semester hour n b1925

special education n b1925

true-false test n b1925

achievement test n

credit n *as in "credit hours"*

credit hour n

dean's list n

dropout n (Am)

exchange student n

hell week n (Am) *hazing*

higher learning n

honor society n (honor roll: b1910)

interdisciplinary adj

minor v (noun use: b1900)

multiple-choice adj

placement test n

term paper n

test n *exam* (verb use: b1970)

tutee n

Religion

Bible Belt n (Am) b1925

fundamentalism n (Am) b1925

last rites n b1925

federated church n

Society/Mores/Culture

kitsch n b1925

middlebrow n b1925

multiracial adj b1925

nonwhite adj/n b1925

social climber n b1925

sophisticate n b1925

genteelism n

lifestyle n (lifeway: b1950)

miz n *miss, mrs.*

preservationist n

pressure group n

pro-family adj

propaganda n *indoctrination* [type of organization: b1720]

Protestant ethic n

socialite n

value n *as in "moral values"*

Government

dual citizenship n b1925

duce n *as in "il duce"* b1925

etatism n *type of socialism* b1925

politburo n b1925

councilwoman n (councilman: b1640; councilperson: b1980)

intergovernmental adj

totalitarian, totalitarianism adj, n

zone v *set municipal growth areas*

Politics

hammer and sickle n b1925

interventionism n b1925 (interventionist: b1870)

isolationism n (Am) b1925

voice vote n b1925

agitprop n *agitation propaganda*

gunboat diplomacy n

multinational adj

Life

antilife adj

Death

box n *coffin* b1925

death benefit n b1925

pesticide n b1925

cool v (Am) *slang murder*

croak v *slang kill* ["die": b1815]

fry v *as in "he'll fry for the murder"*

funeral home n (Am)

gas v

grim reaper n

marble orchard n (Am) *cemetery* (marble town: b1945)

off v *die* ["kill": b1970]

rubout n (Am) *slang murder* (verb use: b1850)

War/Military/Violence

decommission v b1925

destroyer escort n b1925

flight surgeon n b1925

honor guard n b1925

longbowman n b1925

saber rattling n b1925

storm trooper n b1925

tommy gun n b1925 (verb use: b1945)

.30-30 n *type of gun*

airfield n

battlewagon n

BB gun n

chopper n (Am) *automatic gun*

coldcock v

cream v *demolish*

fighter n *type of plane*

fletching n *arrow feathers*

foilist, foilsman n

front n

gunslinger n

half-track n

heater n *gun*

militant n *militarily inclined person* ["combatant": b1610]

paratrooper n (paratroops: b1940)

pocket battleship n

punch-out n

Sunday punch n (Am)

torpedo bomber n

whomp n (verb use: b1945)

Crime/Punishment/Enforcement

aggravated assault n b1925

frog-march v b1925

G-man n b1925

ganef n *swindler* b1925

hijack, highjacker n/v, n (Am) b1925

latent n *as in "latent finger-print"* b1925

police car n b1925

radio car n b1925

scofflaw n b1925

stoolie n b1925 (stool pigeon: b1840; stool: b1910)

triggerman n b1925

bounty hunter n

cease and desist order n

clean adj *slang not guilty* ["drug-free": b1955]

clip v *bilk* (clip joint: b1935)

crookery n

detention home n

false arrest n

front, front man n

fuzz n (Am) *police*

grand theft n

heist n *robbery* (verb use: b1865)

hood n

hustle v *work as a prostitute*

jailbait n (Am)

life n *life imprisonment*

mob n

narcotic n

paddy wagon n

racketeer n/v

record n *as in "criminal record"*

rustle v

score n *crime* (verb use: b1900)

shield n *badge*

sociopath n

sting n *con*

torpedo n *gunman, henchman*

The Law

community property n b1925

small-claims court n b1925

criminalistics n

lip n *slang mouthpiece, lawyer*

notarize v

The Fantastic/ Paranormal

Abominable Snowman n b1925

cryptesthesia n *ESP, etc.* b1925

occult n b1925 (occultism: b1885)

parapsychology n b1925

antigravity adj/n

ectoplasm n

ghoulie n

gremlin n

sasquatch n

voices n

Magic

mojo n (Am) *power*

Interjections

bingo interj b1925

ho hum interj b1925 (adj use: b1970)

hooey interj/n (Am) b1925

hot diggety dog interj b1925

jeez interj (Am) b1925

shush interj/n/v b1925

uh-uh interj (Am) b1925

wahoo interj b1925

wham/whammo adv/interj b1925

yoohoo interj b1925

alley-oop interj

bam interj/n

boy interj

check interj

cheers interj

fuck n

fuck off v

gangway interj

good afternoon interj (good day: b1150; good morning, good-even, good-morrow: b1470; good evening: b1870)

horsefeathers interj/n (Am)

jeepers n (Am)

kayo interj *OK*

la-de-da interj (noun use: b1885; adj use: b1900)

napoo interj *it's over*

oops interj

phooey interj (Am) (phoo: b1700; pfui: b1870)

sis-boom-bah interj

twenty-three skidoo interj (Am)

whoopsie interj

yah boo interj

yeow interj

yessir interj (yes siree: b1850)

zap interj

zing interj

Slang

beaver n b1925

blah adj *bland* b1925

blah-blah-blah adv/n (Am) *etc.; nonsense* b1925

booby hatch n *asylum* b1925 ["jail": b1840]

bugger off v (Brit) *leave* b1925

cat's whiskers, cat's pajamas (Am) b1925 (cat's meow: b1930)

cop v *as in "cop a plea"* b1925 (copout n: b1945)

crash v *intrude* b1925

cuppa n b1925

ditch v *abandon* b1925 ["drive into a ditch": b1830; "defeat": b1900]

dreck/drek n b1925

face-saver n b1925

featherbedding n b1925 (featherbed adj: b1940; featherbed v: b1950)

frigging adj/adv b1925

gassed adj (Brit) *drunk* b1925

go-getter n (Am) b1925

gotta v b1925

hizzoner n b1925

hopped-up adj b1925 (hophead: b1915)

hotshot n b1925

hype n *hypo, or hypo user* (addict) b1925

junkie, junk n (Am) b1925

legman n (Am) b1925

loopy adj b1925

mad money n b1925

meatwagon n *ambulance* b1925 ["hearse": b1945]

milk run n *"routine trip"* b1925

nice-nelly adj/n b1925

ofay n (Am) b1925

palooka n (Am) b1925

patootie n *girl* b1925

rep n *repertory* b1925

revealing adj b1925

right on adj b1925 (interj use: b1970)

shamus n *detective* b1925

shitty adj b1925

squirrel v *as in "squirrel away"* b1925

tearjerker n b1925

truck v *as in "keep on trucking"* b1925

whoopee n b1925

yenta n *meddler* b1925

bad adj

bendy adj *flexible*

bent adj *strange, perverted*

boondoggle n

breeze n *piece of cake*

buy v *accept*

chick n (Am) *girl*

cokehead n

common ground n

cookie n (Am) *as in "tough cookie"*

crocked adj (Am) *drunk*

cut n *share*

dis adj *not operable*

dish n

do n *as in "dos and don'ts"*

do-gooder n (Am)

dogs n *feet*

eye n *as in "private eye"*

finger n *informant, snitch; pickpocket* (verb use: b1970)

fix n *as in "the fix is in"* (verb use: b1790)

flap n *fuss*

flapper n [gen. young woman: b1890]

frame n (verb use: b1910; frame-up: b1900)

fried adj *soused*

fuck n *as in "I don't give a fuck"*

gate-crasher n

go-around n

gruntle v

gussy v (gussy up: b1940)

hackie n

handsome n *as in "hello, handsome"*

haywire adj/adv *wild*

hotsy-totsy adj

hype v *deceive; stimulate*

icky adj

in n *as in "I have an in at the studio"*

jackrabbit adj/v

keen adj *as in "peachy-keen"* [obs. "mentally sharp": b900 to late ME]

kibitz, kibbitzer v, n (Am)

kid stuff n (Am)

lefty n

litterer n

load v *as in "load the dice"*

lowlight n *opp. of highlight*
lube n/v
macho adj (Am)
make v *recognize*
malarkey n (Am)
Mary Jane n
me-too adj
mind-set n
mud n *coffee; opium*
mushroom v *grow quickly*
nah adv *no*
obbo n *observation*
overdog n *opp. of underdog*
parameter n *boundary, definition* (geometric sense: b1660)
peachy adj (peachy-keen: b1960)
pip n *something excellent* (pippin: b1900)
pull for v *cheer*
rap n *incrimination, reputation* b1930
rap v *talk* (noun use: b1970)
rec v *recreation*
rib n/v (Am) *joke, tease*
ride v *harangue*
riot n *as in "a laugh riot"*
rosy adj *drunk*
roundheel n *pushover*
rubber check n (Am)
rumpot n *drunk* (rummy: b1855; rum-hound: b1915)
scram v
shambles n *chaos* ["meat market": b1470]
shoestring n *a little* (adj use: b1880)
sing v *rat out*
sked n *schedule*
smoke v *shoot*
snowball v *grow swiftly*
socko adj/interj
squirrelly adj
sticky wicket n
stinko adj
stool on v *be a stool pigeon*
stuff n *as in "knows his stuff"*
televisionary n
testee n
tomato n *chick*
trip n *as in "drug trip"* (verb use: b1970)
weasel v *as in "weasel out of an obligation"*
weed n *marijuana* ["tobacco": b1610]

weewee n/v
whoop-de-do n (Am)
witch-hunt n
witches' brew n
woman of the street n

Insults

bag n *hag* b1925
bim n *bimbo, girl* b1925 (bimbo: b1920)
birdbrain n b1925
booboisie n b1925
city slicker n (Am) b1925
cold fish n b1925
crow n b1925
dimwit n (Am) b1925 (dimwitted: b1935)
fag n (Am) *homosexual* b1925
fusspot n b1925
goon n b1925 ["hired thug": b1940]
greaseball n b1925
nitwit n b1925
penny pincher n b1925 (penny-pinching: b1935)
schlepp v b1925 (noun use: b1940)
toffee-nosed n (Brit) *narcissistic* b1925
tramp n *slut* b1925
apple-polisher n (apple-polish v: b1935)
crackers adj (Brit)
cunt n *jerk*
deviant n (deviate n: b1915)
dum-dum n *stupid person*
dumb cluck n
fay n
googly-eyed adj
grouch n/v *grouchy person* ["fit of grouchiness": b1895]
grump n *grumpy person* ["grumpy mood": b1845] (verb use: b1845; grumpy: b1780; grumpish: b1800)
ham-fisted adj (ham-handed: b1920)
hotdog n
jughead n
lamebrain n
loogan n (Am) *dolt*
moronic adj
nervous Nelly n
pansy adj/n
pantywaist n

prick n *jerk* [obs. "nice guy": b1570 to 1600s]
ridge-runner n (Am)
ringtail n *bum*
show-off n *showy person* ["display": b1780]
turkey n *jerk*
vegetable n
wetback n (Am)
wetsmack n *party pooper*

Phrases

all wet adj b1925
bear hug n b1925
bee's knees adj b1925
bite the bullet v b1925
bum steer n (Am) b1925
drugstore cowboy n (Am) *urban cowboy* b1925
force of habit n b1925
forgotten man n b1925
from scratch n b1925
hand-wringing n b1925
hot pursuit n b1925
Irish confetti n b1925
learning curve n b1925
life of Riley n b1925
pep talk n b1925
stare down v b1925
stop-and-go adj b1925
triple threat n (Am) b1925
washed-up adj b1925
bad news n
bail out v *duck out*
bed check n
Bronx cheer n (Am)
bull dyke n
bum rap n (Am)
cut out adj *as in "cut out for success"*
double take n (Am)
down-to-earth adj
dummy up v
escape mechanism n
fat cat n (Am)
feel up v
gravy train n
horse around v (horse v: b1905)
horse-and-buggy adj (Am)
hot money n
hot spot n (Am)
long haul n
master plan n
master race n
Mickey Finn n (verb use: b1935)
mixed bag n

never-never adj
no-nonsense adj
pecking order n
period piece n
piece of work n
run-of-the-mill adj (run-of-the-mine: b1905)
running dog n
running start n
see a man about a dog v
shelf life n
shoot the bull v (Am) (shoot the breeze: b1945)
short list n
shouting distance n
snake oil n (Am)
straight and narrow n
straight shooter n
stripped-down adj
sugar daddy n (Am)
toe-to-toe adj/adv
trade up v
under-the-counter adj
up-and-coming adj (Am) *on the rise* ["active": b1850]
warts-and-all adj

General/Miscellaneous

ace n/adj *skilled person* b1925
contaminant n b1925
counselee n b1925
countermeasure n b1925
delectable n b1925
designee n b1925
drop-off n b1925
either-or n b1925 (adj use: b1930)
eye-catching, eye-catcher adj, n b1925
fanfold n b1925
flair n *aptitude* b1925 ["odor": b1390; "instinct, ability to discern": b1885]
gestalt n b1925
masking n b1925
nifty n *something clever* b1925
payload n b1925
titlist n b1925
trailbreaker n b1925
transvestite n b1925 (transvestism: b1930; transvestitism: b1970)
absurd, absurdism n *as in "the absurd"*
basic n *as in "the basics"* (adj use: b1845)
beep n (verb use: b1940)

Gone, But Not Forsaken

English boasts one of the largest vocabularies of all the languages, yet we might consider it to be pretty well streamlined compared to what it might be had so many words not dropped out of the language. Some of them we don't miss, like *trihemitone*, a technical music term from the seventeenth and eighteenth centuries, or *promove*, a verb from the fifteenth and sixteenth centuries that doesn't add any resonance or flexibility to the language than do its synonyms—*promote* and *provoke*.

But I regret having lost *moliminous*, with various meanings of "arduous" and "weighty," literally and figuratively, for a time in the seventeenth and eighteenth centuries. Or *belswagger*, a term for a bully in the sixteenth through eighteenth centuries. Or *stinkibus*, obsolete slang for rotgut from the eighteenth and nineteenth centuries. Or *wraw* out of Middle English—meaning "angry." The wraw belswagger promoved moliminous stinkibus.

What a different cast such now-obsolete words might have put on our everyday speech. For instance, had some Old English words survived, we might be accustomed to seeing such phrases as:

- Grith on earth (*peace* our word for *grith*)
- Ae and order (*law* for *ae*)
- Feorh and limb (*life* for *feorh*)
- Daegred to dusk (*dawn* for *daegred*—literally "day-red")
- Time ece (*eternal* for *ece*)
- Eam Sam (*uncle* for *eam*)

And some of our artistic works might carry such titles as . . .

- *The Power and the Wuldor* (*glory* for *wuldor*)
- *Sigor at Sea* (*victory* for *sigor*)
- *Dryhten of the Rings* (*lord* for *dryhten*)
- *Crime and Wite* (*punishment* for *wite*)
- *Hild of the Bulge* (*battle* for *hild*)

---

black light n

buildup n (Am)

cell n *group, as in "Communist cell"*

checkpoint n

cover n *ground cover*

cover-up n

crossover n

detainee n

dividuality n *sameness, opp. of individuality*

downslide n

downtrend n

downturn n

edge n *advantage*

esoterica n

exclusivity n

gimmick n/v (Am) (gimmickry: b1950)

glop n

grievance committee n

high n *record level*

implementation n (implement v: b1730)

infrastructure n

jump n *as in "parachute jump"*

junior miss n

kudo n

legroom n

low n *low point*

machinofacture n *manufacture*

malfunction n/v

marker n *e.g., headstone*

memorial park n

missionist n

petite n

pilot n *test, as in "TV pilot"* (adj use: b1805)

playback n (play back: b1950)

plug n/v *publicity, as in "a plug for a movie"*

pocket n *as in "pockets of resistance"* (verb use: b1590; adj use: b1600)

pool n *as in "motor pool," "car pool"* (verb use: b1900)

put-on n *deception* (adj use: b1625)

referral n [as in "referral to a specialist": b1935]

reparations n

repercussions n ["repulsion": b1540; "echo": b1600; "reaction": b1630]

schematic n (schema: b1890)

shoo-in n

showdown n *confrontation* ["showing cards in poker": b1850]

slant n *as in "give the story a new slant"* (verb use: b1970)

splash guard n

spot n *situation, as in "a tight spot"*

stablemate n

standout n *something that stands out* ["strike": b1895]

stuff n *miscellanea*

sync n/v

turnaround n

turndown n *rejection*

upside n *the good news* [phys. "upper side": b1615]

Things

doojigger n

polystyrene n

whatchamacallit n

widget n

Description

bouncy adj b1925

cornerways adv b1925

couple adj b1925

crank adj *as in a "crank phone call"* b1925

crashing adj *as in a "crashing success"* b1925

equiprobable adj b1925

exploitive adj b1925 (exploitative: b1885)

extracurricular adj b1925

fairy-tale adj b1925

free-floating adj b1925

handheld adj b1925

hooked adj *addicted* b1925

last-gasp adj b1925

macro adj *large-scale* b1925

mentholated adj b1925

micro adj b1925

picture-book adj b1925

plug-in adj b1925

snap-on adj b1925

water-resistant adj b1925

all-purpose adj

buck adv *as in "buck naked"*

close-knit adj

close-up adj/adv

fixated adj

garden-variety adj

hectic adj [med. sense: b1300]

hellacious adj (Am)
hopefully adv *it is hoped that* [gen. use: b1640]
how-to adj (noun use: b1955)
in-line adj/adv
in-service adj
low-end adj
multi-ply adj
olde adj
omnidirectional adj
one-track adj
outdoorsy adj
paper-thin adj
per capita adj/adv ["individually": b1585]
phallocentric adj
pristine adj *untouched, new* ["original, old": b1535]
shatterproof adj
sunfast adj
terrific adj *good* ["terrifying": b1670]
time-tested adj
true-life adj
walk-in adj (noun use: b1945)
zesty adj

Colors

lime adj *lime-green*
off-white adj/n

teal n *the color* (teal blue: b1940)

Actions/Verbs

antique v b1925
charge off v b1925
compartmentalize v b1925
cue v *give starting signal* b1925
debunk v (Am) b1925
destabilize v b1925
empathize v b1925
finagle v (Am) b1925
fine-tune v b1925
fractionalize v b1925
gang up v b1925
hoke, hokey v, adj *fake* b1925
hook up v b1925
jam-pack v b1925
monitor v b1925 (noun use: b1550)
package v b1925
publicize v b1925
snooker v *dupe* b1925
upstage v b1925
backfire v *blow up in your face*
backslap v (backslapping: b1780)
barrel v
bypass v *go around*
careen v *dash madly* ["tilt": b1600]

celebrate v ["perform a ceremony": b1465; "observe," as in "celebrate an occasion": b1530; "praise": b1570]
chain-smoke v
check v *concur, as in "the story checks out"*
chitter-chatter v (noun use: b1715; chitchat v: b1825)
cite v *single out, praise*
contact v *get in touch with*
copycat v
dead-end v
defreeze v
downgrade v
fishtail v (Am)
high-pressure v (adj use: b1825)
highlight v (noun use: b1855)
hostess v (host v: b1470)
hydrate v *opp. of dehydrate*
liaise v
lift v *copy*
lookit v
option v
outpull v
page v *summon via page* ["serve": b1500]
photocopy v
preview v *see in advance*

["foresee": b1610] (noun use: b1900)
prime v *as in "prime an engine"*
recap v *summarize* (noun use: b1945)
recycle n/v (recycling: b1960)
retool v
rubble v (noun use: b1400)
run v *as in "run water"*
scan v *use a scanning tool*
score v *rebuke*
service v *fix*
shoehorn v (noun use: b1590)
slap v *apply thickly*
slip v *lapse* (noun use: b1600)
slot v *designate*
sweet-talk v
switch v *change, as in "switch positions"*
tell v *tattle*
type v *classify*
vet v *review expertly*
weight v *prorate*
why v
winterize v

IN USE BY
1940

Geography/Places
rangeland n b1935
beachhead n
flash flood n
rip current n (rip: b1775)

Natural Things
deuterium n 1933
antielectron n *positron* b1935
antineutrino n b1935
beta wave n b1935
deuterium oxide n *heavy water* b1935
ecosystem n b1935
microwave n *the wave* b1935
mutagen n b1935
positron n b1935
alpha wave n
carbon 14 n
delta wave n
electromagnetic radiation n
fluorocarbon n
ionic bond n
microevolution n
sound barrier n (sonic barrier: b1945)

Plants
boysenberry n b1935
giant sequoia n b1935
acorn squash n
aloe vera n

Animals
English toy spaniel n b1935
German shorthaired pointer n b1935
giant schnauzer n b1935
great white shark n b1935
howler monkey n b1935

Lhasa apso n *type of dog* b1935
Maine coon n b1935
medfly n b1935 (Mediterranean fruit fly: b1910)
Siamese fighting fish n b1935
strawberry roan n b1935
tetra n *type of fish* b1935
toy poodle n b1935
tropical fish n b1935
woolly mammoth n b1935
giant anteater n
manta ray n (manta: b1770)
mountain gorilla n
neon tetra n *type of fish*
Tennessee walking horse n (Am)

Weather
subzero adj b1935
thermal n *type of air current* b1935
stationary front n
windchill n (windchill factor: b1950)

Heavens/Sky
expanding universe n b1935
neutron star n b1935
ozonosphere n b1935
solar flare n

Science
biomass n b1935
cryogenics n b1935
elementary particle n b1935
Foucault pendulum n b1935
heavy hydrogen, heavy water n b1935
neutrino n b1935
nuclear physics n b1935

psychohistory n b1935
sedimentology n *study of sedimentation* b1935
atom smasher n
earth science n
greenhouse effect n
molecular biology n
oceanarium n
unified field theory n

Technology
cyclotron n *particle accelerator* b1935
light water n b1935
transceiver n b1935
coaxial cable n
fission n *of atoms* [of cells: b1845]

Energy
electrostatic generator n b1935
high-energy adj b1935
hydropower n b1935
luminous energy n b1935
discharge lamp n

Time
atomic clock n
Greenwich mean time n
round-the-clock adj
sweep-second hand n (sweep hand: b1945)

Age/Aging
life expectancy n b1935
senior citizen n

Mathematics
3-D n (Am) b1935
division sign n b1935

econometrics n b1935
scientific notation n b1935
googol n

Measurement
drunkometer n (Am) b1935
mass spectrometer n b1935
meterstick n b1935
Gallup poll n
Mach number n
tenderometer n

The Body
bod n b1935
burp n/v (Am) b1935
DNA n b1935
goose bumps n b1935 (goose-flesh: b1810; goose pimples: b1890)
john n *slang penis* b1935 (Johnson: b1870; John Thomas: b1880)
keister n *bottom* b1935 [type of carrying case: b1885; "safe": b1915]
outer ear n b1935
putz n *penis* b1935 [type of Pennsylvania Dutch Christmas decoration: b1905; "jerk": b1965]
sex gland n b1935
testosterone n b1935
toe jam n b1935
baby tooth n
choppers n (Am) *slang teeth*
five-o'clock shadow n
interneuron n
respiratory system n
sacroiliac n (adj use: b1835)

Physical Description
curvaceous adj (Am) b1935
doe-eyed adj b1935
balding adj

Medicine
antihistamine n/adj b1935
arthroscope, arthroscopy n
  b1935
ascorbic acid n *vitamin C*
  b1935
blood type n b1935
defibrillate v b1935
**electroencephalogram, elec-
  troencephalograph** n b1935
guide dog n b1935
iron lung n (Am) b1935
natural childbirth n b1935
patch test n b1935
physical n b1935
polio n (Am) b1935 (poliomyelitis: b1880)
serum hepatitis n b1935
Typhoid Mary n b1935
water on the knee n b1935
whitehead n b1935
amphetamine n
colonic n
cystic fibrosis n
eyedropper n
family planning n
Guillain-Barre Syndrome n
gurney n [type of carriage:
  b1900]
head cold n
heat cramps n
heat exhaustion n
heat prostration n
hypoallergenic adj
lazy eye n
lethal gene n
leukotomy n *lobotomy*
lobotomy n (lobotomize:
  b1945)
magic bullet n
mammography, mammogram
  n
niacin n
Papanicolaou smear n *pap
  smear* (pap smear: b1955)
pep pill n (Am)
rhythm method n
sulfa drug n
wonder drug n

Everyday Life
candleholder n b1935
courtesy card n (Am) b1935

crapper n *slang toilet* b1935
donnicker n *toilet* b1935
dresser set n *vanity items*
  b1935
dry mop n b1935
filter tip n *of cigarettes* b1935
john n *toilet* b1935
playpen n b1935
potbellied stove n b1935
safety island n b1935
setup n *place setting* b1935
studio couch n b1935
wish book n *catalog* b1935
gents n (Brit) *men's room*
juicer n
laminate n *surfacing material*
loo n (Brit) *toilet*
magnetic tape n
pinking shears n
rollaway adj

Shelter/Housing
breezeway n (Am) b1935
ductwork n b1935
fire truck n b1935 (fire engine: b1680)
rent control n b1935
carport n (Am)
changing room n (Brit)
crash pad n
fiberglass n (verb use:
  b1970)
house trailer n
housing project n
living unit n
motor court n (Am) (motor
  lodge: b1950; motor inn:
  b1955)
picture window n
pressure-treated adj
row house n
rumpus room n (Am)
shotgun house n
widow's walk n (Am)

Drink
gin and tonic n b1935
high-proof adj b1935
white lady n *type of drink*
  b1935
blended whiskey n
pink lady n (Am) *type of
  cocktail*

Food
al dente adj b1935
beef stroganoff n b1935
burrito n (Am) b1935

Canadian bacon n b1935
chess pie n *type of dessert*
  b1935
etouffee n b1935
genoise n *type of cake* b1935
Idaho n *type of potato* b1935
manhattan clam chowder n
  (Am) b1935
polyunsaturated adj b1935
  [polyunsaturate adj/n:
  b1950]
potato pancake n b1935
riboflavin n b1935
shoestring potatoes n b1935
taco n b1935
bubble gum n
burger n
cheeseburger n (Am)
chili powder n (Am)
cioppino n *type of stew*
cook-off n
coq au vin n
dowdy n *pandowdy*
feta n
heart of palm n (Am)
jalapeno n *type of pepper*
kielbasa n
monounsaturated adj *akin to
  polyunsaturated*
oyster cocktail n
oysters Rockefeller n
pastrami n
pesto n
sloppy joe n
tostada n
western omelet n

Agriculture/
Food-Gathering
feedstock n b1935
green fingers n *green thumb*
  b1935 (green thumb:
  b1945)
greenbelt n b1935
cowpat n
crop duster n
dust bowl n (Am)
hydroponics n
subsistence farming n

Cloth/Clothing
skivvy n (Am) b1935 (skiv-
  vies: b1945)
sleepwear n b1935
slide fastener n *zipper* b1935
swimwear n b1935
zip, unzip v b1935

aloha shirt n
babushka n
bra n
bush jacket n
crew neck n (Am)
floor-length adj
houndstooth check n
lederhosen n
Mae West n *life jacket*
nylon n
pressure suit n
rainwear n
saddle shoe n
snowsuit n
tank suit n *type of swimsuit*
tart up v *slang dress up*
wedgie n *type of shoe*

Fashion/Style
bobby pin n (Am) b1935
costume jewelry n (Am)
  b1935
finger wave n *hairstyling term*
  b1935
mudpack n b1935
platinum blonde n b1935
snazzy adj (Am) b1935
snob appeal n b1935
updo n *type of hair style*
  b1935
accessorize v
fancy-dan adj (noun use:
  b1945)
feathercut n *type of hairstyle*
gussy up n
high style n
hipster n (Am) (hippie:
  b1955)
lip gloss n
rug n *slang toupee*

Tools
arc welding n b1935
decompression chamber n
  b1935
electron lens n b1935
electron microscope n b1935
injection molding n b1935
tape recorder n b1935 ["tickertape recorder": b1895]
masking tape n
monocular n *similar to binocular*
plumber's snake n
power mower n
sodium-vapor lamp n

Travel/Transportation

air-traffic control n b1935
auto court n b1935
autocade n b1935
autopilot n b1935 (automatic pilot: b1920)
blacktop n (Am) b1935
cloverleaf n *freeway intersection* b1935
double-park v (Am) b1935
drophead n *convertible* b1935
escape velocity n b1935
ground control n b1935
octane number n b1935
parking meter n b1935
power steering n b1935
puddle jumper n (Am) b1935
railbus n b1935
rent-a-car n b1935
rocket engine n b1935
rotary-wing aircraft n b1935 (rotorcraft: b1940)
scout car n (Am) b1935
seat belt n b1935
seatrain n b1935
soup up v b1935
spaceflight n b1935
spaceport n b1935
starship n b1935
stop sign n b1935
tag n (Am) *license plate* b1935
tourist class n b1935
traffic island n b1935
tune-up n b1935
turbocharger, turbosupercharger n b1935
bumper-to-bumper adj
bush pilot n
celestial navigation n
egg beater n (Am) *helicopter*
feeder road n
flight plan n
flight recorder n
glide path n
glove compartment n (glove box: b1950)
green light n (red light: b1850; yellow light: b1975)
high beam n
instrument landing n
jeep n
landing craft n
leaded gasoline n
panel truck n (Am)
roadblock n

rotorcraft n (rotary-winged aircraft: b1935)
space station n (space platform: b1960)
spaceman n (spacewoman: b1965)
tourist court n *motel*
tourist trap n

Emotions/ Characteristics

cojones n *guts, balls* b1935
conditioned response n b1935
jittery adj (Am) b1935
palsy-walsy adj b1935
scaredy-cat n b1935
send v *as in "you send me"* b1935
snide adj *snippy* b1935 [slang "fake": b1860; "cunning": b1870; "bad": b1905]
stone-faced adj b1935
tizzy n (Am) b1935
uptight adj (Am) b1935
worrywart n b1935
dewy-eyed adj
ludic adj *playfully aimless*
play therapy n
pushy adj (Am)
self-actualization n
slaphappy adj
snit n (Am)
ticked adj *angry, peeved* (tick off v: b1870)

Thoughts/Perception/ The Mind

attention span n b1935
escapism n b1935 (escape n: b1870)
double-dome n *intellectual*
mastermind v
paranoid schizophrenia n
psycho n
psychological warfare n
psychosomatics n
punchy adj *loopy* ["fat": b1800; "vigorous": b1915]

Love/Romance/Sex

call girl n (Am) b1935 (call house: b1930)
chastity belt n b1935
dyke n (Am) b1935
hetero adj/n b1935
lay n/v *as in "get laid"* b1935
lonely hearts adj/n b1935

make time v b1935
undersexed adj b1935
ambisexual adj *bisexual* (ambisextrous: b1930)
boff v *have sex*
hanky-panky n *sex play* [gen. sense: b1845]
make out v *neck, have sex*
pair-bond n *monogamy*
screw around v
stork v (Am) *impregnate*
wolf whistle n

Family/Relations/ Friends

extended family n b1935
gram n b1935
quint n *quintuplet* b1935

Games/Fun/Leisure

bingo n b1935
board game n b1935
eight ball n (Am) b1935
one-armed bandit n (Am) b1935
paddleball n b1935
pinball machine, pintable n (Brit) 1936
beachball n
Chinese checkers n
gift wrap n/v
HO scale n
scavenger hunt n (Am)

Sports

backflip n/v b1935
backhand v b1935 (noun use: b1560)
broomball n b1935
claiming race n b1935
enduro n *type of race* b1935
flutter kick n b1935
freestyle n b1935
headstand n b1935
kegler n *bowler* b1935 (kegling: b1935)
long horse n *gymnastic vaulting horse* b1935
pit stop n b1935
rappel v *descend a cliff* b1935
stickball n (Am) b1935
tennist n b1935
tiebreaker n b1935
touch football n b1935
water ski n b1935
blooper n
chairlift n (Am)

jayvee adj/n
linksman n *golf player*
netminder n
paddleboard n
schuss v *ski fast*
scratch sheet n (Am) *in horseracing*
ski lift n
skin diving n (skin-dive: b1955)
starting block n
synchronized swimming n

Professions/Duties

carny n b1935
gemologist n b1935 (gemology: b1815)
hairstylist n b1935
tillerman n b1935
B-girl n
carhop n
ecdysiast n *stripper*
flack n (Am) *PR person* (verb use: b1965)
interior designer n (interior decorator: b1870; interior design: b1930)
lensman n *cameraman*
private eye n
private investigator n

Business/Commerce/ Selling

commercial n b1935 (commercial traveler "traveling salesman": b1870)
curb service n (Am) b1935
hard goods n b1935
milk bar n b1935
pricey adj b1935
seller's market n b1935
aftermarket n
cafeteria n *eating establishment* ["coffee house": b1840]
cocktail lounge n
Jaycee n
lend-lease n/v
sell-off n
storefront adj
washateria n

The Workplace

careerism n b1935
goof off n b1935
lobster shift n *akin to night shift* b1935

production line n b1935
quality control n b1935
sit-down, sit-down strike n
type of work stoppage b1935
temp n *temporary* b1935
(verb use: b1975)
workstation n b1935
freelancer n (freelance v:
b1905)
semiretired adj
swing shift n
womanpower n

Finances/Money

account executive n b1935
break-even adj (Am) *as in
"break-even point"* b1935
(breakeven n: b1960)
inflationary spiral n b1935
mutual fund n b1935
account payable/receivable n
bread n (Am) *slang money*
death tax n
deficit spending n
dirt-poor adj (Am)
hidden tax n
money adj
single n *dollar*
withholding tax n

Language and Speaking

decrypt v *decode* b1935
dialect atlas n b1935
general semantics n b1935
pig latin n b1935
tag question n *e.g., "isn't it?"*
b1935
double-talk n
metalanguage n (metalin-
guistics: b1950)
pidginize v
pragmatics n

Literature/Writing

dust wrapper n b1935 (dust
jacket: b1930)
field guide n b1935
off-the-record adj b1935
talking book n b1935
column inch n
library card n
pen pal n
photojournalism n

Communication

telex n 1932 (verb use:
b1960)
audiovisual, audiovisual aid
adj (audiovisuals: b1955)

disinformation n
intercom n (intercommuni-
cation system: b1915)
logo n
PA system n
pay phone n
press conference n
press corps n
walkie-talkie n (Am)

Visual Arts/Photography

art director n b1935
art moderne n b1935
flashbulb n b1935 (flash-
tube: b1945; flashcube:
b1965)
nabe n b1935
photoflood n b1935
photomontage n b1935
aesthetic distance n
cel n
doodle n/v
finger painting n (finger
paint: b1950)
hyperrealism n
minicam n
mobile sculpture n (mobile:
b1950)
serigraph n *silkscreen*
single-lens reflex n
time-lapse photography n
visual n *picture*
zoom lens n

Performing Arts

audition v b1935 (noun use:
b1885)
emcee n b1935 (verb use:
b1940)
ham v b1935
revusical n *rev(ue)(m)usical*
b1935
stage left, stage right n b1935
psychodrama n
talent scout n

Music

bazooka n b1935 [type of
weapon: b1945] (bazoo:
b1880)
conga n/v b1935 (conga
line: b1950)
discography n b1935 (dis-
cographer: b1945)
high fidelity n b1935 (hi-fi:
b1950)

jam session n (Am) b1935
(jam n: b1930)
jug band n (Am) b1935
licorice stick n *clarinet* b1935
monaural adj b1935 ["using
one ear": b1890]
platter n *music record* b1935
record changer n b1935
record player n b1935
seventy-eight n *78 RPM*
b1935
swing adj b1935
tweeter n b1935
woofer n b1935
wow n *as in "wow and flutter"* b1935
discophile n
drum majorette n (Am)
groovy adj (Am) *plays jazz
well*
jukebox, juke n
leadman n
reedman n *musician playing a
reed instrument*
sideman n (Am)
skins n *drums*
tonette n
vibes n

Entertainment

fan letter n b1935 (fan mail:
b1925)
gagster n b1935
jitterbug n/v (Am) *type of
dance* b1935
lindy n *type of dance* b1935
nitery n *nightclub* b1935
premiere v b1935 (noun use:
b1900)
shag n *type of dance* b1935
borscht belt/borscht circuit n
merengue n *type of dance*
nightspot n
segue n (verb use: b1855)
striptease n/v (stripteaser:
1930; stripper: b1970)

Movies/TV/Radio

documentary n b1935
dolly shot n *film term* b1935
offscreen adv/adj b1935
rerun n b1935
soundstage n b1935
teleview v *watch TV* b1935
video n/adj b1935
AM, FM n
B picture n

cliff-hanger n (Am) (cliff-
hang v: b1950)
intercut v
key light n
programming n
remake n [occasional use:
b1870]
rough cut n
scripter n (scriptwriter:
b1915)
sneak preview n
soap opera n (Am)
special effects n
station break n
telecast n/v
telefilm n
telegenic adj
telly n (Brit)

Education

chalkboard n
Ivy League n (Ivy Leaguer:
b1945)
postdoctoral adj (postdoc
adj/n: b1970)
schoolkid n (schoolfellow:
b1500; schoolmate:
b1565; schoolboy: b1590;
schoolgirl: b1780; schoolchild: b1840)

Religion

interfaith adj b1935
secular humanism n b1935
Bible-thumper n [Bible-
pounder: b1890; Bible-
banger: b1945]
ecumenics n
Star of David n
storefront church n

Society/Mores/Culture

hepcat, hepster n b1935
(hep: b1910)
Hooverville n b1935
lace-curtain adj *slang middle-
class* b1935
playgirl n b1935 (playboy:
b1630)
bicultural adj
culture shock n
food stamp n
fund-raising n (fund-raiser:
b1960)
glitterati n
Joe Blow n (Am)
white-tie adj

Government
executive privilege n

Politics
absentee vote n b1935
archconservative n b1935
politick v b1935 (politicking: b1930)
write-in n b1935
blimpish adj *reactionary*
Colonel Blimp n *reactionary*
depoliticize v
neo-Nazi n
pollster n (Am)
red-baiting n
sit-in n

Death
mercy killing n b1935
snuff v *murder* b1935 ["die": b1885]
contract n *slang murder*
die-off n
dust off v *kill*

War/Military/Violence
gestapo n 1934
dive-bomb v b1935 (dive bomber: b1940)
dogface n (Am) b1935
double agent n b1935
führer n b1935
Garand rifle n *M-1* b1935
induct v b1935 (inductee: b1940)
martial art n b1935
paramilitary adj/n b1935
powder charge n b1935
rear echelon n b1935
service medal n b1935
shoulder weapon n b1935
throttlehold n b1935
0.38 n *type of gun* b1935
antipersonnel adj
arms race n
blitz, blitzkrieg n
civil defense n
commando n (adj use: b1795)
counterintelligence n
counterspy n
escalation n (Am)
fighter-bomber n
flak n
flying fortress n (Am)
germ warfare n
government issue adj
K ration n (Am)

limited war n
M1 rifle n
machine pistol n
Molotov cocktail n *type of bomb*
motor torpedo boat n
nerve gas n
panzer n
photoreconnaissance n
Russian roulette n
stalag n
thermonuclear adj

Crime/Punishment/Enforcement
approved school n (Brit) *reform school* b1935
black market n b1935
clip joint n b1935
connection n *drug supplier* b1935 (connect: b1930)
dope addict n b1935
gaff v *cheat, con* b1935
pusher n *dealer* b1935 ["prostitute": b1925]
squad car n (Am) b1935
take v *cheat* b1935
funny money n
gangbuster n
house arrest n
illegal n
payola n (Am)
prowl car n (Am)
T-man n (Am)

The Law
family court n b1935
federal district court n b1935
night court n b1935
caseload n
domestic relations court n
show trial n

The Fantastic/Paranormal
Shangri-la n 1933
extrasensory perception/ESP n b1935
silver bullet n b1935
teleportation n b1935 (teleport: b1945)
hobbit n
yeti n

Interjections
dibs interj b1935
drop dead interj b1935

hoo-ha interj/n b1935
nerts interj/n (Am) b1935
nuts interj b1935
okeydoke/okeydokey adv (Am) b1935
shoot interj *damn, shit* b1935
harrumph v
wilco interj

Slang
accident n (Am) *unplanned child* b1935
action n (Am) *as in "where the action is"* b1935
bag it v *quit* b1935
bang n *as in "get a bang out of it"* b1935
big cheese n b1935
big name n b1935
boob n/v *blunder* b1935 (Am boo-boo: b1955)
boss man n b1935 (boss: b1650)
button-down adj/n (Am) b1935
cathouse n b1935
cheesecake n (Am) b1935
coast v *rest on laurels* b1935 [as in "coast on a bicycle": b1775]
corny adj *campy* b1935
cutie-pie n b1935
dig v (Am) *as in "dig that music"* b1935
dilly n (Am) b1935
doghouse n b1935
doodley-squat n (Am) b1935
fancy up v b1935
fix n *hit of drug* b1935
foofaraw n *fuss, finery* b1935
footsie n b1935 (footy: b1970)
freeload v b1935
futz v (Am) b1935
gee-whiz adj b1935
goof v b1935 (noun use: b1915)
gook n *goo* b1935
half-assed adj b1935
high adj b1935 (noun use: b1955)
hip v *inform* b1935
hotfoot n b1935
juke joint n (Am) b1935
kiss off, kissoff v, n b1935
looped adj *drunk* b1935
louse up v b1935
mainline v/n (Am) b1935

man n *as in "hey, man"* b1935
mess around v b1935
nose candy n (Am) b1935
nut n *aficionado* b1935
rat v *inform, betray* b1935 (noun use: b1905)
reefer n *marijuana cigarette* b1935
rope n (Am) *cigar* b1935
rough trade n b1935
schmaltz, schmaltzy n, adj b1935
schmeck n *drugs* b1935 (smack: b1960)
score n/v *buy, procure* b1935
shack up, shackup v, n b1935
shellacking n b1935 [lit. sense: b1885] (shellac: b1930)
shit v *bullshit, deceive* b1935
slug-nutty adj (Am) *slaphappy* b1935
swacked adj (Am) *drunk* b1935
switcheroo n b1935 (switch: b1940)
talkathon n b1935
tops adj b1935
VIP n b1935
wacky adj b1935 (noun use: b1870)
whoopla n b1935
with-it adj b1935
zillion n b1935 (zillionaire: b1950)
baddie n (Am)
belly-up adj *as in "the business went belly-up"*
bollix v (noun use: b1935)
bombed adj *drunk*
crunch n *as in "it's crunch time"*
demo n *demonstration*
dynamite adj
fave n
girl Friday n
groundbreaker n (groundbreaking: b1910)
gutty adj (gutsy: b1895)
Mickey Mouse adj (Am)
oomph n
photo finish n
pickerupper n
pillow talk n
pizzazz n (Am)
pot n *marijuana* (pothead: b1960)

pro n *prostitute*
rifle v *fig. "shoot out"*
sauce n *alcohol*
sharp adj *cool, excellent*
shutterbug n
skinny n
stash n *mustache*
stooge n *yes-man, henchman* ["stagehand": b1910]
toss v *search roughly*
whammy, double whammy n
zaftig adj

Insults
asshole n b1935 [gen. use: b1400]
brownshirt n *Nazi* b1935
ding-a-ling n b1935 [type of sound: b1900]
dip n *nerd* b1935 (dippy: b1900)
drip v b1935
jerk n b1935
layabout n b1935
Milquetoast adj/n b1935
screwball n (Am) b1935 (adj use: b1940; screwy: b1890)
stumblebum n *clod* b1935
twit n (Brit) b1935 ["teasing": b1520]
bad-mouth v (Am)
bitchy adj
blabbermouth n (Am) (blab n: b1375)
brownnose n/v
commie n
dime-store adj
goofball n
pinko n
schnook n (Am)
sourpuss n
spaced-out adj (Am) (spacey: b1700)
wack n (Am) (wacky n: b1870; wacko: b1975)
zombie n *lethargic person* ["living dead": b1830]

Phrases
ace in the hole n (Am) *fig.* b1935 [lit. use: b1915]
American dream n b1935
aw-shucks adj (Am) b1935
banana republic n *backward country* b1935
blow-by-blow adj (Am) b1935

brave new world n b1935
collector's item n b1935
crap out v *fail* b1935
cup of tea n b1935
dirty old man n b1935
dog end n *cigarette butt* b1935
father figure n b1935 (father image: b1940)
Garrison finish n *late come-from-behind finish* b1935
hit the bricks v b1935 (hit the road: b1875)
killer instinct n b1935
moment of truth n b1935
negative feedback n b1935
never mind n *as in "pay no never mind"* b1935
red carpet n b1935
skid row n (Am) b1935
skip it v b1935
sticky fingers n b1935 (sticky-fingered: b1890)
tobacco road n b1935
trial balloon n b1935
tried-and-true adj b1935
united front n b1935
vintage year n b1935
belt-tightening n
blood-and-guts adj
breast-beating n
clamp down, clampdown v/n
dirty pool n
end product n
group dynamics n
hunt-and-peck n
intestinal fortitude n
Jane Doe n (John Doe: b1770)
kissing cousin n
last-in first-out adj
meeting of the minds n
near miss n
on the nose adj
panel discussion n
piece of cake n
postage-stamp adj
powder-puff adj
rat race n
skull session n (Am)
string bean n (Am) *skinny person*
sweater girl n (Am)
war of nerves n
wave of the future n

General/Miscellaneous
buff n *gen. aficionado* b1935 ["firefighting aficionado": b1905]
crackdown n (Am) b1935
kibbutz n b1935
odorant n b1935 (adj use: b1450)
override n b1935
recordholder n b1935
retrospective n b1935
advisory n (adj use: b1780)
attendee n
auslander n *outlander, foreigner*
chromatography n
crewmate n
dressage n
gadgeteer n
hassle n (verb use: b1955)
midsection n
monolith n *fig.* [lit. sense: b1830] (monolithic: b1825)
pratfall n (prat "buttocks": b1570)
quisling n *collaborator*
realia n *artifacts of "real life"*
subsonic adj
walk-through n

Things
whangdoodle n *thingamajig* b1935
decal n (decalcomania: b1865)
foam rubber n

Description
earthbound adj *bound for the earth* b1935 ["bound to the earth": b1605]
full-scale adj b1935
newsworthy adj b1935
one-stop adj b1935
proactive adj b1935
rooftop adj b1935
tongue-in-cheek adj/adv b1935
topflight adj b1935
backroom adj
beat-up adj
capsule adj
coordinated adj
dicey adj
extraordinaire adj
hard-core adj

hypersonic adj
off-the-cuff adj
pearlescent adj
pint-size adj
raunchy adj (Am) *grubby* ["naughty": b1970] (raunch: b1965)
semigloss adj
shock-resistant adj
super-duper adj
unstructured adj
varisized adj

Colors
earth color n b1935 (earth tone: b1975)
kelly green n (Am) b1935
shocking pink n

Actions/Verbs
bop v *hit* b1935 (noun use: b1950)
crew v b1935
hearken back v *hark back* b1935
prefabricate v b1935 (prefab n: b1940)
seal off v b1935
snort v *suck in, as in "snort cocaine"* b1935
tweeze v b1935
cozy up v
cross-check v (noun use: b1955)
de-emphasize v
decontaminate v
dust off v
fill in v
ghetto v
glamorize v (Am)
leverage v
loosen up v
meld v (Am) (noun use: b1955)
phase out v (phaseout: b1960)
plateau v
plummet v
prerecord v (prerecorded: b1960)
pressure v
pressurize v
ramrod v
spearhead v
spell out v
zig v (noun use: b1795; zigzag n: b1715)

IN USE BY
1950

Geography/Places
frost heave n b1945
seamount n b1945
stateside adj b1945
central city n
moonquake n

Natural Things
antineutron n b1945
graviton n b1945
nitrogen balance n b1945
permafrost n b1945
plutonium n b1945
americium n
antimatter n
californium n
chlorofluorocarbon n
fundamental particle n
mesosphere n
replication n

Plants
jade plant n b1945
ming tree n

Animals
ectotherm n *cold-blooded animal* b1945
endotherm n *warm-blooded animal* b1945
feline distemper n b1945
oink n/v b1945
pit bull terrier n b1945
vizsla n *type of dog* b1945
weimaraner n b1945
cat distemper n
coydog n *coyote/dog mix*
English cocker spaniel n
English shepherd n
great ape n
Yorkie n

Weather
electrical storm n b1945
geomagnetic storm n b1945
southerly n b1945
tropical storm n b1945
whiteout n b1945
wind shear n b1945
jet stream n

Heavens/Sky
black dwarf n b1945
outer planet n b1945
big bang n
Coriolis effect n
cosmic noise n
elliptical galaxy n
micrometeorite n (micrometeoroid: b1950)
protogalaxy n
protoplanet n
protostar n

Science
ethnohistory n b1945
genetic drift n b1945
geoscience n b1945
life science n b1945
psi n b1945
audiology n
ergonomics n
gene pool n
information theory n
particle accelerator, particle physics n
radio astronomy n
RNA n
self-replicating adj

Technology
robotics n 1941
echolocation n 1944

blip n *radar image* b1945
computer n b1945 ["calculator": b1900]
CRT n b1945
debug v b1945
digital computer n b1945
photoduplication n b1945
print wheel n b1945
radar n b1945
teleconferencing n b1945
transponder n b1945
cybernetics, cyberneticist n 1948 (cybernetician: b1955)
analog computer n (*Am*)
bit n
chad n *paper scrap from computer tape*
circuit board n
circuitry n
fax n/v
fiche n
hologram n
information retrieval n
linac n *linear accelerator*
machine language n
on-line adj/adv
printed circuit n
readout n
subroutine n
systems analysis n
transistor n
xerography n

Energy
alkaline battery n b1945
atomic reactor n b1945
brownout n b1945
jellied gasoline n b1945
nuclear reactor n b1945
high-voltage adj

nuclear-powered adj
power adj

Time
atomic age n b1945

Mathematics
times sign n (times, as in "four times four": b1450)

Measurement
kiloton n

The Body
beer belly n b1945 (beer gut: b1980)
boob n *slang breast* b1945 (booby, boobies: b1935)
box n *slang female genitalia* b1945
knockers n *slang breasts* b1945
rocks n *slang testicles*

Physical Description
pee n *slang urine* ["urination": b1900]
swivel-hipped adj
yak n/v *talk*

Medicine
anesthesiologist n b1945 (anesthetist: b1885)
antibiotic n b1945 (adj use: b1895)
antifungal adj b1945
battle fatigue n b1945
booster shot n b1945
chemosurgery n b1945
combat fatigue n b1945
crud n *slang disease* b1945

decompression sickness n
  b1945
eye bank n (Am) b1945
eye chart n b1945
farmer's lung n b1945
fluorography n b1945
health care n b1945
hiatal hernia n b1945
infectious hepatitis n b1945
motion sickness n b1945
periodontics n b1945
reconstructive surgery n
  b1945
sedate v b1945
self-medication n b1945
slipped disk n b1945
tunnel vision n b1945
methadone n (Am) 1947
cortisone n 1949
bloodmobile n
decongestant n
delivery room n
dental technician n
euphoriant n
fluoridate v (fluoridation:
  b1930; fluoridize: b1940)
jock itch n
kidney stone n
LPN n Licensed Professional
  Nurse
methamphetimine n
miracle drug n
placebo effect n
plastic surgeon n
postnasal drip n
tubal ligation n

Everyday Life

aerosol can n b1945
antiperspirant n b1945
butcher paper n b1945
day care n b1945
dimout n lesser than blackout
  b1945
dishpan hands n b1945
fire hydrant n b1945 (fireplug: b1715)
grease pencil n b1945
ID card n b1945 (identification card: b1900; identity
  card: b1910)
jerrican/jerry can n type of
  container b1945
penlight n b1945
place setting n b1945
platform rocker n b1945
pot holder n b1945
potty-chair n b1945

stainless n stainless flatware
  b1945
steam iron n b1945
white noise n b1945
backsplash n
ballpoint n
bubble bath n
captain's chair n
clock radio n (Am)
clutch bag n
cocktail table n
compactor n
cooktop n
cosmetic case n
Eames chair n (Am)
extension cord n
Hollywood bed n
ice-cream chair n
launderette n
squeeze bottle n
stepstool n
TV n
welcome mat n

Shelter/Housing

cold-water flat n b1945
cottage curtains n b1945
onion dome n type of roof
  b1945
trailer park n b1945 (trailer
  camp: b1920)
crawl space n
garden apartment n
mobile home n
motor lodge n (motor court:
  b1940; motor inn: b1955)
mudroom n
R-value n
safe house n
shed dormer n
split-level adj/n

Drink

amaretto n b1945
club soda n b1945
espresso n b1945
framboise n raspberry brandy
  or liqueur b1945
Lambrusco n b1945
malted n (Am) b1945
mixed drink n b1945
sauvignon blanc n type of wine
  b1945
spritzer n b1945
triple sec n b1945
Bloody Mary n
cappuccino n
crème fraiche n fresh cream

gewürztraminer n type of wine
Irish coffee n
on the rocks adj
vodka martini n (vodkatini:
  b1970)

Food

Bermuda onion n b1945
butternut squash n b1945
cacciatore adj b1945
chowhound n b1945
coffee roll n b1945
Colby n the cheese b1945
cold cuts n (Am) b1945
cook cheese n b1945
egg roll n b1945
french v style of cutting during
  cooking b1945
hoagie n (Am) b1945
hot pepper n b1945
lox n smoked salmon b1945
luncheon meat/lunchmeat n
  b1945
mahimahi n dolphin meat
  b1945
pareve adj containing no milk
  b1945
quiche n b1945
raw bar n b1945
riblet n b1945
semisweet adj b1945
spring roll n b1945
toke n bit of bread b1945
box lunch n
Caesar salad n
calzone n
chèvre n goat cheese
cookout n (Am)
corn chip n
culinarian n
Denver sandwich n
falafel n
farmer cheese n
food pyramid n
freeze-dried, freeze-dry adj, v
fry bread n
jimmies n ice cream sprinkles
linguine n
London broil n (Am)
manicotti n
marinara adj/n
Monterey Jack n (Am) type of
  cheese
onion ring n
open sandwich n
pablum n
panbroil v
phyllo n

pork belly n
producer goods n
redeye gravy n
scallopini n
snow pea n
Tex-Mex adj (Am)
triple-decker n type of sandwich ["trilogy": b1940]
variety meat n

Agriculture/
Food-Gathering

DDT n b1945
green thumb n b1945 (green
  fingers: b1935)
kibble n animal food b1945
tree farm n b1945
electrofishing n killing fish
  with electricity
farmworker n (farmhand:
  b1845)

Cloth/Clothing

bobby socks n (Am) b1945
boxer shorts n b1945
chino n (Am) type of cloth
  b1945
drag queen n b1945 (drag
  adj/n: b1900)
falsie n (Am) b1945
G suit n (Am) gravity suit
  b1945
garrison cap n (Am) b1945
jumpsuit n b1945 (jumper:
  b1930)
long johns n b1945
pantie girdle n b1945
pedal pushers n (Am) b1945
see-through adj b1945
shirtdress n b1945
shoulder patch n b1945
sundress n b1945
zoot suit n b1945
bikini n
clerical collar n
crew sock n
garter belt n
half-slip n
mandarin collar n
outercoat n
slingback n type of shoe
sports jacket n
tank top n
undershorts n

Fashion/Style

crew cut n (Am) b1945
ear clip n b1945

French provincial n b1945
glamour-puss n b1945
high fashion n b1945
conk v *straighten hair* (noun
  use: b1965)
culture vulture n
decorator adj
ducktail n *type of hairstyle*
eyeliner n
hipness n
neophilia n
Windsor knot n

Tools

Allen wrench n b1945
alligator clip n b1945
bullhorn n b1945
earthmover n b1945
forklift n b1945
wire recorder n b1945
deep fryer n
light pipe n *optical fiber*
sequencer n [in music:
  b1975]
snowblower n

Travel/Transportation

access road n b1945
airlift n b1945
beach buggy n b1945
car pool n b1945 (verb use:
  b1965)
condensation trail, contrail n
  b1945
copter n b1945
ejection seat n b1945
expressway n (Am) b1945
flight suit n b1945
helicopt v b1945
helipad n b1945
heliport n b1945
hot rod n/v (Am) b1945
  (hot rodder: b1950)
island-hop v b1945
jet engine n b1945
jet plane n b1945
limited-access highway n
  b1945
microbus n b1945
motor pool n (Am) b1945
offtrack adj/adv b1945
parking brake n b1945
pedicab n b1945
ramjet n b1945
semi n *semitrailer* b1945
  (semitrailer: b1920)
skimobile n *snowmobile*
  b1945

snow tire n b1945
swamp buggy n b1945
tow truck n b1945 (tow car:
  b1910)
traffic circle n b1945
turbojet, turboprop n b1945
V-8 n b1945
vapor trail n b1945
afterburner n
airboat n
automatic transmission n
convertiplane n
estate car/estate wagon n
  (Brit) *station wagon*
fixed-wing adj
flight attendant n
frontage road n
glove box n (glove compartment: b1940)
hardtop n
inboard n (adj use: b1850)
inertial guidance n
jeepney n
jetliner n
liftgate n
lounge car n
low beam n
median strip n
minicar n
propjet n
retro-rocket n
rooster tail n *boating term*
tailgate v
test-drive v
tollway n
turbocar n
two-way street n

Emotions/ Characteristics

ressentiment n *deep resent-
  ment* 1941
gung ho adj 1942
momism n *dependence on
  mom* 1942
piss and vinegar n b1945
pixie adj *mischievous* b1945
role-playing n b1945
self-worth n b1945
charisma n *aura of authority*
  [rel. sense: b1645; gen.
  "charm": b1965] (charismatic: b1870)
cold-eyed adj
downbeat adj
hepped up adj
piss off v *anger*

spine-chilling adj
stressor n
upbeat adj *cheery*

Thoughts/Perception/ The Mind

dream up v b1945
electroshock n b1945
electroshock therapy n b1945
existentialism, existentialist n
  b1945
group therapy n b1945
schizo adj/n b1945 (schiz:
  b1955)
second-guess v b1945
aversion therapy n
bonkers adj *crazy*
brainwashing n (brainwash:
  b1955)
doublethink n
flip v *go crazy*
futurology n
headshrinker n (Am) *slang
  psychiatrist*
metaethics n
word-association test n

Love/Romance/Sex

Dear John n b1945
hypersexual adj b1945
preggers adj b1945
sexploitation n b1945
skirt-chaser n b1945
straight adj *heterosexual*
  b1945 (noun use: b1970)
sweetheart adj b1945
bedroom eyes n
deep kiss n
dreamboat n (dreamy:
  b1945)
hots, the n
kiss-and-tell adj
missionary position n
sexpot n (Am)
sexual relations n
soul kiss n

Family/Relations/ Friends

nuclear family n

Holidays

trick or treat n b1945
stocking stuffer n

Games/Fun/Leisure

block party n b1945
gin rummy n b1945 (gin:
  b1960)
phillumenist n *matchbook collector* b1945
bumper car n
canasta n
gamesmanship n
spin the bottle n (Am)

Sports

bodysurf v b1945
daily double n b1945
drag race n b1945
extra-base hit n b1945
obstacle course n b1945
rematch n b1945 (verb use:
  b1860)
snorkel n/v b1945
spelunking, spelunker n
  b1945
TKO n b1945
Aqua-Lung n
balance beam n
dead man's float n
drag v *drag race*
driving range n
horseplayer n
locker-room adj
par v *par a hole* (noun use:
  b1900)
pro-am adj/n
racing form n
sweet spot n
swim fin n
time trial n
tote board n
triple-header n
wind sprint n

Professions/Duties

autoworker n b1945
skycap n b1945
executive secretary n
extension agent n

Business/Commerce/ Selling

answering service n b1945
budget adj *inexpensive* b1945
consumerism n (Am) b1945
gift certificate n b1945
layaway n b1945 (lay away v:
  b1930)
mass marketing n b1945
name-brand adj/n b1945

pizzeria n b1945
roll back v b1945 (rollback: b1895)
silicone rubber n b1945
superstore n b1945
thrift shop n b1945
bargain-basement adj (noun use: b1900)
consumer price index n
discount house n
package deal n
presell v
privatize v (privatization: b1970)

The Workplace

deskbound adj b1945
retiree adj (Am) b1945
severance pay n b1945
split shift n b1945
take-home pay n b1945
wildcat strike n (Am) b1945
work stoppage n b1945
workforce n b1945
workload n b1945
automation n
blue-collar adj
fringe benefit n
middle management n
self-employed adj (self-employment: b1745)
stoop labor n
workers' compensation n

Finances/Money

equity capital n b1945
fee splitting n b1945
near money n liquid cash b1945
net national product n b1945
piggy bank n b1945
price support n b1945
risk capital n b1945
rollover n b1945
seed money n b1945
tax base n b1945
venture capital n b1945
zero-sum adj b1945
charge card n
disposable income n
gross national product n
loaded adj rich
macroeconomics n
megabuck n
microeconomics n
savings bond n

Language and Speaking

acronym n b1945
governmentese n b1945
pataphysics n type of jargon b1945
alphanumeric adj
bureaucratese n
buzzword n
contact language n pidgin
federalese n
language arts n
metalinguistics n
newspeak n
protolanguage n
sentence fragment n

Literature/Writing

braillewriter n b1945
comic book n b1945
head rhyme n alliteration b1945
sidebar n b1945
spiral binding, spiral-bound n, adj b1945
think piece n b1945
touch-type v (Am) b1945
trade book n b1945
cover story n
fanzine n (Am)
foreign correspondent n
functional illiterate n
funny book n
gatefold n
hardcover adj/n (hardcase adj: b1900; hardbound adj: b1930; hardback: b1955)
newsweekly n
red-pencil v
repro n
space opera n
story line n
subtext n theme
vanity press n
writer's block n

Communication

conference call n b1945
letter of intent n b1945
microfiche n b1945
mimeo n/v b1945 (mimeograph: b1890)
self-mailer n b1945
squawk box n b1945
citizens band n (Am)
microreader n
news conference n

tape-record, tape v
videophone n
wiretap n (verb use: b1905; wiretapper: b1895)

Visual Arts/Photography

graphic n b1945
photo essay n b1945
photomosaic n b1945
decoupage n
electronic flash n
f-stop n
found object n unintentional art
stick figure n

Performing Arts

arena theater n theater-in-the-round b1945
choreograph v b1945
showbiz n b1945
top billing n b1945
general admission n
ice show n
performing arts n
scene-stealer n
sight gag n
theater-in-the-round n

Music

chorus boy n b1945
deejay n b1945
disc jockey n (Am) b1945
hillbilly music n b1945
lead sheet n (Am) b1945
rhythm band n b1945
up-tempo adj b1945
bop n (Am) bebop
flip side n
hi-fi n (Am) (high fidelity: b1935)
LP n long-playing record
perfect pitch n
rhythm and blues n (Am)
steel drum, steel band n
tape deck n

Entertainment

dead air n b1945
escape artist n b1945 (escapology: b1940)
pinup girl n b1945 (pinup: b1945)
wingding n (Am) party b1945 [type of drug reaction: b1930]

conga line n
DJ n
fun house n
hand puppet n
keynote speaker n
limbo n the dance
mambo n

Movies/TV/Radio

airtime n b1945
fish-eye adj b1945
listenership n b1945
newsbreak n b1945
quiz show n b1945
short subject n b1945
situation comedy n b1945 (sitcom: b1965)
sportscast n b1945
storyboard n b1945
B movie n
closed-circuit television n
freeze-frame n
shoot-'em-up n
simulcast v (Am)
stuntwoman n (Am) (stuntman: b1925)
telethon n
test pattern n
voiceover n

Education

middle school n b1945
academia n
community college n (Am)
elhi n
essay question n
junior varsity n
multidisciplinary adj
nonliterate adj
preschooler n
telecourse n
work-study program n

Religion

theonomous adj subject to God's authority

Society/Mores/Culture

butch adj/n b1945
civic-minded adj b1945
cross-cultural adj b1945
displaced person n b1945
ethnic n b1945 [obs. "heathen": b1375 to 1700s] (ethnicity: b1950)
everywoman n b1945 (everyman: b1910)
gentleperson n b1945

Everything Olde Is Newe Again

How old is *olde*? Not very. In use before 1930.

This is one of many words that have the aura of age, yet are relatively new. On page 186, discussing words that appeared earlier than we might expect, we discuss the word *oldfangled*. To recap: *oldfangled* is quite newfangled, especially compared with *newfangled*. Oldfangled *newfangled* was in use by 1400, while newfangled *oldfangled* didn't arrive until before 1845.

Similarly, *archaic* is surprisingly not a particularly archaic word—in use by 1835 (*archaical* was in use by 1805, and *archaism* is more in line with our expectations, in use by 1645).

Some words are simply slow in coming. For example, *defiance* has been with us since before 1300, yet the adjective *defiant* surfaced only sometime before 1840 (and then it was borrowed from French, not adapted from the noun).

Some other interesting late arrivals:

- *Plan*, as in "plan a strategy" or "plan a picnic," wasn't recorded until before 1770.

- *Medieval* as an adjective wasn't recorded until before 1840 (*Middle Ages*, though, by 1620).

- *Win* as a noun doesn't appear until before 1875.

- The phrase *early American* isn't particularly early—in use by 1895.

- *Empathy* was in use before 1910.

- *Gunslinger*, so much of the Wild West, appeared sometime before 1930. And the staples of cowboys—*cowboy hats* and *cowboy boots*—weren't known by those names until before 1900.

- *Oink* appears before 1945—pigs were apparently mute before then.

Finally, do you also find it something of a surprise that a word so basic to our vocabulary as *basic* is so young?—in use by 1845 as an adjective and by 1930 as a noun.

Joe Public n b1945
latchkey child n b1945
living standard n b1945
multicultural adj b1945 (multiculturalism: b1965)
peer group n b1945
upward mobility n b1945 (upwardly mobile: b1965)
welfare state n b1945
unperson n 1949
elitism n
ethnicity n [obs. "heathenism": b1800]
liberated adj *as in "sexually liberated"*
lifemanship n
lifeway n *lifestyle*
Ms. n (Mr.: b1450; Mrs.: b1615)
postmodern adj
social drinker n
urban renewal n
world-class adj
xenophile adj/n

Government
Capitol Hill n b1945
minority leader n (Am)

Politics
roorback n (Am) *political mud* 1944
globalism n (Am) b1945
pol n (Am) b1945
political action committee n b1945
superpower n *powerful nation* b1945 ["great power": b1925]
apartheid n
Bamboo Curtain n
foreign aid n
free world n
right-to-work adj

Death
death camp n b1945
gas chamber n b1945
genocide n b1945
cremains n

War/Military/Violence
4-F n b1945
air strike n b1945
air-to-air adj b1945 (air-to-surface: b1960)
airstrip n b1945
assault boat n b1945

atom bomb n b1945 (atomic bomb: b1915)
basic training n b1945
bazooka n (Am) b1945 [type of musical instrument: b1935]
blockbuster n b1945
boot camp n (Am) b1945
burp gun n (Am) b1945
buzz bomb n b1945
C ration n b1945
carpet bombing n b1945
clobber v (Am) b1945
clock v *punch* b1945
cold war n b1945 (cold warrior: b1950)
command car n b1945
defoliant n b1945
doughfoot n (Am) *infantry—doughboy on foot* b1945
drop zone n b1945
firestorm n b1945
flying bomb n (Brit) *buzz bomb* b1945
frogman n b1945
GI n b1945 (adj use: b1940; verb use: b1955)
gig n/v *demerit* b1945
guided missile n b1945

gunsel n *gunman* b1945 ["young man": b1915]
kamikaze n/adj b1945
MIA n b1945
napalm n b1945
peacekeeping adj/n b1945
pistolwhip v b1945
proximity fuze n b1945
PT boat n b1945
recoilless adj b1945
robot bomb n b1945
rocket bomb n b1945
Seabee n b1945
servicewoman n b1945 (serviceman: b1900; serviceperson: b1975)
sniperscope n b1945
Sten n *type of gun* b1945
task force n b1945
trigger-happy adj b1945
V sign n b1945
V-1, V-2 n b1945
war-game v b1945 (war game: b1830)
yardbird n b1945
billy club n (billy: b1850)
biological warfare n
chicken colonel n (Am)
duke v *fight* [obs. "shake

---

hands": b1865 to 1900s]
(dukes n: b1875)
enemy alien n
fallout n
fleet admiral n
fusion bomb n
ground zero n
H-bomb n (Am)
hot war n *opp. of cold war*
hydrogen bomb n
law of war n
letter bomb n
militance n [militancy: b1650]
nuclear weapon n
nuke n (verb use: b1970)
shoot-out n
surface-to-air adj
zip gun n
zonk v *hit*

Crime/Punishment/ Enforcement

citizen's arrest n b1945
copshop n (Am) *police station* b1945
lawman n *police officer* b1945 [*type of leg. officer*: b1000; *arch. "lawyer"*: b1570]
sharpie n b1945
squad room n b1945
stakeout n b1945
air piracy n
death row n
dognap v (Am) *akin to kidnap*
gray market n
LSD n *type of hallucinogenic drug*
mug shot n
second-degree murder n
strip search n/v

The Law

escape clause n b1945
friend of the court n b1945
legal eagle n b1945

The Fantastic/ Paranormal

flying saucer n 1947

Magic

incant v *chant* b1945

Interjections

Geronimo interj (Am) b1945
heads up interj b1945

shove it interj b1945
hut interj
ick interj (Am)

Slang

ass n *woman; sex* b1945
bad-mouth v b1945
bobby-soxer n (Am) b1945
brush-off n (Am) b1945
carb n b1945
collision course n b1945
cookbook adj b1945
deep-six v b1945
dive n *intentional loss* b1945
eyepopper n b1945
fence-mending n (Am) b1945
freebie n (Am) b1945
fubar adj b1945
gasser n b1945
gobbledygook n b1945
grind n/v *as in "bump and grind"* b1945
groovy adj *peachy, neat, excellent* b1945
heave-ho n b1945 (interj use: b1470)
hung over adj b1945
hung up adj b1945
hyper adj b1945 (hyperactive: b1870)
jillion n b1945
junker n b1945
kitchen-sink adj *all-inclusive* b1945
klatch/klatsch n b1945
no-hoper n (Brit) b1945
no-no n (Am) b1945
plotz v (Am) b1945
poop n (Am) *inside scoop* b1945
rhubarb n *hubbub* b1945
righteous adj (Am) b1945
road apples n b1945
rundown n *recap* b1945 ["list of horse-racing entries": b1935] (run down: b1965)
rust bucket n b1945
shitlist n b1945
snafu adj/n/v (Am) b1945
specs n *specifications* b1945
spook n *spy* b1945
stacked adj (Am) b1945
toots n *toots(ie)* b1945
whiz kid n b1945
arm-twisting n
beefcake n

benny n (Am) *benzadrine*
big deal n
blooper n *goof-up*
boffo adj
chicken out v (Am)
cock-up n *mess*
college try n
comp v (Am) *(ac)comp(any)*
crud n *gunk* ["curd": b1375; "jerk": b1940] (crut: b1940)
crypto n *secret supporter*
daddy-o n
disincentive n
doo-doo n
finger-pointing n
flyboy n
foot-dragging n (foot-dragger: b1960)
gangbang n/v (Am) (gangshag: b1930)
guck n
heads-up adj
honcho n
horse n *heroin*
hyped-up adj
juiced adj *drunk*
litterbug n
machismo n (Am)
me-tooism n (Am)
mother n
must-see adj/n
name-dropping n
nudnik n (Am)
oater n
panic button n
piss away n
promo adj/n
ream out v *chastise*
rubber n *condom*
ruggedize v
rumble n *fight* (verb use: b1960)
sack out v
scat n *heroin*
shit n *drug*
sloshed adj
stiff v
veep n (Am)
whomp up v
yak n *laugh—yuk*

Insults

sad sack n 1942
fancy-pants adj b1945
fatso n b1945
finger, the n *as in "give him the finger"* b1945

fuckoff n b1945
goof-up n b1945
horse's ass n b1945
knucklehead n b1945
meathead n b1945
oddball adj/n (Am) b1945
party pooper n b1945
pussy n *weakling* b1945
bubblehead n
chickenshit n (Am) (adj use: b1955)
cornball n (Am) (adj use: b1955)
dim bulb n *stupid person*
honky n
nickel-and-dime adj (verb use: b1965)
over-the-hill adj
schmo n (Am)
square adj/n *nerd*

Phrases

across-the-board adj b1945
angry young man n b1945
around-the-clock adj b1945
baby boom n (Am) b1945 (baby bust: b1975; baby boomer: b1975)
back-and-forth n b1945
buddy system n b1945
catbird seat n (Am) b1945
chew out v b1945
common touch n b1945
cop-out n b1945 (verb use: b1965)
crime against humanity n b1945
dry run n (Am) b1945
eager beaver n (Am) b1945
end user n b1945
game plan n b1945
grace period n b1945
hatchet job, hatchet work n b1945
hearts and flowers n (Am) b1945
high ground n b1945
hog heaven n b1945
idiot stick n (Am) *shovel* b1945
jerk around v b1945
kiss of death n b1945
lead time n (Am) b1945
Monday-morning quarterback n b1945
no-holds-barred adj b1945
point of no return n b1945
sack time n b1945

saddle tramp n b1945
seat-of-the-pants adj (Am) b1945
sitting duck n b1945
snow job n (Am) b1945
sock away v b1945
top secret adj b1945
trade down n b1945
back burner n
Big Brother n
blow your stack v
boy wonder n
brass ring n
character assassination n
country mile n
diamond in the rough n
dirty linen n
drunk tank n
family jewels n ["secrets": b1980]
feel no pain v
good life n
inner-directed adj
larger-than-life adj
meat-and-potatoes adj/n
on-again, off-again adj
safety net n
shaggy-dog story n
show-and-tell n
split decision n
sticking point n
tapped out adj
under-the-table adj

General/Miscellaneous

additive n b1945
clunker n (Am) b1945
coproduct n byproduct b1945
critical mass n b1945
deep-freeze v/n b1945 (deep freezer: b1950)
deviance n b1945
ding n small dent b1945
echelon n (Am) level b1945 [mil. use: b1800]

holdout n b1945
in-migrant, in-migrate adj/n, v (Am) immigrant b1945
landfill n (Am) b1945
linkup n b1945
loud-hailer n (Brit) b1945
no-show n (Am) b1945
rehab n/v b1945
returnee n (Am) b1945
service mark n b1945
sonar n b1945
spot-check n/v b1945
staging area n b1945
strobe n b1945
white hunter n b1945
crashworthiness n (crashworthy: b1970)
downside n
foldaway adj
foul-up, foul up, fouled up n, v, adj (Am)
injectant n
loner n
look-alike adj/n
miniaturize, miniaturization v, n
spinoff, spin off n, v
supremacist n
synthetic n
thunk n/v sound
trailhead n
uptick n increase

Things

foamed plastic n b1945
footlocker n (Am) b1945
gizmo n b1945
plastic foam n b1945
polyurethane n b1945
suction cup n b1945

Description

bald-faced adj b1945
best adv as in "you'd best

leave" b1945 (better: b1835)
clutch adj critical b1945
crash adj as in "crash course" b1945
exploded adj as in "an exploded diagram" b1945
irreal adj b1945 (irreality: b1805)
maladapted adj b1945 (maladaptation: b1900)
off-limits adj (Am) b1945
reusable adj b1945
serendipitous adj b1945 (serendipity: 1754)
volume adj b1945
card-carrying adj
fail-safe adj
free-form adj
free-swinging adj
kafkaesque adj
lightfast adj
other-directed adj
soft-line adj opp. of hard-line (noun use: b1970)
space-age adj
subfreezing adj
subminiature adj
tape adj taped
tight-knit adj
wall-to-wall adj

Actions/Verbs

abort v terminate flight or mission prematurely b1945
bat out v turn out quickly b1945
bow out v withdraw b1945
cannibalize v b1945
crash-land v b1945
de-skill v b1945
debrief v b1945
decision v b1945
decondition v b1945
defuse v b1945

double-check v (Am) b1945 (noun use: b1955)
downscale v b1945
doze v bulldoze b1945
escalate v increase, aggravate b1945 ["ride an escalator": b1925]
moisturize v b1945 (moisturizer: b1960)
mothball v repair b1945
orbit v b1945
peel off v b1945
phony v b1945
plink v b1945 (noun use: b1955)
precensor v b1945
prove out v b1945
restructure v b1945
sequence v b1945 (noun use: b1600)
snap back v b1945
spec v b1945
squoosh v b1945
stink up v b1945
tackify v make tacky b1945
tailor v customize b1945
weatherize v b1945
babysit v
barhop v
belly up v
bug v bother
demythologize v
duckwalk v
fast-talk v (Am)
input v
integrate v desegregate
jury v judge
polemicize v
roll over v
surveil v
underwhelm v

IN USE BY
1960

Geography/Places
exurb, exurbia, exurbanite n (Am) *the suburbs' suburbs* b1955
turf n *slang territory* b1955
supercontinent n

Natural Things
ecosphere n b1955
nonhuman adj
quasiparticle n

Animals
choke chain n b1955
foo dog n b1955
Rock Cornish n *type of fowl*
snow crab n

Weather
ice-out n b1955
northerly n b1955
smaze n *sm(oke)(h)aze* b1955

Heavens/Sky
asteroid belt n b1955
deep space n b1955
inner planet n b1955
nightglow n b1955
zero gravity n b1955
extraterrestrial n
moondust n
radio galaxy n
solar wind n
Van Allen belt n

Science
double helix n 1953
behavioral science n b1955
blueshift n b1955

Technology
industrial archaeology n b1955
kinesics n *study of body language* b1955
litmus test n b1955
radiocarbon dating n b1955
artificial intelligence n
bionics n (bionic: b1965)
exobiology n
genetic map n
information science n
International Scientific Vocabulary n
quantum leap n (quantum jump: b1930)
radar astronomy n
urbanology n

Technology
bootstrap v b1955
data processing n b1955
digitize v b1955 (digitalize: b1965)
Doppler radar n b1955
downrange adv b1955
line printer n b1955
orbiter n (Am) b1955
random access memory n b1955 (RAM: b1960)
solid-state adj b1955
terminal n *as in "computer terminal"* b1955
uptime n *opp. of downtime* b1955
Fortran n 1956
byte n 1959
coin-operated adj (coin-op: b1965)
computerize v
cyborg n
fiber optics n

hack, hacker v, n
integrated circuit n
interrupt n (interruption: b1395)
laser n
light pen n
macroinstruction, macro n
microcircuit n
microelectronics n
programming language n
software n
spy satellite n
virtual memory n

Time
real time n b1955
sesquicentenary n b1955
circadian adj *in 24-hour intervals*
nanosecond n

Age/Aging
carbon dating n b1955
preteen adj/n b1955 (preteenager: b1965)
subteen n b1955

Mathematics
hexadecimal adj *base 16 numbering* b1955
innumerate adj/n *mathematically illiterate* 1959
new math n

Measurement
megaton n b1955
tesla n

The Body
digestive system n b1955
limbic system n b1955

interferon n 1957
pheromone n 1959
barf v *slang vomit* (noun use: b1970)
biorhythm n
jugs n *slang breasts*
tinkle v *urinate* (noun use: b1965)

Medicine
broad-spectrum adj b1955
carpal tunnel syndrome n b1955
cat scratch disease n b1955
cortisol n *type of steroid* b1955
defibrillator n b1955
hallucinogen n b1955
hardening n *as in "hardening of the arteries"* b1955
hearing dog n b1955
heart-lung machine n b1955
hydrocortisone n b1955
immune response n b1955
IV n b1955
laetrile n b1955
licensed practical nurse n b1955
major-medical adj b1955
nuclear medicine n b1955
nurse-midwife n b1955
Pap smear/pap test n b1955
paramedic n (Am) b1955 (paramedical: b1925)
perinatal adj b1955
poliovirus n b1955
prescription drug n b1955
rapture of the deep n b1955
Salk vaccine n b1955
script, scrip n *prescription* b1955

stress fracture n b1955
teaching hospital n b1955
tetracycline n b1955
whiplash injury n b1955
amniocentesis n *fetal test*
 (amniotic fluid: b1855;
 amniotic sac: b1885)
anti-inflammatory adj
Asian flu n
cardiac arrest n
cognitive dissonance n
cryobiology n
health spa n
house call n
learning disability n (learning
 disabled: b1975)
life-support adj
Lou Gehrig's disease n
morning-after pill n
noncommunicable adj
nonprescription drug adj
nose job n
oral contraceptive n
pill, the n *birth control*
REM n
sex change n
sonogram n (sonography:
 b1980)
stretch marks n
tab n *tablet*
thalidomide n

Everyday Life
blister pack n b1955
certified mail n b1955
church key n *bottle/can opener*
 b1955
cookware n b1955
director's chair n b1955
dust mop n b1955
flea collar n b1955
library paste n b1955
parfait glass n b1955
pie safe n *type of cupboard*
 b1955
pj's n b1955
plumber's helper n (Am)
 b1955 (plunger: b1800)
rabbit ears n *TV antennae*
 b1955
white pages n b1955
wok n b1955
car wash n
nonstick adj
queen-size adj
three-way bulb n
throw pillow n
tulip chair n

Shelter/Housing
flood wall n b1955
fourplex n b1955
front room n b1955
high-rise adj/n b1955
housing development n b1955
motor inn n b1955 (motor
 court: b1940; motor lodge:
 b1950)
pass-through n (Am) b1955
room and board n b1955
skywalk n b1955 (skybridge:
 b1985)
time-sharing n b1955
geodesic dome n
low-rise adj *opp. of high-rise*
particleboard n
tract house n

Drink
fizzwater n b1955
six-pack n b1955

Food
BLT n b1955
buttercream n b1955
butterfly v b1955
chicken-fried steak n b1955
clams casino n b1955
confit n *type of meat preparation* b1955
coon cheese n b1955
Denver omelet n b1955
devein v b1955
egg cream n (Am) b1955
fast-food adj (Am) b1955
fish stick n b1955 (fish finger: b1965)
hash browns n b1955
hero sandwich n b1955
home fries n b1955
Italian sandwich n b1955
key lime pie n b1955
matzo ball n b1955
nosh n b1955 [nosh bar:
 b1920; noshery: b1965]
 (verb use: b1970)
pita n (Am) *type of bread*
 b1955
rouille n *type of sauce* b1955
tetrazzini adj b1955
TV dinner n (Am) b1955
brown bagging n
chugalug v (Am) (chug v:
 b1970)
crudites n *type of appetizer*
mayo n

oven-ready adj
ploughman's lunch n
prime rib n
refried beans n
reuben n *type of sandwich*
 (reuben sandwich: b1970)
scarf v (Am) *eat* (noun use:
 b1935)
stir-fry v
table sugar n
whole-grain adj

Agriculture/
Food-Gathering
agribusiness n (Am) b1955

Cloth/Clothing
Bermuda shorts n b1955
bomber jacket n b1955
drip-dry v b1955 (adj use:
 b1960)
dry suit, wet suit n *in skin diving* b1955
harem pants n b1955
Hawaiian shirt n b1955
pasties n b1955
safari jacket n b1955
stiletto heel n b1955
sweater-vest n b1955
sweaterdress n b1955
tennies n b1955
tie clasp, tie tack n b1955
capri pants n
car coat n
loungewear n
sack dress n
wash-and-wear adj

Fashion/Style
DA n *hairstyle* b1955
hip n *hipness* b1955
split end n (Am) b1955
tastemaker n *trendsetter*
 b1955
beehive n *type of hairstyle*
dreadlock n
in adj *fashionable*
low-rent adj *subpar*
mod n (adj use: b1965)
moisturizer n (moisturize:
 b1945)
shades n *sunglasses*
trendsetter n (trendy: b1960;
 trends-spotter: b1965)
worry beads n

Tools
maser n *microwave laser*
 b1955
opaque projector n b1955
overhead projector n b1955
saber saw n b1955
snow thrower n b1955
radial saw n
spray can n

Travel/Transportation
beltway n b1955
blastoff, blast off n, v b1955
chopper n/v *helicopter* b1955
commute n b1955
dieseling n b1955 (diesel v:
 b1975)
downshift v b1955
fastback n (Am) *type of car*
 b1955 [type of boat:
 b1975]
flyby n (Am) b1955
holding pattern n b1955
lap belt n *seat belt* b1955
launching pad n b1955
 (launchpad: b1960)
moped n b1955
off-ramp n b1955 (on-ramp:
 b1960)
ragtop n *convertible* b1955
redline n b1955
rocket sled n b1955
roll bar n b1955 (roll cage:
 b1970)
speed shop n b1955
sunroof n b1955
touch-and-go n b1955
traffic cone n b1955
truck stop n (Am) b1955
whirlybird n *helicopter* b1955
whitewall n b1955
aerospace, aerospace plane
 adj/n
boatel n
compact n *compact car*
cosmonaut n
dune buggy n
economy class n
hovercraft n
ion engine n
kart n
launch vehicle n
liftoff n
linear motor n
minibus n
minivan n
moon shot n (Am)

multihull n
on-ramp n (off-ramp: b1955)
plasma jet n
sealift n/v *akin to airlift*
stickshift n
valet parking n
VTOL n

Emotions/ Characteristics
Freudian slip n b1955
go ape v b1955
identity crisis n b1955
kvetch v b1955 (noun use: b1965)
palsy adj *friendly* b1955
teed off adj b1955
unflappable adj b1955
balls n *guts, nerve*
couth n (adj use: b1900)
hang-up n
inner space n
nit-picking adj/n (nitpick n/ v: b1965)

Thoughts/Perception/ The Mind
groupthink n b1955
memory lane n b1955
nonjudgmental adj b1955
split-brain adj

Love/Romance/Sex
ball v *have sex* b1955
bun in the oven n (Am) b1955
nymphet n *sexy young woman* b1955
significant other n b1955
AC/DC adj
adult adj *risqué*
blow job n (blow v: b1935)
double-ring adj *as in "double-ring wedding"*
femme n *the "female" lesbian* [gen. "woman": b1930]
french n/v *oral sex*
homophile adj/n *homosexual*
jack off v *masturbate*
score v *have sex*
sex kitten n
transsexual n

Family/Relations/ Friends
biological clock n b1955
quad n *quadruplet* b1955
parenting n

Holidays
ticker-tape parade n

Games/Fun/Leisure
monkey bars n b1955
whoopee cushion n b1955
gin n
hula hoop n
theme park n (Am)

Sports
demolition derby n b1955
drag strip n (Am) b1955
dragster n (Am) b1955
flag football n b1955
free diver n b1955
motocross n b1955
phys ed n b1955
platoon v b1955 (noun use: b1730)
point spread n (Am) b1955
redshirt n b1955
scuba n b1955 (scuba-diver: b1960; scuba-dive: b1965)
snow bunny n b1955
weight training n b1955
winner's circle n b1955
biathlon n (biathlete: b1970)
ski bum n
skydiving n

Professions/Duties
carmaker n b1955
craftspeople n b1955 (craftsman: b1200; craftswoman: b1890; craftsperson: b1920)
exotic dancer n b1955
press secretary n b1955
trashman n *garbageman* b1955
au pair girl n
meter maid n (Am)
security guard n

Business/Commerce/ Selling
body shop n b1955
common market n b1955
deli n b1955
franchisee n b1955
free-marketeer n b1955
hard sell n (Am) b1955
Madison Avenue n *representing the advertising industry* b1955
mass-market adj b1955

point of purchase adj/n b1955
silent auction n b1955
soft sell n b1955
tag sale n *yard sale* b1955
test-market v b1955
watering hole n b1955
wheeler-dealer n b1955 (wheeler and dealer: b1970)
economy of scale n
full-service adj
growth company n
pitchwoman n (pitchman: b1930)
resale value n
shopping mall n

The Workplace
coffee break n b1955
industrial park n b1955
job-hop, job-hopping v, n b1955
labor-intensive adj b1955
mom-and-pop adj (Am) b1955
overachiever, overachieve n, v b1955
overqualified adj b1955
work ethic n b1955
golden handshake n
moonlight v (moonlighter: b1955)
nine-to-five adj
pension plan n
scut work n

Finances/Money
audit trail n b1955
cash flow n b1955
leveraged adj b1955
S and L n b1955
tax shelter n b1955
tax-deductible adj b1955
trickle-down theory n b1955
capital-intensive adj
credit rating n
double-digit adj
Eurodollar n
prime rate n

Language and Speaking
doublespeak n b1955
educationese n b1955
gadzookery n (Brit) *using archaic words* b1955
computerese n
lexis n

Literature/Writing
centerfold n (Am) b1955
copyedit v b1955
fine print n b1955
hardback n *hardcover* b1955 (hardcase adj: b1900; hardbound adj: b1930; hardcover: b1950)
over-the-transom adj b1955
softbound book n b1955
tell-all n b1955
typestyle n b1955
antinovel n
beatnik, beatster, beat n, n, n/adj

Communication
community antenna television n *cable* b1955
junk mail n (Am) b1955
modem n b1955
speakerphone n (Am) b1955
videotape recorder n b1955
CB, CBer n
picturephone n
press release n
touchtone n

Visual Arts/ Photography
moderne n b1955
moire effect n b1955
auteur n
autofocus adj/n
ghosting n *on a TV*
pop art n

Performing Arts
cattle call n *type of audition* b1955
mistress of ceremonies n b1955
off Broadway n b1955
second banana n b1955
spear-carrier n b1955
talent show n b1955
top banana n b1955
center stage n
dinner theater n
shtik n
street theater n (Am)

Music
rock and roll n 1951
bass fiddle n b1955
country music n b1955
fight song n b1955

hammer dulcimer n b1955
liner notes n b1955
reverb n b1955 (verb use: b1605)
sounds n b1955
bluegrass n
cassette n *as in "audiocassette"* [rare "casket": b1795; for photo film: b1875]
country and western n (country: b1970)
funk n *type of music*
mono n
pops n *as in "Boston Pops"* (pop "popular concert": b1870)
rockabilly n (Am)
session man n *studio musician*
sing-along n
zydeco n

Entertainment
audiophile n b1955
cha-cha n/v b1955
discotheque n b1955
door prize n b1955
grand marshal n b1955
wax museum n b1955
audiotape n
send-up n *parody*

Movies/TV/Radio
art house n b1955
colorcast n/v b1955
educational television n b1955
idiot box n b1955
jock n *disk jockey* b1955
kidvid n b1955
on-screen adj/adv b1955
postproduction n b1955
subscription TV n b1955
teleplay n b1955
videotape n b1955 (verb use: b1960)
anchorman, anchor n (anchorperson, anchorpeople, anchorwoman: b1975)
docudrama n
docutainment n
film clip n
film noir n
game show n
infotainment n
new wave n
pay-TV n

prime time n
residual n *royalty*
small screen n
tube n *as in "boob tube"*

Education
cafetorium n *cafe(teria) (audi)torium* b1955
continuing education n b1955
didact n b1955
ed n b1955
grade point n b1955 (grade point average: b1970)
houseparent n b1955 (housemother: b1840; housefather: b1845)
master class n b1955
oral history n b1955
panty raid n b1955
underachieve, underachiever v, n b1955
pass-fail adj
pop quiz n

Religion
bas mitzvah n b1955 (bar mitvah: b1820)
charismatic n *follower of charismatic religion* b1955

Society/Mores/Culture
desegregate, desegregation v, n b1955
disaster area n b1955
eye contact n b1955
hot line n b1955
househusband n b1955 (housewife: b1225)
jet set n b1955
litterbag n b1955
maid-in-waiting n b1955
population explosion n (Am) b1955
sensitivity training n b1955
urban sprawl n b1955
antiestablishment adj
antinuclear adj (antinuke: b1975)
homophobia n ["gen. fear of men": b1930] (homophobe: b1975)
New Age adj
role model n
status symbol n
unchic adj
WASP n

Government
meritocracy n

Politics
international relations n b1955
kremlinology n
protest rally n

Death
body bag n b1955
hit v b1955 (noun use: b1970)
megadeath n b1955

War/Military/Violence
ballistic missile n b1955
cherry bomb n b1955
deck v *hit* b1955
draft board n b1955
front-end loader n b1955
groundburst n *nuclear explosion* b1955
gunpoint n b1955
ICBM n b1955
karate n b1955
missileman n b1955 (missileer: b1960)
pellet gun n b1955
red alert n b1955
total v *destroy completely* b1955
Uzi n b1955
air-to-surface adj (air-to-air: b1945)
antiballistic missile n
antimissile missile n
cruise missile n
denuclearize v
enlistee n
first strike n
flick-knife n (Brit) *switchblade*
neutron bomb n
search and destroy v
second strike n/adj
test ban n

Crime/Punishment/Enforcement
con game n b1955
con job n b1955
hot-wire v b1955
joint n *marijuana cigarette* b1955
joint, the n *the pen* b1955
juvenile officer n b1955

shooting gallery n *heroin house* b1955
slammer n *jail* b1955 (slam: b1960)
teddy boy n *type of juvenile delinquent* b1955
cellblock n
criminalize v
klepto n
Murphy n *type of con game*
rap sheet n (rap: b1905)
soft drugs n
work-release adj
yardbird n

The Law
character witness n b1955
class action n b1955
prior restraint n b1955

The Fantastic/Paranormal
time warp n b1955
UFO n b1955 (ufology: b1960)
bigfoot n *Sasquatch*

Interjections
cowabunga interj b1955
horseshit interj/n b1955
hup interj b1955
no sweat interj b1955
piss off interj
presto chango n/v
up yours interj
yikes interj

Slang
bazooms n *breasts* b1955
big daddy n b1955
buddy-buddy adj b1955
bug out v (Am) b1955
cool adv *as in "play it cool"* b1955 (adj use: b1950)
cotton-picking adj (Am) b1955
cutting edge n b1955
DIY n b1955
do-good adj b1955
doomsayer n b1955
far-out adj b1955
federal case n b1955
fuck up v b1955 (fuckup: b1960; fucked-up: b1970)
gear adj (Am) *great* b1955
gear up v b1955
goof n b1955

hip-shooting n b1955
joypop v (Am) *irregular drug use* b1955
juice up v b1955
juicehead n *drunk* b1955
just-folks adj b1955
killer adj b1955 (noun use: b1930)
maven n b1955
megillah n *as in "the whole megillah"* b1955
mensch n b1955
mil n b1955
pits, the n b1955
psywar n (Am) b1955
red-carpet adj b1955
schnockered n (Am) *drunk* b1955
skosh n b1955
split v *leave* b1955 [arch. "go fast": b1800]
stoned adj (Am) *drunk* b1955 ["intoxicated by drugs": b1955] (stone v: b1970)
toke v *smoke marijuana* b1955 (noun use: b1970)
uncool adj b1955
veggie n b1955
way-out adj b1955 (way-in: b1960)
wired adj *set for life* b1955
yackety-yack v b1955 (noun use: b1958)
zinger n b1955
psychedelic n/adj 1956 (psychedelia: b1970)
A-OK adj/adv
ace v (Am) *as in "ace a test"*
attrit n/v *wear down*
backgrounder n
badass adj (noun use: b1985)
bag n *lifestyle*
ballsy adj
cancer stick n (Am)
cash cow n
cat n (Am) *good guy*
cloud nine n (Am)
cockamamie adj (Am) [type of decal: b1930]
crock n *as in "crock of bull"*
dullsville n
eighty-six v (noun use: b1940)
Endsville n (Am)
fantabulous adj
fink out v

gas n *something exciting*
gross adj *yucky*
hash n *hashish* (hashish: b1600)
herky-jerky adj
joyjuice n *liquor*
kinky adj *perverted* (kink "kinkiness": b1830; kink "kinky person": b1965)
leadfooted adj
munchies n (munchy: b1930)
OD n (verb use: b1970)
plugola n *akin to payola*
pothead n (Am)
screwup n (Am)
set up v *prepare for a joke; con* (setup: b1970)
shaft n *as in "get the shaft"*
smack n *heroin* [gen. "drug": b1945] (schmeck: b1935)
smashed adj *drunk*
snakebit adj *unlucky*
soul adj/n *pertaining to black experience*
soul brother n (soul sister: b1965)
straight adj *sober; as in "play it straight"*
strung out adj (Am)
swing v *be lively*
upmanship n *one-upmanship*
zonked adj (Am)

Insults

ball buster, ball breaker n b1955 (ball-busting: b1945)
crumbum n *crumb* b1955
fruitcake n *crazy person* b1955
goof-off n b1955
nerd n (Am) b1955
out to lunch adj b1955
skinhead n b1955
sleaze n b1955 ["sleaziness": b1970] (sleazy adj: b1635; sleazo: b1970; sleazebag, sleazeball: b1985)
slumlord n b1955
weirdo n b1955 (weirdie: b1805)
cube n *real square*
fuckup n
hardnose n (hardnosed: b1890)
hatemonger n
jarhead n

klutz n (Am)
kook, kookie n, adj
limp-wristed adj
motherfucker n (mother: b1950)

Phrases

backseat driver n b1955
balancing act n b1955
ball of wax n *as in "the whole ball of wax"* b1955
butt end n b1955
carrot-and-stick adj b1955 (carrot "incentive": b1900)
conflict of interest n b1955
cut-and-paste adj b1955
double whammy n b1955
down-to-the-wire adj b1955
end use n b1955
et alia adv b1955
free rein n b1955
front and center adv b1955
hack it v *manage* b1955
low blow n b1955
mother hen n b1955
mover and shaker n b1955
no contest n b1955
one-upmanship n b1955
security risk n b1955
sonic boom n b1955
standard operating procedure n b1955
tie one on v *get drunk* b1955
track record n b1955
all that jazz n
barn burner n
big picture n
chicken-and-egg adj
gal Friday n
global village n
happy pill n
last hurrah n
laundry list n
lead balloon n
Murphy's law n
no-frills adj
nuts and bolts n (adj use: b1965)
old boy network n
power base n
punch up v
response time n
square one n
think tank n (Am)

General/Miscellaneous

aficionada n b1955 (aficionado: b1845)
countdown n (Am) b1955
deinstitutionalization n b1955
do-it-yourself n b1955
edit n b1955
finest n b1955
hype n *deception* b1955 ["promotion": b1970] (verb use: b1930)
lotus position n b1955
module n *independent section* b1955 [related to measure: b1565] (modular: b1970)
printout/print out n b1955
rollout n b1955
set-in n *inset* b1955
signee n b1955
suction n *sucking* b1955 ["adhesion via vacuum": b1670; arch. "drinking": b1830] (verb use: b1955)
wrap-up n b1955
brinkmanship n
childproof adj/v
clout n ["tiny piece": b700; type of rag: b1200; "blow, strike": b1325]
for instance n
goop n
overkill n/v

Things

float glass n *type of glass*

Description

his/her adj b1955
jive adj *fake* b1955
live-in adj b1955
mini adj b1955
scattershot adj b1955
star-studded adj b1955
take-charge adj b1955
trailblazing adj b1955
vomitous adj *repulsive* b1955
counterproductive adj
in-house adj
multipronged adj
non-negotiable adj
self-adhesive adj

Colors

fire-engine red n b1955
clown white n

Actions/Verbs

automate v b1955 (automatize: b1840; automation: b1950)

bop v *as in "bop into the house"* b1955

bung up v *batter* b1955
cannonball v b1955
claw back v (Brit) *struggle to get back* b1955
downplay v b1955
opt out v b1955

piggyback v b1955
retrofit v (Am) b1955
showboat v *show off* b1955
talk out v b1955
wind down v b1955
crank out v

outperform v
rear-end v

IN USE BY
1970

Geography/Places
core city n b1965
dayside n b1965
inner city n b1965
hood n *neighborhood*
mantle n *Earth layer*
megacity n
plate tectonics n
sanitary landfill n
slurb n *suburban slum*
terraform v

Natural Things
antiquark n b1965
coevolution n b1965
quark n b1965
tachyon n 1967
convergent evolution n *coevolution*
ecocatastrophe n
ecocide n (Am)
threatened species n
weak force n

Plants
kiwifruit n

Animals
German wirehaired pointer n b1965
killer bee n b1965
apso n *type of dog*
bichon frise n
cockapoo n
petting zoo n
walking catfish n

Weather
chill factor n b1965

Heavens/Sky
intragalactic adj b1965
quasar, quasistellar radio source, quasistellar object n b1965
stellar wind n b1965
x-ray star n b1965
pulsar n 1968
black hole n
deep-sky adj
earthrise n
event horizon n

Science
charmed adj *in quantum physics* b1965
genetic code n b1965
high-energy physics n b1965
materials science n b1965
parallel evolution n b1965
R&D n b1965
white room n *clean room* b1965
x-ray astronomy n b1965
astrogeology n
background radiation n
cryptozoology n *study of mysterious creatures*
demographics n (demographic: b1885)
genetic engineering n
holograph n (holography: b1965)
informatics n *information science*
molecular genetics n
planetary science n

potassium-argon dating n
ripple effect n

Technology
ASCII n 1963
assembly language n b1965
central processing unit n b1965
cybernation n *type of automation* b1965
database n b1965
datamation n b1965
dot matrix n b1965
future shock n b1965
fuzzy logic n b1965
glitch n b1965
hardware n b1965
kludge n *jury-rigged computer system* b1965
lidar n *radar using light* b1965
mainframe n *type of computer* b1965
operating system n b1965
optical character recognition n b1965
optical fiber n b1965
program n/v b1965
read-only memory n b1965
technophobia, technofear n b1965
tracking station n b1965
uplink n b1965
voiceprint n b1965
xerox n/v b1965
BASIC n
bubble memory n
CAD/CAM n
chip n *as in "computer chip"*
computer language n
computernik n
CPU n

cursor n ["part of a slide rule": b1595]
data bank n
default n *standard specs*
downlink n
firmware n
hardwired adj
high technology n (high-tech: b1975)
icon n
interface n
light-emitting diode/LED n
magnetic bubble n
megabyte n
microchip n
microprocessor n
minicomputer n
multitasking n
peripheral n
pixel n
port n *as in "computer port"*
ROM n
supercomputer n
technetronic adj
technophile n (technomania: b1970)
thermal printer n
user-friendly adj

Energy
gigawatt n b1965
meltdown n b1965
energy crisis n (Am)
power up v

Age/Aging
golden-ager n b1965 (golden age: b1555)
preteenager n b1965
teenybopper, teenybop n, adj

Mathematics
precalculus n b1965

Measurement
key n (Am) *kilogram*
kilobyte n
klick n *kilometer*
point n *diamond weight*
tidge n *smidgeon*

The Body
dork n *slang penis* b1965
rotator cuff n b1965
spare tire n b1965
tushie, tush n *slang buttocks* b1965
biofeedback n
cellulite n
clit n (clitoris: b1615)
delts n *akin to pecs*
lats n *latissimus dorsi—akin to pecs*
pecs n
quads n *quadriceps*
ticker n *slang heart*

Medicine
anabolic steroid n 1961
antidepressant adj/n b1965
brain death n b1965
candy striper n b1965
cryonics n (Am) b1965
cryosurgery n b1965
denturist n b1965
Down's syndrome n b1965
emergency room n b1965
euphenics n *human improvement* b1965
intensive care n b1965
IUD n b1965
kissing disease n b1965
Lamaze adj b1965
mental illness n b1965 (mental health: b1835)
mono n b1965
Montezuma's revenge n (Am) *slang diarrhea* b1965
mouth-to-mouth resuscitation n b1965
rapid eye movement sleep/ REM sleep n b1965
runs n *diarrhea* b1965
Sabin vaccine n b1965
sperm bank n b1965
walking pneumonia n b1965
zit n b1965
alternative medicine n

aromatherapy n
beta blocker n
big C n *slang cancer*
bypass surgery n (Am)
caplet n
cryopreservation n
family practice n
genital herpes n
ibuprofen n
immunodeficiency n
jet lag n
medevac n
nurse-practitioner n
open-heart surgery n (open-heart adj: b1960)
pacemaker n (pacesetter: b1895)
physician's assistant n
quaalude n
surgicenter n
Tourette's syndrome n

Everyday Life
douche bag n b1965
fabric softener n b1965
garage sale n (Am) b1965
microwave oven, microwave n b1965
pop-top n (Am) b1965
pull tab n b1965
shrink-wrap n/v b1965
toaster oven n b1965
training wheels n b1965
tumble dry v b1965
blow-dry, blow-dryer v, n (blow-dried: b1980)
bumper sticker n
dispenser n *type of container*
epoxy n (adj use: b1920)
head restraint n
highlighter n
identification bracelet n
idiot light n
parsons table n
vanity n

Shelter/Housing
clean room n (Am) b1965
condo, condominium n (Am) b1965 [political sense "common rule": b1715]
gentrification n b1965 (gentrify: b1975)
hospitality suite n b1965
motor home n b1965
rec room n b1965
rent strike n b1965
bi-level n

double-wide n
floatel n
island n *isolated counter, etc.*
mid-rise n *buildings lower than a high-rise*
pullman kitchen n (Am)
sweat equity n
wall unit n
wet bar n

Drink
margarita n b1965 [type of wine: b1930]
cold duck n
eiswein n
rocks n *as in "on the rocks"*
screwdriver n
zombie n *drink*

Food
beef Wellington n b1965
Bibb lettuce n b1965
calamari n b1965
carbonara n b1965
carryout n b1965
doggie bag n (Am) b1965
fettuccini Alfredo n b1965
fish finger n *fish stick* b1965
fish protein concentrate n b1965
foodaholic n b1965
fortune cookie n b1965
meals-on-wheels n b1965
snow cone n b1965
soul food n (Am) b1965
teriyaki n b1965
tree ear n *type of mushroom* b1965
tube steak n *hot dog* b1965
beefsteak tomato n
charbroil v
chili dog n (Am)
chocoholic n
corn dog n (Am)
dirty rice n
empty calorie n (Am)
French dip n
gorp n
junk food n
lo mein n
lo-cal adj
nacho n
nondairy adj
white bean n

Agriculture/ Food-Gathering
landscaper n b1965
tiller n *cultivator*
vinify v

Cloth/Clothing
bolo tie n 1964
baggies n b1965
body stocking n b1965
kneesock n b1965
merry widow n *type of garment* b1965
miniskirt n b1965
pantdress n *dress with legs* b1965
pants suit n b1965 (pantsuit: b1970)
panty hose n b1965
permanent press n b1965
playwear n b1965
skiwear n b1965
support hose n b1965 (support stocking: b1970)
sweetheart neckline n b1965
unitard n *type of garment* b1965
aviator glasses n
body shirt n
dress code n
earth shoes n (Am)
fanny pack n
formalwear n
high-top adj (noun use: b1985)
hiphugger adj
hot pants n
irregular n
love beads n (Am)
maxi/maxiskirt n *type of dress*
micromini n *type of skirt* (micro: b1975)
midi/midiskirt n *type of dress*
negligee n *scanty nightwear* [type of gown: b1770; informal clothing: b1870]
Nehru jacket n
safari suit, safari shirt n (safari jacket: b1955)
ski mask n
thong n
top n

Fashion/Style
blusher n *cosmetic* b1965
body wave n b1965
razor cut n b1965

Afro n *the hair*
designer adj
fat farm n
granny glasses n
hot comb n
radical chic n
today adj

Tools

cherry picker n (Am) *type of crane* b1965
power drill n b1965
disposal n *the machine*
duct tape n
keypad n
portapak n

Travel/Transportation

chopper n (Am) *type of motorcycle* b1965
command module n b1965
fan-jet n b1965
fender bender n b1965
gypsy cab n (Am) b1965
jetport n b1965
jumbo jet n b1965
jump jet n b1965
minibike n b1965
mission control n b1965
oceanaut n (Am) b1965
off-road adj b1965
pace car n b1965
radial tire n b1965
retrofire v (Am) b1965
SST n b1965
standby n b1965
travel trailer n b1965
visitor center n b1965
Wankel engine n b1965
wheelie n b1965
woody n b1965
air bag n
all-terrain vehicle n
boarding pass n
bullet train n
carry-on adj
charter n (verb use: b1800)
choke n *type of valve*
commuter tax n
containership n *type of ship*
cruise control n
Denver boot n
dirt bike n
drive n *as in "four-wheel drive"*
drive time n
funny car n
gas guzzler n

glasphalt n *type of road surface*
grand touring car n
GT n
hatchback n
hog n *type of motorcycle*
interstate n
jet n *jet engine, plane*
limo n (Am)
lunar module n
mag wheel n
midsize adj
monohull n
moonwalk n (Am)
muscle car n
pad n *as in "launch pad"*
people mover n
recreational vehicle/RV n
red-eye n
roll cage n (roll bar: b1955)
rotary n
rumble strip n
scramjet n
shoulder n *of a road*
shoulder belt n
sissy bar n (Am)
space shuttle n (Am)
subcompact n
trail bike n
trunk n *car storage*
vanity plate n
wide-body n *type of airplane*

Emotions/ Characteristics

bummer n b1965
downer n b1965
midlife crisis n b1965
blahs n
conflicted adj
dedication, dedicated n, adj *perseverance, determination*
laid-back adj
outgoing adj *gregarious* ["going out, exiting": b1635]
pop off v *speak angrily*
self-deprecating adj
shell-shocked adj
support group n
survivor syndrome n
tither n *dither*
TLC n
type A, type B adj *describing personality types*

Thoughts/Perception/ The Mind

mind-bending adj b1965
mind-boggling adj b1965
mind-expanding adj b1965
pop psych n b1965
prisoner of conscience n (Am) b1965
psych out v b1965 (noun use: b1975)
streetwise adj b1965 (street-smart: b1975)
transactional analysis n b1965
basket case n
block n *as in "mental block"*
ego trip n
futuristics n
get v *understand*
lateral thinking n
mindblowing adj
read v *understand, as in "do you read me?"*
short-term memory n
shrink n *psychiatrist*
smarts n *intelligence*
transcendental meditation n
wigged-out adj

Love/Romance/Sex

group sex n (Am) b1965
S and M n b1965
score n *prostitute's john* b1965
sex-bomb n b1965
swing, swinging v, n *change sexual partners* b1965
bi adj *bisexual*
cheat v *commit adultery*
escort n *date*
hand job n
item n
live-in lover n
main squeeze n ["muckamuck": b1900]
roll n *as in "a roll in the hay"*
romance v *woo* (noun use: b1830)
sex therapy n
shtup v *slang have sex*
whack off v

Family/Relations/ Friends

empty nester n b1965
single parent n
stepfamily n

Games/Fun/Leisure

exacta n b1965
slot racing, slot car n b1965
blast n *extreme fun* 1966 ["party": b1960]
Frisbee n
hangman n

Sports

floor exercise n b1965
frostbiting n *cold-weather sailing* b1965
isometrics, isometric exercise n b1965
jock n *athlete* b1965
sailboard n (Am) b1965
skateboard n b1965
stationary bicycle n b1965
triple jump n b1965
astroturf n 1966
aerobics n
compulsory n
decathlete n (decathlon: b1915)
downhiller n
instant replay n (Am)
jog, jogging v, n *exercise* ["trudge": b1570] (noun use: b1635)
parasailing n
perfecta n
racquetball n
rally n *type of motor race*
reps n *repetitions*
slow-pitch n
tae kwon do n
team handball n
tuck n *position in diving*
windsurfing, windsurfer n
wrist wrestling n

Professions/Duties

publicist n ["expert in public affairs": b1795; "public affairs writer": b1870]
stripper n

Business/Commerce/ Selling

bar code n b1965
convenience store n b1965
crisis management n b1965
go public v b1965
happy hour n b1965
ma-and-pa adj b1965
nonrefundable adj b1965
power broker n (Am) b1965

pre-owned adj b1965
service center n b1965
swap meet n b1965
bait and switch n
cash bar n
comparison shop v
conglomerate n (Am) *business group*
conglomerateur n
cost-effective/cost-efficient adj
diversify v
generic n *non-brand-name product*
head shop n (Am)
hostile merger n
hypermarket n
market share n
planned obsolescence n
pop for v *slang pay for*
rebate v [obs. "subtract": b1400 to 1700s; obs. "discount": b1530 to 1600s] (noun use: b1570)
service industry n
sticker price n
supermart n
upmarket adj *upscale*

The Workplace
equal opportunity employer n b1965
paper trail n b1965
risk management n b1965
sick day n b1965
working lunch n b1965
blue flu n
job action n (Am)
outplacement n
paperless adj
shitwork n
workaholic n
workfare n *work(wel)fare*

Finances/Money
off-the-books adj b1965
old money n b1965
sin tax n b1965
spreadsheet n *type of ledger* b1965 [computer sense: b1985]
stagflation n b1965
tax shelter n b1965
blind trust n 1969
bottom line n (adj use: b1975)
down-market adj
insider trading n

monetarism n (Am) *type of economic theory*
not-for-profit adj
revolving charge account n
tax break n
top dollar n
user fee n
zero-based adj

Language and Speaking
franglais n b1965
nonword n b1965
oracy n *or(al)(liter)acy* b1965
second language n b1965
Black English n
code word n *euphemism*
interlanguage n *creole*
interrobang n (Am) *?!*

Contractions
'til conj/prep

Literature/Writing
coffee-table book n b1965
datebook n b1965
leaflet v b1965
lit crit n b1965
parajournalism n *subjective journalism* b1965
popup book n b1965
speed-reading n b1965
tab n *tabloid* b1965
advocacy journalism n
aliterate adj (aliteracy: b1985)
faction n *nonfiction with fiction elements*
found poem n
hypertext n
instant book n
large-print adj
legal pad n
metafiction n
micropublishing n
New Journalism n
op-ed n (Am) *opposite the editorial page*
packager n *type of publisher*
police procedural n
pulp n *type of magazine*
shopper n *advertising paper*
word processing, word processor n

Communication
zip code n 1963
answering machine n b1965

area code n b1965
data link n b1965
miscommunication n b1965 (miscommunicate: b1670)
mixed media n b1965
multimedia adj/n b1965
Brand X n
earth station n
exchange n *dialogue*
pager n *beeper*
polylogue n *akin to monologue, dialogue*
press kit n
telecopier n *fax machine*

Visual Arts/Photography
exploded view n b1965
flashcube n b1965 (flashbulb: b1935)
junk art n b1965
kinetic art n b1965
minimal art n b1965
neo-Expressionism n b1965
optical art/op art n b1965
photorealism n b1965
art deco n
conceptual art n
cutaway adj *in drawing*
deco n
decorative art n
minimalism, minimalist n
paparazzo n
soft sculpture n

Performing Arts
cold reading n b1965
guerrilla theater n b1965
schtick n b1965
theater of the absurd n b1965
pancake n *type of makeup*
read v *audition*
stand-up n [type of comedy: b1975]
standing ovation n

Music
amp n b1965
bossa nova n b1965
folk-pop n b1965
folkie n b1965
playlist n b1965
recording engineer n b1965
reel-to-reel adj b1965
ska n *type of music* b1965
soul music n (Am) b1965

third-stream music n b1965
reggae n 1968
acid rock n
axe n *slang guitar* [gen. "musical instrument": b1955] (axeman: b1980)
cover version, cover n *rerecording*
cut n/v *selection, as in "a cut from her latest album"; as in "cut a record"*
doo-wop n
fingerpicking n *style of musicianship*
folk rock n
golden oldie n (Am)
graphic equalizer n
hard rock n
headbanger n *heavy metal fan*
jazz-rock n
jingle n *commercial song*
jive v
lead n
mellotron n *type of musical instrument*
one-hit wonder n
pedal steel n (Am) *type of musical instrument*
quad, quadraphonic adj/n, adj
rap n
rap music n
roadie n
rock n *rock music* (rock and roll: 1951)
single n *single record*
soft rock n
stereo n *stereophonic sound; stereo system*
supergroup n
top 40 adj/n
wa-wa pedal n

Entertainment
a-go-go n/adj b1965
disco n (Am) b1965 ["the music": b1975] (verb use: b1980; discotheque: b1955)
light show n b1965
lip-synch v b1965
black adj *as in "black comedy"*
hootenanny n ["gadget": b1915]
knee-slapper n
one-liner n (Am)
twist n *type of dance*

Movies/TV/Radio

cable television n b1965 (cable, cablevision: b1975)
canned laughter n (Am) b1965
cinema verité n b1965
filmography n b1965
laugh track n b1965
on camera adv b1965
public television n b1965
sitcom n b1965 (situation comedy: b1945)
talk show n b1965
time slot n b1965
airplay n
boob tube n
broadcast journalism n
chat show n (Brit) *talk show*
cinematheque n
coanchor n/v
counterprogramming n
satellite TV n
skinflick n
snow n *bad TV reception*
spaghetti western n
stag film n
televisual adj
toon n *(car)toon*
video disk n
videocassette n
X-rated adj

Education

halls of ivy n b1965
language laboratory n b1965
multiversity n b1965
noncredit adj *as in "noncredit courses"* b1965
programmed instruction n b1965
teach-in n b1965
free university n
grade point average n
magnet school n
minicourse n *type of class*
minischool n
postdoc n/adj *postdoctoral*
women's studies n

Religion

born-again adj b1965
folk mass n b1965

Society/Mores/Culture

beautiful people n b1965
biodegradable adj b1965 (biodegrade v: b1975)
culturati n b1965
hippie n (Am) b1965 ["hipster": b1955]
sexist adj/n b1965 (sexism: b1970)
sexual discrimination n b1965
thermal pollution n b1965
tokenism n b1965
affinity group n
ageism n
anti-utopia n
antidrug adj
chauvinism n *sexism* ["patriotism": b1970]
consciousness-raising n (Am)
counterculture n
downscale adj *lower-end*
encounter group n
first world n
flower child, flower people, flower power n
gender gap n
green card n
lib, libber n (Am)
love-in n (Am)
male chauvinism n
multiethnic adj
peace sign, peace symbol n
recreational drug use n
reverse discrimination n
sophisticate v *enculturate, cultivate* (noun use: b1925; sophistication: b1870; sophisticated: b1900)
street people n
white flight n
women's liberation n
yippie n
youthquake n
zero population growth n

Government

Oval Office n (Am) gen. *"the presidency"* b1965
assemblywoman n (Am) (assemblyman: b1650; assemblyperson: b1975)
Company, the n *CIA*
participatory democracy n

Politics

affirmative action n 1965
domino effect, domino theory n b1965
military-industrial complex n b1965
pro-life adj b1965
third world n b1965
gavel-to-gavel adj
groupuscle n
gun control n
protest singer n
second world n *the communist world*
sisterhood n *feminist sense*
summit n *summit conference*

Death

crib death n b1965
euthanize v b1965
waste v *kill* b1965
autocide n *suicide using a car*
buy the farm v
death squad n
ice v *kill*
off v *kill* ["die": b1930]
pseudocide n
serial killer n
sudden infant death syndrome/SIDS n

War/Military/Violence

claymore mine n b1965
clothesline v b1965
cluster bomb n b1965
counterinsurgency n b1965
de-escalate, de-escalation v b1965
dove n *as in "hawks and doves"* b1965
Green Beret n b1965
grunt n b1965
gunnery sergeant n b1965
hawk n b1965
militaria adj b1965
payload n b1965
surgical strike n b1965
water cannon n b1965
weapons delivery system n b1965
weapons-grade uranium n b1965
agent orange n (Am)
armor n *armored vehicles*
body count n
collateral damage n
firebase n
frag v (Am)
free-fire zone n
gunship n
M16 n
Mace n/v *spray with Mace*
ninja n
nunchaku n
passive restraint n
plastic bullet n
preemptive strike n
presence n
riot shield n
Saturday night special n (Saturday night pistol: b1930)
self-destruct adj/v (Am)
stun gun n
suicide squad n
trash v *destroy* ["insult": b1975]
unit n *as in "military unit"*
urban guerilla n

Crime/Punishment/Enforcement

battered child n b1965
capo n *crime boss* b1965
glue sniffing n (Am) b1965
launder v b1965
man, the n *slang police* b1965 ["authority": b1920]
skyjack v b1965
victimless crime n b1965
yakuza n *Japanese crime syndicate* b1965
angel dust n
decriminalize v (Am)
drug pusher n
family n *mob*
five-finger discount n
gang rape n/v
hard drugs n
hit man n (hit v: b1955; hit n: b1970)
jailhouse lawyer n
narc n (Am) (narco: b1960)
pad n *graft, as in "on the pad"*
PCP n
petnapping n (Am)
policeperson n (policeman: b1805; policewoman: b1855)
push, pusher v, n
skim v
skin search n
skyjack v
speed v *go too fast*
ticket n/v *as in "speeding ticket"*

The Law

deregulate, deregulation v, n b1965
plea bargaining n (Am)

b1965 (plea-bargain v:
b1970)
informed consent n
leash law n
Miranda adj
penalty clause n

The Fantastic/ Paranormal

Bermuda triangle n b1965
tooth fairy n b1965
out-of-body adj
super-real n *surreal, beyond the real*

Interjections

no way interj b1965 (adv use: b1350)
vroom interj/v b1965
yay interj b1965
Chrissake interj
damn interj (adj/adv use: b1775)
tsk interj
yecch interj
yipe interj
yowza interj
yuck interj

Slang

fab adj 1961
bomb n *failure* b1965
camp n *the amusingly out of date* b1965 ["a homosexual": b1935] (adj use: b1910; campy: b1960)
circular file n *wastebasket* b1965
codswallop n (Brit) b1965
come out of the closet v b1965
cookie-cutter adj b1965
diddly, diddly-squat n (Am) b1965
fox n *sensuous woman* b1965 (foxy: b1930)
freak v *as in "freak out"* b1965
freaking adj/adv b1965
grungy, grunge adj, n (Am) b1965
happening n *event* b1965
hotdog v (Am) b1965
lie-in n *akin to sit-in* b1965
loosey-goosey adj b1965
lowball v b1965
nitty-gritty adj/n (Am) b1965

nonevent n b1965
nonissue n b1965
peacenik n (Am) b1965
plotzed adj (Am) *drunk* b1965
pop v *as in "pop pills"* b1965
pseud n (Brit) b1965
pussy-whip n *henpeck* b1965 (pussy-whipped: b1975)
put-down n b1965
scam n/v b1965
snockered adj (Am) *drunk* b1965
speed freak n b1965
sucker punch n/v b1965
unreal adj b1965
upper n *type of drug* b1965
wiped out adj b1965 (wiped: b1960)
x-section n *cross-section* b1965
yuck v *as in "yuck it up"* b1965
z's n *sleep* b1965
acid, acid head n 1966 (acid trip: b1970)
Amerika n (Amerikkka: b1975)
ax v *eliminate, cut*
biker n
bind n *fix, tough spot*
blindside v (noun use: b1610)
blow n *cocaine*
blow it v
broad-brush adj
bubblegum adj *of adolescent interest*
buzz n *drug or alcohol high*
carb/carbo n
charge n *as in "get a charge out of life"*
cheapo adj (noun use: b1975)
closet queen n
crash v *sleep*
crown jewels n
druggie n (Am)
ecofreak n
fantasyland n
feedback n *gen. response*
freak-out n (freak out v: b1965)
front burner n
frontlash n *backlash to a backlash*
fucked-up adj (fuck up: b1955)

gangle v *be gangly* (gangling: b1810; gangly: b1875)
GIGO n *garbage in, garbage out*
glitzy adj (glitz: b1970)
gofer n
grody adj
gross out v (gross-out: b1975)
groupie n
hang in v
humongous adj (Am)
hunk (hunky: b1980)
hype n/v *promote*
into adj *a fan of*
jones n *addiction*
knockoff n *imitation*
main man n
mau-mau v *hostile intimidation*
number n *as in "do a number on someone"*
Panama Red n *type of marijuana*
panda car n (Brit) *black-and-white police car*
pec n
penguin suit n
pop n *power*
psychedelia n (Am)
ralph v *vomit*
rap n *as in "rap session"* (verb use: b1930)
rap group n *discussion group*
revolving-door adj
rip-off, rip off n, v
roach clip n (roach: b1940)
rug rat n (Am) *child*
scag n *heroin* ["cigarette": b1915]
scumbag n *condom* ["low-life": b1975]
sell out v
shitkicker n
sickie, sicko n
sleazy adj *scuzzy*
speed n *amphetamine* (verb use: b1975)
squeaky-clean adj
steal n *bargain*
suss v
touchy-feely adj
toughie n *difficult challenge*
turned-on adj
turnon, turnoff n (Am) (turn on v: b1905)
vibe/vibes/vibrations n (Am)
wasted adj *drunk*
whacked-out adj

whistle-blower n
window n *as in "window of opportunity"*
wired adj *high*
wrecker's ball n (Am)
yucky adj
zilch n
zonk out *fall asleep*

Insults

doofus n (Am) b1965
flaky, flake n/adj *loony tune* b1965
poor-mouth n/v b1965
ratfink n b1965
shithead n b1965
spaz n b1965 (spaz out: b1985)
Ugly American n b1965
weenie n *jerk* b1965 ["tot": b1870; girl: b1929]
bananas adj *crazy*
dickhead n
dirtbag n
gomer n *dimwit*
male chauvinist n
pointy-head n
scuzz, scuzzy n, adj (scuzzbag, scuzzbucket: b1985)
talking head n
yoyo n *loony tune*

Phrases

catch-22 n 1961
all systems go interj (Am) b1965
ballpark, ballpark figure n b1965
beach bum n b1965
brain drain n b1965
brownie point n b1965
can of worms n b1965
case in point n b1965
checkbook journalism n b1965
cop out v b1965 (noun use: b1945)
dog and pony show n b1965
eyeball-to-eyeball adj/adv b1965
fat city n (Am) b1965
fetal position n b1965
fudge factor n b1965
funny farm n b1965
hone in v b1965
no-win situation n b1965
off-the-rack adj b1965
power play n b1965

real time n b1965

real-world, real world adj, n b1965

time frame n b1965

zero out v *factor out* b1965

arm and a leg n

bells and whistles n

benign neglect n

blow your mind v

creative accounting n

credibility gap n

cut it v (Am) *make the grade*

down and dirty adj/adv

dry out v *get sober*

du jour adj

el cheapo adj

fag hag n

good old boy n

high five n/v

high profile adj/n

lighten up v

liquid lunch n

naked ape n

name of the game n

noise pollution n

number cruncher n

off-the-wall adj

one-on-one adj/adv/n

out to lunch adj

quick fix n (adj use: b1980)

security blanket n

straight arrow n

tip of the iceberg n

General/Miscellaneous

boilerplate n *standard* b1965

disposable adj/n *discardable* b1965

in-joke n b1965

matchup n b1965

phasedown n b1965

---

porn adj/v b1965

raunch n (Am) b1965

thrust n *gist* b1965

ticky-tacky adj/n b1965

trade-off n b1965

update n b1965 (verb use: b1910)

zap n b1965 (zappy: b1970)

bricolage n *something jury-rigged*

deck n *as in "tape deck"*

dissensus n *opp. of consensus*

go-ahead n *permission*

no-fault adj/n

overview n [obs. "watching": b1550 to 1600s]

pack n *as in "mudpack"* (verb use: b1800)

project, projection v, n *extrapolate, extrapolation*

sampler n *assortment* (sampler: b1780)

soundalike n

survivalist n

synergy, synergistic n, adj

tight adj *without margin, as in "tight schedule"*

unisex adj/n

vérité n

what-if n

yogini n *woman yogi* [type of demon: b1885] (yogi: b1620)

Things

sleeve n *cover*

two-way mirror n

Description

go-go adj b1965

hard-line adj (Am) b1965

in-depth adj b1965

reclosable adj b1965

---

trendy adj b1965

worst-case adj b1965

ballpark adj *as in "a ballpark estimate"*

Bunyanesque adj

clunky adj

drop-dead adj

earth-shattering adj

exclusive adj *as in "an exclusive club"*

fallaway adj

fast-track adj (verb use: b1975; noun use: b1980)

functional adj *practical*

hands-on adj

heliborne adj *akin to airborne*

ho-hum adj (interj use: b1925)

soft-core adj *as in "soft-core porn"*

spare adj *simple*

tight adj *close, as in "tight friends"*

toll-free adj

zappy adj

Colors

aqua n

Day-Glo adj

Actions/Verbs

demystify v b1965

deselect v b1965

interface v b1965 (noun use: b1885)

keyboard v b1965

log in v b1965

prioritize v b1965

rack up v b1965

skinny-dip v (Am) b1965

access v (noun use: b1300)

---

ace out v

assess v *as in "assess the situation"* (assessment: b1630; assessor: b1870)

audit v *as in "audit a course"* (auditor: b1385; audition: b1600)

bleep v (noun use: b1955)

bobble v *drop* ["bob while moving": b1820]

clear v *approve, as in "clear the idea with the boss"*

compound v *exacerbate*

cover v *substitute, as in "cover for a sick employee"*

double-deal v

fake out v

jive v *jibe*

juke v *fake; move quickly*

latch v *as in "latch onto"* [obs. "grab," "seize": b950 to 1600s; obs. "catch": b1570]

lose v *throw away*

operate, operational v, adj *function, work*

process v *as in "process an application"*

proliferate v *fig. increase* [spec. biological sense: b1875]

pull v *as in "pull a muscle"*

rip off v (Am) (rip v: b1930)

skip v *as in "skip over"*

slap v *as in "slap with a penalty"*

stem v *originate*

swing v *accomplish*

trail v *as in "the home team is trailing 4-3"*

trip v *take a drug trip* (noun use: b1930)

IN USE BY
1980

Geography/Places
burbs n *suburbs* b1975

Natural Things
Gaia hypothesis n b1975
gluon n *type of quark* b1975
green adj *environmental* b1975

Animals
Chinese shar-pei n b1975
snail darter n b1975
tiger shrimp n

Weather
weatherperson n b1975
downburst n

Heavens/Sky
megastar n b1975
singularity n b1975
white hole n b1975
cosmic background radiation n
missing mass n
open universe n

Science
genetic screening n b1975
collider n
garbology n
gene mapping v
gene splicing n
grand unified theory n

Technology
AI n (Am) *artificial intelligence* b1975
computer literacy n b1975
disk drive n b1975
diskette n b1975
floppy, floppy disk n b1975

gigabyte n b1975
high tech adj/n b1975 (high-technology: b1970)
ink-jet adj b1975
LCD n b1975
microcomputer n b1975
motherboard n b1975
pocket calculator n b1975
scroll v b1975
upload v b1975
beta test n
bulletin board n (Am)
computerphobe n
daisy wheel n
download v
graphics tablet n
hard disk n
home computer n
laser disc n
laser printer n
log on v
optical disk n
personal computer/pc n
techie n
touch pad n

Energy
gasohol n
solar energy, solar power n (solar battery, solar cell, solar collector: b1950; solar panel: b1960)
wind farm n

Time
leap second n *akin to leap year* b1975

Age/Aging
bopper n *teeny-bopper*

Mathematics
fractal n 1975

The Body
endorphin n b1975
love handles n *slang folds of fat* b1975
beer gut n (beer belly: b1945)

Medicine
Heimlich maneuver n (Am) 1974
birth defect n b1975
cardiopulmonary resuscitation/CPR n b1975
caregiver n b1975
CAT scan/CAT scanner n b1975
EMT n b1975
extended care n b1975
family practice n b1975
hair transplant n b1975
health maintenance organization/HMO n b1975
in vitro fertilization n b1975
killer cell n b1975
minimum brain dysfunction n b1975
passive smoking n b1975
post-traumatic stress disorder n b1975
postnatal depression n b1975
test-tube baby n b1975
attention deficit disorder n
emergency medical technician n
hearing ear dog n
Legionnaires' disease n
Lyme disease n
quad n *quadriplegic*
radial keratotomy n
secondhand smoke n

sleep apnea n
toxic shock syndrome n

Everyday Life
beanbag chair n b1975
convection oven n b1975
floss v *as in "floss teeth"* b1975
food processor n b1975
hot tub n (Am) b1975
house sitter n b1975 (house sit v: b1980)
paper-train v b1975
pooperscooper n b1975
sleep sofa n b1975
snooze button n b1975
sunblock n b1975
track lighting n b1975
yard sale n b1975
industrial-strength adj
slow cooker n

Shelter/Housing
earth-sheltered adj
starter home n

Drink
shooter n *type of drink* b1975

Food
batter v *coat food with batter* b1975 (noun use: b1385)
beefalo n b1975
chiliburger n (Am) b1975
fork-tender adj *very tender* b1975
gyro n *Greek sandwich* b1975
nouvelle cuisine n b1975
salad bar n b1975
saturated fat n b1975
serrano n *type of pepper* b1975

surf and turf n b1975
tollhouse cookie n b1975
canola oil n
fajita n
trail mix n

Agriculture/ Food-Gathering
leghold trap n b1975

Cloth/Clothing
flares n *type of pants* b1975
jammies n b1975
leisure suit n (Am) b1975
platform shoe n b1975
spaghetti strap n b1975
wafflestomper n (Am) b1975
bustier n
camp shirt n
tube sock n
underwire n

Fashion/Style
cornrow n/v *hairstyle* b1975
hair implant, hair transplant n b1975
mousse n *for hair* b1975 (verb use: b1985)
retro adj b1975
shag n *hair style* b1975
eyelift n *akin to facelift*
hair gel n

Tools
mister n *device that mists* b1975
microcassette n

Travel/Transportation
antilock adj b1975
speed bump n b1975
stretch limo n b1975
ten-speed n b1975
U-ey n *slang U-turn* b1975
vanpool n b1975
yellow light n b1975 (red light: b1850; green light: b1940)
buckle up v
econobox n
eighteen-wheeler n
gridlock n (Am)
performance car n
supersaver n (Am)
ultralight n (adj use: b1975)
V6 n

Emotions/ Characteristics
bummed adj *slang disappointed* b1975
confrontational adj b1975
gut-wrenching adj b1975
support system n

Thoughts/Perception/ The Mind
deprogram v (Am) b1975
head case n b1975
nutso adj (Am) *loony* b1975 (nuts: b1850; nutty: b1900; nutsy: b1945)
primal scream therapy n (Am) b1975
street smarts, street-smart n, adj b1975 (streetwise: b1960)
wacko adj/n (Am) b1975 (wacky n: b1870; wack n: b1940)
knowledge engineering n
right brain n

Love/Romance/Sex
dominatrix n b1975 [limited use: b1565]
get off v (Am) *have orgasm* b1975
open marriage n b1975
relationship n b1975
serial monogamy n b1975 (serial marriage: b1970)
sex clinic n b1975
singlehood n b1975
squeeze n *lover*

Family/Relations/ Friends
natural family planning n b1975
surrogate mother n b1975 (surrogacy: b1985)
domestic partner n
stepparenting n

Games/Fun/Leisure
skybox n b1975
video game n b1975
cruciverbalist n *crossword puzzler*

Sports
arm wrestling n b1975
bench press n/v b1975

color announcer n b1975
colorman n b1975
slam-dunk n b1975
tractor pull n b1975
triathlon n b1975 (triathlete: b1985)
trifecta n b1975
boardsailing n
bungee jumping n
heli-skiing n
minicamp n
pump iron v
T-ball n

Professions/Duties
camerawoman n b1975 (cameraman: b1910; cameraperson: b1980)
chairperson n b1975 (chairman: b1650; chairwoman: b1685)
sanitation engineer n *garbageman* b1975
spokesperson n b1975 (spokespeople: b1975)
waitperson n (waiter: b1530; waitress: b1835; waitron: b1985)

Business/Commerce/ Selling
CEO n b1975
layaway plan n b1975
megacorporation n b1975
open bar n b1975
Universal Product Code n b1975
infomercial n
suit n *slang executive*
telemarketing n

The Workplace
comp n *as in "workman's comp"* b1975
downsize v (Am) b1975
entry-level adj b1975
ESOP n *employee stock option plan* b1975
flextime, flexible time n b1975
paternity leave n b1975
person-hour n b1975
revenue sharing n b1975
telecommuting n b1975
micromanage v
pink-collar adj *akin to blue-collar, white-collar*
quality circle n

terminate v
union scale n

Finances/Money
bean counter n b1975
cashless society n (Am) b1975
individual retirement account, IRA n b1975
petrodollar n b1975
plastic n *credit card* b1975
T-bill n (Am) b1975
tax bracket n b1975
APR n
bracket creep n *in taxes*
debit card n
demand-side adj
electronic banking n
junk bond n
supply-side adj

Language and Speaking
s/he pron b1975
grapholect n *written language*
pound sign n

Literature/Writing
deconstruct, deconstruction v, n b1975
investigative journalism n b1975
page-turner n b1975
procedural n *type of mystery novel* b1975
self-published adj b1975
bodice ripper n
electronic publishing n
freewriting n
interactive fiction n
letter-quality adj/n
videotext n

Communication
teletext n b1975
videoconferencing n b1975
800 number n
car phone n (Am)
electronic mail n
junk call n *akin to junk mail*
signage n

Visual Arts/ Photography
fabric sculpture n b1975
performance art n b1975

Music

art rock n b1975
audiocassette n b1975
crossover n b1975
disco n 1975 [type of club: b1965]
glam-rock n b1975
glitter rock n b1975
heavy metal n b1975
punk rock n b1975
salsa n b1975
sequencer n b1975
western swing n b1975
compact disc/CD n
elevator music n
fusion n
ghetto blaster n
punker, punk n
techno-pop n

Entertainment

prequel n b1975
animatronics n
slam dance n/v

Movies/TV/Radio

blaxploitation n 1972
airdate n b1975
anchorperson, anchorpeople, anchorwoman n b1975 (anchorman, anchor: b1960)
cable n cable TV b1975
cablevision n b1975 (cable television: b1965)
family hour n b1975
happy talk n b1975
maxiseries n akin to miniseries b1975
miniseries n b1975
pay cable n b1975
public-access television n b1975
sensurround n b1975
sound bite n b1975
splatter movie n b1975
videocassette recorder/VCR n b1975
videography, videographer n b1975
closed-captioned adj
colorize v [gen. sense: b1630]
noir adj/n film style; fiction style
pay-per-view adj/n
veejay n

Education

alternative school n b1975
courseware n classroom software b1975
open classroom n b1975
tenure-track adj

Religion

televangelist n b1975
creation science n (creationism: b1850)
fourth world n poorer than third world b1975

Society/Mores/Culture

bicoastal adj b1975
crisis center n b1975
female chauvinism n b1975
free beach n nude beach b1975
herstory n b1975
hyphenate n as in a "hyphenated person" b1975
layperson n b1975
light pollution n b1975
male bonding n b1975
Puritan ethic n b1975
singles bar n b1975
speciesism n b1975
community service n
helpline n
heterosexism n
NIMBY n Not In My BackYard
nonsexist adj
sexual harassment n
womyn n

Government

assemblyperson n (Am) b1975 (assemblyman: b1650; assemblywoman: b1970)
congressperson, congresspeople n b1975
councilperson n (councilman: b1640; councilwoman: b1930)

Politics

pro-choice adj b1975
proabortion adj b1975
right-to-life adj b1975
shuttle diplomacy n b1975
exit poll n
nonvoter n

Death

terminate v b1975
hit squad n
roadkill n (Am)

War/Military/Violence

ABM n (Am) 1972
assault rifle n b1975
autodestruct v b1975
baby batterer n b1975
car bomb n b1975
enlisted woman n b1975 (enlisted man: b1715; enlistee: b1960)
friendly fire n b1975
gulag n b1975
hired gun n b1975
knuckle sandwich n b1975
mail bomb n b1975
nightscope n b1975
punch out v b1975
rubber bullet n b1975
serviceperson n b1975 (serviceman: b1900; servicewoman: b1945)
smart bomb n b1975

Crime/Punishment/Enforcement

child abuse n b1975
correctional facility, corrections officer n (Am) b1975
electronic surveillance n b1975
freebase v/n (Am) b1975
kneecapping n b1975
mechanic n hit man b1975
sinsemilla n type of marijuana b1975
snuff film n b1975
street crime n b1975
chop shop n
graymail n akin to blackmail
prior n prior convictions (previous n: b1935)
pyro n pyromaniac

The Law

foreperson n of a jury b1975 (foreman: b1630; forewoman: b1730)
living will n b1975
paralegal adj/n b1975
shield law n b1975
sunshine law n b1975
palimony n (Am)

The Fantastic/Paranormal

channeling n b1975 (channeler: b1990)

Interjections

uh-oh interj b1975

Slang

factoid n (Am) 1973
baby boomer n b1975 (baby boom: b1945)
blasted adj drunk b1975
bong n b1975
BYOB n b1975
chill, chill out v (Am) b1975
crapshoot n/v b1975
detox adj/n/v (Am) b1975
double-dipper n b1975
ecotage n sabotage of ecology b1975
excess v doublespeak, make excess b1975
foxy adj sexy b1975
gonzo adj b1975
gross-out n b1975 (gross out v: b1970)
hardball n b1975
jay n marijuana cigarette b1975
media event n b1975
mediagenic adj b1975
melons n b1975
motormouth n b1975
munchkin n b1975
no-brainer n b1975
one-note adj b1975
psychobabble n b1975
radwaste n radioactive waste b1975
scope out v b1975
shoot up v take drugs b1975
suck v as in "the TV show sucks" b1975
welfare hotel n b1975
white-knuckle v b1975
awesome adj
bleeping adj
class act n
contempo adj contempo(rary)
crapola n
feel-good adj (Am)
fern bar n (Am)
heartstopper n
malling n
pig out v
veg out v

white-bread adj
wicked adv
wifty adj *dizzy*

Insults
airhead n *dolt* b1975
cornpone adj b1975
ditsy/ditzy adj (Am) b1975
  (ditz n: b1985)
dork n (Am) *twit* b1975
dragon lady n b1975
hard-ass n b1975 (adj use:
  b1975)
ho n *whore* b1975
scumbag n b1975 ["condom": b1975]
wiseass n b1975
candy ass adj/n (Am)
grinch n

Phrases
assertiveness training n 1975
back burner n b1975

bargaining chip n b1975
cheap shot n b1975
day one n b1975
deep throat n b1975
dirty tricks n b1975
empty-nest syndrome n
  b1975
eyes only adj b1975
feeding frenzy n b1975
hidden agenda n b1975
hit list n b1975
hot ticket n b1975
human resources n b1975
keep a low profile v b1975
living history n b1975
low profile n b1975
nail-biter n *close call* b1975
needle park n b1975
photo opportunity n b1975
quick-and-dirty adj b1975
smoking gun n b1975
visual literacy n b1975
wish list n b1975

boat people n 1977
bully pulpit n
bunker mentality n *operating
  as if under siege*
couch potato n
deep pocket n
gender bender n
go for it v
heavy hitter n
loose cannon n
top gun n
touch base v
window of opportunity n
window of vulnerability n

General/Miscellaneous
jump-start n/v b1975
lockdown n b1975
cooldown n
passalong n

Description
complicit adj b1975
cutesy-poo adj b1975

eyeball adj b1975
faux adj *imitation* b1975
in-kind adj b1975
full-bore adj/adv
high-end adj

Colors
earth tone n b1975 (earth
  color: b1935)

Actions/Verbs
bug off v b1975
grandfather v b1975
mainstream v b1975
degenderize v

IN USE BY
1990

Natural Things
force of nature n b1985
biodiversity n
fullerene n
global warming n

Animals
deer tick n b1985

Weather
microburst n *type of storm* b1985

Heavens/Sky
cosmic string n *hypothetical astronomical phenomenon* b1985
dark matter n b1985

Science
biochip n b1985
designer gene n b1985
supercollider n b1985
artificial reality n
cold fusion n
genetic fingerprinting n
Theory of Everything n

Technology
CD-ROM n b1985
desktop computer n b1985
expansion slot n b1985
laptop adj/n b1985
local area network/LAN n b1985
low-tech adj b1985
reverse-engineer v b1985
shareware n *public domain software* b1985
sysop n *systems operator* b1985

vaporware n *software yet to be released* b1985
virus n b1985
WYSIWYG adj b1985
computer virus n
cyberspace n
digital audio tape/DAT n
nanotechnology n
palmtop n *type of small computer*
virtual reality n

The Body
G spot n

Physical Description
challenged adj (Am) *disadvantaged*

Medicine
acquired immune deficiency syndrome/AIDS n 1982
code blue n b1985
magnetic resonance imaging n b1985
orphan drug n *unmarketed drug* b1985
premenstrual syndrome n b1985
underbite n b1985
abortion pill n
chronic fatigue syndrome n
emergicenter n
human immunodeficiency virus/HIV n
liposuction, lipofilling n
shaken baby syndrome n

Everyday Life
area rug n b1985
smokeless tobacco n b1985

static cling n b1985
appliance garage n

Drink
blush wine n b1985
brewski n b1985
decaf adj/n b1985

Food
angel-hair pasta n b1985
blackened adj *as in "blackened redfish"* b1985
chimichanga n b1985
foodie n *akin to junkie* b1985
gelati n *type of ice cream* b1985
ranch dressing n b1985
nuke v *microwave*

Cloth/Clothing
activewear n b1985
high top n *type of shoe* b1985 (adj use: b1970)
stonewashed jeans n b1985
belt bag n *fanny pack*
unisize adj

Fashion/Style
tanning bed n (Am) b1985
eye tuck n

Tools
sneezeguard n b1985

Travel/Transportation
diamond lane n *special street lane*
Humvee n *mil. vehicle*

Emotions/Characteristics
chill out v b1985
stressed-out adj b1985

Love/Romance/Sex
big O n *slang orgasm* b1985
safe sex n b1985

Family/Relations/Friends
quality time n
sandwich generation n

Games/Fun/Leisure
role-playing game n b1985
snowboard n b1985

Sports
blading n
in-line skate n
jazzercise n
Mexican wave n *the wave*

Professions/Duties
waitron n (Am) b1985 (waiter: b1530; waitress: b1835; waitperson: b1980)

Business/Commerce/Selling
cold call n b1985
corporatize v b1985
intrapreneur n *in-company entrepreneur* b1985
microbrewery n b1985
network v *schmooze* b1985
niche market n b1985
poison pill n b1985

teleshopping n b1985
theme restaurant n b1985
brewpub n
infopreneur n

The Workplace

golden parachute n b1985
office park n b1985
outsource/outsourcing v/n
 b1985
quality assurance n b1985
electronic cottage n (Am)
golden handcuffs n
new-collar adj *akin to blue-
 collar, white-collar*

Finances/Money

automated teller n b1985
cash machine n b1985
comparable worth n b1985
program trading n b1985
telebanking n b1985
ATM n

Language and Speaking

sniglet n *made-up word*
 b1985

Literature/Writing

cyberpunk n b1985
desktop publishing n b1985
graphic novel n
splatterpunk n

Communication

e-mail n b1985
voice mail n b1985
caller ID n *type of phone service*
cellphone n (Am)
hypermedia n

Music

ear candy n *gloppy music*
 b1985
hip-hop n b1985
synthpop n b1985
cassingle n
gangsta n *type of rap music*
house n
house music n *type of dance
 music*

New Age music n
sample n/v
speed metal n
world music n

Entertainment

break dancing n b1985
celebrity n (Am) *famous person* b1985
karaoke n b1985
megahit n b1985
celebutante n *cele(brity)(de)
 butante*
lambada n *type of dance*

Movies/TV/Radio

camcorder n b1985
high-concept adj b1985
multiplex n *several theaters in
 one complex* b1985
rock jock n b1985
VHS n b1985
video jockey n b1985
zap n *fast-forward through
 commercials* b1985
cineplex n (Am)
tabloid TV n

Education

SAT n

Society/Mores/Culture

antichoice adj b1985
food bank n b1985
politically correct adj b1985
yuppie n b1985
cocooning n (Am)
mommy track n

Politics

glastnost n
new world order n
perestroika n

Death

drive-by adj/n
suicide machine n

War/Military/Violence

Star Wars n 1983
nuclear winter n b1985

Crime/Punishment/ Enforcement

crack n *type of cocaine* b1985
date rape n b1985
designer drug n b1985
DNA fingerprinting n b1985
kiddie porn n b1985
neighborhood watch n b1985
perp n *perpetrator* b1985
substance abuse n b1985
crack house n
granny battering n
wilding n

The Law

lemon law n b1985

Slang

boom box n b1985
burn out v (Am) b1985
def adj (Am) *excellent* b1985
dis n/v (Am) b1985
ecoterrorist n b1985
fresh adj (Am) *cool* b1985
in-your-face adj b1985
rad adj *cool* b1985 (radical:
 b1970)
serious adj *as in "we will have
 to spend some serious
 money"* b1985
spin n *embellishment* b1985
toyboy n b1985
wanna-be n b1985
wimp out v b1985
young fogie n b1985
camo adj/n *camouflage*
glass ceiling n
hotbutton adj/n
metalhead n *heavy metal fan*
out v *come out of the closet*

rock n *crack cocaine*
tree-hugger n

Insults

bimbette n b1985 (bimbo:
 b1920)
dweeb n b1985
crackhead n
slimeball n

Phrases

level playing field n b1985
over-the-top adj b1985
rust belt n b1985
smoke and mirrors n b1985
spin doctor n b1985
urban legends n b1985
boy toy n
consumer terrorism n (Am)
corporate welfare n (Am)
damage control n
gateway drug n
trophy wife n (Am)

General/Miscellaneous

shark repellent n b1985

Things

tropical oil n

Description

gender-specific adj b1985
picture-perfect adj b1985
101 adj *basic*

Actions/Verbs

broadside v b1985
bulk up v b1985
mentor v b1985 (noun use:
 b1750)

SELECTED BIBLIOGRAPHY

Our Marvelous Native Tongue, by Robert Claiborne (Times Books). The premiere overall English history.

The Roots of English, by Robert Claiborne (Anchor Books). A dictionary of Indo-European rootwords.

A History of English in Its Own Words, by Craig M. Carver (HarperCollins). Word histories explained, in chronological order.

NTC's Dictionary of Changes in Meanings, by Adrian Room (National Textbook Company). Histories of how words have come to new meanings.

The Mother Tongue: English and How It Got That Way, by Bill Bryson (Morrow). An overall history.

The Story of English, by Robert McCrum, William Cran and Robert MacNeil (Viking). The companion to a PBS series by the same name.

Word-Hoard: An Introduction to Old English Vocabulary, by Stephen A. Barney (Yale University Press). Scholarly language text.

Morris Dictionary of Word and Phrase Origins, by William and Mary Morris (Harper & Row). Brief word histories.

NTC's Dictionary of Word Origins, by Adrian Room (National Textbook Company). Brief word histories.

An Etymological Dictionary of Modern English, by Ernest Weekley (Dover). A reprint of a 1921 compilation, in two volumes.

Merriam-Webster's Collegiate Dictionary, Tenth Edition (Merriam-Webster). An excellent overall dictionary.

Random House Webster's College Dictionary (Random House).

The New Shorter Oxford English Dictionary (Clarendon Press-Oxford). The next best thing to having the complete *OED* on your desk.

The Barnhart Concise Dictionary, ed. by Robert K. Barnhart (HarperCollins). Solid etymological reference.

The Oxford Dictionary of Modern Slang, by John Ayto and John Simpson (Oxford University Press). Strong in its international representation of slang.

Neo-Words, by David K. Barnhart (Collier Books). Slim volume of nonce words.

Tuttle's Dictionary of New Words, by Jonathon Green (Charles E. Tuttle Co.). New words since 1960.

Made in America: An Informal History of the English Language in the United States, by Bill Bryson (Morrow). Concentrating on Americanese.

Devious Derivations, by Hugh Rawson (Crown). True stories behind apocryphal etymologies.

Dictionary of Word Origins, by John Ayto (Arcade). Brief word histories.

Our Language, by Simeon Potter (Penguin). Useful overview of the language and how it's created.

The Story Behind the Word, by Morton S. Freeman (ISI Press). Brief word histories.

The Concise Oxford Dictionary of English Etymology, by T.F. Hoad. Technical word etymologies.

The Merriam-Webster New Book of Word Histories (Merriam-Webster). Brief word histories.

A Guide to Chaucer's Language, by David Burnley (University of Oklahoma Press). Scholarly overview of Middle English and how Chaucer wrote in it.

A Dictionary of American Idioms, by Maxine Tull Boatner and John Edward Gates (Barron's Educational Series). A phrase dictionary.

INDEX

Abbreviations Used in This Book

adj adjective • *adv* adverb • *Am* American • *arch.* archaic • *b* by (so that "b1700" means "by 1700") • *Brit* British • *conj* conjunction • *contr* contraction • *esp.* especially • *fig.* figurative • *gen.* general • *geo.* geography • *interj* interjection • *leg.* legal • *LME* Late Middle English • *lit.* literal • *ME* Middle English • *med.* medical • *mil.* military • *n* noun • *obs.* obsolete • *OE* Old English • *opp.* opposite • *phys.* physical • *prep* preposition • *pron* pronoun • *rel.* religion • *spec.* specific • *u* until • *var.* various • *v* verb ❦

advantage n 49
advantage v 49, 96
advent n gen. 20, 205
advent n Christmas season 20
advent n arrival 205
adventure n/v 47
adventurer n 113, 204
adventuresome adj 184
adventuress n 113, 204
adventurous adj 47
adverb n 76
adversarial adj 51, 288
adversary adj 51, 288; n 51
adverse adj 47
adversity n 47
advert v 95
advertent adj 178
advertise v call attention to 95
advertise v commercial sense
95, 185
advertise v obs. pay heed 95
advertisement 95
advertising n 185, 200
advertorial n 263
advice n obs. wisdom 49
advice n gen. 49
advisable adj 91
advise v obs. 49
advise v gen. 49
advisory n 216
advisory adj, n 206, 301
advocacy n 85
advocacy journalism n 318
advocate n/v 51
adz n 16
aegis n shield 155, 205
aegis n fig. 155, 205
aerate v 208
aerator n 208, 242
aerial adj ephemeral 146
aerial n antenna 274
aerial adj happening in the air
146
aerial ladder n on a fire truck
274
aerialist n 276
aerie n 99
aerobatics n 281
aerobic adj 255
aerobics n 317
aerodrome n airport 274
aerodrome n airplane 274
aerodynamics n 220
aerodyne n heavier-than-air
craft 274
aeronaut n 198, 212
aeronautics n 198, 212
aeroplane n 243

aeroplane n obs. aerofoil 243
aerosol n 286
aerosol can n 303
aerospace adj/n 310
aerospace plane n 310
aerostat n lighter-than-air craft
198
aesthete n 214, 265
aesthetic adj/n 214
aesthetic adj/n obs. sensual 214
aesthetic distance n 299
aesthetical adj 214
aesthetics n 214
aesthetics n obs. sensuality 214
afear v 17
afeared adj 17
affable adj 73
affair n tryst 185
affair n gen. 49
affect v arch. show affection 39,
95
affect v change 95
affect v as in "affect airs" 95
affectation n 95
affected adj feigned, adopted
107
affection n 39
affiance n trust 37
affiance v betroth 101
affidavit n 131
affiliate n 207, 269
affiliate v 207, 269; n 207
affiliated 207
affine n relative by marriage 108
affined adj closely related 138
affinity n kindredness 40, 150
affinity n predilection 40, 150
affinity group n 319
affirm v 57
affirmation n 57
affirmative action n 319
affix v 96
afflatus n divine inspiration 173
afflict v obs. deject 116
afflict v trouble 116
affluence n wealth 127
affluence n profuse flow 127
affluent adj 127
afford v have the wherewithal to
93
affordable adj 245
affray v frighten 37
affriended adj obs. befriended
126
affright adj frightened 17
affright v/n 17
affront n/v 37
afghan n 196

afghan hound n 285
aficionada 232, 313
aficionado n 232, 313
aflame adj 137
afloat adj/adv 25
aflower adj 254
aflutter adj 233
afore adv/prep/conj 12
aforehand 12
aforementioned adj 138
aforesaid adj 89
afraid 37
A-frame n 273
African violet n 272
Afro n the hair 317
aft adj/adv 25
after adj/adv/conj/prep 23
after shave n 286
afterbirth n 118
afterburner n 304
aftercare n 195
afterglow n 251
after-hours adj 289
afterimage n 251
afterlife n 129
aftermarket n 298
aftermath n repercussion 176
aftermath n second mowing 176
afternoon n 31
afternoons n (Am) 256
afterpiece n 201
aftershock n 254
aftertaste n 195
afterthought n (Am) late child
283
afterthought n 125
aftertime n the future 119
afterword n 264
afterworld n 129
agape n type of feast 244
agape n nonerotic love 244
agape adj/adv 169
agate n 29
age n how old you are 31
age n as in "Age of Reason" 31
age of consent n 105
age of reason n 195
aged adj as in "aged wine" 65
aged adj 65
ageism n 319
ageless adj 166
agency n 176
agenda n 158, 233
agendum n 158, 233
agent n as in "literary agent"
126
agent n as in "agent of change"
87

agent orange n (Am) 319
agent provocateur n 269
age-old adj 278
aggrandize v 163
aggravate v exacerbate 116
aggravate v burden, worsen
124
aggravate v annoy 116
aggravate v annoy 124
aggravated adj leg. 112
aggravated assault n 291
aggregate adj/n/v 83
aggress v War/Military/Vio-
lence 155, 191
aggress v Emotions/Charac-
teristics 213
aggression n War/Military/Vi-
olence 155
aggression n 212
aggressive adj Emotions/
Characteristics 212
aggressor n War/Military/Vi-
olence 155
aggressor n Emotions/Char-
acteristics 213
aghast adj 37
agile adj 68
agility n 68
agitate v 142
agitprop n agitation propaganda
291
aglare adj 252
agleam adj 251
aglet n part of a shoelace 71
aglimmer adj 233
aglitter adj 233
aglow adj 217
agnail n hangnail 32, 120
agnail n obs. toe corn 120
agnate n male relative on father's side 101
agnostic adj/n 247
ago adj/adv 12
agog adj 73
a-go-go n/adj 318
agone adv/adj ago 65
agony n phys. suffering 74
agony n mental suffering 74
agony column n newspaper
"personals" related to missing
friends and relatives 246
agoraphobia n 239
agree v harmonize 93, 104
agree v concur, accept 93
agreeable 93
agreement n 93
agribusiness n (Am) 310
agricole n obs. farmer 71, 168

anthem n 19
anthill n 30
anthologist n 214
anthologist n 153
anthologize v 153, 214
anthology n *collection of poems* 153
anthology n *gen. collection* 153
anthracite n *type of coal* 209
anthracite n *mineral resembling embers* 209
anthrax n 63
anthropic adj *human* 209
anthropocentric adj 251
anthropoid n 220
anthropoid ape n 220
anthropology n 119
anthropomorph n 233, 270
anthropomorphic adj 233
anthropomorphism n 233
anthropophagy n *cannibalism* 167
anti adj 251
antiaircraft adj 282
anti-American adj (Am) 202
antibacterial adj 257
antiballistic missile n 312
antibiotic adj/n 257, 302
antibody n 256
antibusiness adj 226
antic n 113
anticancer adj 286
antichoice adj 327
Antichrist n 20
anticipate v 116
anticipation 116
anticipatory 116
anticlimactic adj 270
anticlimactic adj 189
anticlimax n 189, 271
anticlockwise adj/adv (Brit) *counterclockwise* 271
anticoagulant adj/n 273
antics n 113
antidemocratic adj 229
antidepressant adj/n 316
antidote n 68
antidrug adj 319
antielectron n *positron* 296
antiestablishment adj 312
antifreeze n 280
antifungal adj 302
antigen n 273
antigravity adj/n 292
antihero n 187, 276
antiheroine n 187, 276
antihistamine n/adj 297
anti-inflammatory adj 310

antilife adj 291
antilock adj 323
antimatter n 302
antimissile missile n 312
antimony n 63
antineutrino n 296
antineutron n 302
antinovel n 311
antinuclear adj 312
antinuke adj 312
antipasto n 122
antipathy n 149
antipersonnel adj 300
antiperspirant n 303
antipope n 78
antiquarian n/adj 126
antiquark n 315
antiquary n *antiquarian* 126
antiquate v 142
antiquate adj *arch.* 142
antiquated 142
antique adj 113; n 113; v 113, 295
antiquity n *as in "times of antiquity"* 31
antiquity n *antique item* 31
antiseptic adj/n 182
antisocial adj 202
antithesis n 113
antithetical 113
antitoxin n 257
antitrust adj (Am) 264
anti-utopia n 319
antler n 64
antonym n 245
antsy adj 225
anus n 66
anvil n 16
anxiety n 107
anxious adj *eager* 150
anxious adj *edgy* 107, 150
any adj 23
anywhither adv 160
anywise adv 25
A-OK adj/adv 313
aorta n 106
apartheid n 306
apartment n 148
apartment building n 241
apartment hotel n 273
apartment house n (Am) 241
apathetic 149
apathy n 149
ape v Slang 156
ape n/v 11
ape-man n 254
aperitif n 259

apert adj *arch. out in the open* 61
aperture n 86
apex n 157
aphasia n *speech loss* 238
aphid n 254
aphorism n *maxim* 127
aphrodisiac n 185
apiary n *beehive* 168
aplenty adj/adv 233
aplomb n 224
apnea n 182
apocalypse n 20
apocalyptic adj 154
apocalyptist n 228
apocrypha n 138
apocryphal adj 138
apogee n 135
Apollonian adj 147
apologetic adj 243
apologetic adj *vindicating* 243
apologia n 205
apologist n 158
apologize v 124, 142, 243
apology n *defense against accusation* 124
apology n *regretful admission* 124, 243
apoplectic adj 68
apoplexy n *stroke* 68
apostle n *arch* 98
apostle n 19
apostless n *obs. female apostle* 19, 98
apostrophe n *punctuation* 110
apostrophe n *obs. the material omitted* 110
apothecary n *druggist* 68
apothegm n *maxim* 127
apotheosis n *gen. triumph* 129
apotheosis n *deification* 129
appall v *shock* 96
appall v *obs. become pale* 96
appalling adj 96, 212
Appaloosa n (Am) 285
apparatus n 158
apparel n *arch. broader equipment, including clothing* 35
apparel n/v 35
apparent adj *obvious* 89
apparent adj *seeming* 89
apparent magnitude n 237
apparently 89
apparition n *ghost* 132
apparition n *gen. unexpected appearance* 132
appeal *gen.* 49, 217; v 49
appeal n *leg.* 49; v 46

appealing adj *attractive* 217, 271
appear v 57
appear v *seem* 57
appearance n *act of appearing* 83
appearance n *how something looks* 57, 83
appease v *placate* 57
appease v *calm* 57
appellate adj 188
append v 93
appendage n 93, 147
appendectomy n 257
appendicectomy n 257
appendicitis n 257
appendix n The Body 147
appendix n *book supplement* 110
appetence n *appetite, desire* 157
appetency n 157
appetite n 32
appetizer n 241
appetizing adj 167
applaud 77
applause n 77
apple n 15
apple butter n (Am) 197
apple pandowdy n (Am) 223
applecart n 197
applejack n 211
apple-knocker n *rustic* 283
apple-pie order n 204
apple-polish v 293
apple-polisher n 293
applesauce n 183
appliance n *application* 123
appliance n *gen. tool* 123
appliance garage n 326
applicable adj 104
applicant n 179
application n 93, 96, 179
applicator n 93
applique n 214
apply v *as in "apply knowledge"; as in "apply oneself"* 96
apply v *have relevance* 93, 104
apply v *as in "apply glue"* 93
apply v *as in "apply for a job"* 93, 179
appoint v 92
appointee n 92, 190
appointment n *scheduled meeting* 85
appointments n *equipment* 136
apportion v 141

appraisal n Thoughts/Perception/The Mind 213

appraisal n 95

appraise v 95

appreciate n *arch.* 150

appreciate v *rise in value* 200

appreciate v *assess* 200

appreciate v *recognize, display gratitude* 124, 200

appreciation 124

appreciation n *assessment* 150, 200

appreciation n *recognition* 150, 200

appreciation n *rise in value* 150, 200

appreciative adj 124

appreciatory adj 124

apprehend v *obs. seize* 93

apprehend v *capture* 93

apprehend v *comprehend* 74

apprehend v *fear* 150

apprehension n *fear* 150

apprentice n/v 41

apprise v 180

apprize v *appraise* 93

approach n/v *phys.* 57

approach v *fig.* 57

approbate v *sanction* 95

appropriate adj 90

appropriate v 96

appropriation n *financial allocation* 200

appropriation n *commandeering* 82

approve n/v 59

approve v *obs. prove* 59

approved school n (Brit) *reform school* 300

approximate v *guess* 208

approximate adj *almost equal* 233

approximate v *bring into phys. proximity* 208

approximation n 208

APR n Finances/Money 323

apricot n 122

April n Time 12

April fool n 175

April Fool's Day n 151

apron n 35

apron string 35

apropos adj/adv 178

apropos adj 178

apso n *type of dog* 315

apt adj *fitting* 137

apt adj *liable, inclined* 115

apt adj *arch. prepared* 137

aptitude n *ability* 120

aptitude n *inclination* 115, 120

aptitude test n 289

aqua n 321

Aqua-Lung n 304

aquamarine n *the rock* 118

aquamarine n *the color* 252

aquanaut n 261

aquaplane n 280

aquarist n 259

aquarium n 220

aquatic adj 99

aquatile adj 99

aqueduct n 114

aqueous adj 161

aquiculture n 241

aquifer n 272

aquiver adj 270

arabesque adj *ornamental style* 149

arabesque n *ballet position* 201

Arabian horse n 181

Arabic alphabet n 227

Arabic numeral n 221

arable adj *suitable for farming* 71

arachnid n 237

arbalest n *type of crossbow* 21

arbiter n 75

arbiter elegantiarum n *lit. "arbiter of refinements"* 212

arbitrage n *arch. arbitration* 245

arbitrage n *type of stock dealing* 245; v 245

arbitrageur n 245

arbitrary adj 89

arbitrate 83

arbitration n 83

arbitration n *obs. authority to make decisions* 83

arbitrator n 83

arbor n *tree* 33

arbor n *obs. lawn* 33

arbor n *spindle, shaft* 177

arbor n *shelter of shrubs or vines* 33

arboreal 33

arboretum n 219

arc n *arch* 136

arc n *obs. path of the sun* 136

arc n/v *curve* 136

arc n *electrical discharge* 221; v 221

arc lamp n 260

arc light n 260

arc welding n 297

arcade n 167

arcane adj 115

arcanum n *arcane knowledge* 125

arch v 93

arch n *gen.* 49; v 49, 93

arch adj *roguish* 169

arch n *foot arch* 49

arch adj *primary, akin to arch-enemy* 169

archaic adj 233

archaical 233

archaism n *use of the archaic; the archaic thing itself* 158

archangel n 20

archbishop n 19

archconservative n 300

archdeacon n 20

archdiocese n 228

archduchess n 111, 154

archduchy 111

archduke n 111, 154

archenemy n 114

archeology n *arch. gen. ancient history* 220

archeology n *scientific study* 220

archer n 45

archery n 45, 80

archetype n 114

archfiend n 176

Archimedes' screw n 242

archipelago n 105

architect n 126

architectonic 126

architectural 126

architecture n 126

archival 157

archive n/v 157, 271

archive v 157

archives n 157

archivist n 157

arctic n *type of overshoe* 242

arctic adj/n 83

arctic circle n 219

arctic fox n 194

ardent adj *lit. and fig. fiery* 54

ardent spirits n *strong liquor* 196

ardor n 72

arduous adj 115

area n 114

area code n 318

area rug n 326

arena n 122

arena theater n *theater-in-the-round* 305

arete n *type of mountain ridge* 219

argon n 254

argonaut n 72

argosy n *type of ship* 123

argot n 245

argue v 58

argue v *contend, as in "argue that"* 58

argue v *as in "argue for" or "argue against"* 58

argufy v 189

argument n *dispute* 51

argument n *argumentation* 51, 58

argumentation n 51

argumentative adj 51

argyle n 197

aria n 187

arid adj 178

arise v 26

aristocracy n *government by the best* 130

aristocracy n *government by the most powerful* 130

aristocrat n 202

aristocratic adj 130, 202

arithmetic adj/n 31

arithmetic progression n 120

arithmetician n 120

ark n *Noah's ark* 31

ark n *coffer* 21

arm n *the appendage* 13

arm n *chair arm* 13

arm n *fig., as in "arm of the government"* 13

arm n *weapon* 45

arm v *equip with weapons* 45

arm and a leg n 321

arm wrestling n 323

armada n *gen. navy* 112

armada n *spec., Spanish Armada* 112

armadillo n 119

Armageddon n 111

armament n *arch. naval force* 188

armament n *war equipment* 188

armband n 197

armchair n 121

armchair adj 233

armed adj *having weapons* 45

armed forces n 174

armhole n 35

armillary sphere n 165

armipotent n *effective as a fighter* 80

armistice n 174

armlock n *hammerlock* 277

armoire n 121

assemblyperson 155, 319, 324
assemblywoman n 155, 319, 324
assent n/v 57
assert v 85, 124
assertion n 85
assertive adj 124
assertiveness training n 325
assess v *as in "assess a tax"* 95
assess v *as in "assess the situation"* 321
assessment n *as in "assessment of a situation"* 321
assessment n *as in "tax assessment"* 95
assessor n *one who assesses* 95
assessor n *tax assessor* 321
asset n 110, 264
assets n 110, 264
asshole n *jerk* 66, 301
asshole n *The Body* 66, 301
assign v 57
assignation n *tryst* 170
assimilate v 87
assimilation n 87
assist v 83, 95, 136; n 95, 136
assistance n 75, 83, 95
assistant n 75, 83
assistant professor n (Am) 246
associate adj *join* 83; n 83
associate adj *as in "criminal associate"* 83; n 83
associate n *colleague* 113
associate professor n 214
association n 83, 113
assoil v *pardon, expiate* 57
assort v 157
assorted adj 157, 207
assortment n 157
assuage v 57
assume v *take for granted* 74
assume v *as in "assume responsibility"* 140
assumed adj 160
assuming adj *presumptuous* 149
assumption n 74, 140
assure v *obs. betroth* 74
assure v *ensure* 162
assure v *comfort, certain* 92
aster n *obs. star* 146
aster n *type of flower* 181
asterisk n *tiny star* 76
asterisk n *Language and Speaking* 76
asterism n *constellation* 119
asteroid n 210
asteroid belt n 309

asthenia n *weakness* 210
asthma n 68
asthmatic adj/n 68, 106
Asti Spumante n 273
astigmatic adj 222
astigmatism n 222
astir adj 207
astonied adj *arch. astonished* 37
astonish v *obs. terrify, stupefy* 107
astonish v *obs. paralyze* 107
astonish v *amaze* 107
astonishing adj 107
astonishment adj 107
astound v *stun* 124
astound v *amaze* 124
astound v *obs. stupefy* 124
astound adj 124
astounding adj 124
astraddle adv *astride* 178
astral adj 146
astride adv 160
astringe v 115
astringent adj *inducing contraction* 115
astringent adj *harsh* 115; n 115
astrogeology n 315
astrolabe n 65
astrologer n *astrologist* 146
astrologer n *obs. astronomer* 146
astrologist n 146
astronaut n 288
astronautics n 288
astronomical unit n 272
astronomy n *obs. astrology* 99
astronomy n 99
astrophysics n 255
astroturf n 317
astute adj 159
asunder adj/adv 54
aswarm adj 251
aswoon adj 14
asylum n *fig. refuge* 69
asylum n *phys. refuge* 69
asylum n *mental institution* 69, 195
asymmetrical adj 179
at bay adj 47
at home n *at-home reception* 188
atavism n 219
atelier n *type of studio* 173
atheism n 111
atheist 111
atheling n *prince, male royalty* 20

athenaeum/atheneum n *library* 201
athenaeum/atheneum n *temple of Athena* 201
athirst adj 13
athlete n 75
athlete's foot n 286
athletic adj 75
athletic supporter n 287
athletics n 75, 151
atingle adj 251
atlas n *book of maps* 153
atlas n *fig. supporter* 153
ATM n 327
atmosphere n *air* 145
atmosphere n *ambience* 145, 205
atmospheric adj *moody* 205
atmospheric adj *of the atmosphere* 145
atmospheric pressure 145
atmospherics n 272
atoll n 145
atom n 99, 210
atom bomb n 282, 306
atom smasher n 296
atomic adj 99, 164
atomic age n 302
atomic bomb n 282, 306
atomic clock n 296
atomic energy n 272
atomic mass 210, 256
atomic number n 210
atomic reactor n 302
atomic theory n 220
atomic weight n 210, 256
atomism 220
atomize 242
atomizer n *sprayer* 242
atomy n *atom* 99, 118
atrabilious adj *melancholy* 169
atrium n 122
atrocious adj *awful* 169, 271
atrocious adj *wicked* 1107, 69
atrocity n *wickedness* 107
atrocity n *wicked deed* 107
atrophy n/v 121
attaboy interj 277
attach v *join together* 96
attach v *seize legally* 46
attach v *join to* 96
attache n 226
attaché case n 273
attachment n *predilection* 158
attack v *assault physically* 131
attack v *assault verbally* 131
attain v 57
attainment 57

attempt n/v 93
attend v *as in "attend a rally"* 96
attend v *heed, listen, deal with* 57
attendee n 301
attention n 74
attention n *as in "at attention"* 203
attention deficit disorder n 322
attention span n 298
attentive adj 74
attenuate adj/v *thin* 95
attest v 116
attic n 167
attic storey n 167
attire n/v 35
attitude n *phys. orientation* 225
attitude n *mental attitude* 225
attorney n 46, 112
attorney general n 111
attorney-at-law n 46, 112
attract v *attract physically* 95
attract v *attract emotionally* 95
attribute n 82, 102; v 102
attrist v *obs. sadden* 169
attrit v *wear down* 82, 313; n 82
attrite v 82
attrition n *wearing down by friction* 82, 284
attrition n *gradual loss* 82, 284
attune v *lit. bring into tune* 142
attune v *fig. bring into tune* 142
atwitter adj 225
atypical adj 251
au courant adj 202
au gratin adj 211
au jus adj 280
au naturel adj 210
au pair girl n 311
au revoir interj/n 175
auburn adj 90
auction n/v 127
auction bridge n 275
auctioneer n 127, 185; v 185
auctorial adj *authorial* 214
audacious adj 73
audacity n *boldness* 73
audacity n *obnoxious boldness* 73
audible adj 103
audience n *spectators* 82, 205
audience n *meeting* 82, 205
audio adj/n 284
audio frequency n 279
audiocassette n 324
audiology n 302

awkward adj obs. backward 106

awl n 16

awning n 148

AWOL adj/adv/n 282

awry adj/adv 88

aw-shucks adj (Am) 301

ax v eliminate, cut 320

ax/axe n 16

ax/axe v 16

axe n slang guitar 318

axe n gen. musical instrument 318

axel n 289

axeman 318

axiom n 102, 207

axiomatic adj 102, 207

axis n 83

axle n 16

axle-tooth n arch. molar 99

axman n (Am) 171

ay interj 47

aye/ay n yes 135

aye/ay adv for ever, continually 53

azalea n 193

azimuth n 65

azure n type of stone 29

azure n the color 103

azure adj 103

azurite n 209

B

B movie n 305

B picture n 299

B vitamin n 279

baa n/v 119

babble n/v 56

babble v as in "babble like a brook" 56

babe n General/Miscellaneous 47

babe n Love/Romance/Sex 244

baboon n obs. grotesque architectural figure 30

baboon n 30

babushka n 297

baby n term of endearment 244

baby n 47, 75

baby v 75, 192

baby batterer n 324

baby blue n (Am) 271

baby boom n (Am) 307, 324

baby boomer n 307, 324

baby bust 307

baby carriage n 239

baby doll n 244

baby grand n 276

baby talk n 227

baby tooth n 296

baby's breath n 254

babysit v 308

baby-snatcher n person who dates someone younger 281

baccalaureate n 154

baccarat n 244

bacchanal n decadent celebration 108

bacchanalia 108

bachelor n 39, 275

bachelorette n 39, 275

bacillus n 257

back v back up, reverse 93

back v arch. clothe 71

back n as in "the back of the house" 51

back v support 116

back n gen. 13

back v 114

back n on the body 51

back and forth adv/adj/n 156

back burner n 308

back door n 106

back room n 122

back talk n 250

back up v 205

backache n 147

back-and-forth n 307

backbeat n 290

backbite v 55

backbiter n 55

backbone n spine 32

backbone n mainstay, courage 32

backbreaking adj 195

backcountry n 181

backdoor adj 217

backdraft n 217

backdrop n (Am) 284

backer n supporter 114, 116

backfill n/v 278

backfire v blow up in your face 295

backfire n (Am) engine irregularity 224; v 224

backflip n/v 298

back-formation n 264

backgammon n 151

background n as in "the background of a photo" 177

background n history 177; v 177

background v 207

background music n 290

background radiation n 315

backgrounder n 207, 313

backhand n/v 170, 298

backhanded adj 204

backhoe n 288

backlash n/v phys. recoil 216

backlash n/v fig. negative reaction 216

backlight n/v 233

backlog n/v stock 270

backlog n log at the back of the fire 177

backpack n/v 281

backpedal v 271

backrest n 239

backroom adj 122

backseat n lit. and fig. 232

backseat driver n 313

backside n hind part 83

backside n buttocks 83

backslap v 206, 295

backslapping adj 206, 295

backslide v/n 134

backspace v/n 281

backspin n 275

backsplash n 303

backstage adj/adv 265

backstairs adj 161

backstitch n/v 149

backstreet n 100

backstretch n 226

backstroke n swimming 171

backswing n 263

back-to-back adj/adv 102

backtrack v (Am) 191

backup n auxiliary 205

backup n as in "traffic backup" 205

backward adj not up to date 175

backwash n 205

backwater n 83

backwoods n/adj (Am) 181

backyard n 167

bacon n 34

bacon n obs. rube 34

bacteria 220

bacterial 220

bacterium n 220

bad adj/adv/n 53

bad adj good 53, 292

bad blood n 216

bad news n 293

badass adj/n 313

baddie n (Am) 300

badge n 83

badger v 208

badger n/v Animals 105

badinage n/v banter 172

badlands n (Am) 236

badling n bad person 21

badminton n 244

badminton n type of drink 244

bad-mouth v (Am) 301, 307

Baedeker n guidebook 246

baffle n 260

baffle v befuddle 142

baffle v obs. swindle 142

baffle v obs. ridicule 142

baffle n obs. confusion 260

bag n hag 293

bag n slang primary interest 52

bag v droop, capture 95

bag n lifestyle 313

bag n sack 52; v 95

bag v kill 95

bag it v quit 300

bag lady n 266

bagatelle n trifle 158, 244

bagatelle n type of game 158, 244

bagel n 280

baggage n 86

baggies n 316

bagman n 203

bagman n tax collector 203

bagpipe n 42

bah interj 132

bail n var. obs. meanings related to jurisdiction 102

bail n/v pail 71

bail n as in "post bail" 102; v 102

bail out v duck out 293

bailiff n 46

bairn n child 18

bait v harass, attack 45

bait n/v 55

bait and switch n 318

bake v fig. cook by heat, as in "bake in the sun" 15

bake v lit. cook by heat 15

baked Alaska n (Am) 274

baked beans n 223

baker n 40

baker's dozen n 120

bakery baker's work 40, 110

bakery type of shop 40, 110, 200

bakeshop 110

bakeshop n 200

baking powder n 223

baking soda n (Am) 259

balance n measuring tool 35

balance n as in "hangs in the balance" 51

balance n equilibrium, stability, as in "mental balance" 176

balance n *aesthetic counterposition* 205

balance n/v *as in "balance sheet"* 127

balance v 35, 205

balance beam n 304

balance of payments n 264

balance of power n 130

balance of trade n 171

balance sheet n 200

balancing act n 313

balcony n 148

balcony n *theatre area* 148

bald adj *worn* 32

bald adj *hairless* 32

bald adj *undisguised* 54

bald adj *obs. round* 32

bald eagle n (Am) 165

balderdash n *nonsense* 177

balderdash n *obs. liquid or concoction of liquids* 177

bald-faced adj 308

balding adj 297

bale n/v *bundle* 53

bale n *great evil* 28

baleen n *whalebone* 30

baleen n *obs. whale* 30

baleen whale n 237

baleful adj 25, 28

baleless *arch.* 25

balk v 96

balk v *obs. plow into ridges* 96

balky adj 96, 234

ball n *round object* 52

ball n *fun, as in "having a ball"* 154

ball v *have sex* 311

ball n *formal dance* 154

ball bearing n 260

ball breaker n 313

ball buster n 313

ball game n (Am) 226

ball joint n 260

ball lightning n 236

ball of fire n 269

ball of wax n *as in "the whole ball of wax"* 313

ballad n 77

balladeer n 154

ballast n 113

ball-busting n 313

ballerina n 173, 201

ballet n 173

ballista *thrower of projectiles* 195

ballistic adj 195

ballistic missile n 312

ballistics n 195

balloon n *obs. type of firework* 244

balloon n *child's toy* 244

balloon v *swell* 235

balloon n *obs. tetherball* 244

balloon n 200

balloon tire n 261

ballooning n *sport* 200

balloonist n 200

ballot n 111

ballot box 111

ballpark n (Am) 262

ballpark adj *as in "a ballpark estimate"* 321; 321

ballpark figure n 320

ballpoint n 303

ballroom n 183

balls interj 267

balls n *testicles* 32

balls n *guts, nerve* 311

ballsy adj 313

ballyhoo n/v (Am) 270

balm n 48

balm v *embalm* 45

balmy adj 91

baloney interj/n (Am) *nonsense* 283

baloney n 287

baloney n *mediocre boxer* 283

balsa n Plants 193

balsa n *type of boat* 193

balsam n *balm* 14

balsam fir n (Am) 209

balsam poplar n 209

bam interj/n 292

bamboo n 118

Bamboo Curtain n 306

bamboo shoot n 259

bamboozle v 189

ban n *arch. official proclamation* 176

ban v *prohibit* 93; n 176

ban v *arch. curse* 93

ban v *obs. call to arms* 93; n 93

ban n *excommunication* 176

banal adj 234

banal adj *related to ban, call to arms* 234

banality 234

banana n 122

banana n *as in "top banana"* 122

banana republic n *backward country* 301

banana split n 280

bananas adj *crazy* 320

band n *troop or group* 102

band n *shackles; obligations* 23

band n *musical group* 102

band n *as in "rubber band"* 52

band v 102

band saw n (Am) 242

band shell n 290

bandage n/v 136

bandana n 184

bandicoot n *type of rat* 209

bandicoot n *type of marsupial* 209

bandit n 131

bandleader n 265

bandstand n 246

bandwagon n (Am) 250

bandy v 141

bandy v *obs. unite* 144

bandy-legged adj *bowed* 166

bane n *arch. killer, something that kills* 136

bane n General/Miscellaneous 136

bane v *arch. kill with poison* 130

bane v *arch. harm* 130

bang n *hair term* 260

bang adv *as in "smack bang in the middle"* 233

bang n/v *noise* 114

bang n *as in "get a bang out of it"* 300

bang v *have sex* 262

bangle n 205

bangs n *hair term* 260

bangtail n *racehorse* 263

bang-up adj *great* 215

banish v 56

banister n 167

banjo n 188

bank n *mound, ridge* 29; v 29

bank n *financial institution, storage place* 101; v 101

bank n *grouping or series* 270

bank holiday n 244

bankbook n 187

banker n 110

banknote n 172

bankroll n/v 264

bankrupt n *bankrupt person* 110

bankrupt adj/v 110

bankruptcy 110

banner n 52

banner adj (Am) *as in "banner year"* 234

banns n *public announcement of proposed marriage* 18

banquet n *obs. between-meal snack* 101

banquet n 101

banshee n 175

bantam n *the fowl* 181

bantam adj 181

bantam-weight n 263

banter n/v 179

banter n 179

bantling n *young child* 130

banyan n 119

baobab n 145

baptism 43

baptism of fire n 216

baptismal name n 247

baptize v 43

bar n *stripe* 87

bar n *rod, pole* 35; v 35

bar v *prevent* 96

bar n *tavern* 101

bar n *counter, as in "snack bar"* 100

bar n *lawyer's organization* 81

bar n *as in "bar of soap"* 136

bar n *musical unit of meter* 173

bar chart n 279

bar code n 317

bar girl n 244

bar graph 279

bar mitzvah n 215, 312; v 215

barb n General/Miscellaneous 50

barb n *fig. pointed remark* 50

barbarian adj/n *savage* 114

barbarian n *infidel* 114

barbarian n *alien* 114

barbaric adj 114

barbarism 114

barbarity 114

barbarous 114

Barbary ape n 237

barbed wire n 241

barbell n 263

barbeque n/v 168

barbeque v *dry on a barbeque* 168

barber n/v 40

barber v 40

barber pole 40

barbershop adj *singing style* 276

barbershop 40

barbiturate n 257

bard n 42

bare adj/v 21

bare bones n 283

bareback adj/adv 123

bare-handed adj/adv 68

bare-knuckle adj/adv 273

barf n/v *slang vomit* 309

barfly n (Am) 277

bargain n/v 51

bargain basement n 263, 305

beach n *the shore area* 118
beach buggy n 304
beach bum n 320
beachball n 298
beachcomber n 226
beachhead n 296
beachwear n 287
beacon n *gen. type of guide light* 42
beacon n *obs. omen* 42
beacon n *signal fire* 42
bead n *obs. prayer* 88
bead n 88
beadsman n *one who prays for another* 43
beagle n 99
beak n *slang nose* 30
beak n *Animals* 30
beaker n 53
be-all and end-all n 156
beam n *wood beam, beam of sunlight* 21
beam v *smile* 95, 268
beam v *direct a beam* 21, 95
beamish adj 243
bean n 15
bean v *hit in the head* 277
bean n *slang head* 15
bean counter n 323
bean curd n 259
bean sprouts n 287
beanbag n 251
beanbag chair n 322
beanery n (Am) 263
beanie n (Am) 287
beanpole n 204
bear v *as in "bear ill will"* 25
bear n 11
bear v *carry; endure; yield; drive* 25
bear v *as in "bear left"* 25
bear hug n 293
bearance 25
bearbaiting n 40
beard v *confront boldly* 116
beard n 16
bearing n *deportment, carriage* 37
bearing n *pertinence, affect* 199
bearing n *as in "ball bearing"* 198
bearings n *awareness of location* 184
bearish adj 187
bearnaise sauce n 259
beast n 30
beast fable n 246
beast of burden n 184

beastie n 205
beastly adj 30
beat adj *exhausted* 195
beat n *musical beat* 265
beat v *pulsate* 59; n 59
beat n *area of concern, as in "police beat," "journalist's beat"* 268
beat v *flap* 96
beat v *win* 59
beat adj/n *as in "beatnik"* 311
beat v *batter, hit* 20
beat a dead horse n 231
beat off v *masturbate* 102
beat the band v 269
beatific adj 150
beatify v 150
beatitude n 150
beatnik 311
beatster *beatnik* 311
beat-up adj 301
beau n 39
beaucoup adj *many* 283
beaut n (Am) 249
beauteous 49
beautician n (Am) 289
beautiful 49
beautiful people n 319
beautify 49
beauty n 49
beauty contest n 265
beauty shop n 275
beauty spot n 168
beaver n *slang female* 11, 292
beaver n *Animals* 11
bebop n (Am) 290
bechance v *befall* 116
beck v *beckon* 26, 61
beckon v 26
become v *suit* 59
become v *come to be* 59
become v *obs. arrive, come* 59
becoming adj 103
bed v 125
bed n/v 14
bed check n 293
bed of roses n 157
bed rest n 239
bed table n 211
bed warmer n 286
bed-and-breakfast n 273
bedbug n 209
bedchamber n 69
bedclothes n 71
bedevil v *bewitch* 132
bedevil v *torment* 132
bedfellow n 86
bedim v *dim* 143

bedlam n *chaos* 158
bedlam n *obs. mentally ill person* 158
bedlamite 158
bedpan n 121
bedpost n 121
bedraggled adj 210
bedridden adj 14
bedrock n 219
bedroll n 177
bedroom n 148
bedroom eyes n 304
bedsheet n 99
bedside manner n 238
bedsore n 238
bedspread n 222
bedspring n 258
bedstead n 69
bedtime n 31
bedtime story n 264
bedwetting n 257
bee n *the insect* 11
bee n *as in "spelling bee"* 205
beech n 10
beechnut n 181
beef n 34
beef v *as in "beef up"* 249
beef n/v *slang gripe* 261
beef stroganoff n 297
beef Wellington n 316
beefalo n 322
beefcake n 307
beefeater n *guard* 155
beefsteak n 183
beefsteak tomato n 316
beehive n *type of hairstyle* 310
beehive n *Animals* 30
beehive n *fig. active environment* 30
beekeeper n 212
beeline n/v (Am) 219
beep n/v 293
beer n 15
beer and skittles n 241
beer belly n 302, 322
beer gut n 302, 322
bee's knees adj 302
beeswax n 165
beet n 15
beet sugar n 223
beetle n *the bug* 11
beetle n *hammering instrument* 16
beeyard n *apiary* 100
befall v *happen* 55
beforesaid adj *obs. aforementioned* 61
beforetime adv *formerly* 61

befriend v 126
befuddle v 271
beg v *lit.* 26
beg v *as in "begs the question"* 26
beg off v 252
begad interj 132
beget v *obs. get* 56
beget v *engender* 56
beggar n/v 43
beggar v 43
begin v 27
beginner n 27, 83
beginning n 27
beglamour v 212
begone v 92
begonia n 193
begorra interj 230
begrudge v 59
beguile v *fascinate* 55
beguile v *delude* 55
behalf n 50
behave v 73
behavior 73
behavioral science n 309
behaviorism n 279
behemoth n 64
behest n *General/Miscellaneous* 47
behest n *obs. guarantee* 47
behind n *buttocks* 195
behindhand adj 115
behind-the-scenes adj 189
behold v 26
beholden adj 54
behoof n *arch.* 25
behoof n *benefit* 28
behoove v 25
beige adj/n 252
being n *something that exists* 49
being n *existence* 49
bejabbers interj/n 215
bejesus interj/n 277
belate v 162
belated adj 160
belay v 26
belch n/v 13
beldam n *obs. grandmother* 82
beldam n *hag* 82
beleaguer v 142
belfry n 33
belie v *distort* 191
belie v *obs. malign* 191
belie v *disprove* 191
belief n 20, 38
believable adj *Religion* 20
believe v *have faith* 20, 259

big band n 290
big bang n 302
Big Brother n 308
big brother n *older brother* 244
big business n (Am) 276
big C n *slang cancer* 316
big cheese n 300
big daddy n 312
big deal n 307
Big Dipper n 237
big game n 237
big house n *slang prison* 283
big name n 300
big noise n *big shot* 283
big O n *slang orgasm* 326
big picture n 313
big shot n 277
big time n (Am) 250
big toe n 256
big top n 246
big wheel n 277
bigamist n 46
bigamous adj 46
bigamy n 46
bigfoot n *Sasquatch* 312
bighearted adj 243
bighorn sheep n (Am) 194
bigmouth n (Am) 268
bigot n *gen.* 173
bigot n *type of religious follower* 173
bigotry n 173
bigwig n Slang 189
bike n/v (Am) 243, 261
biker n 320
bikini n 303
bilateral adj 206
bildungsroman n 276
bile n 106
bi-level n 316
bilge n 102
bilge n *fig. nonsense* 102, 277
bilgewater 102
bilingual adj 227
bilious 106
bilk n/v 158
bill v *applied to people* 119
bill n *unapproved law* 79
bill v *arch.* 42
bill v *as in "bill and coo," applied to birds* 119
bill n *beak* 11
bill n *as in "dollar bill"* 172
bill n *payment due* 76; v 76
bill n *ad, as in "post no bills"* 77
bill n *list, as in "bill of lading"* 42

bill of goods n 281
bill of health n 147
bill of sale n 152
billboard n (Am) 246
billfold n (Am) 258
billiard/billiards n 126
billing n *as in "top billing"* 246
billion n 221
billion n *obs. trillion* 221
billionaire n (Am) 245
billow n/v 133
billow v 133
billy n 229, 306
billy club n 229, 306
billy goat n 237
bim n *bimbo, girl* 283, 293
bimbette n 283, 327
bimbo n *dull woman* 283, 293, 327
bimbo n (Am) *dull man* 283
bin n 23
binary star n 220
binary system 220
bind n *fix, tough spot* 320
bind v *put together, e.g., "bind a book"* 96
bind v *make a formal agreement* 46
bind v *tie* 25
binding adj 46
binge n/v 252
binge v 252
bingo interj 292
bingo n 298
binocular n 242
binoculars n 242
bio 172
biochemical adj 237
biochemistry 237
biochip n 326
biodegradable adj 319
biodegrade v 319
biodiversity n 326
bioengineering n 279
biofeedback n 316
biographee n 172, 187
biographer n 172, 187
biographical 172
biography n 172
biography n *gen. written histories of people* 172
biological adj 210
biological clock n 311
biological warfare n 306
biologist n 237
biology n 210
bioluminescence n 279
biomass n 296

bionic 309
bionics n 309
biophysics n 255
biopsy n 257
biorhythm n 309
biosphere n 254
bipartisan adj 276
biped n 146
biplane n 243
biracial adj 276
birch v *flog* 174, 229
birch n *flogging tool* 174, 229
birch n 10
bird n *spec. young bird* 11
bird n *gen. aviarian* 11
bird v *go birdwatching* 281
bird n *woman* 249
bird n *man* 249
bird dog n/v (Am) 255
bird of paradise n 146
bird of prey n 64
birdbath n (Am) 258
birdbrain n 293
birdcage n 99
birdcall n 146
birdhouse 99
birdhouse n (Am) 239
bird's nest soup n 241
bird's-eye view n 204
birth v/n Love/Romance/Sex 275
birth n/v *applied to living things* 29
birth certificate n 267
birth control n (Am) 279
birth defect n 322
birthday n 40
birthday suit n 195
birthmark n 120
birthplace n 155
birthrate n 247
birthright n 111
birthstone n 278
biscuit n 34
bisexual adj/n 213
bishop n 19
bison n 64
bisque n 148
bistro n 289
bit n *as in "two bits is a quarter"* 172
bit n *as in "drill bit"* 16
bit n *morsel of food* 34
bit n Technology 302
bit n *gen. small portion* 34
bit n *mouthful* 34
bit part n 290
bit player 290

bitch n *as in "life's a bitch"* 215
bitch n *female dog* 11
bitch n *applied to women* 82
bitch v *complain, act surly* 288
bitch n *applied to men* 82
bitch v *bungle* 216
bitch goddess n *success* 277
bitchy adj 82, 301
bite n *portion of food* 102
bite n *act of biting* 102
bite n *piquance* 102
bite v 102
bite the bullet v 293
bitsy adj 278
bitter adj 23
bitter end n 231
bitterroot n (Am) 219
bitters n 183
bitty adj 278
bivouac n 215
biz n (Am) 249
bizarre adj 161
bizarre adj *obs. irascible* 161
bizarrerie 161
blab n *gossipmonger* 47; v 47
blab n *blabbermouth* 301
blabber n/v *blather* 47, 281
blabber n *blather* 281
blabbermouth n (Am) 47, 301
black v 57
black adj *opp. of white* 23
black n *fin. sense* 290
black adj *funereal* 79
black adj *as in "black market"* 289
black n *as in "boot black"* 14
black n *Negro* 154
black adj *as in "black comedy"* 318
black bean n 197
black bear n 181
black belt n 244
black death n 202
black dwarf n 302
Black English n 318
black eye n 147
black gold n *slang oil* 272
black hole n 315
black light n 294
black lung n 221
black mark n 231
black market n 300
black mass n 266
black pepper n 15
black powder n 277
black raspberry n (Am) 197
black rhinoceros n 220
black sheep n 202

black tea n 197
black tie adj/n 241
black widow n 279
black-and-blue adj 33
black-and-white adj/n 133
blackball v 204
blackberry n 10
blackbird n 30
blackboard n 214
blacken v 57
blackened adj *as in "blackened redfish"* 326
black-eyed pea n 183
black-eyed Susan n (Am) 254
blackguard n *rascal* 189
blackhead n 166
black-hearted adj 231
blackjack n *type of card game* 108
blackjack v *hit with a blackjack* 277
blacklist n/v 157
blackmail n *extortion* 229
blackmail n *protection money* 229
blackout n/v 279
blacksmith n 40
blackstrap molasses n (Am) 280
blacktop n (Am) 298
bladder n 13
bladderwort n 209
blade n *spec. to grass, etc.* 10
blade n *flat part of knives, etc.* 51
blade n *gen. leaf* 10
blade n *bon vivant* 51
blading n 326
blah adj *bland* 292
blah n *nonsense* 284
blah n *as in "the blahs"* 284
blah-blah-blah adv/n (Am) *etc.; nonsense* 292
blahs n 317
blame n/v 55
blamed adj/adv *darned, confounded* 230
blanch v *whiten* 59
blanch v *go pale* 59
blanch v *cook* 59
bland adj *applied to things* 124
bland adj *gentle, applied to people* 124
blank n *as in "fill in the blanks"* 133
blank adj *without color* 53
blank adj *not written on* 76
blank adj *as in "blank stare"* 76

blank adj *obs. without color* 76
blank cartridge n 229
blank check n 264
blank verse n 128
blanket adj 270
blanket n *blanketing layer* 33
blanket n 33
blanket v *fig.* 33
blanket v 161
blankety-blank adj/adv 267
blarney n 205
blasé adj 212
blaspheme 42
blasphemous 42
blasphemy n 42
blast n *explosion* 21
blast n *rollicking time* 21
blast n *party* 317
blast n *slang party* 21
blast n *blare* 21
blast n *extreme fun* 317
blast n *as in "blast of cold air"* 21
blast n *explosion* 248
blast off v 310
blasted adj *damned* 132
blasted adj *drunk* 132, 324
blastoff n 310
blatant adj *the blatant beast, coined by Spenser* 139
blatant adj *obvious* 139, 271
blatant adj *noisy* 139, 270
blather n/v 96
blaxploitation n 324
blaze n *outburst, display* 9
blaze n/v *fire* 9
blaze v *as in "blaze a trail"* 192
blazer n 260
blazes n *Hades* 230
bleach v 26
bleach n 258
bleachers n (Am) 263
bleaching boards n 263
bleaching powder n 222, 258
bleak adj *obs. white, pale* 115
bleak adj *barren* 115
bleak adj *hopeless* 115
blear v/adj 89
blear-eyed 89, 286
bleary adj 89
bleary-eyed adj 89, 286
bleat n/v 11
bleed v *lose blood* 13
bleed v *ooze* 13
bleed v *sympathize* 13
bleeder n *foolish person* 204
bleeding adj/adv (Brit) 175, 249

bleep n/v 321
bleep n 321
bleeping adj 324
blemish n/v 58
blend n/v 57, 269
blended whiskey n 297
blender n 239
bless v 19
blessed 19
blessing 19
blight n *gen. pestilence* 122
blight n *as in "plant blight"* 122
blight n *skin rash* 122
blighter n (Brit) 216
blimey interj 267
blimp n 280
blimpish adj *reactionary* 300
blind adj *unsighted* 14; adv/v 14
blind adj *as in "blind alley"* 14
blind n *concealment device* 148
blind alley n 133
blind date n 289
blind side n/v 157
blind spot n 250
blind staggers n (Am) 204
blind tiger n *speakeasy* 245
blind trust n 318
blinder n 212
blindfell v *obs. make blind* 28
blindfelled 116
blindfold n/v 116
blindfold n 116
blindman's bluff n 126
blindside n/v 320
blink n/v 120
blinkers n *blinders* 197
blinkers n *glasses* 197
blintze n 273
blip n *radar image* 302
blirt n *sudden crying* 195
bliss n 17
blister n/v 32
blister pack n 310
blithe adj *careless* 17
blithe adj *carefree* 17
blither v/n 245
blithering 245
blithesome adj 17, 184
blitz n 300
blitzkrieg n 300
blizzard n *violent hit* 237
blizzard n (Am) *snowstorm* 237
blob n/v 189
bloc n 276
block v *plan, as in "block out"* 141

block n *as in "block and tackle"* 72, 224
block n *as in "block of wood"* 51
block n *type of child's toy* 244
block n *as in "mental block"* 317
block v *prevent* 96; n 96
block n *as in "city block"* 205
block and tackle n 224
block letter n 276
block party n 304
blockade n/v 177
blockade-runner n 248
blockage n 251
blockbuster n 306
blockhead n 113
blockhouse n 106
blockish adj 113
bloke n 247
blond/blonde n/adj 99, 195
blond/blonde n *type of silk* 195
blood n *bloodlines, kin* 13
blood n *lit.* 13
blood brother n 75
blood cell n 221
blood heat n *body temperature* 210
blood money n 113
blood plate 256
blood poisoning n 238
blood pressure n 238
blood sausage n 241
blood sport n 269
blood test n 279
blood type n 297
blood vessel n 166
blood-and-guts adj 301
bloodbath n 248
bloodcurdling adj 275
bloodguilt, bloodguilty n, adj 124
bloodhound n 30
bloodletting n 32
bloodline n 275
bloodmobile n 303
bloodshed n 80
bloodshot adj *describing eyes* 147
bloodstock n *thoroughbred horses* 219
bloodstream n 238
bloodsucker n *parasitic person* 64
bloodsucker n 64
bloodthirsty adj 112
bloody adv (Brit) *damned* 175, 249

bloody v 112
Bloody Mary n 303
bloom n/v in flowers 29
bloomer n (Am) as in "bloomers" 241
bloomer n blunder 267
bloomers 241
blooming adj/adv as in "blooming idiot" 267
blooper n Sports 298
blooper n goof-up 307
blossom n/v as in "in blossom" 10
blossom n/v young flower 10
blotter n daily record 121
blotter n for blotting paper 121
blotter n as in "police blotter" 121
blotting paper 121
blotto adj drunk 283
blouse n gen. 223
blouse n spec. to women's clothing 223
blow n cocaine 320
blow n/v blossom 10
blow v squander 268
blow v mess up 132
blow v as in "winds blowing" 25; n 25
blow v leave 283
blow n fig., as in "a blow to the ego" 80
blow v perform oral sex 311
blow n as in "a blow to the head" 80
blow v as in "blow your nose" 140
blow away v kill 202
blow it v 320
blow job n 311
blow up v explode 266
blow your mind v 321
blow your stack v 308
blow-by-blow adj (Am) 301
blow-dried 316
blow-dry v 316
blow-dryer n 316
blower n slang telephone 290
blowfish 255
blowgun n (Am) 215
blowhard n (Am) 249
blowoff n 232
blowout n 216
blowtorch n 260
BLT n 310
blubber v cry 67
blubber n as in "whale blubber" 30

bludgeon n/v 188, 248
blue n the sky, nowhere, as in "out of the blue" 165
blue adj/n colored blue 55
blue adj pornographic 249
blue adj depressed 55, 72, 155; n 55
blue blood n 229
blue cheese n 287
blue chip n (Am) 276
blue devils n despondency 198
blue flu n 318
blue funk n 243
blue jay n (Am) 181
blue jeans n 241
blue law n (Am) 203
blue moon n 216
blue plate adj 287
blue ribbon n 176
blue spruce n 254
blue streak n 231
blue whale n 236
bluebeard n 216
bluebell n 118
blueberry n 183
bluebird n 165
bluebonnet n 164
blue-chipper 276
blue-collar adj 305
blue-devil v 198
bluegill n (Am) 254
bluegrass n (Am) Plants 193
bluegrass n Music 312
bluenose n (Am) 277
blue-plate special 287
blueprint n 269
blues n (Am) depression 72, 185
blues n Music 276
blues n Cloth/Clothing 197
blueshift n 310
blue-sky adj 262
bluesman n 276
bluestocking n learned woman 204
bluff adj frank 160
bluff adj with a smooth front 160
bluff n/v 235
bluff n cliff 164
bluff v 235
blunder v goof up 59; n 189
blunder v as in "blunder about" 59; n 59
blunderbuss n 174
blunt adj frank 36
blunt adj dull, applied to people 36

blunt v 36
blurb n/v (Am) 281
blurt v 141
blush n facial flush 120; v 120
blush n glance, as in "at first blush" 120
blush wine n 326
blusher n cosmetic 316
bluster v lit. and fig. 96
bluster 96
bo obs. boo 215
boa n as in "feather boa" 64, 242
boa n snake 64
boa constrictor n 64, 209
boar n male pig 11
boar n type of wild pig 11
board v enter by force 96
board v gen. enter 96
board n wood plank 23; v 23
board n group, as in "board of directors" 134
board n food, as in "room and board" 34; v 34
board foot n (Am) 256
board game n 298
boarder 183
boarding pass n 317
boarding school n 173
boardinghouse n 183
boardroom n (Am) 226
boardsailing 323
boardwalk n (Am) 241
boast n/v brag 59
boast v feature 59
boast v obs. make threats 59
boat n small boat 16
boat n gen. water vessel 16
boat n gravy container 16
boat people n 325
boatel n 310
boathouse n 184
boatswain's chair n 257
bob v as in "bobbing the head" 57; n 57
bob v arch. cheat/filch 46
bob n as in "plumb bob" 168
bob v trim 179
bob n shilling 200
bob o' lincoln 194
bobbery n hubbub 216
bobbin n 107
bobble v drop 321
bobble v bob while moving 321
bobby n (Brit) policeman 230
bobby pin n (Am) 297
bobby socks n (Am) 303
bobby-soxer n (Am) 307

bobcat n (Am) 255
bobolink n (Am) 194
bobsled n (Am) 224
bobtail n Animals 145
bobtail n type of arrow 145
bobwhite n (Am) 209
bocce n 275
bocci 275
bock n 241
bod n body 296
bodacious adj 231
bode v augur 27
bodement 27
bodice n 123
bodice ripper n 323
body n as in "body of work" 87
body n corpse 13
body n the body 13
body n group, as in "legislative body" 51
body bag n 312
body blow n 203
body cavity n 238
body count n 319
body English n 276
body language 276
body shirt n 316
body shop n 311
body snatcher n 215
body stocking n 316
body wave n 316
bodybuilding n 275
bodyguard n 185
bodysurf v 304
boff v have sex 298
boffo adj 307
bog n/v Geography/Places 29
bog v fig. 142
bogey n as in "bogeyman" 230
bogeyman n 230
bogle n spectre 112
bogus adj (Am) 234
bohemian n artistic person 228
boil v 57
boil n skin inflammation 14
boiled adj drunk 215
boiler n 183
boiler room n 273
boilerplate n 250
boilerplate n standard 321
boiling point n 193
boisterous adj rambunctious 89
boisterous adj obs. physically rough, coarse 89
boistous adj 89
bold adj forward 17
bold adj courageous 17
bolero n 201

boll weevil n (Am) 255
bollix v/n 300
bollocks n *testicles* 182
bolo tie n 316
bologna n 223
bologna sausage 223
bolognian sausage 223
bolster n *type of phys. support* 21; v 21
bolt n *cloth measure* 35
bolt v *move suddenly* 57; n 57
bolt n *crossbow bolt* 21
bolt n *rifle bolt* 248
bolt n *as in "door bolt," "nuts and bolts"* 36
bolt-action adj 248
bomb n/v 174
bomb n *failure* 174, 320
bomb n *obs. type of fire weapon* 174
bombard n *type of cannon* 80
bombard n 80
bombardier n *cannon operator* 130
bombardier n *bomber crewmember* 130
bombardment 80
bombast n 127
bombastic 127
bombastical 127
bombed adj *drunk* 300
bomber n 282
bomber jacket n 310
bombinate v *hum* 256
bombshell n 188
bome 174
bon mot n 187
bon vivant n 174
bon voyage interj 102
bona fide adj 207
bona fides n 204
bonanza n (Am) 232
bonbon n 197
bond n *something that ties, confines* 47
bond n *bail money* 47
bondsman n 188
bone v *debone* 100
bone n 13
bone china n 258
bone of contention n 189
bone up v 252
bone-dry adj 217
bonehead n (Am) 277
bonemeal n (Am) 233
boner n *gaffe* 216
bonesetter n 99
boneyard n (Am) 247

bonfire n 65
bong n *type of pipe* 324
bong n *bell sound* 250
bongo n (Am) *the drum* 282
bonhomie n *congeniality* 198
bonkers adj *crazy* 304
bonnet n *headwear for men* 71
bonnet n *headwear for women* 71
bonny adj *pretty* 99
bonsai n 259
bonus n 205
boo interj/n/v 215
boob n (Am) *simpleton* 277
boob n *slang breast* 302
boob n/v *blunder* 300
boob tube n 319
boobies 302
booboisie n 293
boo-boo (Am) 300
booby *dolt* 277
booby *breast* 302
booby hatch n *asylum* 231, 292
booby hatch n *jail* 231, 292
booby prize n 269
booby trap n 229
booger n 238
boogeyman 230
boogie n/v *Music* 282
boogie-woogie n/v (Am) Music 282
boohoo n/v 107
book n *as in "financial books"* 76
book n 19
book v *process a criminal* 248
book n *applied to betting* 226
book v *schedule* 218
book n *performance script* 129
book n *something bound, as in "matchbook"* 103
book club n 201
book review n 246
book value n 263
bookcase n 183
bookend n 273
bookie n 263
bookish adj 125
bookkeeper n 127
bookkeeping 127
booklet n 246
bookmark n 227
bookmobile n 290
bookseller n 101
bookshelf n 211
bookshop 201
bookstore n (Am) 201
bookworm n 132

Boolean algebra n 256
boom n/v *spar* 107
boom n/v 95
boom n/v *surge* 253
boom box n 327
boomerang n 212
boomtown n 254
boon adj *genial, as in "boon companion"* 72
boon n *blessing* 51
boon n *obs. type of prayer* 51
boondocks n (Am) 277
boondoggle n 292
boonies n 277
boor n 133
boor n *obs. common person* 133
boorish adj 133
boost v (Am) 218
boost n 218
booster n 218
booster shot n 302
boot v *kick, give the boot to* 271
boot n *arch.* 80
boot n *in addition, as in "to boot"* 22; v 22
boot n *footwear* 35; v 35
boot camp n (Am) 306
boot hill n (Am) *slang cemetery* 276
booth n *stall* 33
bootie n (Am) *baby footwear* 197
bootleg n/v 267
bootlegger n 267
bootlick v (Am) 235
bootstrap n 260
bootstrap v 309
booty adj/n 80
booze n/v 34
boozer 34
boozy 34
bop n (Am) *bebop* 305
bop v *as in "bop into the house"* 314
bop n/v *hit* 301
bopeep n *peekaboo* 108
bopper n *teeny-bopper* 322
bordeaux n 122
bordel n 126
bordelaise sauce n 273
bordello n 126
border n/v 82
border line n 82, 250
border line adj 250
border on v 82
borderland n 82, 216
borderline adj/adv 278
bore v *cause boredom* 207

bore v *pierce with a tool* 26
boredom 207
boring adj 207
born adj 23
born-again adj 319
borrow v 26
borrowed time n 269
borscht n 223
borscht belt n 299
borscht circuit n 299
borzoi n *type of dog* 255
bosh n *nonsense* 230
bosh interj 230
bosom v *arch.* 13
bosom n *lit. breast* 13
bosom v *embrace* 144
bosom n *fig. intimate inner portion* 13
bosom adj *as in "bosom buddies"* 138
boss n (Am) *cow* 197
boss n *chief* 158
boss v *as in "boss around"* 252
boss n Slang 300
boss adj *cool* 231
boss n *political leader* 158; v 158
boss man n 158, 300
bossa nova n 318
bossy adj (Am) *domineering* 158, 261
bossy n *cow* 197
Boston baked beans n (Am) 241
Boston cream pie n (Am) 241
Boston terrier n (Am) 255
Boswell n *chronicler* 246
botanical adj 165
botanical garden n 197
botanist 165
botany n 165
botch v *mess up* 116
botch n *boil, blemish* 66
botch v *repair* 116
bother v *annoy* 192; n 192
bother v *confound* 192
botheration interj/n 203
bothersome 203
bottle n *baby's bottle* 33
bottle n/v 33
bottle gourd n 219
bottled gas n 285
bottle-feed v 241
bottleneck adj/n/v 271
bottle-nosed dolphin n 272
bottom n General/Miscellaneous 21
bottom n *buttocks* 21, 256

bottom line adj/n 318
bottom round n *cut of beef* 287
bottomland n 181
bottomless adj 54
botulism n 257
boudoir n 196
bouffant adj/n 224
bough n 10
boughten adj 207
bouillabaisse n 241
bouillon n 167, 287
bouillon cube n 167, 287
boulder n 63
boulderstone 63
boulevard n 149
bounce v *Finances/Money* 264
bounce v *reject a check* 116
bounce v *obs. beat, pound* 116
bounce n/v *rebound* 116
bouncer n *bar guard* 244
bouncer n *braggart* 244
bouncy adj 294
bound n/v *as in "out of bounds"* 49
bound adj *ready, as in "bound and determined"* 89
bound adj *as in "bound for glory"* 89
bound n/v *as in "leaps and bounds"* 113
boundary n 158
bounden adj *beholden* 53
bounder n *knave* 268
bounteous adj *benevolent* 88
bounteous adj *copious* 88
bountied 88
bountiful 88
bounty n *spec. reward for services rendered* 37
bounty n *generosity* 37
bounty hunter n 292
bouquet n 183
bouquet n *fig. compliment* 183
bouquet n *aroma, as in "a wine's bouquet"* 183
bourbon n 241
bourgeois adj 129
bourgeois n 129
bourgeoise n *female bourgeois* 129
bourgeousie n 129
bout n 114
boutique n 200
boutique n *as in "bout of measles"* 200
boutonniere n 242
bovine adj/n 210
bovine n 210

bow n *as in "violin bow"* 129; v 129
bow n *bow of a boat* 72
bow v *bow before someone* 25; v 25
bow n *type of knot* 137
bow n 20
bow out v *withdraw* 308
bow tie n 260
bowdlerize v 227
bowel n 32
bowel n *gen. interior* 32
bowery n (Am) *type of farm* 148
bowie knife n (Am) 229
bowl n 14
bowl n/v *related to bowling* 75
bowl over v 252
bowleg n 120
bowler n *Sports* 75
bowler n *the hat* 242
bowling n *Sports* 75, 101
bowling alley 101
bowls n *Sports* 75, 101
bowman n *archer* 45
bowwow interj *the sound* 132
box n *slang female genitalia* 302
box n *coffin* 291
box n *plant* 10
box n/v *hit* 45
box n/v *as in "container"* 14
box camera n 228
box elder n 194
box kite n 262
box lunch n 303
box office n 201
box seat n 228
box social n (Am) 291
box spring n 258
box turtle n (Am) 209
boxcar n (Am) 242
boxer n *in the sport* 185
boxer n *someone who hits* 45
boxer n *type of dog* 272
boxer shorts n 303
boxing n *the sport* 185
boxing glove 185
boxwood n 164
boxy adj 251
boy interj 292
boy n *young male* 49
boy n *fellow, as in "one of the boys"* 49
boy n *servant* 40
boy n *obs. cad* 49
boy n *derogatory sense* 40
boy scout n 278
boy toy n 327

boy wonder n 308
boycott n/v 263
boyfriend n 262
boyhood n 182
boyo n 249
boysenberry n 296
bozo n (Am) 283
bra n 280, 297
brabble n/v *squabble* 113
brace n *clasp* 36
brace v *prepare for* 59
brace v *support with a brace* 36, 59; n 36
brace v *tighten* 59
bracelet n 71
bracelet n *slang handcuff* 71
bracer n *stiff drink* 196
bracer n *wristband* 71
braces n 257
brachiopod n 220
bracket n *grouping, as in "tax bracket"* 270
bracket n *shelf* 121
bracket n[] 187
bracket n *support for shelf* 121
bracket creep n *in taxes* 323
brackish adj 105
brad n 35
brag v 93
braggadocio n *braggart* 124
braggadocio n *bragging* 124
braggart n 93, 124
bragger 124
braid v *twist into braids* 27; n 27
braid v *obs. move suddenly* 28
braille n/v 245
braillewriter n 305
brain n *slang brainy person* 13
brain n *The Body* 13
brain v *hit in the head* 80
brain n *fig. intelligence* 13
brain coral n 181
brain death n 316
brain drain n 320
brain stem n 256
brain trust n (Am) 277
brain wave n 243
brainchild n 151
brainish adj *hotheaded* 107
brains trust (Brit) 277
brainsick adj *crazy* 17
brainstorm n/v 262
brainteaser n 289
brainwash v 304
brainwashing n 304
brainy adj 225
braise v 207

brake n/v *as in "car brakes"* 198
brakeman n 224
bramble n 10
bran n 34
bran n *obs. dandruff* 34
branch n *subdivision, as in "branch of government"* 49, 177
branch n *tree limb* 49
branch water n 222
brand n *trademark; type* 232
brand n/v *lit. burn mark* 122
brand n *torch, as in "firebrand"* 122
brand n *fig. mark* 122
brand name n 289
Brand X n 318
brandish n/v 58
brand-new adj 137
brandy n 148
brandy-wine 148
brash adj/n *brazen* 213
brash adj/n *fragile* 213
brass n *audacity* 73, 268
brass n *bronze* 23
brass n *the metal* 23
brass band n 228
brass hat n *muckamuck* 268
brass instrument n 246
brass knuckles n (Am) 247
brass ring n 308
brass tacks n 269
brasserie n *type of restaurant* 245
brassiere n 280
brassy adj 249
brassy adj *loud* 138
brassy adj *made of brass* 138, 249
brat n *snotty child* 112
bratling 112
bratwurst n 259
braunschweiger n 287
brava interj/n *"bravo" for women* 203, 215
bravado n 124
brave adj 100; v 117
brave n *one who is brave/bully, arch. assassin* 169
brave n *obs. thug* 169
brave n *warrior* 169, 203
brave v *arch. dare* 117
brave new world n 301
bravery 100
bravo n *thug for hire* 131
bravo interj/n 203, 215
bravura n 201

brawl n/v 93
brawn n *boar meat* 32
brawn n 32
brawny adj 32
brazen adj *made of brass* 137
brazen v 137
brazen adj *hardened by fire* 137
brazen adj *fig. hardened* 137
brazen-faced 137
brazier n *coalpan* 168
brazier n *brassworker* 40
Brazil nut n 223
breach n/v 25
breach of promise n 131
bread n 15
bread n (Am) *slang money* 15, 299
bread v *cover with crumbs* 148
bread and butter n/adj 156
bread and circuses n 283
bread mold n 280
breadboard n 239
breadfruit n 168
breadline n 229
breadstick n 274
breadstuff n (Am) 197
breadth n 66
breadwinner n 213
break v (Am) *as in "breaking news"* 284
break n *as in "coffee break"* 250
break n *gap* 51
break v *fig.* 25
break n/vn 25
break dancing n 327
break down v 232
break in v 248
break out v 217
break through v 284
breakaway adj/n 269
breakbone fever n 238
breakdown n 232
breakeven n 299
break-even adj (Am) *as in "break-even point"* 299
breakfast n/v 70
break-in n 248
breaking and entering n 203
breaking point n 269
breakneck adj 137
breakout n 217
breakthrough n 284
breast n *cut of meat* 13
breast n *mammary gland* 13
breast v *handle boldly* 142
breast n *chest* 13
breast-beating n 301

breastbone n 13
breast-feed v 273
breastplate n 71
breaststroke n 244
breastwork n 155
breath n 31
breath n *obs. aroma, odor* 31
breathe v 31
breathing space n 157
breathless adj *dead* 233
breathless adj *as in "breathless description"* 233
breathtaking adj 270
bred-in-the-bone adj *deep-seated* 102
breech delivery n 257
breech presentation n 211
breech/breeches n *obs. breech-cloth* 35
breech/breeches n *trousers* 35
breechcloth n 197
breechclout n *loincloth* 197
breechloader n 247
breed n *lineage* 75
breed n *line of ancestry* 75
breed v *conceive and bear* 18
breed v *be pregnant* 18
breed v *create hybrids* 18
breeding ground n 250
breeze n *obs. wind from the north* 146
breeze n *slang piece of cake* 146
breeze n 146
breezeway n (Am) 297
breezy adj 249
b'rer n (Am) 267
brethren n 18
breviary n 101
brevity n 102
brew v/n 15
brew v *fig. engender* 15
brewage 15
brewer's yeast n 241
brewery n 15, 41
brewpub n 327
brewski n 326
briar n *type of smoking pipe* 239
bribe n *something given to a beggar* 86
bribe n *obs. something stolen* 86
bribe n/v 86
bribery 86
bric-a-brac n 232
brick adj *brick-colored* 91, 217
brick n *baked clay* 69
brick n *gen. brick-shaped block* 69

brick n *blocks of baked clay* 69; v 69
brick cheese n (Am) 259
brick red 91
brickbat n 133
bricklayer n 75
brickle adj *brittle* 25
bricolage n *something jury-rigged* 321
bridal adj/n 18
bridal wreath n 262
bride v *obs. marry* 18
bride n 18
bridegroom n 18
bride-price n *opp. of dowage* 262
bridesmaid n 125
bridesman 125
bridge n 226
bridge n/v *part of nose* 14
bridge n *ship's control room* 14, 243
bridge n/v *the structure* 14
bridgework n *dental bridge* 257
bridle n/v 15
bridle path n 212
Brie n *the cheese* 241
brief adj 53
brief v 235
brief n *The Law* 175; v 175, 235
brief n *gen. letter* 175
briefcase n 281
briefing n 235
brier n *source of briar pipes* 236
brier n *type of plant* 10
brierroot n 236
brierwood n 236
brig n *the ship* 184
brig n *navy guardhouse, prison* 247
brigade n 155
brigadier n 155
brigand n *obs. type of soldier* 80
brigand n *freebooter* 80
brigantine 184
bright adj 23
bright adj *intelligent* 23
brighten v 23
bright-eyed adj 121
brightwork n (Am) *chrome-work, etc.* 232
brilliance n 179
brilliancy n 179
brilliant adj 179
brilliantine n (Am) *hair dressing* 242

brim n *edge, as in "brim of a cup"* 48
brim n *hat brim* 48
brim n *gen. border* 48
brimstone n *sulfur* 10
brimstone n *fig. passion* 10
brine n/v 10
brine shrimp n 220
bring v 25
brink n 48
brinkmanship n 313
brioche n *type of pastry* 223
briquette n 270
brisk adj *quick* 137
brisk adj *invigorating* 137
brisk adj *brusque* 137
brisk v 137
brisket n 34
bristle v *take offense* 124
bristle n 21
bristlecone pine n 254
britches n 212
British English n 245
British Thermal Unit/BTU n 255
brittle adj 88
brittle n *the candy* 280
bro n *brother* 175
broach v *bring up, address* 141
broach n 48
broach v *phys. pierce* 141
broad adj *overstated* 23
broad adj *wide* 23
broad n *woman* 283
broad adj *wide-ranging* 23
broad jump n 244
broadax/broadaxe n 21
broad-brush adj 320
broadcast n/v *related to radio and TV* 291
broadcast n/v *sow seeds widely* 291
broadcast journalism n 319
broadcasting n *as in TV, radio* 291
broadcloth n 71
broaden v 23, 191
broadloom adj/n *made on a wide loom* 287
broad-minded adj 125
broadside n *part of ship's side* 123; v 123, 327
broadside n *attack from the broadside* 123
broad-spectrum adj 309
broadsword n 21
Brobdingnagian adj 190
brocade n *type of fabric* 122
broccoli n 168

brochure n 187
brogan n type of shoe 223
brogue n type of accent 172
brogue n type of shoe 123
broider v arch. embroider 71
broil n/v brawl 80
broil n/v Food 34
broke adj having no money 187
broken adj not functional 53
broken-down adj 217
brokenhearted adj 108
broken-winded adj having the heaves 121
broker n/v 40
brokerage 40
bromide n 276
bromo n 286
bronc 220
bronchial asthma n 257
bronchial tube n 221
bronchitis n 210
bronco n 220
broncobuster 220
Bronx cheer n (Am) 293
bronze n/v 163
Bronze Age n 237
brooch n 35
brood v sit on to hatch 124
brood n litter 11; n 11
brood v sulk 124
brood mare n 11
brooder n 11
broody adj 124
brook n 9
brook v tolerate 17
brook trout n 220
broom n type of plant 14
broom n/v 14
broomball n 298
broomstick 14
broth n 15
brothel n obs. whore 126
brothel n obs. cur 126
brothel n 126
brother n lit. and fig. 18
brotherhood n group of fellows 44
brotherhood n 44
brother-in-law n 39
brougham n type of carriage 242
brouhaha n 269
brow n obs. eyelash 13
brow n forehead 13
brow n eyebrow 13
browbeat v 141
brown adj of the color brown 23
brown adj tanned, dark complected 23

brown n/v 23
brown bagging n 310
brown bear n 194
brown Betty n (Am) apple pudding 241
brown rice n 280
brown sauce n 259
brown study n 107
brown sugar n 183
brown trout n 255
Brownian motion n 237
brownie n (Am) type of dessert 259
brownie n type of goblin 102
brownie point n 320
brownnose n/v 301
brownout n 302
brownshirt n Nazi 301
brownstone n 222
browse v fig. scan 71
browse n shoots and twigs eaten by animals 107; v 71
browse v scan 252
brrr interj 267
bruin n 99
bruise v crush 55
bruise n/v 55
brume n mist, fog 210
brummagem adj tawdry, spurious 160
brunch n 259
brunette n dark-haired Caucasian 166; adj 166
brunette n dark-skinned Caucasian 166; adj 166
Brunswick stew n 241
brunt n full effect, as in "bear the brunt" 85
brunt n force, attack 85
brush n as in "artist's brush" 71
brush n as in "a brush with the law" 51
brush n/v brushing tool 71
brush n 30
brush fire n (Am) 193
brush up v 142
brushland 30
brush-off n (Am) 307
brusque adj 169
brusquerie 169
brussels sprout n 197
brut adj very dry—to describe wine 259
brutal adj obs. pertaining to animals 91
brutal adj vicious 91
brutal adj brutish 91

brutality n obs. primitiveness 108
brutality n viciousness 91, 108
brutalize 91
brute adj/n 90
BS n (Am) bull 283
bub, bubby n (Am) informal address 231
bubble n/v 50
bubble bath n 303
bubble gum n 297
bubble memory n 315
bubblegum adj of adolescent interest 320
bubblehead n 307
bubbler n water fountain 280
bubbly n (Am) informal address 231
bubbly n champagne 280
bubby n slang breast 166
bubonic adj 257
bubonic plague n 257
buccaneer n French or English pirate 174
buccaneer n gen. pirate 174
buccaneer n obs. boucan cook 174
Bucephalus n riding horse 175
buck adv as in "buck naked" 294
buck n dollar 245
buck v as in "bucking trends" 192, 235
buck v butt with head 235
buck n obs. male goat 11
buck adj as in "buck private" 282
buck v as in "a horse bucking" 235
buck n other male animals 11
buck n male deer 11
buck fever n (Am) nervous excitement 225
buck passer n 284
buck up v 235
buckaroo n (Am) 230
buckboard n (Am) 224
bucket n 35
bucket brigade n 284
bucket seat n 274
bucket shop n (Am) saloon serving alcohol in bucket 245
buckeye n (Am) Plants 193
buckeye n resident of Ohio 193
buckle n/v Cloth/Clothing 35
buckle v collapse 116
buckle v 35
buckle down v get to work 140

buckle up v 323
buckler n small shield 45
bucko n 267
bucksaw n (Am) 242
buckshot n 203
buckskin adj/n 35
bucktooth n 195
buckwheat n 106
bucolic adj 159
bucolic n type of poem 159
bucolical 159
bud n (Am) buddy 226, 249
bud n/v as in "rosebud" 64
bud v fig. spring up 64; n 64
buddy n (Am) 226
buddy v 226
buddy system n 307
buddy-buddy adj 226, 312
budge adj pompous 150
budge v yield 142
budgerigar n 220, 285
budget adj inexpensive 304
budget v/n 187
budget n obs. type of wallet 187
budgeteer n 227
budgie n 220, 285
buff n gen. aficionado 301
buff n birthday suit, as in "in the buff" 147
buff n type of leather 123
buff n firefighting aficionado 301
buff v 232
buff v polish 252
buffalo n Asian buffalo 105
buffalo n American buffalo 105
buffalo v bamboozle 268
buffer n intermediary 232; v 232
buffer state n 266
buffer zone n 277
buffet n/v hit 48
buffet adj in the style of a buffet 197
buffet n sideboard 183
buffoon n obs. type of dance 156
buffoon n clownish person 156
buffoon n professional jester 156
buffoonery 156
bug n any insect 146
bug n obs. bugbear 81
bug v eavesdrop 284
bug n bedbug 146
bug v as in "eyes bugging out" 271
bug v bother 308
bug n germ 146, 286

cabin n *type of building* 33

cabin n *room on a ship, etc.* 33

cabin cruiser n 288

cabin fever n (Am) 281

cabinet n *type of political group* 106, 157

cabinet n *type of furniture* 106

cabinetmaker 106

cabinetry 106

cable n *telegram* 265

cable Communication 246

cable n *cable TV* 324, 319

cable n *type of rope* 35

cable car n (Am) 243

cable television n 319, 324

cablegram n (Am) 246, 265

cablevision n 319, 324

caboodle n (Am) 231, 269

caboose n *ship's kitchen* 242

caboose n *train car* 242

cabriolet n *type of carriage* 198, 224

cabstand n 224

ca'canny n (Brit) *work slow-down* 264

cacao n 118, 183

cacao bean/cocoa bean 118

cacao butter n 122

cacciatore adj 303

cache n 205

cachepot n *flowerpot holder* 239

cachinnate v *laugh loudly* 213

cachinnation n 213

cackle n/v 55

cacography n *badd spelling* 127

cacology n *bad pronunciation* 201

cacophonous 176

cacophony n 176

cactus n 193

cactus n *type of artichoke* 193

cad n *lout* 231

cadaver n 102

cadaverous adj 102

CAD/CAM n 315

caddie n *obs. cadet* 199

caddie n *worker of any odd job* 199

caddie n/v *as in "golf caddie"* 199

caddish adj 231

cadence n *rhythm* 83

cadence n *rhythm in speech* 83

cadency n 83

cadet n 203

cadet n *young son* 203

Cadmean victory n *victory with equal losses* 155

cadmium n 209

caduceus n *Mercury's staff; med. symbol* 135

caducity n *senility* 195

Caesar salad n 303

Caesarism n *totalitarianism* 154

cafe n 200

cafe au lait n 196

café noir n 222

cafeteria n (Am) *coffee house* 226, 298

cafeteria n *type of eating establishment* 226, 298

cafetorium n *cafe(teria) (audi)-torium* 312

caffeine n 211

caftan n 123

cage n/v 48

cageling n 250

cagey n 261

cahoots n (Am) 232

caisson n 188

cajole v 163

cajolery 163

cake v 161

cake n *dessert cake* 34

cake n *type of bread* 34

cakewalk n *type of contest* 246

calabash n *type of gourd* 119

calaboose n (Am) *jail* 203

calamari n 316

calamary n *type of squid* 119

calamine n 69

calamitous 85

calamity n *catastrophe* 85

calamity n *adversity* 85

calash n *type of carriage* 169

calcium n 209

calculate v 96

calculating adj 213

calculation n 83

calculator n *calculating machine* 195

calculen *obs. calculate* 96

calculus n 146

calculus n *obs. gen. calculation* 146

caldera n 164

calendar n *phys. chart of the year, as in "wall calendar"* 31

calendar n *measure of a year* 31; v31

calendar n *schedule, as in "calendar of events"* 31

calendar year n 272

calf n *iceberg portion* 11

calf n *young cow* 11

calf n *back of the leg* 32

calf n *young of other animals* 11

calf's-foot jelly n 197

calf-love n *puppy love* 213

calfskin n 100

caliber n *level* 134

caliber n *on a gun* 131

caliber n *pertaining to guns* 134

calibrate v 238

calibration n 238

calico adj/n *type of cloth* 107

calico bush n (Am) 209

California condor n 220

californium n 302

caliginous adj *misty, dim* 117

caliper n/v 123

calisthenic adj 226

calisthenics n 226

calk *obs. calculate* 96

call v *visit* 25

call v *pertaining to animals* 25

call n/v *as in "telephone call"* 271

call v *telephone* 25

call v *name* 59

call v *pertaining to people* 25

call v *visit* 104

call girl n (Am) 289, 298

call house n *bordello* 289, 298

call letters n 282

call loan n Finances/Money 245

call of nature n 204

call sign n Movies/TV/Radio 282

call slip n (Am) *in libraries* 264

call to quarters n 282

calla n 209

calla lily n 209

callaloo n 168

callant n *lad* 135

callboy n *bellhop* 200

caller ID n *type of phone service* 327

callet n *prostitute* 75

calligrapher n 201

calligrapher n 153

calligraphist n 201

calligraphy n 153

calling n 48

calling card n (Am) 266

calliope n (Am) 246

calliper compasses 123

callous adj *fig. insensitive* 67

callous adj/v 67

callow adj 17

callus n *callosity* 120

callus n/v 120

calm adj/n/v 88

calmative n/adj 238

caloric n *supposed source of heat* 195, 210; adj 195

calorie n 210

calorimeter n 195, 210

calumet n *type of Native American tobacco pipe* 177

calumniate v 73

calumny n 73

calve v 11

calypso n *music style* 290

calzone n 303

cam n *as in "overhead cam"* 195

CAM n 315

camaraderie n 226

camcorder n 327

camel n 11

camel hair/camel's hair n 71

cameleer n 213

camellia n *type of shrub or tree* 193

camelopard n *giraffe* 64

Camembert n 259

cameo n Literature/Writing 245

cameo n *as in "cameo appearance"* 77

cameo n *type of carving* 77

camera n *photographic instrument* 183, 222

camera n *chamber* 183

cameraman n 275, 323

cameraperson n 275

camera-shy adj 288

camerawoman n 275, 323

camerist n *arch.* 275

camion n *type of cart, truck or bus* 261

camisado n *night attack* 112

camise n *type of shirt* 212

camisole n *type of women's garment* 197

camisole n *type of men's garment* 197

camo adj/n *camouflage* 327

camorra n *disreputable organization* 248

camorrista n 248

camouflage adj/n/v 284

camp n *fig. group, as in "the opposing camp"* 106

camp n *temporary residence* 106; v 106

camp n *the amusingly out of date* 277, 320; adj 277, 320

camp n *homosexual* 320

camp follower n 216

camp shirt n 323
campaign n gen. 155
campaign n election use 155, 215
campaign n mil. 155, 215
campanile n bell tower 148
campanology n art of ringing bells 173
campcraft n 258
campfire n 165
campground n (Am) 211
camphor n 29
camphor ball 29
campsite 211
campus n (Am) 205
campy 320
camshaft n 224
can v obs. know 28
can v is able to 28
can n container 14; v 239
can v is allowed 28
can v (Am) stop 277
can n slang buttocks 14, 286
can n (Am) slang jail 283
can n slang toilet 14, 258
can of worms n 320
Canada goose n 181
Canadian bacon n 297
Canadian football n 226
canaille n rabble 130
canal n 169
canal n natural waterway 169
canal n tube 169
canape n 259
canard n falsehood 233
canary n 164
canary n type of wine 164
canary bird 164
canary seed n 118
canary yellow n 252
canasta n 304
cancan n 228
cancel v obliterate 83
cancel v stop 83
cancellation 83
cancer n 147
cancer n obs. type of sore 147
cancer n fig. 147
cancer stick n (Am) 313
cancrene 106
candelabra n 211
candelabrum n 211
candid adj frank 169, 198
candid adj obs. white 169
candid adj arch. pure 169
candidacy n 136
candidate n aspirant 136
candidate n possibility 136

candidature n 136
candied adj 122
candle n 14
candleholder n 297
candlelight n 14
candlelighter n 100
Candlemas n 20
candlepin n 275
candlepower n 256
candlesnuffer n 123
candlestick n 14
can-do adj 275
candor n frankness 198
candor n rare fairness 198
candor n 169
candor n rare whiteness 198
candy n crystallized sugar 34
candy n confection 34; v 34, 106
candy ass adj/n (Am) 325
candy striper n 316
cane n Plants 64
cane n walking aid 64, 123
cane v 123
cane sugar n 223
canine n the tooth 66
canine n dog 66, 237; adj 237
canister/cannister n 167
canker n 14, 273; v 14
canker sore n 14, 273
cannabis n 194
canned laughter n (Am) 319
cannelloni n 223
cannery n (Am) 245
cannibal n 133
cannibalism 133
cannibalize v 308
cannister n 167
cannon n 80
cannon fodder n 266
cannonade n/v 80
cannonball n 80
cannonball v 314
cannot v 93
canny adj cunning 125
canny adj knowing 125
canoe n/v 123
canola oil n 323
canon n 19
canonize v 78
canopy n 69
canopy n pertaining to vehicles 69
canorous adj euphonious 161
can't contr 172
cantaloupe n 183
cantankerous adj 198
cantata n 187

cantatrice n female opera singer 214
canteen n type of establishment 185
canteen 190
canter n/v 184
Canterbury v 184
cantharsis n Spanish fly 74
canticle n 42
cantilever n type of bracket 168; v 168
cantilever n projection 168
cantina n (Am) 227
canto n 128
cantor n 111
canvas n Cloth/Clothing 35
canvas n painting surface 35
canvasback n (Am) type of duck 194
canvass v obs. beat up in a canvas bag 139
canvass v/n poll 139
canyon n (Am) 219
cap v arrest 188
cap n obs. hood 35
cap n sealer 72
cap n as in "cap gun" 229
cap n capital letter 76
cap n headgear 35
cap v 72
cap and gown n 247
cap sleeve n 287
capability n 137
capable adj obs. having sufficient capacity 137
capable adj 137
capacitate v make capable 179
capacity n 85
capacity adj 85, 271
cap-a-pie adv head-to-toe 117
cape n type of religious clothing 123
cape n jutting land 63
cape n type of garment 123
Cape buffalo n 255
Cape Cod cottage n 280
caper n/v leap 135
caper n type of bush 100
caper n scheme 225
caper n garnish 100
capful of wind n 189
capias n warrant 80
capillary n 166
capital n capital letter 76
capital interj 203
capital n related to worth 127
capital n seat of government 174

capital adj as in "capital punishment" 79
capital gain n 289
capital goods n 263
capital letter n 76
capital loss n 289
capital-intensive adj 311
capitalism n 200, 245
capitalist n 200, 245; adj 200
capitalistic 200
capitalize v set value 176
capitalize v benefit 176
capitol n (Am) 167
Capitol Hill n 306
capitulate v cave in 141
capitulate v obs. meanings of negotiate 141
capitulation n 141
caplet n 316
capo n crime boss 319
capon n 11
capote n (Am) long cloak or overcoat 197
cappuccino n 303
capri pants n 310
capricious adj obs. improbable 124
capricious adj whimsical 124
caprine adj relating to goats 64
capriole n type of leap 135; v 135
capsize v 207
capsule adj 301
capsule n med. sense 88, 238
capsule n as in "space capsule" 88
capsule adj/n/v 88
capsulize 88
captain n Sports 244
captain n naval sense 82, 288
captain n gen. 82, 130; v 82
captain n of an airplane 288
captain n War/Military/Violence 130
captain's chair n 303
captivate v obs. control 116
captivate v 116
captive adj/n 50
captivity n 50
captor n 50
capture n/v 208
capture the flag n 289
capuchin n 129
car n as in "train car" 224
car n automobile 36, 224, 261
car n carriage 36
car bomb n 324
car coat n 310

car park n 288
car phone n (Am) 323
car pool n/v 304
car wash n 310
carabineer n 174
carafe n 196
caramel n 183
carapace n 232
carat n 66
caravan n/v 100
caravanner 100
caravansarai n *inn or hotel* 122
caravel n *type of ship* 107
caraway n 34
carb n 307
carb n 320
carbarn n 239
carbine n 155
carbineer n 174
carbo n 320
carbohydrate n 236
carbon n 193
carbon 14 n 296
carbon copy n 258
carbon dating n 309
carbon dioxide n 236
carbon monoxide n 236
carbon paper n 264
carbon steel n 251
carbonado n *style of cooking meat* 122; v 122
carbonara n 316
carbonate v/n 211
carbonation 211
carbonnade n *type of stew* 259
carboy n *type of bottle* 183
carbuncle n *boil* 31
carbuncle n *type of gem* 31
carburet v 242
carburetion n 242
carburetor n 242
carcass n 45
carcass n *fig. remains of inanimate thing* 45
carcinogen n 238
carcinogenesis n 238
carcinogenic adj 238
carcinoma n 182, 238
card n 88
card n (Am) *humorous person* 249
card n *gen., as in "calling card"* 88
card catalog n (Am) 245
card paper n *cardboard* 196
card table n 183
cardamom n 70
cardboard adj/n 222

cardboard adj *flimsy* 222
card-carrying adj 308
cardiac adj 66
cardiac n *cardiac patient* 286
cardiac n *obs. cardiac medicine* 286
cardiac n *type of vein* 286
cardiac arrest n 310
cardigan n 242
cardinal n *type of cloak* 197
cardinal n Religion 20
cardinal n Animals 165, 181
cardinal adj *primary* 54
cardinal adj *red* 271
cardinal bird n 165, 181
cardinal number n 120
cardinal points n *compass points* 118
cardinal virtue n 37
cardiogram n 238
cardiograph n 238
cardiology n 222
cardiopulmonary adj 256
cardiopulmonary resuscitation/ CPR n 322
cardiorespiratory adj 256
cardiovascular adj 256
cardsharp n (Am) 244
cardsharper n 244
care v *as in "I don't care to participate"* 25
care n *as in "health care"* 16, 69; v 69
care n *obs. grief* 17
care n *as in "cares and woes"* 17, 69; v 17
careen v *dash madly* 123, 295
careen v *tilt a ship* 123, 295
career v *gallop* 213
career n *life's calling* 213
career n *obs. lit. course for running, gallop* 213
careerism n 298
carefree adj 198
careful adj 23
careful adj *obs. grieving* 23
caregiver n 322
careless adj *carefree* 124
careless adj *sloppy* 124
caress n/v 157
caress v 157
caret n ^ 172
caretaker n 244
careworn adj 233
cargo n 149
carhop n 298
caribou n (Am) 165
caricature n/v 187

caricature v 187
caries n 121
carillon n 196
carillonneur n 196
cariogenic 121
carking adj *burdensome, vexing* 133
carl n *everyday joe* 20
carl n *churl* 20
carmaker n 311
carmine adj/n 191
carnage n 130
carnal adj 67
carnal adj *blood relative* 67
carnation n 105
carnify v *turn into flesh* 179
carnival n *gen. festival* 111
carnival n *a spec. festival* 111
carnivora n *gen. carnivores* 146, 220
carnivore n 118, 146, 220
carnivorous adj 118, 220
carny n 298
caroche n *type of carriage* 123
carol n *holiday song* 42
carol n *spec. to Christmas* 42
carol n *type of song and dance, then the song* 42
carom n/v 205
carombole 205
carousal 140
carouse n *drinking bout* 140; v 140
carousel n *type of tournament* 151, 173
carousel n *merry-go-round* 173
carp n *complaint* 150; v 36
carp n *the fish* 64
carp n/v *talk* 36
carpal tunnel syndrome n 309
carpe diem n 216
carpenter n/v 40
carpenter ant n 255
carpenter bee n 220
carpentry 40
carpet n *fig. layer* 33
carpet n/v 33
carpet beetle n 255
carpet bombing n 306
carpet sweeper n (Am) 242
carpetbag n/v 222
carpetbagger n (Am) 249
carpeting 33
carport n (Am) 297
carrel n *spec. in library* 135
carrel n 135
carriage n *carrying* 48
carriage n *vehicle* 72

carriage n *obs. type of toll* 48
carriage n *bearing* 124
carriage trade n 185
carriageway n (Brit) 198
carrier pigeon n 146
carrion n *dead flesh* 45
carrion n *obs. carcass* 45
carrion crow n 105
carrot n *fig. incentive* 100
carrot *incentive* 313
carrot n Food 100
carrot-and-stick adj 313
carrottop n 277
carry n *distance of travel* 250
carry v *as in "carry the four"* 195
carry v *keep in stock* 245
carry v 58
carry v *fig. support* 271
carryall n *type of luggage* 222
carryall n (Am) *type of carriage* 184
carrying charge n (Am) 263
carry-on adj 317
carryout n 316
carsick adj 273
cart n/v 16
cart n *obs. chariot* 16
carte blanche n 176
cartel n 278
cartel n *type of agreement* 278
cartel n *type of challenge* 278
carthorse n 70
cartilage n 66
cartiligenous 66
cartography n 219
cartomancy n *telling fortunes with cards* 267
carton n/v 196
cartoon n *type of drawing* 128, 228; v 128
cartoon n *spec. type of humorous drawing* 128, 228; v 128
cartoonist n 228
cartridge n *gen. container* 131
cartridge n War/Military/Violence 131
cartridge belt n 248
cartwheel n 71
cartwheel n *type of gymnastic move* 71, 75; v 75
carve v 25
carven adj *arch.* 25
carving n *act of carving* 42
carving n *carved item* 42
carving knife n 69
casaba n *type of melon* 259
casanova n 262

cascade n/v 158
case n med. sense 48
case n situation 48
case n job, as in "a tough case for a detective" 248
case n box 49
case n example 48
case n argumentation, as in "state your case" 155
case v as in "case the joint" 283
case n casing 49
case n leg. 48, 155
case n as in "nut case" 249
case goods n furniture designed for storage 289
case in point n 320
case law n 248
case study n 251
casebook n 201
cased glass n 222
caseload n 300
casement n window 69
casework 248
cash n obs. cashbox 127
cash v 218
cash adj/n/v 127
cash bar n 318
cash cow n 313
cash crop n (Am) 241
cash discount n 281
cash flow n 311
cash in v die 266
cash machine n 327
cash on delivery n 245
cash register n (Am) 263
cash-and-carry adj/n 281
cashew n 122
cashew nut n 122, 197
cashier v discharge, dismiss 141
cashier n 126
cashier's check n (Am) 245
cashless society n (Am) 323
cashmere n type of fabric 168
cashmere goat n 255
casino n 185
cask n/v 69
casket n coffin 229
casket n box for valuables 229
cassava n type of plant 122
casserole n 183
cassette n as in "audiocassette" 312
cassette n for photo film 246, 312
cassette n rare casket 312
cassimere n type of fabric 184
cassingle n 327

cast n composition, as in "cast of characters" 136
cast v as in "cast a spell" 55
cast n as in "leg cast" 106
cast v throw 55
cast v create with a mold 55
cast n character, as in "the day had a strange cast to it" 134
cast v fling 55
cast v vomit 55
cast v evoke 55
cast n mold 107; v 55
cast v shape 55
cast n/v 55
cast iron n 177
castanet n 154
castaway n/adj 100
caste n breed 154
caste n social level 154
castellan n occupant of a castle 78, 79
caster n type of wheel 184
caster oil n 182
castigate v 161
castigation 161
cast-iron adj 177
castle n 14
castle in the air n 133
castrate v 140
castration 140
castrato n 201
casual adj/n irregular 82
casual adj/n chance 82
casual adj/n unpressured 82
casual adj/n unobligated 82
casual adj/n informal 82
casualty n victim of accident or war 229
casualty n chance, accident 229
cat n (Am) good guy 313
cat n 11
cat n slang dude, as in "hep cat" 11
cat and mouse n 269
cat burglar n 277
cat distemper n 302
CAT scan n 322
CAT scanner n 322
cat scratch disease n 309
catabolism n active metabolism 256
catabolize 256
catachresis n misuse of words 127
cataclysm n 158
catacomb n 14
catafalque n 155
catalepsy n 68

catalog n/v 85
catalysis 278
catalyst n 278
catalyze v 278
catamaran n 149
catamite n youth having sex with a man 131
catamount n type of wild cat 64, 165
catamountain n type of wild cat 64, 165
cataplexy n freezing in fear 261
catapult v/n 131
cataract n 68
cataract n waterfall 68
catastrophe n disaster 111, 190
catastrophe n turn of events in drama 111, 190
catatonia n 257
catatonic n/adj 257
catawba n type of wine 223
catawumpus adj/n 249
catbird n (Am) 181
catbird seat n (Am) 307
catboat n type of boat 261
catcall n raucous noise 190
catcall n noisemaker 190
catch v obs. chase 55
catch v ignite, start 140
catch v fig. as in "catch in the act 162
catch n/v capture 55
catch n type of boat 72
catch v notice, as in "did you catch that?" 142
catch v as in "catch a cold" 55, 96
catch v as in "catch up" 162
catch-22 n 320
catchall n 232
catch-as-catch-can adj 204
catchpenny adj cheap 189
catchphrase n 227
catchup n Food 168
catch-up adj/n (Am) 233
catchword n 187
catchy adj 217
catechesis 111
catechism n 111
catechist 111
categorical adj direct 138
categorization 135
categorize 135
category n 135
catercorner adj/adv 234
catercornered adj 234
cater-cousin n arch. intimate friend 108

caterer n 75
caterpillar n 64
caterwaul v 93
catfight n 283
catfish n 145
catgut n 137
catharsis n Thoughts/Perception/The Mind 151, 243
catharsis n cleansing 243
cathartic adj mentally stimulating 150, 243
cathartic adj med. sense 150
cathedral n gen. large church 129
cathedral n primary diocesan church 129
catheter n 147
cathode n 220, 272
cathode ray tube n 272
catholic adj gen. universal 43
catholic adj pertaining to the Catholic church 43
catholicon n panacea 85
cathouse n 300
catling n 11, 137
catnap n/v (Am) 217
catnip n (Am) 181
cat-o'-nine-tails n 174
cats and dogs adv 189
cat's cradle n 199
cat's meow 292
cat's whiskers, cat's pajamas 292
cat's-eye n type of gem 118
cat's-paw n dupe, puppet 175
cat's-paw n light breeze 175
cattail n type of plant 30
cattalo n 255
cattle n 34
cattle n obs. assets 34
cattle call n type of audition 311
cattle tick n (Am) 237
cattleman n (Am) 244
catty adj 261
cattycorner adj/adv 234
catwalk n 258
caucus n/v (Am) 202
caudle n type of potion 32
caught adj pregnant 249
cauldron n 33
cauliflower n 122
cauliflower ear n (Am) 273
caulk v 93
causative 48
cause n calling, as in "political cause" 48
'cause contr 76

cause n *impetus, as in "cause and effect"* 48

cause v 48

cause célèbre n 204

causerie n 227

causeway n 72

causey n *causeway* 36, 72

causey n *obs. embankment* 36

caustic adj *lit. burning* 83

caustic adj *fig. burning, sarcastic* 83; n 83

cauterization n 68

cauterize v 68

cautery n *cauterizing tool* 68

caution n *carefulness* 49; v 49

caution n *guarantee* 49

caution n *warning* 49

cautionary 49

cautious 49

cavalcade n *obs. horseride* 135

cavalcade n 135

cavalier adj 169

cavalier n 131

cavalier adj *gentlemanly* 169

cavalry 112, 247

cavalryman n 247

cave n 29, 63

cave dweller n 250

cave in v *lit. collapse* 145, 235

cave in v *fig. give in* 145, 235

caveat 110

caveat emptor n 110

cave-in n 145

caveman n 250

caveman, cave dweller n 250

cavern n 29, 63

cavernous adj *huge* 63

cavernous adj *of a cavern* 63

caviar n 122

cavil v 117

caving n *spelunking* 244

cavity n 114

cavort v (Am) 208

caw n/v 119

cay n 164

caye 149

cayenne pepper n 183

cayuse n *type of horse* 220

CB n 311

CBer n 311

C-clamp n 288

CD n *compact disk* 324

CD-ROM n 326

cease n/v 57

cease and desist order n 292

cease-fire n 229

ceaseless adj 138

cedar n *cedar wood* 10

cedar n 10

cedar chest n (Am) 196

cedar waxwing n (Am) 220, 255

cedarbird n 220, 255

cedarwood n 64

cede v 116

ceil v 106

ceiling n *gen. room lining, paneling* 106

ceiling n 106

cel n 299

celeb n 83, 282

celebrant n 226

celebrate v *observe, as in "celebrate an occasion"* 96, 295

celebrate v *perform a ceremony* 96, 295

celebrate v *praise* 96, 295

celebrate v *rejoice, party* 96, 295

celebrated adj 83, 138

celebration n 96

celebrious adj 138

celebrity n *famous person* 83, 327

celebrity n *being famous* 83

celebrity n (Am) *famous person* 327

celebrity n *obs. ceremony* 83

celerity n *speed* 102

celery n 167

celery cabbage n 287

celesta n *musical instrument* 265

celestial adj/n 65

celestial equator n 237

celestial navigation n 298

celestial pole n 237

celestial sphere n 255

celibacy n 170, 225

celibate adj 225

celibate n *arch. celibate person* 225

celibate n *arch. celibacy* 225

cell n *as in "dry cell battery"* 237

cell n *group, as in "Communist cell"* 294

cell n *obs. closet* 15

cell n *unit of life* 219

cell n *small room* 15

cell n *arch. type of biological subsection* 219

cell body n 254

cell division n 254

cell theory n 255

cellar n/v 33

cellarette n *wine storage* 211

cellblock n 312

cellist n 265

cello n 265

cellophane n 280

cellphone n (Am) 327

cellular adj 219

cellulite n 316

celluloid n 251

Celsius adj 221

Celsius's thermometer 221

Celtic cross n 251

cemballo n *harpsichord* 214

cement n *spec. to making concrete* 49; v 49

cement n *gen. gluing agent* 49

cemetery n *obs. churchyard* 79

cemetery n 79

cense v *burn incense* 59

censer n 59

censor n 110

censor n/v 110

censorious 110

censorship 110

censure n/v 83

censure n *leg. judgment* 83

census n *gen. counting* 154

census n *obs. tax* 154

census n *spec. to Roman census* 154

cent n *100* 76

cent n *Finances/Money* 76

centaur n 81

centenarian n 221

centenarian 146

centenary n *century* 146

centenary n *hundredth anniversary* 146

centennial adj 146; n 146, 195

center n/v *core* 82

center n/v *middle* 82

center n *building/area, as in "center of commerce"* 239

center n/v *pivot* 82

center of gravity n 176

center of mass 176

center punch n 260

center stage n 311

centerfold n (Am) 311

centerline n 216

centerpiece n 211

centigrade adj 210

centigram n 195

centiliter n 195

centimeter n 195

centipede n 145

central n 161, 269; adj 161

central city n 302

central heating n 273

central nervous system n 256

central processing unit n 315

central time n (Am) 256

centralize v 208

centric adj 161

centrifugal adj 260

centrifugal force n 182

centrifuge adj/n/v 260

centripetal force n 182

centurion n 45

century n *100 years* 146

century n *obs. type of Roman mil. group* 146

century n *gen. group of 100* 146

century n (Am) *slang $100* 245

century n *obs. land measure* 146

century plant n (Am) 193

CEO n 323

ceorl n *churl* 20

'cept conj/prep 245

ceramic adj/n 233

ceramics 233

ceramist 233

cerate n *type of medicinal ointment* 68

cereal n *breakfast cereal* 223, 241

cereal n *grain* 223, 241; adj 223

cerebellum n 106

cerebral adj *intellectual* 210, 288

cerebral adj *pertaining to the brain* 210, 288

cerebral cortex n 286

cerebral palsy n 257

cerebrate v *think* 281

cerebrum n 147

cerecloth n 79, 155

cerement n *cerecloth* 155, 179

ceremonial adj 83

ceremonious 83

ceremony n 83

cerise n 234

certain adj *fixed* 49

certain adj *inevitable* 49

certain adj *undoubtable, convinced* 49

certainly 61

certainty n *conviction* 49

certainty n *being fixed* 49

certainty n *inevitability* 49

certes adv *certainly, truthfully* 61

certificate n *obs. certification, assurance* 77

certificate n *type of document* 77

certificate v 77
certification n 77
certified adj 59, 159
certified check n (Am) 264
certified mail n 310
certified milk n 259
certified public accountant n (Am) 264
certify v 59
certitude n 74
cerulean adj 178
cerumen n ear wax 166
cervical cap n type of contraceptive 286
cervix n 66
cesarean n 147, 273
cesarean section n 147
cesium n 236
cesspit 178
cesspool n 178
cete n arch. sea creature 30
Chablis n 167
cha-cha n/v 312
chacma baboon n 220
chad n paper scrap from computer tape 302
chador n 149
chafe n/v grate 57
chafe v warm, esp. by rubbing 57
chaff n/v banter 158
chaff n fig. waste 15
chaff n as in "wheat and chaff" 15
chafing dish n 69
chagrin n/v 169
chagrin n obs. despondency 169
chain n franchise, as in "drugstore chain" 227
chain n fig. something that restricts 49
chain n fig. series 49
chain n lit. series of links; bonds 49; v 49
chain n as in "mountain chain" 164
chain gang n 229
chain letter n 276
chain mail n 215
chain of command n 266
chain reaction n 272
chain saw n (Am) 224
chain stitch n 123
chain store n 227, 275
chain-link fence n 286
chain-smoke v 295
chair n position of authority 44; v 44

chair n 33
chair rail n 222
chairbed n 211
chairlift n (Am) 298
chairman 44
chairman n 44, 152, 171, 323; v 152
chairperson 152, 171, 323
chairwoman 44, 152, 171, 323
chaise n 169
chaise longue n 196, 273
chaise lounge 196, 273
chalet n 196
chalice n 14
chalk n the substance 9, 101; v 9
chalk n used for drawing 9, 101
chalk talk n 267
chalk up v 234
chalkboard n 299
challenge n dispute 50, 87
challenge n obs. accusation 50
challenge n dare 50
challenge v 50
challenged adj (Am) disadvantaged 326
challenging adj 234
challis n fabric 223
chamber adj 201
chamber n room 33
chamber n part of a gun 131
chamber n as in "chamber of the heart" 66
chamber n group of rooms 33
chamber music n 201
chamber of commerce n 200
chamber of horrors n 231
chamber orchestra n 290
chamber pot n 106
chamber-fellow n 135
chamberlain n male chambermaid 40
chambermaid n 126
chambray n (Am) fabric 212
chameleon n 30
chameleon n fig. changeable person 30
chamfer v arch. groove 141
chamfer n/v bevel 141
chamois n goat providing chamois leather 122
chamois n type of leather 122
champ n Sports 171, 185
champ v as in "champing at the bit" 93
champagne n Drink 167
champagne n type of color 167
champaign n 63

champers Brit slang 167
champion n winner of competition 48, 185; v 234
champion n/v hero 48, 185
champion v obs. challenge 234
championship n 213
chance n fortune 49
chance n a possibility 49
chance v/adj 49
chanceful adj causal, or eventful 138
chancellery n 20
chancellor n 20
chancellor n of a college 20
chance-medley n related to self-defense 102
chancre n 120
chancy adj 251
chancy adj Scottish lucky 251
chandelier n 183
chandler n 40
change v/n as in "change clothes" 55
change v make change (money) 55; n 55
change v alter 55; n 55
change v/n exchange 55
change of heart n 224
change of life n 221
change of pace n 283
changeful adj variable 138
changeless 138
changeling n traitor 114
changeling n something exchanged 114
changeover n 278
changing room n (Brit) 297
channel n as in "radio channel" 49
channel n/v 49
channeler n 324
channeling n 324
chanson n type of song 101
chant v recite in song 77, 173; n 173
chant v sing 77; v 173
chant v repeat rhythmically 77; n 173
chant n song 173
chanteuse n female singer 246
chantey n as in "sea chanty" 246
chanticleer n rooster 30
Chantilly lace n 223
chanty n as in "sea chanty" 246
chaos n disorder 134
chaos n obs. the void 134
chaotic adj 134

chap n fellow 188
chap n sore or rough skin 68; v 68
chap n customer of a chapman 188
chapajaros n 212
chaparral n (Am) 219
chapbook n 201
chapeau n hat 100
chapel n 42
chaperon n/v 185
chaperon n arch. type of hood 185
chapfallen adj 124
chaplain n 20
chapman n peddler 18
chaps n The Body 120
chaps n (Am) 212
chapter n fig., as in "a chapter in her life" 41
chapter n as in "club chapter" 41
chapter n 41
chapter and verse n 156
chapwoman obs. 18
char v work as a charwoman 187
char n charwoman 275; v 187
char n (Am) tea 283
char v 180
char n 180
charabank n (Brit) type of bus 212
character n quirky person 204
character n as in "character in a novel" 172
character n composite characteristics 150
character n moral fortitude 198
character n reputation 150
character n letter, symbol, etc. 41
character assassination n 308
character sketch n 264
character witness n 312
characterful adj 275
characteristic adj/n 176
characteristical 176
characterization n Literature/Writing 214
characterization n General/Miscellaneous 134
charade n game 199
charade n farce 199
charades 199
charbroil v 316
charcoal n 29
charcoal n type of color 29

charcuterie n *pork store* 245

chardonnay n 287

chare n *chore* 19

charge n/v *as in "electrical charge"* 195

charge n *accusation* 102; v 102

charge n/v *obs. phys. burden* 48

charge n *fee* 227

charge n *as in "get a charge out of life"* 320

charge n *credit* 76; v 76, 227

charge n *as in "explosive charge"* 266

charge n *as in "charge of the Light Brigade"* 130

charge n/v *duty* 48

charge account n (Am) 276

charge card n 305

charge off v 295

charged adj 47

charger n *platter* 33

charger n *horse* 194

chariot n 36

charioteer 36

charisma n *gen. aura of authority* 154, 304

charisma n *God-given talent* 154, 304

charisma n *charm* 154, 304

charismatic adj 304

charismatic n *follower of charismatic religion* 312

charitable adj 49

charity n *contributions* 49

charity n *gen. good will* 49

charity n *Christian love* 49

charivari n *shivaree* 170

charlady n 127

charlatan n *faker* 156

charlatan n *snake-oil salesman* 156

Charleston n *the dance* 291

charley horse n 257

charlotte russe n *type of dessert* 223

charm n *charisma* 47, 124; v 124

charm n/v *spell* 47

charm n *as in "good-luck charm"* 47

charmed adj *in quantum physics* 315

charmed circle n 269

charming adj *charismatic* 169

charming adj *magical* 169

charnel n 79

charnel house 79

charqui n *jerky* 148

chart n/v *map* 118

chart n *type of graph* 118

charter n/v Travel/Transportation 317

charter n *agreement* 48

charter member n (Am) 277

chartreuse n 252

chartreuse n *type of food dish* 252

charwoman n 127

chary adj *obs. grieving* 137

chary adj 137

chase n/v *as in "the chase is on"* 48

chaser n *as in "beer chaser"* 259

chasm n 118

chaste adj *fig. untainted* 39

chaste adj *abstaining* 39

chaste adj *obs. not married* 39

chasten 58

chastien v *chastise* 61

chastise v *obs. reform* 58

chastise v 58

chastity n *no sex* 39

chastity n *singlehood* 39

chastity n *untaintedness* 39

chastity belt n 298

chat v 49, 95; n 95

chat show n (Brit) *talk show* 319

chateau n 183

chateaubriand n 259

chatelain n *occupant of a castle* 79, 229

chatelaine n *mistress of a castle* 79, 229

chatter v/n *as in "chattering teeth"* 48

chatter v 48; n 48, 95

chatterbox n 204

chauffeur n/v 263

chautauqua n 247

chauvinism n *sexism* 243, 319

chauvinism n *patriotism* 243, 319

chaw n/v *chew* 82

chawbacon n 106

cheap adj *inexpensive* 101

cheap adj *flimsy* 101

cheap n *arch.* 101

cheap v *var. meanings of "deal, barter"* 19

cheap shot n 325

cheapen v 101, 179

cheapen v *arch. inquire about price* 179

cheapie n 268

cheapjack n *purveyor of cheap goods* 249; adj 249

cheapo adj/n 320

cheapskate n (Am) 268

cheat n/v 140

cheat v *confiscate* 140

cheat v *commit adultery* 317

cheaters n (Am) *glasses* 286

check v *mark with checkmark* 252; n 252

check n *part of checkered pattern* 83

check v *test, inspect* 180; n 180

check v *hold in check, restrain* 93

check interj 292

check n *ticket, as in "hat check"* 232; v 232

check n *in chess* 40

check 284

check n *bill* 226

check v *concur, as in "the story checks out"* 295

check n *financial instrument* 200

check v *obstruct, stop* 93; n 93

check in v 284

check mark n 252, 284

check off v 235, 252; n 235

check out 284

checkbook n (Am) 200

checkbook journalism n 320

checked adj 89

checkered adj *as in "a checkered past"* 89

checkers n 185

check-in n 284

checking account n (Am) 276

checklist n (Am) 245

checkmate interj/n/v 40

checkmate v 40

checkout n (Am) 289

checkpoint n 294

checkroom n (Am) 258

checks and balances n 204

checkup n (Am) 257

cheddar n 167

cheek n *buttock* 13

cheek n *cheekiness* 13

cheek n *on the face* 13

cheeky adj 224

cheep n/v 115

cheep n 115

cheer v *encourage* 73

cheer n/v *cheeriness* 36, 73

cheer n *disposition* 36

cheer n *audible encouragement* 36

cheer v *cheer up* 73

cheerful 36

cheerio interj (Brit) 277

cheerlead v 275

cheerleader n (Am) 275

cheerless adj 36

cheerly adj *arch. cheerful* 100

cheers interj 292

cheery adj 36

cheese n *bigshot, as in "big cheese"* 277

cheese v *as in "cheese it—the cops!"* 216

cheese n 15

cheeseburger n (Am) 297

cheesecake n (Am) Slang 300

cheesecake n Food 70

cheesecloth n 69

cheeseparing n *penny-pinching, miserliness* 127

cheesy adj *tacky* 268

cheetah n 181

chef n 226

chef d'oeuvre n *masterwork* 153

chemic adj *alchemical, chemical* 119

chemical adj *obs. alchemical* 119

chemical adj/n 119, 182

chemical engineering n 255

chemical warfare n 282

chemiluminescence n 255

chemise n *woman's garment* 35

chemisette n *woman's garment* 212

chemist n 119

chemistry n Science 146

chemistry n *alchemistry* 146

chemosurgery n 302

chemotherapy n 273

chenile n *type of yarn* 184

cherish v *nurture* 58

cherish v *hold dear* 58

cheroot n 167

cherry n (Am) *slang virginity* 289

cherry n 34

cherry n *type of wood* 34

cherry bomb n 312

cherry picker n (Am) *type of crane* 317

cherry picker n 242

cherry tomato n (Am) 223

cherub n *type of angel* 19

cherub n *baby* 19

Chesapeake Bay retriever n *type of dog* 255

chess n *type of grass* 181

chess n *the game* 40
chess pie n *type of dessert* 297
chessboard n 40
chessman n 40
chest n 66
chest n *type of furniture, storage* 14
chest of drawers n 148
chesterfield n *type of sofa* 286
chesterfield n *type of overcoat* 241
chestnut n 64
chestnut n *type of horse* 64
chestnut n *hoary joke* 64
chestnut n *type of color* 64
chestnut adj 137
chestnut blight n (Am) 272
chestnut oak n (Am) 145
chesty adj *big-chested* 261
chesty adj (Am) *haughty* 261
cheval glass n *type of mirror* 222
chevalier n 45
cheviot n *a type of sheep or wool* 194
chèvre n *goat cheese* 303
chew n/v 13
chew out v 307
chew the fat v (Am) 269
chewing gum n (Am) 197
chewing tobacco n (Am) 196
Chianti n 222
chiaroscurist 173
chiaroscuro n 173
chic adj/n 242
chicane v 124
chicanery n 124
chichi adj/n 274
chick n *slang woman* 30
chick n *Animals* 30
chick n (Am) *girl* 292
chick n *arch. child* 30
chickabiddy n *chick* 194
chickadee n 219
chickaree n (Am) *red squirrel* 209
chicken n *coward* 82
chicken n *fig. coward* 11, 82; adj 82
chicken n *Animals* 11
chicken colonel n (Am) 306
chicken feed n 231
chicken hawk n (Am) 219
chicken out v (Am) 82, 307
chicken pox n 182
chicken wire n (Am) 274
chicken-and-egg adj 313
chicken-fried steak n 310

chickenhearted adj (Am) 175
chicken-livered adj (Am) 250
chickenshit adj/n (Am) 307
chickory n *source of coffee flavoring* 64
chickory n 64
chickpea n 183
chickpea n *chickpea plant* 183
chickweed n 30
chide v 59
chide v *argue* 59
chief n 44
chief adj 53
chief executive n (Am) 226
chief petty officer n (Am) 266
chieftain n 44
chiffon n *type of fabric* 260; adj 260
chiffon n *as in "lemon chiffon pie"* 287
chiffon n *arch. type of garment ornamentation* 260
chiffonade n *vegetables cut for garnish* 259
chiffonier n 196
chifforobe n (Am) 273
chigger n (Am) 181
chihuahua n 219
child n *fig., as in "a child of the '60s"* 18
child n *infant; son or daughter* 18
child abuse n 324
childbed n *state of a woman in childbirth* 39
childbed fever n 286
childbirth n 69
childhood n 12
childish adj 17, 23, 124
childlike adj 17, 23, 124
childly adj 17, 23, 124
childproof adj/v 313
child's play n 47
chile relleno n (Am) 259
chili n *the stew* 148, 223
chili n *the pepper* 148, 223
chili con carne n (Am) 223
chili dog n (Am) 316
chili powder n (Am) 297
chiliad n *group of 1,000* 120
chiliad n *1,000 years* 120
chiliburger n (Am) 322
chill v (Am) *Slang* 324
chill v 13, 89; adj 89; n 13
chill factor n 315
chill out v *Slang* 324, 326
chiller n 205
chilly adj 137

chime n/v 59
chime v *indicate time with chimes* 59
chimera n *spec. type of mythical monster* 81
chimera n *gen. monster* 81
chimere n *type of garment* 71
chimerical adj 81
chimes n 77
chimichanga n 326
chimney n *obs. fireplace* 33
chimney n 33
chimney corner n 122
chimney sweep n 151
chimney sweeper 151
chimney swift n 220
chimp n 181, 254
chimpanzee n 181, 254
chin v (Am) *discuss* 249
chin chin interj (Brit) *type of toast* 203
china n 121
china closet n 196
China rose n 181
China-dishes 121
chinaware n 121
chinbone n 13
chinch n *bedbug* 146
chinchilla n 119
chine n/v *spine* 32
Chinese checkers n 298
Chinese lacquer n 258
Chinese lantern n 211
Chinese shar-pei n 322
chink n *money* 127
chink n/v *sound* 135
chink n/v *as in "chink in the armor"* 83
chino n (Am) *type of cloth* 303
chinook salmon n (Am) 236
chintz n *type of fabric* 149
chintzy adj 149, 251
chin-wag n/v *talk* 267
chip n *as in "computer chip"* 315
chip n/v *as in "poker chips"* 244
chip n *as in "fish and chips"* 70
chip v *as in "chip off"* 207
chip n *as in "cowchips"* 241
chip v *as in "the vase was chipped"* 207; n 207
chip n *shard* 51; v 51
chip in v 252
chipmunk n (Am) 220
chipped beef n 241
chipper adj *lively* 225
chippy n (Am) *loose woman* 262

chippy adj *having a chip on the shoulder* 261
chirk v *cheer* 17
chirography n *handwriting* 172
chiromancy n *palm reading* 81
chiropodist n *foot doctor; arch. hand doctor* 196
chiropody 196
chiropractic 257
chirp n/v 95
chirpy adj/adv 232
chirurgeon n *surgeon* 32
chirurgery n 32
chisel n/v *Tools* 36
chisel v *cheat* 215; n 283
chiseler n *cheat* 215, 283
chit n *kid, young woman* 154
chit n *note* 201
chitchat n 172, 187, 218, 295; v 172, 218
chitlings n 34, 223
chitlins n 34, 223
chitmunk n 220
chitter-chatter n 172, 187, 295; v 187, 218, 295
chitterlings n 34, 223
chitty n 201
chiv n/v *knife* 174
chivalresque adj 45
chivalric adj 45
chivalrous adj 45
chivalry n *the code of the knights* 45, 202
chivalry n *gen. knights* 45, 202
chive n 70
chive n *sauce with chives* 70
chloride n 209
chlorinate 209
chlorine n 209
chlorofluorocarbon n 302
chloroform n/v 221
chlorophyll n 209
chock n 51
chock n 212
chock adv/v 51
chockablock adj/adv 234
chock-full adj 89
chocoholic n 316
chocolate n *type of drink* 148
chocolate n *as in "chocolate bar"* 148
chocolatier n 263
choice n *the power to choose* 49
choice n *choosing* 49
choice n *something chosen* 49
choice n *selection, as in "a large choice"* 49
choice adj 49

choir n *place for singing* 77
choir n/v 77
choirboy n 228
choke n *type of valve* 317
choke v *obstruct* 27
choke n/v 27
choke chain 309
chokeberry n (Am) 193
choker n *type of jewelry* 288
choler n *yellow bile* 66
choler n *bilious disposition* 66
cholera n *gen. diarrhetic disease* 121
cholera n *spec. type of disease* 121
cholesterol n 255
cholic n 238
chomp v 235
choo-choo n 274
choose v *decide* 25
choose v *select* 25
choose up v 278
choosy adj (Am) 243
chop n *as in "punch in the chops"* 81
chop v/n 251
chop n/v *mince, as in "chop celery"* 93
chop n *as in "pork chop"* 70
chop n/v *as in "chop wood"* 93
chop n *jowl* 120
chop shop n 324
chop suey n (Am) 259
chop-chop adv/interj 230
chopfallen adj 149
chophouse n 175
chopine n *type of shoe* 123
choplogic adj/n *specious logic* 108
chopper n (Am) *type of motorcycle* 317
chopper n (Am) *automatic gun* 291
chopper n/v *helicopter* 310
choppers n (Am) *slang teeth* 296
chopping block n 182
choppy adj *fickle* 243
choppy adj *as in "choppy seas"* 251
chops n *jowls* 120
chopstick n 167
chopsticks n Music 265
choral adj/n 129
chorale n *type of song* 228
chorale n *choral group* 228
chorale prelude n 290

chord n *cord, as in "spinal chord"* 68
chord n 153
chore n 187
chore n *obs. chorus* 187
choreograph v 201, 305
choreography n *dance notation* 201
choreography n *dance design* 201
chorine n (Am) *chorus girl* 265, 290
chorister n *choir singer* 77
chorizo n *type of sausage* 223
chortle n/v 243
chorus n *singing group* 128
chorus n *something sung or spoken in unison* 129; v 191
chorus n *part of a song* 129
chorus boy n 305
chorus girl n 265
chosen n/adj 49
chow n *type of dog* 194, 255
chow n (Am) *slang food* 197, 241; v 241
chow chow n *type of dog* 194, 255
chow line n 280
chow mein n (Am) 259
chowchow n Food 241
chowchow n *type of relish* 197
chowder n/v (Am) 191
chowderhead n 231
chowhound n 303
chrisom child n *child that dies early* 45
Chrissake interj 320
Christ n 203
Christ n 19
christen v *convert to Christianity* 19
christen v *commemorate a beginning* 19, 78
christen v *baptize* 19
christening n 78
Christian era n 165
Christian name n 114
Christianity n 43
Christmas n 18
Christmas cactus n 254
Christmas card n 262
Christmas club n 276
Christmas Eve n 40
Christmas tree n *type of decoration* 226
Christmastide n 151
Christmastime n 226
Christogram n 266

chromatography n 301
chrome n/v 206
chrome green n 252
chrome yellow n 218
chromium 206
chromosome n 254
chromosome number 254
chronic adj *med. lingering* 68
chronic adj *gen. constantly recurring* 68
chronic fatigue syndrome n 326
chronicle n/v *record* 41
chronicle n *story* 41
chronicle play n 276
chronogram n *type of cryptogram* 151
chronograph n 165
chronologer n 119, 126
chronological adj 119
chronologist 119, 126
chronology n 119, 126
chronometer n 182
chronometer n *obs. metronome* 182
chrysalid n 145
chrysalis n 145
chrysanthemum n 118
chtonic adj *related to the underworld* 267
chub n *type of fish* 64
chubby adj *chuffy* 190
chubby adj *short and thick* 190
chubby adj *resembling a chub* 190
chuck n *as in "drill chuck"* 212
chuck n *cut of beef* 183
chuck v *throw* 142
chuck n *as in "chuck wagon"* 223
chuck v (Am) *stop* 267
chuck n *gen. chunk of meat* 183
chuck wagon n 242
chuckhole n 232
chuckle n *obs. uproarious laughter* 212
chuckle n *quiet laughter* 212
chuckle n 212
chucklehead n 189
chuckwalla n (Am) 237
chuff n *boor* 82
chuff n/v *make exhaust sound* 284
chuffy adj *chubby* 147
chug n (Am) *type of sound* 250; v 250
chug v Food 310
chugalug v (Am) 310
chukker n *polo term* 262

chum n/v *pal* 170
chum n 272
chum n/v (Am) *bait* 241
chum salmon n 272
chummy 170
chump n *fool* 268
chump n *block of wood* 268
chunk n 177
chunky adj (Am) 206
chunter v (Brit) *mutter* 142
church adj/n/v 19
church key n *bottle/can opener* 310
church school n 247
churchgoer n 173
churchianity n 228
churchman n 43, 188
churchwoman n 43, 188
churchyard n 20
churl n *type of freeman* 20
churl n *boor* 20
churn n/v 27
churn out v 284
chute n/v (Am) *parachute* 283
chute n *as in "coal chute"* 211; v 211
chutney n 211
chutzpah n 261
cicada n 64, 210
cicala n *cicada* 64, 210
cider n 34
cider vinegar n 241
cig n 222
cigala n *obs.* 64
cigar n 148, 222
cigarette n 222
cigarillo n 148, 222
cigarito n 222
cilantro n 273
Cimmerian n *mythical people in Homer* 128; adj 128
Cimmerian adj *dark, gloomy* 138
cinch n *sure thing* 268
cinch n *saddle girth* 268
cinder n 9
cinder block n 286
Cinderella n *fig.* 231
cine n 265, 296
cineast n *film enthusiast* 291
cinema n 276
cinema n *type of projector* 276
cinema verité n 319
cinemagoer n 282
cinematheque n 319
cinematic adj 276
cinematize v 276
cinematograph n 265
cinematographer n 265

collaboration n 253
collage n 282
collagen n 238
collapse n/v 191
collapse v fig. 191
collar n as in "dog collar" 35
collar n Cloth/Clothing 35
collar n/v capture 132
collarbone n 99
collard n 196
collateral n 227
collateral damage n 319
collateral security 227
colleague n 113
collect n brief prayer 42
collect v as in "collect one's thoughts" 95
collect v gen. use 95
collect v spec. collect as a hobby 95, 244
collectanea n 176
collectible adj/n 265
collection n 95
collective n collective group, farm 176
collective adj 90
collective bargaining n 264
collective farm n 281
collective noun n 110
collective unconscious n 284
collectivism n 176, 247
collectivize 176, 247
collector's item n 301
colleen n lass 228
college n charity organization 83
college n educational institution 83
college n university 83, 129
college n gen. group 129
college n group, as in "electoral college" 83
college n clerical community 83
college try n 307
collegian n 83
collegiate 83
collide v force a collision 162
collide v experience a collision 162
collider n 322
collie n 165
collier n charcoal maker 40
collier n miner 40
colliery n coal mine and environs 152
collins n type of drink 241
collision n 85, 162
collision course n 307

colloquial adj 201
colloquialism n 201
colloquium n obs. conversation 157
colloquium n conference 157
colloquy n 76
collude v 83
collusion n 83
collywobbles n butterflies in the stomach 213
cologne n 211
colon n part of intestines 66
colon n punctuation 110
colonel n 112
Colonel Blimp n reactionary 300
colonial adj (Am) 79, 202, 247; n 202, 247
colonialism n 202
colonic n 66, 297; adj 66
colonist 79, 188, 247
colonize 79
colonize v 79, 162
colonizer n 188, 247
colonnade n 183
colony n 79
colony n Roman mil. settlement 79
colophon n type of inscription 201
colophon n publisher's imprint 201
color n as in "wearing colors" 71
color n flag, as in "flying the colors" 71
color n tint 55
color n 129
color n paint 55
color n description, flavor, as in "color commentary," "local color" 270
color n skin color 55
color v 55
color announcer n 323
color guard n 215
colorable adj apparently real, true 89
coloration n 157
color-blind adj 221
colorcast n/v 312
colored n 283
colorfast adj 287
colorful adj 270
colorific adj 179, 270
colorimeter n 238
colorist n 173
colorize v 324
colorize v gen. 324

colorless adj 88
colorman n 323
colossal adj huge 190
colossal adj wonderful 190
colossal adj 83
colossus n Colossus of Rhodes 83
colossus n fig. 83
colostomy n 239
colt n 11
colt n spec. to horses 11
coltish adj 73
column n space for copy on a newspaper 77
column n section written by a columnist 77, 282
column n type of architectural feature 69
column n type of troop arrangement 80
column inch n 77, 299
columnist n (Am) 77, 282
coma n 147
comate n mate 126
comatose adj 147, 167
comatose adj fig. sluggish 167
comb n 11
comb n honeycomb 11
comb n/v for hair 14
comb v 14
combat n/v 112; adj 112, 215
combat fatigue n 302
combatant n 102, 112; adj 102
combative adj 233
combo n 9
combination lock n 239
combine v unite 95
combine v harvest with a combine 259, 287; n 259
combine n alliance 269
combo n 290
combust v 65
combustible adj 65, 113; n 113
combustion n obs. med. inflammation 65
combustion n 65
come v 26
come v achieve orgasm 151, 289; n 289
come again? interj 267
come off it interj 283
come out of the closet v 320
comeback n retort 217
comeback n return 217
comedian n 77, 153, 246
comedienne n 153, 246
comedo n blackhead 238
comedown n 133

comedy n story with happy ending 77
comedy n comedic story 77
comedy n gen. humor 77
comedy drama n 265
comedy of manners n 214
come-hither adj 262
comeling n new kid on the block 61
comely adj 13
come-on n (Am) 268
comer n as in "up-and-comer" 268
comestible adj obs. 223
comestible n 223
comestible adj obs. consumable 100
comet n 12
comeuppance n (Am) 249
comfit n type of candy 34
comfort v/n obs. entertain 57
comfort n/v solace, relief 36
comfort v/n 57
comfort n/v being comfortable 36
comfort station n (Am) 273
comfortable n 239
comfortable adj experiencing comfort 198
comfortable adj pleasant 198
comfortable adj comforting 198
comfortable adj as in "comfortable margin" 198
comforter n type of quilt 239
comforter n type of scarf 239
comfy adj 198, 230
comic adj funny 77
comic n comedian 290
comic adj pertaining to comedy 77
comic book n 305
comic opera n 201
comic relief n 216
comic strip n 282
comical 77
comic-opera adj 276
comingle v 161
coming-of-age n 279
coming-out n 216
comity n manners, civility 111
comma n 127
comma n sentence fragment 127
command v 57
command v deserve, as in "command respect" 142
command v be in charge 57
command n commandment, order 83

ENGLISH THROUGH THE AGES

confide v as in "confide a secret" 96

confidence n trust 73

confidence game n (Am) 230, 248

confidence man n (Am) 230, 248

confident adj 138

confident adj obs. gen. trusting 138

confidential adj 206

confidential adj obs. confident 206

configurate v 136

configuration n type of astronomical relationship 136

configuration n 136

configure v 136

confine v restrict 142

confine v border 142

confine, confines n/v 83

confinement n 83, 142, 159

confinement n childbirth 159

confirm v 56

confirmation n Religion 43

confirmation gen. 56

confiscate v take for government treasury 130

confiscate v gen. take 130; adj 130

confiscation n 130

confisk v obs. 130

confit n type of meat preparation 310

conflagrant adj 176

conflagration n gen. fire 176

conflagration n great blaze 176

conflict n/v 80

conflict of interest n 313

conflicted adj 317

conflicting adj 159

confluence n 85

confluent adj 85

conformist n 158

confound v shame 57

confound v confuse 57

confound v bring to ruin 57

confounded adj 57, 88

confrere n obs. fraternity brother 205

confrere n colleague 205

confront v stand before 140

confront v challenge 140

confrontation n hostilities 158

confrontation n meeting 158

confrontational adj 158, 323

confuse v obs. ruin 96

confuse v confound 96

confuse v mistake one for another 96

confusion n 97

confusticate v confuse 271

confusticate confuse 97

conga n/v 299

conga line n 299, 305

congeal v 93

congenial adj pertaining to people 150

congenial adj pertaining to things, situations 150

congenital adj 207

congeries n miscellany 134

congestion n 66

congestion n gen. crowdedness 66

congestive heart failure n 286

conglomerate adj 91

conglomerate n mixture 217

conglomerate n type of rock structure 217

conglomerate n business group 217, 318

conglomerateur n 318

congrats interj/n 267

congratulate v 86

congratulation n 86

congratulations interj 86, 156

congregant n 266

congregate v 111

congregation n General/Miscellaneous 51

congregation n as in "church congregation" 51

congress n governing group 113, 207

congress n group of servants 113

congress n meeting of armies 113

congress n meeting 113

congress n meeting 202

congressman n (Am) 202, 282

congresspeople n 324

congressperson n 202, 282, 324

congresswoman n 202, 282

congruent adj 83

congruity n 83

congruous adj 83

conic adj 106

conical adj 106

conifer n 64

conject obs. 74

conjectural adj 74

conjecture n/v guess 74

conjecture n obs. prophecy 74

conjoin v 92

conjugal adj 108

conjugal rights n 262

conjugate v 110

conjugation n 110

conjunction n 65

conjunction n 76

conjunctivitis n 221

conjure v bind by oath 57

conjure v bring about magically 57, 132

conjurer 57

conk v as in "conk out" 283

conk n/v hit 270

conk v straighten hair 304; n 304

connate adj 118

connatural adj inborn 118

connect v lit. 83, 95

connect v fig. put 2 and 2 together 95

connect v Crime/Punishment/Enforcement 300

connect v in travel 243

connected adj phys. connected 190

connected adj fig. related 190

connection n as in "telephone connection" 250

connection n as in "electrical connection" 250

connection n connecting 83

connection n as in "political connections" 205

connection n transfer Travel/Transportation 243

connection n arch. "lovemaking" 199

connection n drug supplier 300

conning tower n 243

conniption n (Am) 225

connivance 142

connive v 142

connive v arch. ignore 142

conniver n 142

connivery n 142

connoisseur n 188

connotation n 114

connote v 114

connubial adj 170

conquer v fig. overcome 45

conquer v War/Military/Violence 45

conquest n Love/Romance/Sex 39

conquest n War/Military/Violence 45

conquistador n 112

consanguinity n blood relationship 75

consarcination n hodgepodge 180

conscience n obs. deepest feelings 38

conscience n obs. consciousness 38

conscience n 38, 151

conscience money n 232

conscient adj conscious 151

conscientious adj 151

conscientious objector n 266

conscionable adj 108

conscious adj obs. expressing conscience 151

conscious adj 151; n 151, 281

consciousness n being conscious 151

consciousness-raising n (Am) 319

conscribe obs. enlist 203

conscript n 203

conscription n forced enlistment 203

conscription n obs. gen. enlistment 203

conscription n gen. written list 203

consecrate v 78

consecration n 78

consecution n 159

consecutive adj 159

consensual adj related to consent 206, 233

consensual adj by mutual consent 206

consensus n 233

consent n arch. concensus 49

consent v 55

consent n arch. empathy 49

consent n 49

consent n 55

consent decree n 277

consentaneous adj unanimous 139

consequence n weight, importance 83

consequence n result 83

consequent adj 83

consequential adj resulting 160

consequential adj weighty, important 83, 160

conservation n creating fruit preserves 83

conservation n preservation of natural resources 83, 285

conservation n gen. preservation 83

conservation of energy n 237

conservation of mass n 255

conservation of matter n 255

conservationist n 245, 285

conservative adj political sense 88, 229; n 225

conservative adj 88

conservativism n 229

conservatory n botanical building 119

conservatory n obs. preservative 119

conservatory n as in "conservatory of music" 119, 228

conserve v 92

conserve n medicinal fruit perserve 68

conserves n confections 70

consider v 92

considerable adj obs. ponderable 160

considerable adj large 160

considerate adj arch. careful 184

considerate adj thoughtful 184

consideration n 184

consideration n payment 51

consideration n 51

consideration n obs. seeing 51

consideration n 92

considerative obs. 184

considered adj 92, 150

consigliere n 155

consignment n 185

consist v obs. be compatible 116

consist v be consistent 116

consist v as in "this book consists of a lot of words" 116

consist v obs. reside 116

consistency n ability to hold form 176

consistency n being consistent 176, 190

consistency n as in "the consistency of oil" 176

consistent adj 176

consolate v obs. 72

consolation n 72

consolation prize n 263

console n as in "instrument console" 258

console n type of panel 258

console v 72

console n type of cabinet 258

console table n 211

consolidate v 83

consolidated school n (Am) 282

consolidation n gathering 83

consolidation n compacting 83

consolidation n strengthening 83

consomme n 211

consonant n 41

consonant adj fig. harmonious 89

consonant shift n 264

consort n associate 85

consort n obs. association 85

consort n lover 85

consort v 85

consortium n 226

conspicuity 115

conspicuous adj 115

conspicuous consumption n 264

conspicuousness n 115

conspiracy n 82

conspiracy of silence n 250

conspiration n 82

conspire v 82

constable n type of administrator 44

constable n peace officer 44, 229

constable n household administrator 44

constant adj steadfast 88

constant n 221

constant adj gen. 137

constant adj unchanging 88

constellate v join in a group 162

constellate v obs. prophesy horoscopically 162

constellation n astronomical star grouping 31, 65

constellation n astrological star grouping 31

consternate v 149

consternation n 149

constipat adj 116

constipate v fig. clog up 116

constipate v 68, 116

constipated adj 68

constipation n 68

constituency n 229

constituent n 229

constituent adj part of 178

constitute v as in "that constitutes fraud" 95

constitute v form 95

constitute adj 95

constitution n 46

constitution n as in "U.S. Constitution" 174

constitution n build, structure 134

constitution n gen. rule, set of rules 174

constitutional adj Government 174

constitutional adj/n General/Miscellaneous 134

constitutional n type of exercise 226

constrain v force 59

constrain v restrain 59

constrain v obs. strain with effort 59

constraint n 59

constriction n 83

constriction n constrict 83

constrictor n 181

construct v 83

construction n 83

construction paper n 290

constructive adj helpful 251

constructive adj pertaining to construction 251

constructivism n 290

construe n/v 76

consul n 79

consulate n 79

consult v 85

consultancy n 85

consultant n 85, 171

consultation n 85

consulter 171

consultor 171

consumable n 211

consume v spend 93

consume v enthrall 93

consume v eat, drink 93

consume v destroy 68, 93

consume v of tuberculosis 68

consumedly adv excessively 190

consumer n 171

consumer credit n 290

consumer goods n 263

consumer price index n 305

consumer terrorism n (Am) 327

consumerism n (Am) 171, 304

consuming adj deeply felt 213

consuming adj engrossing 213

consummate adj obs. finished 91

consummate adj arch. perfect 91

consummate adj of the highest degree 91

consummate v 91

consummation n 83

consumption n 171

consumption n spending, using 68

consumption n spec. tuberculosis 68

consumptive n tuberculosis victim 166

consumptive adj 68

contact v fig. get in touch with 234, 295

contact v cause to touch 234

contact n 158

contact n as in "a business contact" 158

contact language n pidgin 305

contact lens n 257

contagion n 68

contagious adj 68

contain v quell 57

contain v comprise 57

contain v hold 57

container n 69

containership n type of ship 317

contaminant n 85, 286, 293

contaminate v 85

contamination n 85

contemn v treat with contempt 72, 73

contemplate v 38

contemplation n 38

contemplation n study 38

contemplative adj 38

contempo adj contempo(rary) 158, 324

contemporaneous adj 178

contemporary adj/n 158

contemporary adj/n type of design 158

contempt v obs. 72

contempt n 72

contemptible 72, 125

contemptuous adj contemptible 125

contemptuous adj akin to contempt of court 125

contemptuous 72

contemptuous adj 125

contend v assert 95, 140

contend v rival, be in the running 95

contender n 95

content n as in "the contents of a box" 85

content v sate 73

content adj 73

contented adj 73

contention n 95, 140

contention n battling 83

contentment n 73

cook up v *concoct* 156
cookbook n (Am) 211
cookbook adj 307
cooker *cook* 18, 260
cooker n Tools 260
cookery book (Brit) 211
cookhouse n 33
cookie n Food 183
cookie n (Am) *as in "tough cookie"* 292
cookie cutter n 273
cookie sheet n 286
cookie-cutter adj 320
cook-off n 297
cookout n (Am) 303
Cook's tour n 277
cookshack n 273
cookshop n 127
cookstove n 211
cooktop n 303
cookware n 310
cool v (Am) *slang murder* 291
cool adj *phys. cool; calm* 23; v/ n 23
cool adv *as in "play it cool"* 312
cool adj *fig. unfriendly* 23
cool adj Slang 312
coolant n 288
cooldown n 325
cooler n (Am) *slang jail* 267
cooler n *as in "camping cooler"* 121
cooler n 148
coolheaded adj 198
coolie n 152
coolie hat n 287
cooling tower n 272
coon n (Am) (*rac*)*coon* 181
coon n Insults 249
coon cheese n 310
coonhound n (Am) 279
coon's age n (Am) 231
coonskin n 149
coop n *type of basket* 35
coop n 35
co-op n 232, 250; adj 250
co-op 232
coop v 35
cooper n *wine dealer* 40
cooper n *type of metalworker* 40; v 40
cooperate v *applied to people* 84
cooperate *applied to things* 84
cooperation n 84
cooperative adj 84
cooperative n 232
coordinate v *cause to work together* 179

coordinate n 210
coordinate v *make equal* 179
coordinate geometry n 279
coordinated adj 301
coordinating conjunction n 281
coordinator n 179, 244
coot n Insults 204
coot n *type of bird* 30
cooter n (Am) *type of turtle* 219
cootie n 283
cop n *police officer* 230, 248
cop v *as in "cop a plea"* 292
cop v *steal* 188
cop n *top* 22
cop v (Am) *arrest* 188
cop out v 320
copacetic adj (Am) 283
cope v *obs. hit, fight* 142
cope v *handle* 142
cope n/v *obs. skirmish* 112
cope v *purchase* 142
copilot n 288
coping n *walltop* 122
coping saw n 288
copious adj 54
copout n 292
cop-out n 307
copper n (Am) *police officer* 230, 248
copper n 10
copper v *arrest* 230
copper n *coin* 187
copperhead n (Am) *type of snake* 194
coppersmith n 40
coppice n *group of small trees* 64
coproduct n *byproduct* 308
coprolite n 219
copse n 118
copshop n (Am) *police station* 307
copter n 304
copulate v *obs. link* 151
copulate v 151
copulation 151
copy n *gen.* 42
copy n *spec. document copy* 42
copy n *single copy of a newspaper, etc.* 42
copy v *duplicate* 93
copy n *obs. copiousness* 42
copy v *mimic* 93
copy n *written work* 101
copy v Literature/Writing 42
copy editor n 264
copycat v 268, 295; n 268

copyedit v 101, 311
copying machine n 212
copyist n 172
copyreader n (Am) 264
copyright v 188, 215; n 188
copywriter n 281
coq au vin n 297
coquet n 154
coquette n 154
coral n 30
coral reef n 181
coral snake n 194
coralberry n (Am) 236
corbie n *carrion crow* 30
cord n Measurement 147
cord n *string* 52
cord n *corduroy* 197
cordate adj *obs. savvy* 178
cordate adj *heart-shaped* 178
cordial adj *fig. from the heart* 37
cordial n *drink for the heart* 70
cordial adj *obs. lit. from the heart* 37
cordiality 37
cordless adj 278
cordovan adj/n *type of leather* 123
corduroy n 197
cordwain n *cordovan leather* 71
cordwainer n *shoemaker* 40
cordwainer n *tooler of cordovan leather* 40
cordwood n 146
core n *fig.* 50
core n *of apples, etc.* 50
core n *gen.* 50
core v 50
core city n 315
corgi n *type of dog* 285
coriander n 34
Coriolis effect n 302
Coriolis force n 285
cork n *type of stopper* 123; v 123
cork n Plants 30
corkboard n 258
corker n Slang 231
corking adj Slang 231
corkscrew n 183
corkscrew adj 190
cormorant n *fig. glutton* 30
cormorant n *type of bird* 30
corn n *as in "toe corns"* 66
corn n *grain* 15, 148
corn n *maize* 15, 148
corn borer n 279
corn chip n 303

corn dodger n *type of cornmeal cake* 223
corn dog n (Am) 316
corn flour n (Brit) *cornstarch* 197
corn liquor n (Am) 287
corn oil n 259
corn pone n (Am) 241
corn poppy n 236
corn silk n 236
corn snake n (Am) 165
corn sugar n (Am) 223
corn syrup n (Am) 273
corn whiskey n (Am) 196
cornball n Food 223
cornball adj/n (Am) Insults 307
cornball adj 307
cornbread n (Am) 183
corncob n (Am) 197
corncob pipe n 222
corncrib n 168
cornea n 66
corneous adj *horny* 137
corner v *trap* 218
corner n *as in "a corner of the market"* 245
corner n *as in "far corners of the earth"* 49
corner n *in boxing* 244
corner n 49
corner v 242
cornerstone n General/Miscellaneous 49
cornerstone n *fig.* 49
cornerways adv 294
cornerwise adv 103
cornet n *type of brass instrument* 77
cornet n *made of horn* 77
corn-fed adj 70
cornfield n 34
cornflakes n (Am) 274
cornflower n Plants 105
cornflower n *type of color* 105
cornflower blue n 278
cornhusk n 181
cornhusking n (Am) 168
cornice n 122
corniche n *type of road* 224
cornist n *horn player* 228
cornmeal n 183
cornpone adj 325
cornrow n/v *hairstyle* 323
cornstalk n (Am) 148
cornstarch n (Am) 241
cornucopia n *horn of plenty* 113
cornucopia n *fig.* 113

corny adj *campy* 300
corollary n 65
corona n 165
corona n *type of architectural feature* 165
coronach n *obs. public outcry* 107
coronach n *dirge, lament* 107
coronary adj 166; n 257
coronary artery n 182
coronate 79
coronation n 79
coroner n 45
coronet n *small crown* 71
coronet n *type of headdress* 71
corporal n *mil. rank* 130
corporal adj *pertaining to the body* 66
corporal adj *obs. possessing a body* 66
corporal adj *secular* 66
corporate adj 90
corporate adj *obs. corporal* 90
corporate welfare n (Am) 327
corporation n *trade guild* 86
corporation n 86
corporatism n 263
corporatize v 326
corporator n *part of a corporation* 200
corporeal adj *material* 90
corporeal adj *opp. of spiritual* 90
corporeality n 90
corporeity n 90
corps n *group of people* 131
corps n 131
corps n *Death* 79
corps n *group of knights* 131
corpse v *slang* 79
corpse n *dead body* 79
corpse n *obs. body, dead or alive* 79
corpsman n (Am) 131, 277
corpulence n 67
corpulent adj 67
corpulent adj *obs. gen. solid, corporeal* 67
corpus delecti n 230
corpuscle n 195
corpuscle n *gen. something small* 195
corpuscule *arch.* 195
corral v 122, 235; n 122
correct v 59; adj 59, 139
correct adj *proper* 139
correction n 59

correctional facility n (Am) 324
corrections officer n 324
correctitude n 266
correlate v *make correlated* 192
correlate v *be correlated* 192
correlation n 133
correspond v *Literature/Writing* 153
correspond v *General/Miscellaneous* 85
correspondence n *correlation* 85
correspondence n *letter-writing* 153
correspondence course n 276
correspondence school n 266
correspondency n 85
correspondent n 153
corresponding adj 85
corresponsive adj 85
corridor n *fig., as in "Boston–New York corridor"* 211
corridor n *gen. passageway* 211
corridor n *hallway* 211
corrigible adj *correctable* 91
corrigible adj *obs. needing correction, punishment* 91
corroborant adj *invigorating* 160
corroborate v 191
corroborate v *obs. phys. strengthen* 191
corroboration n 191
corrode v 84
corrosion n 84
corrosive 84
corrugate v 95
corrugated adj 95
corrugated iron n 270
corrugated paper n 270
corrugation n 95
corrupt adj *arch. decayed, morally corrupt* 54
corrupt v 57
corrupt adj *perverted* 54
corruption n *phys., moral decay* 51
corruption n *selling out* 51
corsage n *flower* 223, 280
corsage n *dress bodice* 223, 280
corsage n *obs. the body* 223, 280
corsair n *War/Military/Violence* 112
corsair n *Travel/Transportation* 169
corse n *arch. corpse* 45
corset n *fat inhibitor* 35, 197

corset n *gen. type of clothing* 35, 197
corsetiere n *corsetmaker* 226
cortege n 159
cortisol n *type of steroid* 309
cortisone n 303
corvee n *forced road labor* 41
corvette n *type of ship* 149
cos lettuce n 168
cosh n (Brit) *weapon* 248; v 248
cosher v *pamper* 252
cosine n 146
cosmetic n/adj 149
cosmetic n/adj *art of using cosmetics* 149
cosmetic case n 303
cosmetician n 289
cosmeticize v 212
cosmetology n 288
cosmic adj 220
cosmic adj *obs. earthly* 220
cosmic background radiation n 322
cosmic dust n 255
cosmic noise n 302
cosmic ray n 285
cosmic string n *hypothetical astronomical phenomenon* 326
cosmical adj 220
cosmogony n *beginning of the universe* 165
cosmogony n *study of universal beginnings* 165
cosmography n 65
cosmology n 165
cosmonaut n 310
cosmopolis n 233
cosmopolitan n 154
cosmopolitan adj 154, 229
cosmopolite n 130
cosmopolite 154
cosmos n 31
cossack n 131
cossack n *type of boot* 223
cost v 93
cost n *what is spent* 48
cost v *appraise, estimate* 93
cost n/v 48
cost of living n 264
costar n/v 282
cost-effective adj 318
cost-efficient adj 318
coster 110
costermonger n (Brit) *fruit vendor* 110
costive adj *constipated* 67
costive adj *obs. constipating* 67

cost-of-living index n 281
costume n *gen. dress of a time* 184
costume n *stage costume* 184, 265
costume adj *fake* 270
costume n *style* 184
costume v 184
costume jewelry n (Am) 297
costumer n (Am) 244
costumery n 223
costumier n (Brit) 228
cot n *related to cottage* 14
cot n *gen. type of bed* 148
cot n *portable bed* 148
cotangent n 146
cotemporary adj/n *contemporary* 180
coterie n 190
cotillion n *type of social event* 188
cotillion n *type of dance* 188
cotquean n *loosely, a manly woman or a womanly man* 117
cottage n *housing for the poor* 69
cottage n *gen. type of small house* 69
cottage cheese n (Am) 223
cottage curtains n 303
cottage industry n 289
cottage pie n 197
cottage pudding n 241
cottage tulip n 285
cotter n *type of pin* 36, 260
cotter hole 260
cotter pin n 260
cotton v *succeed* 143
cotton n *the plant* 34
cotton n *the cloth* 34
cotton candy n (Am) 287
cotton flannel n 223
cotton gin n (Am) 197
cotton to v 218
cotton wool n *unprocessed cotton* 71
cottonmouth n (Am) 220, 254
cottonmouth moccasin 220, 254
cotton-picking adj (Am) 312
cottonseed oil n 232
cottontail n (Am) 237
cottonwood n (Am) 209
cotyledon n 193
couch v *lit.* 116
couch n *arch. sleeping place* 69
couch v *as in "couch in delicate terms"* 116

couch n *type of living room furniture* 69
couch potato n 325
couchant adj *reclining* 68
cougar n 194
cough n *one cough* 32
cough v 32
cough n *coughing* 32
cough drop n 221
cough syrup n 257
cough up v *give up* 269
could v 25
couldn't v 152
coulee n (Am) 209
couloir n 209
coulomb n 256
Coulomb's law n 237
coulter n 16
council n *governing body* 20
council n Religion 20
council n *gen. meeting, counseling body* 20
councillor n 40
councilman n 155, 291, 324
councilperson 155, 291, 324
councilwoman 155, 291, 324
counsel n *obs. gen. group of advisors* 81
counsel n *a single leg. advisor* 81
counsel n *leg. advisors* 81
counsel n *secret, as in "keep counsel"* 61
counsel n *advice, advice-giving* 48; v 48, 59
counselee n 293
counselor n 40
counselor The Law 81
counselor-at-law n 155
count v *1,2,3* 31; n 31
count n *title of nobility* 44
count v *as in "counts for something"* 31; n 31
count v/n *as in "I'm counting on it"* 31
count v/n *as in "every little bit counts"* 31
count in v 250
count out v 250
countdown n (Am) 313
countenance n *obs. gen. bearing* 32
countenance n *blessing, support* 32
countenance n *facial expression* 32
countenance n *face* 32
countenance n *calm bearing* 32

countenance v 140
counter n *counting desk* 167
counter n *as in "kitchen counter"* 167
counter v *run counter* 93
counter n *e.g., gamepiece* 33
counter adv/n/adj 93
counteract v 142
counteract v *obs. oppose* 142
counterattack n/v 174
counterbalance n/v 135
counterclockwise adj/adv 270
counterculture n 319
counterespionage n 266
counterfeit adj 53
counterfeit v 57
counterfeit v *obs. impersonate* 57
counterfeit v *pretend* 57
counterfeit adj *var. obs. meanings of deformed, deceiving* 53
counterfeit v/n 53
counterflow n 250
counterfoil n 189
counterinsurgency n 319
counterintelligence n 300
counterirritant n 238
countermand n/v 95
countermeasure n 293
countermelody n 290
counteroffensive n 277
counteroffer n 205
counterpane n *bedspread* 147
counterpart n *complement* 87
counterpart n *duplicate* 87
counterpoint v 253
counterpoint n/v Music 77
counterpoint v 77
counterpose v 142
counterpoynte n 147
counterproductive adj 313
counterprogramming n 319
counterproposal n 269
counterreformation n 228
counterrevolution n 205
countersign v 136
counterspy n 300
countertop n 258
counterweight n 168
countess n 44
counting room n 187
countinghouse n 76
countless adj 138
countrified adj 173
country n *type of municipality; nation; rural area* 44
country n *area, as in "rough country"* 29

country n Music 312
country adj 29
country and western n 312
country club n (Am) 246
country cousin n 204
country gentleman n 154
country house n 69
country mile n 308
country music n 311
country rock n 246
country-dance n 129
countryfolk n 44
countryside n 63
countrywide adj 279
county n *government jurisdiction* 130
county n *obs. count* 111
county n *arch. type of jurisdiction* 130
county n *count's domain* 130
county agent n (Am) 184
county fair n 228
county seat n (Am) 215
coup n/v *blow* 247
coup n *successful move* 247
coup v *overturn* 141; n 155, 247
coup de grace n 176
coup de main n *attack* 203
coup d'etat n 155
coupe n *type of carriage* 224
coupe n *type of automobile* 224
couple n *gen.* 48
couple n *obs. coupling* 48
couple v *have sex* 75
couple n *pertaining to people* 48
couple adj 294
couple v 48
couplement *obs.* 75
coupler n 168
couplet n 128
couplet n *couple* 128
coupon n *investment statement* 214
coupon n *as in "sales coupon"* 214
courage n *bravery* 37
courage n *obs. fig. heart, core, tendencies* 37
courage n *obs. brazenness* 37
courage n *obs. lust* 37
courageous adj 37
courier n 40
course n *golf course* 40
course n *obs. motive power* 36
course n *as in "race course"* 40
course n *obs. gallop* 36
course n Education 129

course n *as in "in the course of time"* 40
course n *as in "the course of the ship"* 36
course v 36
courser n *horse* 30
courser n *type of dog* 30
courser n *type of bird* 30
courses n *menstruation* 120
courseware n *classroom software* 324
coursing n *a type of hunt* 108
court n *royal entourage* 44
court n *royal residence* 44
court n *as in "tennis court"* 33, 108
court v *as in "court disaster"* 108
court n The Law 46
court n *courtyard* 33
court v 108
court of appeals n 203
court of claims n 175
court of common pleas n 175
court of honor n 176
court of law n 81
court order n 155
court reporter n (Am) 267
court tennis n 263
courteous adj 43
courtesan n 79
courtesy n 43
courtesy card n (Am) 297
courtesy title n 247
courthouse n 102
courtier n 44
courtier n *obs. aspiring lover* 44
courtly adj/adv 37
courtly love n 262
court-martial v 80, 247; n 80
courtroom n 175
courtship n *obs. courteousness* 125
courtship n *diplomacy* 125
courtship n Love/Romance/Sex 125
courtyard n 121
couscous n 122
cousin n *pal* 39
cousin n *spec. relative* 39
cousin n *type of royal address* 39
cousin n *gen. relative* 39
cousin n *obs. whore; blockhead* 133
cousin adj 39
cousinage n 39
cousin-german n 39
cousinry n 39

couth n 311
couth adj/n 261
couth adj obs. courteous 261
couth n 261
couth adj obs. known 261
couture n 213, 263, 274
couturier n 213, 263
couturiere n 213, 263
cove n type of closet 118
cove n type of valley 118
cove n bay 118
coven n 173
coven n gen. meeting 173
covenant n/v 49
covenantee n 49
covenanter n 49
cover v substitute, as in "cover for a sick employee" 321
cover v conceal 28
cover n as in "can't judge a book" 128
cover v overlay 28
cover v as in "cover six miles" 224
cover n 28
cover v protect 28
cover n ground cover 294
cover n bedcover 222
cover n place setting 148
cover n assumed identity 132
cover n cover version 318
cover v recover 28
cover n as in "first-day cover" 205
cover v as in "cover a story for a newspaper" 264
cover v as in "five dollars will cover it"; provide insurance coverage 234
cover charge n (Am) 291
cover girl n (Am) 280
cover story n 305
cover version n rerecording 318
coverage n (Am) in insurance 281
coverall n 212
cover-all adj 270
covered bridge n 212
covered wagon n (Am) 184
coverlet n bedspread 33
covert n cover, shelter 54, 70
covert adj 54
coverture n disguise 70
coverture n covering 70
coverture n shelter 70
coverture n cover 70
coverture n bedspread 70
cover-up n 294

covess n female 204
covet v obs. covet sexually 55
covet v 55
covetise n arch. coveting 37
covetous adj 55
covey n 51
cow n applied to nonbovines 11
cow n 11
cow n ugly woman 175
cow v make a coward of 142
cow college n 282
cow horse n (Am) 241
cow pony 241
cow town n 268
cowabunga interj 312
coward n 36
cowardice n 36
cowbell n 168
cowbird n (Am) 209
cowboy n young cowhand 184
cowboy n cowherder 184, 259; v 184
cowboy boot n 260
cowboy hat n 260
cowcatcher n (Am) 224
cower v 37
cowgirl n 259
cowhand n (Am) 241
cowheart n coward 204
cowherd n 15
cowhide n 64
cowl n 16
cowlick n 120
cowling n 280
cowman n 168
coworker n 152
cowpat n 297
cowpea n (Am) 193
cowpoke n 259
cowpox n 196
cowpuncher n 259
cowrie n 165
cowshed n 223
cowslip n 10
coxcomb n jester's cap 132
coxcomb n fool 132
coxcombry n 132
coxswain n 36
coy adj obs. still 72
coy adj 72
coy v arch. 72
coydog n coyote/dog mix 302
coyote n 119
coz n arch. cousin 126
cozen v deceive, cheat 139
cozy adj applied to places 190
cozy adj applied to people 190
cozy n 239

cozy adj friendly 190
cozy up v 301
CPR n 322
CPU n 315
crab v move as a crab 284
crab n crab apple tree 30, 181
crab n complaint 133; v 133
crab n the crustacean 11
crab n grouch 133
crab apple n 181
crab louse n 105
crabber n 133
crabby adj 198
crabgrass n 181
crabgrass n type of marine grass 181
crabmeat n 259
crabs (Brit) 226
crabstick n 183
crack v fig., as in "crack under interrogation" 57
crack n type of cocaine 327
crack n/v snap 57
crack adj as in "a crack shot" 207
crack v make noise 27
crack v put cracks in 57
crack v as in "get cracking" 252
crack v as in "safecracking" 188
crack v as in "crack a whip" 27
crack v as in "his voice cracked"; as in "crack a code" 162
crack n try 230
crack n/v as in "crack a joke" 59
crack n 207
crack house n 327
crack up v as in "not all it's cracked up to be" 234
crackajack adj 268
crackbrain n crackpot 132
crackdown n (Am) 301
cracked adj crazy 151
cracker n as in "nutcracker" 123
cracker n liar 82
cracker n Southern white 204
cracker n 183
cracker-barrel adj (Am) 269
crackerjack adj/n 268
crackers adj (Brit) 151, 293
crackhead 327
cracking adj great 230
cracking adj/adv 230
crackle n/v 96
crackle n 250
crackleware n 257

crackpot n 249
cracksman n safecracker 203
crack-up n 250
cradle n fig. birthplace 14
cradle n/v 14
cradle-snatcher n person who dates young person 289
cradlesong n 77
craft n obs. deceit 21
craft n craftiness 21
craft n skill 21
craft n vehicles, as in "space-craft" 72
craft n obs. magic 21
craft n obs. strength 21
craft n as in "arts and crafts" 21
craft v 21
craft union n 289
craftsman n 40, 263, 281, 311
craftsmanship n 176
craftspeople n 40, 263, 281, 311
craftsperson n 40, 263, 281, 311
craftswoman n 40, 263, 281, 311
crafty adj arch. skilled 38
crafty adj arch. powerful 38
crafty adj sly 38
crag n 29
craggy adj 29
cram v as in "cram for a test" 27, 230
cram v 27
cramfull adj 234
cramp adj cramped 178
cramp n muscle contraction 66; v 66
cramp v obs. apply a type of torture 162; n 162
cramp n clamp 72
cramp v as in "cramp your style" 162
cramped adj 162
cranberry n (Am) 145
cranberry bush n (Am) 193
crane n 11
crane n/v 35
crane n arch. cranium 66
crane v as in "crane your neck" 140
cranial adj 196
craniology n Medicine 238
craniology n phrenology 238
cranium n 66
crank v bend 208
crank n/v Tools 16

crank n *cranky person* 231

crank adj *as in a "crank phone call"* 294

crank n *cranny* 143

crank n 208

crank out v 314

crankcase n 261

crankle n/v *zigzag* 136

crankshaft n 242

cranky adj *infirm* 213

cranky adj *sour* 213

cranny n 86

crap n *rubbish* 268

crap n *dung* 268

crap v *defecate* 221; n 221

crap n *obs. chaff* 268

crap v 268

crap out v *fail* 301

crapola n 324

crapper n *slang toilet* 297

crappie n (Am) 219

crappy adj (Am) 231

craps n (Am) 226

crapshoot n/v 324

crapshooter n 226

crapulous adj *binging* 115

crash v *intrude* 292

crash v *as in "crash a party"* 93

crash v *make noise* 93

crash v *sleep* 320

crash v *go to sleep* 93

crash adj *as in "crash course"* 308

crash v *collide, collapse* 93, 278

crash n/adj/v 93

crash dive n/v 280

crash helmet n 280

crash pad n 297

crashing adj *as in a "crashing success"* 294

crash-land v 308

crashworthiness n 308

crashworthy 308

crass adj *physically coarse* 178

crass adj *fig. coarse* 178

crassitude n 178

crate v 253

crate n *grate* 84

crate n *type of box* 84; v 84

crater n/v 145

craterlet n 254

craunch n/v *crunch* 158, 218

cravat n 168

crave v *yearn for* 32, 92

crave v *obs. demand* 92

crave v *ask for* 92

craving n 32, 92

craw n 83

crawdad n 30, 146, 272

crawfish n 30, 146, 272

crawfish v *back out* 231

crawl n *type of swim stroke* 289

crawl n *act of crawling* 217

crawl n/v *lit.* 55

crawl v *fig. move slow* 55

crawl space n 303

crawlway n 273

crawly adj/n *as in "creepy-crawly"* 250

crayfish n 30, 146, 272

crayon n/v 153

craze v *obs. break* 69

craze v *become physically ill* 69

craze n *fad* 260

craze n *obs. something wrong* 213

craze v *become mentally ill* 69

craze n *state of craziness* 213

crazy n 151, 249

crazy adj *phys. cracked* 151

crazy adj *Thoughts/Perception/The Mind* 151

crazy adj *phys. sick* 151

crazy adj *Medicine* 69

crazy bone n (Am) 238

crazy quilt n 269

crazyweed n *locoweed* 236

creak v/n 141

creak v *speak with a creak* 141

creaky adj 141, 233

cream n 34

cream v *as in "cream off"* 34

cream n *as in "facial cream"* 183

cream n *fig., as in "cream of the crop"* 34

cream n *type of sherry* 259

cream v *demolish* 291

cream n *the color* 207

cream cheese n 122

cream puff n 259

cream soda n (Am) 241

creamery n (Am) 171

crease n/v 86

create adj *arch.* 93

create v 93

create v *invent* 93

creation science n 228, 324

creationism 228, 324

creative adj 93, 100

creative accounting n 321

creative evolution n 272

creativeness n 243

creativity n 243

creator n *Religion* 43

creator n *inventor* 125

creatress n *inventor* 125

creatrix n *inventor* 125

creature n *obs. something created* 30

creature n 30

creature comfort n 156

creche n 202

credence n 51

credent adj 51

credential v 271

credential adj/n/v 176

credenza n 257

credibility n 88

credibility gap n 321

credible adj *obs. believing* 88

credible adj *believable* 88

credit v *as in "credit with success"* 252; n 252

credit n *trust, believability* 114

credit n *as in "credit hours"* 291

credit n *acknowledgement* 114

credit n *opp. of debit* 200; v 200

credit card n (Am) 264

credit hour n 291

credit line n 281

credit rating n 311

credit union n (Am) 264

creditor n 76

creditworthy adj 289

credo n *gen.* 42

credo n *Religion* 42

credulity n 73

credulous 73

creed n *gen.* 20

creed n *Religion* 20

creek n *type of inlet* 145

creek n *type of port* 145

creek n 145

creek n *obs. cleft* 145

creel n 36

creep n *as in "gives me the creeps"* 212

creep v *sneak* 26

creep v *crawl* 26

creep n *Insults* 268

creep v *increase slowly* 26

creeper n 64

creepy adj 233

cremains n 306

cremate v 155, 247

cremation n 155, 247

crematorium n 266

crematory n 266

creme n 211

crème brûlée n 259

crème caramel n 274

crème de cacao n 273

crème de la crème n 232

crème de menthe n 273

crème fraiche n *fresh cream* 303

creole adj/n 191

crepe n 259

crepe n 197

crepe de chine n *type of fabric* 242

crepe paper n 270

crève suzette n 287

crescendo adj/n/v 201

crescent adj *growing, as the moon* 137

crescent n 84

crescent adj *crescent-shaped* 137

crescent roll n 259

cress n 15

crest n *as in "crest of a hill," "crest of a wave"* 87; v 87

crest n 30

crested 30

crestfallen adj 138

cretin n *Medicine* 195

cretin n *slang idiot* 195

cretinism 195

crevasse n (Am) 209

crevice n 29

crew n *as in "road crew," ship crew* 136; v 136

crew n *group* 136

crew n *obs. group of soldiers* 136

crew cut n (Am) 303

crew neck n (Am) 297

crew sock n 303

crewel n *type of embroidery* 100

crewel n *type of yarn* 100

crewman n 289

crewmate n 301

cri de coeur n *cry in the night* 277

crib n *as in "corn crib"* 15; v 15

crib n *as in "baby crib"* 148

crib n *as in "crib notes"* 230

crib n *pad* 239

crib v *Slang* 230

crib death n 319

cribbage n *type of card game* 151

crick n 85

cricket n *the game* 126

cricket n *the insect* 30

crikey interj 230

crim n (Am) 277

crime n *fig.* 80

crime n *obs. accusation* 80

crime n *arch. sin* 80

crime n 80

crucial adj 233

crucial adj *related to the cross* 233

crucible n 72

crucifix n 42

crucifixion n 59, 78

crucify v 59

cruciverbalist n *crossword puzzler* 323

crud n *gunk* 307

crud n *slang disease* 302

crud n 100

crud n *jerk* 307

crud n *curd* 307

crude adj *jury-rigged* 160

crude adj *obs. uncooked* 122

crude adj *natural* 63

crude n *oil* 256

crude adj *boorish* 63

crude adj *arch. not ripe* 63

crude adj *jury-rigged* 63

crudites n *type of appetizer* 310

crudle 163

cruel adj 36

cruelty n 36

cruet n *type of container* 43

cruise v *look for partners* 275

cruise v *in sailing* 168

cruise n/v 168

cruise v *as in "cruising altitude"* 168

cruise control n 317

cruise missile n 312

cruiser n 174

cruller n (Am) 211

crumb n *low person* 283

crumb n/v *Food* 15

crumb n *louse* 283

crumble v 97

crumbs interj 267

crumbum n *crumb* 313

crummy adj 249

crummy adj *arch. slang attractive* 249

crumpet n 168

crumple n/v 59

crunch n/v 218

crunch n *as in "it's crunch time"* 300

crunch v *crush* 218

crunchy adj 270

crusade n 188

crusade n *gen.* 188

crush v *as in "crush against," crush the opposition* 59

crush n/v 59

crush v *arch. drink* 122

crust n *on bread* 34

crust n *outside* 34

crust n *obs. shell* 34

crust n *as in "pie crust"* 34

crust n *as in "crust of a planet"* 34

crustacea n 146

crustacean n 146

crustaceous adj 146

crut n 307

crutch n/v 16

crutch n *fig.* 16

crux n *type of riddle* 189

crux n *gist* 189, 269

crux n *ankh* 189

cry v/n *cry out* 48

cry n *as in "battlecry"* 37

cry v *weep* 48, 124; n 37, 48

cry n *shout, wail, plea* 37

cry v/n *beg* 48

cry n *announcement* 37

cry uncle v 284

crybaby n (Am) 249

cryobiology n 310

cryogen n 237

cryogenic 237

cryogenics n 296

cryonics n (Am) 316

cryopreservation n 316

cryosurgery n 316

cryotherapy n 286

crypt n 174

crypt n *obs. cave* 174

cryptanalysis n (Am) *study of codes and untranslated languages* 290

cryptesthesia n *ESP, etc.* 292

cryptic adj 159

crypto n *secret supporter* 307

cryptogram n 264

cryptograph n 152, 264

cryptographer n 152

cryptology n *codes* 152

cryptology n *mysterious communication* 152

cryptonym n *code name* 264

cryptozoic adj *living in secluded places* 254

cryptozoology n *study of mysterious creatures* 315

crystal n *type of mineral* 10

crystal n *obs. type of ice* 10

crystal n *type of glass* 10

crystal n *electronic sense* 10

crystal n *type of glass* 167

crystal adj 10, 63

crystal ball n 248

crystal gazing n 267

crystal-clear adj 114

crystalline adj 29

crystallize v *form crystals* 10, 118

crystallize v *fig. take form* Geography/Places 118

crystallize v *obs. turn into crystal* Geography/Places 118

cub n *other animal young, including bear* 105

cub n *young fox* 105

cub reporter n 246

cubbyhole n 217

cube n/v 65

cube n *cube-shaped thing* 65

cube adj/n/v 120

cube n *real square* Insults 313

cube root n 166

cube steak n 287

cubic measure n 166

cubicle n 286

cubicle n *obs. bedroom* 286

cubicle n *small bed* 286

cubiculum n *arch. bedroom* 239

cubism n 276

cubit n 31

cubit n *obs. forearm* 31

cuck n *arch. defecate* 66

cucking stool n *type of punishment* 46

cuckold n/v 18

cuckoo n *type of bird* 30; v 30

cuckoo n *looney person* 30, 133, 283; adj 133

cuckoo clock n 195

cuckquean n *female cuckold* 125

cucumber n 70

cucumber tree n (Am) 194

cud n 11

cuddle n/v 213

cuddle v 116

cuddlesome 213

cuddly adj 213

cudgel v 20, 131; n 20

cue v *strike with a pool cue* 207

cue v *queue* 207

cue n *in pool* 185

cue n *pigtail* 184

cue v *give starting signal* 295; n 133

cue v 133

cue ball n 262

cuff v 175

cuff n *obs. type of mitten* 100

cuff n/v *hit* 112

cuff n *as in "pant cuffs"* 100

cuff n/n *as in "shirtcuff"* 100

cuff link n 260

cuffs n *handcuffs* 175

cuirass n *type of armor* 80

cuirassier n 80

cuisine n 197

cuke 70

cuke n *cucumber* 273

cul-de-sac n *blind street* 198

cul-de-sac n *anatomical term* 198

cul-de-sac n *type of container* 198

culinarian n 303

culinary adj 148

cull v 55

cullion n *obs. testicle* 132

cullion n *grouch* 132

cully n *gullible person* 175

cully v *obs.* 175

culminate v 158

culmination n 158

culotte n 280

culotte n *type of breeches* 280

culpable adj *deserving blame* 46

culpable adj *legally guilty* 46

culprit n *defendant* 175

culprit n *guilty person* 175

cult n *fanatical group* 154

cult n *worship* 154

cult n *organized worship* 154

cultivate v *as in "cultivate a relationship"* 179

cultivate v *fig. nurture, as in "cultivate a taste"* 179

cultivate v *lit. and fig.* 148

cultivated adj *refined* 173

cultivation n Agriculture/Food-Gathering 148

cultivation n Society/Mores/Culture 173

cultural adj Society/Mores/Culture 111, 173

cultural adj Agriculture/Food-Gathering 71

cultural anthropology n 285

culturati n 319

culture n *land cultivation* 71

culture n *growing crops, etc.* 71

culture n *personal refinement* 111

culture n *growing bacteria, etc.* 71

culture n *heritage, society* 247

culture shock n 299

culture vulture n 304

cultured pearl n 288

culverin n *type of early gun* 80

cum laude adj/adv (Am) 247

cumber v 88

cumberbund n 149

cumbersome adj 88

cumbrous adj obs. 88

cumin n 15

cummerbund n 149

cumulate n/v 114

cumulative adj 114

cumulonimbus n 255

cumulus n type of cloud 210

cumulus n accumulation 210

cuneiform adj/n 214

cunnilingus n 262

cunning adj knowledgeable; skilled 39

cunning adj intelligent 39

cunning adj crafty 39

cunning n 39

cunt n 32

cunt n jerk 293

cunt-struck adj 262

cup v as in "cup the hands" 234

cup v draw blood 68

cup n cupful 14

cup n Measurement 238

cup n as in "loving cup" 14

cup n 14

cup of tea n 301

cupboard n type of cabinet 33

cupboard n obs. type of table equipment 33

cupboard n sideboard 33

cupcake n (Am) 223

cupidity n greed 73

Cupid's bow n 244

cupola n 106

cuppa n 292

cur n applied to dogs 30

cur n applied to people 30

curacao n 211

curate n 43

curate's egg n (Brit) something with good and bad 277

curative adj curing 68

curative adj medical 68; n 68

curator n museum head 152

curator n type of guardian 152

curator n manager 152

curatrix n 127, 152

curb n gen. restraint 157

curb n as in "street curb" 205

curb n other types of border 205

curb v 157; v 157

curb service n (Am) 298

curbstone n 198

curd n/v 100

curdle v 100, 163

cure v as in "cure a fish" 148

cure n obs. concern 68

cure n/v 68

cure n obs. gen. treatment 68

cure v 68

cure-all n 204

curfew n time to be indoors 31, 256

curfew n lights out 31, 256

curie n unit of radioactivity 273

curio n 239

curiosa n erotic books 264

curiosa n curios 264

curiosity n nosiness 74

curiosity n inquisitiveness 74

curiosity n something curious 74

curiosity n being curious 74

curious adj obs. precise 39

curious adj odd 39

curious adj inquisitive 39, 74

curious adj erotic 262

curious adj obs. careful 39

curious adj odd 190

curious adj obs. excellent, re-markable 190

curious adj inquisitive 190

curl n gen. 120

curl v 93

curl v spec. curl hair 93; n 120

curl n 93

curler n Games/Fun/Leisure 151

curler n Everyday Life 183

curlicue n/v 233

curling n 151

curling iron n 148

curlpaper n 212

curly adj 190

curlycue n/v 233

curmudgeon n 135

currant n 34

currency n gen. flow 172

currency n being up-to-date 137, 190; n 190

currency n circulation of money 172

currency n money 172

current n as in "river current" 84

current adj flowing 61

current adj real 144

current adj accepted, prevalent 137

current n as in "electrical cur-rent" 195

curriculum n 154

curriculum vitae n 276

currier n currier of horses 40

currier n currier of leather 40

curry v comb, groom 57

curry v obs. flatter 116

curry n type of sauce 122

curry v as in "curry favor" 116

curry n spice 122

curry favor v 113

curry powder n 211

currycomb n 123

curse n/v oath 19

curse n cuss 19

curse n gen. bane 47

curse n type of spell 47; v 47

curse, the n slang menstruation 286

cursed adj 19, 47

curses interj 267

cursive adj/n 201

cursor n 315

cursor n part of a slide rule 315

cursory adj 159

curt adj gen. short 150

curt adj 150

curtail v shorten 103

curtail v restrict 103

curtailment n 103

curtain n end of play 129

curtain n stage curtain 33, 129

curtain n 33

curtain n fig. concealing device 33

curtain call n 265

curtain-raiser n 265

curtains n end, doom 283

curtsy n show of respect 111

curtsy n/v type of bow 111

curvaceous adj (Am) 297

curve v 95

cushion n as in "seat cushion" 33

cushion n other types of cushion-ing things 33

cushion v phys. give cushions 33, 191

cushion n as in "pin cushion" 33

cushion v provide fig. cushion 191

cushy adj 283

cuspid n 256

cuspidor n 183

cuss v (Am) 214

cuss n 204

cussed adj (Am) 231

cussword n 214

custard n type of pie 122

custard n 122

custode n 78

custody n incarceration 86

custody n 86

custom adj 233

custom n habit 48

customable adj 159

customary adj normal 159

customary adj by habit instead of by law 159

customer n customs officer 75

customer n 75

customer n fig., as in "a tough customer" 75

customhouse n 101

customize v (Am) 252

customs n 76

cut n as in "haircut," "the cut of one's jib" 136

cut v as in "cut the cards" 126

cut n as in "short cut" 136

cut n selection, as in "a cut from her latest album" 318; v 318

cut n/v lit. and fig. 55

cut v as in "cut through a park-ing lot" 140

cut n as in "price cut" 270

cut n as in "cut of meat" 70

cut v as in "cut a class" 204

cut v dilute 252

cut n edit 158

cut n as in "woodcut" 176

cut n stroke, blow, as in "upper-cut" 188

cut v leave 142

cut v as in "cut a tooth" 180

cut n share 292

cut n as in "roadcut" 134

cut glass n 196

cut it v (Am) make the grade 321

cut out adj as in "cut out for success" 293

cut-and-dried adj 189

cut-and-paste adj 313

cut-and-try adj trial-and-error 277

cutaway adj in drawing 318

cutaway adj/n Cloth/Clothing 223

cute adj acute 226

cute adj adorable 226

cutesy adj 284

cutesy-poo adj 284, 325

cuticle n 273

cuticle n small skin 273

cutie n (Am) 204

cutie-pie n 300

cutlass n 131

cutler n 40

cutlery n 40

cutlet n 183

cutpurse n pickpocket 80

dash n *"long hyphen"* 127

dash n *state of being dashing* 184

dash v *fig. smash* 57

dash n *used in Morse Code* 127

dashboard n 224

dashing adj 184, 207

dastard n *obs. dolt* 82

dastard n *dastardly person* 82

dastardly adj 82

DAT n 326

data n *applied to numbers* 159

data n General/Miscellaneous 159

data bank n 315

data link n 318

data processing n 309

database n 315

datamation n 315

date n *appointment* 31; v 31

date n *spec. time designation* 31

date n *appointment* 256; v 256

date n *the fruit* 34

date v *go out of date* 271

date palm n 64

date rape n 327

datebook n 318

dated adj 191, 271

dateline n 256

datum n 159

daub n/v 59

daughter n 18; adj 18, 159

daughter-in-law n 75

daunt v 57

daunt v *obs. stop* 57

dauntless adj 57, 124

davenport n *couch* 239

davenport n 273

davenport n *writing desk* 239, 273

Davy Jones n 203

Davy Jones's locker n 193, 203

daw n 99

dawdle v 179

dawn n/v *of the sun* 99

dawn v *gen. begin* 99

dawn horse n 285

dawning n 99

day n *24 hours* 12

day n *daylight hours* 12

day n *daylight* 12

day v *obs. dawn* 12

day care n 303

day layborer n 110

day one n 325

day school n 202

day shift n 245

daybed n 121

daybook n 121

daybreak n 105

daydream n/v 170, 213

Day-Glo adj 321

daylight n 10

daylight n *open space, as in "run for daylight"* 10

daylight saving time n 272

daylighting n *opp. of moonlighting* 289

daylily n 119

daymare n 185

dayroom n 211

dayside n 315

daystar n 12

daytime n 105

day-to-day adj 47

day-tripper n 268

daywork n 127

daze n *mica* 164

daze n/v 51

dazzle v *confound* 113

dazzle v *arch. lose eyesight* 113

DDT n 303

de facto adv/adv·159

de rigueur adj 231

deacon n 19, 78

deaconess n 19, 78

deacon's bench n 286

deactivate v 278

dead adj/n *completely* 20

dead v *obs. deaden* 20

dead adj/n *lit. and fig.* 20

dead n *as in "the dead of night"* 22

dead adj/n *obs. deadly, fatal* 20

dead adv 20

dead air n 305

dead bolt n 273

dead center n 249

dead duck n (Am) 231

dead end n 269

dead heat n 200

dead letter n 121

dead man's float n 304

dead men *slang* 284

dead reckoning n 156

dead ringer n 268

dead soldier n *empty bottle* 284

dead weight n 176

dead-air space n 273

deadbeat adj/n 204

deaden v 179

dead-end adj 269; v 269, 295

deadeye n 189

deadhead n *blockhead* 268

deadhead n *obs. death's head figure* 268

deadhead n *free rider* 268

deadline n 250

deadlock n *deadbolt* 239

deadlock n/v *impasse* 205

deadly adj *like death* 20

deadly adj *able to be killed* 20

deadly nightshade n 118

deadly sin n *pride, sloth, etc.* 43

dead-on adj 270

deadpan adj/v (Am) 288

deadwood n *fig. useless things* 99

deadwood n *lit.* 99

deaf adj *as in "tone deaf"* 14

deaf adj 14

deaf v *arch.* 14

deaf adj *fig. unhearing* 14

deafen v 14

deaf-mute n 221

deal v *as in "wheel and deal"* 41; n 227

deal n *portion, quantity, as in "great deal of trouble"* 21; v 21

deal n/v *in cards* 151

dealership n 281

dean n *type of guild leader* 111

dean n *type of religious leader* 111

dean n 111

dean's list n 291

dear interj 175

dear adj *obs. valued* 23

dear adj *obs. noble* 23

dear adj *precious* 25

dear adj *severe, expensive* 23

dear adj *sweet* 25

dear n 49

Dear John n 304

dearth n 49

death n 20

death n *extinction* 20

death interj 156

death benefit n 291

death camp n 306

death cap n *type of mushroom* 285

death house n 282

death instinct n 282

death mask n 266

death rate n 247

death rattle n 215

death ray n 283

death row n 307

death squad n 319

death tax n 299

death trap n 229

death warrant n 174

death wish n 282

deathbed n *grave* 20, 45

deathbed n *the actual bed* 20, 45

deathblow n 202

deathfuladj 20

deathless adj 130

deathly adj/adv *obs. capable of dying* 45

deathly adj/adv *arch. causing death* 45

deathly adj/adv *as in "deathly ill"* 45

death's-head n 130

death's-head moth n 254

deathsman n *executioner* 130

deathwatch n 174

deb n 282

debacle n 233

debacle n *phys. onrush of water* 233

debark v *disembark* 168

debase v *demote, deprecate* 140

debase v 140

debate n *arch. fight* 51

debate n/v 51

debauch n/v 142

debauch v *obs. turn loyalty* 142

debauchee n 142

debauchery n 142

debile adj *debilitated* 121

debilitate v 68

debility n 68

debit n *opp. of credit* 200

debit v 172

debit n *obs. debt* 200

debit n 172; v 200

debit card n 323

debonair adj *obs. gentle* 107

debonair adj 107

debrief v 308

debris n 189

debt adj *obs.* 41

debt n 41

debtee 41

debtor 41

debug v 302

debunk v (Am) 295

debut n/v 204

debutant n 215

debutante n 215

decade n *gen. group of ten* 146

decade n *ten years* 146

decade n *ten books* 146

decadence n 108, 225

decadency n 108

decadent adj/n 108, 225, 261

decaf adj/n 287, 326

decaffeinate v 287

decaffeinated adj 287

decal n 251, 301

decalcomania 251, 301

decalogue n *the Ten Commandments* 78

decant v *transfer to decanter* 163

decant v *pour off* 163

decanter n/v 183

decapitate v 155

decapitation n 155

decapod n 219

decasualization n *hiring permanent employees* 264

decathlete n 281, 317

decathlon n 281, 317

decay n *deteriorating* 86; v 86

decay n *deterioration* 86

decays n *ruins* 144

decease n/v 45

deceased adj/n 45

deceit n 49, 57

deceitful 49

deceive v 49, 57, 85

decelerate, deceleration, v, n 270

December n 12

decency n 174

decency n *honor* 174

decency n *obs. appropriateness* 174

decennial adj 165

decennium n *decade* 146, 165

decent adj *appropriate* 117

decent adj *proper* 117

decent adj *as in "decent wages"* 117

decentralization n 233

decentralize v 233

deception n 85

deception n 57

deceptive adj 85

decern v *obs. decide* 74

decibel n 286

decide v *resolve* 74

decide v *come to a decision* 74

decide v *make a judgment* 74

decided adj 206

deciduous adj 164

decillion n 195

decimal adj *related to ten* 146

decimal n/adj 146

decimal point n 237

decimal system n 166

decimate v *kill one in ten* 142

decimate v *gen. kill a portion of* 142

decision n 74; v 308

decisive adj *determined* 159

decisive adj *deciding* 159

deck n *pack of cards* 126

deck n *gen. platform* 72

deck n *slang, as in "hit the deck"* 72

deck v *hit* 312

deck v 107

deck n *on ships* 72

deck n *as in "tape deck"* 321

deck chair n 196

deck tennis n 289

deckhand n (Am) 224

declaim v 93

declaim v *speak vigorously* 93

declamatory 93

declaration n *marriage proposal* 199

declaration n 59

declare v *state a position* 59

declare v *propose* 199

declare v 59

declasse adj 266

decline n *decay, wither* 51

decline v *say no* 163

decline v 51

deco n 318

decoct v *obs. cook by boiling* 70

decode v 264

decoder n 280

decollate v *behead* 97

decollete adj 223

decommission v 291

decompose v *break down* 207

decompress v 278

decompression chamber n 297

decompression sickness n 303

decondition v 308

decongestant n 303

deconstruct v 323

decontaminate v 301

decor n *stage setting* 265

decor n *as in "residential decor"* 265

decorate v *ornament* 208

decorate v *honor* 208

decorative art n 318

decorator n 200

decorator adj 304

decore v *arch. decorate* 98

decorous adj 124

decorum n 124

decorum n *appropriateness* 124

decoupage n 305

decoy n/v 151

decoy n *place for hunting with decoys* 151

decrease n/v 93

decree n *The Law* 43, 81; v 81

decree n/v *Religion* 43

decrement n 93

decrepit adj 68

decrepitude n 68

decrescent adj 93

decriminalize v (Am) 319

decrypt v *decode* 299

decurtation n *obs. trimming* 98

dedicate adj *arch.* 78

dedicate v *Literature/Writing* 128

dedicate v *Religion* 78

dedicated adj *determined* 317

dedication n 78

dedication n *e.g., "This book is dedicated to my mom"* 128

dedication n *perseverance, determination* 317

deduce v *obs. deduct* 95

deduce v *figure out* 95

deduce v *arch. bring* 95

deduct v 95

deduct v *deduce* 95

deduction n 95

deductive adj 95, 151

deed *as in "good deed"* 21

deed n *type of document* 21

deed n/v *The Law* 46

deejay n 305

deem v 26

de-emphasize v 301

deep n 22, 23; adj 23

deep n *as in "the deep of night"* 22

deep adj *as in "deep feelings"* 23

deep adj *applied to sound, color* 23

deep freezer 308

deep fryer n 304

deep kiss n 304

deep pocket n 325

deep space n 309

deep throat n 325

deep-dish pie n 280

deepen v 23

deep-freeze v/n 308

deep-fry v 287

deep-seated adj 191

deep-six v 307

deep-sky adj 315

deepsome adj 163

deer n *spec. doe, etc.* 11

deer n *gen. animals* 11

deer n *modern sense* 11

deer mouse n (Am) 220

deer tick n 326

deerfly n (Am) 236

deerhound n 209

deerstalker n 212

de-escalate, de-escalation v 319

def adj (Am) *excellent* 327

deface v *obs. defame* 45

deface v *mar* 45

deface v *destroy* 45

defamation n *libel, slander* 37

defamation n 50

defamation n *shame* 37

defamatory adj 138

defame v 50

defamous adj *infamous* 98

defauched adj 142

default n/v 46

default n *fault* 61

default v *as in "default on a loan"* 81

default n *obs. mistake* 61

default n *standard specs* 315

defeat v *obs. deface, demolish* 92

defeat v *as in "defeat the purpose"* 92

defeat v *win over, beat* 92

defeatism, defeatist n 281

defeature n *obs. defeat* 131

defeature n *obs. defeat* 92

defeature n *disfigurement* 208

defecate v *purify* 238

defecate v *go to the bathroom* 238

defecation n 238

defect n 54, 114, 176; v 142

defection n *rare being defective* 114

defection n *switching allegiance* 114

defective adj 54

defector n 176

defeminize v 278

defend v *obs. prevent* 56

defend v 56

defendant adj/n 46

defense n 49

defense mechanism n 261

defensive n 157

defensive n *obs. type of medicine, preventive* 157

defer v *postpone* 92

defer v *delegate* 96

deference n 159

deferent adj 159

deferential adj 159

deferment n 157

defervescence n *fever subsiding* 239

defiance n 225

defiant adj 225

defibrillate v 297

defibrillator n 309

deficiency n 138

deficient adj 138

deficit n 200

deficit spending n 299

defile v *corrupt* 59

defile v *march in single file* 191

define v *as in "define a word"* 127

define v *obs. confine* 92

define v 92

define v *as in "he is defined by his attitude"* 92

define v *obs. end* 92

definite adj 103

definite article n *the* 201

definition n *clarity, as in "photographic definition"* 250

definition n *arbitration, decision* 98

definition n 92

definition n Language and Speaking 127

definitive adj 103

definitude n 232

deflagrate v *burn down* 191

deflate v 271

deflate v *fig. dispirit* 271

deflect v 139

deflection n 139

defloration n Love/Romance/Sex 74

deflower v *take virginity* 74

defoliant n 306

defoliate v 208

defoliation n 208

deforce v *take or keep by force* 46

deforest n 236

deforestation n 236

deform, deformed, deformity v, adj, n 93

defoulen v 59

defraud v 80

defreeze v 295

defrock v 141

defrost v 271

defroster n 288

deft adj 68

deft adj *obs. gentle* 68

defunct adj *dead* 139

defunct adj *no longer used* 139; n 139

defuse v 308

defy v *obs. distrust* 57

defy v *challenge to battle* 57

defy v 57

defy v *as in "I defy you to answer"* 57

degenderize v 325

degenerate adj/n/v 103

degradation n 59

degrade v *demote* 59

degrade v *detract from* 59

degrade v *debase* 59

degrade v *wear out* 59

degree n *as in "first-degree murder"* 175

degree n/v Education 78

degree n *level* 48

degree n *as in "third-degree burns"* 239

degree v *obs.* 48

degree n *step* 48

degressive adj *reducing* 270

degringolade n *rapid decline* 269

degust v *savor* 162

degustate v 162

degustation n 162

dehumanize v 218

dehumidifier n 288

dehumidify v 288

dehydration, dehydrate n, v 250

deicide n 155

deify v *treat as if godlike* 43

deify v *make godlike* 43

deify v *promote to god status* 43

deign v 57

deinstitutionalization n 313

deism n 173

deist n 173

deity n *a spec. god* 43

deity n *divinity* 43

déjà vu n 275

déjà vu entendu *words* 275

déjà vu lu *writing* 275

deject adj *dejected* 98

dejecta n *excrement* 269

dejected adj 73

dejection n *depression* 73, 98

dejection n *obs.* 73, 269

delay v *obs. alleviate* 98

delay n *procrastination* 49; v 49, 57

delay n *obstacle* 49; v 57

dele v/n 135

delectable adj 89; n 89, 293

delectate v *delight* 218

delectate v 89

delectation n *arch. entertainment* 77, 89

delegate n 84; v 84, 97

delegation n *delegating* 157

delegation n *group* 217

delegation n *group of delegates* 157

delegation n 84, 97

delete v 135

deletion n *arch. destruction* 135

deletion n 135

deletorious adj 161

deli n 259, 311

deliber v *arch.* 74

deliberate v/adj 74

deliberation n 74

delible adj *opp. of indelible* 160

delicacy n *gen. fragility* 136

delicacy n *delicate beauty* 136

delicacy n Food 70

delicacy n *obs. hedonism* 72

delicacy n *med. fragility* 68, 136

delicacy n *luxury* 72

delicate adj *subtle* 179

delicate adj *obs. hedonistic, luxurious, indulgent* 72

delicate adj *gen. fragile* 68

delicate adj *sensitive* 137

delicate adj *medically fragile* 68

delicate adj *sticky, as in "a delicate situation"* 206

delicatessen n (Am) *food sold at a delicatessen* 259

delicious adj *obs. hedonistic* 34

delicious adj 34

delicious apple n 273

delict n *minor offense* 80

delight n/v 36

delightable 36

delighted adj 36, 170

delighted adj *obs. delightful* 170

delightful adj 36, 73

delightful adj *obs. delighted* 73

delightsome adj 36, 100

delimit v 252

delineate v 139

delineate v *fig. sketch out* 139

delineation n 139

delinquent adj/n 102

deliquium n *faint* 163

delirancy n *obs.* 121

delire v *obs.* 121

delirious adj 121

delirium n 121

delirium tremens n 211

deliver v *hand over* 55

deliver v *as in "deliver a speech"* 55, 97

deliver v *as in "deliver a punch"* 55

deliver v *arch. rescue* 55

deliver adj *nimble* 61

deliver v *rescue* 55

deliver v *as in "deliver a baby"* 32

delivery n Medicine 32

delivery 97

delivery boy n 280

delivery room n 303

deliveryman n 280

dell n *slang woman* 143

dell n 9

delmonico steak n 287

delouse v 279

delta n 118

delta ray n 272

delta wave n 296

deltoid adj/n 195

delts n *akin to pecs* 316

delude v 85

deluge n/v 63

delusion n *deception* 85

delusion n *hallucination* 85

delusive adj 85

delusory adj 85

deluxe adj 217

delve v *phys. excavate* 26

delve v *investigate* 26

demagogue n/v 155, 247

demagoguery n (Am) 155, 247

demagogy 155, 247

demand v *ask* 93

demand v *require* 93

demand n *inquiry* 98

demand v 93

demanding adj 271

demand-side adj 323

demarcate v 218

demarcation n 218

demark v 218

dematerialize v *make immaterial* 252

dematerialize v *disappear* 252

demean v *degrade* 161

demean v *conduct oneself* 100

demean v *exhibit demeanor* 161

demeanor n 100

demency 151, 199

dement adj/v 151

dementate v 151

demented adj 151

dementia n 151, 199

dementia praecox n *schizophrenia* 262

deuce n *playing card* 101
deuce n *little dickens* 175
deuce n *in tennis* 101
deuced adj *euphemism for "damned"* 204
deus ex machina n 173
deuteragonist n *second banana* 246
deuteranopia n *color blindness to green* 273
deuterium n 296
deuterium oxide n *heavy water* 296
devaluate v 271
devaluation n 271
devalue v 271, 281
devast v *devastate* 163
devastate, devastating v, adj 163
devastation n 163
devein v 310
develop v 192
develop v *unfold* 192
development n *as in "real estate development"* 258
development n 192
deviance n 308
deviant adj 89
deviant n 293
deviate n 283
deviate v 89
deviate n 293
device n *plan, fancy* 49
device n *type of tool* 49
devil n *demon* 19
devil n *Satan* 19
devil v *annoy* 208
devil n *as in "poor devil"* 175
devilfish n 181
devilish adj 73
devil-may-care adj 198
devilment n 205
devilry n 78
devil's advocate n 204
devil's food cake n (Am) 273
deviltry 78
devious adj 150
devious adj *out of the way* 150
devise v 55
devise v *obs. divide* 55
devise v *obs. study* 55
devitalize v 234
devoid adj 89
devote v 36
devoted adj 36
devotee n 36
devotion n 36
devotional adj/n Religion 154

devour v 34
devout adj 42
dew n 9
dew point n 220
dewdrop 9
Dewey decimal classification n 290
dewfall n 145
dewlap n 32
deworm v 287
dewy-eyed adj 298
dexter adj *to the right* 137
dexterity n *mental skill* 108
dexterity n *phys. skill* 108
dexterous adj *convenient* 147
dexterous 108
dexterous adj 147
dharma n 202
diabete n 99
diabetes n 99
diabetic adj/n 99, 221
diablerie n *black magic* 203
diabolic adj 73
diabolical adj 73
diabolify v 179
diabolism n 73
diabolize v 179
diagnose v 147, 238
diagnosis n 147, 167
diagnosis n *gen.* 167
diagnosis v 167
diagnostic adj/n 147
diagnostician n 239
diagonal adj/n 115
diagonal n 115
diagram n/v 153, 235
dial v *as in "dial a telephone"* 214
dial n *compass dial* 31
dial n *gen. meter face* 31
dial n *sundial* 31
dial tone n 265
dialect n *type of examination* 127
dialect n 127
dialect atlas n 299
dialect geography n 290
dialectic n *type of logic* 74
dialectical materialism n 288
dialectology n 245
dialogist n 172
dialogue n/v Literature/Writing 41
dialogue n *gen.* 41
dialysis, dialyze n, v 238
dialysis, dialyze n, v *in logic* 238
diamante n *sparkles* 274
diameter n 65

diamond adj *as in "diamond anniversary"* 252
diamond n *the gem* 29
diamond n *card suit* 126
diamond in the rough n 308
diamond lane n *special street lane* 326
diamondback n 210
diamondback rattler 210
diamondback terrapin n 254
diapasm n *type of scented powder* 144
diaper n 222
diaper n *gen. type of fabric* 222
diaper n *towel* 222
diaphragm n 66
diarist n 214
diarrhea n 68
diary n *keeping a diary* 128
diary n *the book itself* 128
diastema n *gap in teeth* 238
diatonic adj 173
diatribe n *long rebuke* 214
diatribe n *arch. discourse* 214
dibble n 71
dibs n Games/Fun/Leisure 185
dibs interj 300
dice v *chop* 93
dice n 40
dicey adj 301
dichotomy n *division into two* 136
dichotomy n *contrast* 136
dick n *slang detective* 275
dick n *slang penis* 195
dickens n 132
dicker n/v *barter* 213
dickey n 197
dickhead n 320
dictate v *order* 162
dictate v *as in "dictate a letter"* 142
dictate n 162
dictating machine n 274
dictation n *command* 176
dictation n *being a dictator* 130
dictation n 142, 162
dictator n 130
dictator n *type of Roman ruler* 130
dictatorial adj 130
dictatorship n 130
diction n 172
diction n *obs. word* 172
diction n *obs. description* 172
dictionary n *obs. vocabulary* 110
dictionary n 110

dictum n 136
didact n 154, 312
didactic adj/n 154
diddle v *cheat* 207
diddle v *have sex with* 262
diddle v *waste time* 204
diddly, diddly-squat n (Am) 320
didgeridoo n *type of trumpet* 282
dido n *antic* 216
die v *applied to animals, things* 45
die n *as in "die cast"* 168
die v *applied to plants* 45
die v *as in "die laughing," "die for a chance"* 132
die, dice n 40
die, dice v 40
die off v 174
die out v 247
diefenbachia n 219
die-hard adj 234
die-hard adj *conservative* 234
die-off n 300
diesel adj/n 261; v 261, 310
dieseling n 310
diesis n *double dagger* 187
diet n *law-making body* 86
diet n *confab* 86
diet n *regular food* 34; v 34
diet n *type of weight control* 34
dietitian/dietician n 222
dif n *as in "what's the dif?"* 268
differ v *disagree* 92, 140
differ v *rare make different* 92
differ v *be different* 92
difference n 92, 140
different adj/adv 92
differential n 264
differentiate v 216
differentiation n 216
difficile adj *obs. difficult (stubborn sense)* 73
difficult v *obs.* 89
difficult adj *as in "difficult problem"* 89
difficult adj *as in "difficult person"* 89
difficult adj *as in "difficult job"* 89
difficulty n *as in "financial difficulty"* 83
difficulty n 83
diffidence n 150
diffidence n *distrust* 150
diffuse v *scatter* 93
diffuse v *obs. flow* 93

ditch v defeat 292
ditchdigger n 263
dite n obs. writing 42
dither n 212
ditsy adj (Am) 325
ditty n 42
ditty bag n 239
ditty box n (Am) 257
ditz n 325
ditzy adj (Am) 325
diuresis n 68, 167
diuretic adj/n 68
diurnal n diary, journal 121
diurnal adj daily 65
diurnal adj opp. of nocturnal
    255
diva n 265
divan n 183
dive n dumpy drinking establish-
    ment 245
dive v 26
dive n 177
dive n intentional loss 307
dive bomber 300
dive in v get heavily involved
    204
dive-bomb v 300
divell v obs. pull asunder 155
divellicate v 155
diverge v 176
divergence n 176
divergency n 176
divergent adj 176
divers adj various and sundry
    53
divers adj obs. diverse 53
divers adj obs. perverse 53
diverse adj separate 54
diverse adj varied 54
diversification n 54
diversified adj 54
diversify v make diverse 104
diversify v 54
diversify v Business/Com-
    merce/Selling 318
diversify v obs. be diverse 104
diversion n recreation 126
diversion n separation 126
diversionary adj 234
diversity n 54
diversive adj arch. 96
divert v 126
divert, diversion v, n 96
divestiture, divest n, v 157
divide v diverge, separate 60
divide v cut up 60
divide n 219
divide, division v, n 65

dividend n Mathematics 65
dividend n Finances/Money
    172
dividend n the divided portion
    172
dividuality n sameness, opp. of
    individuality 294
divination n 47
divine v 47
divine adj lit. and fig. heavenly
    43; n 43
divine, divination v, n 81
divine right n 130
diviner n 47
diving bell n 168
diving board n 213
diving suit n 275
divinify v 173
divining rod n 203
divinity 43
divinity school n 129
division n as in "sales division,"
    "17th Airborne Division,"
    "Central Division of the
    NFL" 136
division 60
division of labor n 200
division sign n 296
divisive adj 139
divisor 65
divorce n divorced man 213
divorce /vn 74
divorcee n 213
divot n 108
divulge v reveal 162
divulge v obs. publish 162
divvy n/v 249
Dixieland n type of music 290
DIY n 312
dizzard dolt 112
dizzy adj foolish 112
dizzy adj feeling spinning 32
dizzy adj ditzy 112
dizzy adj as in "dizzy heights"
    32
dizzy adj fig. 32
dizzy v 32
DJ n 305
DNA n 296
DNA fingerprinting n 327
do v 26
do v as in "do time," "do
    drugs" 249
do n to-do 136
do v as in "do in" 80
do v be adequate, as in "that
    will do" 142
do n ado 136

do v have sex 262
do n as in "dos and don'ts" 292
do in v 276
dobbin n 119
Doberman pinscher n 279
doc n doctor 222
docent n 266
docile adj tame 207
docile adj teachable 207
dock n applied to land transport
    72
dock v cut short 94
dock n place near the pier 72
dock n part of a tail 31
dock n type of wheat 10
dock n the pier itself 72
dock n The Law 131
dock v 72
dock v 31
dockhand n 281
dockmaster n 184
dockwalloper n (Am) type of
    dockworker 226
dockworker n 281
dockyard n 184
doctor n physician 42, 69, 121;
    v 69
doctor v alter 208
doctor n learned person, teacher
    42
doctorate n person holding a
    doctorate 129
doctorate n 129
doctress 69
doctress n 121
doctrine n obs. teaching 42
doctrine n what is taught 42
docudrama n 312
document n 77
document n obs. something
    taught, documentation 77
document v 191
document v obs. teach 191
documentary adj/n 217
documentary n 299
documentation n 264
docutainment n 312
dodder v 147
doddering adj 147, 175
doddery adj 147, 249
doddypoll n arch. deadhead 82
dodge n fig. 134
dodge v deceive 140; v 140
dodge n act of dodging 134
dodge n 140
dodgeball n 289
dodgery 140
dodo n 146

dodo n dolt 146, 268
doe n 11
doe-eyed adj 297
doesn't contr 245
doff v as in "doff one's hat" 60
dog v 116
dog n Insults 47
dog v as in "I'll be dogged" 249
dog n Animals 11
dog and pony show n 320
dog biscuit n 239
dog collar n 106
dog days n 113
dog end n cigarette butt 301
dog in the manger n 132
dog paddle n 275
dog tag n 282
dog tick n 119
dogbane n 119
dogcart n 169
dogcatcher n (Am) 226
dogdom n 236
doge n 111
dog-eat-dog adj 231
dogess 11
dogface n (Am) 300
dogfish n 99
dogged adj persistent 169
dogged adj obs. mean 169
doggerel adj 76; n 76, 152
doggery n slang tavern 226
doggess n 204
doggie bag n (Am) 316
doggone adj/adv/n/v 230
doggoned adj 230, 249
doggy n 165
doghouse n 121
doghouse n Slang 300
dogie n (Am) as in "get along
    little dogie" 259
dogleg adj/n/v 270
dogma n 125
dogmatic adj 125
dogmatism n 125
dognap v (Am) akin to kidnap
    307
do-good adj 312
do-gooder n (Am) 292
dogs n feet 292
dog's chance n 277
dogsled n (Am) 212
dogtooth n canine tooth 66
dogwatch n night shift 172
dogwood n 119
doily n type of napkin 239
doily n type of ornamentation
    239
doily adj 239

double-u n W 227
double-wide n 316
doubloon n 152
doubt n/v 56
doubt n/v *obs. fear* 56
doubt n/v *obs. reason to fear* 56
doubtful adj *causing doubt* 73
doubtful adj *feeling doubt* 73
doubtful adj *unlikely* 73, 252
doubting Thomas n 269
douche n/v 177
douche bag n 316
dough n *cash* 245
dough n 15
doughboy n (Am) 247
doughfoot n (Am) *infantry—doughboy on foot* 306
doughnut n 211
doughty adj *arch. brave* 17
Douglas fir n 236
dour adj 100
douse n (Brit) *hit* 130
douse v *extinguish* 142
douse v *drench* 142
dove n *symbol of peace* 111
dove n *term of endearment* 75
dove n *as in "hawks and doves"* 319
dove n Animals 30
dovetail n/v 122
dowager n 111
dowd n 133
dowdy adj 133
dowdy n *pandowdy* 297
dowdy n *dowdy woman* 133
dowel n 36
dower n *widow's inheritance* 45
Dow-Jones average n 289
down adv *losing* 263
down n *as in "ups and downs"* 190
down n *on plants* 31
down v *slang drink* 287
down adj *downward* 137
down v *go down* 133
down adv *depressed* 150
down v *put down* 133
down n *on birds* 31
down v *knock down* 133
down and dirty adj/adv 321
down in the mouth adj 150
down payment n 290
down-and-out adj (Am) 269
down-and-out n 269
down-at-the-heels adj 184
downbear v *bear down* 61
downbeat n 265
downbeat adj 304

downburst n 322
downcast adj 150
downcast n 150
down-coming n 61
downdraft n 205
downer n 317
downfall n *rainfall* 49, 210
downfall n General/Miscellaneous 49
downgrade n/v (Am) Geography/Places 236
downgrade v 295
downhearted adj 169
downhiller n 317
down-home adj (Am) 233
downlink n 315
download v 322
down-market adj 318
downplay v 314
downpour n/v 210
downrange adv 309
downs n 29
downs n *type of hill* 29
Down's syndrome n 316
downscale v 308
downscale adj *lower-end* 319
downshift v 310
downside n 308
downsize v (Am) 323
downslide n 294
downspout n 258
downstairs n 222
downtime n 289
down-to-earth adj 293
down-to-the-wire adj 313
downtown adj/adv/n (Am) 232
downtrend n 294
downtrodden adj 137
downturn n 294
downwash n 284
downy mildew n 254
downy woodpecker n (Am) 209
dowry n 39
dowsabel n *sweetheart* 125
dowse v 175
dowser 175
dowser n 230
dowsing rod n 175
doxy n *floozy, bimbo* 112
doyen n *senior member* 176, 250
doyenne n 176, 250
doze v *snooze* 166
doze v *bulldoze* 308
doze v *make sleepy* 166
dozen n 31
dozens n *many* 204

drab n *cloth* 107
drab n *slang prostitute* 108
drab adj *of drab color* 234
drab n *color* 234
drab adj *colorless* 271
drab adj *not bright* 234
drab n *as in "dribs and drabs"* 230
drab v 108
draconian adj 212
draconic adj *related to dragons* 175
draconic adj 212
draft n *as in "first draft"* 201
draft n *conscription* 203
draft n Finances/Money 200
draft v War/Military/Violence 203
draft v/adj Literature/Writing 201
draft board n 312
draftee n 248
draftsman n 171
drafty adj 234
drag adj/n 303
drag v *drag race* 304
drag n (Am) *clout* 268
drag v *as in "drag off a cigarette"* 283
drag v 97
drag n *something boring* 231
drag n 283
drag out v 175
drag queen n 303
drag race n 304
drag strip n (Am) 311
draggle v *bedraggle* 104
draggle v *straggle* 104
draggle-tail n *slut* 133
dragnet n 107
dragon n *obs. python* 46
dragon n *obs. shooting star* 65
dragon n 46
dragon lady n 325
dragon lizard n 285
dragonet n *type of fish* 194
dragonet n The Fantastic/Paranormal 46
dragonfly n 146
dragon's teeth n 250
dragoon n/v 155
dragster n (Am) 311
drain v *as in "drain a glass of beer"* 97
drain n/v 51
drain v *obs. strain* 28
drain n *as in "a drain on the economy"* 51

drainpipe n 239
drake n *male duck* 30
dram v *tipple* 183
dram n 66
drama n Performing Arts 111
drama n *fig.* 111
dramatic irony n 276
dramatic unities n 290
dramatics n 173
dramatis personae n 187
dramatist n 172
dramatize v Performing Arts 201
dramatize v *fig.* 201
dramaturge n 214, 246
dramaturgy n 214
dramshop n *barroom* 185
drape v 235
drape v *obs. weave* 235
draper n (Brit) *cloth dealer* 75
drapery n *curtain* 35
drapery n *cloth* 35
drapes n 286
drastic adj *med. use* 233
drastic adj *gen.* 167
drastic adj 233
drastic adj 167
drat interj/v 215
draughts n (Brit) *checkers* 75
draw v *as in attract* 60
draw v *as in "draw breath"* 60
draw v *as in "quick draw"* 248
draw v *as in "draw the curtains"* 26
draw v *entertainment sense* 60
draw n *tie game* 226
draw v 42
draw v *obs., as in "draw and quarter"* 45
draw v *withdraw* 172
draw v *pull* 26
draw v 226
draw poker n (Am) 226
drawback n *disadvantage* 190
drawback n *type of refund* 172
drawbridge n 33
drawee n 200
drawer n 121
drawers n 123
drawing n *type of artwork* 173
drawing n *act of drawing* 173
drawing n *lottery* 40
drawing board n 187
drawing room n 148
drawknife n 149
drawl v 142
drawl n 142

drawlatch n *arch. type of thief* 46

drawn butter n (Am) 223

drawnwork n 123

drawshave n 224

drawstring n 222

dray n/v *type of wagon* 72

dray horse n 184

dread adj/n/v 17

dreadful adj *dreaded* 36

dreadful adj *obs. in awe* 36

dreadful n *as in "penny dreadful"* 246

dreadful adj *bad* 36

dreadless adj *fearless* 73

dreadless adv *obs.* 73

dreadlock n 310

dreadnought n *type of battleship* 212

dreadnought n *type of overcoat* 212

dream v *hope* 74

dream n *arch. joy* 17

dream n/v *as in "daydream"* 38

dream n/v *as in "the job is a dream"* 38

dream n/v 38

dream n/v *goal* 38

dream n 74

dream up v 304

dream vision n *type of poem* 276

dreamboat n 304

dreamland 216

dreamland n 230

dreamworld n 216

dreamworld 230

dreamy 304

drear adj *dreary* 160, 178

drear n *obs.* 160

dreary adj 178

dreary adj *obs. gory, horrid* 178

dreck/drek n 292

dredge n/v 103

dreg n 49

dreidel n 289

drek n 292

drench v *soak* 27

drench n *type of drink or potion* 15

drench v *force to drink* 27

dress n *clothing* 123; v 123

dress v *as in "dress a wound"* 99

dress n *spec. article of clothing* 123

dress coat n *tail coat* 197

dress code n 316

dress rehearsal n 228

dress shield n 260

dress shirt n 260

dress uniform n 266

dressage n 301

dresser set n *vanity items* 297

dressing gown n 197

dressing room n 167

dressing table n 167

dressing-down n (Am) 249

dressmaker n 213

dressy adj 197

drib n *as in "dribs and drabs"* 182

drib v *dribble* 116

drib v 142

dribble n/ v Sports 244

dribble v 116, 142; n 142

driblet n 127

dried-up adj 217

drier/dryer n 258

drift n *as in "snowdrift"* 49

drift fence n 274

drifter n *transient* 270

driftwood n 145

drill n/v *type of tool* 149

drill v *as in "drill instructions"* 155; n 155

drill n *furrow for seeding* 184; n 184

drill press n (Am) 242

drill team n 290

drink n *as in "in the drink"* 249

drink v/n *toast, drink alcohol* 15

drink v/n *fig. as in "drink in"* 15

drink v/n 15

drinking fountain n 239

drinking song n 129

drip n/v 301

drip v 27

drip-dry adj/v 310

drive v *as in "drive away"* 26

drive v 26

drive v *kill time* 61

drive n *as in "clothing drive"* 270

drive n *as in "four-wheel drive"* 317

drive v *as in "drive a wagon"* 26

drive n *as in "cattle drive"* 177

drive n *ambition* 288

drive n *as in "Sunday drive"* 177

drive time n 317

drive-by adj/n 327

drive-in n (Am) 291

drivel n *type of tool* 61

drivel n 84

drivel n *type of servant* 61

drivel n *arch. drool, dribble* 84

driven adj 288

driver ant n 236

driver's license n 288

driveway n (Am) 239

driving range n 304

drizzle n/v 105

droit n *leg. right* 102

droll adj/n/v *jester* 150

dromedary n 30

drone n Animals 11

drone n *applied to people* 11

drone n *droning speech* 113

drone n *type of missile* 11

drone n *droning sound* 113

drool n/v 210

droop v 57

drop n *as in "cough drop"* 178

drop n *as in "water drop"* 22

drop n *as in "drop in temperature"* 250

drop cloth n 287

drop dead interj 300

drop forge n 260

drop hammer n 242

drop off v *fall asleep* 216

drop zone n 306

drop-dead adj 321

drophead n *convertible* 298

drop-in adj/n 217

droplet 22

drop-off n 293

dropout n (Am) 291

dropped egg n *poached egg* 211

dropper n 260

dropsy n *obs. yen* 32

dropsy n *edema* 32

dross n *gen.* 22

dross n *spec. to metallurgy* 22

drought n *gen. dryness* 31

drought n *fig.* 31

drought n 31

drover n 70

drown v 45

drowse v *obs. droop* 141

drowse n/v 99, 141

drowsy adj 99

drub n/v 155

drub v *fig.* 155

drubly adj *agitated* 28

drudge n/v 60

drudger n 60

drudgery 60

drug n *addictive substance, stimulant* 33

drug n/v 33

drug addict n 283

drug pusher n 319

druggery n *arch. pharmaceuticals* 106

druggie n (Am) 320

druggist n 147

druggist n *obs. drugster* 147

drugstore n (Am) 213

drugstore cowboy n (Am) *urban cowboy* 293

druid n 129

drum n *cathouse, tavern* 245

drum v/n 77

drum n *as in "eardrum"* 147

drum v *as in "drum your fingers"* 252

drum major n 129

drum majorette n (Am) 299

drumble n *slothful person* 132; v 132

drumhead court-martial n 229

drumlin n *glacial feature* 219

drummer n 129, 252

drumroll n 265

drumstick n 197

drumstick n 129

drunk adj 51, 54

drunk n *drunken binge* 205, 250

drunk n *drunken person* 205, 250

drunk tank n 308

drunkard n 51, 251

drunkometer n (Am) 296

druthers n 249

dry adj/v *boring* 23

dry adj/v 23

dry adj *as in "dry wit"* 137

dry adj *alcohol-free* 23, 100; v 23

dry adj/v *thirsty* 23

dry adj/v *applied to wine* 23, 183

dry adj *applied to wine* 183

dry cell n 256

dry dock n 149

dry goods n 171

dry ice n 285

dry measure n 166

dry mop n 297

dry nurse n 121

dry out v *get sober* 321

dry rot n 205

dry run n (Am) 307

dry suit n *in skin diving* 310

dryad n 81

dry-as-dust adj 250

dry-clean v 211

dry-cleaner n 211

eavesdrop v 161
eavesdropper n 161
ebb adj obs. 22
ebb n as in "ebb and flow" 22; v 22
ebb n fig. 22
ebb tide n 219
ebon adj/n 118
ebony n 64
ebony adj 139
ebriety n drunkenness 87
ebrious adj 87
ebullience n 139
ebulliency n 139
ebullient adj lit. boiling 139
ebullient adj fig. 139
eccentric adj describing people 120, 150, 224; n 150, 169, 224
eccentric adj describing circles 120, 150; n 120
eccentricity n 150, 169, 224
ecclesiology n 228
ecdysiast n stripper 298
ecdysis n shedding 236
echelon n (Am) level 308
echelon n mil. use 308
echelon n 203
echelon v 203
echelon n gen. 203
echo v fig. 139
echo n musical sense 29
echo n literary sense 29
echo v 139
echo n 29
echo v 29
echoism n onomatopoeia 264
echolocation n 302
eclair n 241
eclectic adj describing type of philosopher 217
eclectic adj wide-ranging 217; n 217
eclipse v surpass, obscure 97
eclipse n/v 31
ecliptic n 65
ecocatastrophe n 315
ecocide n (Am) 315
ecofreak n 320
ecology n 237
econobox n 323
econometrics n 296
economic adj obs. 69
economic n obs. home economics 69
economic adj Finances/Money 172

economical adj related to economics 207
economical adj/adv thrifty 207
economics n Finances/Money 200
economics n as in "home economics" 200
economist n thrifty person 207, 226
economist n Professions/Duties 226
economist n obs. keeper of the household 226
economize v 207
economy n being thrifty 172
economy n handling resources 86
economy n as in "the nation's economy" 172
economy n thrift 86
economy adj cheap 226
economy class n 310
economy of scale n 311
ecosphere n 309
ecosystem n 296
ecotage n sabotage of ecology 324
ecoterrorist n 327
ecru n type of color 252
ecstasy n obs. type of psychological state 72
ecstasy n 72
ecstatic adj/n 72
ectoplasm n The Fantastic/Paranormal 292
ectoplasm n Animals 255
ectotherm n cold-blooded animal 302
ecumenical adj 129
ecumenics n 299
eczema n 195
ed n Education 312
edacious adj eating 207
Edam n type of cheese 223
eddy v 63, 193; n 63
eddy current n 254
edelweiss n 236
edge v put pan edge on 141
edge n border, extent, rim 87
edge n knife-edge 21
edge n advantage 294
edge n fig. sharpness 21
edge n lit. sharpness 21
edge v 21
edge tool n 36
edging n 133
edgy adj nervous 243
edgy adj phys. sharp 243

edible adj 70, 122; n 122
edict n 49
edifice n 69
edify v build, teach 59
edit v 201
edit n 313
edition n gen. 77
edition n 77
editor n 187, 201
editor 201
editor n publisher 187
editorial adj 187
editorial n 227
editorialist 246, 276
editorialize v (Am) 246
editress n 187, 201
educable adj 228
educate v raise children 129
educate v (Am) teach 111, 129
educated adj 129
education n teaching in school 111, 129
education n gen. rearing 111
educational adj 228
educational adj resulting from education 228
educational television n 312
educationese n 311
educator n (Am) 111, 129, 173
educator n raiser of children 173
eel n 11
eelgrass n (Am) 194
e'en adv 41
e'er adv 41
eerie adj causing fear 17, 198
eerie adj fearful 17, 198
effable adj 160
effect n 83
effect n obs. reality 83
effect v 116
effect n obs. goal 83
effective adj 89
effects n things 190
effectual adj 89
effectuate v 116, 141
effeminacy n/adj 89
effeminate adj/n 89
effeminate n 89
effeminate v obs. 89
effervesce v bubble 207
effervesce v obs. react chemically 207
effervesce v be spirited 225
effervescence n 207, 225
effervescent adj 225
effete adj 202

effete adj obs. no longer unique 202
effete adj obs. infertile 202
efficace n obs. efficacy 61
efficacious adj 85
efficacity n 85
efficacy n 85
efficiency n 158
efficiency n obs. source of efficiency 158
efficiency apartment n 286
efficiency expert n (Am) 281
efficient adj causal 207
efficient adj 158, 207
effigy n 114
efflorescence n blooming 145
effort n 102
effort n obs. power 102
effort n result of effort 102
effortful 102
effortless 102
effrontery n 170
effusion, effuse n, v 84
effusive adj 84, 178
eft adv obs. after, again 28
eftsoons adv obs. again 28
egad interj 175
egalitarian adj 270
egalite 270
egest v opp. of ingest; defecate 99
egesta 99
egestion 99
egg n Slang 156
egg n ovum 30
egg v throw eggs at 252
egg v as in "egg on" 55
egg n 30
egg beater n (Am) helicopter 298
egg beater n (Am) 224
egg cream n (Am) 310
egg roll n 303
egg timer n 256
eggcup n 196
egghead n 283
eggheaded adj 283
eggnog n (Am) 197
eggplant n 197
eggs Benedict n (Am) 259
eggshell n 30
eggshell adj 92
ego n the self 198
ego n conceit 198
ego trip n 317
egocentric adj 198, 262
egoism n 198, 199
egoist n 198, 199

egoistic hedonism n 243

egomania n 198, 213

egotism n 185

egotist n 185

egotistic 213

egotistical adj 213

egotize 198

egregious adj *remarkably bad* 115

egregious adj *remarkably good* 115

egret n 64

Egyptian cotton n 260

eh interj 47

eider n *eiderduck or down* 165

eider duck n 236

eiderdown n 194

eidetic adj *having photographic memory* 288

eidolon n *phantom, spectre* 230

eight n 12

eight ball n (Am) 298

eighteen n 12

eighteen-wheeler n 323

800 number n 323

eightpenny nail n 100

eighty n 12

eighty-six v/n 313

eiswein n 316

either adj/conj/pron *one or the other* 22

either adj/conj/pron *each, both* 22

either adv 22

either-or adj/n 293

ejaculate v *obs. exude* 121

ejaculate v *spout verbally* 121, 179

ejaculate v 121; n 286

ejaculation n 121

eject v 95

ejecta n 95, 269

ejection seat n 304

eke adv *also* 28

eke v *add to* 142

eke out v 142

el n 243, 274

el cheapo adj 321

El Niño n *warm water current* 254

elaborate adj 160

elaborate v *build up* 161

elaborate v *explain in more detail* 161

elaborate v *decide details* 161

elaborate adj *obs. created laboriously* 160

elaborate adj *well-put-together* 160

elan n 243

elapse v *obs. sneak away* 144

elapse v 163

elapse v *obs. kill time* 163

elapsed time n 272

elastic adj 176, 178

elastic n 178, 233

elastic adj *fig. resilient* 178

elastic adj *obs. use describing gas* 178

elastic fabric n 224

elasticity n 176, 178

elate v 185

elated adj 185

elation n *raised spirits* 185

elation n *raised thoughts* 185

elbow n *fig.* 13

elbow v *nudge* 161

elbow n 13

elbow grease n 156

elbowroom n 114

eld n *old age* 12

eld adj *arch.* 12

eld n *obs. the elderly* 12

eld n *elder* 12

eld n *times of old* 12

eld v *obs.* 12

elder n *elderberry* 10

elder n *older person* 12

elder n *authority* 12

elder 12

elder statesman n 276

elderberry n 64

elderly n 12, 237; adj 12

eldest 12

eldress n Religion 154

eldress n Age/Aging 12

eldritch adj 112

elect adj/n/v 57

elect adj/n/v 44

election n 44

Election Day n 101

electioneer n/v 202

elective adj 91

elective n 228

electorate n *voters* 266

Electra complex n 281

electric adj *fig. exhilarating* 146, 230

electric adj *producing electricity* 146

electric adj *using electricity* 146

electric chair n (Am) 266

electric eel n 194

electric eye n 255

electric field n 255

electric organ n 201

electric ray n 194

electric storm n 237

electrical storm n 302

electrician n (Am) 200

electricity n 146

electrify v *lit. and fig.* 182

electrocardiogram n 273

electrocardiograph n 273

electrocute v (Am) 266

electrode n 220

electroencephalogram, electroencephalograph n 297

electrofishing n *killing fish with electricity* 303

electrolysis, electrolyte n 220

electrolysis, electrolyte n *type of hair removal* 220

electromagnet n 210

electromagnetic adj 210

electromagnetic radiation n 296

electromagnetism n 210

electromechanical adj 270

electrometer n 182

electron n 254

electron gun n 288

electron lens n 297

electron microscope n 297

electron tube n 288

electronic adj 272

electronic banking n 323

electronic cottage n (Am) 327

electronic flash n 305

electronic mail n 323

electronic publishing n 323

electronic surveillance n 324

electronics n 272

electroplate v 235

electroshock n 304

electroshock therapy n 304

electrostatic 220

electrostatic generator n 296

electrostatics n 220

electrosurgery n 273

electrotherapy n 262

elegance n 71

elegancy 71

elegant adj *graceful* 71

elegant adj *cultured* 71

elegant adj *natty* 71

elegy n 110

element n *constituent part* 87

element n *obs. celestial object* 31

element n *as in "heating element"* 237

element n *i.e.: earth, fire, water, air* 29

element n *basics* 87

element n *as in "periodic table of elements"* 165

element n *as in "periodic table of elements"* 29

element n *bit, small portion, as in "an element of disgust"* 87

element n *as in "someone is in his element"* 136

elemental n *conjured personification of the elements* 267

elemental adj 29

elementary adj Natural Things 29

elementary adj *basic* 87, 137

elementary particle n 296

elementary school n 228

elements n Weather 31

elephant n 30

elephant bird n 255

elephant grass n 219

elephant seal n 220

elephantiasis n 121

elephantine adj 159

elevate v 104

elevate v *obs. fig. lower* 143

elevated adj 104

elevated n 243

elevated railway n (Am) 243

elevation n *type of drawing* 201

elevation n *altitude* 195

elevation n 104

elevator n *as in "grain elevator"* 197

elevator n *for people* 261

elevator n *airplane steering device* 288

elevator n *type of muscle* 147

elevator music n 324

eleven n 12

elevenses n (Brit) *morning snack* 197

eleventh hour n 231

elf n *dwarf* 21

elf n 21

elfish adj 21

elflock n *type of hair* 123

elhi n 305

elicit v 161

elide v 135

eligible adj/n 87

eliminate v *urinate, defecate* 195

eliminate v *obs. drive away* 191

eliminate v *eradicate* 191

elimination n 191

elision n 135

elite adj/n 202

elitism n 306
elixir n *type of drug* 65
elixir n *alchemical preparation* 65
elk n *arch. length longer than a yard* 12
elk n 11
elkhound n 255
ellipse n Mathematics 166
ellipsis n Language and Speaking 110
elliptical adj Mathematics 166
elliptical adj Language and Speaking 110
elliptical galaxy n 302
elm n 10
elongate v/adj 84
elongation n 84
elope v 151
elope v *gen. escape* 151
eloquence, eloquent n, adj 76
elucidate v *lit. and fig.* 141
elude v 179
elude v *confuse* 179
elusion n 179
elusive adj *tough to catch* 190
elusive adj *uncaught* 190
elven adj 21
elvish 21
elysian adj 137
elysian fields n 132
'em pron 19
emaciate v 162
emaciated adj 162
emaciation n 162
e-mail n 327
emanate v 134
emanation n 134
emancipate v 161
emancipation n 161
emane v *obs. emanate* 180
emasculate adj/v *lit. and fig.* 161
embalm v 45
embank v 193
embankment n 193
embargo n/v Business/Commerce/Selling 200
embargo v *seize* 200
embargo n/v Government 130
embark v 107
embarrass v *humiliate* 234
embarrass v *confuse* 234
embarrass v *make harder* 234
embarrass v *obstruct* 234
embassage n *embassy* 101
embassy n *the job and the home of ambassadors* 111

embattle, embattled adj/n/v 84
embed v 207
embellish v 60
embellishment n *ornament* 60
embellishment n *embellishing* 60
ember n 12
embetter v *make better* 143
embezzle n *obs. waste* 131
embezzle n *make weaker* 131
embezzle v 131
embitter v 104
emblazon v 142
emblem n/v 86
emblematic 86
emblematic adj 86, 161
embodiment n 232
embody v *represent* 271
embody v *give a phys. body to* 271
embolism n 239
embosom v *embrace* 142
emboss v 94
embowel v *disembowel* 112
embrace v *comprise* 142
embrace n/v *hug* 97
embrace v *surround* 60
embrace v *accept* 97
embracer n *jury-tamperer* 81
embrangle v *entangle* 179
embroider, embroidery v, n 71
embroider, embroidery v, n *as in "embroider a tale"* 71
embroil v 161
embryo n 66
embryogenesis n 221
embryology n 220
embryon *obs.* 66
embryonal 66
embryonic adj 66, 221
embryotic adj 66
emcee n/v 299
emerald adj 114
emerald n *the color* 29
emerald n 29
emerald cut n 288
emerald green n 161
emerge v 139
emergence n 139, 189
emergence *obs. emergency* 158
emergence n *emergency* 189
emergency adj/n 158
emergency n *emerging* 158
emergency adj 158
emergency brake n 261
emergency medical technician n 322
emergency room n 316
emergicenter n 326

emerited adj *arch.* 191
emeritus adj 191
emery n 102
emery board n 183
emery wheel n 242
emesis n *throwing up* 222
emigrant n (Am) 202
emigrant adj 202
emigrate v 202
emigration n 154, 202
emigre n 202
eminent adj 139
eminent adj *arch. high-up* 139
eminent adj *high-up* 98
eminent domain n 189
emir n 154
emirate n 154, 247
emission n 87
emit v 87, 162
emit v *obs. publish* 172
emmissary n 157
emolument n *compensation* 76
emote v (Am) 281
emotion n *anger, sorrow, etc.* 224
emotion n *mental commotion* 224
emotion n *arch. commotion* 143, 224
emotional adj 224
emotionless adj 243
empathetic 275
empathic adj 275
empathize v 275, 295
empathy n 275
emperor n 44
emperor penguin n 255
empery n 44
emphasis n 134
emphasize v 134, 218
emphatic adj 134, 190
emphysema n *gen. swelling* 166
emphysema n *spec. type of lung disease* 166, 239
empire n 44
empire, empery n *place ruled* 44
empire, empery n *act of ruling* 44
empiric adj 119
empirical adj 119
emplace v 215
emplacement n 215
employ v *hire* 97, 127; n 127
employ v *use* 97
employe, employee n 127, 213
employer n 127
employment agency n (Am) 264

emperited
empoison v 45
emporium n 127
empower v 163
empress n 44
emprise n *type of enterprise* 61
empt v *arch.* 116
empt v *empty* 61
empty adj/v 23
empty adj *arch. not married* 18
empty adj *without substance* 23
empty adj *obs. penniless* 127
empty adj *without substance, as in "empty argument"* 54
empty v 116
empty calorie n (Am) 316
empty nester n 317
empty-handed adj 121
empty-headed adj 156
empty-nest syndrome n 325
EMT n 322
emu n 219
emu n *applied to other birds* 219
emulate v 114
emulation n 114
emulation n *obs. rival, envy* 114
emulsifier n 252
emulsify v 157, 252
emulsion n 157
en brochette adj 274
en masse adv 204
en route adj/adv 198
enable v *obs. become capable* 141
enable v *empower* 141
enable v *make capable* 141
enact v The Law 81
enact v *obs. record publicly* 81
enact v *act on stage* 77
enactment n 217
enamel n/v 59
enamelware n 273
enamor v 60
encamp v 112
encampment n 112
encapsulate v 252
encapsule v 252
encase v 163
encephalitis n 221
encephalogram n 286
encephalograph n 286
encephalography n 286
encephalon n *the brain* 182
enchant v 47
enchanter n 81
enchanter n 47
enchanting adj 137
enchantment n 47
enchantress n 47, 81

enchantress n *fig.* 81
enchase v 98
encheer v 124
enchilada n 241
enchiridion n *handbook* 77
encircle v 94
enclave n 251
enclose v 59
enclosure n *act of enclosing* 87
enclosure n *type of structure* 87
encoffin v 130
encomiast 134
encomium n 134
encompass v 60
encore n/v 189
encounter v *obs. oppose* 143
encounter v/n *come across* 45
encounter v/n *experience* 45
encounter v/n *battle* 45
encounter group n 319
encounterer n *arch. enemy* 112
encourage v *aid* 96
encourage v *instill courage* 96
encourage v *urge* 96
encouragement n 96
encouraging adj 96
encroach v *obs. take, confiscate* 116
encroach v 116
encrust v 162
encyclopedia n *book of learning* 153
encyclopedia n *learning* 153
encyclopedian adj 217
encyclopedic adj 217
encyclopedist n 153
end n *extent* 22
end n *remnant* 102
end v 27
end v *finish up* 60
end n *final part* 22
end v *ending* 22
end v *obs. kill* 45
end n *termination* 22
end n *goal* 22
end adj 22
end product n 301
end table n (Am) 239
end up v 271
end use n 313
end user n 307
end-all n 156
endangered species n 315
endeavor n/v *labor* 94
endeavor n/v *try* 94
endive n 70
endleaf n 264
endlong adv *lengthwise* 28

endnote n 290
endocrine gland n 279
endoplasm n 255
endorphin n 322
endorse v *support, as in "endorse a candidate"* 104
endorse v *as in "endorse a check"* 104
endorse v 176
endorsee n 205
endorsement n 104, 114, 176
endoscope n 238
endoskeleton n 220
endotherm n *warm-blooded animal* 302
endow v 94
endowment n 94
endpaper n 214
Endsville n (Am) 313
endurance n *ability to endure* 102
endurance n *patience* 102
endurance n *duration* 102
endure v *as in "music that endures"* 59
endure v *as in "endure pain"* 59
endure v *obs. make durable* 59
enduring 59
enduro n *type of race* 298
enema n 69
enemy n 49
enemy alien n 307
energetic adj 207
energetic adj *arch. effective* 207
energetical adj 207
energetics n 237
energic 207
energize v 195
energy n 119
energy n *e.g., electrical energy, kinetic energy* 221
energy n *what's supplied by a utility* 221
energy crisis n (Am) 315
energy level n 272
enervate adj/v 159
enfant terrible n 247
enfeeble v 60
enfever v 163
enfilade n/v 188
enfire v *obs. impassion* 100
enforce v *obs. make forceful* 59
enforce v *as in "enforce a law"* 59
enforce v *obs. use force* 59
enforce v *obs. ravish, conquer* 80

enforcer n 135
enfranchise v 97
engage v *as in "engage the enemy"* 174
engage v *hire* 200
engage v *as in "engage in an activity"* 179
engage v *as in "engage your attention"* 207
engage v *as in "engage a gear"* 253
engaged adj 170
engagement n *Love/Romance/Sex* 170
engagement n *appointment* 232
engagement n *War/Military/Violence* 174
engaging adj 178
engender v *bring about* 60
engine n *as in "steam engine"* 165
engine n *ingenuity* 61
engine n *tool* 61
engine n *weapon* 45
engine company n (Am) *fire squad* 211
engineer n *as in "train engineer"* 149
engineer n *as in "civil engineer"* 152; v 152
engineer v *create* 235
engineer v *orchestrate* 235
engineer v *design* 235
engineering n 182
enginery n *War/Military/Violence* 45
enginery n *engines* 159
English breakfast n 211
English cocker spaniel n 302
English foxhound n 285
English horn n 228
English muffin n 273
English saddle n 213
English setter n 236
English shepherd n 302
English sparrow n (Am) 254
English springer spaniel n 279
English toy spaniel n 296
English walnut n 193
engorge v 104
engram n 273
engrave v 104
engrave v *obs. place in a grave* 130
engraven v *obs.* 104
engraving n *type of artwork* 227
engulf v 139
enhance v *exaggerate* 92

enhance v *obs. lit. and fig. raise up* 92
enhance v *make better* 92
enigma n *mystery, something unknown* 100
enigma n *riddle* 100
enigmatic adj 100
enisle v *make an island of* 161
enisle v *fig. isolate* 161
enjoin v *proscribe* 56
enjoin v *prescribe* 56
enjoy v 73
enjoy v *obs. be joyful* 73
enjoy v *experience* 143
enjoy v *obs. make joyful* 100
enjoyable adj 73
enjoyment n 73
enlarge v *let go, liberate* 98
enlarge v 60
enlighten v *gen.* 78
enlighten v *obs. cause to give off light* 61
enlighten v *lit. and fig.* 142
enlighten v *obs. cure blindness* 69
enlighten v *Religion* 78
enlightenment n 78
enlightenment n *Archaisms* 61
enlist v 130
enlisted man n 188, 324
enlisted woman n 188, 324
enlistee n 188, 312, 324
enliven v *fig. and lit.* 161
enmesh v 161
enmity n 37
ennoble v 103
ennui n 169
enorm n *obs. abomination* 98
enormity n *immensity* 87, 206
enormity n *abomination* 87
enormity n *obs. abnormality* 104
enormous *obs.* 104
enormous adj *obs. abnormal* 115
enormous adj 115, 206
enough adj/adv/pron/n 22
enounce v *announce* 218
enow adj/adv *enough* 25
enrage v 100
enrapt adj 149
enrapture v 149
enrich v *add to* 76
enrich v *make rich* 76
enroll v 60
ensample v *obs. exemplify* 98
ensconce v *obs. mil. sense* 142
ensconce v *gen.* 142

exorbitant adj *obs. crazed, frantic* 91

exorbitant adj *beyond the law* 91

exorbitant adj *excessive* 91

exorcise v *drive away a spirit* 78, 111

exorcise v *call up a spirit* 111

exorcism n 78

exordium n *beginning* 110

exoskeleton n 220

exotic adj *interestingly strange* 139

exotic adj/n *foreign* 139

exotic dancer n 311

exotica n 269

expand v *as in "expand a map"* 96

expand v *elaborate* 96

expand v *enlarge* 96

expanding universe n 296

expanse n 176

expansion n 96

expansion slot n 326

expansionism n 266

expansionist 266

expansive adj 178

expatriate ad/n/v 205

expect v *anticipate* 143

expect v *suspect* 143

expect v *obs. wait, stay* 143

expectant adj 89, 143

expectant adj *pregnant* Medicine 239

expectation n 114

expectorant n 195

expectorate v 166

expedience n 89, 157

expediency n 89, 157

expedient adj 89

expedite v *handle expediently* 103

expedite v *promote* 103

expedition n *obs. expediting* 123

expedition n 123

expeditious adj 103

expel v 84, 94

expellee n 269

expend v *spend* 96

expend v *eplete* 96

expendable adj/n 217

expenditure n *spending* 200

expenditure n *what is spent* 200

expense v 276

expense n 76; v 76, 276

expense account n 245

expensive adj *spending much* 152

expensive adj *costing much* 152

experience v *obs. test, experiment* 143

experience n 84

experience n *skill gained by experience* 84

experience n *knowledge gained by experience* 84

experience v 84

experience n 143

experienced adj 137

experient *obs. experienced* 137

experiential adj 161

experiment v *as in "experiment with drugs"* 207

experiment n/v *try* 207

experiment n 84

experiment v *obs. experience* 207

experiment n *obs. type of medicine* 121

experimental adj *untested* 103

experimental adj *experiential* 103

expert adj/n/v 88

expertise n 243

expertism n 262

expertize v 243

expire v *obs. release the soul* 79

expire v *die* 79

expiry n *expiration, end* 204

explain 84

explanation n 84

explanatory, explanative adj 160

expletive n *filler* 152

expletive n *cussing, interjection* 152

explicable adj 137

explicate v 116

explicatory 116

explicit adj 159

explode v *obs. disapprove noisily* 117

explode v 203

explode v *as in "explode a myth"* 162

exploded adj *as in "an exploded diagram"* 308

exploded view n 318

exploit v 96

exploit n 84

exploit v *perform exploits* 96

exploit n *obs. progress* 84

exploitation n 96

exploitative adj 96, 294

exploitive adj 96, 294

exploration n 232

exploration n *obs. investigation* 232

explorator *obs.* 171

explore v *as in "explore the New World"* 141

explore v *investigate* 141

explorer n 171

explosion n 155

explosive n 248

explosive adj 155

explosive adj/n 178

expo n 284

export n/v 172

export v *obs. carry away* 172

exporter n 172

expose n 216

expose v 97

exposit v *expound* 271

exposition n 42

expositive adj 42

expository adj 42

exposure n 97, 157

exposure meter n 265

expound v 57

express v *press out* 94

express adj/adv 54

express v *state; portray* 94

express n *fast messenger* 153

express n *fast train* 153

expressionism n 276

expressionless adj *unexpressed* 243

expressionless adj 243

expressive adj *communicative* 160

expressman n (Am) 226

expressway n (Am) 304

expugn v *obs. conquer* 98

expulse v 84

expulsion n 84

expunge v 161

expurgate v 180

expurgate v *obs. defecate* 180

exquisite n 216

exquisite adj *obs. exacting, precise* 137

exquisite adj *delicious* 137

exquisite adj *obs. verbose* 137

exquisite adj *at the apex* 137

exquisite adj *intense* 137

exsanguinate v *drain blood* 196

exsanguine adj *bloodless* 161

exscind v *cut off* 179

exsiccate v *dry* 95

exsuccous adj *dry* 180

extant adj 115

extemporal adj 178

extemporaneous adj 178

extemporary *obs.* 178

extempore 178

extemporize v 163

extend v *appraise* 57

extend v *lit. and fig. stretch out* 57

extend v *as in "extend congratulations"* 57

extended adj 91

extended care n 322

extended family n 298

extension n *extending* 84

extension n *expansion* 84

extension n *as in "an extension building"* 251

extension n Education 247

extension agent n 304

extension cord n 303

extension course n 266

extension ladder n 242

extensity n 232

extensive adj *common, wide-ranging* 159

extensive adj *extending* 159

extensor n *type of muscle* 182

extent n *phys. scope* 102

extent n *fig. scope* 102

extent n *land appraisal* 102

exterior adj/n 115

exterminate v *obs. banish* 111

exterminate v 111

exterminator n 111

extermine v *obs.* 111

extern n *opp. of intern* 152

external adj *opp. of internal* 91

external adj *tangible* 91

external combustion engine n 280

externalize v 252

externize v 252

externship n 152

extinct adj *as in "extinct volcano"* 236

extinct adj *wiped out* 79, 91

extinct adj *as in "extinct species"* 174

extinct v *obs.* 91

extinct v *extinguish* 117

extinct adj *obsolete, archaic* 174

extinct adj *obsolete* 91

extinct adj *extinguished* 91, 174

extinction n 79

extinguish v *arch. kill, obliterate* 130

extinguish v 117

extol v 94

extol v *obs. lit. lift up* 94

extort v 46

extortion n 46
extra adj/adv/n 178
extra-base hit n 304
extract n/v 95
extraction n 85
extraction n 101
extracurricular adj 294
extradite v 230
extradition n 230
extragalactic adj 237
extramarital adj 289
extramundane adj *supernatural* 165
extramundane adj *extraterrestrial* 165
extramural adj *educational sense* 236
extramural adj *beyond the city* 236
extraneous adj 160
extraordinaire adj 301
extraordinary adj 91
extrapolate v 243
extrapolate v *obs. delete* 243
extrasensory perception/ESP n 300
extraterrestrial n/adj 237
extraterrestrial n 309
extrauterine adj 182
extravagance n 158
extravagant adj *excessive* 139
extravagant adj *divergent, straying* 139
extravaganza n 206
extravaganza n *extravagance* 206
extravagate v *be extravagant* 143
extravagate v *diverge* 143
extravascular adj 210
extreme adj 82, 91
extreme n 91
extremism n 229
extremity n 82
extremity 82, 91
extricate v 161
extroversion n 281
extroversion n *med. sense* 281
extrovert n 281
extrude 114
extrusion n 114
exuberance n 150
exuberant adj *showing exuberance* 91, 150
exuberant adj *abundant* 91
exude v 141
exult v *obs. jump for joy* 141
exult v 141

exultation 141
exurb, exurbia, exurbanite n (Am) *the suburbs' suburbs* 309
eye v 13, 104
eye n *as in "private eye"* 292
eye n The Body 13
eye v *obs. see* 104
eye n *lit.* 23
eye n *fig. keep an eye on things* 13, 23
eye bank n (Am) 303
eye chart n 303
eye contact n 312
eye dialect n *intentional mispelling to communicate dialect* 290
eye doctor n 257
eye rhyme n 246
eye shadow n 288
eye tuck n 326
eye view n *as in "bird's-eye view"* 204
eyeball adj 325
eyeball n 13, 120
eyeball v 268
eyeball v/adj 120
eyeball-to-eyeball adj/adv 320
eyebar n 260
eyebolt n 198
eyebrow n 66
eyebrow pencil n 260
eye-catching, eye-catcher adj, n 293
eyecup n (Am) 239
eyedropper n 286, 297
eyedrops n 286
eyeful n (Am) 268
eyeful n 232
eyeglass n 168
eyeglass n *obs. eye lens* 168
eyelash n 195
eyelet n 71
eyelid n 31
eyelift n *akin to facelift* 323
eyeliner n 304
eye-opener n (Am) 216
eyepiece n 198
eyepopper n 307
eyes only adj 325
eyeshade n 223
eyeshot n *akin to earshot* 136
eyesight n *obs. range of vision* 31
eyesight n 31
eyesore n *obs. lit. sore in the eye* 113
eyesore n 113

eyestrain n 239
eyestrings n *assumed body parts that don't exist* 120
eyetooth n 106
eyewash n 242
eyewear n 288
eyewitness n 114

F

F clef n 129
fab adj 320
fable n *tale* 42
fable n *lie* 42
fable n *myth* 42
fable n *something legendary* 42
fable v *obs. tell tall tales* 98
fabled adj 159
fabric n 197
fabric n *textile* 104
fabric n *something built* 104
fabric n *factory* 104
fabric v 96
fabric sculpture n 323
fabric softener n 316
fabricant n *manufacturer* 200
fabricate v 96
fabricate v *lie* 96
fabrication n *something fabricated* 102
fabrication n *prevarication* 102
fabular adj 77
fabulist n *teller of fables* 128
fabulist n *liar* 128
fabulize v *obs.* 98
fabulous adj *like a fable* 77, 159
fabulous adj *superlative use* 77, 159
facade n 167
facade n *fig.* 167
face v *confront* 96
face n *as in "type face"* 168
face v *look toward* 96
face n *of a watch* 32
face n The Body 32
face v *boast* 98
face card n 170
face mask n 274
face poser n *type of makeup* 242
face value n 269
facecloth n 147
faceless adj *obs. cowardly* 252
faceless adj *unidentifiable* 252
face-lift n (Am) 288
face-saver n 292
facet n 158
facet n *fig.* 158
facete adj *arch.* 125

facete adj *facetious* 163
facetious adj *sophisticated* 124
facetious adj 124
face-to-face adj/adv 47
facial n 280
facial adj *face-to-face* 159
facial adj *related to the face* 159
facial tissue n 286
facile 161
facile adj 161
facilitate v 161
facility n *gentleness* 108
facility n *aptitude* 108
facility n *as in "health care facility"* 241
facsimile n 176
facsimile n *obs. making of copies* 176
facsimile adj/v 176
fact n 158
fact n *as in "after the fact"* 102
fact n *as in "after the fact"* 158
fact finder n 289
fact of life n 250
faction n *nonfiction with fiction elements* 318
faction n *group* 113
factionalism n 276
factionalize v 276
factitious adj *manmade* 163
factoid n (Am) 324
factory Archaisms 98
factor n *obs. perpetrator* 98
factor n/v 166
factor n *gen. contributing element* 166
factory n *trading post* 152
factory n *job of a factor* 152
factory n 152
factory ship n 289
factual adj 158, 233
facture n *manufacture* 98
facture n *quality of manufacture* 98
faculty n *ability* 83
faculty n *teaching staff* 78
fad n *whim* 224
fad n *craze* 224
fade adj *arch.* 59
fade v 59
fade v *as in "fade away"* 59
fade adj 61
fade-in, fade-out n 282
faerie n 132
fag n *cigarette* 258
fag v *toil* 200
fag n (Am) *homosexual* 293
fag n 200

fag end n (Brit) *cigarette butt* 249

fag hag n 321

faggot n *bundle* 52

faggot n (Am) *homosexual* 283

faggot n *gen. insult* 283

faggot n *woman* 283

fagot/faggot n *bundle* 52

fagoting n *type of embroidery* 242

Fahrenheit adj 195

fail n 55

fail n/v 55

failing n *flaw* 135

faille n *obs. type of hood* 242

faille n *type of fabric* 242

fail-safe adj 308

failure n 55, 158

failure n *person who fails* 158

faineant n *do-nothing* 156; adj 156

faint v 60

faint n 68, 210

faint adj *pretended, feigned* 61

faint adj *as in "faint of heart"* 37

faint v *swoon* 60, 68, 210

faint n *obs. cowardice* 38

faint adj *feeble* 37

faint v *weaken* 68

faint adj *as in "a faint odor"* 37

fainthearted adj 73

fair adj *objective* 37

fair adj *mild, light, as in "fair weather," "fair-haired"* 53

fair n *obs. beauty* 16

fair adj *as in "fair maiden"* 13

fair adj *equal* 37

fair n *as in "county fair"* 41

fair v *obs. beautify* 28

fair market price 276

fair market value n 276

fair play n 133

fair sex n 174

fair shake n 231

fairground n 185

fair-haired adj 147

fairing n *type of boat, airplane structure* 280

fair-minded adj 244

fair-spoken adj 100

fairway n 108

fair-weather adj 191

fairy n 268

fairy n *fig. pixie* 47

fairy n *fairyland* 47

fairy n *homosexual* 47

fairy n *inhabitant of fairyland* 47

fairy godmother n 248

fairy ring n 118

fairy shrimp n 236

fairy tale n 187

fairyism n *magical power* 189

fairyland n 132

fairy-tale adj 294

fait accompli n 231

faith n *obs. promise* 49

faith n *loyalty, belief* 49

faith v *obs.* 49

faith cure, faith healing n 267

faithful adj/n 53

faithful n 53

fajita n 323

fake v 252

fake adj *counterfeit* 206; n 232

fake n *trick* 232

fake n *faker* 232

fake n/v 206, 252

fake v *slang perpetrate* 252

fake out v 321

fakery 232, 269

fakir n 154

falafel n 303

falchion n *type of sword* 45

falcon n 30

falconer n 30, 75

falconet n *type of falcon* 30, 236

falconet n *type of cannon* 130

falcon-gentle n *falcon* 30, 64

falderal/folderol n 189

fall v *fell* 97

fall v *obs. get smaller* 143

fall n *as in "nightfall"* 48

fall n *as in "take the fall"* 268

fall n *as in "rainfall"* 48

fall n *type of hairpiece* 168

fall n/v *drop* 26

fall n *wrestling term* 126

fall v *as in "fall down"* 26

fall n *autumn* 119

fall n *as in "waterfall"* 48

fall v *as in "the temperature is falling"* 271

fall v *as in "fall on hard times"* 26

fall v *be borne* 75

fall v *become quieter* 26

fall n 168

fall n 75

fall guy n (Am) 277

fallacion n 50

fallacious adj 50, 114

fallacy n 50

fallacy n *obs. guile* 50

fallaway adj 321

fallback n (Am) 250

fallibility n 90

fallible adj 90

falling rhythm n 282

falling star n 119

falling-out n 134

fallopian tube n 182

fallout n *War/Military/Violence* 307

fallow adj *brownish, yellowish* 23

fallow adj/n/v 70

fallow deer n 99

false v *obs.* 53

false adv *arch.* 53

false adj *as in "one false move," false hope* 53

false adj 53

false alarm n 133

false arrest n 292

false bottom n 206

false face n 212

false imprisonment n 80

false pregnancy n 238

false pretense n 203

false rib n 99

false start n 213

false-hearted adj 124

falsehood n 49

falsehood n *obs. deceit* 49

falsen v 116

falset 49

falsetto n 201

falsie n (Am) 303

falsify v 116

falsify v *show to be untrue* 116

falsity n 49

falter n/v 60

falter n 60

fame v *famish* 61

fame n 48, 88; v 48

fame n *rumor* 61

fame v 61

famed 48

familial adj 262

familiar adj *obs. polite* 73

familiar adj 54

familiar n 54

familiar spirit n 132

familiarize v 161

familiarize 54

family n *as in "family of nations"* 75

family n *household* 75

family n *type of grouping* 146

family n *lineage* 75; adj 75

family n *mob* 319

family Bible n 188

family court n 300

family doctor n 210, 222

family hour n 324

family jewels n 308

family jewels n *secrets* 308

family man n 199

family name n 170

family physician 210, 222

family planning n 297

family practice n 210, 316, 322

family room n 239

family tree n 213

family way n 204

famine n 70

famish v *obs. starve to death* 67

famish v 67

famished adj 67

famous adj 48, 88

famulus n *type of servant* 226

fan n *device for winnowing grain* 16

fan n (Am) *as in "sports fan"* 269

fan n *cooling device* 69

fan n *gen. abbreviation of fanatic* 269

fan v 16

fan club n 291

fan letter n 291, 299

fan magazine n 290

fan mail n 291, 299

fanatic n *obs. spec. religious madman* 107

fanatic n *madman* 107

fanatic adj 107

fanatical adj 107

fanaticism 107, 169

fanaticize v *be fanatic* 191

fanaticize v *make fanatic* 191

fanatism *obs.* 169

fancied adj *imagined* 137

fancier n 205

fanciful adj 160

fanciful adj *not real, whimsical* 160

fancy n *fanciful thought* 87

fancy n *taste* 87

fancy n *delusion* 87

fancy adj *ornate* 206

fancy adj *fanciful* 161

fancy n *obs., as in "young man's thoughts turning to fancy"* 87

fancy adj *opp. of plain* 161

fancy dress n *costume* 197

fancy man, fancy woman n *slang lover* 213

fancy, the *fandom* 269

fancy up v 300

fancy-dan adj/n 297
fancy-free adj 124
fancy-pants adj 307
fandango n 188
fandom n (Am) 278
fane n temple or church 78
fanfare n 201
fanfaronade n/v bluster 169
fanfold n 293
fang n booty 28
fang n/v Animals 119
fan-jet n 317
fanlight n type of window 211
fanny n buttocks 286
fanny n female genitals 286
fanny pack n 316
fantabulous adj 313
fantasia n 187
fantasie n 248
fantasied adj 132
fantasist n 290
fantasist n visionary 290
fantasize v 288
fantast n visionary 125
fantastic adj 81
fantastic adj whimsical 81
fantastic adj incredible 81
fantasticate v 143
fantastry n 125
fantasy n/v 47
fantasy n obs. phantasm 81
fantasy n daydream 47
fantasyland n 320
fantod n state of apprehension and irritability 225
fanzine n 305
far and away adv 250
far and wide adv 21
farad n unit of measure 238
faraway adj 53
farce n 76
farcical adj 190
fard v paint with cosmetics 71; n 71
fare v 27
fare n obs. travel 72
fare n first a paid journey, then the cost of the journey 72
fare n obs. travelers 72
fare n 15
fare n obs. road 72
fare-thee-well n 205
farewell n 84
farewell adj/n/v 84
farewell adj 178
far-fet arch. 138
far-fet adj obs. fetched from afar 61

farfetched adj straining credibility 138
farfetched adj fetched from afar 138
far-flung adj 270
far-gone adj 206
farina n 70
farkleberry n (Am) 193
farm n 107
farm n leased land 107
farm n type of tax, payment 107
farm v 184
farm v pay rent 184
farmer n rent collector 71
farmer n 71
farmer cheese n 303
farmerette n (Am) 71, 274
farmer's lung n 303
farmery n 107
farmhand n 223, 303
farmhouse n 107, 122
farmstead n 212
farmwife n 259
farmworker n 223, 303
farmyard n 107, 184
far-off adj 103
far-out adj 312
farrago n potpourri 158
far-reaching adj 217
farrier n 101
farry obs. 101
farsighted adj 147
farsightedness n 221
fart v as in "fart around" 268
fart v/n 14
farthing n 19
farthingale n hoop structure for hoop skirts 107
fasces n Roman symbol of authority 130
fascia n 122
fascinate v put under a spell 170
fascinate v captivate attention 170
fascinating adj 151
fascination n arch. spell-casting 156, 243
fascination n ability to fascinate 156
fascination n preoccupation 156, 170, 243
fascination n ability to fascinate 243
fascism n 282
fashion n gen. form 71
fashion n form 49
fashion n 71
fashion v 49

fashion plate n 242
fashionable adj stylish 149
fashionable adj able to be fashioned 149
fashionable n 197
fast adj vigorous 89
fast adj fastened 23
fast adj obs. militarily unassailable 21
fast adj quick, speedy 89
fast adj slang promiscuous 199
fast v decline to eat 15; n 15
fast adj frozen 192
fast adj as in "colorfast" 178
fast and loose adv 132
fast lane n 21
fastback n type of boat 310
fastback n (Am) type of car 310
fasten v obs. stabilize 28
fasten v attach 28
fastener n 136
fastening n 47
fast-food adj (Am) 310
fastidious adj obs. disgusted 150
fastidious adj obs. repulsive, haughty 150
fastidious adj 150
fast-talk v (Am) 308
fast-track adj/n/v 321
fastuous adj arch. arrogant 150
fat adj 13; n 120
fat adj as in "a fat paycheck" 54
fat cat n (Am) 293
fat cell n 221
fat city n (Am) 320
fat farm n 317
fatal adj causing death 79
fatal adj fated, preordained 79
fatalism n belief in fate 184
fatalism n resignation 184
fatalist n 184
fatality n 102
fatback n (Am) 183
fate n/v 82
fateful adj predictive 190
fateful adj deadly 190
fateful adj as in "that fateful day" 190
fathead n 204, 231
fatheaded adj 204
father n/v 18
Father Christmas n 170
father figure n 301
father image 301
father-in-law n 75
fatherland n 20

fathom n arch. 143
fathom v measure 143
fathom v embrace 28, 143; n 28
fathom v fig. understand 143
fathom n 12
fathomless adj 160
fatidic adj prophetic 159
fatigue n duty 229
fatigue n weariness 166; v 166
fatigue n the cause of weariness 166
fatigues n uniform 229
fatiloquent adj 159
fatling n 107
fatso n 307
fatten v 139
fatuity n something fatuous 114
fatuous adj without phys. taste 156
fatuous adj imbecilic 156
fat-witted adj 133
faucet n obs. stopper 71
faucet n 71
faugh interj 112
fault n flaw 49
fault v fail 96
fault v find fault 96
fault n lack 49
fault line, fault n 193
faulty adj 54
faun n 81
fauna n 194
fauteuil n type of chair 183
fauvism n painting style 290
faux adj imitation 325
faux pas n 174
fava n type of bean 287
fave n 300
favor n as in "in good favor" 49
favor n arch. 162
favor n as in "do me a favor" 49
favor v as in "favor a sore leg" 116
favor n as in "party favor" 49
favor v resemble 162
favor v 49
favorable 49
favored 49
favorite adj/n 135
favorite adj 135
favorite son n (Am) 202
favoritism n 135, 198
favors n as in "sexual favors" 126
fawn n Animals 30
fawn n type of color 30
fawn v 56

fax n/v 302
fay n 293
faze v (Am) 225
fealty n 44
fear v instill fear 36
fear n/v 17
fear v worship, as in "God-fear-ing" 20
fear v experience fear 36
fear n obs. danger 17
fearsome adj 198
feasance n obs. opp. of malfea-sance 117
feasibility n 91
feasible adj 91
feast n/v Food 34
feast n Religion 42
feat n 51
feat adj attractive, trim, smart 54
feather n/v 11
feather bed n 14
featherbed adj/v 292
featherbedding n 292
featherbrain n 231
feathercut n type of hairstyle 297
featherhead n 231
featherlight adj 234
featherstitch n 223
featherweight n 213
feature n as in "newspaper fea-ture" 246, 291
feature n arch. shape 82
feature n obs. creature 82
feature n obs. part of the body 82
feature n beneficial part 82
feature story 246
feature-length 291
features n as in "facial fea-tures" 87
featurette n 291
febrific adj 166
febrile adj 166
February n 12
feces n 66
feck n 124
feckless adj 124
fecund adj 90
fecundate v 90
fed up adj 268
federal adj related to a treaty 174
federal adj U.S. type of govern-ment sense 174
federal case n Slang 312
federal court n 203

federal district court n 300
federalese n 305
federalism n 202
federalist n (Am) 202
federate adj 188
federated church n 291
federation n 188
fedity n obs. repulsiveness 143
fedora n (Am) 260
fee n Finances/Money 76
fee n feudal estate 76
fee v obs. bribe 98
fee splitting n 305
feeb n (Am) Insults 283
feeble adj 32
feebleminded adj 112
feeblish adj 179
feed n as in "direct feed" 122
feed n feeding 122
feed v 15
feed n as in "horse feed" 122
feedback n response 279
feedback n electronic sense 279
feedback n gen. response 320
feedbag n (Am) 223
feeder road n 298
feeding frenzy n 325
feedstock n 297
feedstuff n (Am) 241
feel n/v 25
feel no pain v 308
feel up v 293
feelers n 165
feel-good adj (Am) 324
feeling n emotion 25, 72
feelings n 198
feet of clay n 216
feetfirst adv 278
feeze obs. 225
feint v obs. deceive 61
feint adj/n/v 171
feisty adj 261
feldspar n 193
feldspath n 193
felicific adj happy-making 243
felicitate adj happied 149
felicitate v 149
felicitous adj happy 184
felicitous adj appropriate 184
felicity n 72
feline adj 165
feline distemper n 302
fell n (Am) 29
fell v knock down 26
fell n hide, skin 11
fell adj savage 53
fell v obs. lower 26
fell adj obs. angered 53

fella 216
fellate v 262
fellatio n 262
feller n 216
fellow n fella 18
fellow n obs. female companion 61
fellow n obs. African-American 202
fellow n partner 18
fellow n obs. conspirator 98
fellow n equal 18
fellow n Education 78
fellow feeling n common ground 150
fellow feeling n compassion 150
fellow man n 174
felo-de-se n suicide "victim" 155
felon adj/n 46
felon adj/n obs. demon 46
felonious adj 46
felonous adj 46
felonry n 230
felony n obs. evil 46
felony n obs. gen. sin 46
felony n 46
felt n 16
female n 51
female adj 51
female chauvinism n 324
feminal adj 51
femineity n 78
feminine adj 51, 88, 121
femininity n 78
femininity n 78
feminism n 266
feminism n feminine qualities 266
femme n the "female" lesbian 311
femme n gen. woman 311
femme fatale n 283
femur n 195
fen n 9
fence v sell stolen items 155; n 155
fence n/v Shelter/Housing 70
fence v 131
fence v Sports 126
fence n obs. defense 70
fence-mending n (Am) 307
fencerow n 223
fence-sitter/fence-sitting n/adj 277
fencing n Sports 126
fend v defend against 97

fend v as in "fend for yourself" 97
fend v as in "fend off" 97
fender n on a car 280
fender n defender 49
fender n bumper 49
fender bender n 317
fenland n 9
fennel n 15
feracity n prolificity 98
feral adj arch. deadly 155
feral adj bestial 145
fere n mate, spouse 18
fere n companion 18
ferine 145
ferment n 84
ferment, fermentation v, n cause to ferment 84
ferment, fermentation v, n be fermented 84
fermery n arch. infirmary 69
fern adj old, yester 28
fern n 10
fern bar n (Am) 324
ferntickle n arch. skin blemish 66
fernyear n obs. long ago 12
ferocious adj 124
ferocity n 124
ferret n type of animal 31
ferret n detective 156
ferriage n carriage on a ferry 36
ferric adj 193
Ferris wheel n 265
ferrite n 236
ferrotype n type of photo-graph—akin to tintype 228
ferrous adj 193
ferry n 36
ferry n 17, 36; n 17
ferryboat 36
ferryman n 101
fertile adj 63
fertility n 63
fertilization n gen. making fer-tile 236
fertilization n as in "fertilization of an egg" 236
fertilize v as in "fertilize a field" 148
fertilize v as in "fertilize an egg" 148, 236
fertilizer n 148
fervency n 51
fervent, fervor adj, n 51
fess v 230
fest n (Am) as in "filmfest" 249

filmgoer n 282
filmic adj Movies/TV/Radio 291
filmization n (Am) 282
filmland n 282
filmmaker n 276
filmmaking 276
filmography n 319
filmstrip n 291
filter n/v 134
filter n obs. felt 134
filter paper n 224
filter tip n of cigarettes 297
filth n 22
filth n applied to language 22
filthy 22
filtration 133
fimble v fumble with fingers 144
fin n as in "a fish's fin" 11
fin n slang hand 195
fin n (Am) five-dollar bill 245
fin de siecle adj mood at century's end 266
fin whale n 255
finagle v (Am) 295
final adj/n 54
finale n Music 187
finale n gen. 187
finalist n 270
finality n 232
finality n final goal 232
finalize v 278
finance n obs. tax 200
finance v ransom 245
finance v supply money 245
finance n as in "high finance" 200
finance v work in finance 245
finance n obs. payment 200
finance company n 289
finances n 200
financial adj 200
financier n 152
financing n 227
finback n fin whale 181
finch n 11
find n/v 25, 217
fine adj delicate, excellent 53
fine adj very small, as in "fine mist" 53
fine n arch. gen. penalty 80
fine adj large 53
fine v obs. pay a fine 131
fine v obs. end 61
fine n monetary penalty 80; v 80
fine v levy a fine 131
fine n obs. death 45

fine art n 201
fine print n 311
finery n 167
finesse n delicateness 107
finesse n/v 107
finest n 313
fine-tooth comb n 231
fine-tune v 295
finger n informant, snitch 292
finger v Music 77
finger v touch 95
finger n pickpocket 292
finger n/v 13
finger n as in "a finger of scotch" 66
finger v 13
finger bowl n 239
finger food n 287
finger hole n 251
finger paint v 299
finger painting n 299
finger post n sign with finger pointers 198
finger spelling n 281
finger, the n as in "give him the finger" 307
finger wave n hairstyling term 297
fingerboard n Music 173
fingering n Music 77, 173
fingernail n 31
fingerpicking n style of musicianship 318
finger-pointing n 307
fingerprint n/v 251
fingertip n 13, 221
finical adj finicky 124, 213
finick v 213
finicking adj 124, 213
finicky adj 124, 213
finis n gen. 76
finis n Literature/Writing 76
finish n 205
finish v as in "finish a chair" 60
finish v kill 155
finish v 60
finish v obs. die 155
finish line n 263
finishing school n 228
finishment n death 80
finite adj 90
finite adj Mathematics 120
fink n/v (Am) 268
fink out v 313
fipple flute n 282
fir n 10
fire n fig. passion 9
fire n 9

fire v fig. inspire 58
fire v eject 263
fire n as in "gunfire" 131; v 131
fire v 9
fire and brimstone n 47
fire ant n 181
fire away v start talking 230
fire brigade n 183, 211, 222
fire company n (Am) 183, 211, 222
fire department n 183, 211, 222
fire door n 222
fire drill n 258
fire engine n 167, 297
fire escape n 167
fire extinguisher n 222
fire hydrant n 183, 303
fire irons n 149
fire off v 271
fire opal n 209
fire sale n (Am) 263
fire ship n kind of a kamikaze ship 131
fire station n 258
fire tower n 222
fire truck n 167, 297
fire wall n (Am) 196
firearm n 155
firebase n 319
firebird n brightly colored bird 210
fireboat n 222
firebomb n/v 266
firebrand n 35
firebrand n fig. 35
firebreak n 222
firebug n (Am) 248
firecracker n (Am) 233
firedrake n type of dragon 21
fire-eater n 173
fire-engine red n 313
firefight n 266
firefighter n 275
firefly n 165
firehouse n 258
firelight n 9
firelock n type of gun 112
fireman n extinguisher 185
fireman n fire tender 185
fireplace n 167
fireplug n 183, 303
firepower n War/Military/Violence 282
fireproof adj/v 160
fireproof v 160
firestone n 12

firestorm n War/Military/Violence 306
firetrap n 258
firewater n (Am) 211
firewood n 65
firework n type of mil. device 137
firework n 137
firing line n 269
firing pin n 248
firing squad n 277
firm n company 185
firm adj applied to people 54
firm adj 54
firm v 54
firm n obs. company name 185
firm n obs. signature 185
firmament n 31
firmware n 315
first adj 25
first aid n 257
first cause n the creator 78
first class n 187
first cousin n 170
first edition n 227
first lady n 229
first lieutenant n 203
first mortgage n 245
first name n 49
first off adv 270
first offender n 230
first person n 110
first sergeant n 247
first strike n 312
first world n 319
firstborn adj 54
first-class adj/adv 207
first-degree burn n 286
firsthand adj 179
firstling n 114
first-rate adj 178
first-run adj 282
firth n estuary 63
fisc n state treasury, and source of the word "fiscal" 127
fiscal year n 127, 227
fish n 11
fish farm n 241
fish finger n 310
fish finger n fish stick 316
fish fry n 211
fish hawk n (Am) 181
fish pole n 197
fish protein concentrate n 316
fish stick n 310
fish story n (Am) 216
fish-and-chips n 259
fisherfolk n 241

fisherman n 71, 212
fisherwoman n 71, 212
fish-eye adj 305
fishhook n 71
fishing pole n (Am) 122, 197
fishing rod n 122, 197
fishmonger n 40
fishnet n 15
fishpond n 34
fishtail v (Am) 295
fishwife n 75
fishy adj *suspicious* 231
fission n *of atoms* 296
fission n *of cells* 296
fissure n 63
fist n/v 13
fist n *arch. fart* 32
fistfight n 155
fistic adj *pugilistic* 215
fisticuffs n 155
fit n *as in "fit of anger"* 22
fit n 104
fit n *phys.* 22
fit v *as in "fitted for a suit"* 104
fit adj *apt* 88
fit v 88
fitch n *skunk* 64
fitchet 64
fitted adj *apt* 184
fitted adj 184
fitting adj 103
fitting n 184
five n 12
five-and-ten n 263
five-finger discount n 319
five-o'clock shadow n 296
fiver n 227
five-star adj 284
fix n *hit of drug* 300
fix n *as in "the fix is in"* 292; v 292
fix v *repair* 191
fix n *bad situation* 215
fix v *attach* 191
fix v *arrange* 191
fix up v 235
fixate v 271, 275
fixation n *obsession* 275
fixation n 271
fixed star n 119
fixed-wing adj 304
fixity n 206
fixity n *obs. unevaporatability* 206
fixity n *stability* 206
fixture n *process of fixing* 216
fixture n *as in "he's a fixture in the club"* 216

fixture n *fixity* 216
fizgig n *type of firework or noisy toy* 178
fizgig n *arch. flirt* 178
fizz v *cause to fizz* 180
fizz n/v 180
fizzle v/n *fail* 235
fizzle v/n *break wind* 235
fizzle v/n *make a fizz sound* 235
fizzwater n 310
flab n 179
flabbergast v 198
flabby adj 179
flaccid adj 160
flack n (Am) *PR person* 298; v 298
flacon n *type of bottle* 211
flag v 99
flag n *type of stone* 63
flag n *banner* 99
flag v *as in "flagging interest"* 117
flag football n 311
flag of truce n 155
flagellant n 162
flagellate adj/n/v 162
flagellation n 162
flagger 226
flagitious adj *criminal, villainous* 80
flagman n 226
flagon n *type of bottle* 69
flagpole n 148, 257
flagrance n 190
flagrancy 190
flagrant adj 190
flagrant adj *arch. fiery* 190
flagrante delicto adj/adv 230
flagship n 174
flagstaff n 148
flag-waver n 268
flail n/v 21
flail v War/Military/Violence 21
flair n *aptitude* 293
flair n *instinct, ability to discern* 293
flair n *odor* 293
flak n 300
flake n *snowflake* 53
flake n *fluff* 53
flake n *layer* 53
flake n *chip, bit* 53
flake v 53
flaky, flake adj/n *loony tune* 320
flambé adj/v 280

flambé adj *applied to porcelain glaze* 280
flambeau n *torch* 149
flamboyant adj *showy* 270
flamboyant adj *colorful* 270
flamboyant adj *architecturally ornate* 270
flame n/v 29
flame n *as in "old flame"* 29, 170
flamenco n 265
flameproof adj/v 270
flame-retardant 270
flamethrower n 282
flamingo n Animals 119
flamingo n *type of color* 119
flammability n 217
flammable adj 217
flan n 223
flank n/v 112
flank n/v *gen.* 112
flank steak n 273
flannel n *washcloth* 35
flannel n 35
flannelette n 35
flannelmouthed adj (Am) *boastful* 261
flannels n 35
flap n *fuss* 292
flap n *loose woman* 175
flapdoodle n 230
flapjack n 122
flapper n 292
flapper n *gen. young woman* 292
flares n *type of pants* 323
flare-up n 232
flash v *expose* 230
flash v *gen. show off* 230
flash back v 276
flash card n 291
flash flood n 296
flash in the pan n 277
flashback n 276
flashbulb n 299, 318
flashcube n 299, 318
flasher n 230
flash-forward n 276
flashing n 190
flashlight n 260
flashtube 299
flashy adj *showy* 179
flask n 167
flask n *type of case* 167
flat adj *as in "flat beer"* 160
flat n *apartment* 211
flat adj/n Music 129
flat n *type of scenery* 201

flat adj 53
flat adv *as in "flat broke"* 252
flat n *arch. not-sharp person* 204
flat, flats n *flatland* 29
flatboat n 168
flatbread n 259
flatcar n (Am) 242
flatfoot n 248
flat-footed adj 147
flatiron n 183
flatland n 29
flat-out adj 278
flatter v 55
flattery n 55
flatulence n *gastric sense* 238
flatulence n *fig. inflation, pomposity* 238
flatulency n 238
flatulent adj 139, 238
flatuosity n 238
flatware n 239
flatworm n 194
flautist n 246
flavor n *taste* 168
flavor n *aroma* 168
flavoring n 223
flaw n *flake* 135
flaw n 135
flax n *flaxen cloth* 30
flax n Plants 30
flaxen adj *made from flax* 64
flaxen adj *the color of flax* 64
flay v 20
flea n 11
flea collar n 310
flea market n 289
fleabag n 230
fleabane n 105
flea-bitten adj 132
flechette n *type of weapon* 282
fledge v *grow the feathers that allow a bird to fly* 119
fledgling n 119, 219
flee v 26
fleece v *clip a sheep* 117
fleece v *rob* 117
fleece n 11
fleer v *obs. grin* 73
fleer v *sneer* 73
fleer n 73
fleet adj/v 115
fleet n *one ship* 45
fleet n *as in "fleet of trucks"* 45
fleet n (Am) *many ships* 45
fleet v 115
fleet admiral n 307
fleet-footed 115

fleeting adj *obs. not stable, flowing* 137
fleeting adj 137
flesh n *applied to fruit* 13
flesh n *as in "flesh and blood"* 18
flesh n 13
flesh n *as in "in the flesh"* 13
flesh and blood n 18
flesh color n 161
flesh out v 271
flesh wound n 174
fleshen adj *fleshy* 13
fleshly adj *obs. carnal* 20
fleshly adj *corporeal* 20
fleshment n *excitement from getting off to a good start* 149
fleshpot n 108
fleshy adj 13
fleshy fruit n 287
fletcher n 40
fletching n *arrow feathers* 291
fleur-de-lis n 30
flex v 90
flexible adj 90
flexible time n 323
flexile adj 90
flexor n 147
flextime n 323
flibbertigibbet n 82
flick v 218
flick n *movie* 291
flicker n *(Am) type of woodpecker* 209
flicker n/v 55
flickers *obs.* 291
flick-knife n *(Brit) switchblade* 312
flight n *flying* 16, 48
flight n *fleeing* 16, 48
flight v 16
flight attendant n 304
flight deck n 288
flight path n 280
flight plan n 298
flight recorder n 298
flight suit n 304
flight surgeon n 291
flight-test v 288
flighty adj *loony* 198
flighty adj *fast* 198
flighty adj *capricious* 198
flimflam n 114
flimflam v 114
flimsy adj 190
flinch v 141
flinch v *obs. slink away* 141
flinders n *splinters* 86

fling n/v 58
fling n *party, etc.* 226
flint n 9
flintlock n 174
flinty adj 115
flip v *go crazy* 304
flip n *type of drink* 167
flip n/v 116
flip adj *flippant* 225
flip side n 305
flip-flop n/v 168
flippant adj *disrespectful* 184
flippant adj *flexible* 184
flippant adj *obs. loquascious* 184
flipper n Animals 210
flipping adj *(Brit)* Slang 283
flirt v *flick* 151
flirt v 151; n, 185
flirt n *obs. witticism* 117
flirt v *obs. sneer* 151
flirt v *blurt* 180
flirt n 151
flirt n *obs. trollop* 185
flirtation n 151, 185
flirtatious adj 185
flivver n *(Am)* 274
float n Food 287
float v *cause to float* 27
float v *in the air* 27
float v *on water* 27
float glass n *type of glass* 313
floatel n 316
floater n *(Am) dead body* 266
floating rib n 221
floatplane n 288
flock n *as in "flock of geese"* 30
flock n *type of wool* 35; v 35
flock v *as in "flock together"* 58
flock n *applied to people* 30
flock v *obs. bring together* 58
floe, ice floe n 209
flog v *slang sell* 281
flog v 174
flood n *too much water* 92
flood n *gen. water* 9
flood v 9
flood control n *(Am)* 286
flood tide n 181
flood wall n 310
floodgate n 35
floodlight n 288
floodplain n 236
flooey adj *as in "go flooey"* 284
floor n *fig. minimum* 14
floor n 14
floor n *as in "floor of the Senate"* 14

floor v *as in "I was floored by the news"* 224
floor n *as in "3rd-floor apartment"* 14
floor exercise n 317
floor lamp n 258
floor leader n *(Am) political term* 266
floor manager n *(Am)* 263
floor plan n 239
floor show n 291
floorboard n 258
floor-length adj 297
floorwalker n *(Am)* 263
floozy n 277
flop v *make a flopping sound* 161
flop n *failure* 268
flop v *fall* 161
flop v 268
flop n *con* 268
flophouse n 268
floppy, floppy disk n 322
flora n Plants 193
flora n *personification of plant fertility* 193
floral adj 193
florescence n 194
floret n 164
floriculture n 212
florid adj *ruddy* 161
florid adj *covered with flowers* 161
florilegium n *collection, anthology* 152
florist n 152
floss v *as in "floss teeth"* 322
flotation n 216
flotilla n 188
flotsam n 159
flounce v *move broadly* 117; n 117
flounce n *fabric edging* 184; v 184
flounder n 30
flounder v *struggle* 142
flour n 34
flourish v *show off* 30
flourish v *obs. decorate* 30
flourish v *fig.* 30
flourish v *of plants* 30
flow n/v 26
flow diagram n 284
flowchart n 284
flower n/v 29
flower bud n 219
flower child n 319
flower girl n 289

flower people n 319
flower power n 319
flowering dogwood n 219
flowering plant n 181
flowerpot n 121
flu n 221
flub n/v *(Am)* 278
flub n 278
flubdub n *(Am) nonsense* 267
fluctuate v *waver* 163
fluctuate v *undulate* 163
fluctuation n 163
flue n 122
flue pipe n *of organ* 246
flue stop n *of organ* 246
fluff v *goof up* 271
fluff v *as in "fluff a pillow"* 271
fluff n 205
fluff n *flub* 205
fluff n *triviality* 205
flugelhorn n 246
fluid adj/n 90
fluid dram n 238
fluid ounce n 238
fluidify v 234
fluidize v 234
fluke n *type of fish* 11
fluke n *lucky shot, bit of luck* 249; v 249
flumadiddle n *(Am) type of food* 233
flumadiddle n *nonsense* 233
flummery n *nonsense* 148
flummery n Food 148
flummox v 231
flunk v *(Am) gen. fail* 214
flunk v *as in "flunk a course"* 214
flunk out v 282
flunky n 200
flunky n *yes-man* 200
fluorescent lamp n 258
fluoridate v 303
fluoridation n 303
fluoride n 233
fluoridize v 303
fluorine n 217
fluorocarbon n 296
fluorography n 303
fluoroscope n/v *(Am)* 257
flurr v *scatter* 180
flurry n *applied to air* 165
flurry n/v *gen.* 165
flush v *blush* 143
flush adj *perfect* 127
flush adj *rich* 127
flush n *as in "royal flush"* 108

flush v *as in "flush a toilet"* 56, 196
flush adj *even* 127
flush v *as in "flush birds"* 56
flush n 56
fluster v 184
flustrated, flustrate adj 184
flustration n 184
flute n *Music* 42
flute n *flutist* 42, 153
flutist n 42, 153
flutter v *obs. float on water* 27
flutter n/v 27
flutter kick n 298
flux n *change* 158
flux n *outflow* 158
fly v *as in "fly through the sky"* 16
fly v *fig.* 16
fly adj (Brit) *alert, artful* 212
fly n *type of coach* 184
fly n 11
fly n *on pants* 223
fly n *on tents, etc.* 223
fly n 16
fly casting n 126, 263
fly casting 126
fly fisherman n 263
fly rod n 126, 171
fly whisk n 224
flyaway adj 206
flyboat n *speedy boat* 123
flyboy n 307
flyby n (Am) 310
fly-by-night adj/n 204
fly-by-nighter 204
flycast v 263
flycatcher n *type of plant* 119
flycatcher n *type of bird* 119
fly-fish v 126
fly-fishing n 126
flying boat n 280
flying bomb n (Brit) *buzz bomb* 306
flying buttress n 167
flying circus n *air squadron* 282
flying colors n 189
flying fish n 105
flying fortress n (Am) 300
flying fox n 194
flying frog n 165
flying machine n 184
flying saucer n 307
flying squirrel n 146
flying start n 250
flyleaf n 227
flyover n 274
flypaper n 222

flyswatter n 258
flyte v *obs. argue* 28
flytrap n *type of plant* 193
flywheel n 198
FM 209
fnesen v *arch. sneeze* 14
f-number n 265
foal n/v 11
foal n *arch. gen. horse* 11
foam n/v 21
foam rubber n 301
foamed plastic n 308
fob v *cheat, trick* 80
fob n *as in "watch fob"* 167
fob off v 143
focal adj 179
focal point n 187
focus v 207
focus n 146
focus n *fig. point of concentration* 146
fodder n *obs. gen. food* 15
fodder n 15
foe n 20
foeman n 21
fog n *type of grass* 64
fog n/v *Weather* 105
fog bank n 165
fogbound adj 237
fogbow n *similar to rainbow* 220
fogey n *as in "old fogey"* 204
fogger n *pettifogger* 144
foghorn n 242
foible n 169
foible adj *obs. feeble* 144
foible n *fencing term* 169
foie gras n 211
foil v *overthrow* 139
foil n *type of sword* 131
foil v *trample* 61, 139
foil n *counterpoint* 87
foil v *stop* 139
foil n *as in "aluminum foil"* 53
foil n *animal trace* 119
foilist, foilsman n 291
foin n/v *stab at* 80
foison n *cornucopia* 49
foison v *arch.* 49
foist v *impose* 142
foist v *obs. deceive* 142
foist v *obs. perform trickery with dice* 142
fold n *as in "a fold of sheep"* 15
fold v *as in "folding paper"* 26
fold n *Religion* 43
fold v 15
fold n 26
foldaway adj 308

folder n *arch. shepherd* 122
folder n 280
folding money n 290
foliage n *plants* 64
folio n *page* 77
folio n *size of book* 77
folio n *type of book* 77
folk n 20
folk etymology n 264
folk mass n 319
folk medicine n 257
folk music 228
folk rock n 318
folk song n 228
folkie n 318
folklife n 247
folklore n 227
folkmoot/folkmote n *townspeople assembling* 20
folk-pop n *Music* 318
folks n 170
folksinger 228
folksy adj (Am) 251
folktale n 245
folkway n 278
follicle n 66
follow v 25
follow v *occur after* 25
follow v *obs. be similar to* 28
follow v *understand* 25
follower n *servant* 18
follower n *disciple* 18
folly n *type of theatrical revue* 290
folly n *insanity* 61
folly n 48
folly n *obs. crime* 61
foment v *incite* 161
foment v *apply poultice* 161
fon adj/n/v *obs.* 47
fond adj *foolish* 138
fond v *obs. dote on* 108
fond adj *showing fondness* 138
fondant n *type of candy* 168
fondle v/n 206
fondle v/n *obs. pamper* 206
fondling n *loved person* 126
fondue n 241
font n *as in "type font"* 172
font n *act of metal-casting* 172
foo dog n 309
food n *solid food* 15
food n *food and drink* 15
food n *obs. fig. sustenance* 15
food bank n 327
food chain n 287
food poisoning n 257
food processor n 322

food pyramid n 303
food stamp n 299
foodaholic n 316
foodie n *akin to junkie* 326
foodpad n *type of highwayman* 174
foodstuff n 241
foofaraw n *fuss, finery* 300
fool v *obs. be a fool* 142
fool v *deceive* 142
fool v *as in "fool around"* 142
fool adj/n 47
fool around v 235
foolery 100
foolhardy adj 36, 47
foolish adj 47
foolishness n 100
foolproof adj (Am) 278
fool's gold n 236
fool's paradise n 102
foolscap n *type of paper* 149, 172
foolscap n *type of cap* 149, 172
foot v *dance* 77
foot v *kick* 77
foot n *The Body* 13
foot v *walk* 77
foot n *Measurement* 13
foot n *as in "foot of the bed"* 13
foot v *as in "foot the bill"* 234
foot n *poetic beat* 19
foot n *as in "foot of a hill"* 13
foot soldier n 155
footage n *Movies/TV/Radio* 282
footage n *way to determine miners' pay* 264
foot-and-mouth disease n 238
football n 75
footbath n 121
footboy n *page* 126
footbridge n 72
foot-dragger n 307
foot-dragging n 307
footer n *pedestrian* 149
footgear n 223, 260
foothill n (Am) 219
foothold n 158
footle n/v *prattle* 264
footlights n 228
footlocker n (Am) 308
footloose adj 179
footman n *pedestrian* 40
footman n *infantry soldier* 40
footman n *servant* 40
footnote n/v 214
footpath n 107

footrace n 171
footsie n 300
footslog v *march* 261
footstone n *opp. of headstone* 188
footstool n 106
footwear n (Am) 223, 260
footy n 300
foozle n *bungler* 231
foozle v 231
foozle n *instance of bungling* 231
fop n 174
fop n *fool* 174
for ever 146
for instance 313
forage n/v *fodder* 35
foray n/v 45
forayer n *raider* 45
forbear n *ancestor* 101
forbid v 27
forbidden adj 27
forbidden fruit n 173
forbidding adj 190
forbode v 84
force n *as in "gravitational force"* 49
force n *obs. farce* 98
force n/v 49
force v *obs. strengthen* 98
force majeure n 269
force of habit n 293
force of nature n 326
force-feed v 273
forcemeat n *type of stuffing* 168
force-out n (Am) 270
forceps n 123
ford n/v 9
fordo v *kill, destroy* 20
fore interj 248
forearm v *prepare arms* 131
forearm n 182
forebode v 161
foreboding adj/n 84
forecast n *obs. forethought, plan* 74
forecastle n 72
foreclose v *obs. restrain* 188
foreclose v 188
foreclose v *hinder, prevent* 188
foreclosure n 188
foredeck n 123
foredoom v *condemn* 161
foredoom v *preordain* 161
foredoom v 161
forefather n 40, 101
forefeel v *have prescience* 125
forefinger n 66

forefoot n 64
forefront n *fig.* 136
forefront n *building front* 136
forego v *go before* 26
foregone conclusion n 156
foreground n 177
forehanded adj *looking ahead* 151
forehead n 13
foreign adj 53
foreign affairs n 155
foreign aid n 306
foreign correspondent n 305
foreign legion n 266
foreign minister n 188
foreign office n 247
foreign policy n 247
foreknow v 74
foreknowledge n 74
forelady n (Am) 264
foreman n *on a jury* 40, 155, 324
foreman n *primary servant* 40
foreman n *type of supervisor* 40
foremost adj *obs. firstmost* 23
foremost adj 23
foremother n 40, 101
forename n *first name* 114
forenight n *arch. evening* 31
forenoon n *opp. of afternoon* 65
forensic adj 175
forensic n *type of speech* 214
forensic medicine n 221
forensical adj 175
foreordain v *preordain* 96
forepassed/forepast adj *bygone* 119
foreperson n *of a jury* 155, 324
foreplay n 289
forerunner n *predecessor* 49
foresaken adj 26
foresay v *arch. predict* 18, 58
foresee v *obs. prepare for* 17
foresee v 17
foreseeable adj 17, 213
foreshadow n/v 141
foreshadowing n 141
foreshock n *opp. of aftershock* 272
foreshorten v 143
foreshow n *foretell* 97
foreshow v *obs. make provision* 97
foresight n 17, 39
foreskin n 106
forest n 29
forest floor n 219
forest green n 217

forest ranger n 226
forestage n Performing Arts 290
forester n 40
forestry n Agriculture/ Food-Gathering 212
forestry n *the royal forest* 174
foretaste n/v 86
foretell v 58
forethink v *obs.* 39
forethought n 39
forethoughtful adj 39, 213
foretime n 105
foretoken n *harbinger* 22
forever n 237
forever/forevermore adv 146
forewarn v 60
forewoman n 155, 188, 324
foreword n 227
forfeit v *obs. commit a wrong* 60
forfeit n *type of criminal penalty* 46
forfeit v 60
forfend v *obs. forbid* 94
forfend v 94
forgather v 104
forge v 131
forge v *Shape* 60
forge n *smithy* 41
forge v *gen.* 207
forge v *fake* 60
forge v *as in "forge ahead"* 207
forge n *type of tool* 41
forgery n *fakery* 131
forgery n *counterfeiting* 131
forget v 17
forgetive adj *inventive* 125
forget-me-not n 105
forgive v *obs. give* 26
forgive v 26
forgo v 27
forgotten man n 293
fork n *as in "fork in the road"* 87
fork n *obs. gallows* 45
fork n *eating utensil* 16
fork v *arch. slang "pick a pocket"* 175
fork n *pitchfork* 16
fork over, fork out v 249
forked tongue n 231
forklift n 304
fork-tender adj *very tender* 322
forlese v *destroy* 28
forlese v *obs. lose* 28
forlorn adj *pitiful* 137

forlorn adj *obs. morally adrift* 137
forlorn n *obs.* 137
forlorn adj *deserted* 137
forlorn hope n 112
form n *obs. recipe* 70
form n/v 48
form n *mold* 51
form n *as in "form and function"* 246
form n *obs. beauty* 71
form n *something to be filled out* 239
form letter n (Am) 276
formaldehyde n 237
formalwear n 316
format n/v 227
former adj 53
formfitting adj 260
formidable adj 91
formosity n *arch. beauty* 71
formula n 135
formula n *chemical sense* 135
formula n *recipe* 135
formula n *mathematical sense* 135
formulaic adj 270
formulate v 252
fornicate adj *arched* 233
fornication n Love/Romance/ Sex 39
fornicatrix n Love/Romance/ Sex 126
fornix n 166
forold v *arch. age* 12
forridden adj *obs. weary from riding* 107
forsake v 26
forsake v *obs. decline, renounce, steer clear of* 26
forsooth adv 23
forspent adj *exhausted* 120
forstand v *obs. understand* 18
forswear v *renounce, swear falsely* 26
forsythia n 209
fort adj *obs. strong* 98
fort n *fortress* 80
fortalice n *fortress* 80
forte n *strongest part of a sword* 155
forte n *fig. strong point* 170
forte n *applied to people* 155
forte adj/adv/n Music 187
forte n *applied to swords* 170
forte n 187
fortepiano n 201
forthcome v *come forth* 28

forthcoming adj 28

for-thy conj obs. therefore 28

fortification n 80

fortified wine n 273

fortify v 96

fortissimo adj/adv/n 187

fortitude n 48

fortnight n 12

Fortran n 309

fortress v arch. 33

fortress n 33

fortuitous adj 178

fortuity n 190

fortunate adj 49, 89

fortunate v obs. 89

fortunately adv 115

fortune n 49

fortune n a lot of money 127

fortune n rich woman 180

fortune cookie n 316

fortune hunter n 171

fortunes n experiences 158

fortune-teller n 132

forty n 12

forty winks n 216

forty-five n the pistol 277

forty-niner n 244

forum n 87

forward-looking adj 199

forweary adj 61

forworn adj spent 114

forworn adj 61

foryield v pay 28

fosse n ditch 9

fossil n fossilized animal 181

fossil n gen. rock 181

fossil n fossilized fish 181

fossil adj 181

fossil fuel n 221

fossilize v 181

foster home n 258

fosterling n foster child 18

Foucault pendulum n 296

foudroyant adj loud 252

foul adj 23

foul play n 102

foul up v 308

foulard n type of fabric 223

fouled up adj 308

foulmouthed adj 125

foul-up n (Am) 308

found v create, as in a foundry 116

found v start the foundation 58

found object n unintentional art 305

found poem n 318

foundation n various 84

foundation garment n 287

founder n one who founds, as in a city 51, 87

founder v of ships 149

founding father n 283

foundling n orphan 40

foundress n 51, 87

foundry n the founding business 110

foundry n the building 110

fountain n natural spring 63, 106

fountain n manmade 63, 106

fountain v 63, 106, 271

fountain pen n 187

fountainhead n 118

four n 12

four bits n (Am) 227

Four Hundred, the n (Am) high society 266

four-dimensional adj 255

four-eyes n 250

4-F n 306

four-flush/four-flusher v/n, n (Am) 268

four-footed adj 30

fourgon n luggage wagon 224

4-H n 287

four-in-hand n four-horsed vehicle 198

four-leaf clover n 219

four-letter word n 264

fourniture n furniture 258

fourplex n 310

four-poster n 211

four-star 284

fourteen n 12

fourth class n (Am) 246

fourth dimension n 237

fourth world n poorer than third world 324

four-wheel drive n 288

foutre n slang "something worthless" 144

fowl n domestic bird 11

fowl n bird 11

fowling piece n type of shotgun 131

fox n sensuous woman 320

fox n 11

fox n arch. school freshman 247

fox v 163

fox fire n 99

fox terrier n 210

foxed adj stained 234

foxglove n 10

foxhole n 282

foxhound n 194

fox-trot n (Am) the gait and the dance 246

foxy adj Slang 320

foxy adj sexy 324

foxy adj crafty 108

foy n sendoff gift 104

foyer n 239

fracas n 190

fracid adj obs. overripe 180

fractal n 322

fraction n var. meanings of fracture 65

fraction n Mathematics 65

fractional currency n (Am) change from your dollar 245

fractionalize v 295

fractious adj 170

fracture n/n 85

frag v (Am) War/Military/Violence 319

fragile adj 137

fragile adj obs. morally breakable 137

fragment n/v 85

fragmental adj 159

fragmentary adj 159

fragmentation bomb n 282

fragmentize v 85

fragrance n 91, 176

fragrancy n 91, 176

fragrant adj 91

fraidy-cat n 277

frail, frailty adj, n 32

framboise n raspberry brandy or liqueur 303

frame v 267, 277, 292; n 292

frame house n 121

frame of mind n 170

frame of reference n 269

frame-up n (Am) 267, 277, 292

franchisee n 311

franc-tireur n civilian irregular 215

frangible adj breakable 90

frangipane n type of dessert 241

frangipani n type of perfume 242

franglais n 318

frank adj obs. unbound 37

frank n (Am) Food 259, 273

frank adj 37

frankfurter n (Am) 259, 273

frankincense n 64

franklin n landowner 44

Franklin stove n (Am) 196

frankpledge n 44

frantic adj frenzied 73

frantic adj crazy 73

frantic adj 73

frape n obs. riffraff 44

frappé n 273

frappé adj 273

frat n 266

fraternal adj 75

fraternal twin n 275

fraternity n 44

fraternity n college organization 44, 202, 276

fraternize v 161

fratricide n killing a brother 102

fratricide n someone who kills 102

fratry n fraternity 143

fraud n 51

fraudulence n 51

fraudulency n 51

fraudulent adj 51

fraught adj 139

fraught adj arch. laden 139

fray v wear 95

fray v unravel 95

fray v arch. make afraid 37

fray n as in "fracas" 80

frayn v ask 28

frazzle n/v 218

freak v as in "freak out" 320

freak n instance of capriciousness 134

freak n aficionado 277

freak n abnormal 134

freak adj 134

freak of nature n 232

freak out v 320

freak show n 265

freaking adj/adv Slang 320

freakish adj 133

freak-out n 320

freaky adj 133, 217

freck v 66

freckle n/v 66

free n obs. person of nobility 20

free adj/v made free 26

free adj/v 26

free adj/v without financial cost 26

free and easy adj 176

free association n 262

free beach n nude beach 324

free diver n 311

free enterprise n 263

free fall n 280

free lance n mercenary 215

free lance v 215

free love n 213

free lunch n 231

free market n 275
free on board adj/adv 289
free port n 184
free rein n 313
free ride n 269
free speech n 227
free thinker n 170
free trade n 213
free university n 319
free verse n 276
free will n 39
free world n 306
freebase v/n (Am) 324
freebie n (Am) 307
freeboot v 131
freebooter n 131
free-booty obs. 131
freeborn n 44
freedman n 154, 247
freedom n 22
freedom of the seas n 281
freedwoman n (Am) 154, 247
free-fire zone n 319
free-floating adj 294
free-for-all n (Am) 266
free-form adj 308
freehand adj 290
freehanded adj generous 169
freehearted adj frank, generous 73
freelance v The Workplace 299
freelance v War/Military/Violence 215
freelance n mercenary 215
freelancer n The Workplace 299
freelancer n War/Military/Violence 215
free-living adj 212
freeload v 300
freeman n 20
free-marketeer n 311
freemartin n type of calf 165
freemasonry n 79
free-spoken adj 150
freestanding adj 270
freestyle n 298
free-swinging adj 308
freeway n (Am) 288
freewheeling adj 278
freewriting n 323
freeze v freeze solid 27
freeze v cause to freeze 27
freeze v as in "it's freezing out" 27
freeze n/v fig. stop 27

freeze-dried, freeze-dry adj, v 303
freeze-frame n 305
freezer n 224
freezer burn n 286
freezing point n 182
freezing rain n 194
freight n/v 75
freight train n 224
freighter n 243
freighter n person who moves freight 243
french v style of cutting during cooking 303
french n/v oral sex 311
French bread n 100
French cuff n 280
French curve n 260
French dip n 316
French door n 286
French dressing n (Am) 259
french fry n 280
French horn n 173
French kiss n 289
French leave n rapid departure 204
French letter n (Brit) condom 249
French pastry n 287
French provincial n 304
French toast n 241
French window n 211
frenetic adj obs. insane 124
frenetic adj hyper 124
frenzical adj obs. 38
frenzy n craziness 38
frenzy n fig. 38
frenzy v 38
frequence n gathering 98
frequency n 176
frequency modulation n FM 285
frequent v 96
frequent adj 115
fresco n style of painting 128
fresco n a fresco painting 128
fresh adj new 23
fresh adj salt-free 23
fresh adj refreshed 23
fresh adj (Am) cool 327
fresh adj impudent 243
freshman n newcomer 114
freshman n educational sense 114
freshwater adj/n 9
freshwater pearl n 279
fret v obs. eat 124
fret v gnaw physically 124

fret n as in "guitar fret" 101; v 101
fret v as in "fret over a problem" 124
fretsaw n 242
fretwork n 148
Freudian slip n 311
friar n 43
friar's lantern n swamp gas 145
fribble n/v Insults 175
fricassee n/v 122
friction n 134
friction n scientific sense 134
friction match n (Am) 222
friction tape n 280
Friday n 12
fridge n 286
fried adj soused 292
friedcake n (Am) donut 223
friend adj. obs. 18
friend n/v 18
friend of the court n 307
friendlike adj 18
friendly adj 18
friendly n 18
friendly fire n 324
frieze n type of wool 71
frieze n type of architectural detail 122
frig v wiggle 97
frig v fuck 97, 126
frigate n 174
frigate n gen. fast ship 174
frigate bird n 181
frigging adj Love/Romance/Sex 126
fright n something frightful 17
fright n/v 17
fright v 169
fright wig n 260
frighten v 17, 169
frigid adj sexual sense 91, 170
frigid adj 91
frigid zone n 145
frigidity n 91
frijole n 122
frill n gen. luxury 123
frill n spec. type of ornament 123
frill v 123
fringe n gen. 35
fringe n 35
fringe benefit n 305
fripper obs. frippery 167
frippery n finery 167
frippery n obs. clothes 167
Frisbee n 317
friseur n hairdresser 185

frisk adj obs. 115
frisk v/n pat down 204
frisk adj 98
frisk v/n 98
frisky adj 98, 115
frisson n shudder of excitement 198
fritter v as in "fritter away" 191
fritter n 70
fritters n 191
frivol n 100, 199
frivolity n 199
frivolous adj 100, 199
frizz v curl tightly 143; n 143
frizz v groom with pumice stone 143
frizzle v frizz, sizzle 197
frizzly adj 143, 242
frizzy adj 143, 242
frock n 35
frock coat n 184
frog n mouth disease, as in "frog in the throat" 69
frog n 11
frog n base person 47
frog n Frenchman 204
frogman n 306
frog-march v 291
frolic adj/n/v 124
from scratch n 293
frond n 193
frondescence n foliation 219
front n Crime/Punishment/Enforcement 292
front n obs. forehead, face 87
front v opp. of rear 87
front n as in "put on a good front" 87
front n War/Military/Violence 291
front and center adv 313
front burner n 320
front line n 282
front man n 292
front matter n 276
front money n 290
front office n (Am) 263
front room n 310
frontage n 158
frontage road n 304
frontal bone n 182
frontal lobe n 256
front-end loader n 312
frontier adj/n border 84
frontier adj/n unexplored border 84
frontiersman n (Am) 200
frontispiece n 128

frontlash n *backlash to a backlash* 320

frontless adj *shameless* 149

front-page adj/v (Am) 276

front-runner n (Am) 284

front-wheel drive n 288

frore adj *cold, frozen* 53

frosh n 282

frost v *as in "frost hair"* 168

frost n *obs. ice* 9

frost v Food 197

frost n/v Natural Things 9

frost heave n 302

frostbite n/v 211

frostbiting n *cold-weather sailing* 317

frostbitten adj 211

frosting n Food 241

frostline n (Am) 236

froth n/v 84

froth n *scum* 133

frothy adj *frivolous* 84, 133

frown n *phys. expression* 124

frown n *gen. expression of concern* 124

frown v 124

frown n/v 73

frowsy adj 179

frowze n *obs. frizzy wig* 123

fructose n 241

frugal adj 127

fruit n Plants 29

fruit bat n 254

fruit cocktail n 287

fruit cup n (Am) 287

fruit fly n 194

fruit sugar n 259

fruitarian n *fruit vegetarian* 259

fruitcake n *crazy person* 313

fruitcake n Food 223

fruition n 270

fruition n *obs. enjoyment* 270

fruitless adj 54

fruitlet n 254

fruitwood n 285

frumenty n *type of oatmeal* 70

frummagemed adj *obs. slang "hanged"* 174

frump n 216

frump n *instance of mocking* 216

frumpish 216, 234

frumple v *wrinkle* 98

frumpy adj 216, 234

frumpy adj *irascible* 185, 234

frustrate v 96

frustrating adj 96, 243

frustration 96

fry n *spawn* 31, 132

fry v Food 34

fry n *as in "small fry"* 132

fry v *as in "he'll fry for the murder"* 291

fry n 34

fry bread n 303

fryer n 241

frying pan n 71

f-stop n 305

fubar adj 307

fubsy adj (Brit) *fat* 204

fuchsia n 193

fuck n *intercourse partner* 170

fuck n *as in "I don't give a fuck"* 292

fuck v 102

fuck n *act of intercourse* 170; v 102, 170

fuck n 292

fuck v *destroy, spoil* 102

fuck off v 292

fuck up v 312, 320

fucked-up adj 312, 320

fucker n 133

fucking adj/adv 132

fuckoff n 307

fuckup n 312, 313

fud n *fuddy-duddy* 283

fuddle v *befuddle* 132

fuddle v *get drunk* 132; n 132

fuddy-duddy n 277

fudge interj 203

fudge n *nonsense* 175

fudge n (Am) *type of confection* 259

fudge v *fake, dodge* 180

fudge factor n 320

fuel v 37, 142

fuel n Energy 31

fuel n *fig.* 31

fuel v *as in "fuel up"* 142

fuel cell n 285

fuel injection n 261

fuel oil n 256

fuelwood n 65

fug n/v *something stuffy* 269

fugacious adj *quickly gone* 160

fugacity n 160

fugitive adj/n 84

fugleman n *model soldier* 215

fugue n Emotions/Characteristics 288

fugue n Music 129

führer n 300

fulcrum n 168

fulfill v 60

fulfill v *arch. fill up full* 60

fulfillment n 60, 205

fulgent adj *resplendent* 90

fulham n *loaded die* 112

full adj *obs. complete, foresworn, as in "a full enemy"* 28

full adj 23

full v *make full* 23, 97

full v *obs. fulfill* 98

full adj *intoxicated* 132

full blast adv 278

full circle adv 269

full dress 197

full house n *the poker game* 262

full moon n 12

full of beans adj 249

full stop n *period* 127

full tilt adv 139

full-blown adj 159

full-bore adj/adv 325

full-dress adj 197

fuller n *cloth fuller* 18

fuller n *type of hammer* 242; v 242

fullerene n 326

full-fashioned adj 260

full-fledged adj 270

full-length adj 190

fullness of time n 133

full-scale adj 301

full-service adj 311

full-size adj 233

full-time adj 264

full-timer n 264

fulsome adj *plump* 53

fulsome adj *abundant, "full some"* 53

fulsome adj *effusive* 53

fumble v *have bad sex* 112

fumble n/v 97

fume n 84

fume v *express anger* 107

fumigant n 207

fumigate v 207

fumigate v *obs. scent, perfume* 207

fun v *joke with* 230

fun n *obs. trick* 185

fun adj/n/v 185, 226

fun and games n 281

fun house n 305

funambulator n 202

funambulism n 202

funambulist n 202

funambulo n 202

function n Mathematics 195

function n/v 114, 252

function n *ceremony, soiree* 247

functional adj *practical* 114, 321

functional illiterate n 305

functionary n 202

fund n 172

fund v *provide money* 290

fund n *foundation* 172

fund n *obs. bottom* 172

fund v *place in a fund* 290

fundament n *basis* 49

fundament n *foundation* 49, 91

fundament n *buttocks* 49

fundamental n 91, 158; adj 91

fundamental adj *of the buttocks* 204

fundamental law n 283

fundamental particle n 302

fundamentalism n (Am) 291

fundamentals n 158

fund-raiser n 299

fund-raising n 299

funebrial adj 188

funebrious adj 188

funeral adj 79, 80; n 80

funeral director n (Am) 266

funeral home n (Am) 291

funerary adj 80

funereal adj 188

funfest n 283

fungus n 64

funk n *type of music* 312

funk n 150

funk v *retreat, shrink back* 192; n 192

funk hole n 258

funnel n/v 72

funnel cloud n 272

funnies n *comics* 245

funny adj *odd* 198

funny adj *off-kilter, as in "I feel funny"* 198

funny adj *hilarious* 198

funny bone n 221

funny book n 305

funny car n 317

funny farm n 320

funny money n 300

funny paper n (Am) 246

funny/funnies n 245

funnyman n 228

fur n 31

fur seal n 194

furacious adj *thieving* 175

furbelow n 168

furbish v 94

furcate v 218

furcula n *wishbone* 236

furibund adj *furious* 54, 103

furied 54
furious adj 54
furl v 139
furlong n 12
furlong n *obs. running track* 75
furlough n/v 155
furnace n 31
furnish v 96
furnishing n 96
furniture n *var. meanings of equipment* 121
furniture n *obs. act of furnishing* 121
furniture n *chairs, etc.* 121
furor n 100
furor n *obs. madness* 100
furore n *furor* 198
furrier n 40
furriner n *foreigner* 231
furrow n/v 9
furry adj 139
further v 27
furtherance 27
furthersome adj *aiding* 160
furtive adj 103
fury n *inspiration* 72
fury n 72
fuse v *meld* 142
fuse n *as in "dynamite fuse"* 149
fuse n *as in "electrical fuse"* 256
fuselage n 278
fusil, fusilier n *type of flintlock, soldier using a fusil* 174
fusillade n 215
fusion n Music 324
fusionn 142
fusion bomb n 307
fusk adj *dusky* 91
fuss n 189
fuss v 189
fussbudget n (Am) 277
fusspot n 293
fussy adj 189, 225
fustigate v *beat, cudgel* 174
fustigation n 174
fusty adj *musty, out of date* 89
futhark, futhorc n *runic alphabet* 245
futile adj 137
futile adj *chatty* 143
futilitarian adj/n 137, 231
futility n 137
futon n 257
future adj/n 88
future life n *afterlife* 202
future perfect n 264

future shock n 315
futureless adj 251
futures n 245
futurism n 278
futurist adj/n 226
futuristic adj 284
futuristics n 317
futurology n 304
futz v (Am) 300
fuzz n *as in "peach fuzz"* 177
fuzz n (Am) *police* 292
fuzz n *type of fungus* 177
fuzz v 177
fuzzle v *get drunk* 162
fuzzle v *befuddle* 162
fuzzy adj *blurry* 190
fuzzy adj *covered with fuzz* 190
fuzzy logic n 315

G

G, gee n *slang $1,000* 290
G spot n 326
G suit n (Am) *gravity suit* 303
gab n/v *babble* 191
gab v *obs. mock* 61
gab n/v *chat* 191
gabardine n *type of cotton* 107, 274
gabardine n *type of dress* 107, 274
gabber v 191
gabble n/v 141
gabbro n 219
gabfest n (Am) 268
gable n 33
gable roof n 222
gad v *as in "gad about"* 96
gadabout n 96, 232; adj 232
gadbee n 119, 165
gadfly n 119
gadfly n *fig.* 119
gadfly n *gadabout* 144
gad/gads interj 102
gadget n 251
gadgeteer n 251, 301
gadgetry n 251, 284
gadling n *obs. friend* 18
gadso interj *gadzooks* 175
gadzookery n (Brit) *using archaic words* 311
gadzooks interj 175
gaff v *cheat, con* 300
gaff n *type of hook or spur* 36
gaff n *spec. to fish* 36
gaffe n 278
gaffer n *arch. goodfellow, old man; old woman* 130

gaffer, grandfather n 130
gag v *silence* 115
gag n *joke* 244
gag v *retch* 182
gag v 244
gag n *prank* 244
gag law n (Am) 203
gag rule n (Am) 215
gaga adj 281
gaggle n *of geese* 64
gagster n 299
Gaia hypothesis n 322
gaiety n 150
gain v 94
gainful adj 115
gaingiving n *misgiving* 149
gainly adj 251
gainsay v 58
gainstand v *resist* 61
gait n 68
gaiter n *type of shoe* 197
gal n 204
gal Friday n 313
gala n/adj 205
gala n/adj *obs. clothing worthy of a gala* 205
galactic adj 65, 220
galaxy n *gen.* 65
galaxy n *star grouping* 220
galaxy n *Milky Way* 65, 220
gale n 105
galena n 145
galiot n *type of sailing vessel* 72
gall n *gall bladder* 13
gall n *fig.* 13
gall n *bile* 13
gall v *chafe, vex* 143
gall bladder n 166
gallant adj *ostentatious* 73
gallant v *court* 170
gallant adj/n 73
galleass n *type of fighting ship* 112
galleon n *type of ship* 107
galleria n 263
gallery n *theater sense* 153
gallery n *for art display* 128
gallery n 69
gallery n *golf, etc., audience* 263
gallerygoer n 265
galley n 122
galley n *type of ship* 36
galley n Literature/Writing 264
galley proof n 264
galleywest adv *into confusion* 249

galligaskins n *type of loose breeches* 123
gallimaufry n *potpourri* 133
gallinipper n *biting insect* 165
gallipot n *type of pot used by pharmacists* 69
gallivant v 218
gallon n 31
galloon n *type of trim* 149
gallop n/v 72
gallopade n *type of dance* 228
gallous adj *deserving of hanging* 82
gallows n 20
gallows bird n 194
gallows humor n 275
gallows tree n 20
gallstone n 195
Gallup poll n 296
galluses n *suspenders* 223
gally adj *arch. galled* 73
galoot n *oaf* 216
galoot n *rookie marine* 216
galop n *type of dance* 228
galore adv 160
galosh n 71
galp v *obs. gawk* 32
galumph v 253
galvanic battery n 210
galvanism n 195
galvanize v 195, 218
galvanize v *fig.* 218
galvanized iron n 233
galvanometer n 210
gam n *leg* 204
gam n (Am) *school of whales* 220
gam v *talk* 235
gamahuche n/v *oral sex* 244
gamay n *type of wine* 241
gambado n *type of boot* 168
gambeson n *type of tunic* 35
gambit n *chess term* 170, 250
gambit n *gen.* 170, 250
gamble v *risk* 191
gamble n 217
gamble v *wager* 191
gamble n 191
gambol v *make merry* 115, 149
gambol v *leap* 115
gambol n 115
gambol n 149
gambrel roof n (Am) 196
game adj *lame* 196
game n *as in "board game"* 262
game n *fun* 18
game n *as in "play games with the truth"* 175

game n Animals 30
game n Sports 40
game bird n 237
game fish n 237
game fowl n 194
game of chance n 289
game plan n 307
game show n 312
gamecock n 165
gameful obs. 40
gamekeeper n 168
gamesmanship n 304
gamesome adj fun-loving 40
gamete n 255
gamey adj plucky 234
gamey adj 249
gamin n boy urchin 229, 266
gamine n girl urchin 229, 266
gamma radiation n 272
gamma ray n 272
gammer n old woman 130
gamut n General/Miscellaneous 158
gamut n spec. music sense 158
ganch v 155
gander n male goose 11
gander n idiot, fool 132
gander n as in "take a gander" 283
gandy dancer n 281
ganef n swindler 291
gang n 80
gang v as in "gang aft agley" 28
gang n group 51
gang n applied to people 51
gang v 51
gang plow n 223
gang rape n/v 319
gang up v 295
gangbang n/v (Am) 307
gangbuster n 300
gangland n (Am) 283
gangle v be gangly 217, 238, 320
gangling adj 217, 238
gangling adj Slang 320
ganglion n 166
ganglion n type of swelling 166
gangly 217, 238
gangly adj 320
gangplank n (Am) 224
gangrene n 106
gangshag 307
gangsta n type of rap music 327
gangster n (Am) 80, 267
gangway n 178
gangway interj 292

gangway n obs. road 178
ganja n 175
gantelope n gauntlet 163
gap n 51
gape n/v 32
gape-seed n something gaped at 144
gap-toothed adj 120
gar n (Am) 64, 194
gar interj 132
garage n/v 273
garage sale n (Am) 316
Garand rifle n M-1 300
garb n/v 149
garb n obs. fashion 149
garbage n 121
garbage n obs. dung 121
garbageman n (Am) 263
garbanzo n 196
garble v remove garbage 180
garble v miscommunicate 180
garboil n arch. confusion 108
garbology n 322
garcon n 152
garde-manger n preparer of cold foods 289
garden n 15, 34; v 34
garden n as in "Madison Square Gardens" 122
garden apartment n 303
garden city n 222
Garden of Eden n 111
gardener n 15, 34
gardenia n 193
garden-variety adj 294
garderobe n arch. type of storeroom 69
gardyloo interj 156
garefowl n great auk 165
garfish n 64, 194
gargantuan adj 138
gargle n slang alcoholic drink 259
gargle n/v 116
gargoyle n 47
garibaldi n 242
garish adj 115
garland n/v 52
garlic n 15
garment n 35
garner v collect in a granary 94
garner v fig. collect 94
garner n granary, accumulation 34
garnet n 29
garpike n type of fish 194
garret n obs. type of fortified turret 33

garret n 33
garrison n/v 80
garrison n obs. gen. defense 80
garrison v 80
garrison cap n (Am) 303
Garrison finish n late come-from-behind finish 301
garrote v 247
garrote/garote/garotte/garrotte v 247
garrote/garote/garotte/garrotte n 155
garrote/garote/garotte/garrotte n 155
garrulity n 124
garrulous adj 124
garter n 35
garter belt n 303
garter snake n (Am) 194
garth n courtyard, yard 33
gas v 291
gas n flatulence 256
gas n something exciting 313
gas n 181
gas n/v chitchat 249
gas n natural gas 195
gas n gasoline 285
gas n mystical sense 181
gas burner n 210
gas chamber n 306
gas fitter n 244
gas guzzler n 317
gas log n 257
gas main n 211
gas mask n 280
gas meter n 210
gas station n 285
gas turbine n 272
gasbag n 249, 268
gaseous adj 193, 266
gash n/v 51
gash n slang vagina 256
gashouse n (Am) 257
gaslight n 211
gasman n 213
gasohol n 322
gasoline n (Am) 237
gasp n/v 94
gasper n (Brit) cigarette 216
gassed adj (Brit) drunk 292
gasser n 307
gassy adj 193, 206
gast v arch. frighten 17
gastight adj 233
gastralgia n 239
gastrectomy n 257
gastric adj 166

gastric gland n 256
gastric juice n 182
gastric ulcer n 273
gastritis n 210
gastroenterology n 273
gastrointestinal adj 221
gastronome n 211
gastronomy n 211
gastropod n 219
gastroscope n 257
gasworks n 210
gat n (Am) pistol 277
gate n 14
gate n total attendance 265
gate n journey 68
gate v confine by curfew 235
gate-crasher n 292
gatefold n 305
gatehouse n 69
gatekeeper n 126
gateleg table n 273
gateway n 183
gateway drug n 327
gather v deduce, know 141
gather n/v 26
gather n 26
gathering n 22
gathers n Cloth/Clothing 123
gatling gun n (Am) 248
gator n (Am) 220
gauche adj 204
gaucherie n 204
gaucho n 212
gaud n ostentatious trinket 71, 103
gaud v obs. 71
gaudery n 71, 103
gaudy adj 71, 103
gauge n measuring tool 31
gauge n standard 31
gauge v 31
gaunt adj 68
gaunt adj obs. slim 68
gauntlet n as in "run the gauntlet" 176
gauntlet n armored glove 80
gauss n 256
Gaussian curve, Gaussian distribution n 272
gauze n 123
gavel n/v (Am) 242
gavel n type of mallet 242
gavel-to-gavel adj 319
gaw v obs. gape 61
gawd interj 267
gawk n/v 207
gawkish adj 182, 256
gawky adj/n 182

gawp v *gape* 166
gay adj *immoral* 228
gay adj *merry* 37
gay adj *homosexual* 37, 281; n 281
gay adj *light* 37
gaysome adj 37
gaze n/v 84
gaze v *stare blankly* 120
gaze v 120
gazebo n 196
gazehound n *kind of the opp. of bloodhound* 119
gazelle n 119
gazette n 152
gazpacho n 223
geal v *obs. congeal* 98
gear n *individual gear* 107
gear adj *(Am) great* 312
gear n *clothing, equipment* 33
gear n *gear mechanisms* 107
gear up v 312
gearbox n 260
gearshift n 288
gearwheel n 107, 242
gecko n 181
gee interj/v *as in "gee and haw"* 156, 267
gee interj *as in "gee whillikers"* 248
gee whillikins interj 248
gee whiz interj *(Am)* 248, 267; adj 267
gee-ho interj 156
geek n 268
gee-whiz adj 300
geezer n 268
gefilte fish n 259
gegenschein n *light in the night sky* 255
Geiger counter n 285
geir n *obs. vulture* 119
geisha n 263
gel n/v 206, 268
gelate n/v *gelatin* 284
gelati n *type of ice cream* 326
gelatin n *Slang* 268
gelatin n 206
gelatin dynamite n 266
gelato n *type of ice cream* 287
geld v *obs. expurgate, bowdlerize* 128
geld v *castrate* 34
gelding n 34
gelt n *money* 110
gem n 10
gem n *fig.* 10
gemman n *gentleman* 132

gemologist n 210, 298
gemology n 210, 298
gemsbok n *type of antelope* 194
gemstone n 10
gender v *engender* 61
gender n *Language and Speaking* 41
gender n *sex* 66
gender v *arch. copulate* 75
gender bender n 325
gender gap n 319
gender-specific adj 327
gene n 279
gene mapping v 322
gene pool n 302
gene splicing n 322
genealogist n 151, 226
genealogy n *study of ancestry* 40, 226
genealogy n *spec. ancestry* 40, 226
general adj 49
general n *obs. neutral color* 92
general n War/Military/Violence 131
general admission n 305
general delivery n *(Am)* 227
general election n *(Am)* 188
general partnership n 263
general post office n 172
general practitioner n 257
general quarters n 277
general relativity n 279
general semantics n 299
general store n *(Am)* 226
general strike n *(Am)* 213
generaless n War/Military/Violence 131
generalist n 157
generality n 86
generalization n 205
generalize v 97
general-purpose adj 258
generate v 141
generation n 40
generator n 195
generic n *non-brand-name product* 318
generic adj 179
generosity n 138, 157
generosity n *noble birth* 157
generous adj 138
genesis n *Religion* 20
genesis n *fig.* 20
genetic code n 315
genetic drift n 302
genetic engineering n 315
genetic fingerprinting n 326

genetic map n 309
genetic screening n 322
geneticist n 281
genetics n 272
genetrix n *mother* 75
Geneva cross n 270
genial adj *related to reproduction* 124
genial adj *contributing to growth* 124
genial adj *cheerful* 124
genial adj *related to the chin* 221
genie n *jinn* 189
genie n *obs. genius* 189
genital adj 66
genital herpes n 316
genitalia n 66, 256
genitals 66, 256
genitor n *arch. parent* 75
genitories n *arch. testicles* 66
genius n 132
genius n *guardian angel* 81
genius n *type of supernatural guardian* 81
genius n *aptitude* 151
genius loci n 81, 156
genocide n 306
genoise n *type of cake* 297
genotype n 272
genre n 205
gent n 43, 129
gent adj *obs. elegant* 36
gent adj *graceful; genteel* 36
genteel adj *arch. stylish* 123, 154; n 154
genteel adj 154
genteelism n 291
gentile adj/n 78
gentilesse n *arch. courteous manner* 38
gentle adj *kindly, easy* 124
gentle adj *arch. high-born* 43
gentle adj *obs. graceful* 61
gentle adj *highborn* 124
gentle *obs. graceful* 36
gentle n 43
gentlefolk n 130
gentleman n 43, 44, 129
gentleman of fortune n 269
gentleman-at-arms n 247
gentleman-commoner n 174
gentleman-farmer n 188
gentleman's gentleman n 185
gentlemen's agreement n *(Am)* 269
gentleperson n 43, 44, 305
gentler sex n 133
gentlewoman n 43, 44

gentlewoman 43
gentrice n *arch. high birth* 43
gentrification n 316
gentrify v 316
gentry n *noble birth* 44
gentry n *persons of noble birth* 44
gents n *(Brit) men's room* 297
genu n *knee* 238
genuflect v *fig.* 247
genuflect v *bow in worship* 247
genuflect v *obs. bend the knee* 247
genuine adj *real* 160, 252
genuine adj *sincere* 160, 252
genus n 119
geobotany n 272
geocentric adj 164
geochemistry n 272
geochronology n 255
geode n 164
geodesic adj 221
geodesic dome n 310
geographer n 110
geographic adj 99, 118
geographical adj 99, 118
geographical mile n 238
geography n 99
geoid n *hypothetical sphere at earth sea level* 255
geologer n 200
geologic adj 195
geologic time n 237
geological adj 195
geologist n 200
geology n 195
geology n *obs. gen. earth study* 195
geomagnetic storm n 302
geomancy n 81
geometric adj 65
geometric mean n 272
geometric progression n 237
geometric series n *geometric progression* 272
geometrical adj 65
geometrician n 99
geometry n 31
geometry n *obs. land-measurement* 63
geomorphology n 255
geophagy n *eating dirt* 222
geophone n 282
geophysics n 255
geopolitics n 276
georgette n *type of fabric* 280
Georgia pine n *(Am)* 194

georgic adj *agricultural, pastoral* 184

georgic n *poem about agriculture* 110

georgical adj *agricultural* 184

geoscience n 302

geotectonic adj 255

geothermal adj 237

geotropic adj 237

geotropism n 237

geranium n 105

gerbil n 220

geriatric n *old person* 285; adj 273

geriatrician n 286

geriatrics n 273

geriatrist n 286

germ n *something that germinates* 147

germ n *something that can germinate* 64, 147

germ n *Medicine* 147

germ n *fig.* 64

germ cell n 147, 238

germ theory n 239

germ warfare n 300

German measles n 222

German shepherd n 285

German shorthaired pointer n 296

German wirehaired pointer n 315

germane adj 160

germen v 64

germicide n 257

germinate v 143

Geronimo interj (Am) 307

gerrymander n/v (Am) 215

gerund n 110

gest n *gesture* 98

gestalt n 293

Gestalt psychology n 288

gestapo n 300

gestate v 147, 238

gestation n *obs. gen. carrying* 147

gestation n 147

geste n *deportment* 78

gestening n *obs. hospitality* 61

gesticulant adj 270

gesticulate v 87, 147

gesticulation n 87, 147

gesture n/v 68

gesture n *obs. general bodily carriage, motion* 68

gesture language n 245

gesundheit interj (Am) 277

get v *understand* 317

get v *win* 61

get v *as in "the problems got to him"* 253

get v *as in "gotcha"* 249

get v *beget* 60

get n *child* 40

get v *achieve, as in "get drunk"* 143

get v 55

get v *arrive at* 98

get it v (Am) *as in "you're gonna get it!"* 250

get off v (Am) *have orgasm* 323

getatable adj *get-at-able* 207

getaway n 250

get-out n *as in "all get-out"* 249

get-together n 284

getup n 223

get-up-and-go n 249

gewgaw n 52

gewürztraminer n *type of wine* 303

geyser n 164

ghast adj *ghastly* 54, 160

ghastful adj 54

ghastly adj 54

ghee n 167

gherkin n 148

ghetto n *gen.* 148, 254

ghetto n *Jewish quarter* 148, 254

ghetto v 254, 301

ghotto n *Jewish confinement area* 254

ghetto blaster n 324

ghost n *obs. corpse* 28, 45

ghost n *apparition* 81

ghost v *arch. die* 81, 130

ghost n *modern sense* 28, 248

ghost n *obs. gen. spirit* 28

ghost n *obs. soul* 28, 81

ghost n *obs. evil person* 28

ghost v *Literature/Writing* 264; n 264, 290

ghost dance n (Am) 267

ghost story n 215

ghost town n 236

ghostess n 81, 248

ghosting n *on a TV* 311

ghostly adj 21

ghostly adj *spiritual* 28

ghostwrite v 264, 290

ghostwriter n 264, 290

ghoul n 203, 234

ghoulie n 292

ghoulish 203

GI adj *galvanized iron* 282

GI adj/v 306; n 282, 306

giant n Heavens/Sky 279

giant n 47

giant adj 47

giant anteater n 296

giant cactus n 254

giant clam n 255

giant panda n 279

giant schnauzer n 296

giant sequoia n 296

giant squid n 255

giant star n 279

giant tortoise n 272

giantess n 47, 81

giantism n Medicine 257

giantism n *gen.* 257

gib n *gelded cat* 64

gib n *obs. old woman* 112

gibber v/n 110

gibber v 157

gibberish adj *obs.* 110

gibberish n 110

gibbet n 45

gibbet n *gen. execution by hanging* 45

gibbon n 194

gibe n/v 141

giblets n 122

Gibson n *type of martini* 287

Gibson girl n (Am) 260

giddify v 89

giddy adj *obs. crazy* 89

giddy adj *lightheaded* 89

giddy adj *dizzy* 89

giddy v 89

giddyap interj (Am) 267

gift n *obs. bribe* 47

gift n/v 47

gift certificate n 304

gift of gab n 176

gift of tongues n 129

gift wrap n/v 298

gifted adj 151

giftware n 273

gig n *type of fishing gear* 184; v 184

gig n *obs. bimbo* 47

gig n/v *demerit* 306

gig n *as in "whirlygig," light boat* 36; v 36

gig n *musician's job* 290; v 290

gigabyte n 322

gigantean adj 159, 178, 217

gigantesque adj 159, 178, 217

gigantic adj 159, 178, 217

gigantic adj *related to giants* 178

gigantism n 257

gigawatt n 315

giggle v 115

giggle water n (Am) *slang alcohol* 287

giglet n *slut* 47

GIGO n *garbage in, garbage out* 320

gigolo n 289

gigot n *leg of meat* 106

Gila monster n (Am) 254

gild v 28

gild v *"gild" with blood* 144

gilded adj 28

gilden adj *obs. golden* 28

gilden v *obs.* 28

gill n *girl* 82

gill n *as in "fish gills"* 31

gill n *on a mushroom* 181

gillery n *con, trick* 61

gill-flirt n *arch. slut* 175

gilt n *gold* 28, 144

gimcrack n 88, 205

gimcrackery n 88, 205

gimlet n 36

gimlet adj 206

gimlet n *type of drink* 287

gimlet eye n *sharp eye, look* 195, 216

gimlet-eyed adj *sharp-eyed* 195, 216

gimme n/v 267

gimmick n/v (Am) 294

gimmickry 294

gimp n *bravura, spirit* 277

gimp n (Am) *slang cripple* 286; v 286

gin n Drink 183

gin n *as in "cotton gin"* 197

gin n *obs. stone-thrower* 45

gin n 304, 311

gin v *begin* 55

gin and tonic n 297

gin mill n (Am) 245

gin rummy n 304

gingall n *type of gun* 229

ginger n/adj 10

ginger adj/n *the color* 252

ginger ale n 259

ginger beer n 211

ginger jar n 257

gingerade n 241

gingerbread n 34

gingerly adj 114

gingerroot n 219

gingersnap n 211

gingham n 149

gingiva n 256

gingivitis n 239

gingko n 193

gink n (Am) *person* 277

ginseng n 164

gipser n *belt-hung bag* 71

giraffe n *type of piano* 129

giraffe n Animals 119

gird v *fig.* 27

gird v *as in "girding one's loins"* 27

gird v *obs. hit* 117

gird v *mock* 117

girder n 148

girdle n *corset* 16, 287

girdle n *gen.* 16, 287

girl n 244

girl n *female worker* 171

girl n *girlfriend* 170

girl n 134

girl n *male or female child* 134

girl Friday n 300

girleen n 251

girlfriend n 170, 244

girlish adj 137

gist n The Law 188

gist n *gen.* 188

gittern n *a medieval guitar* 77

give v *yield* 143

give v 26

give v *as in "give a damn"* 180

give v 143

give-and-take n 204

giveaway n (Am) 251

given name n (Am) 232

gizmo n 308

gizzard n 64

glabella n *area between the eyebrows* 120

glace adj *candied, frosted* 223

glacial adj *cold* 178

glacial adj *related to glaciers* 178

glaciarium n *type of skating rink* 244

glaciate v 236

glaciate v *freeze* 236

glacier n 181

glaciology n 255

glad v *obs. be glad* 17

glad adj *obs. bright* 17

glad 11

glad adj 17

glad n Plants 285

glad v *arch. gladden* 17

glad v *arch.* 37

glad hand n/v 269

glad rags n 269

gladden v 37

glade n 63

gladful adj 17, 38

gladiator n 80

gladiola n 11, 285

gladiolus n 11, 285

gladsome adj 17, 72

gladstone n *type of suitcase* 258

glair n *egg white* 34

glaive n *type of sword* 45

glamorize v (Am) 301

glamour n 247

glamour n *magic* 247

glamour-puss n 304

glam-rock n 324

glance v *as in "glance off"* 96

glance n/v *as in "glance at"* 96, 136

gland n 166

glans n *head of penis or clitoris* 147

glare n/v 58

glare n (Am) *smooth surface, as in "glare ice"* 134

glare v *stare* 58, 152

glasphalt n *type of road surface* 317

glass n *hourglass* 120

glass n *mirror* 69

glass n 14

glass n *as in "eyeglass"* 106

glass v *look into a mirror* 143

glass n *as in "drinking glass"* 14

glass n *telescope* 149

glass ceiling n 327

glass eye n 147

glass fiber n 270

glass harmonica n 276

glass jaw n 283

glassblowing n 226

glassie n *type of marble* 262

glassmaker n 126

glassware n 183

glassy-eyed adj 257

glastnost n 327

glaucoma n 147

glaze v *install glass* 92

glaze v *apply glassy layer* 92

glaze n 92

glazier n 40

gleam n/v 22

gleam v 22

glean v 60

glee n *happiness* 38

glee n *obs. fun* 38

glee n *type of song* 173, 214

glee club n 214

gleed n *arch. ember* 14

gleeful adj 38

gleek n *obs.* 126

gleek v *joke* 126

gleeman n *roving minstrel* 19

gleesome adj 38

gleimy adj *obs. sticky* 98

glen n 99

glen plaid n 287

glengarry n *type of cap* 223

glib adj 124

glide v 26

glide path n 298

glider n 261

glim n *type of lamp* 167

glimmer v *obs. shine brightly* 60

glimmer v *shine dimly* 60

glimpse v *see briefly* 208

glimpse v *glimmer* 208

glisten n/v 27

glister v *glisten* 94

glitch n 315

glitter n/v 60

glitter rock n 324

glitterati n 299

glitz n 320

glitzy adj 320

gloam n *twilight* 10, 209

gloaming n *twilight* 10, 209

gloat v 198

gloat v *glance at* 198

glob n 270

global adj *worldwide* 271

global adj *related to globes* 271

global village n 313

global warming n 326

globalism n (Am) 306

globe n *our planet* 86

globe n *round map* 86

globe n *sphere* 86

globe-trotter n 249

globular cluster n 237

glockenspiel n 214

glogg n *type of drink* 287

glom v 277

gloom v *look gloomy* 60; n 60

gloom n 158

gloomy adj 60, 138

glop n 294

glorify v 60

glorious adj 51, 53

glory n/v 51

glory/glory be interj 215

gloss n *explanation—related to glossary* 41, 76

gloss n *glaze* 114; v 114

gloss v 41

glossarist n Literature/Writing 76, 201

glossary n *a collection of glosses* 41, 76

glossator n *gloss writer* 76, 201

glossy n 290

glottis n 120

glout v *scowl, frown* 73

glove n 15

glove box n 298

glove compartment n 298, 304

glove leather n 184

glover n 75

glow v *arch. glower* 73

glow n/v 27

glow lamp n 256

glower v 184

glower v *gaze* 184

glowworm n 31

glucose n 232

glue n/v 53

glue sniffing n (Am) 319

glum v *obs.* 108

glum adj 108

gluon n *type of quark* 322

glut v *eat greedily* 122

glut v *as in "glut the market"* 59

gluteus n 166

gluteus maximus n 166, 256

glutton n 34

glutton v *obs.* 34

gluttonous 34

gluttony n 34

glycerine n 219

glycerol n 219

glyph n 227

G-man n 291

gnar v *snarl* 98

gnarl v *obs.* 98

gnash v 97

gnast v *obs. gnash* 61

gnat n 11

gnatcatcher n *type of bird* 220

gnatter v 232

gnaw v 27

gnocchi n *type of dumpling* 259

gnome n 175

gnome n *aphorism* 127

gnomon n *sundial pointer* 105

gnosis n 129

gnostic n 129

gnosticism n 129

gnu n 194

go n *as in "on the go"* 190

go n *the game* 262

go v 26

go v *as in "how the story goes"* 143

go v *die* 80

go ape v 311

go down v (Am) *perform oral sex* 281

go for it v 325

go public v 317

go to interj 102

go up v (Brit) *attend a university* 101

goad n/v 16, 141

go-ahead n *permission* 233, 321

go-ahead adj (Am) *energetic* 233

goal n 108

goal n *fig.* 108

goal n *obs. border* 108

goalie n 171, 289

goalkeeper n 170, 289

goalpost n 244

goaltender n 170, 275, 289

go-around n 292

goat n 11

goat cheese n 259

goatee n (Am) 224

goatherd n 15

gob v *spit* 268

gob n 84

gobble v *make turkey noises* 180; n 180

gobble v *eat quickly* 148

gobbledygook n 307

gobbler n *turkey* 181

go-between n 136

goblet n *stemmed glassware* 33, 258

goblet n *drinking bowl* 33, 258

goblin n 47

go-cart n *baby carriage* 169

god v 19, 129

god n 19, 78

god-awful adj (Am) 270

godchild n 18, 39

goddamned, goddamn adj/adv 284

goddaughter n 18

goddaughter 18

goddaughter 18, 39

goddess n *fig.* 78

goddess n 19, 78

godet n *clothing term* 242

go-devil n (Am) *type of sled* 224

godfather n 18

God-fearing adj 228

godforsaken adj 251

godhead n 43

godless adj 111

godling n 101

God-man n *God in human form* 129

godmother n 18

godparent n 18, 244

God's acre n *churchyard* 154

godsend n 216

godson n 18, 39

Godspeed interj 47

goety n *type of magic* 132

gofer n 320

go-getter n (Am) 292

goggle v 94

goggle-eye n *type of fish* 220

goggle-eyed adj 67

goggles n 123

go-go adj 321

going-over n (Am) 250

goings-on n 204

goiter n 147

gold n *the color* 9

gold n 9

gold certificate n (Am) 245

gold coast n *upperclass residential area* 254

gold digger n (Am) 231

gold dust n 181

gold medal n 275

gold mine n 101

gold reserve n (Am) 245

gold rush n 269

gold standard n (Am) 227

goldarn adj 230, 248

goldarned 230

goldbrick n/v (Am) 245

goldbug n (Am) 266

gold-dig v 231

golden age n 120, 315

golden handcuffs n 327

golden handshake n 311

golden oldie n (Am) 318

golden parachute n 327

golden plover n 194

golden retriever n 279

golden rule n 215

golden-ager n 120, 315

goldenrod n 118

goldfinch n 11

goldfish n 165

goldsmith n 18

golem n 267

golf n 75

golf ball n 108

golf cart n 263

golf course n 263

golly interj 203

gomer n *dimwit* 320

Gomorrah n *a place of sin* 277

gonad n 256

gondola n 107

gondolier n 107, 149

gone adj 139

gone goose n (Am) *dead duck* 231

goner n 229

gonfalon n *type of banner* 137

gong n 129

gongoozler n (Am) 277

gonna v 283

gonorrhea n 106

gonzo adj 324

goo n (Am) 270

goober n *peanut* 223

good adj/n 23

good afternoon 21, 81, 248, 292

good book n Religion 247

good day interj 21, 81, 248, 292

good deal n 269

good evening interj 21, 81, 248, 292

good faith n 269

good fellow n 47

good humor n 150

good life n 308

good morning interj 21, 81, 248, 292

good nature n 73

good old boy n 321

Good Samaritan n 231

goodbye interj/n 132

good-natured 73

good-even interj 81, 248, 292

good-for-nothing adj/n 112

good-hearted adj 123

good-humored adj 150

goodie two-shoes n/adj 204

goodlike adj 143

good-looking adj 197

goodly adj *handsome* 54

goodly adj 54

goodman n *Master, Mr.* 43

good-morrow interj 21, 81, 248, 292

good-tempered adj 198

goodwife n *Mrs.* 43, 44

goodwill n 17

goody interj 203

goody n 44

goody n Insults 249

goody n *goodwife* 132

goody n *as in "goodies"* 204

goody-goody n 249

gooey adj 278

goof n 312

goof n/v 300

goof n *dolt* 283

goof v 283

goof n *mistake* 283

goof off n 298

goofball n 283, 301

goof-off n 313

goof-up n 307

goofy adj 284

googly-eyed adj 293

googol n 296

goo-goo eyes n 268

gook n *goo* 300

goon n Insults 293

goon n *hired thug* 293

gooney bird n 255

goop n 313

goose v 267

goose n 11

goose bumps n 212, 261, 296

goose egg n *slang zero* 237

goose pimples n 212, 261, 296

goose step n/v 215

gooseberry n 105

gooseflesh n 212, 261, 296

gooseflesh n *lit.* 212

gooseherd n 34

gopher n 194

gopher snake n (Am) 220

gorblimey interj 267

Gordian knot n 133

gore v *pierce* 80

gore n *triangular piece of cloth or land* 22

gore n *obs. dung, offal* 130

gore n *blood, esp. clotted blood* 130

gore n 80

gore v War/Military/Violence 130

gorge n 193

gorge n *throat* 32

gorge v *stuff yourself* 34

gorgeous adj 103

gorgon n 81

gorgonize v *mesmerize, petrify* 150

gorgonzola n *type of cheese* 259

gorilla n Animals 194

gorilla n *fig.* 194

gormandize v *gorge* 107

gorp n 316

gory adj 130

gosh interj 203

gosling n 11, 31

gospel n *fig.* 19

gospel n Religion 19

gossamer adj 51, 217; n 51

gossip n *gossipy person* 134, 232

gossip n *result of gossiping* 134, 232

gossip n *obs. godparent* 134

gossip v 134, 162, 232

gossipmonger n 231

gothic adj 149

Gothic arch n 183

Gothic revival n 239

gotta v 292

gouache n 265

Gouda n 241

gouge v *cheat, soak* 248

gouge v 141

gouge n/v Tools 36

goulash n 241

gourd n *head* 221

gourd n 30

gourmand n *gourmet* 70

gourmand n *glutton* 70

gourmet adj/n 211

gout n 32

gouts n *arch. akin to oats* 11

govern v 44

governance n 44, 79

governess n 75

government n 44, 79

government issue adj 300

governmentese n 305

governor n 44

governor, guvner n Slang 268

gowk n *idiot* 133

gowk n *type of bird* 133

gown n *robe* 35

gown n *in hospitals* 33, 35

gown n *dress* 35

gownsman n 126

grab v 141

grab bag n (Am) 249

grabble v 141

grace v 141

grace n Physical Description 32

grace n Religion 20, 43

grace n *obs. graces gen. thanks* 43

grace cup n 130

grace period n 307

graceful adj Physical Description 68

graceful Religion 78

graceless adj Religion 78

graceless adj *inelegant* 68, 78

gracile adj *slim* 147

gracious adj 37

grackle n 194

grad n 78, 247; adj 247

gradation n 114

grade n *as in "first grade"* 247

grade n *stage, level* 206

grade v *arrange into grades or categories* 179

grade n *slope, gradation* 232

grade n *as in "grade A"* 247

grade n *as in "gradation in color"* 206

grade point n 312

grade point average n 312, 319

grade school n (Am) 247

gradely adj *worthy of praise* 61

grader n (Am) 224

gradient n 232

gradual n *type of hymnal* 78

gradual adj 178

gradual adj *obs. in stages, gradated* 178

graduate v *earn a degree* 228

graduate n 78

graduate v *earn a degree* 78

graduate v *award a degree* 228

graduate v *award a degree* 78

graduate n *type of measuring glass* 256

graduation n Education 78, 228

graffito/graffiti n 245

graft v/n 100

graft n *illicit profiteering* 248; v 248

graft n *as in "skin graft"* 257; v 257

graham cracker n (Am) 211

graham flour n (Am) *whole wheat flour* 223

grail n 43

grain n *as in "grain of truth"* 49

grain n Measurment 66

grain n *graininess* 87

grain n *as in "grain of sand"* 49

grain n *oats, etc.* 35

grain n *as in "wood grain"* 158

grain n *kernel* 49

grain n *spec. to photos* 87

grain alcohol n 259

grain elevator n 241

grain of salt n 157

grain sorghum n 280

grainfield n 212

gram n Measurement 195

gram n *gramma* 298

gram n *chickpea and other such plants* 181

gram calorie n 273

gram-atomic weight n 286

gramercy interj *mercy me!* 47, 156

gramercy interj *thanks* 47, 156

grammar n *study of grammar* 76, 245

grammar n *grammar rules* 76, 245

grammar school n 77

grammarian n 76

gramophone n 265

gramp n*grampa* 262

grampus n *type of dolphin* 105

granary n 107

grand n *$1,000* 289

grand adj *awe-inspiring, large* 191

grand n *grand piano* 228

grand dame n 188

grand duchess n 174, 202, 229

grand duchy n 174, 202, 229

grand duke n 174, 202, 229

grand finale n 201

grand jury n 102

grand larceny n 229

grand mal n *type of epilepsy* 257

grand marshal n 312

grand old man n 250

grand opera n 214

grand piano n 228

grand prix n 244

grand theft n 292

grand tour n 176

grand touring car n 317

grand unified theory n 322

grandaunt n 75, 226

grandbaby n 126, 281

grandchild n 126

granddad n 75, 199, 262

granddaddy n 75, 199, 262

granddaughter n 126, 151

grandee n 132

grandeur n 168

grandeur n *power* 168

grandeur n *phys. height* 168

grandfather n 75, 199, 262

grandfather v 325

grandfather clause n (Am) 267

grandfather clock n 272

grandiloquence, grandiloquent n, adj 135

grandiose adj 234

grandity *obs.* 168

grandity n *obs. grandeur* 144

grandkid n 126

grandma n 75, 170, 199

grandmamma n 75, 170, 199

grandmother n 75, 170, 199

grandnephew n 151, 226

grandniece n 151, 226

grandpa n 75, 199, 262

grandpapa n 75, 199, 262

grandpappy n 75, 199, 262

grandparent n 226

grandpop n 75, 199, 262

grandsire n *grandfather* 262

grandsire n *animal's grandparent* 34

grandson n 126, 151

grandstand n/v 226, 284

granduncle n 75, 226

granita n *type of drink* 241

granite n *fig.* 145

granite n 145

granny n 75, 145, 199

granny battering n 327

granny dress n 274

granny glasses n 317

granny knot n 251

Granny Smith n *type of apple* 259

granola n 241

grant n/v 56

grantee n 86

grant-in-aid n 247

granula n *obs.* 176

granular adj 176

granule n 176

grape n Plants 29

grape n War/Military/Violence 174, 188

grape sugar n 223

grapefruit n 209

grapeshot n War/Military/Violence 174, 188

grapevine n 164

graph n/v Mathematics 256

graph paper n 285

graphic adj 160

graphic n 305

graphic arts n 173

graphic equalizer n 318

graphic novel n 327

graphics n 265

graphics tablet n 322

graphite n 193

grapholect n *written language* 323

graphologist 246

graphology n *study of writing* 246

graphology n *study of handwriting* 246

grapple n 36, 107; v 36, 116

grappling iron n 107

grasp v *as in "grasp at"* 94

grasp v *take hold* 94; n 94

grass n Plants 10

grass n *the time when grass grows* 99
grass cloth n 241
grass court n 263
grass roots n 277
grass snake n (Am) 220
grass widow n *unmarried woman who has enjoyed the "fruits" of marriage* 113
grasshop n *obs.* 30
grasshopper n 30
grassland n (Am) 164
grassroots adj 277
grate n *grating* 84
grate v 94
grate adj *obs. pleasing* 117
grate v *fig.* 94
grateful adj 123
gratification 117
gratify v 117
gratify v *obs. grate, make pleasant* 117
gratifying adj 117
gratin n *the crust on au gratin* 168
gratine adj *au gratin* 287
gratine v 287
grating adj *irritating* 137
grating n 148
gratis adj/adv 91
gratitude n 73
gratuitous adj *unnecessary* 178
gratuitous adj *gratis* 178
gratuity n 110
gratulate v *congratulate* 141
gratulate v *greet* 141
grave n *burial place* 20
grave v *arch.* 20
grave n *type of accent mark* 152
grave v *engrave, dig* 27
grave adj *somber* 107
gravedigger n 130
gravel n 29
gravel n *obs. sand* 29
graveless adj *without a grave, deathless* 155
graven image n *engraved, sculpted image* 82
graver n *engraver* 18
gravesite n 229
gravestone n 45
graveyard n 202
graveyard shift n (Am) 276
graving dock n *dry dock* 224
gravitas n *deadly seriousness* 288
gravitate v 145, 180

gravitate v *obs. affect with gravity* 180
gravitation n 145
gravitational wave n 272
graviton n 302
gravity n *seriousness* 100
gravity n 164
gravure n 264
gravy n *type of dressing* Food 34
gravy n *modern sense* Food 34
gravy train n 293
gray n *gray clothing* 35
gray adj/n 25
gray fox n 165
gray market n 307
gray matter n 221
gray squirrel n (Am) 146
gray whale n 236
gray wolf n 209
graybeard n 132
graymail n *akin to blackmail* 324
graze v *brush against* 143
graze v *eat grass, etc.* 15
grazier n 40
grease v *as in "grease his palm"* 112; n 112
grease n *obs. animal fat* 34; v 34
grease n *melted fat* 34
grease monkey n 289
grease pencil n 303
greaseball n 293
greasepaint n 265
greasy spoon n 289
great adj *talented* 23, 160
great adj *grand* 23
great adj *comparatively large* 23
great adj *myriad* 98
great adj *as in "the great one"* 54
great adj *large* 23
great adj *very good, exceptional* 23
great adj *pregnant* 32
great adj *texturally coarse* 23
great ape n 302
great auk n 219
great dane n 194
great divide n 236
great horned owl n 209
great laurel n 194
great power n *superpower* 266
great room n 167
great seal n 101
great vowel shift n 276
great white shark n 296
great-aunt n 170

greatcoat n 168
greaten 32
great-grandchild n 185, 199
great-granddaughter 185
great-grandfather n 108, 262
great-grandmother n 108, 262
great-grandparent n 108, 262
great-grandson n 185, 199
greathearted adj 73
great-nephew n 126, 262
great-niece n 126
great-uncle n 170
greave n *piece of armor* 45
grebe n *type of bird* 194
gree n *arch. goodwill* 37
gree n *degree* 61
gree v 37
greed n 17, 125
greedy adj 17
Greek cross n 190
Greek fire n 215
Greek Revival n 280
green adj *environmental* 322
green n *Sports* 199
green adj 23
green n *as in "village green"* 29
green n *slang money* 289
green adj *inexperienced* 54
green adj *jealous* 38
green n *Colors* 55
green adj *verdant* 63
green alga n 272
green bean n (Am) 223
Green Beret n 319
green card n 319
green corn n (Am) 145
green fingers 303
green fingers n *green thumb* 297
green flash n *green light at sunrise/set* 279
green light n 224, 298, 323
green onion n 223
green pepper n 168
green snake n (Am) 181
green soap n 221
green tea n 183
green thumb n 297, 303
green turtle n 165
green vegetable n 259
greenback n (Am) *Finances/Money* 245
greenbelt n 297
greenbrier n (Am) 196
green-eyed monster n 125
greenfinch n 99
greengrocer n 185, 226
greengrocery n 185, 226

greenhorn n *young animal* 99, 175
greenhorn n *fig.* 99, 175
greenhouse n 168
greenhouse effect n 296
greenroom n 187
greens n *Food* 183
greenskeeper n 184
greenstick fracture n 257
greenstuff n *green foodstuff* 241
Greenwich mean time n 296
greet v *lament* 17
greet, greeting v, n 20
greeting card n 258
gregarious adj *describing animals* 165, 202
gregarious adj *describing people* 165, 202
Gregorian calendar n 146
Gregorian chant n 201
gremlin n 292
grenade n *obs. pomegranate* 112
grenade n 112
grenadier n 174
grenadine n *type of syrup* 241
grenadine n *poultry dish* 183
Gresham's law n *economic theory* 245
grey friar n 78
greyhound n 11
grid n 232
grid 35
grid n *on paper* 232
griddle n *grill* 71
griddle n 71
griddle cake n 197
gride v *hurt, wound* 98
gridiron n 35, 232
gridlock n (Am) 323
grief n *obs. grievance* 36
grief n 36
grief n *obs. phys. pain* 36
grief-stricken adj 275
grievance n *obs. distress* 49
grievance n 49
grievance n *obs. hardship* 49
grievance n *obs. disease* 69
grievance committee n 294
grieve v 56
grieve v *obs. cause grief, hurt* 56
griffin/griffon/gryphon n 47
grift n/v *graft* 283
grig n *obs. little person* 82
grill n/v 167, 168
grill n *food that has been grilled* 167

grill n *type of restaurant* 167, 263
grille/grill n *grate* 167
grillroom n 263
grim v *arch.* 23
grim adj 23
grim reaper n 291
grimace n/v 169
grimalkin n *type of cat* 119
grime n 49
grimoire n *book of magic* 248
grimy adj 49
grin n/v 17
grin v *display teeth in anger* 17
grinch n 325
grind v 27
grind n/v *as in "bump and grind"* 307
grind v 60
grind v *as in "organ grinder"* 201
grind v *grind at* 27
grind n *spec. to coffee* 70
grind n/v *hard work* 245
grind v *obs. grind with your teeth* 60
grind v *as in "grind down"* 162
grind v *have sex* 151
grind away v *Slang* 249
grind house n 291
grind out v *Slang* 249
grinder n 168
grinders n *slang teeth* 66
grindle stone n *arch. grindstone* 33
grindstone n 35
gringo n 231
grip v/n 26
grip n *in films* 265
grip n *type of baggage* 258
griph n *obs. conundrum* 180
gripman n *cable car driver* 261
grippe n *the flu* 195
gripple adj *arch. penurious* 19
gripsack n (Am) 270
grisly adj *obs. touched by grisliness* 25
grisly adj 25
grist n 15
gristle n 13
gristmill n 148
grisy n *obs. grisly* 144
grit n *determination* 224
grit n *slang* 22
grit n 22
grits n 122
grizzly bear n 194
groan v/n 22

grocer n 75
grocer n *obs. wholesaler* 75
grocery n *groceries* 226
grocery n *type of store* 226
grody adj 320
grog n 196
groggy adj *cloudy* 208
groggy adj 225
groggy adj *drunk* 208, 225
grogram n 123
groin n 66
groom n 151, 170
groom n *boy, man* 61
groomsman 151, 170
groove n 249
groove n/v 176
groove n *fig.* 176
groove n *mine shaft* 176
groovy adj *peachy, neat, excellent* 307
groovy adj (Am) *plays jazz well* 299
grope v *obs. investigate* 61
grope v *obs. gen. feel* 26
grope v *cop a feel* 47
grope n/v 26
grosbeak n *type of bird* 165
gross adj *yucky* 313
gross n *144* 66
gross n *as opposed to net* 127
gross anatomy n 257
gross national product n 305
gross-out n/v 324
grot n *grotto* 105, 145
grotesque n/adj 175
grotesque n *art style* 123; adj 123
grotto n 105, 145
grouch n *grouchy mood* 261, 293; v 261, 293
grouch n *grouchy person* 261, 293; v 261, 293
grouchy adj/v 261
ground n *God, soul* 19
ground n *earth's surface* 9
ground n *base coat, as in of paint* 87
ground n *obs. dry land* 9
ground n *soil* 9
ground cloth 273
ground control n 298
ground cover n 254
ground floor n 148
ground glass n 222
ground ivy n 30
ground pine n 118
ground plan n 183
ground sloth n 236

ground wire n 256
ground zero n 307
groundbreaker n 277, 300
groundbreaking adj 277, 300
groundburst n *nuclear explosion* 312
groundhog n (Am) 165
groundkeeper n 259
groundless adj *without foundation* 160
groundless adj *obs. bottomless* 160
groundling n 153
grounds n *as in "palace grounds"* 63
grounds n *obs. phys. sense* 51
grounds n *obs. tenets* 51
grounds n *as in "coffee grounds"; as in "grounds for divorce"* 51
groundsheet n 273
groundskeeper n 259, 274
groundspeed n 281
groundswell n 209
groundwater n 254
groundwood n 269
groundwork n *fig.* 87
groundwork n 87
group n/v 177
group dynamics n 301
group sex n (Am) 317
group therapy n 304
grouper n 146
groupie n 320
groupthink n 311
groupuscle n 319
grouse n/v 105
grouse n/v *grumble* 224, 281
grout n 149
grove n 9
grovel n/v 73
groveling adv/adj 73
groves of academe n 228
grow v 26
grow v *as in "grow plants"* 26
growing pains n 216
growl n/v 94
grown-up adj/n 65, 210
growth company n 311
growth hormone n 286
growth ring n 272
growthy adj 270
grub n *arch. pimple* 195
grub n *obs. short person* 82
grub n *food* 167
grub n 65
Grub Street n 152
grubberyn 167

grubby adj *dirty* 82, 252
grubstake n/v (Am) 245
grudge n 100
grudge v/n *begrudge* 98
grudge v/n *complain* 98
grue v 137
gruel n *obs. flour, etc.* 70
gruel n *something grueling* 208
gruel n *Food* 70
grueling adj/n 251
gruesome adj 137
gruff adj 170
gruff adj *physically coarse* 170
grumble v/n 124
grume n *clot* 147
grump n *grumpy person* 225, 293; v 225, 293
grump n *grumpy mood* 225, 293; v 225, 293
grumpish adj 198, 225, 293
grumpy adj 198, 225, 293
grungy, grunge adj, n (Am) 320
grunion n *type of fish* 279
grunt n *War/Military/Violence* 319
grunt n *scut worker* 289
grunt n/v 26
grunt work n 289
gruntle v *complain* 125
gruntle v 292
grutch v *begrudge* 98
Gruyere n *type of cheese* 211
gryphon n 47
G-string n (Am) *Cloth/Clothing* 242
G-string n *musical sense* 242
GT n *Travel/Transportation* 317
guacamole n 280
guano n 145
guarantee n/v 200
guarantee n *guarantor* 200
guarantor n 226
guaranty n 110
guard n *group of guards* 174
guard n *obs. guardianship* 75
guard n *person or thing that guards* 75
guard n *safeguard* 75
guard v 75
guard of honor n 266
guarded adj *on one's guard* 184
guardhouse n 131
guardian adj/n 85
guardian angel n 154
guardrail n 222
guardroom n 203

guardsman n 215
guava n 122
gubernatorial adj (Am) 188
guck n 307
guernsey n *type of cow* 223
guerrilla n/adj 215
guerrilla theater n 318
guess v *as in "I guess"* 97
guess v/n 39
guesstimate n (Am) 288
guesswork n 185
guest n *obs. stranger* 14
guest n 14
guesthouse n 15
guff n 267
guff n *bit of wind* 267
guffaw n/v 184
guggle v *gurgle* 161
guidance 82
guide n/v General/Miscella-
neous 82
guide n Literature/Writing
152
guide dog n 297
guidebook n 152, 214
guided missile n 306
guidepost n 205
guild n 18
guild hall n 18
guild socialism n 282
guildsman n 245
guile n 36
guileful adj 36, 184
guileless 36
guileless adj 36, 184
Guillain-Barre Syndrome n 297
guillotine n 203
guilt n *obs. the act producing the
guilt* 17
guilt n *being guilty* 17
guilt n *emotional sense* 17
guinea fowl n 194
guinea hen n 119
guinea pig n 165
guipure n *type of lace* 223
guise n *obs. gen. style* 48
guise n 48
guitar n 154
gul n *rose* 209
gulag n 324
gulch n 219
gulf v *engulf* 218
gulf n 29
gulf n *fig.* 29
gull n 64
gull n/v *a gullible person* 113,
212
gullet n *throat* 64

gullet n 64
gullible adj 113, 212
gullish adj 113
gully n *gullet* 145
gully n *trench* 145
gully erosion n 285
gullywasher n 210
gulp v *as in "gulp down"* 67
gulp v *swallow hard in fear* 67;
n 67
gum v *as in "gum up the works"*
143
gum n *chewing gum* 241
gum n *as in "tree gum"* 30
gum v *chew with gums* 197
gum n *type of tree* 164
gum interj *as in "by gum"* 230
gum n *interior of mouth* 32
gum arabic n 88
gum boot n (Am) 224
gumbo n *type of stew, soup* 211
gumbo n (Am) *creole* 227
gumdrop n (Am) 241
gump n *idiot* 216
gumption n 184
gums n *as in "dental gums"* 32
gumshoe n *detective* 275; v 275
gumshoe n *type of shoe* 275
gun v *hunt* 155
gun n *as in "hired gun"* 229
gun n *obs. any large weapon* 45
gun n War/Military/Violence
45
gun v *as in "gun down"* 155
gun control n 319
gun down v 174
gun for v 269
gun it v *give it gas* 281
gun moll n 277
gunboat n 203
gunboat diplomacy n 291
gundog n *hunting dog* 185
gunfight n 174
gunfire n 215
gunflint n 188
gung ho adj 304
gunk n (Am) 231
gunman n 155, 229
gunnel n 100
gunner n 45
gunnery n 102
gunnery n *all guns* 102
gunnery sergeant n 319
gunny n 239
gunnysack n 239
gunplay n (Am) 266
gunpoint n 312
gunpowder n 80

gunrunner, gunrunning n 267
gunsel n *young man* 283, 306
gunsel n *young man* 306
gunsel n *young homosexual* 283
gunsel n *gunman* 306
gunship n 319
gunshot n 80
gun-shy adj 261
gunslinger n 291
gunsmith n 127
gunwale n 100
guppy n 285
gurgitate v 114
gurgitation n 114
gurgle n/v 87
gurney n 297
gurney n *type of carriage* 297
gurney cab n 261
guru n 157
gush n/v 94
gush v *speak gushingly* 243
gusher n 237
gushy adj 243
gussy v Slang 292
gussy up Slang 292
gust v/n *as in "gust of wind"*
119
gust n *gusto* 98
gust n *liking, taste* 98
gusto n 157
gut n *as in "catgut"* 66
gut n *as in "beergut"* 66
gut v 60
gutbucket n *type of jazz* 290
gutless adj 268
guts n/adj *courage* 261
guts n 13
gutsy adj 261, 300
gutter n 33
guttersnipe n 249
gutty adj 261, 300
gut-wrenching adj 323
guv n (Brit) 249
guvnor 249, 268
guy n *guyline* 71
guy n *effigy, man* 216
guzzle v 122
gym n 126, 244
gymnasiast n *gymnast* 126, 244
gymnasium n 126, 244
gymnast n 126, 244
gymnastic adj 170
gymnastics n 170
gymnosperm n 219
gynarchy n 130, 154
gynecocracy n 154
gynecologist, gynecology n 222
gynocracy n 130

gyp n/v (Am) 267
gypsum n 63
Gypsy n gen. 114
Gypsy n 114
gypsy cab n (Am) 317
gypsy moth n 210
gyrate v 157, 234
gyration n 157, 234
gyro n *Greek sandwich* 322
gyro n *gyroscope* 274
gyrocompass n 274
gyropilot n *automatic pilot* 288
gyroplane n 274
gyroscope n 242, 274
gyrostabilizer n 288
gyve n/v *fetter* 48

H

ha interj 21, 47
ha ha interj 21, 47
habeas corpus n 81
haberdasher n 152
haberdasher n *gen. vendor* 152
habergeon n *type of armor* 35
habit n *obs. gen. bearing* 73
habit n *clothing* 35
habit v *clothe* 71
habit n *gen. character, repeated
act* 73
habit v *obs. reside* 98
habit n *as in "drug habit"* 229
habit v 73
habitat n 193
habit-forming adj 771
habitual adj 91
habitude n *arch. character* 73
habitue n 217
hacienda n 183
hack v 309
hack n *type of cough* 257
hack n *drudge worker* 110, 172
hack n *type of horse* 31
hack n *taxi* 149, 184; v 184
hack n/v *cut* 21
hack n Literature/Writing 214
hack it v *manage* 313
hack off v *tick off* 261
hack writer n 227
hacker n Technology 309
hackie n 184, 292
hackney n *obs. scutworker* 110
hackney adj 191
hackney v *create cliches* 128
hackney n *type of horse* 31
hackney n 36
hackney coach n 149
hackneyed adj 191

hacksaw n 168
haddock n 30
hades n 19
Hades n 129
haft n *weapon handle* 21
hag n *gen. insult* 46, 82
hag n *fantastic creature* 46, 82
haggard n *male hawk* 119
haggard adj *drawn, gaunt* 166
haggard n *an intractable person* 119
haggard adj *applied to hawks* 166
haggis n 70
haggle v *obs. hack at* 127
haggle v/n *barter* 127, 250
hagride v *torment, harass* 179
haiku n 264
hail interj 47
hail v *greet* 58
hail v *as in "hail a cab"* 58
hail n/v Weather 12
Hail Mary n 43
hail-fellow adj *hail-fellow-well-met* 135
hailstone n 12
hailstorm n 99
hair n 13
hair ball n 189
hair cell n 256
hair follicle n 195
hair gel n 323
hair implant n 323
hair shirt n 71
hair transplant n 322, 323
hair trigger adj/n 215
hairbreadth n 66
hairbrush n 121
haircloth n 100
haircut n 260
hairdo n 280, 288
hairdresser n 200
hairpiece n 288
hairpin n 196
hairpin adj 270
hair-raiser, hair-raising n, adj 270
hair-splitter n 230, 231
hair-splitting n 230, 231
hairspring n *type of fine spring* 232
hairstyle 280, 288
hairstylist n 298
hair-trigger adj 233
hairy adj *difficult, rough* 231
hake n *type of fish* 30
halberd n *type of weapon* 102
halcyon adj 115

halcyon n 81
hale adj 13
half n 22
half bath n 258
half blood n 126
half boot n 197
half brother n 39, 40
half dime n 200
half disme n *type of coin* 200
half eagle n (Am) *$5 coin* 200
half hour n 65
half note n 129
half shell n (Am) 241
half sister n 39, 40
half-and-half n 183
half-assed adj 300
half-baked adj 156
half-blood 204
half-breed n (Am) 126, 204
half-cocked adj 217
half-dollar n 200
halfhearted adj 73
half-life n 272
half-light n 145
half-moon n/adj 65
halfpenny n 41
half-pint n 147
half-slip n 303
half-track n 291
half-truth n 176
halfway adj 54
halfway house n 175
half-wit n 156
halibut n 64
halite n *rock salt* 236
halitosis n 238
hall n *as in "dining hall"* 33
hall n *as in "concert hall"* 14
hall n *hallway* 33, 167, 258
hall n *mansion* 15
Hall of Fame n 275
hallelujah interj/n 112
hallmark n *fig.* 176, 187
hallmark n *mark to establish purity* 187
hallmark n *type of seal* 176
hallo interj/n/v b1570 132, 248
halloo interj 175
hallow v 19
Halloween n 126
halls of ivy n 319
hallucinate v 170
hallucinate v *obs. trick* 170
hallucination n 170
hallucinogen n 309
hallway n (Am) 167, 258
halo n *religious sense* 119, 154

halo n Weather 119, 154
halo effect n 285
halogen n 219
halt adj *arch. lame* 14
halt n/v *stop* 136
halt v *vacillate* 97
halt n/v 14
halter n 15
halterbreak v 223
halting adj 97
halvah n 168
halve v 58
halyard n 72
ham n Food 100
ham n *arch. area behind the knee* 13
ham n Performing Arts 265; v 265, 299
ham radio operator v 290
hambone n Performing Arts 265
hamburger n 259
hamfatter n *hamhanded musician* 265
ham-fisted adj 283, 293
ham-handed adj 283, 293
hamlet n 20
hammer n Sports 263
hammer n/v Tools 16
hammer n *on a gun* 80
hammer and sickle n 291
hammer and tongs adv/adj 189
hammer dulcimer n 312
hammer out v 133
hammer throw n 263
hammerlock n 263
hammock n *hummock* 118
hammock n 121
hamper v 92
hamper n 33
hams n *as in "hamstrings"* 99
hamster n 145
hamstring v War/Military/Violence 120, 155
hamstring n 99, 120
hamstring muscle n 256
hand v *handle* 98
hand n 13
hand n *obs. hand and arm* 147
hand n *as in "poker hand"* 126
hand n *applause* 129
hand v *as in "hand over"* 179
hand n *on a clock* 119
hand n *as in "farmhand"* 171
hand and foot adv 21
hand ax n 16
hand brake n 224
hand glass n *small mirror* 196

hand grenade n 174
hand job n 317
hand lens n 288
hand organ n (Am) Music 201
hand out v 232
hand over fist adv 216
hand puppet n 305
hand towel n 33
hand truck n 280
handbag n 239
handball n *in a game similar to football* 75
handball n 75, 263
handbarrow n 72
handbasket n 100
handbill n 201
handbook n *gen.* 19, 214
handbook n *religious sense* 19, 214
handcar n (Am) 224
handcart n 149
handcuff n/v 149
handfast n *arch. contract* 46
hand-feed v 211
handgun n 45
handheld adj 294
handhold n 159
hand-holding n 277
handicap n *type of horserace* 200
handicap n *gen. "encumbrance"* 269
handicap n *arch. type of game* 151
handicap n *fig.* 200
handicap v 252
handicap n/v 252
handicapped adj 279
handicapper n Sports 199
handicuffs n *arch. fisticuffs* 188
handiwork n 22
handkerchief n 106, 258
handle v *fig.* 26
handle v 26
handle n *how something handles* 270
handle n 22
handlebar n 258
handlebar mustache n 260
handmade adj 159
handmaiden n 44
hand-me-down adj/n 231
handoff n 270
handout n 232
handpick v 235
handrail n 196
hands down adj/adv 250
handsaw n 71

handset n 284
handshake n 247
hands-off adj 278
handsome n as in "hello, hand-some" 292
handsome adj attractive 121
handsome adj large 121
handsome adj handy 121
hands-on adj 321
handspring n 251
handstand n 263
hand-to-hand adj 82
hand-to-mouth adj 113
handwoven adj 260
hand-wringing n 293
handwrite v 77, 227
handwriting n 77, 227
handwrought adj 263
handy adj dexterous 32
handy adj nearby 161
handyman n 245
hang v as in "keeping the crowd hanging" 204
hang v as in "hang around, hang out" 216
hang v Slang 230
hang v 26
hang n as in "the hang of a dress" 206
hang v Death 20
hang about v 235
hang around v 230
hang back v 141
hang glider n 288
hang in v 320
hangar n/v 242
hangdog adj/n 175
hanger n hangman 45
hanger-on n 114
hangman n Death 45
hangman n Games/Fun/Lei-sure 317
hangment n arch. execution by hanging 80
hangnail n 32
hangout n (Am) 250
hangover n (Am) 257
hang-up n 311
hank n 35
hanker v 161
hankering n 161
hankie n 106, 258
hanky-panky n sex play 231, 298
hansom n 224
hap n luck, happening 61; v 61
hap v 60
hap n 133

ha'penny n 110
haphazard adj/n chance 134
haphazard adj 134
hapless adj 89
happen v find, as in "happen upon" 141
happen v 60
happenchance n 269, 270
happening n 133
happening n event 320
happen-so 269, 270
happenstance n 269, 270
happiness n prosperity, success 98
happiness n gladness 98
happy adj as in "happy acci-dent" 88
happy adj tipsy 204
happy adj lucky 107
happy adj joyful, satisfied 107
happy hour n 317
happy hunting ground n (Am) 229
happy pill n 313
happy talk n 324
happy-go-lucky adj 169
hara-kiri n 229
harangue n/v 86, 179
harass v 161
harbinger n omen 134
harbinger n obs. servant fore-runner 40
harbor n spec. to the sea 29
harbor n any refuge 29
harbormaster n 200
hard adj as in "hard water" 178
hard adj as in "hard currency" 187
hard adj as in "hard G" 201
hard adj difficultly accomplished 54
hard adj physically hard 23
hard adj as in "hard news" 290
hard v obs. harden 28, 55
hard adj as in "hard liquor" 196
hard candy n 287
hard cider n (Am) 197
hard coal n 193
hard copy n 264
hard disk n 322
hard drugs n 319
hard goods n 298
hard hat n 287
hard knocks n 283
hard labor n 245
hard maple n (Am) 193
hard pine n 254
hard put adj 270

hard rock n 318
hard sauce n type of dessert top-ping 259
hard sell n (Am) 311
hard up adj 217
hard wheat n 211
hard-and-fast adj 250
hard-ass adj/n 325
hardback n hardcover 264, 290, 305, 311
hardball n Slang 324
hard-bitten adj 206
hard-boil v 259
hard-boiled adj 184
hardbound adj 264, 290, 305, 311
hardcase adj 264, 290, 305, 311
hard-core adj 301
hardcover 264, 290, 305, 311
harden v 55
hardening n as in "hardening of the arteries" 309
hardfisted adj 172
hardhanded adj 138
hardhead n 102
hardheaded adj 102
hardhearted adj 47
hard-hitting adj 234
hard-line adj (Am) 321
hardmouthed adj stubborn 150
hardnose 268, 313
hardnosed adj 268, 313
hard-of-hearing adj 121
hard-on n Love/Romance/Sex 262
hard-pressed adj 217
hardscrabble adj (Am) meager 217
hard-shell clam n (Am) 194
hard-shell crab n 272
hard-shell/hard-shelled adj 204
hardship n 48
hardtack n 223
hardtop n 304
hardware n General/Miscella-neous 113
hardware n in computing 113, 315
hardwired adj 315
hard-won adj 234
hardwood n 118
hardy adj 54
hare v obs. harass 117
hare n 11
hare and hounds n type of game 226
harebrained adj 112

harelip n 121
harem n 199
harem n secluded house quarters 199
harem pants n 310
hark v 27, 55
hark back v 234
harken v 27, 55
harlequin n 128
harlequinade n 201
harlot n obs. vagabond 82
harlot n 82
harlot n obs. male worker 82
harm n obs. insult 22
harm n/v 22
harmful 22
harmless adj not causing harm 22, 137
harmless adj unharmed 137
harmonic adj Music 173
harmonic adj obs. musical 173
harmonica n 201
harmonical obs. 111
harmonics n 187
harmonious adj gen. 111
harmonious adj Music 111
harmonium n 228
harmonize v 101
harmony n 83
harm's way n 176
harness v fig. 271
harness v 35, 272; n 35
harness horse n 241
harness racing/harness race n 275
harp v as in "harp on" 116
harp n/v 19
harp seal n 194
harping-iron obs. 131
harpoon v 131
harpsical adj obs. 154
harpsichord n 154
harpy n gen. as insult 81
harpy n The Fantastic/Paranormal 81
harquebus n type of gun 112
harridan n 175
harried adj 284
harrier n type of hawk 105
harrow n/v plunder 21
harrow n cultivating tool 35
harrowing adj 21, 217
harrumph v 300
harry v raid 20
harry v harrass 20
harsh adj to the touch 54
harsh adj strict 54
harsh adj to other senses 54

harshen v 218
hart n 11
hartebeest n type of antelope 194
harum-scarum adj/adv reckless 191
harvest n arch. autumn 12, 34
harvest n/v 34
harvest v 34
harvest ant n 255
harvest fly n cicada 194
harvest home n 122
harvest mite n (Am) chigger 220
harvest moon n 182
harvestman n reaper 71
has-been n 156
hasenpfeffer n 259
hash n as in "corned beef hash" 167
hash n hashish 131, 313
hash v 167
hash browns n 310
hash house n (Am) 245
hash joint 245
hash mark n 277
hash slinger 245
hashish n 131, 313
hasp n 16
hassle n/v 301
haste n 48
haste v make haste 48, 61
hasten 48, 61
hastive obs. 89
hasty adj 48, 89
hasty adj arch. speedy 89
hasty pudding n 122
hat n 15
hat in hand adv 250
hat tree n (Am) 211
hat trick n 269
hatband n 71
hatbox n 196
hatch v as in "hatch an egg" 29; n 29
hatch n type of door 15
hatch v fig. 29
hatchback n 317
hatchery n 259
hatchet n 36
hatchet face n 156
hatchet job n 307
hatchet man n (Am) 204
hatchet work n 307
hatchling n 255
hate n/v 17, 36
hatemonger n 313
hatmaker n 40, 101

hatpin n 258
hatred n 17, 36
hatter n 40, 101
hauberk n type of chain mail 45
haught adj arch. haughty 73, 100
haughty adj 73, 100
haughty adj noble 100
haul off v 253
haunch n 31
haunt v weigh upon 55
haunt v frequent 55; n 55
haunt v The Fantastic/ Paranormal 132
haunt n 55
haut bourgeoisie 202
haut monde n high society 174
haut noblesse 202
hautbois n oboe 129
haute adj 197
haute couture n 274
haute cuisine n 287
hauteur n haughty airs 150
have v cheat, con 215
have v have sex with 126
have n possessions 61
have n as in "haves and have-nots" 202
have v 26
have n 231
have a baby v 82
have at v 97
haveless adj obs. having nothing 28, 202
haven n safe place for ships 15
haven n gen. 15
have-not n 202, 231
haversack n 184
having n owning 61
havings n possessions 61
haviour 61
havoc n type of battle cry 102
havoc n/v 102
haw n/v as in "hem and haw" 163
haw interj similar to ha! 175
haw interj/v as in "gee and haw" 230
Hawaiian guitar n 290
Hawaiian shirt n 310
hawhaw interj 230
hawk v as in "hawk up phlegm" 133
hawk n War/Military/Violence 319
hawk v as in "hawking wares" 75
hawk v hunt with a hawk 35

hawk n the bird 11
hawker n hawkhandler 15
hawker n vendor 75
hawkeyed adj 217
hawkish adj 231
hawksbill turtle n 181
hawkshaw n detective 263
hawthorn n 10
hay n/v Agriculture/ Food-Gathering 15
hay n type of dance 111
hay fever n 221
haycock n 34, 100
hayfork n 123
hayloft n 122
haymaker n type of punch 282
hayride n (Am) 242
hayseed n 133
haystack n 100
haywire n 274
haywire adj/adv wild 274, 292
hazard n type of game 49
hazard v venture, as in "hazard a guess" 143
hazard n dangerous obstacle 49; v 49
hazardous adj 137
haze n fig. 146
haze v nautical sense 228
haze n Weather 146
haze v gen. terrify 228
haze v make hazy 218
haze v as in "frat hazing" 228
hazel adj 89; n 10
hazel n the color 10
hazel n the tree 10
hazelnut n 10
hazing 228
hazy adj Weather 146
hazy adj 160
H-bomb n (Am) 307
he interj 21
head n bathroom 196
head n as in "come to a head" 51
head n as in "heads and tails" 87
head n source 51
head n as in "drughead," "motorhead" 47
head adj 25
head n akin to foot Measurement 120
head v behead 45
head n as in "16 head of cattle" 107
head n as in "the head on a beer" 122

head n leader 22
head n as in "a head for figures" 82
head n headline 290
head n The Body 13
head and shoulders adv 250
head case n 323
head cold n 297
head for v 253
head louse n 105
head off v 235
head over heels adv 204
head restraint n 316
head rhyme n alliteration 305
head shop n (Am) 318
head start n 269
headache n 14
headband n 107
headbanger n heavy metal fan 318
headboard n 183
headcheese n 223
headdress n 184
headfirst adv 233
headforemost 233
headgear n 100
headhunt v 245
headhunter n 245
headlamp n 242, 260
headland n 9
headlight n (Am) 242
headline n 214
headline v Entertainment 265
headlock n 277
headlong adj/adv 88
headmaster n 129, 247
headmistress n 129, 247
headnote n 245
head-on adj 278
head-on adj/adv (Am) 234, 278
headphone n 280
headpiece n 107
headpin n in bowling 289
headquarter v 278
headquarters n gen. 155, 206
headquarters n mil. 155, 206
headrest n 239
headroom n 239
heads up interj 307
headset n 288
headshrinker n (Am) slang psychiatrist 304
headsman n leader 98
headsman n beheader 45, 155
headstand n 298
headstone n 111
headstrong adj 73

heads-up adj 307
head-to-head adj/adv 189
headwaiter n 213
headway n progress 190
headway n type of mining passage 190
headway n type of road 190
headwind n 194
headword n 214
headwork n 225
heal v 14
healer n 32
healsome adj obs. 121
health n 14
health care n 303
health food n 259
health insurance n 275
health maintenance organization/HMO n 322
health spa n 310
healthful adj 89
healthless adj 121
healthy adj 121
heap n rattletrap car 288
heap n/v 21
heap n many, a lot, as in "a heap of trouble" 51
hear v as in "hear of" 143
hear v as in "hear about" 60
hear v 26
hear him, hear hear interj 175
hearing n 132
hearing aid n 286
hearing dog n 309
hearing ear dog n 322
hearken v 27
hearken back v hark back 301
hearsay n 86
hearsay evidence n 203
hearse n type of coffin cover 45
hearse n type of vehicle 45
heart v 107
heart n as in "dear heart" 39
heart n fig. core 13
heart n The Body 13
heart v hearten 17
heart attack n 286
heart disease n 238
heart failure n 257
heart of palm n (Am) 297
heartache n fig. 14, 151
heartache n lit. 14, 151
heartbeat n 221
heartbreak n 74, 170
heartbreaker n 74, 170
heartbreaking adj 74
heartbroken adj 108, 126
heartburn n obs. passion 121

heartburn n 121
heartburning adj obs. 121
heartburnings n jealousy 73
hearten v 17, 107
heartfelt adj 184
heart-free adj not in love 101, 185
heartful adj arch. with all my heart 73
hearth n 14
heartland n 272
heartless adj 38
heart-lung machine n 309
heartrending adj 124
hearts n 262
hearts and flowers n (Am) 307
heartsease n serenity 73
heartsick adj 108, 126
heartsore adj 126
heartstopper n 324
heartstring n 99
heartthrob n 226
heart-to-heart adj/n 243, 278
heartwarming adj 261
heart-whole adj not in love 101, 185
heartwood n 209
heartworm n 255
hearty adj 72
heat n hot spiciness Food 70
heat n/v Energy 12
heat n as in "in heat" Love/Romance/Sex 39
heat n as in "the heat of the moment" 136
heat n Sports 171
heat v 12
heat cramps n 297
heat engine n 256
heat exchanger n 272
heat exhaustion n 297
heat lightning n 220
heat prostration n 297
heat pump n 256
heat rash n 257
heat wave n 255
heated adj fig. 270
heater n gun 291
heath n 9
heathen adj/n 20
heather n 11
heathland n 209
heatproof adj 278
heatstroke n 239
heave ho interj 81, 307
heave-ho n 307
heaven n Heavens/Sky 12
heaven n Religion 20

heaven n sky 12, 20
heavenly adj fig. 20
heavenly adj Religion 20
heavens interj 21
heaven-sent adj 157
heavier-than-air adj 274
heavy n 21
heavy adj lit. and fig. 23
heavy cream n 287
heavy hitter n 325
heavy hydrogen n 296
heavy metal n 324
heavy water n 296
heavy wet n type of alcohol 241
heavy-duty adj 284
heavy-footed adj 160
heavy-handed adj 160
heavy-hearted adj 73
heavyset adj 286
heck n 249
heckle v 179
heckler n 179
hectic adj gen. 294
hectic adj med. sense 294
hectograph n type of duplicating machine 260
hector v swagger 175
hector n Slang 175
hedge v as in "hedge a bet" 180; n 180
hedge n/v Plants 10
hedge v dodge 143
hedgehog n 64, 145
hedgehop v 280
hedgepig n 64, 145
hedgerow n 10
hedonic adj 169, 213, 243
hedonism n 169, 213, 243
hedonist n 169, 213, 243
heebie-jeebies n (Am) 275
heed n/v 25
heehaw n/v (Am) 209
heel n (Am) jerk 283
heel v follow 271
heel n The Body 13
heel n/v tip, lean 141
heel n on a sock, shoe 13
heel-and-toe adj 216
heelbone n 120
heeltop n liquor remaining after drinking 175
heft n 252
hefty adj 252
hegemon n 130
hegemony n leadership, domination 130
hegira n exodus 204

hegira n spec. exodus of Muhammed 204
heh interj 81
hehe interj/v 21, 243
heifer n 15
heigh interj used to call attention, give encouragement 47
heigh-ho interj 81
height n arch. altitude 66
height n 12
heighten v 96
heighten v intensify 96
heighten v obs. exalt 96
Heimlich maneuver n (Am) 322
heinous adj 80
heir n 39, 151
heir apparent n 82
heir presumptive n 151
heiress n 39, 151
heirloom n 85
heist n/v (Am) 229, 292
heliborne adj akin to airborne 321
helicon n type of tuba 246
helicopt v 261, 304
helicopter n 261; v 261, 288
heliocentric adj 164
heliolatry n worship of the sun 228
heliotherapy n 286
heliotropism n 237
helipad n 304
heliport n 304
heli-skiing n 323
helium n 236
helix n 158
helix n architectural sense 158
hell n Religion 19, 129
hell interj 132
hell n fig. 19
hell on wheels n 231
hell week n (Am) hazing 291
hellacious adj (Am) 295
hellbender n (Am) type of salamander 209
hell-bent adj (Am) 233
hellbroth n 156
hellcat n 156
heller n (Am) hellion 204, 268
hellfire n Religion 20
hell-for-leather adj/adv 269, 284
hellhole n 81
hellhound n 21
hellion n (Am) 204, 268
hello interj/n 132, 248
hell-raiser n 283

hell's bells interj 283
helluva adj/adv 277
helm n *as in "helm of boat"* 16
helm n *helmet* 20
helmet n 80
help v/n 21
help n *as in "the help"* The Workplace 41
helper n 151, 185
helping n *as in "2nd helpings"* 259
helping hand n 102
helpline n 324
helpmate n 151, 185
helpmeet n *helper* 151, 185
helter-skelter adj/adv/n 177
hem interj/v *as in "hem and haw"* 102
hem n *stitched edge* 168
hem n *gen. edge* 168
hematology n 211
hematoma n *collection of blood internally* 222
hemidemisemiquaver n 228
hemisphere n 29
hemline n 287
hemlock n 10
hemoglobin n 238
hemophilia n 238
hemophiliac adj 238
hemophilic adj 238
hemorrhage n/v 68, 286
hemorrhoid n 66
hemorrhoidectomy n 280
hemostat n 257
hemp n 10
hemp n *the fiber* 10
hen n 11
hen fruit n (Am) *eggs* 241
hen party n 269
henbane n *type of plant* 30
henchman n 40, 231
henchman n *pejorative sense* 40
hencoop n 107, 168
henhouse n 107, 168
henna n/v 280
henna n *Plants* 119
henotheism n 247
henpeck v 132
henten v *tell* 157
hep adj 274
hepatitis n 182
hepatoma n 286
hepcat n 299
hepped up adj 304
hepster n 299
herald n *messenger* 45

herald n/v War/Military/Violence 45
herald v 93
heraldry n 131
heraldy obs. 131
herb n 30
herb doctor n 221
herbal n 110
herbalist n 127
herbarist n 127
herbarium n 193
herbicide n 259
herbivore n 236
herbivorous adj 236
herculean adj 138
herd v 34
herd n *group* 15; v 15
herd n *herder* 15
herd-boy n 15, 197
herder n 15, 35
herdman n obs. 71
herdsman n 15, 71, 223
herdswoman n 15, 71, 223
here and how n 231
here and there adv 82
hereditarian n *genetic theorist* 255
hereditary adj 90
heredity n 237
heredity n *inheritance* 90
Hereford n *type of cattle* 209
heresy n 42
heretic n 42
heriot n *feudal death tax* 20
heritage n 48
herky-jerky adj 313
hermaphrodite n 63
hermit n *gen.* 42, 174
hermit n *religious use* 42, 174
hermit crab n 181
hermitage n 49
hernia n 68
hero n *protagonist* 173, 188
hero n 84, 157, 188
hero sandwich n 310
hero worship n 204
heroic couplet n 128, 172, 276
heroic poem n 128, 172, 276
heroic verse n 128, 172, 276
heroicomic adj 202
heroicomical adj 202
heroin n 267
heroine n General/Miscellaneous 84, 157
heroine n *protagonist* Entertainment 173, 188
heron n 30
heroon n *hero's monument* 202

hero-worship n/v 261
herpes n 68, 210, 273, 286
herpes simplex n 68, 210, 273, 286
herpes zoster n 68, 210, 273, 286
herpesvirus n 68, 210, 273, 286
herpetology n 210
herring n 11
herringbone n 242
herstory n 324
hertz n *measurement of energy* 285
hesitance n 84
hesitancy n 84
hesitate v 162
hesitation n 84
hesitation n *pause* 84
Hessian boot n 212
hest n *command* 28
hestern n obs. 165
hesternal adj arch. *yesterday* 165
het adj *heated* 98
het up adj *excited, heated up* 243
hetero adj/n 262, 298
heterogeneal adj 160
heterogeneous adj *opp. of homogeneous* 160
heterogeny n *spontaneous generation* 237
heteronym n *e.g., bow "gesture" and bow "front of ship"* 264
heterosexism n 324
heterosexual adj/n 262, 281
hethen adv obs. *hence* 61
heuristic adj 213
hew v 26
hex v *perform witchcraft* 230, 248, 277
hex n *witch* 248, 267, 277
hex n *type of spell* 277
hex n *type of spell* 230, 248, 277
hexadecimal adj *base 16 numbering* 309
hexagon n 120
hexagonal adj 120
hexagram n 237
hexapod n *insect* 165
hexerei n *witchcraft* 230, 267
hey interj 47
hey presto interj (Brit) *kind of "voila"* 189
heyday n *high spirits, excitement* 124

heyday interj *hey!* 112
heyday n *best of times* 124, 204
hi interj *hello* 102
hi interj *used to get attention, akin to hey* 102
hiatal hernia n 303
hiatus n phys. *gap* 134
hiatus n gen. *gap* 134
hibachi n 239
hibernate v 218
hibernation n 218
hibiscus n 181
hic n *hiccup* 267
hiccup/hiccough n 133
hick adj/n 132, 283
hicket n obs. *hiccup* 106
hickey n *as in "doohickey"* 278
hickey n (Am) *bitemark* 275
hickory n (Am) 164
hid adj 26
hidden adj 26
hidden agenda n 325
hidden tax n 299
hide v *conceal* 26
hide n *unit of land measure, usually 120 acres* 12
hide v *flog* 215
hide n *skin* 11
hide-and-seek n 170
hideaway n *hiding place* 251
hideaway n *hiding person* 251
hideosity n 54
hideous adj 54
hideout n 241
hidey-hole n 211
hierarch n Religion 43
hierarchic adj Religion 43
hierarchical Religion 43
hierarchize v *prioritize* 271
hierarchy n 43
hierarchy n gen. 43
hieroglyph n 127
hieroglyphic, hieroglyphics adj, n 127
hi-fi 299
hi-fi n (Am) 299, 305
higgle v *haggle* 163
higgledy-piggledy adv/adj 139
high n Weather 255
high adj *as in "living high"* 156
high adj *as in "high noon"* 54
high n *record level* 294
high adj 23
high adj/n Slang 300
high and dry n 216
high and low adv 82
high beam n 298
high blood pressure n 280

Hobson's choice n *no choice at all* 156

hock n *as in "ham hocks"* 64

hock n/v *pawn* 245

hock n *arch. type of plant, as in "hollyhock"* 10

hockey n 108

hockey stick n 226

hockshop n 245

hocus v *trick or hoax* 180, 208

hocus-pocus interj/n/v 156

hod n 123

hod carrier n 198

hodgepodge, hotchpotch n 83

Hodgkin's disease n 238

hoe n/v 36

hoecake n (Am) *type of pancake* 183

hoedown n (Am) 228

hog n *type of motorcycle* 317

hog n 12

hog n/v Slang 267

hog heaven n 307

hogback n 219

hogshead n *type of cask* 88

hogtie v (Am) 259

hogwash n 189

hogwash n *lit.* 189

hog-wild adj (Am) 275

ho-hum adj 321

hoi polloi n 174

hoity-toity adj *playful* 170, 266

hoity-toity adj *haughty* 170, 266

hoke, hokey v, adj *fake* 295

hokeypokey n *type of ice cream* 259

hokeypokey interj 156

hokum n 283

hold v 26

hold n *as in "ship's hold"* 123

holding company n 275

holding pattern n 310

holdout n *device for cheating at cards* 268

holdout n 308

holdover n (Am) 269

holdup n (Am) *delay* 232

holdup n *robbery* 267

hole n 21

hole up v 249

hole-and-corner adj *secret* 231

hole-in-the-wall adj/n 250

holiday n/v 40, 244

holiday n *vacation day* 40

holiday n *holy day* 40

holier-than-thou adj 250

holiness n 19

holiness n *form of address* 19

holism, holistic n, adj 286

hollandaise n 241

holler n/v *yell* 180, 218

hollo interj 132

hollow adj *fig., as in "hollow promises"* 115

hollow n 29

hollow-hearted 115

holly n 10

hollyhock n 29

Hollywood n *American movie industry* 291; adj 291

Hollywood bed n 303

holocaust n *conflagration* 49

holocaust n *mass destruction* 49

hologram n 302

holograph n Science 315

holograph n *related to handwriting* 152

holography n 315

holography n 152

holstein n 241

holster n 168

holus-bolus adv *all at once* 234

holy adj 19

holy city n 78

Holy Communion n 111

holy day n 19

Holy Ghost n 19

holy ghost 78

Holy Grail n 129

Holy Joe n *chaplain* 247

Holy Roller n 228

holy spirit 19

Holy Spirit n 78

holy war n 174

holy water n 19

holystone n 212

homage n 48

homage v *obs.* 48

hombre n 229

homburg n *type of hat* 260

home v 207

home n 14

home brew n 241

home builder n 263

home computer n 322

home economics n (Am) 258

home fries n 310

home front n 284

home rule n 247

homebody n (Am) 216

homeboy n (Am) 289

homecoming n 82

homegirl n (Am) 289

homegrown adj 233

homeling n *native* 144

homely adj 54

homemade adj 178

homemaker n 257

homeopathic, homeopathy adj, n 211

homeothermic adj *warm-blooded* 237

homeroom n 282

homesick adj 199

homespun adj *lit. "made at home"* 121

homespun adj *homey, simple* 121

homestead n/v 14, 241

homestead n *gen. home* 14

homestead law n (Am) 230

homestretch n (Am) 226

hometown n (Am) 279

homework n 173

homey adj 239

homicidal adj 188

homicide n *murderer* 45, 79

homicide n *murder* 45, 79

homing pigeon n 255

hominid adj/n 255

hominoid 255

hominy n (Am) 148

hominy grits n (Am) 197

homo n Love/Romance/Sex 262, 289

Homo sapiens n 210

homoerotic, homoeroticism adj/n 281

homogeneous adj 161

homogenize v 271

homogenize v *prepare milk* 271, 287

homonym n 152

homonymy n 152

homophile adj/n *homosexual* 275, 311

homophobe n 312

homophobia n 312

homophobia n *gen. fear of men* 312

homosexual n 262, 275

homosexualist n 275

homosexuality n 262

hon n Slang 277

honcho n 307

hone n/v 36, 234

hone n *gen. stone* 36

hone n *whetstone* 36

hone in v 320

honest adj *truthful* 37

honest adj *chaste* 75

honest adj *worthy of honor* 37

honest broker n 263

honest injun interj (Am) 249

honest-to-goodness/honest-to-God adj/adv 284

honesty n 125

honey n Food 15

honey n *as in "a honey of a day"* 268

honey n *term of endearment* 75

honey n *the color* 234

honey locust n 181

honeybee n 99

honeycomb v 207

honeycomb n 11

honeycomb n *obs. honey* 11

honeydew n 118

honeydew melon n 280

honeymoon n/v *lit.* 108

honeymoon n/v *fig.* 108

honeysuckle n 29

honk v (Am) *make a honking sound* 208; n 208

honk v *as in "honk a horn"* 271

honky n 307

honkytonk n/v (Am) 268

honor n/v 43, 56, 191

honor n *something awarded* 51

honor n *arch. promise made on honor* 169

honor v *adhere to* 56

honor v *bequeath honor* 191

honor guard n 291

honor roll n 276, 291

honor society n 276, 291

honor system n (Am) 277

honorable mention n 250

honorarium n 172

honorary adj 159

honors n 202

hooch n *slang liquor* 259

hood n *type of headgear* 15

hood n *neighborhood* 315

hood n 292

hoodlum n *criminal* 248

hoodlum n (Am) *juvenile delinquent* 248

hoodman-blind n *blindman's bluff* 126

hoodoo n/v (Am) 248

hoodwink v 162

hoodwink v *blindfold* 162

hooey interj/n (Am) 292

hoof v Performing Arts 282

hoof n 11

hoof v Slang 156

hoof-and-mouth disease n (Am) 257

hoofer n (Am) *dancer* 282

hoofprint n 209

hoo-ha interj/n 300
hook n *pickpocket* 248
hook v *fig. catch* 180
hook v *catch with a hook* 58
hook n *as in "phone off the hook"* 258
hook n 16
hook v 226
hook v *lit. catch* 180
hook v 258
hook and eye n *type of fastener* 149
hook and ladder truck n (Am) 222
hook it v *play hookey* 77
hook, line and sinker adv 231
hook up v 295
hooked adj *addicted* 294
hooker n *prostitute* 226
hooker n *type of drink* 241
hookup n 278
hookworm n 272
hooky n (Am) 228
hooligan, hooliganism n 267
hoop n 35
hoopla n 248, 251
hoopskirt n (Am) 242
hooray interj 204
hooroosh n *confused noise* 251
hoosegow n 248
hoot n *as in "I don't give a hoot"* 268
hoot v 55
hootchy-kootchy n 265
hootenanny n *Entertainment* 318
hootenanny n *gadget* 318
Hooverville n 299
hop n *as in "barley and hops"* 71
hop n *narcotic* 268
hop n/v *leap* 27
hop n *type of dance* 188
hop, skip and a jump n 204
hop, step and jump n *triple jump* 185
hope n/v 26
hope chest n 280
hopeful adj/n 184
hopefully adv *gen.* 295
hopefully adv *it is hoped that* 295
hopeless adj *undeserving of hope* 107
hopeless adj *without hope* 107
hophead n *druggie* 283, 292
hop-o'-my-thumb n *small person* 112

hopped-up adj 283, 292
hopper n 35
hopperdozern n *insect killer* 259
hopping adv *as in "hopping mad"* 271
hop-scot 213
hopscotch n/v 213
horde n 133
horizon n 63
horizontal adj *opp. of vertical* 133
horizontal adj *related to horizon* 133
horizontal bar n 226
hormone n 273
horn n *slang erection* 195
horn n *type of drinking container* 14
horn n *Music* 19
horn adj/n/v *Animals* 11
horn in v 283
horn of plenty n 133
hornbill n 194
hornblende n 193
hornbook n 128
horned lizard n (Am) 209
horned owl n 64
hornet n 11
hornet n *type of beetle* 11
hornet's nest n 189
hornist n 228
horn-mad adj 124, 262
horn-mad adj *horny* 124
hornpipe n 64
horn-rims n 286
hornswoggle v 216
horny adj *seeking sex* 195, 262
horologe n *any timekeeping device* 65
horology n 210
horoscope n 23
horrendous adj 178
horrible adj 53
horrid adj 159
horrid adj *unpleasant* 159
horrid adj *bristling* 159
horrific adj 178
horrify v 208
horripilation n 158
horror n 37
horrors interj 267
horrors, the n *depression* 198
horror-struck/horror-stricken adj 212
hors d'oeuvre adv/n 183
horse n 11
horse n *heroin* 307
horse v 293

horse around v 293
horse chestnut n 119
horse latitudes n 193
horse opera n 291
horse sense n (Am) 225
horse trade n 227
horse-and-buggy adj (Am) 293
horsecar n (Am) 224
horsefeathers interj/n (Am) 292
horseflesh n 71
horsefly n 64
horselaugh n 184
horseless carriage n 261
horsemanship n 126
horseplay n 126
horseplayer n 304
horsepower n 210
horseradish n 122
horse's ass n 307
horseshit interj/n 312
horseshoe n 35
horseshoe crab n 194
horsetail n *type of plant* 119
horsewhip n 36
horticulture n 168
hosanna interj/n/v 21
hose v 271
hose n/v *as in "water hose"* 36
hose n 16
hosier n 40
hosiery n 16, 40, 197
hospice n 211
hospice n *med. sense* 211
hospitable adj 122
hospital n 106
hospital n *guest house* 106
hospital obs. *hospitality* 69
hospitality n 69
hospitality obs. *hospital* 106
hospitality suite n 316
hospitalize v 166
hoss n 230
host n *large army* 84
host v 84, 295
host n *the eucharistic bread* 43
host n 44; v 44, 295
host n *large group* 84
host n *obs. sacrifice* 43
hostage n *obs. hostel* 70
hostage n 51
hostage n *hosted lodger* 51
hostel n 33
hosteler n 40
hostess n 44; v 44, 85, 295
hostile adj 131
hostile merger n 318

hostility n *hostile act* 80
hostility n *hostile feelings* 80
hot adj *excited* 39
hot adj 25
hot adj *erotic* 39
hot adj *popular, good* 260
hot adj *fig. fresh* 25
hot adj *stolen* 215
hot v 25
hot air n *empty talk* 250
hot comb n 317
hot cross bun n 183
hot diggety dog interj 267, 292
hot dog n (Am) 259
hot dog interj 267
hot flash n 273
hot line n 312
hot money n 293
hot pants n 316
hot pepper n 303
hot plate n 224
hot potato n 232
hot pursuit n 293
hot rod n/v (Am) 304
hot rodder n 304
hot seat n 284
hot spot n 293
hot spring n 164
hot stuff n 204
hot ticket n 325
hot tub n (Am) 322
hot war n *opp. of cold war* 307
hot water n *trouble* 113
hotbed n 148, 204
hotbed n *fig.* 148, 204
hotbed n *lit.* 148, 204
hotblood n 125
hot-blooded adj 125
hotbutton adj/n 327
hotcake n (Am) 168
hotdog n *Insults* 293
hotdog v (Am) 320
hotel n 196
hotelier n 275, 276
hotelkeeper n (Am) 226, 275
hotfoot adv/v 268; n 300
hothead n 150
hotheaded adj 150
hothouse n *obs. bordello* 108
hothouse n 197
hots, the n 304
hotshot n 292
hotspur n *hothead* 82
hotsy-totsy adj 292
hot-wire v 312
hound v *fig. pursue doggedly* 143
hound n/v *Animals* 11

hound n *hunting dog* 11
houndstooth check n 297
houp-là interj 248, 251
hour n 31
hour hand n 165
hourglass adj 233
hourglass n 99
hours n *as in "1300 hours"* 65
house n Music 327
house n/v 14
house n *audience* 173
house arrest n 300
house call n 310
house cat n 145
house detective n (Am) 263
house girl n 226
house mouse n 220
house music n *type of dance music* 327
house of cards n 277
house of correction n 131
house party n 265
house sit v 322
house sitter n 322
house sparrow n 165
house trailer n 297
houseboat n 196
houseboy n 226, 263
housebreaking n *as in "breaking and entering"* 155
housebroken adj 258
houseclean/housecleaning v 239
housecoat n 280
housedress n (Am) 260
housefather n Education 228, 266, 312
housefly n 64
housegirl n 263
houseguest n 280
household n 69
household art n *household skill* 286
householdry n *arch.* 106
househusband n 43, 312
housekeep v 222
housekeeper n 126
housekeeper n *obs. householder* 126
housekeeping n 106
houselights n 282
housemaid n 171
housemaid's knee n 221
housemaster n 263
housemate n 211
housemother n Education 228, 266, 312
housepainter n 171

houseparent n Education 228, 266, 312
houseplant n 236
housewares n 286
housewarming n 129
housewife n 43, 312
housewifery n 43
housework n 121
housing n *for a machine* 102
housing n *ornamental enclosure* 102
housing n *accommodations* 33
housing development n 310
housing project n 297
hovel n 69
hoven n 94
hover v 94
hovercraft n 310
howbeit conj *although* 98
how-do-you-do n *as in "that's a fine how-do-you-do"* 156
howdy interj 189
howitzer n 174
howl v *applied to animals* 30
howl v *applied to things* 30
howl n 30
howler n *big goof* 267
howler n Animals 194
howler n *big storm* 237
howler monkey n 296
how-to adj/n 295
how-to n 295
hoy interj 81
hoy n *type of ship* 36
hoyden adj/n *obs. rude man* 175
hoyden adj/n *tartish woman* 175
huarache n *type of sandal* 260
hub n 149
hub n *fig. center* 149
hubble-bubble n 133
hubbub n 133
hubby n 170
hubcap n 274
hubris n 261
huckleberry n (Am) 119
huckster n *pejorative sense* 41
huckster n *salesperson* 41; v 41
huddle v *obs. hide* 141
huddle adv/n/v 141
hue n *arch. outcry* 36
hue n 21
hue and cry n *gen. commotion* 46, 102
hue and cry n *leg. sense* 46
huff n/v 141
huff interj 81

huffish adj 169
huffy adj 141, 169
hug n/v 141, 151
hug n *used in wrestling* 151
hug n *gen.* 151
huge adj 25
hugeous adj 25
hugger-mugger n *secrecy* 113
hug-me-tight n (Am) *type of women's jacket* 242
huh interj 156
hula n 214
hula hoop n 311
hulk v 208
hulk n *rotting ship* 16
hulk n *type of ship* 16
hulk n *huge person* 16
hulking adj 179
hull n/v *husk* 10
hull n *as in "ship's hull"* 72
hullabaloo n 205
hulled corn n 197
hum v *slang "con"* 208
hum v 265
hum n/v *music sense* 60
hum v *um* 60
human adj *exhibiting human foibles* 89
human adj/n 89, 114
human adj *related to homo sapiens* 89
human being n 114, 206
human ecology n 272
human engineering n (Am) 279
human immunodeficiency virus/ HIV n 326
human nature n 169
human relations n 284
human resources n 325
human rights n 202
humane adj 100
humane adj *human* 100
human-interest adj 290
humanitarian n 229
humanitarian n *obs. believer in nondivine Christ* 229
humanity n 78
humanize v 161
humankind n 78, 154
humanoid adj 279
humble adj *not grand* 37
humble adj *self-deprecating* 37
humble v *humiliate* 78
humble v *bow* 78
humble pie n 157
humblebee n *bumblebee* 64
humblesse n *obs. humility* 73

humbug interj/n/v *nonsense* 190
humbug interj/n/v *fraud* 190
humdinger n 267
humdrum adj 137
humid adj 65
humidifier, humidify n, v 260
humidity n 65
humidor n 273
humiliate v 72
humiliation n 72
humility n 37
hummer n Slang 267
hummingbird n (Am) 146
humongous adj (Am) 320
humor n *state of mind* 100
humor n *type of body fluid* 125
humor n *whim* 142
humor n *type of body fluid* 32, 100
humor v 142
humor n *mood* 32, 100, 125
humor n *funny perspective* 32, 100, 125
humoresque n *type of musical composition* 265
humorist n *1599* 129
humorous adj *funny* 125, 184
hump v *slang work hard* 227
hump n 189
hump v *have sex* 199; n 199
humpback whale n 181
humph interj 132, 218; v 218
humus n 193
Humvee n *mil. vehicle* 326
hunch v *as in "hunch your shoulders"* 141
hunch n *inkling* 262
hunch v *push* 141
hunch n *hint* 262
hunchback n 182
hunchbacked adj 182
hundred n 12
hundredweight n 106
hung jury n (Am) 230
hung over adj 307
hung up adj 307
hunger n *nonfood sense* 13
hunger n/v 13
hunger strike n 266
hungry adj 13
hunk n 216
hunk n Slang 320
hunker v 191
hunkers n *haunches* 195
hunks n *a Scrooge* 156
hunky adj Slang 320
hunky-dory adj (Am) 252

hunt n/v 15, 34, 70
hunt v fig. 15
hunt obs. hunter 34
hunt n obs. hunter 70, 122
hunt-and-peck n 301
hunter n 34, 70
hunter green n 252
hunting horn n 168
huntress n 34, 70
huntsman n 34, 70, 122
huntswoman n 34, 70, 122
hup interj 312
hurdle v fig. 271
hurdle n 16
hurdle n fig. 16
hurdle n sports sense 16
hurdle v create a hurdle 271
hurdy-gurdy n 188
hurl v 56
hurly n hurlyburly 51, 135
hurly-burly n 51, 135
hurrah/hurray interj/n/v 175
hurricane n 119
hurricane lamp n 258
hurroo interj 230
hurry n/v 176
hurry n commotion 136
hurry-scurry adj/adv/n/v 190, 218
hurt v feel pain 45, 239
hurt v cause pain 45, 239
husband n obs. head of household 39
husband n married to wife 39
husband n obs. farmer 35
husbandman n farmer 35
husbandry n 34
hush adj hushed 163
hush v 94
hush interj 156
hush money n 189
hush puppy n 280
hushaby interj 203
hush-hush adj 284
husht interj 156
husk n/v 64
husking bee n 212
husk-tomato n (Am) 254
husky adj burly, strong 238
husky n type of dog 236
husky adj as in "a husky voice" 182
hussy n 156
hussy n housewife 156
hustle n/v con 218
hustle v shake 218
hustle v hurry 218

hustle n as in "hustle and bustle" 216
hustle v push 218
hustle v work as a prostitute 292
hustler n con 215
hut interj 307
hut n 167
hut n mil. 167
hutch n chest 167
hutch n as in "rabbit hutch" 167
hutch n piece of furniture 167
hutment n group of huts or a single hut 258
huzzah interj/n/v 132, 175
hyacinth n type of gem 119
hyacinth n Plants 119
Hydra n 81
Hydra n fig. 81
hydra n 194
hydrant n 211
hydrate v opp. of dehydrate 295
hydraulic adj 159
hydraulic brake n 243
hydraulics n 165
hydro n 256
hydrocarbon n 219
hydrochloric acid n 232
hydrocortisone n 309
hydroelectric adj 256
hydroelectric adj type of steam generator 256
hydrofoil n 281
hydrogen n 193
hydrogen bomb n 307
hydrogen peroxide n 251
hydrolysis n 255
hydrometeor, hydrometeorology n precipitation 237
hydropathy n 221, 257
hydroplane n 274
hydroponics n 297
hydropower n 296
hydrosphere n 254
hydrotherapy n 221, 257
hydrozoan n 237
hyena n 30
hygiene n 121
hygienic adj 121
hygienist n 245
hymn v 20, 173; n 20
hymnal n 19, 101, 266
hymnal 266
hymnary n hymnal 19, 101, 266
hymnbook n 19, 101, 266
hype v stimulate 292
hype v deceive 292; n 313
hype n/v promote 313, 320

hype n hypo, or hypo user (addict) 292
hype n deception 313
hyped-up adj 307
hyper adj Slang 239, 307
hyperactive adj Medicine 239, 307
hyperactivity 239
hyperbola n 166
hyperbole n 76
hypercorrect adj using pretty English 290
hyperextend v 257
hyperinflation n 290
hyperirritability n 279
hyperkinesis/hyperkinesia n 222
hypermarket n 318
hypermedia n 327
hyperparasite n the parasite's parasite 220
hyperpituitarism n 273
hyperrealism n 299
hypersensitive adj 238
hypersexual adj 304
hypersonic adj 301
hyperspace n 248
hypertension n 257
hypertext n 318
hyperthermia n 257
hyperthyroidism n 257
hyperventilate 286
hyperventilation n 286
hyphen n 152; v 152, 214
hyphenate n as in a "hyphenated person" 324
hyphenate v 214
hyphenize v 214
hypnosis n mesmerization 262
hypnosis n coaxing to sleep 262
hypnotherapy n 262
hypnotic adj 151
hypnotism n 225
hypnotist n 225
hypnotize v 225
hypo n hypodermic needle 273
hypoallergenic adj 297
hypocenter n 272
hypochondria n self-convinced illness 169, 221
hypochondria n unexplained melancholia 169, 221
hypocrisy n 38
hypocritical adj 38
hypocrite n 38
hypocritic adj 38
hypocritical adj 38

hypodermic n the needle itself 239
hypodermic n type of treatment 239
hypodermic adj/n 238, 239, 273
hypodermic injection n 239
hypodermic needle n 257, 273
hypodermic syringe n 257, 273
hypoglycemia n 257
hypomania n 262
hypotenuse n 120
hypothesis n scientific sense 136
hypothesis n 136
hypothesize v 136
hypothetic adj 138
hypothetical adj 136, 138
hysterectomy n 257
hysteria n of women only 210
hysteria n gen. 210
hysterical adj 210

I

I beam n 258
iamb n 227
iambus n 227
ibex n 145
ibis n 64
ibuprofen n 316
ICBM n 312
ice n icing 183
ice n type of ice cream 183
ice n 9
ice n diamonds 277
ice v kill 319
ice age n 237
ice ax n 212
ice cap n 236
ice chest n (Am) 222
ice cream n Food 183
ice cream n ice cream cone 183
ice cube n 280
ice dancing n 289
ice floe n 209
ice fog n 237
ice hockey n 263
ice milk n 223
ice pack n 239
ice pick n 242
ice point n point when water freezes 272
ice sheet n 236
ice show n 305
ice storm n 255
ice water n 181
iceberg n 193

iceberg n *obs. type of glacier* 193

iceberg lettuce n 259

iceboat n 198

icebox n 222

icebreaker n *fig.* 243

icebreaker n (Am) *fig. ship* 243

ice-cold adj 25

ice-cream chair n 303

ice-cream cone n 273

icehouse n 171

ice-out n 309

ice-skate n/v 171

ice-skate n 171

ichor n *blood* 99

ichthyosaur n 219

icicle n 9

icing n 183

ick interj (Am) 307

icky adj 292

icky-boo, icky-poo adj *sick* 283

icon n 315

iconoclasm n 202

iconoclast n *gen.* 129

iconoclast n Religion 129

icthyology n *study of birds* 146

I'd contr 172

id n 288

ID card n 273, 303

Idaho n *type of potato* 297

idea n *thought* 74

idea n *ideal* 74

ideal adj/n 90

idealism n 185

idealist n 185

identical adj 160

identical twin n 262

identification n 158

identification bracelet n 316

identification card n 258, 273, 303

identify v 179

identify v *emphathize* 179

identify v *view as identical* 179

identity n 176

identity n *being identical* 176

identity card n 258, 273, 303

identity crisis n 311

ideograph n 227

ideology n 275

ideology n *speculation* 275

ideology n *arch. study of ideas* 275

ides n 12

idiocy n 107

idiom n 127

idiomatic adj 127, 187

idiosyncrasy n *personality quirk* 147, 169

idiosyncrasy n *phys. quirk* 147, 169

idiot n *med.* 32

idiot n *gen.* 32

idiot box n 312

idiot light n 316

idiot savant n 286

idiot stick n (Am) *shovel* 307

idiotism n *idiom* 127

idiotism n 107

idle adj 23

idlesse n *idleness* 102

idol n *gen.* 43

idol n Religion 43

idolatrize v 143

idolatry n 43

idolize v 143

idyll n 128

idyllian adj 128, 251

idyllic adj 128, 251

iffy adj 283

igloo n 211

igneous adj 178

igneous adj *geologic sense* 178

ignis fatuus n *"foolish fire"—swamp gas* 118

ignite v 157

ignition n 157

ignoble adj *not of noble birth* 139

ignoble adj 139

ignominy n 108

ignoramus n 156

ignorance n 38

ignorant adj 38

ignore v 218

ignore v *be unintentionally ignorant* 218

iguana n 119

ilk n *kind, sort* 21

ill adj *bad* 25

I'll contr 128

ill adj *sick* 25; n 25

ill at ease adj 73

ill will n 37

ill-being n 221

ill-boding adj 138

ill-bred adj 154

illegal adj 112; n 300

illegalize v 215

illegible adj 152

illegitimate adj *gen.* 111

illegitimate adj *bastard* 111

ill-fated adj 190

ill-gotten adj 131

illicit adj 111

illiteracy n 77, 172

illiterate adj/n 77

ill-natured adj 149

ill-starred adj *ill-fated* 159

ill-tempered adj 149

illume v 95

illuminate v Religion 43

illuminate v *fig.* 95

illuminate v 95

illuminati n 132

illumination n *enlightening with light* 43

illumination n *spiritual enlightenment* 43

illumination n *enlightening with knowledge* 43

illumine v 95

ill-use v 235

illusion n *mockery* 51

illusion n *something deceptive* 51

illusionary adj 270

illusionist n *magician* 230

illusive adj 139

illusory adj 139

illustrate v *create art* 116

illustrate v *obs. enlighten* 116

illustrate n/v Visual Arts/ Photography 153, 227

illustrate v *illuminate* 116

illustrate v *give examples* 116

illustrious adj 137

I'm contr 128

image n *mental sense* 48

image n *outward impression* 48

image n *as in "corporate image"* 278

image n *phys.* 48

image v 48

imagemaker n 278, 289

imaginary adj 74

imaginary number n 272

imagination n 39

imagine v 39

imagism n *type of poetry* 281

imbalance n 269

imbecile n 216

imbecile adj *physically mentally weak* 216

imbibe v *drink* 167

imbibe v *fig. absorb* 167

imbroglio n 217

imbroglio n *hodgepodge* 217

imbrute v *become brutish* 150

imburse v *save, store, place in pocket* 143

imitate v 84

imitation adj 84, 234

imitation n 84

imitation n *counterfeit* 84

immaculate adj 91

Immaculate Conception n 173

immane adj *huge, monstrous* 159

immaterial adj 89

immature adj *premature* 115

immediate adj 90

immedicable adj *incurable* 106

immemorial adj 146

immense adj *great, swell* 204

immense adj 91

immerge v *immerse* 161

immerse v 161

immersion heater n 279

immigrant n (Am) 154, 202

immigrate v 154

immigration n 154

imminent adj 91

immingle v *intermingle* 161

immix v *commingle* 96

immobile adj 54, 253

immobilize v 54, 253

immoderate adj 89

immodest adj 124

immolate v 117

immoral adj 130, 173

immorality n 130, 173

immortal adj/n 45, 79, 174

immortality n 45, 79

immortalize v 141

immune adj 68

immune response n 309

immune system n 279

immunity n 68, 257

immunize, immunization v, n 257

immunochemistry n 273

immunodeficiency n 316

immunology n 273

immunotherapy n 273

immutable adj 90

impact v *make phys. impact* 161

impact v *as in "impacted tooth"* 161

impact v *make fig. impact* 161

impact n/v 161, 205

impact crater n 254

impair, impairment v, n 50

impala n 237

impale v War/Military/Violence 155

impale v *fence in* 155

impartial adj 138

impassable adj 137

impasse n 250

impassion v 142

inheritress n 81, 102, 112
inheritrix n 81, 102, 112
inhiate v *arch. gape open-mouthedly* 124
inhibit v *hinder* 116
inhibit v *forbid* 116
inhibition n 261
in-house adj 313
inhuman adj 91
inhumanism n 91
inhumanity n 91
inhume n *opp. of exhume* 155
inique *obs.* 50
iniquitous 50
iniquity n 50
iniquous *obs.* 50
initial v Literature/Writing 246
initial adj 115
initial n Language and Speaking 152
initial rhyme n *alliteration* 227
initialism n *acronym* 264
initiate v *as in "initiate a frat member"* 141
initiate n 216
initiate v *gen. begin* 141
initiate adj/n/v 141
initiation n 141
initiative n *action of initiation* 205
initiative n *will to initiate* 205, 288
inject v 85, 162
inject v *obs. throw* 162
injectant n 308
injection n 85
injection molding n 297
in-joke n 321
injunct v 85
injunction n *leg.* 85
injunction n 85
injure v 80
injurious adj 80
injury n 80
injust adj *obs.* 78
injustice n 78
ink n Everyday Life 33
ink n *in squid* 33
inkblot test n 288
inkhorn n 71
inkhorn adj *learned, pedantic* 111
in-kind adj 325
ink-jet adj 322
inkle n *type of cloth* 107
inkling n *obs. suggestion made in low voice* 108

inkling n 108
inkwell n 242
inland n 118
inlander n 157
inlaw n *opp. of outlaw* 46
in-law n Family/Relations/Friends 262
inlay n/v 143
inlay v *obs. hide* 143
inlet n *letting in* 61
inlet n Geography/Places 118
in-line adj/adv 295
in-line engine n 288
in-line skate n 326
inly adv *obs. inwardly* 28
inmate n *roommate* 122, 229
inmate n *prisoner* 122, 229
in-migrant, in-migrate adj/n, v (Am) *immigrant* 308
inn n *public lodging* 70
inn n *hotel* 15
inn n *student residence* 15
inn n *gen. dwelling* 15
innards n The Body 210
innards n *gen. insides* 210
innate adj 90
inner circle n 250
inner city n 315
inner ear n 286
inner light n 247
inner planet n 309
inner space n 311
inner tube n 260
inner-directed adj 308
innersole n *insole* 256
innervate v *furnish with nerves* 238
innerve v *invigorate* 234
inning n 185
innkeeper n 101
innocence n 46
innocency n 46
innocent adj *not guilty* 46
innocent adj *untainted* 46
innocent n 46
innocuous adj 139
innovate v 86
innovation n 86
innovative adj 86, 159
innoxious adj *obs. innocent* 163
innuendo n 170
innuendo n *leg. phrases* 170
innumerate adj/n *mathematically illiterate* 309
inoculate v 182
inoculate v *obs. graft* 182
inoculation n 182
inoperable adj 257

inopinate adj *obs. unexpected* 144
inordinate adj 89
inorganic adj 193
inorganic chemistry n 220
inpatient n Medicine 166
input n/v 270, 308
inquest n 46
inquiet adj *obs. anxious* 107
inquiet adj *obs. tumultuous* 98
inquire v 58
inquiry n 58, 86
inquiry n *official sense* 86
inquisition n 83
inquisition n *as in "Spanish Inquisition"* 83
inquisitive adj 74
inquisitor n 75
inroad n War/Military/Violence 112
inroad n *gen.* 112
inrush n 217
ins and outs n 176
insalubrious adj *unhealthy* 147
insane adj/n 108
insane adj *fig.* 108
insanitary adj 252
insanity n 108
inscribe v 97
inscription n 76
inscroll v *arch. write on a scroll* 128
inseam n 260
insect n 145
insectarium n 255
insectary n 259
insecticide n 247
insectivore n 165, 220
insectivorous adj 165, 220
inselberg n *type of mountain* 279
inseminate v *implant with semen* 148, 285
inseminate v *implant seed* 148
insemination n 148, 285
insense v *impart understanding* 74
insert n/v 104
insert n 269
in-service adj 295
inside job n 277
inside track n (Am) 250
inside/insides n 66
insider n 233
insider trading n 318
insides n 66
insidious adj 115
insight n 38

insightful adj 275
insignia n *gen. badges* 159
insignia n *one badge* 159
insincerity n *lack of sincerity* 117
insincerity n *corruption* 117
insinuate, insinuation v, n 113
insipid adj *without flavor* 159
insipid adj *fig. dull* 159
insist v 8, 252
insistence n 86, 252
insistency n 86
insistent adj 86, 252
insole n 241
insolency n 72
insolent, insolence adj, n 72
insolvent adj Finances/Money 127
insomnia n 147, 273
insomniac n 147, 273
insouciance n 199, 224
insouciant n 199, 224
inspect n *obs.* 83
inspect v 162
inspection n 83, 162
inspector n *in the police* 151, 248
inspector n *gen.* 151, 248
inspector general n 185
inspectress n 151
inspiration n *gen.* 43
inspiration n Religion 43
inspire v *religious sense* 43, 97
inspire v 97
instability, instable n, adj 85
install v *of people* 95
install v *of things* 95
installation n 95
installment n Literature/Writing 227
installment n Finances/Money 200
installment plan n 264
instance n *urgency* 61
instance n *gen.* 61
instancy n 61
instant adj 89
instant n 65
instant adj *urgent* 89
instant book n 318
instant replay n (Am) 317
instantaneous adj 161
instanter adv 179
instate v 161
instep n 66
instigate v 253
instigate v *urge* 253
instill v *gen. introduce* 95

jackstraw n *a nobody* 126
jackstraws n *pick-up-sticks* 213
jack-tar n *sailor* 204
jaconet n *type of cloth* 197
jactation n *bragging* 135
jade n *the stone* 118
jade v *wear out or dull* 143
jade n *useless horse* 64
jade green n 271
jade plant n 302
jaded adj 143, 178
jag n *something jagged* 135
jag n *spree, fling* 268
jag n *ornamental cut in clothing* 135
jagged adj 138
jaggery n *type of sugar* 122
jaguar n 145
jai alai n 275
jail n/v 46
jailbait n (Am) 292
jailbird n 155
jailbreak n (Am) 277
jailer n 46
jailhouse n (Am) 46, 215
jailhouse lawyer n 319
jakes n *bathroom* 106
jalapeno n *type of pepper* 297
jalopy n (Am) 288
jalousie n *type of shutter* 122
jam n *as in "peach jam"* 183
jam n *musical improv* 290
jam n/v 191
jam n *fig. tight spot* 283
jam n 299, v 290
jam n *as in "traffic jam"* 216
jam v *as in "jam radio signals"* 191
jam v 216
jam session n (Am) 290, 299
Jamaica rum n 196
jamb n 33
jambalaya n (Am) 241
jamboree n (Am) 244
jammies n 323
jam-pack v 295
jam-up 216
jane n (Am) *female* 277
Jane Doe n 204, 301
janitor n 185
janitor n *doorman* 185
January n 12
Janus-faced adj *two-faced* 175
Japanese beetle n 255
Japanese cedar n 254
Japanese maple n 254
jar n *type of container* 121
jar v 116

jar v *clash, phys. grate against* 116
jardiniere n *ornamental plant stand* 222
jargon n *pidgin* 172
jargon n *nonsense* 172
jargon n *arch. warbling* 172
jargon n *obs. type of code* 172
jargon n *argot, industry-specific terms* 172
jargonize v 214
jarhead n 313
jarring adj 116
jasm n *energy* 238
jasmine n Plants 118
jasmine n *type of perfume* 118
jasper n *type of mineral* 29
jaunce v *prance* 144
jaundice n Medicine 32
jaundice n *fig.* 32
jaundice v *affect* 208
jaundiced adj Medicine 32
jaunt v *trudge about* 123
jaunt n *short trip* 123, 169
jaunt v *take a short trip* 123
jaunt n *tiresome trip* 123, 169
jaunt n/v 123
jaunting car n 212
jaunty adj *obs. stylish* 169
jaunty adj *devil-may-care* 169
java n *coffee* 223
javelin n 75
javelot n 75
jaw n 66
jaw v *slang* 66, 189
jawbone n 99
jawbreaker n 223
jay adj (Am) *crude, backwater* 268
jay n *type of bird* 30
jay n *marijuana cigarette* 324
jaybird n (Am) 165
Jaycee n 298
jayvee adj/n 298
jaywalk v (Am) 283
jazz n *nonsense* 283
jazz n Music 282
jazz v *as in "jazz up a car"* 284
jazz v *slang have sex* 281; n 281
jazzercise n 326
jazzman n 290
jazz-rock n 318
jazzy adj (Am) 283
je ne sais quoi n 176
jealous adj 36
jealous adj *obs. zealous, desirous* 36

jealous adj *protective, as in "jealous of my time"* 36
jealousy n 36
jean *denim* 242
jeans n 242
jeep n 298
jeepers n (Am) 292
jeepney n 304
jeer n/v 124
jeez interj (Am) 292
jefe n *chief, boss* 277
jeff n *backwater rube* 268
Jehovah n 111
jejune adj *not nutritive, not significant, dull* 159
jejune adj *obs. starved* 159
Jekyll and Hyde n 267
jell v 207
jell v *fig. take shape, come together* 207
jellied gasoline n 302
jellify v 207
jelly n *gen. jelly-like material* 70
jelly n Food 70
jelly v 207
jelly bean n (Am) 273
jelly roll n (Am) 259
jellyfish n 220
jellyfish n *fig. wimp* 220
jenny n *female animal* 119
jenny n *as in "spinning jenny"* 196
jeopard v *jeopardize* 51, 98
jeopardize v 51, 163
jeopardy n 51
jeopardy n *obs. puzzle* 51
jeopardy n *obs. scheme* 51
jerboa n *type of rodent* 165
jeremiad n 198
jerk n/v 197, 223
jerk n *obs. whip lash* 134
jerk n *twitch* 134
jerk n *quick motion* 134
jerk n 134, 301
jerk around v 307
jerk off v 277
jerkin n *type of jacket* 107
jerkwater adj (Am) 250
jerky n (Am) *as in "beef jerky"* 134, 148, 323
jeroboam n *type of bottle* 211
jerrican/jerry can n *type of container* 303
jerry n *chamber pot* 249
jerry can n 303
jerry shop n *public house* 245
jerry-build v 251
jerry-built n 251

jersey n *type of cloth* 123
jersey n *top made of jersey* 123
Jerusalem artichoke n 148
jest n/v 108
jester n 108, 110
Jesus n 111
jet n *jet engine, plane* 317
jet n *jets of air* 177
jet n *type of coal* 29
jet v *obs. strut* 98
jet engine n 304
jet lag n 316
jet plane n 304
jet propulsion n 243
jet set n 312
jet stream n 302
jet-black adj 103
jetliner n 304
jetport n 317
jet-propelled adj 261
jetsam n 137
jettison v 86, 235; n 86
jetty n 88
jewel n *gem* 35
jewel n *piece of jewelry* 35
jeweler n 35, 40
jewelry n 35
Jew's harp n 129
jib n/v *type of sail* 168
jibe n/v *related to ship movement* 169
jibe v (Am) *agree, confirm* 218
jiff n *jiffy* 195
jiffy n *very short period of time* 195
jig n *game, as in "the jig is up"* 132
jig n *type of dance* 129
jig n/v *as in "fishing jigs"* 244
jig-a-jig n 158
jigger n *chigger* 194, 235
jiggered adj *as in "I'll be jiggered"* 231
jiggery-pokery n *trickery* 268
jiggle n/v 235
jiggle n 235
jigsaw n/v 242
jigsaw puzzle n 275
jihad n 247
jillion n Slang 307
jilt v/n Love/Romance/Sex 170
jilt v/n *be disloyal* 170
jim-dandy adj/n 267
jimjams n *nervousness* 243
jimmies n *ice cream sprinkles* 303

jimmy n *type of crowbar* 224; v 224
jingle n *commercial song* 318
jingle n/v 94
jingo interj *as in "by jingo"* 175
jingo, jingoism n 266
jink v *move quickly, jerk* 207
jinx n/v 284
jism n *slang semen* 238
jitney adj *two-bit* 274
jitney n (Am) 274
jitter n/v (Am) 288
jitterbug n/v (Am) *type of dance* 299
jittery adj (Am) 298
jive v *Music* 318
jive n (Am) *jargon, blather* 290
jive adj *fake* 313
jive v *jibe* 321
job n *occupation* 127
job n *duty, challenge* 127
job n *crime* 188
job v 127
job action n (Am) 318
job lot n 245
jobber n 171
jobe v *obs. upbraid* 180
jobholder n (Am) 275
job-hop, job-hopping v, n 311
jock n *athlete* 289, 317
jock n *jockey* 200
jock n *slang genitals, male or female* 195
jock n *disk jockey* 312
jock n 260
jock itch n 303
jockey n/v *Sports* 171
jockey v *as in "jockey for position"* 156
jockey n *horse trader* 171
jockstrap n 260
jocose adj 150
jocoserious adj *semi-serious* 169
jocular adj 150
jocund adj 73
jodhpur n *type of riding breeches* 260
joe n *as in "average joe"* 229
joe n *coffee* 223
Joe Blow n 299
Joe Public n 306
joey n *baby kangaroo* 220
jog v *shake* 117
jog v *nudge* 117
jog v *trudge* 317
jog n *as in "jog in the road"* 251
jog n/v 317

jogging n *exercise* 317
john n (Am) *whorer* 283
john n *slang policeman* 267
john n *toilet* 297
john n *slang penis* 296
John Barleycorn n 148
John Bull n *English Uncle Sam* 188
John Doe n 204, 301
John Hancock n *signature* 227
John Henry n *signature* 227, 281
John Thomas n 296
johnboat n (Am) 274
johnny n *guy, chap* 174
Johnny Reb n (Am) 248
johnnycake n (Am) 183
johnny-come-lately n 231
johnny-on-the-spot n 249
Johnson 296
join v 58
join v *as in "join a club"* 58
join v *take up battle* 58
join in 58
join with 58
joint n *as in "let's blow this pop joint"* 216
joint n *in bodies* 32
joint n *gen.* 32
joint n *marijuana cigarette* 216
joint v 216
joint adj *The Body* 32
joint, the n *the pen* 216, 312
joist n 69
joke n/v *jest* 170
joke n/v *something trivial* 170
joke n/v *something mockable* 170
joker n 170
joker n *in cards* 262
joker n 190
jokist n 170
jollification n 213
jollify v 37, 213
jolliment n 37
jollity n 37
jolly adj 37
jolly adj *obs. lustful* 37
jolly adv *very* 115
jolly adj *fat* 37
jolly n *as in "get your jollies"* 268
jolly adj *attractive* 37
jolly adj *obs. youthfully exuberant* 37
jolly boat n 169
Jolly Roger n 203
jolt n *slang drink* 273
jolt n/v 143

jolt v *fig.* 143
jolt-head n *dolt* 133
jones n *addiction* 320
jorum n *type of drinking vessel* 183
josh n/v (Am) 231
Joshua tree n (Am) 254
joskin n *rube* 204
jostle v *have sex with* 117
jostle n/v 117
jot v *Literature/Writing* 187
jot n *little bit* 99
joule n *measure of energy* 256
jounce n/v *bounce* 96
jouncy adj 96
journal n *financial books* 101, 152
journal n *newspaper, etc.* 152, 187
journal n *obs. traveler's guide* 152
journal n *diary* 152
journalese n 264
journalism n 172, 227
journalist n 172, 227
journalize v 201
journey n *obs. distance traveled in a day* 36
journey n *other things done in a day, such as work* 36
journey n *obs. day* 36
journey n/v 36
journeyman n *tyro* 76, 200
journeywoman n 76, 200
journeywork n 152
joust n/v 40
jovial adj *obs. astrological Jovian* 124
jovial adj 124
jowl n *head* 13
jowl n *dewlap, jaw* 13
jowl n *as in "hog jowls"* 15
jowly adj 238
joy n/v 36
joyance n 36
joyful adj 36
joyjuice n *liquor* 313
joyless 36
joyous adj 36
joypop v (Am) *irregular drug use* 313
joyride n/v (Am) 274
joystick n 275
jubilance n 169, 244
jubilant adj 73, 169
jubilarian n *celebrant* 199
jubilate v 73
jubilation n 73

jubilee n *type of celebration* 75
jubilee n *time of celebration* 75
jubilee n *celebratory joy* 75
jubilize v 73
Judas tree n 164
judge v *sit in judgment* 38
judge n *as in "let me be the judge"* 46
judge v *opine, evaluate* 38
judge n *The Law* 46
judge advocate n 189
judger n 46
judgess n 46, 131
judgmatic adj *judicious* 225
judgmatical adj 225
judgment n *judiciousness* 125
judgment n *decision* 39
judgment n *The Law* 46
judgment n *Religion* 43
judgment call n 232
judgment day n 129
judgmental adj 275
judicial adj 81
judiciary n 230
judicious adj 125
judo n 263
jug n *type of container* 106
jug n *prison* 204
jug v *as in "jugged chicken"* 183
jug band n (Am) 299
juggernaut n *fig.* 154
juggernaut n *referring to Krishna* 154
juggle n/v *magic trick* 173
juggle v *var. gen. meanings of entertain* 265
juggle v *as in "juggle balls"* 265
jugglery n 173
jughead n *Insults* 293
jugs n *slang breasts* 309
jugular vein n 120
juice n (Brit) *gasoline* 274
juice n *slang electricity* 256
juice n 50
juice n *arch. bodily fluid* 50
juice v 50
juice up v 313
juiced adj *drunk* 307
juicehead n *drunk* 313
juicer n 297
juicy adj *titillating* 268
juicy adj 50
jujitsu n 244
jujube n 34
juke v *fake* 321
juke n *jukebox* 299
juke v *move quickly* 321
juke joint n (Am) 300

jukebox n 299

julep n *drink spiked with medicine* 68

julep n *type of alcoholic drink* 68

July n 12

jumble v *mix together* 116

jumble n/v 157

jumble v *be confused* 116

jumbo adj/n 216

jumbo jet n 317

jump n/v 116

jump v *start in surprise, as in "jump to conclusions"* 116

jump n *something to jump* 251

jump v *as in "train jumping the tracks"* 271

jump v *rise quickly, as in "a price jumping"* 116

jump n *as in "parachute jump"* 294

jump v *as in "jump ship"* 271

jump n 271

jump jet n 317

jump rope n 213

jumper n 303

jumper cables n 288

jumping bean n (Am) 254

jumping jack n (Am) 244

jumping-off place n (Am) 231

jump-start n/v 325

jumpsuit n 303

jumpy adj *vacillating* 252

jumpy adj *nervous* 252

junction n *crossing* 243

junction n *act of joining* 243

juncture n 84

June n 12

june bug n 219

jungle n 194

jungle n *fig.* 194

jungle fever n 210

jungle gym n 289

junior adj/n *as in "John Smith, Junior"* 40

junior n *Age/Aging* 105

junior n *Education* 202

junior adj *for kids, as in "junior sizes"* 237

junior college n (Am) 266

junior high school n 276

junior miss n 294

junior varsity n 305

juniority n *opp. of seniority* 136

juniper n 64

junk v *discard* 284

junk n *heroin* 292

junk n *type of ship* 123

junk n/v *trash* 239

junk n *arch. type of splint* 147

junk n *obs. bad rope* 239

junk n *type of shipboard food* 239

junk art n 318

junk bond n 323

junk call n *akin to junk mail* 323

junk food n 316

junk mail n (Am) 311

junker n 307

junket n *type of cream dish* 70

junket n/v 123

junkie n *addict* 292

junkman n (Am) 245

junkyard n (Am) 257

junta n 154

jurisdiction n *The Law* 46

jurisdiction n *gen. province* 46

jurisprudence n 155

jurisprudent n *jurist* 155

jurist n *leg. expert* 102

jurist n 102

juror n *obs. false accusor* 46

juror n 46

jury adj *makeshift* 160

jury n *nonlegal sense* 46

jury v *judge* 308

jury n 46

jury-rig v 208

jurywoman n 215

just adj *obs. precise* 72

just adj *deserved* 72

just adj *fair* 72

just adj *legal* 72

just adj *righteous* 72

just-folks adj 313

justice n *spec. legal system* 20

justice n *judge, etc.* 46

justice n *being just* 39

justice n *leg. system* 46

justice n *getting what you deserve* 20

justice of the peace n 80

justifiable adj 137

justifiable adj *subject to adjudication* 137

justification n *law* 100

justification n *reason, rationalization* 100

justify v *clear of wrongdoing* 141

justify v *show reason* 141

justify v *prove true* 141

justify v *obs. mete justice* 46

jut v 139

juvenal obs. 182

juvenescence n 195

juvenescent adj 195

juvenile adj *immature* 146

juvenile adj *young* 146

juvenile adj/n 146, 182

juvenile court n (Am) 267

juvenile delinquency n 215

juvenile delinquent n 215

juvenile officer n 312

juvenilia n 152

juvenility 146

juxtapose v 176, 252

juxtaposition n 176

K

K ration n (Am) 300

kabob n 168

Kabuki n 265

kaddish n *type of prayer* 154

kaffeeklatsch n 258

kafkaesque adj 308

kahuna n *Hawaiian witch doctor* 267

kaiser roll n 259

kale n 34

kaleidoscope n 213

kaleyard n 34

kame n *glacial feature* 193

kamikaze n/adj 306

kangaroo n 194

kangaroo court n (Am) 250

kangaroo rat n 194

kapellmeister n *choir director* 228

kaput adj 268

karaoke n 327

karat n 99

karate n 312

karma n 228

kart n 310

kashruth n *Jewish dietary laws* 276

katydid n (Am) 194

katzenjammer n *hangover, clamor* 231

katzenjammer n *confusion* 231

kayak n 198

kayo n/v (Am) 281

kayo interj *OK* 292

kazoo n (Am) 265

keel n *type of boat* 36

keel n *as in "ship's keel"* 36

keel v *as in "keel over"* 234

keelboat n 169

keelhaul v 179

keen adj *intense* 53

keen adj *sharp* 53

keen adj *as in "peachy-keen"* 292

keen n *funeral lament* 215; v 215

keen adj *obs. mentally sharp* 292

keep n *as in "for keeps"* 205

keep v *as in "keep a promise"* 28

keep n *as in "earn your keep"* 232

keep v *store, maintain possession* 60

keep v *as in "shopkeeper"* 110

keep v *var. obs. meanings of take, acquire* 60

keep v *as in "keep Christmas"* 28

keep v *"maintain," as in "keep the books"* 141

keep v *akin to "kept woman"* 125

keep v *continue, as in "keep talking"* 60

keep n *part of a castle* 122

keep v *as in "housekeeper"* 110

keep n *custody, charge* 61

keep a low profile v 325

keep back v 235

keepsake n 205

keg n 121

kegler n *bowler* 298

kegling n *bowling* 298

keister n *bottom* 296

keister n *safe* 296

keister n *type of carrying case* 296

kelly green n (Am) 301

kelp n 64

kelpie n *folklore spirit* 175

kelpie n *type of dog* 272

Kelvin adj/n *thermometer scale* 273

kempt adj 14

ken v *tell* 39

ken v *obs. tell* 28

ken v *know* 39, 125

ken n *range of knowledge* 125

ken v *arch. see* 39

ken n *obs. range of sight* 125

Kendal green n *type of cloth* 107

kennel n *pet shelter* 35; v 35

kennel n *street gutter* 99

kennel n *animal den* 35

keno n (Am) 213

kenspeckle adj *conspicuous* 137

Kentucky bluegrass n 220

Kentucky rifle n 229

kercher n 35

kerchief n 35

kerchief n as in "handkerchief" 35

kerfuffle n (Brit) disturbance, commotion 230

kernel n as in "kernel of grain" 30

kernel n gen. core 30

kernel n inside of nut 30

kerosene n 237

kerplunk adv 267

kersey n type of fabric 71

kerseymere n type of fabric 197

ketch n type of boat 100

ketchup n 168

kettle n 14

kettle n geo. sense 14, 236

kettle of fish n 189

kettledrum n 129

Kewpie n 289

key n as in "piano key" 77, 101, 242

key n as in "key of G" 77

key n type of island, reef 164

key n type of winding or grasping tool 149

key adj crucial 271

key n as in "typewriter key" 101, 242

key n (Am) kilogram 316

key n lit. and fig. something that unlocks 16

key light n 299

key lime n 285

key lime pie n 310

key ring n 258

keyboard n as in "piano key board" 214, 242

keyboard n as in "typewriter keyboard" 214, 242

keyboard v 321

keyboard v 242, 321

keyhole n 121

keyhole saw n 198

keynote v 284

keynote n 201

keynote n gen. 201

keynote address n 276

keynote speaker n 305

keypad n 317

keypunch n/v 280

keystroke n/v 278

K.G. adj (Am) no go 231

khaki adj/n pertaining to the color and the cloth 242

khakis n 242

kibble n type of dog 119

kibble v grind 208

kibble n animal food 303

kibbutz n 301

kibitz, kibitzer v, n (Am) 292

kibosh n/v 230

kick n as in "kick of a gun" 229

kick v fig., as in "kick yourself" 94

kick n fig. "shock, thrill," as in "getting your kicks" 243

kick n fig. 113

kick n fad 168

kick v 94

kick n/v 113

kick v as in "kick the bucket" 174

kick around v 235

kick in v 278

kick out v 180

kick the bucket v 202

kickback n (Am) 284

kickoff n 250

kicks n shoes 277

kickshaw n fancy chow 122

kickstart v 280

kid n young child 30

kid n young goat 30

kid n/v josh 216

kid n 168

kid glove n 260

kid leather n 168

kid stuff n (Am) 292

kidder n 216

kiddie n 30, 130, 132, 251

kiddo n 267

kidnap v 174

kidnapper n 174

kidney n bodily part 32

kidney n fig. "temperament" 32

kidney bean n 107

kidney stone n 303

kidskin n 71

kidvid n 312

kielbasa n 297

kill v as in "kill a case of beer," "kill the lights," "kill a story" 249

kill n (Am) creek, channel 164

kill v 45

kill n result of killing 215

kill v fig., as in "this job is killing me" 45

kill v as in "kill time" 45

kill n 45

kill off v 155

killdeer n (Am) 181

killer n 249

killer adj 313

killer n 313

killer bee n 315

killer cell n 322

killer instinct n 301

killer whale n 255

killing n 268

killjoy n 204

kiln n 16

kilo n 238

kilobyte n 316

kilocycle n kilohertz 285

kilogram n 195

kilohertz n 286

kiloliter n 210

kilometer n 195

kiloton n 302

kilowatt n 256

kilt n/v 35, 184

kilt v tuck up 35

kilter n (Am) 158

kiltie n person in kilts 223

kimono n 168

kin adj 18, 126

kin n descendents 18

kin 40

kin n arch. single relative 18

kin n relatives 18, 40

kind n grouping 23

kind n obs. gender 18

kind n natural condition 28

kind adj obs. natural 28

kind adj obs. of good ancestry 38

kind n arch. ancestry 18

kind n variety 23

kind n kin 18

kind adj loving 38

kind n nature 28

kind n place of ancestry 18

kind adj compassionate 38

kind adj obs. semen 18

kind adj obs. amiable 38

kindergarten n 247

kindhearted adj 108

kindle v 31

kindless adj obs. unnatural 61

kindling n act of starting fires 105

kindling n material to start fires 105

kindly adv obs. naturally 28

kindly adv/adj 38

kindly adj obs. natural 28

kindness 38

kindred adj similar 54

kindred adj related, kin 54

kindred n kinship 54

kinematics n study of motion 220

kinesics n study of body language 309

kinesiology n study of anatomy and movement 255

kinesis n study of body reactions 239, 272

kinetic adj 237, 251

kinetic art n 318

kinetic energy n 237

kinetics n 237

kinetoscope n 265

kinfolk n 18, 244

king n in cards 75, 126

king n fig. leader, ruler 20

king n obs. queen bee 64

king n in chess 75, 126

king n/v 20

king cobra n 255

king crab n 165

king mackerel n 285

king of beasts n 64

king penguin n 255

king salmon n (Am) 255

king snake n 181

kingcraft n 20

kingdom n Government 44

kingdom n as in "animal kingdom" 44, 165

kingdom n ruling as a king 44

kingdom come n 202

kingfish n type of fish 181

kingfisher n 31

kinglet n 156

kingmaker n 102

kingpin n 249

King's English n 110

king's evil n type of disease 68

king's ransom n 133

king-size adj 217

kink n kinkiness 313

kink n kinky person 313

kink n 177

kink v 177

kinkajou n 194

kinkle 177

kinky adj perverted 313

kinsfolk n 18, 244

kinship n 226

kinship n fig. being related 226

kinsman n 18, 40, 199

kinspeople n 18, 40, 199, 244

kinswoman 18

kinswoman n 18, 40, 199

kiosk n 159

kipper n 11

kirsch n type of brandy 211

kismet n fate 232

kiss n/v 18

kiss n Food 223
kiss ass v 189
kiss my ass interj 189
kiss of death n 307
kiss of peace n 269
kiss off, kissoff v, n 300
kiss-and-tell adj 304
kisser n *slang mouth* 238
kissing cousin n 301
kissing disease n 316
kit n *kitten or small animal* 64, 119
kit n *type of violin* 111
kit n *group of items* 196
kit v 196
kit n *type of container* 196
kit n *as in "model kit"* 196
kit and caboodle n 269
kit bag n 258
kitchen n 15
kitchen n *cuisine* 15
kitchen cabinet n (Am) 222
kitchen garden n 122
kitchen midden n *refuse heap* 239
kitchen police n 282
kitchenette n 273
kitchen-sink adj *all-inclusive* 307
kite n/v *as in "kite a check"* 245
kite n *type of bird* 11
kite n/v *as in "fly a kite"* 170
kite n *arch. predatory person* 11
kith n *obs. things known* 18
kith n 18
kith n *obs. conventions of behavior* 18
kith n *obs. home* 18
kithara n *type of stringed instrument* 77
kitsch n 291
kitten n *girl* 268
kitten n *applied to other animals* 64, 119
kitten n *applied to cats* 64, 119
kittenish adj 64, 198
kittiwake n 146
kitty n *Brit slang jail* 262
kitty n *as in "poker kitty"* 262
kitty n *kitten* 64, 181
kitty-corner adj 270
kiwi n 219
kiwifruit n 315
klatch/klatsch n 307
klaxon n (Am) 278
klepto n 312
kleptomania n 229
kleptomaniac n 229

klick n *kilometer* 316
kludge n *jury-rigged computer system* 315
klutz n (Am) 313
knack n *trick* 136
knack n *talent* 136
knapsack n 159
knave n *obs. boy* 18
knave n *arch. servant* 18, 47
knave n *in cards: jack* 126
knave n *rascal* 18, 47
knavery n 47
knead v 27
knee n 13
knee v *bend the knee* 28
knee v *obs. kneel* 28
knee v *hit with the knee* 267
knee breeches n 223
knee jerk n 256
kneecap n 66, 238
kneecap n *knee covering* 238
kneecapping n 324
knee-deep adj 103
knee-high adj (Am) 191
knee-jerk adj 262
kneel v 27
kneepad n 242
kneepan n *kneecap* 66, 238
knee-slapper n 318
kneesock n 316
knell n/v *ring a bell* 97
knell n 23
knell v *obs. hit* 97
knelt v 271
knickerbockers n 224
knickers n 224, 260
knickers n *type of women's clothing* 260
knicknack n 167
knife n *as in "under the knife"* 16
knife n/v 16
knife v 252
knife v *as in "knife through the crowd"* 252
knight n *in chess* 40
knight n 20
knight n *obs. meanings of knave, boy* 20
knight-errantry n 44
knight-errant n 44
knighthood n 40
knightly adj 40
knish n 280
knit v *arch. knot* 35
knit v *as in "knitted brow"* 97
knit v *as in "knit a sweater"* 35
knit v *obs. method of gelding* 35

knit v *heal* 99
knit v *fig.* 35
knit n *Cloth/Clothing* 123
knitwear n 287
knob n 23
knobble v 23
knobby adj 23
knock Love/Romance/Sex 170
knock v *as in "knock around"* 141
knock n 51
knock v *as in "an engine knocking"* 27
knock v *insult* 268
knock v *hit, collide, as in "knees knocking"* 60
knock n/v 27
knock off v *rob* 283
knock off v *quit* 277
knock out v 247
knock over v *rob* 283
knock up v *slang impregnate* 170
knockabout adj/n 269
knock-down-drag-out adj 231
knockers n *slang breasts* 302
knock-knee n 221
knockoff n *imitation* 320
knockout n 266
knockout n *slang type of auction* 266
knockout drops n 269
knockwurst n 287
knoll n/v *sound a knell* 51
knoll n *obs. mountaintop* 9
knoll n *small hill* 9
knot n *Measurement* 166
knot n *obs. obligation* 23
knot n *as in "tree knot"* 32, 64
knot n *type of tied ribbon* 23
knot n *in rope* 23
knot n *tense muscle* 32
knot n *fig. bond* 23
knot v 23
knot garden n *elaborate garden* 107
knothole n 190
knotty adj *knotted* 53
knotty adj *fig. intricate* 53
knotty pine n 254
know v *as in "know a friend"; as in "know pain"; be aware; have sex; learn; be educated; understand* 39
know n 39
know-all n (Brit) *know-it-all* 249
know-nothingism n 216
know-how n (Am) 225

know-it-all n 268
knowledge n 39
knowledge engineering n 323
knowledgeable adj *obs. perceivable* 225
knowledgeable adj 225
know-nothing n 216
knuckle n 66
knuckle n *as in "pig's knuckles"* 146
knuckle down v 252
knuckle sandwich n 324
knuckle under v 207
knuckle-duster n (Am) 249
knucklehead n 307
KO n/v 289
koala n 209
kobold n *type of gnome* 156
Kodiak bear n 255
kohlrabi n 211
koine n *dialect* 264
kola nut n 236
kola tree n 181
komoda dragon n 285
kook, kookie n, adj 313
kookaburra n 220
Koran n 154
kosher adj/n/v Religion 247
kosher adj *slang OK* 247
kowtow n/v 216
KP n (Am) 282
kraken n *mythical monster* 203
kraut n *sauerkraut* 241
kremlinology n 312
krill n *type of crustacean* 272
Kriss Kringle n 226
krummholz n *timberline forest* 272
krummhorn n *type of woodwind instrument* 173
kuchen n *type of coffee cake* 241
kudo n 294
kudos n 206
kudzu n 254
kugel n *type of pudding* 223
kultur n 282
kumquat n 168
kung fu n 263
kvetch n/v 311
kyle n *obs. boil* 69
kymograph n *measurer of fluid pressure* 238
kyrie n *type of prayer* 43

L

la interj 132
lab n 268

label n *ribbon* 51
label n *arch. band, esp. around a document* 51
label n *identifier* 51
label v *characterize, stereotype* 161
label v *attach label* 161
label n *brand name* 289
label v 51
labial adj *related to the lip* 127
labor n *the result of hard work* 41
labor n *hard work* 41
labor n *workingpeople* 41, 245
labor v *obs.* 121
labor n *in childbirth* 41, 121
labor n *workingpeople* 245
labor v 41
labor camp n 264
labor force n 263
labor of love n 176
labor union n 245
laboratory n 146
labored adj *difficult* 115
labored adj *obs. worn* 115
labored adj *obs. well worked* 115
labor-intensive adj 311
laborious adj 41
laborsaving adj 200
Labrador retriever n 272
labyrinth n *fig.* 84
labyrinth n/v 84
labyrinthian adj 84
labyrinthine adj 84
lace v *as in "lace a drink with strychnine"* 180
lace n *as in "shoelace"* 33
lace v *as in "lace up shoes"* 33, 56; n 33, 56
lace n 122
lace pillow n 196
lace-curtain adj *slang middle-class* 299
lacerate adj/v 97
laceration n 97
lacewing n *type of insect* 236
lacework n 233
lack n *obs. offense* 51
lack n 51
lack n *gen. want, need* 51
lack n/v 55
lackadaisical adj 198
lackadaisy interj 175, 203
lackadaisy adj 198
lackaday interj *expression of regret* 175, 203
lackey n/v 113

lackey v 113
lackluster adj/n 136
laconic adj 138
laconism n 138
lacquer n/v 177
lacquer n/v *obs. type of secretion* 177
lacquerware n 167
lacrosse n (Am) 185
lactate v 164
lactation n 164
lactic adj *related to milk* 196
lad n 44
ladder n 16
ladder n *fig. hierarchy* 16
ladder truck n 274
ladder-back adj 273
laddie n 44, 111
lade v *load* 26
la-de-da adj/interj/n 292
laden adj 25, 26; v 26
ladies' man n 199
ladies' room n 239
ladle n/v 16
lady n *as in "behave like a lady"* 20
lady n *akin to gentleman* 20
lady n *akin to lord* 20
lady n *type of formal rank* 20
lady n *head of a household* 20
lady of the evening n 249
lady of the house n 196
ladybeetle n 254
ladybug n 165
ladyfinger n 168
lady-in-waiting n 247
lady-killer n 213
ladykin n 247
ladylike adj 130
ladylove n 185
lady's man/ladies' man n 199
lady's slipper n (Am) 119
laetrile n 309
lag n *result of lagging* 251
lag adj *obs. last* 251
lag n *barrel stave* 168
lag n *obs. last person* 251
lag v 251
lager n 222
laggard adj/n 190
lagniappe n (Am) 233
lagoon n *tropical lagoon* 164
lagoon n *type of standing water* 164
laid-back adj 317
lair n *gen. sleeping place* 70
lair n *animal den* 70
lair n 14

laissez-faire n 215
laity n 78
lake n *small pool* 29
lake n 29
lake n *obs. stream* 29
lake dwelling n 239
lake herring n 220
lake trout n 165
lakeport n (Am) 243
lakeshore n 193
lallygag n (Am) 252
lam v *thrash* 142
lam n/v *as in "on the lam"* 268
lama n *lamaist monk* 173
Lamaze adj 316
lamb n *fig. and lit.* 11
lamb n 70
lambada n *type of dance* 327
lambaste v *beat, hit* 155
lambkin n 119
Lambrusco n 303
lambskin n 71
lame n *armorplates* 131
lame adj *crippled* 14; v 45
lame n *type of fabric* 287
lame adj *as in "lame excuse"* 14
lame v 14
lame duck n 202
lamebrain n 293
lament v/n 72
lamentation n 72
lamia n *witch* 81
lamia n *type of monster* 81
laminate adj/v 179
laminate n *surfacing material* 297
lamination n 179
lammergeier n *type of vulture* 210
lamp n 33
lampblack n 136
lamper eel n 30, 105
lamplight n 69
lamplighter n 185
lampoon n/v 158
lamppost n 196
lamprey n 30
lamps n Slang 132
lampshade n 239
lamster n *someone on the lam* 277
LAN n *local area network* 326
lanai n *porch* 211
lance n 45, 131
lance v *as in "lance a boil"* 104
lance n *type of soldier* 45
lance corporal n 203

lance-knight n 112
lancer n 131
lancet n *type of surgical instrument* 68
lancet n *obs. small lance* 68
lancinate v *pierce* 161
land v *as in "land a good job"* 162
land v *as in "land a plane"* 36
land v *as in "land a ship"* 36
land n *nation* 9
land n *as in "land a fish"* 36, 162
land n *ground* 9
land n *as in "meadowland"* 9
land v 9
land bank n 172
land mine n 266
land of Nod n *sleepland* 189
land yacht n 288
landau n *type of carriage* 184
landaulet n *small carriage* 198
landed adj 25
landfall n *landing* 149
landfill n (Am) 308
landform n 254
landholder n 79
landing n *type of platform* 86
landing n *landing place* 86
landing craft n 298
landing field n 281
landing strip n 288
landlady n 18, 110
landlocked adj 145
landlord n 18, 110
landlubber n 175
landmark n *fig. prominent point* 9
landmark n *phys. prominent feature* 9
landmark n *lit. something marking land* 9
landmark adj 9
landmass n 236
land-office business n (Am) 227
land-poor adj (Am) 252
landscape v *as in "landscape a yard"* 284
landscape n *the land being painted* 128
landscape n 128
landscape architect n 226
landscape gardener n 200
landscaper n 284, 316
landscapist n *type of painter* 128, 228

landslide n *big political victory* 219

landslide n Geography/Places 164, 219; v 219

landslip n 164, 219

lane n *as in "fast lane"* 17

lane n *path, street* 17

lane n *as in "shipping lane"* 17

language n *cursing* 41

language n *as in "body language"* 41

language n 41

language n *jargon* 41

language arts n 305

language laboratory n 319

languid adj 58

languish v 58

lank adj 25, 166

lanky adj 25, 166

lanolin n 254

lantern n 35

lantern fish n 194

lantern jaw n 176

lantern slide n 246

lap n/v *once around the track* 244

lap v *as in "lapping waves"* 27; n 27

lap n *flap, as in "earlap"* 15

lap n *as in "sit on Santa's lap"* 32

lap v *overlap* 162; n 206

lap n *obs. bosom* 32

lap v *as in "dog lapping up water"* 27

lap belt n *seat belt* 310

lap robe n (Am) 242

lapboard n 216

lapdog n 146

lapel n 168

lapidary n *obs. gem expert* 75

lapidary n *gem cutter* 75

lapse n/v *something that has lapsed* 87

lapse n/v *inattentive goof* 87

laptop adj/n 326

larboard adj/n *port* 51

larcener n 102

larcenist n 102

larcenous adj 102

larceny n 102

larch n 105

lard n/v 34

lard n/v *obs. bacon* 34

larder n *type of storage* 69

larder n *what is stored* 69

large adv *obs.* 91

large adj *not strict, unrestrained* 98

large adj *big* 91

large intestine n 210

largehearted adj 150

large-minded adj 185

largemouth bass n (Am) 254

large-print adj 318

larger-than-life adj 308

large-scale adj 270

largesse n 36

lariat n 224

lark n *type of bird* 11

lark n/v *whim* 212

larkspur n *type of plant* 118

larky adj 212, 224

larrigan n *type of moccasin* 260

larum n *alarm* 87

larva n *arch. type of ghost* 175

larva n 194

laryngitis n 211

larynx n 120

lasagna n 223

lascivious adj 74

laser n 309

laser disc n 322

laser printer n 322

lash v *lace, as in "lash a corset"* 96; n 96

lash n/v 51

lash v *as in "lash a rope"* 96

lash v *dish out liberally* 60

lash v *as in "lash a tail," "rain that lashes"* 60

lashes n *eyelashes* 195

lash-up n *something jury-rigged* 270

lass n 44

lassie n 44, 188

lasso n/v 197

last v *continue* 26

last adj *most recent* 53

last v *as in "as long as supplies last"* 26

last adj *final* 53

last adj/n 26

last hurrah n 313

Last Judgment n 78

last minute n 284

last name n 266

last rites n 291

last straw n 232

last word n 133

last-ditch adj 278

last-gasp adj 294

last-in first-out adj 301

lasting adj 53

lasting adj 26

latch v *obs. catch* 321

latch n 52

latch v *obs. grab, seize* 321

latch v *obs. grab* 28

latch v *as in "latch onto"* 321

latch v 52

latchkey n 211

latchkey child n 306

late adj *as in "late in the day"* 12

late adj *as in "late in the Victorian era"* 12

late adj *behind the time* 12

late adj *as in "the late Mr. Smith"* 12

late adj *slow* 12

late adv 12

latecomer n 251

lated adj *belated* 138

laten v *get late* 271

latency n 91

latent adj 91

latent n *as in "latent fingerprint"* 292

later adv 12

lateral adj 91

lateral thinking n 317

latest n 269

latex n *type of plant secretion* 164

latex n *obs. bodily fluids* 164

latex n *type of artificial mixture* 164

lathe n 36

lather n *consternation, tizzy* 136, 249

lather n *as in "soap lather"* 136

lather n *heavy sweat* 68, 136; v 68

lather n *obs. type of froth* 136

lather v 136

latitude n *leeway* 66

latitude n *gen. area* 66

latitude n *opp. of longitude* 66

latitude n *variance range* 66

latrine n 33

latrociny n *obs. robbery* 80

lats n *latissimus dorsi—akin to pecs* 316

latter adj 54

latter adj *obs. slower* 54

latter-day adj 234

latterly adv *later, lately* 191

lattermost adj 217

lattice n 51

latticework 51

laud n *gen. praise* 43

laud n Religion 43

laud, laudable v, adj 95

laudanum n *morphine medication* 121

laudation n 95

laudative n 95

laudatory adj 95

laugh n/v 17

laugh n *as in "that's a laugh"* 169

laugh line n *wrinkle* 286

laugh off v 191

laugh track n 319

laughable adj 17, 139

laughful adj 224

laughing gas n 233

laughing jackass n 204

laughing matter n 133

laughingstock n 112

laughsome adj 17, 139

laughter n 17

laughworthy adj 17, 139

launch v *set off, introduce* 60

launch v *begin* 60

launch v *as in "launch a boat"* 60

launch n *type of boat* 169

launch v *propel* 60

launch n *the result of launching* 190

launch n 60

launch vehicle n 310

launching pad n 310

launchpad n 310

launder v Crime/Punishment/Enforcement 319

launder v Everyday Life 69

launderette n 303

laundress n 110

laundry n *washing clothes* 69

laundry n *place to wash clothes* 69

laundry n *clothes to be washed* 69

laundry v 69

laundry list n 313

laundryman n 185, 244

laundrywoman n 185, 244

laurel n *honor* 30

laurel n *type of tree* 30

lava n 181

lavation n 167

lavatory n *bathing room* 167

lavatory n *toilet* 167

lavatory n *rest room* 167

lavatory n *bath* 69, 167

lave v *wash, bathe* 14, 167

lavender n *type of potpourri* 29

lavender n *type of color* 29, 252

lecture n *arch. reading* 128
lecture n/v 128
lecturess n 84, 270
LED n *light-emitting diode* 315
lederhosen n 297
ledge n 114
ledge n *obs. type of barring device* 114
ledger n *obs. type of bible* 127
ledger n *gen. recordbook* 127
ledger n Finances/Money 127
lee n *protection* 14
lee n *the protected side* 14
lee adj 14
lee shore n *shore at ship's leeward side* 118
leech n *fig.* 10
leech n *physician* 14
leech n 10
leech v *act as a parasite* 221
leech v *cure* 14
leech v *apply leeches* 221
leek n *type of plant* 10
leer n/v 107
leery adj 190
leeway n 176
left adj *obs. weak* 53
left adj *on the weak side* 53
left n *in boxing* 248
left adj *on the left side* 53
left n Politics 247
left wing n Politics 266
left-hand adj 53
left-handed adj *using the left* 53, 67
left-handed adj *obs. disabled* 69
left-handed adj *awkward* 53, 67
left-hander n *left-handed person* 256
left-hander n *blow from the left hand* 256
leftism, leftist n Politics 282
leftover adj/n 270
leftover adj 270
lefty n 256, 267, 292; adj 267
leg n Cloth/Clothing 71
leg n *in furniture* 32, 148
leg v *run* 149
leg n The Body 32
leg n *as in "second leg of the race"* 286
leg v 32
leg up n 231
leg warmer n 260
legacy n *fig.* 82
legacy n *something bequeathed* 82
legal adj *allowed by law* 102

legal n 112
legal adj *pertaining to law* 102
legal age n 277
legal aid n 267
legal eagle n 307
legal holiday n (Am) 244
legal pad n 318
legal tender n 187
legalese n 281
legality n 81
legalize v 155
legend n *motto* 101
legend n *as in "the legend of the Lone Ranger"* 51
legend n *tale of saint's life* 51
legendary adj 138
legerdemain n *gen. trickery* 81
legerdemain n *magic tricks* 81
leggings n 197
leggy adj 204
leghold trap n 323
leghorn n 237
legible adj 76
legion n 45; adj 45
legion adj 45, 179
legionary n *legionnaire* 131
legionnaire n 215
Legionnaires' disease n 322
legislate v 215
legislation n *a law itself* 175
legislation n *making laws* 175
legislator n 102
legislature n 175
legist n *leg. expert* 81
legit adj/n 277
legitimate adj *as in "a legitimate child"* 75
legitimate v 208
legitimate adj *gen.* 75
legitimate v Family/Relations/ Friends 75
legitimatize v 208
legitimize v 208
legman n (Am) Slang 292
leg-of-mutton adj *describing a shape* 231
legroom n 294
legume n 164
legwork n (Am) 268
lei n 223
leister n/v *spear used to catch fish* 107
leisure n 40
leisure suit n (Am) 323
leitmotif n 265
lemming n 145
lemon n *bad car* 274
lemon n *loser* 250

lemon n 64
lemon adj/n *the color* 207
lemon n *crabby person* 250
lemon balm n *type of mint* 254
lemon drop n 211
lemon law n 327
lemon sole n 259
lemon yellow n 217
lemonade n 148
lemongrass n 209
lemur n 194
lend v 26
lending library n 187
lend-lease n/v 298
length n 12
length n *swimming measure* 289
lengthen v 94
lengthways 138
lengthwise adv 138
lengthy adj (Am) 179
lenience n 74
leniency n 74
lenient adj 199
lenient adj *soothing* 180
lenient adj *arch. soothing* 199
lenity n *leniency* 74
lens n 178
lens n *applied to the eye* 178
lensman n *cameraman* 298
lenticular adj 90
lentil n *type of legume* 34
leonine adj 89
leopard n 30, 119
leopard frog n (Am) 220
leopard seal n 255
leopardess n 30, 119
leotard n 260
leper adj *obs.* 68
leper n *fig.* 68
leper n Medicine 32, 68
leper n *obs. leprosy* 68
lepidopterology n *study of moths and butterflies* 255
leprechaun n 156
leprosarium n *leprosy sanitarium* 222
leprosy n 22, 99
leprous adj 32
lesbian adj/n 244
lesbian adj/n *of Lesbos* 262
lesbian adj/n *gay* 244, 262
lesbianism n 244
lesion n 69
less v 58
lessee n 81
lessen v 58
lesser adj/adv 53

lesson n *obs. lecture* 42
lesson n *as in "let that be a lesson to you"* 42
lesson n Education 42
lesson v *arch.* 42
lessor n 81
let v *permit* 27
let v *hinder* 26
let n *in tennis* 226
let v *lease* 27
letch v 204, 283
letdown n 205
lethal adj 155
lethal adj *describing spiritual death* 155
lethal gene n 297
lethargic adj 72
lethargy n 72
letter n *type of correspondence* 42
letter n *e.g., ABC . . .* 41
letter n *as in "letter of the law"* 51
letter bomb n 307
letter box n 201
letter carrier n 126
letter of credit n 152
letter of intent n 305
lettered adj *educated* 42
letterhead n 258
letterless adj Education 42
letterman n Sports 185
letter-perfect adj 234
letterpress n 201
letter-quality adj/n 323
letters n Education 266
lettuce n *slang cash* 290
lettuce n 34
letup n (Am) 232
leukemia n 222
leukotomy n *lobotomy* 297
levee n (Am) 183
level v *raze, destroy* 155
level adj 262
level adj *even* 91
level n *as in "sea level"* 134
level v *as in "let me level with you"* 283
level n 36
level n *as in "the topmost level"* 134
level adj *horizontal* 91
level v 91
level off v 284
level playing field n 327
levelheaded adj (Am) 262
leveling rod n 260

lever n *type of control device* 35, 242

lever n *type of pry* 35, 242

lever v 35, 242

leverage n/v 232, 301

leverage n *using a lever* 232

leverage n *fig.* 232

leveraged adj 311

leviathan adj/n 47

levitate v 176

levitation n 176

levity n *lightness* 176

levity n 134

levy n/v *as in "tax levy"* 41

lewd adj *obs. secular* 75

lewd adj *lascivious, vulgar* 75

lewd adj *obs. bumbling* 75

lew-warm adj *lukewarm* 91

lex n *law* 102

lexical adj *related to words* 227

lexicographer n *creator of dictionaries* 172

lexicography n 172

lexicology n 227

lexicon n *vocabulary* 172

lexicon n *type of dictionary* 172

lexis n 311

Lhasa apso n *type of dog* 296

liability n *accountability* 205

liability n *debit* 205

liable adj *as in "liable to explode"* 139

liable adj 76

liaise v 295

liaison n *tryst* 226

liaison n 226

liar n 22

lib n (Am) 319

libate v 70

libation n *pouring* 70

libation n *drink* 70

libber n 319

libel n/v 155

libel v *obs. sue* 81

libel n/v *type of document* 155

libel n/v *obs. libelous publication* 155

liberal adj 54

liberal arts n 77

liberal, liberalism n Politics 215

liberated adj *as in "sexually liberated"* 306

liberation n 86

libertarian adj/n Politics 202

libertine n *free spirit* 124

liberty n 82

libidinal adj 262

libidinous adj 74, 262

libido n 262

librarian n 185

librarian n *obs. copier* 185

library n 42

library card n 299

library paste n 310

library science n 276

librettist n *composer of librettos* 246

libretto n *the book of a musical* 188

license n *written permission* 80

license n *approval* 80

license n *as in "poetic license"* 128

license n *freedom* 80

license v 80

license plate n 288

licensed practical nurse n 309

licensee n 248

licentiate v *arch. license* 98

licentious adj 108

lichen n 145

licit adj *opp. of illicit* 103

lick n/v *drub* 131

lick n/v 27

lick v *as in "lick a problem"* 204

lickerish adj *greedy, hungry* 73

lickety-split adv (Am) 231

licking n 131

lickspittle n *brownnoser* 156

licorice n *the food* 34

licorice n *the plant* 34

licorice stick n *clarinet* 299

lid n *slang hat* 260

lid n 22

lidar n *radar using light* 315

lido n *chichi resort* 173

lie v *prevaricate* 26

lie v *as in "lie in bed"* 26

lie v *arch. have sex* 39

lie v *as in "lie down"* 26

lie n 26

lie detector n 274

liebfraumilch n *type of wine* 222

lief adv *gladly* 37

lief adj *dear, beloved* 18

liege adj/n 44

liege man n *vassal* 44

lie-in n *akin to sit-in* 320

lien n 110

lieu n 50

lieutenant n *type of mil. title* 75, 131

lieutenant n 75

lieutenant governor n 130

life n 20

life n *liveliness* 130

life n *life imprisonment* 292

life belt n *life preserver* 239

life belt 149

life buoy n 149

life buoy n 211

life cycle n 236

life expectancy n 296

life force n 254

life history n 251

life insurance n 213

life jacket n 149, 239

life of Riley n 293

life preserver n 149

life raft n 212

life ring n *lifepreserver* 149, 273

life science n 302

life span n 279

life vest n (Am) 149, 280

life zone n 272

life-and-death/life-or-death adj 176

lifeblood n 120

lifeboat n 211

life-form n 270

lifeful adj *lively* 44

life-giving adj 130

lifeguard n *in swimming* 152

lifeguard n 152

lifeless adj 20

lifelike adj 79

lifeline n 167

lifelong adj 206

lifelong adj *livelong* 206

lifemanship n 306

lifer n Slang 230

life-size adj 234

lifesome 44

lifestyle n 291

life-support adj 310

lifetime n 48

lifetime adj 276

lifeway n *lifestyle* 291, 306

lifework n 245

lift n *as in "give your spirits a lift"* 199

lift v *steal* 112

lift n *sky, heavens* 12

lift n *in elevator shoes* 168

lift n *elevator* 239

lift v *raise up* 58

lift v *copy* 295

lift n *upward force on a wing* 288

lift truck n 288

liftgate n 304

liftman n (Brit) *elevator operator* 263

liftoff n 310

ligament n *type of binding* 66

ligament n *type of body section* 66

light v *as in "light a room," "light a match"* 60

light n *e.g., matches* 167

light v *obs. be bright* 60

light n *as in "skylight"* 70

light n *illumination* 22; v 22

light adj *obs. bright* 28

light adj *below weight* 25

light v *alight* 26

light adj *as in "a light color"* 25

light adj *as in "light reading"* 42

light v *make lighter* 98

light adj *not heavy* 25

light v *dismount* 26

light adj *as in "a light pastry"* 54

light heavyweight n 275

light housekeeping n 273

light meter n 286

light opera n (Am) 265

light out v 249

light pen n 309

light pipe n *optical fiber* 304

light plane n 288

light pollution n 324

light show n 318

light water n 296

lightbulb n 258

light-emitting diode/LED n 315

lighten v *make lighter* 94

lighten v *unload* 94

lighten v *illuminate* 60

lighten up v 321

lighter n *something that lights* 224

lighter n *type of barge* 72

lighter-than-air adj 274

lightfast adj 308

light-fingered adj 112

light-footed adj 90

lightful adj 98

light-headed adj *frivolous* 106

light-headed adj *dizzy* 106

lighthearted adj 73

lighthouse n 148

lightness n *obs. light* 28

lightness n *opp. of heaviness* 48

lightning v *lighten* 278

lightning n 31

lightning arrester n 242

lightning bug n (Am) 194

lightning rod n (Am) 198

light-o'-love n *lover, whore* 125

lightship n *floating lighthouse* 224

lightsome adj *elegant* 54

lightsome adj *lighthearted* 54

lightsome adj *illuminated* 91

lights-out n 239

lightweight n Sports 200

lightweight adj 217

lightweight n *fig.* 200

light-year n 256

ligneous adj *woody* 145

likable adj 191

like n *as in "the likes of you"* 50

like n *liking* 206

like v *appreciate* 17

like v *obs. liken* 98

like v *arch. please, suit* 17

like adv *equally* 98

likelihood n 53, 84

likelihood n *obs. likeness* 84, 98

likely adj/adv 53

likely adj *obs. similar* 53, 98

like-minded adj 108

liken v *obs. grow similar* 59

liken v 59

likeness n 22

lilac n Plants 145

lilac n *the color* 145, 207

lilliputian adj 190

lilt n 251

lilt n *type of song* 251

lilting adj 207

lily adj 103

lily n 10

lily of the valley n 118

lily pad n (Am) 209

lily-livered adj 149

lily-white adj 55

lily-white adj *slang Caucasian* 55

lima bean n 196

limb n 21

limber v 192

limber adj 137

limbic system n 309

limbo n *fig.* 43

limbo n Religion 43

limbo n *the dance* 305

Limburger n *type of cheese* 211

lime adj *lime-green* 295

lime n *the powder* 10

lime n *citrus fruit* 148

lime n *type of tree* 145

limeade n 259

limekiln n 35

limelight n/v Performing Arts 228

limelight n *fig.* 228

limerick n 264

limestone n 63

limewater n 99

liminal adj *perceptible, as in "subliminal"* 234

limit n/v 82

limitation n *something that limits* 84

limitation n *obs. territory* 84

limitation n *limiting* 84

limited adj 159

limited adj *obs. fixed* 159

limited edition n 276

limited liability n 248

limited partner n 275

limited war n 300

limited-access highway n 304

limiting adj 138

limitless adj 138

limo n (Am) 274, 317

limousine n 274

limp adj 190

limp n/v 137, 211

limpet n *type of sea creature* 11

limpid adj 91

limp-wristed adj 313

linac n *linear accelerator* 302

linchpin n 35

linden n *type of tree* 118

lindy n *type of dance* 299

line n *as in "learn your lines"* Performing Arts 265

line n *as in "telephone line"* 246

line n *queue* 134

line n *as in "family lines"* 40

line n *as in "drop me a line"* 172

line n *as in "pickup line"* 290

line n *rope* 16

line v *as in "line a coat"* 94

line n *as in "line of poetry"* 128

line n *as in "railroad line"* 200

line n *as in "draw a line"* 42; v 42

line drawing n 265

line graph n 285

line of credit n 281

line of duty n 284

line of fire n 247

line of sight n 133

line printer n 309

line squall n 255

line storm n 220

line up v 252

lineage n 40

lineal adj 89

linear adj 161

linear algebra n 256

linear equation n 210

linear measure n 256

linear motor n 310

linear space n 256

linecut n *type of engraving* 276

linen adj 15

linen n *the cloth* 15, 35

linen n *linen clothing* 35

linen closet n 258

liner n *lining* 148

liner notes n 312

lineup n (Am) 269

linger v *stay* 104

linger v *as in "lingering illness"* 104

linger v *dawdle* 104

lingerie n 223

lingo n 172

lingua n *tongue* 172, 221

lingua franca n 152

linguine n 303

linguist n *gen. language expert* 127

linguist n *foreign language expert* 127

linguistic atlas n 290

linguistician n *linguist* 127, 264

linguistics n 227

liniment n 68

lining n 71

link n *fig.* 86

link n *as in "link in a chain"* 86

link n *as in "sausage links"* 70

link v 86

linkage n 251

linkboy n *type of servant* 171

linkman n 171

linksman n *golf player* 298

linkup n 308

linoleum n 239

linseed n 10

linseed oil n 100

linsey-woolsey n *type of fabric* 71

lint n *flax* 71, 148

lint n *type of cloth* 71

lint n *fuzz* 71, 148

lint n *flax* 71

lintel n 33

linter n (Am) *lint-removing machine* 260

lion n 30

lioness n 30

lionhearted adj 184

lionize v 218

lion's share n 204

lip n *as in "lip of a cup"* 13

lip n/v The Body 13

lip n *backtalk* 216

lip n *slang mouthpiece, lawyer* 292

lip gloss n 297

lip service n 157

Lipizzaner n 285

liposuction, lipofilling n 326

lip-read v 246

lipreading n 246

lipstick n/v (Am) 260

lip-synch v 318

liquate *obs.* 86

liquefied petroleum gas n 285

liquefy, liquefaction v, n 86

liqueur n 183

liquid adj/n Finances/Money 264

liquid adj 89

liquid lunch n 321

liquid measure n 238

liquidate v 127

liquidize v 235

liquor n/v 34

lisp n/v 147

lissome adj 195

list v *listen* 26

list v *please* 26

list n *narrow strip* 22

list n/v *tilt* 162

list v 27

list n *as in "grocery list"* 128

list n 26

list price n 245

listen n *as in "give a listen"* 205

listen v 27

listen n *obs. sense of hearing* 205

listen in v 278

listenable adj 284

listenership n 305

listless adj *without craving* 73

lit adj *drunk* 277

lit n *short for "literature"* 227

lit crit n 318

lit up 277

litany n *fig.* 19

litany n Religion 19

lite adj 25

liter n 195

literacy n 77, 264

literal adj *opp. of figurative* 206

literal adj *as in "literal translation"* 89

literary adj 187

literary adj *obs. of the alphabet* 187

literate adj/n 77

literati n 152
literature n 201
literature n *learnedness* 201
literatus n 152
lithe adj *gentle* 32
lithe adj 32
lithesome adj *lissome* 195
lithium n 209
litho n 214
lithograph n/v 214
lithography n 214
lithy n 32
litigant n 175
litigate v 175
litigation n 175
litigious adj 81
litmus n 30
litmus paper n 210
litmus test n 309
litter n Medicine 32
litter n Animals 65
litter n *obs. gen.* bed 32
litter n *garbage* 205; v 205
litter n *as in "kitty litter"* 87
litterateur n *writer* 214
litterbag n 312
litterbug n 307
litterer n 292
little adj/adv/n/v 22
little bitty adj (Am) 277
little finger n 13
little guy n 250
little magazine n *magazine of the small press* 264
little people n 189
little theater n 214
little toe n 13
little woman n 156
liturgy n 129
livability n 284
livable adj 160
live v *as in "live it up"* 162
live adj *alive* 111
live v 26
live v *reside* 33
live adj *as in "real live"* 111
live v *survive* 26
live down v 235
live trap n 241
live wire n (Am) 272
lived-in adj 252
live-in adj 313
live-in lover n 317
livelihead n *obs. liveliness* 98
livelihood n 41
livelihood n *obs. lifetime* 28, 41
livelong adj 89
lively adj 32

lively adj *obs. living* 32
liven v *enliven* 191
liver n *source of cowardliness* 132
liver n The Body 13
liver fluke n 194
liver sausage n 241
liver spots n 238
liverwort n *type of moss* 11
liverwurst n (Am) 241
livery stable n 185
livestock n 168
livid adj 68
livid adj *enraged* 68, 281
living n *livelihood* 41
living death n 176
living fossil n 285
living history n 325
living room n 211
living standard n 306
living unit n 297
living wage n 264
living will n 324
livingly adv *vitally* 102
lizard n 64
'll contr *will* 128
llama n 119
lo interj 21
lo and behold interj 215
lo mein n 316
load v *as in "load a gun"* 155
load n *obs. act of carrying* 48
load n/v 48
load v *as in "load the dice"* 292
loaded adj *rich* 305
loaded adj *drunk* 249
loaf n *as in "loaf of bread"* 22
loaf n 231
loafer n (Am) *slaggard* 231
loam n *type of clay* 164
loam n *gen. soil* 164
loan n/v 48
loan shark n (Am) 277
loaner n 263
loanword n 245
loath adj *obs. loathsome* 36
loath adj *deeply reluctant* 36
loath adj *obs. belligerent* 36
loathe v *obs. be loathsome* 38
loathe v 38
loathful adj 38
loathing n 38
loathly 38
loathsome 38
lob n/v *type of throw* 250
lobby n 122
lobby n/v Politics 229

lobbygow n (Am) *errand boy* 275
lobbyist n Politics 247
lobe n 66
loblolly n *gruel, mire* 122
loblolly pine n (Am) 193
lobo n *type of wolf* 220
lobotomize v 297
lobotomy n 297
lobster n 11
lobster pot n 197
lobster shift n *akin to night shift* 298
lobster thermidor n *lobster dish* 287
local n *type of train route* 261
local n *resident* 217
lo-cal adj 316
local n *someone assigned to a locality* 217
local area network/LAN n 326
local color n 189
local time n 221
locale n 193
locality n *neighborhood* 158
locality n *being local* 158
locate v *find* 271
location n *place* 135
location n *being located* 135
location n Movies/TV/Radio 291
loch n *lake* 63
lochan n 63
lock v *jam up* 253
lock n *on a waterway* 123
lock n *as in "door lock"* 14; v 14
lock n *as in "lock of hair"* 13
lock n *obs. under-bridge passage* 123
lock n *little bit* 13
lock n *obs. water barrier* 123
lock out v *mainly in the employee relations sense* 245
lock, stock and barrel adv 231
lockbox n (Am) 241
lockdown n 325
locker n 88
locker room n 263; adj 263, 304
locket n 168
locket n *obs. type of locking device* 168
lockjaw n 210
locknut n 242
lockout n 245
locksmith n 40
lockstep n 216
lockstitch n 242

lockup n 232
loco v *make crazy* 267; adj 267
loco n (Am) *locoweed* 219
locomobile n 261
locomote v 230
locomotion n 149
locomotive n 224
locomotory adj 212
locoweed n (Am) 254
locus n 189
locust n *type of insect* 30
locust n *type of tree* 145
locution n 76
lode n *vein of ore* 16
lode n *road* 16
lodesman n *obs. leader* 61
lodestar n 31
lodestone n 105
lodge v *wedge* 162
lodge n/v 33
lodgement n *lodging* 122
lodger n 122
lodger n *obs. tent-dweller* 122
lodging house 122, 196
loess n *type of loam* 219
loft n *obs. heavenly vault* 33
loft n 33
loft v *lob* 253
lofty adj 54
log v *as in "become water-logged"* 207
log n/v *as in "ship's log"* 227
log n *as in "tree stem"* 30; v 30
log n *type of punishment* 248; v 248
log n *logarithm* 146
log in v 321
log on v 322
logarithm n 146
logarithmic function n 285
logbook n 172
loge n *booth* 183
logged adj 207
logger n (Am) 185
loggerhead n 133
loggerhead turtle n (Am) 209
logic n 38
logical adj *related to logic* 38, 74
logical adj *reasonable* 74
logical adj *reasoning* 74
logician n 75
logistics n 243
logjam n 269
logo n 299
logodaedalist n *articulate person* 187
logodiarrhea n *diarrhea* 182

louden v *get louder* 207
loud-hailer n (Brit) 308
loudmouth n 156
loudmouthed adj 156
loudness n 23
loudspeaker n 260
lounge v *lay about* 115; n 115
lounge n *type of furniture* 196
lounge v *dally* 115
lounge n 258
lounge v *slouch about* 115
lounge car n 304
lounge lizard n 283
loungewear n 310
loupe n *type of magnifier* 198
loup-garou n *werewolf* 132
louse n *Animals* 11
louse v *delouse* 97
louse n *fig.* 11, 156
louse up v 300
lousy adj *bad* 68, 82
lousy adj *infested with lice* 68
lousy with adj *as in "the stands were lousy with hecklers"* 231
lout v *bow before respectfully* 28
lout v *be sarcastic* 124
lout n/v 113
loutish adj 113
louver n 33
lovable adj 39
love n/v *sex* 75
love n *obs. lover* 75
love n *term of endearment* 226
love n *Love/Romance/Sex* 199
love n/v 18
love v *as in "I love to play poker"* 38
love affair n 126
love apple n *tomato* 118
love beads n (Am) 316
love child n *illegitimate child* 213
love handles n *slang folds of fat* 322
love knot n 74
love life n 281
love potion n 156
love seat n 273
lovebird n *type of bird* 119
loved one n 244
love-in n (Am) 319
lovelock n *lock of hair of a loved one* 126
lovelorn adj 151
lovely adj *obs. passionate* 18
lovely adj *obs. loving* 18
lovely adj *attractive* 18
lovely adj *lovable* 18

lovely n 18
lovemaking n 74
lover n 39
loverly adj 249
lovesick adj 75
lovesome adj *loving* 18
lovesome adj *lovable* 18, 39
lovey n 226
lovey-dovey n *term of endearment* 213, 226; adj 213
loving cup n 213
loving-kindness n 108
low n *low point* 294
low n *Weather* 255
low adj/n *lit. and fig.* 47
low n/v *moo* 11
low adj *arch. dead* 45
low adj/n *applied to prices* 47
low v *lower, diminish* 60
low adj/n *applied to rivers, sound, temperature, etc.* 47
low beam n 304
low blood pressure n 286
low blow n 313
low comedy n 153
low country n 99
low profile n 325
low relief n *bas relief* 187
low tide n 219
lowball v 320
lowborn adj 44
lowboy n *type of furniture* 183
lowbred adj 44, 202
lowbrow adj/n 276
lowdown n 283
low-down adj 231
low-end adj 295
lower adj 53
lower v *make physically lower* 116
lower v *reduce* 116
lower n *part of dentures* 257
lower class n/adj 202
lowercase adj/n 172
lowercase v 172, 276
lower/lour n/v *frown* 37
lowest common denominator, lowest common multiple n 285
low-grade adj 270
low-key adj 270
lowland adj/n 99
lowlander n 177
low-level adj 270
lowlife adj/n 204, 283
lowlight n *opp. of highlight* 293
lowlihead n *lowliness* 98
low-lying adj 236
low-minded adj 185

lowmost adj *lowest* 143
low-pressure adj 233
low-rent adj *subpar* 310
low-rise adj *opp. of high-rise* 310
low-spirited adj 124
low-tech adj 326
lox n *smoked salmon* 303
lox n *liquid oxygen explosive* 285
loyal adj *gen.* 111
loyal adj *loyal to country* 73, 111
loyalist n *Politics* 155
loyalty n 73
lozenge n *type of shape* 51
lozenge n *obs. type of pastry* 51
lozenge n *tablet* 51, 121
LP n *long-playing record* 305
LPN n *Licensed Professional Nurse* 303
LSD n *type of hallucinogenic drug* 307
luau n 223
lubber n *clumsy person* 82
lubber n *as in "landlubber"* 82
lubberly adj 82
lube n/v 293
lubric adj 101, 162
lubric adj *smooth* 104
lubricant n 217
lubricate v 162
lubricious adj 101
lubricity n *loose bowels* 121
lubricity n *lust* 101
lucent adj *shining* 91
lucid adj *sane* 138
lucid adj *transparent* 138
lucid adj *easy to understand* 138
lucid adj *luminous* 138
lucidity n 170
luciferous adj *illuminating* 161
luck n 86
lucky adj *experiencing good luck* 91
lucky adj *bringing good luck* 91
lucrative adj 76, 90
lucre n 76
lucriferous adj *obs. lucrative* 90
lucrous adj *obs.* 76
luculent adj *clearly understood* 138
luculent *luminous* 138
ludic adj *playfully aimless* 298
ludicrous adj *ridiculous* 206
ludicrous adj *obs. witty, frivolous* 206
lues n *syphilis* 147

lug n/v *carry* 60
luge n/v 275
luggage n *baggage* 121
luggage n *suitcases* 121
luke adj *as in "lukewarm"* 61
lukewarm adj 89
lull n/v 60
lull n *something that lulls* 232
lull n *quiet period* 232
lullaby n 112, 129
lullaby interj 112
lulu n 249
lumbago n *type of rheumatism* 167
lumbar adj 166
lumber v *move clumsily* 60
lumber n *timber* 133
lumber n *furniture discards* 133
lumberjack n 213, 226
lumberman n (Am) 213
lumbermill n (Am) 226
lumbersome adj *cumbersome* 235
lumberyard n (Am) 200
luminary n *lit. and fig.* 86
lumine v *illuminate* 98
luminesce v 269
luminescence n 269
luminosity n 91
luminous adj 91
luminous energy n 296
luminous paint n 217
lump v (Am) *as in "like it or lump it"* 204
lump n *as in "a cancerous lump"* 50
lump v *as in "lump together"* 162
lump adj 179
lump n *mass* 50
lump n *as in "a lump in my throat"* 249
lump, the n *workhouse* 268
luna moth n (Am) 236
lunacy n 37
lunar adj *related to the moon* 91
lunar adj *shaped like a crescent* 91
lunar eclipse n 182
lunar module n 317
lunarian n *lunar native* 189
lunatic adj/n 37
lunatic fringe n 283
lunch n 122, 211; v 211
lunch n *chunk* 144
lunch v 211
lunch counter n 245
lunchbox n 239

luncheon n obs. 144
luncheon n 122
luncheon meat/lunchmeat n 303
luncheonette n (Am) 289
lunchmeat n 303
lunchpail n (Am) 258
lunchroom n 211
lunchtime n 237
lunes n arch. lunatic spells 150
lung n 13
lunge v 218
lunge n/v weapon thrust 188
lunge n gen. 188
lungfish n 255
lunker n 279
lunkhead n (Am) 249
lupine adj wolflike 165
lurch v arch. steal 98, 131
lurch v obs. lurk 98
lurch v arch. steal 131
lurch n sudden movement 177
lurch n as in "in the lurch" 134
lurch n 177
lurch v 134
lurcher n thief 112
lurdane adj/n 47
lure n in falconry 51
lure n/v gen. 51
lurid adj pale 166
lurid adj graphic 166
lurid adj vividly red 166
lurk v obs. be lazy 58
lurk v 58
lurk v obs. peek 58
luscious adj 90
luscious adj cloyingly luscious 90
luscious adj sexual sense 90
lush n drunkard 196, 267
lush n alcohol 196
lush adj 159
lush v 196
lush n drunk 196
lush adj obs. soft 159
lush n drinking 196
lushy adj 196
lust v sexual sense 18
lust n obs. gen. pleasure 18
lust n 18
lust v gen. 18
lust n obs. gen. affinity 18
luster n half a decade 65
luster n/v 113
lustrous adj 113
lusty adj robust 36
lusty adj arch. merry 36
lusty adj obs. lustful 36
lute n 42

lutenist n lute player 129
luthier n maker of stringed instruments 265
lutist n lute player 129
lutulent adj clouded, muddied 144
lux n measure of illumination 256
luxe n luxury 133
luxe 176
luxuriate v 176
luxury n obs. lust 176
luxury n obs. lechery 39
luxury n item of luxury 176
luxury n as in "life of luxury" 176
lyam n leash 87
lyamhound n bloodhound 99
lycanthrope n 124
lycanthropy n werewolfism 124, 248
lycanthropy n delusions of being an animal 124, 248
lye n 22
lyke-wake n watch over the dead 80
Lyme disease n 322
lymph n 166
lymph n gen. water 166
lymph gland n 238
lymph node n 256
lymphatic adj frantic, crazed 150
lymphocyte n type of cell 256
lynch v 215, 229
lynch law n (Am) 215
lynx n 31
lynx-eyed adj sharpsighted 121
lyre n type of stringed instrument 42
lyrebird n 220
lyric n type of poetry 128
lyric n song's words 128, 265
lyric adj 128
lyrical 128
lyrical adj pertaining to lyric poetry 227
lyrical adj fig. poetic 227
lyricism n 201
lyricist n master of lyric poetry 290
lyricist n type of songwriter 290
lyrism n 201

M

'm contr am 128
M1 rifle n 300

M16 n 319
ma n 230
maa interj sheep sound 230
ma'am n 172
ma-and-pa adj 317
mab adj arch. slut 132
mac n 223
macabre adj/n 252
macadam n macadamized road 212
macadamia nut n 287
macaque n 165
macaroni n 122
macaroon n type of cookie 148
macaroon n obs. dimwit 133
macaw n type of parrot 146
Mace n/v spray with Mace 319
mace v bamboozle 204
mace n type of weapon 45
mace n type of spice 34
macedoine n potpourri 217
Mach number n 296
machete n 131
Machiavellian adj/n 130
Machiavellian adj 130
machination n 86
machine n penis 204
machine n mechanical device 168
machine v obs. 144
machine n arch. type of war machine 174
machine n gen. something built 114, 168
machine v 242
machine n fig. 168
machine n obs. vehicle 169
machine n obs. machination 144
machine gun n 248
machine language n 302
machine, machinery n plot device 172
machine pistol n 300
machine shop n (Am) 224
machine tool n 242
machine-gun adj 277
machinery n 198
machinist n 185
machinofacture n manufacture 294
machismo n (Am) 307
macho adj (Am) 293
mackerel n type of fish 30
mackerel n pimp, madam 82
mackerel shark n 210
mackerel sky n type of cloud formation 165

mackinaw n (Am) type of blanket 222
mackintosh n 223
macon n type of wine 241
macrame n 246
macro adj large-scale 294
macrobiotic adj 193
macrocosm n opp. of microcosm 119
macrocosm n the universe 119
macroeconomics n 305
macroinstruction, macro n 309
macula n spot 90
maculate adj spotted 90
macule blemish 90
mad adj crazed 17
mad adj obs. maddening 17
mad n madness, bad mood 225
mad adj as in "I'm mad about ice cream" 17
mad v arch. be mad 38
mad v madden 38
mad adj angry 37
mad money n 292
madam n female pimp 267
madam n 44
madame n 130
mad-brained adj 132
madcap adj/n 135
madden v make mad 184
madden v get mad 184
maddening adj 213
madder n type of herbs 10
madding adj frenzied 38
mademoiselle n 79
made-to-order adj 278
made-up adj 159
madhouse n 175
Madison Avenue n representing the advertising industry 311
madman n 39, 74
madras n type of kerchief 223
madrigal n type of poem, song 129
maduro adj/n type of cigar 222
madwoman n 39, 74
Mae West n life jacket 297
maelstrom n 118
maestro n Music 187
maestro n fig. 187
maffick v celebrate 262
Mafia n 248
mafioso n 248
mag n 230
mag n chitchat 204
mag wheel n 317
magazine n armory 131

magazine n Literature/Writing 201

magazine n *storehouse* 122

magazine n *as in "gun magazine"* 131

magazine n *type of book* 201

magazinist n 290

magdalen n *former prostitute* 125

mage n 81

Magen David n *star of David* 276

magenta adj/n 252

maggot n 64

maggot n *erratic person* 175

Magian n 129

magic adj/n/v 81

magic v 277

magic bullet n 297

magic lantern n *type of projector* 173

magic realism n 290

magical adj 81

magician n *fig.* 81

magician n 81

magistrate n 79

magistrate's court n 248

magma n *obs. dregs* 236

magma n *molten rock* 236

magna cum laude adj/adv 266

magnanimity n *being magnanimous* 169

magnanimity n *magnanimity because of feelings of superiority* 169

magnanimous adj 174

magnate n 75

magnesium n 209

magnet n *magnetized item* 63

magnet n *magnetic rock* 63

magnet school n 319

magnetic adj *magnetized* 147

magnetic adj *attractive* 147

magnetic bubble n 315

magnetic field n 220

magnetic north n 209

magnetic pole n 181

magnetic resonance imaging n 326

magnetic storm n 237

magnetic tape n 297

magnetical adj 147

magnetism n 63

magnetize v 218

magnetize v *arch. attract, fascinate* 218

magneto n *type of generator* 256

magnetograph n 221

magnetometer n 221

magnific adj *magnificent* 103

magnification n 87, 94

magnification n *something magnified* 87

magnificence n *tasteful spending* 52

magnificence n *grandeur* 52

magnificence n *obs. plentitude, glory* 52

magnificency n 52

magnificent adj 52

magnifico n *bigshot* 132

magnifier n 107

magnify v *glorify* 94

magnify v *as with a magnifying glass* 94

magnify v *make larger* 94

magnify v *exaggerate* 94

magnifying glass n 168

magniloquence n *bombast* 150

magniloquent adj 150

magnitude n 84

magnitude n *astronomic sense* 84

magnolia n 181

magnolious adj *wonderful* 249

magnum n *type of wine bottle* 196

magnum opus n 201

magpie adj *black and white* 217

magpie n *type of bird* 119

magpie n *fig.* 119

magsman n *con man* 229

magus n 47

mahimahi n *dolphin meat* 303

mah-jongg n *type of game* 281

mahogany n 164

maid n *servant* 43

maid n *virgin* 43

maid n *as in "old maid"* 43

maid n 20

maid n *girl* 43

maid n *obs. virgin man* 44

maid of honor n *compare matron of honor* 126

maiden adj *as in "maiden voyage"* 137

maiden n *servant* 20

maiden n *girl* 20

maiden n 43

maiden adj 20

maiden name n 170

maidenhair fern n 64

maidenhair tree n 193

maidenhead n *hymen* 39

maidenhead n *virginity* 39

maidenhood n 20

maidhood n 20

maid-in-waiting n 312

maidservant n 101

mail n *arch. film in the eye* 66

mail n *related to postal* 172

mail n/v *type of armor* 45

mail n *payment, as in "blackmail"* 28

mail v *send via the mail* 227

mail n/v *obs. mail armor piece* 45

mail n *type of bag* 172

mail v 172

mail bomb n 324

mail carrier n (Am) 200

mail order n (Am) 245

mail order house n (Am) 245, 275

mailbag n 214

mailbox n 211

mailed fist n 267

maillot n *type of clothing* 260

mailman n 245

maim adj/n/v 45

main adj *var. obs. meanings of large, powerful, great* 103

main n *obs. goal* 143

main n *as in "water main"* 158

main adj *primary* 103

main n *as in "the Spanish Main"* 63, 118

main adj *obs. flowing* 158

main n *main railroad line* 243

main n *as in "might and main"* 22

main n *the main part* 136

main line n 224

main man n 320

main squeeze n Love/Romance/Sex 317

main squeeze n *muckamuck* 317

Main Street n 188

Maine coon n 296

mainframe n *type of computer* 315

mainland n 63

mainline v/n (Am) 300

mainmast n 100

mainsail n *sailing term* 100

mainsheet n 100

mainspring n 135

mainstay n 102

mainstream v 325

mainstream adj/n 176

maintain v 56

maintenance n 51

maitre d' n 213

maize n 122

majestatic adj *divinely majestic* 173

majestic adj *gen.* 159

majestic adj Religion 43

majestical adj Religion 43

majestuous adj Religion 43

majesty n *grand dignity* 43

majesty n *as in "his majesty"* 43

majesty n *majesty of god* 43

major adj Music 173

major adj/n 54

major n 266; v 266, 282

major league, minor league adj/n (Am) 263

major, major-general n 174

majority n *larger part* 133

majority n *as in "age of majority"* 120

majority n *obs. state of being major* 133

majority rule n 266

major-medical adj 309

majuscule n *CAPITAL LETTER* 187

make v *construct* 26

make v *slang bed, seduce* 281

make v *achieve* 141

make v *behave* 28

make n *as in "on the make"* 249

make v *as in "make a mess"* 26

make v *recognize* 293

make v *obs. entertain* 42

make v *obs. do* 28

make v *force, as in "make me do that"* 179

make n *brand* 41

make n *making, manufacture* 208

make n *mate, match* 28

make mincemeat of v 176

make out v *neck, have sex* 298

make time v Love/Romance/Sex 298

makebate n *inciter* 117

make-belief adj 213

make-believe adj/n 213

make-do adj/n 270

makefast n 270

make-game n *target of ridicule* 208

make-or-break adj 284

makepeace n 117

makeshift adj *obs.* 132

makeshift adj *obs. shifty person* 132

makeshift adj/n 179

manifestation n 54, 248
manifesto n 153
manifold v *reproduce, publish* 253
manifold adj 25
manifold n 261
Manila hemp n 219
manila paper n 239
manioc n 118
manipulate v 232
manipulation n 232
manipulation n *chemical experimentation* 232
manipulation n *technical use* 232
manitou n (Am) *type of supernatural spirit* 132
mank v *arch. maim* 46
mankind n 44
mankind n *men as a group* 44
mankind n *obs. being human* 44
manly adj *obs. human* 44
manly adj 44
man-made adj 190
manna n Food 15
manna n *fig.* 15
mannequin n 190
manner n 48
mannerable adj *mannered* 44
mannered adj 44
mannerism n 212
mannerless adj 44
manners n 44
man-of-war n *type of warship* 102
man-of-war n *type of jellyfish* 181
manor n *obs. gen. shelter* 33
manor n 33
manor house n 122
manpower n *available workforce* 238, 289
manpower n *akin to horsepower* 238, 289
manque adj *failed in aspirations* 206
man's man n 269
manse n *obs. mansion* 100
manservant n 75
mansion n *obs. stopover place* 33
mansion n *obs. act of dwelling* 33
mansion n 33
manslaht n 45
manslaughter n 45
manslayer n 46
mansuete adj 73

mansuetude n *arch. docility* 73
manswear v *lie under oath* 28
manta n 296
manta ray n 296
man-tailored adj 287
manteau n *type of outerwear* 168
mantel n *support beam* 106
mantel n *mantelshelf* 106
mantelet n *type of cloak* 71
mantelpiece n 167
mantelshelf n 106, 222
manteltree 106
mantic adj *related to divination* 230
mantical adj 230
manticore n *type of legendary beast* 47
mantid n 165, 255
mantilla n *type of scarf* 184
mantis n 165
mantle n *type of cloak, hood* 16
mantle n *in lanterns, etc.* 260
mantle v *cover up, cloak* 58
mantle n *Earth layer* 315
man-to-man adj 277
mantra n 202
mantrap n 203
manual adj 91
manual n 77
manual alphabet n 246
manuary n 91
manuductor n *obs. conductor* 180
manufactory n *factory* 152
manufactory n *obs. something manufactured* 152
manufacture v *create* 180
manufacture n *arch. factory* 171
manufacture v *make usable* 180
manufacture n *act of creating* 158
manufacture n *something created* 158
manufacturer n *obs. laborer* 187, 200
manufacturer n 200
manumit v *emancipate* 96
manure v *obs. dwell* 71
manure v *obs. cultivate mentally* 71
manure v 71
manure n 107
manure v *obs. manage land* 71
manuscript adj/n 128
manuscript adj 128
Manx cat n 236
many adj 23

man-year n 281
many-sided adj 137
map n/v 113
map v 113
maple n 10
maple sugar n (Am) 183
maple syrup n 223
mapmaker n 200
mappemonde n *arch. world map* 63
maquette n *small preliminary model* 278
maquillage n 260
mar n 133
mar v *obs. spoil* 26
mar n/v 26
mar v *obs. confound* 26
maraca n 214
maraschino n 197
maraschino cherry n 273
marathon adj/n Sports 263
marathon n *gen.* 263
marathoner n 289
maraud v 174
marauder n 174
marble n Games/Fun/Leisure 170
marble v 180
marble n Natural Things 29
marble cake n (Am) 241
marble orchard n (Am) *cemetery* 291
marble town n *cemetery* 291
marbleize v 180
marbles n *as in "lost your marbles"* 288
marcel n/v *type of hair wave* 260
March n 31
march n *border* 49
march n/v 80
march n Music 154
march v *fig.* 80
march out v 141
marching orders n 203
marchpane n *marzipan* 100
mare n *female horse* 12
mare n *horse* 12
mare n *as in "nightmare"* 21
mare n *lunar and martian "seas"* 236
mare n *woman* 47
mare n *obs. melancholy* 107
mare's nest n 132
margarin n *source of margarine* 241
margarine n (Am) 241
margarita n 316

margarita n *type of wine* 316
margarite n *arch. pearl* 10
marge General/Miscellaneous 84
marge 241
margent 84
margin n *as in "profit margin," "margin for error"* 251
margin n *as in "margin of a page"* 77
margin n *border* 84
marginal adj 84
marginal adj 251
marginal adj 77
marginal adj *barely productive* 271
marginalia n 77, 227
mariachi n 290
marigold n 30
marijuana n (Am) 267
marimba n 187
marina n 212
marinade n/v 148, 183
marinade v 183
marinara adj/n 303
marinate v 148, 183
marine adj *describing shipping* 63
marine adj 63
marine n War/Military/Violence 131
mariner n 36
mariner's compass n 149
marionette n 151
marital adj 101
maritime adj 107
marjoram n *type of mint* 70
mark n *English, Scottish monetary* 19
mark n *obs. trace* 61
mark n *as in "trademark"* 42, 200
mark n *evidence* 42
mark n *as in "high water mark"* 205
mark n *as in "trademark"* 42
mark n *victim* 267
mark n *obs. type of marker* 62
mark n *German unit* 19
mark n *goal* 52
mark n/v *as in "landmark"* 23
mark n *indicator* 42
mark n *grade* 228
mark n *target, as in "hit your mark"* 52
mark n/v *border* 28
mark n *substitute for signature* 42

media n *as in "mass media"* 290

media event n 324

mediagenic adj 324

median adj 146

median n *geometric sense* 87

median n *type of vein* 87

median adj 87

median strip n 304

mediate adj *intermediate* 90

mediate v *divide* 90

mediate v *moderate* 90

mediation n 84

medic n 166

medical adj 147

medical examiner n 222

medicament n *medication* 69

medicaster n *arch. phony doctor* 147

medicate v 147

medication n *medicine* 68

medication n *use of medicine* 68

medicinable adj 33

medicinal adj 33

medicinal leech n 257

medicine n/v 32

medicine ball n 263

medicine dropper n 257

medicine man n 210

medicine show n (Am) 273

mediciner n *arch. doctor* 69

medico n 167

medieval adj/n 221

mediocre adj 86, 138

mediocrity n *moderate success* 86

mediocrity n *being mediocre* 86

mediocrity n *in the middle* 86

meditate v 38

meditation n 38

Mediterranean fruit fly 296

medium n *psychic* 248

medium n *as in "the medium of television"* 153

medium n *average* 135

medium adj 135, 190

medium of exchange n 187

medium-sized adj 270

medley n 52

meed n *reward* 28

meek adj *obs. kindly* 36

meek adj *obs. nonviolent* 36

meek adj 36

meeken v 36

meerschaum n 196

meet n 226

meet v 26

meeting of the minds n 301

meetinghouse n 148

megabuck n 305

megabyte n 315

megacity n 315

megacorporation n 323

megadeath n 312

megahit n 327

megalith n 236

megalomania n 262

megalopolis n 219

megaphone n/v (Am) 260

megastar n 322

megaton n 309

megillah n *as in "the whole megillah"* 313

megrim n 68

melancholia n 33, 167

melancholic adj 32

melancholious adj 32

melancholize v 32

melancholy v *obs.* 32

melancholy n *gen. depression* 32

melancholy adj/n 32

melancholy adj 32

melange n 176

melanin, melanism n *type of pigment* 221

melanoma n 221

melba toast n 287

meld n/v (Am) 301

melee n 155

meliorate v 117

melioration n 117

meliorative adj 117

mellay *arch.* 155

mellifluent adj 90, 159

mellifluous adj 90

mellophone n *type of musical instrument* 290

mellotron n *type of musical instrument* 318

mellow adj *ripe, mature* 91

mellow adj *fig. mature* 91

mellow adj *drunk* 91

mellow adj *easy-going, laid-back* 91, 184

mellow v 91

melodeon n (Am) *type of musical instrument* 228

melodic adj 77, 214

melodious adj 77, 214

melodist n 201

melodrama n 214

melodramatics n 214

melody n 42

melody n *obs. song* 42

melody n *primary song line* 42

melon n 64

melons n Slang 324

melt n *obs. succumb to grief* 17

melt n/v 26, 250

melt v *fig. dissipate* 26

meltdown n 315

melting point n 219

melting pot n 282

melton n *type of fabric* 212

meltwater n 285

member n The Body 32

member n *as in "member of the party"* 52

membership n 52

membership n *group of members* 52, 159

membership n *being a member* 52, 159

membrane n The Body 66

memento n *type of prayer* 206

memento n *reminder* 206

memento n *souvenir* 206

memento mori n *reminder of death* 130

memo n 187

memoir n *official notation* 172

memoir n *autobiography* 172

memorabilia n 206

memorable adj 38, 74

memorables n *memorabilia* 163

memorandum adj/n *note* 264

memorandum n *memory jogger* 264

memorial adj/n 79; v 202

memorial park n 294

memorialize v 79, 202

memorize v *make memorable* 225

memorize v *learn by heart* 225

memory n 38

memory lane n 311

menace n/v *endangerment* 50

menace n/v *threat* 50

ménage à trois n 262

menagerie n 165

menarche n *start of menstruation* 256

mend v 55

mendacious adj 150

mendacity n 150

Mendel's law n *genetic theory* 272

menestral n *arch. servant* 40

menfolk n 215

menial adj/n *servant* 75

meningitis n 221

menopause n 238

menorah n 266

menorrhagia n *heavy menstruation* 196

menorrhea n *menstrual flow* 238

mens rea n *criminal motive* 248

men's room n 286

mensch n 313

menses n 238

menstrual adj 66

menstruate adj/v 195

menstruation n 195, 238

menstruum n *arch.* 147, 238

menswear n 274

mental adj 74

mental age n 281

mental deficiency n 238

mental health n 221, 316

mental illness n 221, 316

mental retardation n 279

mentality n 243

mentation n 225

menthol n 254

mentholated adj 294

mention n/v 50, 116

mentor n/v 177, 327

menu n 223

meow n/v 119

mercantile adj 152

mercantile system n 200

mercantilism n 245

Mercator projection n *type of map form* 164

mercenary n *hired gun* 75, 112

mercenary n *hired hand* 75, 112

mercenary adj 75

mercer n *fabric seller* 40

merchandise n/v 41

merchandry n 76

merchant n/v 41

merchant marine n 245

merchant ship n 100

merchantman n *type of ship* 100

merciful adj 36, 38

merciless adj *obs. receiving no mercy* 38

merciless adj 36, 38

mercurial adj 139

mercuric adj 139

mercury n *the metal* 63

mercury-vapor lamp n 273

mercy n 36, 38

mercy killing n 300

merde n 283

merengue n *type of dance* 299

meretricious adj *related to prostitution* 156

merge v *obs. be immersed* 191

merge v *intertwine, coalesce* 191

merger n *leg.* 188

merger n *corporate sense* 188

meridian n 65

meringue n 183

merit n *obs. just deserts* 48

merit n/v 48

merit system n 269

meritocracy n 312

meritorious adj 48

merlin n *type of falcon* 31

mermaid n 47, 156, 230

merman n 47, 156, 230

merriment n 17, 124

merriment n *obs. type of entertainment* 124

merriness n 17

merry adj/v 17

merry widow n *type of garment* 316

merry-andrew n *clowning person* 170

merry-go-round n 185

merrymaker n 226

merry-making 226

merwoman n 47, 156, 230

mesa n (Am) 193

mesalliance n *marriage to someone of lower status* 199

mescaline n 257

meseems v *it seems to me, methinks* 28, 98

mesh n *the spaces in a net* 83

mesh n *the net itself* 83

meshuga adj 268

meshuggener n *crazy person* 268

mesmerian n 199

mesmeric adj 199

mesmerism n 199, 225

mesmerize v 199, 225

mesne lord n *lord subserviant to another lord* 154

mesosphere n 302

mesquite n (Am) 193

mess n *something dirty* 232

mess n *entanglement* 232

mess n *something jumbled* 232

mess n/v *food* 34

mess v 232

mess around v 300

mess hall n 239

mess jacket n 260

mess kit n 259

message n/v 42

messenger n 42

messiah n 43, 228

messianic adj 43, 228

Messie Religion 43

messy adj 234

Messyass Religion 43

metabolic adj 238

metabolism n 238

metabolize v 238

metaethics n 304

metafiction n 318

metagalaxy n 285

metal n 29

metalanguage n 299

metalhead n *heavy metal fan* 327

metalinguistics n 299, 305

metallic adj 29

metallophone n *type of musical instrument* 265

metallurgy n 189

metalsmith n 75

metalware n 258

metalwork n 233

metalworking n 233

metamathematics n 256

metamorphism n 219

metamorphose v 114, 141

metamorphosis n 114

metamorphosis n *biological sense* 114

metaphor n 101

metaphrase n *type of translation* 152

metaphysic adj 74

metaphysical adj 74

metaphysician n 74

metaphysics n 74

metapolitics n 202

metapsychology n 275

mete v *arch. measure* 28

mete v 28

meteor n 119, 210

meteor n *arch. weather phenomenon* 99, 119, 146

meteor shower n 255

meteorite n 119, 210

meteoroid n 119, 210

meteorolite n 119, 210

meteorology n 146

meter n *in metrics* 195

meter n *as in "musical meter"* 19

meter n *as in "water meter"* 210; v 210

meter maid n (Am) 311

meterstick n 296

methadone n (Am) 303

methamphetimine n 303

methane n 236

methanol n 254

metheglin n *type of mead* 106

methinks n *it seems to me* 28, 98

method n *spec. to medicine* 68, 135

method n *gen.* 68, 135

methodology n 195

methyl alcohol n 219

meticulous adj 233

meticulous adj *obs. timid* 233

metier n 205

me-too adj 293

me-tooism n (Am) 307

metric adj 238

metric system n 238

metric ton n 256

metro n 274

metronome n 214

mettle n 124

mew n *type of enclosure* 35

mew n *type of gull* 10

mew v *make a mewing sound* 59; n 59

Mexican hairless n 255

Mexican jumping bean n 254

Mexican wave n *the wave* 326

mezzanine n *gen.* 183, 290

mezzanine n *in a theater* 183, 290

mezzo n 201

mezzo-soprano n 201

mezzotint n *obs. half tint* 228

mezzotint n *type of engraving style* 228

MIA n 306

miasma n Medicine 166

miasma n *fig.* 166

mica n 193

mica n *obs. type of crystal* 193

mick, micky n 250

Mickey Finn n/v 293

Mickey Mouse adj (Am) 300

micrify v *trivialize* 253

micro adj 294

micro n *type of dress* 316

microanatomy n 256

microbe n 254

microbiology n 255

microbrewery n 326

microburst n *type of storm* 326

microbus n 304

microcassette n 323

microchip n 315

microcircuit n 309

microclimate n 285

microcomputer n 322

microcosm n 86

microcosmos n 86

microeconomics n 305

microelectronics n 309

microevolution n 296

microfiche n 305

microfilm n/v 290

micrology n *picking nits* 169

micromanage v 323

micromania n *self-depreciation* 261

micrometeorite n 302

micrometeoroid n 302

micrometeorology n 285

micrometer n *type of measuring instrument* 166, 256

micromini n *type of skirt* 316

micron n *unit of length* 256

microorganism n 254

microphone n *in telephone* 264

microphone n *in radio* 264

microphone n *arch. ear trumpet* 167, 264

microphysics n 255

microprocessor n 315

micropublishing n 318

microreader n 305

microscope n 168

microscopic adj 191

microscopic adj *related to the microscope* 191

microscopy n 168

microsecond n 272

microsurgery n 286

microtome n 242

microwave n *the wave* 296

microwave oven, microwave n 316

mid adj 23

midafternoon adj/n 256

Midas touch n 269

midcourse adj 137

midday n 12

midday n *obs. south* 12

midden n 52

middle adj/n 23

middle n 23

middle age n 65, 146, 256

middle ages n 146

middle class n 202

middle ear n 238

Middle English n 227

middle finger n 13

middle game n *in chess* 262

middle ground n 216

middle management n 305

middle name n 232

middle of the road adj/ n 284

middle school n 305

middle-aged adj 65, 146
middlebrow n 291
middle-class adj 229
middleman n 200
middle-of-the-road adj/n (Am) 269
middleweight adj/n 244
middy n War/Military/Violence 215
middy blouse n 280
midge n type of fly 11
midget adj/n 250
midi/midiskirt n type of dress 316
midlatitudes n 285
midlife n 65, 256
midlife crisis n 317
midnight n 12
midnight n fig. 12
midnight blue n 284
midnight sun n 237
midnoon n 120
midpoint n 82
midriff n 13
mid-rise n buildings lower than a high-rise 316
midsection n 301
midshipman n 155
midsize adj 317
midst n 51
midstream n 29
midsummer n 12
midterm adj/n 247
midtown adj/n 285
midway adj/adv 25
midway n 265
midweek adj/adv/n 182
midwife adj/n/v Medicine 32
midwife adj/n fig. 32
midwifery 32
midwinter n 12
midyear adj/n 65
mien n 107
miff n tiff 150
miff n/v a state of miffment 150
might n 22
might v 26
mightful adj 23, 62
mightiness n as in "Your Mightiness" 136
mightiness n 22
mightless adj 62
mightn't contr 264
mighty adv as in "I'm mighty cold" 54
mighty adj 23
migraine n 68
migrant adj/n 177

migrant n 177
migrate v 162
migrate v spec. to animals 162
migration n 162
migratory adj 162
mike n/v 290
mil n 313
mil n 182
milady n 130, 202
mild adj 23
milden v make mild 23, 163
mildew n/v 33
mildew n honeydew 33
mile n 12
milepost n (Am) 195
miler n Sports 263
milestone n 182
milieu n 202
militance n militancy 80, 307
militancy n 80
militant n fig. 155
militant adj in battle 80; n 80, 291
militant adj aggressive 80; n 255, 291
militaria adj 319
militarism n 248, 277
militaristic adj 248, 277
militarize v 266
military adj/n 80
military academy n (Am) 203
military police n 229
military school n (Am) 202
military science n 229
military-industrial complex n 319
militate v fig. 131
militate v War/Military/Violence 131
militia n 131
militiaman 131, 203
milk v fig. 116
milk v lit. 116
milk n/v 15
milk bar n 298
milk chocolate n 183
milk glass n 239
milk house n 122
milk of magnesia n 257
milk run n "routine trip" 292
milk sickness n (Am) 211
milk sugar n 223
milk tooth n 182
milk-and-water adj weak 206
milking stool n 224
milk-livered adj arch. cowardly 149
milkmaid n 126, 127

milkman n 126, 127
milkshake n (Am) 259
milksop n 82
milksop n obs. milk and break 82
milkweed n 119
Milky Way n our galaxy 65, 237
Milky Way n stars in the Milky Way 65, 237
mill v rob 132
mill n 15
mill v as in "mill about" 271
mill n as in "textile mill" 15
mill wheel n 16
millefleur adj flowered background 274
millenium n 146
miller n 40
millet n type of grass 64
millhouse n 34
millimeter, milliliter n 210
milliner n 110
millinery n 110
milling machine n 260
million n 65
millionaire n 227, 264
millionairess n 227, 264
millipede n 145
millpond n 63
millstone n 16
millward obs. 40
milo n (Am) type of grain 259
milord n 130, 202
Milquetoast adj/n 301
mime n/v 153
mimeo n/v 265, 305
mimeograph n/v 265, 305
mimic n/v 180
mimic n 153
mimic adj/n/v 135
mimicry n 135, 177
mimosa n type of plant 193
mince v as in "don't mince words" 143
mince v 93
minced meat 241
mincemeat n 241
mind v pay attention to 170
mind v object 150
mind n 17
mind reader n 267
mind reading n 267
mind-bending adj 317
mindblowing adj 317
mind-boggling adj 317
mind-expanding adj 317
mindful adj 39
mindless adj 17

mindly adv obs. 39
mind's eye n 74
mind-set n 293
mine n as in "gold mine" 41
mine n 80, 266; v 80
minefield n 80, 266
minelayer n 277
mineral n/adj 63
mineral kingdom n 164
mineral oil n 216
mineral spirits n 269
mineral water n 121
mineralogy n 165
minestrone n type of soup 259
minesweeper n 277
ming tree n 302
mingle v 97
mingy adj 267
mini adj 313
miniature adj/n 135, 190
miniature golf n 281
miniature pinscher n 285
miniature schnauzer n 285
miniaturize, miniaturization v, n 308
minibike n 317
minibus n 310
minicam n 299
minicamp n 323
minicar n 304
minicomputer n 315
minicourse n type of class 319
minify v opp. of magnify 180
minikin n slight or insignificant thing 134
minimal adj 178
minimal art n 318
minimalism, minimalist n 318
minimalist n Menshevik 276
minimize v make small 218
minimize v regard as insignificant 218
minimum n 136
minimum n obs. atom 136
minimum brain dysfunction n 322
minimum wage n 245
minion n lover 101
minischool n 319
miniseries n Movies/TV/Radio 324
miniskirt n 316
minister n 50
minister n 188
minister n Religion 43, 101
ministress n Religion 43, 101
ministry n Religion 78
minivan n 310

miniver n *type of fur* 35
mink n *type of fur* 71
mink n *the animal* 71
mink n *type of fur* 71, 146
mink n 71, 146
minnow n 64
minor adj/n Music 173
minor n *underage person* 146
minor adj/n 53
minor n Education 266; v 266, 291
minor league adv/n 263
minor planet n 237
minority adj/n *a minority group* 114
minority adj/n *being in the minority* 114
minority leader n (Am) 306
minster n *type of church* 19
minstrel n 42
minstrel show n (Am) 246
mint n *as in "peppermint"* 10
mint n *obs. coin* 75
mint n *coin factory* 75
mint adj *newly made* 278
mint v 75
mint julep n (Am) 211
minuet n 173
minus sign n 166
minuscule adj 270
minuscule n *type of writing style* 187
minuscule adj *typographical sense* 270
minute adj *small* 160
minute adj *chopped small* 160
minute n 65
minute hand 165
minute steak n 287
minuteman n (Am) 203
minutes n *as in "minutes of a meeting"* 77
minutia n 205
minx n *type of dog* 132
minx n Slang 132
miracle n 23
miracle drug n 303
miracle play n 246
miracular *obs.* 90
miraculous adj *fig.* 90
miraculous adj 90
mirage n 209
Miranda adj 320
mire n/v 29
mirepit n 29
mirific adj *wonderful* 104
mirifical adj *obs.* 104
mirror n/v 33

mirror image n 269
mirth n 38
misadventure n 50
misagree v 143
misandry n *hatred of men* 150, 288
misanthrope n 169, 204
misanthropic adj 169, 204
misanthropical adj 204
misanthropy n 169
misapprehension n 158
misbecome v 116
misbegotten adj 102
misbehave v 73
misbehavior n 73
misbelief, misbelieve n, v 42
miscarriage n 106, 166
miscarriage n *as in "miscarriage of justice"* 158
miscarriage n *obs. misbehavior* 124
miscarry v 106, 166
miscarry v *obs. get hurt or destroyed* 61
miscast adj/v 290
miscegenation n (Am) *integration* 250
miscellanea n 136
miscellaneal adj *obs.* 160
miscellaneous adj 160
miscellany n 136, 160
miscellany adj *obs.* 160
miscellany n 172
mischance n/v 50
mischief n *misfortune, evil* 177
mischief n *as in "malicious mischief"* 155
mischief, the n *the devil* 129
mischiefful adj 169
mischieve v *obs. harm* 62
mischievous adj *naughty* 169, 177
mischievousness n 177
miscommunicate v 318
miscommunication n 318
misconduct n/v 189
miscreancy n 131
miscreant n *heathen* 131
miscreant adj/n *criminal* 131
miscue n/v 251
misdeal n/v 226
misdeal n/v *distribute poorly* 226
misdeem v *deem wrongly* 62
misdemean v *arch. have a bad demeanor* 100

misdemeanant n *perp of misdemeanor* 102, 215
misdemeanor n 102, 215
misdiagnose v 286
misdo v 27
misdoing n 27
mise-en-scène n 228
miser n 127
miser n *obs. miserable person* 66, 127
miserable adj *in mental misery* 125
miserable adj 66
miserable adj *in phys. misery* 125
misery n *phys. misery* 66, 107
misery n *mental misery* 66, 107
misfire n/v 203, 229
misfit n 217
misfortunate adj 86
misfortune n 86
misgive v 107, 149
misgiving n 149
mishap n 49
mishmash n 102
misinterpret v 108
misknow v 39
mislike v *displease* 28
mismarriage n 213
misnomer n 76
miso n *type of food paste* 183
misogamy n 170
misogynism n 224
misogynist n 150
misogyny n 150, 288
misology n *hatred of knowledge* 228
misplay n/v (Am) 244
misplay v 244
misprint n/v 101
misrepresent v 163
miss n *lack* 28
miss v *as in "miss the bus"* 25
miss v *as in "an engine missing"* 288
miss v *rue absence* 38
miss n *unmarried woman* 174
miss n/v 25
miss n 163
miss n *opp. of hit* 133
miss v 133
miss out v *eliminate* 253
missal n 43
missile n *long-range weapon* 174, 188
missile n *thrown weapon* 174, 188
missile adj 174

missileer 312
missileman n 312
missilery n 266
missing adj/n 115
missing link n 250
missing mass n 322
mission n 136
mission n *seat of missionaries* 202
mission adj *describing a type of architecture* 274
mission control n 317
missionary adj/n 173
missionary position n 304
missioner n 173
missionist n 173, 294
missive adj/n 110
misspeak v *obs. insult* 47
misspeech n *obs.* 47
misspell v 172
misspend v 94
misstep n 206
missus n 204
missy adj/n 177
mist n/v Weather 12
mistake n/v *make a mistake* 93, 158
mistaken 158
mistaken adj 93, 158
mister n *device that mists* 323
mister n Mr. 129
misthink v *obs. have lewd thoughts* 39
misthink v *think mistakenly* 108
misthink v *obs. have lewd thoughts* 108
misthrive v 143
mistletoe n 10
mistreading n *obs. transgression* 144
mistress n *concubine* 44
mistress n *female master* 44
mistress of ceremonies n 311
mistrial n 155
misty-eyed adj 288
misventure n 143
mite n *a bit* 31
mite n *type of arachnid* 11
miter n/v 168
miter n *type of hat* 43
miter joint n 168
miter, miter box n *in construction* 168
miter square n 168
mithridate n 106
mitigate v *as in "mitigating circumstances"* 92
mitigate v 92

moneyed adj 76
money-grubber n 231
mong n *mixture* 65
monger n/v 18, 200
mongolism n 257
mongoloid adj 257
mongoose n 165
mongrel adj/n 65
mongrel n *applied to people* 65
monies n 76
monies n *coins* 76
moniker n 249
monish v *admonish* 61
monitor n *ironclad* 248
monitor n 111
monitor n/v 295
monk n *monkey* 105, 231
monk n *type of religious figure* 19
monkery n 19, 111
monkey n 105
monkey v *mimic* 249
monkey n *slang $500* 245
monkey v *as in "monkey around"* 267
monkey bars n 311
monkey business n (Am) 269
monkey jacket n 223
monkey wrench n 242
monkeyshines n (Am) 230
monkfish n 145
monk's cloth n 224
mono n *Music* 312
mono n *Medicine* 316
monochord n *type of musical instrument* 77
monochromat n *color-blind person* 273
monochromatic adj 217
monochrome adj 234
monochrome adj/n 173
monocle n 166
monocracy n 174
monocrat n 174
monocular n *similar to binocular* 297
monocycle n *unicycle* 243
monodrama n 201
monogamist n 151
monogamy n *faithfulness to one person at a time* 151
monogamy n *marrying only once* 151, 262
monoglot adj *unilingual* 227
monogram n/v 177
monogram n *type of sketch* 177
monograph n/v 214

monogyny n *having only one wife at a time* 262
monogyny n *monogamy in this sense* 262
monohull n 317
monolingual adj 290
monolith n *lit.* 232
monolith n *fig.* 232
monolithic adj 301
monologue n *person who controls conversation* 173
monologue n 173
monomania n 213
monomial n 182
mononucleosis n 280
monoplane n *type of airplane* 274
monopolist n 110, 152
monopolize v 110, 162
monopoly n 110
monorail adj/n 261
monosodium glutamate n 287
monotheism n 173
monotheist n 173
monotheistic adj 173
monotone n 158
monotonous adj *characterized by monotone* 206, 233
monotonous adj *boringly repetitious* 206, 233
monotony n *boringly repetitious* 233
monounsaturated adj *akin to polyunsaturated* 297
monoxide n 236
mons pubis n 256
mons veneris n 166
monsignor n 129
monsoon n 119
monster n *fantastic creature* 30, 81
monster n *applied to people* 30
monster n *deformed creature* 30, 81
monster adj 231
monstrosity n *abnormality* 85
monstrosity n *monstrous creature* 85
monstrous adj *obs. unnatural* 114
monstrous adj *obs. unnatural* 98
monstrous adj *egregiously villainous* 131
monstrous adj *huge* 114
monstrous adj *huge* 131
monstrous adj *egregiously villainous* 114

monstrous adj *obs. unnatural* 131
montage n/v 291
monte n *type of card game* 213
Monterey cypress n 236
Monterey Jack n (Am) *type of cheese* 303
Monterey pine n 219
montero n *type of hunting cap* 149
Montessori method n 282
Montezuma's revenge n (Am) *slang diarrhea* 316
month n 12
monthly n Literature/Writing 227
monument n *obs. burial vault* 45, 87
monument n 87
monumental adj 159
monumentalize v 252
moo n/v 105
mooch n/v 250
mooch n/v *obs. feign destitution* 250
mooch n/v *sneak* 250
mood n *as in "bad mood"* 17
moody adj *dour* 124
moody adj *obs. angry* 124
moody adj *obs. brave* 17, 124
moola n (Am) *money* 276
moon n *our moon* 12
moon v *as in "moon over a lover"* 225
moon n *gen. planetary moon* 12
moon n *slang buttocks* 256
moon n *slang month* 65
moon v *as in "moon about"* 225
moon blindness n 176
moon shot n (Am) 310
moonbeam n 118
moondust n 309
moon-eyed adj *drunk* 204
moonlet n 220
moonlight v 311
moonlight n 31, 65
moonlighter n 311
moonquake n 302
moonrise n 182, 220
moonscape n 279
moonset n 182, 220
moonshine n *illegally created liquor* 241
moonshine n *moonlight* 31, 65
moonshine n *smuggled liquor* 241
moonshine v 241
moonshiner n 241

moonstone n 145
moonstruck adj 169
moonwalk n (Am) 317
moor n 9
moor v 100
moorland n 9
moose n (Am) 145
moot adj *open to argument* 252
moot n *assembly for discussion* 28
moot adj *not relevant* 252
moot n The Law 203
moot case 203
moot court n 203
moot point n 157
mop *obs.* 157
mop n *arch. fool, child* 47
mop n *cleaning tool* 99
mop up v 216
mopboard n 239
mope n *moper* 169
mope v *arch. act dazed* 142
mope n/v *sulk* 142
mope n *idiot* 169
moped n 310
mopes, the n 224
moppet n 157
mopsy 157
mop-up n 268
moraine n *glacial feature* 193
moral n 243
moral v 78
moral adj 39
moral n 101
moral v 39
morale n *attitude* 243
morale n *morals* 243
moralism n 228
moralist n 228
moralistic 228
morality n 78, 154
morality play n 290
moralize *obs.* 101
moralize v *preach* 78
moralize v *discuss moral aspects* 78
morals n 78, 154
morass n *fig.* 63
morass n *marsh* 63
morass n *lit. and fig. swamp* 63, 249
moratorium n The Law 248
moratorium n *gen.* 248
moratory n 248
moray eel n (Am) 146
morbid adj *dark, funereal* 243
morbid adj *diseased* 243
morbid adj 166

ENGLISH THROUGH THE AGES

nascent adj 177
nasturtium n 118
nasturtium n *earlier type of plant* 118
nasty adj/n 83
natal v *obs.* 63
natal adj 63
natatorium n *swimming pool* 258
natch adv 249
natheless adv *nonetheless* 23
nation n 44
nation adj *very large* 206
national adj 44
national n *citizen* 266
national bank n (Am) 200
national cemetery n (Am) 247
national church n 173
national debt n (Am) 200
national forest n 272
national monument n 278
national park n (Am) 244
nationalism n 188
nationalist n 188
nationalist adj 188
nation-state n 282
nationwide adj/adv 282
native adj *as in "native of Nebraska"* 88
native adj *innate* 79, 88
native n 114
native adj *born in slavery* 79, 88
native n 79
native son n (Am) 229
native-born adj 103
nativity n *astrological sense time of birth* 42
nativity n 42
natter n/v *nibble* 232
natter n/v *grumble* 232
natter n/v *chatter* 232
natty adj 197
natural n *talented person* 51
natural adj *as in "natural father"* 63
natural n 51
natural adj *physical* 29
natural adj *of nature* 29
natural adj *uncorrupted* 29
natural childbirth n 297
natural family planning n 323
natural food n 280
natural gas n 210
natural history n 129
natural law n 63
natural resource n 236
natural science n 65
natural selection n 236

naturalist n 118
naturalistic adj 234
naturalize v 139
nature n The Body 31
nature n *as in "human nature"* 31
nature n *natural surroundings* 164
nature worship n 236
naught n *zero* 12
naught n *obs. evil* 12
naughty adj *mischievous* 111, 150
naughty adj *saucy* 111, 150
naughty adj *arch. evil* 150
naughty adj *obs. inferior* 150
naughty adj *obs. needy* 150
nausea n 68, 147
nauseate v *create nausea* 147
nauseate v *feel nausea* 147
nauseating adj 147
nauseous adj *feeling nausea, causing nausea* 147
nauseous adj *creating nausea* 147
nautic adj 123
nautical adj 123
nautical mile n 147
nautilus n *type of mollusk* 145
naval adj 72
navel n 13
navel orange n 254
navigate v 107
navigation n 107
navigator n 127
navy n *navy blue* 271
navy n *obs. gen. ships* 45
navy n 45
navy bean n 236
nay adv *no* 53
nay n 53
naysayer n 189
ne *applied to men* 206
Neanderthal n 236
Neanderthal man n 236
Neapolitan ice cream n 259
near v 104
near adj *fig. close by* 53
near adj *lit. close by* 53
near adv 53
near beer n (Am) 273
near miss n 301
near money n *liquid cash* 305
nearsighted adj 167
neat adj *tidy* 114, 138
neat adj *pure* 115, 138
neat n *a bovine* 11
neat adj *obs. clean* 138

neat adj *straight, as in "scotch neat"* 122, 138
neaten 138
neaten v 138, 271
neatherd n 70
neat's foot oil n 135
nebbish n 268
nebula n 182
nebula n *eye film* 182
nebula n *cloudiness* 182
nebulous adj *indistinct* 233
nebulous adj *cloudy* 233
nebulous adj *pertaining to nebulas* 233
necessary adj/n 88
necessitate v 162
necessity n *as in "by necessity"* 82
necessity n *state of need* 82
necessity n *something necessary* 82
neck n *area, as in "this neck of the woods"* 193
neck n *narrow passage, as in "bottleneck"* 87
neck n 13
neck v Love/Romance/Sex 213
neck v *hit in the neck* 213
neck and neck adj/adv 204
neckerchief n 71
necklace n 123
neckline n 274
necktie n 223
necrology n *obituary* 188
necrology n *list of the dead* 188
necromancy n *conjuring spirits* 47
necrophilia n 266
necrophilism n 266
necrophobia n 266
necropolis n *burial ground* 215
necropsy n/v *autopsy* 247
nectar n *drink fit for gods* 122
nectar n *spec. drink of the gods* 122
nectarine n 148
nee adj *female ne* 206
need n 22
need v 55
needcessity n 134
needful adj 53
needle n *stylus* 290
needle n *evergreen leaf* 194
needle n *as in "knitting needle"* 99
needle v *annoy* 268

needle n *as in "hypodermic needle"* 257
needle n *as in "compass needle"* 88
needle n *penis* Slang 175
needle n *as in "pins and needles"* 22
needle park n 325
needlepoint adj/n/v 167
needs adv 25
needy adj/n 47
ne'er adv 41
ne'er-do-well n 189
nefarious adj 159
negate v 86
negation n 86
negative n *photographic negative* 246
negative adj *pessimistic* 124
negative adj/adv *saying no* 89
negative n *negative statement* 87
negative adj *electrical term* 195
negative feedback n 301
negativism n 213
neglect n/v 97
neglect n 97
negligee n *scanty nightwear* 316
negligee n *informal clothing* 316
negligee n *type of gown* 316
negligence n 52
negligible adj 233
negotiable 143, 253
negotiable n 172
negotiable adj *liquid, as in "negotiable bonds"* 200
negotiate v *discuss compromise* 143
negotiate v *convert negotiable assets* 172
negotiate v *maneuver through* 253
negotiate v *arrange, as in "negotiate a deal"* 162
negotiation n 143, 253
Nehru jacket n 316
neigh n/v *horse noise* 11
neighbor n 22
neighbor adj/n/v 22
neighborhood n *vicinity* 63
neighborhood n 63
neighborhood n *proximity* 63
neighborhood watch n 327
neighborly adj 111
neither adj/adv 25

nelson n *type of wrestling hold* 263

nemesis n *persistent foe* 135

nemesis n *avenger* 135

neoclassic adj 265

neo-Expressionism n 318

neo-gothic adj 265

neo-impressionism n 265

neolith n *stone tool* 237

neolithic adj 237

neolithic adj fig. *out of date* 237

neologism n *creation of a word, the word itself* 201

neon adj/n 254

neon adj *bright* 271

neon tetra n *type of fish* 296

neonatal adj *related to newborns* 257

neonate n *newborn* 257

neo-Nazi n 300

neophilia n 304

neophyte n gen. *beginner* 78

neophyte n *religious convert* 78

neorealism n 282

neoteric adj *modern, trendy* 128

nephew n obs. *niece* 40

nephew n 40

nephew n obs. *grandson* 40

nepotism n 170

nepotism n spec. *favoring the Pope's nephew* 170

nerd n (Am) 313

nerts interj/n (Am) 300

nerve n *gall* 261

nerve n *part of nervous system* 66

nerve n *courage* 261

nerve n *sinew* 66

nerve n *strength* 261

nerve cell 66

nerve center n 250

nerve gas n 300

nerve net 66

nerveless adj 184

nerve-wracking adj 212

nervine adj arch. *medically soothing nerves or tendons* 166

nervosity n 66

nervous adj *anxious* 66, 184

nervous adj *pertaining to nerves* 66

nervous adj *suffering nerve problems* 184

nervous adj *sinewy* 66

nervous breakdown n (Am) 273

nervous Nelly n 293

nervous system 66

nescience n *ignorance* 151

nesing n *sneeze* 147

nest n gen. *animal's home* 11

nest n *bird's home* 11

nest v *create a nest* 12

nest n *fit snugly together* 12

nest egg n 76

nestle v *settle in snugly* 11

nestle v *make a nest* 11, 12

nestling n fig. *baby of the family* 64

nestling n *bird that hasn't left the nest* 64

net n *network* 16

net n as in *"butterfly net"* 16

net adj as in *"net earnings"* 76

net n as in *"hair net"* 16

net v/n Finances/Money 76

net income 76

net national product n 305

nether adj 23

nethermost adj 23

netherworld n 156

netminder n 298

nettle n/v *type of plant* 10

nettle v 10

nettle rash n 182

nettlesome adj *irritable* 198

nettlesome adj *irritating* 198

network n fig. *interconnected things* 133

network n *netting* 133

network n as in *"TV network"* 133

network v *schmooze* 326

neural adj 66

neuralgia n 211

neurologist n 167

neurology n 167

neuromuscular adj 238

neuron n 256

neurosis n 199

neurosurgery n 273

neurotic adj/n 199, 244

neuter adj/n 89; v 274

neutral adj/n 86

neutral adj/n *asexual* 86

neutral spirits n 280

neutralism n 102

neutrality n 86, 102

neutralize v *make chemically neutral* 195

neutralize v *nullify* 195

neutralize v obs. *stay neutral* 195

neutrino n 296

neutron n 285

neutron bomb n 312

neutron star n 296

never adv 23

never mind n as in *"pay no never mind"* 301

nevermore adv 25

never-never n 293

never-never land n 269

nevertheless adv 54

new adj/adv 23

New Age adj 312

New Age music n 327

New Journalism n 318

new math n 309

new moon n 12

new wave n 312

New World n 118

new world order n 327

newborn n 45, 262; adj 45

new-collar adj *akin to blue-collar, white-collar* 327

newcomer n 87

newel n *staircase post* 69

newel post 69

newfangled adj *new* 81, 234

newfangled adj *impressed with new things* 81

newfanglement n 82

new-fashioned adj 138

newfound adj 103

newly adv 23

newly adv obs. *right now* 23

newlywed n 281

news n *broadcast news program* 87

news n obs. *something new* 87

news n 87

news agency n (Am) 246

news conference n 305

newsboy n 201

newsbreak n 305

newscast n 290

newsdealer n 245

newshound n 282

newsie n 201

newsletter n 276

newsmagazine n (Am) 290

newsman n 128

newsmonger n 128

newspaper n/v 172

newspaper n *pulp paper* 172

newspaperman n 214, 264

newspaperwoman n 214, 264

newspeak n 305

newspeople n 128

newsperson n 128

newsreel n 282

newsstand n (Am) 200

newsweekly n 305

newswoman n 128

newsworthy adj 301

newsy n *newspaper dealer* 245

newsy adj 233

newt n 64

next door adv 138

next of kin n 199

next-door adj 138

niacin n 297

nib n 158

nib n *beak* 158

nibble v *eat* 70

nibble n 70

nibs n as in *"his nibs"* 216

nice adj 53

nice-nelly adj/n 292

niche n/v 157

niche market n 326

nick n/v as in *"shaving nick"* 87

nick n as in *"the nick of time"* 87

nick n 87

nickel n *the metal* 193

nickel n *five cents, but once meant one cent* 245

nickel-and-dime adj/v 307

nickelodeon n (Am) 265

nickname n 86

nickname v *use a nickname, use a wrong name* 86

nicotine n 209

nictitate v *wink* 210

niece n obs. *nephew, granddaughter* 40

niece n 40

nifty n *something clever* 293

nifty adj (Am) 251

niggard adj/n 72

niggardly adj/adv 72

nigger n Insults 133

niggle v 162

niggle v slang *have sex with* 162

niggle v *nag* 162

niggling adj 139

niggling adj 162

night n *time of darkness* 10

night n *the darkness itself* 10

night and day adv 21

night court n 300

night crawler n (Am) 285

night owl n 232

night school n 111

night shift n 187

night table n 196

night terror n 257

night watch n 22

night watch n *night watchman* 22

night watchman n 22, 245

nightcap n 222

nightcap n *type of nightwear* 71, 222

nightclothes n 149

nightclub n (Am) 265

nightdress n 184

nightfall n 146

nightglow n 309

nightgown n 71, 242

nighthawk n 145

nightie n 71, 242

nightingale n *fig. good singer* 11

nightingale n 11

nightlife n 246

night-light n 148

nightmare n *feelings of suffocation during sleep* 225

nightmare n *spectre bringing bad sleep* 47

nightmare n *bad dream* 47, 255

nightscope n 324

nightshade n *type of poisonous plant* 10

nightshirt n 224

nightspot n 299

nightstand n 258

nightstick n (Am) 266

nighttime n 65

nightwalker n 101

nighty-night interj 267

nihilism n 213

nihilist n 213

nil n 251

nill v *won't* 28

nim n *type of game* 275

nimble adj *physically quick* 13

nimble adj *mentally quick* 13

nimbostratus n Weather 146

nimbus n Weather 146

NIMBY n *Not In My BackYard* 324

nimiety n *excess* 134

niminy-piminy adj 204

nincompoop n 175

nincompoopery n Insults 175

nine n 12

nine day's wonder n *flash in the pan* 133

ninepin n 126

nineteen n 12

nineteenth hole n 277

nine-to-five adj 311

ninety adj/n 12

ninja n 319

ninny 175

ninny, ninnyhammer n 133

nip n/v *drink* 167

nip n/v *bite* 94

nip and tuck adj/adv 231

nipper n *as in "little nipper"* 205

nipperkin n *type of liquor bottle* 148

nipple n *nipple for baby bottle* 106, 258

nipple n *on body* 106, 258

nirvana n 215

nit n (Brit) *nitwit* 133

nit n *louse egg* 11

nitery n *nightclub* 299

nithing n *arch. cur* 21

nitpick n/v 311

nit-picking adj/n 311

nitrate n 195

nitric acid n 195

nitro n 237

nitrogen n 193

nitrogen balance n 302

nitrogen cycle n 272

nitroglycerin n 237

nitrous oxide n 195

nitty-gritty adj/n (Am) 320

nitwit n 293

nix v 278

nix adv/n/v 205

nixie, nix n *mythical water sprite* 230

no adv 22

no n 135

no contest n 313

no man's land n 46

no siree interj (Am) 230

no sweat interj 312

no way interj 53, 320; adv 320

no-account adj 231

nobby adj (Brit) 204

nobility 44

noble n 44

noble adj 44

noble adj *virtuous* 44

noble savage n 176

nobleman n 44

noblesse n 44

noblesse oblige n 229

noblewoman n 44

nobody n 130

no-brainer n 324

nocent adj *harmful* 103

noctambulism n 182

noctambulist n *sleepwalker* 182

noctambulo *obs. noctambulist* 182

nocturnal adj *pertaining to animals* 103

nocturnal adj *of the night* 103

nocturnal emission n 221

nocturne n 246

nocuous adj *opp. of innocuous* 160

nod v *nod off* 67

nod n/v *give phys. assent* 67

noddle n *simpleton* 66

noddle n *head* 66

noel n Religion 215

noetic adj *intellectual* 170

no-fault adj/n 321

no-frills adj 313

nog n 197

noggin n *head* 195

noggin n *mugful of drink* 195

noggin n *mug* 195

no-go adj/n 249

no-good adj/n (Am) 278

no-holds-barred adj 307

no-hoper n (Brit) 307

nohow adv *anyhow* 206

noir adj/n *fiction style* 324

noir adj/n *film style* 324

noise n 48

noise pollution n 321

noisemaker n 134

noisome adj 89

noisy adj 179

nolo 248

nolo contendere n 248

nom de guerre n 174

nom de plume n 214

nomad n 130

nomadic adj 130

nomenclator n *creator of names* 128

nomenclator n *book listing words* 128

nomenclature n *name* 152

nomenclature n *terminology* 152

nomenclature n *creation of names* 152

nomenclature n *system of names* 152

nominal adj *pertaining to names* 160

nominal adj *pertaining to nouns* 160

nominal adj *in name only* 160

nomination n *obs. a name* 86

nomination n *proposing for a post or honor* 86

nominee n *one nominated* 176

nominee n *person named* 176

non compos mentis adj *not of sound mind* 150

non sequitur n 110

nonage n *being under legal age* 65

nonage n *fig. youth* 65

nonagenarian n *someone in their nineties* 210

nonagon n *nine-sided polygon* 146

nonce n 48

nonce words n 264

nonchalance n 169

noncom n 188

noncommissioned officer n 188

noncommunicable adj 310

nonconform v 154

nonconformist n *spec. rel. sense* 154

nonconformist n *gen.* 154

noncredit adj *as in "noncredit courses"* 319

nondairy adj 316

nondescript adj 179

nondescript adj *obs. scientific not easily classified* 179

nondrinker n 259

nonentity n 130

nonessential adj 206

nonetheless adv 234

non-euclidean adj 237

nonevent n 320

nonfat adj 287

nonfeasance n 132

nonfiction n 276

nonflammable adj 284

nonhuman adj 309

nonissue n 320

nonjudgmental adj 311

nonliterate adj 305

non-negotiable adj 313

no-no n (Am) 307

no-nonsense adj 293

nonpareil adj/n *without equal* 91

nonperson n 276

nonplus n/v 135

nonprescription drug adj 310

nonprofit adj 276

nonreader n 291

nonrefundable adj 317

nonreturnable adj 278

nonscience n 237

nonsectarian adj Religion 228

nonsense n 157

nonsense verse n 201

nonsexist adj 324

nonstick adj 310

nonstop adj/adv 278
nonunion adj 245
nonverbal adj 290
nonviolence n 283
nonvoter n 324
nonwhite adj/n 291
nonword n 318
noodle n *the pasta* 197
noodle n *simpleton/head* 204
noodle n *the head* 279
nook n 34
nooky n *Love/Romance/Sex* 289
noon n 31
noon n *obs. nine hours after daybreak* 31
noonday n 105
noontide 31
noontime 31
noose n *spec. hanging rope* 88
noose n/v 88
nope adv (Am) 270
norm, normal n, adj 217
north n 29
North Pole 63
North Star n 65
northeast n 29
northeaster n Weather 194
norther n (Am) Weather 194
northerly n Weather 309
Northern Cross n 272
northern hemisphere 145
northern hemisphere n 193
northern lights n 65
northern pike n (Am) 237
northland n 9
northwester n Weather 182
Norway maple n 194
Norway pine n 181
Norway rat n 194
Norway spruce n 181
nose n *informant* 204
nose n *ability to sense things, as in "a nose for news"* 47
nose n *front of ship, etc.* 13
nose v 121
nose n The Body 13
nose bag n *feedbag* 197
nose bag n *slang food* 197
nose candy n (Am) 300
nose job n 310
nose paint n *alcohol* 269
nose ring n 197
nosebleed n 222
nosedive n/v 284
no-see-um n *type of insect* 220
nosegay n *type of bouquet* 71
nosh n/v 310

nosh n *nosh bar* 310
no-show n (Am) 308
nostalgia n *homesickness for a place* 198
nostalgia n *homesickness for a time* 198
nostalgist n 198
nostril n 13
nostrum n *snake oil* 147
nosy adj 261
not adv 53
nota bene v 189
notabilia n *things notable, akin to memorabilia* 251
notable n *someone notable* 216
notable adj 54
notarize v 40, 292
notary n 40
notary n *obs. secretary* 40
notary public n 40
notch n *level, as in "take it up a notch"* 135
notch n/v 135
note n/v *as in "make a note"* 87
note n Music 42
note n *official IOU* 172
note n *explanation, as in "footnote"* 128
note n/v *notableness* 52
note n *brief letter* 128
note of hand 172
notebook n 128
notepad 227
notepaper n 227
noteworthy adj 137
not-for-profit adj 318
nothing n *as in "that is nothing"* 87
nothing n *as in "he is a nothing"* 87
nothing doing interj 277
nothingness n 87
notice n *sign* 232
notice n *awareness of something* 125; v 125
notice n *as in "give notice"* 205
notice n *warning* 86
noticeable adj 207
notify, notification v, n 82
notify, notification v, n *obs. notice* 82
notion n *concept* 74
notion n *inkling* 74
notions n *goods* 200
notoriety n *someone with notoriety* 134
notoriety n 134

notorious adj *obs. obvious* 115
notorious adj 115
notoriously adv 115
nougat n *type of confection* 223
nought adj/adv/v *zero* 12
nought adj/adv/n *nothing* 12
noun n 76
nourish v 32
nourish v *obs. nurture* 32
nourishing adj 32
nourishment n 32
nouveau adj 217
nouveau riche n 215
nouvelle adj *novel* 197
nouvelle cuisine n 322
nova n 255
novel adj 103
novel n *book-length fiction* 153
novel n *fiction of shorter length* 153
novel adj *obs. freshly created* 103
novelette n 153, 201
novelist n 153, 187
novelist n *obs. creator of the new* 187
novelize v 227
novelize v *obs. create novel things* 227
novella n 153, 264
novelty n 84
novelty n *gadget, doodad* 84
November n 12
novice n 52
novitiate n *apprenticeship* 127
novitiate n *neophyte* 127
novocaine n 273
now adj *slang modern, hip* 89
now adj 89
now and then adv 102
nowadays adv 88
noway adv 53
nowhence adv/pron 206
nowhere adv/n 25
nowhere n 25
nowheres 25
nowhither adv *toward nowhere* 23
no-win situation n 320
nowise adv 89
nowness n 154
noxious adj 103
nozzle n *spout* 159
nozzle n *projection* 159
nuance n 205
nubile adj *marriageable* 151
nubile adj *attractive* 151

nuclear adj *pertaining to atomic energy* 220
nuclear adj *pertaining to the atomic nucleus* 220
nuclear adj *gen. pertaining to the nucleus* 220
nuclear energy n 285
nuclear family n 304
nuclear medicine n 309
nuclear physics n 296
nuclear reactor n 302
nuclear weapon n 307
nuclear winter n 327
nuclear-powered adj 302
nucleus n (Am) *center of cell* 182, 219
nucleus n *biological center of cell* 182
nucleus n *center of atom* 179, 182
nucleus n *gen. central part* 182
nucleus n *core of a comet* 182
nude adj/n *naked* 242
nude adj *obs. plain, obvious* 242
nude n 242
nudge n/v 180, 267
nudism n 287
nudnik n (Am) 307
nuff said interj (Am) 230
nugget n 250
nuisance n *leg., as in "public nuisance"* 177
nuisance n *annoyance* 177
nuke n 220
nuke v *microwave* 326
nuke n/v War/Military/Violence 307
null adj *as in "null and void"* 137
null n 137
null and void adj 137, 176
nullify v 117
null-space n 255
numb adj/n 89
number n/v 31
number n *as in "do a number on someone"* 320
number n *as in "I've got your number"* 249
number cruncher n 321
number one adj/n 189
number one, number two *bathroom references* 273
numbing adj 160
numen n *type of supernatural force* 156
numeral adj 89

numeral n *word representing a number* 166

numeral n *number* 166

numerator n 106

numerical adj 146

numero uno 189

numerology n 279

numerous adj *copious, multi-faceted* 103

numerous adj 103

numinous adj 156

numismatic adj 199

numismatics n 199

numps n *arch. dolt* 133

numskull n 189

nun n 19

nunchaku n 319

nunnery n *arch. slang bordello* 43

nunnery n *Religion* 43

nuptial adj/n 101

nuptial n 101

nurse v *as in "nurse a drink"* 70

nurse v *breast-feed* 70

nurse n *nanny* 40

nurse v *help as a med. nurse* 70

nurse n *med. employee* 40

nursemaid n 171

nurse-midwife n 309

nurse-practitioner n 316

nursery n *nurturing* 100

nursery n 100

nursery rhyme n 227

nursery school n 228

nursing home n 257

nursle v *arch.* 99

nursling n 99

nurture n/v 52

nurture v 52

nut n *head* 231

nut n *as in "nuts and bolts"* 149

nut n *aficionado* 300

nut n 15

nut n *loony person* 277

nut college 268

nutcase n 277

nutcracker n 106

nuthatch n *type of bird* 31

nuthouse n 268

nutmeat n 280

nutmeg n 34

nutpick n 258

nutrient adj/n 161

nutriment n *nourishment* 70

nutrition n 70

nutritionist n 289

nutritious adj 70, 178

nutritive 178

nuts adj *loony* 225, 268, 277, 323

nuts n *testicles* 279

nuts adj *enthusiastic* 204

nuts interj 300

nuts and bolts adj/n 313

nutso 225, 268, 323

nutsy *crazy* 225, 268, 323

nuttery n 268

nutty *crazy* 225, 268, 323

nuzzle n/v *obs. grovel* 113

nuzzle n/v 113

nyctalopia n 167

nylon n 297

nymph n *The Fantastic/Paranormal* 81

nymph n *young woman* 81

nymphet n *sexy young woman* 311

nympho n 199

nympholepsy n *possessed by nymphs* 203

nympholept n 203

nymphomania n 199

O

O interj/n *as in "O ye of little faith"* 47, 112

o' prep *as in "o'clock"* 41

oaf n 156

oafish adj 156

oak adj/n 10

oak adj 10

oak apple/oak gall n 64

oaken adj 10

oakmoss n 285

oar n 16

oarsman n 72, 212

oarswoman n 72, 212

oasis n 145

oasis n *fig. refuge* 145

oat n 15

oatcake n 70

oater n *horse* 307

oath n *promise* 21

oath n *profanity* 21

oatmeal n 70

obbo n *observation* 293

obedience, obedient n, adj 36

obeisance n *type of bow* 78

obeisance n *obs. obedience* 78

obelisk n 114

obese adj 147

obesity n 147

obey v 58

obfuscate v 97

obfuscation n 97

obit n *obs. funeral* 79

obit n *obituary notice* 79, 188

obit n *obs. death* 79

obit n *memorial service* 79

obituary n *newspaper item* 188

obituary n *list of obit-days* 188

obituary adj 188

object v *obs. create an obstacle* 97

object n *objective* 86

object v *express disagreement* 97

object n *thing* 88

object n *obs. obstacle* 88

object v 83

object lesson n 231

objection n 83

objection n *obs. attack* 83

objectionable adj 206

objective n *goal* 269

objective adj *unbiased* 243

objective adj *obs. related to objects* 243

objectivism n 243

objectivity n 213

objet d'art n 246

oblate n 247

oblectation n 117

obligate v 57

obligation n 50, 57

obligatory adj 57

oblige v *make necessary* 57

oblige v *bind* 57

oblige v *perform a favor* 57

obliging adj 150

oblique adj/adv *lit. and fig.* 90

obliterate v 143

obliterative adj 143

oblivion n 83

oblivious adj 74, 83

obliviscence n *forgetfulness* 199

oblong adj 90

obnoxious adj 169

obnoxious adj *obs. submissive* 169

obnoxious adj *susceptible to injury* 169

oboe n 173

obscene adj 135

obscenity n 135

obscure adj *dark* 89

obscure v 89

obscurity n *gen. indistinctness* 84

obscurity n *something obscure* 84

obscurity n 89

obsequious adj *gen. serving* 73

obsequious adj *servile* 73

obsequy n *type of funeral rite* 79

observance n 48

observant adj *perceptive* 125

observant adj *obs. servile* 125

observatory n 165

observe v *as in "observe a holiday"* 93

observe v *watch* 141

observe v *state an observation* 162

observer n 141

obsess v *besiege* 108

obsess v 108

obsess v *rare possess* 108

obsession n 170

obsession n 108

obsession n *obs. siege* 170

obsession n *something haunted* 170

obsessive adj 275

obsessive adj 108

obsessive-compulsive adj 288

obsidian n 164

obsolesce v 206

obsolescence n 206

obsolescent adj 206

obsolete adj/v 138

obstacle n 51

obstacle course n 304

obstepterous adj *clamorous* 115

obstetricate v *help a birth* 147

obstetrician n 221

obstetric/obstetrical adj 182

obstetrics n 211

obstetrix n *midwife* 239

obstinate adj 54

obstipation n *obsti(nate) (consti)pation* 121

obstreperous adj 139

obstruct v *lit. get in the way* 142

obstruct v *fig.* 142

obstruct v 114

obstruction n *something that obstructs* 114

obstruction n *act of obstructing* 114

obstrupescence n *stupefication* 125

obtain v 95

obtain v *obs. win* 95

obtrude v 178

obtrusion n 178

obtrusive adj 178

obtuse adj *dull-witted* 100

obtuse adj *geometry sense* 100

obtuse angle n 120

obviate v *dispose of* 143

obvious adj 138
ocarina n 265
Occam's razor n 231
occasion n/v 83
occasion n *special event* 83
occasional adj *pertaining to an occasion* 160
occasional adj *every once in a while* 160
occlude v 143
occlusion n 143
occult adj *pertaining to mystical arts* 103
occult adj *hidden* 103
occult n 292
occultation n 103
occultism n 292
occupant n *resident* 148
occupation n *profession* 40
occupation n *forceful occupation* 40
occupation n *owning* 40
occupational adj 40, 244
occupational therapy n 279
occupy v *obs. have sex with* 59
occupy v *keep busy* 59
occupy v *seize* 59
occupy v *reside in* 59
occur v *as in "it occurs to me"* 104
occur v 104
occurrence n 104
occurrent adj 104
ocean n 29
ocean n *fig. expanse, a lot* 29
oceanarium n 296
oceanaut n (Am) 317
oceanfront adj/n 279
oceanography n 237
oceanology n (Am) 237
ocelot n 194
ocher n 29
ochlocracy n *mob rule* 101
o'clock adv 187
octagon n 120
octagonal adj 120
octahedron n 120
octane n 237
octane number n 298
octangle *obs.* 120
octave n 129
octaves n *8 days following a celebration* 65
October n 12
octogenarian adj/n 210
octopus n 194
ocularist n *maker of artificial eyes* 239

oculist 239
oculist n 121
OD n/v *overdose* 313
odd adj *obs. unique, remarkable* 138
odd adj *occasional, as in "the odd complaint"* 91
odd adj *left over* 53
odd adj *opp. of even* 65
odd adj *unusual* 138
odd lot n 263
odd man out n 269
oddball adj/n (Am) 307
oddity n 189
oddment n 206
odds and ends n 189
odds-on adj 270
ode n 128
odeum n 153
odious adj 88
odium n *odiousness* 157
od/odd interj 132
odometer n (Am) 195
odor n 50
odorant n 301
odorant adj 301
odoriferous adj 50
odorous 50
odso interj 21
odyssey n 261
Oedipal 275
Oedipus complex n 275
oeillade n *glance* 144
oenophile n *wine lover* 287
oeuvre n *body of work* 246
of course 113
of the clock 187
ofay n (Am) 292
off v *take off, remove* 116
off adj 178
off v *kill* 116, 291, 319
off v *die* 291, 319
off v *be off* 116
off adj *not working* 227
off and on adv 113
off Broadway n 311
off year n 250
off your nut adj 277
off your rocker adj 262
offal n 84
offbear v *take away* 271
offbeat n/adj 290
off-color adj 251
offend, offense v, n 51
offender n 102
offensive adj 51
offensive adj *grating, insulting* 138

offensive adj/n War/Military/Violence 112
offer n *bid, attempt* 86
offer v *offer to give* 19
offer v *attempt* 19
offer n *result of offering* 86
offer v *make an offering* Religion 19; n 19
offer v *as in "offer a ride"* 95
offer v *propose* 19
offering 19
office n *company, workplace, as in "branch office"* 171
office n *arch. bodily function* 68
office n *job, esp. in public service* 44
office n *workroom* 76
office n *responsibility* 50
office park n 327
officer n *as in "police officer"* 112
officer n *officeholder* 44
officer n *as in "club officer"* 44
officer n *mil. leader* 80
official n Government 130
official n Religion 43
officialdom n 247
officialese n 264
officiate v 180
officiate v *rel. sense* 180
officinal adj *medicinal* 182
officious adj *obs. helpful* 125
officious adj *obnoxiously official* 125
offing n *type of nautical term* 205
offing n *as in "in the offing"* 205
offish adj (Am) *standoffish* 225
off-key adj/adv 290
off-limits adj (Am) 308
off-load v 235
offput v 233
off-putting adj 233
off-ramp n 310
off-road adj 317
offscouring n *discards* 113
offscreen adv/adj 299
offscum n *scum* 136
off-season adj/adv/n 226
offset v 180
offset n *outset* 143
offshoot n 189
offspring n *gen. descendents* 18
offspring n *a spec. descendent* 18
offstage adj/adv 290
off-the-books adj 318

off-the-cuff adj 301
off-the-rack adj 320
off-the-record adj 299
off-the-wall adj 321
offtrack adj/adv 304
off-white adj/n 295
ofhungered adj *obs. starved* 14
ogle n/v 180
ogre, ogress n 189
oh 47, 112
ohm n 238
ohmmeter n 238
oho interj 47
oh-oh interj 112, 189
oh-so adv *as in "it was oh-so cute"* 271
oil n *petroleum* 105
oil n *oil painting* 128
oil n *olive oil* 29
oil n *oil paint* 128
oil n *gen. grease* 29
oil color n 110
oil of wintergreen n 251
oil paint n 128, 196
oil painting n 201
oil shale n 236
oil slick n 270
oil well n (Am) 224
oilcan n 224
oilcloth n *waterproofed cloth* 167
oilcloth n *type of covering* 167
oilstone n *whetstone* 123
oink n/v 302
ointment n 32
OK interj 248
OK adj 234
OK n/v/adv 233
okapi n 255
okeydoke/okeydokey adv (Am) 300
okra n *type of plant* 168
old adj 12
old adj *as in "old friend"* 12
old boy interj 156
old boy network n 313
old country n 204
Old English n 41
Old English sheepdog n 255
old fogey n 231
Old Glory n 247
old guard n 232
old hand n 204
old hat n 204
old lady n *wife, mother* 250
old lady n 204
old maid n Society/Mores/Culture 111

old maid n Games/Fun/Leisure 244

old man n 250

old man n *father, husband* 204

old master n 214

old money n 318

Old Nick n *the devil* 173

old school n 189

Old Testament n 43

old wives' tale n 176

Old World adj/n 130

Old World monkey n 237

olde adj 295

olden adj 89

oldfangled adj 81, 234

old-fashioned adj 139

oldie n 249

old-time adj 207

old-timer n 207

old-timey adj 207

ole adj *old* 12, 231

olé interj/n 248

oleander n *type of shrub* 105

oleo n 241

oleomargarine n 241

olfaction n *sense of smell* 166, 221

olfactory adj 166

oligarch n 101

oligarchy n 101

oligopoly n *akin to monopoly* 263

olive adj 160

olive n 122

olive n *olive tree* 122

olive branch n *token of peace* 47

olive drab n 160, 271

olive green adj/n 160, 207

olympiad n 75

Olympian Games 151

Olympic Games n 151

ombudsman n 281

omelette n 148

omen n/v 135

ominate v *predict* 125

ominous adj *obs. indicating good signs* 138

ominous adj *gen. predictive* 138

ominous adj *indicating bad signs* 138

omission n 52

omnibus adj *varied* 234

omnibus n 224

omnicompetent adj 233

omnidirectional adj 295

omnificent adj *having ultimate power to create* 179

omnipotence n 54

omnipotent adj 54

omnipresent, omnipresence adj 139

omniscience n 150

omniscient adj 150

omniverous adj 165

omnivore 165

on and off adj/adv 250

on camera adv 319

on tenterhooks n 185

on the fritz adj (Am) 189

on the nose adj 301

on the rocks adj *ruined* 269

on the rocks adj 303

on-again, off-again adj 308

onanism n 185

once-over n (Am) 283

oncology n *study of tumors* 238

oncome n 234

oncoming adj/n 234

one adj/n 12

one-armed bandit n (Am) 298

one-dimensional adj 270

one-hit wonder n 318

one-liner n (Am) 318

one-man adj 234

oneness n 22

one-night stand n (Am) Love/Romance/Sex 262

one-nighter n Love/Romance/Sex 289

one-note adj 324

one-on-one adj/adv/n 321

101 adj *basic* 327

onerous adj 89

one-shot adj/n 278

one-sided adj 217

one-step n/v *type of dance* 282

one-stop adj 301

onetime adj/adv 234

one-track adj 295

one-two n 215

one-upmanship n 313

onewhere adv *akin to everywhere, nowhere* 163

ongoing adj/n 251

onion n 34

onion dome n *type of roof* 303

onion ring n 303

onionskin n (Am) *type of paper* 257

on-line adj/adv 302

onlooker n 157

only adj/adv/conj 23

only child n 101

only-begotten adj *arch. being the only child* 75

onomatop n 127

onomatopoeia n 127

onomatopoesis n 127

onomatopy n 127

on-ramp n 310, 311

on-screen adj/adv 312

onset n *attack* 134

onset n 134

onslaught n 158

ontological argument n 262

ontology n 185

onus n 158

onyx n 29

oodles n 249

ooh interj 283

oologist n 220

oology n 220

oolong n *type of tea* 223

oomph n 300

oons interj 132

oops interj 292

ooze n *act of oozing* 10

ooze n *muck* 10

ooze v 10

opal n 63

opalescent adj 217

opaque adj 161

opaque adj *obs. in the dark* 161

opaque adj *rare nonreflecting* 161

opaque projector n 310

ope adj 74

op-ed n (Am) *opposite the editorial page* 318

open adj *not clogged, not obstructed, clear* 24

open adj *not covered* 24

open adj *as in "open for business"* 24

open adj *frank* 38

open adj *not closed* 24

open adj *receptive* 38

open adj *unprotected, as in "open to attack"* 103

open v 24

open bar n 323

open classroom n 324

open house n 102

open letter n 264

open marriage n 323

open sandwich n 303

open season n (Am) 263

open secret n 231

open sesame n 189

open shop n 264

open universe n 322

open up v 141

open-air adj 222

open-and-shut adj (Am) 231

open-eyed adj 159

open-heart adj 316

open-heart surgery n 316

openhearted adj 150

opening n *gap, hole* 47

opening n *opportunity, chance* 206

opening n *as in "opening of a play"* 173

opening n *gen. beginning* 173

opening n *first chess move* 173

open-minded adj 225

opera n *opera company* 154

opera n *the form* 154

opera glass n 184

opera hat n 212

opera house n 187

operable adj *med. able to be operated on* 115

operable adj *working* 115

operant adj 91

operate v *control* 253

operate v *Medicine* 167

operate v *function, work* 321

operate v 142

operating system n 315

operation n War/Military/Violence 203

operation n Medicine 167

operation n 253

operational adj *functional* 321

operative adj *significant* 91

operative adj *as in "the operative clause"* 91

operetta n 201

operose adj *hardworking* 171

ophthalmologist n 221

ophthalmology n 221

opiate n 87

opiate adj 87

opiniatre n *opinionated person* 151

opiniatre v *obs.* 151

opinion n 39

opinion n *type of formal declaration* 39

opinionated adj 39, 150

opium n 46

opium poppy n 236

opossum n (Am) 145

oppone v 62

opponent n *someone with an opposing point of view* 135

opponent adj 135

opportune adj *obs. useful* 90

opportune adj *timed well* 84, 90

opportunism n 251

opportunistic 251

opportunity n 84
oppose v 94
opposed adj *against* 139
opposeless adj *incapable of being opposed* 159
opposite adj *on the other side* 89
opposite adj *reversed* 89
opposite n/adv/prep 89
opposite number n 278
oppress v *obs. surprise, rape* 97
oppress v *subjugate* 97
oppress v *obs. suppress* 97
oppression n 97
oppressive adj *fig., as in "oppressive heat"* 139
oppressive adj 97, 139
oppugn v *obs. to fight against* 116
oppugn v *impugn* 116
opt v 134, 271
opt out v 314
optic adj *arch. optical* 66
optic adj 66
optical adj 134
optical art/op art n 318
optical character recognition n 315
optical disk n 322
optical fiber n 315
optical illusion n 204
optician n 195
optician n *rare optical expert* 195
optics n 119
optimal adj 270
optimism n *positive outlook* 224
optimism n *type of philosophy* 224
optimist n 224
optimization n 234
optimize v 234
optimum n 269
option n *act of choosing* 134
option n *as in "stock option," "movie option"* 200; v 200
option n *ability to choose* 134
option v 295
option n *accessory* 134
optional adj *not necessary* 207
optional adj *pertaining to choice* 207
optometrist n 257
optometry n 257
opulence n 113
opulent adj 113
opus n 187
opuscule n *minor opus* 172, 187
opusculum n *minor work* 172

or adv/conj/prep *before, ere* 28
or what? interj 203
oracle n 84
oracy n *or(al)(liter)acy* 318
oral adj *pertaining to the mouth* 147
oral adj *verbal* 152
oral contraceptive n 310
oral history n 312
orang n 165
orange n 34
orange adj/n *color* 115
orange pekoe n *type of tea* 259
orangeade n 183
orangery n 168
orangutan n 165
orate *speak* 113
oration n 113
oration n *obs. type of prayer* 113
oratorical adj 113
oratory 113
orb n *spec. spheres that carry the planets* 114
orb n *circle* 114
orb n *sphere* 114
orbit n/v *as in "a planet's orbit"* 165
orbit n *eyesocket* 66
orbit v 308
orbiter n (Am) 309
orc n *obs. type of sea creature* 132
orc n *type of land creature* 132
orca n 237
orchard n 15
orchardist n 197
orchardist 15
orchestra n *arch. part of the theater* 187
orchestra n *group of musicians* 187
orchestra n *place in theater where musicians sit* 187
orchestral adj 187
orchestrate v 187, 246, 265
orchestrate v *fig. organize* 265
orchestration n 246, 265
orchid n 219
ordain v *obs. arrange* 43
ordain v *decree* 43
ordain v *appoint to ministry* 43
ordeal n *gen. trying circumstance* 21
ordeal n *as in "trial by ordeal"* 21
order n *as in "religious order"* 43

order n/v *sequence* 52
order n *normal, tidy state* 134
order n *as in "law and order"* 102
order n/v *as in "place an order"* 245
order v 56
order n *rank, level, as in "on the order of . . ."* 177
order n/v *command* 131
order n *as in "money order"* 175
order of business n 269
orderly n *hospital aide* 196
orderly n *mil. aide* 196
orderly adj 137
ordinance n *law* 46
ordinary adj *plain* 91
ordinary adj *normal* 91
ordnance n 80
ore n 10
oregano n 197
Oregon fir n 272
organ n *publication* 201
organ n *internal body part* 66
organ n *gen. musical instrument* 19
organ n *internal organ* 273
organ n *penis* 66, 273
organ n *spec. type of keyboard instrument* 19
organdy n *type of muslin* 223
organ-grinder n 214
organic adj *of a whole* 66
organic adj *arch. instrumental* 66
organic adj *biological* 66
organic adj *pertaining to body organs* 66
organic chemistry n 237
organism n *organization* 236
organism n *living thing* 236
organism n *something that resembles the living* 236
organist 19, 129
organist n *obs. organ-maker* 129
organistrum n *type of hurdy-gurdy* 265
organization n *organic internal structure* 206
organization n *organism* 206
organization n *act or result of organizing* 206
organization n *group* 206, 232
organization v 206
organized adj *orderly* 217
orgasm n 151

orgasm n *fig.* 151
orgulous adj *proud* 37
orgy n *decadent celebration* 126
orgy n *type of ancient worship* 126
orient v *position to face East* 191
Oriental rug n 258
orientate v 191
orientation n 191
orientation n *introduction* 232
orientation n *fig. position* 232
orientation n *phys. position* 232
orifice n 87
oriflamme n *spec. banner of St. Dennis* 103
oriflamme n *type of banner* 103
origami n 290
origanum n *type of seasoning* 34
origin n 84
original adj *originative* 89
original adj *clever, creative* 89
original adj *native* 89
original sin n 43
originality 84, 89, 190
originate v 84, 179
oriole n 194
orison n *arch. prayer* 42
ornament n/v 48
ornament n *obs. useful accessory, such as furniture* 48
ornamental adj 48
ornate adj *lit. and fig.* 90
ornery adj 199
ornithology n 165
ornithopter n 274
orogeny, orogenesis n *creation of mountains* 254
orography n *mountain geology* 219
orotund adj *clear, pertaining to voice* 207
orphan n 75; v 75, 218
orphan drug n *unmarketed drug* 326
orphanage n 239
orphanage n *obs. caring for orphans* 239
orphanage n *state of being an orphan* 239
orphic adj *prophetic* 170
ort n *scraps* 86
orthodontia n 222, 273
orthodontics n 222, 273
orthodox adj 91
orthodoxy n 91
orthographic projection n 164
orthography n *spelling* 76

overdrive n 288
overdue adj 234
overexpose v 253
overflow n/v 26
overgarment 242
overgraze v 280
overhand adj/adv 166
overhaul v 191
overhaul v overtake 191
overhead 281
overhead projector n 310
overhear v eavesdrop 117
overhear obs. ignore 116, 117
overhear v obs. hear 117
overjoy n too much joy 124
overjoy, overjoyed v, adj 124
overkill n/v 313
overlap n/v 191
overlay n/v 87
overload n/v 139
overlook v look over 92
overlook n vantage point 92
overlook v ignore 116
overlord n/v 44
overnight v 271
overnight bag n 286
overnighter n 286
overpass n 288
overplus n overage 84
overpopulate v 215
overpopulation n 215
overpower v phys. overwhelm 142
overpower v fig. 142
overprice v 152
overqualified adj 311
override v overrule 141
override v ride over 141
override v take over manually 141
override n 301
overripe adj 164
oversee v 26
oversee v spy 26
overseer n supervisor 110
overseer n watcher 110
oversexed adj 262
overshadow v steal the spotlight 143
overshadow v cast a shadow over 143
overshirt n 212
overshoe n 123
oversight n overseeing 52
oversight n negligence 52
overslop n type of loose garment 16
oversoul n (Am) 228

overt adj 54
overt adj rare not closed 54
overtake v 56
over-the-counter adj 289
over-the-hill adj 307
over-the-top adj 327
over-the-transom adj 311
overthrow v knock down 60
overthrow v depose 60
overtime adv/n 110
overtone n akin to undertone 251
overtone n musical term 251
overture n obs. gen. beginning 173
overture n proposal, suggestion 173
overture n proposal, suggestion 52
overture n musical beginning 52, 173
overturn v 56
overturn v obs. revolve 56
overview n 321
overview n obs. watching 321
overwade n wade across 28
overwatch v 139
overwhelm v phys. bury 60
overwhelm v fig. bury 60
overwhelming adj 60
overwork n/v 213
overwork n overtime 213
overwrought adj 91
ovine adj/n relating to sheep 219
ovulate adj/v 221
ovulation n 221
ow interj 283
owe v is the result of 60
owe v 60
owe v obs. own 60
owl n 11
owlet n small owl 11, 105
owlish adj 147
own v obs. obtain 27
own v 27
ownership n 135
ox n 11
ox n fig. clod 11
oxblood n type of color 191
oxbow adj/n type of river feature 35, 193
oxbow adj/n type of yoke 35
oxcart n 184
oxford n type of shoe 260
oxidate v 193
oxidation n 193
oxidize v 193
oxygen mask n 280

oxygen, oxygenate n, v 193
oxygen tent n 286
oxymoron n 172
oy interj 203, 267
oyez interj 81
oyster n 30
oyster cocktail n 297
oyster crab n 194
oyster cracker n 241
oysters Rockefeller n 297
ozone n 220
ozone hole n 255
ozone layer n 285
ozone shield n 285
ozonosphere n 296

P

pa n pa(pa) 213
PA system n 299
pablum n 303
pabulum n 168
pabulum n fig. food for the soul 168
pabulum n insipidity 168
pace v step 116
pace n rate, as in "keeping pace" 31
pace v as in "pace off" 116
pace n a step 31
pace v set the pace, maintain a speed 116
pace car n 317
pace egg 213
pacemaker n 316
pacemaker n leader 233, 270
pacesetter n 270, 316
pachisi n type of board game 199
pachyderm n 220
pacific adj peaceful 115
pacific adj peace-making 115
pacific time n (Am) 256
pacification n 87
pacificism n 276
pacifier n 106
pacifism n 276
pacifist n 276
pacify v 103
pack n backpack 286
pack n as in "mudpack" 321
pack n as in "pack of cards" 48
pack v as in "pack your bags" 180
pack n packet, as in "pack of cigarettes" 48
pack n as in "pack of dogs" 87
pack n/v package 48

pack animal n 220
pack rat n 231
package v 295
package n parcel 190
package n/v the action of packing 190
package deal n 305
package store n 281
packager n type of publisher 318
packer n 75
packet n 102
packhorse n 71
packman n peddler 127
packsack n (Am) 239
packsaddle n 72
pact n 81
pad n as in "launch pad" 317
pad v supply with a pad 234
pad n as in "mattress pad" 121
pad n as in "knee pad" 148
pad n bed, residence 183
pad n/v travel on foot 123
pad n graft, as in "on the pad" 319
paddle n type of oar 72
paddle n stirring tool 72
paddle n gaming device 72
paddle tennis n (Am) 289
paddle wheel n 169
paddle wheeler n 288
paddleball n 298
paddleboard n 298
paddleboat n 243
paddy n where rice is grown 122
paddy n rice 122
paddy wagon n 292
padlock n/v 100
paean n type of song 111
pagan n 78
paganism n 78
page n errand boy 40
page v summon via page 295
page n servant 40
page n as in "page of a book" 128
page n knight in training 40
page v serve 295
pageant n 77
pageantry n 77
pager n beeper 318
page-turner n 323
pah interj 132
pail n 16
pain v obs. hurt someone else 67
pain n 32
pain v feel pain 67
painful adj causing physical pain 38

painful adj *arch. painstaking* 38

painful adj *causing mental pain* 38

painkiller n (Am) 238

painstaking adj 179

paintbrush n 224

painted lady n *type of butterfly* 194

painted turtle n 254

painted/carved leaves n 64

painter n *one who paints* 41

painter n (Am) *type of cougar* 194

painteress n 41

painter's colic n *lead poisoning* 211

painting n 42

pair n/v 50

pair-bond n *monogamy* 298

pairing n 50

paisley n 212

pajama n 260

pajamas n 197

pal v 271

pal n/v 170

palace n 33

paladin n 131

palatable adj *tasty* 168

palatable adj *fig. enjoyable* 168

palate n 66

palate n *liking, preference* 66

palatial adj 33

palaver n/v 190

pale adj *pertaining to colors* 32

pale adj *pertaining to people* 32

pale n *area enclosed by pales* 52

pale n *stake, fence, as in "beyond the pale"* 52

paleface n 216

paleography n *study of ancient writings* 210

paleontology n 220

palette n *artist's tool* 153

palette n *range of color* 153

palette knife n 198

palfrey n *horse other than a war-horse* 30

palimony n (Am) 324

palimpsest n *type of writing material* 172

palimpsest n *obs. type of parchment writing service* 172

palindrome n 152

palisade n *row of pales* 136; v 136

pall n *type of cloth* 15

pall n *fig. gloom* 15

pallbearer n 188

pallid adj 138

pall-mall n *type of game* 126

pallor n 87

pally adj *being pals* 268

palm v *as in "palm a coin"* 180

palm n *part of the foot* 32

palm n *part of the hand* 32

palm n *type of tree* 10

palm off v 218

palm sugar n 241

palmetto n *type of palm tree* 10, 118

palmist n 263

palmistry n 81, 263

palmtop n *type of small computer* 326

palmyra n *type of palm tree* 10, 164

palomino n (Am) *type of horse* 279

palooka n (Am) 292

palpable adj 89

palpate v *diagnose by touch* 222

palpitate v 162

palsy adj *friendly* 311

palsy n/v *paralysis, the shakes* 32

palsy-walsy adj 298

palter v *waffle* 161

paltry adj/n 134

pamper v *spec. feed well* 70

pamper v *gen. treat well* 70

pamphlet n 76

pamphleteer n 76, 128; v 128

pan v *give a bad review* 281

pan n *pan(orama)* Movies/TV/Radio 291

pan n *as in "brain pan"* 16

pan v *as in "pan gold"* 235

pan n *type of cooking device* 16

pan out v 253

panace n *nonexistent cure-all herb* 106

panacea n 106

panache n *suaveness* 261

panache n *type of feather decoration* 261

panama n *type of hat* 223

Panama Red n *type of marijuana* 320

panatela/panetela n *type of cigar* 222

panbroil v 303

pancake v *flatten* 271

pancake n 34

pancake n *type of makeup* 318

pancake v *land an airplane flatly* 271

panchestron n *obs. cure-all* 180

pancreas n 120

panda n 220

panda car n (Brit) *black-and-white police car* 320

pandect n *body of law* 112

pandemic adj *gen. universal* 166

pandemic adj *sweeping through the population* 166

pandemic n 166

pandemonium n *hell (in Paradise Lost)* 251

pandemonium n *chaos* 251

pander n *matchmaker, pimp* 82

pander v 161

pander v 82

Pandora's box n 133

pandowdy n (Am) *type of dessert* 211

pane n *gen. panel* 50

pane n *section of cloth* 50

pane n *as in "window pane"* 50

panegyric n *tribute, eulogy* 130

panegyrist 130

panel n *as in "panel of inquiry"* 136

panel n *gen. jury, group* 81

panel n *pane* 87

panel n *jury list* 81, 136

panel n *distinct part of a surface* 87

panel v 87

panel discussion n 136, 301

panel truck n (Am) 298

paneling n 87

panelist n 135, 136

panfish n (Am) 209

panfry v 287

pang n/v 102

pangolin n 194

panhandle n *as in "Texas panhandle"* 236

panhandle v 263

panhandler n/v (Am) 263

panic n *panicked emotion* 189

panic adj 159

panic n 169

panic n *commotion* 189

panic v 189

panic n *commotion* 169

panic button n 307

panic-stricken adj 212

panjandrum n *big wheel* 204

panoplied adj 135

panoply n 135

panorama n *gen. scenic view* 201

panorama n *type of photograph* 201

panpipe n 214

pansexual adj 289

pansy n *the flower* 64

pansy adj/n 64, 293

pansy n *the color* 64

pant v *breathe heavily* 32

pant n 32

pantalets n *type of drawers* 223

pantaloon n *type of clown* 123

pantaloon n 123

pantdress n *dress with legs* 316

pantheism n 188

pantheon n 43

panther n 30

pantie n *trousers* 274

pantie n (Am) 274

pantie girdle n 303

pantograph n *earlier copying tool* 184

pantomime n *type of performance* 129

pantomime n *type of performer* 129

pantomime v 129

pantomimist n 129

pantry n 33

pantryman n *butler* 126

pants n *as in "pair of pants"* 223

pants singular use 223

pants suit n 316

panty hose n 316

panty raid n 312

pantywaist n 293

panzer n 300

pap n 70

pap n *gen. pablum* 70

pap smear 297

Pap smear/pap test n 309

papa n 170

papacy, papal n, adj 78

Papanicolaou smear n *pap smear* 297

paparazzo n 318

papaw/pawpaw n *type of tree* 118

papaya n *type of tree* 119

paper n *(news)paper* 172

paper n 33

paper v *put on paper, write* 128

paper adj *flimsy* 138

paper n *type of document* 33

paper v *wallpaper* 128

paper adj *existing only on paper* 138

paper chase n 249

paper clip n 242
paper cutter n 224
paper doll n 226
paper money n 76
paper tiger n 231
paper trail n 318
paper wasp n (Am) 236
paperback n 264
paperboy n 263
paperhanger n *forger* 283
paperless adj 318
papermaker n 126
papers n *credentials* 33
paper-thin adj 295
paper-train v 322
paperweight n 239
paperwork n 127
papess n 154
papier-mâché adj/n 201
papist, papistry n 111
papoose n (Am) 151
pappy n 170, 199
paprika n 259
papyrus n *type of plant* 187
papyrus n *writing material* 187
par n *equality* 136
par n/v *golf average* 136, 304
par n *average* 136
par excellence adj 176
parable n/v 42
parabola n 120
parachute n/v 198
parachutist n 198
parade n *type of procession* 176
parade n *mil. display* 176
parade n/v *showiness* 176
paradiddle n *drumroll* 290
paradigm n 102
paradisal adj 22
paradise n *gen. heavenly place* 22
paradise n 22
paradisiac adj 22
paradisiacal adj 22
paradox n 114
paradoxical adj 114
paraffin n 222
paragon n 114
paragon n *foe* 114
paragon n *obs. companion* 114
paragraph n 101
parajournalism n *subjective journalism* 318
parakeet n 119
paralegal adj/n 324
parallax n 119
parallel adj/adv 106

parallel n *mapping convention* 133
parallel n/v *parallel line* 133
parallel n/v *close analogy* 133
parallel adj *fig. closely similar* 106
parallel bars n 244
parallel evolution n 315
parallelogram n 120
paralogism n *false argument* 125
paralysis n *fig.* 14
paralysis n *Medicine* 14
paralysis agitans n *shaking palsy* 211
paralyze v 14, 208
paramedic n (Am) 286, 309
paramedical adj 286, 309
parameter n *geometric sense* 166
parameter n *boundary, definition* 166, 293
paramilitary adj/n 300
paramount adj/n 115
paramour n *lover* 75
paramour adv *obs. for love* 75
paranoia n 213
paranoid adj/n 213, 275
paranoid schizophrenia n 298
paranormal adj/n 283
parapet n 122
paraphernalia n *miscellanea* 205
paraphernalia n *type of leg. allocation* 205
paraphrase n/v 110
paraphrastic adj 110
paraplegia n 166
paraplegic adj/n 166
parapsychology n 292
parasailing n 317
parasite n *parasitic person* 112, 181
parasite n *parasitic animal* 112, 181
parasitic adj 112
parasitical adj 112
parasitism n 112
parasitology n 255
parasol n 148
paratrooper n 291
paratroops n 291
parbake v 259
parboil v *obs. boil completely* 70
parboil v *par(tially)boil* 70
parcel n *as in "parcel of land"* 87
parcel n *package* 87

parcel n *obs. thing* 87
parcel post n 227
parch v 60
parched 60
parchment n *animal skin for writing* 42
parchment n *paper for writing* 42
pard n *leopard* 30
pardie interj *by God* 47
pardner n (Am) 204
pardon n/v 46
pare v 59
paregoric n *type of elixer* 222
paregoric adj *soothing* 222
parent v *rear* 170
parent n 75
parent v *sire or bear* 170
parent adj 75
parental adj 75
parenthesis n *parenthetical material* 114
parenthesis n *type of punctuation* 114
parenthesize v 235
parenthetic adj 114, 160
parenthetical adj 114, 160
parenthood n 244
parenting n 311
parent-in-law n 262
parent-teacher association n 282
paresis n *partial paralysis* 167
paresthesia n *skin sensation without apparent cause* 238
pareve adj *containing no milk* 303
parfait n 259
parfait glass n 310
parhelion n *sun dog* 146
pariah n *gen. shunned person* 154
pariah n *spec. Indian caste* 154
parietal lobe n *part of the brain* 256
pari-mutuel n 263
paring knife n 121
parish n *gen. governmental district* 43
parish n 43
parishioner n 43
parity n *parenthood* 262
parity n *equality* 134
park v *as in "park a car"* 243
park n *as in "city park"* 34
park n *hunting area* 34
park n *as in "ballpark"* 34

park n *as in "industrial park"* 34
parka n 197
parking brake n 304
parking lot n (Am) 288
parking meter n 298
parkinsonism n 257, 286
Parkinson's disease n 257
parkland n 34
parkway n (Am) 261
parlance n *idiom, phrasing* 201
parlance n *gen. speech, parlaying* 201
parlay n/v (Am) 234
parlay n 278
parley n *meeting* 135
parley n *arch. conversation* 135
parliament n 44
parliament n *obs. conversation* 44
parliamentary adj 44
parliamentary law n 267
parlor n *business, as in "beauty parlor"* 42
parlor n *room in a church* 42, 69
parlor n *type of room in a home* 42, 69
parlor car n 242
parlor game n 244
parlor grand n (Am) 246
parlous adj/adv *perilous* 89
Parmesan n 106
parmigiana adj 259
parochial adj *of a parish* 78
parochial adj *provincial* 78
parochial school n 202
parochialism n 225
parodist n 128, 187
parody n *fig. unintentionally funny imitation* 128
parody n/v 128
parole n/v 102
parolee n 102, 277
paronomasia n *punning* 127
paroxysm n 69
paroxysm n *gen. outburst* 69
parquet n/v *type of flooring* 211
parricide n *murder of parents or close relative* 130
parrot n 105
parrot n/v *fig. mimic* 105
parrot fish n 181
parry v *fig. defend* 131
parry v *in swordplay* 131
parsec n 279
parsimonious adj 73
parsimony n *cheapness* 73

pathetic adj *obs. stirring emotions* 198

pathetic fallacy n *personifying inanimate things* 250

pathfinder n (Am) 232

pathobiology n 273

pathogen n 238

pathogenic adj 238

pathological adj *pertaining to pathology* 121, 125

pathological adj *as in "pathological liar"* 125

pathologist n 121

pathology n 121

pathos n 169

pathos n *rare something pathetic* 169

pathway 16

patience n *perseverance* 48

patience n *endurance* 48

patience n *willingness to wait* 48

patient adj 48

patient n *Medicine* 68

patina n 190

patio n (Am) 222

patois n *type of dialect* 152

patootie n *girl* 292

patriarch n 44

patriarchy n 44, 155

patrician n 79

patricide n *act of killing a parent* 130

patricide n *victim of patricide* 130

patrilineage n 275

patrilineal adj 275

patriot n 130

patriotic adj 130

patriotism n 130

patrol n *something that patrols* 176

patrol n *patroling* 176

patrol v 176

patrol wagon n (Am) 267

patrolman n (Am) 226

patron saint n 188

patronize v *shop at* 142

patronize v *support* 142

patronymic n *name derived patrilineally* 151

patsy n (Am) 268

patter n *as in "pitter-patter"* 233

patter v/n *pat* 162

patter n/v 94

patter song n 214

pattern n *repeated design* 136

pattern n 52

pattern n *spec., as in "dress pattern"* 52

pattern n *repeated actions, etc., as in "pattern of violence"* 136

patternmaker n 213

patty n *as in "hamburger patty"* 287

patty-cake n 262

paucify v *obs.* 86

paucity n 86

paunch n 66

paunchy adj 66

pauper n 101

pauperize v 101

pause n/v 86

pave v 33

pavement n 33

pavid adj *timid* 169

pavillion n *type of building* 33

pavillion n *type of tent* 33

pavior n *road paver* 41

paw n (Am) *dad* 275

paw v *handle rudely* 162

paw n *animal foot* 31

pawn n *in chess* 75

pawn n/v *as in "pawn shop"* 101

pawn n *gen. tool* 75

pawn off v 235

pawn ticket 227

pawnbroker n 171

pawnshop n 227

pay n/v 41

pay v *obs. satisfy* 41

pay adj *as in "pay toilet"* 245

pay cable n 324

pay dirt n (Am) 249

pay envelope n 276

pay phone n 299

pay-as-you-go adj (Am) 227

paycheck n 264

payday n 110

payee n 82, 200

payer n 82

payload n *General/Miscellaneous* 293

payload n *War/Military/Violence* 319

paymaster n 110

payment n *act of paying* 41

payment n *what is paid* 41

payoff adj/n 278

payola n (Am) 300

pay-per-view adj/n 324

payroll n 187

pay-TV n 312

PC n *personal computer* 322

PCP n 319

PDQ adv 249

pea adj/n 148

pea bean n 259

pea green n 207

pea jacket n (Am) 184

pea soup n *Food* 183

pea soup n *fog* 183

peace v *silence* 60

peace n 23

peace offering n 113

peace officer n 188

peace pipe n 204

peace sign, peace symbol n 319

peaceable adj 54

peaceable adj *obs. quiet* 54

peaceful adj 53

peacekeeping adj/n *War/Military/Violence* 306

peacemaker n *War/Military/Violence* 248

peacemaker n *General/Miscellaneous* 86

peacenik n (Am) 320

peacetime n 119

peach n *something good* 204

peach n *type of fruit* 34

peach n *as in "a peach of a person"* 34

peach Melba n 274

peachblow n (Am) *type of color* 234

peachy adj *slang* 139, 293

peachy-keen 293

peacoat n (Am) 197

peacock n 30

peacock v 142

peacock blue n 271

peafowl n *type of pheasant* 209

peahen n 30

peak v 221

peak adj *utmost* 278

peak n *mountaintop* 145

peak n *as in "mountain peak"* 107

peak n *fig.* 107

peak n *peak of a hat* 107

peaked adj *pale* 221

peaky adj 221

peal n 84

peal n/v 84

peanut n (Am) 197

peanut adj *worthless* 231

peanut butter n (Am) 259

peanut gallery n (Am) 265

peanut oil n 259

pear n 15

pearl n 29

pearl n *the color* 29

pearl essence n *fake pearl* 274

pearl gray n 207

pearl onion n 259

pearlescent adj 29, 301

pearly adj 91

pear-shaped adj 206

peasant n *fig. insult* 79

peasant n 79

peasantry 79

pease n *arch. pea* 15

peasecod n *arch. peapod* 15, 98

peashooter n 213

peat n 29

peat moss n 254

pebble n 10

pec n 320

pecan n (Am) 183

peccable adj *opp. of impeccable* 160

peccadillo n 132

peck v/n *kiss* 60

peck v *nag* 60

peck n *measure* 31

peck v 60

pecker n *slang penis* 273

pecking order n 293

peckish adj *ornery* 261

pecs n 99, 147, 316

pectoral adj/n 99

pectoral muscle n 147

peculate v *obs. steal public money* 215

peculate v *embezzle* 215

peculiar adj *distinguished* 91

peculiar adj *odd* 91

peculiarity n 91

pecuniary adj 110

pecunious *rich* 110

pedagogue n 78

pedagogy n 78

pedal v 261

pedal adj *of the foot* 147

pedal n/v 159

pedal pushers n (Am) 303

pedal steel n (Am) *type of musical instrument* 318

pedant n *obs. teacher* 129

pedant n *learned showoff* 129

pedantic adj 129

pedanticism n 129

pedantism n 129

pedantry n 129

peddle v 41

peddler n 41

pederast n 151

pederasty n 151

pedestal n 137

pedestal n fig. 137
pedestrian adj by foot 198
pedestrian adj dull 190
pedestrian n 198
pedestrious obs. 198
pediatrician 257, 273
pediatrics n 257
pediatrist n 257, 273
pedicab n 304
pediculosis n lice infestation 221
pediculous adj lousy 221
pedicure n 260
pedicure n person who gives pedicures 260
pedigree n 86
pedology n study of soils 279
pedometer n 182
pedophile n 277
pedophilia n 277
pee v 256
pee n slang urine 256, 302
pee n urination 256, 302
peek n/v 92, 233
peekaboo adj 260
peekaboo n 126
peel n as in "orange peel" 134
peel v 27
peel v obs. pillage 27
peel n type of shovel 134
peel v as in "sunburned skin peeling" 27
peel v remove clothes 27
peel n 27
peel off v 308
peen n 168
peen v work with a peen hammer 107
peep v as in "peep out" 97
peep n/v sound 86
peep n dawn 105
peep v peek 97
peep show n 246
peeper n peeping Tom 174
peeper n type of frog 237
peepers n slang eyes 166
peephole n 177
peeping Tom n 203
peer v gaze 142
peer n social equal 44
peer n obs. companion or foe 44
peer n age equal 44
peer group n 306
peeress 44, 174
peerless adj 54
peeve n/v 275
peeved adj 73, 275
peeved n 275

peevish adj obs. silly 73
peevish adj malevolent 73
peevish adj irritable 73
peewee n small marble 213
peewee n small person 213
peewee adj 213
peg v hit 117
peg v stereotype, describe 117
peg n fig. level 86
peg n/v 86, 117
peg leg n 195
peg top n type of toy 185
peignoir n type of negligee 223
pejorative adj/n 264
Peking duck n 241
pekoe n type of tea 183
pelican n 11
pellet n globule; type of shot 88
pellet n animal dropping 88
pellet v 88
pellet gun n 312
pelt n hide 30
pelt n/v hit 102
pelting adj paltry 117
peltry n pelts 30
pelvic adj 147
pelvis n 147
pemmican n type of rations 183
pen n female swan 105
pen n obs. feather 41
pen n (Am) prison 267
pen n writing instrument 41
pen v shut in 27
pen and ink n type of drawing 246
pen name n 227
pen pal n 299
pen pusher n 277
penal adj incurring penalty 81
penal adj 81
penal code n 230
penalty n 103
penalty clause n 320
penance n/v 37
pence n 41
penchant n 177
pencil n slang penis 128
pencil n type of brush 128
pencil n 128
pencil pusher n (Am) 268
pendant n type of jewelry 71
pendant n type of architectural feature 71
pendular adj 177
pendulous adj 159, 177
pendulous adj obs. overhanging 159
pendulum n 159, 177

penetrate v begin intercourse 116
penetrate v 116
penetration n 116
penguin n obs. great auk 119
penguin n 119
penguin suit n 320
penholder n 211
penicillin n 286
penicillium n 286
penicillum n 236
penile adj 166, 238
peninsula n 105
penis 166, 238
penis envy n 288
penitence n 100
penitence n rare penance 100
penitentiary n prostitute's halfway house 267
penitentiary n (Am) prison 80, 267
penitentiary n obs. ecclesiastic place of punishment 267
penitentiary adj 267
penknife n 69
penlight n 303
penman n 110
penmanship n 172
pennant n 178
penniless adj 41
penny n 19
penny ante n (Am) 244
penny arcade n 275
penny dreadful n 246
penny pincher n 293
penny stock n (Am) 281
penny-ante adj 244, 250
penny-pinching 293
pennyweight n measure of weight 66
pennywhistle n 214
penny-wise adj 152
pennyworth n bargain 18
penology n 230
pension n 76
pension n obs. wages 76
pension plan n 311
pensive adj 74
pentagon/pentagonal n/adj 120
pentagram n 221
pentangle n 84, 221
pentathlete n 151, 226
pentathlon n 151
penthouse n room at the top 34
penthouse n type of building 34
pent-roof n shed roof 241
pent-up adj 190
penult n next to last 114

penultimate adj/n 177
penurious adj stingy 127
penurious adj poor 127
penury n stinginess 76
penury n poverty 76
peon n 154
peony n type of flower 10
people n/v 44
people mover n 317
peoplehood n 266
pep n/v 221
pep pill n (Am) 297
pep talk n 293
pepper v sprinkle, spray 117
pepper n/v 15
pepper mill n 239
pepper shaker n 258
pepper-and-salt adj salt-and-pepper 252
peppercorn adj/n 15
peppermint n 164
peppermint n oil of peppermint 164
peppermint n peppermint-flavored candy 164
pepperoni n (Am) 287
peppy adj 221
peptic ulcer n 257
per accidens adv opp. of per se 113, 133
per annum adv 113
per capita adj/adv 295
per capita adj/adv individually 295
per diem n 213
per diem adj/adv 113; n 113, 213
per mensem adv 146
per se adv 113, 133
peradventure adv/n perchance 61
perambulate v 72
perambulator n baby buggy 239
percale n type of cloth 149
perceive v sense 58
perceive v hold an opinion of 58
percent n 166
percent adj/adv/n 120
percentage n 120, 195
percentile n 256
percept n 232
perceptible adj 159
perceptible adj obs. able to perceive 159
perception n perceiving 84
perception n opinion, image 84
perceptive adj able to perceive 243

perspiration n obs. respiration 147

perspire v 147, 166

perspire v obs. evaporate 166

persuade v convince 104

persuade v 84, 104

persuasion n type, as in "of the human persuasion" 84, 249

persuasion n 84

persuasive adj 84, 89

persue n obs. trail of a wounded deer 143

pcrt adj perky 107

pert adj attractive, jaunty 107

pert adj obs. adept 107

pertain v 60

pertinent adj 89

pertinent adj obs. belonging to 89

perturb v 72

pertussis n whooping cough 68

peruke n hair 149

peruke n type of wig 149

peruse v 110

peruse v obs. use up 110

pervade v 179

pervasive adj 179

perverse adj 88

perversion n 60; 84

pervert v obs. overturn 60

pervert n/v 60, 176

pervious adj 160

pesky adj 206

pessimism n 198

pessimism n obs. bad conditions 198

pessimist n 198

pessimistic adj 198

pest n 113

pest n pestilence 113

pester v 117

pesthole n 277

pesthouse n 147

pesticide n 291

pestiferous adj causing pestilence 91

pestiferous adj 51

pestilence n 51

pestilent adj 51

pestle n/v 36

pesto n 297

pet v caress 162

pet v treat with favoritism 162

pet n peeve 125

pet n/adj 113, 121

pet n favorite 113

pet peeve n (Am) 281

petal n 181

peter n slang penis 273

peter v as in "peter out"; stop 218

Peter Pan collar n 274

petit four n type of cake 259

petit jury n 102

petite adj 206

petite n 294

petition n/v request 52

petition n type of document 52

petnapping n (Am) 319

petri dish n 255

petrify v lit. "turn to stone" 63

petrify v fig. scare 63

petrochemical adj/n 279

petrodollar n 323

petroglyph n 246

petrol n (Brit) gasoline 256

petrol n petroleum 256

petrolatum n (Am) petroleum jelly 257, 258

petroleum n 99

petroleum jelly n 257, 258

petrology n study of rocks 210

petronel n type of gun 131

petticoat n obs. type of men's garment 71

petticoat n type of skirt 71

petticoat n slang woman 71

petticoat adj 171, 178

pettifogger adj 133

petting zoo n 315

pettish adj 125

pettitoes n 122

petty adj small; not of primary importance 88

petty adj frivolous 88

petty cash n 227

petty larceny n 215

petunia n 209

pew n 78

pewter n 33

pewterer n 41

peyote n (Am) 233

pfui interj 248, 292

pH n 272

phaeton n type of carriage 123

phaeton n type of charioteer 123

phalanx n 130

phallic adj 195

phallicism n 269

phallocentric adj 295

phallus n 147

phantasm n obs. something deceptive 81

phantasm n obs. charlatan 81

phantasm n 81

phantasma n 132

phantasmagoria n 189

phantom adj/n 47

phantom n obs. something illusionary 47

phantom adj 47

pharaoh n 20

pharmaceutical adj/n 147, 257

pharmaceutist n 221

pharmacist n 221

pharmacology n 182

pharmacy n the profession 166

pharmacy n using drugs 166

pharmacy n apothecary 166

pharynx n 166

phase n as in "phase of the moon" 216

phase n stage, as in "he's going through a phase" 216

phase out v 301

phasedown n 321

phaseout n 301

pheasant n 30

phenobarbital n 280

phenom n 267

phenomena n 136

phenomenal adj extraordinary 234

phenomenal adj related to phenomena 234

phenomenon n 136

pheromone n 309

phew interj 156

Philadelphia lawyer n (Am) 204

philander n obs. lover 170

philander v 170

philanderer n 170, 226

philanthropic adj 154

philanthropism n 154

philanthropy n 154

philatelist, philately n 244

philharmonic n Music 228

philharmonic n music lover 228

philistia n the class of philistines 249

philistia n Education 228

philistine n someone not educated 228

phillumenist n matchbook collector 304

philodendron n 254

philogynist n 151

philogyny n love of women 151

philology n study of language 152

philology n love of learning 152

philomel n type of bird 65

philosophe n philosopher 39

philosopher n 39

philosopher n obs. conjurer 39

philosopher's stone n 81

philosophess n 39, 170

philosophical adj 39

philosophical adj educated 78

philosophical adj pertaining to philosophy 78

philosophism n specious philosophy 199

philosophize v 39

philosophy n 39

philosophy of life n 243

philter n/v type of potion 121

phlebitis n 211

phlebotomy n blood-letting 68

phlegm n 32

phlegmatic adj pertaining to phlegm 125

phlegmatic adj 125

phlogiston n arch. fire as a substance 181

phlox n type of flower 181

phobia n 199

phobic adj/n 262

phoenix n fig. something resurrected 21

phoenix n 21

phoenix n fig. standard of beauty 21

phonate v 251

phone n a sound 251

phone n/v telephone 264

phone book n 273

phoneme n 264

phonetic adj 245

phonetic alphabet n 227

phonics n 245

phonics n obs. gen. study of sounds 245

phono n Music 276

phonograph n Music 265

phonography n phonetic spelling 187

phony adj/n (Am) 268; v 268, 308

phoo interj 292

phooey interj (Am) 248, 292

phosphate n 205

phosphor n 181

phosphor n Satan 181

phosphoresce v 158

phosphorescence n 158

phosphorescent adj 158

phosphoric acid n 205

phosphorus n 158

phosphorus n anything phosphorescent 158

photo adj/n/v 246
photo essay n 305
photo finish n 300
photo opportunity n 325
photocopier n 288
photocopy v 295; n 273
photodrama n 282
photoduplication n 302
photoelectric cell, photocell n 256
photoengraving n 246
photoflash n 290
photoflood n 299
photog n 276
photogenic adj 288
photogenic adj obs. photographic 288
photogram n photograph 228, 246
photograph, photographic, photography n/v, adj, n 228
photographer n 228
photogravure n 265
photojournalism n 299
photomontage n 299
photomosaic n 305
photomural n 290
photon n 279
photoplay n (Am) 282
photorealism n 318
photoreconnaissance n 300
photostat n/v 280
photosynthesis n 254
phototelegraphy n transmission of pictures 265
phototropism n 254
photovoltaic adj 256
phrase n/v phraseology 110
phrase n type of linguistic unit 110
phrase n as in "a phrase of music" 110
phrase book n 127
phrasemaker n 214
phrasemonger n 214
phraseology n 110, 172
phrasing n 110, 152
phrenology n skull reading 215
phthisis n type of consumptive disease 106
phyllo n 303
phylum n 254
phys ed n 311
physiatrics n 238
physiatrist n 238
physiatry n 238
physic n obs. natural science 32
physic n the art of healing 32

physic n a spec. medicine 32
physic n people in medicine 32
physic v 32
physical adj 32
physical adj bodily; material 195
physical adj medical 195
physical n 297
physical anthropology n 237
physical education n 228
physical examination n 257
physical science n 210
physical therapy n 286
physician n 32
physician n obs. physicist 32
physician's assistant n 316
physicist n 220
physics n 182
physics n gen. science 182
physiognomy n 66
physiology n gen. science 146
physiology n 146
physiotherapy n 273
physique n 210
phytochemistry n plant chemistry 220
phytology n botany 165
phytoplankton n 254
pi n 182
pianism n 228
pianist n 228
piano n 214
piano adj/adv 173
piano accordian n 246
piano roll n 290
piazza n public square 118
pic n 267
pica n abnormal food craving 121
pica n unit of measure 120
picador n 200, 289
picara n female picaro 200, 289
picaresque adj/n 214, 264
picaroon n/v pirate, rascal 155
picayune adj/n small coin 200, 233
piccolo n 246
pick v as in "pick your way through the mess" 58
pick v steal 58
pick v pick at 58
pick v as in "pick a fight," "pick a lock" 58
pick n as in "pickax" 36
pick v hit with a pick 58
pick v choose 58
pick n selection 205

pick v play a stringed instrument 58
pick v pluck 58
pickaback adj/adv/v piggyback 134
pick-and-shovel adj 264
pickax n 36
pickerupper n 300
picket n stake 190
picket v fence in 192
picket v as in "picket a business" 192, 245; n 190
picket n guard 190
picket n 190
picket n type of mil. punishment 190
picket fence n (Am) 196
picket line n 245
picketboat n 243
pickfork n arch. pitchfork 35
pickle n 70
pickle n slang jam, predicament 70
pickle n/v bleach 70
pickled adj drunk 231
pickled adj 70
picklock n tool of the picklock 131
picklock n akin to pickpocket 131
pick-me-up n 249
pickpocket n/v 131
pickpocket v 131
pickpurse n arch. pickpocket 80, 131
pickthank n sycophant 104
picky adj 243
picnic n 183
picnic v 234
picnic n slang piece of cake 183
pictogram n 245, 276
pictograph n 245, 276
pictography n 245
pictorial n 227
pictorial adj 161
picture v create a picture 101
picture v imagine 101
picture n/v motion picture 265
picture n 101
picture book n 227
picture hat n type of hat 260
picture window n 297
picture writing n 187
picture-book adj 294
pictureize v make pictures 228
picture-perfect adj 327
picturephone n 311
picture-postcard adj 278

picturesque adj 190
picturesque adj descriptive 190
piddle v 117
piddle v slang urinate 117
piddling adj 117
piddly adj 117
pidgin n 264
pidgin English n 227
pidginize v 264, 299
pie n fig. treat 34
pie n magpie 30
pie n baked dish 34
pie chart n 290
pie in the sky n (Am) 283
pie safe n type of cupboard 310
piebald n mongrel 237
piebald adj motley 54, 138
piebald n motley animal 237
piece n as in "down the road a piece" 48, 66
piece n sexual object, as in "piece of ass" 48
piece n section, part 48
piece n as in "game piece" 48
piece n part of a collection, as in "piece of furniture" 48
piece n gun 48, 131
piece by piece adv 133
pièce de résistance n main entree 204
pièce de résistance n 204
piece goods n 171
piece of cake n 301
piece of eight n 152
piece of work n 293
piecework n 110
piecrust n 122
pied adj piebald 54, 138
pied piper n 231
pied-à-terre n temporary residence 222
piedmont adj related to foothills 236
pie-eyed adj (Am) 257
pie-faced adj 273
pieplant n (Am) 219
pier n landing 15
pier n piering 15
pier glass n type of mirror 183
pier table n used with pier glass 211
pierce v 58
piety n obs. pity 78
piety n Religion 78
piezoelectricity n 256
piffle n/v 235
piffling adj 235
pig n slang police officer 30

poke v *slang* have sex 60, 244; n 244

poke n *as in "a poke in the eye"* 136; v 60

poke v *jab* 60

poke n *pokeweed* 119

poke n *sack, as in "pig in a poke"* 52

poke n 60

poke around v 204

poke bonnet n 212

poker n *type of goblin* 132

poker n (Am) 226

poker n/v *type of fire tool* 107

poker face n (Am) 261

poker-faced adj 261

pokerish 132

pokeweed 119

pokey n *jail* 283

pol n (Am) 155, 306

polar adj 63

polar bear n 194

polarize, polarization v, n 210

polarize, polarization v, n *fig.* divide 210

pole n *ski pole* 23, 263

pole n *in pole vault* 23, 263

pole n *racing pole position* 23, 263

pole n *type of tree* 23

pole n *stick* 23

pole n 63

pole bean n 197

pole hammer n *war hammer* 248

pole jump n *pole vault* 263

pole vault n/v 263

poleax n/v *War/Military/Violence* 46

poleax n *type of butcher's tool* 46

polecat n 30

polemic n 158

polemicize v 158, 308

polestar n 119

police n 188

police n *obs. government* 101, 188

police action n 266

police blotter n 267

police car n 292

police dog n 277

police force n 230

police officer n 44, 203

police procedural n Literature/Writing 318

police reporter n 229

police state n 247

police station n 230

policeman n 215, 248, 319

policeperson n 215, 248, 319

policewoman n 215, 248, 319

policy n *as in "insurance policy"* 134

policy n *obs. government* 84

policy n *political shrewdness* 84

policy n *obs. deception* 84

policy n *gen. shrewdness* 84

policy n *stated way of handling things* 84

policyholder n (Am) 250

polio n (Am) 257, 297

poliomyelitis n 257, 297

poliovirus n 309

polish n/v 58

polish n 58

polish off v 231

politburo n 291

polite adj 100

polite adj *obs. phys. polished* 100

polite adj *obs. phys. clean* 100

politesse n *formal politeness* 188

politic adj 79, 111

political adj *pertaining to government* 130

political adj *pejorative sense* 130

political adj 111

political action committee n 306

political science n 202

politicalize v *make political* 202, 229

politically correct adj 327

politician n *obs. cunning schemer* 155

politician n 111, 155

politicize v *be a politician* 202

politicize v *give a political twist* 202

politick v 111, 300

politicking n 300

politico n 155

politics n *political maneuvering* 111, 174

politics n *administration of government* 111, 174

polka n/v 228

polka dot n (Am) 260

poll n *vote* 154

poll n *obs. census, headcount* 154

poll n *head* 154

poll n *survey* 154

poll n *counting votes* 154

poll tax n 174

pollen n 193

pollen n *obs. gen. powder* 193

pollen grain n 193, 219

pollex n *thumb* 221

pollinate v 193, 236

pollination 193, 236

pollster n (Am) 154, 300

pollutant n 78, 270

pollute v *corrupt morally* 78

pollute v *corrupt physically* 78

polluted adj 78

polluted adj *drunk* 283

pollution n *polluted state* 84

pollution n *ejaculation without sex* 84

pollution n 78

Pollyanna n (Am) 288

pollywog n 64

polo n 226

polo coat n 274

polo shirt n 280

polonaise n *type of overdress* 197

polrumptious adj *cocky* 199

poltergeist n 230

poltroon adj/n *wretch, coward* 112

poltroonery n 112

polyandrist n 170

polyandrous n 170

polyandry n *marrying multiple husbands* 126, 170, 199

polychromatic adj *multicolored* 234

polydipsia n *abnormal thirst* 166, 167

polyester n/adj 287

polygamist n 126

polygamous adj 126

polygamy n 126, 170, 199

polyglot adj *multilingual* 152

polygon n 120

polygraph n *lie detector* 248

polygraph n *type of drawing instrument* 248

polygyny n *having more than one wife* 126, 170, 199

polyhedron n 120

polylogue n *akin to monologue, dialogue* 318

polymer n 251

polymorph n 193

polymorphism n 193

polymorphous adj 193

polynomial n 166

polyp n 68

polyphagia n *abnormal appetite* 166, 167

polystyrene n 294

polytechnic adj/n 214

polytheism n 154

polyunsaturated adj 297

polyurethane n 308

pomade n *type of ointment* 121

pomander n 99

pome n *type of fruit* 70

pomegranate n 34

pomelo n 241

Pomeranian n 194

pommel horse n 275

pomology n *science of growing fruit* 212

pomp n/v 37

pompadour n *hairstyle* 260

pompadour n *gen. fashions from the reign of Marquise de Pompador* 260

pompano n *type of fish* 194

pom-pom n *as in "pom-pom guns"* 267

pom-pom/pom-pon n *obs. type of hair ornament* 270

pom-pom/pom-pon n *as in "pom-pom girls"* 270

pomposity n 37, 72, 150

pomposity n *stateliness* 72, 150

pomposity n *arrogance* 72, 150

pompous adj *stately; arrogant* 37, 72

poncho n 184

pond n 29

pond lily n (Am) 181

pond scum n 254

pond skater n 255

ponder v 74

ponder v *var. obs. meanings of evaluate, weigh* 74

ponderate v *obs.* 74

ponderosa pine n (Am) 254

ponderous adj 74

ponderous adj *fig. difficult* 90

ponderous adj *heavy* 90

pondweed n 118

pone n (Am) *as in "corn pone"* 148

poniard n *type of dagger* 131

pontiff n *high-ranking priest* 129

pontiff n *the Pope* 129

pontificate v *be a blowhard* 218

pontificate n 129

pontificate v *serve as a pontiff* 218

pontoon n *type of boat, sometimes used as bridge support* 123

pontoon bridge n 123, 184

ENGLISH THROUGH THE AGES

preggers adj *pregnant* 304

pregnable adj *opp. of impregnable* 90

pregnancy n 68, 106

pregnancy n *fig. fertility, creativity* 106

pregnant adj *meaningful* 88

pregnant adj *with child* 68, 88

pregnant adj *convincing* 88

prehensile adj 194

prehistorian n 237

prehistoric adj 237

prehistory n 237

prejudge v 74

prejudice n *harm because of a judgment* 73

prejudice n *negative prejudgment* 73

prejudice v 73

prejudiced adj 74

prejudicial adj 73

prelate n 42, 173

prelatess n 42, 173

prelim adj/n 267

preliminary adj/n 176

preliminary n *sports sense* 176

preliterate adj 290

prelude n *used in music* 134, 173

prelude n 134, 173

prelude v 134

prelusion n 173

preman n 285

premarital adj 262

premature adj 115

premature adj *med. sense* 114

premeditate v 108

premeditated adj 108

premeditation n 108

premenstrual adj 256

premenstrual syndrome n 326

premier n 188

premier adj *foremost* 91

premiere adj/n/v 270

premiere n/v Entertainment 299

premiere n 299

premise n 82

premises n *gen.* 81

premises n *property, as in "occupy the premises"* 81

premium n *bonus* 177

premium adj 157, 234

premium n *prize* 157

premium n *surcharge* 157, 177

premium n *as in "insurance premium"* 157, 171

premium n *purchase enticement* 289

premonish v 100

premonition n 100

premonitory 100

prenatal adj 221

prenominate adj *obs. aforementioned* 117

prenotion n *premonition* 125

prentice n *apprentice* 41

prenuptial adj 244

preoccupation n 125, 150

preoccupation n *something that preoccupies* 150

preoccupation n *being preoccupied* 150

preoccupied adj 125, 225

preoccupy v 125

pre-owned adj 318

prep as in *"prep school"* 247

prep n Slang 249, 283

prep school n 266

preparation n *getting ready* 84

preparation n *study* 247

preparation n *as in "Preparation H"* 166

preparatory adj 84, 90

preparatory school n 214

prepare v Medicine 166

prepare v *as in "prepare dinner"* 97

prepare v Education 247

prepare v *make ready* 84, 97

preparedness n 84

prepay v *gen.* 226

prepay v *referring to postage* 227

preponderant adj 92

preposition n *obs. prefix* 76

preposition n 76

preposterous adj 115

preposterous adj *rare reversed* 115

preppy adj (Am) *pertaining to prep school* 266

preppy adj *of a type of fashion* 266

prepubertal adj 286

prepuberty n 279, 286

prepubescence n 279, 286

prepubescent adj/n 272, 279, 286

prequel n 324

prerecord v 301

prerecorded adj 301

prerequire v 158

prerequisite adj/n 158

prerogative n 84

presage n/v *omen* 84

presbyter n Religion 129, 173

presbyteress n Religion 129

presbytery n 78

preschool adj/n 291

preschooler n 291, 305

prescience n 81

prescient adj 81

prescribe v *decree* 103

prescribe v 121

prescription n Medicine 121

prescription n 103

prescription drug n 309

prescriptive adj 103, 191

presell v 305

presence n *someone with presence* 100

presence n *bearing, stature, as in "stage presence"* 100

presence n *obs. group of people* 52

presence n *as in "ghostly presence"* 175

presence n *being here/there* 52

presence n War/Military/Violence 319

presence of mind n 170

present adj/n *now* 31

present v *as in "present oneself"* 60

present adj *as in "the present topic of discussion"* 92

present adj/n *obs. presence, something that is present* 31, 48, 52

present n *gift, presentation* 48

present v *introduce; give a present* 60

present adj *here* 53

present obs. *having presence of mind* 170

present adj *obs. having presence of mind* 92

present arms n 203

present tense n 76

presentable adj 60

presentation n 60, 84

presentation n *manner of presenting* 84

presentation n *speech, demonstration* 84

present-day adj 256

presentiment n *a touch of prescience* 185

preservation n 87

preservationist n 291

preservative adj/n 90

preservative n *obs. preventive medicine* 87

preservative n 87

preserve n *as in "wildlife preserve"* 222

preserve n/v *jam* 122

preserve v *retain* 92

preserve v *maintain* 92

preserve v *protect* 92

preshrink v 287

preside v 161

presidency n 79

president n 79, 202

president adj *rare* 79

presidentess n 79, 202

presidential adj 79

presoak n/v 280

press n *printing press* 123

press n *journalism business* 201

press n/v *arch. troubles* 48

press n/v *as in "press down"* 94

press n *journalists as a group* 123, 201, 290

press n/v *spec. printing press* 72

press n *the journalism business* 123, 201, 290

press n/v *fig. pressure* 48

press n/v *as in "garlic press"* 72

press n *publishing house* 123, 128

press n/v *as in "the press of the crowd"* 48

press agent n 263

press box n (Am) 265

press conference n 299

press corps n 299

press gallery n 153

press kit n 318

press release n 311

press secretary n 311

pressboard n *type of pasteboard* 273

pressboard n *ironing board* 222

pressing adj *urgent* 160

pressing adj *oppressive* 160

pression n *pressure* 85

pressure n *lit. and fig.* 84

pressure v 301

pressure v 84

pressure cooker n 280

pressure gauge n 238

pressure group n 291

pressure sore n 257

pressure suit n 297

pressure-treated adj 297

pressurize v 301

prestidigitation n 248

prestidigitator n 248

progress n *arch. type of journey, as in "Pilgrims' Progress"* 87

progress n *improvement* 87; v 117

progress n *headway* 87; v 117

progress v 87, 117

progression n *series of steps* 87, 117, 134, 159

progressive adj *involving steps in a progression* 87, 159

progressive adj/n *Politics* 229

progressive education n 228

progressivism n 229

prohibit v *fig. prohibit* 96

prohibit v *phys. prohibit* 96

prohibit v 51

prohibition n 51

prohibitionist n *someone seeking alcohol bans* 229

prohibitory adj 51, 229

project v *protrude* 97

project n *enterprise* 85

project v *engage in psychological projection* 288

project n *obs. plan, design* 85

project v *cause to protrude* 97

project v *as in "project a picture"* 179

project v *obs.* 85

project v *throw* 143

project n *obs. vision* 85

project, projection v, n *extrapolate, extrapolation* 321

projectile n 143, 174

projection n *type of map* 118

projection n *arch. type of alchemical process* 99

projection 143, 179

projectionist n 291

projector n *Movies/TV/Radio* 265

prole n 173, 266; adj 266

proletaire n 173

proletarian adj/n 173

proletarian adj 173

proletariat n 173, 247

pro-life adj 319

proliferate v *fig. increase* 321

proliferate v *spec. biological sense* 321

prolific adj 161

prolific adj *applied to people* 161

prolificacy n 161

prolificity n 161

prolix adj 90

prologue n/v 41

prolusion n *prelude* 157

prom n (Am) 265

promenade n *walk* 134

promenade n *place to walk* 134, 149

promenade v 134

promethean adj 138

prominence n *being prominent* 136

prominence n *something prominent* 136

prominent adj *protruding* 92

prominent adj *obtrusive* 92

promiscuity n 262

promiscuous adj *Love/Romance/Sex* 262

promiscuous adj *mixed* 262

promise n *portent* 86

promise n *commitment* 86

promise v *be promising* 97

promise v *foreshadow* 97

promise v 97

promised land n 176

promissory adj 86, 92

promissory note n 187

promo adj/n 307

promontory n 105

promote v *help, publicize* 94

promote v *as in "promote an employee"* 94

promotion n *publicizing* 94

promotion n *elevation* 94

prompt v 60

prompt adj *on time* 92

promptbook n 214

promptitude n 92

promulgate v 116

promulge v *arch.* 116

prone adj *tending toward* 90

prone adj *opp. of supine* 90

prong n *tine* 178

prong n *tined utensil* 178

pronghorn n *type of antelope* 209

pronoun n 76

pronounce v *articulate* 60

pronounce v *declare* 60

pronounced adj *noticeable* 191

pronouncement n 60

pronunciation n 76

proof n *result* 48

proof n *confirming evidence* 48

proof n *in alcohol* 183

proof n *test run in printing* 153

proof v *proofread; create a proof* 264

proof n *in coinage* 153

proof n *in photography* 153

proof v *as in "waterproof"* 271

proof n *in engraving* 153

proof spirit n *liquor with 50% plus ethanol* 183

proofread v 227, 282

proofreader n 227

prop n *propeller* 280

prop n *support* 86

prop n *property* 228

propaganda n *type of organization* 291

propaganda n *indoctrination* 225, 291

propagandize v 225

propane n 237

propel v *cause to move* 143

propel v *obs. expel* 143

propellant adj/n 143, 210

propeller n 224

propense adj 134

propension n 134

propensity n 134

proper adj *as in "prim and proper"* 188

proper adj *decorous, decent* 53

proper adj *suitable* 53

proper adj *appropriate* 53

proper adj *as in "proper name"* 53

proper noun n 101

property n *characteristic* 51

property n *something owned* 51

property n *spec. land owned* 51

property n *theatrical prop* 51

property n *obs. being proper* 51

property tax n 214

prophecy n 38, 42

prophesy n 38

prophet n *something prophetic* 42

prophet n 42, 43

prophetess n 42, 43

prophetic adj 42

prophetize v *obs.* 38

prophylactic n *slang condom* 147

prophylactic adj *Medicine* 121; n 147

propitious adj 91

propjet n 304

proponent n 135

proportion n/v 85

proportional adj 85

proportionate adj 85

proposal n *marriage proposal* 170, 176

proposal n *contractual proposal* 176

proposal n *suggestion* 176

propose v *present* 60

propose v *propose marriage* 60, 170

propose v *suggest* 60

propose v *nominate* 60

proposition v *suggest sex* 289

proprietor n 101, 171

proprietress n 101, 171

proprietrix n 171

propriety n *true nature* 154

propriety n *properness* 154

propulsion n 206

propulsion n *obs. repelling* 206

prorate v (Am) 237

proruption n *erupting forth* 180

prosaic adj *bland* 206

prosaic adj *pertaining to prose* 206

prosaist n 214

prosateur n *prose writer* 264

proscenium n *stage Performing Arts* 153

proscenium n *forestage Performing Arts* 153

prosciutto n *type of ham* 287

proscribe v 85

proscription n 85

prose n *fig. unpoetic writing* 42

prose n 42

prose poem n 227

prosecute v *obs. pursue* 132

prosecute v *practice, execute* 132

prosecute v *gen. persist* 132

prosecute v 132

prosecuting attorney n 230

prosecution n *The Law* 132

prosecutor n 132, 230

proselyte n 82, 158; v 82

proselyte 158

proselytess n 82, 158

proselytize v 82

prosit interj *toast to health* 230

prosody n 77

prospect n *fig. chance of happening* 134

prospect n *what is viewed* 134

prospect n *obs. mentally viewing* 177

prospect n *view* 134

prospect v *search, mine* 235

prospect n *obs. viewing* 134

prospect n 289

prospect v *obs. see, view* 235

prospect v 134

prospective n 134; adj 177

prospects n *chances, potential* 177

pubescent adj 66

pubic adj 120, 221

public n *as in "out in public"* 103

public adj *related to government* 78

public n *people* 103

public adj *opp. of private* 78

public adj/n 78

public assistance n 258

public defender n 283

public domain n (Am) 230

public health n 154

public house n *public building* 122

public house n *hotel* 122

public house n *pub* 122

public opinion n 130

public relations n 214

public school n 129

public servant 130

public service n 130

public speaking n 201

public television n 319

public utility n 272

public-access television n 324

public-address system n 290

publication n *gen. dissemination* 77

publication n *spec., as in "magazine publication"* 77

publication n Literature/Writing 128

publicist n 201, 317

publicist n *expert in public affairs* 317

publicist n *public affairs writer* 317

publicity n 201

publicize v 295

public-spirited adj 174

publish v *obs. create a public—populate* 62

publish v *gen. make known, distribute* 110

publish v *obs. accuse* 110

publish v *as in "publish a book"* 110

publisher n 110

puce n 207

pucelage n *obs. female virginity* 125

puck n 18

puck n *as in "hockey puck"* 263

pucker n/v 136

puckish adj 18, 243

pud n 189

pudding n *penis* 189

pudding n Food 122

pudding n *animal intestines as food* 122

puddle n 52

puddle jumper n (Am) 298

pudendum n 66

pudge n 221

pudgy adj 221

puerile adj 125

puff v *smoke cigarettes, etc.* 27

puff v *praise* 27

puff n *as in "cheese puff"* 70

puff n/v 27

puff adder n 194

puff paste n 122

puff pastry n 148

puffball n 145

puffery n 205

puffin n 30

puft n *obs. bit of wind* 65

pug nose n 195

pugilism n 200

pugilist n 200

pugnacious adj 150

puke n/v 120

pulchritude n 68

pull n *lit. and fig. the power to pull* 136

pull n/v 27

pull n *the force of pulling* 136

pull v *as in "pull taffy"* 253

pull v *as in "pull a muscle"* 321

pull v *restrain, as in "pull punches"* 208

pull for v *cheer* 293

pull in v 156

pull off v *accomplish* 269

pull tab n 316

pullback n 135

pullen n *arch. poultry* 35

pullet n 64

pulley n 36

Pullman n *type of railroad car* 243

pullman kitchen n (Am) 316

pull-on n 280

pullout n 217

pullover n 287

pull-up n 289

pull-up n *sudden stop* 289

pulmonary artery/pulmonary vein n 182

pulp n/v 64

pulp n *type of magazine* 318

pulp n *gen. goo* 64

pulpit n 43

pulpwood n 254

pulsar n 315

pulsate v 32, 86

pulsation n 32, 86

pulse n *gen. beat* 32

pulse n *fig. heart* 32

pulse n *as in "take your pulse"* 32

pulse v 32, 97

pulver n *obs.* 97

pulverize v *fig. destroy* 97

pulverize v 97

puma n 194

pummel v 117

pump v 115

pump v *as in "pump for information"* 115

pump n *as in "water pump"* 72; v 72

pump v *slang have sex* 115, 185

pump n *type of shoe* 122

pump n *heart* 195

pump iron v 323

pump up v 204

pumpernickel n 197

pumpkin n 145

pun n/v 172

pun v 172

punch n/v *hit* 131

punch n *type of drink* 148

punch v *poke, stab* 131

punch n/v *as in "metal punch"* 107

punch bowl n 167

punch card 279

punch in n 289

punch line n (Am) 291

punch out v 324

punch up v 313

Punch-and-Judy show n 265

punch-drunk adj (Am) 281

punched card n 279

punchinello n *type of clown* 173

punching bag n 263

punch-out n 291

punchy adj *loopy* 298

punchy adj *vigorous* 298

punchy adj *fat* 298

puncion n *obs. puncture* 85

punctual adj *punctilious* 139

punctual adj 139

punctual adj *exact* 139

punctuate v Language and Speaking 214

punctuate v *point out* 214

punctuation mark n 245

puncture n *act of puncturing; the hole itself* 85

pundigrion obs. 172

pundit n *gen.* 232

pundit n *Hindu expert* 232

pungency n 139

pungent adj *sharp-tasting* 139

pungent adj *painful* 139

pungitive obs. 139

pungle v *pay* 249

punish v 60

punish v *gen.* 60

punishment n 60

punition n 60

punitive adj 60, 155

punitive damages n 267

punitory adj 155

punk n *thug* 283

punk n Music 324

punk n (Am) *stick for lighting fuses* 168

punk n *arch. prostitute* 126

punk adj *inferior* 270

punk n *prostitute* 283

punk n *homosexual* 283

punk rock n 324

punker n Music 324

punkie n (Am) *type of insect* 194

punster 172

puny adj *junior* 115

puny adj *obs. callow* 115

puny adj *small* 115

pup n 194

pup n *obnoxious man* 194

pup tent n (Am) 239

pupil n *student* 78

pupil n *part of the eye* 66

pupil n *orphan* 78

puppet n *doll* 111

puppet n *marionette* 111

puppet n *fig.* 111

puppeteer n 111, 289

puppy n Animals 119

puppy n *obnoxious man* 119

puppy n *obs. wench* 119

puppy dog 119

puppy love n 226

purblind adj *mentally blind* 32

purblind adj/v 32

purchase n *obs. hunt* 127

purchase v *var. obs. meanings of procure by var. means* 76

purchase n *foothold* 190

purchase n *buying; the thing bought* 127

purchase v *buy* 76

purchase n *obs. procurement, attempt to procure* 127

purchase n 76

pure v *obs.* 44

pure adj/adv *unadulterated, physically and morally* 53
pure v *obs.* 53
pure adj/adv *as in "pure mathematics"* 53
pureblood n/v 202
pure-blooded adj 213
purebred adj 241
puree n 183; v 287
purehearted adj 225
purfle n/v *ornament* 35
purgation n 82
purgation n *obs. laxative* 82
purgation n *obs. menstruation* 82
purgative n 69
purgatory adj/n 42
purge n 130
purge v *clean phys. and morally* 58
purify v *clean morally* 44
purify v 53
purify v *clean physically* 44
purist n 53, 189
puritan adj/n 111
Puritan ethic n 324
puritanical adj 111
puritanism adj 111
purity n *spiritual cleanness* 42
purity n *phys. cleanness* 42
purloin v *obs. put away* 80
purloin v 80
purple adj *as in "purple prose"* 20, 128
purple adj *of royal fabric; royal* 20
purple adj/n/v *of the color* 20, 92
purple martin n (Am) 181
purport n/v 86
purported adj 86, 270
purpose n *intent* 50
purpose n *goal* 50
purpose n *reason for existence* 50
purposeful adj 251
purpurine adj *obs. purple* 25
purr n Animals 145
purse n *obs. gen. bag* 14
purse v *as in "purse your lips"* 162
purse n *obs. scrotum* 14
purse n *pocketbook* 14
purse n *prize* 14
purse n 14
purse strings n 69
purse-proud adj 169
purser n 76

pursue v *fig. follow* 58
pursue v *hunt* 58
pursuit n 58
pursy adj 169
purveyor n 52
pus n 66
push v *arch. stab at* 58
push n/v *shove* 58
push v *prod* 143
push v *fig. drive, press, as in "push it to the limit"* 58
push v *promote, sell* 191; n 199
push v *as in "sprouts pushing up"* 162
push v *make effort* 143
push v *sell drugs* 319
push broom n 288
push button n (Am) 257
push-button adj (Am) 269
pushcart n 261
pusher v 300, 319
pusher n *prostitute* 300
pushful adj 271
pushover n 277
pushover n *something done easily, a piece of cake* 277
pushpin n 273
pushpin n *type of game* 273
push-up n 281
pushy adj 298
pusillanimous adj 74
puss n *slang girl* 105
puss n *slang face* 256
puss n *cat* 105
pussy n *cat* 119
pussy n *female sex organs* 256
pussy n *weakling* 307
pussy willow n (Am) 236
pussycat n 209
pussycat n *fig.* 209
pussyfoot v (Am) 268
pussy-whip v *henpeck* 320
pussy-whipped adj 320
put v *place* 55
put n *as in "shot put"* 40
putative adj 91
put-down n 320
put-on adj/n 160, 294
putrefy v *obs. type of alchemical process* 94
putrefy v 90, 94
putrid adj 90
putsch n 283
putt n/v 171
putter v *as in "putter around"* 271
putter n *golf club* 185

putty n *type of mortar* 148; v 148
putty n *type of cement* 148
putty knife n 242
put-upon adj 284
putz n *penis* 296
putz n *type of Pennsylvania Dutch Christmas decoration* 296
putz n *jerk* 296
puzzle n *challenge* 157
puzzle n *as in "crossword puzzle"* 157
puzzle n *puzzlement* 157
puzzle n/v 142
puzzleheaded adj 204
puzzlement n 172, 217
puzzling adj 142, 178
pygmy n 85
pyramid n 88
pyre n 176
pyrexia n *fever* 195
pyro n *pyromaniac* 324
pyrography n *woodburning* 128
pyrogravure n 128
pyrolatry n *fire worship* 173
pyromancy n *divining by fire* 81
pyromania n 230
pyrotechnic adj 182, 217; n 232
pyrotechnics n *art of fireworks* 189
pyrotechnics n *the fireworks themselves* 189
Pyrrhic victory n 266
Pythagorean theorem n 272
python n 220
pythoness n *diviner* 81

Q

q.t. n 267
quaalude n 316
quabbe n *bog* 29
quack n *fake doctor* 133, 147; adj 147
quack n/v 30
quack grass n 209
quackery n 147
quackle v *choke* 163
quacksalver n *charlatan* 133
quad n *quadriplegic* Medicine 322
quad n *quadruplet* Family/Relations/Friends 199, 311
quad n *type of bicycle* 261
quad n *quadrangle* 209
quad 199
quad adj/n Music 318

quadragenerian n *40-year-old* 221
quadrangle n *courtyard* 65, 118
quadrangle n Mathematics 65
quadrant n *a quarter day* 105
quadrant n *square* 105
quadraphonic adj Music 318
quadrennial adj *every four years* 146
quadrennial adj *lasting four years* 146
quadriceps n 120
quadrilateral adj/n 147
quadrille n *type of square dance* 202
quadrille n *type of card game* 185
quadrillion n 166
quadriplegia, quadriplegic n, adj/n 286
quadruped n 146
quadruple adj/n/v 65
quadruplet n Family/Relations/Friends 199
quads n *quadriceps* 120, 316
quads 120
quaere n/v *question* 117
quaff n/v 106
quaff n 106
quag n 118
quaggy adj 118
quagmire n Geography/Places 118
quagmire n *complex situation* 118
quahog n *type of clam* 194
quail v *wither* 123
quail v *intimidate* 123
quail v *shy away* 123
quail n 30
quaint adj *obs. wise, skilled* 54
quaint adj 54
quaint adj *arch. cunning* 54
quake v 26; n 51
quake n *earthquake* 51
Quaker gun n *fake gun* 215
quaking aspen n 194
quaky adj 26
qualification n 142
qualified adj *euphemism for "damn"* 268
qualified adj 117, 142
qualify v *as in "qualify a statement"* 117
qualify v *as in "qualify for a job"* 142
quality adj *high-quality* 190
quality n 37

rabbi n 20
rabbinic adj 20
rabbinical adj 20
rabbit n 64
rabbit interj *drat it* 203
rabbit n *rabbit fur* 64
rabbit ears n *TV antennae* 310
rabbit punch n 282
rabble n *obs. verbal babble* 111
rabble n/v 111
rabble n *obs. animal pack* 111
rabblement n 111
rabblerous adj 111
rabblerouser n 233
rabid adj *"furious"* 150
rabid adj *afflicted with rabies* 150
rabid adj *Medicine* 121
rabies n *Medicine* 121
raccoon n 145
race n *gen. kindred group* 202
race n *family, descendents* 202
race n *as in "the human race"* 202
race v *as in "race the engine," my heart races* 40
race n *competition* 108; v 40
race n *type of channel* 63
race n *as in "space race"* 108
race n *as in "race relations"* 202
race n *fast current* 63
race n *moving forward* 108
race n *journey* 98
race v 108
racecourse n 199
racehorse n 151
racer n *snake* 219
racetrack n 244
raceway n *racecourse* 226
raceway n *channel* 226
racial adj 202, 247
racialism n *racism* 202, 276
racing form n 304
racism n 202, 247
rack n *as in "hatrack"* 52
rack n *as in "off the rack"* 52
rack v *wine-making term* 100
rack n *instrument of torture* 52
rack v *as in "rack pool balls"* 101
rack n *cut of meat* 122
rack n *as in "rack and ruin"* 136
rack up v 321
racket n *scam* 215
racket n *Sports* 101
racket n *occupation* 215

racket n *game played with rackets* 108
racket n *noise* 134
racket n *sports gear* 108
racketeer n/v 215, 292
rackety adj 206
raconteur n 226
racquet n 101, 134
racquetball n 317
racy adj *blue* 151
rad n *dose of radiation* 279
rad adj *cool* 327
radar n 302
radar astronomy n 309
radial keratotomy n 322
radial saw n 310
radial symmetry n 269
radial tire n 317
radiancy n 91
radiant adj/n 91
radiant adj *fig., as in "a radiant personality"* 91
radiant energy n 256
radiant heating n 195
radiate v *emit light* 162
radiate v *fan out from a single source* 162
radiate v *emit heat, energy* 162
radiate 119
radiation n *radiating* 87
radiation n *as in "energy radiation"* 87, 119
radiation sickness n 286
radiator n 222
radical adj *Politics* 229
radical *Slang* 327
radical chic n 317
radicalism n 222
radio n *type of communication* 276
radio n *radio receiver* 276
radio adj/v 276
radio astronomy n 302
radio car n 292
radio frequency n 282
radio galaxy n 309
radio telescope n 285
radioactivate v 256
radioactive adj 256
radioactivity n 256
radiocarbon dating n 309
radiocast n 290
radiologist n 257
radiology n 257
radiophone n 264
radiotelegraph n 265
radious adj *obs. radiant* 98
radish n 15

radium n 254
radius n *type of bone* 120
radius n *in geometry* 120
radon n 279
radwaste n *radioactive waste* 324
raffish adj 212
raffle n 199; v 143
raffle n/v 143
raffle n *type of dice game* 199
raft n *arch. rafter* 100
raft n *a lot* 230
raft n/v *boat* 100
rafter n 14
raftsman n 198
rag n/v *scold* 192
rag n *money* 216
rag n *ragtime song* 265
rag n *as in "rags to riches"* 53
rag n *bad newspaper* 187
rag v *tease* 192
rag doll n 244
rag trade n *clothing business* 227, 263
ragamuffin adj/n 44
ragbag n 216
rage v 37
rage v *as in "raging battle"* 37
rage n *anger* 37
rage n *obs. foolishness* 37
rage n *fad* 37, 197
rage n *obs. madness* 37
rage n *lust, passion* 37
ragged adj *unfinished, rough* 53
ragged adj 53
ragged edge n 267
raggedy adj 270
raggedy 53
raggletaggle adj 278
ragman n *raggedy person* 127
ragman n *Professions/Duties* 127
ragout n *Food* 167
ragpicker n *Professions/Duties* 244
rags n *slang clothes* 242
ragtag adj/n 270
ragtag and bobtail n 216
ragtime n *Music* 265
ragtop n *convertible* 310
ragweed n 194
rah interj 249
rah-rah adj *enthusiastic* 249, 281
raid n/v 80, 248
raid n *nonmilitary sense* 80
raider n 80, 248
rail v *obs. joke around* 74

rail v *erupt verbally* 74; n 74
rail n *as in "fence rail"* 52
rail n *as in "ride the rails"* 149
rail n *type of bird* 65
rail n *for railroads* 52
railbird n *horserace fan* 262
railbus n 298
railcar n 224
raillery n *repartee* 172
railroad v *Slang* 268
railroad n/v *for trains* 212
railroad n *for wagons* 212
railroad flat n 287
railsplitter n 244
railway n 169
raiment n 71
rain n/v 12
rain check n 269
rain forest n 272
rainbow n *fig. gamut* 12
rainbow n *Weather* 12
rainbow trout n 255
raincoat n (Am) 223
rainfall n 220
rainmaker/rainmaking n (Am) 200
rainspout n 286
rainstorm n 210
rainwater n 12
rainwear n 297
rainy adj 12
rainy day n 133
raise v *as in "raise kids"* 168
raise v *as in "raise your voice in song"* 154
raise v *rise* 97
raise v *as in "raise flowers"* 168
raise v *pay increase* 187
raise v *in cards* 226
raise v *as in "raise a question"* 179
raise v *conjure* 81
raise n *Games/Fun/Leisure* 226
raisin n *obs. grapes* 34
raisin n *Food* 34
raison d'être n 250
rake n/v *as in "leaf rake"* 16
rake n *incline* 158
rake n/v *libertine* 173
rake v *as in "fingernails raking the blackboard"* 143
rakehell adj/n *rake* 173
rakish adj *jaunty* 173, 212
rally v *as in "rally courage"* 142, 179
rally v *as in "rally the troops"* 142

rally n *as in "pep rally"* 251
rally n *type of motor race* 317
rally v *as in "rally round a friend"* 142, 234
rally n/v *recover from illness* 142, 239
ralph v *vomit* 320
ram v *pack with a ram* 60
ram v *as in "ram the wall"* 60
ram n 11
ram n *ramming machine* 21
RAM 309
ramble v *travel aimlessly* 97, 149
ramble v *express yourself wanderingly* 97
ramble n 149
rambunctious adj (Am) 225
ramification n *consequence* 205
ramification n 97
ramification n *organic branch* 205
ramify v *branch out* 97
ramjet n 304
ramp n *type of wild onion* 119
ramp v *arch. be rampant* 94
ramp v *menace* 94, 170
ramp n *as in "launch ramp"* 196
ramp n 94
rampage n/v 170
rampageous adj 170
rampallion n *obs. rapscallion* 144
rampant adj *applied to plants* 90
rampant adj *fierce* 90
rampant adj *obs. lusting* 170
rampant adj *on hind legs* 90
rampant adj *not restrained* 90
rampart n 106
rampion n 118
rampire *arch.* 106
ramrod adj *unbending* 278
ramrod n *leader* 270
ramrod v 301
ramrod n *for loading guns* 203
ramshackle adj *describing people* 210
ramshackle adj *describing buildings* 210
ranch n/v (Am) 212
ranch n *as in "ranch house"* 212
ranch dressing n 326
ranch house n (Am) 239
rancher n 226
ranch-style adj 239
rancid adj 160
rancor n *obs. bad smell* 37

rancor n/v 37
rancorous 37
random n *as in "select a contestant at random"* 134
random n *obs. speed, power* 134
random n *obs. gun range* 134
random adj/adv 134
random access memory n 309
random sampling n 256
randy adj *crude* 169
randy adj *unruly* 169
randy adj *bawdy* 169
range n *as in "mountain range"* 145
range n *as in "target range"* 251
range n 237
range n/v *as in "home on the range"* 63
range n *distance, extent, as in "range of sight"* 136
range v *run a gamut, vary* 253
range n *cooking device* 69
range v *arrange* 98
range n 174
range n *as in "range of discussion"* 177
range v *roam* 72
rangefinder n 242
rangeland n 296
ranger n *as in "forest ranger"* 75
rangy adj *describing animals* 237
rangy adj *describing people* 237
rank adj *gen. offensive* 115
rank v *arrange in an order* 141
rank n *informal position achieved* 85
rank adj *gen. foul* 115
rank adj *obs. arrogant* 17
rank adj *luxuriant, excessive* 53
rank adj *foul-smelling* 115
rank n *formal position achieved* 85
rank and file n *gen. group members* 131
rank and file n *type of formation* 131
ranking adj *senior* 251
rankle v *bother* 149
rankle v *fester, cause wounds* 149
ranks n *arrangement of soldiers* 131
ransack v 57
ransack v *obs. frisk* 57
ransackle v *obs.* 57

ransom n/v 46
rant n/v *as in "rant and rave"* 143
rant v *be unruly* 143
rap n *type of knock* 46; v 46, 97
rap n *as in "rap sheet"* 277, 312
rap n/v *hit* 46
rap v *obs. testify against* 188
rap n *incrimination, reputation* 204, 293
rap n/v *as in "rap session"* 293, 320
rap n *Music* 318
rap n/v *critical remark* 204
rap n *as in "don't care a rap"* 230
rap n 97
rap group n *discussion group* 320
rap music n 318
rap sheet n 312
rapacious adj 169
rape v *taking away by force* 102
rape n *type of herb* 64
rape n/v *sexual assault* 102
rapeseed n 64
rapeseed oil n 217
rapid adj 160
rapid eye movement n 280
rapid eye movement sleep/REM sleep n 316
rapid transit n (Am) 243
rapid-fire adj 270
rapidity n 160
rapids n 193
rapier n 112
rapine n *plundering* 80
rappel v *descend a cliff* 298
rapport n 169
rapprochement n 215
rapscallion n 175
rapt adj *obs. phys. carried away, raped* 74
rapt adj *fig. carried away, to heaven* 74
rapt adj *mesmerized* 74
rapture n *intense joy* 125
rapture n/v *religious rapture* 125
rapture n *obs. seizing, carrying off, rape* 125
rapture of the deep n 309
rare adj *scarce* 90
rare adj *obs. far apart* 90
rare adj *obs. describing eggs* 167
rare adj *obs. spaced out* 90
rare adj *describing meat* 167

rare bird n 269
rare posterior n 65
rarebit n 183
rarefied 94
rarefy v 94
raring adj *eager* 277
rascal n *obs. rabble* 134
rascal n 134
rascality n 134
rascallion n 177
rascally adv 134
rascalry n 134, 251
rash adv *obs.* 73
rash adj *describing actions* 73
rash adj *describing people* 73
rash n *Medicine* 182
rash n *fig., as in "a rash of injuries"* 182
rasp *arch. raspberry* 148
rasp n/v *Tools* 107
rasp n/v *speak with a rasp* 57, 251
rasp v 107
raspberry n 148
raspberry n *slang fart* 257
raspis n *obs. type of wine* 70
rat n *informant* 277, 300
rat n *as in "you dirty rat"* 133
rat n 11
rat v *inform, betray* 277, 300
rat v *desert* 216
rat race n 301
rat snake n 237
rataplan n *beating sound* 233
ratatat n 177
ratatouille n 259
ratchet n 168
rate n *as in "rate of speed"* 166
rate v *berate* 94
rate v *rank* 191
rate v *obs. allot, divide* 104
rate n/v *grade, value* 86
rate n *charge, as in "the going rate"* 101
rate v *fig. regard* 191
rate v *as in "that rates a second look"* 191
rate of exchange n 187
ratfink n 320
rathe adj *eager* 17
rather *sooner* 17
rather interj 249
rathskeller n (Am) 263
ratify v 92
ratio n 146
ratiocinate v 151
ration n/v 183
ration n *reasoning* 144

riot n as in "a laugh riot" 293
riot act n 216
riot act n lit. leg. use 216
riot gun n 283
riot shield n 319
riotous adj 80
rip 296
rip n/v 97
rip v 321
rip n/v tear 189
rip n worthless person, horse 204
rip v steal 277
rip cord n 274
rip current n 296
rip off v (Am) 277, 320, 321
ripe adj 10
ripe adj drunk 216
ripe v 10
ripen v make ripe 118
ripen v 10
ripen v get ripe 118
rip-off n 320
riposte n counter in fencing 185
riposte n retort 185
ripped adj high 216
ripped adj drunk 216
ripple n 164
ripple v 180
ripple effect n 315
rip-roaring adj (Am) 233
riproarious adj 233
ripsaw n 224
ripsnorter n 231
ripsnorting adj 231
riptide n 236
rise v 27
risk n/v 176, 233
risk capital n 305
risk management n 318
risky adj 176, 233
risque adj 252
rite n 51
rite of passage n 276
ritual adj/n 51, 137
ritz n/v 280
ritzy adj (Am) 280
rival n equal 135
rival v be approximately equal 104
rival adj/n 135
rival adj 104
rivality n 136
rivalry n 136
rivalship n 136
river n 29
river horse n 145
riverbank n 118

riverbed n 219
riverboat n 123
riverfront n 236
rivet n/v Tools 71
riveting adj 170
rivulet n 118
RNA n 302
roach n Slang 320
roach n type of fish 30
roach clip n 320
road v obs. travel by horseback 123
road n 123
road agent n 244
road apples n Slang 307
road company n (Am) 265
road gang n 264
road hog n 261
road map n 261
road racing n 226
road show n 276
road test n 275
roadability n 280
roadblock n 298
roadhouse n 239
roadie n 318
roadkill n (Am) 324
roadrunner n 237
roadster n type of car 275
roadster n hobo 266, 275
roadster n type of horse 212, 275
roadster n type of ship 184, 275
roadster n type of carriage 261, 275
roadway n 123
roadwork n 243
roadworthy adj 212
roam v 60
roan adj/n 115
roar n/v 26
roaring boy n type of ruffian 132
roast n as in "wienie roast" 265
roast n/v 34
roast v upbrade 189
roaster n type of cooking pan 167
roasting ear n 148
rob v 46
Rob Roy n type of canoe 243
Rob Roy n type of drink 280
robber n 46
robber baron n 263
robbery n 46
robe n 35
robin n 105
robin redbreast n 65
robot n 279

robot bomb n 306
robotics n 302
robust adj 115
robusta n type of coffee 273
roc n 132
rock n crack cocaine 327
rock n rock music 318
rock n distaff 71
rock n diamond 277
rock n stone material 29
rock v as in "rock the boat" 27
rock n piece of rock 29
rock n massive stone feature 29
rock and roll n 311, 318
rock and rye n 259
rock bass n 209
rock bottom adj/n (Am) 250
rock candy n 183
rock climbing n 263
Rock Cornish n type of fowl 309
rock garden n 222
rock hound n (Am) 283
rock jock n Movies/TV/Radio 327
rock lobster n 255
rock oil n 164
rock salt n 181
rockabilly n (Am) Music 312
rockaway n (Am) type of carriage 224
rocker n Tools 198
rocker n rocking chair, rocking horse 185, 196, 239
rocker arm n 242
rocket v launch a rocket 224
rocket n type of plant 99
rocket n 159
rocket v travel fast 224
rocket bomb n 306
rocket engine n 298
rocket plane n 288
rocket ship n 288
rocket sled n 310
rocketeer n 224
rocketry n 288
rockfall n 285
rockfish n 119
rocking chair n (Am) 196
rocking horse n 185
rocks n slang testicles 302
rocks n as in "on the rocks" 316
rocky adj shaky 189
Rocky Mountain goat n (Am) 220
Rocky Mountain sheep n (Am) 194

Rocky Mountain spotted fever n (Am) 257
rococo n/adj 228
rod n penis 277
rod n in fishing 75
rod n gun 277
rod n 23
rodent n 220
rodeo n roundup 223, 289
rodeo n type of exhibition 289
rodeo n type of competition 223
roe n fish eggs 65
roe n doe 11
roe deer n 11
roebuck n 11, 64
roentgen adj/n Measurement 286
roentgen ray n 255
roger n obs. penis 166; v 166
roger v 166
rogue n vagrant 134
rogue n rascal 134
rogue adj 252
rogue elephant n 250
roguery n 134
rogues' gallery n 250
roil n/v 142
roil n obs. type of horse 64
roister n carouser 143
roister v 143
roke n smoke, fog, etc. 62
role n 157
role model n 312
role-playing n 304
role-playing game n 326
roll n Food 70
roll v 60
roll n register, as in "roll call" 41
roll n as in "drum roll" 173
roll v as in "roll the r" 127
roll v move on rollers 107
roll n scroll, list 41
roll n as in "a roll in the hay" Love/Romance/Sex 317
roll n as in "bankroll" Finances/Money 245
roll v rob 248
roll back v 263, 305
roll bar n 310, 317
roll cage n 310, 317
roll call n 204
roll film n 265
roll out v 271
roll over v 308
roll up v 252
rollaway adj 297
rollback n 263, 305

roundabout n *type of jacket* 223
roundabout n *type of chair* 196
roundabout n *rotary* 288
roundabout adj 115
roundelay n Music 77
rounders n Games/Fun/Leisure 226
roundheel n *pushover* 293
roundhouse n *locomotive switcher* 243
roundhouse n *arch. prison* 80
roundhouse n *type of punch* 283
round-robin n 114
roundsman n *someone who makes rounds* 200
round-the-clock adj 296
round-trip n (Am) 242
roundup n 197
roundworm n 119
roustabout n (Am) 245
rout v/n *defeat* 131
route n 48
router n 224
routine adj/n 177, 217
routine n *as in "dance routine"* 290
rove v 107
row n *as in "ducks in a row"* 23
row v *as in "row a boat"* 16
row n/v *disturbance* 188
row house n 297
rowboat n 107
rowdy adj/n (Am) 217
rowdyism n (Am) 233
rowing machine n 226
royal adj *as in "he's a royal pain"* 132
royal adj 79
royal blue n 207
royal flush n 244
royal purple n 179
royal we pron 227
royalty n Government 79
royalty n Finances/Money 245
rub n *as in "there's the rub"* 144
rub v 60
rub in v 249
rub out n/v *kill* 229
rubber n *condom* Slang 307
rubber n *as in material* 193
rubber n *as in "rubber game"* 126
rubber band n 258
rubber bullet n 324
rubber cement n 258
rubber check n (Am) 293

rubber plant n 254
rubber stamp n 260
rubber tree n 219
rubberneck n/v (Am) 268
rubbers n *galoshes* 242
rubber-stamp v 283
rubbery adj 278
rubbing n Visual Arts/ Photography 228
rubbing alcohol n 286
rubbish interj 156
rubbish n 69
rubble n/v 85, 295
rube n (Am) 268
rubella n Medicine 257
rubeola n *measles* 210
rubout n/v (Am) *slang murder* 291
rubric n 42
ruby adj 103
ruby n 29
rubythroat n 194
rubythroated hummingbird n 194
rucksack n 242
ruckus n (Am) 217, 268
ruction n 217, 268
rudder n 36
rudder n *obs. oar* 36
ruddy adj 25
rude adj *simple* 54
rude adj *insolent, uneducated* 54
rudiment n 114, 234
rudimentary adj 114, 234
rue v *obs. cause rue* 55
rue n/v 55
rue n 55
rueful adj 55
ruffed grouse n (Am) 194
ruffian n 102
ruffle v 58
rug n *carpet* 222
rug n *blanket* 222
rug n *slang toupee* 297
rug n *obs. type of cloth* 222
rug rat n (Am) *child* 320
rugby n 244
rugged adj *rough around the edges* 137
rugged adj *rough* 137
rugged adj *obs. rough like a rug (blanket)* 137
rugged adj *manly* 137
rugged adj *obs. shaggy* 137
ruggedize v 307
ruin n/v 48
ruin n *fig.* 48

ruin v *destroy* 131
ruin v *spoil* 131
ruin n War/Military/Violence 131
ruination n 48
ruins n 87
rule n/v *reign, control* 44
rule n *regulation* 46
rule n *measure, as in "as a rule"* 31
rule n *as in "rules and regulations"* 46
rule n *type of printing line* 172
rule v 44
rule of the road n 243
rule of thumb n 176
rule out v 250
ruler n Measurement 31
ruler n Government 44
ruling n 81
ruly adj *opp. of unruly* 92
rum n 167
rumba n 291
rumble n/v 92
rumble n/v *fight* 307
rumble seat n 224
rumble strip n 317
rumbullion n *arch. rum* 167
rumbustious adj 198
rumdum adj/n 268
rum-hound 293
ruminate v *chew cud* 108
ruminate v *ponder* 108
rummage v *arrange* 142
rummage sale n 239
rummer n *type of drinking glass* 167
rummy n (Am) *type of card game* 275
rummy n *drunk* 249, 293
rummy adj *odd* 230
rumor n/v 82
rumormonger n 268
rump n 64
rumple n/v 113
rumpot n *drunk* 293
rumpus n 205
rumpus room n (Am) 297
rumrunner n (Am) 283
run n *as in "a run in my hose"* 286
run n *as in "a run on the bank"* 172
run n/v *as in "the run of a play"* 187
run n/v 26
run n *score* Sports 244
run n *regular route* 184

run n *as in "run of good luck"* 177
run v *as in "run for office"* 229
run v *as in "run water"* 295
run v *as in "it runs in the family"* 208
run v 184
run along v 277
run down v 307
run in v *arrest* 248
run off at the mouth v 278
runabout n 107
runagate n *obs. renegade* 117
runagate n *vagabond* 117
runaround n (Am) 249
runaway adj/n 113
run-down adj 252
rundown n *recap* Slang 307
rundown n *list of horse-racing entries* 307
run-down adj *downtrodden* 252
run-down adj *shabby* 252
rune n Magic 203
rune n Language and Speaking 19
rung n 16
run-in n 250
run-in n *rugby term* 250
runner-up n 233
running board n (Am) 212
running dog n 293
running light n 261
running mate n (Am) 247
running start n 293
running water n 280
runny adj 217
runoff n (Am) 247
run-of-the-mill adj 293
run-of-the-mine adj 293
run-on sentence n 281
runs n *diarrhea* 316
runt n *smallest in litter* 181
runt n *small cow* 181
runt n *type of tree stump* 181
runt n *small person* 181
run-through n Performing Arts 290
runway n *for airplanes* 261
runway n (Am) *gangway* 261
runway n *deer tracks* 261
rupture n/v 88
rural adj 63
rural n *arch.* 63
rural free delivery n 265
rural route n 265
rurban adj 279
ruse n 232
rush v *force to hurry* 92

satire n/v *work of satire* 111
satire n *gen. mockery* 111
satiric adj 111
satirical adj 111
satirist n 128
satirize v 161
satisfaction n *as in "can't get no satisfaction"* 43
satisfaction n *contentment* 83
satisfaction n *as in "satisfaction of debts"* 43
satisfactory adj *adequate* 160
satisfy v Religion 43
satisfy v 83
saturate v *drench* 207
saturate v *obs. satisfy* 117
saturate v *obs. satisfy* 207
saturated fat n 322
saturation n *obs.* 117
Saturday n 12
Saturday night pistol n 319
Saturday night special n 319
Saturn n 12
saturnalia n *gen. bacchanal* 126
saturnalia n *type of festival* 126
saturnine adj *related to Saturn* 73
saturnine adj *given to inertia* 73
saturnism n *lead poisoning* 238
satyr n *fig. horny guy* 81
satyr n *type of ape* 81
satyr n 81
satyr play n 290
satyriasis n *male nymphomania* 75
sauce n *alcohol* 301
sauce n/v 34
sauceboat n 183
saucebox n *naughty person* 132
saucepan n 167
saucer n *obs. type of condiment holder* 147
saucer n 147
saucery n *spec. type of kitchen* 34
saucy adj *bawdy* 112
saucy adj *tasty* 112
saucy adj *insolent* 112
sauerbraten n (Am) 259
sauerkraut n 148
sauna n *saunabath* 258
sauna n *saunahouse* 258
saunter v *obs. talk ramblingly* 169
saunter v *walk ramblingly* 169
sausage n 70
sauté n/v 211
sauternes n *type of wine* 183

sauvignon blanc n *type of wine* 303
savage adj *frenzied* 53
savage adj *uncivilized* 53
savage adj *of the wild* 53
savage n 53
savagery n 53, 135
savagism n 53
savanna n 118
savant n 188
save v *rescue* 55
save v *store, keep* 55, 58
save v *obs. spare* 55
save-all n 158
saving grace n 133
savings account n 281
savings and loan association n 290
savings bank n 214
savings bond n 305
savior n *gen. and rel.* 50
savoir faire n 212
savor v *relish* 93
savor v *give pleasure* 93
savor v *season* 93
savor n 48
savor n/v 48, 93
savor v 48
savory n *type of mint* 34
savoy cabbage n 183
savvy adj 199, 275
savvy n/v *knowledge/know* 199
saw n/v 16
saw n *obs. gen. speech* 19
saw n *as in "old saw"* 19
saw grass n 209
sawbones n 221
sawbuck n (Am) 227
sawdust n 114
sawed-off adj (Am) 252
sawhorse n 198
sawmill n 127
saw-toothed adj 138
sawyer n 40
sax n Music 290
sax n *type of knife* 21
saxhorn n 228
saxophone n 246
saxtuba n 246
say n *obs. food-testing* 70
say v *as in "the speedometer says 45"* 25
say v *as in "the details say luxury"* 25
say interj 249
say v *obs. test* 62
say n/v 25
say n *as in "have your say"* 157

say v *as in "say mass"* 60
saying n 41
sayonara interj 249
say-so n *permission* 152, 277
say-well n *saying nice things* 98
'sblood interj 132
'sbodikins interj 175
'sbud 132
scab n *rascal* 133
scab n *type of disease* 32
scab n/v 66
scab n/v *strikebreaker* 200
scabbard n 45
scabies n *obs. type of disease* 211
scabies n *type of rash* 211
scabland n 272
scads n *many* 249
scaffold n *place of execution* 130
scaffold n *execution itself* 130
scaffold, scaffolding n 36
scag n *heroin* 320
scag n *cigarette* 320
scalawag n (Am) 231
scald v 55
scald n *rascal* 133
scale n *pan on a scale* 72
scale v *as in "scale up, scale down"* 208
scale n/v 72
scale n 129
scale n *obs. ladder rung* 71
scale n *part of scale armor* 80
scale n *as in "4:1 scale"* 166
scale n *measurement standard* 66
scale n *as in "the scale of a production"* 103
scale n *type of bowl* 72
scale v *as in "scale a wall"* 93
scale n/v *as in "fish scales"* 30
scale n *e.g., Fahrenheit scale* 66
scale armor n 229
scallion n *leek* 70
scallion n 70
scallop v 183
scallop n *type of shell* 64
scallop n 64
scallopini n 303
scalp n *fig. type of trophy* 120
scalp n *hair and skin* 120
scalp n *obs. pate* 120
scalp v *as in "scalp tickets"* 263
scalp n *lit. type of trophy* 120
scalp v War/Military/Violence 174
scalpel n 182

scalper n 263
scaly anteater n *pangolin* 220
scam n/v 320
scamp n *rascal* 216
scamp v 235
scamp n *obs. highwayman* 216
scamp v *roam* 235
scamper v 180
scamper n/v *obs. escape* 180
scan v *as in "scan poetry"* 76
scan v *as in "the poetry scans"* 76
scan v *skim* 201
scan v *use a scanning tool* 295
scandal n/v 136
scandal n *spec. to rel.* 136
scandal v 142
scandal n *cause of scandal* 136
scandal n *obs. slander* 136
scandal sheet n 276
scandalize v *publicize a scandal* 104
scandalize v *offend* 104
scandalmonger n 189
scandalous adj 136
scanner n 288
scant v *skimp* 141
scant adj/adv 54
scanties n 287
scanty adj 54, 139
scape n *as in "city scape"* 193
scape v *escape* 58
scapegoat n/v *blame-taker* 216
scapegoat n *lit.* 216
scapegrace n *rascal* 216
scapula n 120
scar n *fig.* 66
scar n/v 66
scar tissue n 238
scarab n 119
scarab n *type of gem* 119
scaramouche n *rascal* 175
scarce adj/adv 92
scarce adj *obs. stingy* 92
scarce adv 92
scarce adj *obs. sparse* 92
scarcity n 50, 92
scarcity n *obs. stinginess* 50
scare n *obs. being scared* 108
scare v *as in "I scare easily"* 36
scare n 108
scare v 36
scare up v 231
scarecrow n 122
scarecrow n *person who scares crows* 122
scaredy-cat n 298

scarehead n *alarming headline* 264

scaremonger n 269

scarf v (Am) *eat* 310; n 310

scarf n *sash, headscarf* 122

scarf n *type of joint* 49

scarf v 49

scarify v *scare* 204

scarify v *scratch, lacerate* 93

scarlatina n *scarlet fever* 210

scarlet n *type of cloth* 35

scarlet n *red* 35

scarlet adj/n *red* 55

scarlet n *type of official dress* 35

scarlet fever n *scarlatina* 167

scarlet letter n (Am) 174

scarlet tanager n (Am) 209

scary adj *scaring* 124

scary adj *scared* 124

scat interj/v (Am) *scoot* 230

scat n/v *type of jazz* 290

scat n *heroin* 307

scat n *slang feces* 286

scat v 290

scathe n/v *injury, harm* 21

scathing adj *phys. injurious* 207

scathing adj *harsh, caustic* 207

scatological adj 269

scatology n 269

scatter n/v 55

scatter rug n 286

scatteration n 55, 205

scatterbrain n 189

scatterbrained adj 189

scattergood n *arch. spendthrift* 127

scattershot adj 313

scavager n 110

scavenge v 110

scavenger n *garbageman* 110

scavenger n *garbage picker* 110

scavenger n *applied to animals* 110, 165

scavenger hunt n (Am) 298

scenario n *Performing Arts* 265

scenario n *gen.* 265

scenarist n 282

scene n *gen. location, as in "scene of the crime"* 111

scene n *Performing Arts* 111

scene n *as in "make a scene"* 204

scenery n *Performing Arts* 201

scenery n *as in "viewing the scenery"* 193

scenery n *obs. stage action* 201

scene-stealer n 305

scenic adj *Geography/Places* 193

scenic adj *Performing Arts* 111, 137

scenic adj *dramatic* 137

scenic adj *pretty* 137

scenic adj *fake* 137

scenic railway n 261

scenical adj 111

scent n *gen. odor* 82

scent v *smell* 82

scent n *as in "bloodhound following a scent"* 82

scent v *feel* 82

scent n *spec. perfume* 197; v 197

scented 197

scepter n 52

sceptered adj *endowed with authority* 114

schedule n *obs. note* 76

schedule n *list* 76

schedule n/v *timetable* 76, 237

schedule n *appendix* 76

schema 294

schematic adj 190

schematic n 90, 294

scheme n/v *plan* 159

scheme n *describing related elements* 205

scheme n *obs. map of the heavens* 159

scheming adj 225

schemist n *astrologer* 180

scherzo n *Music* 246

schilling n 200

schism n *Religion* 78

schist n *type of rock* 193

schiz 288

schiz n 288, 304

schizo adj/n 288, 304; n 304

schizoid adj/n 288

schizophrene n *schizophrenic* 275, 288

schizophrenia n 275

schizophrenic adj/n 275

schizy adj *schizo* 288

schlemiel n 268

schlepp n/v 293

schlepp n 293

schlock adj/n 283

schmaltz, schmaltzy n, adj 300

schmeck n *drugs* 300, 313

schmo n (Am) 307

schmooze n/v (Am) 266

schmuck n 268

schnapps n 211

schnauzer n 285

schnitzel n (Am) 241

schnockered n (Am) *drunk* 313

schnook n (Am) 301

schnozz n *nose* 286

schnozzle n *slang nose* 286

scholar n *learned person* 19

scholar n *student* 19

scholarity n *obs. being a scholar* 129

scholarly adj/adv 154

scholarly adv 154

scholarship n *scholarliness* 111

scholarship n *financial aid* 111

school v *teach* 19, 78

school n/v *as in "school of fish"* 64

school n *schooling* 19

school v *attend school* 78

school n *school building* 19, 247

school n *as in "school of thought," "the deco school of architecture"* 251

school board n 228

school day n 129

school district n 214

school year n 247

school-age adj 182

schoolbag n 258

schoolbook n 187

schoolboy n 129, 202, 228, 299

schoolboyish adj 175

schoolchild n 129, 202, 228, 299

schoolfellow n 101, 129, 202, 228, 299

schoolgirl adj 175

schoolgirl n 129, 202, 228, 299

schoolhouse n 78

schoolkid n 129, 202, 228, 299

schoolmarm n (Am) 42, 228

schoolmaster n 42

schoolmate n 101, 129, 202, 228, 299

schoolmistress n 42

schoolroom n 202

schoolteacher n 228

schoolwork n 247

schoolyard n 247

schoon n *move like a schooner* 243

schooner n (Am) *Travel/Transportation* 184

schooner n *type of beer glass* 258

schottische n *type of dance* 228

schtick n 318

schuss v *ski fast* 298

schwa n 214

sciamachy n *fighting an imaginary enemy* 155

sciatic nerve n 182

sciatica n *Medicine* 68

science n *as in "arts and sciences"* 129

science n 182

science n *knowledge* 39

science n *knowledge* 182

science fiction n 245

sciential adj 65

scientific adj *not mechanical* 144

scientific adj 165

scientific method n 237

scientific notation n 296

scientist n 220

scientize v 255

scimitar n 112

scintilla n *trace, bit* 158, 166

scintilla 158

scintillant adj 191, 207

scintillant 207

scintillate v 158

scintillating adj 207

scintillation n 158

sciolism n *pretending to learn* 214

sciolist n 214

scion n 50

scissor n/v 71

scissors n 71

scissors kick n 289

sclerosis n *Medicine* 68

scoff v *slang eat greedily* 197

scoff n/v 38

scoff v 38

scofflaw n 292

scold v *quarrel* 21, 93

scold n *quarrelsome person* 21

scold v *reprove* 21, 93

scoliosis n 182

sconce n *wall light* 70

sconce n *obs. type of candle* 70

sconce n *arch. head, sense or wit* 125

sconce n *detached defensive work* 131

scone n *type of bread* 106

scoop n/v *breaking story* 246

scoop n *as in "ice cream scoop"* 36

scoop n *as in "sugar scoop"* 36

scoop n *ladle* 36

scoop n *scoopful* 36

scoot v 207

scooter n *type of plow* 281

scooter n *type of boat, toy* 281

scuba n 311
scuba-dive v 311
scuba-diver n 311
scuff v (Am) as in "scuff a shoe" 271
scuff n type of hit 131
scuff v walk scuffingly 271
scuffle n/v 131
scullery n area of kitchen responsibility 70
scullery n spec. place 70
scullion n scullery worker 101
sculpt v 17, 153, 173, 246
sculptor n 153, 173
sculptress n 153, 173
sculpture v 246
sculpture n/v 77, 246
sculpturesque adj 221
scum n fig. 51
scum n obs. foam 51
scum n 51
scum n Insults 133
scumbag n condom 320, 325
scumbag n low-life 320, 325
scuppernong n (Am) type of grape 211
scurry n/v 218
scurvy n 121
scut work n 311
scuttle v scrap 163
scuttle n type of platter 14
scuttle n gen. basket 14
scuttle n/v quick shuffle 158
scuttle n obs. dish 14
scuttle n coal bucket 221
scuttlebutt n rumor 212, 277
scuttlebutt n type of cask 212, 277
scuzz adj Insults 320
scuzzbag Insults 320
scuzzbucket Insults 320
scuzzy adj 320
scythe n 16
'sdeath interj God's death 156
sea n 9
sea n on the moon 9
sea anemone n 181
sea bass n 194
sea biscuit n hardtack 168
sea captain n 149
sea change n 156
sea cow n 145
sea cucumber n 145
sea devil n 156
sea eagle n 165
sea fire n ocean bioluminescence 209
sea grass n 118

sea green n 139
sea horse n 99
sea legs n 184
sea level n 209
sea lily n 254
sea lion n 48, 165
sea mew n 99
sea mile n 195
sea otter n 165
sea power n 229
sea robber n pirate 131
sea rover n 131
sea salt n 145
sea serpent n 156
sea slug n 194
sea snake n 194
sea star n starfish 119
sea trout n 181
sea turtle n 145
sea urchin n 119
sea wrack n seaweed 105
seabag n 280
seabed n 219
Seabee n 306
seabird n 119
seacoast n 29
seafarer n 36
seafaring adj/n 36
seafloor n 236
seafood n (Am) 223
seagoing adj 36, 224
seagull n 105
seal n sea lion 11, 165
seal n/v as in "seal of approval" 48
seal off v 301
sealift n/v akin to airlift 311
sealing wax n 36
seam n/v 16
seam n geo. sense 16
seaman n obs. merman 132
seaman n 16
seamanship n 198
seamless adj 16
seamount n 302
seamster n 18, 127
seamstress n 18, 127
seamy adj fig. 159
seamy adj lit. seamed 159
seance n 215
seance n portrait sitting 215
seance n gen. governmental or royal meeting 215
seaplane n 280
seaport n 123
seaquake n 164
sear v burn 26
sear v become parched 26

sear v parch 26
sear v cook 26
search n/v 60
search and destroy v 312
search warrant n 189
searchless adj impenetrable 159
searchlight n 260
seascape n Visual Arts/Photography 201
seashell n 10
seashore n 105
seasick adj 121
seasickness n 121
season v 70
season n 31
season n arch. year 221
season v make mature, experienced 141
season ticket n 214
seasonal adj 221
seasoning n 122
seastrand n seashore 9
seat n as in "seat of the pants" 33, 147
seat n center 88
seat n/v 33
seat n Cloth/Clothing 242
seat n buttocks 33, 147, 242
seat n sitting place 147, 242
seat belt n 298
seat-of-the-pants adj (Am) 308
seatrain n 298
seawater n 9
seaway n 17
seaweed n 118
sec adj somewhat dry (of champagne) 34
sec n second 256
secant n Mathematics 120
secede v 207
secessionist n (Am) 247
secluded adj 159
secluse adj secluded 144
seclusion n 159, 206
seclusion n exclusion 206
second n unit of time 120
second v as in "I second the motion" 142
second adj after the first 54
second n the one after first 85
second n unit of measurement 66
second banana n 311
second base n 226
second best adj/n 82
second childhood n 157
second class adj/n 212

Second Coming n 154
second cousin n 170
second fiddle n Music 214
second fiddle n slang 214
second hand n 165
second language n 318
second mortgage n 281
second nature n 176
second person n Language and Speaking 172
second strike n/adj War/Military/Violence 312
second thought n 151
second wind n 216
second world n the communist world 319
secondary adj 90
secondary cell n storage battery 272
secondary color n 234
secondary road n 274
secondary school n 228
second-best adj 90
second-class adj/n 234
second-degree burn 286
second-degree murder n 307
second-guess v 304
secondhand adj/adv 178
secondhand smoke n 322
second-rate adj 178
seconds n Food 197
seconds n manufacturer's rejects 127
second-story man n Crime/Punishment/Enforcement 267
second-string adj 161
secrecy n 85
secret v obs. 85
secret adj/n/v 85
secret partner n 226, 275
secret police n 215
secret service n 188
secret society n 231
secretary n 75
secretary n obs. confidant 75
secretary n type of writing desk 222
secretary bird n 194
secretary-general n 188
secrete v secret away 192
secrete v exude 191
secretion n 191
sect n Religion 43
section n/v 88, 218
sectional n type of furniture 273
secular adj 43
secular humanism n 299

secure v Finances/Money 227
secure v *make safe* 142
secure adj *safe* 108
secure adj/v 108
securities n 172
security n Finances/Money 227
security n 142
security blanket n 321
security guard n 311
security risk n 313
sedan n *sedan chair* 149
sedan n 288
sedan n *type of car* 149
sedan chair 149
sedate v 69, 303
sedation n 69, 106
sedative adj 69
sedentary adj *lethargic* 147
sedentary adj *not migratory* 147
seder n *type of Jewish service* 247
sedge n *type of plant* 10
sediment n 114
sediment n *geological sense* 114
sedimentary adj 219
sedimentology n *study of sedimentation* 296
sedition n *anti-authority action* 79
seditious adj 79
seduce v *sexual sense* 103
seduce v 103
seducement n 103
seduction n 103
seductor n Love/Romance/Sex 101
seductress n *obs. seductor* 213
seductress Love/Romance/Sex 101
seductress n 213
sedulity n 108
sedulous adj *perseverant* 108
see v *in poker* 126
see v *as in "seeing a girlfriend"* Love/Romance/Sex 101
see v 26
see a man about a dog v 293
seed n *sperm* 10
seed n/v Plants 10
seed v *rank in a tournament* 263
seed v Agriculture/Food-Gathering 71
seed money n 305
seed plant n 184
seed stock n 287
seedcake n 100

seeder n 242
seedling n 164
seedtime n 15
seedy adj Slang 189
seedy adj *lit.* 189
seek v 26
seem v 55
seem v *obs. be appropriate* 55
seemly adj *opp. of unseemly* 61
seep n/v 208
seepage n 208
seer n 47, 230
seeress n 47, 230
seersucker n 184
seesaw n/v Games/Fun/Leisure 226
seesaw n *gen. back and forth* 226
seethe v *arch. cook, boil* 60
seethe v *applied to things* 60
seethe v *applied to people* 60
seething adj 90
see-through adj 303
segment n 205; v 205, 252
segment n *geometry sense* 205
segregate adj/v 117
segregation n 117
segregationist n 282
segue n/v 246, 299
seidel n *type of beer glass* 273
seine n 16, 223; v 223
seismic adj 236
seismogram n 238
seismograph n 238
seismology n 237
seismometer n 238
seize v 58
seize up v 271
seizure n Medicine 196
seizure n 58, 271
selcouth adj 28
select adj/n/v 137
select v/n 137
selected adj 137
selection n *selecting* 158
selection n *something selected* 158
selective adj 160
selective service n 282
selenology n *study of the moon* 210
self n 50
self-absorbed adj 225
self-abuse n 190
self-abuse n *self-deceiving* 190
self-actualization n 243, 298
self-actualize v 243
self-addressed adj 227

self-adhesive adj 313
self-appointed adj 207
self-assertive adj 243
self-assured adj 184
self-aware adj 262
self-awareness n 262
self-centered adj 169
self-centering adj 169
self-respecting adj 125
self-conceit n 149
self-confidence n 150
self-confident adj 150
self-congratulation n 270
self-congratulatory adj 270
self-conscious adj *feeling awkward* 170, 243
self-conscious adj *self-aware* 170, 243
self-contempt n 125
self-control n 184
self-defense n 174
self-dependence n 243
self-dependent adj 243
self-deprecating adj 317
self-destroying adj 169
self-destruct v 169, 319
self-destruction n 169
self-destructive adj 169
self-discipline n 199
self-discovery n 288
self-disgust n 288
self-doubt n 225
self-employed adj 187, 305
self-employment n 187, 305
self-esteem n 169
self-evidencing adj 177
self-evident adj/n 177
self-explanatory adj 271
selfful adj *arch. selfish* 150, 169
self-fulfillment n 243
self-government n 184, 188
self-heal n *type of plant* 30
self-help adj/n 232
self-homicide n *suicide* 155
selfhood n 150
self-hypnosis n 275
self-importance n 198
self-important adj 198
self-indulgence n 198
self-indulgent adj 198
self-involved adj 225
selfish adj 150
selfless adj 199
self-love n 125
self-made adj 160
self-mailer n 305
self-medication n 303
self-murder *suicide* 155

self-mutilation n 248
self-perception n 170
self-perpetuating adj 217
self-pity n 150
self-portrait n 228
self-possessed adj 212
self-preservation n 150
self-propelled adj 261
self-published adj 323
self-realization n 243
self-reliance n 225
self-reliant adj 225
self-replicating adj 302
self-respect n 125
self-righteous adj 169
self-rising flour n (Am) 241
self-rule n 247
self-sacrifice n 212
self-satisfaction n 184
self-serve adj 281
self-service adj/n 281
self-serving adj 233
self-slaughter n *suicide* 155
self-starter n 261
self-styled adj 217
self-subsistent adj 124
self-sufficiency n 124
self-sufficient adj 124
self-sufficing adj 124
self-taught adj 188
self-treatment n 257
self-violence n 155
self-worth n 304
sell v *obs. give* 18
sell v 18
sell n *saddle* 88
sell n *hoax* 231
sell off v 171
sell out v 320
seller's market n 298
selling point n 289
sell-off n 298
sellout n (Am) 249
seltzer n 183
semantic adj 264
semantic adj *arch. related to weather* 165
semantician n 276
semanticist n 264, 276
semantics n 264
semaphore n/v 214
semblable adj *obs. similar* 62
semblance n 50
semblant n *obs.* 50
semble v *obs. resemble* 62
semble v *obs.* 50
semen n 66
semester n 221

semester hour n 291
semi 281
semi n *semitrailer* 281, 304
semiannual adj 195
semiautomatic adj/n War/Military/Violence 266
semicircle n 105
semicolon n 152
semiconductor n 224
semiconscious adj 225
semifinal adj/n 263
semigloss adj 301
semigod n 78
seminal adj 178
seminal adj *related to semen* 178
seminal fluid n 286
seminal vesicle n 256
seminar n (Am) 266
seminarian n Religion 129
seminary n Religion 129
seminate v *disseminate* 144
semiprecious adj 270
semipro adj/n 275
semiprofessional adj 275
semiretired adj 299
semiskilled adj 289
semisweet adj 303
semitrailer n 281
semitropical adj 236
senate, senator n 44
send v *as in "you send me"* 298
send v 26
send-off n (Am) 250
send-up n *parody* 312
senesce v 166
senescence n *old age* 166
senescent adj 166
senile adj *mentally decrepit* 243
senile adj *related to agedness* 243
senile dementia n 243
senility n 243
senior n Education 154
senior adj/n Age/Aging 65
senior citizen n 296
senior high school n 276
sennight n *arch. a week* 12
sensate adj *arch.* 157
sensate adj 98
sensation n *sensing* 157
sensational adj 233, 234
sensationalism n 233
sensationalize v 233
sense n *as in "common sense"* 125
sense n *as in "that makes sense"* 151

sense n/v *taste, etc.* 106
sense n *as in "the sense of a word"* 76
sense n *perception* 125
sense organ n 238
senseful adj *obs. sensible, reasonable* 144
senseless adj 137
senses n *as in "come to your senses"* 125
sensibilia n *that which can be sensed* 250
sensibilities n 199
sensitive adj 90, 235
sensitive n 230
sensitivity training n 312
sensor n 286
sensorium n 147
sensory adj 160
sensual adj *carnal* 91
sensual adj 91
sensuous adj 161
sensurround n 324
sentence n Language and Speaking 76
sentence n *obs. sense, significance* 62
sentence v *obs. gen. judge, opine* 132
sentence n/v The Law 132, 248
sentence n *obs. opinion* 248
sentence fragment n 305
sentience n 225
sentient adj/n 225
sentiment n *obs. sensation* 150
sentiment n *gen. feeling* 150
sentiment n *emotional feeling* 150, 185
sentimental adj 185
sentimentalism n 185
sentimentality n 185
sentinel n/v 126
sentry n/v 155
sentry box n 188
separate adj/v 96
separate n *a la carte clothing* 260
separate adj 103
separate v *prelude to divorce* 170
separate adj *obs. separated* 103
separationist n 229
separator n 157
sepia n *ink of cuttlefish* 209
sepia n *cuttlefish* 65
sepia n *color* 209
September n *unit of a clan* 108

September n 12
septet n *group of 7* 232
septic adj 159
septic sore throat n *strep throat* 286
septic tank n 273
septuagenarian adj/n 210
sepulchral adj 155
sepulchre n *tomb* 45, 130
sepulchre v *bury* 45, 130
sepulture n *burial* 45
sequel n *sycophant* 113
sequel n *as in "sequel to a book"* 111
sequel n *consequence* 113
sequence n 136
sequence n *gen.* 78
sequence n *religious use* General/Miscellaneous 136
sequence n Religion 78
sequence n/v 308
sequencer n Music 304, 324
sequencer n Tools 304
sequin n *gaudery* 260
sequin n *type of coin* 260
sequitur n *consequence* 232
sequoia n 219
serape n (Am) 223
seraph n *type of angel* 19, 20
seraphim n *type of angel* 19, 20
sere adj *dried, withered* 24
serenade n/v Music 154
serendipitous adj 204, 308
serendipity n 204, 308
serene adj *applied to people* 92
serene adj 92
serenity n 92
serf n *obs. slave* 101
serf n 101
serge n *type of fabric* 71
sergeant n *in the police* 248
sergeant n *obs. servant* 45
sergeant n *mil. sergeant* 45, 248
sergeant n *police sergeant* 45, 248
sergeant at arms n 82
serial adj 234
serial n Movies/TV/Radio 291
serial n *magazine* 227
serial killer n 319
serial marriage n 323
serial monogamy n 323
serial number n 258
serialize v 265
serialize v *arrange serially* 265
series n 157

series n Literature/Writing 201
serif n 227
serigraph n *silkscreen* 299
seriocomic adj 202
serious adj *critical* 73
serious adj *devout* Religion 202
serious adj *solemn* 73
serious adj *as in "we will have to spend some serious money"* 327
serious-minded adj 225
sermon n *fig. preaching* 42
sermon n *obs. gen. speech, discussion* 42
sermon n Religion 42, 215
sermonette n 42, 215
serology n *study of serums* 273
serpent n Animals 30
serpent adj 90
serpent n *the Devil* 43
serpentiform adj 90
serpentine adj 90
serpentine adj *curving* 90
serpentine v 90
serrano n *type of pepper* 322
serrate v *obs. amputate* 69
serrated adj 190
serried adj 141
serry v *press together* 141
serum n Medicine 257
serum n *gen. fluid* 257
serum hepatitis n 297
serum sickness n 279
servant n 40
servant n Love/Romance/Sex 101
serve n/v *in tennis* 151
serve v 55
serve v *as in "serve food"* 60
serve v *as in "if memory serves"* 180
serve v *as in "serve papers"* 81
service n *military* 188
service n 40
service n *fix* 295
service n 20
service n *set of utensils* 167
service book n 129
service center n 318
service charge n 281
service industry n 318
service mark n 308
service medal n 300
service road n 288
service station n 279
service stripe n 283

shit n *worthless person* 120
shit n *drug* 307
shit n *obs. diarrhea* 120
shit v *bullshit, deceive* 300
shithead n Insults 320
shithouse n *outhouse* 196
shitkicker n Slang 320
shitlist n Slang 307
shitter n 196
shitty adj Slang 292
shitwork n 318
shiv n *knife* 174
shivaree n (Am) 226
shiver n/v *tremble* 60
shiver n/v *splinter* 48
shoal n *crowd* 135
shoal adj/n *shallows* 29
shock n *as in "shock of hair"* 52, 217
shock n/v *electrical jolt* 195
shock n Medicine 221
shock n *jolt, blow* 158
shock n *arch. type of battle* 130
shock n/v *surprise* 169
shock v *obs.* 130
shock n *items drawn together* 52
shock v 52
shock absorber n 275
shock therapy n 280
shock troops n 283
shock wave n 278
shocker n 216
shocking adj 179
shocking pink n 301
shockproof adj/v 284
shock-resistant adj 301
shod adj *wearing shoes* 35
shoddy adj *second-rate* 234
shoddy n *reclaimed wool* 223
shoe n *on horses* 16
shoe n/v 16
shoe tree n 222
shoeblack n *bootblack* 196
shoehorn n/v 123, 295
shoelace n 149
shoemaker n 75
shoestring n 149
shoestring adj/n Slang 267
shoestring adj/n *a little* 293
shoestring potatoes n 297
shoo v 163
shoo interj 81
shoofly interj 249
shoofly n *type of rocker* 262
shoofly pie n (Am) 287
shoo-in n 294
shook-up adj *agitated* 261
shoot v Sports 263

shoot v Movies/TV/Radio 265
shoot n *shooting* 112
shoot interj *damn, shit* 267, 300
shoot v *go fast* 26
shoot n *as in "turkey shoot"* 112
shoot interj *go ahead* 283
shoot n/v 64
shoot v War/Military/Violence 112
shoot down v 235
shoot the breeze 293
shoot the bull v (Am) 293
shoot up v *take drugs* 324
shoot up v 266
shoot your mouth off v 250
shoot-'em-up n 305
shooter n *gun* 229
shooter n *type of drink* 322
shooting gallery n Games/Fun/Leisure 199
shooting gallery n *heroin house* 312
shooting iron n (Am) 174
shooting script n 291
shooting star n 118
shooting stick n *portable seat* 137
shoot-out n 307
shoot-the-chutes n Games/Fun/Leisure 281
shop v *as in "go shopping"* 196
shop n 41
shop n *as in "workshop"* 76
shop steward n 276
shop window n 101
shopkeeper n 110
shoplift v 174
shoplifter n 174
shopper n *one who shops* 245
shopper n *advertising paper* 318
shopping bag n 263
shopping center n 263
shopping list n 280
shopping mall n 311
shoptalk n 264
shopworn adj 234
shore n *coast* 10
shore v *prop—as in "shore up"* 60; n 52
shore dinner n 259
shore leave n 266
shore patrol n 283
shorebird n 165
shorefront n 279
shoreless adj *limitless* 160
shoreline n 236

short v 237
short n *as in "the long and the short"* 135
short adj *opp. of long* 24
short circuit n 237
short cut/shortcut n *obs. short journey* 123
short division n *opp. of long division* 256
short end n *as in "short end of the stick"* 277
short list n 293
short ribs n 280
short run n 269
short shrift n 133
short sight n *myopia* 257
short story n Literature/Writing 264
short subject n Movies/TV/Radio 305
shortage n 251
shortbread n 183
shortcake n 122
shortchange v (Am) Finances/Money 264
short-circuit v Energy 237
shortcoming n 103
shortcut v 284; n 123
shorten v 60
shortening n Food 197
shortfall n 270
shorthair n *type of cat* 272
shorthand n/adj 153
shorthanded adj *understaffed* 152
shorthanded adj *obs. inefficient* 163
short-lived adj 130
short-order cook n 281
short-range adj 252
shortsighted adj 151
short-tempered adj 261
short-term adj 278
short-term memory n 317
shortwave adj/n 272
short-winded adj 68
shorty n 268
shot n *shotgun ammunition* 203
shot n *nasty remark* 20
shot n *injection* 286
shot n *act of shooting* 20
shot put n 263
shotgun n (Am) 203
shotgun house n 297
shotgun wedding n (Am) 289
should v 28
shoulder n Food 34

shoulder v *assume responsibility* 32
shoulder n 13
shoulder n *of a road* 317
shoulder v *press against with shoulder* 32
shoulder bag n 280
shoulder belt n 317
shoulder blade n 32
shoulder patch n 303
shoulder strap n 168
shoulder weapon n 300
shouldn't contr 227
shout n/v 85
shout song n 290
shouting distance n 293
shove v 26; n 85
shove it interj 307
shove off v (Am) *leave* 231
shovel n/v 16
shovel-nosed adj 182
show n *formal entertainment* 50
show v *obs. inspect, read* 55
show n/v *display* 55
show n *pageant* 50
show bill n 214
show business n 228
show off v 204
show trial n 300
show up v 234
show window n (Am) 226
show-and-tell n 308
showbiz n 228, 305
showboat v *show off* 314
showboat n/v (Am) 246
showcase n/v 232
showdown n *showing cards in poker* 294
showdown n *confrontation* 294
shower n *shower bath* 196
shower n/v *as in "rain shower"* 12
shower n *as in "baby shower"* 289
shower bath n 196
showgirl n 228
showman n 187
show-me adj (Am) 278
show-off n *display* 293
show-off n *showy person* 293
showplace n 135, 269
showroom n 152
showstopper n 290
showy adj 190
shrapnel n 215
shred n/v 22
shredded wheat n 259

shrew n *arch. villain of either sex* 47

shrew n 11

shrew n *shrewish woman* 47

shrewd adj *var. obs., arch. meanings of ominous, evil* 108

shrewd adj *mischievous* 108

shrewd adj *sagacious* 108

shrewish adj 47

shriek n/v 104

shriekmark n *!* 245

shrike n *type of bird* 105

shrill adj 90

shrill n/v *shriek* 58

shrimp n Animals 31

shrimp n Insults 82

shrimp pink n 271

shrine n 20

shrink v 26

shrink n *psychiatrist* 317

shrink away v 26

shrinking violet n *shy person* 102

shrink-wrap n/v 316

shrivel v 141

shroud n *as in "death shroud"* 123

shroud v 94

shroud n *obs. clothes* 123

shroud n *covering* 123

shroud n *obs. shelter* 123

shrub n 10

shrubbery n 181

shrug v *obs. fidget* 68

shrug v *as in "shrug your shoulders"* 68

shrug n 68

shrug off 68

shtik n Performing Arts 311

shtup v *slang have sex* 317

shuck n/v *husk* 164

shucks interj 230

shudder n/v 58

shuffle n/v *rearrange, walk slowly* 141

shuffleboard n 108

shun v *var. meanings of hide from* 60

shun v *avoid* 60

shunpike n (Am) 242

shush interj/n/v 292

shut adj/v 27

shut-eye n 268

shut-in adj/n (Am) 233

shut-in adj 233

shutter n *photographic shutter* 167

shutter n *as in "window shutters"* 167

shutterbug n 301

shuttle n/v 117

shuttle n *bobbin* 33

shuttle n *type of vehicle* 261; v 261

shuttle diplomacy n 324

shuttlecock n 108

shy adj *bashful* 169

shy v *as in "shy away"* 150

shy adj *skittish* 169

shy adj *cautious* 169

shyster n (Am) 230

Siamese cat n 237

Siamese fighting fish n 296

Siamese twin n 226

sib adj/n *kin* 18

Siberian husky n 285

sibilant adj 178

sibilate v 178

sibilous adj 178

sibling n *brother or sister* 275

sibling n *obs. gen. relative* 275

sic v *as in "sic the dogs"* 235

sic adv *as in "keeping the piece (sic)"* 251

sick adj *mental sense* 14

sick adj *phys. sense* 14

sick and tired adj 204

sick bay n 211

sick day n 227, 318

sick headache n *migraine* 196

sick leave n 227

sick pay n 264

sickbed n 68

sicken v *disgust* 32

sicken v *make ill* 14, 32

sickening adj 14, 32

sickie n Slang 320

sickle adj/n Tools 16

sickle-cell anemia n 286

sickly adj 33

sickness n 14

sicko n Slang 320

side v *as in "side with"* 142

side n 22

side arm n 174

side by side adv 47

side dish n 183

side drum n *snare drum* 201

side effect n 269

side road n 242

side street n 149

sidearm adj *as in "a sidearm throw"* 273

sidebar n Literature/Writing 305

sideboard n 69

sideburns n (Am) Fashion/Style 260

sidecar n *on a motorcycle* 224

sidekick n (Am) 278

sidelong adj 92

sideman n (Am) 299

sidereal adj *astral* 146

sidereal time n 210

sidesaddle adv/n 100

sideshow n (Am) 228

sidesplitting adj 243

sidestep v (Am) 278

sideswipe n/v (Am) 278

sidetrack v 271

sidetrack n (Am) 224

sidewalk n 184

side-whiskers n 212

sidewinder n Animals 255

sidewinder n *type of punch* 229

sidle v 180

siege n/v *type of attack* War/Military/Violence 45

siege mentality n 262

sierra n 118

siesta n 167

sieve n/v 16

sift v 26

sift v 26

sigh v 37

sight n *ability to see* 22; v 22

sight n *something to be seen* 22

sight n *pupil of the eye* 22

sight n/v *as in "gunsight"* 123

sight gag n 305

sightless adj *blind* 32

sightless adj *invisible* 32

sightly adj 92

sight-read v 276

sightsee v 213

sightseeing n 213

sign n *as in "street sign"* 77

sign v *portent* 42

sign v *place signature on* 41

sign n *gesture* 42

sign v *mark with a sign* 41

sign language n 227

sign of the cross n 43

sign of the zodiac n 250

signage n 323

signal n/v 85

signal v 85

signalman n 185

signatory n 250

signature n 110

signboard n 153

signee n 313

signet n *official seal* 44

signet ring n 174

significance n 50

significancy n 50

significant adj 50

significant other n 311

significantly adv 50

signify v 57

signpost n *the post itself* 157

signpost n *post and sign* 157

silage n 259

silence n/v 48

silencer n 136

silent n *type of movie* 291

silent adj 103

silent auction n 311

silent partner n (Am) 226

silentious adj *typically silent* 103

silhouette n *type of portrait* 201; v 201

silicon n 209

silicone n 272

silicone rubber n 305

silk n *jockey's gear* 16

silk n *type of fiber, cloth* 16

silk hat n 223

silk stocking n *bigshot* 269

silken adj 24

silkscreen n/v 290

silk-stocking adj 269

silkweed n (Am) *milkweed* 194

silkworm n 11

silky adj 24

sill n 14

silly adj *foolish* 124

silly adj *blessed* 124

silly adj *ignorant* 124

silly adj *weak* 124

silly adj *innocent* 124

silly n 124

silly season n 246

silo n 223

silt n/v 63

silt v 63

silver adj *dulcet* 115

silver adj/n *the metal* 10

silver n *the color* 103

silver bullet n 300

silver certificate n 264

silver lining n 250

silver maple n 193

silver paper n *tin foil* 206

silver perch n (Am) 210

silver salmon n 254

silver screen n 282

silver spoon n 216

silver standard n (Am) 227

silverfish n 181

ENGLISH THROUGH THE AGES

solicit v 96

solicit v obs. cause anxiety 96

solicit v as in "solicit prostitutes" 96

solicitation n 96

solicitor n lawyer 131

solicitous adj 96

solicitress n woman who solicits 131

solicitrix n prostitute 151

solid adj as in "solid color" 191

solid adj as opposed to liquid, or hollow 88, 90

solid n 88

solid adj strong, as in "solid support" 252

solid adj as in "solid food" 90

solid adj pure, as in "solid gold" 191

solid geometry n 182

solidarism n 177

solidarity n 177

solidify v 90

solid-state adj 309

soliloquacity n 42

soliloquize v 42

soliloquy n 42

solipsism n 244

solitaire n type of gem setting 71

solitaire n Games/Fun/Leisure 199

solitaire n reclusive person 199

solitary adj/n 55

solitary n 203

solitary confinement n 203

solitude n 52

solo n composition for one 173

solo n performance of solo 173

solo v 173

soloist n 173

solstice n 31

solution n "solid dissolved in liquid" 82

solution n as in "solution to a problem" 82

solve v dissolve 117

solve v obs. untie 117

solve v as in "solve a problem" 117

solvency n 187

solvent n 177

solvent adj 152

somber adj 198

sombrero n 197

sombrero n type of umbrella 197

sombrous adj 198

somebody n someone of note 130

somedeal adv somewhat 28

somersault n/v 108

something n as in "isn't that something?" 136

somewhere n 159

somewhither adv 98

somnambulant adj 196

somnambulate v 196

somnambulism n 196

somnolent adj 92

son n 18

son of a bitch interj/n 175

son of a gun interj 189

sonar n 308

sonata n 173

song n 19

song and dance n (Am) 201

song cycle n 265

song sparrow n (Am) 209

song thrush n 165

songbird n 194

songbird n slang songstress 194

songfest n 282

songsmith n 201

songster n 19, 187

songstress 19, 187

songwriter n 214

sonhood n 126

sonic adj 285

sonic barrier n 296

sonic boom n 313

son-in-law n 40

sonnet n 128

sonneteer n 128

sonny n 233

sonogram n 310

sonography n 310

sonship n 126

sooey interj 267

sooner or later adv 133

soot n 22

sooth adj/n true/truth 22

soothe v 180

soothe v obs. flatter 180

soothe v obs. prove 180

soothfast adj truthful 17

soothing adj 17

soothsayer n prognosticator 52

soothsayer n obs. truthteller 52

sop v 27

sophisticate n 291, 319

sophisticate v dilute, adulterate 94

sophisticate v corrupt with devious reasoning 143

sophisticate v rob of simplicity 94, 163

sophisticate v bring culture to 94, 319

sophisticated adj 94, 163, 319

sophistication n 94, 163, 319

sophistry n 39

sophomore n Education 173

sophomoric adj (Am) 217

sopor n sleep 178

soporific adj causing sleep 178

soporific adj sleepy 178

soporific n 178

sopping adj 115

soprano adj/n Music 188

sorbet n 122

sorcerer n 47

sorceress n 47

sorcerous adj 47

sorcery n 47

sordid adj 139

sordid adj obs. lowly 139

sordid adj obs. med. discharging pus, etc. 139

sore adj great, as in "sore amazement" 24

sore n 14

sore adj 24

sore n var. obs. meanings of gen. pain 14

sore adj angry 24, 170

sore throat n 167

sorehead n 231

sorghum n 119

sororal adj Family/Relations/Friends 244

sorority n 111, 202, 276

sorority n gen. women's group 111

sorority n spec. university women's group 111

sorrel n type of horse 31

sorrel adj 55; n 31, 55

sorrel n type of plant 64

sorrow n/v 17

sorry adj remorseful, apologetic 17

sorry adj sorrow-making, pitiful 17

sorry adj as in "feel sorry for" 17

sort v obs. assign 94

sort n 49

sort v 94

sortie n 203

sortilege n 81

SOS n 276

sot n 20

sot n dullard 20

sottery n 144

sottish adj 144

soufflé n 211

soufflé n med. type of body sound 211

soul n obs. life itself 22

soul n embodiment, as in "soul of wit" 22

soul n 22

soul n person, as in "poor soul" 22

soul adj/n pertaining to black experience 313

soul brother n 313

soul food n (Am) 316

soul kiss n 304

soul mate n 213

soul music n (Am) 318

soul sister n 313

soulful adj 178

soul-searching adj 151

sound adj valid, well-reasoned, as in "a sound decision" 54

sound adj financially sound 54

sound v make sound 58

sound n type of inlet 9

sound n 50

sound n obs. music 50, 290

sound v fathom 97

sound adj in good shape 54

sound n musical style 50, 290

sound v cause to make sound 58

sound barrier n 296

sound bite n 324

sound effects n 276

sound off v 278

soundalike n 321

sounding board n 189

soundman n 289

sounds n 312

soundstage n 299

soundtrack n 290

soundwave n 219

soup n 34

soup kitchen n 222

soup up v 298

soup-and-fish n slang formalwear 280

soupcon n 195

soupspoon n 183

sour adj opp. of sweet 25

sour n (Am) type of drink 241

sour adj spoiled, cantankerous 25

sour v 241

sour ball n 259

sour cream n (Am) 212

sour grapes n 198
sour mash n (Am) 259
sourcebook n (Am) 264
sourdough n 34
sourpuss n 301
sousaphone n 265
souse n *drinking spree* 283
souse n *drunk* 283
soused adj 283
south n 9
South Pole 63
southeaster n Weather 194
southerly n Weather 302
southern hemisphere 145, 193
southern lights n 194
southpaw n (Am) 267
southwester n Weather 220
souvenir n 202
sou'wester n *type of raingear* 223
sovereign n *ruler* 44
sovereign n *type of coin* 110
sovereignty n 44
soviet n Government 282
sow v 26
sow n *fat woman* 11
sow n Animals 11
sowbelly n 241
soy n 168
soy sauce n 197
soybean n 211
sozzled adj Slang 267
spa n 148
space n *outer space* 165
space n *unoccupied place* 63
space n *break between words* 172
space n *area* 29
space heater n 285
space opera n 305
space platform 298
space shuttle n (Am) 317
space station n 298
space-age adj 308
spacecraft n 288
spaced-out adj (Am) 301
spaceflight n 298
spaceman n 298
spaceport n 298
spaceship n 261
spacesuit n 288
spacewoman 298
spacey adj 301
spacious adj 90
spack adj *arch. quick and wise* 39
spade n/v 16
spade n *on cards* 126

spadework n *legwork* Slang 204
spaghetti n 241
spaghetti strap n 323
spaghetti western n 319
spaghettini n 287
span n *time, distance from one end to another* 120
span n *space between thumb and little finger* 120
span n *part of a bridge* 120
spang adv (Am) *directly, smack* 234
spangle n/v 86
spaniel n 31
Spanish moss n (Am) 210
Spanish omelette n 259
Spanish rice n 287
spank v 191
spanking n 191
spanking adv *as in "brand spanking new"* 178; adj 178
spanking n *corporal punishment* 248
span-new adj 54
spar n *pole* 52
spar v *box* 200
spar v *fight with spurs, as in a cockfight* 200
spare v *refrain from killing, punishing, etc.* 26
spare adj *extra, in excess* 137
spare adj *simple* 321
spare v *refrain from other things, as in "spare me the details"* 26
spare adj *duplicate, in reserve* 92
spare n *something extra* 158
spare v *forgo, as in "spare expense"* 26
spare adj *spartan* 25
spare tire n 316
spareribs n 122
sparge v *spatter* 139
sparge v *splash* 139
sparhawk 65
spark *arch.* 143
spark n/v *love* 185
spark n 22
spark *arch.* 103
spark n/v *catalyst* 22
spark v 185
spark plug n (Brit) 274
sparking plug n (Brit) 274
sparkle n *fig. ebullience* 103
sparkle v 143
sparkle n 103
sparkler n *type of firework* 262

sparkling wine n 167
sparrow n 11
sparrow hawk n 65
sparse adj 206
spartan adj 178
spasm n/v 68
spasm n *fig.* 68
spasmatic adj 167
spasmodic adj *irregular* 167
spasmodic adj *pertaining to spasm* 167
spastic adj/n *med. sense* 195
spastic adj 167
spat n General/Miscellaneous 216
spat n Cloth/Clothing 212
spate n *lit. flood* 63
spate n *fig.* 63
spatial adj 234
spatter v 141
spatula n 106
spawl v *arch. spit* 121
spawn v *fig. engender* 64
spawn n/v Animals 64
spay v 71
spaz n *slang* 195, 320
spaz out 320
speak v *give a speech* 19
speak v *converse* 19
speak v 263
speak v *talk* 19
speak v *indicate relevance, as in "speak to a need"* 19
speakeasy n (Am) 263
speakerphone n (Am) 311
speaking tube n 227
speako n Business/Commerce/Selling 263
spear adj *opp. of distaff* 244
spear n *as in "broccoli spear"* 21
spear n/v War/Military/Violence 21
spear-carrier n Performing Arts 311
speargun n 131
spearhead n 21
spearhead n 80
spearhead v 301
spearmint n 105
spec v 308
special adj/adv 53
special n *as in "blue plate special"* 245
special delivery n (Am) 265
special education n 291
special effects n 299
special theory of relativity n 279

specialist n 250
specialization n 162
specialize v 250
specialize v *concentrate on a specialty* 162
specialize v *make special* 162
specialized adj 251
specialty n *state of being special* 251
specialty n *area of expertise* 251
specialty n *special quality* 251
specialty n 250
speccie n 115
species n *spec. biological grouping* 145
species n *gen. grouping* 145
speciesism n 324
specific adj *peculiar, as in "specific to" someone or something* 160
specific adj *concrete, exact* 206
specific n 160
specify v 58
specimen n *sample* 178
specimen n *scientific use* 178
specimen n *model* 178
specimen n *fig., as in "a fine specimen of a man"* 178
specious adj *ultimately false* 114
specious adj *obs. beautiful* 114
speck n/v 22
speckle n/v 22, 86
speckled trout n (Am) 209
specs n *specifications* 307
specs n *glasses* 69, 210
spectacle n 52
spectacles n *glasses* 69
spectacular adj/n 52, 179
spectate v *see* 135
spectate v *watch a spectator sport* 244
spectate v *gen. watch* 244
spectator n 135
specter n The Fantastic/Paranormal 156
specter n *fig., as in "the specter of bankruptcy"* 156
spectral adj 156, 215
spectral adj *able to see specters* 215
spectrograph n 256
spectrometer n 238
spectroscope n 238
spectroscopy n 238
spectrum n *range of color* 165
spectrum n *arch. specter* 156
speculate v 143

splint n med. sense 53, 68
splinter n/v 53
split v leave 313
split n/v obs. splinter 135
split n/v 135
split v share 180
split adj 135
split v arch. go fast 313
split decision n 308
split end n (Am) 310
split infinitive n 264
split personality n 286
spllt rall n 233
split second n 279
split shift n 305
split-brain adj 311
split-level adj/n 303
split-new adj brand-new 179
split-up n 232
splodge n/v 157
splotch n/v 157
splotch v 157
splurge n spending spree 232
splurge n (Am) big show 232
splurge v 232
spoil v as in "spoil for a fight" 248
spoil v as in "spoil a child" 134
spoil v go bad 168
spoil n gen. reward 46
spoil v ruin 134
spoil n war booty 46
spoilage n 168
spoilsport n 216
spoke n 22
spokeshave n 107
spokesman n 110, 171
spokespeople n 110, 171, 323
spokesperson n 110, 171, 323
spokeswoman n 110, 171
spoliate v 88
spoliation n plunder 88
sponge n/v 14
sponge v 14
sponge bath n 239
sponge cake n 168
sponge rubber n 270
sponsor n financial supporter 176
sponsor n nominator 176
sponsor n esp. godparent 176
sponsor n supporter 176
sponsor v 176, 271
sponsor v 176
spontaneity n 176
spontaneous adj 176
spontaneous combustion n 193
spontaneous generation n 165

spoof n/v type of card game 265
spoof n/v parody 265
spook n/v (Am) The Fantastic/Paranormal 215
spook n spy 215, 307
spook v startle 261
spook v 215
spookery adj 215
spooky 215
spool n/v 33
spool v 33
spoon n/v 33
spoon n obs. splinter 33
spoon v pitch woo 226
spoon bread n (Am) 274
spoonbill n 165
spoonerism n 264
spoon-feed v 148
sporadic adj gen. intermittent 233
sporadic adj med. isolated 233
spore n 219
sporozoan n 254
sport n gaming 126
sport n arch. jest 126
sport n pastime 126
sport adj 126, 244
sport n sportsperson, as in "good sport" 126
sport adj 126
sport shirt n 280
sportfishing n 275
sportif adj 270
sporting adj fair 207
sporting adj obs. playful 207
sporting chance n 269
sporting dog n 200
sporting house n 249
sports car n 288
sports jacket n 303
sports medicine n 238
sportscast n 305
sportsman 199
sportsman n 171, 199
sportsmanship n 185
sportswear n 280
sportswoman n 171, 199
sportswriter n 276
sporty adj sporting 270
sporty adj flashy 270
spot v see 253
spot n situation, as in "a tight spot" 294
spot n pimple 48
spot n little bit, as in "a spot of trouble" 66
spot n blotch 48
spot n small place 63

spot v 48
spot-check n/v 308
spotlight n/v 274
spotted fever n 147
spotted owl n 272
spotty adj intermittent 55
spotty adj spotted 55
spouse v obs. marry 61
spouse n obs. fiancee/fiancee 39
spouse n 39
spout n 85
sprain n/v 147
sprawl v pertaining to things 27
sprawl v pertaining to people 27
sprawl 27
spray n/v as in "water spray" 158
spray gun n 280
spread v 55
spread eagle adj/n/v 133
spreadsheet n type of ledger 318
spreadsheet n computer sense 318
spree n 206
sprig n 30
sprightful adj 139
sprightly adj 139
spring n metal coil 72
spring n effluent water source 29
spring n water source 10
spring v release Slang 268
spring v as in "spring forth," 26
spring n springiness 177
spring n type of season 65
spring n/v leap 61
spring n give, elasticity 177
spring v "spring up"; sprout; bound 26
spring v pay Slang 277
spring n 61
spring chicken n (Am) 221
spring cleaning n 239
spring fever n (Am) 225
spring roll n 303
springboard n lit. and fig. 206
springer spaniel n 255
Springfield rifle n 266
springform pan n 286
springhouse n (Am) cooling-house 197
springtime n fig. beginning 99
springtime n 99
springwater n 99
sprinkle v 94
sprinkler system n 258
sprinkling n smattering 86

sprinkling n the result of sprinkling 86
sprint n/v obs. spring 238
sprint n/v run fast 238
sprite n arch. fig. spriteliness 47
sprite n ghost, pixie 47
spritz n/v (Am) 278
spritzer n 303
sprocket n part of a gear 182
sprocket n element of construction 182
sprout n/v 55
spruce v as in "spruce up" 142
spruce n 64
spruce adj 142
spruce beer n 100
spruce pine 64
spry adj 191
spud n Slang 231
spud n/v 168
spud n potato 168
spumoni n 287
spun glass n 205
spun silk n 197
spun sugar n 70
spun yarn n 71
spunk n tinder 198
spunk n spirit 198
spunk v 198
spunky adj 198
spur n lit. "horse prod" 16
spur n as in "railroad spur" 16
spur n animal claw 16
spur v 16
spurious adj false 160
spurious adj lit. bastard 160
spurn v reject 28
spurn v obs. trip with the foot 28
spur-of-the-moment adj 216
spurt v squirt 141
spurt n/v as in "spurt of energy" 135
sputter v pertaining to things 143
sputter v come to a halt 143
sputter v speak with a sputter 143
sputter n 143
sputum n 166
spy n/v 45
spy satellite n 309
spyglass n 184
squab n 165
squab squat person 195
squab n obs. tyro 165
squabble n/v 157
squabby adj squat 195

squad n 131, 159
squad n *gen. group* 159
squad car n (Am) 300
squad room n 307
squadron n 131
squalid adj 138
squall n/v *squawk* 163
squall n *lit.* 165
squall n *fig. squabble* 165
squalor n 138, 158
squander v *spend* 117
squander v *scatter* 117
squander n 117
square n/v *as in "2 × 2"* 120; adj/v 65
square n *as in "town square"* 164
square n *type of shape* 65
square n *obs. fight* 229
square adj/n *nerd* 307
square adj/n 35
square v *reconcile, jibe* 143
square dance n 246
square knot n 251
square meal n 223
square off v 229
square one n 313
square root n 120
square shooter n 284
square-rigger n 242
squash v *quash* 140
squash n 145
squash v 140
squash n 262
squat v 97
squat adj *short and stocky* 147
squat adj *squatting* 147
squat n 97
squatter v *splash about* 207
squatter n 205
squawk n/v 218
squawk v *slang complain* 218, 230
squawk n 218
squawk box n 305
squeak n 177
squeak v *pertaining to things* 94
squeak v *pertaining to living things* 94
squeak v 230
squeaky-clean adj 320
squeal n/v 58
squeal v *slang tattle* 58
squeal v *inform* 230
squealer n 230
squeam v/n *rare* 73
squeamish adj 73
squeege v *arch.* 224

squeegee n 224
squeeze n/v 141
squeeze v *extract money from* 141
squeeze n *lover* 323
squeeze bottle n 303
squeezebox n (Am) 276
squelch v 162
squench v *quench, extinguish* 97
squib n *lit. firework* 110
squib n *fig. fiery remark* 110
squid n 119
squidge n *the sound mud makes* 254
squiffed adj *drunk* 249
squiffy adj 249
squiggle v 218
squinny v *cry* 253
squint v *look through partially closed eyes* v *look cross-eyed* 143
squint n 143
squire n *servant* 44
squire n *escort* 44
squire n *nobleman* 44
squirearchy n 202
squirm v *lit. wriggle* 180
squirm v *fig.* 180
squirrel v *as in "squirrel away"* 292
squirrel n 31
squirrel monkey n 194
squirrel rifle n 229
squirrelly adj 293
squirt v *squirt into* 61
squirt v *squirt out* 61
squirt n 61
squirt gun n (Am) 213
squish n/v *smoosh* 159
squish n/v *make a squishing sound* 159
squishy adj 159
squizzed adj *drunk* 249
squoosh v 308
SST n 317
st interj *shh* 132
St. Elmo's Fire n 210
stab n *attempt* 134
stab n/v *lit. stabbing* 80
stab n/v *fig. stabbing* 80
stability n *fig.* 52
stability n *lit. fixed* 52
stabilize v 252
stabilizer n 278
stable n/v *lit.* 34
stable n *fig. collection* 34
stable adj 53
stableboy n 185

stablemate n 294
staccato adj 190
stack n/v 50
stack up v 271
stacked adj (Am) Slang 307
stadium n 241
stadium n *stadium-length race course* 241
stadium n *type of distance measure* 241
staff n *type of stick* 16
staff n *group of assistants* 19
staff n 173
staff n *worker pool* 19
staff v 19
staff of life n 156
staff officer n 188
staffer n 172
stag n *male deer* 30
stag adj *male-only* 231
stag beetle n 165
stag film n 319
stage n *boxing ring* 128
stage n *as in "theatrical stage"* 128; v 128, 265; adj 128
stage n *fig. phase, step* 50
stage n *rare story of a building* 128
stage n *phys. phase, step* 50
stage door n 201
stage fright n 265
stage left, stage right n 299
stage whisper n 246
stagecoach n 149
stagecraft n 265
stagestruck adj 214
stagflation n 318
stagger v *arrange in a staggered way* 97
stagger v *astonish* 97
stagger v 97
staggering adj *astonishing* 169
staghound n 181
staging area n 308
stagnant adj *lit. motionless* 178
stagnant adj *fig. undeveloping* 178
stagnate v 178
staid adj 129
stain n/v *spot* 135
stain v *spot; taint* 94
stain v *obs. bleach* 94
stain n *staining material* 205
stain v *color, dye* 94
stain v 94
stained glass n 201
stainless adj *unstained* 138
stainless adj *stainproof* 271

stainless n *stainless flatware* 303
stainless steel n 280
stair n *stairway* 15
stair n *individual stair* 15
staircase n 148
stairstep n 15, 222
stairway 148
stairway n 148, 196
stairwell n 148, 280
stake n/v *savings* 245
stake n/v *wager* 75
stake n/v *spike* 23
stake n *interest, as in "a stake in the outcome"* 75
stake race n 262
stake truck n 275
stakeout n 307
stalactite n 164
stalag n 300
stalagmite n 164
stale adj *aged, pertaining to liquor* 92
stale adj 92
stale n/v *urinate* 68
stale v 92
stalemate n/v *spec. to chess* 199
stalemate n/v *gen. impasse* 199
stalk v *walk haughtily* 58
stalk n 51
stalk v *pursue* 58
stalking horse n 108
stall n *obs. gen. place* 14
stall n/v *delay* 103
stall n *cell* 14
stall n *hesitation, as in "an airplane stall"* 284
stallion n *male horse* 39
stallion n 64
stallion n *promiscuous person* 39, 64
stalwart adj/n 90
stamina n 114
stammer n/v 14
stamp n/v *imprint* 141
stamp n *as in "rubber stamp"* 88
stamp v *as in "stamp a coin"* 97
stamp n *influence, affect, as in "shows the stamp of oppression"* 136
stamp v *crush* 55
stamp v *place a stamp on* 207
stamp v *walk heavily* 97
stamp n *as in "postage stamp"* 239

stroll n/v *walk* 169

stroll v *obs. move nomadically* 169

strong adj *powerful* 24

strong adv *as in "come on strong"* 24

strong adj *pertaining to pulse* 24

strong adj *healthy* 24

strong adj *able* 24

strong adj *harsh, as in "strong measures"* 24

strong adj *pertaining to language* 24

strong adj *defensible* 24

strong adj *as in "strong drink"* 24

strong room n 196

strong suit n 250

strong-arm adj (Am) 233

strongbox n 178

stronghold n 69

strongman n 246

strong-minded adj 199

strong-willed 199

strop n/v *for sharpening razors* 184

structural adj 233

structure n *organization, composition* 148

structure n *obs. process of construction* 148

structure n *building* 148

structure v 148, 180

strudel n 259

struggle v *fig. and lit. fight* 94

struggle v *try hard* 94

struggle n 94

strum v 201

strumpet n *prostitute* 39

strung out adj (Am) 313

strut v *obs. bloat* 97

strut v *obs. protrude* 97

strut n *support* 122

strut v *swagger* 97

strychnine n 209

stub n *as in "cigar stub," etc.* 10

stub n *as in "check stub"* 10

stub n *tree stump* 10

stubble n *cut growth of grain* 35

stubble n *other types of stubble, as in "beard stubble"* 35

stubborn adj 38

stubby adj *squat* 120

stuc n 122

stucco n *type of exterior covering* 122

stucco n *type of plaster* 122

stuck on adj (Am) *in love with* 262

stuck-up adj 230

stud n *type of ornament* 71

stud n *type of building device* 16

stud n *sexual man* 15

stud n (Am) *attractive man* 262

stud v *as in "star-studded"* 253

stud n Agriculture/ Food-Gathering 15

stud poker n (Am) 244

student n 78

student body n 276

student lamp n (Am) 239

student teacher n 276

studentess rare 78

studhorse n 15

studhorse n *sexual man* 15

studhorse poker 244

studied adj 100

studio n *as in "artist's studio"* 211

studio n *place for filmmaking* 211

studio apartment n 273

studio couch n 297

studious adj Education 42

studious adj *very careful* 42

study n *type of room* 34

study n/v *examination, scrutiny* 74

study n/v *learning* 42

study n/v *obs. uncertainty* 39

study n *preliminary* 201

study n *the thing studied* 42

study n/v *revery* 39

study hall n 228

stuff v *cram* 104

stuff n *what composes, as in "the stuff of dreams"* 136

stuff v 122

stuff n *miscellanea* 294

stuff n *as in "knows his stuff"* 293

stuff n *obs. edible stuffing* 70

stuff n *as in "the right stuff"* 134

stuffed shirt n (Am) 283

stuffing n 122

stuffing n *as in "knock the stuffing out of"* 113

stuffy adj *unventilated* 217

stuffy adj *haughty* 217

stuffy adj *obs. stuffed* 217

stumble n/v 59

stumblebum n *clod* 301

stumbling block n 133

stump v *puzzle, confound* 225

stump n *stub* 32

stump n *as in "tree stump"* 71

stump v *dare* 225

stump n *remains of amputated limb* 32

stump v *campaign* 247

stumpy adj 139

stun n/v 58

stun gun n 319

stunner n *good-looker* 230

stunning adj *confounding* 169

stunning adj *gorgeous* 169

stunt n/v (Am) *as in "motorcycle stunt"* 265

stunt v *inhibit* 179

stunt v 265

stunt v *irk* 179

stuntman n (Am) 291, 305

stuntwoman n (Am) 291, 305

stupe n *blockhead* 204

stupefy v *make stupid* 74

stupefy v *stun* 74

stupendous adj 137

stupid 108, 189

stupid adj 108

stupor n 85

stuporous adj 85

sturdy adj *solid* 92

sturdy adj *obs. fierce* 92

sturgeon n 30

stut n *arch. stutter* 69

stutter n/v 116

sty n *type of inflammation* 147

sty n *pen* 15

styglan adj 137

style n *way of doing things* 52

style n *fashionable way of doing things* 52

style n *stylus* 53

style n *as in "impressionist style"* 187

style adj/n *fashion* 197

stylist n 201

stylize v 271

stymie n/v 252

styptic adj 90

styptic pencil n 273

suasible adj 98

suasion n *persuasion* 98

suave adj *nice* 107

suave adj 107

suaviloquence n *suave talk* 107

sub n *sub(marine)* 283

sub n *sub(ordinate)* 230

sub n/v *sub(stitute)* 230

subatomic adj 272

subbasement n 273

subchaser n 283

subclass n 217

subcompact n 317

subconscious adj/n 225

subconscious n 225

subcontinent n 236

subcontract n/v 215

subcontractor n 215

subculture n *sociological sense* 254

subculture n *biological sense* 254

subcutaneous adj 166

sub-deb 282

subdebutante n 282

subdivide v 96

subdivision n *gen* 241

subdivision n *housing development* 241

subdolous adj *arch. cunning* 125

subduce v *obs. subtract* 144

subdue v 94

subdued adj 94

subfreezing adj 308

subgum n *type of Chinese dish* 287

subheading, subhead n 264

subhuman n/adj 207

subhuman n 207

subject n *topic* 88

subject n *grammatical sense* 172

subject adj/n/v *as in "subject of the crown"* 44

subject matter n *phys. source material* 133

subject matter n *topic* 133

subjective adj *opp. of objective* 206

subjugate v *take control over* 96

subjugate v *defeat* 96

sublease n/v 196, 222

sublet n/v 196

subliminal adj 270

submachine gun n 283

submarine n 160

submarine n/v 188

submariner n 188

submerge v 161

submerse v 97

submersible adj/n 252

subminiature adj 308

submiss adj *submissive* 144

submission n 82

submissive adj 138

submit v 82

subordinate adj 92

subplot n 282

summate v *sum up* 205, 256
summation n *summary* 205
summation n *addition* 205
summer n 12
summer cypress n 193
summer kitchen n 241
summer school n (Am) 247
summer squash n 193
summer stock n 290
summer theater n 214
summerhouse n 15
summertime n 65
summit n *phys. top* 88
summit n *summit conference* 319
summit n *fig. top* 88
summon v 56
summons n *gen. and leg.* 46
summons v 46
sumo n 263
sump n *pit* 164
sump n *swamp* 164
sump pump n 261
sumptuous adj *luxurious* 103
sumptuous adj *obs. expensive* 103
sun n *gen. star* 12
sun n *sunlight* 12
sun v *sunbathe* 61
sun n *the star* 12
sun dog n *parhelion* 146
sun parlor 280
sunbathe v 143
sunbeam n 10
sunblock n 322
sunbow n *akin to rainbow* 210
sunburn n/v 69
sunburnt 69
sunburst n 210
sun-cured adj (Am) 259
sundae n 259
Sunday n 12
Sunday best n 149
Sunday punch n (Am) 291
Sunday school n 202
Sunday-go-to-meeting adj (Am) 231
sunder v 21
sundial n 119
sundown n 146
sundress n 303
sundries n *miscellanea* 196
sundry adj *obs. discrete* 54
sundry adj *miscellaneous* 54
sunfast adj 295
sunfish n 146
sunflower n 118
sunglass n 212

sunlamp n 258
sunlight n 29
sunny-side up adj 274
sunporch n (Am) 280
sunrise n 31
sunroof n 310
sunroom n (Am) 280
sunscreen n 183
sunset n *fig.* 65
sunset n 65
sunshine n 29
sunshine law n 324
sunspot n *skin spot caused by the sun* 194
sunspot n *spot on the sun* 194
sunstroke n 238
sunsuit n 287
suntan n/v 273
sunup n (Am) 182
sup v *eat* 34
sup v *sip* 15
super adj 271
super n *superintendent, supervisor* 226
superable adj *overcomeable* 160
superb adj *stately* 191
superb adj *excellent* 191
supercharger n 285
supercilious adj 107
supercluster n 285
supercollider n 326
supercomputer n 315
superconductivity n 279
supercontinent n 309
supercool v 271
super-duper adj 301
superego n 281
superficial adj 91
superficiality n 91
superfluous adj 91
supergalaxy n 285
supergroup n 318
superhero n 282
superhighway n (Am) 288
superhuman adj 160
superimpose v 208
superintendent n 126
superior adj/n 90
superior n 88
superior court n 175
superioress n 88
superlative adj/n 90
superliner n 281
superman n 278
supermarket n (Am) 289
supermart n 318
supernatural adj 81
supernatural, the 203

supernaturalism n 203
supernaturals n *supernatural beings* 203
supernature n 203
supernature n *the supernatural* 230
supernova n 285
superordinate adj *opp. of subordinate* 160
superpower n *great power* 306
superpower n *powerful nation* 306
super-real n *surreal, beyond the real* 320
supersaver n (Am) 323
supersensible adj *supernatural* 203
supersensory adj 203
supersensual adj 203
superstar n (Am) 291
superstition n 47
superstore n 305
superstructure n 148
supertanker n 288
superterranean adj *opp. of subterranean* 164
supervise v *be a supervisor* 142
supervise v 75
supervise v *obs. read over* 142
supervision n 75, 142
supervisor n 75, 142
superwoman n 278
supine adj 92
supper n 34
supper club n 289
supplant v *obs. overthrow* 58
supplant v 58
supple adj/v 54
supplement n/v 85, 234
supplemental adj 85
supply n *stock* 136
supply v *obs. supply troops* 93
supply v *provide supplies, etc.* 93
supply v *obs. assist* 93
supply n *supplying* 136
supply-side adj 323
support v *provide fig. support* 61
support v *tolerate* 61
support v *as in "support a family"* 97
support n *phys. support* 177
support v *provide evidence for, as in "support a claim"* 207
support n 61, 97, 207
support group n 317
support hose n 316
support stocking 316

support system n 323
supporter n 86
supporter n Cloth/Clothing 260
supportive adj 61, 138
supposable adj *conceivable* 161
suppose v *obs. believe* 125
suppose v *obs. suspect* 125
suppose v *assume, as in "suppose you do go"* 39
suppose v *as in "you're supposed to be on time"* 180
suppose v *presume* 39, 125
supposed adj 100
suppository n 68
suppress v *stop* 94
suppress v *restrain, as in "suppress laughter"* 94
suppression n 94
suppressor n 94
supremacist n 308
supremacy n 114
supreme adj 103
Supreme Being n 173
supreme court n 188
surcease v 96
surcharge n/v 76
surcoat n *type of outer coat* 35
sure adj *certain* 54
sure adj *obs. safe, protected* 54
sure adj *guaranteed* 54
sure adj *reliable* 54
sure adv 54
sure enough adv/adj 113
sure thing n (Am) 231
surefire adj 278
surefooted adj 147
surehanded adj 286
surely adv *as in "surely you jest"* 92
surely adj *obs. without risk* 92
surety bond n 281
surf v Sports 289
surf n Natural Things 164
surf and turf n 323
surf casting n 289
surf fish n (Am) 255
surface n 157
surface v *apply a surface* 207
surface v *fig. arise* 207
surface v *come to the surface* 207
surface adj 157
surface n *fig.* 157
surface tension n 255
surface-to-air adj 307
surfbird n (Am) 220
surfboard n 226

tax stamp n 290
taxation n 41
tax-deductible adj 311
tax-exempt adj 290
taxi n (Am) 275
taxi v 275, 280
taxi dancer n *dancer on the meter* 291
taxi stand n 288
taxicab n/v 275
taxidermy n 213
taximeter n 261
taxing adj 207
taxonomy n *study of classification* 210
taxpayer n 214
TB n 279
T-ball n 323
T-bill n (Am) 323
T-bone n 280
tea n 167
tea n *type of social event* 202
tea bag n 274
tea ball n 258
tea caddy n 196
tea cake n (Am) 223
tea garden n 211
tea gown n *gown for afternoon entertaining* 260
tea party n 202
tea room n 196
tea rose n 219
tea service n 106
tea set n 222
tea table n 167
tea time n 202
tea towel n 239
tea tray n 196
tea wagon n 286
teaberry n 194
teach v *educate, show, demonstrate* 19
teacher n 19
teachers college n 276
teacher's pet n 282
teach-in n 319
teaching hospital n 310
teacup n 167
teahouse n 171
teak n 164
teakettle n 184
teakwood n 164
teal n *the color* 30, 295
teal n *type of duck* 30
teal blue 295
team n *applied to people* 21
team n *as in "team of horses"* 21

team n (Am) *arch. descendents* 18
team v/adj 21
team handball n 317
team player n (Am) 269
teammate n 284
teamster n *horse-team driver* 200
teamster n *truck driver* 200
teamwork n 232
teapot n 167
tear n/v fig. 17
tear v *as in "the loss tears him up"* 26
tear v fig., *as in "tear yourself away"* 26
tear n/v *in crying* 17
tear v *as in "tear down"* 26
tear v *as in "tear around"* 26
tear n *spree, binge, as in "on a tear"* 249
tear v *rip* 26
tear gas n/v 283
tear sheet n 290
tearaway n (Brit) *rebel* 270
tearaway adj 270
teardrop n 198
tearjerker n 292
teary adj 17
tease n 177
tease v *tease sexually* 262
tease v *as in "tease hair"* 27
tease n/v *fray* 27
tease n/v *make fun* 162
tease v *be a sexual tease* 27, 162, 262; n 262
tease v *bait, provoke* 27
teaspoon n 167
teaspoon n *teaspoonful* 167
teat n *artificial teat* 31
teat n *The Body* 31
tec n *detective* 267
teched adj 288
techie n 322
technetronic adj 315
technic n *arch. pertaining to art* 153
technical adj *detailed* 252
technical adj *knowledgeable* 252
technical adj *using technical terms* 252
technical knockout n *TKO* 289
technicality n 217
technician n *knowledgeable person* 226
technician n *operator of technical equipment* 226
technician n *skilled person* 226

technique n 217
technobabble n 264
technocracy n 282
technocrat n 282
technofear n 315
technological 237
technology 237
technology, technological n, adj *describing the arts* 153
technomania n 315
technophile n 315
technophobia n 315
techno-pop n 324
techous adj *touchy* 132
tectonic adj 254
tectonic adj *gen. of building* 254
tectonics n 245, 255
tectonics n *architectural science* 255
teddy n (Am) *type of lingerie* 287
teddy bear n 275
teddy boy n *type of juvenile delinquent* 312
tedious adj 90
tedium n 90
tee n/v *golf tee* 171
tee off v 262
teed off adj 311
teem v obs. *give birth* 143
teem v 143
teen adj/n *teenager* 210, 285
teen n obs. *injury* 14
teen v *annoy* 14
teenage adj 285
teenaged 285
teenager n 285
teener n *teenager* 256
teener 285
teens n 120
teensy adj 268
teensy-weensy 267, 268
teeny adj 216
teenybop n 315
teenybopper n, adj 315
teeny-weeny adj 267
teeter n/v 51
teeter-totter n/v (Am) 275
teethe v 66
teething ring n (Am) 258
teetotal, teetotaler, teetotalism adj/v, n, n 229
tehee interj 47
tehee v/n 47
tektite n *type of meteorite* 272
telebanking n 327
telecast n/v 299
telecommunication n 227

telecommuting n 323
teleconferencing n 302
telecopier n *fax machine* 318
telecourse n 305
telefilm n 299
telegenic adj 299
telegram n (Am) 201, 246
telegram 201
telegram v 246
telegraph n 201
telegraph n *type of semaphore* 201
telegraphese n 264
telekinesis n 267
telemarketing n 323
telemeter n/v 238
telemetry n 238
teleology n 182
telepath 267
telepathy, telepathic n, adj 267
telephone n *type of ship communication device* 264
telephone n *type of loudspeaker* 264
telephone n *modern sense* 264
telephone v 264
telephone book n 282
telephone booth n (Am) 265
telephone box n (Brit) 276
telephone number n 265
telephoto adj/n 265
telephotography n 265
teleplay n 312
teleport v 300
teleportation n 300
teleprinter n 288
telescope n 149
telescope v 253
teleshopping n 327
teletext n 323
telethon n 305
teletypewriter, teletype n 276
televangelist n 324
teleview v *watch TV* 299
televise v 291
television n 291
television n *seeing at a distance* 291
televisionary n 293
televisual adj 319
telex n/v 299
telex v 299
tell v *count* 28
tell n *mound, hill* 236
tell v obs. *list* 27
tell v *as in "tell him what to do"* 27
tell v *tattle* 27

tell v *tattle* 295
tell v *recognize* 27
tell v 27
tell off v 218
tell-all n 311
teller n 101
telling adj 139
telltale adj/n 114
telluric adj *earthly* 234
tellurium n 234
telly n (Brit) 299
telpherage n *electrical transportation* 261
temblor n (Am) *earthquake* 254
temerarious adj 72
temerity n 72
temerity n *chance* 72
temp n/v *temporary* 299
temper n *arch. compromise* 73
temper n *calmness* 73
temper n *tendency toward anger* 73, 225
temper n *placidity* 225
temper v 27
temper n *gen. mood* 73, 225
temper tantrum n 288
tempera n 228
temperament n Emotions/Characteristics 213
temperament n *obs. blend* 213
temperament n *obs. temperature* 213
temperament n *weather conditions* 213
temperamental adj Emotions/Characteristics 213
temperance n *not drinking alcohol* 229
temperance n *obs. nice weather* 37
temperance n *self-discipline* 37
temperance movement n 247
temperate adj *not extreme, physically or emotionally* 88
temperate adj *of mild temperature* 88
temperate adj 37
temperate rain forest n 285
temperate zone n 118
temperature n *arch. complexion* 166
temperature n 166
temperature n *obs. something mixed* 166
temperature n *obs. temperament* 166
tempest n/v Weather 31

tempestuous adj 31
template n *shaping tool* 212
temple n *template* 212
temple n *Mormon church* 19
temple n *synagogue* 19
temple n *facial feature* 32
temple n *place of worship* 19
tempo n 173
tempo n *gen. pace* 173
temporal The Body 256
temporal adj *describing time* 43 65
temporal adj *secular* 43, 65
temporal adj *of present life* 43
temporal lobe n 256
temporaneous *arch.* 43
temporaries n *obs. temporal things* 137
temporary adj 115
temporary n 227
temporary adj *obs. temporal* 115
temporize v *delay* 141
temporize v *compromise* 141
tempt v *test* 36
tempt v, n *entice* 36
temptation n 36
tempter n 126
tempting adj 92
temptress n 126
tempura n 280
ten n 12
tenable adj *fig.* 138
tenable adj *defensible* 138
tenacious adj 73
tenacity n *toughness* 73
tenacity n 73
tenant n 33
tenant n *property owner* 33
tenant v 33
tenant farmer n 184
ten-cent store n (Am) 275
tend v *pay attention to* 55
tend v *fig. be inclined* 59
tend v *obs. listen to* 55
tend v *obs. offer, tender* 59
tend v *cultivate, take care of* 55
tend v *phys. lean, be inclined* 59
tendance n 55
tendency n 158
tender adj *gentle, loving* 53
tender n *as in "legal tender"* 200
tender adj *soft* 53
tender adj *immature* 53
tender v 183
tender adj *frail* 53
tender n/v *offer* 117

tender v 53
tenderfoot n (Am) 231
tenderhearted adj 108
tenderize v 53, 183
tenderloin n (Am) *as in "tenderloin district"* Slang 268
tenderloin n (Am) 223
tender-minded adj 150
tenderometer n 296
tendinitis n 257
tendon n 66
tendon of Achilles n 256
tendril n 105
tenebres *obs. darkness* 98
tenebrific *arch.* 98
tenebrous adj *dark, gloomy* 98
tenement n *leg. property* 69
tenement n *residence building* 69
tenement n *spec. type of building* 69
tenement house n 239
tenet n 85
ten-gallon hat n 287
Tennessee walking horse n (Am) 296
tennies n Cloth/Clothing 260, 310
tennis n *modern form of the game* 40
tennis n *arch. form of the game* 40
tennis elbow n 257
tennis shoe n 260
tennist n 298
tenor n *tenor singer* 77, 246
tenor n *gist, tone* 50
tenorist n 246
tenpenny nail n 100
tenpin n 126
tenpins n 126
tense n *as in "verb tense"* 41
tense adj 106
tense adj *applied to people* 178, 213
tense adj *applied to things* 178, 213
tense v 178, 213
tensiometer n 279
tension n *as in "high-tension wire"* 210
tension n *mental tension* 106
tension v 106, 271
tension n *bodily tension* 106
tension 178, 198
tensity n 178
ten-speed n 323
tent n 33

tentacle n 194
tentative adj 138
tenth n 12
tenuous adj 139
tenure n Education 129
tenure n *owning a tenement* 129
tenure-track adj Education 324
tepee n (Am) 183
tepid adj 90
tequila n 223
tercel n *male hawk* 31
tergiversate 134
tergiversation n *equivocation, lying* 134
teriyaki n 316
term v *obs. terminate* 98
term n *length of pregnancy* 31, 247
term n *length of time* 31
term n *arch. end* 31
term n Language and Speaking 76, 214; v 76
term insurance n 258
term paper n 291
termagant adj/n *shrew, bully* 112
terminable adj *endable* 139
terminable adj *obs. determinable* 139
terminal adj *at the end* 217
terminal n *as in "railroad terminal"* 261
terminal n *as in "electrical terminal"* 233
terminal adj *at the boundary* 217
terminal adj *fatal* 257
terminal adj 62
terminal adj *final, last* 217
terminal n *as in "computer terminal"* 309
terminate v *end* 95
terminate v *form a border* 95
terminate v *be part of the end* 95
terminate v *obs. determine* 144
terminate adj 92
terminate v *fire* 95, 323
terminate v *kill* 324
termination n 95
terminator n *nightline* 194
terminology n 214
terminus n 224
terminus n *gen. end* 224
termitarium n 220
termitary n *termite's nest* 194, 219
termite n 194

termless adj *endless* 115
terms n *conditions* 51
terms n *obs. menstruation* 62
terms n *boundary* 62
tern n 165
ternary adj/n *threefold* 65
terra firma n *land* 145
terra incognita n *unexplored territory* 145
terrace n *type of geog. feature* 106
terrace n/v 106
terra-cotta n 183
terra-cotta n *the color* 183
terraculture n 241
terraform v 315
terrain n 193
terrain n *place for horse training* 193
terrain n *fig.* 193
terranean adj *of the earth* 164
terrapin n (Am) 145
terrarium n 254
terrazzo n 258
terrestrial adj *resembling Earth* 89
terrestrial adj *of the Earth* 89
terrestrial adj *land-living* 89
terrestrial adj *of the real world* 89
terrestrial n 89
terrestrious *obs.* 89
terrible adj *atrocious* 72
terrible adj *terrifying* 72
terrible adj *inspiring dread* 72
terrier n 64
terrific adj *very good* 169, 295
terrific adj *terrifying* 169, 295
terrific adj *huge* 169
terrification n 169
terrify v 124
terrifying adj 138
territorial adj *pertaining to territory* 160
territorial adj *protecting territory* 160
territorial court n 247
territorial waters n 229
territory n *as in "sales territory"* 63
territory n *gen. area* 63
territory n *animal's range* 63
territory n *city property* 63
territory n *akin to state* 63
terror n *fig., as in "a terror on the golf course"* 72
terror n 72
terrorism n 203, 248

terrorism n *government by terror* 203
terrorist n 203, 248
terrorize v 203
terry n *as in "terry cloth"* 197
terse adj *curt* 206
terse adj *obs. cultured* 206
terse adj *obs. neat and clean* 206
tertiary adj 178
tesla n 309
tesseract n *cube in four dimensions* 256
test n/v *exam* 291
test n/v *as in "drug test"* 255
test n/v *as in "a test of accuracy"* 135
test n *type of container* 135
test ban n 312
test case n 269
test pattern n 305
test pilot n 281
test tube n 220
testament n *as in "last will and testament"* 45
testament n *as in "Old Testament"* 43
testament n *covenant between God and man* 43
testament n *testimony* 88
testate adj/n 46
testator n 132
testator n *one who dies testate* 46
testatrix n *woman who dies testate* 46, 132
test-drive v 304
testee n 293
testicle n *female ovary* 66
testicle n 66
testify v 93
testimonial adj *as in "testimonial dinner"* 252
testimonial n *honor* 252
testimonial adj *arch. related to testimony, evidentiary* 252
testimonial n *written reference* 252
testimony n Religion 129
testimony n The Law 46
testis n 166
testis n *obs. female ovary* 166
test-market v 311
testosterone n 296
test-tube baby n 322
testy adj *obstinate* 107
testy adj *irritable* 107
tetanus n 68

tetchy adj *touchy* 132
tête-à-tête n *type of sofa* 239
tête-à-tête n *talk* 177
tête-à-tête adv/adj 177
tether n *fig. limit* 88
tether n *fig. shackle* 88
tether n *type of rope* 88
tether v 88
tetherball n 262
tetra n *type of fish* 296
tetracycline n 310
tetralogy n Literature/Writing 172
tetralogy n Medicine 286
tetrapod n 220
tetrazzini adj 310
Texas longhorn n (Am) 272
Tex-Mex adj (Am) 303
text n *textbook* 202, 264
text n *writing* 42
textbook n 202
textbook adj 278
textbookish adj 284
textile n 107
texture n *obs. weaving* 177
texture n *character* 177
texture n *surface feel* 177
texture v 177
thalassocracy n *"maritime supremacy"* 229
thalidomide n 310
thanatology n 229
thanatophobia n *fear of death* 247
thank, thanks n/v *obs. nice thoughts* 17
thank, thanks n/v 17
thankee interj 230
thankful adj *obs. warranting gratitude* 17
thankful adj *giving thanks* 17
thankfully adv *obs. done to garner thanks* 25
thankfully adv *as in "thankfully, the storm quit"* 25
thankfully adv *as in "he thankfully returned the favor"* 25
thankless adj 17
thanksgive v 108
thanksgiving n 108
thankworthy adj 90
thank-you n 205
thank-you-ma'am n 231
thataway n 231
thatch v/n 69
thatch v/n *obs. cover* 69
thatch n *type of grass* 69

thatch n *covering, such as hair* 69
thatch n *type of roofing* 69
thatch n *as in "lawn thatch"* 69
thaumaturge n *magician* 189, 230
thaumaturgist n 189, 230
thaumaturgy n 189
thaw v *fig. get warmer* 27
thaw n/v 27
theater n *the building* 77
theater n *the art* 77
theater n *histrionics* 77
theater of operations n 266
theater of the absurd n 318
theater of war n 266
theatergoer n 246
theater-in-the-round n 305
theatrical adj *demonstrative* 128
theatrical adj 77, 128
theatricalize v 201
theatricals n 77, 173
theatrics n 77, 214
theft n 21
their adj 53
theirn pron 249
theism n Religion 173
thematic adj 179
theme n *in music* 50
theme n *type of essay* 50
theme n *subject* 50
theme park n (Am) 311
theme restaurant n 327
theme song n (Am) 290
then and there adv 102
theocentric adj 266
theocracy n 155
theocrat n 155
theodicy n Religion 202
theogony n *origins of the gods* 154
theologaster n *bad theologian* 154
theologian n 101
theologician n 101
theology n *non-Christian theology* 78
theology n 78
theomorphic adj *in God's image* 266
theonomous adj *subject to God's authority* 305
theonomy n *being theonomous* 266
theophany n *appearance of God to a person* 20
theorbo n *type of stringed instrument* 153

theorem n 120
theoretical adj 170
theoretical adj obs. theorizing 170
theoretician n 125, 262
theorician n 125
theorist n 125
theorize v 125
theory n 125
theory n as in "music theory" 125
theory n guess 125
theory n obs. contemplation 125
Theory of Everything n 326
theosophy n type of way of seeing God 154
therapeusis n arch. therapeutics 238
therapeutic adj 106
therapeutics n 106
therapist n 263
therapy n 222
there interj 132
thereinafter adv 217
therm n unit of heat 256
thermal adj pertaining to hot springs 193
thermal n type of air current 296
thermal adj pertaining to heat 193
thermal pollution n 319
thermal printer n 315
thermic adj 193
thermocouple n 256
thermodynamic adj 220
thermodynamics n 220
thermoelectricity, thermoelectric n, adj 210
thermometer n 147
thermonuclear adj 300
thermos n 273
thermostat n/v 221
thesaurus n dictionary 214
thesaurus n as in "Roget's" 214
thesis n supposition 125
thespian adj/n 228
theurgist n 132
theurgy n type of magic 132
they them 175
they'd contr 172
they'll contr 152
they're contr 128
they've contr 152
thiamine n vitamin B2 273
thick adj slang excessive 24
thick adj as in "thick as thieves" 204
thick adj as in "thick accent" 92

thick v 95
thick adj congealed 24
thick adj 133, 189
thick adj obs. frequent 24
thick adj broad 24
thick adj obs. deep 24
thick adj stuffy 24
thick adj dense 24
thick n Insults 133
thick adv/n 24
thick and thin n 82
thicken v get wider 95
thicken v 95
thicken v as in "the plot thickens" 95
thicken v obs. compact 95
thicket n 10
thickhead n 189
thickheaded adj 189
thickset adj fat 191
thickset adj close together 191
thick-skinned adj 108
thick-witted adj 156
thief n 21
thieve v 21
thievery n 21
thievish adj 21
thigh n in animals 13
thigh n in people 13
thighbone n 66
thimble n 69
thimblerig n/v the shell game 213
thin adj of sound or color 25
thin adj of crowds 25
thin adj meager 25
thin adj obs. few 25
thin adj slim 25
thin adj watery 25
thin v/adv 25
thine adj 25
thing n as in "do your own thing" 231
thing n as in "gather your things" 23
thing n slang penis 66
thing n obs. type of meeting, matter brought before a meeting 23
thing n as in "music is my thing" 23
thing n as in "sweet thing" 23
thing n 23
thingamabob n 206
thingamajig n 206
thingness n being 270
thingummy n 206
thingy n 270

think v remember 17
think v consider 17
think n 17, 225
think v cogitate 17
think v believe 17
think v opine 17
think v as in "think of me if you want to sell" 170
think v conceive 17
think v picture, imagine 17
think v experience 28
think n 17
think piece n 305
think tank n (Am) 313
thinking cap n 250
thin-skinned adj 125
third n/v as in "divide into thirds" 85
third n/v in music 85
third adj/n 25
third degree n (Am) 267
third dimension n 237
third person n Language and Speaking 127
third world n 319
third-class adj/n 234
third-class n 234
third-degree burn 286
third-rate adj type of naval designation 217
third-rate adj inferior 217
third-stream music n 318
thirst n/v lit. 13
thirst n/v fig. 13
thirsty adj 13
thirteen n 12
thirty n 12
thirty n the end Literature/Writing 264
.30-30 n type of gun 291
0.38 n type of gun 300
0.32 n type of gun 277
thistle n 10
thistledown n 118
this-worldliness n 270
this-worldly adj 270
thong n strap 23
thong n 316
thorax n 66
thorn n on animals 10
thorn n/v on plants 10
thorn v 10
thorn apple n 118
thorny adj 10
thorny adj fig. sticky 10
thorough adj carried through 103
thorough adv/prep through 28

thoroughbred adj of people 154
thoroughbred adj of horses 154
thoroughbred adj/n 220
thoroughbred adj 220
thoroughfare n main highway 72
thoroughfare n pathway 72
thorp n arch. village 9
thou n thousand 245
thought n spec. idea 17
thought n act of thinking 17
thoughtful adj cogitative 38
thoughtful adj considerate 38
thoughtless adj 38
thousand n 12
Thousand Island dressing n 280
thrall v arch. enthrall 37
thrall n 22
thrash v beat 27
thrash v thresh 27
thrashing n 232
thread n/v Cloth/Clothing 16
thread n/v sequence 177
thread n continuity 177
threadbare adj lit. 71
threadbare adj fig. worn 71
threads n Cloth/Clothing 287
threat n menace 52
threat n gen. oppression 52
threat v obs. 52
threaten n 52
threatened species n 315
threatening adj 115
three n 12
3-D n (Am) 296
three R's n 228
three-card monte n (Am) 244
three-dimensional adj 270
three-legged race n 275
three-ring circus n (Am) 265
threesome n 83
three-toed sloth n 254
three-way bulb n 310
three-wheeler n 261
threnody n elegy 154
thresh v 15
threshing machine n 197
threshold n point of perception or activity, as in "threshold of hearing" 22
threshold n lit. and fig. border 22
thrift n obs. thriving, hard work 41
thrift n savings 41
thrift shop n 305
thriftless adj useless 90
thrifty adj thriving 110

thrifty adj *frugal* 110
thrill v *obs. pierce* 37
thrill n/v 37
thriller n 269
thrive v 58
thriveless adj 90
thriving adj 159
throat n *gen. passage* 13
throat n 13
throaty adj 13
throb n/v 93
throe n *phys. spasm* 31
throe n *fig. spasm* 31
thrombosis n *blood clot* 182
thrombosis n *gen. coagulation* 182
throne n *representing power* 33
throne n Shelter/Housing 33
throne n *slang toilet* 286
throne room n 239
throng v *obs. crush* 116
throng v 116
throng n 22
throttle n/v 94
throttle v *mechanical sense* 94
throttle n *type of valve* 106
throttle n *throat* 106
throttle v *choke* 106
throttlehold n 300
through and through adv 102
through street n *opp. of dead end* 288
throughput n *akin to input and output* 284
throw n/v *fling, toss* 61
throw v *fashion, shape* 94
throw n *as in "50 cents a throw"* 268
throw v *lose on purpose* 244
throw pillow n 310
throw rug n 286
throw up v *vomit* 182
throwaway adj/n 278
throwaway adj 278
throwback n 250
throw-in n 269
thrum n *obs. crowd* 28
thrush n *type of disease* 166
thrush n 11
thrust n *gist* 321
thrust n *force* 190
thrust v 55
thrust n *attack* 190
thrust n *gist* 190
thruway n 288
thud n/v 113
thug n *member of Indian crime organization* 215

thug n *gen. hooligan* 215
thuggee n 215
thuggery n 215
thuggism n 215
thumb n 13
thumb n *obs. big toe* 13
thumb index n 276
thumbless adj *inept* 175
thumbling n *little person* 250
thumbnail n *thumbnail sketch* 147
thumbnail adj 251
thumbnail adj/n The Body 147
thumbnail adj 147
thumbscrew n 188
thumbs-down n 269
thumb-sucker n 270
thumbs-up n 269
thumbtack n (Am) 260
thump v 117
thumping adj 138
thunder n/v Weather 12
thunderation interj (Am) 230
thunderbird n The Fantastic/Paranormal 230
thunderbolt n 65
thunderbolt n *zigzag drawing* 65
thunderclap n 65
thundercloud n 165
thunderhead n 237
thunderlight n *arch. lightning* 31
thunderpeal n Weather 210
thundershower n 165
thunderstorm n 165
thunderstrike v 142
thunk n/v *sound* 308
Thursday n 12
thurse n *arch. type of giant* 21
thwack n/v 97
thwack n 97
thwart v *arch. gen. oppose* 104
thwart v *oppose successfully* 104
thy adj 53
thyme n 34
thymus n *obs. type of growth* 147
thymus n *type of gland* 147
thyroid adj/n 166
tiara n 122
Tibetan spaniel n 285
Tibetan terrier n 272
tibia n 66
tic n *spasm, twitch* 195
tick n *as in "ticktock"* 177
tick n *obs. touch* 177
tick n *type of arachnid* 11
tick n *ticking* 69
tick v 177

tick fever n 257
tick off v 281
tick-a-tick 233
ticked adj *angry, peeved* 298
ticker n *slang heart* 316
ticker n *producer of tickertape* 224
ticker tape n (Am) 278
ticker-tape parade n 311
ticket n/v *as in "speeding ticket"* 319
ticket n *pass, as in "meal ticket," "airline ticket"* 167
ticket n *as in "party ticket"* 188
ticket n *note* 113
ticket n/v *tag, designate* 134
ticket v 167
ticket office n 167
ticking n *type of fabric* 148
tickle n/v 61
tickled pink adj 275
tickler file n (Am) 213
ticklish adj *susceptible to tickling* 138
ticklish adj *fig. sensitive, as in "a ticklish situation"* 138
ticktack 233
ticktock n 233
ticky-tacky adj/n 321
tic-tac-toe n 244
tidal basin n 236
tidal wave n 219
tidbit n 158
tiddlywinks n 226
tiddlywinks n *game using dominoes* 226
tide n *time, as in "eventide"* 12
tide n 64
tide v *happen* 28
tide over v 218
tideland n 209
tidewater n 193
tidge n *smidgeon* 316
tiding n *as in "glad tidings"* 23
tidy adj *neat* 191
tidy v 191, 218
tidy adj *obs. timely* 191
tidy adj *attractive* 191
tidy adj *ordered* 191
tie n/v *draw, as in "a 10-10 tie"* 171
tie v *bind with something* 28
tie n *rope* 16
tie n *as in "necktie," "bowtie"* 197
tie v *as in "tie a shoelace"* 28
tie n *bond, as in "family ties"* 134

tie clasp n 310
tie one on v *get drunk* 313
tie tack n 310
tiebreaker n 298
tie-dyed adj 274
tie-in n 291
tier n/v 103
tier n *fig. rank* 103
tiff n/v *quarrel* 180
tiff v *drink* 180
tiffany n 149
tiger n 11
tiger lily n 209
tiger moth n 210
tiger shark n 194
tiger shrimp n 322
tiger swallowtail n *type of butterfly* 255
tight adj *close, as in "tight race"* 233
tight adj *lacking maneuvering space, as in "tight curve"* 206
tight adj *tight-fitting* 207
tight adj *hard to handle, as in "tight spot"* 206
tight adj *taut* 139
tight adj *compacted, close* 92
tight adj *without margin, as in "tight schedule"* 321
tight adj *concise* 271
tight adj *drunk* 230
tight adj *cheap* 216
tight adj *close, as in "tight friends"* 321
tight adj *penurious* Insults 268
tight adj *as in "watertight"* 92
tight adv 92
tightfisted adj 231
tight-knit adj 308
tight-lipped adj 261
tightrope n 214
tights n *akin to leggings* 223
tights n *type of breeches* 223
tightwad n (Am) 216, 268
'til conj/prep 318
tilde n 245
tile n/v 14
tile n *type of game piece* 14
till n *gen. compartment* 178
till n *tray, as in "cash register till"* 178
till v *obs. work hard* 35
till v *cultivate* 35
tiller n *part of steering mechanism* 72
tiller n *cultivator* 316
tillerman n 298
tilt n/v *joust* 108

torpedo n *type of fish* 105
torpedo v *lit. and fig.* 266
torpedo boat n (Am) 215
torpedo bomber n 291
torpefy v 74
torpid adj 74
torpor n 74
torque n/v *type of force* 256
torrefy v *scorch* 161
torrent n 118
torrent adj 118
torrential adj 118
torrid adj *lit. hot* 115
torrid adj *fig. hot, passionate* 115
torrid zone n 118
torso n 182
tort n *The Law* 131
torte n 122
tortellini n 274
tortilla n 168
tortoise n 64
tortoiseshell n 161
tortuous adj 90
torture n War/Military/Violence 131
torture n *type of punishment* 69
torture n *agony* 69
torture v 69
torturous adj 69
tosh n *nonsense* 112
toss v *search roughly* 301
toss v *as in "toss a salad"* 115, 183
toss v *fling or overturn* 115
toss v *buffet* 115
toss v *as in "toss your head"* 115
toss v *throw* 115
toss n 115
toss-up n 190
tostada n 297
tot n *child* 170
total adj 90
total v *destroy completely* 312
total n/adv 90
total recall n 288
totalitarian, totalitarianism adj, n 291
totality n 136
totalize v 90
tote v (Am) 180
tote bag n (Am) 258
tote board n 304
totem n (Am) 202
totem pole n 266
totemism n (Am) 202
tother adj/pron *t(he)other* 41

totter n/v 97
totter v *obs. swing* 97
toucan n 119
touch n 52
touch n *little bit, as in "a touch of spring"* 52
touch v 58
touch n *as in "lose touch"* 52
touch and go adj 176
touch base v 325
touch down v Travel/Transportation 242
touch football n 298
touch off v 207
touch pad n 322
touch system n *typing system* 282
touch up v *fix* 191
touch up v *seek a loan* 191
touch-and-go n 310
touchdown n *landing* 244
touchdown n *football score* 244
touché interj 277
touched adj *crazy* 74
touching adj 107
touchous adj 149
touchstone n *type of stone* 99
touchstone n *fig. standard, benchmark* 99
touchtone n 311
touch-type v (Am) 305
touch-up n 269
touchy adj 149
touchy-feely adj 320
tough v *as in "tough it out"* 234
tough n *ruffian* 251
tough adj *strenuous* 25
tough adj *stringent* 25
tough adj *like a ruffian, as in "tough guy"* 271
tough adj *difficult* 25
tough adj *phys. tough* 25
tough v/n 25
toughen v 25
toughie n *difficult challenge* 251, 320
tough-minded adj 275
toupee n 184
tour n *turn, as in "tour of duty"* 50
tour n *inspection* 169
tour n *as in "tour of the country"* 50
tour n *visit* 169
tour de force n 216
tour of duty n 248
tourbillion n *whirlwind, vortex* 63

Tourette's syndrome n 316
touring car n 274
tourism n 198, 212
tourist n 198
tourist class n 298
tourist court n *motel* 298
tourist trap n 298
touristy adj 243
tournament n 40
tournedos n 259
tourney n/v 40
tourniquet n 167
touse n/v *tousle* 61, 96
tousle v 96
tow n/v 27
tow car n (Am) *towtruck* 261, 304
tow truck n 304
towardly adj 98
towboat n 212
towel n 33
towelette n 273
tower v 141
tower n 15
Tower of Babel n 269
towering adj 91
towhead n (Am) 221
town n *municipality* 20
town car n 275
town crier n 151
town hall n 101
town house n 106
town meeting n 155
townie n (Am) 247
townlet n 130
townsfolk n 188
township n *type of municipality* 174
townsman n 20
townspeople n 154
townswoman n 174
toxic adj *caused by poison* 166
toxic adj *poisonous* 166
toxic n 166, 257
toxic shock syndrome n 322
toxicant n 257
toxicity n 257
toxicology n 195
toxin n 257
toy n *arch. joke* 126
toy n *something trivial* 126
toy n *child's toy* 126
toy adj 217
toy v *phys. fiddle with* 116
toy n *obs. friskiness* 126
toy v *as in "toy with the prey"* 116
toy v/adj 126

toy poodle n 296
toyboy n Slang 327
to-year adv *arch. akin to tonight* 31
toyful adj *arch. playful* 261
trace n *evidence* 50
trace n *type of harness gear* 36
trace n *instance of tracking* 50
trace v *copy by tracing* 94, 207
trace n *tiny remaining amount* 50
trace v *as in "trace a chronology"* 94
trace v *track* 94
trace n *track* 50; v 94
trace v *obs. walk about* 94
trace v *gen. draw, diagram* 207
trace element n 118
trachea n 66
tracheotomy n 182
tracing paper n 207, 214
track n *course for runners, horses* 103, 244
track v *as in "track dirt into the house"* 253
track n *route* 123
track n *as in "animal track"* 103
track n *as in "tank tracks"* 261
track n *song* Music 290
track n *as in "railroad tracks"* 103, 224
track n *track-and-field sports* 244, 289
track n *as in "railroad tracks"* 224
track n *gen. route* 103
track n *as in "tank tracks"* 103, 261
track v 103
track lighting n 322
track meet n (Am) 275
track record n 313
track shoe n 275
track-and-field adj 275
tracking station n 315
tracklayer n (Am) 245
trackless trolley n 288
tracksuit n 287
tract n *area, etc.* 118
tract n *as in "religious tract"* 78
tract n *as in "digestive tract," etc.* 118
tract n *type of Scripture* 78
tract n *obs. length of time* 118
tract house n 310
tractor n 259
tractor pull n 323

ENGLISH THROUGH THE AGES

vindication n obs. 117
vindictive adj 180
vindictive adj Archaisms 117
vine n/v 30
vinegar n 34
vinegar n fig. 34
vinegarish adj 34
vinegary adj 34
vinery n 35
vineyard n 35
viniculture n wine-making 241
vinification n 259
vinify v 316
vino n 259
vint v arch. sell wine 185
vintage n good wine 71
vintage n wine harvest 71
vintage adj 71, 139
vintage n wine crop 71
vintage n fig. 71
vintage adj 71
vintage year n 301
vinter n obs. 71
vintner n 71
vinyl n 239
viol n 101
viola n 187
violate adj 98
violate, violation v, n 87
violence n 45
violet adj/n the color 92
violet n Plants 30
violin n 129
violinmaker n 173
violoncello n 187
VIP n 300
viper n type of snake 105
viper n fig. mean person 105
virago n 82
virago n arch. virile woman 82
virago n obs. gen. woman 82
virgin n Love/Romance/Sex 39
virgin adj pure 90
virgin adj chaste 39, 90
virgin birth n 173
virgin wool n 280
virginal adj 39, 90
virginal n type of spinet 111
Virginia creeper n (Am) 164
Virginia reel n (Am) 214
virginity n 39
virgule n / 227
virid adj verdant 139
viridescent adj green 234
virile adj arch. describing manly attire 101

virile adj able to father children 101
virile adj lusty 101
virile adj 101
virility n 101
virtual adj 90
virtual adj arch. related to virtue 78
virtual memory n 309
virtual reality n 326
virtue n obs. act of God 44
virtue n obs. power, magical power 62
virtue n 44
virtue n chastity 125
virtuous adj obs. manly 38
virtuous adj 38
virulent adj 90
virus n Animals 255
virus n Technology 326
virus n snake venom 255
visa n/v The Law 230
visage n 32
vis-à-vis n type of carriage 198
viscera n 166
visceral adj deeply felt 138
viscid adj 90
viscosity n 90
viscount n 79, 101
viscountess n 79, 101
viscous adj 90
vise n/v 36
visible adj 55
vision n imagination, goal 74
vision n foresight 74
vision n ability to see 68
vision v 199
vision n as in "a vision of radiance" 125
vision n something supernatural 47
vision n dream 125
visionary n 185
visionary adj able to envision 151
visionary adj futuristic 151
visionary adj pertaining to visions 151
visionary n 151
visions n 125
visit n/v 56
visitator n 87, 144
visiting card n 202
visitor n 56, 87, 232
visitor center n 317
visitress n 87, 232
visive adj obs. seeing 98
visor n on a helmet 35

visor n on a hat 35
vista n 158
visual n picture 299
visual adj meant to be seen 68
visual adj optical 68
visual adj pertaining to seeing 68
visual acuity n 257
visual aid n 284
visual literacy n 325
visuality n ability to see 243
visuality n mental picture 243
visualization n 213
visualize v 213
vital adj necessary 90
vital adj 90
vital signs n Medicine 280
vital statistics n 231
vitalism n 210
vitality n 90
vitalize v 90
vitals n 147
vitamin n 279
vitamin A, B, C n 280
vitriol n type of chemical 63
vitriol n fig. acrimony 63, 205
vitriolic adj 205
vittles n 70
vituperate v 74
vituperation n 74
vituperative adj 74
vituperatory adj 74
viva interj 175
vivacious adj 73
vivacity n 73
vivarium n obs. habitat 118
vivarium n type of terrarium 118
vivid adj clear 161
vivid adj bright 161
vivid adj vivacious 161
vivid adj as in "vivid memory" 161
vivific adj making vivacious 137
vivify v 97
vivisect v 182
vivisection n 182
vixen n Insults 133
vixen n female fox 12
vizsla n type of dog 302
vocabulary n words available 110, 201
vocabulary n type of word list 110, 201
vocal adj opp. of instrumental 129
vocal adj able to speak 90
vocal adj 90
vocal adj articulate 90, 262
vocal adj outspoken 90

vocal n Music 129
vocal cords n 238
vocalist n Music 228
vocalist n speaker 228
vocalize v 180
vocation n The Workplace 101
vocation n religious calling 78
vocational adj 101
vociferant adj 160
vociferate v 143
vociferous adj 143
vociferous adj 160
vodka n 211
vodka martini n 303
vodkatini n 303
vogue n fashion 123
vogue n obs. inclination 123
voguish adj 288
voice n obs. speech 98
voice n lit. and fig. 50
voice n Music 129
voice v 50
voice box n 279
voice mail n 327
voice vote n 291
voiceover n 305
voiceprint n 315
voices n The Fantastic/ Paranormal 292
void n Heavens/Sky 165
void adj/v The Law 81
void adj vacant 54
void v 69
void n as in "feeling a void" 165
voila interj 189
voir dire n The Law 175
volatile n obs. birds 30
volatile adj/n 139
volatility n 139
volcanic adj/n 193
volcanic glass n 219
volcanicity n 236
volcanism n 236
volcano n 145
volcanology n 255
volition n as in "of his own volition" 170
volition n arch. wishing 170
volley n War/Military/Violence 131
volley n/v 126
volleyball n (Am) 262
volt n 237
voltage n 237
voltameter n 256
voltmeter n 256
voluble adj changeable 138

wallop n/v *blow* 215

wallop n/v *gen. boiling* 215

walloping adj 233

wallow v *fig., as in "wallow in glory"* 27

wallow n/v 27

wallow n *as in "hog wallow"* 122

wallpaper n 222; v 222, 286

wall-to-wall adj 308

walnut n 10

walnut n *the color* 271

walnut n *the tree* 10

walrus n 165

walter v *wallow* 98

waltz n/v 201

waltz v *dance* 202

waltz v *cavort, move* 202

wamble n *arch. stomach trouble* 121

wampum n 152

wampumpeag n 152

wan adj *describing the sea* 32

wan adj *describing heavenly bodies* 32

wan adj *morose* 32

wander v 27

wander v *as in "mind wandering"* 27

wander v *as in "wandering gaze"* 27

wander v *as in "wandering river"* 27

wanderlust n 242

wane n/v 25

wangle n/v 218

wanhope n *lack of hope* 38

Wankel engine n 317

wanna v 268

wanna-be n 327

want v/n *as in "wanted by the police"* 48 203

want v/n *lack, need* 48

want n *dire need* 48

wa'n't contr 187

want v/n *desire, yearn* 48

want n *as in "for want of a nail"* 48

want ad n (Am) 264

wanta v 268

wanton adj *uncontrolled* 37

wanton adj *lewd, extravagant* 37

wanton v 37

want-wit adj/n *arch. dimwit* 82

war n *a spec. conflict* 21

war n *section of a prison* 46

war n *obs. invasion* 21

war n *arch. part of a castle* 46

war n *warfare* 21

war n *prison* 46

war v 21

war baby n 276

war bride n 281

war chest n (Am) 277

war correspondent n (Am) 246

war crime n 277

war cry n 188

war dance n (Am) 188

war game n 229, 306

war hawk n 203

war of nerves n 301

war paint n (Am) 229

war party n (Am) 203

war room n 282

war zone n 282

warble n/v 52

warbler n *Animals* 194

warbler n *singer* 154

warbonnet n 215

ward v *as in "ward off"* 143

ward n *section of a hospital* 147

ward n *guardianship* 22

ward n *surveillance* 22

ward n *arch. guard* 143

ward n *child under care, as in "ward of the court"* 22

ward n *district* 44

wardrobe n *obs. dressing room* 121

wardrobe n *type of furniture* 71, 121

wardrobe n *piece of furniture* 121

wardrobe n *clothing* 71, 121

wardrobe n *obs. bedroom* 121

wardroom n 203

ware adj/v/n *arch. aware/beware/wariness* 17

warehouse n/v 41

warehouse n *outlet store* 41

wareless adj *not careful* 144

wareroom n 213

ware/wares n *merchandise* 18

ware/wares n *slang genitals* 18

warfare n 80

war-game v 229, 306

warhead n 174, 267

wark n *pain* 28

warlike adj *obs. prepared for war* 80

warlike adj 80

warlock n *male witch* 47

warlock n *obs. evil person, demon, Satan* 47

warlock n *magician* 47

warlord n 248

warm adj/adv/v *protecting from cold* 25

warm adj *rich* 132

warm adj/adv/v *as in "a warm welcome"* 25

warm adj *as in "a warm blue"* 206

warm adj *saucy, blue* 230

warm v *as in "warm up to someone"* 97

warm v *obs. as in "house warming"* 163

warm v 206

warm n 25

warm spot n *as in "a warm spot in my heart"* 288

warm up v 226

warm-blooded adj 194

warmed-over adj 270

warmfront n 285

warmhearted adj 100

warming pan n *bedmate* Slang 175

warming pan n *bedwarmer* 100

warming pan n *slang fill-in* 175

warmonger n 229

warmonger n *mercenary* 229

warm-up n 226

warning n *portent* 21

warning n *type of signal, as in "tornado warning"* 21

warning n *obs. precaution* 21

warning n *being warned* 21

warning adj 21

warp n *Cloth/Clothing* 15

warp v *pervert* 97

warp v *propel* 28

warp v *bend, distort* 97

warp v *throw* 28

warp v *hit* 28

warp n 97

warpath n (Am) 203

warplane n 282

warrant v 57

warrant n *type of directive* 46

warrant n *as in "search warrant"* 46

warrantee n 177

warrantor n 177

warranty n *type of legal guarantee* 46

warranty n *gen. guarantee* 46

warren n *breeding ground* 70

warrener n *gamekeeper* 35

warrior n 45, 131

warrioress n 45, 131

warship n 112

wart n *The Body* 13

wart n *fig.* 13

warthog n 220

wartime n 80

warts-and-all adj 293

wary adj 74

wary v *obs. curse* 28

wash v *fig. make pure* 27

wash v *clean* 27

wash n *washing laundry* 183

wash v *as in "wash ashore"* 163

wash v *be understood, get approval, as in "his alibi will wash"* 249

wash n *the laundry itself* 183

wash n *as in "hogwash"* 71

wash n/v *in painting* 128

wash n/v *as in "eye wash"* 148

wash n 27

wash away v *erode* 143

wash down v *as in "wash it down with water"* 122

wash out v *rinse* 139

wash out v *clean* 139

wash up v 207

wash-and-wear adj 310

washateria n 298

washbasin n 211

washboard n 196

washboard n *type of ship protection* 196

washbowl n 106

washcloth n (Am) 258

washday n 222

washed-out adj *faded* 207

washed-out adj *pale* 207

washed-up adj 293

washer n *connecting disk* 35

washer n *Everyday Life* 211

washerman n 152, 185

washerwoman n 127, 152, 185

washhouse n *laundry* 121

washing machine n 196

washout n *lit.* 251

washout n *slang failure* 251

washrag n (Am) 258

washroom n (Am) 211

washtub n 147

washwoman n 127, 152

wasn't contr 227

wasp n *fig. annoying person* 11

WASP n 312

wasp n *Animals* 11

wasp waist n 250

waspish adj 124

wassail n/v 23

wassail bowl 23

wassailer n 23

waste adj/n *refuse, overage* 88

waste n *misuse, overuse* 50

waste adj *obs. wasted, destroyed* 62

waste n *as in "lay waste"* 102

waste v *kill* 319

waste n *wasteland* 29

waste v *discard* 271

waste v *as in "waste a chance"* 253

waste v *as in "waste away"* 61

waste n 61

wastebasket n 222

wasted adj *drunk* 320

wasted adj 91

wasteful adj *destructive* 54

wasteful adj *squanderous* 54

wasteland n 63

wastepaper n 121

waster n 231

wastethrift n *arch. spendthrift* 152

wastewater n 87

wastrel n *bit of wasteland* 231

wastrel n *spendthrift* 231

watch n *obs. alarm clock* 119

watch n 119

watch v *remain on watch* 55

watch n *obs. types of clock works* 119

watch v *guard* 55

watch v *keep abreast of* 143

watch v *as in "watch the kids"* 55

watch v *obs. stay awake* 55

watch v *observe* 143

watch v *"watch for"* 55

watch v *as in "watch out"* 253

watch n 55

watch out v 235

watch pocket n 223

watchdog n 145; v 145, 278

watchdog n *fig.* 145

watchmaker n 152

watchman n *guard* 75

watchtower n 106

watchword n 187

watchword n *obs. password* 187

water v *as in "water down a drink"* 82

water n/v 10

water ballet n 290

water bed n 222

water beetle n 165

water blister n 257

water boatman n *type of insect* 209

water buffalo n 255

water bug n 181

water cannon n 319

water chestnut n 241

water closet n 196

water cure n 222

water down v 235

water flea n 119

water glass n 121

water heater n 257

water hole n 164

water level n Tools 123

water level n *level of groundwater, gen. water* 236

water lily n 99

water main n 211

water meter n 238

water moccasin n 210

water nymph n 81

water on the knee n 297

water pipe n 70

water pistol n 275

water polo n 263

water rat n 119

water ski n 298

water snake n 145

water spaniel n 119

water sprite n 203

water strider n 220

water supply n 258

water table n 254

water taxi n 288

water tower n 258

water vapor n 254

water wagon n 211

water wings n 275

water witch n (Am) 215

waterbiscuit n 197

watercolor n *type of painting* 128

watercolor n *type of paint* 128

watercooler n (Am) 222

watercress n 30

watered-down adj 271

waterfall n 9

waterfowl n 30

watering can n 167

watering hole n 311

watering place n 63

waterjet n 232

waterlog 206

waterlogged adj 206

waterloo n 216

watermelon n 122

waterpower n 210

waterproof adj 191

waterproof n 197

waterproof n/v 191

water-repellent adj 191, 271

water-resistant adj 191, 294

watershed n Geography/Places 209

watershed n *fig.* 209

waterspout n Natural Things 181

waterspout n Tools 71

waterthrush n (Am) 210

watertight adj 89

waterwheel n 65

waterworks n 122

watt n 256

wave n/v *as in "wave of the hand"* 177

wave v *vacillate* 93

wave n/v *on the ocean* 99

wave v *obs. waver* 98

wave n *as in "sound waves"* 193

wave v *as in "a flag waving"* 28

wave v *fashion into waves* 93

wave n *gen. surge* 99

wave of the future n 301

wavelength n 221

wavelength n *fig.* 221

waver v *quaver* 57

waver v *sway* 57

waver n/v 57

wavy adj 191

wa-wa pedal n 318

wax n (Brit) *anger* 243

wax n *music* 291

wax n *beeswax* 9

wax v *opp. of wane* 25

wax v *thrash* Slang 249

wax n *other waxes* 9

wax n *phonograph record* 291

wax v 9

wax n 25

wax bean n 259

wax light n *candle* 121

wax museum n 312

wax paper n 222

waxwing n 210

way v *obs.* 21

way n 21

way n *as in "go this way"* 51

way v 144

way adv 'way 41

way adv *very* 234

way point n (Am) 261

way station n (Am) 198

wayfare n/v *arch.* 72

wayfarer n 72

wayfaring adj *arch. traveling* 17

wayfaring adj 72

way-in adj Slang 313

waylay v 112

wayless adj 25

way-out adj Slang 313

ways n *as in "the ways of the wild"* 205

wayside n 72

wayward adj 88

wayworn adj *tired because of traveling* 198

weak adj *phys. weak* 17, 32

weak v *obs.* 17

weak adj *as in "a weak drink"* 90

weak adj *weak-minded* 17

weak adj *weak-willed* 17, 32

weak force n 315

weak sister n 249

weaken v 17

weakheaded adj 170

weakhearted adj 108

weak-kneed adj 249

weakling n 113

weakling n *unreligious person* Insults 113

weakling n *obs. effeminate person* Insults 113

weal n 22

weald n *gen. forest* 9

weald n *spec. forest* 9

wealth n 41

wealthy adj *obs. happy* 76

wealthy adj *prosperous* 76

wealthy adj 41

wealthy adj *rich* 76

wean v 15

weanling n 15

weapon n *slang penis* 13

weapon n *obs. weaponry* 20

weapon n/v 20

weaponry n 20, 229

weapons delivery system n 319

weapons-grade uranium n 319

wear v *irritate* 253

wear v *continue, as in "the idea wears well"* 141

wear v *as in "wear your hair long"* 16

wear n/v *as in "wear away"* 57

wear n *as in "sportswear"* 123

wear v *as in "wear a coat"* 16; n 16

wear v *erode* 57

wear and tear n 176

weariful adj *wearied* 13, 92

weariful adj *wearying* 92

weariless adj 13

wearing adj *tiring* 217

wearisome adj *wearying* 91

wet v *drink* 70
wet adj *able to sell alcohol* 200
wet adj/n/v 22
wet bar n 316
wet blanket n 216
wet dream n 250
wet nurse n/v 151
wet suit n *310*
wetback n (Am) *Insults* 293
wether n 15
wetland n 193
wetsmack n *party pooper* 293
we've contr 187
whack n *as in "I'll take a whack at it"* 268
whack v 191
whack n 191
whack off v 317
whacked-out adj 320
whacking adj/adv 217
whacking adv 217
whale n/v 11
whale v *as in "whale on your head"* 203
whale shark n 255
whaleboat n 168
whalebone n 30
whalebone whale n 181
whalefish *obs.* 11
whaler n *something huge* 249
whaler n 171
whaler n *whaling ship* 171
wham n/v 190
wham v 190
whammy, double whammy n 301
wham/whammo adv/interj 292
whangdoodle n *thingamajig* 301
wharf n 17
what interrogative *how much?* 28
what interrogative *obs. why?* 28
what for n *as in "I'll give him what for"* 250
what ho interj 81
what the hell? interj 249
whatchamacallit n 294
what-if n 321
whatness n 157
whatnot n 136
whatnot pron 136
whatsit n 267
whatso pron *whatever* 62
wheat n 15
wheat bread n 70
wheat cake n 197
wheat germ n 259
whee interj 267

wheedle v 179
wheel n/v 16
wheel of fortune n 199
wheelbarrow n 36
wheelchair n 167
wheeler and dealer n 311
wheeler-dealer n 311
wheelhouse n 212
wheelie n 317
wheelwright n 40
wheeze n *old joke* 230
wheeze v 98
whelm v 58
whelp n/v 11
wherewithal n 136
whet n/v 27
whet v *obs. foment* 27
whetstone n 16
whew n *obs. type of musical instrument* 77
whew interj 81
whey n 15
whey-face n 156
whiff v 180
whiff n/v *small breeze* 119
while n 22
while conj/v 22
whiles conj 61
whillikers interj (Am) 248
whilom adv *formerly* 61
whilom adv *obs. while* 61
whilom adj 92
whim n *obs. wordplay* 125
whim n 125
whim n *obs. quirky idea* 125
whimp v *whine* 116, 144
whimper n/v 116
whimsy n *whim* 150
whimsy n *whimsical thing* 150
whim-wham n 73
whine v *make a whining sound* 28
whine v *obs. applied to arrows* 28
whine v *grouse* 28
whine n 28
whinny n/v 116
whinny n 116
whip n *as in "dairy whip"* 197
whip v *go fast* 94
whip v *drink fast* 121
whip n 247
whip n/v *Tools* 36
whip v *Food* 168
whip n 168
whip hand n 175
whip up v *create fast* 156
whip up v *excite* 156

whiplash n 135
whiplash injury n 310
whippersnappper n 175
whippet n *type of wine* 145
whippet n *small person* 145
whippet n *type of dog* 145
whipping boy n 157
whipping cream n 287
whipping post n 131
whippoorwill n (Am) 181
whipsaw n 107; v 107, 235
whipsaw v 235
whipsaw v 107
whirl n/v 58
whirl n 58
whirligig n 75
whirligig beetle n 181
whirlpool n 105
whirlpool bath n 280
whirlwind adj 160
whirlwind adj/n *Weather* 31
whirlwind n *fig.* 31
whirlwind adj 31
whirlybird n *helicopter* 310
whirr v *make whirring sound* 94
whirr v *obs. throw* 94
whisk n/v 33, 168
whisk broom n 242
whisker n 66
whisker n *obs. whisking tool* 66
whiskey n 183
whiskey sour n (Am) 259
whisper v *speak quietly* 19
whisper v *gen. make quiet sounds* 19
whisper n 19
whist n 170
whistle n *type of sound* 14
whistle n *noisemaker* 14
whistle n *as in "wet your whistle"* 82
whistle v 14
whistle-blower n 320
whistle-stop n/v (Am) 288
whistling swan n 194
whit n *as in "not a whit"* 88
white adj *describing hair, wine* 25
white n *as in "egg white"* 15
white n *Cloth/Clothing* 35
white adj/n 25
white v *obs. whiten* 28
white adj/n *Caucasian* 160
white n *money* 76
white adj *obs. plausible* 98
white ant n *termite* 165
white ash n *type of tree* 164
white bean n 316

white blood cell 238
white bread n 34
white cell n 238
white chocolate n 287
white corpuscle 238
white dwarf n 285
white elephant n 102
white flag n 131
white flight n 319
white fox n 165
white gas n 285
white gold n 164
white goods n 239
white heat 217
white hole n 322
white hunter n 308
white knight n 269
white lady n *type of drink* 297
white lightning n (Am) 280
white list n *opp. of blacklist* 270
white matter n *akin to gray matter* 221
white mule n *type of alcohol* 259
white noise n 303
white pages n 310
white paper n *report* 264
white pepper n 70
white pine n (Am) 164
white rice n 287
white room n *clean room* 315
white sale n 281
white sauce n 183
white shark n 165
white slave n 248
white trash n (Am) 231
white whale n 165
white wine n 34
whitebeard n *old man* 65
white-bread adj 325
whitecap n 164
white-collar adj 281
whitefish n 65
whitehead n 297
white-hot adj 217
white-knuckle v 324
white-livered adj *lily-livered* 108
whiten v 25, 58
whitener n 157
whiteout n 302
whitesmith n 40
whitetail 220
white-tailed deer n 220
white-tie adj 299
whitewall n 310
whitewash n/v 135
whitewash n/v *fig.* 135
whitewater n 118
whitey n *Insults* 231

windbag n *part of a bagpipe* 101

windbags n *lungs* 120

wind-bell n *wind chime* 273

windbreak n 193

windbreaker n Cloth/Clothing 280

windburn n 285

windchill n 296

windchill factor 296

windchime n 286

windfall n *unexpected gain* Slang 132

windfall n *something blown down by the wind* 132

winding adj 115

windjammer n (Am) 261

windlass n 71

windmill n 35

windmill v 284

window n *as in "window of opportunity"* 320

window n *gen., as in "window envelope"* 33

window n 33

window blind n 183

window box n 258

window dressing n 196

window envelope n 282

window of opportunity n 325

window of vulnerability n 325

window seat n 184

window shade n 211

windowpane n 211

window-shop v 289

windowsill n 183

windpipe n 106

windshield n 274

Windsor chair n 183

Windsor knot n 304

Windsor tie n 260

windstorm n 65

windsurfing, windsurfer n 317

windup n 135

wine n *the color* 271

wine v 222

wine n *from grapes* 15

wine cellar n 69

wine steward n 263

wine taster n 152

winebibber n 122

wineglass n 121

winemaking n 212

winery n (Am) 259

wineskin n 211

wing n 80

wing n *as in "wing of a building"* 106

wing n 30

wing v *wound* 229

wing chair n 273

wing collar n 280

wing it v *improvise* 268

wing nut n 261

wing tip n 242

wingding n *type of drug reaction* 305

wingding n (Am) *party* 305

wingspan n 281

wingspread n 255

wink v *obs. close eyes* 13

wink v *obs. sleep* 52

wink n/v *as in "wink at a friend"* 13

wink n *as in "40 winks"* 52

wink v *blink* 13

winner's circle n 311

winnow v *applied to wheat* 15

winnow v *gen.* 15

wino n (Am) 283

winter n/v 12

winter solstice n 146

wintergreen n 105

wintergreen n *type of flavor* 105

winterize v 295

winter-kill v 212

winterly adj 12

wintersquash n 181

wintertide n 12

wintertime n 12

wintry adj 12

wipe n/v *sweeping blow* 112

wipe n/v 27

wipe v *trounce* 112

wipe v 112

wipe out v *destroy* 112

wiped adj Slang 320

wiped out adj Slang 320

wire n/v 23

wire v *as in "wire a house for electricity"* 259

wire n/v *telegram* 246

wire n *as in "wire to wire"* 263

wire recorder n 304

wired adj *set for life* 313

wired adj *high* 320

wirehair n 220

wirehaired adj 217

wireless n 276

wireless telegraphy n 265

wireless telephone n 265

wire-puller n (Am) *influence peddler* 230

wiretap v/n 265, 276, 305

wiretapper n 265, 276, 305

wiry adj *describing people* 221

wis, wist v *arch. know—be wise* 108

wisdom n 17

wisdom tooth n 166

wise v *as in "wise up"* 275

wise adj 17

wise guy n (Am) 268

wise man n 20, 78

wiseacre n 133

wiseass n 325

wisecrack n/v (Am) 283

wisenheimer n (Am) 277

wisewoman n 20, 78

wish n *making a wish* 74

wish n/v 27

wish n *something desired* 74

wish book n *catalog* 297

wish for v 27

wish list n 325

wishbone n 241

wishful thinking n 288

wish-wash n *swill* 169

wishy-washy adj 169

wisp n *as in "wisp of smoke"* 36

wisp n 36

wisp n 251

wispish adj 190, 271

wispy adj 190

wisteria n 209

wistful adj 169

wistful adj *obs. attentive* 169

wit n *the mind itself* 17

wit n *arch. sanity* 17

wit n *humorous person* 39

wit v *arch. know, learn* 17

wit n *as in "have your wits about you"* 74

wit n *mental agility, penchant for humor* 39

wit n/v *obs. skill* 17

wit n *humor* 39

witch n/v 21

witch n *fig. crone* 21

witch v *enchant* 47

witch v *bewitch* 47

witch v *obs. use magic* 47

witch doctor n 182

witch hazel n 105

witchcraft n 21

witchery n 112

witches' brew n 293

witches' Sabbath n 175

witch-hunt n *fig.* 293

witch-hunt n 267

witching hour n 221

withdraw v Finances/Money 200

withdraw v 56

withdraw v War/Military/Violence 80

withdrawal n 56

withdrawal n Emotions/Characteristics 150

withdrawal n *as in "heroin withdrawal"* 257

withdrawal n Finances/Money 200

withdrawing room n *drawing room* 122

withdrawment n 56

withdrawn adj 150

wither v 58

withering adj 138

withhold v 55

withholding tax n 299

withindoors, withinside adv *indoors* 138

with-it adj 300

withoutdoors adv 138

withstand v 27

witless adj 21

witling n *arch. lesser wit* 170

witness v *gen. see* 98

witness n/v *as in "witness to a murder"* 52

witness n *giving testimony* 23

witness v *as in "witness a wedding"* 98

witness n *obs. wisdom* 17

witness n/v *person who watches* 23

witness stand n (Am) 248

witticism n 39, 170

wittol n *arch. knowing cuckold* 74

wittol n *gen. fool* 74

wive v *marry* 18

wizard n *arch. wise man* 132

wizard n 132

wizard n *skilled person* 156

wizard adj/v 156

wizen adj/v 27

wizen adj 27

wobble n/v 139

woe interj 21

woe n 37

woebegone adj 38

woeful adj 37, 38

woelmist n *mist of death* 20

wok n 310

wold n 10

wolf n/v *masher* 231

wolf n 11

wolf v *eat quickly* 238

wolf pack n War/Military/Violence 266

wolf spider n 145

wolf whistle n 298

wolfhound n 194

wolverine n 119

woman n 22

woman of the street n 293

woman of the world n 130

woman suffrage n 229

womanfully adv 217

womanhood n 22

womanism n *type of feminism* 247

womanize v *pursue women* 262

womanize v *feminize* 142

womankind n 78

womankind n *obs. an individual woman* 78

womanpower n The Workplace 299

woman's rights n 154, 229

womanthrope n *misogynist* 268

womb n 13

womb n *obs. gen. stomach* 13

wombat n 194

womenfolk n 229

womenkind n 78

women's liberation n 319

women's rights n 154

women's room n 239

women's studies n 319

women's wear n 280

womyn n 324

won v *dwell* 28

wonder v *obs. make wonder* 39

wonder v *ponder, speculate* 39

wonder n *something wonderful* 22

wonder v *express wonder* 18

wonder n *as in "sense of wonder"* 22

wonder v 22

wonder adj 18

wonder drug n 297

wonderful adj *obs. expressing wonder* 25

wonderful adj 22, 25

wonderland n 205

wonderment n 22

wonders adj *obs. wondrous* 103

wondrous adj 22, 103

won't contr 172

wont adj 25

won't n 172

wont n/v 25

wontless adj *not usual* 144

woo v *gen.* 18

woo n/v 18

wood adj *wild; crazy* 28

wood n/v *obs.* 28

wood n *obs. a single tree* 11

wood n *fig. the composition of a person* 10

wood adj *in a rage* 28

wood n *forest* 11

wood n *tree composition* 10

wood alcohol n 239

wood carving n 228

wood duck n (Am) 194

wood engraving n 214

wood fiber n 236

wood louse n 146

wood nymph n 132

wood pussy n *skunk* 255

wood thrush n 194

wood tick n 165

woodbine n *type of vine* 10

woodblock n *woodcut* 173, 228

woodblock 173

woodchuck n (Am) 165

woodcut n 173

woodcutter n (Am) 200

wooded adj 11, 145

wooden adj *lit. and fig.* 115

wooden overcoat n *coffin* 276

woodenhead n Insults 231

woodenheaded adj Insults 231

wooder n 200

woodhenge n 287

woodland adj/n 9

woodlore n 280

woodmonger n 41

woodnote n *natural music* 105

woodpecker n 105

woodpecker n *slang machine gun* 267

woodpile n 121

woodshed n 222

woodsman n 171

woodstove n 221

woodwind n *woodwind section* 265

woodwind n *woodwind instrument* 265

wood/wooden adj 10

woodworking, woodworker n 241

woody n *type of car* 317

woof n/v *bark* 209

woofer n 299

wool n *clothing made of wool* 16

wool n 16

woolen adj/n 16

woolly bear n *type of caterpillar* 220

woolly mammoth n 296

woolward adj *obs. wearing wool* 35

woozy adj (Am) 257

Worcestershire sauce n 168

word v *choose words* 152

word n *notification, news as in "receive word"* 23

word v *speak* 61

word n *single word* 19

word n *promise, as in "give your word"* 88

word n *speech* 19

word v *arch.* 19

word for word adv 76

word of mouth n 128

word processing, word processor n 318

word salad n Slang 283

word-association test n 304

wordbook n 128

word-hoard n 246

wording n *obs. having words* 82

wording n *arch.* 61

wording n *phrasing* 128

wordmonger n 127

word-of-mouth adj 214

wordplay n 245

words n *argument, as in "have words"* 82

wordsmith n 264

wordy adj 19

work v *function properly* 61

work v *create needlework* 33

work v *ache* 98

work n *commotion* 28

work n *job, workplace* 127; v 41

work v *have a job* 41

work n/v The Workplace 41

work n *work done; work to do* 19

work v *as in "work the controls"* 98

work v *as in "work it so he can attend"* 271

work n *as in "work of art"* 42

work v *write* 19

work n Literature/Writing 19

work ethic n 311

work of art n 228

work song n 282

work stoppage n 305

workable adj *able to be worked* 115

workable adj *doable* 115

workaday n *workday* 41, 76

workaday adj 127

workaholic n 318

workbench n 198

workbook n 276

workday n 76

worked up adj 275

workers' compensation n 305

workfare n *work(wel)fare* 318

workfolk n 101

workforce n 305

workful adj *dedicated to work* 245

workful obs. *functional* 62

workhorse n 107

workhouse n *poorhouse* 155

working capital n 276

working class n 200

working day n 101

working girl n Slang 249

working lunch n 318

working papers n 289

working stiff n 289

working-class adj 227

workingman n 152

workingwoman n 245

workload n 305

workman n *laborer* 19

workman n 19, 110

workman n *skilled worker* 19

workmanly adj 110

workmanship n *craftsmanship* 76

workmanship n *obs. work done* 76

workmen's compensation insurance n 281

workout n Sports 263

workpeople n 187

workplace n 227

work-release adj 312

workroom n 127

works n *mechanism* 149

works, the n Slang 268

workshop n 127

workstation n 299

work-study program n 305

worktable n 200

workweek n 289

workwoman n 110

world n 22

world n *as in "the animal world"* 177

world n *fig.* 22

world beat n Music 265

world music n 327

world power n Politics 247

world premiere n Movies/TV/Radio 291

world war n 277

world-beater n 268

ENGLISH THROUGH THE AGES

Z

More Great Books for Writers!

"Behind the Scenes" Series:

Inside Hollywood: A Writer's Guide to the World of Movies and TV—Behind the glitz and glamor, Hollywood insider John Morgan Wilson gives fiction and screen writers an honest portrayal of America's entertainment capitol. This sourcebook presents crucial information in an easy-to-reference format, featuring charts, trivia, glossaries, and sidebars. You'll get a the complete history of Hollywood, a close-up look at studios, job profiles of industry professionals, insider information on marketing films and TV shows, and also the inside language of showbiz.
#10551/$16.99/paperback/240 pages

Howdunit Series:

Missing Persons: A Writer's Guide to Finding the Lost, the Abducted and the Escaped—Now your characters can go beyond the phone book to search for missing relatives, old friends and vanishing villains! Professional PI, Fay Faron, shows you why people turn up missing and the search procedures used to find them.
#10511/$16.99/272 pages/paperback

Murder One: A Writer's Guide to Homicide—Build believable homicide scenarios—from accidental murders to crimes of passion. Prosecuting investigators Mauro Corvasce and Joseph Paglino take you step by step through motives, weapons and disposals of bodies—illustrated with scene-by-scene accounts from real life cases.
#10498/$16.99/240 pages/paperback

Amateur Detectives: A Writer's Guide to How Private Citizens Solve Criminal Cases—Make your amateur-crime-solver novels and stories accurate and convincing! You'll investigate what jobs work well with sleuthing, information-gathering methods, the law as it relates to amateur investigators and more!
#10487/$16.99/240 pages/paperback

Body Trauma: A Writer's Guide to Wounds and Injuries—Bring realism to your work using this detailed examination of serious bodily injury. You'll learn what happens to organs and bones maimed by accident or intent—from the 4 steps in trauma care to the "dirty dozen" dreadful—but survivable—chest injuries.
#10488/$16.99/240 pages/20 b&w illus./paperback

Malicious Intent: A Writer's Guide to How Criminals Think—Create unforgettable villains with the help of this guide to criminal psychology. You'll explore the fact and fiction of who these people are, why they commit their crimes, how they choose their victims and more! *#10413/$16.99/240 pages/paperback*

Modus Operandi: A Writer's Guide to How Criminals Work—From murder to arson to prostitution, two seasoned detectives show you how to create masterful crimes while still dropping enough clues to let the good guys catch the bad guys.
#10414/$16.99/224 pages/paperback

Police Procedural: A Writer's Guide to the Police and How They Work—Learn how police officers work, when they work, what they wear, who they report to, and how they go about controlling and investigating crime.
#10374/$16.99/272 pages/paperback

Private Eyes: A Writer's Guide to Private Investigators—How do people become investigators? What procedures do they use? What tricks/tactics do they use? This guide gives you the "inside scoop" on the world of private eyes!
#10373/$15.99/208 pages/paperback

Scene of the Crime: A Writer's Guide to Crime-Scene Investigations—Save time with this quick reference book! You'll find loads of facts and details on how police scour crime scenes for telltale clues. #10319/$15.99/240 pages/paperback

Cause of Death: A Writer's Guide to Death, Murder & Forensic Medicine—Discover how to accurately "kill-off" your characters as you are led step-by-step through the process of trauma, death and burial. #10318/$16.99/240 pages/paperback

Armed & Dangerous: A Writer's Guide to Weapons—You'll learn how to arm your characters with weapons to perfectly suit their crime. Hundreds of examples and easily understood language make complicated details completely accessible. #10176/$15.99/186 pages/paperback

Deadly Doses: A Writer's Guide to Poisons—You'll discover creative ways for your villains to poison their victims, authentically. Includes key characteristics of common and not-so-common poisons. #10177/$16.99/298 pages/paperback

Books to help you write better and sell more:

1998 Writer's Market: Where & How to Sell What You Write—Get your work into the right buyers' hands and save yourself the frustration of getting manuscripts returned in the mail. You'll find more than 4,000 listings loaded with submission information, as well as real life interviews on scriptwriting, networking, freelancing and more! #10512/$27.99/paperback/1088 pages

1998 Novel & Short Story Writer's Market—For years, fiction writers have relied on this trusted guide to the best opportunities to get fiction published. You get more than 2,000 listings, including accurate, up-to-date information on each market to help you find the right publisher for your work. #10525/$22.99/paperback/656 pages

The Writer's Digest Guide to Manuscript Formats—Don't take chances with your hard work! Learn how to prepare and submit books, poems, scripts, stories and more with the professional look editors expect from a good writer. #10025/$19.99/200 pages

Grammatically Correct: The Writer's Guide to Punctuation, Spelling, Style, Usage and Grammar—Write prose that's clear, concise and graceful! This comprehensive desk reference covers the nuts-and-bolts basics of punctuation, spelling and grammar, as well as essential tips and techniques for developing a smooth, inviting writing style. #10529/$19.99/352 pages

How to Write Attention-Grabbing Query & Cover Letters—Use the secrets John Wood reveals to write queries perfectly tailored, too good to turn down! In this guidebook, you will discover why boldness beats blandness in queries every time, ten basics you *must* have in your article queries, ten query blunders that can destroy publication chances and much more. #10462/$17.99/208 pages

How to Write a Book Proposal, Revised Edition—Get your nonfiction published as you learn the basics of creating effective book proposals with experienced literary agent, Michael Larsen. From test marketing potential book ideas to creating a professional-looking proposal package, you'll cover every step that's essential for breaking into the publishing market! #10518/$14.99/224 pages/paperback

Building Fiction: How to Develop Plot & Structure—Even with the most dynamic language, images and characters, no piece of fiction will work without a strong infrastructure. This book shows you how to build that structure using such tools as point of view, characterization, pacing, conflict, and transitional devices such as flashbacks. With Jesse Lee Kercheval's guidance, you will build a work of fiction just as an architect would design a house—with an eye for details and how all the parts of a

story or novel interconnect. *#48028/$16.99/208 pages/paperback*

Writing the Private Eye Novel: A Handbook by the Private Eye Writers of America—Discover pages of advice on writing and publishing PI novels—from authors whose fiction flies off the shelves. You'll find 23 tip-filled chapters on topics that include plot structure, character development, setting and short stories. Plus, specific advice on finding ideas, keeping readers on edge, creating slam-bang endings and more! *#10519/$18.99/240 pages*

Elements of the Writing Craft—Apply the techniques of the masters in your own work! This collection of 150 lessons reveals how noted writers have "built" their fiction and nonfiction. Each exercise contains a short passage of work from a distinguished writer, a writer's-eye analysis of the passage and a wealth of innovative writing exercises. *#48027/$19.99/272 pages*

Writer's Digest Handbook of Making Money Freelance Writing—Discover promising new income-producing opportunities with this collection of articles by top writers, editors and agents. Over 30 commentaries on business issues, writing opportunities and freelancing will help you make the break to a full-time writing career. *#10501/$19.99/320 pages*

The Writer's Digest Dictionary of Concise Writing—Make your work leaner, crisper and clearer! Under the guidance of professional editor Robert Hartwell Fiske, you'll learn how to rid your work of common say-nothing phrases while making it tighter and easier to read and understand. *#10482/$19.99/352 pages*

The 30-Minute Writer—Write short, snappy articles that make editors sit up and take notice. Full-time freelancer Connie Emerson reveals the many types of quickly written articles you can sell—from miniprofiles and one-pagers to personal essays. You'll also learn how to match your work to the market as you explore methods for expanding from short articles to columns and even books! *#10489/$14.99/256 pages/paperback*

Writing to Sell, 4th Edition—You'll discover high-quality writing and marketing counsel in this classic writing guide from well-known agent Scott Meredith. His timeless advice will guide you along the professional writing path as you get help with creating characters, plotting a novel, placing your work, formatting a manuscript, deciphering a publishing contract—even combating a slump! *#10476/$17.99/240 pages*

Writer's Encyclopedia, 3rd Edition—Rediscover this popular writer's reference—now with information about electronic resources, plus more than 100 new entries. You'll find facts, figures, definitions and examples designed to answer questions about every discipline connected with writing and help you convey a professional image. *#10464/$22.99/560 pages/62 b&w illus.*

Writing and Selling Your Novel—Write publishable fiction from start to finish with expert advice from professional novelist Jack M. Bickham! You'll learn how to develop effective work habits, refine your fiction writing technique, and revise and tailor your novels for tightly targeted markets. *#10509/$17.99/208 pages*

The Writer's Digest Handbook of Short Story Writing, Volume II—Orson Scott Card, Dwight V. Swain, Kit Reed and other noted authors bring you sound advice and timeless techniques for every aspect of the writing process. *#10239/$13.99/252 pages/paperback*

The Writer's Legal Guide, Revised Edition—Now the answer to all your legal questions is right at your fingertips! The updated version of this treasured desktop companion contains essential information on business issues, copyright protection and

registration, contract negotiation, income taxation, electronic rights and much, much more. #10478/$19.95/256 pages/paperback

The Writer's Digest Sourcebook for Building Believable Characters—Create unforgettable characters as you "attend" a roundtable where six novelists reveal their approaches to characterization. You'll probe your characters' backgrounds, beliefs and desires with a fill-in-the-blanks questionnaire. And a thesaurus of characteristics will help you develop the many other features no character should be without. #10463/$17.99/288 pages

Get That Novel Written: From Initial Idea to Final Edit—Take your novel from the starting line to a fabulous finish! Professional writer Donna Levin shows you both the basics and the finer points of novel writing while you learn to use words with precision, create juicy conflicts, master point of view and more! #10481/$18.99/208 pages

Travel Writing: A Guide to Research, Writing and Selling—Bring your travels home in print as you discover the many types of articles there are to write—and how to do it. You'll learn how to make your journey into a salable article by finding information, verifying it and bringing it to life on paper. #10465/$18.99/256 pages

Romance Writer's Sourcebook: Where to Sell Your Manuscripts—Get your romance manuscripts published with this new resource guide that combines how-to-write instruction with where-to-sell direction. You'll uncover advice from established authors, as well as detailed listings of publishing houses, agents, organizations, contests and more! #10456/$19.99/475 pages

Science Fiction and Fantasy Writer's Sourcebook, 2nd Edition—Discover how to write and sell your science fiction and fantasy! Novel excerpts, short stories and advice from pros show you how to write a winner! Then over 300 market listings bring you publishers hungry for your work! Plus, you'll get details on SF conventions, online services, organizations and workshops. #10491/$19.99/480 pages

Writing for Money—Discover where to look for writing opportunities—and how to make them pay off. You'll learn how to write for magazines, newspapers, radio and TV, newsletters, greeting cards and a dozen other hungry markets! #10425/$17.99/256 pages